CENSUS OF INDIA 1911

CENSUS OF INDIA, 1911

VOLUME - X

CENTRAL PROVINCES AND BERAR

PART II - TABLES

J. T. MARTEN

GYAN

Published by

GYAN

Gyan Publishing House
5, Ansari Road
Daryaganj, New Delhi-110002
Phone: 011-47034999, 9811692060
E-mail: books@gyanbooks.com

Distribution Network
gyanbooks.com
India, USA, Canada, UK, Australia

ISBN: 978-81-212-7127-1 (Set) 23 Vols. In 41 Bindings

ISBN: 978-81-212-7467-8 (PB) Vol. X, Pt. II

First Published, 1912

2nd Impression 2024

Printed at: Gyan Press, Delhi.

CENSUS OF INDIA 1911

CENSUS OF INDIA, 1911.

VOLUME X.

CENTRAL PROVINCES & BERAR.

PART II—TABLES.

BY

J. T. MARTEN, M.A., I.C.S.,

SUPERINTENDENT OF CENSUS OPERATIONS, CENTRAL PROVINCES AND BERAR.

ALLAHABAD
PRINTED AT THE PIONEER PRESS

1912

TABLE OF CONTENTS.

TABLE I.

Area, Houses and Population.

THIS table shows for each district the area, the number of towns and villages, the number of occupied houses and the total urban and rural population, male and female. Similar figures are given for the Feudatory States.

The difference between some of the areas here shown and those in the corresponding table of 1901 is due to inter-district transfers, as explained on the title-page of Table II.

For the purpose of column 3 (number of towns) Cantonments have been treated as forming part of the Municipalities which they adjoin.

The main statistics for Tahsils will be found in Provincial Tables I and II at the end of the Volume.

TABLE I.—Area,

Serial No.	DISTRICT or STATE.	Area in square miles.	Number of Towns.	Number of Villages.	Occupied houses. Total.	Occupied houses. In towns.	Occupied houses. In villages.
	1	2	3	4	5	6	7
	Central Provinces and Berar ...	**130,997**	**117**	**47.668**	**3,246.873**	**268,731**	**2,976.142**
	C. P. British Districts and Berar	**99,823**	**112**	**39.005**	**2,858.302**	**260.151**	**2,598.151**
	C. P. British Districts	**82,057**	**65**	**33.156**	**2.203.068**	**177.602**	**2.025.466**
	Jubbulpore Division	*18,953*	*13*	*8,794*	*606,706*	*53,571*	*451,535*
1	Saugor	3,962	5	1,809	115,712	16,074	99,638
2	Damoh	2,816	1	1,148	68,597	3,374	65,223
3	Jubbulpore	3,912	4	2,350	164,794	29,483	135,311
4	Mandla	5,057	1	1,918	74,877	2,030	72,847
5	Seoni	3,206	1	1,569	81,726	2,910	78,816
	Nerbudda Division	*18,388*	*17*	*6,433*	*418,853*	*31,898*	*356,955*
6	Narsinghpur	1,976	3	1,009	69,433	4,133	65,300
7	Hoshangabad	3,682	6	1,326	93,979	9,098	84,881
8	Nimar	4,227	2	1,019	74,066	9,876	64,690
9	Betul	3,872	2	1,242	75,789	2,746	73,043
10	Chhindwara	4,631	4	1,842	105,585	6,545	99,040
	Nagpur Division	*23,677*	*29*	*7,796*	*628,606*	*71,749*	*556,857*
11	Wardha	2,428	7	920	99,211	13,680	85,531
12	Nagpur	3,840	12	1,689	167,374	42,175	125,199
13	Chanda	9,312	5	2,419	134,556	8,561	125,995
14	Bhandara	3,965	4	1,633	148,920	5,648	143,272
15	Balaghat	3,132	1	1,135	78,545	1,685	76,860
	Chhattisgarh Division	*22,039*	*7*	*10,128*	*649,904*	*20,084*	*629,820*
16	Raipur	9,776	3	4,271	271,504	11,151	260,353
17	Bilaspur	7,618	3	3,345	218,760	7,393	211,367
18	Drug	4,645	1	2,512	159,640	1,540	158,100
	Berar	**17,766**	**47**	**5,849**	**655,234**	**82.549**	**572,685**
19	Amraoti	4,733	20	1,627	187,321	34,119	153,202
20	Akola	4,097	12	1,481	171,040	23,085	147,955
21	Buldana	3,731	9	1,174	144,586	16,152	128,434
22	Yeotmal	5,205	6	1,567	152,287	9,193	143,094
	Feudatory States	**31.174**	**5**	**8.663**	**388,571**	**8.580**	**379,991**
23	Makrai	155	...	68	3,097	...	3,097
24	Bastar	13,062	...	2,475	75,616	...	75,616
25	Kanker	1,429	...	510	24,064	...	24,064
26	Nandgaon	871	1	525	32,590	2.474	30,116
27	Khairagarh	931	1	497	30,290	1,682	28,608
28	Chhuikhadan	154	...	107	6,538	...	6,538
29	Kawardha	798	1	372	17,475	1,479	15,996
30	Sakti	138	...	125	6,767	...	6,767
31	Raigarh	1,486	1	709	41,829	1,966	39,863
32	Sarangarh	540	1	453	16,868	979	15,889
33	Chang Bhakar	906		123	4,711		4,711
34	Korea	1,631	...	301	11,686	...	11,686
35	Surguja	6,055	...	1,598	76,587	...	76,587
36	Udaipur	1,055	...	210	10,808	...	10,808
37	Jashpur	1,063	...	530	29,645	...	29,645

Houses and Population.

POPULATION.									
PERSONS.			MALES.			FEMALES.			Serial No.
Total.	Urban.	Rural.	Total.	Urban.	Rural.	Total.	Urban.	Rural.	
8	9	10	11	12	13	14	15	16	
16,033,310	**1,213,049**	**14,820,261**	**7,984,022**	**628,375**	**7,355,647**	**8,049,288**	**584,674**	**7,464,614**	
13,916,308	**1,176,225**	**12,740,083**	**6,930,392**	**610,417**	**6,319,975**	**6,985,916**	**565,808**	**6,420,108**	
10,859,146	**806,431**	**10,052,715**	**5,379,778**	**418,090**	**4,961,688**	**5,479,368**	**388,341**	**5,091,027**	
2,421,064	*241,948*	*2,179,616*	*1,210,980*	*128,809*	*1,082,171*	*1,210,084*	*112,630*	*1,097,445*	
541,410	75,663	465,747	276,233	40,136	236,097	265,177	35,527	229,650	1
333,047	17,042	316,005	168,060	8,732	159,328	164,987	8,310	156,677	2
745,892	125,525	620,367	373,173	68,561	304,612	372,719	56,964	315,755	3
405,234	9,379	395,855	200,872	4,640	196,232	204,362	4,739	199,623	4
395,481	13,839	381,642	192,642	6,740	185,902	202,839	7,099	195,740	5
2,081,477	*143,557*	*1,938,920*	*1,043,239*	*73,244*	*969,995*	*1,038,238*	*69,313*	*968,925*	
325,677	18,749	306,928	161,795	9,444	152,351	163,882	9,305	154,577	6
457,395	35,903	421,492	230,632	18,873	211,759	226,763	17,030	209,733	7
391,071	44,381	346,690	200,765	23,135	177,630	190,306	21,246	169,060	8
390,386	12,927	377,459	194,163	6,461	187,702	196,223	6,466	189,757	9
516,948	30,597	486,351	255,884	15,331	240,553	261,064	15,266	245,798	10
3,109,838	*332,533*	*2,777,305*	*1,548,737*	*171,043*	*1,377,694*	*1,561,101*	*161,490*	*1,399,611*	
459,796	60,665	399,131	231,871	31,315	200,556	227,925	29,350	198,575	11
809,901	194,903	614,998	408,843	101,188	307,655	401,058	93,715	307,343	12
677,544	41,704	635,840	337,540	20,813	316,727	340,004	20,891	319,113	13
773,677	27,861	745,816	380,014	14,062	365,952	393,663	13,799	379,864	14
388,920	7,400	381,520	190,469	3,605	186,804	198,451	3,735	194,716	15
3,246,767	*89,893*	*3,156,874*	*1,576,822*	*44,994*	*1,531,828*	*1,669,945*	*44,899*	*1,625,046*	
1,324,856	51,615	1,273,241	645,186	26,039	619,147	679,670	25,576	654,094	16
1,146,223	31,230	1,114,993	558,477	15,366	543,111	587,746	15,864	571,882	17
775,688	7,048	768,640	373,159	3,589	369,570	402,529	3,459	399,070	18
3,057,182	**369,794**	**2,687,368**	**1,550,614**	**192,327**	**1,358,287**	**1,506,548**	**177,467**	**1,329,081**	
875,904	155,946	719,958	447,216	80,825	366,391	428,688	75,121	353,567	19
788,863	103,146	685,717	400,893	53,915	346,978	387,970	49,231	338,739	20
669,182	67,822	601,360	337,179	35,347	301,832	332,003	32,475	299,528	21
723,213	42,880	680,333	365,326	22,240	343,086	357,887	20,640	337,247	22
2,117,002	**36,824**	**2,080,178**	**1,053,630**	**17,958**	**1,035,672**	**1,063,372**	**18,866**	**1,044,506**	
15,021	...	15,021	7,530	...	7,530	7,491	...	7,491	23
433,310	...	433,310	218,015	...	218,015	215,295	...	215,295	24
127,014	...	127,014	63,010	...	63,010	64,004	...	64,004	25
167,362	11,979	155,383	80,293	6,041	74,252	87,069	5,938	81,131	26
155,471	6,249	149,222	74,742	2,965	71,777	80,729	3,284	77,445	27
31,150	...	31,150	15,117	...	15,117	16,033	...	16,033	28
77,654	5,180	72,474	37,488	2,341	35,147	40,166	2,839	37,327	29
34,547	...	34,547	16,871	...	16,871	17,676	...	17,676	30
218,860	8,041	210,819	107,850	3,986	103,864	111,010	4,055	106,955	31
102,071	5,375	96,696	49,851	2,625	47,226	52,220	2,750	49,470	32
24,421	...	24,421	12,462	...	12,462	11,959	...	11,959	33
62,107	...	62,107	31,856	...	31,856	30,251	...	30,251	34
428,703	...	428,703	217,749	...	217,749	210,954	...	210,954	35
64,853	...	64,853	32,790	...	32,790	32,063	...	32,063	36
174,458	...	174,458	88,006	...	88,006	86,452	...	86,452	37

TABLE II.

Variation in Population since 1872.

This table compares the population as now ascertained with that of the four previous Censuses. The figures for the latter differ from those shown in the old Census reports. This is due to subsequent transfers of territory from one Province to another, and also from one District to another. The effect of these changes on the population of the Districts concerned has been calculated, and the figures have been adjusted accordingly.

The following are the Districts of which transfers of territory have taken place:—

Between 1872 and 1881—

Seoni, Balaghat, Betul, Hoshangabad, Chanda, Chhindwara.

Between 1881 and 1891—

Mandla, Balaghat, Seoni.

Between 1891 and 1901—

Nagpur, Seoni, Chhindwara, Hoshangabad, Nimar, Betul, Mandla, Balaghat.

Between 1901 and 1911—

Saugor, Narsinghpur, Mandla, Balaghat, Hoshangabad, Nimar, Betul, Chhindwara, Chanda, Drug, Raipur, Bilaspur, Amraoti, Akola, Buldana, Yeotmal.

The total population of the Province lost 27,695 persons by the transfer of the Talukas of Bhadrachalam and Rakapalli to the Madras Presidency between 1872 and 1881.

On the other hand, it received a nett addition of 1,729,563 persons between 1901 and 1911 by changes which added Berar and the Chota Nagpur States (Chang Bhakar, Korea, Surguja, Udaipur and Jashpur) to the Province and transferred almost the whole of the Sambalpur District and the Oriya States (Bamra, Rairakhol, Sonpur, Patna and Kalahandi) to Bengal and a portion of Chanda to Madras.

The first census of Berar was taken in 1867. The figures given under 1872 in this and subsequent statements are those of the 1867 census.

TABLE II.—Variation in

Serial No.	DISTRICT OR STATE	PERSONS. 1911.	1901.	1891	1881.	1872.	MALES. 1911.	1901.	1891.	1881.
	1	2	3	4	5	6	7	8	9	10
	Central Provinces and Berar ...	**16,033,310**	**13,602,592**	**14,761,534**	**13,330,657**	**10,879,384**	**7,984,022**	**6,738,327**	**7,436,060**	**6,757,203**
	C. P. British Districts and Berar...	**13,916,308**	**11,971,452**	**13,048,972**	**11,943,363**	**9,951,268**	**6,930,392**	**5,926,357**	**6,573,559**	**6,056,311**
	C. P. British Districts ...	**10,859,146**	**9,217,436**	**10,151,481**	**9,270,690**	**7,723,614**	**5,379,778**	**4,532,057**	**5,081,733**	**4,675,819**
	JUBBULPORE DIVISION	*2,521,063*	*2,081,480*	*2,374,809*	*2,300,170*	*1,824,665*	*1,210,980*	*1,032,478*	*1,204,693*	*1,127,310*
1	Saugor ...	541,410	469,479	589,837	562,829	525,976	276,233	237,972	304,737	293,684
2	Damoh	333,047	285,326	325,613	312,957	269,642	168,660	143,488	167,329	162,570
3	Jubbulpore ...	745,892	680,585	748,146	687,233	528,859	373,173	335,552	375,964	349,251
4	Mandla ...	405,234	318,381	340,443	301,377	213,056	200,872	157,050	171,822	153,343
5	Seoni ...	395,481	327,709	370,767	335,774	287,132	199,642	158,416	184,841	168,462
	NERBUDDA DIVISION...	*2,031,477*	*1,785,008*	*1,883,053*	*1,765,526*	*1,592,056*	*1,043,230*	*886,029*	*951,672*	*901,841*
6	Narsinghpur ...	325,677	315,518	363,932	367,294	341,144	161,795	154,694	185,092	187,746
7	Hoshangabad ...	457,395	440,645	493,941	464,384	435,264	230,632	222,893	252,048	239,480
8	Nimar ...	391,071	327,173	286,176	253,921	224,517	200,765	167,994	148,215	133,076
9	Betul ...	390,386	287,807	326,581	306,796	275,830	194,163	141,113	164,287	155,407
10	Chhindwara ...	516,948	407,865	407,423	372,831	315,901	255,884	199,335	202,090	186,132
	NAGPUR DIVISION ...	*3,109,838*	*2,659,236*	*2,909,322*	*2,697,252*	*2,370,081*	*1,548,737*	*1,312,807*	*1,557,530*	*1,352,635*
11	Wardha ...	459,796	385,103	400,854	387,221	354,720	231,871	193,815	203,286	195,564
12	Nagpur ..	809,991	751,844	757,862	697,356	631,109	408,843	377,612	382,963	351,756
13	Chanda ...	677,544	583,887	625,495	589,000	511,171	337,540	263,562	314,605	296,012
14	Bhandara ...	778,677	663,062	742,850	683,779	564,813	380,014	320,648	366,696	340,811
15	Balaghat ...	358,920	325,390	382,261	339,896	315,168	190,469	157,170	190,060	168,492
	CHHATTISGARH DIVISION	*3,246,767*	*2,691,662*	*2,984,300*	*2,608,042*	*1,929,312*	*1,576,822*	*1,300,743*	*1,477,838*	*1,293,033*
16	Raipur ...	1,324,856	1,096,858	1,125,019	990,689	700,308	645,186	532,675	555,753	493,557
17	Bilaspur ...	1,146,223	918,491	1,046,606	880,878	621,201	558,477	446,405	515,267	436,853
18	Drug ..	775,688	676,313	812,675	736,475	607,713	373,159	321,663	406,818	363,623
	Berar ...	**3,057,162**	**2,754,016**	**2,897,491**	**2,672,673**	**2,227,654**	**1,550,614**	**1,394,300**	**1,491,826**	**1,380,492**
19	Amraoti ...	875,904	809,499	849,604	778,167	675,302	447,216	413,013	439,741	403,076
20	Akola ...	788,863	754,187	758,323	734,846	610,501	400,893	383,120	391,442	381,163
21	Buldana ...	669,182	614,373	679,015	642,507	526,894	337,179	309,460	347,804	330,682
22	Yeotmal ...	723,213	575,957	610,098	517,153	414,957	365,326	289,707	312,513	265,571
	Railway Passengers	...	...	451	—	...	...	...	326	...
	Feudatory States ...	**2,117,002**	**1,631,140**	**1,712,562**	**1,387,294**	**928,116**	**1,053,630**	**811,970**	**862,501**	**700,892**
23	Makrai ...	15,021	13,035	18,549	16,764	13,648	7,530	6,492	9,339	8,521
24	Bastar ...	433,310	306,501	310,884	196,248	78,856	218,015	155,683	159,656	103,046
25	Kanker ..	127,014	103,536	82,379	63,610	43,542	63,010	51,596	42,306	32,131
26	Nandgaon ...	167,362	126,365	183,866	164,339	148,454	80,293	60,110	90,558	81,717
27	Khairagarh ..	155,471	137,554	181,184	166,138	122,264	74,742	65,699	89,076	82,677
28	Chhuikhadan ..	31,150	26,368	36,288	32,979	29,590	15,117	12,596	17,672	16,267
29	Kawardha ...	77,654	57,474	91,813	86,362	75,462	37,488	27,962	46,063	42,706
30	Sakti ...	34,547	22,301	25,374	22,819	8,394	16,871	10,885	12,582	11,352
31	Raigarh ...	218,860	174,929	168,525	128,943	63,304	107,850	86,548	84,227	64,767
32	Sarangarh ..	102,071	79,900	83,210	71,274	37,091	49,851	38,738	41,034	35,221
33	Chang Bhakar ...	24,421	19,548	18,526	13,466	8,919	12,462	10,003	9,708	6,826
34	Korea ...	62,107	35,113	36,240	29,846	21,127	31,856	17,948	18,586	15,162
35	Surguja ...	428,703	351,011	324,552	270,311	182,831	217,749	177,961	165,294	137,359
36	Udaipur ..	64,853	45,391	37,536	33,955	27,708	32,790	23,107	19,121	17,111
37	Jashpur ...	174,458	132,114	113,636	90,240	66,926	88,006	66,047	57,279	45,999

Population since 1872.

	FEMALES.					VARIATION. Increase (+) Decrease (—)				Net variation in period 1872—1911. Increase (+) Decrease (—)	Serial No.
1872.	1911.	1901.	1891.	1881.	1872.	1901—1911.	1891—1901.	1881—1891.	1872—1881.		
11	12	13	14	15	16	17	18	19	20	21	
5,552,860	8,049,288	6,864,265	7,325,474	6,573,454	5,326,524	+ 2,430,718	— 1,158,942	+ 1,430,877	+ 2,451,273	+ 5,153,926	
5,082,986	6,985,916	6,045,095	6,475,413	5,887,052	4,868,282	+ 1,944,856	— 1,077,520	+ 1,105,609	+ 1,992,095	+ 3,965,040	
3,930,804	5,479,368	4,685,379	5,069,748	4,594,871	3,792,810	+ 1,641,710	— 934,045	+ 880,791	+ 1,547,076	+ 3,135,532	
944,064	*1,210,084*	*1,049,003*	*1,170,113*	*1,072,860*	*830,601*	+ *339,584*	— *293,326*	+ *174,636*	+ *375,505*	+ *596,399*	
277,443	265,177	231,507	285,100	269,145	248,533	+ 71,931	— 120,358	+ 27,008	+ 36,853	+ 15,434	1
139,962	164,987	141,838	158,284	150,387	129,680	+ 47,721	— 40,387	+ 12,656	+ 43,315	+ 63,405	2
270,237	372,719	345,033	372,182	337,982	258,622	+ 65,307	— 67,561	+ 60,913	+ 158,374	+ 217,033	3
110,477	204,362	161,331	168,621	148,034	102,579	+ 86,853	— 22,062	+ 39,066	+ 88,321	+ 192,178	4
145,945	202,830	169,293	185,926	167,312	141,187	+ 67,772	— 43,058	+ 34,993	+ 48,642	+ 108,349	5
824,817	*1,038,838*	*898,979*	*931,381*	*863,385*	*767,839*	+ *296,469*	— *98,045*	+ *117,837*	+ *172,570*	+ *488,821*	
177,460	163,882	160,824	183,900	179,548	163,684	+ 10,159	— 53,414	+ 1,638	+ 26,150	— 15,467	6
228,827	226,763	228,752	241,893	224,904	208,437	+ 10,750	— 47,296	+ 29,557	+ 29,120	+ 22,131	7
119,371	190,306	159,179	137,961	120,845	105,146	+ 63,898	+ 40,997	+ 32,255	+ 29,404	+ 166,554	8
140,141	196,223	146,694	162,294	151,389	135,689	+ 102,579	— 38,774	+ 19,785	+ 30,960	+ 114,556	9
159,018	361,064	206,530	205,333	186,699	156,883	+ 109,083	+ 442	+ 34,592	+ 56,930	+ 201,047	10
1,193,924	*1,561,101*	*1,346,479*	*1,451,792*	*1,344,617*	*1,183,057*	+ *450,568*	— *250,036*	+ *212,070*	+ *330,271*	+ *732,857*	
180,899	227,925	191,288	197,568	191,657	173,821	+ 74,693	— 15,751	+ 13,633	+ 32,501	+ 105,076	11
321,440	401,058	374,232	374,999	345,600	309,660	+ 58,057	— 6,018	+ 60,566	+ 66,247	+ 178,792	12
256,118	340,004	270,325	310,890	292,988	255,053	+ 143,657	— 91,608	+ 36,495	+ 77,829	+ 166,373	13
279,284	393,063	342,414	376,154	342,968	285,529	+ 110,615	— 79,788	+ 59,071	+ 118,966	+ 208,864	14
156,188	198,451	168,220	192,181	171,404	158,985	+ 63,530	— 56,871	+ 42,365	+ 24,728	+ 73,752	15
867,999	*1,609,945*	*1,390,919*	*1,516,462*	*1,314,003*	*961,313*	+ *555,105*	— *293,638*	+ *376,258*	+ *673,730*	+ *1,317,455*	
351,893	679,670	564,183	569,266	497,132	348,505	+ 227,998	— 23,161	+ 134,330	+ 290,291	+ 624,458	16
313,729	587,746	472,086	531,339	444,025	307,472	+ 227,732	— 128,115	+ 165,728	+ 259,677	+ 525,022	17
302,377	402,529	354,650	415,857	372,852	305,336	+ 99,375	— 136,362	+ 76,200	+ 128,762	+ 167,975	18
1,152,182	1,506,548	1,359,716	1,405,665	1,292,181	1,075,472	+ 303,146	— 148,475	+ 224,818	+ 445,019	+ 829,508	
350,291	428,688	396,486	409,863	375,091	325,011	+ 66,405	— 40,105	+ 71,437	+ 102,865	+ 200,602	19
315,220	387,970	371,067	366,881	353,683	295,281	+ 34,676	— 4,136	+ 23,477	+ 124,348	+ 178,362	20
273,376	332,003	305,913	331,211	311,825	253,518	+ 54,809	— 64,642	+ 36,508	+ 115,613	+ 142,288	21
213,295	357,887	286,250	297,585	251,582	201,662	+ 147,256	— 34,141	+ 92,945	+ 102,196	+ 308,256	22
...	...	...	125	...	...	...	— 451	+ 451	...	...	
469,874	1,063,372	819,170	850,061	686,402	458,242	+ 485,862	— 81,422	+ 325,268	+ 459,178	+ 1,188,886	
7,115	7,491	6,543	9,210	8,243	6,533	+ 1,986	— 5,514	+ 1,785	+ 3,116	+ 1,373	23
40,745	215,295	150,818	151,228	93,202	38,111	+ 126,809	— 4,383	+ 114,636	+ 117,392	+ 354,454	24
22,758	64,004	51,940	49,073	31,479	20,787	+ 23,478	+ 21,157	+ 18,769	+ 20,068	+ 83,472	25
74,456	87,069	66,255	93,308	82,622	73,998	+ 40,997	— 57,501	+ 19,527	+ 15,885	+ 18,008	26
61,085	80,729	71,855	92,108	83,461	61,229	+ 17,917	— 43,630	+ 15,046	+ 43,874	+ 33,207	27
14,984	16,083	13,772	18,616	16,712	14,606	+ 4,782	— 9,920	+ 3,309	+ 3,380	+ 1,560	28
38,092	40,166	29,512	45,750	43,656	37,370	+ 20,180	— 34,339	+ 5,451	+ 10,900	+ 2,192	29
4,585	17,676	11,416	12,792	11,467	3,809	+ 12,246	— 3,073	+ 2,555	+ 14,425	+ 26,153	30
31,233	111,010	88,386	84,208	64,176	32,071	+ 43,981	+ 6,404	+ 39,582	+ 65,639	+ 155,556	31
19,345	52,220	41,162	42,176	36,053	17,741	+ 22,171	— 3,310	+ 11,930	+ 34,183	+ 64,980	32
4,498	11,959	9,545	8,818	6,640	4,421	+ 4,873	+ 1,022	+ 5,000	+ 4,547	+ 15,502	33
11,093	30,251	17,165	17,654	14,684	10,034	+ 26,994	— 1,127	+ 6,394	+ 8,719	+ 40,980	34
91,291	210,954	173,050	159,258	132,922	91,540	+ 77,692	+ 26,450	+ 54,241	+ 87,480	+ 245,872	35
13,999	32,063	22,284	18,415	16,844	13,709	+ 10,462	+ 7,855	+ 3,581	+ 6,247	+ 37,145	36
34,648	86,452	65,467	56,357	44,241	32,278	+ 42,344	+ 18,478	+ 23,396	+ 23,314	+ 107,532	37

TABLE III.

Towns and Villages classified by population.

In this table, as in Tables I and IV, Cantonments have been treated as forming part of the Municipalities which they adjoin. Small outlying hamlets have been treated as part of the main residential village to which they appertain.

TABLE III.—Towns and

Serial No.	DISTRICT OR STATE.	Total number of inhabited towns and villages.	Population.	Under 500. Number.	Under 500. Population.	500—1,000. Number.	500—1,000. Population.	1,000—2,000. Number.	1,000—2,000. Population	2,000— Number.
	1	2	3	4	5	6	7	8	9	10
	Central Provinces and Berar	**47,785**	**16.033,310**	**39,758**	**7,806,247**	**6,099**	**4,085,639**	**1,464**	**1,930,519**	**365**
	C. P. British Districts and Berar ...	**39,117**	**13,916,308**	**31,980**	**6,391,120**	**5,339**	**3,590,470**	**1,350**	**1,790,200**	**354**
	C. P. British Districts...	**33,221**	**10,859,146**	**27,898**	**5,502,364**	**4,116**	**2,743,305**	**922**	**1,202,428**	**227**
	JUBBULPORE DIVISION ...	*8,806*	*2,421,064*	*7,881*	*1,420,556*	*736*	*490,429*	*150*	*193,571*	*29*
1	Saugor ...	1,814	541,410	1,584	269,424	172	117,329	47	62,719	6
2	Damoh ...	1,149	333,047	993	174,008	118	81,506	29	37,980	8
3	Jubbulpore ...	2,354	745,892	2,050	375,821	239	158,852	53	65,759	9
4	Mandla ...	1,919	405,234	1,833	327,963	74	47,775	6	7,222	5
5	Seoni ...	1,570	395,481	1,421	273,340	132	84,907	15	19,891	1
	NERBUDDA DIVISION ...	*6,455*	*2,081,477*	*5,469*	*1,059,138*	*738*	*499,362*	*177*	*237,219*	*58*
6	Narsinghpur ...	1,012	325,677	836	154,335	127	85,333	37	46,630	11
7	Hoshangabad ...	1,332	457,395	1,093	214,281	180	124,206	42	56,468	13
8	Nimar ...	1,021	391,071	830	171,693	148	100,935	27	36,495	14
9	Betul ...	1,244	390,386	1,056	207,900	138	93,394	41	55,019	7
10	Chhindwara ...	1,846	516,948	1,654	310,929	145	95,494	30	42,607	13
	NAGPUR DIVISION ...	*7,825*	*3,109,838*	*6,105*	*1,195,825*	*1,240*	*840,363*	*353*	*457,743*	*100*
11	Wardha ...	927	459,796	670	154,856	177	123,417	55	72,084	18
12	Nagpur ...	1,701	809,901	1,376	294,801	216	143,389	66	83,867	32
13	Chanda ...	2,424	677,544	2,086	308,174	240	165,240	68	89,034	25
14	Bhandara ...	1,637	773,677	1,082	253,012	402	272,423	132	171,354	18
15	Balaghat ...	1,136	388,920	891	184,982	205	135,894	32	41,404	7
	CHHATTISGARH DIVISION	*10,135*	*3,246,767*	*8,443*	*1,826,845*	*1,403*	*913,151*	*242*	*313,395*	*40*
16	Raipur	4,274	1,324,856	3,607	747,100	554	367,468	98	125,540	12
17	Bilaspur	3,348	1,146,223	2,728	607,725	489	309,836	104	137,656	24
18	Drug	2,513	775,688	2,108	472,020	360	235,847	40	50,659	4
	Berar	**5,896**	**3,057,162**	**4,082**	**888,756**	**1,223**	**847,165**	**428**	**587,772**	**127**
19	Amraoti	1,647	875,904	1,189	235,267	277	194,524	118	163,634	48
20	Akola	1,493	788,863	1,036	210,034	303	206,414	114	166,412	30
21	Buldana	1,183	669,182	759	181,282	286	200,804	100	132,350	32
22	Yeotmal	1,573	723,213	1,098	262,173	357	245,423	96	125,576	17
	Feudatory States ...	**8,668**	**2,117,002**	**7,778**	**1,415,127**	**760**	**495,169**	**114**	**140,319**	**11**
23	Makrai	68	15,021	62	9,234	4	2,917	2	2,870	...
24	Bastar	2,475	433,310	2,312	307,229	138	90,800	22	28,088	3
25	Kanker	510	127,014	462	91,657	43	26,865	3	8,119	2
26	Nandgaon	526	167,362	455	105,935	64	42,028	6	7,420	...
27	Khairagarh	499	155,471	426	97,391	64	39,401	5	5,797	2
28	Chhuikhadan ...	107	31,150	98	23,529	7	4,087	1	1,211	1
29	Kawardha	873	77,654	347	54,322	23	15,414	2	2,738	...
30	Sakti	125	34,547	112	23,807	11	7,321	1	1,005	1
31	Raigarh	770	218,860	682	140,353	78	50,702	9	13,764	...
32	Sarangarh	454	102,071	421	71,311	25	16,672	7	8,713	...
33	Chhang Bhakar ...	123	24,421	116	20,295	7	4,126	...	...	...
34	Korea	301	62,107	280	46,458	18	12,343	3	3,306	...
35	Surguja	1,598	428,703	1,398	288,579	178	112,703	21	23,641	1
36	Udaipur	210	64,853	172	34,865	32	22,832	6	7,156	—
37	Jashpur	530	174,458	435	94,162	68	46,778	26	31,491	1

Villages classified by population.

5,000.	5,000—10,000.		10,000—20,000.		20,000—50,000.		50,000—100,000		100,000 and over.		
Population.	Number.	Population.	Number.	Population.	Number.	Population.	Number.	Population.	Number.	Population.	Serial No.
11	12	13	14	15	16	17	18	19	20	21	
1,073,314	**68**	**436,824**	**23**	**312,981**	**6**	**185,720**	...	...	**2**	**202,066**	
1,043,751	**64**	**411,979**	**22**	**301,002**	**6**	**185,720**	...	...	**2**	**202,066**	
633,716	**38**	**246,879**	**14**	**202,764**	**4**	**125,624**	...	...	**2**	**202,066**	
78,690	*6*	*44,566*	*3*	*46,693*	*1*	*45,908*	...	...	*1*	*100,651*	
16,275	4	29,755	...	...	1	45,908	...	...	...	...	1
22,451	...	...	1	17,042	...	...	...	...	...	...	2
23,565	1	5,432	1	15,812	...	...	...	...	1	100,651	3
12,895	1	9,379	...	...	...	...	...	...	...	...	4
3,504	...	...	1	13,839	...	...	...	...	...	...	5
159,572	*9*	*58,303*	*2*	*23,502*	*2*	*44,381*	...	...	...	...	
28,749	...	...	1	10,630	...	...	...	...	...	...	6
34,789	4	27,651	...	...	...	...	...	...	...	...	7
37,567	...	...	...	...	2	44,381	...	...	...	...	8
21,146	2	12,927	...	...	...	...	...	...	...	...	9
37,321	3	17,725	1	12,872	...	...	...	...	...	...	10
292,471	*19*	*119,762*	*7*	*102,259*	...	...	...	...	*1*	*101,415*	
48,774	4	23,279	3	37,386	...	...	...	...	...	...	11
97,660	8	53,984	2	34,785	...	...	...	...	1	101,415	12
73,392	4	21,838	1	19,866	...	...	...	...	...	...	13
53,405	2	13,261	1	10,222	...	...	...	...	...	...	14
19,240	1	7,400	...	...	...	...	...	...	...	...	15
102,983	*4*	*24,248*	*2*	*30,310*	*1*	*35,335*	...	...	...	...	
33,133	1	5,820	1	10,460	1	35,335	...	...	...	...	16
59,776	2	11,380	1	19,850	...	...	...	...	...	...	17
10,074	1	7,048	...	...	...	...	...	...	...	...	18
410,035	**26**	**165,100**	**8**	**98,238**	**2**	**60,096**	...	...	...	...	
147,713	12	75,480	2	25,007	1	34,270	...	...	...	...	19
111,153	7	48,794	2	25,230	1	25,826	...	...	...	...	20
99,898	3	20,372	3	34,476	...	...	...	...	...	...	21
51,271	4	25,445	1	13,525	...	...	...	...	...	...	22
29,563	**4**	**24,845**	**1**	**11,979**	...	...	...	...	...	...	
...	...	...	...	...	...	...	...	...	...	...	23
7,103	...	...	...	...	...	...	...	...	...	...	24
5,373	...	...	...	...	...	...	...	...	...	...	25
...	...	...	1	11,979	...	...	...	...	...	...	26
6,633	1	6,249	...	...	...	...	...	...	...	...	27
2,323	...	...	...	...	...	...	...	...	...	...	28
...	1	5,180	...	...	...	...	...	...	...	...	29
2,414	...	...	...	...	...	...	...	...	...	...	30
...	1	8,041	...	...	...	...	...	...	...	...	31
...	1	5,375	...	...	...	...	...	...	...	...	32
...	...	...	...	...	...	...	...	...	...	...	33
...	...	...	...	...	...	...	...	...	...	...	34
3,690	...	...	...	...	...	...	...	...	...	...	35
...	...	...	...	...	...	...	...	...	...	...	36
2,027	...	...	...	...	...	...	...	...	...	...	37

TABLE IV.

Population of towns with variation since 1872.

The population of Cantonments has been added to that of the Municipalities or Towns which they adjoin. The Cantonment population is shown below separately:—

Cantonment.	Muncipality or Town with which included.	1911.			1901.		
		Persons.	Males.	Females.	Persons.	Males.	Females.
Jubbulpore ...	Jubbulpore ...	21,642	14,252	7,390	13,157	7,780	5,377
Saugor ...	Saugor ...	11,032	6,510	4,522	10,918	6,388	4,530
Kamptee(Military area	Kamptee ...	2,286	1,731	555	Not available.		
Pachmarhi ...	Pachmarhi ...	3,287	1,842	1,445	Not available.		

The urban population was much affected by the prevalence of plague at the time of census. A recensus of 12 principal towns shows an increase of 82,650 persons (males 41,945, females 40,705) in the urban population. Detailed figures of the recensus are given in the Report Volume. The town population for previous years has been adjusted as far as possible.

TABLE IV.—Towns Classified by

Serial No.	TOWN.	DISTRICT OR STATE.	Town, Municipality or Cantonment.	POPULATION. 1911.	1901.	1891.	1881.	1872.
	1	2	3	4	5	6	7	8
		Central Provinces and Berar ...		**1.213.049**	**1.307.072**	**1.200.787**	**1.089.219**	**867.166**
		British Districts and Berar ...		**1.176.225**	**1.273.759**	**1.171.968**	**1.063.062**	**854.794**
								Class I.—
1	Nagpur ...	Nagpur ...	Municipality ...	101,415	127,734	117,014	98,299	84,441
2	Jubbulpore ...	Jubbulpore ...	Do. and Cantonment.	100,651	90,533	84,082	76,023	55,469
								Class II.—
								Class III.—
3	Saugor ...	Saugor ...	Do. do. ...	45,908	42,330	44,674	44,416	45,655
4	Raipur ...	Raipur ...	Municipality ...	35 335	32,114	23,759	24,948	15,116
5	Amraoti ...	Amraoti ...	Do. ...	34,270	34,216	28,946	23,550	23,410
6	Akola ...	Akola ...	Do. ..	25,826	20,289	21,470	16,614	14,606
7	Burhanpur ...	Nimar ...	Do. ...	22,777	33,341	32,252	30 017	20,303
8	Khandwa ...	Do. ...	Do. ...	21,604	19,401	15,589	15,142	14,119
								Class IV.—
9	Chanda ...	Chanda ...	Do. ...	19.866	17,803	16,175	16,137	16.233
10	Bilaspur ...	Bilaspur ..	Do. ...	19.850	18,937	11,122	7,775	4,898
11	Umrer ...	Nagpur ...	Do. ..	17,630	15,043	15,180	14,747	11,394
12	Kamptee ...	Do. ...	Cantonment ...	17,155	38,888	43,159	50,987	48,831
13	Damoh ...	Damoh ...	Municipality ...	17,042	13,355	11,753	8.665	8,189
14	Murwara ...	Jubbulpore ...	Do. ...	15,812	14,137	9.460	8.612	2.885
15	Hinganghat ...	Wardha ...	Do. ...	14,943	12.062	10,934	9,000	9,415
16	Ellichpur ...	Amraoti ...	Do. ...	13,909	26,082	26,637	26.728	27,782
17	Seoni ...	Seoni ...	Do. ...	13,839	11,864	11.976	10,263	9.557
18	Yeotmal ...	Yeotmal ...	Do. ...	13,525	10,545	6,464	4,445	...
19	Chhindwara ...	Chhindwara ...	Do. ...	12,872	9.736	8,973	8,220	8,626
20	Karanja ...	Akola ...	Do. ...	12,617	16,535	14,436	10,923	11,750
21	Akot ...	Do. ...	Do. ...	12,593	18,252	15,995	16,137	14,006
22	Malkapur ...	Buldana ...	Do. ...	12,391	13,112	9,222	8,152	7,988
23	Shegaon ...	Do. ...	Do. ...	11,962	15,057	11,422	11,079	7,450
24	Arvi ...	Wardha ...	Do. ...	11,902	10,676	8,615	8,072	6,732
25	Badnera ...	Amraoti ...	Town ...	11,008	10,859	9,016	6,460	6,876
26	Narsinghpur ...	Narsinghpur ...	Municipality ...	10,630	11,233	10,220	10,222	7,554
27	Wardha ...	Wardha ...	Do. ..	10,541	9,872	8,322	5,816	3,562
28	Dhamtari ...	Raipur ...	Do. ...	10,460	9,151	6,726	6,647	6,023
29	Pauni ...	Bhandara ...	Do. ...	10,222	9,366	9,869	9.773	8,973
30	Khamgaon ...	Buldana ...	Do. ...	10,123	18,341	15,598	12,300	8,472
								Class V.—
31	Ramtek ...	Nagpur ...	Do. ...	9,806	8,732	7,584	7,814	7,045
32	Mandla ...	Mandla ...	Do. ...	9,379	5,428	5,057	4,732	4,636
33	Basim ...	Akola ...	Do. ...	9,068	13,823	12,389	11,576	8,625
34	Etawa ...	Saugor ...	Town ...	8,968	6,418	3,982	2,177	2,015
35	Anjangaon ...	Amraoti ...	Do. ...	8,628	8,783	10,598	9,842	11,389
36	Harda ...	Hoshangabad ...	Municipality ...	8,341	16.300	13,556	11,203	9,170
37	Khapa ...	Nagpur ...	Do. ...	8,233	7,615	9.383	8,465	8,007
38	Garhakota ...	Saugor ...	Town ...	8,180	8,508	9,525	11,414	9,085

Population with variation since 1872.

Variation. Increase + Decrease (—) 1901—1911	1891—1901	1881—1891	1872—1881	Variation in period 1872—1911 Increase (+) Decrease (—)	Males. 1911.	1901.	1891.	Females. 1911.	1901.	1891.	Serial No.
9	10	11	12	13	14	15	16	17	18	19	
−94,023	+106,285	+111,568	+222,053	+345,883	628,375	667,403	620,043	584,874	639,669	580,744	
−90,512	+101,791	+108,906	+208,268	+321,431	610,417	651,120	605,175	565,804	622,639	566,793	
100,000 and over.											
− 26,319	+ 10,720	+ 18,715	+ 13,858	+ 16,974	53,698	66,255	60,640	47,719	61,479	56,374	1
+ 10,118	+ 5,851	+ 8,659	+ 20,551	+ 45,182	56,035	46,989	45,045	44,610	43,544	39,637	2
50,000 to 100,000.											
None.											
20,000 to 50,000.											
+ 3,578	− 2,344	+ 258	− 1,229	+ 253	24,330	21,981	23,725	21,578	20,349	20,949	3
+ 3,221	+ 8,355	− 1,189	+ 5,832	+ 16,219	18,088	16,573	11,983	17,297	15,541	11,770	4
+ 54	+ 5,270	+ 5,30[illegible]	+ 140	+ 10,86[illegible]	18,147	18,295	15,833	16,123	15,921	13,113	5
− 3,463	+ 7,819	+ 4,850	+ 2,008	+ 11,220	14,006	16,038	11,814	11,320	13,251	9,656	6
− 10,564	+ 1,089	+ 2,235	+ 714	− 6,526	11,624	16,792	16,532	11,153	16,549	15,720	7
+ 2,203	+ 3,81[illegible]	+ 447	+ 1,023	+ 7,485	11,511	10,388	8,302	10,098	9,013	7,287	8
10,000 to 20,000.											
+ 2,063	+ 1,628	+ 38	− 96	+ 3,633	10,077	8,842	7,837	9,789	8,961	8,338	9
+ 913	+ 7,815	+ 3,347	+ 2,877	+ 14,952	9,983	9,705	5,753	9,867	9,232	5,369	10
+ 1,687	+ 762	+ 933	+ 2,853	+ 6,236	8,600	7,858	7,388	9,030	8,085	7,792	11
− 21,733	− 4,271	− 7,828	+ 2,156	− 31,676	9,348	19,879	22,660	7,807	19,009	20,409	12
+ 3,687	+ 1,602	+ 3,18[illegible]	+ 476	+ 8,853	8,732	6,746	6,002	8,310	6,609	5,751	13
+ 1,675	+ 4,677	+ 848	+ 5,727	+ 12,927	8,173	7,350	5,165	7,039	6,787	4,292	14
+ 2,281	+ 1,698	+ 1,964	− 415	+ 5,528	7,690	6,486	5,044	7,253	6,176	5,320	15
− 12,173	− 555	− 91	− 1,054	− 13,873	7,027	12,914	13,389	6,882	13,168	13,248	16
+ 1,975	− 112	+ 1,773	+ 646	+ 4,282	6,740	5,693	6,037	7,009	6,171	5,939	17
+ 2,980	+ 4,081	+ 2,010	...	...	7,249	5,547	3,548	6,276	4,998	2,016	18
+ 3,136	+ 763	+ 753	− 406	+ 4,246	6,503	4,711	4,355	6,369	5,025	4,618	19
− 3,888	+ 2,099	+ 3,513	− 827	+ 897	6,556	8,567	7,612	6,091	7,968	6,824	20
− 5,669	+ 2,257	− 142	+ 2,131	− 1,423	6,523	9,315	8,417	6,060	8,937	7,578	21
− 721	+ 3,890	+ 1,070	+ 184	+ 4,403	6,463	6,762	4,773	5,928	6,350	4,449	22
− 3,095	+ 3,635	+ 343	+ 3,629	+ 4,512	6,290	7,815	6,036	5,672	7,242	5,386	23
+ 1,226	+ 2,061	+ 543	+ 1,340	+ 5,170	6,134	5,681	4,562	5,768	4,995	4,053	24
+ 239	+ 945	+ 3,456	− 416	+ 4,222	5,898	5,648	5,360	5,200	5,211	4,656	25
− 603	+ 1,013	− 2	+ 2,668	+ 3,076	5,407	5,645	5,052	5,223	5,588	5,169	26
+ 669	+ 1,550	+ 2,506	+ 2,254	+ 6,979	5,719	5,105	4,583	4,822	4,767	3,739	27
+ 1,309	+ 2,425	+ 79	+ 624	+ 4,437	5,170	4,340	3,151	5,290	4,811	3,575	28
+ 856	− 503	+ 96	+ 800	+ 1,249	5,037	4,568	4,859	5,185	4,798	5,010	29
− 8,218	+ 2,748	+ 3,208	+ 3,918	+ 1,651	5,545	9,470	8,769	4,578	8,871	6,829	30
5,000 to 10,000.											
+ 1,074	+ 1,148	− 230	+ 769	+ 2,761	4,840	4,394	3,630	4,966	4,338	3,954	31
+ 3,951	+ 371	+ 325	+ 96	+ 4,743	4,640	2,756	2,547	4,730	2,672	2,510	32
− 4,755	+ 1,434	+ 813	+ 2,951	+ 448	4,562	7,072	6,434	4,506	6,751	5,956	33
+ 2,550	+ 2,436	+ 1,805	+ 162	+ 6,953	4,897	3,626	2,250	4,071	2,792	1,732	34
− 155	− 1,810	+ 751	− 1,547	− 2,761	4,394	4,434	5,431	4,234	4,349	5,102	35
− 7,959	+ 2,744	+ 2,353	+ 2,033	− 829	4,303	8,468	7,232	4,038	7,832	6,324	36
+ 618	− 1,708	+ 918	+ 458	+ 226	4,140	3,781	4,738	4,093	3,834	4,645	37
− 828	− 1,017	− 1,889	+ 2,329	− 905	4,590	4,671	4,924	3,590	3,837	4,001	38

TABLE IV.—Towns Classified by

Serial No.	TOWN.	DISTRICT or STATE.	Town, Municipality or Cantonment.	POPULATION. 1911.	1901.	1891.	1881	1872.
	1	2	3	4	5	6	7	8
								Class V.—
39	Jalgaon ...	Buldana ...	Town ...	7,552	8,487	9,307	10,392	8,763
40	Badnur ...	Betul ...	Municipality ...	7,454	5,566	5,014	2,881	2,881
41	Bhandara ...	Bhandara ...	Do. ...	7,414	14,023	13,348	11,150	11,433
42	Balaghat ...	Balaghat ...	Do. ...	7,400	6,223	5,138	4,136	...
43	Sohagpur ...	Hoshangabad ...	Do. ...	7,239	7,420	7,306	7,027	7,552
44	Warud ...	Amraoti ...	Town ...	7,089	7,179	7,291	6,607	7,065
45	Pandhurna ...	Chhindwara ...	Municipality ...	7,058	8,904	8,172	7,469	5,218
46	Drug ...	Drug ...	Town ...	7,048	4,002	4,151	3,797	...
47	Shendurjana ...	Amraoti ...	Do. ...	6,948	6,860	10,043	8,501	8,680
48	Khurai ...	Saugor ...	Municipality ...	6,868	6,012	6,272	5,370	4,965
49	Pusad ...	Yeotmal ...	Town ...	6,862	6,742	5,144	5,047	3,497
50	Nandura ...	Buldana ...	Do. ...	6,794	6,669	6,471	6,743	6,035
51	Talegaon Dashasahasra	Amraoti ...	Do. ...	6,692	6,220	6,440	5,506	4,198
52	Saoner ...	Nagpur ...	Municipality ...	6,636	5,821	5,555	5,023	5,295
53	Seoni-Malwa ...	Hoshangabad ...	Do. ...	6,568	7,531	6,779	6,998	7,579
54	Digras ...	Yeotmal ...	Town ...	6,479	6,084	5,081	4,235	...
55	Hiwarkhed ...	Akola ...	Do. ...	6,404	6,143	6,520	7,300	6,648
56	Amraoti Camp ...	Amraoti ...	Municipality ...	6,340	5,295	4,709	...	...
57	Morsi ...	Do. ...	Town ...	6,336	8,313	7,104	5,592	5,332
58	Wun ...	Yeotmal ...	Do. ...	6,282	6,109	4,856	4,206	...
59	Katol ...	Nagpur ...	Do. ...	6,260	7,313	4,560	4,137	...
60	Ashti ...	Wardha ...	Town ...	6,257	5,237	5,898	5,245	4,262
61	Narkher ...	Nagpur ...	Do. ...	6,203	7,726	8,256	7,061	7,159
62	Warora ...	Chanda ...	Municipality ...	6,174	10,626	10,018	8,042	3,584
63	Mangrul Pir ...	Akola ...	Town ...	6,072	5,793	5,241	4,900	—
64	Shirasgaon ...	Amraoti ...	Do. ...	6,039	6,537	5,776	5,408	5,599
65	Dewalgaon Raja ...	Buldana ...	Do. ...	6,026	6,293	7,382	7,025	9,298
66	Sindi ...	Wardha ...	Do. ...	5,981	4,533	5,463	4,644	...
67	Balapur ...	Akola ...	Do. ...	5,953	10,486	10,250	11,244	12,631
68	Ner Pinglai ...	Amraoti ...	Do. ...	5,935	5,408	6,848	6,644	5,419
69	Mungeli ...	Bilaspur ...	Do. ...	5,881	5,907	4,755	4,757	4,392
70	Gondia ...	Bhandara ...	Do ...	5,847	4,457	2,770	...	...
71	Umarkhed ...	Yeotmal ...	Do. ...	5,822	4,570	6,414	5,959	5,753
72	Arang ...	Raipur ...	Do. ...	5,820	6,499	5,250	4,608	3,868
73	Kelod ...	Nagpur ...	Do. ...	5,785	5,141	5,200	4,481	...
74	Deori ...	Saugor ...	Municipality ...	5,739	4,980	6,306	7,414	3,994
75	Barsi Takli ...	Akola ...	Town ...	5,696	6,288	5,046	5,377	5,336
76	Karasgaon ...	Amraoti ...	Do. ...	5,581	7,456	6,846	7,330	7,369
77	Deoli ...	Wardha ...	Municipality ...	5,575	5,008	5,450	5,126	5,558
78	Kalmeshwar ...	Nagpur ...	Do. ...	5,575	5,340	5,921	5,318	4,738
79	Hoshangabad ...	Hoshangabad ...	Do. ...	5,503	14,940	13,495	15,863	11,613

Population with variation since 1872.

VARIATION. Increase (+) Decrease (—)				Variation in period 1872—1911 Increase (+) Decrease (—)	MALES.			FEMALES.			Serial No.
1901—1911	1891—1901	1881—1891	1872—1881		1911.	1901.	1891.	1911.	1901.	1891.	
9	10	11	12	13	14	15	16	17	18	19	
5,000 to 10,000—(contd.)											
— 935	— 820	— 1,085	+ 1,620	— 1,211	3,851	4,217	4,705	3,701	4,270	4,602	39
+ 1,888	+ 552	+ 2,133	...	+ 4,573	3,839	2,790	2,597	3,615	2,776	2,417	40
— 6,609	+ 675	+ 2,198	— 283	— 4,019	3,787	6,840	6,593	3,627	7,183	6,755	41
+ 1,177	+ 1,085	+ 1,002	...	...	3,665	3,057	2,589	3,735	3,166	2,549	42
— 181	+ 114	+ 279	— 525	— 313	3,513	3,625	3,700	3,726	3,795	3,606	43
— 90	— 112	+ 684	458	+ 24	3,634	3,582	3,709	3,455	3,597	3,582	44
— 1,846	+ 732	+ 703	+ 2,251	+ 1,840	3,507	4,354	4,000	3,551	4,550	4,172	45
+ 3,046	— 149	+ 354	...	...	3,589	1,889	2,001	3,459	2,113	2,150	46
+ 88	— 3,183	+ 1,542	— 179	— 1,732	3,522	3,452	5,090	3,426	3,408	4,953	47
+ 856	— 260	+ 902	+ 405	+ 1,903	3,437	3,027	3,170	3,431	2,985	3,102	48
+ 120	+ 1,598	+ 97	+ 1,550	+ 3,365	3,448	3,441	2,627	3,414	3,301	2,517	49
+ 125	+ 198	— 272	+ 708	+ 759	3,464	3,430	3,254	3,330	3,239	3,217	50
+ 472	— 220	+ 934	+ 1,308	+ 2,494	3,355	3,109	3,284	3,337	3,111	3,156	51
+ 815	+ 206	+ 532	— 212	+ 1,341	3,425	2,966	2,787	3,211	2,855	2,768	52
— 963	+ 752	— 219	— 581	— 1,011	3,396	3,835	3,383	3,172	3,696	3,396	53
+ 445	+ 952	+ 846	...	...	3,355	3,077	2,677	3,124	2,957	2,404	54
+ 261	— 377	— 780	+ 652	— 244	3,209	2,995	3,226	3,195	3,148	3,294	55
+ 1,045	+ 586	...	...	...	3,334	2,928	2,671	3,006	2,372	2,038	56
— 1,977	+ 1,209	+ 1,512	+ 260	+ 1,004	3,229	4,238	3,653	3,107	4,075	3,451	57
+ 173	+ 1,253	+ 650	...	...	3,273	3,506	2,297	3,009	2,603	2,559	58
— 1,044	+ 2,753	+ 423	...	...	3,252	3,556	2,284	3,017	3,757	2,276	59
+ 1,020	— 661	+ 653	+ 983	+ 1,995	3,144	2,664	2,939	3,113	2,573	2,959	60
— 1,523	— 530	+ 1,195	— 98	— 956	3,065	3,689	4,078	3,138	4,037	4,178	61
— 4,452	+ 608	+ 1,996	+ 4,438	+ 2,590	3,196	5,599	5,650	2,978	5,027	4,368	62
+ 279	+ 552	+ 341	...	...	3,074	2,948	2,646	2,998	2,845	2,595	63
— 498	+ 761	+ 368	— 191	+ 440	3,048	3,322	2,835	2,991	3,215	2,941	64
— 267	— 1,089	+ 357	— 2,273	— 3,272	3,012	3,144	3,649	3,014	3,149	3,733	65
+ 1,448	— 930	+ 819	...	...	2,950	2,297	2,766	3,031	2,236	2,697	66
— 4,533	+ 236	— 994	— 1,387	— 6,678	2,939	5,165	4,970	3,014	5,321	5,280	67
+ 527	— 1,440	+ 204	+ 1,225	+ 516	3,046	2,772	3,607	2,889	2,636	3,241	68
— 26	+ 1,152	— 2	+ 365	+ 1,489	2,839	2,823	2,282	3,042	3,084	2,473	69
+ 1,390	+ 1,687	...	...	...	3,115	2,354	1,367	2,732	2,103	1,403	70
+ 1,252	— 1,844	+ 455	+ 206	+ 69	2,908	2,274	3,231	2,914	2,296	3,183	71
— 679	+ 1,249	+ 642	+ 740	+ 1,952	2,831	3,076	2,406	2,989	3,423	2,754	72
+ 644	— 59	+ 719	...	...	2,945	2,632	2,654	2,840	2,509	2,546	73
+ 759	— 1,326	— 1,108	+ 3,420	+ 1,745	2,882	2,408	3,179	2,857	2,572	3,127	74
— 592	+ 1,242	— 331	+ 41	+ 360	2,889	3,097	2,553	2,807	3,191	2,493	75
— 1,875	+ 610	— 484	— 39	— 1,788	2,808	3,789	3,397	2,773	3,667	3,449	76
+ 567	— 442	+ 324	— 432	+ 17	2,808	2,455	2,722	2,767	2,553	2,728	77
+ 235	— 581	+ 603	+ 580	+ 837	2,868	2,673	2,917	2,707	2,667	3,004	78
— 9,437	+ 1,445	— 2,368	+ 4,250	— 6,110	2,993	7,578	7,076	2,510	7,362	6,419	79

TABLE IV.—Towns Classified by

Serial No.	TOWN.	DISTRICT OR STATE.	Town, Municipality or Cantonment.	POPULATION. 1911.	1901.	1891.	1881.	1872.
	1	2	3	4	5	6	7	8
								Class V.—
80	Kholapur ...	Amraoti ...	Town ..	5,501	5,373	5,725	6,452	6,169
81	Patur ...	Akola ...	Do. ...	5,500	5,990	6,156	7,219	6,011
82	Ratanpur ...	Bilaspur ...	Do. ...	5,499	5,479	6,389	5,615	5,111
83	Mohpa ...	Nagpur ...	Do. ...	5,477	5,336	5,638	5,515	5,572
84	Betul ...	Betul ...	Do. ...	5,473	4,789	5,260	4,693	4,593
85	Pulgaon ...	Wardha ...	Municipality ...	5,466	4,710	1,979	...	...
86	Sausar ...	Chhindwara ...	Do. ...	5,442	4,785	4,707	4,311	...
87	Sihora ...	Jubbulpore ...	Do. ...	5,432	5,595	5,798	5,736	3,988
88	Brahmpuri ...	Chanda ...	Town ...	5,359	4,328	4,685	4,818	...
89	Pusla ...	Amraoti ...	Do. ...	5,261	4,837	5,687	...	...
90	Mohgaon ...	Chhindwara ...	Do. ...	5,225	5,730	5,565	5,180	4,921
91	Chimur ...	Chanda ...	Do. ...	5,218	4,085	5,096	4,846	...
92	Mangrul Dastgir ...	Amraoti ...	Do. ...	5,139	6,588	6,221	6,122	5,381
93	Murtizapur ...	Akola ...	Do. ...	5,101	6,156	4,438	4,887	...
94	Nawargaon ...	Chanda ...	Do. ...	5,087	4,100	5,086	4,304	...
								Class VI.—
95	Wadegaon ...	Akola ...	Do. ...	4,890	5,825	5,872	6,096	5,431
96	Dattapur ...	Amraoti ...	Do. ...	4,776	5,187	3,225	1,090	...
97	Chikhli ...	Buldana ...	Do. ...	4,731	5,889	4,672	4,396	...
98	Mowar ...	Nagpur ...	Municipality ...	4,719	4,799	4,581	4,054	...
99	Gadarwara ...	Narsinghpur ...	Do. ...	4,715	8,198	8,815	8,100	6,068
100	Chandur Railway ...	Amraoti ...	Town ...	4,508	5,700	4,794	3,578	...
101	Itarsi ...	Hoshangabad ...	Do. ...	4,430	5,769	3,090	2,138	1,701
102	Mehkar ...	Buldana ...	Do. ...	4,423	5,330	5,102	4,374	...
103	Tumsar ...	Bhandara ...	Municipality ...	4,378	8,116	7,566	7,388	7,367
104	Balgaon Jagir ...	Amraoti ...	Town ...	4,045	5,284	5,939	4,905	...
105	Paratwara ...	Do. ...	Municipality ...	4,001	10,410	9,603	9,445	11.269
106	Darwha ...	Yeotmal ...	Town ...	3,910	5,168	4,972	4,052	–
107	Chandur Bazar ...	Amraoti ...	Do. ...	3,850	5,208	4,974	4,816	...
108	Pachmarhi ...	Hoshangabad ...	Municipality and Cantonment.	3,822	3,020	1,823	2,054	...
109	Buldana ...	Buldana ...	Municipality ...	3,820	4,137	3,243	2,979	...
110	Panagar ...	Jubbulpore ...	Town ...	3,630	4,082	4,457	4,915	...
111	Telhara ...	Akola ...	Do. ...	3,406	2,528	2,291	...	...
112	Chhindwara ...	Narsinghpur ...	Municipality ...	3,404	4,216	3,814	3,519	2,211
		Feudatory States	...	**36,824**	**33,313**	**28,819**	**26,157**	**12,372**
								Class IV.—
113	Rajnandgaon ...	Nandgaon State ...	Town ...	11,979	11,094	8,850	5,849	2,949
								Class V.—
114	Raigarh ...	Raigarh State ...	Do. ...	8,041	6,764	4,552	4,860	1,916
115	Dongargarh ...	Khairagarh State ...	Do. ...	6,249	5,856	5,675	5,543	917
116	Sarangarh ...	Sarangarh State ...	Do. ...	5,375	5,227	4,393	4,220	...
117	Kawardha ...	Kawardha State ...	Do. ...	5,180	4,872	5,349	5,685	6,590

Population with variation since 1872.

VARIATION. Increase (+) Decrease (—) 1901—1911	1891—1901	1881—1891	1872—1881	Variation in period 1872—1911 Increase (+) Decrease (—).	MALES. 1911.	1901.	1891.	FEMALES. 1911.	1901.	1891.	Serial No.
9	10	11	12	13	14	15	16	17	18	19	
5 000 to 10 000—(concld.)											
+ 128	— 352	— 727	+ 283	— 668	2,790	2,814	2,837	2,702	2,559	2,888	80
490	— 166	— 1,063	+ 1,208	— 511	2,818	3,072	3,108	2,682	2,918	3,048	81
+ 20	— 910	+ 774	+ 504	+ 388	2,544	2,456	3,006	2,955	3,023	3,383	82
+ 141	- 302	+ 123	- 57	— 95	2,702	2,511	2,772	2,775	2,825	2,866	83
+ 734	— 521	+ 567	+ 100	+ 580	2,622	2,189	2,514	2,851	2,550	2,746	84
+ 756	+ 2,731	...	...	...	2,870	2,611	1,002	2,596	2,099	977	85
+ 657	+ 78	+ 396	...	...	2,729	2,325	2,340	2,713	2,460	2,367	86
— 163	— 203	+ 63	+ 1,748	+ 1,444	2,620	2,661	2,948	2,812	2,934	2,850	87
+ 1,031	— 557	+ 67	...	...	2,585	2,058	2,429	2,774	2,270	2,456	88
+ 424	— 850	...	...	...	2,093	2,413	2,872	2,598	2,424	2,815	89
— 505	+ 165	+ 385	+ 259	+ 304	2,592	2,717	2,687	2,633	3,013	2,878	90
+ 1,133	— 1,011	+ 260	...	...	2,520	1,984	2,577	2,698	2,101	2,519	91
— 1,449	+ 367	+ 99	+ 741	— 242	2,635	3,426	3,212	2,504	3,182	3,009	92
— 1,055	+ 1,718	— 449	...	...	2,988	3,414	2,391	2,113	2,742	2,047	93
+ 987	— 986	+ 782	...	...	2,435	1,968	2,072	2,652	2,132	2,514	94
Under 5,000.											
— 935	— 47	— 224	+ 665	— 541	2,639	2,821	2,922	2,358	3,004	2,950	95
— 411	+ 1,962	+ 2,135	...	...	2,631	2,789	1,904	2,145	2,398	1,321	96
— 1,158	+ 1,217	+ 276	...	...	2,406	3,029	2,426	2,325	2,860	3,246	97
— 80	+ 218	+ 527	...	...	2,307	2,374	2,282	2,412	2,425	2,299	98
— 3,483	— 617	+ 715	+ 2,032	— 1,353	2,350	4,068	4,603	2,365	4,130	4,212	99
— 1,192	+ 906	+ 1,216	...	...	2,392	2,986	2,557	2,116	2,714	2,237	100
— 1,339	+ 2,679	+ 952	+ 437	+ 2,729	2,506	3,203	1,762	1,924	2,466	1,328	101
— 907	+ 228	+ 728	...	...	2,279	2,706	2,598	2,144	2,624	2,504	102
— 3,738	+ 550	+ 178	+ 21	— 2,989	2,123	3,885	3,664	2,255	4,231	3,902	103
— 1,239	— 655	+ 1,[illegible]54	...	...	2,129	2,711	3,168	1,916	2,573	2,771	104
— 6,409	+ 807	+ 158	— 1,824	— 7,268	2,136	5,654	5,852	1,865	4,756	4,251	105
— 1,268	+ 196	+ 920	...	...	2,007	2,645	2,593	1,903	2,523	2,379	106
— 1,358	+ 234	+ 158	...	...	1,998	2,638	2,505	1,852	2,570	2,469	107
+ 802	+ 1,197	— 231	...	...	2,162	1,598	1,037	1,660	1,422	786	108
— 317	+ 894	+ 264	...	...	2,037	2,225	1,700	1,783	1,[illegible]2	1,453	109
— 453	— 375	— 458	...	...	1,738	1,851	2,265	1,897	2,[illegible]	[illegible],192	110
+ 878	+ 237	...	...	...	1,819	1,379	1,327	1,587	1,149	964	111
— 812	+ 402	+ 295	+ 1,308	+ 1,193	1,687	2,131	1,927	1,717	2,085	1,887	112
+ 3,511	+4,494	+2,662	+13,785	+24,452	17,958	16,283	14,868	18,866	17,030	13,951	
10,000 to 20,000.											
+ 885	+ 2,244	+ 3,001	+ 2,900	+ 9,030	6,041	5,447	5,072	5,938	5,647	3,778	113
5,000 to 10,000.											
+ 1,277	+ 2,212	— 308	+ 2,944	+ 6,125	3,986	3,396	2,308	4,055	3,868	2,244	114
+ 393	+ 181	+ 132	+ 4,626	+ 5,332	2,965	2,794	2,879	3,284	3,062	2,7[illegible]6	115
+ 148	+ 834	+ 173	...	...	2,625	2,590	2,133	2,75[illegible]	2,637	2,260	116
+ 808	- 977	- 336	— 905	— 1,410	2,341	2,056	2,476	2,839	2,316	2,873	117

TABLE V.

Towns arranged territorially with population by Religion.

In this table the column "Others" includes the following:—

Serial No. in the Table.	Town.	Hindu (Arya).			Hindu (Brahmo).			Sikh.			Buddhist.			Zoroastrian.			Jew.		
		P.	M.	F.	P.	M.	F.	P.	M.	F.	P.	M.	F.	P.	M.	F.	P.	M.	F.
1	Saugor	93	45	48	2	2	...	624	560	64	...	...	...	3	3	...	4	3	1
5	Etawa	4	4	...	...	...	...	3	3	...	...	...	...	82	50	32	5	5	...
6	Damoh	...	...	...	...	...	...	19	12	7	...	...	...	12	9	3	...	...	...
7	Jubbulpore	113	72	41	7	3	4	602	538	64	2	2	...	116	65	51	8	7	1
9	Murwara	27	13	14	...	...	...	7	5	2	...	...	...	11	5	6	1	1	...
10	Sihora	...	...	...	...	...	...	...	...	...	...	...	...	6	4	2	...	...	...
11	Mandla	1	1	...	...	...	...	7	4	3	...	...	...	...	...	...	...	...	...
12	Seoni	23	13	10	...	...	...	...	...	...	7	2	5	8	3	5	...	...	...
15	Narsinghpur	70	48	22	...	...	...	...	...	...	...	...	...	...	...	...	...	...	...
16	Hoshangabad	...	...	...	...	...	...	...	...	...	...	...	...	3	3	...	...	...	...
17	Itarsi	...	...	...	...	...	...	...	...	...	...	...	...	3	3	...	...	...	...
18	Harda	5	2	3	...	...	...	...	...	...	...	...	...	71	41	30	4	2	2
19	Sohagpur	17	7	10	...	...	...	...	...	...	...	...	...	3	3	...	...	...	...
20	Pachmarhi	...	...	...	...	...	...	28	24	4	...	...	...	...	...	...	3	1	2
21	Seoni-Malwa	14	9	5	...	...	...	6	5	1	...	...	...	...	...	...	...	...	...
22	Khandwa	3	2	1	...	...	...	...	...	...	1	1	...	80	47	33	19	7	12
23	Burhanpur	...	...	...	...	...	...	...	...	...	...	...	...	6	5	1	...	...	...
24	Badnur	6	6	...	...	...	...	12	8	4	...	...	...	3	3	...	...	...	...
26	Chhindwara	11	7	4	...	...	...	2	2	...	...	...	...	...	...	...	...	...	...
30	Wardha	...	...	...	5	...	5	12	7	5	...	...	...	36	24	12	...	...	...
31	Arvi	...	...	...	1	1	...	...	...	...	...	...	...	...	...	...	...	...	...
33	Ashti	...	...	...	...	...	...	2	2	...	...	...	...	...	...	...	...	...	...
36	Pulgaon	...	...	...	...	...	...	...	...	...	...	...	...	4	...	4	...	...	...
37	Nagpur	...	...	...	...	...		143	94	49	2	2	...	547	321	226	44	23	21
39	Kamptee	...	...	...	...	...	...	1	...	1	...	...	...	15	11	4	5	5	...
40	Ramtek	...	...	...	...	...	...	2	2	...	...	...	...	...	...	...	...	...	...
43	Katol	...	...	...	...	...	...	...	...	...	...	...	...	1	1	...	...	...	...
44	Narkher	...	...	...	...	...	...	...	...	...	...	...	...	1	1	...	...	...	...
49	Chanda	...	...	...	1	1	...	3	3	...	...	...	...	10	4	6	...	...	...
50	Warora	...	...	...	...	...	...	5	5	...	...	...	...	1	1	...	...	...	...
54	Bhandara	12	6	6	...	...	...	...	...	...	...	...	...	5	4	1	...	...	...
56	Gondia	3	2	1	...	...	...	6	6	...	...	...	...	2	2	...	...	...	...
58	Balaghat	...	...	...	...	...	...	7	2	5	...	...	...	3	1	2	...	...	...
59	Raipur	9	6	3	...	...	...	21	8	13	...	...	...	44	27	17	...	...	...
61	Dhamtari	1	1	...	...	...	...	3	2	1	...	...	...	1	1	...	...	...	...
62	Bilaspur	55	33	22	6	2	4	3	3	...	...	...	...	4	4	...	...	...	...
64	Mungeli	13	6	7	...	...	...	...	...	...	...	...	...	...	...	...	...	...	...
65	Drug	16	9	7	...	...	...	...	...	...	...	...	...	...	...	...	...	...	...
66	Amraoti	...	...	...	...	...	...	7	7	...	...	...	...	26	14	12	12	9	3
67	Amraoti Camp	...	...	...	...	...	...	2	2	...	...	...	...	18	7	11	...	...	...
69	Badnera	...	...	...	...	...	...	...	...	...	...	...	...	210	125	85	...	...	...
76	Ner Pinglai	...	...	...	...	...	...	...	...	...	...	...	...	1	...	1	...	...	...
79	Pusla	...	...	...	...	...	...	2	2	...	...	...	...	...	...	...	...	...	...
82	Dattapur	...	...	...	...	...	...	...	...	...	...	...	...	4	4	...	9	6	3
83	Chandur Railway	...	...	...	...	...	...	6	5	1	...	...	...	...	...	...	4	4	...
84	Paratwara	...	...	...	...	...	...	...	...	...	...	...	...	3	3	...	...	...	...
85	Chandur Bazar	...	...	...	...	...	...	...	...	...	...	...	...	3	3	...	...	...	...
86	Akola	7	4	3	...	...	...	...	...	...	...	...	...	94	65	29	...	...	...
87	Karanja	...	...	...	...	...	...	...	...	...	...	...	...	8	8	...	...	...	...
88	Akot	...	...	...	1	1	...	55	25	30	...	...	...	5	5	...	3	3	...
89	Basim	...	...	...	...	...	...	...	...	...	...	...	...	5	3	2	...	...	...
92	Balapur	...	...	...	...	...	...	...	...	...	...	...	...	6	5	1	...	...	...
94	Patur	1	1	...	...	...	...	...	...	...	...	...	...	...	...	...	...	...	...
95	Murtizapur	8	6	2	...	...	...	...	...	...	...	...	...	14	8	6	...	...	...
96	Buldana	...	...	...	...	...	...	...	...	...	...	...	...	2	2	...	...	...	...
100	Shegaon	...	...	...	...	...	...	...	...	...	...	...	...	24	19	5	...	...	...
101	Khamgaon	...	...	...	...	...	...	...	...	...	...	...	...	30	15	15	...	...	...
102	Jalgaon	...	...	...	...	...	...	...	...	...	...	...	...	2	1	1	...	...	...
103	Nandura	...	...	...	...	...	...	...	...	...	...	...	...	6	3	3	...	...	...
105	Chikhli	...	...	...	...	...	...	...	...	...	...	...	...	1	...	1	...	...	...
106	Mehkar	...	...	...	...	...	...	21	10	11	...	...	...	...	...	...	...	...	...
107	Yeotmal	...	...	...	...	...	...	8	7	1	...	...	...	4	4	...	...	...	...
111	Umerkhed	...	...	...	...	...	...	3	1	2	...	...	...	...	...	...	...	...	...
112	Darwha	...	...	...	...	...	...	...	...	...	...	...	...	1	1	...	...	...	...
113	Rajnandgaon	...	...	...	...	...	...	...	...	...	...	...	...	17	10	7	...	...	...
114	Dongargarh...	...	...	...	...	...	...	7	5	2	2	2	...	5	5	...	...	...	...
115	Kawardha	...	...	...	...	...	...	5	5	...	...	...	...	...	...	...	...	...	...
116	Raigarh	...	...	...	...	...	...	3	1	2	...	...	...	...	...	...	...	...	...

TABLE V.—Towns arranged territorially

	DISTRICT OR STATE.	Town, Municipality or Cantonment.	POPULATION.			INDO-ARYAN.					
						HINDU (BRAHMANIC).			JAIN.		
			Persons.	Males.	Females.	Persons.	Males	Females.	Persons.	Males.	Females.
	1	2	3	4	5	6	7	8	9	10	11
											BRITISH
	Central Provinces and Berar ...		1,213,049	628,375	584,674	938,786	483,612	455,174	18,390	9,600	8,790
	C. P. British Districts and Berar ...		1,176,225	610,417	565,808	907,722	468,472	439,250	17,928	9,330	8,598
	C. P. British Districts ...		806,431	418,090	388,341	629,283	323,283	306,000	12,370	6,463	5,907
	JUBBULPORE DIVISION ...		*241,448*	*128,809*	*112,639*	*174,818*	*91,853*	*83,965*	*6,379*	*3,295*	*3,084*
1	Saugor ...	Saugor M & C ...	45,908	24,330	21,578	33,793	17,077	16,116	1,244	668	576
2		Deori M ...	5,739	2,882	2,857	4,581	2,292	2,289	357	189	168
3		Garhakota T ...	8,180	4,590	3,590	6,375	3,508	2,867	372	200	172
4		Khurai M ...	6,868	3,437	3,431	4,981	2,472	2,509	597	291	306
5		Etawa T ...	8,968	4,897	4,071	6,329	3,459	2,870	599	324	275
6	Damoh ...	Damoh M ...	17,042	8,732	8,310	13,034	6,606	6,428	662	327	335
7	Jubbulpore ...	Jubbulpore M & C ...	100,651	56,035	44,616	68,902	37,334	31,568	1,364	720	644
8		Panagar T ...	3,630	1,733	1,897	2,910	1,408	1,502	227	98	129
9		Murwara M ...	15,812	8,173	7,639	12,730	6,663	6,067	245	125	120
10		Sihora M ...	5,432	2,620	2,812	4,477	2,126	2,351	117	64	53
11	Mandla ...	Mandla M ...	9,379	4,640	4,739	7,684	3,833	3,851	75	33	42
12	Seoni ...	Seoni M ...	13,839	6,740	7,099	9,022	4,475	4,547	520	256	264
	NERBUDDA DIVISION		*142,557*	*73,244*	*69,313*	*101,049*	*51,736*	*49,313*	*2,229*	*1,184*	*1,045*
13	Narsinghpur	Narsinghpur M ...	10,630	5,407	5,223	7,633	3,815	3,818	343	178	165
14		Chhindwara M ...	3,404	1,687	1,717	2,746	1,367	1,379	301	152	149
15		Gadarwara M ...	4,715	2,350	2,365	3,946	1,970	1,976	156	87	69
16	Hoshangabad	Hoshangabad M ...	5,503	2,993	2,510	3,952	2,153	1,799	20	16	4
17		Itarsi T ...	4,430	2,506	1,924	3,384	1,898	1,486	51	28	23
18		Harda M ...	8,341	4,303	4,038	5,586	2,890	2,696	84	43	41
19		Sohagpur M ...	7,239	3,511	3,728	4,937	2,475	2,462	69	32	37
20		Pachmarhi M & C ...	3,822	2,162	1,660	2,669	1,490	1,179	...	...	...
21		Seoni-Malwa M ...	6,568	3,396	3,172	5,197	2,663	2,534	89	50	39
22	Nimar ...	Khandwa M ...	21,604	11,511	10,093	13,657	7,319	6,338	366	207	159
23		Burhanpur M ...	22,777	11,624	11,153	12,144	6,119	6,025	61	35	26
24	Betul ...	Badnur M ...	7,454	3,839	3,615	5,343	2,751	2,592	111	59	52
25		Betul T ...	5,473	2,622	2,851	5,047	2,413	2,644	54	25	29
26	Chhindwara	Chhindwara M ...	12,872	6,503	6,369	9,034	4,573	4,461	307	170	137
27		Pandhurna M ...	7,058	3,507	3,551	6,284	3,108	3,176	71	40	31
28		Sausar M ...	5,442	2,729	2,713	4,873	2,443	2,430	15	7	8
29		Mohgaon T ...	5,225	2,592	2,633	4,617	2,299	2,318	131	55	76
	NAGPUR DIVISION ...		*332,533*	*171,043*	*161,490*	*279,065*	*142,640*	*136,425*	*3,046*	*1,583*	*1,463*
30	Wardha ...	Wardha M ...	10,541	5,719	4,822	8,444	4,603	3,841	213	106	107
31		Arvi M ...	11,902	6,134	5,768	10,124	5,236	4,888	140	75	65
32		Hinganghat M ...	14,943	7,690	7,253	12,255	6,280	5,975	420	214	206
33		Ashti T ...	6,257	3,144	3,113	5,148	2,618	2,530	53	28	25
34		Sindi T ...	5,981	2,950	3,031	5,198	2,555	2,643	132	57	75
35		Deoli M ...	5,575	2,808	2,767	5,120	2,560	2,560	35	17	18
36		Pulgaon M ...	5,466	2,870	2,596	4,605	2,411	2,194	99	52	47
37	Nagpur ...	Nagpur M ...	101,415	53,696	47,719	80,141	42,187	37,954	624	354	270
38		Umrer M ...	17,630	8,600	9,030	16,633	8,122	8,511	14	4	10
39		Kamptee C ...	17,155	9,348	7,807	10,434	5,430	5,004	54	28	26

with Population by Religion—(*contd.*)

PRIMITIVE.			SEMITIC.						OTHERS.			
ANIMIST.			MUSALMAN.			CHRISTIAN.						
Persons.	Males.	Females.	Persons.	Males.	Females.	Persons.	Males.	Females.	Persons.	Males.	Females.	
12	13	14	15	16	17	18	19	20	21	22	23	
DISTRICTS AND BERAR.												
12,914	6,420	6,494	217,719	113,306	104,413	21,363	12,718	8,645	3,877	2,719	1,158	
11,801	5,922	5,879	213,956	111,468	102,488	20,980	12,534	8,446	3,838	2,691	1,147	
9,943	4,971	4,972	132,256	69,317	62,939	19,357	11,753	7,604	3,222	2,303	919	
1,646	*813*	*833*	*48,500*	*26,011*	*22,489*	*8,308*	*5,403*	*2,905*	*1,797*	*1,434*	*363*	
11	6	5	9,520	5,054	4,466	614	312	302	720	613	113	1
141	71	70	657	328	329	3	2	1	...	...	...	2
43	36	7	1,378	835	543	12	11	1	...	...	...	3
...	...	...	1,268	660	608	22	14	8	...	...	...	4
...	...	...	1,656	890	766	290	162	128	94	62	32	5
20	12	8	2,891	1,452	1,439	404	314	90	31	21	10	6
195	118	77	23,032	12,827	10,205	6,310	4,349	1,961	848	687	161	7
...	...	...	474	225	249	19	2	17	...	...	...	8
147	71	76	2,268	1,185	1,083	376	105	271	46	24	22	9
30	13	17	789	406	383	13	7	6	6	4	2	10
286	139	147	1,210	564	646	116	66	50	8	5	3	11
773	347	426	3,357	1,585	1,772	129	59	70	38	18	20	12
1,803	*914*	*889*	*34,447*	*17,683*	*16,764*	*2,659*	*1,491*	*1,168*	*370*	*236*	*134*	
183	104	79	2,116	1,040	1,076	285	222	63	70	48	22	13
31	14	17	292	139	153	34	15	19	...	...	...	14
54	24	30	559	269	290	...	...	...	...	...	...	15
10	6	4	1,447	777	670	71	38	33	3	3	...	16
200	102	98	644	379	265	148	96	52	3	3	...	17
68	35	33	2,126	1,072	1,054	397	218	179	80	45	35	18
159	73	86	1,853	848	1,005	201	75	126	20	10	10	19
17	9	8	936	529	407	169	109	60	31	25	6	20
7	4	3	1,099	558	541	156	107	49	20	14	6	21
8	5	3	6,812	3,587	3,225	658	336	322	103	57	46	22
...	...	...	10,544	5,454	5,090	22	11	11	6	5	1	23
407	205	202	1,486	765	721	86	42	44	21	17	4	24
57	26	31	315	168	147	...	...	...	...	...	...	25
355	192	163	2,732	1,338	1,394	431	221	210	13	9	4	26
42	21	21	661	338	323	...	...	...	...	...	...	27
204	93	111	349	185	164	1	1	...	...	...	...	28
1	1	...	476	237	239	...	...	...	...	...	...	29
4,790	*2,362*	*2,428*	*38,416*	*20,084*	*18,332*	*6,337*	*3,843*	*2,494*	*579*	*531*	*348*	
350	174	176	1,352	720	632	129	85	44	53	31	22	30
282	145	137	1,353	677	676	2	...	2	1	1	...	31
328	168	160	1,915	1,011	904	25	17	8	...	...	...	32
68	29	39	986	467	519	...	...	...	2	2	...	33
126	60	66	525	278	247	...	...	...	...	...	...	34
63	36	27	357	195	162	...	...	...	...	...	...	35
136	66	70	622	341	281	...	...	...	4	...	4	36
1,365	703	662	14,589	7,854	6,735	3,960	2,158	1,802	736	440	296	37
6	4	2	967	462	505	10	8	2	...	...	...	38
93	46	47	4,839	2,533	2,306	1,714	1,295	419	21	16	5	39

TABLE V.—Towns arranged territorially

	DISTRICT OR STATE.	Town, Municipality or Cantonment.		POPULATION.			INDO-ARYAN.					
							HINDU (BRAHMANIC).			JAIN.		
				Persons.	Males.	Females.	Persons.	Males.	Females.	Persons.	Males.	Females.
	1	2		3	4	5	6	7	8	9	10	11
												BRITISH
40	Nagpur (concld.)	Ramtek	M ...	9,806	4,840	4,966	8,959	4,408	4,551	102	41	61
41		Khapa	M ...	8,233	4,140	4,093	7,594	3,814	3,780	50	21	29
42		Saoner	M ...	6,636	3,425	3,211	6,093	3,124	2,969	9	7	2
43		Katol	T ...	6,269	3,252	3,017	5,807	2,997	2,810	65	32	33
44		Narkher	T ...	6,203	3,065	3,138	5,865	2,897	2,968	100	55	45
45		Kelod	T ...	5,785	2,945	2,840	5,306	2,697	2,609	120	63	57
46		Kalmeshwar	M ...	5,575	2,868	2,707	5,223	2,677	2,546	77	40	37
47		Mohpa	T ...	5,477	2,702	2,775	5,184	2,574	2,610	...	...	...
48		Mowar	M ...	4,719	2,307	2,412	4,313	2,109	2,204	18	10	8
49	Chanda ...	Chanda	M ...	19,806	10,077	9,780	17,694	8,955	8,739	127	70	57
50		Warora	M ...	6,174	3,196	2,978	4,696	2,430	2,266	218	114	104
51		Brahmpuri	T ...	5,359	2,585	2,774	4,711	2,275	2,436	...	...	...
52		Chimur	T ...	5,218	2,520	2,698	4,693	2,278	2,415	5	3	2
53		Nawargaon	T ...	5,087	2,435	2,652	4,500	2,156	2,344	...	...	...
54	Bhandara ...	Bhandara	M ...	7,414	3,787	3,627	6,393	3,268	3,125	19	9	10
55		Pauni	M ...	10,222	5,037	5,185	9,182	4,510	4,672	...	...	...
56		Gondia	T ...	5,847	3,115	2,732	4,743	2,537	2,206	124	58	66
57		Tumsar	M ...	4,378	2,123	2,255	4,094	1,983	2,111	...	...	...
58	Balaghat ...	Balaghat	M ...	7,400	3,665	3,735	5,913	2,949	2,964	228	125	103
	CHHATTISGARH DIVISION		...	*89,803*	*44,994*	*44,809*	*74,351*	*37,054*	*37,297*	*716*	*401*	*315*
59	Raipur ...	Raipur	M ...	35,335	18,038	17,297	28,196	14,421	13,775	388	209	179
60		Arang	T ...	5,820	2,831	2,989	5,434	2,648	2,786	17	6	11
61		Dhamtari	M ...	10,460	5,170	5,290	8,625	4,159	4,466	132	86	46
62	Bilaspur ...	Bilaspur	M ...	19,850	9,983	9,867	16,038	8,106	7,932	7	2	5
63		Ratanpur	T .	5,499	2,544	2,955	4,880	2,242	2,638	...	...	...
64		Mungeli	T ...	5,881	2,839	3,042	5,201	2,471	2,730	51	32	19
65	Drug ...	Drug	T ...	7,048	3,589	3,459	5,977	3,007	2,970	121	66	55
	Berar		...	**369,794**	**192,327**	**177,467**	**278,439**	**145,189**	**133,250**	**5,558**	**2,867**	**2,691**
66	Amraoti ...	Amraoti	M ...	34,270	18,147	16,123	26,015	13,860	12,155	666	344	322
67		Amraoti Camp	M ...	6,340	3,334	3,006	5,066	2,680	2,386	7	4	3
68		Ellichpur	M ...	13,909	7,027	6,882	8,851	4,553	4,298	54	26	28
69		Badnera	T ...	11,098	5,898	5,200	8,145	4,308	3,837	93	45	48
70		Anjangaon	T ...	8,628	4,394	4,234	5,960	3,070	2,890	175	83	92
71		Warud	T ...	7,089	3,634	3,455	6,134	3,136	2,998	99	53	46
72		Shendurjana	T ..	6,948	3,522	3,426	5,904	2,970	2,934	216	107	109
73		Talegaon Dashasahasra	T	6,692	3,355	3,337	5,116	2,583	2,533	...	...	...
74		Morsi	T ...	6,336	3,229	3,107	5,172	2,647	2,525	3	3	...
75		Sirasgaon	T ...	6,039	3,048	2,991	4,846	2,462	2,384	91	46	45
76		Ner Pinglai	T ...	5,935	3,046	2,889	5,045	2,586	2,459	53	27	26
77		Karasgaon	T ...	5,581	2,808	2,773	5,081	2,562	2,519	70	35	35
78		Kholapur	T ...	5,501	2,799	2,702	3,469	1,775	1,694	94	47	47
79		Pusla	T ...	5,261	2,663	2,598	4,893	2,493	2,400	43	17	26
80		Mangrul-Dastgir	T ...	5,139	2,635	2,504	4,599	2,363	2,236	3	1	2
81		Balgaon Jagir	T ...	4,045	2,129	1,916	3,458	1,830	1,628	26	11	15
82		Dattapur	T ...	4,776	2,631	2,145	3,998	2,197	1,801	52	20	32
83		Chandur Railway	T ...	4,508	2,392	2,116	4,067	2,145	1,922	102	49	53
84		Paratwara	M ...	4,001	2,136	1,865	2,757	1,470	1,287	51	26	25
85		Chandur Bazar	T ...	3,850	1,998	1,852	2,793	1,435	1,358	72	44	28
86	Akola ...	Akola	M ...	25,826	14,006	11,820	18,891	10,285	8,606	227	133	94
87		Karanja	M ...	12,647	6,556	6,091	8,043	4,166	3,877	716	355	361
88		Akot	M ...	12,583	6,523	6,060	9,600	5,014	4,586	91	44	47
89		Basim	M ...	9,068	4,562	4,506	6,697	3,374	3,323	199	103	96
90		Hiwarkhed	T ...	6,404	3,209	3,195	5,136	2,595	2,541	97	51	46
91		Mangrul Pir	T ...	6,072	3,074	2,998	3,670	1,867	1,803	89	43	46
92		Balapur	T ...	5,953	2,939	3,014	2,734	1,353	1,381	198	96	102
93		Barsi Takli	T ...	5,696	2,889	2,807	3,630	1,839	1,791	21	8	13
94		Patur	T ...	5,500	2,818	2,682	3,573	1,842	1,731	35	20	15
95		Murtizapur	T ...	5,101	2,988	2,113	3,437	1,965	1,472	137	92	45
96		Wadegaon	T ...	4,890	2,532	2,358	4,448	2,292	2,156	14	8	6
97		Telhara	T ...	3,406	1,819	1,587	3,104	1,655	1,449	5	2	3

with Population by Religion—(*contd.*)

PRIMITIVE.			SEMITIC.						OTHERS.			
ANIMIST.			MUSALMAN.			CHRISTIAN.						
Persons.	Males.	Females.	Persons.	Males.	Females.	Persons.	Males.	Females.	Persons.	Males.	Females.	
12	13	14	15	16	17	18	19	20	21	22	23	
DISTRICTS AND BERAR—(*contd.*)												
128	70	58	600	311	289	15	8	7	2	2	...	40
5	4	1	584	301	283	...	...	...	...	...	...	41
34	17	17	466	256	210	34	21	13	...	...	...	42
26	12	14	367	208	159	3	2	1	1	1	...	43
...	...	...	237	112	125	...	...	...	1	1	...	44
...	...	...	359	185	174	...	...	...	...	...	...	45
...	...	...	275	151	124	...	...	...	...	...	...	46
...	...	...	293	128	165	...	...	...	...	...	...	47
1	1	...	387	187	200	...	...	...	...	...	...	48
392	183	209	1,402	719	683	237	142	95	14	8	6	49
201	102	99	1,053	544	509	...	...	...	6	6	...	50
303	131	172	338	177	161	7	2	5	...	...	...	51
115	58	57	404	180	224	1	1	...	...	...	...	52
361	173	188	226	106	120	...	...	...	...	...	...	53
55	23	32	842	432	410	88	45	43	17	10	7	54
12	5	7	1,028	522	506	...	...	...	...	...	...	55
99	43	56	825	449	376	45	18	27	11	10	1	56
38	16	22	244	123	121	2	1	1	...	...	...	57
203	93	110	981	455	526	65	40	25	10	3	7	58
1,704	*882*	*822*	*10,893*	*5,539*	*5,354*	*2,053*	*1,016*	*1,037*	*170*	*103*	*74*	
233	127	106	5,888	2,962	2,926	556	278	278	74	41	33	59
220	99	121	145	76	69	4	2	2	...	...	...	60
704	375	329	653	354	299	341	192	149	5	4	1	61
66	41	25	2,796	1,410	1,386	875	382	493	68	42	20	62
315	162	153	303	139	164	1	1	...	...	...	...	63
34	18	16	362	184	178	220	128	92	13	6	7	64
132	60	72	746	414	332	56	33	23	16	9	7	65
1,858	**951**	**907**	**81,700**	**42,151**	**39,549**	**1,623**	**781**	**842**	**616**	**388**	**228**	
15	8	7	7,436	3,855	3,581	93	50	43	45	30	15	66
26	12	14	882	492	390	839	137	202	20	9	11	67
123	75	48	4,881	2,373	2,508	...	...	...	...	...	...	68
151	79	72	2,340	1,260	1,080	159	81	78	210	125	85	69
1	1	...	2,492	1,240	1,252	...	...	...	...	...	...	70
5	3	2	846	438	408	5	4	1	...	...	...	71
4	2	2	824	443	381	...	...	...	...	...	...	72
323	156	167	1,247	613	634	6	3	3	...	...	...	73
151	69	82	1,008	509	499	2	1	1	...	...	...	74
1	...	1	1,101	540	561	...	...	...	...	...	...	75
75	38	37	761	395	366	...	...	...	1	...	1	76
...	...	...	430	211	219	...	...	...	...	...	...	77
2	1	1	1,936	970	960	...	...	...	...	...	...	78
3	..	3	320	151	169	...	...	...	2	2	...	79
117	61	56	420	210	210	...	...	...	...	...	...	80
20	10	10	541	278	263	...	...	...	...	...	...	81
68	33	35	694	365	269	11	6	5	13	10	3	82
2	2	...	310	179	131	17	8	9	10	9	1	83
46	20	26	1,126	569	557	68	48	20	3	3	...	84
19	9	9	964	507	457	...	...	...	3	3	...	85
131	71	60	6,238	3,305	2,933	238	143	95	101	69	32	86
126	66	60	3,741	1,953	1,788	13	8	5	8	8	...	87
9	5	4	2,814	1,423	1,391	5	3	2	64	34	30	88
...	...	...	1,993	1,005	988	174	77	97	5	3	2	89
1	1	...	1,170	562	606	...	...	...	...	...	...	90
...	...	...	2,310	1,163	1,147	3	1	2	...	...	...	91
...	...	...	3,015	1,485	1,530	...	...	...	6	5	1	92
...	...	...	2,045	1,042	1,003	...	...	...	...	...	...	93
...	...	...	1,890	954	936	1	1	...	1	1	...	94
36	21	15	1,432	880	552	37	16	21	22	14	8	95
...	...	...	428	232	196	...	...	...	...	...	...	96
2	1	1	295	161	134	...	...	...	...	...	...	97

TABLE V.—Towns arranged territorially

	DISTRICT OR STATE.	Town, Municipality or Cantonment.		POPULATION.			INDO-ARYAN. HINDU (BRAHMANIC.)			INDO-ARYAN. JAIN.		
				Persons.	Males.	Females.	Persons.	Males.	Females.	Persons.	Males.	Females.
	1	2		3	4	5	6	7	8	9	10	11
												BRITISH
98	Buldana	Buldana	M ...	3,820	2,037	1,783	2,943	1,555	1,388	60	35	25
99		Malkapur	M ...	12,391	6,463	5,928	7,558	3,998	3,560	355	182	173
100		Shegaon	M ...	11,962	6,290	5,672	10,068	5,297	4,771	41	20	21
101		Khamgaon	M ...	10,123	5,545	4,578	7,349	4,066	3,283	196	118	78
102		Jalgaon	T ...	7,552	3,851	3,701	6,262	3,194	3,068	...	...	...
103		Nandura	T ...	6,794	3,464	3,330	5,167	2,615	2,552	63	28	35
104		Deulgaon Raja	T ...	6,026	3,012	3,014	4,726	2,367	2,359	419	216	203
105		Chikhli	T ...	4,731	2,406	2,325	3,595	1,821	1,774	50	25	25
106		Mehkar	T ...	4,423	2,279	2,144	3,486	1,798	1,688	1	...	1
107	Yeotmal	Yeotmal	M ...	13,525	7,249	6,276	11,203	6,007	5,196	185	110	75
108		Pusad	T ...	6,862	3,448	3,414	4,963	2,516	2,447	174	80	94
109		Digras	T ...	6,479	3,355	3,124	4,607	2,327	2,280	79	40	39
110		Wun	T ...	6,282	3,273	3,009	5,275	2,744	2,531	11	7	4
111		Umarkhed	T ...	5,822	2,908	2,914	4,272	2,142	2,130	58	29	29
112		Darwha	T ...	3,910	2,007	1,903	2,683	1,370	1,313	67	34	33
	Feudatory States		...	**36,824**	**17,958**	**18,866**	**31,064**	**15,140**	**15,924**	**462**	**270**	**192**
113	Nandgaon State	Rajnandgaon	T ...	11,979	6,041	5,938	10,014	5,024	4,990	351	215	136
114	Khairagarh State	Dongargarh	T ...	6,249	2,965	3,284	4,710	2,235	2,475	60	27	33
115	Kawardha State	Kawardha	T ...	5,180	2,341	2,839	4,348	1,970	2,378	49	26	23
116	Raigarh State	Raigarh	T ...	8,041	3,986	4,055	7,034	3,483	3,551	1	1	...
117	Sarangarh State	Sarangarh	T ...	5,375	2,625	2,750	4,958	2,428	2,530	1	1	...

with Population by Religion—(*concld.*)

Primitive. Animist. Persons.	Animist. Males.	Animist. Females.	Semitic. Musalman. Persons.	Musalman. Males.	Musalman. Females.	Christian. Persons.	Christian. Males.	Christian. Females.	Others. Persons.	Others. Males.	Others. Females.	
12	13	14	15	16	17	18	19	20	21	22	23	
DISTRICTS AND BERAR—(*concld.*)												
2	2	...	756	408	348	57	35	22	2	2	...	98
...	...	...	4,467	2,274	2,195	11	9	2	...	...	...	99
1	1	...	1,781	923	858	47	30	17	24	19	5	100
...	...	...	2,379	1,296	1,083	169	50	119	30	15	15	101
...	...	...	1,288	656	632	...	...	...	2	1	1	102
...	...	...	1,540	8[illegible]9	737	12	9	3	6	3	3	103
...	...	...	870	426	450	5	3	2	...	...	...	104
...	...	...	1,085	560	525	...	...	...	1	...	1	105
...	...	...	915	471	444	...	...	...	21	10	11	106
220	104	116	1,770	967	803	135	50	85	12	11	1	107
...	...	...	1,725	852	873	...	...	...	...	...	...	108
...	...	...	1,793	988	805	...	...	...	...	...	...	109
178	100	78	806	415	391	12	7	5	...	...	...	110
1	...	1	1,488	736	752	...	...	...	3	1	2	111
...	...	...	1,155	601	554	4	1	3	1	1	...	112
1,113	**498**	**615**	**3,763**	**1,838**	**1,925**	**383**	**184**	**199**	**39**	**28**	**11**	
171	82	89	1,282	652	630	144	58	86	17	10	7	113
329	136	193	906	435	471	230	120	110	14	12	2	114
213	90	123	558	246	312	7	4	3	5	5	...	115
235	114	121	766	385	381	2	2	...	3	1	2	116
165	76	89	251	120	131	...	...	...	...	...	...	117

TABLE VI.

Religion.

TABLE VI.

Serial No.	DISTRICT OR STATE.	TOTAL POPULATION.			INDO-ARYAN. HINDU (BRAHMINIC).		
		Persons.	Males.	Females.	Persons.	Males.	Females.
	1	2	3	4	5	6	7
	Central Provinces and Berar	**16.033.310**	**7.984.022**	**8.049,288**	**12.807.874**	**6.382.743**	**6,425,131**
	C. P. British Districts and Berar ...	**13.916.308**	**6.930.392**	**6.985.916**	**11,496,486**	**5.731.936**	**5.764.550**
	C. P. British Districts ...	**10.859.146**	**5,379.778**	**5,479.368**	**8,828.377**	**4.379.540**	**4,448.837**
	JUBBULPORE DIVISION ...	*2,421,064*	*1,210,980*	*1,210,084*	*1,743,763*	*875,450*	*868,312*
1	Saugor	541,410	276,233	265.177	471,650	240,356	231,294
2	Damoh	333,047	168,060	164,987	303,189	152,873	150,316
3	Jubbulpore	745,892	373,173	372,719	598,960	298,484	300,476
4	Mandla	405,234	200,872	204,362	155,006	77,986	77,020
5	Seoni	395,481	192,642	202,839	214,957	105,751	109,206
	NERBUDDA DIVISION ...	*2,081,477*	*1,043,239*	*1,038,238*	*1,568,391*	*790,633*	*777,858*
6	Narsinghpur	325,677	161,795	163,882	278,048	138,622	139,426
7	Hoshangabad	457,395	230,632	226,763	382,775	193,785	188,990
8	Nimar	391,071	200,765	190,306	340,030	174,111	165,919
9	Betul	390,286	184,163	196,223	259,318	129,817	129,501
10	Chhindwara	516,948	255,884	261,064	308,320	154,298	154,022
	NAGPUR DIVISION ...	*3,109,838*	*1,548,737*	*1,561,101*	*2,637,913*	*1,315,027*	*1,322,886*
11	Wardha	459,796	231,871	227,925	391,063	197,583	193,480
12	Nagpur	809,901	408,843	401.058	725,399	365,125	360,274
13	Chanda	677.544	337,540	340,004	539,713	269,465	270,248
14	Bhandara	773,677	380,014	393,663	685,342	337,335	348,007
15	Balaghat	388,920	190,469	198,451	296,396	145,519	150,877
	CHHATTISGARH DIVISION ...	*3,246,767*	*1,576,822*	*1,669,945*	*2,378,311*	*1,398,430*	*1,479,781*
16	Raipur	1,324,856	645,186	679,670	1,126,497	549,378	577,119
17	Bilaspur	1,146,223	558,477	587,746	1,077,338	524,724	552,614
18	Drug	775,688	373,159	402,529	674,376	324,328	350,048
	Berar	**3.057.162**	**1.550.614**	**1.506.548**	**2,668.109**	**1.352.396**	**1.315,713**
19	Amraoti	875,904	447,216	428,688	738,294	377,352	360,942
20	Akola	788,863	400,893	387,970	711,025	360,644	350,381
21	Buldana	669,182	337,179	332,003	608,609	305,993	302,616
22	Yeotmal	723,213	365,326	357,887	610,181	308,407	301,774
	Feudatory States ...	**2,117,002**	**1,053.630**	**1,063,372**	**1,311,388**	**650,807**	**660,581**
23	Makrai	15,021	7,530	7,491	10,036	5,006	5,030
24	Bastar	433,310	218,015	215,295	141,987	71,965	70,022
25	Kanker	127,014	63,010	64,004	57,065	28,275	28,790
26	Nandgaon	167,362	80,293	87,069	138,738	66,851	71,887
27	Khairagarh	155,471	74,742	80,729	144,249	69,477	74,772
28	Chhuikhadan	31,150	15,117	16,033	25,564	12,457	13,107
29	Kawardha	77,654	37,488	40,166	60,040	28,998	31,042
30	Sakti	34,547	16,871	17,676	29,293	14,330	14,963
31	Raigarh	218,860	107,850	111,010	199,085	98,116	100,969
32	Sarangarh	102,071	49,851	52,220	99,494	48,630	50,864
33	Chang Bhakar	24,421	12,462	11,959	11,446	5,948	5,498
34	Korea	62,107	31,856	30,251	21,387	11,269	10,118
35	Surguja	428,703	217,749	210,954	267,193	135,879	131,314
36	Udaipur	64,853	32,790	32,063	16,397	8,303	8,094
37	Jashpur	174,458	88,006	86,452	89,414	45,303	44,111

—Religion.

INDO-ARYAN.												
Sects included among Hindus (Brahmanic).						Hindu (Arya).			Hindu (Brahmo).			Serial No.
Kabirpanthi.			Satnami.									
Persons.	Males.	Females.	Persons.	Males.	Females.	Persons.	Males.	Females.	Persons.	Males.	Females.	
8	9	10	11	12	13	14	15	16	17	18	19	
597,199	291,093	306,106	460,280	224,577	235,703	974	554	420	32	19	13	
489,725	238,373	251,352	394,595	191,888	202,707	944	538	406	30	17	13	
488,576	237,757	250,819	392,808	190,985	201,823	906	514	392	29	16	13	
113,844	*56,812*	*57,032*	*4,537*	*2,272*	*2,265*	*291*	*168*	*123*	*12*	*8*	*4*	
7,172	4,183	2,989	108	44	64	101	53	48	2	2	...	1
5,383	2,632	2,751	2,296	1,170	1,126	3	3	...	...	...	...	2
75,113	36,770	38,343	1,026	506	520	153	93	60	8	4	4	3
17,263	8,937	8,326	907	461	446	...	...	...	2	2	...	4
8,913	4,290	4,623	200	91	109	34	19	15	...	...	...	5
29,908	*14,840*	*15,068*	*1,530*	*821*	*709*	*355*	*196*	*159*	*2*	*2*	...	
2,278	1,184	1,094	149	70	79	162	88	74	1	1	...	6
16,650	8,304	8,346	331	162	169	89	49	40	1	1	...	7
5,375	2,428	2,947	342	181	161	74	40	34	...	...	...	8
1,577	825	752	436	252	184	16	9	7	...	...	...	9
4,028	2,009	1,929	272	156	116	14	10	4	...	...	...	10
31,999	*14,622*	*17,377*	*2,890*	*1,488*	*1,402*	*73*	*42*	*31*	*9*	*4*	*5*	
178	83	95	...	...	...	...	...	...	6	1	5	11
7,536	3,829	3,707	696	354	342	6	4	2	...	...	...	12
520	248	272	914	449	465	...	...	...	1	1	...	13
6,005	2,953	3,052	685	367	318	20	11	9	1	1	...	14
17,760	7,509	10,251	695	318	277	47	27	20	1	1	...	15
312,825	*151,483*	*161,342*	*383,851*	*186,404*	*197,447*	*187*	*108*	*79*	*6*	*2*	*4*	
124,885	60,547	64,338	182,462	88,229	94,233	55	33	22	...	...	...	16
100,108	48,675	51,433	100,647	47,839	52,808	82	49	33	6	2	4	17
87,832	42,261	45,571	100,742	50,336	50,406	50	26	24	...	...	...	18
1,149	616	533	1,787	903	884	38	24	14	1	1	...	
907	479	428	20	14	6	11	6	5	...	...	...	19
152	91	61	68	43	25	27	18	9	1	1	...	20
29	13	16	1,479	732	747	...	...	...	...	...	...	21
61	33	28	220	114	106	...	...	...	...	...	...	22
107,474	52,720	54,754	65,685	32,689	32,996	30	16	14	2	2	...	
1,910	1,000	910	33	13	20	...	...	...	...	...	...	23
4,101	2,063	2,038	1,308	712	596	25	13	12	...	...	...	24
2,667	1,314	1,353	1,257	647	610	...	...	...	...	...	...	25
21,519	10,405	11,114	16,864	8,208	8,656	...	...	...	...	...	...	26
21,806	10,498	11,308	17,280	8,538	8,742	2	...	2	2	2	...	27
3,713	1,826	1,887	2,454	1,233	1,221	...	...	...	...	...	...	28
6,690	2,974	3,716	9,987	4,558	5,429	1	1	...	...	...	...	29
4,103	1,983	2,120	418	192	226	2	2	...	...	...	...	30
13,314	6,492	6,822	906	444	462	...	...	...	...	...	...	31
7,299	3,569	3,730	78	44	34	...	...	...	...	...	...	32
86	41	45	18	10	8	...	...	...	...	...	...	33
589	306	283	105	42	63	...	...	...	...	...	...	34
8,368	4,379	3,989	7,802	4,125	3,677	...	...	...	...	...	...	35
3,389	1,677	1,712	28	12	16	...	...	...	...	...	...	36
7,920	4,193	3,727	7,147	3,911	3,236	...	...	...	...	...	...	37

TABLE VI.

Serial No.	DISTRICT OR STATE.	INDO ARYAN—(concld.)								
		SIKH.			JAIN.			BUDDHIST.		
		Persons.	Males.	Females.	Persons.	Males.	Females.	Persons.	Males.	Females.
		20	21	22	23	24	25	26	27	28
	Central Provinces and Berar	**2,337**	**1,802**	**535**	**71,417**	**36,780**	**34,637**	**9**	**8**	**1**
	C. P. British Districts and Berar	**2,201**	**1,730**	**471**	**70,258**	**36,109**	**34,149**	**9**	**8**	**1**
	C. P. British Districts ...	**1,997**	**1,626**	**371**	**51,358**	**26,434**	**24,924**	**9**	**8**	**1**
	JUBBULPORE DIVISION ...	*1,295*	*1,152*	*143*	*32,702*	*16,727*	*15,975*	*3*	*3*	...
1	Saugor	634	570	64	16,713	8,627	8,086	...	...	...
2	Damoh	19	12	7	7,270	3,685	3,585	...	...	...
3	Jubbulpore	629	558	71	6,233	3,163	3,070	2	2	...
4	Mandla	10	10	...	730	389	341	1	1	...
5	Seoni	3	2	1	1,756	863	893	...	...	...
	NERBUDDA DIVISION ...	*319*	*211*	*108*	*9,098*	*4,661*	*4,437*	*4*	*3*	*1*
6	Narsinghpur	...	...	...	2,288	1,163	1,125	...	...	...
7	Hoshangabad	50	36	14	1,784	867	917	...	...	...
8	Nimar	144	80	64	1,664	921	743	1	1	...
9	Betul	117	89	28	1,360	669	691	...	...	...
10	Chhindwara	8	6	2	2,002	1,041	961	3	2	1
	NAGPUR DIVISION ...	*239*	*173*	*66*	*7,423*	*3,813*	*3,610*	*2*	*2*	...
11	Wardha	15	10	5	2,488	1,255	1,233	...	...	...
12	Nagpur	149	98	51	3,040	1,564	1,476	2	2	...
13	Chanda	24	22	2	708	376	332	...	...	...
14	Bhandara	11	11	...	625	295	330	...	...	...
15	Balaghat	40	32	8	561	322	239	...	...	...
	CHHATTISGARH DIVISION ...	*144*	*90*	*54*	*2,136*	*1,234*	*902*	...	...	...
16	Raipur	98	51	47	977	557	420	...	...	...
17	Bilaspur	24	20	4	366	200	166	...	...	...
18	Drug	22	19	3	793	477	316	...	...	...
	Berar	**204**	**104**	**100**	**18,900**	**9,675**	**9,225**	...	...	...
19	Amraoti	39	19	20	5,254	2,735	2,519	...	...	...
20	Akola	57	26	31	5,844	2,896	2,948	...	...	...
21	Buldana	25	13	12	4,459	2,308	2,151	...	...	...
22	Yeotmal	83	46	37	3,343	1,736	1,607	...	...	...
	Feudatory States ...	**136**	**72**	**64**	**1,159**	**671**	**488**	...	...	...
23	Makrai	...	...	...	67	29	38	...	...	...
24	Bastar	...	...	...	52	26	26	...	...	...
25	Kanker	...	...	...	71	35	36	...	...	...
26	Nandgaon	...	...	...	541	330	211	...	...	...
27	Khairagarh	5	5	...	217	125	92	...	...	...
28	Chhuikhadan	...	...	...	115	71	44	...	...	...
29	Kawardha	5	5	...	63	36	27	...	...	...
30	Sakti	1	1	...	...	...	...	...	...	...
31	Raigarh	125	61	64	13	6	7	...	...	...
32	Sarangarh	...	...	...	7	4	3	...	...	...
33	Chang Bhakar	...	...	...	...	...	...	...	...	...
34	Korea	...	...	...	...	...	...	...	...	...
35	Surguja	...	...	...	13	9	4	...	...	...
36	Udaipur	...	...	...	...	...	...	...	...	...
37	Jashpur	...	...	...	...	...	...	...	...	...

—Religion.

PRIMITIVE.			SEMITIC.						
ANIMIST.			MUSALMAN.			*Sects included among Musalmans.* Sunni.			
Persons.	Males.	Females.	Persons.	Males.	Females.	Persons.	Males.	Females.	Serial No.
29	30	31	32	33	34	35	36	37	
2.490.355	1.219.551	1.270.804	585.029	302.227	282.802	550.425	284.287	266,138	
1.744.921	847.167	897,754	564.909	292.047	272.862	536.525	277.304	259.221	
1,617.060	784.072	832.988	326.244	168.594	157.650	307.624	159.060	148.564	
530,920	*257,700*	*273,220*	*101,952*	*53,341*	*48,611*	*98,746*	*51,721*	*47,025*	
24.924	12,154	12,770	25,835	13,632	12.203	25,195	13,208	11,927	1
11,115	5,461	5,654	11,002	5.680	5,322	10,343	5,365	4,978	2
91,543	44,113	47,430	41,339	22,117	19,222	40,234	21.553	18,681	3
242,261	118.656	123,605	6,342	3,329	3,013	5,759	3.089	2,670	4
161,077	77,816	83,761	17,434	8,583	8,851	17,215	8,446	8,709	5
400,134	*193,920*	*206,214*	*95,378*	*49,450*	*45,928*	*90,906*	*47,143*	*43,763*	
32,902	15,714	17,278	11,707	5,888	5,819	11,151	5,583	5,568	6
49,915	24,157	25,758	20,799	10,640	10,159	20,234	10,319	9,915	7
6,803	3.434	3,369	38,428	20,109	18.319	36,141	18,983	17,158	8
121,175	58,947	62,228	7,849	4.354	3.495	7,273	4,047	3,226	9
189,249	91,668	97,581	16,595	8,459	8,136	16,107	8,211	7,896	10
364,175	*177,747*	*186,428*	*91,453*	*46,883*	*44,570*	*83,296*	*42,702*	*40,594*	
47.831	23,549	24,282	18,174	9,331	8,843	17,419	8,934	8,485	11
36,003	17.870	18,133	38,434	20,047	18,387	32,863	17,138	15,725	12
124,356	61,161	63,195	12,172	6,205	5,967	11,596	5,926	5,670	13
72.424	34,669	37,755	14,707	7,434	7.273	13,594	6,898	6,696	14
83,561	40,498	43,063	7,966	3,866	4,100	7,824	3,806	4,018	15
321,831	*154,705*	*167,126*	*37,461*	*18,920*	*18,541*	*34,676*	*17,494*	*17,183*	
177,300	85,106	92,194	16,515	8,393	8,122	14.853	7.502	7,351	16
52,425	25,455	26,970	13,964	7,049	6,915	13,104	6,612	6,492	17
92,106	44,144	47,962	6,982	3,478	3,504	6,719	3,380	3,339	18
127,861	63.095	64,766	238,665	123,453	115,212	228,901	118,244	110,657	
57,191	28,198	28,903	73,311	37,896	35,415	69,547	35,928	33,619	19
934	491	443	70,148	36,342	33,806	67,606	34,982	32,624	20
382	204	178	55,257	28.435	26,822	54,028	27,764	26,264	21
69,354	34.202	35,152	39,949	20,780	19,169	37,730	19,570	18.150	22
745.434	372,384	373.050	20.120	10.180	9,940	13.900	6,983	6.917	
4,089	2,077	2,012	829	418	411	600	300	300	23
288,323	144,541	143,782	1,646	826	820	1,567	785	782	24
69,232	34,389	34,843	636	306	330	584	282	302	25
25,763	11,982	13,781	2,149	1,055	1,094	2,044	994	1,050	26
8,487	3,919	4,568	2,249	1,074	1,175	2,047	968	1,079	27
4,558	2,133	2,425	903	452	451	877	442	435	28
16,000	7,702	8,298	1,517	734	783	1,505	726	779	29
4,882	2,353	2,529	352	176	176	346	174	172	30
18,210	8,939	9.271	1,376	701	675	1,329	670	659	31
2,197	1,039	1.158	356	168	188	280	141	148	32
12,915	6,477	6,438	60	37	23	57	35	22	33
40,176	20,284	19,892	540	300	240	534	296	238	34
155,921	78,950	76,971	5,576	2,911	2,665	1,135	638	497	35
48,163	24,325	23,838	285	156	129	282	154	128	36
46,518	23,274	23,244	1,646	866	780	704	378	326	37

TABLE VI.—Religion—*concld.*

Serial No.	DISTRICT OR STATE.	SEMITIC—*concld.*									IRANIAN.		
		Sects included among Musalmans—(concld.) Shia.			CHRISTIAN.			JEW.			ZOROASTRIAN.		
		Persons.	Males.	Females.	Persons.	Males.	Females.	Persons	Males.	Females.	Persons.	Males.	Females.
		38	39	40	41	42	43	44	45	46	47	48	49
	Central Provinces and Berar	**18,631**	**10,017**	**8,614**	**73,401**	**39,208**	**34,193**	**125**	**78**	**47**	**1,757**	**1,052**	**705**
	C. P. British Districts and Berar	**16,567**	**8,841**	**7,726**	**34,697**	**19,731**	**14,966**	**125**	**78**	**47**	**1,728**	**1,031**	**697**
	C. P. British Districts ...	**11,890**	**6,311**	**5,579**	**31,874**	**18,210**	**13,664**	**95**	**54**	**41**	**1,197**	**710**	**487**
	JUBBULPORE DIVISION ...	*1,630*	*908*	*722*	*9,844*	*6,259*	*3,585*	*18*	*16*	*2*	*265*	*156*	*109*
1	Saugor	348	219	129	1,454	777	677	9	8	1	88	54	34
2	Damoh	151	92	59	437	837	100	...	...	...	12	9	3
3	Jubbulpore	763	387	376	6,880	4,554	2,326	9	8	1	136	77	59
4	Mandla	180	103	77	871	491	380	...	...	...	11	8	3
5	Seoni	188	107	81	202	100	102	...	...	...	18	8	10
	NERBUDDA DIVISION ...	*2,743*	*1,480*	*1,263*	*7,463*	*4,025*	*3,438*	*23*	*9*	*14*	*210*	*129*	*81*
6	Narsinghpur	182	95	87	471	315	156	...	...	...	8	4	4
7	Hoshangabad	491	293	198	1,897	1,044	853	4	2	2	81	51	30
8	Nimar	1,455	764	691	3,793	1,994	1,799	19	7	12	115	68	47
9	Betul	322	169	153	547	274	273	...	...	...	4	4	...
10	Chhindwara	293	159	134	755	398	357	...	...	...	2	2	...
	NAGPUR DIVISION ...	*5,308*	*2,777*	*2,531*	*7,832*	*4,631*	*3,201*	*54*	*29*	*25*	*666*	*387*	*279*
11	Wardha	459	244	215	178	117	61	...	...	...	41	25	16
12	Nagpur	4,306	2,254	2,052	6,245	3,764	2,481	49	28	21	574	341	233
13	Chanda	291	160	131	541	304	237	5	1	4	24	5	19
14	Bhandara	185	88	97	538	250	288	...	...	...	9	8	1
15	Balaghat	67	31	36	330	196	134	...	...	...	18	8	10
	CHHATTISGARH DIVISION ...	*2,209*	*1,146*	*1,063*	*6,735*	*3,295*	*3,440*	...	...	...	*56*	*38*	*18*
16	Raipur	1,498	804	694	3,365	1,637	1,728	...	...	...	49	31	18
17	Bilaspur	477	254	223	2,011	971	1,040	...	...	...	7	7	...
18	Drug	234	88	146	1,359	687	672	...	...	...	...	...	...
	Berar	**4,677**	**2,530**	**2,147**	**2,823**	**1,521**	**1,302**	**30**	**24**	**6**	**531**	**321**	**210**
19	Amraoti	2,176	1,177	999	1,489	827	662	27	21	6	288	162	126
20	Akola	790	423	367	666	365	301	3	3	...	158	107	51
21	Buldana	628	330	298	378	183	195	...	...	...	72	43	29
22	Yeotmal	1,083	600	483	290	146	144	...	...	...	13	9	4
	Feudatory States ...	**2,064**	**1,176**	**888**	**38,704**	**19,477**	**19,227**	...	...	...	**29**	**21**	**8**
23	Makrai	...	...	...	...	...	...	...	...	...	...	...	...
24	Bastar	70	39	31	1,277	644	633	...	...	...	...	...	...
25	Kanker	27	10	17	10	5	5	...	...	...	...	...	...
26	Nandgaon	95	56	39	154	65	89	...	...	...	...	...	...
27	Khairagarh	25	9	16	252	132	120	...	...	...	17	10	7
28	Chhuikhadan	8	4	4	10	4	6	...	...	...	8	8	...
29	Kawardha	12	8	4	28	12	16	...	...	...	...	...	...
30	Sakti	5	1	4	14	7	7	...	...	...	...	...	...
31	Raigarh	44	31	13	51	27	24	...	...	...	3	2	1
32	Sarangarh	60	22	38	16	9	7	...	...	...	...	...	...
33	Chang Bhakar	3	2	1	...	...	...	...	...	...	1	1	...
34	Korea	2	2	...	4	3	1	...	...	...	...	...	...
35	Surguja	1,028	593	435	...	...	...	...	...	...	...	...	...
36	Udaipur	3	2	1	8	6	2	...	...	...	...	...	...
37	Jashpur	682	397	285	36,880	18,563	18,317	...	...	...	...	...	...

TABLE VII.

Age, Sex and Civil Condition.

THIS table is divided into three parts. Part A (pp. 36 to 39) shows the distribution, for the Province as a whole of the total population and of each religion by age, sex and civil condition. Part B (pp. 40 to 50) shows the distribution in Districts and States of the total population and of the main religions by age, sex and civil condition; but in this Part, in order to economise space, the age statistics have been given in less detail than in the Provincial Summary. Part C (p. 51) gives similar details for Cities.

TABLE VII.—Age, Sex and Civil Condition.
Part A.—Provincial Summary.

Religion.	Age.	Population.			Unmarried.			Married.			Widowed.		
		Persons.	Males.	Females.	Persons.	Males.	Females.	Persons.	Males.	Females.	Persons.	Males.	Females.
	1	2	3	4	5	6	7	8	9	10	11	12	13
ALL RELIGIONS	0—1 ...	606,641	303,465	303,176	605,302	302,912	302,390	1,293	542	751	46	11	35
	1—2 ...	370,432	180,343	190,089	368,603	179,722	188,881	1,771	599	1,172	58	22	36
	2—3 ...	511,617	246,906	264,711	506,540	245,409	261,131	4,958	1,456	3,502	119	41	78
	3—4 ...	580,542	275,511	305,031	571,417	273,309	298,108	8,885	2,118	6,767	240	84	156
	4—5 ...	504,529	249,707	254,822	489,890	246,106	243,784	14,113	3,497	10,616	526	104	422
	Total 0—5	*2,573,761*	*1,255,932*	*1,317,829*	*2,541,752*	*1,247,458*	*1,294,294*	*31,020*	*8,212*	*22,808*	*989*	*262*	*727*
	5—10 ...	2,199,406	1,102,907	1,096,499	1,969,430	1,052,170	917,260	223,871	49,267	174,604	6,105	1,470	4,635
	10—15 ...	1,475,895	802,769	673,126	923,861	625,621	298,240	539,306	173,171	366,135	12,728	3,977	8,751
	15—20 ...	1,079,162	545,341	533,821	330,781	278,893	51,888	730,299	259,649	470,650	18,082	6,793	11,289
	20—25 ...	1,368,979	613,621	755,358	175,554	155,764	19,790	1,151,442	441,874	709,568	41,983	15,983	26,000
	25—30 ...	1,545,920	759,960	785,960	91,017	81,248	9,769	1,381,004	649,731	731,273	73,899	28,981	44,918
	30—35 ...	1,465,574	746,165	719,409	46,369	38,598	7,771	1,299,729	670,827	628,902	119,476	36,740	82,736
	35—40 ...	967,878	509,920	457,958	20,099	16,592	3,507	836,536	463,465	373,071	111,243	29,863	81,380
	40—45 ...	1,035,420	528,871	506,549	18,402	14,560	3,842	804,507	472,227	332,280	212,511	42,084	170,427
	45—50 ...	539,095	283,131	255,964	7,161	5,814	1,347	396,405	249,460	146,945	135,529	27,857	107,672
	50—55 ...	718,020	356,692	361,428	9,240	7,190	2,050	432,675	300,509	132,166	276,105	48,893	227,212
	55—60 ...	227,883	114,119	113,764	2,703	2,098	605	136,842	93,239	43,603	88,338	18,782	69,556
	60—65 ...	490,265	216,393	273,872	5,662	4,255	1,407	208,636	163,800	44,836	275,967	48,338	227,629
	65—70 ...	98,293	46,062	52,231	1,210	910	300	43,104	33,146	9,958	53,979	12,006	41,973
	70 and over	247,759	102,239	145,520	3,411	2,496	915	80,226	64,998	15,228	164,122	34,745	129,377
	Total ...	*16,033,310*	*7,984,025*	*8,049,285*	*6,146,652*	*3,533,667*	*2,612,985*	*8,295,602*	*4,093,575*	*4,202,027*	*1,591,056*	*356,780*	*1,234,276*
HINDU (BRAHMANIC)	0—1 ...	490,297	245,362	244,935	489,149	244,889	244,260	1,120	468	652	28	5	23
	1—2 ...	293,042	143,000	150,042	291,468	142,465	149,003	1,530	517	1,013	44	18	26
	2—3 ...	406,998	196,941	210,057	402,498	195,661	206,837	4,410	1,248	3,162	90	32	58
	3—4 ...	452,606	215,303	237,303	444,375	213,419	230,956	8,042	1,816	6,226	189	68	121
	4—5 ...	391,487	194,155	197,332	377,919	190,956	186,963	13,140	3,109	10,031	428	90	338
	Total 0—5	*2,034,430*	*994,761*	*1,039,669*	*2,005,409*	*987,390*	*1,018,019*	*28,242*	*7,158*	*21,084*	*779*	*213*	*566*
	5—10 ...	1,729,725	867,333	862,392	1,511,199	819,671	691,528	213,076	46,339	166,737	5,450	1,323	4,127
	10—15 ...	1,179,164	641,833	537,331	675,299	476,568	198,731	492,322	161,646	330,676	11,543	3,619	7,924
	15—20 ...	865,560	438,742	426,818	229,653	202,984	26,669	620,616	229,841	390,775	15,291	5,917	9,374
	20—25 ...	1,095,927	492,207	603,720	120,262	108,586	11,676	941,249	370,389	570,860	34,416	13,232	21,184
	25—30 ...	1,234,184	609,941	624,243	63,659	57,686	5,973	1,109,815	528,404	581,411	60,710	23,851	36,859
	30—35 ...	1,164,261	593,690	570,571	33,899	28,663	5,236	1,032,633	534,762	497,871	97,729	30,265	67,464
	35—40 ...	779,474	410,046	369,428	15,109	12,700	2,409	671,536	372,223	299,313	92,829	25,123	67,706
	40—45 ...	827,677	419,715	407,962	13,887	11,184	2,703	639,623	373,491	266,132	174,167	35,040	139,127
	45—50 ...	441,989	231,302	210,687	5,592	4,650	942	322,814	202,948	119,866	113,583	28,704	89,879
	50—55 ...	583,432	289,394	294,038	7,240	5,752	1,488	349,519	242,819	106,700	226,673	40,823	185,850
	55—60 ...	188,859	94,614	94,245	2,125	1,676	449	112,564	76,935	35,629	74,170	16,003	58,167
	60—65 ...	398,821	176,581	222,240	4,389	3,436	953	169,295	133,073	36,222	225,137	40,072	185,065
	65—70 ...	82,238	38,792	43,446	958	733	225	35,974	27,837	8,137	45,306	10,222	35,084
	70 and over	202,133	83,792	118,341	2,658	2,002	656	64,984	52,999	11,985	134,491	28,791	105,700
	Total ...	*12,807,874*	*6,382,743*	*6,425,131*	*4,691,338*	*2,723,681*	*1,967,657*	*6,804,262*	*3,360,864*	*3,443,398*	*1,312,274*	*298,195*	*1,014,079*
HINDU (ARYA)	0—1 ...	31	12	19	31	12	19	...	...	...	...	...	...
	1—2 ...	23	13	10	23	13	10	...	...	...	...	...	...
	2—3 ...	31	17	14	31	17	14	...	...	...	...	...	...
	3—4 ...	25	18	7	25	18	7	...	...	...	...	...	...
	4—5 ...	16	6	10	16	6	10	...	...	...	...	...	...
	Total 0—5	*126*	*66*	*60*	*126*	*66*	*60*	...	...	...	...	...	...
	5—10 ...	133	64	69	130	64	66	2	...	2	1	...	1
	10—15 ...	126	84	42	107	82	25	19	2	17	...	...	...
	15—20 ...	83	48	35	32	29	3	50	19	31	1	...	1
	20—25 ...	101	52	49	23	21	2	71	31	40	7	...	7
	25—30 ...	104	67	37	6	6	...	93	58	35	5	3	2
	30—35 ...	67	37	30	3	3	...	57	34	23	7	...	7
	35—40 ...	73	48	25	1	1	...	66	43	23	6	4	2
	40—45 ...	55	36	19	...	...	...	48	35	13	7	1	6
	45—50 ...	34	18	16	...	...	...	30	17	13	4	1	3
	50—55 ...	20	9	11	1	1	...	10	7	3	9	1	8
	55—60 ...	15	11	4	...	...	...	8	8	...	7	3	4
	60—65 ...	17	8	9	...	...	...	10	8	2	7	...	7
	65—70 ...	8	4	4	...	...	...	2	2	...	6	2	4
	70 and over	12	2	10	...	...	...	2	1	1	10	1	9
	Total ...	*974*	*554*	*420*	*429*	*273*	*156*	*468*	*265*	*203*	*77*	*16*	*61*

TABLE VII.—Part A.—Provincial Summary—*continued.*

Religion.	Age.	Population.			Unmarried.			Married.			Widowed.		
		Persons.	Males.	Females.	Persons.	Males.	Females.	Persons.	Males.	Females.	Persons.	Males.	Females.
	1	2	3	4	5	6	7	8	9	10	11	12	13
HINDU (BRAHMO)	0—1 ...	...	...	...	...	...	...	...	...	...	...	...	...
	1—2 ...	...	...	...	...	...	...	...	...	...	...	...	...
	2—3 ...	1	...	1	1	...	1	...	...	...	...	...	...
	3—4 ...	...	...	...	...	...	...	...	...	...	...	...	...
	4—5 ...	1	...	1	1	...	1	...	...	...	...	...	...
	Total 0—5	*2*	...	*2*	2	...	*2*	...	...	...	...	...	...
	5—10 ...	2	...	2	2	...	2	...	...	...	...	...	...
	10—15 ...	2	1	1	1	1	...	1	...	1	...	...	...
	15—20 ...	2	...	2	...	...	...	2	...	2	...	...	...
	20—25 ...	3	1	2	...	...	...	3	1	2	...	...	...
	25—30 ...	1	1	...	...	...	...	1	1	...	...	...	...
	30—35 ...	6	5	1	1	1	...	5	4	1	...	...	...
	35—40 ...	2	2	...	...	...	...	2	2	...	...	...	...
	40—45 ...	2	1	1	...	...	...	1	...	1	1	1	...
	45—50 ...	1	...	1	...	...	...	1	...	1	...	...	...
	50—55 ...	5	5	...	...	...	...	5	5	...	...	...	...
	55—60 ...	2	2	...	...	...	...	1	1	...	1	1	...
	60—65 ...	2	1	1	...	...	...	...	...	...	2	1	1
	65—70 ...	...	...	...	...	...	...	...	...	...	...	—	...
	70 and over	...	...	...	...	...	...	...	...	...	...	...	...
	Total ...	*32*	*19*	*13*	*6*	*2*	*4*	*22*	*14*	*8*	*4*	*3*	*1*
SIKH	0—1 ...	51	24	27	51	24	27	...	...	...	...	...	...
	1—2 ...	25	13	12	25	13	12	...	...	...	...	...	...
	2—3 ...	39	21	18	39	21	18	...	...	...	...	...	...
	3—4 ...	52	22	30	50	21	29	2	1	1	...	...	...
	4—5 ...	25	14	11	25	14	11	...	...	...	...	...	...
	Total 0—5	*192*	*94*	*98*	*190*	*93*	*97*	*2*	*1*	*1*	...	...	...
	5—10 ...	118	58	60	115	57	58	3	1	2	...	...	...
	10—15 ...	116	74	42	82	57	25	34	17	17	...	...	...
	15—20 ...	211	156	55	116	111	5	93	44	49	2	1	1
	20—25 ...	572	492	80	268	265	3	286	210	76	18	17	1
	25—30 ...	412	349	63	127	127	...	266	205	61	19	17	2
	30—35 ...	263	217	46	37	37	...	210	165	45	16	15	1
	35—40 ...	189	167	22	16	16	...	158	136	22	15	15	...
	40—45 ...	119	96	23	8	8	...	105	82	23	6	6	...
	45—50 ...	45	32	13	3	8	...	32	25	7	10	4	6
	50—55 ...	47	38	9	...	...	...	34	31	3	17	7	6
	55—60 ...	13	8	5	...	...	...	10	7	3	3	1	2
	60—65 ...	19	10	9	...	...	...	12	9	3	7	1	6
	65—70 ...	3	1	2	...	...	...	...	...	...	3	1	2
	70 and over	18	10	8	...	...	...	10	8	2	8	2	6
	Total ...	*2,337*	*1,801*	*536*	*962*	*774*	*188*	*1,355*	*941*	*314*	*120*	*87*	*33*
JAIN	0—1 ...	2,369	1,178	1,191	2,359	1,173	1,186	10	5	5	...	...	...
	1—2 ...	1,174	557	617	1,165	554	611	9	3	6	...	...	...
	2—3 ...	1,898	901	997	1,884	897	987	12	3	9	2	1	1
	3—4 ...	1,985	938	1,047	1,966	928	1,038	15	8	7	4	2	2
	4—5 ...	1,705	869	836	1,681	861	820	22	8	14	2	...	2
	Total 0—5	*9,131*	*4,443*	*4,688*	*9,055*	*4,413*	*4,642*	*68*	*27*	*41*	*8*	*3*	*5*
	5—10 ...	8,534	4,300	4,284	7,963	4,244	3,719	541	51	490	30	5	25
	10—15 ...	7,227	4,037	3,190	4,684	3,586	1,098	2,447	435	2,012	96	16	80
	15—20 ...	5,697	3,131	2,566	1,929	1,884	45	3,572	1,207	2,365	196	40	156
	20—25 ...	6,878	3,453	3,425	1,288	1,248	40	5,105	2,091	3,014	485	114	371
	25—30 ...	6,721	3,606	3,115	752	733	19	5,286	2,694	2,592	683	179	504
	30—35 ...	6,355	3,236	3,119	459	435	24	4,842	2,570	2,272	1,054	231	823
	35—40 ...	4,470	2,307	2,103	220	205	15	3,327	1,972	1,355	923	190	733
	40—45 ...	4,737	2,374	2,363	206	192	14	3,041	1,907	1,134	1,490	275	1,215
	45—50 ...	2,764	1,565	1,199	94	89	5	1,675	1,210	465	995	266	729
	50—55 ...	3,553	1,730	1,823	128	125	3	1,674	1,229	445	1,751	376	1,375
	55—60 ...	1,339	733	606	33	29	4	655	527	128	651	177	474
	60—65 ...	2,313	1,036	1,277	73	70	3	747	606	141	1,493	360	1,133
	65—70 ...	558	279	279	20	20	...	186	158	28	352	101	251
	70 and over	1,140	490	650	26	22	4	291	245	46	823	223	600
	Total ...	*71,417*	*36,780*	*34,637*	*26,930*	*17,295*	*9,635*	*33,457*	*16,929*	*16,528*	*11,030*	*2,556*	*8,474*

TABLE VII.—Part A.—Provincial Summary—*continued.*

Religion.	Age.	Population. Persons.	Males.	Females.	Unmarried. Persons.	Males.	Females.	Married. Persons.	Males.	Females.	Widowed. Persons.	Males.	Females.
	1	2	3	4	5	6	7	8	9	10	11	12	13
BUDDHIST	0—20 ...	...	...	...	...	...	...	...	...	...	...	...	...
	20—25 ...	3	3	...	2	2	...	1	1	...	...	...	...
	25—30 ...	1	1	...	...	...	...	1	1	...	...	...	...
	30—35 ...	2	2	...	1	1	...	1	1	...	...	...	...
	35—40 ...	1	1	...	...	...	...	...	...	...	1	1	...
	40—45 ...	...	...	...	...	...	...	...	...	...	...	...	...
	45—50 ...	...	...	...	...	...	...	...	...	...	...	...	...
	50—55 ...	1	1	...	...	...	...	...	...	...	1	1	...
	55—60 ...	...	...	...	...	...	...	...	...	...	...	...	...
	60—65 ...	...	...	...	--	...	...	...	...	...	...	...	...
	65—70 ...	...	...	...	...	...	...	...	...	...	...	...	...
	70 and over	1	...	1	...	...	...	...	...	...	1	...	1
	Total ...	*9*	*8*	*1*	*3*	*3*	...	*3*	*3*	...	*3*	*2*	*1*
ANIMIST	0—1 ...	90,952	45,448	45,504	90,821	45,396	45,425	120	48	72	11	4	7
	1—2 ...	63,507	30,542	32,965	63,334	30,489	32,845	165	51	114	8	2	6
	2—3 ...	82,900	39,462	43,438	82,479	39,311	43,168	401	146	255	20	5	15
	3—4 ...	103,946	48,831	55,115	103,301	48,608	54,693	613	212	401	32	11	21
	4—5 ...	91,757	45,039	46,718	90,957	44,725	46,232	733	306	427	67	8	59
	Total 0—5	*433,062*	*209,322*	*223,740*	*430,892*	*208,529*	*222,363*	*2,032*	*763*	*1,269*	*138*	*30*	*108*
	5—10 ...	371,008	186,204	184,804	362,912	183,948	178,964	7,649	2,166	5,483	447	90	357
	10—15 ...	224,623	120,547	104,076	189,938	111,432	78,506	33,960	8,883	25,077	725	232	493
	15—20 ...	160,240	78,282	81,958	75,640	54,455	21 185	82,741	23,175	59,566	1,859	652	1,207
	20—25 ...	202,633	85,705	116,928	36,881	30,264	6,617	160,933	53,605	107,328	4,819	1,836	2,983
	25—30 ...	241,192	112,358	128,834	18,177	15,347	2,830	214,079	93,483	120,596	8,936	3,528	5,408
	30—35 ...	235,198	117,697	117,501	8,346	6,458	1,888	211,631	106,670	104,961	15,221	4,569	10,652
	35—40 ...	146,282	76,160	70,122	3,240	2,471	769	130,310	70,474	59 836	12,732	3,215	9,517
	40—45 ...	159,780	84,312	75,468	2,984	2,171	813	129,230	77,140	52,090	27,566	5,001	22,565
	45—50 ...	74,093	38,804	35,289	1,021	751	270	57,238	35,211	22,027	15,834	2,842	12,992
	50—55 ...	100,744	49,860	50,884	1 288	902	386	63,377	43,317	20,060	36,079	5,641	30,438
	55—60 ...	28,877	13,820	15,057	380	280	100	18,380	11,731	6,649	10,117	1,809	8,308
	60—65 ...	68,349	29,065	39,284	858	523	335	29,454	22,687	6,767	38,037	5,855	32,182
	65—70 ...	11,362	4,849	6,513	165	114	51	5,046	3,618	1,428	6,151	1,117	5,034
	70 and over	32,912	12,566	20,346	491	308	183	10,895	8,266	2,629	21,526	3,992	17,534
	Total ...	*2,490,355*	*1,219,551*	*1,270,804*	*1,133,213*	*617.953*	*515,260*	*1,156,955*	*561,189*	*595,766*	*200,187*	*40,409*	*159,778*
MUSALMAN	0—1 ...	20,128	10,045	10,083	20,080	10,023	10.057	42	21	21	6	1	5
	1—2 ...	10,323	5,042	5,281	10,254	5,015	5,239	63	25	38	6	2	4
	2—3 ...	17,406	8,444	8,962	17,260	8,384	8,882	133	57	76	7	3	4
	3—4 ...	18,609	8,959	9,950	18,687	8,878	9.809	208	79	129	14	2	12
	4—5 ...	17.052	8,406	8,646	16,812	8,327	8,485	211	73	138	29	6	23
	Total 0—5	*83,818*	*40,896*	*42,922*	*83,099*	*40,627*	*42,472*	*657*	*255*	*402*	*62*	*14*	*48*
	5—10 ...	78,831	39,355	39.476	76.206	38,635	37,571	2,458	673	1,785	167	47	120
	10—15 ...	56.729	31,722	25,007	46,621	29,626	16,995	9.771	1,994	7,777	337	102	235
	15—20 ...	41,059	21,845	19,214	19,461	16,875	2.586	20,923	4,800	16,123	675	170	505
	20—25 ...	54,301	26,647	27,654	13,166	12,177	989	39,045	13,736	25,309	2,090	734	1,356
	25—30 ...	55,684	29,111	26,573	6,230	5,520	710	46.125	22,268	23,857	3,329	1,323	2,006
	30—35 ...	53,540	27,987	25,553	2,938	2,462	476	45,475	23,956	21,519	5,127	1,569	3,558
	35—40 ...	33,257	18,817	14,440	1,202	996	206	27,652	16,602	11,050	4,403	1,219	3,184
	40—45 ...	39,556	20,402	19,154	1,125	887	238	29,722	17,863	11,859	8,709	1,652	7,057
	45—50 ...	18,201	10,323	7,878	375	280	95	13,076	9,080	3,996	4,750	963	3,787
	50—55 ...	28,081	14,455	13,626	513	373	140	16,631	12,148	4,483	10,937	1,984	9,003
	55—60 ...	7,844	4,467	3,377	124	94	30	4,642	3,649	993	3,078	724	2,354
	60—65 ...	19,383	9,075	10,308	313	214	99	8,508	6,930	1,578	10,562	1,931	8,631
	65—70 ...	3,810	2,009	1,810	60	39	21	1,758	1,442	316	2,001	528	1,473
	70 and over	10,926	5,116	5,810	222	155	67	3,821	3,308	513	6,853	1,658	5,230
	Total ...	*585,029*	*302,227*	*282,802*	*251,655*	*148,960*	*102,695*	*270,264*	*138,704*	*131 ,560*	*63,110*	*14,563*	*48,547*
CHRISTIAN	0—1 ...	2,754	1,366	1,388	2,753	1,365	1,388	...	...	...	1	1	...
	1—2 ...	2,314	1,158	1,156	2,313	1,158	1,155	1	...	1	...	...	...
	2—3 ...	2,311	1,101	1,210	2,309	1,099	1,210	2	2	...	...	...	...
	3—4 ...	2,966	1,414	1,552	2,962	1,412	1,550	3	1	2	1	1	...
	4—5 ...	2,452	1,198	1,254	2,445	1,197	1,248	7	1	6	—	...	...
	Total 0—5	*12,797*	*6,237*	*6,560*	*12,782*	*6,231*	*6,551*	*13*	*4*	*9*	*2*	*2*	...

TABLE VII.—Part A.—Provincial Summary—*concluded.*

Religion.	Age.	Population.			Unmarried.			Married.			Widowed.		
		Persons.	Males.	Females.	Persons.	Males.	Females.	Persons.	Males.	Females.	Persons.	Males.	Females.
	1	2	3	4	5	6	7	8	9	10	11	12	13
CHRISTIAN—(concld.)	5—10 ...	10,853	5,484	5,369	10,705	5,443	5,262	138	36	102	10	5	5
	10—15 ...	7,774	4,405	3,369	7,000	4,206	2,794	747	191	556	27	8	19
	15—20 ...	6,167	3,074	3,093	3,828	2,495	1,333	2,281	560	1,721	58	19	39
	20—25 ...	8,354	4,932	3,422	3,526	3,096	430	4,683	1,786	2 897	145	50	95
	25—30 ...	7,406	4,397	3,009	1,972	1,752	220	5,219	2,565	2,654	215	80	135
	30—35 ...	5,698	3,175	2,523	639	499	140	4,744	2,589	2,155	315	87	228
	35—40 ...	3,978	2,215	1,763	300	195	105	3,354	1,930	1,424	324	90	234
	40—45 ...	3,327	1,821	1,506	186	112	74	2,590	1,608	982	551	101	450
	45—50 ...	1,879	1,025	854	74	39	35	1,462	914	548	343	72	271
	50—55 ...	2,061	1,041	1,020	67	35	32	1,365	902	463	629	104	525
	55—60 ...	891	436	455	40	18	22	554	360	194	297	58	239
	60—65 ...	1,330	599	731	29	12	17	594	476	118	707	111	596
	65—70 ...	293	119	174	7	4	3	131	88	48	155	32	123
	70 and over	593	248	345	12	7	5	211	162	49	370	79	291
	Total ...	*73,401*	*39,208*	*34,193*	*41,167*	*24,144*	*17,023*	*28,086*	*14,166*	*13,920*	*4,148*	*898*	*3,250*
JEW	0—1 ...	7	3	4	7	3	4	...	...	...	...	...	...
	1—2 ...	2	2	...	1	1	...	1	1	...	...	...	...
	2—3 ...	4	3	1	4	3	1	...	...	...	...	...	...
	3—4 ...	6	4	2	5	4	1	1	...	1	...	...	...
	4—5 ...	2	2	...	2	2	...	...	...	...	...	...	...
	Total 0—5	*21*	*14*	*7*	*19*	*13*	*6*	*2*	*1*	*1*	...	...	...
	5—10 ...	16	8	8	16	8	8	...	...	...	...	...	...
	10—15 ...	11	7	4	11	7	4	...	...	...	...	...	...
	15—20 ...	8	4	4	7	4	3	1	...	1	...	...	...
	20—25 ...	15	12	3	10	9	1	5	3	2	...	...	...
	25—30 ...	12	6	6	1	1	...	11	5	6	...	...	...
	30—35 ...	12	6	6	...	...	...	10	5	5	2	1	1
	35—40 ...	9	8	1	1	1	...	8	7	1	...	...	...
	40—45 ...	7	4	3	...	...	...	7	4	3	...	...	...
	45—50 ...	4	2	2	...	...	...	4	2	2	...	...	...
	50—55 ...	1	1	...	...	...	...	1	1	...	—	...	...
	55—60 ...	3	3	...	...	...	...	2	2	...	1	1	—
	60—65 ...	3	1	2	...	...	...	1	1	...	2	...	2
	65—70 ...	1	1	...	...	...	...	—	...	...	1	1	...
	70 and over	2	1	1	...	...	...	...	...	...	2	1	1
	Total ...	*125*	*78*	*47*	*66*	*43*	*22*	*52*	*31*	*21*	*8*	*4*	*4*
ZOROASTRIAN	0—1 ...	52	27	25	51	27	24	1	...	1	...	...	...
	1—2 ...	22	16	6	20	14	6	2	2	...	...	...	...
	2—3 ...	29	16	13	29	16	13	...	...	...	...	...	...
	3—4 ...	47	22	25	46	21	25	1	1	...	...	...	...
	4—5 ...	32	18	14	32	18	14	...	...	...	—	...	...
	Total 0—5	*182*	*99*	*83*	*178*	*96*	*83*	*4*	*3*	*1*	...	...	...
	5—10 ...	186	101	85	182	100	82	4	1	3	...	...	...
	10—15 ...	123	59	64	118	56	62	5	3	2	...	...	...
	15—20 ...	135	59	76	115	56	59	20	3	17	...	...	...
	20—25 ...	192	117	75	128	96	32	61	21	40	3	...	3
	25—30 ...	203	123	80	93	76	17	108	47	61	2	...	2
	30—35 ...	172	113	59	46	39	7	121	71	50	5	3	2
	35—40 ...	143	89	54	10	7	3	123	76	47	10	6	4
	40—45 ...	160	110	50	6	6	...	140	97	43	14	7	7
	45—50 ...	85	60	25	2	2	...	73	53	20	10	5	5
	50—55 ...	75	58	17	3	2	1	59	50	9	13	6	7
	55—60 ...	40	25	15	1	1	...	26	19	7	13	5	8
	60—65 ...	28	17	11	...	...	...	15	10	5	13	7	6
	65—70 ...	11	8	3	...	...	...	7	6	1	4	2	2
	70 and over	23	14	8	2	2	...	12	9	3	8	3	5
	Total ...	*1,757*	*1,058*	*706*	*884*	*539*	*345*	*778*	*469*	*309*	*95*	*44*	*51*

TABLE VII.—Part B.—Details for Districts.

District or State.	Age.	Population.			Unmarried.			Married.			Widowed.		
		Persons.	Males.	Females.	Persons.	Males.	Females.	Persons.	Males.	Females.	Persons.	Males.	Females.
	1	2	3	4	5	6	7	8	9	10	11	12	13
SAUGOR	ALL RELIGIONS.	*541,410*	*276,233*	*265,177*	*223,448*	*135,882*	*87,566*	*255,795*	*127,264*	*128,531*	*62,167*	*13,087*	*49,080*
	0—5 ...	85,142	42,365	42,777	84,968	42,306	42,662	162	58	104	12	1	11
	5—10 ...	74,792	38,290	36,502	72,271	37,944	34,327	2,447	333	2,114	74	13	61
	10—15 ...	47,297	26,772	20,525	32,450	23,403	9,047	14,601	3,334	11,267	246	35	211
	15—20 ...	39,626	21,955	17,671	14,057	13,420	637	24,845	8,390	16,455	724	145	579
	20—40 ...	191,593	96,708	94,885	17,602	16,911	691	156,515	75,579	80,936	17,476	4,218	13,258
	40—60 ...	83,102	41,227	41,875	1,752	1,592	160	50,707	34,035	16,672	30,643	5,600	25,043
	60 and over	19,858	8,916	10,942	348	306	42	6,518	5,535	983	12,992	3,075	9,017
	HINDU (BRAHMANIC)	*471,650*	*240,256*	*231,394*	*193,713*	*118,087*	*75,626*	*223,551*	*110,812*	*112,739*	*54,386*	*11,457*	*42,929*
	0—5 ...	74,465	37,188	37,277	74,302	37,132	37,170	151	55	96	12	1	11
	5—10 ...	65,451	33,606	31,845	63,119	33,281	29,838	2,266	313	1,953	66	12	54
	10—15 ...	41,190	23,319	17,871	27,738	20,202	7,536	13,225	3,084	10,141	227	33	194
	15—20 ...	34,481	19,140	15,341	11,879	11,478	401	21,961	7,537	14,424	641	125	516
	20—40 ...	166,856	83,726	83,130	14,900	14,374	526	136,613	65,692	70,921	15,343	3,660	11,683
	40—60 ...	72,194	35,747	36,447	1,490	1,364	126	43,809	29,439	14,370	26,895	4,944	21,951
	60 and over	17,013	7,630	9,383	285	256	29	5,526	4,692	834	11,202	2,682	8,520
	ANIMIST ...	*24,924*	*12,154*	*12,770*	*10,596*	*5,828*	*4,768*	*12,022*	*5,864*	*6,158*	*2,306*	*462*	*1,844*
	0—5 ...	4,396	2,113	2,283	4,389	2,111	2,278	7	2	5	...	...	...
	5—10 ...	3,529	1,746	1,783	3,500	1,738	1,762	26	7	19	3	1	2
	10—15 ...	1,775	962	813	1,465	896	569	308	66	242	2	...	2
	15—20 ...	1,630	813	817	636	538	98	971	265	706	23	10	13
	20—40 ...	8,731	4,119	4,612	540	493	47	7,602	3,470	4,132	589	156	433
	40—60 ...	3,988	1,980	2,008	55	43	12	2,763	1,764	999	1,170	173	997
	60 and over	875	421	454	11	9	2	345	290	55	519	122	397
	MUSALMAN	*25,835*	*13,632*	*12,203*	*10,906*	*6,624*	*4,372*	*12,149*	*6,424*	*5,725*	*2,690*	*584*	*2,106*
	0—5 ...	3,793	1,817	1,976	3,789	1,816	1,973	4	1	3	...	...	...
	5—10 ...	3,423	1,719	1,704	3,338	1,707	1,631	84	12	72	1	—	1
	10—15 ...	2,355	1,332	1,023	1,849	1,232	617	500	98	402	6	2	4
	15—20 ...	1,939	1,108	831	888	817	71	1,028	286	742	23	5	18
	20—40 ...	9,302	5,144	4,158	1,048	988	60	7,574	3,931	3,643	680	225	455
	40—60 ...	3,900	2,017	1,883	62	51	11	2,555	1,747	808	1,283	219	1,064
	60 and over	1,123	495	628	22	13	9	404	349	55	697	133	564
	JAIN ...	*16,713*	*8,627*	*8,086*	*6,882*	*4,517*	*2,365*	*7,151*	*3,571*	*3,580*	*2,680*	*539*	*2,141*
	0—5 ...	2,213	1,118	1,095	2,213	1,118	1,095	...	...	...	...	...	...
	5—10 ...	2,165	1,107	1,058	2,091	1,107	984	70	...	70	4	...	4
	10—15 ...	1,825	1,071	754	1,252	988	264	562	83	479	11	...	11
	15—20 ...	1,310	747	563	468	459	9	805	283	522	37	5	33
	20—40 ...	5,568	2,870	2,698	709	698	11	4,044	2,025	2,019	815	147	668
	40—60 ...	2,822	1,362	1,460	121	119	2	1,446	991	455	1,255	252	1,003
	60 and over	810	352	458	28	28	...	224	189	35	558	135	423
DAMOH	ALL RELIGIONS.	*333,047*	*168,060*	*164,987*	*139,876*	*83,475*	*56,401*	*157,202*	*77,351*	*79,851*	*35,969*	*7,234*	*28,735*
	0—5 ...	51,419	25,744	25,675	51,269	25,692	25,577	134	47	87	16	5	11
	5—10 ...	47,907	24,778	23,129	46,412	24,485	21,927	1,446	279	1,167	49	14	35
	10—15 ...	31,719	17,679	14,040	23,061	15,342	7,719	8,500	2,303	6,197	158	34	124
	15—20 ...	23,816	13,034	10,782	8,366	7,758	608	14,996	5,166	9,830	454	110	344
	20—40 ...	116,374	57,070	59,304	9,521	9,080	441	96,949	45,801	51,148	9,904	2,189	7,715
	40—60 ...	50,018	24,298	25,720	988	891	97	31,007	20,284	10,723	18,023	3,123	14,900
	60 and over	11,794	5,457	6,337	259	227	32	4,170	3,471	699	7,365	1,759	5,606
	HINDU (BRAHMANIC)	*303,189*	*152,873*	*150,316*	*127,139*	*75,769*	*51,370*	*143,303*	*70,533*	*72,770*	*32,748*	*6,572*	*26,176*
	0—5 ...	46,850	23,445	23,405	46,712	23,395	23,317	122	45	77	16	5	11
	5—10 ...	43,698	22,587	21,111	42,341	22,309	20,032	1,310	264	1,046	47	14	33
	10—15 ...	28,918	16,090	12,828	20,849	13,872	6,977	7,922	2,186	5,736	147	32	115
	15—20 ...	21,661	11,828	9,833	7,483	6,948	535	13,773	4,788	8,985	405	92	313
	20—40 ...	105,973	51,941	54,032	8,606	8,215	391	88,304	41,720	46,584	9,063	2,006	7,057
	40—60 ...	45,491	22,080	23,411	912	822	90	28,160	18,416	9,744	16,419	2,842	13,577
	60 and over	10,598	4,902	5,696	236	208	28	3,711	3,113	598	6,651	1,581	5,070
	ANIMIST ...	*11,115*	*5,461*	*5,654*	*4,756*	*2,594*	*2,162*	*5,450*	*2,664*	*2,786*	*909*	*203*	*706*
	0—5 ...	1,890	918	972	1,882	917	965	8	1	7	...	—	...
	5—10 ...	1,656	833	823	1,640	830	810	14	3	11	2	...	3
	10—15 ...	879	468	411	754	437	317	124	31	93	1	...	1
	15—20 ...	743	373	370	279	228	51	451	141	310	13	4	9
	20—40 ...	3,861	1,807	2,054	180	172	17	3,474	1,581	1,893	198	54	144
	40—60 ...	1,666	840	826	8	7	1	1,179	749	430	479	84	395
	60 and over	420	222	198	4	3	1	200	158	42	216	61	155

TABLE VII.—Part B.—Details for Districts—*continued.* [Jubbulpore Mandla]

District or State.	Age.	Population.			Unmarried.			Married.			Widowed.		
		Persons.	Males.	Females.	Persons.	Males.	Females.	Persons.	Males.	Females.	Persons.	Males.	Females.
	1	2	3	4	5	6	7	8	9	10	11	12	13
DAMOH—(concld.)	MUSALMAN	*11,002*	*5,680*	*5,332*	*4,751*	*2,945*	*1,806*	*5,094*	*2,396*	*2,698*	*1,157*	*239*	*918*
	0—5 ...	1,676	872	804	1,672	871	801	4	1	3	...	...	...
	5—10 ...	1,555	795	760	1,466	787	679	89	8	81	...	...	...
	10—15 ...	1,043	603	440	844	565	279	196	38	158	3	...	3
	15—20 ...	732	417	315	324	304	20	391	102	289	17	11	6
	20—40 ...	3,925	2,002	1,923	417	394	23	3,212	1,527	1,685	296	81	215
	40—60 ...	1,643	800	843	21	19	2	1,048	698	350	574	83	491
	60 and over	428	181	237	7	5	2	154	122	32	267	64	203
JUBBULPORE	ALL RELIGIONS.	*745,892*	*373,173*	*372,719*	*297,551*	*174,563*	*122,988*	*366,583*	*181,286*	*185,297*	*81,758*	*17,324*	*64,434*
	0—5 ...	116,204	57,204	59,000	115,230	56,929	58,301	931	266	665	43	9	34
	5—10 ...	101,733	51,471	50,262	94,401	49,444	44,957	7,188	1,986	5,197	149	41	108
	10—15 ...	71,423	39,585	31,838	47,006	31,216	15,790	23,884	8,168	15,716	533	201	332
	15—20 ...	52,700	28,312	24,388	17,692	15,493	2,199	34,065	12,460	21,605	943	359	584
	20—40 ...	261,318	130,667	130,651	20,991	19,594	1,397	219,745	105,200	114,545	20,582	5,873	14,700
	40—60 ...	113,887	54,002	59,885	1,863	1,591	272	71,051	45,270	25,781	40,973	7,141	33,832
	60 and over	28,627	11,932	16,695	368	296	72	9,724	7,936	1,788	18,535	3,700	14,835
	HINDU (BRAHMANIC)	*598,960*	*298,484*	*300,476*	*232,350*	*136,504*	*95,846*	*298,077*	*147,399*	*150,678*	*68,533*	*14,581*	*53,952*
	0—5 ...	92,007	45,283	46,814	91,217	45,051	46,166	842	224	618	38	8	30
	5—10 ...	81,164	41,052	40,112	74,556	39,208	35,347	6,484	1,810	4,674	130	39	91
	10—15 ...	58,547	32,563	25,984	36,990	24,997	12,002	21,092	7,404	13,688	456	162	294
	15—20 ...	42,380	23,953	18,427	13,378	12,154	1,224	28,229	10,512	17,717	773	287	486
	20—40 ...	209,452	103,631	105,821	14,408	13,539	869	177,459	85,185	92,274	17,585	4,907	12,678
	40—60 ...	92,512	43,565	48,947	1,508	1,322	186	56,541	36,136	20,405	34,463	6,107	28,356
	60 and over	22,808	9,437	13,371	290	238	52	7,430	6,128	1,302	15,088	3,071	12,017
	ANIMIST...	*91,543*	*44,113*	*47,430*	*40,353*	*22,125*	*18,228*	*43,567*	*20,708*	*22,859*	*7,523*	*1,280*	*6,243*
	0—5 ...	16,887	8,349	8,538	16,819	8,319	8,500	63	29	34	5	1	4
	5—10 ...	13,818	7,045	6,773	13,404	6,931	6,473	404	113	291	10	1	9
	10—15 ...	7,766	4,123	3,643	6,068	3,617	2,451	1,657	490	1,177	41	26	15
	15—20 ...	5,886	2,859	3,027	2,144	1,549	595	3,668	1,278	2,390	74	32	42
	20—40 ...	30,409	14,119	16,290	1,818	1,572	246	27,135	12,156	14,979	1,456	391	1,065
	40—60 ...	13,264	6,214	7,050	162	115	47	9,262	5,598	3,664	3,840	501	3,339
	60 and over	3,513	1,404	2,100	38	22	16	1,378	1,054	324	2,097	328	1,769
	MUSALMAN	*41,339*	*22,117*	*19,222*	*16,682*	*10,273*	*6,409*	*20,198*	*10,661*	*9,537*	*4,459*	*1,183*	*3,276*
	0—5 ...	5,696	2,828	2,868	5,670	2,815	2,855	26	13	13	...	...	...
	5—10 ...	5,344	2,713	2,631	5,064	2,650	2,414	272	62	210	8	1	7
	10—15 ...	3,924	2,271	1,653	2,926	1,992	934	966	266	700	32	13	19
	15—20 ...	3,236	1,870	1,366	1,386	1,268	118	1,774	565	1,209	76	37	39
	20—40 ...	14,802	8,175	6,627	1,521	1,449	72	12,116	6,247	5,869	1,165	479	686
	40—60 ...	6,485	3,369	3,116	90	77	13	4,286	2,876	1,410	2,109	416	1,693
	60 and over	1,852	891	961	25	22	3	756	632	126	1,069	237	832
	CHRISTIAN	*6,880*	*4,554*	*2,326*	*5,050*	*3,673*	*1,377*	*1,623*	*832*	*791*	*207*	*49*	*158*
	0—5 ...	647	320	327	647	320	327	...	...	...	...	...	...
	5—10 ...	567	248	319	553	237	316	4	1	3	...	...	...
	10—15 ...	498	231	267	496	229	267	2	2	...	...	...	...
	15—20 ...	564	242	322	491	238	253	71	4	67	2	...	2
	20—40 ...	3,986	3,181	805	2,796	2,606	190	1,138	561	577	52	14	38
	40—60 ...	513	277	236	61	38	23	352	219	133	100	20	80
	60 and over	115	65	50	6	5	1	56	45	11	53	15	38
MANDLA	ALL RELIGIONS.	*405,234*	*200,872*	*204,362*	*172,734*	*96,432*	*76,302*	*200,976*	*97,934*	*103,042*	*31,524*	*6,506*	*25,018*
	0—5 ...	70,498	34,575	35,923	69,824	34,339	35,485	632	228	404	42	13	29
	5—10 ...	61,066	30,764	30,302	57,760	29,782	27,978	3,247	988	2,259	89	24	65
	10—15 ...	35,640	19,230	16,410	26,168	16,112	10,056	9,298	3,054	6,244	174	64	110
	15—20 ...	26,930	13,268	13,662	9,107	7,461	1,646	17,356	5,624	11,732	467	183	284
	20—40 ...	139,727	67,675	72,052	8,762	7,812	950	123,499	57,333	66,166	7,466	2,530	4,936
	40—60 ...	56,813	29,644	27,169	935	787	148	41,449	26,417	15,032	14,429	2,440	11,989
	60 and over	14,530	5,686	8,844	178	139	39	5,495	4,295	1,200	8,857	1,252	7,605
	HINDU (BRAHMANIC)	*155,006*	*77,986*	*77,020*	*63,817*	*36,710*	*27,107*	*76,827*	*38,243*	*38,584*	*14,362*	*3,033*	*11,329*
	0—5 ...	25,920	12,816	13,104	25,475	12,661	12,814	424	146	278	21	9	12
	5—10 ...	22,636	11,365	11,271	20,708	10,781	9,927	1,881	568	1,313	47	16	31
	10—15 ...	14,549	7,937	6,612	9,810	6,353	3,457	4,644	1,553	3,091	95	31	64
	15—20 ...	10,811	5,624	5,187	3,495	3,022	473	7,121	2,537	4,584	195	65	130
	20—40 ...	53,863	26,962	26,901	3,815	3,451	364	46,293	22,313	23,980	3,755	1,198	2,557
	40—60 ...	21,716	11,153	10,563	439	374	65	14,558	9,593	4,965	6,719	1,186	5,533
	60 and over	5,511	2,129	3,382	75	68	7	1,906	1,533	373	2,530	528	3,002

Seoni
Narsinghpur] TABLE VII.—Part B.—Details for Districts—*continued.*

District or State.	Age.	Population. Persons.	Population. Males.	Population. Females.	Unmarried. Persons.	Unmarried. Males.	Unmarried. Females.	Married. Persons.	Married. Males.	Married. Females.	Widowed. Persons.	Widowed. Males.	Widowed. Females.
	1	2	3	4	5	6	7	8	9	10	11	12	13
MANDLA—(concld.)	ANIMIST ...	*242,261*	*118,656*	*123,605*	*105,616*	*57,712*	*47,904*	*120,301*	*57,648*	*62,653*	*16,344*	*3,296*	*13,048*
	0—5 ...	43,429	21,158	22,271	43,205	21,079	22,126	204	75	129	20	4	16
	5—10 ...	37,472	18,916	18,556	36,098	18,494	17,604	1,333	414	919	41	8	33
	10—15 ...	20,412	10,923	9,489	15,804	9,417	6,387	4,530	1,474	3,056	78	32	46
	15—20 ...	15,554	7,358	8,196	5,355	4,227	1,128	9,936	3,016	6,920	263	115	148
	20—40 ...	82,784	39,029	43,755	4,582	4,031	551	74,719	33,738	40,981	3,483	1,260	2,223
	40—60 ...	33,874	17,828	16,046	476	396	80	26,078	16,244	9,834	7,320	1,188	6,132
	60 and over	8,736	3,444	5,292	96	68	28	3,501	2,087	814	5,139	689	4,450
SEONI	ALL RELIGIONS.	*395,481*	*192,642*	*202,839*	*163,894*	*91,262*	*72,632*	*195,768*	*94,692*	*101,076*	*35,819*	*6,688*	*29,131*
	0—5 ...	62,442	30,344	32,098	62,173	30,260	31,913	264	83	181	5	1	4
	5—10 ...	56,753	28,265	28,488	54,215	27,563	26,652	2,491	692	1,799	47	10	37
	10—15 ...	35,457	19,118	16,339	27,312	16,589	10,723	8,049	2,502	5,547	96	27	69
	15—20 ...	25,165	12,868	12,297	9,824	7,986	1,838	15,074	4,789	10,285	267	93	174
	20—40 ...	135,061	64,060	71,001	9,141	7,910	1,231	118,890	53,850	65,040	7,030	2,300	4,730
	40—60 ...	62,399	31,010	31,389	1,009	798	211	44,221	27,567	16,654	17,169	2,645	14,524
	60 and over	18,204	6,977	11,227	220	156	64	6,779	5,209	1,570	11,205	1,612	9,593
	HINDU (BRAHMANIC)	*214,957*	*105,751*	*109,206*	*85,524*	*48,395*	*37,129*	*109,363*	*53,420*	*55,943*	*20,070*	*3,936*	*16,134*
	0—5 ...	33,582	16,423	17,159	33,394	16,372	17,022	184	50	134	4	1	3
	5—10 ...	30,798	15,290	15,508	28,607	14,665	13,942	2,159	619	1,540	32	6	26
	10—15 ...	20,269	10,978	9,291	13,898	8,908	4,990	6,297	2,051	4,246	74	19	55
	15—20 ...	14,123	7,328	6,795	4,549	3,944	605	9,407	3,318	6,089	167	66	101
	20—40 ...	72,490	35,181	37,309	4,454	4,009	445	64,119	29,885	34,234	3,917	1,287	2,630
	40—60 ...	33,689	16,620	17,069	516	422	94	23,478	14,595	8,883	9,695	1,603	8,092
	60 and over	10,006	3,931	6,075	106	75	31	3,719	2,902	817	6,181	954	5,227
	ANIMIST...	*161,077*	*77,316*	*83,761*	*69,603*	*37,803*	*31,800*	*77,737*	*37,085*	*40,652*	*13,737*	*2,428*	*11,309*
	0—5 ...	26,001	12,515	13,486	25,931	12,487	13,444	60	28	41	1	...	1
	5—10 ...	23,074	11,502	11,572	22,770	11,433	11,337	291	65	226	13	4	9
	10—15 ...	13,329	7,121	6,208	11,768	6,704	5,064	1,542	411	1,131	19	6	13
	15—20 ...	9,786	4,882	4,904	4,647	3,527	1,120	5,052	1,329	3,723	87	26	61
	20—40 ...	55,998	25,700	30,298	3,909	3,261	708	49,332	21,533	27,799	2,697	906	1,791
	40—60 ...	25,600	12,900	12,700	424	323	101	18,703	11,665	7,038	6,473	912	5,561
	60 and over	7,289	2,696	4,593	94	68	26	2,748	2,054	694	4,447	574	3,873
	MUSALMAN	*17,434*	*8,583*	*8,851*	*7,895*	*4,574*	*3,321*	*7,770*	*3,729*	*4,041*	*1,769*	*280*	*1,489*
	0—5 ...	2,558	1,275	1,283	2,547	1,270	1,277	11	5	6	...	...	...
	5—10 ...	2,636	1,355	1,281	2,594	1,347	1,247	40	8	32	2	...	2
	10—15 ...	1,654	916	738	1,488	884	604	163	30	133	3	2	1
	15—20 ...	1,106	574	532	558	456	102	536	117	419	12	1	11
	20—40 ...	5,911	2,844	3,067	635	565	70	4,920	2,187	2,733	356	92	264
	40—60 ...	2,762	1,303	1,459	54	39	15	1,817	1,151	666	891	113	778
	60 and over	807	316	491	19	13	6	283	231	52	505	72	433
NARSINGHPUR	ALL RELIGIONS.	*325,677*	*161,795*	*163,882*	*124,094*	*74,178*	*49,916*	*161,998*	*78,551*	*83,447*	*39,585*	*9,066*	*30,519*
	0—5 ...	49,701	25,047	24,654	49,520	24,998	24,522	171	45	126	10	4	6
	5—10 ...	43,406	22,167	21,239	40,540	21,504	19,036	2,813	643	2,170	53	20	33
	10—15 ...	29,973	16,419	13,554	18,544	13,117	5,427	11,131	3,213	7,918	298	89	209
	15—20 ...	22,047	11,889	10,158	6,855	6,419	436	14,716	5,292	9,424	476	178	298
	20—40 ...	113,935	55,485	58,450	7,684	7,308	376	96,238	44,854	51,384	10,013	3,323	6,690
	40—60 ..	54,158	25,974	28,184	806	715	91	33,255	21,424	11,831	20,097	3,835	16,262
	60 and over	12,457	4,814	7,643	145	117	28	3,674	3,080	594	8,638	1,617	7,021
	HINDU (BRAHMANIC)	*278,048*	*138,622*	*139,426*	*105,160*	*63,320*	*41,840*	*138,702*	*67,354*	*71,348*	*34,186*	*7,948*	*26,238*
	0—5 ...	42,205	21,315	20,890	42,039	21,271	20,768	156	40	116	10	4	6
	5—10 ...	37,106	18,991	18,115	34,418	18,372	16,046	2,639	601	2,038	49	18	31
	10—15 ...	26,071	14,333	11,738	15,567	11,217	4,350	10,234	3,038	7,196	270	78	192
	15—20 ...	19,141	10,355	8,786	5,715	5,408	307	13,001	4,786	8,215	425	161	264
	20—40 ...	96,945	47,462	49,483	6,566	6,290	276	81,673	38,303	43,370	8,706	2,869	5,837
	40—60 ...	45,976	22,017	23,959	730	657	73	27,886	17,957	9,929	17,360	3,403	13,957
	60 and over	10,604	4,149	6,455	125	105	20	3,113	2,629	484	7,366	1,415	5,951
	ANIMIST...	*32,992*	*15,714*	*17,278*	*12,845*	*7,137*	*5,708*	*16,465*	*7,851*	*8,614*	*3,682*	*726*	*2,956*
	0—5 ...	5,257	2,593	2,664	5,246	2,589	2,657	11	4	7	...	...	...
	5—10 ...	4,384	2,165	2,219	4,265	2,126	2,139	115	37	78	4	2	2
	10—15 ...	2,461	1,291	1,170	1,913	1,184	729	530	97	433	18	10	8
	15—20 ...	1,842	922	920	668	585	83	1,139	325	814	35	12	23
	20—40 ...	12,019	5,556	6,463	686	607	79	10,476	4,636	5,840	857	313	544
	40—60 ...	5,770	2,770	3,000	56	41	15	3,824	2,463	1,361	1,890	266	1,624
	60 and over	1,259	417	842	11	5	6	370	289	81	878	123	755

TABLE VII.—Part B.—Details for Districts—*continued.* [Hoshangabad Nimar

District or State.	Age.	Population. Persons.	Population. Males.	Population. Females.	Unmarried. Persons.	Unmarried. Males.	Unmarried. Fmales.	Married. Persons.	Married. Males.	Married. Females.	Widowed. Persons.	Widowed. Males.	Widowed. Females.
	1	2	3	4	5	6	7	8	9	10	11	12	13
NARSINGHPUR—(concld.)	MUSALMAN	*11,707*	*5,888*	*5,819*	*4,776*	*2,848*	*1,928*	*5,581*	*2,732*	*2,849*	*1,350*	*308*	*1,042*
	0—5 ...	1,823	928	895	1,819	927	892	4	1	3	...	...	...
	5—10 ...	1,544	809	735	1,494	804	690	50	5	45	...	...	...
	10—15 ...	1,088	590	498	806	519	287	276	70	206	6	1	5
	15—20 ...	778	427	351	334	294	40	433	129	304	11	4	7
	20—40 ...	3,996	1,956	2,040	301	286	15	3,355	1,552	1,803	340	118	222
	40—60 ...	1,997	985	1,012	16	14	2	1,302	841	461	679	130	549
	60 and over	481	193	288	6	4	2	161	134	27	314	55	259
HOSHANGABAD	ALL RELIGIONS.	*457,395*	*230,632*	*226,763*	*176,380*	*105,543*	*70,837*	*228,343*	*113,196*	*115,147*	*53,672*	*11,893*	*40,779*
	0—5 ...	66,027	32,550	33,477	65,737	32,477	33 260	269	69	200	21	4	17
	5—10 ...	57,914	29,521	28,393	55,183	28,989	26,194	2,661	514	2,147	70	18	52
	10—15 ...	44,519	24,814	19,705	30,826	21,420	9,406	13,467	3,319	10,148	226	75	151
	15—20 ...	32,644	17,938	14,706	11,804	10,773	1,031	20,386	6,993	13,393	454	172	282
	20—40 ...	155,429	77,382	78,047	11,175	10,443	732	132,953	63,416	69,537	11,301	3,523	7,778
	40—60 ...	79,071	39,064	40,007	1,370	1,213	157	51,128	32,719	18,409	26,573	5,132	21,441
	60 and over	21,791	9,363	12,428	285	228	57	7,479	6,166	1,313	14,027	2,969	11,058
	HINDU (BRAHMANIC)	*382,775*	*193,785*	*188,990*	*145,199*	*87,794*	*57,405*	*192,801*	*95,658*	*97,143*	*44,775*	*10,333*	*34,442*
	0—5 ...	55,031	27,265	27,766	54,779	27,209	27,570	237	52	185	15	4	11
	5—10 ...	48,452	24,798	23,654	45,865	24,305	21,560	2,529	477	2,052	58	16	42
	10—15 ...	37,981	21,232	16,749	25,219	18,020	7,199	12,557	3,139	9,418	205	73	132
	15—20 ...	27,758	15,378	12,380	9,263	8,780	483	18,079	6,432	11,647	416	166	250
	20—40 ...	129,010	64,619	64,391	8,695	8,254	441	110,657	53,326	57,331	9,658	3,039	6,619
	40—60 ...	66,219	32,593	33,626	1,133	1,024	109	42,499	27,075	15,424	22,587	4,494	18,093
	60 and over	18,324	7,900	10,424	245	202	43	6,243	5,157	1,086	11,836	2,541	9,295
	ANIMIST...	*49,915*	*24,157*	*25,758*	*20,948*	*11,637*	*9,311*	*24,010*	*11,648*	*13,362*	*4,957*	*872*	*4,085*
	0—5 ...	7,711	3,686	4,025	7,686	3,675	4,011	23	11	12	2	...	2
	5—10 ...	6,462	3,275	3,187	6,389	3,251	3,138	68	23	45	5	1	4
	10—15 ...	4,104	2,207	1,897	3,628	2,115	1,513	468	91	377	8	1	7
	15—20 ...	3,152	1,577	1,575	1,627	1,221	406	1,509	353	1,156	16	3	13
	20—40 ...	17,902	8,360	9,542	1,483	1,272	211	15,416	6,816	8,600	1,003	272	731
	40—60 ...	8,498	4,242	4,256	123	95	28	5,806	3,779	2,027	2,569	368	2,201
	60 and over	2,086	810	1,276	12	8	4	720	575	145	1,354	227	1,127
	MUSALMAN	*20,799*	*10,640*	*10,159*	*8,432*	*5,045*	*3,437*	*9,821*	*5,021*	*4,800*	*2,496*	*574*	*1,922*
	0—5 ...	2,773	1,334	1,439	2,762	1,330	1,432	7	4	3	4	...	4
	5—10 ...	2,575	1,257	1,318	2,508	1,242	1,266	61	14	47	6	1	5
	10—15 ...	2,072	1,180	892	1,684	1,103	581	376	76	300	12	1	11
	15—20 ...	1,387	817	570	718	638	80	648	176	472	21	3	18
	20—40 ...	7,087	3,598	3,489	711	655	56	5,831	2,766	3,065	545	177	368
	40—60 ...	3,718	1,894	1,824	80	67	13	2,441	1,600	841	1,197	227	970
	60 and over	1,187	560	627	19	10	9	457	385	72	711	165	546
NIMAR	ALL RELIGIONS.	*391,071*	*200,765*	*190,306*	*150,124*	*89,307*	*60,817*	*201,351*	*100,872*	*100,479*	*39,596*	*10,586*	*29,010*
	0—5 ...	59,304	29,052	30,252	59,057	28,989	30,068	234	61	173	13	2	11
	5—10 ...	51,376	26,006	25,370	48,317	25,600	22,717	2,979	387	2,592	80	19	61
	10—15 ...	38,834	21,279	17,555	24,058	17,666	6,392	14,546	3,559	10,987	230	54	176
	15—20 ...	28,369	14,029	14,340	8,283	7,509	774	19,661	6,377	13,284	425	143	282
	20—40 ...	134,792	69,001	65,791	9,092	8,434	658	116,173	57,472	58,701	9,527	3,095	6,432
	40—60 ...	59,687	32,257	27,430	1,027	883	144	40,426	26,977	13,449	18,234	4,397	13,837
	60 and over	18,709	9,141	9,568	290	226	64	7,332	6,039	1,293	11,087	2,876	8,211
	HINDU (BRAHMANIC)	*340,030*	*174,111*	*165,919*	*128,263*	*76,435*	*51,728*	*177,047*	*88,401*	*88,646*	*34,720*	*9,225*	*25,495*
	0—5 ...	51,722	25,299	26,423	51,498	25,245	26,253	212	53	159	12	1	11
	5—10 ...	44,550	22,525	22,025	41,642	22,139	19,503	2,834	368	2,466	74	18	56
	10—15 ...	33,695	18,479	15,216	20,019	15,096	4,923	13,470	3,339	10,131	206	44	162
	15—20 ...	24,507	12,109	12,398	6,587	6,102	485	17,544	5,879	11,665	376	128	248
	20—40 ...	117,628	59,967	57,661	7,433	6,959	474	101,857	50,350	51,507	8,338	2,658	5,680
	40—60 ...	51,847	27,940	23,907	851	754	97	34,905	23,281	11,624	16,091	3,905	12,186
	60 and over	16,081	7,792	8,289	233	190	43	6,225	5,131	1,094	0,623	2,471	7,152
	MUSALMAN	*33,436*	*20,109*	*18,319*	*16,338*	*9,581*	*6,741*	*18,333*	*9,433*	*8,900*	*3,773*	*1,095*	*2,678*
	0—5 ...	5,587	2,786	2,801	5,570	2 781	2,789	16	4	12	1	1	...
	5—10 ...	5,074	2,565	2,509	4,978	2,554	2,424	90	10	80	6	1	5
	10—15 ...	3,902	2,098	1,804	3,097	1,944	1,153	784	144	640	21	10	11
	15—20 ...	2,900	1,448	1,452	1,269	1,081	188	1,598	357	1,241	33	10	23
	20—40 ...	12,823	6,778	6,045	1,234	1,110	124	10,678	5,316	5,362	911	352	559
	40—60 ...	5,994	3,309	2,685	124	82	42	4,250	2,846	1,404	1,620	381	1,239
	60 and over	2,148	1,125	1,023	50	29	21	917	750	161	1,181	340	841

 TABLE VII.—Part B.—Details for Districts—*continued.*

District or State.	Age.	Population.			Unmarried.			Married.			Widowed.		
		Persons.	Males.	Females.	Persons.	Males.	Females.	Persons.	Males.	Females.	Persons.	Males.	Females.
	1	2	3	4	5	6	7	8	9	10	11	12	13
BETUL	ALL RELIGIONS.	*390,386*	*194,165*	*196,223*	*171,531*	*95,167*	*76,364*	*185,285*	*91,617*	*93,668*	*33,570*	*7,379*	*26,191*
	0—5 ...	66,018	31,971	34,047	65,749	31,896	33,853	257	73	184	12	2	10
	5—10 ...	56,716	28,360	28,356	54,277	27,896	26,381	2,365	451	1,914	74	13	61
	10—15 ...	36,154	19,410	16,744	28,146	16,955	11,191	7,883	2,413	5,470	125	42	83
	15—20 ...	24,731	12,291	12,440	10,970	7,920	3,050	13,490	4,273	9,223	265	98	167
	20—40 ...	128,151	62,504	65,647	11,108	9,502	1,606	110,615	50,892	59,723	6,428	2,110	4,318
	40—60 ..	59,125	30,985	28,140	1,014	813	201	42,756	27,301	15,455	15,355	2,871	12,484
	60 and over	19,491	8,642	10,849	267	185	82	7,913	6,214	1,699	11,311	2,243	9,068
	HINDU (BRAHMANIC)	*259,318*	*129,817*	*129,501*	*106,731*	*60,516*	*46,216*	*129,157*	*64,156*	*65,001*	*23,400*	*5,116*	*18,284*
	0—5 ...	42,559	20,715	21,843	42,368	20,662	21,706	182	51	131	8	2	6
	5—10 ...	37,385	18,611	18,774	35,085	18,177	16,908	2,237	423	1,814	63	11	52
	10—15 ...	23,739	12,968	10,771	16,543	10,724	5,819	7,086	2,206	4,880	110	38	72
	15—20 ...	16,392	8,413	7,979	5,759	4,758	1,001	10,430	3,580	6,850	203	75	128
	20—40 ...	84,689	41,659	43,030	6,184	5,551	633	74,017	34,632	39,385	4,488	1,476	3,012
	40—60 ...	40,550	21,232	19,318	628	523	105	29,429	18,733	10,696	10,493	1,976	8,517
	60 and over	14,005	6,219	7,786	164	120	44	5,806	4,561	1,245	8,035	1,538	6,497
	ANIMIST...	*121,175*	*58,947*	*62,228*	*60,591*	*32,055*	*28,536*	*51,110*	*24,567*	*26,543*	*9,174*	*2,025*	*7,149*
	0—5 ...	22,161	10,636	11,525	22,088	10,616	11,472	69	20	49	4	...	4
	5—10 ...	18,134	9,140	8,994	18,043	9,121	8,922	82	18	64	9	1	8
	10—15 ...	11,486	5,910	5,576	10,842	5,738	5,104	636	169	467	8	3	5
	15—20 ...	7,699	3,528	4,171	4,885	2,893	1,992	2,762	614	2,148	52	21	31
	20—40 ...	39,746	18,692	21,054	4,318	3,396	922	33,718	14,756	18,963	1,710	541	1,169
	40—60 ...	17,004	8,871	8,133	322	235	87	12,249	7,824	4,425	4,433	812	3,621
	60 and over	4,945	2,170	2,775	93	56	37	1,894	1,467	427	2,958	647	2,311
CHHINDWARA	ALL RELIGIONS.	*516,948*	*255,884*	*261,064*	*220,727*	*123,067*	*97,660*	*251,069*	*123,492*	*127,577*	*45,152*	*9,325*	*35,827*
	0—5 ...	83,739	41,018	42,721	83,176	40,858	42,318	537	155	382	26	5	21
	5—10 ...	75,526	37,361	38,165	71,679	36,564	35,115	3,714	766	2,948	133	31	102
	10—15 ...	49,334	26,303	23,031	37,820	22,810	15,010	11,267	3,422	7,845	247	71	176
	15—20 ...	32,652	16,826	15,826	13,717	10,617	3,101	18,587	6,069	12,518	348	140	208
	20—40 ...	170,093	82,418	87,675	12,593	10,814	1,770	148,782	68,799	79,983	8,718	2,805	5,913
	40—60 ...	79,136	40,590	38,536	1,436	1,183	253	57,526	35,855	21,671	20,164	3,552	16,612
	60 and over	26,478	11,368	15,110	306	221	85	10,656	8,426	2,230	15,516	2,721	12,795
	HINDU (BRAHMANIC)	*308,320*	*154,298*	*154,022*	*123,326*	*70,260*	*53,066*	*157,391*	*78,059*	*79,332*	*27,603*	*5,979*	*21,624*
	0—5 ...	49,260	24,261	24,999	48,815	24,149	24,666	426	108	318	19	4	15
	5—10 ...	44,253	21,893	22,360	40,751	21,222	19,529	3,400	646	2,754	102	25	77
	10—15 ..	29,901	16,045	13,856	20,149	13,009	7,140	9,544	2,977	6,567	208	59	149
	15—20 ...	19,677	10,297	9,380	6,535	5,571	964	12,899	4,624	8,275	243	102	141
	20—40 ...	100,372	49,640	50,732	6,101	5,497	604	89,034	42,388	46,646	5,237	1,755	3,482
	40—60 ...	47,996	24,674	23,322	782	665	117	35,044	21,727	13,317	12,170	2,282	9,888
	60 and over	16,801	7,488	9,373	193	147	46	7,044	5,589	1,455	9,624	1,752	7,872
	ANIMIST	*189,249*	*91,668*	*97,581*	*88,667*	*47,692*	*40,975*	*84,947*	*41,050*	*43,894*	*15,638*	*2,926*	*12,712*
	0—5 ..	31,622	15,320	16,302	31,522	15,277	16,245	95	42	53	5	1	4
	5—10 ...	28,519	14,114	14,405	28,219	13,993	14,226	276	115	161	24	6	18
	10—15 ...	17,566	9,214	8,352	16,034	8,801	7,233	1,503	404	1,099	29	9	20
	15—20 ...	11,718	5,825	5,893	6,506	4,478	2,028	5,118	1,315	3,803	94	32	62
	20—40 ...	63,217	29,510	33,707	5,721	4,639	1,082	54,421	23,941	30,480	3,075	930	2,145
	40—60 ...	28,119	14,319	13,800	572	446	126	20,345	12,749	7,506	7,202	1,124	6,078
	60 and over	8,488	3,366	5,122	93	58	35	3,186	2,484	702	5,209	824	4,385
	MUSALMAN	*16,595*	*8,459*	*8,136*	*7,523*	*4,378*	*3,145*	*7,499*	*3,752*	*3,747*	*1,573*	*329*	*1,244*
	0—5 ...	2,489	1,242	1,247	2,472	1,238	1,234	15	4	11	2	...	2
	5—10 ...	2,428	1,198	1,230	2,386	1,188	1,198	31	5	26	6	...	6
	10—15 ...	1,582	885	697	1,406	849	557	16[illegible]	33	136	7	3	4
	15—20 ...	1,011	565	446	543	459	84	460	101	359	8	5	3
	20—40 ...	5,549	2,772	2,777	629	569	60	4,590	2,102	2,488	330	101	229
	40—60 ...	2,589	1,368	1,221	69	61	8	1,955	1,194	661	665	113	552
	60 and over	952	434	518	18	14	4	379	313	66	555	107	448
WARDHA	ALL RELIGIONS.	*459,796*	*231,871*	*227,925*	*155,174*	*93,288*	*61,886*	*252,244*	*125,316*	*126,928*	*52,378*	*13,267*	*39,111*
	0—5 ...	66,987	32,600	34,387	66,078	32,333	33,745	858	247	611	51	20	31
	5—10 ...	56,505	27,783	28,722	48,543	26,867	21,676	7,774	869	6,905	188	47	141
	10—15 ...	41,803	22,657	19,146	23,215	17,976	5,239	18,051	4,549	13,502	537	132	405
	15—20 ...	30,288	14,876	15,412	7,298	6,947	351	22,436	7,735	14,701	554	194	360
	20—40 ...	152,307	76,014	76,293	8,641	8,008	633	133,206	64,599	68,607	10,460	3,407	7,053
	40—60 ...	81,378	42,615	38,763	1,075	888	187	57,080	36,604	20,476	23,223	5,123	8,100
	60 and over	30,528	15,326	15,202	324	269	55	12,835	10,713	2,126	17,365	4,344	3,021

TABLE VII.—Part B.—Details for Districts—*continued.* [Wardha Nagpur

District or State.	Age.	Population.			Unmarried.			Married.			Widowed.		
		Persons.	Males.	Females.	Persons.	Males.	Females.	Persons.	Males.	Females.	Persons.	Males.	Females.
	1	2	3	4	5	6	7	8	9	10	11	12	13
WARDHA—(concld.)	HINDU (BRAHMANIC).	*391,063*	*197,583*	*193,480*	*129,367*	*78,292*	*51,075*	*216,703*	*107,736*	*108,967*	*44,993*	*11,555*	*33,438*
	0—5 ...	57,061	27,841	29,220	56,260	27,629	28,631	755	195	560	46	17	29
	5—10 ...	47,985	23,621	24,364	40,420	22,787	17,633	7,394	795	6,599	171	39	132
	10—15 ...	35,900	19,447	16,453	18,896	14,975	3,921	16,493	4,347	12,146	511	125	386
	15—20 ...	25,928	12,717	13,211	5,649	5,430	219	19,787	7,105	12,682	492	182	310
	20—40 ...	120,367	64,853	64,514	6,976	6,500	476	113,429	55,418	58,011	8,962	2,935	6,027
	40—60 ..	68,976	36,117	32,859	906	759	147	48,054	30,858	17,196	20,016	4,500	15,516
	60 and over	25,846	12,987	12,859	260	212	48	10,791	9,018	1,773	14,795	3,757	11,038
	ANIMIST ...	*47,831*	*23,549*	*24,282*	*16,911*	*9,724*	*7,187*	*25,981*	*12,689*	*13,292*	*4,939*	*1,136*	*3,803*
	0—5 ...	7,006	3,383	3,623	6,929	3,342	3,587	74	38	36	3	3	...
	5—10 ..	5,753	2,781	2,972	5,452	2,725	2,727	291	52	239	10	4	6
	10—15 ...	3,870	2,081	1,789	2,634	1,928	706	1,215	147	1,068	21	6	15
	15—20 ...	2,926	1,412	1,514	977	930	47	1,917	474	1,443	32	8	24
	20—40 ...	16,012	7,557	8,455	809	716	93	14,262	6,549	7,713	941	202	649
	40—60 ...	8,890	4,624	4,266	81	58	23	6,688	4,164	2,524	2,121	406	1,715
	60 and over	3,374	1,711	1,663	29	25	4	1,534	1,269	265	1,811	417	1,394
	MUSALMAN	*18,174*	*9,331*	*8,843*	*7,930*	*4,655*	*3,275*	*8,203*	*4,190*	*4,013*	*2,041*	*486*	*1,555*
	0—5 ...	2,602	1,228	1,374	2,576	1,217	1,359	24	11	13	2	...	2
	5—10 ...	2,451	1,220	1,231	2,380	1,195	1,185	65	21	44	6	4	2
	10—15 ...	1,766	979	787	1,513	936	577	250	42	208	3	1	2
	15—20 ...	1,237	644	593	610	528	82	606	112	494	21	4	17
	20—40 ...	5,954	3,107	2,847	751	699	52	4,751	2,250	2,501	452	158	294
	40—60 ...	3,028	1,009	1,419	71	54	17	2,041	1,369	672	916	186	730
	60 and over	1,136	544	592	29	26	3	466	385	81	641	133	508
NAGPUR.	ALL RELIGIONS.	*809,901*	*408,843*	*401,058*	*286,431*	*171,202*	*115,229*	*436,842*	*216,641*	*220,201*	*86,628*	*21,000*	*65,638*
	0—5 ..	117,640	57,930	59,710	116,229	57,467	58,762	1,388	454	934	23	9	14
	5—10 ...	103,924	51,966	51,958	92,108	50,592	41,516	11,520	1,321	10,199	296	53	243
	10—15 ...	76,759	41,419	35,340	44,984	33,370	11,614	30,767	7,853	22,914	1,008	196	812
	15—20 ...	52,354	26,480	25,874	14,587	13,294	1,293	36,742	12,823	23,919	1,025	363	662
	20—40 ..	261,692	131,043	130,649	15,960	14,480	1,480	228,573	111,025	117,548	17,150	5,538	11,612
	40—60 ..	138,151	71,018	67,133	1,941	1,518	423	101,127	62,194	38,933	35,083	7,306	27,777
	60 and over	59,381	28,987	30,394	613	481	132	26,725	20,971	5,754	32,043	7,535	24,508
	HINDU (BRAHMANIC)	*725,399*	*365,125*	*360,274*	*250,233*	*149,710*	*100,523*	*397,345*	*196,622*	*200,723*	*77,821*	*18,793*	*59,028*
	0—5 ...	105,928	52,208	53,720	104,633	51,788	52,845	1,280	415	865	15	5	10
	5—10 ...	93,200	46,678	46,522	81,751	45,400	36,351	11,186	1,235	9,951	263	43	220
	10—15 ...	69,120	37,178	31,942	38,571	29,383	9,188	29,597	7,612	21,985	952	183	769
	15—20 ...	46,653	23,548	23,105	11,695	10,974	721	34,038	12,230	21,808	920	344	576
	20—40 ...	232,818	115,915	116,903	11,492	10,482	1,010	206,150	100,561	105,589	15,176	4,872	10,304
	40—60 ...	124,051	63,416	60,635	1,557	1,249	308	90,904	55,633	35,271	31,590	6,534	25,056
	60 and over	53,623	26,182	27,441	534	434	100	24,190	18,936	5,254	28,899	6,812	22,087
	ANIMIST ...	*36,003*	*17,870*	*18,133*	*14,264*	*8,070*	*6,194*	*18,393*	*9,023*	*9,370*	*3,346*	*777*	*2,569*
	0—5 ...	5,316	2,545	2,771	5,259	2,528	2,731	57	17	40	...	...	...
	5—10 ...	4,644	2,354	2,290	4,504	2,314	2,190	120	36	93	11	4	7
	10—15 ...	2,847	1,563	1,284	2,389	1,474	915	447	86	361	11	3	8
	15—20 ...	2,111	1,029	1,082	992	799	193	1,096	228	838	23	2	21
	20—40 ...	11,917	5,615	6,302	996	869	128	10,335	4,578	5,757	586	169	417
	40—60 ...	6,467	3,428	3,039	104	74	80	5,062	3,075	1,987	1,301	279	1,022
	60 and over	2,701	1,336	1,365	20	13	7	1,267	1,003	264	1,414	320	1,094
	MUSALMAN	*38,434*	*20,047*	*18,387*	*16,551*	*9,810*	*6,782*	*17,316*	*9,054*	*8,262*	*4,567*	*1,174*	*3,393*
	0—5 ...	5,210	2,570	2,640	5,170	2,554	2,616	37	15	22	3	1	2
	5—10 ...	5,091	2,441	2,650	4,929	2,395	2,534	153	43	110	9	3	6
	10—15 ...	3,853	2,160	1,693	3,229	2,014	1,215	588	137	451	36	9	27
	15—20 ...	2,559	1,339	1,220	1,225	1,046	179	1,272	282	990	62	11	51
	20—40 ...	12,831	6,861	5,970	1,779	1,646	133	9,915	4,801	5,114	1,137	414	723
	40—60 ..	6,251	3,414	2,837	176	138	38	4,250	2,884	1,366	1,825	392	1,433
	60 and over	2,639	1,262	1,377	43	26	17	1,101	892	209	1,495	344	1,151
	CHRISTIAN	*6,245*	*3,764*	*2,481*	*3,982*	*2,704*	*1,378*	*1,876*	*949*	*937*	*387*	*111*	*276*
	0—5 ...	733	360	373	727	357	370	4	1	3	2	2	...
	5—10 ...	527	259	268	515	254	261	8	2	6	4	3	1
	10—15 ...	588	338	250	572	337	235	14	1	13	2	...	2
	15—20 ...	720	397	323	553	374	179	160	21	139	7	2	5
	20—40 ...	2,800	1,942	858	1,520	1,338	182	1,163	568	595	117	36	81
	40—60 ...	695	373	322	85	41	44	451	295	156	159	37	122
	60 and over	182	95	87	10	3	7	76	61	15	96	31	65

Chanda
Bhandara]

TABLE VII.—Part B —Details for Districts—*continued.*

District or State.	Age.	Population.			Unmarried.			Married.			Widowed.		
		Persons.	Males.	Females.	Persons.	Males.	Females.	Persons.	Males.	Females.	Persons.	Males.	Females.
	1	2	3	4	5	6	7	8	9	10	11	12	13
CHANDA	ALL RELIGIONS.	*677,544*	*337,540*	*340,004*	*253,207*	*147,950*	*105,257*	*356,812*	*176,357*	*180,455*	*67,525*	*13,333*	*54,292*
	0—5 ...	111,074	54,256	57,718	109,997	53,975	56,022	1,928	273	1,655	49	8	41
	5—10 ...	89,810	45,246	44,564	76,754	42,605	34,149	12,763	2 571	10,192	293	70	223
	10—15 ...	62,748	34,121	28,627	36,688	26,115	10,573	25,493	7,867	17,626	567	139	428
	15—20 ...	42,358	20,579	21,779	12,976	10,974	2,002	28,828	9,440	19,388	554	165	389
	20—40 ...	221,544	108,463	113,081	15,005	12,934	2,071	194,122	92,375	101,747	12,417	3,154	9,263
	40—60 ...	106,486	56,380	52,106	1,424	1,086	338	77,053	50,152	26,901	30,009	5,142	24,867
	60 and over	40,624	18,495	22,129	363	261	102	16,625	13,679	2,946	23,636	4,555	19,081
	HINDU (BRAHMANIC)	*539,713*	*269,465*	*270,248*	*192,158*	*113,855*	*78,303*	*292,562*	*144,910*	*147,652*	*54,993*	*10,700*	*44,293*
	0—5 ...	88,736	43,209	45,527	86,987	42,991	43,996	1,714	211	1,503	35	7	28
	5—10 ...	71,379	35,932	35,447	58,983	33,436	25,547	12,130	2,430	9,700	266	66	200
	10—15 ...	50,492	27,496	22,996	26,668	19,947	6,721	23,294	7,419	15,875	530	130	400
	15—20 ...	33,622	16,507	17,115	8,591	7,843	748	24,559	8,518	16,041	472	146	326
	20—40 ...	175,516	86,240	89,276	9,616	8,638	978	155,809	75,085	80,724	10,091	2,517	7,574
	40—60 ...	86,926	44,994	41,932	1,034	794	240	61,522	40,077	21,445	24,370	4,123	20,247
	60 and over	33,042	15,087	17,955	279	206	73	13,534	11,170	2,364	19,229	3,711	15,518
	ANIMIST...	*124,356*	*61,161*	*63,195*	*55,214*	*30,599*	*24,615*	*58,111*	*28,289*	*29,822*	*11,031*	*2,273*	*8,758*
	0—5 ...	21,363	10,164	11,199	21,161	10,108	11,053	190	55	135	12	1	11
	5—10 ...	16,610	8,393	8,217	15,992	8,254	7,738	592	136	456	26	3	23
	10—15 ...	10,929	5,864	5,065	8,910	5,439	3,471	1,987	416	1,571	32	9	23
	15—20 ...	7,868	3,621	4,247	3,960	2,766	1,194	3,836	838	2,998	72	17	55
	20—40 ...	41,463	19,843	21,620	4,780	3,742	1,038	34,689	15,552	19,137	1,994	549	1,445
	40—60 ...	19,369	10,246	9,123	339	247	92	14,062	9,066	4,996	4,968	933	4,035
	60 and over	6,754	3,030	3,724	72	43	29	2,755	2,226	529	3,927	761	3,166
	MUSALMAN.	*12,172*	*6,205*	*5,967*	*5,259*	*3,131*	*2,128*	*5,564*	*2,846*	*2,718*	*1,349*	*228*	*1,121*
	0—5 ...	1,736	805	931	1,713	799	914	21	6	15	2	...	2
	5—10 ...	1,660	838	822	1,624	834	790	36	4	32	...	...	...
	10—15 ...	1,188	670	518	995	646	349	188	24	164	5	...	5
	15—20 ...	740	390	350	354	316	38	380	73	307	6	1	5
	20—40 ...	4,075	2,111	1,964	520	486	34	3,268	1,544	1,724	287	81	206
	40—60 ...	1,992	1,035	957	43	40	3	1,349	923	426	600	72	528
	60 and over	781	356	425	10	10	...	322	272	50	449	74	375
BHANDARA	ALL RELIGIONS.	*773,677*	*380,014*	*393,663*	*291,624*	*165,736*	*125,888*	*407,220*	*198,662*	*208,558*	*74,833*	*15,616*	*59,217*
	0-5 ...	122,133	59,582	62,551	120,559	59,010	61,549	1,551	568	983	23	4	19
	5—10 ...	102,372	51,250	51,122	92,308	48,810	43,498	9,852	2,397	7,455	212	43	169
	10—15 ...	70,662	37,866	32,796	44,643	29,499	15,144	25,490	8,248	17,242	520	119	410
	15—20 ...	50,934	25,352	25,582	16,842	13,639	3,203	33,458	11,519	21,939	634	194	440
	20-40 ...	253,217	121,536	131,681	15,279	13,386	1,893	224,895	104,530	120,365	13,043	3,620	9,423
	40—60 ...	125,338	62,666	62,672	1,530	1,062	477	91,474	55,573	35,901	32,325	6,031	26,294
	60 and over	49,021	21,762	27,259	454	330	124	20,500	15,827	4,673	28,067	5,605	22,462
	HINDU (BRAHMANIC)	*685,342*	*337,335*	*348,007*	*254,777*	*145,360*	*109,417*	*365,372*	*178,335*	*187,037*	*65,193*	*13,640*	*51,553*
	0—5 ...	109,038	53,238	55,800	107,592	52,734	54,858	1,429	502	927	17	2	15
	5—10 ...	91,767	45,988	45,779	81,935	43,605	38,330	9,629	2,342	7,287	203	41	162
	10—15 ...	63,487	33,989	29,498	38,176	25,812	12,364	24,827	8,071	16,756	484	106	378
	15-20 ...	45,080	22,514	22,506	13,385	11,323	2,062	31,117	11,024	20,003	578	167	411
	20 40 ...	222,786	107,134	115,652	12,050	10,745	1,305	199,380	93,234	106,155	11,347	3,155	8,192
	40—60 ...	110,138	55,214	54,924	1,265	862	403	80,776	49,106	31,670	28,097	5,246	22,851
	60 and over	43,046	19,258	23,788	374	279	95	18,205	14,056	4,149	24,467	4,923	19,544
	ANIMIST...	*72,424*	*34,669*	*37,755*	*29,754*	*16,227*	*13,527*	*34,822*	*16,797*	*18,025*	*7,848*	*1,645*	*6,203*
	0—5 ...	10,961	5,326	5,635	10,851	5,268	5,583	106	57	49	4	1	3
	5—10 ...	8,475	4,183	4,292	8,290	4,140	4,150	179	42	137	6	1	5
	10—15 ...	5,638	3,017	2,621	5,116	2,868	2,248	503	137	366	19	12	7
	15—20 ...	4,762	2,257	2,505	2,817	1,829	988	1,896	402	1,494	49	26	23
	20-40 ...	25,077	11,664	13,413	2,427	1,938	489	21,319	9,350	11,969	1,331	376	955
	40—60 ...	12,619	6,205	6,414	197	146	51	8,979	5,399	3,580	3,443	660	2,783
	60 and over	4,892	2,017	2,875	56	38	18	1,840	1,410	430	2,996	569	2,427
	MUSALMAN	*14,707*	*7,434*	*7,273*	*6,552*	*3,868*	*2,684*	*6,502*	*3,264*	*3,238*	*1,653*	*302*	*1,351*
	0—5 ...	1,986	955	1,031	1,970	945	1,025	14	9	5	2	1	1
	5—10 ...	2,009	1,027	982	1,969	1,014	955	37	12	25	3	1	2
	10—15 ...	1,439	811	628	1,273	775	498	140	35	105	26	1	25
	15—20 ...	968	541	427	559	454	105	403	86	317	6	1	5
	20—40 ...	4,882	2,488	2,394	693	624	69	3,856	1,783	2,073	333	81	252
	40—60 ...	2,411	1,152	1,259	65	44	21	1,620	994	626	726	114	612
	60 and over	1,012	460	552	23	12	11	432	345	87	557	103	454

TABLE VII.—Part B.—Details for Districts—*continued.* [Balaghat Raipur

District or State.	Age.	Population.			Unmarried.			Married.			Widowed.		
		Persons.	Males.	Females.	Persons.	Males.	Females.	Persons.	Males.	Females.	Persons.	Males.	Females.
	1	2	3	4	5	6	7	8	9	10	11	12	13
BALAGHAT.	ALL RELIGIONS.	*388,920*	*190,469*	*198,451*	*152,178*	*85,205*	*66,973*	*200,131*	*97,642*	*102,489*	*36,011*	*7,622*	*28,989*
	0—5 ...	62,873	30,906	31,967	62,502	30,739	31,713	361	112	249	10	5	5
	5—10 ...	52,678	26,126	26,552	48,687	24,813	23,874	3,897	1,292	2,605	94	21	73
	10—15 ...	33,511	17,970	15,541	22,627	14,129	8,498	10,723	3,791	6,932	161	50	111
	15—20 ...	25,617	12,843	12,774	9,099	7,258	1,841	16,256	5,476	10,780	262	109	153
	20—40 ...	128,925	62,375	66,550	8,246	7,394	852	114,142	52,828	61,319	6,537	2,158	4,379
	40—60 ...	62,384	31,142	31,242	800	656	144	45,619	27,474	18,145	15,965	3,012	12,953
	60 and over	22,932	9,107	13,825	217	166	51	9,133	6,674	2,459	13,582	2,267	11,315
	HINDU (BRAHMANIC)	*296,396*	*145,519*	*150,877*	*112,133*	*63,033*	*49,100*	*156,309*	*76,609*	*79,700*	*27,954*	*5,877*	*22,077*
	0—5 ...	48,255	23,788	24,467	47,040	23,096	24,244	308	88	220	7	4	3
	5—10 ...	40,234	19,961	20,273	36,395	18,704	17,691	3,762	1,239	2,523	77	18	59
	10—15 ...	26,303	14,160	12,143	16,142	10,476	5,666	10,013	3,638	6,375	148	46	102
	15—20 ...	19,789	9,932	9,857	5,812	4,899	913	13,764	4,939	8,825	213	94	119
	20—40 ...	97,193	47,283	49,910	5,151	4,691	460	87,092	40,955	46,137	4,950	1,637	3,313
	40—60 ...	47,104	23,456	23,648	554	463	91	34,392	20,687	13,705	12,158	2,300	9,852
	60 and over	17,518	6,939	10,579	139	104	35	6,978	5,063	1,915	10,401	1,772	8,629
	ANIMIST...	*83,561*	*40,494*	*43,063*	*36,161*	*19,889*	*16,272*	*39,791*	*19,055*	*20,736*	*7,609*	*1,554*	*6,055*
	0—5 ...	13,407	6,509	6,898	13,353	6,484	6,869	52	24	28	2	1	1
	5—10 ...	11,228	5,570	5,658	11,007	5,521	5,576	118	46	72	13	3	10
	10—15 ...	6,391	3,369	3,022	5,773	3,237	2,536	607	129	478	11	3	8
	15—20 ...	5,245	2,573	2,672	2,955	2,080	875	2,245	478	1,767	45	15	30
	20—40 ...	28,604	13,526	15,078	2,695	2,342	353	24,550	10,722	13,828	1,359	462	897
	40—60 ...	13,812	7,000	6,812	219	170	49	10,256	6,198	4,058	3,337	632	2,705
	60 and over	4,874	1,951	2,923	69	55	14	1,963	1,458	505	2,342	438	2,404
RAIPUR.	ALL RELIGIONS.	*1,324,856*	*645,180*	*679,676*	*513,547*	*284,182*	*229,355*	*691,790*	*338,932*	*352,858*	*119,519*	*22,066*	*97,453*
	0—5 ...	222,491	108,304	114,187	220,386	107,667	112,719	2,087	624	1,413	68	13	55
	5—10 ...	178,704	89,945	88,759	162,281	84,561	77,720	16,014	5,280	10,734	409	104	305
	10—15 ...	118,764	64,638	54,126	78,129	49,988	28,141	40,215	14,476	25,739	420	174	246
	15—20 ...	88,321	45,181	43,140	27,080	22,215	4,865	60,320	22,587	37,733	915	379	536
	20—40 ...	441,949	212,753	229,196	22,807	17,736	5,071	397,213	187,266	209,947	21,929	7,751	14,178
	40—60 ...	203,056	98,665	104,391	2,178	1,571	607	148,968	88,983	59,985	51,910	8,111	43,799
	60 and over	71,571	25,700	45,871	686	450	236	27,017	19,716	7,301	43,868	5,534	38,334
	HINDU (BRAHMANIC)	*1,126,497*	*549,378*	*577,119*	*425,204*	*235,650*	*189,545*	*600,655*	*294,644*	*306,041*	*100,600*	*19,079*	*81,530*
	0—5 ...	189,527	92,334	97,193	187,545	91,750	95,795	1,923	572	1,351	59	12	47
	5—10 ...	151,667	76,520	75,147	135,579	71,229	64,350	15,709	5,192	10,517	379	99	280
	10—15 ...	100,214	54,561	45,653	61,701	40,388	21,321	38,119	14,008	24,111	380	165	221
	15—20 ...	75,247	38,406	36,841	20,411	17,222	3,189	54,018	20,844	33,174	816	340	478
	20—40 ...	376,813	181,459	195,354	17,652	13,437	4,216	340,687	161,320	179,367	18,473	6,702	11,771
	40—60 ...	172,488	84,082	88,406	1,742	1,259	483	127,185	75,829	51,356	43,561	6,904	36,567
	60 and over	60,541	22,016	38,525	565	371	194	23,044	16,879	6,165	36,932	4,706	32,166
	ANIMIST...	*177,300*	*85,106*	*92,194*	*79,442*	*43,332*	*36,110*	*81,173*	*39,151*	*42,022*	*16,686*	*2,623*	*14,062*
	0—5 ...	30,111	14,614	15,497	30,013	14,566	15,447	90	47	43	8	1	7
	5—10 ...	24,562	12,203	12,359	24,282	12,126	12,156	251	72	179	29	5	24
	10—15 ...	16,616	9,004	7,612	14,737	8,570	6,167	1,852	426	1,426	27	8	19
	15—20 ...	11,313	5,847	5,466	5,722	4,257	1,465	5,507	1,553	3,954	84	37	47
	20—40 ...	57,551	27,266	30,285	4,225	3,493	732	50,397	22,867	27,530	2,929	906	2,023
	40—60 ...	27,293	12,921	14,372	356	252	104	19,548	11,692	7,856	7,389	977	6,412
	60 and over	9,854	3,251	6,603	107	68	39	3,528	2,494	1,034	6,219	689	5,530
	MUSALMAN	*16,515*	*8,393*	*8,122*	*6,796*	*4,029*	*2,767*	*7,861*	*4,087*	*3,774*	*1,858*	*277*	*1,681*
	0—5 ...	2,165	1,027	1,138	2,141	1,022	1,119	23	5	18	1	...	1
	5—10 ...	1,960	963	997	1,907	948	959	52	15	37	1	...	1
	10—15 ...	1,529	852	677	1,317	815	502	206	36	170	6	1	5
	15—20 ...	1,244	685	559	635	538	97	600	145	455	9	2	7
	20—40 ...	5,928	3,155	2,773	727	656	71	4,777	2,392	2,385	424	107	317
	40—60 ...	2,652	1,335	1,317	56	40	16	1,806	1,187	621	788	108	680
	60 and over	1,037	376	661	13	10	3	895	307	88	629	59	570
BILASPUR.	ALL RELIGIONS.	*1,146,223*	*558,477*	*587,746*	*440,031*	*244,802*	*195,229*	*593,749*	*291,774*	*306,975*	*107,443*	*21,901*	*86,542*
	0—5 ...	194,801	94,702	100,099	191,889	93,953	97,936	2,818	726	2,092	94	23	71
	5—10 ...	170,916	85,479	85,437	149,143	78,680	70,463	21,190	6,597	14,593	583	202	381
	10—15 ...	100,562	53,867	46,695	58,005	38,277	19,728	41,793	15,242	26,551	764	348	416
	15—20 ...	78,624	39,240	39,384	19,564	16,415	3,149	57,675	22,202	35,473	1,385	623	762
	20—40 ...	382,199	183,592	198,607	18,202	15,175	3,028	338,987	160,377	178,610	25,009	8,040	16,969
	40—60 ...	165,230	80,478	84,752	2,568	1,853	715	115,884	70,992	44,892	46,778	7,633	39,145
	60 and over	53,891	21,119	32,772	659	449	210	20,402	15,638	4,764	32,830	5,032	27,798
	HINDU (BRAHMANIC)	*1,077,338*	*524,724*	*552,614*	*411,554*	*228,903*	*182,651*	*565,298*	*275,285*	*290,010*	*100,486*	*20,533*	*79,953*
	0—5 ...	183,598	89,262	94,336	180,777	88,546	92,231	2,735	697	2,038	86	19	67
	5—10 ...	160,679	80,301	80,378	139,538	73,629	65,909	20,580	6,476	14,104	561	196	365
	10—15 ...	95,071	50,892	44,179	53,761	35,698	18,063	40,576	14,859	25,717	734	335	399

TABLE VII.—Part B.—Details for Districts—*continued.*

District or State.	Age.	Population. Persons.	Population. Males.	Population. Females.	Unmarried. Persons.	Unmarried. Males.	Unmarried. Females.	Married. Persons.	Married. Males.	Married. Females.	Widowed. Persons.	Widowed. Males.	Widowed. Females.
	1	2	3	4	5	6	7	8	9	10	11	12	13
BILASPUR—(concld.)	15-20 ...	74,160	37,056	37,113	17,898	15,086	2,812	54,967	21,378	33,589	1,304	592	71[illegible]
	20—40 ...	358,405	172,005	186,400	16,565	13,703	2,772	318,498	150,746	167,752	23,342	7,460	15,87[illegible]
	40—60 ...	154,901	75,358	79,543	2,404	1,735	669	108,753	66,438	42,315	43,744	7,185	36,55[illegible]
	60 and over	50,515	19,850	30,665	611	416	195	19,189	14,694	4,495	30,715	4,740	25,97[illegible]
	ANIMIST ...	*52,425*	*25,455*	*26,970*	*21,865*	*12,143*	*9,722*	*25,389*	*12,300*	*13,089*	*5,171*	*1,012*	*4,15[illegible]*
	0—5 ...	8,912	4,329	4,583	8,845	4,305	4,540	62	21	41	5	3	[illegible]
	5—10 ...	8,086	4,136	3,950	7,557	4,033	3,524	512	97	415	17	6	11
	10—15 ...	4,057	2,204	1,853	3,097	1,885	1,212	936	307	629	24	12	1[illegible]
	15—20 ...	3,219	1,575	1,644	1,133	927	206	2,034	624	1,410	52	24	2[illegible]
	20—40 ...	17,820	8,493	9,327	1,080	886	194	15,608	7,173	8,335	1,232	434	79[illegible]
	40—60 ...	7,807	3,782	4,025	119	84	35	5,415	3,374	2,041	2,273	324	1,94[illegible]
	60 and over	2,524	936	1,588	34	23	11	922	704	218	1,568	209	1,35[illegible]
	MUSALMAN	*13,964*	*7,049*	*6,915*	*5,491*	*3,165*	*2,326*	*6,953*	*3,603*	*3,350*	*1,520*	*281*	*1,23[illegible]*
	0—5 ...	1,891	918	973	1,867	909	958	21	8	13	3	1	[illegible]
	5—10 ...	1,845	898	947	1,746	874	872	96	24	72	3	...	[illegible]
	10—15 ...	1,238	679	559	973	604	309	260	74	186	5	1	[illegible]
	15—20 ...	1,032	532	500	418	350	68	587	176	411	27	6	2[illegible]
	20—40 ...	5,055	2,604	2,451	439	393	46	4,248	2,092	2,156	368	119	24[illegible]
	40—60 ...	2,175	1,137	1,038	36	27	9	1,484	1,019	465	655	91	56[illegible]
	60 and over	728	281	447	12	8	4	257	210	47	459	63	39[illegible]
DRUG	ALL RELIGIONS.	*775,688*	*373,159*	*402,529*	*275,057*	*152,308*	*122,749*	*427,644*	*207,895*	*219,749*	*72,987*	*12,956*	*60,03[illegible]*
	0—5 ...	131,846	64,083	67,813	130,725	63,703	67,022	1,078	321	757	43	9	3[illegible]
	5—10 ...	96,904	49,019	47,885	85,706	45,342	40,364	10,973	3,611	7,362	225	66	15[illegible]
	10—15 ...	61,662	33,478	28,184	34,549	23,004	11,455	26,837	10,250	16,587	270	134	1[illegible]
	15—20 ...	51,811	26,045	25,766	12,648	10,563	2,085	38,698	15,238	23,460	465	244	22[illegible]
	20—40 ...	263,712	126,035	137,677	9,962	8,580	1,382	241,339	113,018	128,321	12,411	4,437	7,97[illegible]
	40—60 ...	125,666	59,314	66,352	1,093	798	295	92,247	53,677	38,570	32,326	4,839	27,48[illegible]
	60 and over	44,087	15,235	28,852	374	228	146	16,472	11,780	4,692	27,241	3,227	24,01[illegible]
	HINDU (BRAHMANIC)	*674,376*	*324,328*	*350,048*	*233,784*	*129,557*	*104,227*	*377,646*	*183,575*	*194,070*	*62,947*	*11,196*	*51,75[illegible]*
	0—5 ...	115,174	55,995	59,179	114,114	55,690	58,424	1,020	296	724	40	9	3[illegible]
	5—10 ...	84,041	42,472	41,569	73,300	38,924	34,376	10,532	3,486	7,046	209	62	14[illegible]
	10—15 ...	53,972	29,288	24,684	28,400	19,397	9,003	25,319	9,765	15,554	253	120	1[illegible]
	15—20 ...	45,315	22,743	22,572	9,631	8,424	1,207	35,280	14,101	21,179	404	218	1[illegible]
	20—40 ...	228,511	109,178	119,333	7,166	6,301	865	210,795	99,081	111,714	10,550	3,796	6,75[illegible]
	40—60 ...	108,996	51,367	57,629	847	623	224	80,308	46,571	33,737	27,841	4,173	23,66[illegible]
	60 and over	38,367	13,285	25,082	326	198	128	14,391	10,275	4,116	23,650	2,812	20,83[illegible]
	ANIMIST ...	*92,106*	*44,144*	*47,962*	*37,489*	*20,547*	*16,942*	*45,635*	*22,045*	*23,550*	*8,959*	*1,549*	*7,4[illegible]*
	0—5 ...	15,882	7,430	7,052	15,834	7,408	7,926	45	22	23	3	...	[illegible]
	5—10 ...	11,811	6,035	5,776	11,395	5,913	5,482	401	118	283	15	4	11
	10—15 ...	6,968	3,790	3,178	5,623	3,321	2,202	1,423	461	962	22	8	1[illegible]
	15—20 ...	5,819	2,927	2,892	2,650	1,843	816	3,101	1,058	2,043	59	26	3[illegible]
	20—40 ...	31,778	15,032	16,746	2,335	1,894	441	27,825	12,574	15,251	1,618	564	1,05[illegible]
	40—60 ...	15,128	7,182	7,946	202	142	60	10,943	6,468	4,475	3,983	572	3,41[illegible]
	60 and over	5,220	1,748	3,472	41	26	15	1,890	1,347	543	3,289	375	2,91[illegible]
AMRAOTI	ALL RELIGIONS.	*875,904*	*447,216*	*428,688*	*302,717*	*182,302*	*120,415*	*467,532*	*234,900*	*232,632*	*105,655*	*30,014*	*75,64[illegible]*
	0—5 ...	128,109	62,688	65,421	125,980	61,873	64,107	2,074	796	1,278	55	19	3[illegible]
	5—10 ...	109,250	53,874	55,376	94,111	52,134	41,977	14,700	1,651	13,049	439	89	35[illegible]
	10—15 ...	77,670	42,237	35,433	43,645	33,494	10,151	32,885	8,448	24,437	1,140	295	84[illegible]
	15—20 ...	60,135	29,032	31,103	16,246	14,802	1,444	42,430	13,740	28,690	1,459	490	96[illegible]
	20—40 ...	286,574	145,008	141,566	18,735	16,786	1,949	244,042	119,846	124,196	23,797	8,376	15,42[illegible]
	40—60 ...	156,345	84,644	71,701	2,916	2,347	569	107,281	70,091	37,190	46,118	12,206	33,91[illegible]
	60 and over	57,821	29,733	28,088	1,054	866	188	24,120	20,328	3,792	32,617	8,539	24,10[illegible]
	HINDU (BRAHMANIC)	*738,294*	*377,352*	*360,942*	*241,176*	*147,089*	*94,087*	*404,757*	*203,512*	*201,245*	*93,361*	*26,751*	*66,61[illegible]*
	0—5 ...	105,621	51,678	53,943	103,771	50,972	52,799	1,802	689	1,113	48	17	3[illegible]
	5—10 ...	89,996	44,175	45,821	75,410	42,584	32,826	14,182	1,513	12,669	404	78	32[illegible]
	10—15 ...	64,871	35,194	29,677	32,934	26,868	6,066	30,862	8,048	22,814	1,075	278	79[illegible]
	15—20 ...	50,854	24,591	26,263	11,934	11,303	631	37,599	13,833	24,766	1,321	455	86[illegible]
	20—40 ...	242,796	123,460	119,336	13,832	12,641	1,191	208,170	103,344	104,826	20,704	7,475	13,31[illegible]
	40—60 ...	134,442	72,625	61,817	2,396	1,959	430	91,561	59,678	31,881	40,483	10,988	29,49[illegible]
	60 and over	49,714	25,629	24,085	897	702	135	20,581	17,407	3,171	28,230	7,400	20,77[illegible]
	ANIMIST...	*57,191*	*28,198*	*28,993*	*26,465*	*14,398*	*12,067*	*26,848*	*12,906*	*13,942*	*3,878*	*594*	*2,98[illegible]*
	0—5 ...	11,043	5,387	5,656	10,908	5,346	5,563	132	42	90	3	...	[illegible]
	5—10 ...	8,405	4,299	4,106	8,202	4,229	3,973	191	69	125	9	1	[illegible]
	10—15 ...	5,060	2,689	2,371	4,311	2,532	1,779	734	154	590	15	3	1[illegible]
	15—20 ...	3,289	1,302	1,927	1,430	1,021	409	1,835	334	1,501	24	7	1[illegible]
	20—40 ...	18,280	8,424	9,856	1,423	1,141	282	16,039	7,007	9,022	768	216	55[illegible]
	40—60 ...	8,557	4,729	3,828	140	100	40	6,633	4,250	2,374	1,784	370	1,41[illegible]
	60 and over	2,557	1,308	1,249	51	30	21	1,231	981	250	1,275	207	97[illegible]

TABLE VII.—Part B.—Details for Districts—*continued.* [Akola Buldana

District or State.	Age.	Population. Persons.	Population. Males.	Population. Females.	Unmarried. Persons.	Unmarried. Males.	Unmarried. Females.	Married. Persons.	Married. Males.	Married. Females.	Widowed. Persons.	Widowed. Males.	Widowed. Females.
	1	2	3	4	5	6	7	8	9	10	11	12	13
AMRAOTI—(concld.)	MUSALMAN.	*73,311*	*37,896*	*35,415*	*32,325*	*19,124*	*13,201*	*32,479*	*16,656*	*15,823*	*8,507*	*2,116*	*6,391*
	0— 5 ...	10,489	5,158	5,331	10,363	5,097	5,266	122	59	63	4	2	2
	5—10 ...	9,944	4,911	5,033	9,685	4,843	4,842	238	58	180	21	10	11
	10—15 ...	7,081	3,987	3,094	6,018	3,819	2,199	1,021	156	865	42	12	30
	15—20 ...	5,400	2,754	2,646	2,649	2,293	356	2,657	444	2,213	94	17	77
	20—40 ...	23,138	11,899	11,239	3,171	2,756	415	17,977	8,523	9,454	1,900	620	1,370
	40—60 ...	12,092	6,567	5,525	340	252	94	8,278	5,574	2,704	3,468	741	2,727
	60 and over	5,167	2,620	2,547	93	64	29	2,186	1,842	344	2,888	714	2,174
AKOLA	ALL RELIGIONS.	*758,863*	*400,893*	*357,970*	*240,809*	*147,083*	*93,726*	*452,015*	*226,090*	*225,925*	*95,136*	*26,830*	*68,310*
	0— 5 ...	115,625	55,990	59,635	112,057	55,227	56,830	3,482	735	2,747	86	28	58
	5—10 ...	97,653	48,195	49,458	73,237	44,768	28,469	23,737	3,290	20,447	679	137	542
	10—15 ...	72,121	39,389	32,732	30,192	24,504	5,688	40,361	14,358	26,003	1,568	527	1,041
	15—20 ...	52,151	24,828	27,323	9,949	9,160	789	40,722	15,037	25,685	1,480	631	849
	20—40 ...	262,312	132,963	129,349	12,827	11,343	1,484	227,527	113,219	114,308	21,958	8,401	13,557
	40—60 ...	140,475	75,637	64,838	2,025	1,653	372	96,815	63,533	33,282	41,635	10,451	31,184
	60 and over	48,526	23,891	24,635	522	428	94	20,274	16,818	3,456	27,730	6,645	21,085
	HINDU (BRAHMANIC)	*711,025*	*360,644*	*350,381*	*207,163*	*127,323*	*79,840*	*417,431*	*208,684*	*208,747*	*86,431*	*24,637*	*61,794*
	0— 5 ...	104,623	50,706	53,917	101,174	49,983	51,191	3,374	697	2,677	75	26	49
	5—10 ...	87,117	42,971	44,146	63,147	39,662	23,485	23,316	3,175	20,141	654	134	520
	10—15 ...	64,362	35,058	29,304	23,854	20,457	3,397	38,992	14,083	24,909	1,516	518	998
	15—20 ...	46,656	21,989	24,667	7,345	6,934	411	37,952	14,447	23,505	1,359	608	751
	20—40 ...	237,018	119,906	117,112	9,453	8,474	979	207,698	103,692	104,006	19,867	7,740	12,127
	40—60 ...	127,837	68,698	59,139	1,742	1,437	305	88,052	57,624	30,428	38,043	9,637	28,406
	60 and over	43,412	21,316	22,096	448	376	72	18,047	14,966	3,081	24,917	5,974	18,943
	MUSALMAN.	*70,148*	*36,342*	*33,806*	*30,990*	*18,141*	*12,849*	*31,550*	*16,305*	*15,245*	*7,608*	*1,896*	*5,712*
	0— 5 ...	9,992	4,810	5,182	9,892	4,774	5,118	90	34	56	10	2	8
	5—10 ...	9,669	4,823	4,846	9,353	4,720	4,633	297	100	197	19	3	16
	10—15 ...	7,050	3,932	3,118	5,900	3,709	2,191	1,117	215	902	33	8	25
	15—20 ...	4,913	2,559	2,354	2,427	2,081	346	2,397	463	1,934	89	15	74
	20—40 ...	22,642	11,682	10,960	3,110	2,628	482	17,728	8,484	9,244	1,804	570	1,234
	40—60 ...	11,303	6,222	5,081	245	187	58	7,917	5,329	2,588	3,141	706	2,435
	60 and over	4,579	2,314	2,265	63	42	21	2,004	1,680	324	2,512	592	1,920
BULDANA	ALL RELIGIONS.	*669,182*	*337,179*	*332,003*	*207,123*	*136,691*	*80,432*	*383,237*	*190,037*	*193,199*	*78,822*	*20,450*	*58,372*
	0— 5 ...	103,783	50,225	53,558	100,442	49,559	50,883	3,285	646	2,639	56	20	36
	5—10 ...	85,568	42,789	42,779	62,987	39,883	23,104	21,959	2,812	19,147	622	94	528
	10—15 ...	63,446	34,156	29,290	25,221	20,888	4,333	36,804	12,831	23,973	1,421	437	984
	15—20 ...	46,618	22,473	24,145	7,650	7,050	600	37,511	14,813	22,698	1,457	610	847
	20—40 ...	221,190	111,083	110,107	8,837	7,717	1,120	192,930	96,403	96,527	19,423	6,963	12,460
	40—60 ...	111,914	58,873	53,041	1,460	1,158	302	76,027	50,273	25,754	34,427	7,442	26,985
	60 and over	36,663	17,580	19,083	526	430	90	14,721	12,260	2,461	21,416	4,884	16,532
	HINDU (BRAHMANIC)	*608,609*	*305,993*	*302,616*	*180,467*	*111,003*	*69,464*	*355,693*	*176,116*	*179,577*	*72,459*	*18,874*	*53,585*
	0— 5 ...	94,654	45,859	48,795	91,414	45,234	46,180	3,191	612	2,579	49	13	36
	5—10 ...	77,078	38,516	38,562	54,800	35,688	19,112	21,687	2,747	18,940	591	81	510
	10—15 ...	57,219	30,666	26,553	20,247	17,621	2,626	35,605	12,629	22,976	1,367	416	951
	15—20 ...	42,296	20,274	22,022	5,708	5,349	359	35,215	14,331	20,884	1,373	594	779
	20—40 ...	201,745	101,135	100,610	6,593	5,727	866	177,327	88,918	88,409	17,825	6,490	11,335
	40—60 ...	102,423	53,727	48,696	1,235	995	240	69,456	45,899	22,557	31,732	6,833	24,899
	60 and over	33,194	15,816	17,378	460	389	71	13,212	10,980	2,232	19,522	4,447	15,075
	MUSALMAN	*55,257*	*28,436*	*26,824*	*24,734*	*14,486*	*10,248*	*24,908*	*12,590*	*13,318*	*5,620*	*1,359*	*4,261*
	0— 5 ...	8,447	4,046	4,401	8,360	4,013	4,347	82	28	54	5	5	...
	5—10 ...	7,885	3,961	3,924	7,650	3,894	3,756	210	57	153	25	10	15
	10—15 ...	5,701	3,202	2,499	4,661	3,027	1,634	997	157	840	43	18	25
	15—20 ...	3,855	1,985	1,870	1,790	1,579	211	2,004	392	1,612	61	14	47
	20—40 ...	17,507	9,000	8,507	2,038	1,815	223	14,169	6,770	7,399	1,390	415	975
	40—60 ...	8,575	4,621	3,954	178	120	58	6,019	3,978	2,041	2,378	523	1,855
	60 and over	3,197	1,620	1,577	57	38	19	1,422	1,208	214	1,718	374	1,344
	ALL RELIGIONS.	*723,213*	*365,326*	*357,887*	*241,847*	*143,763*	*98,084*	*407,658*	*203,535*	*204,123*	*73,708*	*18,028*	*55,680*
	0— 5 ...	117,674	57,262	60,412	113,414	56,420	56,994	4,188	824	3,364	72	18	54
	5—10 ...	95,623	47,402	48,221	73,700	42,409	31,297	21,286	4,799	16,487	631	194	437
	10—15 ...	65,102	35,064	30,038	29,737	22,567	7,170	34,335	12,082	22,253	1,030	415	615
	15—20 ...	44,612	21,215	23,397	9,776	8,949	827	33,982	11,879	22,103	854	387	467
	20—40 ...	239,084	119,830	119,254	12,931	11,606	1,325	211,357	103,163	108,194	14,796	5,061	9,735
	40—60 ...	119,768	64,764	55,004	1,809	1,454	355	85,203	56,442	28,761	32,756	6,868	25,888
	60 and over	41,350	19,789	21,561	474	358	116	17,307	14,346	2,961	23,569	5,085	18,484

 TABLE VII.—Part B.—Details for Districts—*concluded.*

District or State.	Age.	Population.			Unmarried.			Married.			Widowed.		
		Persons.	Males.	Females.	Persons.	Males.	Females.	Persons.	Males.	Females.	Persons.	Males.	Females.
	1	2	3	4	5	6	7	8	9	10	11	12	13
YEOTMAL—(concld.)	HINDU (BRAHMANIC.)	610,181	308,407	301,774	195,542	117,407	78,135	350,791	175,061	175,730	63,848	15,939	47,909
	0—5 ...	98,658	48,100	50,558	94,697	47,349	47,348	3,917	734	3,183	44	17	27
	5—10 ...	80,000	39,691	40,309	59,125	34,990	24,135	20,305	4,520	15,785	570	181	389
	10—15 ...	55,018	29,576	25,442	22,519	17,676	4,843	31,555	11,510	20,045	944	390	554
	15—20 ...	37,782	18,014	19,768	7,403	6,879	524	29,630	10,779	18,851	749	356	393
	20—40 ...	202,030	101,375	100,655	9,948	8,994	954	179,169	87,878	91,291	12,913	4,503	8,410
	40—60 ...	101,705	54,918	46,787	1,469	1,213	256	71,811	47,607	24,204	28,425	6,098	22,327
	60 and over	34,988	16,733	18,255	381	306	75	14,404	12,033	2,371	20,203	4,394	15,809
	ANIMIST ...	69,364	34,202	35,162	27,732	15,322	12,410	36,077	17,730	18,347	5,545	1,150	4,395
	0—5 ...	12,348	5,914	6,434	12,167	5,864	6,303	174	50	124	7	...	7
	5—10 ...	9,778	4,822	4,956	9,180	4,708	4,472	578	112	466	20	2	18
	10—15 ...	5,961	3,203	2,758	4,060	2,816	1,244	1,853	381	1,472	48	6	42
	15—20 ...	3,891	1,727	2,164	1,115	971	144	2,730	740	1,990	46	16	30
	20—40 ...	22,313	10,649	11,664	1,060	880	180	20,313	9,481	10,832	940	288	652
	40—60 ...	11,209	6,024	5,185	107	68	39	8,613	5,550	3,063	2,489	406	2,083
	60 and over	3,854	1,863	1,991	43	15	28	1,816	1,416	400	1,995	432	1,563
	MUSALMAN.	39,949	20,780	19,169	17,174	10,172	7,002	18,939	9,796	9,143	3,836	812	3,024
	0—5 ...	6,163	3,017	3,146	6,056	2,981	3,075	88	35	53	19	1	18
	5—10 ...	5,430	2,682	2,748	5,040	2,515	2,525	351	158	193	39	9	30
	10—15 ...	3,781	2,108	1,673	2,954	1,928	1,026	801	168	633	26	12	14
	15—20 ...	2,658	1,337	1,321	1,143	1,009	134	1,465	317	1,148	50	11	39
	20—40 ...	13,370	7,053	6,317	1,732	1,558	174	10,829	5,259	5,570	809	236	573
	40—60 ...	6,235	3,480	2,755	207	151	56	4,383	3,019	1,364	1,645	310	1,335
	60 and over	2,312	1,103	1,209	42	30	12	1,022	840	182	1,248	233	1,015
FEUDATORY STATES	ALL RELIGIONS.	2,117,002	1,053,630	1,063,372	946,548	520,273	426,275	1,008,455	498,638	509,817	161,999	34,719	127,280
	0—5 ...	367,331	177,584	189,747	364,791	176,738	188,053	2,381	806	1,575	159	40	119
	5—10 ...	332,280	166,820	165,460	314,804	160,935	153,869	16,860	5,738	11,122	616	147	469
	10—15 ...	210,735	115,298	95,437	156,835	97,090	59,745	52,926	17,889	35,037	974	319	655
	15—20 ...	146,659	74,787	71,872	56,391	42,271	14,120	88,053	31,727	56,326	2,215	789	1,426
	20—40 ..	667,173	336,001	351,172	47,928	39,249	8,679	600,019	284,057	315,962	39,226	12,695	26,531
	40—60 ...	284,841	147,466	137,375	4,448	3,152	1,296	212,125	131,598	80,527	68,268	12,716	55,552
	60 and over	87,983	35,674	52,309	1,851	838	513	36,091	26,823	9,268	50,541	8,013	42,528
	HINDU (BRAHMANIC)	1,311,386	650,807	660,581	546,565	302,654	243,914	657,423	325,708	331,715	107,397	22,445	84,952
	0—5 ...	219,867	106,533	113,334	217,906	105,881	112,025	1,858	626	1,232	103	26	77
	5—10 ...	199,083	99,789	99,294	183,730	94,579	89,151	14,925	5,100	9,825	428	110	318
	10—15 ...	128,275	70,384	57,891	86,631	55,472	31,159	40,999	14,680	26,319	645	232	413
	15—20 ...	91,238	47,026	44,212	29,548	23,153	6,395	60,246	23,319	36,927	1,444	554	890
	20—40 ...	431,570	211,153	220,417	25,272	21,073	4,199	380,994	181,752	199,242	25,304	8,328	16,976
	40—60 ...	183,780	93,432	90,348	2,702	1,987	715	135,437	83,234	52,203	45,641	8,211	37,430
	60 and over	57,575	22,490	35,085	779	509	270	22,964	16,997	5,967	33,832	4,984	28,848
	ANIMIST	745,434	372,384	373,050	370,357	201,139	169,218	324,846	159,834	165,012	50,231	11,411	38,820
	0—5 ...	136,513	65,752	70,761	136,964	65,564	70,400	495	174	321	54	14	40
	5—10 ...	123,559	62,151	61,408	121,599	61,531	60,068	1,780	587	1,193	180	33	147
	10—15 ...	75,816	41,172	34,644	64,507	38,095	26,412	11,018	3,002	8,016	291	75	216
	15—20 ...	51,269	25,576	25,693	24,885	17,594	7,291	25,677	7,764	17,913	707	218	489
	20—40 ...	236,928	115,560	121,368	21,280	17,007	4,273	202,841	94,526	108,315	14,807	4,027	8,780
	40—60 ...	93,271	49,958	43,313	1,584	1,038	546	70,868	44,690	26,178	20,819	4,225	16,594
	60 and over	28,078	12,220	15,858	538	310	228	12,167	9,091	3,076	15,373	2,819	12,554
	MUSALMAN	20,120	10,180	9,940	8,091	4,787	3,304	9,869	4,947	4,922	2,160	446	1,714
	0—5 ...	2,727	1,320	1,407	2,701	1,315	1,386	24	5	19	2	...	2
	5—10 ...	2,618	1,355	1,263	2,510	1,321	1,189	103	31	72	5	3	2
	10—15 ...	1,906	1,034	872	1,467	918	549	423	112	311	16	4	12
	15—20 ...	1,435	790	645	618	526	90	788	255	533	29	7	22
	20—40 ...	7,265	3,639	3,626	686	615	73	5,971	2,831	3,140	606	193	413
	40—60 ...	3,159	1,630	1,529	87	77	10	2,175	1,421	754	897	132	765
	60 and over	1,010	412	598	20	13	7	385	292	93	605	107	498
	CHRISTIAN.	38,704	19,377	19,327	20,976	11,326	9,650	15,674	7,780	7,894	2,054	371	1,683
	0—5 ...	8,053	3,902	4,151	8,050	3,901	4,149	3	1	2	...	...	...
	5—10 ...	6,908	3,475	3,433	6,854	3,454	3,400	51	20	31	3	1	2
	10—15 ...	4,592	2,619	1,973	4,117	2,524	1,593	453	87	366	22	8	14
	15—20 ...	2,605	1,319	1,286	1,286	943	343	1,284	366	918	35	10	25
	20—40 ...	10,841	5,289	5,552	589	457	132	9,801	4,707	5,094	451	125	326
	40—60 ...	4,428	2,343	2,085	66	41	25	3,521	2,169	1,352	841	133	708
	60 and over	1,277	530	747	14	6	8	561	430	131	702	94	608

TABLE VII.—Part C.—Details for Cities.

City.	Age.	Population.			Unmarried.			Married.			Widowed.		
		Persons.	Males.	Females.	Persons.	Males.	Females.	Persons.	Males.	Females.	Persons.	Males.	Females.
	1	2	3	4	5	6	7	8	9	10	11	12	13
JUBBULPORE	ALL RELIGIONS.	*100,651*	*56,035*	*44,616*	*40,267*	*26,156*	*14,111*	*48,926*	*26,539*	*22,387*	*11,458*	*3,340*	*8,118*
	0—5 ...	12,890	6,341	6,549	12,831	6,316	6,515	55	25	30	4	...	4
	5—10 ...	10,991	5,564	5,427	10,541	5,488	5,053	432	74	358	18	2	16
	10—15 ...	8,973	5,371	3,602	6,593	4,803	1,790	2,313	542	1,771	67	26	41
	15—20 ...	7,997	4,578	3,419	3,347	2,994	353	4,462	1,490	2,972	188	94	94
	20—40 ...	39,943	23,728	16,215	6,559	6,215	344	30,075	16,176	13,899	3,309	1,337	1,972
	40—60 ...	15,385	8,422	6,963	338	291	47	9,928	6,862	3,066	5,119	1,269	3,850
	60 and over	4,472	2,031	2,441	58	49	9	1,661	1,370	291	2,753	612	2,141
	HINDU (BRAHMANIC).	*68,902*	*37,334*	*31,568*	*25,207*	*15,911*	*9,296*	*35,100*	*18,949*	*16,151*	*8,595*	*2,474*	*6,121*
	0—5 ...	9,116	4,480	4,636	9,067	4,462	4,605	45	18	27	4	...	4
	5—10 ...	7,490	3,791	3,708	7,132	3,727	3,405	353	63	290	14	1	13
	10—15 ...	6,221	3,752	2,469	4,347	3,306	1,041	1,819	426	1,393	55	20	35
	15—20 ...	5,252	3,014	2,238	1,899	1,808	91	3,226	1,142	2,084	127	64	63
	20—40 ...	26,528	14,851	11,677	2,500	2,377	123	21,505	11,499	10,006	2,523	975	1,548
	40—60 ...	11,099	6,065	5,034	224	201	23	7,041	4,887	2,154	3,834	977	2,857
	60 and over	3,187	1,381	1,806	38	30	8	1,111	914	197	2,038	437	1,601
	MUSALMAN	*23,032*	*12,827*	*10,205*	*9,438*	*5,987*	*3,451*	*11,190*	*6,102*	*5,088*	*2,414*	*738*	*1,676*
	0—5 ...	3,012	1,492	1,520	3,002	1,485	1,517	10	7	3	...	...	...
	5—10 ...	2,791	1,440	1,351	2,715	1,429	1,286	72	10	62	4	1	3
	10—15 ...	2,171	1,295	876	1,716	1,182	534	443	107	336	12	6	6
	15—20 ...	1,999	1,160	839	888	836	52	1,059	296	763	52	28	24
	20—40 ...	8,464	4,976	3,488	1,040	995	45	6,780	3,668	3,112	644	313	331
	40—60 ...	3,488	1,905	1,583	52	45	7	2,354	1,620	734	1,082	240	842
	60 and over	1,107	559	548	15	15	...	472	394	78	620	150	470
	CHRISTIAN	*6,310*	*4,349*	*1,961*	*4,680*	*3,558*	*1,122*	*1,451*	*752*	*699*	*173*	*33*	*140*
	0—5 ...	554	276	278	551	276	278	...	...	...	...	...	...
	5—10 ...	491	215	276	480	214	275	2	1	1	...	...	...
	10—15 ...	409	221	188	407	219	188	2	2	...	...	...	...
	15—20 ...	499	284	265	435	230	205	62	4	58	2	...	2
	20—40 ...	3,801	3,095	706	2,738	2,580	158	1,019	504	515	44	11	33
	40—60 ...	461	255	206	52	35	17	318	202	116	91	18	73
	60 and over	95	53	42	5	4	1	48	39	9	42	10	32
NAGPUR	ALL RELIGIONS.	*101,415*	*53,696*	*47,719*	*36,713*	*22,659*	*14,054*	*51,356*	*27,430*	*23,926*	*13,346*	*3,607*	*9,739*
	0—5 ...	12,706	6,320	6,386	12,548	6,245	6,303	148	69	79	10	6	4
	5—10 ...	11,107	5,599	5,508	10,426	5,471	4,955	643	116	527	38	12	26
	10—15 ...	8,701	4,858	3,843	6,166	4,257	1,909	2,406	565	1,841	129	36	93
	15—20 ...	7,410	3,935	3,475	2,941	2,621	320	4,281	1,251	3,030	188	63	125
	20—40 ...	36,777	20,123	16,654	4,079	3,654	425	29,247	15,275	13,972	3,451	1,194	2,257
	40—60 ...	17,552	9,408	8,144	425	323	102	11,719	7,827	3,892	5,408	1,258	4,150
	60 and over	7,162	3,453	3,709	128	88	40	2,912	2,327	585	4,122	1,038	3,084
	HINDU (BRAHMANIC)	*80,141*	*42,187*	*37,954*	*27,420*	*16,990*	*10,430*	*41,886*	*22,306*	*19,580*	*10,835*	*2,891*	*7,944*
	0—5 ...	10,109	5,038	5,071	9,972	4,974	4,998	131	60	71	6	4	2
	5—10 ...	8,737	4,453	4,284	8,127	4,350	3,777	578	94	484	32	9	23
	10—15 ...	6,660	3,672	2,988	4,412	3,151	1,261	2,138	491	1,647	110	30	80
	15—20 ...	5,613	2,931	2,682	1,923	1,787	136	3,534	1,088	2,446	156	56	100
	20—40 ...	29,219	15,914	13,305	2,606	2,424	182	23,832	12,553	11,279	2,781	937	1,844
	40—60 ...	13,990	7,424	6,566	285	235	50	9,339	6,166	3,173	4,866	1,023	3,843
	60 and over	5,818	2,756	3,058	95	69	26	2,334	1,854	480	3,384	832	2,552
	MUSALMAN	*14,591*	*7,856*	*6,735*	*5,925*	*3,605*	*2,320*	*6,804*	*3,723*	*3,081*	*1,860*	*526*	*1,334*
	0—5 ...	1,759	880	879	1,748	875	873	10	5	5	1	...	1
	5—10 ...	1,731	827	904	1,675	804	871	51	20	31	5	3	2
	10—15 ...	1,418	818	600	1,183	747	436	223	66	157	10	3	7
	15—20 ...	1,047	570	477	481	441	40	545	125	420	21	4	17
	20—40 ...	5,058	2,800	2,258	749	676	73	3,837	1,935	1,902	472	189	283
	40—60 ...	2,511	1,412	1,099	65	48	17	1,682	1,199	483	764	165	599
	60 and over	1,067	549	518	24	14	10	456	373	83	587	162	425
	CHRISTIAN	*3,960*	*2,158*	*1,802*	*2,337*	*1,436*	*901*	*1,312*	*651*	*661*	*321*	*81*	*240*
	0—5 ...	511	239	272	507	237	270	2	...	2	2	2	...
	5—10 ...	365	170	195	357	169	188	7	1	6	1	...	1
	10—15 ...	422	262	160	407	258	149	10	1	9	5	3	2
	15—20 ...	531	320	211	427	308	119	97	10	87	7	2	5
	20—40 ...	1,443	816	627	559	422	137	789	371	418	95	23	72
	40—60 ...	544	281	263	64	30	34	346	221	125	134	30	104
	60 and over	144	70	74	6	2	4	61	47	14	77	21	56

TABLE VIII.

Education by Religion and Age.

This table, like Table VII, is divided into three parts. Part A (pp. 54 and 55) shows the extent of literacy in the Province as a whole amongst the total population and for each religion returned. Part B (pp. 56 to 65) gives details for districts for the total district population and for each main religion, and Part C (p. 66) gives similar details for cities.

Columns 6, 7, 8 of the table show the number of persons literate in their vernacular. The number of persons literate in English has also been shown. Some of these have returned English as their only language, while others are also literate in a vernacular, and have accordingly been entered twice—once in the column referring to the vernacular, and again in the columns "Literate in English." The latter columns must, therefore, be left out of account in calculating the total number of literate persons.

The following statement distributes the total number of literate Christians in the Provinces in each category between Europeans and Anglo-Indians on the one side and Indian Christians on the other side :—

TOTAL LITERATE	TOTAL.			0—10.			10-15.			15—20.			20 and over.		
	Persons.	Males.	Females	Persons.	Males.	Females	Persons.	Males.	Females.	Persons.	Males.	Females.	Persons.	Males.	Females.
Europeans and Anglo-Indians.	9,633	6,804	2,829	636	345	291	619	336	283	605	331	274	7,773	5,792	1,981
Indian Christians ...	8,621	5,148	3,473	477	251	226	1,327	737	590	2,019	1,010	1,009	4,798	3,150	1,648
Literate in English—															
Europeans and Anglo-Indians.	9,579	6,772	2,807	619	337	282	615	333	282	598	327	271	7,747	5,775	1,972
Indian Christians ...	2,682	1,926	756	69	39	30	260	171	89	537	347	190	1,816	1,369	447

TABLE VIII.—Education by Religion and Age.

Part A.—Provincial Summary.

Religion.	Age.	POPULATION.									LITERATE IN ENGLISH		
		TOTAL.			LITERATE.			ILLITERATE.					
		Persons.	Males.	Females.	Persons.	Males.	Females.	Persons.	Males.	Females.	Persons.	Males.	Females.
1	2	3	4	5	6	7	8	9	10	11	12	13	14
ALL RELIGIONS	Total ...	*16,033,310*	*7,984,023*	*8,049 288*	*521,187*	*497,541*	*23,646*	*15,512,123*	*7,486,481*	*8,035,642*	*47,350*	*43,101*	*4,1*
	0—10 ...	4,773,167	2,358,839	2,414,328	11,465	9,742	1,723	4,761,702	2,349,097	2,412,605	793	469	3
	10—15 ...	1,475,895	802,769	673,126	59,025	55,034	3,991	1,416,870	747,735	669,135	3,067	2,621	4
	15—20 ...	1,079,162	545,341	533,821	63,446	59,426	4,020	1,015,716	485,915	529,801	6,693	6,118	5
	20 and over	8,705,086	4,277,073	4,428,013	387,251	373,339	13,912	8,317,835	3,903,734	4,414,101	36,697	33,893	2,8
HINDU (BRAHMANIC)	Total ...	*12,807,874*	*6,382,743*	*6,425,131*	*422,888*	*410,019*	*12,869*	*12,384,986*	*5,972,724*	*6,412,262*	*28,379*	*28,068*	*3*
	0—10 ...	3,764,155	1,862,094	1,902,061	8,553	7,665	888	3,755,602	1,854,429	1,901,173	72	68	
	10—15 ...	1,179,164	641,833	537,331	48,796	46,419	2,377	1,130,368	595,414	534,954	1,821	1,777	
	15—20 ...	865,560	438,742	426,818	51,357	49,269	2,088	814,203	389,473	424,730	4,571	4,513	
	20 and over	6,998,995	3,440,074	3,558,921	314,182	306,666	7,516	6,684,813	3,133,408	3,551,405	21,915	21,710	2
HINDU (ARYA)	Total ...	*974*	*554*	*420*	*434*	*356*	*78*	*540*	*198*	*342*	*153*	*146*	
	0—10 ...	259	130	129	20	13	7	239	117	122	1	1	...
	10—15 ...	126	84	42	74	56	18	52	28	24	10	9	
	15—20 ...	83	48	35	49	39	10	34	9	25	21	18	
	20 and over	506	292	214	291	248	43	215	44	171	121	117	
HINDU (BRAHMO)	Total ...	*32*	*19*	*13*	*19*	*13*	*6*	*13*	*6*	*7*	*12*	*8*	
	0—10 ...	4	...	4	...	...	...	4	...	4	...	...	...
	10—15 ...	2	1	1	1	1	...	1	...	1	...	...	...
	15—20 ...	2	...	2	...	...	...	2	...	2	...	...	...
	20 and over	24	18	6	18	12	6	6	6	...	12	8	
SIKH	Total ...	*2,337*	*1,802*	*535*	*986*	*958*	*28*	*1,351*	*844*	*507*	*138*	*134*	
	0—10 ...	310	152	158	6	5	1	304	147	157	...	...	...
	10—15 ...	116	74	42	22	18	4	94	56	38	1	1	...
	15—20 ...	211	156	55	76	75	1	135	81	54	9	9	...
	20 and over	1,700	1,420	280	882	860	22	818	560	258	128	124	
JAIN	Total ...	*71,417*	*36,780*	*34,637*	*18,610*	*17,573*	*1,037*	*52,807*	*19,207*	*33,600*	*547*	*537*	
	0—10 ...	17,665	8,743	8,922	364	291	73	17,301	8,452	8,849	1	1	...
	10—15 ...	7,227	4,037	3,190	2,035	1,816	219	5,192	2,221	2,971	47	45	
	15—20 ...	5,697	3,131	2,566	2,270	2,117	153	3,427	1,014	2,413	113	112	
	20 and over	40,828	20,889	19,959	13,941	13,349	592	26,887	7,520	19,367	386	379	

TABLE VIII.—Part A.—Provincial Summary—*concluded.*

Religion.	Age.	POPULATION. Total. Persons.	Total. Males.	Total. Females.	Literate. Persons.	Literate. Males.	Literate. Females.	Illiterate. Persons.	Illiterate. Males.	Illiterate. Females.	Literate in English. Persons.	Literate in English. Males.	Literate in English. Females.
1	2	3	4	5	6	7	8	9	10	11	12	13	14
BUDDHIST	Total ...	*9*	*8*	*1*	*6*	*6*	...	*3*	*2*	*1*	*4*	*4*	...
	0—10 ...	...	...	...	...	...	...	...	...	...	...	...	...
	10–15 ...	...	...	...	...	...	...	...	...	...	...	...	...
	15–20 ...	...	...	...	...	...	...	...	...	...	...	...	...
	20 and over	9	8	1	6	6	...	3	2	1	4	4	...
ANIMIST	Total ...	*2,490,355*	*1,219,551*	*1,270,804*	*5,441*	*5,341*	*100*	*2,484,914*	*1,214,210*	*1,270,704*	*42*	*42*	...
	0—10 ...	804,070	395,526	408,544	136	132	4	803,934	395,394	408,540	...	...	...
	10—15 ...	224,623	120,547	104,076	725	704	21	223,898	119,843	104,055	3	3	...
	15—20 ...	160,240	78,282	81,958	920	903	17	159,320	77,379	81,941	10	10	...
	20 and over	1,301,422	625,196	676,226	3,660	3,602	58	1,297,762	621,594	676,168	29	29	...
MUSALMAN	Total ...	*585,029*	*302,227*	*282,802*	*53,181*	*50,445*	*2,736*	*531,848*	*251,782*	*280,066*	*4,780*	*4,728*	*52*
	0—10 ...	162,649	80,251	82,398	1,205	1,008	197	161,444	79,243	82,201	11	11	...
	10—15 ...	56,729	31,722	25,007	5,324	4,900	424	51,405	26,822	24,583	263	260	3
	15—20 ...	41,059	21,845	19,214	6,021	5,624	397	35,038	16,221	18,817	753	737	16
	20 and over	324,592	168,409	156,183	40,631	38,913	1,718	283,961	129,496	154,465	3,753	3,720	33
CHRISTIAN	Total ...	*73,401*	*39,208*	*34,193*	*18,254*	*11,952*	*6,302*	*55,147*	*27,256*	*27,891*	*12,261*	*8,698*	*3,563*
	0—10 ...	23,650	11,721	11,929	1,113	596	517	22,537	11,125	11,412	688	376	312
	10—15 ...	7,774	4,405	3,369	1,946	1,073	873	5,828	3,332	2,496	875	504	371
	15—20 ...	6,167	3,074	3,093	2,624	1,341	1,283	3,543	1,733	1,810	1,135	674	461
	20 and over	35,810	20,008	15,802	12,571	8,942	3,629	23,229	11,066	12,173	9,563	7,144	2,419
JEW	Total ...	*125*	*78*	*47*	*66*	*46*	*20*	*59*	*32*	*27*	*38*	*32*	*6*
	0—10 ...	37	22	15	7	2	5	30	20	10	1	...	1
	10—15 ...	11	7	4	7	5	2	4	2	2	3	2	1
	15—20 ...	8	4	4	7	3	4	1	1	...	3	1	2
	20 and over	69	45	24	45	36	9	24	9	15	31	29	2
ZOROASTRIAN	Total ...	*1,757*	*1,052*	*705*	*1,302*	*833*	*470*	*455*	*220*	*235*	*896*	*705*	*191*
	0—10 ...	368	200	168	61	30	31	307	170	137	19	12	7
	10—15 ...	123	59	64	95	42	53	28	17	11	44	20	24
	15—20 ...	135	59	76	122	55	67	13	4	9	78	44	34
	20 and over	1,131	734	397	1,024	706	319	107	29	78	755	629	126

TABLE VIII.—Part B.—Details for Districts.

District.	Age.	POPULATION. Total. Persons.	Males.	Females.	Literate. Persons.	Males.	Females.	Illiterate. Persons.	Males.	Females.	Literate in English. Persons.	Males.	Females.
1	2	3	4	5	6	7	8	9	10	11	12	13	14
SAUGOR	ALL RELIGIONS	*541,410*	*276,233*	*265,177*	*26,001*	*24,291*	*1,710*	*515,409*	*251,942*	*263,467*	*2,193*	*1,981*	*212*
	0—10 ...	159,934	80,655	79,279	575	480	95	159,359	80,175	79,184	42	27	15
	10—15 ...	47,297	26,772	20,525	3,035	2,710	319	44,262	24,056	20,206	161	129	32
	15—20 ...	39,626	21,955	17,671	3,515	3,189	326	36,111	18,766	17,345	376	346	30
	20 and over	294,553	146,851	147,702	18,876	17,906	970	275,677	128,946	146,732	1,614	1,479	135
	HINDU (BRAHMANIC)	*471,650*	*240,356*	*231,294*	*18,115*	*17,308*	*807*	*453,535*	*223,048*	*230,487*	*1,294*	*1,281*	*13*
	0—10 ...	139,916	70,794	69,122	397	351	46	139,519	70,443	69,076	3	3	...
	10—15 ...	41,190	23,319	17,871	2,099	1,949	150	39,091	21,370	17,721	98	95	3
	15—20 ...	34,481	19,140	15,341	2,488	2,342	146	31,993	16,798	15,195	278	272	6
	20 and over	256,063	127,103	128,960	13,131	12,666	465	242,932	114,437	128,495	915	911	4
	ANIMIST...	*24,924*	*12,154*	*12,770*	*17*	*15*	*2*	*24,907*	*12,139*	*12,768*	...	...	...
	0—10 ...	7,925	3,859	4,066	...	...	...	7,925	3,859	4,066	...	...	...
	10—15 ...	1,775	962	813	1	1	...	1,774	961	813	...	...	...
	15—20 ...	1,630	813	817	2	2	...	1,028	811	817	...	...	...
	20 and over	13,594	6,520	7,074	14	12	2	13,580	6,508	7,072	...	...	...
	MUSALMAN	*25,835*	*13,632*	*12,203*	*2,422*	*2,316*	*106*	*23,413*	*11,316*	*12,097*	*296*	*295*	*1*
	0—10 ...	7,216	3,536	3,680	48	43	5	7,168	3,493	3,675	...	...	...
	10—15 ...	2,355	1,332	1,023	242	221	21	2,113	1,111	1,002	10	9	1
	15—20 ...	1,939	1,108	831	276	260	16	1,663	848	815	45	45	...
	20 and over	14,325	7,656	6,669	1,856	1,792	64	12,469	5,864	6,605	241	241	...
	CHRISTIAN	*1,454*	*777*	*677*	*827*	*463*	*364*	*627*	*314*	*313*	*476*	*284*	*192*
	0—10 ...	411	196	215	43	24	19	368	172	196	38	23	15
	10—15 ...	118	60	58	92	41	51	26	19	7	43	15	28
	15—20 ...	185	81	104	141	53	88	44	28	16	36	15	21
	20 and over	740	440	300	551	345	206	189	95	94	359	231	128
	JAIN ...	*16,713*	*8,627*	*8,086*	*4,157*	*3,764*	*393*	*12,556*	*4,863*	*7,693*	*43*	*43*	...
	0—10 ...	4,378	2,225	2,153	80	57	23	4,298	2,168	2,130	...	...	...
	10—15 ...	1,825	1,071	754	580	486	94	1,245	585	660	8	8	...
	15—20 ...	1,310	747	563	562	493	69	748	254	494	7	7	...
	20 and over	9,200	4,584	4,616	2,935	2,728	207	6,265	1,856	4,409	28	28	...
DAMOH	ALL RELIGIONS.	*333,047*	*168,060*	*164,987*	*15,389*	*14,730*	*659*	*317,658*	*153,330*	*164,328*	*847*	*809*	*38*
	0—10 ...	99,326	50,522	48,804	488	437	51	98,838	50,085	48,753	5	3	2
	10—15 ...	31,719	17,679	14,040	2,103	1,986	117	29,616	15,693	13,923	62	58	4
	15—20 ...	23,816	13,034	10,782	1,975	1,889	86	21,841	11,145	10,696	117	114	3
	20 and over	178,186	86,825	91,361	10,823	10,418	405	167,363	76,407	90,956	663	634	29
	HINDU (BRAHMANIC)	*303,189*	*152,873*	*150,316*	*12,124*	*11,736*	*388*	*291,065*	*141,137*	*149,928*	*619*	*614*	*5*
	0—10 ...	90,548	46,032	44,516	340	311	29	90,208	45,721	44,487	1	1	...
	10—15 ...	28,918	16,090	12,828	1,625	1,559	66	27,293	14,531	12,762	49	47	2
	15—20 ...	21,661	11,828	9,833	1,537	1,480	57	20,124	10,348	9,776	74	74	...
	20 and over	162,062	78,923	83,139	8,622	8,386	236	153,440	70,537	82,903	495	492	3
	ANIMIST ...	*11,115*	*5,461*	*5,654*	*41*	*40*	*1*	*11,074*	*5,431*	*5,653*	...	...	...
	0—10 ...	3,546	1,751	1,795	...	...	...	3,546	1,751	1,795	...	...	...
	10—15 ...	879	468	411	6	5	1	873	463	410	...	...	...
	15—20 ...	743	373	370	4	4	...	739	369	370	...	...	...
	20 and over	5,947	2,869	3,078	31	31	...	5,916	2,838	3,078	...	...	...
	MUSALMAN	*11,003*	*5,680*	*5,323*	*1,114*	*1,030*	*84*	*9,885*	*4,650*	*5,235*	*104*	*104*	...
	0—10 ...	3,231	1,667	1,564	39	32	7	3,192	1,635	1,557	...	...	...
	10—15 ...	1,043	603	440	163	150	13	880	453	427	10	10	...
	15—20 ...	732	417	315	118	108	10	614	309	305	17	17	...
	20 and over	5,996	2,993	3,003	794	740	54	5,202	2,253	2,949	77	77	...

TABLE VII.—Part B.—Details for Districts—*continued.*

Jubbulpore
Mandla
Seoni

District.	Age.	Population. Total. Persons.	Total. Males.	Total. Females.	Literate. Persons.	Literate. Males.	Literate. Females.	Illiterate. Persons.	Illiterate. Males.	Illiterate. Females.	Literate in English. Persons.	Literate in English. Males.	Literate in English. Females.
1	2	3	4	5	6	7	8	9	10	11	12	13	14
JUBBULPORE	ALL RELIGIONS	*745,892*	*373,173*	*372,719*	*44,985*	*41,652*	*3,333*	*700,907*	*331,521*	*369,386*	*8,402*	*7,198*	*1,204*
	0—10 ..	217,937	108,675	109,262	1,277	997	280	216,660	107,678	108,982	231	131	100
	10—15 ..	71,423	39,585	31,838	5,068	4,537	531	66,355	35,048	31,307	592	431	158
	15—20 ..	52,700	28,312	24,388	5,698	5,154	544	47,002	23,158	23,844	916	742	174
	20 and over	403,832	196,601	207,231	32,942	30,964	1,978	370,890	165,637	205,253	6,663	5,891	772
	HINDU (BRAHMANIC)	*598,960*	*298,484*	*300,476*	*32,186*	*30,840*	*1,346*	*566,774*	*267,644*	*299,130*	*2,739*	*2,691*	*48*
	0—10 ...	173,261	86,335	86,926	807	694	113	172,454	85,641	86,813	9	9	...
	10—15 ...	58,547	32,563	25,984	3,916	3,681	235	54,631	28,882	25,749	228	223	5
	15—20 ..	42,380	22,953	19,427	4,221	4,017	204	38,159	18,936	19,223	424	416	8
	20 and over	324,772	156,633	168,139	23,242	22,448	794	301,530	134,185	167,345	2,078	2,043	35
	ANIMIST...	*91,543*	*44,113*	*47,430*	*331*	*331*	...	*91,212*	*43,782*	*47,430*	*1*	*1*	...
	0—10 ...	30,705	15,394	15,311	4	4	...	30,701	15,390	15,311	...	...	...
	10—15 ...	7,766	4,123	3,643	43	43	...	7,723	4,080	3,643	...	...	...
	15—20 ...	5,886	2,859	3,027	61	61	...	5,825	2,798	3,027	...	...	...
	20 and over	47,186	21,737	25,449	223	223	...	46,963	21,514	25,449	1	1	...
	MUSALMAN	*41,339*	*22,117*	*19,222*	*4,779*	*4,456*	*323*	*36,560*	*17,661*	*18,899*	*692*	*682*	*10*
	0—10 ...	11,040	5,541	5,499	126	106	20	10,914	5,435	5,479	3	3	...
	10—15 ...	3,924	2,271	1,653	452	412	40	3,472	1,859	1,613	45	44	1
	15—20 ...	3,236	1,870	1,366	646	603	43	2,590	1,267	1,323	132	130	2
	20 and over	23,139	12,435	10,704	3,555	3,335	220	19,584	9,100	10,484	512	505	7
	CHRISTIAN	*6,880*	*4,554*	*2,326*	*5,442*	*3,939*	*1,503*	*1,438*	*615*	*823*	*4,749*	*3,635*	*1,114*
	0—10 ...	1,204	558	646	284	149	135	920	409	511	214	115	99
	10—15 ...	498	231	267	433	204	229	65	27	38	304	155	149
	15—20 ...	564	242	322	488	212	276	76	30	46	324	165	159
	20 and over	4,614	3,523	1,091	4,237	3,374	863	377	149	228	3,907	3,200	707
MANDLA	ALL RELIGIONS	*405,235*	*200,872*	*204,363*	*8,494*	*8,112*	*382*	*396,740*	*192,760*	*203,980*	*744*	*700*	*44*
	0—10 ...	131,594	65,369	66,225	231	196	35	131,363	65,173	66,190	8	4	4
	10—15 ...	35,640	19,230	16,410	1,101	1,025	76	34,539	18,205	16,334	34	32	2
	15—20 ...	26,930	13,268	13,662	1,119	1,063	56	25,811	12,205	13,606	109	105	4
	20 and over	211,070	103,005	108,065	6,043	5,828	215	205,027	97,177	107,850	593	559	34
	HINDU (BRAHMANIC)	*155,006*	*77,986*	*77,020*	*6,694*	*6,451*	*243*	*148,312*	*71,535*	*76,777*	*477*	*475*	*2*
	0—10 ...	48,556	24,181	24,375	187	163	24	48,369	24,018	24,351	...	...	...
	10—15 ...	14,549	7,937	6,612	934	872	62	13,615	7,065	6,550	28	27	1
	15—20 ...	10,811	5,624	5,187	901	869	32	9,910	4,755	5,155	82	82	...
	20 and over	81,090	40,244	40,846	4,672	4,547	125	76,418	35,697	40,721	367	366	1
	ANIMIST...	*242,261*	*118,656*	*123,605*	*428*	*420*	*8*	*241,833*	*118,236*	*123,597*	*1*	*1*	...
	0—10 ..	80,901	40,074	40,827	15	15	...	80,886	40,059	40,827	...	...	...
	10—15 ...	20,412	10,923	9,489	52	50	2	20,360	10,873	9,487	...	...	...
	15—20 ...	15,554	7,358	8,196	70	69	1	15,484	7,289	8,195	...	...	...
	20 and over	125,394	60,301	65,093	291	286	5	125,103	60,015	65,088	1	1	...
SEONI	ALL RELIGIONS	*395,481*	*192,642*	*202,839*	*10,099*	*9,576*	*523*	*385,382*	*183,066*	*202,316*	*551*	*535*	*16*
	0—10 ...	119,195	58,609	60,586	207	165	42	118,988	58,444	60,544	1	1	...
	10—15 ...	35,457	19,118	16,339	1,187	1,081	106	34,270	18,037	16,233	26	26	...
	15—20 ...	25,165	12,868	12,297	1,284	1,210	74	23,881	11,658	12,223	65	65	...
	20 and over	215,664	102,047	113,617	7,421	7,120	301	208,243	94,927	113,316	459	443	16
	HINDU (BRAHMANIC)	*214,957*	*105,751*	*109,206*	*7,765*	*7,427*	*338*	*207,192*	*98,324*	*108,868*	*358*	*357*	*1*
	0—10 ...	64,380	31,713	32,667	168	132	36	64,212	31,581	32,631	1	1	...
	10—15 ...	20,269	10,978	9,291	911	844	67	19,358	10,134	9,224	18	18	...
	15—20 ...	14,123	7,328	6,795	971	925	46	13,152	6,403	6,749	40	40	...
	20 and over	116,185	55,732	60,453	5,715	5,526	189	110,470	50,206	60,264	299	298	1

TABLE VIII.—Part B.—Details for Districts—*continued.*

District.	Age.	Population. Total. Persons.	Population. Total. Males.	Population. Total. Females.	Population. Literate. Persons.	Population. Literate. Males.	Population. Literate. Females.	Population. Illiterate. Persons.	Population. Illiterate. Males.	Population. Illiterate. Females.	Literate in English. Persons.	Literate in English. Males	Literate in English. Females.
1	2	3	4	5	6	7	8	9	10	11	12	13	14
SEONI—(concld.)	ANIMIST...	*161,077*	*77,316*	*83,761*	*376*	*358*	*18*	*160,701*	*76,958*	*83,743*	*2*	*2*	...
	0—10 ...	49,075	24,017	25,058	4	2	2	49,071	24,015	25,056	...	...	...
	10—15 ...	13,329	7,121	6,208	52	51	1	13,277	7,070	6,207	...	...	...
	15—20 ...	9,786	4,882	4,904	59	59	...	9,727	4,823	4,904	1	1	...
	20 and over	88,887	41,296	47,591	261	246	15	88,626	41,050	47,576	1	1	...
	MUSALMAN	*17,434*	*8,583*	*8,851*	*1,323*	*1,260*	*63*	*16,111*	*7,323*	*8,788*	*113*	*112*	*1*
	0—10 ...	5,194	2,630	2,564	21	21	...	5,173	2,609	2,564	...	...	...
	10—15 ...	1,654	916	738	132	121	11	1,522	795	727	5	5	...
	15—20 ...	1,106	574	532	162	154	8	944	420	524	15	15	...
	20 and over	9,480	4,463	5,017	1,008	964	44	8,472	3,499	4,973	93	92	1
NARSINGHPUR	ALL RELIGIONS.	*325,677*	*161,795*	*163,882*	*16,114*	*15,494*	*620*	*309,563*	*146,301*	*163,262*	*848*	*816*	*32*
	0—10 ...	93,107	47,214	45,893	232	212	20	92,875	47,002	45,873	4	4	...
	10—15 ...	29,973	16,419	13,554	1,833	1,730	103	28,140	14,689	13,451	64	61	3
	15—20 ...	22,047	11,889	10,158	2,243	2,144	99	19,804	9,745	10,059	179	177	2
	20 and over	180,550	86,273	94,277	11,806	11,408	398	168,744	74,865	93,879	601	574	27
	HINDU (BRAHMANIC)	*278,046*	*138,622*	*139,426*	*14,290*	*13,831*	*459*	*263,756*	*124,791*	*138,967*	*556*	*549*	*7*
	0—10 ...	79,311	40,306	39,005	181	170	11	79,130	40,136	38,994	1	1	...
	10—15 ...	26,071	14,333	11,738	1,578	1,500	78	24,493	12,833	11,660	43	43	...
	15—20 ...	19,141	10,356	8,786	1,927	1,855	72	17,214	8,500	8,714	101	100	1
	20 and over	153,525	73,628	79,897	10,604	10,306	298	142,921	63,322	79,599	411	405	6
	ANIMIST...	*32,992*	*15,714*	*17,278*	*77*	*72*	*5*	*32,915*	*15,642*	*17,273*	...	...	...
	0—10 ...	9,641	4,758	4,883	2	2	...	9,639	4,756	4,883	...	...	...
	10—15 ...	2,461	1,291	1,170	9	9	...	2,452	1,282	1,170	...	...	...
	15—20 ...	1,842	922	920	12	11	1	1,830	911	919	...	...	...
	20 and over	19,048	8,743	10,305	54	50	4	18,994	8,693	10,301	...	...	...
	MUSALMAN	*11,707*	*5,888*	*5,819*	*827*	*761*	*66*	*10,880*	*5,127*	*5,753*	*128*	*125*	...
	0—10 ...	3,367	1,737	1,630	29	23	6	3,338	1,714	1,624	...	...	...
	10—15 ...	1,088	590	498	124	113	11	964	477	487	8	8	...
	15—20 ...	778	427	351	143	130	13	635	297	338	32	32	...
	20 and over	6,474	3,134	3,340	531	495	36	5,943	2,639	3,304	88	88	...
HOSHANGABAD	ALL RELIGIONS.	*457,395*	*230,632*	*226,763*	*25,392*	*24,366*	*1,036*	*432,003*	*206,266*	*225,737*	*2,273*	*2,048*	*225*
	0—10 ...	123,941	62,071	61,870	393	343	50	123,548	61,728	61,820	15	12	3
	10—15 ...	44,519	21,814	19,705	3,113	2,974	139	41,406	21,840	19,566	143	126	17
	15—20 ...	32,644	17,038	14,706	3,234	3,040	194	29,410	14,898	14,512	423	395	28
	20 and over	256,291	125,809	130,482	18,652	18,009	643	237,639	107,800	129,839	1,692	1,515	177
	HINDU (BRAHMANIC)	*382,775*	*193,785*	*188,990*	*21,494*	*20,999*	*495*	*361,281*	*172,786*	*188,495*	*1,399*	*1,386*	*13*
	0—10 ...	103,483	52,063	51,420	321	291	30	103,162	51,772	51,390	4	4	...
	10—15 ...	37,981	21,232	16,749	2,726	2,639	87	35,255	18,593	16,662	94	90	4
	15—20 ...	27,758	15,378	12,380	2,755	2,679	76	25,003	12,699	12,304	325	325	...
	20 and over	213,553	105,112	108,441	15,692	15,390	302	197,861	89,722	108,139	976	967	9
	ANIMIST...	*49,915*	*24,157*	*25,758*	*87*	*85*	*2*	*49,828*	*24,072*	*25,756*	*1*	*1*	...
	0—10 ...	14,173	6,961	7,212	...	...	...	14,173	6,961	7,212	...	...	...
	10—15 ...	4,104	2,207	1,897	9	9	...	4,095	2,198	1,897	...	...	...
	15—20 ...	3,152	1,577	1,575	10	8	2	3,142	1,569	1,573	...	...	...
	20 and over	28,486	13,412	15,074	68	68	...	28,418	13,344	15,074	1	1	...
	MUSALMAN	*20,799*	*10,640*	*10,159*	*2,194*	*2,096*	*98*	*18,605*	*8,544*	*10,061*	*241*	*239*	*2*
	0—10 ...	5,348	2,591	2,757	39	33	6	5,309	2,558	2,751	...	...	...
	10—15 ...	2,072	1,180	892	218	201	17	1,854	979	875	17	17	...
	15—20 ...	1,387	817	570	239	227	12	1,148	590	558	38	38	...
	20 and over	11,992	6,052	5,940	1,698	1,635	63	10,294	4,417	5,877	186	184	2

TABLE VIII.—Part B.—Details for Districts—*continued.* [Nimar Betul Chhindwara

District.	Age.	POPULATION.									Literate in English.		
		Total.			Literate.			Illiterate.					
		Persons.	Males.	Females.	Persons.	Males.	Females.	Persons.	Males.	Females.	Persons.	Males.	Females.
1	2	3	4	5	6	7	8	9	10	11	12	13	14
NIMAR	ALL RELIGIONS.	*391,071*	*200,765*	*190,306*	*21,718*	*20,885*	*833*	*369,353*	*179,880*	*189,473*	*1,650*	*1,553*	*97*
	0—10 ...	110,680	55,058	55,622	393	349	44	110,287	54,709	55,578	9	7	2
	10—15 ...	38,834	21,279	17,555	2,306	2,171	135	36,528	19,108	17,420	98	90	8
	15—20 ...	28,369	14,029	14,340	2,381	2,231	150	25,988	11,798	14,190	242	221	21
	20 and over	213,188	110,399	102,789	16,638	16,134	504	196,550	94,265	102,285	1,301	1,235	66
	HINDU (BRAHMANIC)	*340,030*	*174,111*	*165,919*	*17,374*	*16,930*	*444*	*322,656*	*157,181*	*165,475*	*1,156*	*1,146*	*10*
	0—10 ...	96,272	47,824	48,448	298	269	29	95,974	47,555	48,419	3	3	...
	10—15 ...	33,695	18,479	15,216	1,875	1,801	74	31,820	16,678	15,142	74	73	1
	15—20 ...	24,507	12,109	12,398	1,843	1,775	68	22,664	10,334	12,330	190	185	5
	20 and over	185,556	95,699	89,857	13,358	13,085	273	172,198	82,614	89,584	889	885	4
	MUSALMAN	*38,428*	*20,109*	*18,319*	*3,078*	*2,920*	*158*	*35,350*	*17,189*	*18,161*	*184*	*183*	*1*
	0—10 ...	10,661	5,351	5,310	65	56	9	10,596	5,295	5,301	1	1	...
	10—15 ...	3,902	2,098	1,804	286	266	20	3,616	1,832	1,784	8	8	...
	15—20 ...	2,900	1,448	1,452	324	300	24	2,576	1,148	1,428	22	22	...
	20 and over	20,965	11,212	9,753	2,403	2,298	105	18,562	8,914	9,648	153	152	*1*
	CHRISTIAN	*3,793*	*1,994*	*1,799*	*501*	*324*	*177*	*3,292*	*1,670*	*1,622*	*212*	*141*	*71*
	0—10 ...	1,236	615	621	15	12	3	1,221	603	618	5	3	2
	10—15 ...	458	277	181	70	35	35	388	242	146	14	7	7
	15—20 ...	358	186	172	121	76	45	237	110	127	10	3	7
	20 and over	1,741	916	825	295	201	94	1,446	715	731	183	128	55
BETUL	ALL RELIGIONS.	*390,386*	*194,163*	*196,223*	*10,676*	*10,325*	*351*	*379,710*	*183,838*	*195,872*	*822*	*781*	*41*
	0—10 ...	122,734	60,331	62,403	267	247	20	122,467	60,084	62,383	7	4	3
	10—15 ...	36,154	19,410	16,744	1,200	1,154	46	34,954	18,256	16,698	65	65	...
	15—20 ...	24,731	12,291	12,440	1,078	1,032	46	23,653	11,259	12,394	110	104	6
	20 and over	206,767	102,131	104,636	8,131	7,892	239	198,636	94,239	104,397	640	608	32
	HINDU (BRAHMANIC)	*259,318*	*129,817*	*129,501*	*8,801*	*8,632*	*169*	*250,517*	*121,185*	*129,332*	*580*	*576*	*4*
	0—10 ...	79,943	39,326	40,617	214	201	13	79,729	39,125	40,604	1	1	...
	10—15 ...	23,739	12,968	10,771	989	964	25	22,750	12,004	10,746	50	50	...
	15—20 ...	16,392	8,413	7,979	910	889	21	15,482	7,524	7,958	86	83	3
	20 and over	139,244	69,110	70,134	6,688	6,578	110	132,556	62,532	70,024	443	442	1
	ANIMIST...	*121,175*	*58,947*	*62,228*	*89*	*87*	*2*	*121,086*	*58,860*	*62,226*	*1*	*1*	...
	0—10 ...	40,295	19,776	20,519	1	1	...	40,294	19,775	20,519	...	...	...
	10—15 ...	11,486	5,910	5,576	15	15	...	11,471	5,895	5,576	...	...	...
	15—20 ...	7,699	3,528	4,171	7	6	1	7,692	3,522	4,170	...	...	...
	20 and over	61,695	29,733	31,962	66	65	1	61,629	29,668	31,961	1	1	...
CHHINDWARA	ALL RELIGIONS.	*516,948*	*255,884*	*261,064*	*13,997*	*13,491*	*506*	*502,951*	*242,393*	*260,558*	*899*	*831*	*68*
	0—10 ...	159,265	78,379	80,886	399	354	45	158,866	78,025	80,841	2	1	1
	10—15 ...	49,334	26,303	23,031	1,958	1,848	110	47,376	24,455	22,921	74	70	4
	15—20 ...	32,652	16,826	15,826	1,746	1,671	75	30,906	15,155	15,751	171	164	7
	20 and over	275,697	134,376	141,321	9,894	9,618	276	265,803	124,758	141,045	652	596	56
	HINDU (BRAHMANIC)	*308,320*	*154,298*	*154,022*	*11,135*	*10,912*	*223*	*297,185*	*143,386*	*153,799*	*572*	*565*	*7*
	0—10 ...	93,513	46,154	47,359	305	284	21	93,208	45,870	47,338	...	...	...
	10—15 ...	29,901	16,045	13,856	1,579	1,531	48	28,322	14,514	13,808	49	49	...
	15—20 ...	19,677	10,297	9,380	1,457	1,377	80	18,270	8,920	9,350	103	103	...
	20 and over	165,229	81,802	83,427	7,844	7,720	124	157,385	74,082	83,303	420	413	7
	ANIMIST...	*189,249*	*91,668*	*97,581*	*279*	*276*	*3*	*188,970*	*91,392*	*97,578*	*3*	*3*	...
	0—10 ...	60,141	29,434	30,707	4	4	...	60,137	29,430	30,707	...	...	...
	10—15 ...	17,566	9,214	8,352	41	40	1	17,525	9,174	8,351	...	...	...
	15—20 ...	11,718	5,825	5,893	40	40	...	11,678	5,785	5,893	2	2	...
	20 and over	99,824	47,195	52,629	194	192	2	99,630	47,003	52,627	1	1	...

TABLE VIII.—Part B.—Details for Districts —*continued.*

District.	Age.	Population. Total. Persons.	Total. Males.	Total. Females.	Literate. Persons.	Literate. Males.	Literate. Females.	Illiterate. Persons.	Illiterate. Males.	Illiterate. Females.	Literate in English. Persons.	Literate in English. Males.	Literate in English. Females.
1	2	3	4	5	6	7	8	9	10	11	12	13	14
CHHINDWARA—(concld.)	MUSALMAN	*16,595*	*8,459*	*8,136*	*1,580*	*1,525*	*55*	*15,015*	*6,934*	*8,081*	*100*	*100*	...
	0—10 ...	4,912	2,435	2,477	39	39	...	4,873	2,396	2,477	1	1	..
	10—15 ...	1,582	885	697	187	176	11	1,395	709	686	8	8	...
	15—20 ...	1,011	565	446	157	150	7	854	415	439	2	20	...
	20 and over	9,090	4,574	4,516	1,197	1,160	37	7,893	3,414	4,479	77	77	...
WARDHA	ALL RELIGIONS.	*459,796*	*231,871*	*227,925*	*21,656*	*21,122*	*534*	*438,140*	*210,749*	*227,391*	*1,562*	*1,547*	*35*
	0—10 ...	123,492	60,383	63,109	487	458	29	123,005	59,925	63,080	5	5	...
	10—15 ...	41,803	22,657	19,146	2,535	2,441	94	39,268	20,216	19,052	107	104	3
	15—20 ...	30,288	14,876	15,412	2,556	2,481	75	27,732	12,395	15,337	257	253	4
	20 and over	264,213	133,955	130,258	16,078	15,742	336	248,135	118,213	129,922	1,193	1,185	28
	HINDU (BRAHMANIC)	*391,063*	*197,583*	*193,480*	*18,934*	*18,543*	*391*	*372,129*	*179,040*	*193,089*	*1,336*	*1,326*	*10*
	0—10 ...	105,046	51,462	53,584	413	394	19	104,633	51,068	53,565	4	4	...
	10—15 ...	35,900	19,447	16,453	2,256	2,185	71	33,644	17,262	16,382	99	96	3
	15—20 ...	25,928	12,717	13,211	2,243	2,181	62	23,685	10,536	13,149	235	234	1
	20 and over	224,189	113,957	110,232	14,022	13,783	239	210,167	100,174	109,993	998	992	6
	ANIMIST ...	*47,831*	*23,549*	*24,282*	*86*	*84*	*2*	*47,745*	*23,465*	*24,280*	*3*	*3*	...
	0—10 ...	12,759	6,164	6,595	5	5	...	12,754	6,159	6,595	...	...	...
	10—15 ..	3,870	2,081	1,789	11	10	1	3,859	2,071	1,788	...	...	...
	15—20 ...	2,926	1,412	1,514	17	16	1	2,909	1,396	1,513	..	...	...
	20 and over	28,276	13,892	14,384	53	53	...	28,223	13,839	14,384	3	3	...
	MUSALMAN	*18,174*	*9,331*	*8,843*	*1,836*	*1,771*	*65*	*16,338*	*7,560*	*8,778*	*99*	*98*	*1*
	0—10 ..	5,053	2,448	2,605	60	51	9	4,993	2,397	2,596	...	...	...
	10—15 ...	1,766	979	787	180	168	12	1,586	811	775	3	3	...
	15—20 ..	1,237	644	593	214	205	9	1,023	439	584	11	10	1
	20 and over	10,118	5,260	4,858	1,382	1,347	35	8,736	3,913	4,823	85	85	...
NAGPUR	ALL RELIGIONS.	*809,901*	*408,843*	*401,058*	*43,450*	*40,090*	*3,360*	*766,451*	*368,753*	*397,698*	*9,415*	*8,250*	*1,165*
	0—10 ...	221,564	109,896	111,668	1,587	1,234	353	219,977	108,662	111,315	290	162	128
	10—15 ...	76,759	41,419	35,340	5,179	4,690	489	71,580	36,729	34,851	700	565	135
	15—20 ...	52,354	26,480	25,874	4,857	4,375	482	47,497	22,105	25,392	1,215	1,037	178
	20 and over	459,224	231,048	228,176	31,827	29,791	2,036	427,397	201,257	226,140	7,210	6,486	724
	HINDU (BRAHMANIC)	*725,399*	*365,125*	*360,274*	*33,283*	*31,725*	*1,558*	*692,116*	*333,400*	*358,716*	*4,849*	*4,760*	*89*
	0—10 ...	199,134	98,886	100,248	1,051	918	133	198,083	97,968	100,115	18	16	2
	10—15 ...	69,120	37,178	31,942	4,202	3,954	248	64,918	33,224	31,694	320	306	14
	15—20 ...	46,653	23,548	23,105	3,785	3,557	228	42,868	19,991	22,877	692	679	13
	20 and over	410,492	205,513	204,979	24,245	23,296	949	386,247	182,217	204,030	3,819	3,759	60
	ANIMIST ...	*36,003*	*17,870*	*18,133*	*85*	*85*	...	*35,918*	*17,785*	*18,133*	*4*	*4*	...
	0—10 ...	9,960	4,899	5,061	5	5	...	9,955	4,894	5,061	...	...	...
	10—15 ...	2,847	1,563	1,284	10	10	...	2,837	1,553	1,284	1	1	...
	15—20 ...	2,111	1,029	1,082	12	12	...	2,099	1,017	1,082	2	2	...
	20 and over	21,085	10,379	10,706	58	58	...	21,027	10,321	10,706	1	1	...
	MUSALMAN	*38,534*	*20,097*	*18,387*	*4,679*	*4,367*	*312*	*33,755*	*15,680*	*18,075*	*675*	*671*	*4*
	0—10 ...	10,301	5,011	5,290	132	108	24	10,169	4,903	5,266	1	1	...
	10—15 ...	3,853	2,160	1,693	433	385	48	3,420	1,775	1,645	25	25	...
	15—20 ...	2,659	1,339	1,220	414	382	32	2,145	957	1,188	76	75	1
	20 and over	21,721	11,537	10,184	3,700	3,492	208	18,021	8,045	9,976	573	570	3
	CHRISTIAN	*6,245*	*3,764*	*2,481*	*4,139*	*2,853*	*1,286*	*2,106*	*911*	*1,195*	*3,511*	*2,518*	*993*
	0—10 ...	1,260	619	641	352	174	178	908	445	463	261	140	121
	10—15 ..	588	338	250	434	267	167	154	71	83	327	221	106
	15—20 ...	720	397	323	515	320	195	205	77	128	409	259	150
	20 and over	3,677	2,410	1,267	2,838	2,092	746	839	318	521	2,514	1,898	616

TABLE VIII.—Part B.—Details for Districts—*continued.*

District.	Age.	POPULATION. Total. Persons.	Total. Males.	Total. Females.	Literate. Persons.	Literate. Males.	Literate. Females.	Illiterate. Persons.	Illiterate. Males.	Illiterate. Females.	Literate in English. Persons.	Literate in English. Males.	Literate in English. Females.
1	2	3	4	5	6	7	8	9	10	11	12	13	14
CHANDA	ALL RELIGIONS.	*677,544*	*337,540*	*340,004*	*16,002*	*15,496*	*506*	*661,542*	*322,044*	*339,498*	*1,316*	*1,274*	*42*
	0—10 ...	201,784	99,502	102,282	346	300	46	201,438	99,202	102,236	6	5	1
	10—15 ...	62,748	34,121	28,627	1,793	1,727	66	60,955	32,394	28,561	88	88	...
	15—20 ...	42,358	20,579	21,779	1,725	1,635	90	40,633	18,944	21,689	189	184	5
	20 and over	370,654	183,338	187,316	12,138	11,834	304	358,516	171,504	187,012	1,033	997	36
	HINDU (BRAHMANIC)	*539,713*	*269,465*	*270,248*	*13,399*	*13,103*	*296*	*526,314*	*256,362*	*269,952*	*1,047*	*1,043*	*4*
	0—10 ...	160,115	79,141	80,974	267	245	22	159,848	78,896	80,952	4	4	...
	10—15 ...	50,492	27,496	22,996	1,537	1,491	46	48,955	26,005	22,950	76	76	...
	15—20 ...	33,622	16,507	17,115	1,429	1,379	50	32,193	15,128	17,065	164	164	...
	20 and over	295,484	146,321	149,163	10,166	9,988	178	285,318	136,333	148,985	803	799	4
	ANIMIST...	*124,356*	*61,161*	*63,195*	*364*	*362*	*2*	*123,992*	*60,799*	*63,193*	*3*	*3*	...
	0—10 ...	37,973	18,557	19,416	14	14	...	37,959	18,543	19,416	...	...	...
	10—15 ...	10,929	5,864	5,065	39	39	...	10,890	5,825	5,065	...	...	—
	15—20 ...	7,868	3,621	4,247	51	50	1	7,817	3,571	4,246	...	...	...
	20 and over	67,586	33,119	34,467	260	259	1	67,326	32,860	34,466	3	3	...
	MUSALMAN	*12,172*	*6,205*	*5,967*	*1,697*	*1,632*	*65*	*10,475*	*4,573*	*5,902*	*110*	*110*	...
	0—10 ...	3,396	1,643	1,753	28	27	1	3,368	1,616	1,752	...	...	...
	10—15 ...	1,188	670	518	157	147	10	1,031	523	508	3	3	...
	15—20 ...	740	390	350	162	156	6	578	234	344	11	11	...
	20 and over	6,848	3,502	3,346	1,350	1,302	48	5,498	2,200	3,298	96	96	...
BHANDARA	ALL RELIGIONS	*773,677*	*380,014*	*393,663*	*21,267*	*20,691*	*576*	*752,410*	*359,323*	*393,087*	*1,165*	*1,084*	*81*
	0—10 ...	224,505	110,832	113,673	410	376	34	224,095	110,456	113,639	17	9	8
	10—15 ...	70,662	37,866	32,796	2,482	2,400	82	68,180	35,466	32,714	51	46	5
	15—20 ...	50,934	25,352	25,582	2,402	2,286	116	48,532	23,066	25,466	162	146	16
	20 and over	427,576	205,964	221,612	15,973	15,629	344	411,603	190,335	221,268	935	883	52
	HINDU (BRAHMANIC)	*685,342*	*337,335*	*348,007*	*18,215*	*17,876*	*339*	*667,127*	*319,459*	*347,668*	*832*	*827*	*5*
	0—10 ...	200,805	99,226	101,579	342	323	19	200,463	98,903	101,560	2	1	1
	10—15 ...	63,487	33,989	29,498	2,210	2,149	61	61,277	31,840	29,437	37	36	1
	15—20 ...	45,080	22,514	22,566	2,031	1,976	55	43,049	20,538	22,511	120	119	1
	20 and over	375,970	181,606	194,364	13,632	13,428	204	362,338	168,178	194,160	673	671	2
	ANIMIST...	*72,424*	*34,669*	*37,755*	*334*	*333*	*1*	*72,090*	*34,336*	*37,754*	*2*	*2*	...
	0—10 ...	19,436	9,509	9,927	7	7	...	19,429	9,502	9,927	...	...	...
	10—15 ...	5,638	3,017	2,621	34	34	...	5,604	2,983	2,621	...	...	...
	15—20 ..	4,762	2,257	2,505	48	48	...	4,714	2,209	2,505	1	1	...
	20 and over	42,588	19,886	22,702	245	244	1	42,343	19,642	22,701	1	1	...
	MUSALMAN	*14,707*	*7,434*	*7,273*	*2,189*	*2,140*	*49*	*12,518*	*5,294*	*7,224*	*119*	*119*	...
	0—10 ...	3,995	1,982	2,013	32	32	...	3,963	1,950	2,013	...	...	...
	10—15 ...	1,439	811	628	197	194	3	1,242	617	625	5	5	...
	15—20 ...	968	541	427	239	231	8	729	310	419	15	15	...
	20 and over	8,305	4,100	4,205	1,721	1,683	38	6,584	2,417	4,167	99	99	...
BALAGHAT	ALL RELIGIONS.	*388,920*	*190,469*	*198,451*	*11,389*	*10,987*	*402*	*377,531*	*179,482*	*198,049*	*725*	*685*	*40*
	0—10 ...	115,551	57,032	58,519	312	278	34	115,239	56,754	58,485	3	1	2
	10—15 ...	33,511	17,970	15,541	1,655	1,596	59	31,856	16,374	15,482	52	47	5
	15—20 ...	25,617	12,843	12,774	1,559	1,491	68	24,058	11,352	12,706	115	109	6
	20 and over	214,241	102,624	111,617	7,863	7,622	241	206,378	95,002	111,376	555	528	27
	HINDU (BRAHMANIC)	*296,396*	*145,519*	*150,877*	*9,093*	*8,840*	*253*	*287,303*	*136,679*	*150,624*	*504*	*498*	*6*
	0—10 ...	88,489	43,749	44,740	260	234	26	88,229	43,515	44,714	1	1	...
	10—15 ...	26,303	14,160	12,143	1,395	1,356	39	24,908	12,804	12,104	44	43	1
	15—20 ...	19,789	9,932	9,857	1,203	1,158	45	18,586	8,774	9,812	93	89	4
	20 and over	161,815	77,678	84,137	6,235	6,092	143	155,580	71,586	83,994	366	365	1

TABLE VIII.—Part B.—Details for Districts—*continued.*

District.	Age.	Population. Total. Persons.	Total. Males.	Total. Females.	Literate. Persons.	Literate. Males.	Literate. Females.	Illiterate. Persons.	Illiterate. Males.	Illiterate. Females.	Literate in English. Persons.	Literate in English. Males.	Literate in English. Females.
1	2	3	4	5	6	7	8	9	10	11	12	13	14
BALAGHAT—(concld.)	ANIMIST...	*83,561*	*40,498*	*43,063*	*651*	*645*	*6*	*82,910*	*39,853*	*43,057*	*6*	*6*	...
	0—10 ...	24,635	12,079	12,556	18	18	...	24,617	12,061	12,556	...	...	...
	10—15 ...	6,391	3,369	3,022	94	94	...	6,297	3,275	3,022	...	...	...
	15—20 ...	5,245	2,573	2,672	154	152	2	5,091	2,421	2,670	2	2	...
	20 and over	47,290	22,477	24,813	385	381	4	46,905	22,096	24,809	4	4	...
RAIPUR	ALL RELIGIONS.	*1,324,856*	*645,186*	*679,670*	*27,721*	*26,174*	*1,547*	*1,297,135*	*619,012*	*678,123*	*2,125*	*2,031*	*94*
	0—10 ...	401,195	198,249	202,946	567	460	107	400,628	197,789	202,839	9	9	...
	10—15 ...	118,764	64,638	54,126	3,456	3,156	300	115,308	61,482	53,826	187	183	4
	15—20 ...	88,321	45,181	43,140	3,870	3,558	312	84,451	41,623	42,828	358	347	11
	20 and over	716,576	337,118	379,458	19,828	19,000	828	696,748	318,118	378,630	1,571	1,492	79
	HINDU (BRAHMANIC)	*1,126,497*	*549,378*	*577,119*	*23,498*	*21,697*	*801*	*1,103,099*	*527,681*	*576,318*	*1,465*	*1,450*	*15*
	0—10 ...	341,194	168,854	172,340	439	377	62	340,755	168,477	172,278	...	...	...
	10—15 ...	100,214	54,561	45,653	2,883	2,704	179	97,331	51,857	45,474	131	131	...
	15—20 ...	75,247	38,406	36,841	3,051	2,942	109	72,196	35,464	36,732	262	259	3
	20 and over	609,842	287,557	322,285	16,125	15,674	451	593,717	271,883	321,834	1,072	1,060	12
	ANIMIST...	*177,300*	*85,106*	*92,194*	*703*	*680*	*23*	*176,598*	*84,426*	*92,172*	*2*	*2*	...
	0—10 ...	54,673	26,817	27,856	5	4	1	54,668	26,813	27,855	...	...	...
	10—15 ...	16,616	9,004	7,612	81	74	7	16,535	8,930	7,605	...	...	...
	15—20 ...	11,313	5,847	5,466	117	116	1	11,196	5,731	5,465	...	...	...
	20 and over	94,098	43,438	51,260	499	486	13	94,199	42,952	51,247	2	2	...
	MUSALMAN	*16,516*	*8,393*	*8,123*	*2,941*	*2,732*	*209*	*13,575*	*5,661*	*7,914*	*371*	*366*	*5*
	0—10 ...	4,125	1,990	2,135	53	42	11	4,072	1,948	2,124	3	3	...
	10—15 ...	1,529	852	677	282	253	29	1,247	599	648	31	31	...
	15—20 ...	1,244	685	559	359	318	41	885	367	518	60	58	2
	20 and over	9,617	4,866	4,751	2,247	2,119	128	7,370	2,747	4,623	277	274	3
	CHRISTIAN	*3,365*	*1,637*	*1,728*	*1,055*	*594*	*461*	*2,311*	*1,043*	*1,267*	*229*	*160*	*69*
	0—10 ...	950	464	486	47	21	26	903	443	460	5	5	...
	10—15 ...	302	167	135	161	86	75	141	81	60	17	13	4
	15—20 ...	393	174	219	280	125	155	113	49	64	29	23	6
	20 and over	1,720	832	888	566	358	208	1,154	474	680	178	119	59
BILASPUR	ALL RELIGIONS.	*1,146,223*	*558,477*	*587,746*	*22,341*	*21,234*	*1,107*	*1,123,882*	*537,243*	*586,639*	*1,273*	*1,118*	*155*
	0—10 ...	365,717	180,181	185,536	410	371	39	365,307	179,810	185,497	21	9	12
	10—15 ...	100,562	53,867	46,695	2,691	2,475	216	97,871	51,392	46,479	69	51	18
	15—20 ...	78,624	39,240	39,384	3,111	2,873	238	75,513	36,367	39,146	141	126	15
	20 and over	601,320	285,189	316,131	16,129	15,515	614	585,191	269,674	315,517	1,042	932	110
	HINDU (BRAHMANIC)	*1,077,335*	*524,724*	*552,611*	*19,648*	*18,957*	*691*	*1,057,690*	*505,767*	*551,923*	*806*	*796*	*10*
	0—10 ...	344,277	169,563	174,714	351	330	21	343,926	169,233	174,693	1	1	...
	10—15 ...	95,071	50,892	44,179	2,438	2,302	136	92,633	48,590	44,043	34	33	1
	15—20 ...	74,169	37,056	37,113	2,755	2,611	144	71,414	34,445	36,969	90	89	1
	20 and over	563,821	267,213	296,608	14,104	13,714	390	549,717	253,499	296,218	681	67	8
	ANIMIST...	*52,425*	*25,455*	*26,970*	*100*	*100*	...	*52,325*	*25,355*	*26,970*	...	...	...
	0—10 ...	16,998	8,465	8,533	5	5	...	16,993	8,460	8,533	...	...	...
	10—15 ...	4,057	2,204	1,853	1	12	...	4,045	2,192	1,853	...	...	...
	15—20 ...	3,219	1,575	1,644	14	14	...	3,205	1,561	1,644	...	...	...
	20 and over	28,151	13,211	14,940	69	69	...	28,082	13,142	14,940	...	...	...
	MUSALMAN	*13,964*	*7,049*	*6,915*	*1,782*	*1,704*	*78*	*12,182*	*5,345*	*6,837*	*113*	*110*	*3*
	0—10 ...	3,736	1,816	1,920	26	22	4	3,710	1,794	1,916	...	...	...
	10—15 ...	1,238	679	559	146	133	13	1,092	546	546	3	3	...
	15—20 ...	1,032	532	500	202	195	7	830	337	493	14	14	...
	20 and over	7,958	4,022	3,936	1,408	1,354	54	6,550	2,668	3,882	96	93	3

TABLE VIII.—Part B.—Details for Districts—*continued.*

District.	Age.	POPULATION.									LITERATE IN ENGLISH.		
		TOTAL.			LITERATE.			ILLITERATE.					
		Persons.	Males.	Females.	Persons.	Males.	Females.	Persons.	Males.	Females.	Persons.	Males.	Females.
1	2	3	4	5	6	7	8	9	10	11	12	13	14
DRUG	ALL RELIGIONS.	*775,688*	*373,159*	*403,529*	*13,932*	*13,488*	*444*	*761,756*	*359,671*	*403,085*	*610*	*589*	*21*
	0—10 ...	228,750	113,052	115,698	215	196	19	228,535	112,856	115,679	3	2	1
	10—15 ..	61,662	33,478	28,184	1,407	1,312	95	60,255	32,166	28,089	21	21	...
	15—20 ...	51,811	26,045	25,766	1,771	1,70	69	50,040	24,343	25,697	66	64	2
	20 and over	433,465	200,584	232,881	10,539	10,278	261	422,926	190,306	232,620	520	502	18
	HINDU (BRAHMANIC)	*674,376*	*324,328*	*350,048*	*12,101*	*11,838*	*263*	*662,275*	*312,490*	*349,785*	*400*	*400*	...
	0—10 ...	199,215	98,467	100,748	184	168	16	199,031	98,299	100,732	2	2	...
	10—15 ..	53,972	29,288	24,684	1,243	1,178	65	52,729	28,110	24,619	16	16	...
	15—20 ...	45,315	22,743	22,572	1,539	1,496	43	43,776	21,247	22,529	45	45	...
	20 and over	375,874	173,830	202,044	9,135	8,996	139	366,739	164,834	201,905	343	343	...
	ANIMIST..	*92,106*	*44,144*	*47,962*	*260*	*259*	*1*	*91,846*	*43,885*	*47,961*	*2*	*2*	...
	0—10 ...	27,193	13,465	13,728	5	5	...	27,188	13,460	13,728	...	...	...
	10—15 ..	6,968	3,790	3,178	23	23	...	6,945	3,767	3,178	...	...	...
	15—20 ...	5,819	2,927	2,892	33	33	...	5,786	2,894	2,892	...	...	...
	20 and over	52,120	23,962	28,134	199	198	1	51,927	23,761	28,163	2	2	...
AMRAOTI	ALL RELIGIONS.	*875,904*	*447,216*	*428,688*	*44,450*	*43,772*	*1,078*	*831,454*	*404,444*	*427,010*	*3,694*	*3,429*	*265*
	0—10 ...	237,359	116,562	120,797	662	514	148	236,697	116,048	120,649	52	26	26
	10—15 ..	77,670	42,237	35,433	3,821	3,560	261	73,849	38,677	35,172	195	157	38
	15—20 ..	60,135	29,032	31,103	5,074	4,796	278	55,061	24,236	30,825	544	518	26
	20 and over	500,740	259,385	241,355	34,893	33,902	991	465,847	225,483	240,364	2,903	2,728	175
	HINDU (BRAHMANIC)	*738,294*	*377,352*	*360,942*	*37,265*	*36,220*	*1,045*	*701,029*	*341,132*	*359,897*	*2,647*	*2,614*	*33*
	0—10 ...	195,617	95,853	99,764	460	376	84	195,157	95,477	99,680	4	3	1
	10—15	64,871	35,194	29,677	3,114	2,937	177	61,757	32,257	29,500	104	98	6
	15—20 ...	50,854	24,591	26,263	4,184	4,007	177	46,670	20,584	26,086	375	370	5
	20 and over	426,952	221,714	205,238	29,507	28,900	607	397,445	192,814	204,631	2,164	2,143	21
	ANIMIST...	*57,191*	*28,198*	*28,993*	*39*	*39*	...	*57,152*	*28,159*	*28,993*	...	...	...
	0—10 ...	19,448	9,686	9,762	1	1	...	19,447	9,685	9,762	...	...	...
	10—15 ...	5,060	2,689	2,371	6	6	...	5,054	2,683	2,371	...	...	...
	15—20 ...	3,289	1,362	1,927	7	7	...	3,282	1,355	1,927	...	...	...
	20 and over	29,394	14,461	14,933	25	25	...	29,369	14,436	14,933	...	...	...
	MUSALMAN	*73,311*	*37,896*	*35,415*	*5,090*	*4,868*	*222*	*68,221*	*33,028*	*35,193*	*443*	*438*	*5*
	0—10 ..	20,433	10,069	10,364	110	90	20	20,323	9,979	10,344	1	1	...
	10—15 ..	7,081	3,987	3,094	533	505	28	6,548	3,482	3,066	43	43	...
	15—20 ...	5,400	2,754	2,646	616	572	44	4,784	2,182	2,602	110	108	2
	20 and over	40,397	21,086	19,311	3,831	3,701	130	36,566	17,385	19,181	289	286	3
	CHRISTIAN	*1,489*	*827*	*662*	*647*	*358*	*289*	*842*	*469*	*373*	*416*	*223*	*193*
	0—10 ...	538	302	236	73	34	39	465	268	197	46	22	24
	10—15 ...	163	102	61	65	30	35	98	72	26	35	12	23
	15—20	147	74	73	9.	54	43	54	20	30	38	21	17
	20 and over	641	349	292	412	240	172	229	109	120	297	168	129
AKOLA	ALL RELIGIONS.	*758,563*	*400,593*	*357,970*	*34,240*	*33,221*	*1,019*	*754,623*	*367,672*	*356,951*	*2,338*	*2,255*	*83*
	0—10 ...	213,278	104,185	109,093	742	642	100	212,536	103,543	108,993	32	26	6
	10—15 ..	72,121	39,389	32,732	3,448	3,273	175	68,673	36,116	32,557	85	85	...
	15—20 ...	52,151	24,828	27,323	3,572	3,361	211	48,579	21,467	27,112	359	349	10
	20 and over	451,313	232,491	218,822	26,478	25,945	533	424,835	206,546	218,289	1,862	1,795	67
	HINDU (BRAHMANIC)	*711,025*	*360,645*	*350,381*	*28,089*	*27,539*	*550*	*682,936*	*333,105*	*349,831*	*1,792*	*1,787*	*5*
	0—10 ..	191,740	93,677	98,063	566	524	42	191,174	93,153	98,021	9	9	...
	10—15 ..	64,362	35,058	29,304	2 811	2,710	101	61,551	32,348	29,203	70	70	...
	15—20 ...	46,656	21,989	24,667	2,908	2,767	141	43,748	19,222	24,526	297	296	1
	20 and over	408,267	209,920	198,347	21,804	21,538	266	386,463	188,382	198,081	1,416	1,412	4

TABLE VIII.—Part B.—Details for Districts—*continued.*

District.	Age.	Population.									Literate in English.		
		Total.			Literate.			Illiterate.					
		Persons.	Males.	Females.	Persons.	Males.	Females.	Persons.	Males.	Females.	Persons.	Males.	Females.
1	2	3	4	5	6	7	8	9	10	11	12	13	14
AKOLA—(concld.)	MUSALMAN	*70,148*	*36,342*	*33,806*	*4,331*	*4,052*	*269*	*65,827*	*32,290*	*33,537*	*251*	*243*	*8*
	0–10 ...	19,661	9,633	10,028	115	71	44	19,546	9,562	9,984	...	...	...
	10–15 ...	7,050	3,932	3,118	471	417	54	6,579	3,515	3,064	10	10	...
	15–20 ...	4,913	2,559	2,354	475	435	40	4,438	2,124	2,314	42	36	6
	20 and over	38,524	20,218	18,306	3,260	3,129	131	35,264	17,089	18,175	199	197	2
BULDANA	ALL RELIGIONS.	*669,182*	*337,179*	*332,003*	*27,533*	*26,694*	*839*	*641,649*	*310,485*	*331,164*	*1,689*	*1,630*	*59*
	0–10 ...	189,351	93,014	96,337	443	404	39	188,908	92,610	96,298	5	4	1
	10–15 ...	63,446	34,156	29,290	2,652	2,512	140	60,794	31,644	29,150	83	80	3
	15–20 ...	46,618	22,473	24,145	3,092	2,950	142	43,526	19,523	24,003	266	251	15
	20 and over	369,767	187,536	182,231	21,346	20,828	518	348,421	166,708	181,713	1,335	1,295	40
	HINDU (BRAHMANIC)	*608,609*	*305,993*	*302,616*	*23,423*	*22,846*	*577*	*585,186*	*283,147*	*302,039*	*1,355*	*1,344*	*11*
	0–10 ...	171,732	84,375	87,357	363	336	27	171,369	84,039	87,330	...	...	...
	10–15 ...	57,219	30,666	26,553	2,245	2,146	99	54,974	28,520	26,454	68	68	...
	15–20 ...	42,296	20,274	22,022	2,608	2,520	88	39,688	17,754	21,934	224	221	3
	20 and over	337,362	170,678	166,684	18,207	17,844	363	319,155	152,834	166,321	1,063	1,055	8
	MUSALMAN	*55,257*	*28,435*	*26,822*	*2,782*	*2,663*	*119*	*52,475*	*25,772*	*26,703*	*156*	*149*	*7*
	0–10 ...	16,332	8,007	8,325	58	52	6	16,274	7,955	8,319	1	1	...
	10–15 ...	5,701	3,202	2,499	295	274	21	5,406	2,928	2,478	9	8	1
	15–20 ...	3,855	1,985	1,870	317	298	19	3,538	1,687	1,851	20	18	2
	20 and over	29,369	15,241	14,128	2,112	2,039	73	27,257	13,202	14,055	126	122	4
YEOTMAL	ALL RELIGIONS.	*723,213*	*365,326*	*357,887*	*19,390*	*18,825*	*565*	*703,823*	*346,501*	*357,322*	*961*	*930*	*31*
	0–10 ...	213,297	104,664	108,633	355	329	26	214,942	104,335	108,607	5	5	...
	10–15 ...	65,102	35,064	30,038	1,812	1,720	92	63,290	33,344	29,946	37	36	1
	15–20 ...	44,612	21,215	23,397	2,006	1,902	104	42,606	19,313	23,293	120	113	7
	20 and over	400,202	204,383	195,819	15,217	14,874	343	384,985	189,509	195,476	799	776	23
	HINDU (BRAHMANIC)	*610,181*	*308,407*	*301,774*	*15,750*	*15,384*	*366*	*594,431*	*293,023*	*301,408*	*805*	*801*	*4*
	0–10 ...	178,658	87,791	90,867	266	252	14	178,392	87,539	90,853	1	1	...
	10–15 ...	55,018	29,576	25,442	1,457	1,394	63	53,561	28,182	25,379	32	32	...
	15–20 ...	37,782	18,014	19,768	1,595	1,533	62	36,187	16,481	19,706	110	108	2
	20 and over	338,723	173,026	165,697	12,432	12,205	227	326,291	160,821	165,470	662	660	2
	ANIMIST ...	*69,354*	*34,202*	*35,152*	*78*	*78*	...	*69,276*	*34,124*	*35,152*	*1*	*1*	...
	0–10 ...	22,126	10,736	11,390	4	4	...	22,122	10,732	11,390	...	...	...
	10–15 ...	5,961	3,203	2,758	15	15	...	5,946	3,188	2,758	...	...	...
	15–20 ...	3,891	1,727	2,164	11	11	...	3,880	1,716	2,164	1	1	...
	20 and over	37,376	18,536	18,840	48	48	...	37,328	18,488	18,840	...	...	...
	MUSALMAN	*39,949*	*20,780*	*19,169*	*2,625*	*2,536*	*89*	*37,324*	*18,244*	*19,080*	*65*	*65*	...
	0–10 ...	11,593	5,699	5,894	68	59	9	11,525	5,640	5,885	...	...	...
	10–15 ...	3,781	2,108	1,673	265	249	16	3,516	1,859	1,657	1	1	...
	15–20 ...	2,658	1,337	1,321	289	275	14	2,369	1,062	1,307	3	3	...
	20 and over	21,917	11,636	10,281	2,003	1,953	50	19,914	9,683	10,231	61	61	...
FEUDATORY STATES	ALL RELIGIONS.	*2,117,003*	*1,053,630*	*1,063,372*	*24,951*	*23,825*	*1,126*	*2,092,051*	*1,029,805*	*1,062,246*	*1,148*	*1,047*	*101*
	0–10 ...	699,611	344,404	355,207	467	400	67	699,144	344,004	355,140	21	12	9
	10–15 ...	210,735	115,298	95,437	3,190	2,950	240	207,545	112,348	95,197	73	67	6
	15–20 ...	146,659	74,787	71,872	3,578	3,393	185	143,081	71,394	71,687	193	188	5
	20 and over	1,059,997	519,141	540,856	17,716	17,082	634	1,042,281	502,059	540,222	861	780	81
	HINDU (BRAHMANIC)	*1,311,388*	*650,807*	*660,581*	*21,212*	*20,385*	*837*	*1,290,176*	*630,482*	*659,754*	*785*	*776*	*9*
	0–10 ...	418,950	206,322	212,628	373	322	51	418,577	206,000	212,577	3	3	...
	10–15 ...	128,275	70,384	57,891	2,773	2,573	200	125,502	67,811	57,691	59	57	2
	15–20 ...	91,238	47,026	44,212	3,066	2,934	132	88,172	44,092	44,080	161	160	1
	20 and over	672,925	327,075	345,850	15,000	14,556	444	657,925	312,519	345,406	562	556	6

TABLE VIII.—Part B.—Details for Districts—*concluded*. [Feudatory States —(concld.)

District.	Age.	POPULATION.									LITERATE IN ENGLISH.		
		TOTAL.			LITERATE.			ILLITERATE.					
		Persons.	Males.	Females.	Persons.	Males.	Females.	Persons.	Males.	Females.	Persons.	Males.	Females.
1	2	3	4	5	6	7	8	9	10	11	12	13	14
FEUDATORY STATES—(concld.)	ANIMIST ...	*745,434*	*372,384*	*373,050*	*995*	*970*	*25*	*744,439*	*371,414*	*373,025*	*10*	*10*	...
	0—10 ...	260,072	127,903	132,169	37	36	1	260,035	127,867	132,168	...	...	...
	10—15 ...	75,816	41,172	34,644	171	163	8	75,645	41,009	34,636	2	2	...
	15—20 ...	51,269	25,576	25,693	184	177	7	51,085	25,399	25,686	1	1	...
	20 and over	358,277	177,733	180,544	603	594	9	357,674	177,139	180,535	7	7	...
	MUSALMAN	*20,120*	*10,180*	*9,940*	*1,807*	*1,698*	*109*	*18,313*	*8,482*	*9,831*	*109*	*107*	*2*
	0—10 ...	5,345	2,675	2,670	28	23	5	5,317	2,652	2,665	...	...	...
	10—15 ...	1,906	1,034	872	164	146	18	1,742	888	854	4	4	...
	15—20 ...	1,435	790	645	222	203	19	1,213	587	626	15	15	...
	20 and over	11,434	5,681	5,753	1,393	1,326	67	10,041	4,355	5,686	90	88	2
	CHRISTIAN	*38,704*	*19,477*	*19,227*	*411*	*266*	*145*	*38,293*	*19,211*	*19,082*	*226*	*136*	*90*
	0—10 ...	14,961	7,377	7,584	22	13	9	14,939	7,364	7,575	18	9	9
	10—15 ...	4,592	2,619	1,973	27	16	11	4,565	2,603	1,962	8	4	4
	15—20 ...	2,605	1,319	1,286	41	17	24	2,564	1,302	1,262	14	10	4
	20 and over	16,546	8,162	8,384	321	220	101	16,225	7,942	8,283	186	113	73

TABLE VIII.—Part C.—Details for Cities.

City.	Age.	Population.									Literate in English.		
		Total.			Literate.			Illiterate.					
		Persons.	Males.	Females.	Persons.	Males.	Females.	Persons.	Males.	Females.	Persons.	Males.	Females.
1	2	3	4	5	6	7	8	9	10	11	12	13	14
JUBBULPORE	ALL RELIGIONS.	*100,651*	*56,035*	*44,616*	*19,298*	*16,815*	*2,483*	*81,353*	*39,220*	*42,133*	*7,519*	*6,468*	*1,051*
	0—10 ..	23,881	11,905	11,976	773	563	210	23,108	11,342	11,766	228	131	97
	10—15 ..	8,973	5,371	3,602	1,873	1,546	327	7,100	3,825	3,275	507	393	114
	15—20 ..	7,997	4,578	3,419	2,231	1,824	407	5,766	2,754	3,012	802	664	138
	20 and over	59,800	34,181	25,619	14,421	12,882	1,539	45,379	21,209	24,080	5,982	5,280	702
	HINDU .. (BRAHMANIC)	*68,902*	*37,334*	*31,568*	*9,893*	*9,039*	*854*	*59,009*	*28,295*	*30,714*	*2,238*	*2,197*	*41*
	0—10 ..	16,615	8,271	8,344	387	315	72	16,228	7,956	8,272	10	10	...
	10—15 ..	6,221	3,752	2,469	1,136	1,012	124	5,085	2,740	2,345	199	195	4
	15—20 ..	5,252	3,014	2,238	1,226	1,093	133	4,026	1,921	2,105	364	357	7
	20 and over	40,814	22,297	18,517	7,144	6,619	525	33,670	15,678	17,992	1,665	1,635	30
	MUSALMAN	*23,032*	*12,827*	*10,205*	*3,350*	*3,059*	*291*	*19,682*	*9,768*	*9,914*	*576*	*566*	*10*
	0—10 ..	5,803	2,932	2,871	103	83	20	5,700	2,849	2,851	3	3	...
	10—15 ...	2,171	1,295	876	316	278	38	1,855	1,017	838	39	38	1
	15—20 ...	1,999	1,160	839	450	412	38	1,549	748	801	118	116	2
	20 and over	13,059	7,440	5,619	2,481	2,286	195	10,578	5,154	5,424	416	409	7
	CHRISTIAN	*6,310*	*4,349*	*1,961*	*5,068*	*3,815*	*1,253*	*1,242*	*534*	*708*	*4,533*	*3,556*	*977*
	0—10 ...	1,045	491	554	253	142	111	792	349	443	210	114	96
	10—15 ...	409	221	188	350	196	154	59	25	34	256	148	108
	15—20 ...	499	234	265	428	205	223	71	29	42	288	162	126
	20 and over	4,357	3,403	954	4,037	3,272	765	320	131	189	3,779	3,132	647
NAGPUR	ALL RELIGIONS.	*101,415*	*53,696*	*47,719*	*13,854*	*11,686*	*2,168*	*87,561*	*42,010*	*45,551*	*5,591*	*4,732*	*859*
	0—10 ...	23,813	11,919	11,894	632	407	225	23,181	11,512	11,669	185	111	74
	10—15 ...	8,701	4,858	3,843	1,243	954	289	7,458	3,904	3,554	467	381	86
	15—20 ...	7,410	3,935	3,475	1,573	1,257	316	5,837	2,678	3,159	761	628	133
	20 and over	61,491	32,984	28,507	10,406	9,068	1,338	51,095	23,916	27,169	4,178	3,612	566
	HINDU ... (BRAHMANIC)	*80,141*	*42,187*	*37,954*	*8,670*	*7,710*	*960*	*71,471*	*34,477*	*36,994*	*2,771*	*2,696*	*75*
	0—10 ..	18,846	9,491	9,355	319	235	84	18,527	9,256	9,271	15	13	2
	10—15 ...	6,660	3,672	2,988	731	586	145	5,929	3,086	2,843	187	175	12
	15—20 ...	5,613	2,931	2,682	930	792	138	4,683	2,139	2,544	347	336	11
	20 and over	49,022	26,093	22,929	6,690	6,097	593	42,332	19,996	22,336	2,222	2,172	50
	MUSALMAN	*14,589*	*7,854*	*6,735*	*1,947*	*1,856*	*91*	*12,642*	*5,998*	*6,644*	*443*	*440*	*3*
	0—10 ...	3,490	1,707	1,783	41	37	4	3,449	1,670	1,779	...	...	...
	10—15 ...	1,416	816	600	138	123	15	1,278	693	585	12	12	...
	15—20 ...	1,047	570	477	153	146	7	894	424	470	48	47	1
	20 and over	8,636	4,761	3,875	1,615	1,550	65	7,021	3,211	3,810	383	381	2
	CHRISTIAN	*3,960*	*2,158*	*1,802*	*2,520*	*1,570*	*950*	*1,440*	*588*	*852*	*2,049*	*1,341*	*708*
	0—10 ...	876	409	467	238	117	121	638	292	346	162	94	68
	10—15 ...	422	262	160	320	214	106	102	48	54	243	182	61
	15—20 ...	531	320	211	413	267	146	118	53	65	331	223	108
	20 and over	2,131	1,167	964	1,549	972	577	582	195	387	1,813	842	471

TABLE IX.

Education by Selected Castes, Tribes or Races.

This table repeats the information given in Table VIII in respect of education with this difference that, whereas in that table the population is distributed by age and religion, it is here arranged according to caste or tribe. Moreover in Table VIII the whole population is dealt with, while this table refers only to selected castes and tribes; the minor castes and tribes have been left out of account altogether and even those selected for inclusion have been taken only for the districts where they were specially numerous. To save space figures have been given not for each district separately but for groups of districts the local conditions of which may be presumed to be fairly uniform. These groups as a rule correspond to the Natural Divisions whose constitution is explained in Chapter I of the Report Volume. Thus the Divisions for purposes of this table are as follows :—

Nerbudda Valley.—Saugor, Damoh, Jubbulpore, Narsinghpur, Hoshangabad and Nimar.

Maratha Division.—Nagpur, Wardha, Bhandara, Chanda and the Berar Districts.

Plateau Division.—Mandla, Seoni, Betul, Chhindwara and Balaghat.

Chhattisgarh Division.—Raipur, Bilaspur and Drug.

It may be explained that the total district strength of a caste in this table does not necessarily tally with that in Table XIII, as the latter includes figures added in the course of classification.

TABLE IX.—Education by Selected Castes, Tribes or Races.

Caste, Tribe or Race.	Locality.	Population. Total. Persons.	Total. Males.	Total. Females.	Literate. Persons.	Literate. Males.	Literate. Females.	Illiterate. Persons.	Illiterate. Males.	Illiterate. Females.	Literate in English. Persons.	Literate in English. Males.	Literate in English. Females.
1	2	3	4	5	6	7	8	9	10	11	12	13	14
Agaria ...	Chhattisgarh Division	2,622	1,302	1,320	119	117	2	2,503	1,185	1,318	...	...	...
Ahir ...	Province ...	727,733	361,600	366,133	5,262	5,076	186	722,471	356,524	365,947	163	163	...
Andh ...	Berar ...	52,376	25,501	26,815	80	80	...	52,296	25,481	26,815	...	...	...
Are ...	Chanda District ...	2,286	1,123	1,163	12	12	...	2,274	1,111	1,163	...	...	...
Bahna ...	Nerbudda Valley ...	23,398	11,096	11,702	781	646	135	22,617	11,050	11,567	16	15	1
Baiga ...	Total ...	*25,977*	*12,875*	*13,102*	*9*	*8*	*1*	*25,968*	*12,867*	*13,101*	...	...	...
	Jubbulpore ...	2,223	1,099	1,124	1	1	...	2,222	1,098	1,124	...	...	...
	Mandla ...	18,684	9,311	9,373	5	5	...	18,679	9,306	9,373	...	...	...
	Balaghat ...	5,070	2,465	2,605	3	2	1	5,067	2,463	2,604	...	...	...
Bairagi ...	Province ...	37,984	19,649	18,335	3,470	3,392	78	34,514	16,257	18,257	31	31	...
Balahi ...	Total ...	*50,859*	*25,108*	*25,751*	*266*	*260*	*6*	*50,593*	*24,848*	*25,745*	*2*	*2*	...
	Hoshangabad ...	20,142	9,927	10,215	83	83	...	20,059	9,844	10,215	2	2	...
	Nimar ...	28,814	14,243	14,571	180	174	6	28,634	14,069	14,565	...	...	...
	Makrai ...	1,903	938	965	3	3	...	1,900	935	965	...	...	...
Bania ...	Province ...	194,820	100,683	94,137	47,641	45,883	1,758	147,179	54,800	92,379	1,560	1,543	17
Banjara ...	Total ...	*129,636*	*67,343*	*62,293*	*920*	*909*	*11*	*128,716*	*66,434*	*62,282*	*9*	*9*	...
	Plateau Division ...	9,379	4,844	4,535	62	60	2	9,317	4,784	4,533	1	1	...
	Maratha Division ...	87,953	45,708	42,245	708	701	7	87,245	45,007	42,238	7	7	...
	Chhattisgarh Division	11,487	5,400	6,087	37	36	1	11,450	5,364	6,086	1	1	...
	Nimar ...	15,570	8,544	7,032	107	107	...	15,463	8,437	7,032	...	...	...
	Bastar ...	5,241	2,847	2,394	6	5	1	5,235	2,842	2,393	...	...	...
Barai ...	Province ...	59,158	29,640	29,518	3,467	3,327	140	55,691	26,313	29,378	157	157	...
Barhai ...	Province ...	108,815	56,297	52,518	4,817	4,763	84	103,998	51,534	52,434	141	140	1
Basor ...	Nerbudda Valley ...	31,331	15,542	15,789	38	34	4	31,293	15,508	15,785	...	...	...
Bedar ...	Akola ...	1,481	680	801	143	134	9	1,338	546	792	22	21	1
Beldar ...	Total ...	*6,265*	*3,167*	*3,098*	*262*	*259*	*3*	*6,003*	*2,908*	*3,095*	*17*	*17*	...
	Saugor ...	968	521	447	36	36	...	932	485	447	...	...	...
	Jubbulpore ...	1,149	586	563	41	40	1	1,108	546	562	3	3	...
	Nimar ...	1,116	583	533	5	5	...	1,111	578	533	...	...	...
	Wardha ...	2,078	981	1,097	117	116	1	1,961	865	1,096	10	10	...
	Nagpur ...	954	496	458	63	62	1	891	434	457	4	4	...
Bharbhunja ...	Raipur ...	347	133	214	38	35	3	309	98	211	1	1	...
Bharia (Bhumia)	Total ...	*37,263*	*17,864*	*19,399*	*53*	*51*	*2*	*37,210*	*17,813*	*19,397*	*1*	*1*	...
	Jubbulpore ...	26,982	12,882	14,100	48	47	1	26,934	12,835	14,099	1	1	...
	Narsinghpur ...	2,544	1,230	1,314	2	2	...	2,542	1,228	1,314	...	...	...
	Chhindwara ...	7,737	3,752	3,985	3	2	1	7,734	3,750	3,984	...	...	...
Bhat ..	Total ...	*12,430*	*6,110*	*6,320*	*1,127*	*1,096*	*31*	*11,303*	*5,014*	*6,289*	*31*	*31*	...
	Nerbudda Valley ...	7,939	3,976	3,963	742	718	24	7,197	3,258	3,939	20	20	...
	Nagpur ...	1,613	795	818	165	164	1	1,448	631	817	9	9	...
	Raipur ...	1,631	788	843	133	128	5	1,498	660	838	3	3	...
	Drug ...	1,247	551	696	87	86	1	1,160	465	695	2	2	...
Bhil ...	Nimar ...	23,737	11,804	11,933	33	33	...	23,704	11,771	11,933	...	...	...
Bhilala ...	Total ...	*15,274*	*7,717*	*7,557*	*196*	*193*	*3*	*15,078*	*7,524*	*7,554*	*2*	*2*	...
	Hoshangabad ...	2,733	1,393	1,340	24	24	...	2,709	1,369	1,340	...	...	...
	Nimar ...	12,541	6,324	6,217	172	169	3	12,369	6,155	6,214	2	2	...
Bhoyar ...	Total ...	*58,551*	*28,943*	*29,608*	*1,137*	*1,130*	*7*	*57,414*	*27,813*	*29,601*	*4*	*4*	...
	Betul ...	22,792	11,256	11,536	409	403	6	22,383	10,853	11,530	1	1	...
	Chhindwara ...	20,743	10,173	10,570	466	466	...	20,277	9,707	10,570	1	1	...
	Wardha ...	11,705	5,850	5,855	225	224	1	11,480	5,626	5,854	1	1	...
	Nagpur ...	3,311	1,664	1,647	37	37	...	3,274	1,627	1,647	1	1	...

TABLE IX.—Education by Selected Castes, Tribes or Races—*contd.*

CASTE, TRIBE OR RACE.	LOCALITY.	POPULATION.									LITERATE IN ENGLISH.		
		TOTAL.			LITERATE.			ILLITERATE.					
		Persons.	Males.	Females.	Persons.	Males.	Females.	Persons.	Males.	Females.	Persons.	Males.	Females.
1	2	3	4	5	6	7	8	9	10	11	12	13	14
Bhulia ...	Raipur ...	2,813	1,441	1,372	31	30	1	2,782	1,411	1,371	3	3	...
Bidur ...	Maratha Division ...	17,191	8,507	8,684	3,308	3,235	73	13,883	5,272	8,611	321	319	2
Bohra ...	Nimar ...	1,345	703	642	436	385	51	909	318	591	11	11	...
Brahman ...	Province ...	445,627	237,567	208,060	107706	102404	5,302	337,831	135,163	202,668	16,200	16,038	171
Chadar ...	*Total* ...	*27,456*	*13,627*	*13,829*	*231*	*227*	*4*	*27,225*	*13,400*	*13,825*	*3*	*3*	...
	Saugor ...	14,638	7,305	7,333	92	88	4	14,546	7,217	7,329	3	3	...
	Damoh ...	7,197	3,516	3,681	52	52	...	7,145	3,464	3,681	...	...	...
	Jubbulpore ...	2,686	1,327	1,359	56	56	...	2,630	1,271	1,359	...	...	...
	Narsinghpur ...	2,935	1,479	1,456	31	31	...	2,904	1,448	1,456	...	...	...
Chamar ...	Province ...	901,522	443,017	458,505	2,060	2,025	35	899,462	440,992	458,470	33	33	...
Chauhan ...	Bilaspur ...	2,074	1,019	1,055	46	46	...	2,028	973	1,055	...	...	...
Chhipa ...	*Total* ...	*2,145*	*985*	*1,160*	*230*	*227*	*3*	*1,915*	*758*	*1,157*	*2*	*2*	...
	Jubbulpore ...	1,363	637	726	150	149	1	1,213	488	725	2	2	...
	Narsinghpur ...	782	348	434	80	78	2	702	270	432	...	...	...
Chitari ...	Maratha Division ...	954	542	412	41	41	...	913	501	412	3	3	...
Dahayat ...	Jubbulpore ...	8,997	4,423	4,574	303	301	2	8,694	4,122	4,572	2	2	...
Dangi ...	*Total* ...	*24,006*	*12,180*	*11,826*	*1,038*	*1,026*	*12*	*22,968*	*11,154*	*11,814*	*1*	*1*	...
	Saugor ...	22,895	11,608	11,287	954	945	9	21,941	10,663	11,278	1	1	...
	Damoh ...	1,111	572	539	84	81	3	1,027	491	536	...	...	...
Daraiha ...	Bilaspur ...	2,513	1,179	1,334	177	176	1	2,336	1,003	1,333	...	...	...
Darji ...	Province ...	51,282	26,109	25,173	4,745	4,626	119	46,537	21,483	25,054	181	181	...
Deswali ...	*Total* ...	*7,021*	*3,599*	*3,422*	*125*	*124*	*1*	*6,896*	*3,475*	*3,421*	...	...	...
	Hoshangabad ...	4,490	2,314	2,176	81	80	1	4,409	2,234	2,175	...	...	...
	Nimar ...	2,531	1,285	1,246	44	44	...	2,487	1,241	1,246	...	...	...
Dhanagar ...	*Total* ...	*17,170*	*8,607*	*8,563*	*300*	*296*	*4*	*16,870*	*8,311*	*8,559*	*5*	*5*	...
	Wardha ...	7,064	3,598	3,466	92	92	...	6,972	3,506	3,466	...	...	...
	Nagpur ...	7,565	3,721	3,844	147	144	3	7,418	3,577	3,841	4	4	...
	Chhindwara ...	1,140	567	573	43	43	...	1,097	524	573	...	...	...
	Nimar ...	1,401	721	680	18	17	1	1,383	704	679	1	1	...
Dhimar ...	Province ...	283,413	140,734	142,679	1,967	1,893	74	281,446	138,841	142,605	99	96	3
Dhobi ...	Province ...	164,573	80,673	83,900	1,784	1,737	47	162,789	78,936	83,853	31	30	1
Dhuri ...	Bilaspur ...	2,105	1,016	1,089	57	52	5	2,048	964	1,084	1	1	...
Dohor ...	Buldana ...	2,955	1,508	1,447	3	3	...	2,952	1,505	1,447	...	...	...
Gadaria ...	*Total* ...	*30,385*	*15,349*	*15,036*	*329*	*314*	*15*	*30,056*	*15,035*	*15,021*	*22*	*22*	...
	Chhattisgarh Division	11,975	5,821	6,154	104	98	6	11,871	5,723	6,148	2	2	...
	Nerbudda Valley ...	18,410	9,528	8,882	225	216	9	18,185	9,312	8,873	20	20	...
Ganda ...	*Total* ...	*104,119*	*50,834*	*53,285*	*314*	*309*	*5*	*103,805*	*50,525*	*53,280*	...	...	...
	Chhattisgarh Division	90,766	44,184	46,582	277	275	2	90,489	43,909	46,580	...	...	...
	Surguja ...	3,114	1,559	1,555	7	5	2	3,107	1,554	1,553	...	...	...
	Jashpur ...	10,239	5,091	5,148	30	29	1	10,209	5,062	5,147	...	...	...
Gandhi ...	Maratha Division ...	138	63	75	16	16	...	122	47	75	...	...	...
Gandli ...	Chanda ...	2,375	1,154	1,221	201	201	...	2,174	953	1,221	1	1	...

TABLE IX.—Education by Selected Castes, Tribes or Races—*contd.*

Caste, Tribe or Race.	Locality.	Population. Total. Persons.	Total. Males.	Total. Females.	Literate. Persons.	Literate. Males.	Literate. Females.	Illiterate. Persons.	Illiterate. Males.	Illiterate. Females.	Literate in English. Persons.	Literate in English. Males.	Literate in English. Females.
1	2	3	4	5	6	7	8	9	10	11	12	13	14
Ghosi ...	Total ...	*7,596*	*3,914*	*3,682*	*135*	*133*	*2*	*7,461*	*3,781*	*3,680*	*3*	*3*	...
	Saugor ...	4,908	2,530	2,378	85	84	1	4,823	2,446	2,377	1	1	...
	Damoh ...	1,824	936	888	38	37	1	1,786	899	887	1	1	...
	Narsinghpur ...	864	448	416	12	12	...	852	436	416	1	1	...
Gond ...	Province ...	2,227,540	1,085,536	1,142,004	7,177	7,006	171	2,220,363	1,078,530	1,141,833	81	80	1
Gosain ...	Total ...	*19,953*	*10,176*	*9,777*	*1,568*	*1,547*	*21*	*18,385*	*8,629*	*9,756*	*29*	*26*	*3*
	Balaghat ...	965	483	482	140	140	...	825	343	482	5	5	...
	Narsinghpur ...	1,600	832	768	75	72	3	1,525	760	765	...	...	...
	Jubbulpore ...	2,063	1,011	1,052	158	154	4	1,905	857	1,048	6	4	2
	Hoshangabad ...	2,781	1,481	1,300	134	134	...	2,647	1,347	1,300	3	3	...
	Nagpur ...	2,972	1,529	1,443	249	248	1	2,723	1,281	1,442	7	7	...
	Wardha ...	1,408	769	639	177	175	2	1,231	594	637	1	1	...
	Bhandara ...	1,124	587	537	123	123	...	1,001	464	537	...	...	...
	Raipur ...	2,407	1,228	1,179	252	247	5	2,155	981	1,174	3	3	...
	Bilaspur ...	2,998	1,445	1,553	144	139	5	2,854	1,306	1,548	4	3	1
	Drug ...	1,635	811	824	116	115	1	1,519	696	823	...	...	...
Gowari ...	Maratha Division ...	119,709	58,732	60,977	440	427	13	119,269	58,305	60,964	15	15	...
Gujar ...	Total ...	*51,845*	*26,539*	*25,306*	*1,878*	*1,866*	*13*	*49,967*	*24,674*	*25,293*	*18*	*18*	...
	Narsinghpur ...	4,940	2,503	2,437	85	85	...	4,855	2,418	2,437	1	1	...
	Hoshangabad ...	23,496	12,080	11,416	910	900	10	22,586	11,180	11,406	9	9	...
	Nimar ...	23,409	11,956	11,453	883	880	3	22,526	11,076	11,450	8	8	...
Gurao ...	Total ...	*4,215*	*2,099*	*2,116*	*771*	*755*	*16*	*3,444*	*1,344*	*2,100*	*63*	*63*	...
	Wardha ...	1,579	771	808	279	279	...	1,300	492	808	22	22	...
	Nagpur ...	1,665	845	820	319	309	10	1,346	536	810	27	27	...
	Chanda ...	971	483	488	173	167	6	798	316	482	14	14	...
Halba ...	Total ...	*31,475*	*15,645*	*15,830*	*475*	*461*	*14*	*31,000*	*15,184*	*15,816*	*3*	*3*	...
	Chanda ...	2,398	1,217	1,181	59	59	...	2,339	1,158	1,181	...	...	...
	Bastar ...	15,849	7,966	7,883	237	236	1	15,612	7,730	7,882	1	1	...
	Raipur ...	4,499	2,186	2,313	69	68	1	4,430	2,118	2,312	1	1	...
	Kanker ...	8,729	4,276	4,453	110	98	12	8,619	4,178	4,441	1	1	...
Hatgar ...	Yeotmal ...	10,371	5,117	5,254	221	220	1	10,150	4,897	5,253	...	...	...
Jat ...	Total ...	*5,779*	*2,902*	*2,877*	*291*	*281*	*10*	*5,488*	*2,621*	*2,867*	*11*	*10*	*1*
	Narsinghpur ...	935	496	439	89	79	10	846	417	429	7	6	1
	Hoshangabad ...	4,844	2,406	2,438	202	202	...	4,642	2,204	2,438	4	4	...
Jingar ...	Maratha Division ...	1,555	790	765	81	80	1	1,474	710	764	7	7	...
Jogi ...	Total ...	*2,859*	*1,492*	*1,367*	*76*	*75*	*1*	*2,783*	*1,417*	*1,366*	...	...	...
	Mandla ...	1,121	557	564	14	14	...	1,107	543	564	...	...	...
	Hoshangabad ...	1,738	935	803	62	61	1	1,676	874	802	...	...	...
Julaha ...	Chota Nagpur States	937	481	456	16	16	...	921	465	456	...	...	...
Kachera ...	Province ...	2,225	1,084	1,141	91	87	4	2,134	997	1,137	2	2	...
Kachhi ...	Total ...	*115,930*	*58,181*	*57,749*	*1,417*	*1,374*	*43*	*114,513*	*56,807*	*57,706*	*27*	*27*	...
	Plateau Division ...	7,745	3,977	3,768	282	274	8	7,463	3,703	3,760	3	3	...
	Nerbudda Valley ...	108,185	54,204	53,981	1,135	1,100	35	107,050	53,104	53,946	24	24	...
Kadera ...	Nerbudda Valley ...	2,050	1,009	1,041	108	101	7	1,942	908	1,034	6	6	...
Kahar ...	Total ...	*14,681*	*7,368*	*7,313*	*212*	*210*	*2*	*14,469*	*7,158*	*7,311*	*6*	*6*	...
	Narsinghpur ...	2,174	1,053	1,121	7	7	...	2,167	1,046	1,121	...	...	...
	Hoshangabad ...	5,944	2,997	2,947	47	46	1	5,897	2,951	2,946	3	3	...
	Nimar ...	2,582	1,338	1,244	56	56	...	2,526	1,282	1,244	1	1	...
	Bilaspur ...	3,981	1,980	2,001	102	101	1	3,879	1,879	2,000	1	1	...

TABLE IX.—Education by Selected Castes, Tribes or Races—*contd.*

CASTE, TRIBE OR RACE.	LOCALITY.	POPULATION.									LITERATE IN ENGLISH.		
		TOTAL.			LITERATE.			ILLITERATE.					
		Persons.	Males.	Females.	Persons.	Males.	Females.	Persons.	Males.	Females.	Persons.	Males.	Females.
1	2	3	4	5	6	7	8	9	10	11	12	13	14
Kalar ...	Province ...	195,295	96,393	98,902	11,095	10,888	207	184,200	85,505	98,695	365	362	3
Karan ...	Raigarh ...	312	216	96	67	64	3	245	152	93	4	4	...
Kasar ...	*Total* ...	*1,803*	*883*	*920*	*280*	*275*	*5*	*1,523*	*608*	*915*	*11*	*11*	...
	Wardha ...	858	443	415	158	157	1	700	286	414	1	1	...
	Nagpur ...	945	440	505	122	118	4	823	322	501	10	10	...
Katia ...	*Total* ...	*39,266*	*19,177*	*20,089*	*547*	*525*	*22*	*38,719*	*18,652*	*20,067*	*19*	*19*	...
	Plateau Division ...	29,854	14,600	15,254	401	385	16	29,453	14,215	15,238	13	13	...
	Narsinghpur ...	2,101	958	1,143	55	53	2	2,046	905	1,141	1	1	...
	Hoshangabad ...	7,311	3,619	3,692	91	87	4	7,220	3,532	3,688	5	5	...
Kawar ...	*Total* ...	*89,280*	*43,814*	*45,466*	*379*	*368*	*11*	*88,901*	*43,446*	*45,455*	*5*	*4*	*1*
	Chanda ...	1,447	751	696	5	5	...	1,442	746	696	...	...	...
	Chhattisgarh Division	87,833	43,063	44,770	374	363	11	87,459	42,700	44,759	5	4	1
Kayasth ...	Province ...	33,571	17,580	15,991	10,916	10,111	805	22,655	7,469	15,186	2,206	2,161	45
Kewat ...	*Total* ...	*11,567*	*5,574*	*5,993*	*53*	*52*	*1*	*11,514*	*5,522*	*5,992*	*2*	*2*	...
	Jubbulpore ...	5,424	2,557	2,867	45	44	1	5,379	2,513	2,866	2	2	...
	Narsinghpur ...	1,296	668	628	6	6	...	1,290	662	628	...	...	...
	Chanda ...	4,847	2,349	2,498	2	2	...	4,845	2,347	2,498	...	...	...
Kharwar ...	*Total* ...	*3,841*	*1,873*	*1,968*	*48*	*47*	*1*	*3,793*	*1,826*	*1,967*	*1*	*1*	...
	Bilaspur ...	2,607	1,260	1,347	6	6	...	2,601	1,254	1,347	1	1	...
	Jashpur ...	1,234	613	621	42	41	1	1,192	572	620	...	...	...
Khangar ...	*Total* ...	*11,663*	*5,845*	*5,818*	*417*	*405*	*12*	*11,246*	*5,440*	*5,806*	*13*	*13*	...
	Saugor ...	5,803	2,903	2,900	138	134	4	5,665	2,769	2,896	8	8	...
	Damoh ...	2,116	1,050	1,066	77	75	2	2,039	975	1,064	2	2	...
	Jubbulpore ...	2,743	1,398	1,345	149	143	6	2,594	1,255	1,339	1	1	...
	Narsinghpur ...	1,001	494	507	53	53	...	948	441	507	2	2	...
Khatik ...	Jubbulpore ...	1,544	768	776	26	25	1	1,518	743	775	...	...	...
Khatri ...	Jubbulpore ...	285	172	113	133	114	19	152	58	94	33	33	...
Kir	*Total* ...	*6,086*	*3,226*	*2,860*	*11*	*10*	*1*	*6,075*	*3,216*	*2,859*	...	...	...
	Narsinghpur ...	852	453	399	1	1	...	851	452	399	...	...	...
	Hoshangabad ...	5,234	2,773	2,461	10	9	1	5,224	2,764	2,460	...	...	...
Kirar ...	*Total* ...	*46,298*	*23,267*	*23,031*	*1,335*	*1,318*	*17*	*44,963*	*21,949*	*23,014*	*11*	*11*	...
	Plateau Division ...	19,719	9,845	9,874	513	505	8	19,206	9,340	9,866	...	...	...
	Narsinghpur ...	11,943	6,046	5,897	317	312	5	11,626	5,734	5,892	1	1	...
	Hoshangabad ...	10,359	5,204	5,155	336	335	1	10,023	4,869	5,154	...	...	...
	Nagpur ...	4,277	2,172	2,105	169	166	3	4,108	2,006	2,102	10	10	...
Kohli ...	*Total* ...	*22,090*	*11,044*	*11,046*	*917*	*916*	*1*	*21,173*	*10,128*	*11,045*	*1*	*1*	...
	Chanda ...	8,312	4,135	4,177	277	277	...	8,035	3,858	4,177	1	1	...
	Bhandara ...	13,778	6,909	6,869	640	639	1	13,138	6,270	6,868	...	...	...
Kol	*Total* ...	*68,318*	*32,797*	*35,521*	*68*	*63*	*5*	*68,250*	*32,734*	*35,516*	...	...	...
	Jubbulpore ...	52,321	24,810	27,511	57	52	5	52,264	24,758	27,506	...	...	...
	Mandla ...	10,104	5,023	5,081	11	11	...	10,093	5,012	5,081	...	...	...
	Chota Nagpur States	5,893	2,964	2,929	...	...	...	5,893	2,964	2,929	...	...	...
Koli ...	Berar ...	33,352	16,715	16,637	519	513	6	32,833	16,202	16,631	4	4	...
Kolta ...	Raigarh ...	11,830	5,838	5,992	243	243	...	11,587	5,595	5,992	...	...	...
Komti ...	Chanda ...	3,840	2,019	1,821	845	843	2	2,995	1,176	1,819	16	16	...
Kori ...	Nerbudda Valley ...	30,621	15,339	15,282	488	467	21	30,133	14,872	15,261	26	24	2

TABLE IX.—Education by Selected Castes, Tribes or Races—*contd.*

CASTE, TRIBE OR RACE.	LOCALITY.	POPULATION.									LITERATE IN ENGLISH.		
		TOTAL.			LITERATE.			ILLITERATE.					
		Persons.	Males.	Females.	Persons.	Males.	Females.	Persons.	Males.	Females.	Persons.	Males.	Females.
1	2	3	4	5	6	7	8	9	10	11	12	13	14
Korku ...	Total ...	*95,035*	*47,307*	*47,728*	*99*	*97*	*2*	*94,936*	*47,210*	*47,726*	...	...	...
	Hoshangabad ...	20,204	10,014	10,190	27	27	...	20,177	9,987	10,190	...	...	...
	Amraoti ...	2,240	1,124	1,116	...	...	...	2,240	1,124	1,116	...	...	...
	Nimar ...	36,917	18,549	18,368	43	42	1	36,874	18,507	18,367	...	...	...
	Betul ...	35,674	17,620	18,054	29	28	1	35,645	17,592	18,053	...	...	...
Koshti ...	Total ...	*133,835*	*69,501*	*69,334*	*7,284*	*7,112*	*172*	*131,551*	*62,389*	*69,162*	*85*	*84*	*1*
	Jubbulpore ...	2,351	1,156	1,195	67	61	6	2,284	1,095	1,189	2	2	...
	Chhindwara ...	3,547	1,769	1,778	298	296	2	3,249	1,473	1,776	4	4	...
	Chhattisgarh Division	36,692	17,893	18,799	2,132	2,034	98	34,560	15,859	18,701	10	9	1
	Maratha Division ...	94,200	47,635	46,565	4,696	4,633	63	89,504	43,002	46,502	64	64	...
	Nimar ...	760	390	370	58	55	3	702	335	367	4	4	...
	Seoni ...	1,285	658	627	33	33	...	1,252	625	627	1	1	...
Koskati ...	Chanda ...	1,090	534	556	113	113	...	977	421	556	3	3	...
Kumhar ...	Province ...	118,501	60,047	58,454	1,650	1,615	35	116,851	58,432	58,419	24	24	...
Kunbi ...	Total ...	*1,342,000*	*675,302*	*666,698*	*41,681*	*41,261*	*420*	*1,300,319*	*634,041*	*666,278*	*923*	*916*	*7*
	Maratha Division ...	1,241,859	625,398	616,461	38,605	38,212	393	1,203,254	587,186	616,068	868	861	7
	Chhindwara ...	26,991	13,503	13,488	904	899	5	26,087	12,604	13,483	19	19	...
	Nimar ...	27,958	14,195	13,763	1,287	1,269	18	26,671	12,926	13,745	18	18	...
	Betul ...	45,192	22,206	22,986	885	881	4	44,307	21,325	22,982	18	18	...
Kundera ...	Nerbudda Valley ...	102	45	57	13	13	...	89	32	57	1	1	...
Kuramwar ...	Chanda ...	3,776	1,884	1,892	...	...	...	3,776	1,884	1,892	...	...	...
Kurmi ...	Total ...	*284,311*	*141,079*	*143,232*	*9,961*	*9,836*	*125*	*274,350*	*131,243*	*143,107*	*150*	*149*	*1*
	Nerbudda Valley ...	113,301	57,295	56,006	4,980	4,936	44	108,321	52,359	55,962	52	52	...
	Plateau Division ...	30,904	15,377	15,527	1,216	1,197	19	29,688	14,180	15,508	38	37	1
	Chhattisgarh Division	140,106	68,407	71,699	3,765	3,703	62	136,341	64,704	71,637	60	60	...
Lakhera ...	Nerbudda Valley ...	1,716	865	851	227	209	18	1,489	656	833	...	...	...
Lodhi ...	Province ...	312,374	155,174	157,200	7,159	7,051	108	305,215	148,123	157,092	58	58	...
Lohar ...	Province ...	181,311	90,929	90,382	3,541	3,445	96	177,770	87,484	90,286	109	108	1
Lonari ...	Berar ...	997	510	487	4	4	...	993	506	487	...	...	...
Madgi ...	Chanda ...	5,395	2,677	2,718	7	7	...	5,388	2,670	2,718	...	...	...
Mala ...	Chanda ...	3,820	1,935	1,885	15	15	...	3,805	1,920	1,885	4	4	...
Mali ...	Province ...	561,232	279,589	281,643	9,504	9,207	297	551,728	270,382	281,346	234	234	...
Mallah ...	Total ...	*3,395*	*1,686*	*1,709*	*15*	*15*	...	*3,380*	*1,671*	*1,709*	...	...	...
	Jubbulpore ...	1,801	898	903	10	10	...	1,791	888	903	...	...	...
	Narsinghpur ...	1,594	788	806	5	5	...	1,589	783	806	...	...	...
Mana ...	Nagpur Division ...	42,849	20,985	21,864	229	225	4	42,620	20,760	21,860	3	3	...
Mang ...	Maratha Division ...	77,150	37,943	39,207	283	282	1	76,867	37,661	39,206	11	11	...
Manihar ...	Nerbudda Valley ...	278	134	144	24	23	1	254	111	143	1	1	...
Maratha ...	Province ...	93,879	46,701	47,178	7,072	6,825	247	86,807	39,876	46,931	550	543	7
Mehra ...	Province ...	1,164,383	575,028	589,355	9,933	9,775	158	1,154,450	565,253	589,197	219	213	6
Mehtar ...	Total ...	*18,852*	*9,558*	*9,294*	*178*	*174*	*4*	*18,674*	*9,384*	*9,290*	*7*	*7*	...
	Nerbudda Valley ...	13,668	6,948	6,720	107	103	4	13,561	6,845	6,716	...	...	...
	Nagpur ...	2,810	1,447	1,363	55	55	...	2,755	1,392	1,363	7	7	...
	Raipur ...	2,374	1,163	1,211	16	16	...	2,358	1,147	1,211	...	...	...
Mhali ...	Maratha Division ...	36,946	18,843	18,103	1,129	1,112	17	35,817	17,731	18,086	32	32	...
Mochi ...	Nerbudda Valley ...	1,503	760	743	102	95	7	1,401	665	736	9	9	...
Nai ...	Province ...	146,090	72,797	73,293	4,182	4,047	135	141,908	68,750	73,158	119	118	1

TABLE IX.—Education by Selected Castes, Tribes or Races—*concld.*

CASTE, TRIBE OR RACE.	LOCALITY.	POPULATION.									LITERATE IN ENGLISH.		
		TOTAL.			LITERATE.			ILLITERATE.					
		Persons.	Males.	Females.	Persons.	Males.	Females.	Persons.	Males.	Females.	Persons.	Males.	Females.
1	2	3	4	5	6	7	8	9	10	11	12	13	14
Oraon (Hindu and Animist.)	Total ...	*77,099*	*38,901*	*38,198*	*49*	*49*	...	*77,050*	*38,852*	*38,198*	...	...	...
	Raigarh ...	6,108	3,004	3,104	2	2	...	6,106	3,002	3,104	...	...	...
	Chota Nagpur States	70,991	35,897	35,094	47	47	...	70,944	35,850	35,094	...	...	...
Oraon (Christian)	Jashpur ...	36,362	18,302	18,060	80	75	5	36,282	18,227	18,055	7	7	...
Otari ...	Maratha Division ...	2,260	1,086	1,174	39	39	...	2,221	1,047	1,174	1	1	...
Panchal ...	Maratha Division ...	8,564	4,179	4,385	1,041	1,021	20	7,523	3,158	4,365	35	34	1
Panka ...	Total ...	*132,978*	*63,642*	*69,336*	*1,236*	*1,218*	*18*	*131,742*	*62,424*	*69,318*	*3*	*3*	...
	Mandla ...	17,619	8,706	8,913	160	156	4	17,459	8,550	8,909	...	...	...
	Seoni ...	2,439	1,185	1,254	25	25	...	2,414	1,160	1,254	...	...	...
	Balaghat ...	2,961	1,451	1,510	76	76	...	2,885	1,375	1,510	1	1	...
	Chhattisgarh Division	109,959	52,300	57,659	975	961	14	108,984	51,339	57,645	2	2	...
Parbhu ...	Maratha Division ...	1,252	641	611	527	395	132	725	246	479	236	229	7
Pathrat ...	Maratha Division ...	876	421	455	2	2	...	874	419	455	...	...	...
Patwa ...	Total ...	*4,970*	*2,436*	*2,534*	*362*	*340*	*22*	*4,608*	*2,096*	*2,512*	*4*	*4*	...
	Nerbudda Valley ...	3,318	1,655	1,663	254	241	13	3,064	1,414	1,650	4	4	...
	Chhattisgarh Division	1,652	781	871	108	99	9	1,544	682	862	...	...	...
Rajput ...	Province ...	440,323	223,103	217,220	27,840	27,032	808	412,483	196,071	216,412	1,464	1,445	19
Rangari ...	Total ...	*2,166*	*1,118*	*1,048*	*280*	*275*	*5*	*1,886*	*843*	*1,043*	*5*	*5*	...
	Nimar ...	953	486	467	119	114	5	834	372	462	2	2	...
	Wardha ...	1,213	632	581	161	161	...	1,052	471	581	3	3	...
Sali ...	Total ...	*3,249*	*1,602*	*1,647*	*290*	*290*	...	*2,959*	*1,312*	*1,647*	*2*	*2*	...
	Amraoti ...	2,006	990	1,016	203	203	...	1,803	787	1,016	1	1	...
	Buldana ...	1,243	612	631	87	87	...	1,156	525	631	1	1	...
Sawara ...	Total ...	*54,143*	*26,414*	*27,729*	*139*	*137*	*2*	*54,004*	*26,277*	*27,727*	7	7	...
	Saugor ...	18,527	9,062	9,465	12	11	1	18,515	9,051	9,464	...	...	...
	Damoh ...	6,705	3,243	3,462	1	1	...	6,704	3,242	3,462	...	...	...
	Chhattisgarh Division	28,911	14,109	14,802	126	125	1	28,785	13,984	14,801	7	7	...
Sunar ...	Province ...	126,864	63,830	63,034	15,990	15,629	361	110,874	48,201	62,673	379	371	8
Takari ...	Akola ...	3,323	1,720	1,603	44	42	2	3,279	1,678	1,601	...	...	...
Tamera ...	Total ...	*2,604*	*1,333*	*1,171*	*455*	*443*	*12*	*2,049*	*890*	*1,159*	*13*	*12*	*1*
	Saugor ...	687	379	308	176	170	6	511	209	302	6	6	...
	Jubbulpore ...	831	435	396	166	163	3	665	272	393	1	1	...
	Raipur ...	215	122	93	69	67	2	146	55	91	3	2	1
	Maratha Division ...	771	397	374	44	43	1	727	354	373	3	3	...
Teli ...	Province ...	869,336	427,124	442,212	19,615	19,247	368	849,721	407,877	441,844	272	270	2
Waddar ...	Yeotmal ...	4,172	2,181	1,991	2	2	...	4,170	2,179	1,991	...	...	...
Wanjari ...	Berar ...	32,787	16,367	16,420	249	249	...	32,538	16,118	16,420	10	10	...

TABLE X.

Language.

In this table, the languages and dialects have been arranged according to their family affinity. The principal vernaculars of the Province are :—

Hindi	...	...	...	Columns 5—7
Marathi	...	...	...	" 20—22
Gondi	...	...	...	" 44—46

the other minor vernaculars being Oriya (cols. 26—28), Oraon (cols. 50—52), Telugu (cols. 59—61), Kolami (cols. 62—64), Kherwari (cols. 68—70), Korku (cols. 83—85), Kharia (cols. 89—91), and Gadaba (cols. 92—94).

Dialects were not asked for in the instructions to enumerators and the figures for dialects cannot, therefore, be taken as accurate. A better estimate of the distribution of dialects will be found in the subsidiary tables appended to Chapter IX (Language) in Part I of the report.

The dialect Marwari properly belongs to the group Rajasthani which Dr. Grierson holds to be linguistically distinct from Hindi. The two other dialects of that group in these Provinces, *viz.*, Nimari and Malwi have been returned by the enumerators as Hindi, and as it is not therefore possible to make a complete group of the Rajasthani languages Marwari has also been included in the figures of Hindi. The matter is elaborately dealt with in the Chapter on language in the Report Volume.

TABLE X.—

Serial number.	DISTRICT OR STATE.	TOTAL POPULATION.			TOTAL HINDI.			LANGUAGES OF — DIALECTS INCLUDED — Chhattisgarhi.			Pon
		Persons.	Males.	Females.	Persons.	Males.	Females.	Persons.	Males.	Females.	Persons.
	1	2	3	4	5	6	7	8	9	10	11
	Central Provinces and Berar ...	**16,033,310**	**7,984,022**	**8,049,288**	**8,906,073**	**4,423,682**	**4,482,391**	**999,472**	**483,568**	**515,904**	**34,011**
	C. P. British Districts and Berar	**13,916,308**	**6,930,392**	**6,985,916**	**7,439,143**	**3,697,526**	**3,741,617**	**998,821**	**483,225**	**515,596**	**34,011**
	C. P. British Districts ...	**10,859,146**	**5,379,778**	**5,479,368**	**7,076,977**	**3,501,649**	**3,575,328**	**998,821**	**483,225**	**515,596**	**34,005**
	JUBBULPORE DIVISION ...	*2,421,064*	*1,210,980*	*1,210,084*	*2,166,338*	*1,083,257*	*1,085,081*	*2,507*	*1,202*	*1,305*	...
1	Saugor ...	541,410	276,233	265,177	537,356	275,477	263,879	...	...	...	...
2	Damoh ...	333,047	168,060	164,987	332,218	167,590	164,628	...	...	...	...
3	Jubbulpore ...	745,892	373,173	372,719	728,483	362,380	366,103	...	...	...	...
4	Mandla ...	405,234	200,872	204,362	307,711	153,243	154,468	2,505	1,201	1,304	...
5	Seoni ...	395,481	192,642	202,839	260,570	124,567	136,003	2	1	1	...
	NERBUDDA DIVISION	*2,081,477*	*1,043,239*	*1,038,238*	*1,413,993*	*712,987*	*701,006*	*2*	...	*2*	...
6	Narsinghpur ...	325,677	161,795	163,882	324,353	161,151	163,202	...	...	...	...
7	Hoshangabad ...	457,395	230,632	226,763	419,886	211,950	207,936	...	...	...	...
8	Nimar ...	391,071	200,765	190,306	256,791	133,001	123,790	...	...	...	...
9	Betul ...	390,386	194,163	196,223	151,979	77,012	74,967	1	...	1	...
10	Chhindwara ...	516,948	255,884	261,064	260,984	129,873	131,111	1	...	1	...
	NAGPUR DIVISION ...	*3,109,838*	*1,548,737*	*1,561,101*	*531,542*	*270,709*	*260,833*	*478*	*267*	*211*	*34,005*
11	Wardha ...	459,796	231,871	227,925	48,323	24,965	21,358	...	...	...	43
12	Nagpur ...	800,901	408,843	401,058	107,401	56,808	50,593	24	18	6	4
13	Chanda ...	677,544	337,540	340,004	27,066	14,346	12,720	105	55	50	...
14	Bhandara ...	773,677	380,014	393,663	123,431	62,723	60,708	345	190	155	33,956
15	Balaghat ...	388,920	190,469	198,451	227,321	111,867	115,454	4	4	...	2
	CHHATTISGARH DIVISION ...	*3,246,767*	*1,576,822*	*1,669,945*	*2,965,104*	*1,436,696*	*1,528,408*	*995,834*	*481,756*	*514,078*	...
16	Raipur ...	1,324,856	645,186	679,670	1,115,136	541,096	574,040	1,570	711	859	...
17	Bilāspur ...	1,146,223	558,477	587,746	1,115,872	543,269	572,603	994,216	481,015	513,201	...
18	Drug ...	775,688	373,159	402,529	734,096	352,331	381,765	48	30	18	...
	Berar ...	**3,057,162**	**1,550,614**	**1,506,548**	**362,166**	**195,877**	**166,289**	...	...	...	**6**
19	Amraoti ...	875,904	447,216	428,688	128,634	69,600	59,034	...	...	...	4
20	Akola ...	788,863	400,893	387,970	99,757	54,262	45,495	...	...	...	...
21	Buldana ...	669,182	337,170	332,003	78,576	41,919	36,657	...	...	...	...
22	Yeotmal ...	723,213	365,326	357,887	55,190	30,096	25,103	...	...	...	2
	Feudatory States ...	**2,117,002**	**1,053,630**	**1,063,372**	**1,466,930**	**726,156**	**740,774**	**651**	**343**	**308**	...
23	Makrai ...	15,021	7,530	7,491	11,255	5,599	5,656	...	...	...	...
24	Bastar ...	433,310	218,015	215,295	26,587	13,371	13,216	265	130	135	...
25	Kanker ...	127,014	63,010	64,004	90,410	44,234	46,176	10	5	5	...
26	Nandgaon ...	167,362	80,293	87,069	160,324	76,822	83,502	26	12	14	...
27	Khairagarh ...	155,471	74,742	80,729	150,552	72,301	78,251	67	43	24	...
28	Chhuikhadan ...	31,150	15,117	16,033	30,979	15,030	15,949	...	...	...	...
29	Kawardha ...	77,654	37,488	40,166	77,420	37,387	40,033	...	...	...	...
30	Sakti ...	34,547	16,871	17,676	33,815	16,490	17,325	9	5	4	...
31	Raigarh ...	218,860	107,850	111,010	178,237	87,632	90,605	28	13	15	...
32	Sarangarh ...	102,071	49,851	52,220	76,527	37,300	39,227	20	9	11	...
33	Chang-Bhakar ...	24,421	12,462	11,959	24,421	12,462	11,959	...	...	...	...
34	Korea ...	62,107	31,856	30,251	61,590	31,565	30,025	1	...	1	...
35	Surguja ...	428,703	217,749	210,954	389,469	197,727	191,742	127	72	55	...
36	Udaipur ...	64,853	32,790	32,063	56,169	28,454	27,715	76	43	33	...
37	Jashpur ...	174,458	88,006	86,452	99,175	49,782	49,393	22	11	11	...

Language.

INDIA: A.—ARYAN.

in Hindi.									Total Marathi.			Dialect included in Marathi.			
wari.		Urdu.			Marwari.							Halbi.			
Males.	Females.	Persons.	Males.	Females.	Persons.	Males.	Females.	Persons.	Males.	Females.	Persons.	Males.	Females.	Serial number.
12	13	14	15	16	17	18	19	20	21	22	23	24	25	
18,507	**15,504**	**292,485**	**149,669**	**142,816**	**73,941**	**42,756**	**31,185**	**5,012,099**	**2,500,954**	**2,511,145**	**141,969**	**71,676**	**70,293**	
18,507	**15,504**	**290,896**	**148,891**	**142,005**	**71,231**	**41,214**	**30,017**	**4,865,980**	**2,427,510**	**2,438,470**	**13,667**	**6,964**	**6,703**	
18,502	**15,503**	**77,078**	**39,504**	**37,574**	**26,373**	**14,649**	**11,724**	**2,465,187**	**1,221,414**	**1,243,773**	**13,479**	**6,824**	**6,655**	
...	...	*8,366*	*4,699*	*3,667*	*908*	*572*	*336*	*33,504*	*16,750*	*16,754*	...	...	...	
...	...	4,806	2,661	2,145	55	23	32	1,369	749	620	...	...	...	1
...	...	1,485	775	710	320	163	157	367	208	159	...	...	...	2
...	...	1,069	785	284	365	289	76	1,373	803	570	...	...	—	3
...	...	26	17	9	94	54	40	635	336	299	...	...	...	4
...	...	980	461	519	74	43	31	29,760	14,654	15,106	...	...	...	5
...	...	*19,244*	*9,814*	*9,430*	*10,923*	*5,907*	*5,016*	*245,575*	*121,809*	*123,766*	*40*	*24*	*16*	
...	...	817	399	418	80	40	40	495	233	262	...	...	...	6
...	...	826	376	450	5,847	2,920	2,927	3,403	1,621	1,782	...	...	...	7
...	...	15,382	7,942	7,440	3,801	2,342	1,549	54,318	27,332	26,986	40	24	16	8
...	...	1,916	970	946	226	134	92	89,833	44,112	45,721	...	...	—	9
...	...	303	127	176	879	471	408	97,526	48,511	49,015	...	...	—	10
18,502	*15,503*	*42,188*	*21,354*	*20,834*	*9,992*	*5,516*	*4,476*	*2,158,809*	*1,069,472*	*1,089,337*	*5,693*	*3,024*	*2,669*	
22	21	6,775	3,446	3,329	4,307	2,432	1,875	363,146	182,618	180 528	403	212	191	11
2	2	19,214	9,922	9,292	2,577	1,377	1,200	636,619	317,823	318,796	1,543	800	743	12
...	...	6,738	3,350	3,388	721	437	284	486,241	242,197	244,044	3,445	1,864	1,581	13
18,478	15,478	5,888	2,967	2,921	2,161	1,146	1,015	573,690	278,689	295,001	302	148	154	14
...	2	3,573	1,669	1,904	226	124	102	99,113	48,145	50,968	—	...	—	15
...	...	*7,280*	*3,637*	*3,643*	*4,550*	*2,654*	*1,896*	*27,299*	*13,383*	*13,916*	*7,746*	*3,776*	*3,970*	
...	...	5,073	2,478	2,595	1,857	1,075	782	13,776	6,593	7,183	7,673	3,703	3,970	16
...	...	1,297	637	660	1,532	884	648	3,668	1,834	1,834	58	58	...	17
...	...	910	522	388	1,161	695	466	9,855	4,956	4,899	15	15	...	18
5	**1**	**213,818**	**109,387**	**104,431**	**44,858**	**26,565**	**18,293**	**2,400,793**	**1,206,096**	**1,194,697**	**188**	**140**	**48**	
3	1	66,365	33,904	32,461	13,439	7,827	5,612	671,424	339,621	331,803	89	46	43	19
...	...	62,906	32,199	30,707	13,837	8,358	5,479	657,274	329,091	328,183	...	...	...	20
...	...	48,990	25,009	23,981	12,323	7,356	4,967	571,180	285,742	285,438	...	...	...	21
2	—	35,557	18,275	17,282	5,259	3,024	2,235	500,915	251,642	249,273	99	94	5	22
...	...	**1,589**	**778**	**811**	**2,710**	**1,542**	**1,168**	**146,119**	**73,444**	**72,675**	**128,302**	**64,712**	**63,590**	
...	...	...	...	...	47	25	22	46	24	22	...	...	...	23
...	...	18	12	6	32	15	17	133,622	67,309	66,313	127,047	64,069	62,978	24
...	...	85	40	45	192	99	93	2,804	1,397	1,407	1,248	638	610	25
...	...	368	167	201	871	531	340	5,147	2,489	2,658	...	...		26
...	...	812	393	419	703	401	302	3,130	1,546	1,584	1	1	...	27
...	...	...	...	...	65	40	25	155	79	76	...	...	...	28
...	...	6	6	...	31	20	11	205	80	119	...	...	...	29
—	...	3	2	1	1	1	...	17	9	8	...	...	...	30
...		11	6	5	650	348	302	487	238	249	6	4	2	31
...	...	98	48	50	54	31	23	435	227	208	...	...	...	32
...	...	...	...	...	...	...	...	...	...	...	...	...	...	33
...	...	...	...	...	2	2	...	1	1	...	...	...	...	34
...	...	81	42	39	1	1	...	24	13	11	...	...	...	35
...	...	82	46	36	61	28	33	30	19	11	...	...	...	36
...	...	25	16	9	...	—	...	16	7	9	...	...	...	37

TABLE X.—

Serial number.	District or State.	Languages of India: A.—Aryan—(concld.)														
		Oriya.			Total Gujarati.			Dialect included in Gujarati. Bhili.			Bengali.			Punjabi.		
		Persons.	Males.	Females.	Persons.	Males.	Females.	Persons.	Males.	Females.	Persons.	Males.	Females.	Persons.	Males.	Females.
	1	26	27	28	29	30	31	32	33	34	35	36	37	38	39	40
	Central Provinces and Berar ...	**302,635**	**150,981**	**151,654**	**69,388**	**37,943**	**31,445**	**23,263**	**11,514**	**11,749**	**2,540**	**1,496**	**1,044**	**4,531**	**3,746**	**785**
	C. P. British Districts and Berar.	**200,181**	**99,666**	**100,515**	**68,947**	**37,615**	**31,332**	**23,263**	**11,514**	**11,749**	**2,386**	**1,396**	**990**	**4,486**	**3,713**	**773**
	C. P. British Districts ...	**200,178**	**99,663**	**100,515**	**42,796**	**23,686**	**19,110**	**22,139**	**10,975**	**11,164**	**2,189**	**1,295**	**894**	**4,064**	**3,439**	**625**
	Jubbulpore Division ...	*243*	*186*	*57*	*1,650*	*1,067*	*583*	...	...	...	*570*	*320*	*250*	*2,590*	*2,325*	*265*
1	Saugor ...	9	6	3	425	265	160	...	...	...	68	39	29	1,077	968	109
2	Damoh ...	5	5	...	303	169	134	...	...	...	28	13	15	6	4	2
3	Jubbulpore ...	184	151	33	570	377	193	...	...	...	405	228	177	1,385	1,257	128
4	Mandla ...	3	3	...	196	153	43	...	...	...	42	22	20	86	67	19
5	Seoni ...	42	21	21	156	103	53	...	...	...	33	24	9	36	29	7
	Nerbudda Division	*33*	*19*	*14*	*34,278*	*17,872*	*16,403*	*22,137*	*10,973*	*11,164*	*383*	*217*	*166*	*656*	*471*	*185*
6	Narsinghpur ...	4	4	...	135	93	42	...	...	...	24	9	15	13	13	...
7	Hoshangabad ...	7	6	1	788	505	283	...	...	...	114	66	48	76	61	15
8	Nimar ...	...	...	...	31,240	15,777	15,463	22,137	10,973	11,164	81	32	49	308	211	92
9	Betul ...	20	8	12	949	660	289	...	...	...	102	73	29	218	154	64
10	Chhindwara ...	2	1	1	1,166	837	329	...	...	...	62	37	25	46	32	14
	Nagpur Division ...	*464*	*273*	*191*	*4,951*	*3,272*	*1,679*	...	...	...	*772*	*453*	*319*	*498*	*359*	*139*
11	Wardha ...	2	2	...	1,072	688	384	...	...	...	15	9	6	30	15	15
12	Nagpur ...	116	68	48	1,969	1,326	643	...	...	...	576	332	244	230	166	64
13	Chanda ...	208	119	89	1,099	669	430	...	...	...	81	52	29	124	98	26
14	Bhandara ...	108	70	38	375	265	110	...	...	...	58	31	27	30	25	5
15	Balaghat ...	30	14	16	436	324	112	...	...	...	42	20	13	84	55	29
	Chhattisgarh Division ...	*199,438*	*99,185*	*100,253*	*1,917*	*1,475*	*442*	*2*	*2*	...	*458*	*299*	*159*	*320*	*284*	*36*
16	Raipur ...	180,713	89,883	90,830	909	713	196	2	2	...	102	109	53	121	110	11
17	Bilaspur ...	18,575	9,231	9,344	786	596	190	...	...	...	259	163	96	133	120	13
18	Drug ...	150	71	79	222	166	56	...	...	...	37	27	10	66	54	12
	Berar ...	**3**	**3**	...	**26,151**	**13,929**	**12,222**	**1,124**	**539**	**585**	**197**	**101**	**96**	**422**	**274**	**148**
19	Amraoti ...	1	1	...	6,812	3,736	3,076	31	1	30	154	79	75	124	69	55
20	Akola ...	1	1	...	6,496	3,980	2,516	47	26	21	17	10	7	59	37	22
21	Buldana ...	1	1	...	9,422	4,170	5,252	41	19	22	11	7	4	82	45	37
22	Yeotmal ...	...	...	...	3,421	2,043	1,378	1,005	493	512	15	5	10	157	123	34
	Feudatory States ..	**102,454**	**51,315**	**51,139**	**441**	**328**	**113**	...	...	...	**154**	**100**	**54**	**45**	**33**	**12**
23	Makrai ...	...	...	...	...	...	...	...	...	...	...	...	...	5	5	...
24	Bastar ...	39,361	19,936	19,425	17	16	1	...	...	...	1	1	...	...	...	...
25	Kanker ...	92	44	48	46	31	15	...	...	...	24	14	10	...	...	...
26	Nandgaon ...	11	5	6	142	95	47	...	...	...	15	11	4	...	...	...
27	Khairagarh ...	15	7	8	52	44	8	...	...	...	21	15	6	20	13	7
28	Chhuikhadan ...	1	1	...	15	7	8	...	...	...	...	...	...	...	...	...
29	Kawardha ...	2	2	...	8	8	...	...	...	...	1	1	...	...	...	...
30	Sakti ...	105	50	55	30	24	6	...	...	...	2	2	...	3	3	...
31	Raigarh ...	30,626	15,241	15,385	100	87	13	...	...	...	42	25	17	8	4	4
32	Sarangarh ...	22,629	11,165	11,464	17	9	8	...	...	...	7	4	3	3	3	...
33	Chang-Bhakar ...	...	...	...	...	...	...	...	...	...	...	...	...	...	...	...
34	Korea ...	...	...	...	...	...	...	...	...	...	...	...	...	...	...	...
35	Surguja ...	206	118	88	...	...	...	...	...	...	8	6	2	4	3	1
36	Udaipur ...	2,225	1,096	1,129	8	7	1	...	...	...	10	5	5	...	...	...
37	Jashpur ...	7,181	3,650	3,531	...	...	...	...	...	...	23	16	7	2	2	...

Language—*continued.*

Languages of India: B.—Dravidian.																		
Minor Languages of the Aryan Sub-Family.			Total Gondi.			Dialect included in Gondi. Parja or Parji.			Kurukh or Oraon.			Tamil.			Kanarese.			
Persons.	Males.	Females.	Persons.	Males.	Females.	Persons.	Males.	Females.	Persons.	Males.	Females.	Persons.	Males.	Females.	Persons.	Males.	Females.	Serial number.
41	42	43	44	45	46	47	48	49	50	51	52	53	54	55	56	57	58	
4,507	3,587	920	1,167,015	574,919	592,096	15,110	7,904	7,206	103,764	52,425	51,339	5,209	2,747	2,462	4,400	2,020	2,380	
4,248	3,442	806	917,113	449,449	467,664	...	...	...	2,940	1,432	1,508	5,063	2,673	2,390	4,397	2,020	2,377	
2,574	2,055	519	832,736	408,169	424,567	...	...	...	2,940	1,432	1,508	4,679	2,471	2,208	3,776	1,700	2,076	
683	*597*	*86*	*204,880*	*101,788*	*103,092*	...	...	...	...	...	...	*911*	*563*	*348*	*58*	*31*	*27*	
345	292	53	49	31	18	...	...	...	...	...	...	67	43	24	...	...	...	1
25	21	4	4	3	1	...	...	...	...	...	...	7	6	1	4	4	...	2
197	183	14	7,029	3,476	3,553	...	...	...	...	...	...	774	476	298	15	8	7	3
26	19	7	95,494	46,447	49,047	...	...	...	...	...	...	29	17	12	4	2	2	4
90	82	8	102,304	51,831	50,473	...	...	...	...	...	...	34	21	13	35	17	18	5
820	*623*	*197*	*278,212*	*134,987*	*143,225*	...	...	...	*1*	*1*	...	*401*	*221*	*180*	*85*	*44*	*41*	
36	26	10	484	192	292	...	...	...	...	...	...	11	6	5	19	10	9	6
98	76	22	20,450	9,986	10,464	...	...	...	...	...	...	139	71	68	32	17	15	7
172	132	40	5,779	2,868	2,911	...	...	...	1	1	...	161	94	67	27	15	12	8
407	296	111	111,183	54,129	57,054	...	...	...	...	...	...	25	15	10	...	...	...	9
107	93	14	140,316	67,812	72,504	...	...	...	...	...	...	65	35	30	7	2	5	10
859	*647*	*212*	*313,810*	*153,597*	*160,213*	...	...	...	*1*	*1*	...	*2,968*	*1,485*	*1,483*	*3,625*	*1,620*	*2,005*	
132	106	26	43,365	20,470	22,895	...	...	...	...	...	...	33	18	15	19	11	8	11
484	330	154	47,167	23,614	23,553	...	...	...	...	...	...	2,525	1,284	1,241	63	49	14	12
133	116	17	92,809	45,698	4,711	...	...	...	...	...	...	167	96	71	3,430	1,517	1,913	13
83	74	9	70,608	34,825	35,783	...	...	...	...	...	...	70	36	34	103	39	64	14
27	21	6	59,861	28,990	30,871	...	...	...	1	1	...	173	51	122	10	4	6	15
212	*188*	*24*	*35,834*	*17,797*	*18,037*	...	...	...	*2,938*	*1,430*	*1,508*	*399*	*202*	*197*	*8*	*5*	*3*	
124	117	7	4,107	2,069	2,038	...	...	...	1,037	503	534	251	110	141	2	2	...	16
68	52	16	739	346	393	...	...	...	1,893	919	974	89	69	20	5	2	3	17
20	19	1	30,988	15,382	15,606	...	...	...	8	8	...	59	23	36	1	1	...	18
1,674	1,387	287	84,377	41,280	43,097	...	...	...	...	...	...	384	202	182	621	320	301	
498	416	82	20,809	10,381	10,428	...	...	...	...	...	...	162	87	75	149	87	62	19
576	472	104	2,267	1,170	1,097	...	...	...	...	...	...	100	52	48	192	95	97	20
223	201	22	744	386	358	...	...	...	...	...	...	82	41	41	159	71	88	21
377	298	79	60,557	29,343	31,214	...	...	...	...	...	...	40	22	18	121	67	54	22
259	145	114	249,902	125,470	124,432	15,110	7,904	7,206	100,824	50,993	49,831	146	74	72	3	...	3	
...	...	...	967	480	481	...	...	...	...	...	...	...	...	...	...	...	...	23
53	36	17	212,605	106,388	106,217	15,110	7,904	7,206	2	2	...	31	14	17	...	...	...	24
...	...	...	33,188	17,081	16,107	...	...	...	...	...	...	...	...	...	3	...	3	25
8	6	2	1,509	753	756	...	...	...	...	...	...	59	32	27	...	...	...	26
23	14	9	1,330	640	690	...	...	...	...	...	...	43	20	23	...	...	...	27
...	...	...	...	...	...	...	...	...	...	...	...	...	...	...	...	...	...	28
...	...	...	14	2	12	...	...	...	...	...	...	...	...	...	...	...	...	29
...	...	...	1	1	...	...	...	...	398	203	195	13	8	5	...	...	...	30
6	6	...	67	20	47	...	...	...	5,822	2,865	2,957	...	...	...	...	...	...	31
2	2	...	126	57	69	...	...	...	909	433	476	...	...	...	...	...	...	32
...	...	...	...	...	...	...	...	...	...	...	...	...	...	...	...	...	...	33
...	...	...	45	21	24	...	...	...	383	210	173	...	...	...	...	...	...	34
43	36	7	24	13	11	...	...	...	27,385	13,865	13,520	...	...	...	...	...	...	35
...	...	...	1	...	1	...	...	...	6,025	3,029	2,996	...	...	...	...	...	...	36
124	45	79	16	8	8	...	...	...	59,900	30,386	29,514	...	...	...	...	...	...	37

TABLE X.—

Serial number.	DISTRICT OR STATE.	LANGUAGES OF INDIA: B.—DRAVIDIAN—(concld.)									LANGUAGES OF INDIA: C—MUNDA.								
		Telugu.			Kolami.			Minor Languages of the Dravidian Family.			Total Kherwari.			Dialects included					
														Mundari.			Turi.		
		Persons.	Males.	Females.	Persons.	Males.	Females.	Persons.	Males.	Females.	Persons.	Males.	Females.	Persons.	Males.	Females.	Persons.	Males.	Females.
	1	59	60	61	62	63	64	65	66	67	68	69	70	71	72	73	74	75	76
	Central Provinces and Berar ...	**140,413**	**70,327**	**70,086**	**24,074**	**12,151**	**11,923**	**36**	**12**	**24**	**17,649**	**9,289**	**8,360**	**1,029**	**732**	**297**	**1,202**	**605**	**597**
	C. P. British Districts and Berar.	**125,033**	**62 571**	**62,462**	**24,074**	**12,151**	**11,923**	**36**	**12**	**24**	**673**	**316**	**357**	**158**	**77**	**81**	**170**	**69**	**101**
	C. P. British Districts ...	**85,688**	**43,062**	**42,626**	**2,067**	**1,041**	**1,026**	**14**	**12**	**2**	**671**	**314**	**357**	**158**	**77**	**81**	**170**	**69**	**101**
	Jubbulpore Division	*1,869*	*895*	*974*	...	...	...	*11*	*9*	*2*	...	...	...	...	...	...	...	...	...
1	Saugor ...	107	65	42	...	...	...	...	...	...	...	...	...	...	...	...	...	...	...
2	Damoh ...	4	1	3	...	...	...	...	...	...	...	...	...	...	...	...	...	...	...
3	Jubbulpore ...	777	301	476	...	...	...	8	7	1	...	...	...	...	...	...	...	...	...
4	Mandla ...	84	57	27	...	...	...	...	...	...	...	...	...	...	...	...	...	...	...
5	Seoni ...	897	471	426	...	...	...	3	2	1	...	...	...	...	...	...	...	...	...
	Nerbudda Division	*1,117*	*583*	*534*	...	...	...	...	...	...	...	...	...	...	...	...	...	...	...
6	Narsinghpur ...	31	17	14	...	...	...	...	...	...	...	...	...	...	...	...	...	...	...
7	Hoshangabad ...	107	50	57	...	...	...	...	...	...	...	...	...	...	...	...	...	...	...
8	Nimar ...	436	226	210	...	...	...	...	...	...	...	...	...	...	...	...	...	...	...
9	Betul ...	254	139	115	...	...	...	...	...	...	...	...	...	...	...	...	...	...	...
10	Chhindwara ...	289	151	138	...	...	...	...	...	...	...	...	...	...	...	...	...	...	...
	Nagpur Division ...	*80,724*	*40,591*	*40,133*	*2,067*	*1,041*	*1,026*	*3*	*3*	...	...	...	...	...	...	...	...	...	...
11	Wardha ...	1,953	1,053	900	2,063	1,037	1,026	...	...	...	...	...	...	...	...	...	...	...	...
12	Nagpur ...	7,475	3,732	3,743	4	4	...	2	2	...	...	...	...	...	...	...	...	...	...
13	Chanda ...	65,012	32,000	33,012	...	...	...	1	1	...	...	...	...	...	...	...	...	...	...
14	Bhandara ...	4,959	3,146	1,813	...	...	...	...	...	...	...	...	...	...	...	...	...	...	...
15	Balaghat ...	1,325	660	665	...	...	...	...	...	...	...	...	...	...	...	...	...	...	...
	Chhattisgarh Division ...	*1,978*	*993*	*985*	...	...	...	...	...	...	*671*	*314*	*357*	*158*	*77*	*81*	*170*	*69*	*101*
16	Raipur ...	1,359	685	674	...	...	...	...	...	...	140	65	75	40	28	12	100	37	63
17	Bilaspur ...	507	248	259	...	...	...	...	...	...	531	249	282	118	49	69	70	32	38
18	Drug ...	112	60	52	...	...	...	...	...	...	...	...	...	...	...	...	...	...	...
	Berar ...	**39,345**	**19,509**	**19,836**	**22,007**	**11,110**	**10,897**	**22**	...	**22**	**2**	**2**	...	...	...	...	...	...	...
19	Amraoti ...	2,992	1,545	1,447	105	53	52	...	...	...	...	...	...	...	...	...	...	...	...
20	Akola ...	3,934	1,966	1,968	...	...	...	22	...	22	2	2	...	...	...	...	...	...	...
21	Buldana ...	3,231	1,651	1,580	...	...	...	...	...	...	...	...	...	...	...	...	...	...	...
22	Yeotmal ...	29,188	14,347	14,841	21,902	11,057	10,845	...	...	...	...	...	...	...	...	...	...	...	...
	Feudatory States	**15,380**	**7,756**	**7,624**	...	...	...	...	...	...	**16,976**	**8,973**	**8,003**	**871**	**655**	**216**	**1,032**	**536**	**496**
23	Makrai ...	...	...	...	...	...	...	...	...	...	...	...	...	...	...	...	...	...	...
24	Bastar ...	15,076	7,603	7,473	...	...	...	...	...	...	436	434	2	436	434	2	...	...	...
25	Kanker ...	35	18	17	...	...	...	...	...	...	...	...	...	...	...	...	...	...	...
26	Nandgaon ...	113	60	53	...	...	...	...	...	...	...	...	...	...	...	...	...	...	...
27	Khairagarh ...	87	41	46	...	...	...	...	...	...	...	...	...	...	...	...	...	...	...
28	Chhuikhadan ...	...	...	...	...	...	...	...	...	...	...	...	...	...	...	...	...	...	...
29	Kawardha ...	...	...	...	...	...	...	...	...	...	...	...	...	...	...	...	...	...	...
30	Sakti ...	8	5	3	...	...	...	...	...	...	55	28	27	55	28	27	...	...	...
31	Raigarh ...	34	16	18	...	...	...	...	...	...	15	6	9	12	6	6	...	...	...
32	Sarangarh ...	18	8	10	...	...	...	...	...	...	244	119	125	136	63	73	108	56	52
33	Chang-Bhakar ...	—	...	...	...	...	...	...	...	...	...	—	...	...	...	...	...	...	...
34	Korea ...	...	...	...	...	...	...	...	...	...	84	56	28	13	13	...	21	14	7
35	Surguja ...	8	4	4	...	...	...	...	...	...	11,417	5,902	5,515	132	67	65	...	...	...
36	Udaipur ...	1	1	...	...	...	...	...	...	...	62	29	33	...	...	...	...	...	...
37	Jashpur ...	...	...	...	...	...	...	...	...	...	4,663	2,399	2,264	87	44	43	903	466	437

Language—*continued.*

LANGUAGES OF INDIA: C.—MUNDA—(*concld.*)

IN KHERWARI.						TOTAL KORKU.			DIALECT INCLUDED IN KORKU.			KHARIA.			GADABA.			
Korwa.			Other Kherwari dialects.						Muwasi.									
Persons.	Males.	Females.	Persons.	Males.	Females.	Persons.	Males.	Females.	Persons.	Males.	Females.	Persons.	Males.	Females.	Persons.	Males.	Females.	Serial Number
77	78	79	80	81	82	83	84	85	86	87	88	89	90	91	92	93	94	
15,232	7,858	7,374	186	94	92	134,829	66,965	67,864	11,314	6,036	5,278	8,238	4,060	4,178	306	141	165	
343	168	175	2	2	...	132,078	65,546	66,532	11,314	6,036	5,278	985	447	538	...	...	...	
343	168	175	...	...	...	90,004	44,906	45,098	11,301	6,023	5,278	985	447	538	...	...	...	
...	...	...	...	...	...	*5*	*2*	*6*	...	...	...	...	...	...	...	...	...	
...	...	...	...	...	...	4	1	3	...	...	...	...	...	...	...	...	...	1
...	...	...	...	...	...	...	...	...	...	...	...	...	...	...	...	...	...	2
...	...	...	...	...	...	4	1	3	...	...	...	...	...	...	...	...	...	3
...	...	...	...	...	...	...	...	...	...	...	...	...	...	...	...	...	...	4
...	...	...	...	...	...	...	...	...	...	...	...	...	...	...	...	...	...	5
...	...	...	...	...	...	*89,885*	*44,796*	*45,092*	*11,301*	*6,023*	*5,278*	...	...	...	...	...	...	
...	...	...	...	...	...	...	...	...	...	...	...	...	...	...	...	...	...	6
...	...	...	...	...	...	11,719	5,874	5,845	...	...	...	...	...	...	...	...	...	7
...	...	...	...	...	...	28,021	13,713	14,308	...	...	...	...	...	...	...	...	...	8
...	...	...	...	...	...	35,028	17,358	17,670	...	...	...	...	...	...	...	...	...	9
...	...	...	...	...	...	15,120	7,851	7,269	11,301	6,023	5,278	...	...	...	...	...	...	10
...	...	...	...	...	...	*108*	*108*	...	...	...	...	...	...	...	...	...	...	
...	...	...	...	...	...	...	...	...	...	...	...	...	...	...	...	...	...	11
...	...	...	...	...	...	...	...	...	...	...	...	...	...	...	...	...	...	12
...	...	...	...	...	...	13	13	...	...	...	...	...	...	...	...	...	...	13
...	...	...	...	...	...	...	...	...	...	...	...	...	...	...	...	...	...	14
...	...	...	...	...	...	95	95	...	...	...	...	...	...	...	...	...	...	15
343	*168*	*175*	...	...	...	...	...	...	...	...	...	*985*	*447*	*538*	...	...	...	
...	...	...	...	...	...	...	...	...	...	...	...	58	20	38	...	...	...	16
343	168	175	...	...	...	...	...	...	...	...	...	927	427	500	...	...	...	17
...	...	...	...	...	...	...	...	...	...	...	...	...	...	...	...	...	...	18
...	...	...	2	2	...	42,074	20,640	21,434	13	13	...	...	...	...	...	...	...	
...	...	...	...	...	...	41,484	20,317	21,167	13	13	...	...	...	...	...	...	...	19
...	...	...	2	2	...	78	49	29	...	...	...	...	...	...	...	...	...	20
...	...	...	...	...	...	512	274	238	...	...	...	...	...	...	...	...	...	21
...	...	...	...	...	...	...	...	...	...	...	...	...	...	...	...	...	...	22
14,889	7,690	7,199	184	92	92	2,751	1,419	1,332	...	...	...	7,253	3,613	3,640	306	141	165	
...	...	...	...	...	...	2,748	1,416	1,332	...	...	...	...	...	...	...	...	...	23
...	...	...	...	...	...	...	...	...	...	...	...	...	...	...	306	141	165	24
...	...	...	...	...	...	...	...	...	...	...	...	...	...	...	...	...	...	25
...	...	...	...	...	...	...	...	...	...	...	...	...	...	...	...	...	...	26
...	...	...	...	...	...	...	...	...	...	...	...	...	...	...	...	...	...	27
...	...	...	...	...	...	...	...	...	...	...	...	...	...	...	...	...	...	28
...	...	...	...	...	...	...	...	...	...	...	...	...	...	...	...	...	...	29
...	...	...	...	...	...	3	3	...	...	...	...	91	42	49	...	...	...	30
...	...	...	3	...	3	...	...	...	...	...	...	2,784	1,393	1,391	...	...	...	31
...	...	...	...	...	...	...	...	...	...	...	...	836	392	444	...	...	...	32
...	...	...	...	...	...	...	...	...	...	...	...	...	...	...	...	...	...	33
20	10	7	24	10	14	...	...	...	...	...	...	...	...	...	...	...	...	34
11,280	5,832	5,448	5	3	2	...	...	...	...	...	...	9	8	1	...	...	...	35
4	2	2	58	27	31	...	...	...	...	...	...	236	107	129	...	...	...	36
3,579	1,837	1,742	94	52	42	...	...	...	...	...	...	3,297	1,671	1,626	...	...	...	37

TABLE X.—Language—(*concluded*).

Serial number.	DISTRICT OR STATE.	LANGUAGES OF INDIA: D.—GIPSY. Total Gipsy. Persons.	Males.	Females.	Dialect included in Gipsy. Banjari. Persons.	Males.	Females.	LANGUAGES FOREIGN TO INDIA: E. Other Asiatic Languages. Persons.	Males.	Females.	Non-Asiatic Languages. English. Persons.	Males.	Females.	Other non-Asiatic Languages. Persons.	Males.	Females.	Serial number.
	1	95	96	97	98	99	100	101	102	103	104	105	106	107	108	109	
	Central Provinces and Berar ...	**113,410**	**58,381**	**55,029**	**109,828**	**56,616**	**53,212**	**569**	**361**	**208**	**11,307**	**7,617**	**3,690**	**318**	**218**	**100**	
	C. P. British Districts and Berar.	**106,726**	**54,918**	**51,808**	**103,158**	**53,160**	**49,998**	**450**	**294**	**156**	**11,058**	**7,482**	**3,576**	**311**	**213**	**98**	
	C. P. British Districts ...	**30,603**	**15,473**	**15,130**	**30,180**	**15,260**	**14,920**	**242**	**175**	**67**	**10,500**	**7,192**	**3,308**	**276**	**183**	**93**	
	JUBBULPORE DIVISION	*2,255*	*1,211*	*1,044*	*2,255*	*1,211*	*1,044*	*61*	*34*	*27*	*5,350*	*3,877*	*1,473*	*77*	*62*	*15*	
1	Saugor ...	...	...	...	...	...	...	28	15	13	490	271	219	16	11	5	1
2	Damoh ...	...	...	...	...	...	...	...	...	...	74	36	38	2	...	2	2
3	Jubbulpore ...	5	4	1	5	4	1	8	6	2	4,617	3,465	1,152	58	50	8	3
4	Mandla ...	771	412	359	771	412	359	23	11	12	129	82	47	1	1	...	4
5	Seoni ...	1,479	795	684	1,479	795	684	2	2	...	40	23	17	...	...	...	5
	NERBUDDA DIVISION	*14,898*	*7,924*	*6,974*	*14,684*	*7,828*	*6,856*	*112*	*78*	*34*	*936*	*553*	[illegible]	*90*	*54*	*36*	
6	Narsinghpur ...	...	...	...	...	...	...	...	...	...	67	38	29	5	3	2	6
7	Hoshangabad ...	...	...	...	...	...	...	7	5	2	562	338	224	7	6	1	7
8	Nimar ...	13,522	7,223	6,299	13,308	7,127	6,181	6	6	...	182	108	74	31	26	5	8
9	Betul ...	282	138	144	282	138	144	20	26	...	64	35	29	16	8	8	9
10	Chhindwara ...	1,094	563	531	1,094	563	531	73	41	32	60	34	26	31	11	20	10
	NAGPUR DIVISION...	*4,905*	*2,586*	*2,319*	*4,771*	*2,512*	*2,259*	*26*	*21*	*5*	*3,629*	*2,450*	*1,179*	*77*	*49*	*28*	
11	Wardha ...	1,586	841	745	1,512	783	729	2	2	...	53	34	19	2	2	...	11
12	Nagpur ...	1,909	1,008	901	1,886	999	887	9	6	3	3,276	2,242	1,034	63	36	27	12
13	Chanda ...	1,086	575	511	1,061	575	486	11	10	1	71	41	30	5	5	...	13
14	Bhandara ...	6	6	...	6	6	...	...	...	...	153	82	71	3	3	...	14
15	Balaghat ...	318	156	162	306	149	157	4	3	1	76	51	25	4	3	1	15
	CHHATTISGARH DIVISION ...	*8,545*	*3,752*	*4,793*	*8,470*	*3,709*	*4,761*	*43*	*42*	*1*	*586*	*313*	*273*	*32*	*18*	*14*	
16	Raipur ...	6,789	3,008	3,781	6,777	3,003	3,774	26	25	1	124	66	58	22	13	9	16
17	Bilaspur ...	1,732	723	1,009	1,669	685	984	7	7	...	426	221	205	6	1	5	17
18	Drug ...	24	21	3	24	21	3	10	10	...	36	26	10	4	4	...	18
	Berar ...	**76,123**	**39,445**	**36,678**	**72,978**	**37,900**	**35,078**	**208**	**119**	**89**	**558**	**290**	**268**	**35**	**30**	**5**	
19	Amraoti ...	2,094	996	1,098	1,668	801	867	122	69	53	321	143	178	19	16	3	19
20	Akola ...	17,947	9,614	8,333	16,352	8,788	7,564	30	24	6	104	62	42	7	6	1	20
21	Buldana ...	4,818	2,582	2,236	4,459	2,386	2,073	50	22	28	82	59	23	9	8	1	21
22	Yeotmal ...	51,264	26,253	25,011	50,499	25,925	24,574	6	4	2	51	26	25	...	...	...	22
	Feudatory States	**6,684**	**3,463**	**3,221**	**6,670**	**3,456**	**3,214**	**119**	**67**	**52**	**249**	**135**	**114**	**7**	**5**	**2**	
23	Makrai ...	...	...	...	...	...	...	...	...	...	...	...	...	...	...	...	23
24	Bastar ...	5,195	2,752	2,443	5,195	2,752	2,443	6	6	...	12	6	6	...	...	...	24
25	Kanker ...	412	191	221	412	191	221	...	...	...	...	...	...	...	...	...	25
26	Nandgaon ...	...	...	...	...	...	...	...	...	...	34	20	14	...	...	...	26
27	Khairagarh ...	...	...	...	...	...	...	...	...	...	188	100	88	1	1	...	27
28	Chhuikhadan ...	...	...	...	...	...	...	...	...	...	...	...	...	...	...	...	28
29	Kawardha ...	...	...	...	...	...	...	...	...	...	...	...	...	4	2	2	29
30	Sakti ...	...	...	...	...	...	...	...	...	...	6	3	3	...	...	...	30
31	Raigarh ...	622	313	309	622	313	309	4	4	...	...	...	...	...	...	...	31
32	Sarangarh ...	317	132	185	303	125	178	...	...	...	1	...	1	...	...	...	32
33	Chang-Bhakar ...	...	...	...	...	...	...	...	...	...	...	...	...	...	...	...	33
34	Korea ...	...	...	...	...	...	...	...	...	...	3	2	1	1	1	...	34
35	Surguja ...	...	...	...	...	...	...	106	54	52	...	...	...	...	...	...	35
36	Udaipur ...	80	38	42	80	38	42	...	...	...	5	4	1	1	1	...	36
37	Jashpur ...	58	37	21	58	37	21	3	3	...	...	...	...	...	...	...	37

APPENDIX TO TABLE X

DETAILS OF MINOR LANGUAGES AND DIALECTS.

MINOR LANGUAGES OF THE ARYAN SUB-FAMILY—(A).

See column 41 of Table X.

Language		Number	Distribution
(1) Sanskrit ...	Persons ... M. 1, F. 0.	1	Jubbulpore (1).
(2) Sindhi ...	Persons ... M. 37, F. 7.	44	Damoh (1), Jubbulpore (8), Mandla, (2), Hoshangabad (2), Nimar (4), Betul (7), Wardha (9), Nagpur (2), Akola (9).
(3) Kachchhi ...	Persons ... M. 1,113, F. 442	1,555	Saugor (1), Damoh (14), Mandla (14), Seoni (7), Narsinghpur (30), Hoshangabad (51), Nimar (90), Betul (73), Chhindwara (6), Wardha (56), Nagpur (312), Chanda (63), Bhandara (52), Balaghat (16), Raipur (41), Bilaspur (10), Amraoti (272), Akola (267), Buldana (35), Yeotmal (120), Khairagarh (13), Raigarh (3).
(4) Bihari ...	Persons ... M. 40, F. 79	119	Nagpur (1), Jashpur (118).
(5) Assamese ...	Persons ... M. 1, F. 3.	4	Bilaspur (4).
(6) Central Pahari ...	Persons ... M. 21, F. 0.	21	Hoshangabad (7), Nimar (3), Betul (2), Bilaspur (2), Akola (3), Surguja (4).
(7) Naipali ...	Persons ... M. 66, F. 43.	109	Saugor (83), Hoshangabad (5), Betul (5), Chhindwara (1), Bilaspur (6), Khairagarh (9).
(8) Kashmiri ...	Persons ... M. 9, F. 12.	21	Saugor (19), Drug (2).
(9) Balochi ...	Persons ... M. 104, F. 44.	148	Betul (108), Wardha (3), Nagpur (2), Amraoti (2), Akola (4), Buldana (10), Yeotmal (19).
(10) Pashto ...	Persons ... M. 2,194, F. 290.	2,484	Saugor (242), Damoh (10), Jubbulpore (188), Mandla (10), Seoni (83), Narsinghpur (6), Hoshangabad (33), Nimar (66), Betul (212), Chhindwara (100), Wardha (64), Nagpur (166), Chanda (70), Bhandara (31), Balaghat (11), Raipur (83), Bilaspur (46), Drug (18), Amraoti (224), Akola (203), Buldana (178), Yeotmal (238), Bastar (53), Nandgaon (8), Khairagarh (1), Raigarh (3), Sarangarh (2), Surguja (39), Jashpur (6).
(11) Burmese* ...	Persons ... M. 1, F. 0.	1	Nagpur (1).

MINOR DIALECT OF MARATHI INCLUDED IN COLUMN 20 OF TABLE X.

Dialect		Number	Distribution
Goanese ...	Persons ... M. 174, F. 86.	260	Saugor (6), Damoh (2), Jubbulpore (44), Mandla (3), Seoni (1), Narsinghpur (6), Hoshangabad (24), Nimar (22), Betul (4), Chhindwara (1), Wardha (5), Nagpur (69), Chanda (4), Bhandara (7), Bilaspur (4), Drug (1), Amraoti (29), Akola (11), Buldana, (13), Bastar (2), Kawardha (2).

SUB-DIALECT OF BHILI INCLUDED IN COLUMN 32 OF TABLE X.

Dialect		Number	Distribution
Naikidi ...	Persons ... M. 463, F. 487.	950	Yeotmal (950).

MINOR LANGUAGES OF THE DRAVIDIAN FAMILY—(B).

See column 65 of Table X.

Language		Number	Distribution
(1) Malayalam ...	Persons ... M. 10, F. 24.	34	Jubbulpore (6), Seoni (3), Nagpur (2), Chanda (1), Akola (22)
(2) Kodagu or Coorgi ...	Persons ... M. 2, F. 0.	2	Jubbulpore (2).

MINOR DIALECTS OF GONDI INCLUDED IN COLUMN 44 OF TABLE X.

Dialect		Number	Distribution
(1) Gotte ...	Persons ... M. 430, F. 413.	843	Chanda (843).
(2) Koi or Koya ...	Persons ... M. 1,738, F. 1,788.	3,526	Chanda (3,526)

DIALECT OF TELUGU INCLUDED IN COLUMN 59 OF TABLE X.

Dialect		Number	Distribution
Holia or Golari ...	Persons ... M. 2,256, F. 826.	3,082	Chhindwara (17), Nagpur (546), Bhandara (2,519).

OTHER KHERWARI DIALECTS OF THE MUNDA FAMILY—(C).

See column 80 of Table X.

Dialect		Number	Distribution
(1) Asuri ...	Persons ... M. 58, F. 47.	105	Surguja (5), Udaipur (6), Jashpur (94).
(2) Santali or Har ...	Persons ... M. 12, F. 14.	26	Akola (2), Korea (24).
(3) Birhor	Persons ... M. 24, F. 31.	55	Raigarh (3), Udaipur (52).

Note.—Burmese really belong to the Tibeto-Burman sub-family, but as there is only one speaker it has been included under the Aryan sub-family to which all the other languages under this heading belong.

Sub-dialect of Korwa included in column 77 of Table X.

Language		Persons	Total	Distribution
Kudaku	...	Persons ... M. 2,623, F. 1,109.	3,732	Surguja (3,732).

Dialect of Korku included in column 83 of Table X.

Language		Persons	Total	Distribution
Nahali	...	Persons ... M. 249, F. 220.	469	Betul (1), Amraoti (31), Buldana (437).

Minor Gipsy Languages—(D).

See column 95 of Table X.

Language		Persons	Total	Distribution
(1) Bavri	...	Persons ... M. 98, F. 94.	192	Akola (192).
(2) Beldari	...	Persons ... M. 493, F. 437.	930	Nimar (84), Amraoti (126), Akola (410), Buldana (183), Yeotmal (127).
(3) Bhamti	...	Persons ... M. 21, F. 23.	44	Wardha (7), Nagpur (19), Yeotmal (18).
(4) Ghisadi	...	Persons ... M. 62, F. 64.	126	Akola (49), Buldana (56), Yeotmal (21).
(5) Kaikadi	...	Persons ... M. 403, F. 385.	788	Nimar (115), Wardha (2), Amraoti (151), Akola (371), Buldana (90), Yeotmal (59).
(6) Kolhati	...	Persons ... M. 22, F. 51.	73	Nimar (15), Wardha (18), Akola (17), Buldana (14), Yeotmal (9).
(7) Nati	...	Persons ... M. 34, F. 25.	59	Bilaspur (30), Akola (15), Sarangarh (14).
(8) Pardhi	...	Persons ... M. 430, F. 523.	953	Wardha (47), Nagpur (4), Chanda (25), Balaghat (12), Raipur (12), Bilaspur (33), Amraoti (114), Akola (162), Buldana (16), Yeotmal (528).
(9) Takankari	...	Persons ... M. 172, F. 169.	341	Amraoti (7), Akola (334).
(10) Tirguli	...	Persons ... M. 12, F. 29.	41	Amraoti (28), Akola (10), Yeotmal (3).
(11) Waghri	...	Persons ... M. 18, F. 17.	35	Akola (35).

Other Asiatic Languages—(E).

See column 101 of Table X.

Indo-European Family.

Language		Persons	Total	Distribution
(1) Persian	...	Persons ... M. 292, F. 195.	487	Saugor (28), Jubbulpore (1), Mandla (23), Seoni (2), Hoshangabad (6), Betul (26), Chhindwara (73), Wardha (1), Nagpur (9), Chanda (8), Raipur (19), Bilaspur (5), Drug (9), Amraoti (117), Akola (5), Buldana (48), Raigarh (4), Surguja (102), Jashpur (1).
(2) Armenian	...	Persons ... M. 2, F. 0.	2	Jubbulpore (1), Jashpur (1).
(3) Turkish	...	Persons ... M. 1, F. 0.	1	Chanda (1).

Mongolian Family.

Language		Persons	Total	Distribution
(1) Chinese	...	Persons ... M. 5, F. 0.	5	Nimar (5).
(2) Japanese	...	Persons . M. 3, F. 2.	5	Jubbulpore (4), Nimar (1).

Semitic Family.

Language		Persons	Total	Distribution
Arabic	...	Persons ... M. 58, F. 11.	69	Jubbulpore (2), Hoshangabad (1), Wardha (1), Chanda (2), Balaghat (4), Raipur (7), Bilaspur (2), Drug (1), Amraoti (5), Akola (25), Buldana (2), Yeotmal (6), Bastar (6), Surguja (4), Jashpur (1).

Other Non-Asiatic Languages—(E).

See column 107 of Table X.

Language		Persons	Total	Distribution
(1) French	...	Persons ... M. 12, F. 5.	17	Jubbulpore (1), Nimar (9), Chhindwara (2), Nagpur (2), Raipur (3).
(2) German	...	Persons ... M. 23, F. 7.	30	Nimar (16), Betul (3), Raipur (7), Drug (4).
(3) Portuguese	...	Persons ... M. 142, F. 48.	190	Saugor (4), Damoh (2), Jubbulpore (47), Mandla (1), Narsinghpur (5), Hoshangabad (7), Nimar (3), Betul (3), Wardha (2), Nagpur (44), Chanda (5), Bhandara (3), Balaghat (4), Raipur (12), Bilaspur (6), Amraoti (19), Akola (7), Buldana (9), Khairagarh (1), Kawardha (4), Korea (1), Udaipur (1).
(4) Italian	...	Persons ... M. 12, F. 9	21	Saugor (4), Nagpur (17).
(5) Swedish	...	Persons ... M. 16, F. 31.	47	Saugor (8), Betul (10), Chhindwara (29).
(6) Irish	...	Persons ... M. 10, F. 0.	10	Jubbulpore (10).
(7) Greek	...	Persons ... M. 3, F. 0.	3	Nimar (3).

TABLE XI.

Birthplace.

This Table is divided into two parts:—

Part A. contains the statistics of birthplace for the Province as a whole, for each District and for all the Feudatory States combined.

Part B. contains similar information for cities.

TABLE XI.—Birthplace.

District, State, Province or Country where born.	Total Central Provinces and Berar.			District where enumerated.					
				Saugor.			Damoh.		
	Persons.	Males.	Females.	Persons.	Males.	Females.	Persons.	Males.	Females.
1	2	3	4	5	6	7	8	9	10
Total Population ...	**16,033,310**	**7,984,022**	**8,049,288**	**541,410**	**276,233**	**265,177**	**333,047**	**168,060**	**164,987**
A.—Born in C. P. and Berar ...	**15,283,325**	**7,579,109**	**7,704,216**	**498,735**	**255,952**	**242,783**	**316,642**	**160,455**	**156,187**
(1)—British Districts and Berar.	**13,285,281**	**6,585,972**	**6,699,309**	**498,717**	**255,942**	**242,775**	**316,621**	**160,439**	**156,182**
Jubbulpore Division ...	*2,289,140*	*1,144,019*	*1,145,121*	*495,024*	*254,236*	*240,788*	*315,646*	*159,938*	*155,708*
Saugor	512,474	261,991	250,483	486,910	251,169	235,741	12,156	4,138	8,018
Damoh	317,369	161,616	155,753	7,042	2,490	4,552	298,379	153,779	144,600
Jubbulpore	688,009	342,751	345,258	893	487	406	4,988	1,958	3,030
Mandla	379,420	186,984	192,436	108	50	58	54	32	22
Seoni	391,868	190,677	201,191	71	40	31	69	31	38
Nerbudda Division	*1,969,343*	*984,327*	*985,016*	*3,190*	*1,428*	*1,762*	*778*	*378*	*400*
Narsinghpur	327,299	163,827	163,472	2,508	1,078	1,430	527	220	307
Hoshangabad	469,379	237,737	231,642	463	237	226	139	95	44
Nimar	298,283	152,535	145,748	72	35	37	44	28	16
Betul	385,732	189,896	195,836	61	35	26	28	15	13
Chhindwara	488,650	240,332	248,318	86	43	43	40	20	20
Nagpur Division	*3,138,153*	*1,556,490*	*1,581,663*	*294*	*165*	*129*	*118*	*72*	*46*
Wardha	418,143	209,829	208,314	15	12	3	10	7	3
Nagpur	824,512	411,455	413,057	200	109	91	54	34	20
Chanda	678,219	336,985	341,234	16	9	7	24	15	9
Bhandara	835,699	412,146	423,553	33	18	15	20	9	11
Balaghat	381,580	186,075	195,505	30	17	13	10	7	3
Chhattisgarh Division ...	*3,145,328*	*1,517,279*	*1,628,049*	*163*	*85*	*78*	*67*	*45*	*22*
Raipur	1,284,151	621,439	662,712	105	61	44	29	19	10
Bilaspur	1,071,298	515,488	555,810	53	21	32	34	23	11
Drug	789,879	389,352	400,527	5	3	2	4	3	1
Berar	**2,743,317**	**1,383,857**	**1,359,460**	**46**	**28**	**18**	**12**	**6**	**6**
Amraoti	805,666	406,780	398,886	17	8	9	8	4	4
Akola	729,575	367,490	362,085	20	15	5	2	1	1
Buldana	612,225	309,968	302,257	7	4	3	2	1	1
Yeotmal	505,851	209,619	296,232	2	1	1	...	...	...
(2)—Feudatory States ...	**1,998,044**	**993,137**	**1,004,907**	**18**	**10**	**8**	**21**	**16**	**5**
B.—Born in other parts of India	**743,067**	**399,009**	**344,058**	**42,222**	**19,915**	**22,307**	**16,383**	**7,589**	**8,794**
(1)—British Territory ...	**371,073**	**210,822**	**160,251**	**17,028**	**8,978**	**8,050**	**2,420**	**1,461**	**959**
(*a*) Provinces adjacent to C. P. and Berar—									
Bihar and Orissa (including Sambalpur)	123,076	64,951	58,125	104	63	41	44	30	14
Sambalpur District ...	*99,433*	*51,279*	*48,154*	*7*	*3*	*4*	*3*	*1*	*2*
United Provinces of Agra and Oudh.	130,799	82,777	48,022	14,572	7,021	7,551	2,126	1,269	857
Bombay	86,003	42,863	43,140	466	312	154	114	78	36
Madras	10,219	5,452	4,767	68	42	26	13	8	5
(*b*) Provinces remote from C. P. and Berar.									
Ajmer-Merwara	2,673	1,664	1,009	38	24	14	20	13	7
Andamans and Nicobars ...	19	7	12	...	...	...	...	...	...
Assam	151	72	79	...	...	...	...	...	...
Baluchistan	1,064	971	93	1	1	...	1	...	1
Bengal	5,792	3,374	2,418	80	47	33	33	13	20
Burma	236	143	93	7	3	4	2	1	1
Coorg	15	11	4	...	...	...	...	...	...
North-West Frontier Province	697	588	109	61	58	3	4	3	1
Punjab	10,329	7,949	2,380	1,631	1,407	224	63	46	17
(2)—States and Agencies ...	**371,994**	**188,187**	**183,807**	**25,194**	**10,937**	**14,257**	**13,963**	**6,128**	**7,835**
(*a*) States and Agencies adjacent to C. P. and Berar—									
Central India Agency (including Rewah, Panna, Bhopal and Indore)	198,560	95,464	103,096	23,692	10,006	13,686	13,488	5,874	7,614
Rewah	*83,046*	*46,529*	*41,517*	*145*	*99*	*46*	*144*	*89*	*55*
Panna	*20,202*	*8,809*	*11,393*	*2,302*	*817*	*1,485*	*7,246*	*2,815*	*4,431*
Bhopal	*31,812*	*12,321*	*19,491*	*7,778*	*3,092*	*4,686*	*204*	*81*	*123*
Indore	*18,969*	*8,592*	*10,377*	*188*	*96*	*92*	*20*	*6*	*14*
Hyderabad	92,731	40,701	52,030	138	92	46	15	9	6

PART A.—Districts and States.

DISTRICT, STATE, PROVINCE OR COUNTRY WHERE BORN.	TOTAL CENTRAL PROVINCES AND BERAR.			DISTRICT WHERE ENUMERATED.					
				SAUGOR.			DAMOH.		
	Persons.	Males.	Females.	Persons.	Males.	Females.	Persons.	Males.	Females.
1	2	3	4	5	6	7	8	9	10
B.—(2)—*concluded.*									
(*b*) States and Agencies remote from C. P. and Berar—									
Assam State	40	20	20	1	1	...	1	1	...
Baroda	409	258	151	20	14	6	3	3	...
Bihar and Orissa States ...	5,522	2,520	3,002	...	...	...	...	...	...
Bengal States	6	2	4	...	...	...	...	...	...
Bombay States	15,064	11,658	3,406	217	156	61	59	50	9
Kashmir	105	62	43	18	5	13	1	...	1
Madras States (including Cochin and Travancore).	31	20	11	...	...	...	...	...	...
Cochin	*12*	*9*	*3*	...	...	...	...	...	...
Travancore	*15*	*11*	*7*	...	...	...	...	...	...
Mysore	748	398	350	24	13	11	...	...	...
North-West Frontier Province States.	1	...	1	...	...	...	...	...	...
Punjab States	1,326	887	439	92	68	24	2	1	1
Rajputana Agency	55,861	35,068	20,793	866	503	363	340	164	176
Sikkim	2	1	1	...	...	...	...	...	...
United Provinces States ...	768	539	229	98	61	37	53	25	28
(3)—French and Portuguese Settlements.	**820**	**589**	**231**	**28**	**18**	**10**	**1**	**1**	...
C.—Born in other Asiatic countries	**1,533**	**1,301**	**232**	**294**	**256**	**38**	**3**	**3**	...
Afghanistan	1,064	1,007	57	222	214	8	1	1	...
Arabia	74	59	15	...	...	...	...	...	...
Bhotan	2	2	...	2	2	...	...	...	...
Ceylon	22	11	11	...	...	...	...	...	...
China	35	12	23	...	...	...	...	...	...
Hongkong	1	1	...	...	...	...	...	...	...
Japan	4	4	...	...	...	...	...	...	...
Nepal	253	156	97	70	40	30	1	1	...
Persia	61	39	22	...	...	...	...	...	...
Straits Settlements and Malaya	3	2	1	...	...	...	1	1	...
Turkey in Asia	8	7	1	...	...	...	...	...	...
Asia unspecified	6	1	5	...	...	...	...	...	...
D.—Born in Europe	**5,132**	**4,438**	**694**	**156**	**108**	**48**	**17**	**11**	**6**
United Kingdom	4,846	4,275	571	138	98	40	17	11	6
England and Wales ...	*4,442*	*3,968*	*474*	*114*	*83*	*31*	*17*	*11*	*6*
Scotland	*186*	*139*	*57*	*20*	*12*	*8*	...	...	...
Ireland	*208*	*168*	*40*	*4*	*3*	*1*	...	...	...
Channel Islands and Isle of Man.	*10*	*10*	...	...	...	...	...	...	...
Belgium	5	4	1	...	...	...	...	...	...
Denmark	2	2	...	...	...	...	...	...	...
France	101	29	72	3	...	3	...	...	...
Germany	74	47	27	4	...	4	...	...	...
Greece	10	10	...	...	...	...	...	...	...
Holland	2	2	...	1	1	...	...	...	...
Iceland	1	...	1	...	...	...	...	...	...
Italy	39	36	3	9	8	1	...	...	...
Malta	1	...	1	...	...	...	...	...	...
Norway	4	4	...	...	...	...	...	...	...
Sweden	35	19	16	1	1	...	...	...	...
Portugal	6	5	1	...	...	...	...	...	...
Russia	2	1	1	...	...	...	...	...	...
Spain	1	1	...	...	...	...	...	...	...
Switzerland	2	2	...	...	...	...	...	...	...
Europe unspecified	1	1	...	...	...	...	...	...	...
E.—Born in Africa	**46**	**38**	**8**	**2**	**1**	**1**	**1**	**1**	...
Egypt	3	2	1	...	...	...	1	1	...
Mauritius	2	...	2	...	...	...	...	...	...
Somaliland	1	1	...	...	...	...	...	...	...
Africa unspecified	40	35	5	2	1	1	...	...	...
F.—Born in America	**145**	**71**	**74**	...	...	...	**1**	**1**	...
Canada	19	13	6	...	...	...	...	...	—
United States	9	3	6	...	...	...	...	...	...
America unspecified	117	55	62	...	...	...	1	1	...
G.—Born in Australasia ...	**60**	**54**	**6**	**1**	**1**	...	...	...	...
Australia	50	47	3	...	...	...	...	...	...
Java	1	...	1	...	...	...	...	...	...
New Zealand	5	5	...	1	1	...	...	...	...
Philippines	8	1	2	...	...	...	...	...	...
Tasmania	1	1	...	...	...	...	...	...	...
H.—Born at Sea	**2**	**2**	...	...	...	...	...	...	...

TABLE XI.—Birthplace.

DISTRICT, STATE, PROVINCE OR COUNTRY WHERE BORN.	DISTRICT WHERE ENUMERATED.								
	JUBBULPORE.			MANDLA.			SEONI.		
	Persons.	Males.	Females.	Persons.	Males.	Females.	Persons.	Males.	Females.
11	12	13	14	15	16	17	18	19	20
Total Population ...	**745,892**	**373,173**	**372,719**	**405,234**	**200,872**	**204,362**	**395,481**	**192,642**	**202,839**
A.—Born in C. P. and Berar ...	**673,558**	**334,071**	**339,487**	**392,394**	**193,981**	**198,413**	**391,575**	**190,211**	**201,364**
(1)—British Districts and Berar	**673,422**	**334,009**	**339,413**	**392,255**	**193,930**	**198,325**	**391,561**	**190,204**	**201,357**
JUBBULPORE DIVISION ...	*664,045*	*329,724*	*334,321*	*381,982*	*188,667*	*193,315*	*368,101*	*179,960*	*188,141*
Saugor	3,297	1,725	1,572	562	326	236	438	234	204
Damoh	8,676	3,636	5,040	309	173	136	215	119	96
Jubbulpore	646,868	321,947	324,921	10,995	5,506	5,489	3,998	1,876	2,122
Mandla	3,467	1,564	1,903	363,265	179,603	183,662	5,095	2,196	2,899
Seoni	1,737	852	885	6,851	3,059	3,792	358,355	175,535	182,820
NERBUDDA DIVISION	*7,038*	*3,023*	*4,015*	*1,106*	*641*	*465*	*10,018*	*4,375*	*5,643*
Narsinghpur	5,296	2,058	3,238	556	309	247	3,687	1,697	1,990
Hoshangabad ...	1,108	660	538	179	111	68	140	71	69
Nimar	243	142	101	32	25	7	35	22	13
Betul	111	67	44	16	6	10	98	50	48
Chhindwara	190	96	94	323	190	133	6,058	2,535	3,523
NAGPUR DIVISION	*1,416*	*746*	*670*	*4,016*	*2,086*	*1,930*	*13,258*	*5,791*	*7,467*
Wardha	50	29	21	22	11	11	44	21	23
Nagpur	1,038	544	494	327	195	132	1,337	627	710
Chanda	96	46	50	61	38	23	35	20	15
Bhandara	100	55	45	167	96	71	2,481	1,153	1,328
Balaghat	132	72	60	3,439	1,746	1,693	9,361	3,970	5,391
CHHATTISGARH DIVISION ...	*687*	*372*	*315*	*5,081*	*2,492*	*2,589*	*124*	*49*	*75*
Raipur	371	207	164	500	258	242	80	38	51
Bilaspur	299	151	148	4,542	2,204	2,338	32	10	22
Drug	17	14	3	39	30	9	3	1	2
Berar	**236**	**144**	**92**	**70**	**44**	**26**	**60**	**29**	**31**
Amraoti	153	94	59	55	35	20	44	22	22
Akola	69	41	28	9	8	1	11	5	6
Buldana	8	5	3	1	1	...	2	1	1
Yeotmal	6	4	2	5	...	5	3	1	2
(2)—Feudatory States ...	**136**	**62**	**74**	**139**	**51**	**88**	**14**	**7**	**7**
B.—Born in other parts of India.	**69,204**	**36,243**	**32,961**	**12,795**	**6,859**	**5,936**	**3,849**	**2,380**	**1,469**
(1).—British Territory ...	**26,471**	**16,460**	**10,011**	**2,479**	**1,668**	**811**	**2,144**	**1,339**	**805**
(a) Provinces adjacent to C. P. and Berar—									
Bihar and Orissa (including Sambalpur)	825	504	321	115	64	51	40	25	15
Sambalpur District ...	*52*	*31*	*21*	*22*	*12*	*10*	*10*	*3*	*7*
United Provinces of Agra & Oudh	20,011	12,095	7,916	1,927	1,326	601	1,743	1,086	657
Bombay	1,350	774	576	82	45	37	87	44	43
Madras	887	500	387	44	29	15	53	34	19
(b) Provinces remote from C. P. and Berar—									
Ajmer-Merwara	75	50	25	4	3	1	6	4	2
Andamans and Nicobars ...	2	1	1	...	...	...	...	...	...
Assam	5	5	...	8	4	4	4	4	...
Baluchistan	2	2	...	13	13	...	19	19	...
Bengal	530	289	241	98	55	43	65	42	23
Burma	89	58	31	1	...	1	3	3	...
Coorg	10	8	2	...	...	...	...	...	...
North-West Frontier Province ...	149	113	36	12	10	2	4	4	...
Punjab	2,536	2,061	475	175	119	56	120	74	46
(2)—States and Agencies ...	**42,733**	**19,783**	**22,950**	**10,316**	**5,191**	**5,125**	**1,705**	**1,041**	**664**
(a) States and Agencies adjacent to C. P. and Berar—									
Central India Agency (including, Rewah, Panna, Bhopal and Indore)	39,574	17,631	21,943	9,677	4,739	4,938	1,225	717	508
Rewah	*22,701*	*10,181*	*12,520*	*8,943*	*4,304*	*4,639*	*603*	*376*	*227*
Panna	*6,346*	*2,646*	*3,700*	*276*	*155*	*121*	*192*	*103*	*89*
Bhopal	*422*	*251*	*171*	*78*	*48*	*30*	*54*	*31*	*23*
Indore	*355*	*261*	*94*	*40*	*13*	*27*	*13*	*6*	*7*
Hyderabad	662	319	343	33	24	9	17	13	4

PART A.—Districts and States.

District, State, Province or Country where born.	Jubbulpore. Persons.	Jubbulpore. Males.	Jubbulpore. Females.	Mandla. Persons.	Mandla. Males.	Mandla. Females.	Seoni. Persons.	Seoni. Males.	Seoni. Females.
11	12	13	14	15	16	17	18	19	20
B.—(2)—*concluded.*									
(*b*) States and Agencies remote from C. P. and Berar—									
Assam State	16	5	11	1	1	...	...	...	...
Baroda	45	35	10	6	5	1	1	...	1
Bihar and Orissa States ...	3	1	2	...	...	...	1	...	1
Bengal States	...	...	...	...	...	...	...	...	...
Bombay States	490	375	115	259	216	43	117	98	19
Kashmir	15	7	8	1	1	...	...	...	...
Madras States (including Cochin and Travancore).	8	5	3	...	...	—	...	...	...
Cochin	...	...	...	...	...	...	...	...	...
Travancore	*7*	*5*	*2*	...	...	—	...	...	...
Mysore	142	69	73	6	2	4	...	...	...
North-West Frontier Province States.	...	...	...	...	...	—	1	...	1
Punjab States	27	22	5	12	10	2	23	17	6
Rajputana Agency ...	1,596	1,195	401	308	185	123	313	190	123
Sikkim	...	...	...	...	...	...	...	...	...
United Provinces States ...	36	24	12	8	3	5	6	5	1
(3)—French and Portuguese Settlements.	119	95	24	5	5	...	1	1	...
C.—Born in other Asiatic countries	**114**	**107**	**7**	**11**	**10**	**1**	**44**	**42**	**2**
Afghanistan	89	84	5	5	5	—	37	37	...
Arabia	14	14	...	3	2	1	...	...	...
Bhotan	...	...	...	...	...	...	...	...	...
Ceylon	1	...	1	...	...	...	...	...	...
China	...	...	...	...	...	...	4	2	2
Hongkong	...	...	...	...	...	...	1	1	...
Japan	2	2	...	—	...	...	...	...	...
Nepal	5	5	...	3	3	...	1	1	...
Persia	3	2	1	...	...	...	1	1	...
Straits Settlements and Malaya	...	...	...	...	...	...	...	...	...
Turkey in Asia	...	...	...	...	...	...	...	...	...
Asia unspecified	...	...	...	...	...	...	...	...	...
D.—Born in Europe	**2,974**	**2,721**	**253**	**33**	**21**	**12**	**11**	**7**	**4**
United Kingdom	2,956	2,716	240	31	20	11	10	6	4
England and Wales ...	*2,771*	*2,566*	*205*	*27*	*17*	*10*	*7*	*6*	*1*
Scotland	*58*	*47*	*11*	*1*	*1*	...	*3*	...	*3*
Ireland	*127*	*103*	*24*	*3*	*2*	*1*	...	...	...
Channel Islands and Isle of Man.	...	...	...	...	...	...	...	...	...
Belgium	1	...	1	...	...	...	...	...	...
Denmark	...	—	...	...	...	...	...	...	...
France	8	...	8	1	1	...	1	1	...
Germany	8	5	3	1	...	1	...	...	...
Greece	...	...	...	...	...	...	...	...	...
Holland	...	...	...	...	...	...	...	...	...
Iceland	1	—	1	...	...	...	...	...	...
Italy	...	...	...	...	...	...	...	...	...
Malta	...	...	...	...	...	...	...	...	...
Norway	...	...	...	...	...	...	...	...	...
Sweden	...	...	...	...	...	...	...	...	...
Portugal	...	...	...	...	...	...	...	...	...
Russia	...	...	...	...	...	...	...	...	...
Spain	...	...	...	...	...	...	...	...	...
Switzerland	...	...	...	...	...	...	...	...	...
Europe unspecified ...	...	...	...	...	...	...	...	...	...
E.—Born in Africa	**3**	**1**	**2**	...	...	...	**1**	**1**	...
Egypt	...	...	...	...	...	...	...	...	...
Mauritius	2	...	2	...	...	...	...	...	...
Somaliland	1	1	...	...	...	...	...	...	...
Africa unspecified... ...	...	...	...	...	...	...	1	1	...
F.—Born in America	**25**	**17**	**8**	...	...	...	...	...	...
Canada	3	2	1	...	—	...	...	...	...
United States	...	...	...	...	...	...	...	...	...
America unspecified ...	22	15	7	...	...	...	...	...	...
G.—Born in Australasia ...	**14**	**13**	**1**	...	—	...	**1**	**1**	...
Australia	13	12	1	...	...	...	1	1	...
Java	...	...	...	...	...	...	...	...	...
New Zealand	...	...	...	...	...	...	...	...	...
Philippines	1	1	...	...	...	...	...	...	...
Tasmania	...	...	...	...	...	...	...	...	...
H.—Born at Sea	—	...	...	1	1	...	...	...	...

(Column groups: DISTRICT WHERE ENUMERATED — Jubbulpore, Mandla, Seoni.)

TABLE XI.—Birthplace.

DISTRICT, STATE, PROVINCE OR COUNTRY WHERE BORN.	DISTRICT WHERE ENUMERATED. Narsinghpur. Persons.	Narsinghpur. Males.	Narsinghpur. Females.	Hoshangabad. Persons.	Hoshangabad. Males.	Hoshangabad. Females.	Nimar. Persons.	Nimar. Males.	Nimar. Females.
21	22	23	24	25	26	27	28	29	30
Total Population ...	**325,677**	**161,795**	**163,882**	**457,395**	**230,632**	**226,763**	**391,071**	**200,765**	**190,306**
A.—Born in C. P. and Berar ...	**317,141**	**158,023**	**159,118**	**427,166**	**216,174**	**210,992**	**337,563**	**172,941**	**164,622**
(1)—British Districts and Berar	**317,119**	**158,011**	**159,108**	**425,256**	**215,575**	**209,681**	**335,554**	**171,927**	**163,627**
JUBBULPORE DIVISION	*9,692*	*3,894*	*5,798*	*2,546*	*1,309*	*1,237*	*951*	*505*	*446*
Saugor	3,465	1,361	2,104	1,190	589	601	398	208	190
Damoh	1,392	651	741	153	87	66	65	42	23
Jubbulpore	3,625	1,372	2,253	1,099	584	515	380	189	191
Mandla	89	44	45	45	19	26	24	18	6
Seoni	1,121	466	655	59	30	29	84	48	36
NERBUDDA DIVISION ...	*307,136*	*153,989*	*153,147*	*421,879*	*213,815*	*208,064*	*326,790*	*167,450*	*159,340*
Narsinghpur	301,546	152,023	149,523	4,842	1,816	3,026	1,173	688	485
Hoshangabad	4,370	1,406	2,964	411,274	209,264	202,010	34,173	17,571	16,602
Nimar	185	99	86	2,356	1,053	1,303	289,688	148,322	141,366
Betul	69	23	46	2,681	1,336	1,345	1,670	829	841
Chhindwara	966	438	528	726	346	380	86	40	46
NAGPUR DIVISION	*198*	*94*	*104*	*475*	*252*	*223*	*932*	*465*	*467*
Wardha	22	11	11	32	17	15	19	11	8
Nagpur	118	55	63	316	169	147	650	338	312
Chanda	12	5	7	34	16	18	46	17	29
Bhandara	25	13	12	58	31	27	204	93	111
Balaghat	21	10	11	35	19	16	13	6	7
CHHATTISGARH DIVISION ...	*64*	*22*	*42*	*119*	*73*	*46*	*90*	*49*	*41*
Raipur	48	19	29	63	40	23	70	38	32
Bilaspur	15	3	12	55	32	23	20	11	9
Drug	1	...	1	1	1	...	...	...	...
Berar	**29**	**12**	**17**	**228**	**117**	**111**	**6,791**	**3,458**	**3,333**
Amraoti	18	6	12	131	71	60	5,433	2,781	2,652
Akola	10	5	5	47	20	27	910	459	451
Buldana	1	1	...	45	23	22	434	210	224
Yeotmal	...	...	...	5	3	2	14	8	6
(2)—Feudatory States ...	**22**	**12**	**10**	**1,910**	**599**	**1,311**	**2,009**	**1,014**	**995**
B.—Born in other parts of India ...	**8,498**	**3,750**	**4,748**	**30,034**	**14,315**	**15,719**	**53,411**	**27,752**	**25,659**
(1)—British Territory ...	**2,004**	**1,258**	**746**	**8,217**	**5,247**	**2,970**	**29,110**	**15,346**	**13,764**
(a) Provinces adjacent to C. P. and Berar—									
Bihar and Orissa (including Sambalpur).	54	31	23	133	86	47	55	36	19
Sambalpur District ...	*9*	*4*	*5*	*10*	*6*	*4*	*7*	*6*	*1*
United Provinces of Agra & Oudh	1,634	1,039	595	6,061	3,873	2,188	8,115	5,270	2,845
Bombay	187	102	85	1,137	690	447	20,064	9,447	10,617
Madras	14	12	2	142	71	71	140	82	58
(b) Provinces remote from C. P. and Berar—									
Ajmer-Merwara	12	7	5	113	64	49	186	128	58
Andamans and Nicobars ...	...	...	...	...	...	...	...	...	...
Assam	...	...	...	12	1	11	8	3	5
Baluchistan	...	...	...	18	18	...	50	45	5
Bengal	28	14	14	117	58	59	95	54	41
Burma	...	...	...	2	1	1	3	1	2
Coorg	...	...	...	1	...	1	...	...	...
North-West Frontier Province ...	5	3	2	37	28	9	35	34	1
Punjab	70	50	20	444	357	87	359	246	113
(2)—States and Agencies ...	**6,494**	**2,492**	**4,002**	**21,817**	**9,068**	**12,749**	**24,301**	**12 406**	**11,895**
(a) States and Agencies adjacent to C. P. and Berar—									
Central India Agency (including Rewah, Panna, Bhopal and Indore)	6,098	2,258	3,840	18,464	6,881	11,583	19,107	9,101	10,006
Rewah	*367*	*225*	*142*	*367*	*124*	*243*	*338*	*190*	*148*
Panna	*382*	*212*	*170*	*298*	*179*	*119*	*200*	*120*	*80*
Bhopal	*4,435*	*1,322*	*3,113*	*12,949*	*4,432*	*8,517*	*3,372*	*1,711*	*1,661*
Indore	*74*	*33*	*41*	*3,431*	*1,341*	*2,090*	*13,311*	*6,004*	*7,307*
Hyderabad	45	37	8	109	58	51	634	334	300

PART A.—Districts and States.

District, State, Province or Country where born.	District where enumerated.								
	Narsinghpur.			Hoshangabad.			Nimar.		
	Persons.	Males.	Females.	Persons.	Males.	Females.	Persons.	Males.	Females.
21	22	23	24	25	26	27	28	29	30
B.—(2)—*concluded.*									
(*b*) States and Agencies remote from C. P. and Berar—									
Assam State	6	...	6	...	...	...	...	...	...
Baroda	1	...	1	15	10	5	44	29	15
Bihar and Orissa States	...	...	...	2	2	...	1	...	1
Bengal States	...	...	...	...	...	...	...	...	...
Bombay States	115	89	26	497	400	97	632	444	188
Kashmir	2	2	...	2	2	...	10	2	8
Madras States (including Cochin and Travancore).	1	1	...	...	...	...	...	...	...
Cochin	...	...	...	...	...	...	...	...	...
Travancore	*1*	*1*	...	...	...	...	...	...	...
Mysore	2	2	...	30	21	9	25	23	2
North-West Frontier Province States.	...	...	...	...	...	...	...	...	...
Punjab States	1	1	...	8	5	3	44	33	11
Rajputana Agency	212	94	118	2,605	1,631	974	3,763	2,412	1,351
Sikkim	...	...	...	...	...	...	1	1	...
United Provinces States	1	1	...	19	13	6	13	10	3
(3)—French and Portuguese Settlements	10	7	3	66	45	21	27	17	10
C.—Born in other Asiatic countries.	18	11	7	26	23	3	26	15	11
Afghanistan	11	4	7	11	11	...	9	9	...
Arabia	6	6	...	...	...	...	...	...	...
Bhotan	...	...	...	...	...	...	...	...	...
Ceylon	...	...	...	...	...	...	...	...	...
China	...	...	...	4	3	1	...	...	...
Hongkong	...	...	...	...	...	...	...	...	...
Japan	...	...	...	...	...	...	—	...	...
Nepal	1	1	—	11	9	2	17	6	11
Persia	—	...	...	...	...	...	...	...	...
Straits Settlements and Malaya	...	...	...	...	...	...	...	...	...
Turkey in Asia	...	...	...	...	...	...	...	...	...
Asia unspecified	...	...	...	...	...	...	...	...	...
D.—Born in Europe	18	10	8	156	111	45	62	51	11
United Kingdom	17	10	7	150	100	44	32	24	8
England and Wales	*12*	*7*	*5*	*129*	*98*	*36*	*25*	*19*	*6*
Scotland	*5*	*3*	*2*	*14*	*10*	*4*	*7*	*5*	*2*
Ireland	...	...	...	*7*	*3*	*4*	...	...	...
Channel Islands and Isle of Man.	...	...	...	...	—	...	...	...	...
Belgium	...	...	—	...	...	—	...	...	...
Denmark	—	...	...	...	...	...	...	...	...
France	1	...	1	8	2	1	9	6	3
Germany	...	...	...	1	1	...	19	19	...
Greece	...	...	...	...	...	...	2	2	...
Holland	...	...	...	...	...	...	—	...	...
Iceland	...	...	...	—	...	—	...	...	...
Italy	...	...	...	...	...	...	...	...	...
Malta	...	...	...	...	...	...	...	...	...
Norway	...	...	...	—	—	...	...	...	...
Sweden	...	...	...	—	...	...	...	...	...
Portugal	...	...	...	2	2	...	...	...	...
Russia	...	...	...	...	—	...	...	...	...
Spain	...	...	...	...	—	...	...	...	...
Switzerland	...	...	...	...	...	...	...	...	...
Europe unspecified	...	...	...	...	...	...	...	...	...
E.—Born in Africa	...	...	...	6	5	1	...	...	...
Egypt	...	...	...	...	...	...	...	...	...
Mauritius	...	...	...	...	...	...	...	...	...
Somaliland	...	...	...	...	...	...	...	...	...
Africa unspecified	...	...	...	6	5	1	...	...	...
F.—Born in America	2	1	1	6	3	3	7	4	3
Canada	...	...	...	1	1	...	...	...	...
United States	...	...	...	...	...	...	...	...	...
America unspecified	2	1	1	5	2	3	7	4	3
G.—Born in Australasia	...	...	...	1	1	...	2	2	...
Australia	...	...	...	1	1	...	2	2	...
Java	...	...	...	...	...	...	...	...	...
New Zealand	...	...	...	...	...	...	...	...	...
Philippines	...	...	...	...	...	...	...	...	...
Tasmania	...	...	...	—	...	...	...	...	...
H.—Born at Sea	...	...	...	...	...	...	...	—	...

TABLE XI.—Birthplace.

District, State, Province or Country where born.	District where enumerated. Betul. Persons.	Betul. Males.	Betul. Females.	Chhindwara. Persons.	Chhindwara. Males.	Chhindwara. Females.	Wardha. Persons.	Wardha. Males.	Wardha. Females.
31	32	33	34	35	36	37	38	39	40
Total Population	390,386	194,163	196,223	516,948	255,884	261,064	459,796	231,871	227,925
A.—Born in C. P. and Berar ...	379,238	186,894	192,344	508,048	250,049	257,999	447,272	223,651	223,621
(1)—British Districts and Berar	379,147	186,847	192,300	508,033	250,044	257,989	447,251	223,643	223,608
Jubbulpore Division... ...	*2,297*	*1,328*	*969*	*11,073*	*5,313*	*5,760*	*771*	*414*	*357*
Saugor	542	301	241	871	200	171	159	73	86
Damoh	94	61	33	106	54	52	29	14	15
Jubbulpore	1,461	886	575	3,262	2,070	1,192	273	152	121
Mandla	53	28	25	202	97	105	34	25	9
Seoni	147	52	95	7,132	2,892	4,240	276	150	126
Nerbudda Division	*371,077*	*182,820*	*188,257*	*481,047*	*238,688*	*242,359*	*2,097*	*1,040*	*1,057*
Narsinghpur	689	358	331	4,827	2,599	2,228	115	87	28
Hoshangabad	6,179	3,094	3,085	4,076	2,016	2,060	182	116	66
Nimar	527	252	275	39	26	13	157	96	61
Betul	360,709	177,866	182,843	6,803	3,041	3,762	762	360	402
Chhindwara	2,973	1,250	1,723	465,302	231,006	234,296	881	381	500
Nagpur Division	*1,161*	*664*	*597*	*13,264*	*4,939*	*8,325*	*406,944*	*207,118*	*199,826*
Wardha	168	87	81	470	197	273	353,808	182,440	171,368
Nagpur	836	407	429	11,602	4,184	7,418	28,160	12,417	15,743
Chanda	75	34	41	109	37	72	11,604	5,242	6,362
Bhandara	35	15	20	595	271	324	11,433	5,973	5,460
Balaghat	47	21	26	488	250	238	1,939	1,046	893
Chhattisgarh Division ...	*284*	*164*	*120*	*485*	*271*	*214*	*536*	*307*	*229*
Raipur	223	127	96	302	163	139	415	217	198
Bilaspur	42	27	15	73	52	21	103	78	25
Drug	19	10	9	110	56	54	18	12	6
Berar	4.328	1,971	2.357	2.164	833	1.331	36.903	14.764	22,139
Amraoti	4,231	1,925	2,306	2,107	807	1,300	22,681	8,878	13,803
Akola	67	28	39	23	10	13	717	294	423
Buldana	7	1	6	17	7	10	179	88	91
Yeotmal	23	17	6	17	9	8	13,326	5,504	7,822
(2)—Feudatory States ...	91	47	44	15	5	10	21	8	13
B.—Born in other parts of India ...	11,045	7,189	3,856	8,820	5,786	3,034	12,504	8,204	4,300
(1)—British Territory ...	4,690	3,082	1,608	3,080	2.054	1,026	5,825	3,743	2.082
(a) Provinces adjacent to C. P. and Berar—									
Bihar and Orissa (including Sambalpur)	104	52	52	79	51	28	76	50	26
Sambalpur District ...	*2*	*1*	*1*	*9*	*3*	*6*	*6*	*4*	*2*
United Provinces of Agra and Oudh.	3,127	2,069	1,058	2,372	1,572	800	3,435	2,348	1,087
Bombay	518	278	240	183	110	73	1,882	1,057	825
Madras	31	15	16	70	37	33	74	46	28
(b) Provinces remote from C. P. and Berar—									
Ajmer-Merwara	44	27	17	4	2	2	120	64	56
Andamans and Nicobars ...	...	...	...	...	...	...	...	...	...
Assam ...	1	1	...	2	1	1	2	1	1
Baluchistan	191	119	72	69	69	...	47	46	1
Bengal	82	56	26	90	54	36	58	31	27
Burma	2	1	1	2	2	...	1	1	...
Coorg	...	...	...	...	...	...	...	...	...
North-West Frontier Province	36	33	3	24	20	4	1	1	...
Punjab	554	431	122	185	136	49	129	98	31
(2.—States and Agencies ...	6,355	4,107	2,248	5,740	3,732	2,008	6,679	4,461	2,218
(a) States and Agencies adjacent to C. P. and Berar—									
Central India Agency (including Rewah, Panna, Bhopal and Indore)	3,846	2,365	1,481	4,030	2,506	1,524	2,788	1,958	830
Rewah	*2,313*	*1,469*	*844*	*2,716*	*1,776*	*940*	*2,034*	*1,477*	*557*
Panna	*133*	*78*	*55*	*306*	*182*	*124*	*303*	*207*	*96*
Bhopal	*531*	*290*	*241*	*562*	*306*	*256*	*48*	*25*	*23*
Indore	*130*	*83*	*47*	*20*	*9*	*11*	*103*	*60*	*43*
Hyderabad	91	50	41	74	37	37	486	288	198

PART A.—Districts and States.

DISTRICT, STATE, PROVINCE OR COUNTRY WHERE BORN.	DISTRICT WHERE ENUMERATED.								
	BETUL.			CHHINDWARA.			WARDHA.		
	Persons.	Males.	Females.	Persons.	Males.	Females.	Persons.	Males.	Females.
31	32	33	34	35	36	37	38	39	40
B.—(2)—*concluded.*									
(*b*) States and Agencies remote from C. P. and Berar—									
Assam State	...	...	...	...	...	...	...	...	...
Baroda	3	3	...	6	3	3	23	17	6
Bihar and Orissa States ...	...	...	...	...	...	...	1	...	1
Bengal States	...	...	...	...	...	...	...	...	...
Bombay States	843	640	203	1,040	793	247	611	453	158
Kashmir	11	11	...	2	1	1	5	3	2
Madras States (including Cochin and Travancore).	...	...	...	...	...	...	2	...	2
Cochin	...	...	...	...	...	...	*2*	...	*2*
Travancore	...	...	...	...	...	...	...	...	...
Mysore	36	18	18	43	34	9	8	6	2
North-West Frontier Province States.	...	...	...	...	...	...	...	...	...
Punjab States	99	97	2	15	7	8	5	4	1
Rajputana Agency	1,079	645	434	525	348	177	2,724	1,718	1,006
Sikkim	...	...	...	...	...	...	...	...	...
United Provinces States ...	340	272	68	3	1	2	13	8	5
(3)—French and Portuguese Settlements.	7	6	1	2	2	...	13	6	7
C.—Born in other Asiatic countries	71	67	4	34	17	17	7	5	2
Afghanistan	60	59	1	9	8	1	3	2	1
Arabia	1	1	...	2	1	1	1	1	...
Bhotan	...	...	...	...	...	...	...	...	...
Ceylon	...	...	...	...	...	...	...	...	...
China	...	...	...	...	...	...	...	...	...
Hongkong	...	...	...	...	...	...	...	...	...
Japan	...	...	...	...	...	...	...	...	...
Nepal	8	5	3	5	4	1	3	2	1
Persia	2	2	...	18	4	14	...	...	...
Straits Settlements and Malaya...	...	...	...	...	...	...	...	...	...
Turkey in Asia	...	...	...	...	...	...	...	...	...
Asia unspecified	...	...	...	...	...	...	...	...	...
D.—Born in Europe	32	13	19	45	31	14	13	11	2
United Kingdom	14	8	6	22	17	5	12	10	2
England and Wales ...	*12*	*7*	*5*	*20*	*15*	*5*	[illegible]	*7*	*1*
Scotland	...	...	...	...	...	...	*4*	*3*	*1*
Ireland	*2*	*1*	*1*	*2*	*2*	...	...	...	...
Channel Islands & Isle of Man	...	...	...	...	...	...	...	...	...
Belgium	...	...	...	...	...	...	1	1	...
Denmark	...	...	...	...	...	...	...	...	...
France	2	...	2	...	...	...	...	...	...
Germany	6	2	4	...	...	...	...	...	...
Greece	...	...	...	...	...	...	...	...	...
Holland	...	...	...	...	...	...	...	...	...
Iceland	...	...	...	...	...	...	...	...	...
Italy	...	...	...	...	...	...	...	...	...
Malta	...	...	...	...	...	...	...	...	...
Norway	...	...	...	...	...	...	...	...	...
Sweden	10	3	7	23	14	9	...	...	...
Portugal	...	...	...	...	...	...	...	...	...
Russia	...	...	...	...	...	...	...	...	...
Spain	...	...	...	...	...	...	...	...	...
Switzerland	...	...	...	...	...	...	...	...	...
Europe unspecified	...	...	...	...	...	...	...	...	...
E.—Born in Africa	...	...	...	1	1	...	...	...	...
Egypt	...	...	...	...	...	...	...	...	...
Mauritius	...	...	...	...	...	...	...	...	...
Somaliland	...	...	...	...	...	...	...	...	...
Africa unspecified	...	...	...	1	1	...	...	...	...
F.—Born in America	...	...	...	...	...	...	...	...	...
Canada	...	...	...	...	...	...	...	...	...
United States	...	...	...	...	...	...	...	...	...
America unspecified... ...	...	...	...	...	...	...	...	...	...
G.—Born in Australasia ...	...	...	...	...	...	...	...	...	...
Australia	...	...	...	...	...	...	...	...	...
Java	...	...	...	...	...	...	...	...	...
New Zealand	...	...	...	...	...	...	...	...	...
Philippines	...	...	...	...	...	...	...	...	...
Tasmania	...	...	...	...	...	...	...	...	...
H.—Born at Sea	...	...	...	...	...	...	...	...	...

TABLE XI.—Birthplace.

DISTRICT, STATE, PROVINCE OR COUNTRY WHERE BORN.	DISTRICT WHERE ENUMERATED.								
	NAGPUR.			CHANDA.			BHANDARA.		
	Persons.	Males.	Females.	Persons.	Males.	Females.	Persons.	Males.	Females.
41	42	43	44	45	46	47	48	49	50
Total Population ...	**809,901**	**408,843**	**401,058**	**677,544**	**337,540**	**340,004**	**773,677**	**380,014**	**393,663**
A.—Born in C. P. and Berar ...	**783,901**	**392,027**	**391,874**	**658,537**	**327,373**	**331,164**	**768,069**	**376,582**	**391,487**
(1)—British Districts and Berar ...	**783,700**	**391,928**	**391,772**	**656,009**	**326,007**	**330,002**	**765,560**	**375,461**	**390,099**
JUBBULPORE DIVISION ...	*6,571*	*3,524*	*3,047*	*806*	*449*	*357*	*2,788*	*1,336*	*1,452*
Saugor	468	294	174	103	57	46	103	62	41
Damoh	140	80	60	61	36	25	46	22	24
Jubbulpore	3,068	1,723	1,345	550	310	240	806	411	395
Mandla	91	51	40	14	7	7	59	24	35
Seoni	2,804	1,376	1,428	78	39	39	1,774	817	957
NERBUDDA DIVISION	*10,042*	*3,758*	*6,284*	*317*	*194*	*123*	*635*	*318*	*317*
Narsinghpur	319	185	134	61	46	15	169	96	73
Hoshangabad	524	305	219	51	35	16	66	34	32
Nimar	332	208	124	71	42	29	56	30	26
Betul	799	330	469	34	20	14	34	23	11
Chhindwara	8,068	2,730	5,338	100	51	49	310	135	175
NAGPUR DIVISION	*754,706*	*379,326*	*375,380*	*640,251*	*318,476*	*321,775*	*755,476*	*370,396*	*385,080*
Wardha	12,335	4,746	7,589	5,332	2,201	3,041	867	405	462
Nagpur	706,905	358,831	348,074	5,363	2,179	3,184	12,654	5,123	7,531
Chanda	6,926	2,876	4,050	621,486	310,675	310,811	6,421	2,258	4,163
Bhandara	24,423	10,846	13,577	7,810	3,201	4,609	719,887	356,926	362,961
Balaghat	4,117	2,027	2,090	260	130	130	15,647	5,684	9,963
CHHATTISGARH DIVISION ...	*2,115*	*1,070*	*1,045*	*5,631*	*3,022*	*2,609*	*3,965*	*2,008*	*1,957*
Raipur	1,680	833	847	2,345	1,238	1,107	3,253	1,644	1,609
Bilaspur	286	147	139	152	85	67	140	65	75
Drug	149	90	59	3,134	1,699	1,435	572	299	273
Berar	**10,266**	**4,250**	**6,016**	**9,004**	**3,866**	**5,138**	**2,696**	**1,403**	**1,293**
Amraoti	8,168	3,138	5,030	807	397	410	2,130	1,109	1,021
Akola	611	296	315	140	69	71	193	111	82
Buldana	389	241	148	56	30	26	32	18	14
Yeotmal	1,098	575	523	8,001	3,370	4,631	341	165	176
(2)—Feudatory States ...	**201**	**99**	**102**	**2,528**	**1,366**	**1,162**	**2,509**	**1,121**	**1,388**
B.—Born in other parts of India ...	**24,508**	**15,515**	**8,993**	**18,942**	**10,119**	**8,823**	**5,556**	**3,394**	**2,162**
(1)—British Territory ...	**16,945**	**10,610**	**6,335**	**4,335**	**2,917**	**1,418**	**2,658**	**1,607**	**1,051**
(a) Provinces adjacent to C. P. and Berar—									
Bihar and Orissa (including Sambalpur).	255	160	95	246	231	15	120	67	53
Sambalpur District ...	*86*	*50*	*36*	*16*	*5*	*5*	*58*	*21*	*37*
United Provinces of Agra and Oudh.	9,026	5,965	3,061	1,971	1,435	536	1,574	988	586
Bombay	4,592	2,646	1,946	1,045	608	437	421	211	210
Madras	1,509	827	682	506	350	156	157	85	72
(b) Provinces remote from C. P. and Berar—									
Ajmer-Merwara ...	212	126	86	65	39	26	24	17	7
Andamans and Nicobars ...	2	...	2	3	2	1	2	1	1
Assam	3	3	...	...	...	...	1	...	1
Baluchistan	35	34	1	70	69	1	14	14	...
Bengal	654	403	251	287	78	209	131	67	64
Burma	82	47	35	2	1	1	3	1	2
Coorg	...	...	...	...	...	...	...	...	...
North-West Frontier Province	48	44	4	1	1	...	10	10	...
Punjab	527	355	172	139	103	36	201	146	55
(2)—States and Agencies ...	**7,563**	**4,905**	**2,658**	**14,607**	**7,202**	**7,405**	**2,898**	**1,787**	**1,111**
(a) States and Agencies adjacent to C. P. and Berar—									
Central India Agencies (including Rewah, Panna, Bhopal and Indore)	3,100	2,070	1,030	1,497	1,094	403	1,054	619	435
Rewah	*1,875*	*1,249*	*626*	*1,198*	*965*	*233*	*704*	*418*	*286*
Panna	*298*	*221*	*77*	*122*	*28*	*94*	*186*	*110*	*76*
Bhopal	*137*	*74*	*63*	*24*	*19*	*5*	*37*	*15*	*22*
Indore	*209*	*125*	*84*	*35*	*16*	*19*	*31*	*10*	*21*
Hyderabad	1,311	740	571	11,616	5,129	6,487	119	69	50

PART A.—Districts and States.

DISTRICT, STATE, PROVINCE OR COUNTRY WHERE BORN.	DISTRICT WHERE ENUMERATED.								
	NAGPUR.			CHANDA.			BHANDARA.		
	Persons.	Males.	Females.	Persons.	Males.	Females.	Persons.	Males.	Females.
41	42	43	44	45	46	47	48	49	50
B.—(2)—*concluded.*									
(b) States and Agencies remote from C. P. and Berar—									
Assam State	12	9	3	...	...	...	...	...	...
Baroda	25	11	14	3	1	2	13	9	4
Bihar and Orissa States ...	3	1	2	...	...	...	1	1	...
Bengal States	...	...	...	...	...	...	...	...	...
Bombay States	1,052	819	233	908	631	277	314	239	75
Kashmir	3	3	...	2	2	...	1	...	1
Madras States (including Cochin and Travancore).	1	1	...	4	2	2	...	...	...
Cochin	...	...	...	*2*	*2*	...	...	...	...
Travancore	*1*	*1*	...	*2*	...	*2*	...	...	...
Mysore	198	100	98	58	17	41	20	10	10
North-West Frontier Province States.	...	...	...	...	...	...	...	...	...
Punjab States	40	22	18	2	2	...	191	115	76
Rajputana Agency	1,540	922	618	475	312	163	1,181	721	460
Sikkim	1	...	1	...	...	...	...	...	...
United Provinces States ...	10	7	3	31	3	28	...	...	—
(3)—French and Portuguese Settlements.	267	200	67	11	9	2	4	4	...
C.—Born in other Asiatic countries.	140	101	39	28	27	1	28	24	4
Afghanistan	66	64	2	25	24	1	21	21	...
Arabia	14	7	7	...	...	...	1	1	...
Bhotan	...	...	...	...	...	...	...	...	...
Ceylon	12	6	6	2	2	...	3	...	3
China	18	1	17	1	1	...	1	...	1
Hongkong	...	...	—	...	...	...	...	...	...
Japan	...	...	...	...	...	...	...	...	...
Nepal	10	9	1	...	...	...	2	2	...
Persia	11	11	...	...	...	...	...	...	...
Straits Settlements and Malaya	...	...	...	...	...	...	...	...	...
Turkey in Asia	3	2	1	...	...	...	...	...	...
Asia unspecified	6	1	5	...	...	...	...	...	...
D.—Born in Europe	1,282	1,139	143	33	18	15	24	14	10
United Kingdom	1,193	1,084	109	27	17	10	23	13	10
England and Wales ...	*1,091*	*1,001*	*90*	*23*	*13*	*10*	*16*	*11*	*5*
Scotland	*46*	*29*	*17*	*4*	*4*	...	*4*	*1*	*3*
Ireland	*46*	*44*	*2*	...	...	...	*3*	*1*	*2*
Channel Islands and Isle of Man	*10*	*10*	...	...	...	...	...	...	...
Belgium	1	1	...	...	...	...	1	1	...
Denmark	1	1	...	...	...	...	...	...	...
France	42	15	27	4	...	4	...	...	...
Germany	13	9	4	2	1	1	...	...	...
Greece	8	8	...	...	...	—	...	...	...
Holland	...	...	...	...	...	...	...	...	...
Iceland	...	...	...	...	...	...	...	...	...
Italy	14	13	1	...	...	...	...	...	...
Malta	...	...	...	...	...	...	...	...	...
Norway	4	4	...	...	...	...	...	...	...
Sweden	...	...	...	...	...	...	...	...	...
Portugal	3	2	1	...	...	...	...	...	...
Russia	1	...	1	...	...	...	...	...	...
Spain	1	1	...	...	...	—	...	...	...
Switzerland	1	1	...	...	...	...	...	...	...
Europe unspecified — ...	...	—	...	...	...	...	...	...	...
E.—Born in Africa	21	19	2	...	...	...	...	...	...
Egypt	1	...	1	...	...	...	...	...	...
Mauritius	...	...	...	...	...	...	...	...	...
Somaliland	...	...	...	...	...	...	...	...	...
Africa unspecified	20	19	1	...	...	...	...	...	...
F.—Born in America	20	13	7	4	3	1	...	...	...
Canada	1	1	...	2	2	...	...	...	...
United States	1	1	...	1	1	...	...	...	...
America unspecified... ...	18	11	7	1	...	1	...	...	...
G.—Born in Australasia ..	29	29	...	...	...	...	...	...	...
Australia	24	24	...	..	...	...	...	...	...
Java	...	...	...	...	...	...	...	...	...
New Zealand	4	4	...	...	...	...	...	...	...
Philippines	...	...	...	...	...	...	...	...	...
Tasmania	1	1	...	...	...	...	...	...	—
H.—Born at Sea	—	...	...	...	...	...	...	...	...

TABLE XI.—Birthplace.

DISTRICT, STATE, PROVINCE OR COUNTRY WHERE BORN.	DISTRICT WHERE ENUMERATED.								
	BALAGHAT.			RAIPUR.			BILASPUR.		
	Persons.	Males.	Females.	Persons.	Males.	Females.	Persons.	Males.	Females.
51	52	53	54	55	56	57	58	59	60
Total Population ...	**388,920**	**190,469**	**198,451**	**1,324,856**	**645,186**	**679,670**	**1,146,223**	**558,477**	**587,746**
A.—Born in C. P. and Berar ...	**384,681**	**187,697**	**196,984**	**1,283,314**	**622,603**	**660,711**	**1,049,009**	**505,927**	**543,082**
(1)—British Districts and Berar	**382,836**	**186,816**	**196,020**	**1,265,896**	**614,652**	**651,244**	**1,013,991**	**492,075**	**521,916**
JUBBULPORE DIVISION ...	*15,722*	*7,415*	*8,307*	*1,494*	*829*	*665*	*3,566*	*1,896*	*1,670*
Saugor	240	137	103	355	196	159	425	213	212
Damoh	66	32	34	177	96	81	154	84	70
Jubbulpore	991	532	459	689	383	306	1,514	847	667
Mandla	3,895	1,858	2,037	120	66	54	1,382	696	686
Seoni	10,530	4,856	5,674	153	88	65	91	56	35
NERBUDDA DIVISION ...	*642*	*356*	*286*	*638*	*355*	*283*	*444*	*257*	*187*
Narsinghpur	133	74	59	179	100	70	203	123	80
Hoshangabad	68	38	30	150	85	65	102	63	39
Nimar	31	20	11	143	73	70	40	24	16
Betul	16	8	8	43	24	19	47	26	21
Chhindwara	394	216	178	123	64	59	52	21	31
NAGPUR DIVISION	*359,399*	*175,749*	*183,650*	*4,953*	*2,463*	*2,490*	*2,017*	*1,044*	*973*
Wardha	144	75	69	129	61	68	80	38	42
Nagpur	1,665	830	835	2,939	1,414	1,525	1,236	628	608
Chanda	173	78	95	339	175	164	142	73	69
Bhandara	19,843	8,007	11,836	1,218	647	571	369	194	175
Balaghat	337,574	166,759	170,815	328	166	162	190	111	79
CHHATTISGARH DIVISION ...	*6,706*	*3,118*	*3,588*	*1,258,611*	*610,911*	*647,700*	*1,007,871*	*488,838*	519,033
Raipur	2,532	1,118	1,414	1,208,791	589,119	619,672	14,161	5,675	8,486
Bilaspur	1,005	478	527	23,746	10,515	13,231	985,974	480,064	505,910
Drug	3,169	1,522	1,647	26,074	11,277	14,797	7,736	3,099	4,637
Berar	**367**	**178**	**189**	**200**	**94**	**106**	**93**	**40**	**53**
Amraoti	227	109	118	100	46	54	37	18	19
Akola	66	38	28	74	37	37	20	10	10
Buldana	26	14	12	17	6	11	9	3	6
Yeotmal	48	17	31	9	5	4	27	9	18
(2)—Feudatory States ...	**1,845**	**881**	**964**	**17,418**	**7,951**	**9,467**	**35,018**	**13,852**	**21,166**
B.—Born in other parts of India ...	**4,194**	**2,739**	**1,455**	**41,391**	**22,462**	**18,929**	**97,093**	**52,464**	**44,629**
(1)—British Territory ...	**1,754**	**1,181**	**573**	**30,072**	**16,282**	**13,790**	**77,906**	**42,625**	**35,281**
(*a*) Provinces adjacent to C. P. and Berar—									
Bihar and Orissa (including Sambalpur).	76	48	28	22,248	11,154	11,094	68,437	36,747	31,690
Sambalpur District ...	*13*	*6*	*7*	*18,336*	*9,336*	*9,000*	*67,628*	*36,229*	*31,399*
United Provinces of Agra and Oudh.	1,150	793	357	5,937	3,890	2,047	8,039	5,003	3,036
Bombay	186	111	75	337	221	116	322	193	129
Madras	82	42	40	663	344	319	125	75	50
(*b*) Provinces remote from C. P. and Berar—									
Ajmer-Merwara	2	2	...	21	14	7	3	1	2
Andamans and Nicobars ...	...	...	...	3	1	2	...	—	...
Assam	8	5	3	15	8	7	64	27	37
Baluchistan	1	1	...	25	25	...	3	3	...
Bengal	86	56	30	306	203	103	398	218	180
Burma	3	...	3	1	...	1	4	2	2
Coorg	...	...	...	...	...	—	...	...	...
North-West Frontier Province	9	9	...	16	14	2	27	19	8
Punjab	151	114	37	500	408	92	484	337	147
(2)—States and Agencies ...	**2,440**	**1,558**	**882**	**11,319**	**6,180**	**5,139**	**19,187**	**9,839**	**9,348**
(*a*) States and Agencies adjacent to C. P. and Berar—									
Central India Agency (including Rewah, Panna, Bhopal and Indore)	1,369	782	587	1,304	890	414	17,124	8,438	8,686
Rewah	*1,036*	*580*	*456*	*846*	*603*	*243*	*16,346*	*8,006*	*8,340*
Panna	*71*	*41*	*30*	*138*	*82*	*56*	*204*	*98*	*106*
Bhopal	*70*	*32*	*38*	*49*	*33*	*16*	*53*	*31*	*22*
Indore	*15*	*9*	*6*	*54*	*28*	*26*	*47*	*26*	*21*
Hyderabad	45	31	14	272	150	122	42	26	16

PART A.—Districts and States.

DISTRICT, STATE, PROVINCE OR COUNTRY WHERE BORN.	DISTRICT WHERE ENUMERATED.								
	BALAGHAT.			RAIPUR.			BILASPUR.		
	Persons.	Males.	Females.	Persons.	Males.	Females.	Persons.	Males.	Females.
51	52	53	54	55	56	57	58	59	60
B.—(2)—(*concluded*).									
(*b*) States and Agencies remote from C. P. and Berar—									
Assam State	...	...	...	1	1	...	...	...	...
Baroda	...	...	...	10	9	1	14	11	3
Bihar and Orissa States ...	...	...	...	4,776	2,133	2,643	87	16	71
Bengal States	...	...	...	...	...	...	1	...	1
Bombay States	420	336	84	842	729	113	735	606	129
Kashmir	2	2	...	2	2	...	14	9	5
Madras States (including Cochin and Travancore) ...	...	...	...	2	1	1	6	6	...
Cochin	...	...	...	*2*	*1*	*1*	*2*	*2*	...
Travancore	...	...	...	...	...	...	*4*	*4*	...
Mysore	14	7	7	34	19	15	19	8	11
North-West Frontier Province States.	...	...	...	...	...	...	...	...	...
Punjab States	13	7	6	59	37	22	83	60	23
Rajputana Agency ...	485	302	183	3,976	2,180	1,796	985	628	357
Sikkim	...	...	...	...	...	...	...	...	...
United Provinces States ...	86	86	...	8	1	7	1	1	...
(3)—French and Portuguese Settlements.	6	5	1	33	28	5	76	30	46
C.—Born in other Asiatic countries.	9	8	1	97	92	5	60	48	12
Afghanistan	7	6	1	82	80	2	38	38	...
Arabia	1	1	...	2	2	...	1	1	...
Bhotan	...	...	...	...	...	...	...	...	...
Ceylon	...	...	...	...	...	...	...	...	...
China	...	...	...	...	...	...	2	...	2
Hongkong	...	...	...	...	...	...	...	...	...
Japan	...	...	...	...	...	...	...	...	...
Nepal	1	1	...	10	7	3	17	7	10
Persia	...	...	...	1	1	...	1	1	...
Straits Settlements and Malaya	...	...	...	...	...	...	1	1	...
Turkey in Asia	...	...	...	2	2	...	...	...	...
Asia unspecified	...	...	...	...	...	...	...	...	...
D.—Born in Europe	33	22	11	44	29	15	43	29	14
United Kingdom	30	19	11	28	17	11	35	23	12
England and Wales ...	*25*	*18*	*7*	*24*	*13*	*11*	*31*	*20*	*11*
Scotland	*3*	*1*	*2*	*4*	*4*	...	*1*	*1*	...
Ireland	*2*	...	*2*	...	...	...	*3*	*2*	*1*
Channel Islands and Isle of Man	...	...	...	...	...	...	...	...	...
Belgium	...	...	...	...	...	...	...	...	...
Denmark	...	...	...	...	...	...	1	1	...
France	...	...	...	...	...	...	...	...	...
Germany	...	...	...	5	1	4	6	4	2
Greece	...	...	...	...	...	...	...	...	...
Holland	...	...	...	...	...	...	...	...	...
Iceland	...	...	...	...	...	...	...	...	...
Italy	3	3	...	10	10	...	...	...	...
Malta	...	...	...	...	...	...	...	...	...
Norway	...	...	...	...	...	...	...	...	...
Sweden	...	...	...	1	1	...	...	...	...
Portugal	...	...	...	...	...	...	...	...	...
Russia	...	...	...	...	...	...	1	1	...
Spain	...	...	...	...	...	...	...	...	...
Switzerland	...	...	...	...	...	...	...	...	...
Europe unspecified	...	...	...	...	...	...	...	...	...
E.—Born in Africa	...	...	...	...	...	...	...	...	...
Egypt	...	...	...	...	...	...	...	...	...
Mauritius	...	...	...	...	...	...	...	...	...
Somaliland	...	...	...	...	...	...	...	...	...
Africa unspecified	...	...	...	...	...	...	...	...	...
F.—Born in America	1	1	...	9	...	9	17	8	9
Canada	1	1	...	...	...	...	7	3	4
United States	...	...	...	...	...	...	...	...	...
America unspecified ...	...	...	...	9	...	9	10	5	5
G.—Born in Australasia ...	2	2	...	1	...	1	1	1	...
Australia	2	2	...	...	...	...	1	1	...
Java	...	...	...	1	...	1	...	...	...
New Zealand	...	...	...	...	...	...	...	...	...
Philippines	...	...	...	...	...	...	...	...	...
Tasmania	...	...	...	...	...	...	...	...	...
H.—Born at Sea	...	...	...	...	...	...	...	...	...

TABLE XI.—Birthplace.

DISTRICT, STATE, PROVINCE OR COUNTRY WHERE BORN.	DISTRICT WHERE ENUMERATED. Drug. Persons.	Drug. Males.	Drug. Females.	Amraoti. Persons.	Amraoti. Males.	Amraoti. Females.	Akola. Persons.	Akola. Males.	Akola. Females.
61	62	63	64	65	66	67	68	69	70
Total Population ...	**775,688**	**373,159**	**402,529**	**875,904**	**447,216**	**428,688**	**788,863**	**400,893**	**387,970**
A.—Born in C. P. and Berar ...	**770,674**	**369,961**	**400,713**	**837,783**	**422,907**	**414,876**	**734,536**	**370,825**	**363,711**
(1)—British Districts and Berar	**731,671**	**354,209**	**377,462**	**837,714**	**422,869**	**414,845**	**734,500**	**370,812**	**363,688**
JUBBULPORE DIVISION ...	*669*	*364*	*305*	*1,218*	*704*	*514*	*737*	*484*	*253*
Saugor	183	107	76	382	213	169	99	52	47
Damoh	60	42	18	37	20	17	15	13	2
Jubbulpore	204	106	98	570	364	215	561	376	185
Mandla	139	57	82	31	14	17	7	6	1
Seoni	83	52	31	189	93	96	55	37	18
NERBUDDA DIVISION ...	*229*	*123*	*106*	*16,858*	*8,215*	*8,643*	*933*	*482*	*451*
Narsinghpur	89	49	40	128	65	63	45	26	19
Hoshangabad	60	32	28	1,728	895	833	347	202	145
Nimar	16	10	6	2,037	1,014	1,023	420	184	236
Betul	22	12	10	11,324	5,629	5,695	77	45	32
Chhindwara	42	20	22	1,641	612	1,029	44	25	19
NAGPUR DIVISION	*3,835*	*1,993*	*1,842*	*75,876*	*35,360*	*40,516*	*10,538*	*5,498*	*5,040*
Wardha	66	40	26	17,888	7,131	10,757	593	278	315
Nagpur	613	310	303	29,030	13,200	15,830	4,452	2,293	2,159
Chanda	1,524	767	757	1,857	950	907	357	199	158
Bhandara	718	428	290	24,734	12,857	11,877	4,467	2,372	2,095
Balaghat	914	448	466	2,367	1,222	1,145	669	356	313
CHHATTISGARH DIVISION ...	*726,879*	*351,697*	*375,182*	*352*	*212*	*140*	*149*	*98*	*51*
Raipur	23,051	8,452	14,599	224	135	89	74	36	38
Bilaspur	11,045	3,888	7,157	77	49	28	48	35	13
Drug	692,783	339,357	353,426	51	28	23	27	27	...
Berar	**59**	**32**	**27**	**743,410**	**378,378**	**365,032**	**722,143**	**364,250**	**357,893**
Amraoti	29	19	10	711,719	365,915	345,804	23,151	9,843	13,308
Akola	8	3	5	21,472	8,200	13,272	667,524	341,963	325,561
Buldana	4	2	2	1,515	740	775	20,609	7,795	12,814
Yeotmal	18	8	10	8,704	3,523	5,181	10,859	4,649	6,210
(2)—Feudatory States ...	**39,003**	**15,752**	**23,251**	**69**	**38**	**31**	**36**	**13**	**23**
B.—Born in other parts of India ...	**4,977**	**3,166**	**1,811**	**37,947**	**24,193**	**13,754**	**54,129**	**29,904**	**24,225**
(1)—British Territory ...	**2,495**	**1,748**	**747**	**18,418**	**11,845**	**6,573**	**22,966**	**13,523**	**9,443**
(a) Provinces adjacent to C. P. and Berar—									
Bihar and Orissa (including Sambalpur) ...	168	113	55	110	91	19	84	54	30
Sambalpur District ...	*51*	*27*	*24*	*17*	*13*	*4*	*28*	*5*	*23*
United Provinces of Agra and Oudh	1,853	1,302	551	9,831	7,120	2,711	5,989	4,251	1,738
Bombay	120	70	50	7,440	3,908	3,532	15,611	8,332	7,279
Madras	77	53	24	289	158	131	156	86	70
(b) Provinces remote from C. P. and Berar—									
Ajmer-Merwara	14	12	2	142	82	60	540	341	199
Andamans and Nicobars ...	...	...	...	4	1	3	3	1	2
Assam	7	2	5	2	2	...	4	...	4
Baluchistan	2	2	...	157	156	1	75	74	1
Bengal	73	53	20	87	46	41	151	116	35
Burma	2	2	...	10	8	2	8	6	2
Coorg	...	...	...	1	...	1	...	...	...
North-West Frontier Province	14	12	2	20	18	2	31	30	1
Punjab	165	127	38	325	255	70	314	232	82
(2)—States and Agencies ...	**2,482**	**1,418**	**1,064**	**19,529**	**12,348**	**7,181**	**31,163**	**16,381**	**14,782**
(a) States and Agencies adjacent to C. P. and Berar—									
Central India Agency (including Rewah, Panna, Bhopal and Indore)	894	347	547	6,252	4,032	2,220	1,916	1,314	602
Rewah	*308*	*221*	*87*	*3,590*	*2,488*	*1,102*	*1,102*	*825*	*277*
Panna	*45*	*28*	*17*	*775*	*440*	*335*	*100*	*70*	*30*
Bhopal	*82*	*18*	*64*	*483*	*283*	*200*	*128*	*62*	*66*
Indore	*25*	*14*	*11*	*349*	*185*	*164*	*158*	*76*	*82*
Hyderabad	31	18	13	3,096	1,653	1,443	18,659	7,807	10,852

PART A.—Districts and States.

DISTRICT, STATE, PROVINCE OR COUNTRY WHERE BORN.	DISTRICT WHERE ENUMERATED.								
	DRUG.			AMRAOTI.			AKOLA.		
	Persons.	Males.	Females.	Persons.	Males.	Females.	Persons.	Males.	Females.
61	62	63	64	65	66	67	68	69	70
B—(2)—*concluded.*									
(*b*) States and Agencies remote from C. P. and Berar—									
Assam State	...	...	...	...	...	...	2	2	...
Baroda	2	1	1	53	19	34	36	17	19
Bihar and Orissa States ...	14	8	6	...	...	...	...	...	...
Bengal States	1	...	1	...	...	...	...	...	...
Bombay States	238	191	47	1,239	965	274	1,823	1,437	386
Kashmir	2	2	...	6	2	4	2	2	...
Madras States (including Cochin and Travancore).	...	...	...	...	...	...	...	...	...
Cochin	...	...	...	...	...	...	...	...	...
Travancore	...	...	...	...	...	...	...	...	...
Mysore	4	4	...	23	12	11	13	10	3
North-West Frontier Province States.	...	...	...	...	...	...	...	...	...
Punjab States	15	6	9	74	46	28	59	36	23
Rajputana Agency	1,279	839	440	8,710	5,563	3,147	8,630	5,741	2,889
Sikkim	...	...	...	...	...	...	...	...	...
United Provinces States ...	2	2	...	8	4	4	4	1	3
(3)—**French and Portuguese Settlements.**	...	...	...	**68**	**52**	**16**	**19**	**14**	**5**
C.—Born in other Asiatic countries.	**22**	**22**	...	**93**	**84**	**9**	**164**	**144**	**20**
Afghanistan	...	...	...	62	61	1	130	115	15
Arabia	...	...	...	6	6	...	9	9	...
Bhotan	...	...	...	...	...	...	...	...	...
Ceylon	...	...	...	...	...	...	2	1	1
China	...	...	...	1	1	...	2	2	...
Hongkong	...	...	...	...	...	...	...	...	...
Japan	...	...	...	...	...	...	2	2	...
Nepal	22	22	...	11	8	3	7	5	2
Persia	...	...	...	12	7	5	12	10	2
Straits Settlements and Malaya	...		...	...	...	...	...	...	...
Turkey in Asia	...	...	...	1	1	...	...	...	...
Asia unspecified ...	...	...	...	...	...	...	...	...	...
D.—Born in Europe	**11**	**7**	**4**	**74**	**30**	**44**	**15**	**9**	**6**
United Kingdom ...	6	4	2	40	22	18	13	7	6
England and Wales ...	*6*	*4*	*2*	*33*	*18*	*15*	*10*	*5*	*5*
Scotland	...	...	...	*3*	*1*	*2*	*2*	*1*	*1*
Ireland	...	...	...	*4*	*3*	*1*	*1*	*1*	...
Channel Islands and Isle of Man.	...	...	...	...	...	...	...	...	...
Belgium	...	...	...	1	1	...	...	...	...
Denmark	...	...	...	...	...	...	...	...	...
France	...	...	...	27	4	23	...	...	...
Germany	5	3	2	2	1	1	...	...	...
Greece	...	...	...	...	...	...	...	...	...
Holland	...	...	...	...	...	...	...	...	...
Iceland	...	...	...	...	...	...	...	...	...
Italy	...	...	...	1	...	1	2	2	...
Malta	...	...	...	1	...	1	...	...	...
Norway	...	...	...	...	...	...	...	...	...
Sweden	...	...	...	...	...	...	...	...	...
Portugal	...	...	...	...	...	...	...	...	...
Russia	...	...	...	...	...	...	...	...	...
Spain	...	...	...	...	...	...	...	...	...
Switzerland	...	...	...	1	1	...	...	...	...
Europe unspecified ...	...	...	...	1	1	...	...	...	...
E.—Born in Africa	**1**	**1**	...	**2**	**1**	**1**	**3**	**3**	...
Egypt	...	...	...	...	...	...	1	1	...
Mauritius	...	...	...	...	...	...	...	...	...
Somaliland	...	...	...	...	...	...	...	...	...
Africa unspecified ...	1	1	...	2	1	1	2	2	...
F.—Born in America ...	**1**	**1**	...	**3**	...	**3**	**16**	**8**	**8**
Canada	1	1	...	...	...	...	...	...	...
United States	...	...	...	...	...	...	...	...	...
America unspecified ...	...	...	...	3	...	3	16	8	8
G.—Born in Australasia ...	**2**	**1**	**1**	**2**	**1**	**1**	...	...	...
Australia	2	1	1	2	1	1	...	...	...
Java	...	...	...	...	...	...	...	...	...
New Zealand	...	...	...	...	...	...	...	...	...
Philippines	...	...	...	...	...	...	...	...	...
Tasmania	...	...	...	...	...	...	...	...	...
H.—Born at Sea	...	...	...	...	...	...	...	...	...

TABLE XI.—Birthplace.

DISTRICT, STATE, PROVINCE OR COUNTRY WHERE BORN.	DISTRICT OR STATE WHERE ENUMERATED.								
	BULDANA.			YEOTMAL.			FEUDATORY STATES.		
	Persons.	Males.	Females.	Persons.	Males.	Females.	Persons.	Males.	Females.
71	72	73	74	75	76	77	78	79	80
Total Population ...	**669,182**	**337,179**	**332,003**	**723,213**	**365,326**	**357,887**	**2,117,002**	**1,053,630**	**1,063,372**
A.—Born in C. P. and Berar ...	**614,832**	**311,353**	**303,479**	**670,054**	**338,267**	**331,787**	**2,038,603**	**1,011,185**	**1,027,418**
(1)—British Districts and Berar	**614,545**	**311,101**	**303,444**	**670,007**	**338,256**	**331,751**	**143,916**	**61,215**	**82,701**
JUBBULPORE DIVISION ...	*175*	*107*	*68*	*318*	*183*	*135*	*2,939*	*1,431*	*1,508*
Saugor	87	48	39	74	33	41	458	240	212
Damoh	3	1	2	25	13	12	125	71	54
Jubbulpore	74	51	23	190	128	62	941	493	448
Mandla	1	1	...	12	1	11	1,233	527	706
Seoni	10	6	4	17	8	9	182	94	88
NERBUDDA DIVISION ...	*1,539*	*741*	*798*	*399*	*202*	*197*	*4,611*	*1,679*	*2,832*
Narsinghpur	61	38	23	15	12	3	131	71	60
Hoshangabad	187	105	82	59	25	34	3,064	1,277	2,387
Nimar	1,244	581	663	99	56	43	416	193	223
Betul	6	4	2	72	36	36	250	111	139
Chhindwara	41	13	28	154	73	81	50	27	23
NAGPUR DIVISION ...	*1,249*	*636*	*613*	*76,823*	*37,658*	*39,164*	*10,955*	*6,599*	*5,356*
Wardha	104	45	59	25,805	11,825	14,040	80	51	29
Nagpur	778	377	401	12,420	6,247	6,179	1,813	944	869
Chanda	42	25	17	23,752	11,871	11,881	3,088	1,559	1,529
Bhandara	285	167	118	12,912	6,743	6,169	3,882	2,031	1,851
Balaghat	40	22	18	1,807	972	805	2,092	1,014	1,078
CHHATTISGARH DIVISION ...	*34*	*18*	*16*	*149*	*58*	*91*	*135,166*	*62,300*	*72,866*
Raipur	28	10	12	113	39	74	25,684	11,947	13,737
Bilaspur	2	1	1	36	19	17	43,519	17,530	25,989
Drug	4	1	3	...	...	...	55,963	22,823	33,140
Berar	**611,548**	**309,599**	**301,949**	**592,319**	**300,155**	**292,164**	**345**	**206**	**139**
Amraoti	2,396	1,080	1,316	21,734	10,300	11,434	290	175	115
Akola	21,524	8,297	13,227	16,046	7,572	8,474	12	8	4
Buldana	587,280	300,053	287,227	1,575	721	854	10	3	7
Yeotmal	348	169	179	552,964	281,562	271,402	33	20	13
(2)—Feudatory States ...	**287**	**252**	**35**	**47**	**11**	**36**	**1,894,687**	**949,970**	**944,717**
B.—Born in other parts of India ...	**54,237**	**25,732**	**28,505**	**53,074**	**26,994**	**26,080**	**78,254**	**42,345**	**35,909**
(1)—British Territory ...	**24,247**	**11,762**	**12,485**	**15,377**	**8,832**	**6,545**	**50,432**	**27,254**	**23,178**
(a) Provinces adjacent to C. P. and Berar—									
Bihar and Orissa (including Sambalpur).	23	19	4	389	315	74	29,291	14,960	14,331
Sambalpur District ...	*1*	*1*	...	*23*	*3*	*20*	*13,045*	*5,512*	*7,533*
United Provinces of Agra and Oudh.	2,512	1,905	607	5,101	3,503	1,598	12,693	7,654	5,039
Bombay	20,511	9,015	11,496	8,987	4,395	4,592	361	216	145
Madras	100	57	43	157	86	71	4,862	2,413	2,449
(b) Provinces remote from C. P. and Berar—									
Ajmere-Merwara	741	470	271	258	157	101	29	17	12
Andamans and Nicobars ...	...	...	...	...	...	...	...	...	...
Assam	...	...	...	...	...	...	5	5	...
Baluchistan	140	135	5	131	126	5	...	...	...
Bengal	26	13	13	65	24	41	2,352	1,384	868
Burma	2	1	1	...	...	...	7	4	3
Coorg	...	...	...	...	...	...	3	3	...
North-West Frontier Province ...	26	25	1	47	37	10	80	62	18
Punjab	166	122	44	242	189	53	849	536	313
(2)—States and Agencies ...	**29,990**	**13,970**	**16,020**	**37,697**	**18,162**	**19,535**	**27,822**	**15,091**	**12,731**
(a) States and Agencies adjacent to C. P. and Berar—									
Central India Agency (including Rewah, Panna, Bhopal & Indore).	583	361	222	635	439	196	20,843	11,042	9,801
Rewah	*117*	*89*	*28*	*268*	*225*	*43*	*20,005*	*10,553*	*9,452*
Panna	*13*	*8*	*5*	*115*	*68*	*47*	*158*	*99*	*54*
Bhopal	*56*	*37*	*19*	*46*	*28*	*18*	*214*	*100*	*114*
Indore	*128*	*58*	*70*	*89*	*39*	*50*	*142*	*91*	*51*
Hyderabad	21,632	8,541	13,091	31,651	14,140	17,511	1,953	1,136	817

PART A.—Districts and States.

DISTRICT, STATE, PROVINCE OR COUNTRY WHERE BORN.	DISTRICT OR STATE WHERE ENUMERATED.								
	BULDANA.			YEOTMAL.			FEUDATORY STATES.		
	Persons.	Males.	Females.	Persons.	Males.	Females.	Persons.	Males.	Females.
71	72	73	74	75	76	77	78	79	80
B.—(2)—*concluded.*									
(*b*) States and Agencies remote from C. P. and Berar—									
Assam State	...	...	...	...	...	...	...	...	...
Baroda	23	17	6	29	23	6	34	21	13
Bihar and Orissa	...	...	...	...	...	...	633	358	275
Bengal States	...	...	...	...	...	...	4	2	2
Bombay States	815	638	177	1,440	1,050	390	349	294	55
Kashmir	...	...	...	2	2	...	2	2	...
Madras States (including Cochin and Travancore).	4	4	...	...	...	...	3	...	3
Cochin	*4*	*4*	...	...	...	...	...	...	...
Travancore	...	...	...	...	...	...	*3*	...	*3*
Mysore	14	5	9	3	1	2	32	17	15
North-West Frontier Province States.	...	...	...	...	...	...	...	...	...
Punjab States	18	11	7	48	32	16	396	248	148
Rajputana Agency	6,867	4,366	2,501	3,872	2,463	1,409	3,530	1,946	1,584
Sikkim	...	...	...	...	...	...	...	...	...
United Provinces States ...	...	...	...	6	1	5	22	10	12
(3)—French and Portuguese Settlements.	**34**	**27**	**7**	**2**	**2**	...	**21**	**15**	**6**
C.—Born in other Asiatic countries.	**81**	**72**	**9**	**61**	**53**	**8**	**102**	**70**	**32**
Afghanistan	63	58	5	53	49	4	60	57	3
Arabia	3	2	1	6	3	3	4	2	2
Bhotan	...	...	...	...	...	...	...	...	...
Ceylon	...	...	...	...	...	...	2	2	...
China	2	2	...	...	...	...	...	...	...
Hongkong	...	...	...	...	...	...	...	...	...
Japan	...	...	...	...	...	...	...	...	...
Nepal	11	8	3	2	1	1	35	9	26
Persia	...	...	...	...	...	...	...	...	...
Straits Settlements and Malaya	...	...	...	...	...	...	1	...	1
Turkey in Asia	2	2	...	...	...	...	...	...	...
Asia unspecified	...	...	...	...	...	...	...	...	...
D.—Born in Europe	**16**	**13**	**3**	**8**	**8**	...	**32**	**25**	**7**
United Kingdom	14	12	2	7	7	...	31	24	7
England and Wales ...	*11*	*10*	*1*	*6*	*6*	...	*25*	*19*	*6*
Scotland	*1*	...	*1*	*1*	*1*	...	*5*	*5*	...
Ireland	*2*	*2*	...	*1*	*1*	...	*1*	...	*1*
Channel Islands and Isle of Man.	...	...	...	...	...	...	...	...	...
Belgium	...	...	...	...	...	...	...	...	...
Denmark	...	...	...	...	...	...	...	...	...
France	...	...	...	...	...	...	...	...	...
Germany	1	...	1	1	1	...	...	...	...
Greece	...	...	...	...	...	...	...	...	...
Holland	...	...	...	...	...	...	1	1	...
Iceland	...	...	...	...	...	...	...	...	...
Italy	...	...	...	...	...	...	...	...	...
Malta	...	...	...	...	...	...	...	...	...
Norway	...	...	...	...	...	...	...	...	...
Sweden	...	...	...	...	...	...	...	...	...
Portugal	1	1	...	...	...	...	...	...	...
Russia	...	...	...	...	...	...	...	...	...
Spain	...	...	...	...	...	...	...	...	...
Switzerland	...	...	...	...	...	...	...	...	...
Europe unspecified ...	...	...	...	...	...	...	...	...	...
E.—Born in Africa	**1**	**1**	...	...	...	...	**4**	**3**	**1**
Egypt	...	...	...	...	...	...	...	...	...
Mauritius	...	...	...	...	...	...	...	...	...
Somaliland	...	...	...	...	...	...	...	...	...
Africa unspecified... ...	1	1	...	...	...	...	4	3	1
F.—Born in America	**14**	**7**	**7**	**14**	**4**	**10**	**5**	...	**5**
Canada	3	2	1	...	...	...	...	...	...
United States	...	...	...	7	1	6	...	...	...
America unspecified ...	11	5	6	7	3	4	5	...	5
G.—Born in Australasia ...	**1**	**1**	...	**2**	...	**2**	**1**	**1**	...
Australia	1	1	...	...	...	...	1	1	...
Java	...	...	...	...	...	...	...	...	...
New Zealand	...	...	...	...	...	...	...	...	...
Philippines	...	...	...	2	...	2	...	...	...
Tasmania	...	...	...	...	...	...	...	...	...
H.—Born at Sea	...	...	...	...	...	...	**1**	**1**	...

TABLE XI.—Birthplace.

DISTRICT, STATE, PROVINCE OR COUNTRY WHERE BORN.	TOTAL CENTRAL PROVINCES AND BERAR.			CITY WHERE ENUMERATED. JUBBULPORE.			NAGPUR.		
	Persons.	Males.	Females.	Persons.	Males.	Females.	Persons.	Males.	Females.
1	2	3	4	5	6	7	8	9	10
Total City Population ...	**202,066**	**109.731**	**92,335**	**100,651**	**56.035**	**44.616**	**101,415**	**53,696**	**47.719**
A.—Born in C. P. and Berar ...	**155.714**	**79.923**	**75.791**	**67,493**	**34,751**	**32.742**	**88,221**	**45.172**	**43,049**
(1)—British Districts and Berar	**155.473**	**79.811**	**75,662**	**67.370**	**34.696**	**32.674**	**88,103**	**45.115**	**42.988**
JUBBULPORE DIVISION ...	*64,037*	*32,946*	*31,091*	*62,295*	*31,963*	*30,332*	*1,742*	*983*	*759*
Saugor	2,734	1,489	1,245	2.440	1,294	1,146	294	195	90
Damoh	1,254	665	589	1,176	616	560	78	49	29
Jubbulpore	58,466	29,900	28,566	57,556	29,397	28,159	910	503	407
Mandla	519	272	247	470	243	227	49	29	20
Seoni	1,064	620	444	653	413	240	411	207	204
NERBUDDA DIVISION ...	*4,513*	*2,482*	*2,031*	*3,190*	*1,714*	*1,476*	*1,323*	*768*	*555*
Narsinghpur	1,971	1,037	934	1,801	931	870	170	106	64
Hoshangabad	1,233	709	524	932	519	413	301	190	111
Nimar	453	286	167	210	128	82	243	158	85
Betul	206	136	70	98	59	39	108	77	31
Chhindwara	650	314	336	149	77	72	501	237	264
NAGPUR DIVISION	*83,476*	*42,389*	*41,087*	*1,196*	*621*	*575*	*82,280*	*41,765*	*40,512*
Wardha	1,100	519	581	39	19	20	1,061	500	561
Nagpur	73,785	37,449	36,336	882	454	428	72,903	36,995	35,908
Chanda	1,133	629	504	84	42	42	1,049	587	462
Bhandara	6,021	3,037	2,984	77	45	32	5,944	2,992	2,952
Balaghat	1,437	755	682	114	61	53	1,323	694	629
CHHATTISGARH DIVISION ...	*1,377*	*724*	*653*	*497*	*275*	*222*	*880*	*449*	*431*
Raipur	956	486	470	267	150	117	689	336	353
Bilaspur	375	206	169	216	112	104	159	94	65
Drug	46	32	14	14	13	1	32	19	13
Berar	**2.070**	**1,270**	**800**	**192**	**123**	**69**	**1,878**	**1.147**	**731**
Amraoti	1,148	686	462	131	81	50	1,017	605	412
Akola	361	193	168	50	34	16	311	159	152
Buldana	270	199	71	5	4	1	265	195	70
Yeotmal	291	192	99	6	4	2	285	188	97
(2)—Feudatory States ...	**241**	**112**	**129**	**123**	**55**	**68**	**118**	**57**	**61**
B.—Born in other parts of India ...	**42.912**	**26.758**	**16.154**	**30,071**	**18.456**	**11.615**	**12,841**	**8.302**	**4.539**
(1)—British Territory ...	**29.551**	**18,786**	**10.765**	**19.603**	**12,345**	**7.258**	**9.948**	**6,441**	**3.507**
Bihar and Orissa	748	424	324	638	346	292	110	78	32
Bengal	953	577	376	440	242	198	513	335	178
United Provinces of Agra and Oudh.	18,878	11,903	6,975	13,881	8,506	5,375	4,997	3,397	1,600
Bombay (including Aden) ...	4,200	2,524	1,676	1,348	775	573	2,852	1,749	1,103
Madras	1,773	986	787	793	453	340	980	533	447
Ajmer-Merwara	143	99	44	71	47	24	72	52	20
Andamans	2	1	1	2	1	1	...	...	...
Baluchistan	11	10	1	2	2	...	9	8	1
Burma	114	88	26	69	55	14	45	33	12
Coorg	10	8	2	10	8	2	...	...	...
Assam	17	12	5	11	7	4	6	5	1
North-West Frontier Province	141	104	37	126	90	36	15	14	1
Punjab	2,561	2,050	511	2,212	1,813	399	349	237	112

PART B.—Cities.

District, State, Province or Country where born.	Total Central Provinces and Berar.			City where enumerated.					
				Jubbulpore.			Nagpur.		
	Persons.	Males.	Females.	Persons	Males.	Females.	Persons.	Males.	Females.
1	2	3	4	5	6	7	8	9	10
B.—*concluded.*									
(2)—Feudatory States ...	**13,361**	**7,972**	**5,389**	**10,468**	**6,111**	**4,357**	**2,893**	**1,861**	**1,032**
Central India Agency ...	8,971	5,166	3,805	7,942	4,451	3,491	1,029	715	314
Hyderabad	1,409	732	677	645	309	336	764	423	341
Baroda	63	41	22	38	30	8	25	11	14
Bihar and Orissa States ...	3	2	1	1	1	...	2	1	1
Bengal States	...	...	...	...	...	...	...	...	...
Bombay States	172	124	48	82	46	36	90	78	12
Assam State	28	14	14	16	5	11	12	9	3
Kashmir	12	5	7	11	4	7	1	1	...
Madras States (including Travancore).	4	3	1	3	2	1	1	1	...
Travancore	*4*	*3*	*1*	*3*	*2*	*1*	*1*	*1*	...
Mysore	299	154	145	142	69	73	157	85	72
Punjab States	31	24	7	24	19	5	7	5	2
Rajputana Agency	2,013	1,437	576	1,415	1,061	354	598	376	222
Sikkim	1	...	1	...	...	...	1	...	1
United Provinces States ...	43	29	14	33	22	11	10	7	3
(3)—French and Portuguese Settlements	**312**	**241**	**71**	**116**	**92**	**24**	**196**	**149**	**47**
C.—Born in other Asiatic countries	**140**	**121**	**19**	**99**	**93**	**6**	**41**	**28**	**13**
Afghanistan	95	89	6	78	74	4	17	15	2
Arabia	23	16	7	13	13	...	10	3	7
Ceylon	8	4	4	1	...	1	7	4	3
Japan	2	2	...	2	2	...	...	...	...
Nepal	7	7	...	3	3	...	4	4	...
Persia	2	1	1	2	1	1	...	...	...
Turkey in Asia	2	1	1	...	...	...	2	1	1
Asia unspecified	1	1	...	...	...	...	1	1	...
D.—Born in Europe	**3,250**	**2,894**	**356**	**2,950**	**2,707**	**243**	**300**	**187**	**113**
United Kingdom	3,184	2,872	312	2,933	2,702	231	251	170	81
England and Wales ...	*2,970*	*2,710*	*260*	*2,756*	*2,558*	*198*	*214*	*152*	*62*
Scotland	*81*	*54*	*27*	*56*	*46*	*10*	*25*	*8*	*17*
Ireland	*133*	*108*	*25*	*121*	*98*	*23*	*12*	*10*	*2*
Belgium	1	...	1	1	...	1	...	...	...
France	44	11	33	8	...	8	36	11	25
Germany	14	7	7	8	5	3	6	2	4
Italy	2	1	1	...	...	...	2	1	1
Portugal	3	2	1	...	...	...	3	2	1
Russia	1	...	1	...	...	...	1	...	1
Spain	1	1	...	...	...	...	1	1	...
E.—Born in Africa	**4**	**1**	**3**	**1**	...	**1**	**3**	**1**	**2**
Egypt	1	...	1	...	...	...	1	...	1
Mauritius	1	...	1	1	...	1	...	...	...
Africa unspecified	2	1	1	...	...	...	2	1	1
F.—Born in America	**31**	**20**	**11**	**24**	**16**	**8**	**7**	**4**	**3**
Canada	4	3	1	3	2	1	1	1	...
America unspecified... ...	27	17	10	21	14	7	6	3	3
G.—Born in Australasia ...	**15**	**14**	**1**	**13**	**12**	**1**	**2**	**2**	...
Australia	15	14	1	13	12	1	2	2	...

TABLE XII.

Infirmities.

This table is divided into two parts. Part I shows the distribution of the persons afflicted according to age, and Part II their distribution according to locality. No cases of double infirmities were recorded.

TABLE XII.—Infirmities. Part I.—Distribution by Age.

Age.	Population afflicted.			Insane.			Deaf-Mutes.			Blind.			Lepers		
	Persons.	Males.	Females.	Persons.	Males.	Females.	Persons.	Males.	Females.	Persons.	Males.	Females.	Persons.	Males.	Females.
1	2	3	4	5	6	7	8	9	10	11	12	13	14	15	16
0—1 ...	188	111	77	...	...	...	5	2	3	183	109	74	...	...	...
1—2 ...	148	97	51	1	...	1	3	1	2	143	95	48	1	1	...
2—3 ...	269	148	121	4	3	1	30	17	13	229	126	103	6	2	4
3—4 ...	440	253	187	10	6	4	125	61	64	287	175	112	18	11	7
4—5 ...	496	287	209	15	8	7	189	117	72	281	157	124	11	5	6
Total 0—5 ...	*1,541*	*896*	*645*	*30*	*17*	*13*	*353*	*198*	*154*	*1,123*	*662*	*461*	*36*	*19*	*17*
5—10 ...	2,861	1,704	1,157	166	92	74	1,221	745	476	1,407	845	562	67	22	45
10—15 ...	2,746	1,609	1,137	272	167	105	1,118	659	459	1,147	684	463	209	99	110
15—20 ...	2,475	1,359	1,116	298	170	128	839	490	349	1,081	569	512	287	160	127
20—25 ...	3,220	1,754	1,466	288	183	105	920	505	415	1,535	796	739	477	270	207
25—30 ...	3,731	2,025	1,706	302	216	86	784	459	325	1,920	890	1,030	715	460	255
30—35 ...	4,364	2,304	2,060	286	193	93	757	422	335	2,406	1,097	1,309	915	592	323
35—40 ...	3,229	1,732	1,497	188	118	70	391	252	139	1,856	848	1,008	794	514	280
40—45 ...	4,475	2,320	2,155	218	137	81	398	228	170	2,813	1,240	1,573	1,046	715	331
45—50 ...	2,793	1,409	1,384	123	86	37	214	125	89	1,769	721	1,048	687	477	210
50—55 ...	4,696	2,080	2,616	129	78	51	206	106	100	3,487	1,334	2,153	874	562	312
55—60 ...	1,784	792	992	40	30	10	66	36	30	1,388	538	850	290	188	102
60—65 ...	5,646	2,034	3,612	76	35	41	122	63	59	4,871	1,590	3,281	577	346	231
65—70 ...	1,374	543	831	23	15	8	38	22	16	1,212	444	768	101	62	39
70 and over	5,438	1,792	3,646	27	14	13	66	38	28	5,113	1,593	3,520	232	147	85
Total ...	*50,403*	*24,383*	*26,020*	*2,466*	*1,551*	*915*	*7,502*	*4,348*	*3,154*	*33,128*	*13,851*	*19,277*	*7,307*	*4,633*	*2,674*

TABLE XII.—Infirmities. Part II.—Distribution by Districts.

Serial number.	DISTRICT OR STATE.	Population Afflicted. Persons.	Population Afflicted. Males.	Population Afflicted. Females.	Insane. Persons.	Insane. Males.	Insane. Females.	Deaf-Mutes. Persons.	Deaf-Mutes. Males.	Deaf-Mutes. Females.	Blind. Persons.	Blind. Males.	Blind. Females.	Lepers. Persons.	Lepers. Males.	Lepers. Females.	Serial number.
	1	2	3	4	5	6	7	8	9	10	11	12	13	14	15	16	
	Central Provinces and Berar ...	**50,403**	**24,383**	**26,020**	**2,466**	**1,551**	**915**	**7,502**	**4,348**	**3,154**	**33,128**	**13,851**	**19,277**	**7,307**	**4,633**	**2,674**	
	C. P. British Districts and Berar ...	**45,602**	**21,958**	**23,644**	**2,205**	**1,391**	**814**	**6,620**	**3,849**	**2,771**	**30,494**	**12,621**	**17,873**	**6,283**	**4,097**	**2,186**	
	C. P. British Districts ...	**35,136**	**16,250**	**18,886**	**1,750**	**1,103**	**647**	**5,281**	**3,085**	**2,196**	**23,805**	**9,438**	**14,367**	**4,300**	**2,624**	**1,676**	
	JUBBULPORE DIVISION ...	*8,355*	*3,750*	*4,605*	*359*	*214*	*145*	*1,268*	*783*	*485*	*6,360*	*2,508*	*3,852*	*368*	*245*	*123*	
1	Saugor ...	2,146	960	1,186	71	42	29	275	172	103	1,673	651	1,022	127	95	32	1
2	Damoh ...	1,209	546	663	43	25	18	180	103	77	965	407	558	21	11	10	2
3	Jubbulpore ...	2,659	1,213	1,446	93	50	43	370	240	130	2,131	880	1,251	65	43	22	3
4	Mandla ...	1,317	617	700	99	61	38	281	168	113	815	311	504	122	77	45	4
5	Seoni ...	1,024	414	610	53	36	17	162	100	62	776	259	517	33	19	14	5
	NERBUDDA DIVISION ...	*6,182*	*2,918*	*3,264*	*290*	*161*	*129*	*1,071*	*623*	*448*	*4,464*	*1,878*	*2,586*	*357*	*256*	*101*	
6	Narsinghpur	1,227	534	693	39	21	18	207	120	87	935	355	580	46	38	8	6
7	Hoshangabad	1,531	742	789	54	31	23	228	146	82	1,181	517	604	68	48	20	7
8	Nimar ...	1,304	670	634	63	39	24	148	98	50	928	417	511	165	116	49	8
9	Betul ...	902	395	507	67	34	33	196	97	99	610	240	370	29	24	5	9
10	Chhindwara	1,218	577	641	67	36	31	292	162	130	810	349	461	49	30	19	10
	NAGPUR DIVISION ...	*7,563*	*3,779*	*3,783*	*687*	*464*	*223*	*1,458*	*814*	*644*	*4,742*	*2,034*	*2,708*	*675*	*467*	*208*	
11	Wardha ...	1,442	732	710	80	50	30	220	122	98	994	450	544	148	110	38	11
12	Nagpur ...	2,253	1,209	1,044	377	280	97	357	207	150	1,329	587	742	190	135	55	12
13	Chanda ...	1,621	739	882	87	48	39	342	189	153	1,008	385	623	184	117	67	13
14	Bhandara ...	1,498	727	771	82	53	29	334	177	157	976	423	553	106	74	32	14
15	Balaghat ...	748	372	376	61	33	28	205	119	86	435	189	246	47	31	16	15
	CHHATTISGARH DIVISION.	*13,037*	*5,803*	*7,234*	*414*	*264*	*150*	*1,484*	*865*	*619*	*8,239*	*3,018*	*5,221*	*2,900*	*1,656*	*1,244*	
16	Raipur ...	5,222	2,284	2,938	163	101	62	619	369	250	3,439	1,238	2,201	1,001	576	425	16
17	Bilaspur ...	3,969	1,837	2,132	161	116	45	553	308	245	2,507	976	1,531	748	437	311	17
18	Drug ...	3,846	1,682	2,164	90	47	43	312	188	124	2,293	804	1,489	1,151	643	508	18
	Berar ...	**10,466**	**5,708**	**4,758**	**455**	**288**	**167**	**1,339**	**764**	**575**	**6,689**	**3,183**	**3,506**	**1,983**	**1,473**	**510**	
19	Amraoti ...	3,050	1,733	1,317	140	86	54	433	254	179	1,816	891	925	661	502	159	19
20	Akola ...	2,707	1,478	1,229	144	91	53	297	159	138	1,826	891	935	440	337	103	20
21	Buldana ...	2,735	1,447	1,288	90	59	31	282	161	121	1,806	826	980	557	401	156	21
22	Yeotmal ...	1,974	1,050	924	81	52	29	327	190	137	1,241	575	666	325	233	92	22
	Feudatory States ...	**4,801**	**2,425**	**2,376**	**261**	**160**	**101**	**882**	**499**	**383**	**2,634**	**1,230**	**1,404**	**1,024**	**536**	**488**	
23	Makrai ...	40	14	26	1	1	...	9	3	6	26	8	18	4	2	2	23
24	Bastar ...	1,091	560	531	62	40	22	214	118	96	358	176	182	457	226	231	24
25	Kanker ...	511	233	278	28	20	8	83	52	31	328	130	198	72	31	41	25
26	Nandgaon ...	535	235	300	10	9	1	41	27	14	366	125	241	118	74	44	26
27	Khairagarh...	656	378	278	22	7	15	71	32	39	437	295	142	126	44	82	27
28	Chhuikhadan	105	40	65	...	...	...	14	7	7	78	29	49	13	4	9	28
29	Kawardha ...	232	95	137	3	2	1	19	9	10	184	68	116	26	16	10	29
30	Sakti ...	104	54	50	7	4	3	13	7	6	66	28	38	18	15	3	30
31	Raigarh ...	295	171	124	17	14	3	83	44	39	135	75	60	60	38	22	31
32	Sarangarh ...	217	115	102	15	8	7	70	42	28	85	38	47	47	27	20	32
33	Chang Bhakar ...	68	33	35	6	1	5	17	11	6	44	20	24	1	1	...	33
34	Korea ...	102	49	53	8	5	3	15	7	8	75	33	42	4	4	...	34
35	Surguja ...	422	232	190	40	26	14	124	79	45	237	115	122	21	12	9	35
36	Udaipur ...	94	57	37	7	4	3	31	19	12	46	26	20	10	8	2	36
37	Jashpur ...	329	159	170	35	19	16	78	42	36	169	64	105	47	34	13	37

TABLE XII-A.

Infirmities by Selected Castes, Tribes or Races.

TABLE XII-A.—Infirmities by Selected Castes, Tribes or Races.

Serial number.	CASTE, TRIBE OR RACE.	POPULATION DEALT WITH.			INSANE.			DEAF-MUTES.			BLIND.			LEPERS.			Serial number.
		Persons.	Males.	Females.	Persons	Males.	Females.	Persons.	Males.	Females.	Persons.	Males.	Females.	Persons	Males.	Females.	
	1	2	3	4	5	6	7	8	9	10	11	12	13	14	15	16	
	Central Provinces and Berar.	**16,033,310**	**7,984,022**	**8,049,288**	**2,466**	**1,551**	**915**	**7,502**	**4,348**	**3,154**	**33,128**	**13,851**	**19,277**	**7,307**	**4,633**	**2,674**	
1	Ahir ...	738,192	366,815	371,377	95	63	32	294	170	124	1,510	541	969	332	174	158	1
2	Bairagi ...	38,059	19,093	18,866	6	5	1	10	8	2	111	61	50	16	9	7	2
3	Balahi ...	52,314	25,857	26,457	5	3	2	17	13	4	151	53	98	16	13	3	3
4	Bania, Hindu...	131,718	68,395	63,323	21	17	4	73	47	26	261	131	130	27	24	3	4
5	Bania, Jain ...	67,618	34,895	32,723	18	14	4	44	27	17	200	103	97	20	18	2	5
6	Barai ...	59,461	29,764	29,697	20	10	10	42	23	19	112	48	64	52	42	10	6
7	Barhai ...	108,834	56,297	52,537	18	12	6	85	54	81	258	121	137	31	18	13	7
8	Basor ...	52,947	26,148	26,799	12	3	9	22	11	11	118	45	73	18	14	4	8
9	Bhil ...	27,785	13,768	14,017	2	...	2	14	7	7	76	27	49	5	3	2	9
10	Bhoyar ...	58,638	28,990	29,648	8	5	3	61	31	30	97	37	60	5	4	1	10
11	Brahman ...	445,744	237,605	208,139	133	103	30	212	131	81	980	472	508	90	62	28	11
12	Chadar ...	28,129	13,968	14,161	5	3	2	16	10	6	116	44	72	4	2	2	12
13	Chamar ...	901,594	443,059	458,535	95	45	50	278	173	105	2,733	1,035	1,698	399	270	129	13
14	Darji ...	51,301	26,113	25,188	6	2	4	18	12	6	113	49	64	9	7	2	14
15	Dhanagar ...	96,283	48,797	47,486	19	11	8	42	25	17	252	125	127	54	38	16	15
16	Dhimar ...	283,684	140,853	142,831	38	26	12	199	104	95	608	238	370	105	69	36	16
17	Dhobi ...	165,427	81,127	84,300	13	9	4	84	51	33	320	116	204	112	73	39	17
18	Gadaria ...	40,207	20,244	19,963	5	3	2	22	14	8	122	42	80	9	6	3	18
19	Ganda ...	151,787	74,285	77,502	10	8	2	72	40	32	210	85	125	46	20	26	19
20	Gond ...	2,333,893	1,138,157	1,195,736	307	182	125	1,035	582	453	4,444	1,575	2,869	801	478	323	20
21	Gujar ...	55,798	28,607	27,191	6	3	3	21	13	8	143	60	83	15	11	4	21
22	Halba ...	100,211	48,836	51,375	11	7	4	45	29	16	155	61	94	69	37	32	22
23	Kachera ...	2,844	1,362	1,482	...	...	...	...	...	...	4	3	1	2	...	2	23
24	Kachhi ...	119,553	60,287	59,266	18	10	8	61	38	23	359	149	210	25	14	11	24
25	Kalar ...	195,450	96,426	99,024	38	27	11	137	75	62	392	162	230	86	50	36	25
26	Kawar ...	229,412	113,563	115,849	26	16	10	100	57	43	288	125	163	75	48	27	26
27	Kayasth ...	33,584	17,580	16,004	7	7	...	16	11	5	56	30	26	1	1	...	27
28	Kewat ...	169,395	81,704	87,691	19	12	7	78	47	31	376	132	244	169	93	76	28
29	Kirar ...	47,793	24,036	23,757	5	4	1	30	19	11	98	41	57	10	8	2	29
30	Kol ...	82,598	40,857	41,741	11	6	5	24	21	3	206	80	126	11	7	4	30
31	Kori ...	39,628	20,397	19,231	13	11	2	22	12	10	112	44	68	4	1	3	31
32	Korku ...	152,363	75,559	76,804	13	8	5	39	24	15	170	66	104	51	34	17	32
33	Koshti ...	153,388	76,712	76,676	16	9	7	64	43	21	244	100	144	51	35	16	33
34	Kumhar ...	118,520	60,054	58,466	6	5	1	72	39	33	217	85	132	42	27	15	34
35	Kunbi ...	1,356,734	682,737	673,997	204	130	74	585	344	241	2,898	1,361	1,537	710	544	166	35
36	Kurmi ...	302,588	150,109	152,479	41	30	11	188	122	66	910	351	559	184	121	63	36
37	Lodhi ...	313,900	155,922	157,978	46	29	17	165	100	65	733	293	440	64	45	19	37
38	Lohar ...	181,590	91,183	90,407	27	18	9	123	64	59	332	143	189	81	47	34	38
39	Mali ...	563,528	279,868	283,660	79	46	33	247	153	94	1,181	530	651	385	266	119	39
40	Mana ...	49,037	23,835	25,202	3	1	2	24	13	11	75	29	46	28	20	8	40
41	Maratha ...	93,901	46,716	47,185	22	15	7	39	16	23	213	103	110	37	26	11	41
42	Mehra ...	1,165,177	575,449	589,728	170	105	65	467	248	219	2,175	909	1,266	494	323	171	42
43	Nai ...	148,750	74,078	74,672	40	30	10	102	64	38	487	212	275	76	50	26	43
44	Oraon ...	83,099	41,916	41,183	10	7	3	34	16	18	46	17	29	9	7	2	44
45	Panka ...	214,894	104,032	110,862	28	18	10	73	43	30	497	207	290	100	65	35	45
46	Rajput ...	441,231	223,581	217,650	68	50	18	239	149	90	780	355	425	129	92	37	46
47	Sunar ...	126,878	63,844	63,034	33	24	9	89	55	34	259	137	122	33	22	11	47
48	Teli ...	869,370	427,126	442,244	135	74	61	450	251	199	2,132	819	1,313	737	459	278	48
49	Musalman ...	585,029	302,227	282,802	169	107	62	269	145	124	1,018	477	541	180	135	45	49
50	Christian ...	73,401	39,208	34,193	34	12	22	35	16	19	119	59	60	619	302	317	50
51	Others ...	2,130,051	1,061,381	1,068,670	332	206	126	1,024	588	436	3,661	1,763	1,898	679	399	280	51

TABLE XIII.

Caste, Tribe, Race or Nationality.

THIS table shows caste and the religion to which a caste belongs. In cases where large numbers of the caste profess various religions, separate figures have been given for each. Where figures for other religions than the main religions were very small, they have been added to those for the main religion and the number so added has been noted in the column of remarks.

As a rule, persons converted from Hinduism or Muhammadanism to Christianity were returned as 'Indian Christians' and their caste of origin was not mentioned in the census schedules. In the case of the aboriginal Oraons of the Jashpur State, however, the name of the tribe was frequently given and the number so returned has been noted in the remarks column.

Sub-divisions of castes were returned in the case of Banias and Rajputs only and have been duly entered. As far as possible groups that are not true castes have been added to the castes to which they appeared to belong after such enquiries, local or otherwise, as it was possible to make. Castes with small numbers have been massed together under 'Minor Castes' in columns 680 and 681, and their details have been given in an appendix. The unclassed castes have been similarly dealt with in columns 682 and 683.

The four principal races of Musalmans, so far as they were returned, have been entered in columns 684 to 691, other Musalmans who did not return their race being put in columns 693 and 694. The remaining population belonging to casteless religions has been entered in columns 695 to 702, the nationality of Christians being omitted as it will be found in Table XVII.

The Divisions mentioned in the remarks column and in the appendices are the administrative Divisions of this Province.

TABLE XIII.—Caste,

Serial number.	DISTRICT OR STATE.	AGARIA. Hindu. Males.	AGARIA. Hindu. Females.	AGARIA. Animist. Males.	AGARIA. Animist. Females.	AGHARIA. Hindu. Males.	AGHARIA. Hindu. Females.	AHIR. Hindu. Males.	AHIR. Hindu. Females.	AHIR. Animist. Males.	AHIR. Animist. Females.
	1	2	3	4	5	6	7	8	9	10	11
	Central Provinces and Berar ...	3,446	3,583	1,264	1,207	13,413	13,644	359,071	363,366	7,744	8,011
	C. P. British Districts and Berar ...	1,474	1,548	374	350	6,093	6,301	279,066	283,051	7,329	7,546
	C. P. British Districts	1,474	1,548	374	350	6,093	6,301	269,428	274,835	7,325	7,541
	JUBBULPORE DIVISION	*298*	*326*	*228*	*232*	...	...	*64,791*	*63,004*	*5,387*	*5,340*
1	Saugor	...	...	...	...	...	...	14,443	13,210	2	2
2	Damoh	10	8	...	...	...	...	7,815	7,288	3	...
3	Jubbulpore	130	143	...	...	...	...	17,139	16,614	462	478
4	Mandla	158	175	228	232	...	...	10,268	10,393	4,723	4,667
5	Seoni	...	...	...	...	...	...	15,126	15,499	197	203
	NERBUDDA DIVISION	*6*	*4*	...	...	...	...	*43,910*	*42,840*	*1,821*	*2,109*
6	Narsinghpur	5	4	...	...	...	...	4,579	4,600	1	2
7	Hoshangabad	...	...	...	...	...	...	5,718	5,499	50	57
8	Nimar...	...	...	...	...	...	...	5,291	4,717	1	...
9	Betul	1	...	...	...	—	...	8,873	8,514	77	68
10	Chhindwara	...	...	...	...	...	...	19,449	19,510	1,692	1,982
	NAGPUR DIVISION	*14*	*16*	...	...	...	...	*11,580*	*10,823*	*29*	*28*
11	Wardha	...	...	...	...	...	...	2,427	2,231	...	...
12	Nagpur	...	...	...	...	...	...	2,384	1,873	3	9
13	Chanda	...	...	...	...	...	...	1,376	1,300	1	...
14	Bhandara	...	...	...	...	...	...	1,240	1,194	...	...
15	Balaghat	14	16	...	...	...	...	4,203	4,216	25	19
	CHHATTISGARH DIVISION	*1,156*	*1,202*	*146*	*118*	*6,093*	*6,301*	*149,147*	*158,168*	*88*	*64*
16	Raipur	...	...	...	...	2,712	2,880	66,905	70,468	55	36
17	Bilaspur	1,155	1,200	146	118	3,381	3,421	48,211	50,803	22	17
18	Drug	1	2	...	...	...	...	34,031	36,897	11	11
	Berar	...	...	...	...	...	...	9,638	8,216	4	5
19	Amraoti	...	...	...	...	...	...	3,442	2,833	4	5
20	Akola	...	...	...	...	...	...	2,444	1,992	...	...
21	Buldana	...	...	...	...	...	...	764	674	...	...
22	Yeotmal	...	...	...	...	...	...	2,988	2,717	...	...
	Feudatory States	1,972	2,035	890	857	7,320	7,343	80,005	80,315	415	465
23	Makrai	...	...	...	...	...	...	16	16	...	...
24	Bastar	...	...	...	...	...	...	9,054	8,781	53	35
25	Kanker	27	37	...	...	...	...	4,315	4,449	34	44
26	Nandgaon	...	...	...	...	...	...	8,087	9,011	9	4
27	Khairagarh	...	...	...	...	...	...	7,430	8,173	1	...
28	Chhuikhadan	...	...	...	...	...	...	1,649	1,739	...	...
29	Kawardha	4	5	58	62	...	...	2,862	3,044	10	11
30	Sakti	...	...	...	...	...	...	1,514	1,551	...	...
31	Raigarh	370	499	1	...	3,751	3,656	9,485	9,730	5	2
32	Sarangarh	...	...	...	...	3,569	3,687	4,260	4,523	...	...
33	Chang Bhakar	238	219	16	9	...	...	1,215	1,053	4	7
34	Korea	13	17	471	455	...	...	2,626	2,374	21	12
35	Surguja	1,296	1,228	30	38	...	...	17,565	16,857	175	229
36	Udaipur	16	17	300	275	...	...	2,865	2,934	82	100
37	Jashpur	8	13	14	18	...	...	6,962	6,580	21	21

Tribe, Race or Nationality.

ANDH.		AHIR.		BAHELIA.				BAHNA.				Remarks.	Serial No.
Hindu.		Hindu.		Hindu.		Animist.		Hindu.		Musalman.			
Males.	Females.	Males.	Females.	Males.	Females.	Males.	Females.	Males.	Females.	Males.	Females.		
12	13	14	15	16	17	18	19	20	21	22	23	24	
25,563	26,815	1,125	1,164	1,099	1,020	41	45	610	636	23,435	23,726		
25,563	26,815	1,125	1,164	839	794	14	18	605	634	23,270	23,557		
2	...	1,125	1,164	796	767	14	18	598	631	20,336	20,736		
...	...	...	...	*309*	*299*	*1*	...	*21*	*15*	*9,281*	*9,234*	Agharia includes—	
...	...	...	...	14	10	...	...	4	1	2,360	2,340	M. F.	1
...	...	...	...	12	13	...	...	10	10	1,799	1,682	*Animist.* Bilaspur 20 17	2
...	...	...	...	165	142	...	...	...	...	3,373	3,459		3
...	...	...	...	78	83	1	...	...	1	339	363		4
...	...	...	...	45	51	...	...	7	3	1,410	1,390		5
...	...	...	...	*70*	*53*	...	...	*42*	*28*	*6,535*	*6,780*	Ahir includes—	
...	...	...	...	2	3	...	...	...	2	1,538	1,686	*Musalman.* Nagpur 23 22	6
...	...	...	...	17	9	...	...	1	5	1,137	1,223	Amraoti 45 18	7
...	...	...	...	9	5	...	...	31	14	1,443	1,449	Akola 657 648	8
...	...	...	...	8	5	...	...	1	...	168	142	Buldana 80 60	9
...	...	...	...	39	31	...	...	9	7	2,249	2,280	Yeotmal 227 214	10
												Arya. Narsinghpur 2 1	
2	...	*1,123*	*1,163*	*31*	*33*	...	...	*28*	*36*	*4,475*	*4,695*	*Jain.* Nagpur 2 0	
1	...	...	...	...	...	...	...	...	...	597	589		11
...	...	...	...	5	3	...	...	3	15	2,307	2,495		12
1	...	1,123	1,168	...	...	...	...	17	19	227	256		13
...	...	...	...	17	23	...	...	8	2	806	846		14
...	...	...	...	9	7	...	...	...	...	448	309		15
...	...	*2*	*1*	*356*	*332*	*13*	*18*	*507*	*552*	*45*	*27*		
...	...	1	1	115	96	3	6	489	539	10	9		16
...	...	...	...	256	275	10	12	...	...	34	17		17
...	...	1	...	15	11	...	...	18	13	1	1		18
25,561	26,815	...	...	43	27	...	...	7	3	2,934	2,821		
...	1	...	...	35	22	...	...	2	2	1,893	1,713		19
9,504	10,036	...	...	8	3	...	...	2	...	144	169		20
2,091	2,301	...	...	...	2	...	...	1	1	302	419		21
13,966	14,477	...	...	...	...	...	...	2	...	505	520		22
...	...	...	...	260	226	27	27	5	2	165	169		
...	...	...	...	...	...	...	...	1	...	31	33		23
...	...	...	...	75	61	...	...	...	...	7	4		24
...	...	...	...	...	...	...	...	...	...	...	...		25
...	...	...	...	13	11	...	...	...	...	3	3		26
...	...	...	...	1	1	...	...	...	...	1	...		27
...	...	...	...	...	...	...	...	1	2	...	...		28
...	...	...	...	...	...	...	...	...	...	...	...		29
...	...	...	...	8	9	...	...	...	...	...	...		30
...	...	...	...	21	10	...	...	...	...	...	...		31
...	...	...	...	1	...	...	...	...	...	1	...		32
...	...	...	...	5	5	...	...	...	...	...	...		33
...	...	...	...	19	8	...	...	...	...	...	...		34
...	...	...	...	115	121	4	7	3	...	132	129		35
...	...	...	...	2	...	17	13	...	...	...	...		36
...	...	...	...	...	...	6	7	...	...	...	...		37

TABLE XIII.—Caste,

Serial No.	DISTRICT OR STATE.	BAIGA.				BAIRAGI.		BALAHI.		BA *Including*	
		HINDU.		ANIMIST.		HINDU.		HINDU.		HINDU.	
		Males.	Females.	Males.	Females.	Males.	Females.	Males.	Females.	Males.	Females.
		25	26	27	28	29	30	31	32	33	34
	Central Provinces and Berar ...	935	952	14,110	14,394	19,693	18,366	25,857	26,457	68,395	63,323
	C. P. British Districts and Berar ...	536	589	12,944	13,205	15,596	14,366	24,919	25,484	63,559	59,166
	C. P. British Districts	536	589	12,944	13,205	14,787	13,790	24,351	24,857	39,549	37,304
	JUBBULPORE DIVISION	*177*	*195*	*10,678*	*10,824*	*2,201*	*1,738*	*34*	*11*	*12,100*	*11,774*
1	Saugor	...	...	...	...	535	351	1	...	2,393	2,250
2	Damoh	...	...	...	...	194	135	...	...	1,876	1,829
3	Jubbulpore	48	41	1,051	1,086	934	782	33	11	5,988	6,026
4	Mandla	99	106	9,212	9,267	352	297	...	...	828	746
5	Seoni	30	48	415	471	186	173	...	...	1,015	923
	NERBUDDA DIVISION	*6*	*3*	*3*	*1*	*2,233*	*1,905*	*24,339*	*24,844*	*12,049*	*11,132*
6	Narsinghpur	6	3	...	...	522	443	...	...	3,371	3,407
7	Hoshangabad	...	...	...	...	985	838	9,927	10,215	2,841	2,609
8	Nimar	...	...	...	...	356	260	14,243	14,571	4,119	3,671
9	Betul	...	...	...	...	104	101	69	58	478	374
10	Chhindwara	...	...	3	1	206	263	..	...	1,240	1,071
	NAGPUR DIVISION	*219*	*241*	*2,246*	*2,364*	*1,070*	*948*	*77*	*2*	*8,082*	*7,295*
11	Wardha	...	...	...	...	150	127	...	...	2,524	2,304
12	Nagpur	...	...	...	...	285	230	3	...	3,082	2,695
13	Chanda	...	...	...	...	135	143	...	...	537	399
14	Bhandara	...	...	...	...	329	201	73	...	1,396	1,351
15	Balaghat	219	241	2,246	2,364	171	157	1	2	543	546
	CHHATTISGARH DIVISION	*134*	*150*	*17*	*16*	*9,283*	*9,199*	*1*	...	*7,318*	*7,103*
16	Raipur	71	70	10	8	236	3,129	...	...	2,394	2,259
17	Bilaspur	63	79	7	8	407	4,503	1	...	3,717	3,582
18	Drug	...	1	...	...	1,640	1,567	...	...	1,207	1,262
	Berar	...	...	...	...	809	576	568	627	24,010	21,862
19	Amraoti	...	...	...	...	308	232	568	627	6,170	5,624
20	Akola	...	...	...	...	186	140	...	...	7,103	6,349
21	Buldana	...	...	...	...	253	158	...	...	6,812	6,247
22	Yeotmal	...	...	...	...	63	46	...	...	3,925	3,642
	Feudatory States	399	363	1,166	1,189	4,097	4,000	938	973	4,836	4,157
23	Makrai	...	...	1	...	8	9	938	972	151	155
24	Bastar	193	174	34	40	207	204	...	...	65	38
25	Kanker	147	143	53	59	100	89	...	...	89	71
26	Nandgaon	...	...	...	...	751	740	...	...	417	354
27	Khairagarh	...	...	...	...	559	487	...	...	454	426
28	Chhuikhadan	...	...	...	...	271	263	...	...	77	75
29	Kawardha	...	...	1,077	1,090	185	183	...	...	431	457
30	Sakti	...	...	...	...	240	245	...	...	144	107
31	Raigarh	57	46	...	...	701	691	...	...	909	778
32	Sarangarh	...	...	...	...	451	462	...	...	227	184
33	Chang Bhakar	...	...	...	...	2	7	...	1	131	92
34	Korea	...	...	...	...	33	31	...	...	95	52
35	Surguja	...	...	...	...	431	442	...	...	1,306	1,166
36	Udaipur	...	...	...	...	101	92	...	...	68	25
37	Jashpur	2	...	1	...	54	55	...	...	272	177

Tribe, Race or Nationality.

NIA. subcastes.		SUBCASTES OF BANIA.											
		AGARWAL.		AGRAHARI.		AJUDHYA-BASI.		ASATHI.		BADNORE.		REMARKS.	
JAIN.		*Hindu.*		*Hindu.*		*Hindu.*		*Hindu.*		*Jain.*			
Males.	Females.	Males.	Females.	Males.	Females.	Males.	Females.	Males.	Females.	Males.	Females.		Serial No.
35	36	37	38	39	40	41	42	43	44	45	46	47	
34,895	32,723	13,387	11,760	972	1,021	800	929	1,280	1,288	145	166		
34,224	32,235	11,936	10,645	655	723	749	871	1,279	1,288	145	166		
25,943	24,470	8,539	7,628	619	683	743	862	1,279	1,288	31	27		
16,726	*15,975*	*2,649*	*2,391*	*309*	*393*	*205*	*180*	*1,190*	*1,188*	...	...	BAIRAGI includes— *Animist.* M. F. Chhindwara ... ... 1 0 Nagpur ... ... 2 1 Chhattisgarh Division ... 4 2 *Sikh.* Amraoti ... ... 2 0 *Jain.* Chanda ... ... 1 1 Drug ... ... 2 2 Buldana 3 3	
8,627	8,086	397	414	...	1	32	27	180	177	...	...		1
8,684	3,585	374	336	...	...	...	...	540	411	...	...		2
3,163	3,070	1,283	1,130	280	378	134	133	461	588	...	...		3
389	341	238	220	20	14	37	17	15	12	...	...		4
863	893	357	291	...	...	2	3	...	...	...	...		5
4,649	*4,431*	*2,742*	*2,552*	*24*	*22*	*295*	*370*	*8*	*2*	...	...	BALAHI includes— *Animist.* Bhandara ... ... 73 0 Amraoti ... ... 165 191 Makrai 0 10	
1,163	1,125	979	965	9	6	150	167	8	2	...	...		6
867	917	1,003	1,027	6	7	91	134	...	...	...	...		7
915	742	508	308	2	2	3	2	...	...	...	...		8
669	691	159	93	...	...	50	67	...	...	...	...		9
1,035	956	93	69	7	7	1	...	...	...	...	...		10
3,337	*3,165*	*922*	*767*	*69*	*65*	*141*	*168*	*75*	*94*	*31*	*27*	BANIA includes— *Arya.* Jubbulpore Division .. ... 3 8 Nerbudda Division ... ... 7 8 Chhattisgarh Division ... 17 11 Akola ... ... 3 8 Khairagarh ... ... 0 2 *Sikh.* Betul 2 0	
1,218	1,192	258	229	4	8	...	...	...	...	31	27		11
1,239	1,161	843	280	33	24	15	12	...	...	...	...		12
314	276	55	27	...	...	...	...	...	...	...	...		13
244	297	195	163	32	33	...	...	70	87	...	...		14
322	239	71	68	...	...	126	156	5	7	...	...		15
1,231	*899*	*2,226*	*1,918*	*217*	*203*	*102*	*144*	...	*4*	...	...	AGARWAL includes— *Jain.* Jubbulpore Division ... 79 47 Nerbudda Division ... 80 94 Nagpur Division ... ... 54 32 Chhattisgarh Division ... 90 69 Amraoti ... ... 36 31 Akola ... ... 14 11 Buldana ... ... 154 134 Yeotmal ... ... 38 20 Feudatory States 147 118	
557	420	952	840	93	98	31	17	...	...	...	...		16
200	166	858	630	113	90	53	95	...	4	...	...		17
474	318	416	448	11	15	18	32	...	...	...	...		18
8,281	7,765	3,397	3,017	36	40	6	9	...	...	114	139	AGRAHARI includes— *Jain.* Mandla 3 2	
2,461	2,265	926	742	30	37	6	9	...	...	38	51		19
2,571	2,555	1,138	1,079	2	...	...	...	...	...	47	60		20
1,776	1,617	924	817	1	...	...	...	...	...	1	...		21
1,473	1,328	409	379	3	3	...	...	...	...	28	28		22
671	488	1,451	1,115	317	298	51	58	1	...	...	...	AJUDHYABASI includes— *Jain.* Saugor ... ... 5 0 Hoshangabad ... ... 63 62 ASATHI includes— *Jain.* Saugor ... ... 15 11 Damoh ... ... 42 41 Jubbulpore 78 113	
29	38	37	38	...	...	...	...	...	...	...	...		23
20	26	10	7	2	2	...	...	1	...	...	...		24
35	36	14	8	...	...	...	...	...	...	...	...		25
330	211	166	131	1	...	47	58	...	...	...	...		26
125	92	230	198	...	...	...	...	...	...	...	...		27
71	44	67	48	...	...	...	...	...	...	...	...		28
36	27	38	31	...	...	...	...	...	...	...	...		29
...	...	129	93	...	...	...	...	...	...	...	...		30
6	7	506	498	98	105	...	...	...	...	...	...		31
4	3	58	31	...	...	...	...	...	...	...	...		32
...	...	1	...	3	2	...	...	...	...	...	...		33
...	...	13	2	47	35	4	...	...	...	...	...		34
9	4	47	24	163	154	...	...	...	...	...	...		35
...	...	37	12	...	...	...	...	...	...	...	...		36
...	...	8	4	3	...	...	...	...	...	...	...		37

TABLE XIII.—Caste,

Serial No.	DISTRICT OR STATE.	SUB-CASTES: Baghelwal. Jain. Males.	Baghelwal. Jain. Females.	Bania (unspecified). Hindu. Males.	Bania (unspecified). Hindu. Females.	Bania (unspecified). Jain. Males.	Bania (unspecified). Jain. Females.	Benaikaya. Jain. Males.	Benaikaya. Jain. Females.	Bhatia. Hindu. Males.	Bhatia. Hindu. Females.	Charnagar. Jain. Males.	Charnagar. Jain. Females.
		48	49	50	51	52	53	54	55	56	57	58	59
	Central Provinces and Berar ...	**240**	**234**	**17,644**	**16,682**	**4,804**	**4,356**	**572**	**609**	**155**	**111**	**1,302**	**1,219**
	C. P. British Districts and Berar ...	**240**	**234**	**16,876**	**16,111**	**4,802**	**4,353**	**565**	**600**	**155**	**111**	**1,143**	**1,124**
	C. P. British Districts	...	...	**6,855**	**6,330**	**2,334**	**2,187**	**538**	**586**	**29**	**17**	**1,143**	**1,124**
	JUBBULPORE DIVISION	...	...	*1,663*	*1,536*	*509*	*495*	*475*	*504*	...	...	*771*	*759*
1	Saugor	...	...	87	49	136	135	445	474	...	...	20	18
2	Damoh	...	...	384	408	227	250	18	23	...	...	669	629
3	Jubbulpore	...	...	595	542	113	85	12	7	...	...	9	26
4	Mandla	...	...	340	325	14	10	...	...	...	...	2	...
5	Seoni	...	...	256	212	19	15	...	...	...	...	71	86
	NERBUDDA DIVISION	...	...	*1,660*	*1,289*	*444*	*412*	*9*	*2*	...	...	*372*	*365*
6	Narsinghpur	...	...	141	176	6	8	...	...	...	...	...	...
7	Hoshangabad	...	...	285	145	71	86	2	2	...	...	...	...
8	Nimar	...	...	825	697	25	9	6	...	...	...	...	...
9	Betul	...	...	125	82	141	164	1	...	...	...	...	...
10	Chhindwara	...	...	284	189	201	145	...	...	...	...	372	365
	NAGPUR DIVISION	...	...	*2,467*	*2,544*	*1,291*	*1,205*	*48*	*73*	*29*	*17*	...	...
11	Wardha	...	...	589	636	557	490	5	45	27	15	...	...
12	Nagpur	...	...	742	804	531	514	39	26	1	2	...	...
13	Chanda	...	...	248	165	102	87	...	...	...	...	...	...
14	Bhandara	...	...	618	601	96	113	...	...	1	...	...	...
15	Balaghat	...	...	270	248	5	1	4	2	...	...	...	...
	CHHATTISGARH DIVISION	...	...	*1,066*	*961*	*90*	*75*	*6*	*7*	...	...	...	...
16	Raipur	...	...	292	409	40	32	...	...	...	...	...	...
17	Bilaspur	...	...	627	440	43	38	6	7	...	...	...	...
18	Drug	...	...	147	112	7	5	...	...	...	...	...	...
	Berar	**240**	**234**	**10,021**	**9,781**	**2,468**	**2,166**	**27**	**14**	**126**	**94**	...	...
19	Amraoti	79	88	2,599	2,574	889	783	9	1	4	4	...	...
20	Akola	149	146	3,982	3,614	621	540	...	...	35	25	...	...
21	Buldana	12	...	1,282	1,648	589	516	13	13	71	54	...	...
22	Yeotmal	...	...	2,158	1,945	369	327	5	...	16	11	...	...
	Feudatory States	...	...	**768**	**571**	**2**	**3**	**7**	**9**	...	...	**159**	**95**
23	Makrai	...	...	44	44	...	...	...	...	...	...	10	6
24	Bastar	...	...	43	23	...	...	...	...	...	...	6	9
25	Kanker	...	...	50	42	2	3	1	...	...	...	5	5
26	Nandgaon	...	...	92	53	...	...	...	...	...	...	49	45
27	Khairagarh	...	...	34	25	...	...	3	2	...	...	46	15
28	Chhuikhadan	...	...	...	...	...	...	...	...	...	...	30	6
29	Kawardha	...	...	34	18	...	...	1	6	...	...	5	6
30	Sakti	...	...	5	...	...	...	...	...	...	...	...	...
31	Raigarh	...	...	34	72	...	...	...	...	...	...	2	1
32	Sarangarh	...	...	39	6	...	...	...	...	...	...	...	1
33	Chang Bhakar	...	...	72	52	...	...	2	1	...	...	...	...
34	Korea	...	...	10	7	...	...	...	...	...	...	...	...
35	Surguja	...	...	163	158	...	...	...	...	...	...	6	1
36	Udaipur	...	...	16	3	...	...	...	...	...	...	...	...
37	Jashpur	...	...	132	68	...	...	...	...	...	...	...	...

Tribe, Race or Nationality.

OF BANIA.—(*contd.*)

Chhatrapuri.		Chitora.		Dasora.		Deshwal.		Dhakar.		Dhusar.		Dikshawant.		Remarks.	Serial No.
Hindu.		*Hindu.*		*Hindu.*		*Hindu.*		*Hindu.*		*Hindu.*		*Hindu.*			
Males.	Females.	Males.	Females.	Males.	Females.	Males.	Females.	Males.	Females.	Males.	Females.	Males.	Females.		
60	61	62	63	64	65	66	67	68	69	70	71	72	73	74	
111	77	139	115	371	430	163	169	95	87	154	168	102	100		
111	77	139	115	371	430	162	169	95	87	154	168	102	100		
49	30	139	115	359	419	162	169	95	87	154	168	...	...		
...	...	...	...	...	...	...	...	...	...	*61*	*79*	...	...	BEHRAIKAYA includes—	
														Hindu. M. F.	
...	...	...	...	...	...	...	...	...	...	24	20	...	...	Jubbulpore Division 35 36	1
...	...	...	...	...	...	...	...	...	...	1	4	...	...	Nerbudda Division 17 0	2
...	...	...	...	...	...	...	...	...	...	10	38	...	...	Nagpur Division 48 73	3
...	...	...	...	...	...	...	...	...	...	11	12	...	...	Chhattisgarh Division ... 6 7	4
...	...	...	...	...	...	...	...	...	...	15	5	...	...	Berar 27 14	5
...	...	...	...	...	...	...	...	...	...			...	...	Feudatory States 7 9	
3	*3*	*139*	*115*	*359*	*419*	*160*	*169*	*94*	*87*	*28*	*28*	...	...	BHATIA includes—	
														Jain.	
...	...	...	...	...	...	...	...	...	...	3	3	...	...	Nagpur Division 4 4	6
...	...	...	...	2	40	...	...	8	7	2	1	...	...	Berar 68 32	7
...	...	139	115	357	379	95	100	86	80	...	3	...	...		8
...	...	...	...	...	...	...	...	...	...	19	20	...	...		9
3	3	...	...	...	...	65	60	...	...	4	1	...	...		10
46	*27*	...	...	...	...	...	...	...	...	*11*	*3*	...	...	CHARNAGAR includes—	
														Hindu.	
33	23	...	...	...	...	...	...	...	...	...	...	...	...	Jubbulpore Division 54 43	11
10	...	...	...	...	...	...	...	...	...	10	1	...	...	Nerbudda Division 6 5	12
...	...	...	...	...	...	...	...	...	...	...	...	...	...		13
3	4	...	...	...	...	...	...	...	...	...	...	...	...		14
...	...	...	...	...	...	...	...	...	...	1	2	...	...		15
...	...	...	...	...	...	*2*	...	*1*	...	*54*	*58*	...	...		
...	...	...	...	...	...	...	...	1	...	46	56	...	...		16
...	...	...	...	...	...	2	...	...	...	4	2	...	...		17
...	...	...	...	...	...	...	...	...	...	4	...	...	...		18
62	47	...	...	12	11	...	...	...	...	...	...	102	100		
55	44	...	...	...	...	...	...	...	...	...	...	...	1		19
...	...	...	...	...	...	...	...	...	...	...	...	...	...		20
...	...	...	...	12	11	...	...	...	...	...	...	...	...		21
7	3	...	...	...	...	...	...	...	...	...	...	102	99		22
...	...	...	...	...	...	1	...	...	...	...	...	...	...		
...	...	...	...	...	...	...	...	...	...	...	...	...	...		23
...	...	...	...	...	...	...	...	...	...	...	...	...	...		24
...	...	...	...	...	...	...	...	...	...	...	...	...	...		25
...	...	...	...	...	...	...	...	...	...	...	...	...	...		26
...	...	...	...	...	...	...	...	...	...	...	...	...	...		27
...	...	...	...	...	...	...	...	...	...	...	...	...	...		28
...	...	...	...	...	...	...	...	...	...	...	...	...	...		29
...	...	...	...	...	...	...	...	...	...	...	...	...	...		30
...	...	...	...	...	...	...	...	...	...	...	...	...	...		31
...	...	...	...	...	...	...	...	...	...	...	...	...	...		32
...	...	...	...	...	...	...	...	...	...	...	...	...	...		33
...	...	...	...	...	...	...	...	...	...	...	...	...	...		34
...	...	...	...	...	...	...	...	...	...	...	...	...	...		35
...	...	...	...	...	...	...	...	...	...	...	...	...	...		36
...	...	...	...	...	...	1	...	...	...	...	...	...	...		37

TABLE XIII.—Caste,

Serial No.	DISTRICT OR STATE.	SUB-CASTES													
		DOSAR.		GAHOI.		GANGRADA.		GOLAPURAB.		GUJRATI.		GULARE.		JAUNPURI.	
		Hindu.		*Hindu*		*Hindu.*		*Jain.*		*Hindu.*		*Hindu.*		*Hindu.*	
		Males.	Females.	Males.	Females.	Males.	Females.	Males.	Females.	Males.	Females.	Males.	Females.	Males.	Females.
		75	76	77	78	79	80	81	82	83	84	85	86	87	88
	Central Provinces and Berar ...	**397**	**306**	**3,402**	**3,373**	**615**	**550**	**2,952**	**2,849**	**99**	**95**	**119**	**168**	**150**	**118**
	C. P. British Districts and Berar ...	**381**	**287**	**3,369**	**3,340**	**615**	**550**	**2,880**	**2,829**	**99**	**95**	**119**	**168**	...	...
	C. P. British Districts	**344**	**249**	**3,363**	**3,335**	**615**	**550**	**2,875**	**2,822**	**65**	**49**	**119**	**168**	...	...
	JUBBULPORE DIVISION	*100*	*68*	*2,445*	*2,465*	...	...	*2,498*	*2,441*	*10*	*10*	*2*	*4*	...	...
1	Saugor	19	17	780	744	...	...	1,587	1,546	2	6	2	4	...	...
2	Damoh	...	...	243	221	...	...	608	570	...	...	...	...	...	...
3	Jubbulpore	62	25	1,269	1,311	...	...	264	282	8	4	...	...	...	...
4	Mandla	...	...	49	79	...	...	8	2	...	...	...	...	...	...
5	Seoni	19	26	104	110	...	...	31	41	...	...	...	...	...	...
	NERBUDDA DIVISION	*74*	*50*	*821*	*792*	*615*	*550*	*377*	*381*	*38*	*30*	*46*	*53*	...	...
6	Narsinghpur	1	...	737	724	...	...	314	339	2	...	...	...	...	...
7	Hoshangabad	7	5	40	25	80	69	3	...	12	8	...	...	...	...
8	Nimar	9	1	30	27	532	479	...	...	23	19	...	...	...	...
9	Betul	55	40	8	15	3	2	3	...	...	3	...	...	...	...
10	Chhindwara	2	4	6	1	...	...	57	42	1	...	46	53	...	...
	NAGPUR DIVISION	*106*	*105*	*23*	*11*	...	...	...	...	15	9	*71*	*111*	...	...
11	Wardha	35	26	7	5	...	...	...	...	...	...	...	...	...	...
12	Nagpur	64	73	1	...	...	...	...	...	15	5	71	111	...	...
13	Chanda	...	2	...	...	...	...	...	...	...	...	...	...	...	...
14	Bhandara	7	4	...	...	...	...	...	...	...	...	...	...	...	...
15	Balaghat	...	...	14	6	...	...	...	...	...	4	...	...	...	...
	CHHATTISGARH DIVISION	*64*	*26*	*75*	*67*	...	...	...	...	*2*	...	...	...	...	...
16	Raipur	37	9	56	48	...	...	...	...	2	...	...	...	...	...
17	Bilaspur	26	12	10	9	...	...	...	...	...	...	...	...	...	...
18	Drug	1	5	9	10	...	...	...	...	...	...	...	...	...	...
	Berar	**37**	**38**	**6**	**5**	...	...	**5**	**7**	**34**	**46**	...	...	...	...
19	Amraoti	7	6	5	5	...	...	5	7	26	44	...	...	...	...
20	Akola	27	28	1	...	...	...	...	...	4	2	...	...	...	...
21	Buldana	...	...	...	...	...	...	...	...	4	...	...	...	...	...
22	Yeotmal	3	4	...	...	...	...	...	...	...	...	...	...	...	...
	Feudatory States	**16**	**19**	**33**	**33**	...	...	**72**	**20**	...	...	...	...	**150**	**118**
23	Makrai	...	...	1	...	...	...	...	...	...	...	...	...	...	...
24	Bastar	...	...	...	1	...	...	...	...	...	...	...	...	...	...
25	Kanker	...	...	3	...	...	...	...	...	...	...	...	...	...	...
26	Nandgaon	3	2	12	22	...	...	72	20	...	...	...	...	...	...
27	Khairagarh	5	5	2	1	...	...	...	...	...	...	...	...	...	...
28	Chhuikhadan	...	...	7	4	...	...	...	...	...	...	...	...	...	...
29	Kawardha	...	...	4	3	...	...	...	...	...	...	...	...	...	...
30	Sakti	3	3	2	2	...	...	...	...	...	...	...	...	...	...
31	Raigarh	1	4	1	...	...	...	...	...	...	...	...	...	...	...
32	Sarangarh	...	...	1	...	...	...	...	...	...	...	...	...	136	114
33	Chang Bhakar	4	5	...	...	...	...	...	...	...	...	...	...	...	...
34	Korea	...	...	...	...	...	...	...	...	...	...	...	...	...	...
35	Surguja	...	...	...	...	...	...	...	...	...	...	...	...	...	...
36	Udaipur	...	...	...	...	...	...	...	...	...	...	...	...	...	...
37	Jashpur	...	...	...	...	...	...	...	...	...	...	...	...	14	4

Tribe, Race or Nationality.

OF BANIA.—(*contd.*)

Jhamaiya. Hindu. Males.	Jhamaiya. Hindu. Females.	Kapari. Hindu. Males.	Kapari. Hindu. Females.	Kasarwani. Hindu. Males.	Kasarwani. Hindu. Females.	Kasaundha. Hindu. Males.	Kasaundha. Hindu. Females.	Khandayat. Hindu. Males.	Khandayat. Hindu. Females.	Khandelwal. Hindu. Males.	Khandelwal. Hindu. Females.	Remarks.	Serial No.
89	90	91	92	93	94	95	96	97	98	99	100	101	
75	96	81	11	3,339	3,240	2,598	2,969	138	145	828	669		
75	96	...	...	2,455	2,400	2,235	2,563	138	145	812	658		
75	96	...	...	2,438	2,389	2,233	2,563	138	145	609	494		
21	*18*	...	...	*938*	*795*	*662*	*828*	...	...	*102*	*82*	DOSAR includes— M. F.	
...	...	...	...	391	315	...	...	...	...	6	9	*Jain.* Amraoti 1 0	1
...	...	...	...	13	10	...	...	...	...	4	2	Akola 0 2	2
21	18	...	...	468	438	650	822	...	...	41	37		3
...	...	...	...	37	12	12	5	...	...	7	2		4
...	...	...	...	19	20	...	1	...	...	44	32		5
39	*57*	...	...	*80*	*44*	*7*	*3*	*138*	*140*	*283*	*248*	GAHOI includes—	
38	57	...	...	26	26	...	...	...	...	1	...	*Jain.* Jubbulpore Division 4 4	6
...	...	...	...	33	4	5	3	...	...	140	143		7
1	...	...	...	14	9	...	...	138	140	46	20		8
...	...	...	...	2	5	2	...	...	...	40	42		9
...	...	...	...	5	...	...	...	...	...	56	40		10
...	...	...	...	*42*	*22*	*22*	*14*	...	...	*172*	*129*	GOLAPURAB includes—	
...	...	...	...	9	8	3	...	...	...	29	23	*Hindu.* Jubbulpore Division ... 29 37	11
...	...	...	...	25	6	4	4	...	...	67	52	Narsinghpur 268 296	12
...	...	...	...	...	...	7	5	...	...	...	...	Hoshangabad 2 0	13
...	...	...	...	8	8	8	5	...	...	73	52	Chhindwara 5 1	14
...	...	...	...	...	...	...	...	...	...	3	2		15
15	*21*	...	...	*1,388*	*1,538*	*1,542*	*1,718*	...	*5*	*52*	*38*	KASARWANI includes—	
5	8	...	...	227	173	369	401	...	5	11	2	*Jain.* Jubbulpore Division 8 13	16
10	13	...	...	932	1,108	1,024	1,155	...	...	6	1	Drug 2 0	17
...	...	...	...	229	247	149	162	...	...	35	35		18
...	...	...	...	17	11	2	...	...	...	203	164	KHANDELWAL includes—	
...	...	...	...	1	6	2	...	...	...	119	94	*Jain.* Jubbulpore Division 26 20	19
...	...	...	...	15	5	...	...	...	...	28	16	Nerbudda Division 85 57	20
...	...	...	...	...	...	...	...	...	...	56	54	Nagpur Division 32 32	21
...	...	...	...	1	...	...	...	...	...	...	...	Chhattisgarh Division 21 9	22
												Berar 17 20	
...	...	81	11	884	840	363	406	...	...	16	11		
...	...	...	...	...	...	...	...	...	...	...	...		23
...	...	...	...	3	...	4	7	...	...	...	...		24
...	...	...	...	...	...	22	20	...	...	...	...		25
...	...	...	...	2	1	64	65	...	...	16	11		26
...	...	...	...	37	36	62	80	...	...	...	...		27
...	...	...	...	...	...	18	18	...	...	...	...		28
...	...	...	...	200	225	160	181	...	...	...	...		29
...	...	81	11	5	9	...	...	...	...	...	...		30
...	...	...	...	84	82	...	...	...	...	...	...		31
...	...	...	...	127	120	...	...	...	...	...	...		32
...	...	...	...	49	32	...	...	...	...	...	...		33
...	...	...	...	18	7	...	...	...	...	...	...		34
...	...	...	...	345	309	33	35	...	...	...	...		35
...	...	...	...	...	...	...	...	...	...	...	...		36
...	...	...	...	14	10	...	...	...	...	...	...		37

TABLE XIII.—Caste,

Serial No.	DISTRICT OR STATE.	SUB-CASTES													
		LINGAYAT.		LOD.		LOHANA.		MAHESHRI.		MAHURE.		MARWADI.		MITHKAR.	
		Hindu.		*Hindu.*		*Hindu.*		*Hindu.*		*Hindu.*		*Hindu.*		*Hindu.*	
		Males.	Females.	Males.	Females.	Males.	Females.	Males.	Females.	Males.	Females.	Males.	Females	Males.	Females.
		102	103	104	105	106	107	108	109	110	111	112	113	114	115
	Central Provinces and Berar ...	**4,204**	**3,589**	**2,691**	**2,692**	**58**	**194**	**7,443**	**6,664**	**69**	**56**	**2,481**	**1,688**	**107**	**110**
	C. P. British Districts and Berar	**4,203**	**3,588**	**2,690**	**2,690**	**55**	**192**	**7,292**	**6,490**	**69**	**56**	**2,475**	**1,688**	**107**	**110**
	C. P. British Districts... ...	**1,872**	**1,523**	**1,303**	**1,280**	**31**	**34**	**2,919**	**2,611**	**69**	**56**	**618**	**330**	**107**	**110**
	JUBBULPORE DIVISION	*7*	*1*	...	...	*1*	...	*188*	*157*	*37*	*26*	*43*	*35*	...	...
1	Saugor	4	...	...	...	...	...	84	76	21	17	...	...	...	...
2	Damoh	...	...	...	...	...	...	8	4	...	...	3	4	...	...
3	Jubbulpore	1	1	...	...	1	...	84	71	14	6	26	23	...	...
4	Mandla	2	...	...	...	...	...	5	1	2	3	8	4	...	...
5	Seoni	...	...	...	...	...	...	7	5	...	...	6	4	...	...
	NERBUDDA DIVISION	*334*	*360*	*595*	*528*	*25*	*17*	*1,309*	*1,183*	*32*	*30*	*60*	*21*	...	...
6	Narsinghpur	...	...	...	...	...	...	76	50	...	...	1	...	...	...
7	Hoshangabad	...	...	...	...	2	1	736	655	32	30	2	1	...	...
8	Nimar	49	52	582	518	4	6	287	270	...	...	41	13	...	...
9	Betul	7	6	...	...	15	10	8	5	...	...	2	...	...	...
10	Chhindwara	278	302	13	10	4	...	202	197	...	...	14	7	...	...
	NAGPUR DIVISION	*1,522*	*1,157*	*701*	*752*	*5*	*3*	*1,110*	*945*	...	...	*403*	*259*	*107*	*110*
11	Wardha	713	609	50	94	...	...	606	559	...	...	135	81	28	24
12	Nagpur	660	357	482	492	5	3	354	265	...	...	185	130	15	17
13	Chanda	74	87	19	24	...	...	72	26	...	...	24	17	64	69
14	Bhandara	57	78	150	142	...	...	69	84	...	...	54	29	...	...
15	Balaghat	18	26	...	...	...	...	9	11	...	...	10	2	...	...
	CHHATTISGARH DIVISION ...	*9*	*5*	*7*	...	...	*14*	*312*	*326*	...	...	*107*	*15*	...	...
16	Raipur	...	...	1	...	...	3	119	149	...	...	99	...	...	...
17	Bilaspur	8	5	6	...	...	...	15	9	...	...	3	2	...	...
18	Drug	1	...	...	...	...	11	178	168	...	...	5	13	...	...
	Berar	**2,331**	**2,065**	**1,387**	**1,410**	**24**	**158**	**4,373**	**3,879**	...	...	**1,857**	**1,358**	...	...
19	Amraoti	367	311	141	142	...	...	1,417	1,336	...	...	374	221	...	...
20	Akola	338	339	570	653	5	3	901	657	...	...	526	474	...	...
21	Buldana	1,000	764	500	456	...	...	1,626	1,546	...	...	881	614	...	...
22	Yeotmal	626	651	176	159	19	155	429	340	...	...	76	40	...	...
	Feudatory States	**1**	**1**	**1**	**2**	**3**	**2**	**151**	**174**	...	...	**6**	...	...	...
23	Makrai	...	...	...	...	...	...	65	73	...	...	...	...	...	...
24	Bastar	1	1	...	...	...	...	...	...	...	...	2	...	...	...
25	Kanker	...	...	...	...	...	...	1	1	...	...	...	...	...	...
26	Nandgaon	...	...	...	...	2	2	23	36	...	...	2	...	...	...
27	Khairagarh	...	...	1	2	1	...	62	51	...	...	2	...	...	...
28	Chhuikhadan	...	...	...	...	...	...	...	13	...	...	...	...	...	...
29	Kawardha	...	...	...	...	...	...	...	...	...	...	...	...	...	...
30	Sakti	...	...	...	...	...	...	...	...	...	...	...	...	...	...
31	Raigarh	...	...	...	...	...	...	...	...	...	...	...	...	...	...
32	Sarangarh	...	...	...	...	...	...	...	...	...	...	...	...	...	...
33	Chang Bhakar	...	...	...	...	...	...	...	...	...	...	...	...	...	...
34	Korea	...	...	...	...	...	...	...	...	...	...	...	...	...	...
35	Surguja	...	...	...	...	...	...	...	...	...	...	...	...	...	...
36	Udaipur	...	...	...	...	...	...	...	...	...	...	...	...	...	...
37	Jashpur	...	...	...	...	...	...	...	...	...	...	...	...	...	...

Tribe, Race or Nationality.

OF BANIA—(*contd.*)															
MOD.		NAGAR.		NEMA.		OSWAL.		PALLIWAL.		PANCHAM.		PARWAR.			
Hindu.		*Hindu.*		*Hindu.*		*Jain.*		*Hindu.*		*Hindu.*		*Jain.*		REMARKS.	
Males.	Females.	Males.	Females.	Males.	Females.	Males.	Females.	Males.	Females.	Males.	Females.	Males.	Females.		Serial No.
116	117	118	119	120	121	122	123	124	125	126	127	128	129	130	
54	63	105	59	1,840	1,867	5,498	4,114	245	223	93	62	14,874	14,103		
54	63	105	59	1,839	1,867	5,276	3,922	245	223	93	62	14,714	13,955		
54	63	103	59	1,818	1,847	2,823	2,078	245	223	77	60	14,437	13,717		
...	...	...	...	*753*	*772*	*232*	*176*	*7*	*5*	...	...	*11,887*	*11,219*		
...	...	...	...	307	290	52	38	7	5	...	...	6,151	5,615		1
...	...	...	...	124	147	16	18	...	...	...	...	2,153	2,111		2
...	...	...	...	89	79	115	81	...	...	...	...	2,555	2,474		3
...	...	...	...	3	2	13	5	...	...	...	...	391	359		4
...	...	...	...	230	245	36	34	...	...	...	...	637	660		5
57	*61*	*103*	*59*	*1,051*	*1,068*	*821*	*613*	*209*	*216*	*77*	*60*	*2,006*	*1,936*		
...	...	...	...	849	860	135	116	11	7	...	...	985	953		6
28	28	103	59	2	3	211	177	31	53	...	...	406	439		7
19	33	...	...	46	39	381	257	146	133	...	...	435	400		8
...	...	...	...	...	...	71	51	...	...	...	...	26	22		9
...	...	...	...	154	166	23	12	21	23	77	60	154	122		10
2	...	...	...	*10*	*6*	*945*	*728*	*29*	*2*	...	...	*306*	*344*		
...	...	...	...	...	...	311	274	...	2	...	...	53	34		11
...	...	...	...	...	...	172	117	29	...	...	...	102	154		12
2	...	...	...	...	...	171	150	...	...	...	...	1	2		13
...	...	...	...	2	1	93	47	...	...	...	...	30	51		14
...	...	...	...	8	5	198	140	...	...	...	...	120	103		15
5	*2*	...	...	*4*	*1*	*825*	*661*	...	...	...	...	*238*	*213*		
5	2	...	...	4	1	382	282	...	...	...	...	118	112		16
...	...	...	...	...	...	46	20	...	...	...	...	90	84		17
...	...	...	...	...	...	307	250	...	...	...	...	30	22		18
...	...	2	...	21	20	2,453	1,844	...	...	16	2	277	238		
...	...	...	...	16	20	528	398	...	...	2	2	199	178		19
...	...	...	...	...	...	211	188	...	...	...	...	10	7		20
...	...	...	...	5	...	874	584	...	...	4	...	43	40		21
...	...	2	...	...	...	840	674	...	...	10	...	25	13		22
...	...	...	...	1	...	222	192	...	...	...	...	160	148		
...	...	...	...	...	...	15	26	...	...	...	...	8	6		23
...	...	...	...	...	...	11	6	...	...	...	...	8	7		24
...	...	...	...	...	...	14	19	...	...	...	...	12	9		25
...	...	...	...	...	...	92	40	...	...	...	...	94	72		26
...	...	...	...	...	...	28	41	...	...	...	...	27	29		27
...	...	...	...	...	...	26	20	...	...	...	...	...	10		28
...	...	...	...	...	...	18	5	...	...	...	...	7	9		29
...	...	...	...	...	...	...	...	...	...	...	...	...	...		30
...	...	...	...	1	...	9	12	...	...	...	...	2	3		31
...	...	...	...	...	...	5	19	...	...	...	...	2	1		32
...	...	...	...	...	...	...	...	...	...	...	...	...	...		33
...	...	...	...	...	...	1	...	...	...	...	...	...	...		34
...	...	...	...	...	...	...	1	...	...	...	...	...	2		35
...	...	...	...	...	...	...	...	...	...	...	...	...	...		36
...	...	...	...	...	...	8	3	...	...	...	...	...	...		37

Remarks (column 130):

LINGAYAT includes—

	M.	F.
Jain.		
Chhindwara	0	1
Nagpur Division	7	10
Berar	5	0

LOD includes—

	M.	F.
Jain.		
Nerbudda Division	13	10
Nagpur Division	121	197
Amraoti	83	86
Akola	559	637
Buldana	40	50
Yeotmal	160	149

MAHESHRI includes—

	M.	F.
Jain.		
Jubbulpore	1	2
Nerbudda Division	6	13
Nagpur Division	25	30
Drug	7	8
Berar	65	45

MITHKAR includes—

	M.	F.
Jain.		
Chanda	6	2

NEMA includes...

	M.	F.
Jain.		
Jubbulpore Division	48	63
Nerbudda Division	49	70
Amraoti	16	20

OSWAL includes—

	M.	F.
Hindu.		
Jubbulpore Division	24	14
Nerbudda Division	115	88
Nagpur Division	96	69
Chhattisgarh Division ...	99	71
Amraoti	89	68
Akola	34	39
Buldana	339	152
Yeotmal	170	98
Feudatory States	80	80

PALLIWAL includes—

	M.	F.
Jain.		
Saugor	7	5
Nerbudda Division	28	30
Nagpur Division	29	2

PARWAR includes—

	M.	F.
Hindu.		
Jubbulpore Division	84	84
Nerbudda Division	103	67
Nagpur Division	14	27
Chhattisgarh Division ...	15	20
Amraoti	101	88
Akola	5	9
Buldana	43	40
Yeotmal	24	13
Feudatory States	11	8

TABLE XIII.—Caste,

Serial No.	DISTRICT OR STATE.	SUB-CASTES: Pokhar. Hindu. Males.	Pokhar. Hindu. Females.	Raswant. Hindu. Males.	Raswant. Hindu. Females.	Raunihar. Hindu. Males.	Raunihar. Hindu. Females.	Saitwal. Jain. Males.	Saitwal. Jain. Females.	Samaiya. Jain. Males.	Samaiya. Jain. Females.	Saraogi. Jain. Males.	Saraogi. Jain. Females.
		131	132	133	134	135	136	137	138	139	140	141	142
	Central Provinces and Berar ...	**28**	**74**	**127**	**128**	**553**	**502**	**3,426**	**3,591**	**262**	**308**	**556**	**519**
	C. P. British Districts and Berar ...	**28**	**74**	**127**	**128**	**18**	**31**	**3,425**	**3,591**	**262**	**308**	**549**	**515**
	C. P British Districts	...	**37**	...	...	**18**	**31**	**1,119**	**1,233**	**262**	**308**	**502**	**426**
	JUBBULPORE DIVISION	...	...	...	...	*3*	*21*	...	...	*247*	*296*	*34*	*11*
1	Saugor	...	...	...	...	...	21	...	...	213	270	19	...
2	Damoh	...	...	...	...	...	...	...	...	...	...	4	5
3	Jubbulpore	...	...	...	...	3	...	...	...	34	26	1	...
4	Mandla	...	...	...	...	...	...	...	...	...	...	...	...
5	Seoni	...	...	...	...	...	...	...	...	...	...	10	6
	NERBUDDA DIVISION	...	*37*	...	...	...	...	*542*	*597*	*15*	*12*	*333*	*309*
6	Narsinghpur	...	...	...	...	...	...	5	9	5	...	...	...
7	Hoshangabad	...	...	...	...	...	...	...	...	10	12	140	170
8	Nimar	...	...	...	...	...	...	25	21	...	...	170	133
9	Betul	...	37	...	...	...	...	403	432	...	...	5	3
10	Chhindwara	...	...	...	...	...	...	109	135	...	...	9	3
	NAGPUR DIVISION	...	...	...	...	...	...	*577*	*636*	...	...	*54*	*57*
11	Wardha	...	...	...	...	...	...	219	241	...	...	25	29
12	Nagpur	...	...	...	...	...	...	330	308		...	13	9
13	Chanda	...	...	...	...	...	...	10	10	...	...	1	1
14	Bhandara	...	...	...	...	...	...	18	77	...	...	13	17
15	Balaghat	...	...	...	...	...	...	...	...	...	...	2	1
	CHHATTISGARH DIVISION	...	...	...	...	*15*	*10*	...	...	...	...	*81*	*49*
16	Raipur	...	...	...	...	11	10	...	...	...	...	29	11
17	Bilaspur	...	...	...	...	4	...	...	...	...	...	17	7
18	Drug	...	...	...	...	...	...	...	...	...	...	35	31
	Berar	**28**	**37**	**127**	**128**	...	...	**2,306**	**2,358**	...	...	**47**	**89**
19	Amraoti	...	...	...	...	...	...	747	758	...	...	10	...
20	Akola	28	37	1	...	...	...	942	943	...	...	5	5
21	Buldana	...	...	...	...	...	...	406	430	...	...	30	84
22	Yeotmal	...	...	126	128	...	...	211	227	...	...	2	...
	Feudatory States	...	...	...	...	**535**	**471**	**1**	...	...	...	**7**	**4**
23	Makrai	...	...	...	...	...	...	...	...	...	...	...	...
24	Bastar	...	...	...	...	...	...	...	...	...	...	...	...
25	Kanker	...	...	...	...	...	...	...	...	...	...	...	...
26	Nandgaon	...	...	...	...	...	...	...	...	...	...	6	4
27	Khairagarh	...	...	...	...	...	...	...	...	...	...	...	...
28	Chhuikhadan	...	...	...	...	...	...	...	...	...	...	...	...
29	Kawardha	...	...	...	...	...	...	...	...	...	...	...	...
30	Sakti	...	...	...	...	...	...	...	...	...	...	...	...
31	Raigarh	...	...	...	...	...	...	1	...	...	...	1	...
32	Sarangarh	...	...	...	...	...	...	...	...	...	...	...	...
33	Chang Bhakar	...	...	...	...	...	...	...	...	...	...	...	...
34	Korea	...	...	...	...	2	1	...	...	...	...	...	...
35	Surguja	...	...	...	...	421	372	...	...	...	...	...	...
36	Udaipur	...	...	...	...	15	10	...	...	...	...	...	...
37	Jashpur	...	...	...	...	97	88	...	...	...	...	...	...

Tribe, Race or Nationality.

OF BANIA—(concld.)						BANJARA.							
SHRIMALI.		SURSENI.		UMRE.		HINDU.		ANIMIST.		MUSALMAN.		REMARKS.	Serial No.
Hindu.		*Hindu.*		*Hindu.*									
Males.	Females.	Males.	Females.	Males.	Females.	Males.	Females.	Males.	Females.	Males.	Females.		
143	144	145	146	147	148	149	150	151	152	153	154	155	
326	**302**	**97**	**85**	**924**	**943**	**69,469**	**64,320**	**438**	**437**	**569**	**558**		
322	**299**	**97**	**85**	**881**	**902**	**65,032**	**60,355**	**319**	**326**	**569**	**558**		
206	**190**	**95**	**84**	**872**	**894**	**23,732**	**22,085**	**302**	**313**	**508**	**510**		
1	*1*	*88*	*77*	*693*	*716*	*2,801*	*2,679*	*34*	*26*	*312*	*336*	SAITWAL includes— M. F.	
...	...	...	...	56	43	104	62	...	...	267	278	*Hindu.* Nerbudda Division 19 28	1
...	...	...	...	271	261	207	265	2	3	...	...	Nagpur Division 27 33	2
...	...	88	77	349	390	123	95	...	...	45	58	Berar ... — ... 160 117	3
...	...	...	...	3	3	1,247	1,130	29	23	...	...	Raigarh 1 0	4
1	1	...	...	14	19	1,120	1,127	3	...	...	...		5
200	*188*	*1*	*4*	*83*	*84*	*10,891*	*9,166*	*125*	*113*	*185*	*168*	SAMAIYA includes—	
...	...	...	...	52	58	49	60	...	...	...	...	*Hindu.* Jubbulpore Division 13 18	6
190	186	...	...	7	6	478	399	...	...	16	20	Narsinghpur 5 0	7
...	...	1	4	9	8	8,381	6,888	...	...	169	148		8
1	2	...	...	1	1	555	504	79	71	...	...		9
...	...	...	...	14	11	1,428	1,315	46	42	...	...		10
2	...	...	...	*61*	*70*	*4,774*	*4,312*	*9*	*14*	*11*	*6*	SARAOGI includes—	
2	...	...	...	13	14	1,623	1,464	5	12	...	...	*Hindu.* Jubbulpore Division 5 5	11
...	...	...	...	3	...	1,164	1,023	...	...	11	6	Nerbudda Division 58 47	12
...	...	...	...	1	3	1,526	1,397	2	...	...	...	Nagpur Division... ... ... 4 2	13
...	...	...	...	43	52	90	100	...	...	...	...	Chhattisgarh Division 13 0	14
...	...	...	...	1	1	371	323	2	2	...	...	Berar ... ... 13 21 Feudatory States 7 4	15
3	*1*	*6*	*3*	*35*	*24*	*5,266*	*5,928*	*134*	*161*	...	...	SHRIMALI includes—	
...	...	...	...	21	11	3,798	4,235	134	159	...	...	*Jain.* Betul 1 2	16
...	...	6	3	8	5	1,347	1,614	...	2	...	...	Wardha 2 0	17
3	1	...	...	6	8	121	79	...	...	...	...	Drug ... ... 8 1 Berar 93 82	18
116	**109**	**2**	**1**	**9**	**8**	**41,300**	**38,270**	**17**	**13**	**61**	**48**	BANJARA includes—	
28	27	2	1	...	...	1,598	1,461	...	...	...	...	*Sikh.* Jubbulpore 24 8	19
88	82	...	...	...	...	10,351	9,378	...	...	31	29	Nerbudda Division ... 74 61	20
...	...	...	...	9	8	6,600	6,548	...	...	20	15		21
...	...	...	...	...	...	22,751	20,883	17	13	10	4		22
4	**3**	...	...	**43**	**41**	**4,437**	**3,965**	**119**	**111**	...	...		
...	...	...	...	...	...	3	5	...	...	...	...		23
...	...	...	...	...	1	2,750	2,318	88	76	...	...		24
...	...	...	...	...	...	348	368	...	...	...	...		25
4	3	...	...	...	...	12	14	...	...	...	...		26
...	...	...	...	39	38	14	16	...	...	...	...		27
...	...	...	...	...	...	...	...	...	...	...	...		28
...	...	...	...	...	...	...	...	...	...	...	...		29
...	...	...	...	...	...	7	3	1	...	...	...		30
...	...	...	...	4	2	593	591	...	...	...	...		31
...	...	...	...	...	...	254	247	...	...	...	...		32
...	...	...	...	...	...	41	51	...	...	...	...		33
...	...	...	...	...	...	77	57	17	15	...	...		34
...	...	...	...	...	...	6	6	...	...	...	...		35
...	...	...	...	...	...	226	241	3	8	...	...		36
...	...	...	...	...	...	97	48	10	12	...	...		37

TABLE XIII.—Caste, Tribe,

Serial No.	DISTRICT OR STATE.	BARAI.		BARGAHA.		BARHAI.		BASOR.			
		HINDU.		HINDU.		HINDU.		HINDU.		ANIMIST.	
		Males.	Females.	Males.	Females.	Males.	Females.	Males.	Females.	Males.	Females.
		156	157	158	159	160	161	162	163	164	165
	Central Provinces and Berar ...	**29.764**	**29.697**	**1.567**	**1,565**	**56.297**	**52,537**	**24,666**	**25.288**	**1,482**	**1,511**
	C. P. British Districts and Berar ...	**28,010**	**27,850**	**921**	**929**	**55,741**	**52,067**	**23.872**	**24,485**	**1,472**	**1,502**
	C. P. British Districts	**13,640**	**13.840**	**921**	**929**	**38.556**	**37.076**	**22,930**	**23.573**	**1,385**	**1,418**
	JUBBULPORE DIVISION	*3,933*	*3,934*	*180*	*182*	*9,486*	*9,147*	*14,047*	*14,364*	*6*	*11*
1	Saugor	1,288	1,274	...	...	3,066	2,878	4,652	4,605	...	...
2	Damoh	931	928	...	...	2,220	2,227	3,827	3,919	...	...
3	Jubbulpore	1,030	1,023	177	180	3,349	3,193	4,080	4,252	1	9
4	Mandla	386	396	3	2	165	167	590	617	5	1
5	Seoni	298	313	..	...	686	682	898	971	...	1
	NERBUDDA DIVISION	*2,968*	*3,102*	*4*	*2*	*12,305*	*11,914*	*4,138*	*4,238*	*21*	*28*
6	Narsinghpur	491	465	...	...	2,814	2,762	1,642	1,691	...	...
7	Hoshangabad	591	634	...	...	3,671	3,606	1,201	1,169	...	...
8	Nimar	621	641	...	...	1,978	1,782	178	177	...	...
9	Betul	307	337	...	...	1,722	1,643	478	500	...	...
10	Chhindwara	958	1,025	4	2	2,120	2,121	639	691	21	28
	NAGPUR DIVISION	*5,443*	*5,431*	*1*	...	*16,271*	*15,711*	*2,717*	*2,742*	*1,278*	*1,301*
11	Wardha	1,248	1,259	...	...	4,048	3,895	149	136	41	44
12	Nagpur	2,453	2,378	...	...	7,252	6,98[illegible]	464	483	13	21
13	Chanda	1,204	1,168	1	...	2,448	2,369	997	1,014	598	595
14	Bhandara	360	423	...	...	2,357	2,309	879	865	452	475
15	Balaghat	178	203	...	...	166	138	228	244	174	166
	CHHATTISGARH DIVISION	*1,296*	*1,373*	*736*	*745*	*494*	*304*	*2,028*	*2,239*	*80*	*78*
16	Raipur	369	365	81	88	241	106	673	711	...	...
17	Bilaspur	746	810	634	637	222	182	692	748	9	5
18	Drug	181	198	21	20	31	16	663	780	71	73
	Berar	**14,370**	**14,010**	...	...	**17.185**	**14,991**	**942**	**912**	**87**	**84**
19	Amraoti	7,101	6,901	...	...	5,197	4,801	453	475	2	19
20	Akola	1,891	1,781	...	...	3,997	3,258	149	154	...	...
21	Buldana	3,560	3,439	.	...	3,639	3,081	55	55	...	...
22	Yeotmal	1,818	1,889	...	...	4,352	3,851	285	228	85	65
	Feudatory States	**1.754**	**1.847**	**646**	**636**	**556**	**470**	**794**	**803**	**10**	**9**
23	Makrai	25	21	...	...	102	110	46	38	...	...
24	Bastar	1,275	1,322	...	...	23	8	25	21	...	...
25	Kanker	13	17	...	...	...	...	97	93	...	...
26	Nandgaon	104	119	...	...	43	13	173	213	...	...
27	Khairagarh	26	38	...	...	15	10	161	185	...	...
28	Chhuikhadan	100	106	...	...	...	...	16	17	...	...
29	Kawardha	18	14	...	...	28	33	30	37	...	...
30	Sakti	18	18	..	...	4	1	1	...	...	...
31	Raigarh	56	64	...	...	16	10	70	77	...	...
32	Sarangarh	84	87	...	...	6	4	70	20	...	...
33	Chang Bhakar	...	1	18	18	3	1	74	72	2	2
34	Korea	2	1	271	256	4	3	27	24	6	6
35	Surguja	31	35	356	362	282	252	4	6	...	...
36	Udaipur	...	1	...	...	10	4	...	...	2	1
37	Jashpur	2	3	1	...	20	21	...	...	...	...

Race or Nationality.

BEDAR.		BELDAR.		BHAINA.		BHAMTA.		BHANGI.		BHAR-BHUNJA.		Remarks.	Serial No.
Hindu.		Hindu.		Hindu.		Hindu.		Hindu.		Hindu.			
Males.	Females.	Males.	Females.	Males.	Females.	Males.	Females.	Males.	Females.	Males.	Females.		
166	167	168	169	170	171	172	173	174	175	176	177	178	
1,893	1,936	12,905	12,711	8,489	8,898	2,120	2,150	3,735	3,825	1,722	1,526		
1,893	1,934	12,822	12,642	7,132	7,390	2,120	2,150	3,690	3,746	1,635	1,454		
81	45	6,053	5,952	7,132	7,390	1,193	1,170	3,665	3,716	1,206	1,165		
19	*2*	*1,617*	*1,601*	*462*	*506*	*2*	...	*1,745*	*1,745*	*587*	*538*		
3	2	521	457	...	...	...	...	784	800	184	179		1
...	...	356	382	...	...	...	...	456	477	46	48		2
2	...	628	639	...	...	...	...	423	379	293	240		3
14	...	12	15	462	506	...	...	4	2	42	34		4
...	...	100	108	...	...	2	...	78	78	23	27		5
2	*1*	*1,212*	*1,056*	...	*1*	*28*	*25*	*1,623*	*1,677*	*207*	*193*		
...	...	102	70	...	...	...	...	526	514	32	27		6
1	1	243	236	...	...	...	...	792	862	46	59		7
...	...	583	533	...	...	21	19	233	236	52	52		8
...	...	121	123	...	1	...	...	56	56	33	28		9
1	...	163	124	...	...	7	6	15	9	44	26		10
58	*42*	*2,267*	*2,309*	...	...	*1,163*	*1,144*	*5*	*9*	*185*	*146*		
16	8	981	1,097	..	...	558	549	...	...	55	50		11
24	25	496	458	...	...	418	400	...	...	90	75		12
...	...	653	614	...	...	183	189	...	...	24	12		13
18	9	73	84	...	...	4	6	...	...	6	3		14
...	...	64	56	...	...	...	..	5	9	10	6		15
2	...	*957*	*956*	*6,670*	*6,883*	...	*1*	*293*	*255*	*227*	*299*		
2	...	654	639	127	104	...	...	128	134	133	214		16
...	...	117	144	6,543	6,779	...	1	102	111	88	77		17
...	...	186	173	...	...	...	...	63	40	6	8		18
1,812	**1,889**	**6,769**	**6,690**	...	...	**927**	**980**	**25**	**30**	**429**	**289**		
586	532	1,161	1,183	...	...	331	354	...	...	253	185		19
680	801	1,652	1,643	...	...	245	276	25	30	84	54		20
354	378	1,611	1,609	...	...	...	...	...	...	46	25		21
192	178	2,345	2,255	...	...	351	350	...	...	44	25		22
...	**2**	**83**	**69**	**1,357**	**1,508**	...	...	**45**	**79**	**87**	**72**		
...	...	2	3	...	...	...	...	21	24	...	...		23
...	...	13	6	7	...	...	...	...	17	7	3		24
...	...	34	33	1	...	...	...	...	...	...	...		25
...	...	7	3	...	...	...	...	4	5	5	8		26
...	...	5	5	...	...	...	...	...	3	...	...		27
...	...	9	10	...	...	...	...	...	...	...	...		28
...	...	...	...	...	...	...	...	17	20	1	1		29
...	...	...	...	...	19	...	...	...	...	5	5		30
...	...	2	2	909	977	...	...	...	...	6	6		31
...	...	...	...	415	486	...	...	...	...	...	...		32
...	...	3	4	...	...	...	...	...	...	...	...		33
...	...	2	3	25	20	...	...	1	1	1	...		34
...	...	...	...	...	...	...	...	2	...	50	45		35
...	...	...	...	...	...	...	...	...	...	3	3		36
...	2	6	...	...	...	...	...	...	...	9	1		37

Remarks (column 178):

		M.	F.
Barai includes—			
Animist.	Feudatory States	3	1
Musalman.	Berar	19	24
Arya.	Narsinghpur	3	5
Bargaha includes—			
Animist.	Korea	107	98
	Surguja	5	5
Barhai includes—			
Animist.	Jubbulpore	3	0
	Nerbudda Division	6	4
	Nagpur Division	26	16
	Surguja	31	32
Musalman.	Yeotmal	1	0
Arya.	Jubbulpore	3	1
	Hoshangabad	3	6
Jain.	Berar	20	8
Sikh.	Jubbulpore Division	30	7
	Nerbudda Division	3	2
Basor includes—			
Musalman.	Amraoti	0	1
	Buldana	1	0
Bedar includes—			
Musalman.	Amraoti	1	0
Beldar includes—			
Animist.	Yeotmal	3	3
	Korea	0	1
Bhaina includes—			
Animist.	Mandla	4	112
	Bilaspur	111	146
	Feudatory States	33	53
Bhangi includes—			
Animist.	Damoh	1	0
Musalman.	Jubbulpore Division	114	130
	Nerbudda Division	48	50
	Chhattisgarh Division	2	5
Sikh.	Saugor	0	1
	Damoh	1	1
	Hoshangabad	4	4
	Akola	25	30
Bharbhunja includes—			
Musalman.	Saugor	0	1
	Yeotmal	1	2
Arya.	Jubbulpore	2	2

TABLE XIII.—Caste,

Serial No.	DISTRICT OR STATE.	BHARIA OR BHUMIA. Hindu. Males.	BHARIA OR BHUMIA. Hindu. Females.	BHARIA OR BHUMIA. Animist. Males.	BHARIA OR BHUMIA. Animist. Females.	BHARUD. Hindu. Males.	BHARUD. Hindu. Females.	BHAT. Hindu. Males.	BHAT. Hindu. Females.	BHIL. Hindu. Males.	BHIL. Hindu. Females.
		179	180	181	182	183	184	185	186	187	188
	Central Provinces and Berar ...	11,005	11,797	13,583	14,621	1,087	1,049	14,629	14,483	12,264	12,480
	C. P. British Districts and Berar ...	10,620	11,350	13,548	14,607	1,087	1,049	13,618	13,362	12,200	12,380
	C. P. British Districts	10,620	11,350	13,548	14,607	1,087	1,049	9,929	10,380	11,163	11,300
	Jubbulpore Division	*8,340*	*8,966*	*7,023*	*7,733*	...	...	*3,028*	*3,126*	*43*	*33*
1	Saugor	8	1	...	...	...	...	755	693	41	32
2	Damoh	600	634	168	173	...	...	630	668	1	...
3	Jubbulpore	7,518	8,106	5,364	5,994	...	...	1,089	1,136	1	1
4	Mandla	40	40	788	796	...	...	262	294	...	...
5	Seoni	174	185	703	770	...	...	292	335	...	5
	Nerbudda Division	*453*	*426*	*5,030*	*5,339*	*1,087*	*1,049*	*2,164*	*2,200*	*11,097*	*11,255*
6	Narsinghpur	113	119	1,117	1,195	...	...	457	516	...	...
7	Hoshangabad	22	25	370	372	1	...	657	614	20	17
8	Nimar	...	...	...	...	1,086	1,049	388	350	11,046	11,236
9	Betul	104	62	5	7	...	...	155	171	28	2
10	Chhindwara	214	220	3,538	3,765	...	...	507	549	3	...
	Nagpur Division	*85*	*80*	...	...	—	...	*2,433*	*2,468*	*18*	*7*
11	Wardha	...	...	...	...	...	...	508	438	1	...
12	Nagpur	...	3	...	...	...	...	795	819	17	7
13	Chanda	...	...	...	...	...	...	485	514	...	...
14	Bhandara	46	41	...	...	...	...	445	468	...	...
15	Balaghat	39	36	...	...	...	...	200	229	...	...
	Chhattisgarh Division	*1,742*	*1,878*	*1,495*	*1,535*	...	...	*2,304*	*2,586*	5	...
16	Raipur	4	4	1	...	...	...	825	874	5	...
17	Bilaspur	1,738	1,874	1,494	1,535	...	—	928	1,016	...	...
18	Drug	...	...	...	...	...	...	551	696	...	...
	Berar	...	—	...	...	...	...	3,689	2,982	1,037	1,080
19	Amraoti	...	...	...	...	...	...	1,213	1,018	55	75
20	Akola	...	...	...	...	...	...	816	521	91	90
21	Buldana	...	...	...	...	...	...	827	679	431	434
22	Yeotmal	...	...	...	...	...	...	833	764	460	481
	Feudatory States	385	447	35	14	...	...	1,011	1,121	64	100
23	Makrai	...	—	...	...	...	...	10	8	...	...
24	Bastar	...	...	13	6	...	...	128	116	...	...
25	Kanker	1	...	...	...	...	...	21	29	...	...
26	Nandgaon	...	...	...	...	...	...	130	121	7	5
27	Khairagarh	...	...	...	...	...	...	98	112	...	...
28	Chhuikhadan	...	...	...	...	...	...	20	26	...	...
29	Kawardha	...	...	...	...	...	...	56	55	...	...
30	Sakti	...	...	...	...	...	...	57	79	...	...
31	Raigarh	308	384	...	...	...	...	104	99	4	3
32	Sarangarh	5	3	...	...	...	...	92	121	...	...
33	Chang Bhakar	63	53	3	3	—	—	18	18	...	...
34	Korea	3	5	19	5	...	...	21	20	4	...
35	Surguja	1	...	...	—	...	...	134	159	49	92
36	Udaipur	2	...	...	...	...	...	5	17	...	...
37	Jashpur	2	2	...	...	...	...	117	140	...	...

Tribe, Race or Nationality.

		BHILALA.		BHOYAR.		BHUINHAR.					
MUSALMAN.		HINDU.		HINDU.		HINDU.		ANIMIST.		REMARKS.	
Males.	Females.	Males.	Females.	Males.	Females.	Males.	Females.	Males.	Females.		Serial No.
189	190	191	192	193	194	195	196	197	198	199	
1,504	**1,537**	**7,800**	**7,637**	**28,990**	**29,648**	**8,515**	**7,955**	**5,611**	**5,539**		
1,504	**1,537**	**7,747**	**7,584**	**28,988**	**29,648**	**984**	**804**	**13**	**10**		
760	**719**	**7,747**	**7,584**	**28,958**	**29,622**	**974**	**792**	**13**	**10**		
...	...	*11*	*2*	...	...	*2*	...	...	...	BHAT includes— M. F. *Animist.* Nagpur Division ... ... 10 10 Drug ... ... 5 3 *Musalman.* Jubbulpore ... ... 4 3 Hoshangabad ... ... 3 7 Nagpur Division ... ... 20 34 Chhattisgarh Division ... 14 6 Berar ... ... 25 33 Feudatory States 11 11	
...	...	...	...	...	...	...	...	...	...		1
...	...	...	...	...	...	...	...	...	...		2
...	...	11	2	...	...	2	...	...	...		3
...	...	...	...	...	...	...	...	...	...		4
...	...	...	...	...	...	...	...	...	...		5
760	*719*	*7,731*	*7,577*	*21,435*	*22,112*	*3*	*3*	...	...	BHIL includes— *Animist.* Nerbudda Division ... ... 3 3 Wardha ... ... 1 0 Berar 57 42	
...	...	...	...	...	...	...	...	...	...		6
...	...	1,393	1,340	8	5	...	...	...	...		7
760	719	6,324	6,220	1	...	...	...	...	...		8
...	...	14	17	11,256	11,536	...	...	...	...		9
...	...	...	...	10,175	10,571	3	3	...	...		10
...	...	*5*	*5*	*7,523*	*7,508*	*119*	*9*	...	...	BHOYAR includes— *Animist.* Nerbudda Division ... ... 4 4 Bilaspur 0 2	
...	...	...	...	5,850	5,855	...	...	...	...		11
...	...	...	...	1,664	1,647	...	...	...	...		12
...	...	...	...	9	6	115	7	...	...		13
...	...	...	...	...	...	...	...	...	...		14
...	...	5	5	...	...	4	2	...	...		15
...	...	...	...	...	*2*	*850*	*780*	*13*	*10*		
...	...	...	...	...	...	2	1	...	...		16
...	...	...	...	...	2	848	779	13	10		17
...	...	...	...	...	...	...	...	...	...		18
744	**818**	...	...	**30**	**26**	**10**	**12**	...	...		
392	388	...	...	30	21	6	9	...	...		19
...	...	...	...	...	5	...	...	...	...		20
352	430	...	...	...	...	...	...	...	...		21
...	...	...	...	...	...	4	3	...	...		22
...	...	**53**	**53**	**2**	...	**7,531**	**7,151**	**5,598**	**5,529**		
...	...	53	53	...	...	...	...	...	...		23
...	...	...	...	...	...	19	13	...	...		24
...	...	...	...	...	...	...	...	...	...		25
...	...	...	...	...	...	...	...	...	...		26
...	...	...	...	...	...	...	...	...	...		27
...	...	...	...	...	...	...	...	...	...		28
...	...	...	...	...	...	...	...	...	...		29
...	...	...	...	...	...	35	44	2	...		30
...	...	...	...	...	...	1,134	1,118	3	3		31
...	...	...	...	...	...	6	16	...	...		32
...	...	...	...	...	...	...	...	26	27		33
...	...	...	...	3	...	1	2	1,300	1,271		34
...	...	...	...	...	...	3,009	2,619	3,502	3,451		35
...	...	...	...	...	...	8	8	421	454		36
...	...	...	...	...	...	8,319	8,331	344	323		37

TABLE XIII.—Caste,

Serial No	DISTRICT OR STATE.	BHULIA. Hindu. Males.	BHULIA. Hindu. Females.	BHUNJIA. Hindu. Males.	BHUNJIA. Hindu. Females.	BIDUR. Hindu. Males.	BIDUR. Hindu. Females.	BINJHWAR. Hindu. Males.	BINJHWAR. Hindu. Females.	BINJHWAR. Animist. Males.	BINJHWAR. Animist. Females.
		200	201	202	203	204	205	206	207	208	209
	Central Provinces and Berar ...	**2,450**	**2,387**	**3,466**	**3,455**	**10,377**	**10,610**	**26,010**	**26,852**	**2,888**	**2,983**
	C. P. British Districts and Berar ...	**2,203**	**2,196**	**3,463**	**3,450**	**9,893**	**10,138**	**21,129**	**21,768**	**2,317**	**2,368**
	C. P. British Districts	**2,203**	**2,196**	**3,463**	**3,450**	**5,517**	**5,855**	**21,020**	**21,648**	**2,317**	**2,368**
	JUBBULPORE DIVISION	...	...	...	...	*160*	*141*	*119*	*146*	...	...
1	Saugor	...	...	...	...	36	35	...	...	...	...
2	Damoh	...	...	...	...	10	11	...	...	...	...
3	Jubbulpore	...	...	...	...	2	3	...	...	...	...
4	Mandla	...	...	...	...	75	62	10	9	...	...
5	Seoni	...	...	...	...	37	30	109	137	...	...
	NERBUDDA DIVISION	...	...	...	...	*739*	*782*	*3*	...	...	...
6	Narsinghpur	...	...	...	...	5	1	...	...	...	...
7	Hoshangabad	...	...	...	...	5	3	...	...	...	...
8	Nimar	...	...	...	...	86	101	...	...	...	...
9	Betul	...	...	...	...	278	307	3	...	...	...
10	Chhindwara	...	...	...	...	355	370	...	...	...	...
	NAGPUR DIVISION	...	...	...	...	*4,201*	*4,492*	*5,742*	*6,191*	...	*1*
11	Wardha	...	...	...	...	1,109	1,192	3	2	...	...
12	Nagpur	...	...	...	...	1,410	1,415	59	66	...	...
13	Chanda	...	...	...	...	1,026	1,129	199	187	...	...
14	Bhandara	...	...	...	...	596	673	2,641	2,772	...	...
15	Balaghat	...	...	...	...	60	83	2,840	3,164	...	1
	CHHATTISGARH DIVISION	*2,203*	*2,196*	*3,463*	*3,450*	*427*	*440*	*15,156*	*15,311*	*2,317*	*2,367*
16	Raipur	1,441	1,372	3,463	3,450	226	234	9,790	9,924	2,292	2,352
17	Bilaspur	762	824	...	...	176	177	5,365	5,387	25	15
18	Drug	...	...	...	...	25	29	1	...	...	...
	Berar	...	...	...	...	**4,376**	**4,283**	**109**	**120**	...	...
19	Amraoti	...	...	...	...	1,820	1,692	66	64	...	...
20	Akola	...	...	...	...	903	942	43	56	...	...
21	Buldana	...	...	...	...	574	586	...	...	...	...
22	Yeotmal	...	...	...	...	1,070	1,063	...	...	...	...
	Feudatory States	**247**	**191**	**3**	**5**	**484**	**472**	**4,881**	**5,084**	**571**	**615**
23	Makrai	...	...	...	...	3	3	...	...	...	...
24	Bastar	...	...	3	4	424	406	...	...	...	...
25	Kanker	...	...	...	...	1	...	...	...	...	...
26	Nandgaon	...	...	...	...	16	14	...	...	...	...
27	Khairagarh	...	...	...	...	15	15	2	1	...	...
28	Chhuikhadan	...	...	...	...	5	9	...	...	...	...
29	Kawardha	...	...	...	...	...	...	6	1	...	...
30	Sakti	...	...	...	...	1	4	1	4	...	1
31	Raigarh	189	130	...	...	...	3	34	17	237	265
32	Sarangarh	58	61	...	...	...	...	3,239	3,505	9	11
33	Chang Bhakar	...	...	...	...	...	...	...	...	...	...
34	Korea	...	...	...	...	...	...	5	1	321	337
35	Surguja	...	...	...	...	16	14	1,594	1,539	4	1
36	Udaipur	...	...	...	...	3	3	...	...	...	...
37	Jashpur	...	...	...	1	...	1	...	16	...	...

Tribe, Race or Nationality.

BISNOI. Hindu. Males.	BISNOI. Hindu. Females.	BOHRA. Musalman. Males.	BOHRA. Musalman. Females.	BRAHMAN. Hindu. Males.	BRAHMAN. Hindu. Females.	CHADAR. Hindu. Males.	CHADAR. Hindu. Females.	CHAMAR. Hindu. Males.	CHAMAR. Hindu. Females.	Serial No.
210	211	212	213	214	215	216	217	218	219	
563	531	2,852	2,133	237,605	208,139	13,968	14,161	443,059	458,535	
563	531	2,783	2,074	227,262	199,258	13,842	14,053	402,099	416,891	
563	531	2,108	1,576	183,170	165,518	13,840	14,053	385,704	401,102	
...	...	*257*	*223*	*76,399*	*71,249*	*12,314*	*12,550*	*82,679*	*81,764*	
...	...	65	52	22,187	20,305	7,303	7,333	35,914	35,219	1
...	...	23	16	12,527	11,452	3,516	3,081	21,757	21,562	2
...	...	175	143	32,969	31,689	1,327	1,359	19,999	19,966	3
...	...	1	1	4,506	3,894	26	22	2,376	2,303	4
...	...	23	10	4,210	3,909	140	155	2,633	2,714	5
557	*527*	*1,097*	*838*	*45,376*	*40,275*	*1,522*	*1,501*	*29,849*	*29,243*	
...	...	120	19	11,860	11,151	1,480	1,456	9,219	9,238	6
518	506	156	99	17,091	15,518	29	30	11,097	10,719	7
34	21	728	642	8,911	7,123	...	1	3,041	2,971	8
5	...	80	66	2,725	2,228	3	3	2,495	2,398	9
..	...	13	12	4,789	4,255	10	11	3,997	3,917	10
5	*2*	*487*	*363*	*27,377*	*22,411*	*2*	...	*12,638*	*11,852*	
...	1	146	114	6,839	5,267	...	...	1,953	1,711	11
2	1	254	179	11,612	9,519	1	...	4,201	4,014	12
...	...	35	40	8,458	2,905	...	...	1,734	1,587	13
3	...	37	19	3,724	3,373	...	...	3,210	3,053	14
...	...	15	11	1,744	1,347	1	...	1,540	1,487	15
1	*2*	*237*	*153*	*34,018*	*31,553*	*2*	*2*	*260,538*	*278,243*	
1	2	137	78	11,492	10,393	...	...	98,701	104,377	16
...	...	88	69	15,711	14,834	...	1	103,768	110,553	17
...	...	12	6	6,815	6,350	2	1	58,069	63,313	18
...	...	675	498	44,092	33,740	2	...	16,395	15,789	
...	...	390	269	13,915	10,416	2	...	3,940	3,821	19
...	...	76	52	12,535	9,600	...	...	5,266	5,097	20
...	...	108	93	10,916	8,863	...	...	4,578	4,335	21
...	...	101	90	6,726	4,861	...	...	2,605	2,530	22
...	...	69	59	10,343	8,881	126	108	40,960	41,644	
...	...	...	...	590	591	...	...	200	192	23
...	...	...	2	1,227	1,075	125	108	1,234	1,132	24
...	...	5	11	381	337	...	...	684	653	25
...	...	42	22	1,341	1,171	...	...	8,633	9,158	26
...	...	8	16	1,159	1,090	...	...	8,573	8,839	27
...	...	1	...	171	164	...	...	1,376	1,380	28
...	...	...	...	688	690	...	...	5,569	5,876	29
...	...	...	...	170	155	...	...	1,229	1,310	30
...	...	13	8	1,315	1,188	...	...	3,430	3,406	31
...	...	...	...	795	711	...	...	4,412	4,394	32
...	...	...	...	228	211	...	...	296	258	33
...	...	...	...	475	230	...	...	643	605	34
...	...	...	...	1,406	1,088	...	...	4,263	4,052	35
...	...	...	...	126	46	...	...	198	181	36
...	...	...	...	271	134	1	...	220	208	37

Remarks (220).

	M.	F.
Bhunjia includes—		
Animist.		
Raipur	2,083	2,116
Bidur includes—		
Animist.		
Jubbulpore Division	2	4
Nagpur Division	5	7
Bilaspur	0	1
Bastar	2	0
Brahmo.		
Akola	1	0
Jain.		
Nagpur	1	4
Berar	0	2
Bohra includes—		
Hindu.		
Nagpur	8	1
Yeotmal	26	51
Brahman includes—		
Animist.		
Bastar	2	0
Arya		
Jubbulpore Division	59	48
Nerbudda Division	23	16
Balaghat	3	2
Chhattisgarh Division	40	30
Feudatory States	5	2
Sikh.		
Jubbulpore	1	1
Jain.		
Nagpur Division	30	13
Drug	1	1
Berar	49	79
Chadar includes—		
Animist.		
Damoh	2	0
Narsinghpur	1	0
Bastar	2	2
Chamar includes—		
Animist.		
Jubbulpore Division	6	5
Chhindwara	2	0
Balaghat	1	0
Chhattisgarh Division	9	8
Feudatory States	15	10

TABLE XIII.—Caste,

Serial No.	DISTRICT OR STATE	CHAUHAN.		CHHIPA.				CHITARI.		DAHAYAT.		DANGI.	
		HINDU.		HINDU.		MUSALMAN.		HINDU.		HINDU.		HINDU.	
		Males.	Females.	Males.	Females.	Males.	Females.	Males.	Females.	Males.	Females.	Males.	Females.
		221	222	223	224	225	226	227	228	229	230	231	232
	Central Provinces and Berar ...	3,265	3,485	3,170	3,202	1,229	1,198	677	550	7,212	7,473	12,327	11,956
	C. P. British Districts and Berar ...	2,767	2,974	3,115	3,153	1,229	1,198	669	534	7,151	7,409	12,308	11,945
	C. P. British Districts	2,767	2,974	2,990	3,043	1,207	1,190	401	288	7,144	7,403	12,308	11,945
	JUBBULPORE DIVISION	...	...	*825*	*937*	*822*	*840*	*95*	*99*	*5,162*	*5,359*	*12,210*	*11,864*
1	Saugor	...	...	331	348	353	376	61	60	5	...	11,608	11,287
2	Damoh	...	...	21	24	92	107	1	2	482	495	572	539
3	Jubbulpore	...	...	297	395	345	332	32	37	4,423	4,574	29	38
4	Mandla	...	...	10	4	14	14	1	...	93	113	1	...
5	Seoni	...	...	166	156	18	11	...	...	159	177	...	...
	NERBUDDA DIVISION	...	...	*1,732*	*1,629*	*383*	*349*	*7*	...	*591*	*604*	*98*	*80*
6	Narsinghpur	...	...	338	428	10	6	2	...	250	272	67	56
7	Hoshangabad	...	...	370	384	45	49	...	...	208	220	...	...
8	Nimar	...	...	349	305	252	234	...	...	2	6	31	24
9	Betul	...	...	322	192	...	...	...	...	18	12	...	...
10	Chhindwara	...	...	353	320	76	60	5	...	113	94	...	...
	NAGPUR DIVISION	...	...	*373*	*439*	*2*	*1*	*274*	*166*	*52*	*51*	...	*1*
11	Wardha	...	...	1	2	...	...	79	67	12	10	...	...
12	Nagpur	...	...	52	59	1	1	53	54	8	4	...	1
13	Chanda	...	...	20	34	1	...	28	30	22	33	...	...
14	Bhandara	...	...	124	139	...	...	114	15	8	3	...	...
15	Balaghat	...	...	176	205	...	...	...	...	2	1	...	...
	CHHATTISGARH DIVISION	*2,767*	*2,974*	*60*	*48*	...	...	*25*	*23*	*1,339*	*1,389*	...	...
16	Raipur	802	868	3	6	...	...	13	13	6	10	...	...
17	Bilaspur	1,019	1,100	56	42	...	...	12	10	1,332	1,379	...	...
18	Drug	946	1,006	1	...	...	...	...	...	1	...	...	...
	Berar	...	...	125	110	22	8	268	246	7	6	...	...
19	Amraoti	...	...	84	81	10	6	52	40	6	6	...	...
20	Akola	...	...	32	24	8	1	202	205	1	...	...	...
21	Buldana	...	...	9	5	4	1	1	...	...	...	...	...
22	Yeotmal	...	...	...	...	...	...	13	1	...	...	...	...
	Feudatory States	498	511	55	49	...	...	8	16	61	64	19	11
23	Makrai	...	...	...	...	...	...	...	...	...	...	19	11
24	Bastar	4	15	6	8	...	...	2	6	...	...	...	...
25	Kanker	8	8	...	...	...	...	...	...	...	...	...	...
26	Nandgaon	92	113	9	6	...	...	6	10	...	...	...	...
27	Khairagarh	122	129	4	3	...	...	...	...	...	...	...	...
28	Chhuikhadan	...	...	...	...	...	...	...	...	...	...	...	...
29	Kawardha	271	243	36	30	...	...	...	...	31	35	...	...
30	Sakti	...	...	...	...	...	...	...	...	...	...	...	...
31	Raigarh	...	...	...	...	...	...	...	...	...	...	...	...
32	Sarangarh	...	...	...	...	...	...	...	...	...	...	...	...
33	Chang Bhakar	...	...	...	...	...	...	...	...	...	...	...	...
34	Korea	1	...	...	...	...	...	...	...	...	...	...	...
35	Surguja	...	3	...	2	...	...	...	...	30	29	...	...
36	Udaipur	...	...	...	...	...	...	...	...	...	...	...	...
37	Jashpur	...	...	...	...	...	...	...	...	...	...	...	...

Tribe, Race or Nationality.

DARAIHA.		DARJI.		DESWALI.		DHANAGAR.		DHANUK.		Remarks.	Serial No.
Hindu.		Hindu.		Hindu.		Hindu.		Hindu.			
Males.	Females.	Males.	Females.	Males.	Females.	Males.	Females.	Males.	Females.		
233	234	235	236	237	238	239	240	241	242	243	
1,294	1,446	26.113	25,188	3.978	3,783	48.797	47,486	3.215	3,386		
1,265	1,415	25.699	24.749	3.708	3.495	48,710	47,434	3,215	3.386		
1,265	1.415	18,001	17,524	3.708	3,495	11.073	11,045	3,211	3.381		
...	...	*6,812*	*6,485*	*44*	*30*	*9*	*6*	*25*	*20*	Chhipa includes— *Arya.* Bastar ... — ... M. 3 F. 4 *Sikh.* Saugor ... ... M. 1 F. 0	
...	...	1,967	1,835	42	30	...	...	6	7		1
...	...	1,179	1,067	1	...	...	...	...	...		2
...	...	2,655	2,574	...	...	8	4	22	13		3
...	...	426	418	1	...	...	2	...	...		4
...	...	585	591	...	...	1	...	...	...		5
...	...	*3,501*	*3.679*	*3,610*	*3,431*	*1,291*	*1,253*	*3,150*	*3,359*	Chitari includes— *Animist.* Bastar 1 0	
...	...	1,068	1,114	3	3	...	...	2,411	2,583		6
...	...	994	954	2.314	2,176	2	..	322	404		7
...	...	928	844	1,285	1,246	721	680	431	356		8
...	...	311	275	8	6	1	..	3	...		9
...	...	500	492	...	...	567	573	13	16		10
...	...	*6,400*	*6,305*	*1*	*2*	*9,745*	*9,745*	*3*	*2*	Dahayat, includes— *Animist.* Jubbulpore Division 2 3	
...	...	1,255	1,177	...	...	3.598	3,466	...	...		11
—	...	2,080	2.039	...	1	3,721	3,844	3	2		12
...	...	1,556	1,536	...	...	1,906	1,874	...	...		13
...	...	1,217	1,201	...	...	519	561	...	...		14
...	...	342	352	1	1	...	...	...	...		15
1,265	*1,415*	*988*	*1,055*	*53*	*32*	*29*	*41*	...	...	Darji includes— *Animist.* Mandla ... ... 0 1 Narsinghpur ... ... 1 0 *Musalman* Jubbulpore Division ... 5 11 Nerbudda Division ... 3 3 Raipur ... ... 8 5 Berar ... ... 0 3 Feudatory States 3 0	
62	74	292	302	...	2	22	80	...	...		16
1,179	1,334	568	610	53	20	7	8	...	...		17
24	7	128	143	...	...	...	3	...	...		18
...	...	7,698	7,225	...	...	37,637	36.389	4	5	*Arya.* Akola ... ... 2 2 *Sikh.* Jubbulpore — ... ... 1 0 *Jain.* Nimar ... ... 6 1 Nagpur Division ... ... 3 5 Amraoti ... ... 29 30 Akola ... ... 241 295 Buldana ... ... 420 412 Yeotmal 103 98	
—	...	2,122	2,036	...	...	9,910	9,367	—	...		19
—	—	1,889	1.601	...	...	10,863	10,586	2	...		20
—	...	2,219	2,123	...	...	9,290	8,988	...	...		21
...	—	1,518	1,465	...	...	7,574	7,448	2	5		22
29	31	414	439	270	288	87	52	—	...	Deswali includes— *Animist.* Sakti ... ... 11 0 Dhanagar includes— *Animist.* Feudatory States 3 3	
...	...	3J	35	200	223	1	...	...	...		23
—	...	25	17	...	...	59	41	...	...		24
...	...	3	6	..	...	...	...	...	...		25
...	...	49	51	...	—	2	2	...	...		26
...	...	75	83	...	...	1	3	...	...		27
...	...	19	25	...	...	...	...	...	...		28
...	...	42	64	...	...	...	...	...	...		29
...	...	1	1	70	64	...	...	...	...		30
29	31	67	62	...	...	...	...	...	...		31
...	...	42	57	...	..	..	...	...	...		32
...	...	15	13	...	...	...	...	...	...		33
...	...	5	4	...	...	...	...	...	...		34
...	...	32	21	...	1	1	1	...	...		35
...	...	...	...	...	...	...	...	...	...		36
...	...	...	...	...	...	23	5	...	...		37

TABLE XIII.—Caste,

Serial No.	DISTRICT OR STATE.	DHANWAR.				DHIMAR.		DHOBI.		DHO	
		HINDU.		ANIMIST.		HINDU.		HINDU.		HINDU.	
		Males.	Females.	Males.	Females.	Males.	Females.	Males.	Females.	Males.	Females.
		244	245	246	247	248	249	250	251	252	253
	Central Provinces and Berar ...	**7.074**	**7,183**	**2.107**	**2,273**	**140.853**	**142.831**	**81,127**	**84.300**	**1.759**	**1.621**
	C. P. British Districts and Berar ...	**4.924**	**5,168**	**502**	**594**	**139.674**	**141.638**	**72,093**	**74.600**	**1.644**	**1.509**
	C P. British Districts	**4,924**	**5,168**	**502**	**594**	**122.534**	**125.333**	**59.141**	**61,925**	**1.644**	**1,506**
	JUBBULPORE DIVISION	*3*	*3*	*1*	...	*35,349*	*36,561*	*13,963*	*14,351*	*726*	*754*
1	Saugor	...	...	..	...	5,522	5,534	3,967	4,017	...	...
2	Damoh	...	...	...	...	5,532	5,494	2,377	2.374	...	...
3	Jubbulpore	...	...	...	...	16,216	16,970	4,553	4,796	9	3
4	Mandla	3	3	1	...	5,184	5,416	1,369	1,314	649	675
5	Seoni	..	...	..	...	2,895	3,147	1,696	1,880	68	76
	NERBUDDA DIVISION	*8*	...	...	...	*16,460*	*16,518*	*8,184*	*8,543*	*353*	*134*
6	Narsinghpur	...	...	..	...	6,626	6,887	2,385	2,516	...	...
7	Hoshangabad	7	...	...	...	3,965	3,962	2,278	2,427	267	73
8	Nimar	1	...	...	...	835	830	1,012	1,059	74	52
9	Betul	...	...	...	...	1,634	1,648	903	860	...	...
10	Chhindwara	...	...	...	...	3,400	3,191	1,606	1,681	12	9
	NAGPUR DIVISION	...	...	...	...	*54,976*	*55,435*	*11,436*	*11,452*	*316*	*356*
11	Wardha	...	...	...	...	5,483	5,253	2,172	2,193	...	7
12	Nagpur	...	...	...	...	9,747	9,764	4,070	4,039	18	26
13	Chanda	...	...	...	...	17,030	17,253	2,588	2,606	24	28
14	Bhandara	...	...	...	...	18,759	19,129	1,977	1,928	...	...
15	Balaghat	...	...	...	...	3,957	4,035	629	686	274	295
	CHHATTISGARH DIVISION	*4,913*	*5,165*	*501*	*594*	*15,749*	*16,820*	*25,559*	*27,549*	*249*	*262*
16	Raipur	362	389	...	...	9,009	9,554	7,809	8,576	7	4
17	Bilaspur	4,546	4,775	501	594	4,022	4,384	11,716	12,358	241	258
18	Drug	5	1	...	...	2,718	2,882	6,034	6,615	1	...
	Berar	...	...	...	...	**17.140**	**16,305**	**12,952**	**12,675**	...	**3**
19	Amraoti	...	...	...	...	6,509	6,088	4,238	4,095	...	...
20	Akola	...	...	...	...	3,280	3,097	3,677	3,549	...	...
21	Buldana	...	...	...	...	1,810	1,710	2,233	2,194	...	...
22	Yeotmal	...	...	...	...	5,641	5,460	2,804	2,837	...	3
	Feudatory States	**2,150**	**2,015**	**1,605**	**1,679**	**1.179**	**1.193**	**9.034**	**9.700**	**115**	**112**
23	Makrai	...	...	...	...	24	19	70	85	...	...
24	Bastar	...	...	...	...	229	227	567	578	...	...
25	Kanker	...	...	...	...	185	178	364	377	...	...
26	Nandgaon	...	...	...	...	332	368	1,172	1,348	...	...
27	Khairagarh	...	...	..	...	211	198	1,370	1,409	...	...
28	Chhuikhadan	...	...	...	...	...	...	219	247	...	...
29	Kawardha	1	...	..	...	44	32	605	672	2	3
30	Sakti	177	159	5	6	22	28	541	574	...	...
31	Raigarh	35	37	1,098	1,182	17	19	1,212	1,331	...	...
32	Sarangarh	54	46	3	3	6	7	1,128	1,200	...	...
33	Chang Bhakar	...	...	...	...	88	96	11	9	75	71
34	Korea	...	...	233	235	4	...	142	132	6	8
35	Surguja	1,881	1,739	4	2	...	...	1,135	1,114	32	30
36	Udaipur	...	...	262	251	...	...	209	212	...	...
37	Jashpur	2	34	...	...	17	21	289	322	...	...

Tribe, Race or Nationality.

LI.		DHURI.		DOHOR.		DOM.		FAKIR.				Remarks.	Serial No.
Animist.		Hindu.		Hindu.		Hindu.		Hindu.		Musalman.			
Males.	Females.	Males.	Females.	Males	Females.	Males.	Females	Males.	Females.	Males.	Females.		
254	255	256	257	253	259	260	261	262	263	264	265	266	
749	**785**	**1,521**	**1,683**	**3,181**	**3,152**	**4,660**	**4,684**	**38**	**17**	**4,488**	**4,552**		
734	**768**	**1,464**	**1,621**	**3,181**	**3,152**	**3,745**	**3,745**	**29**	**17**	**4,321**	**4,370**		
734	**768**	**1,464**	**1,621**	**170**	**158**	**3,657**	**3,677**	**18**	**10**	**2,312**	**2,460**		
649	*701*	*11*	*9*	...	...	*2,293*	*2,345*	*1*	...	*901*	*978*	DHIMAR includes— *Animist.* M. F. Jubbulpore Division ... ... 3 2 Nagpur Division ... ... 13 15 Bilaspur ... ... 2 0 Yeotmal ... ... 1 0 Feudatory States ... ... 2 2 *Musalman.* Nimar 28 26	
...	...	2	3	...	...	104	97	...	...	169	131		1
...	...	...	...	...	...	...	...	...	...	141	163		2
...	...	9	5	...	...	1,939	1,965	...	...	277	277		3
649	701	...	1	...	...	206	245	...	...	57	57		4
...	...	...	...	...	...	44	38	1	...	257	350		5
...	...	...	...	...	...	*64*	*52*	*11*	*9*	*738*	*699*	DHOBI includes— *Animist.* Jubbulpore Division ... ... 4 1 Nagpur Division ... ... 2 33 Chhattisgarh Division ... ... 1 1 Feudatory States ... ... 12 10 *Musalman.* Jubbulpore ... ... 19 0 Nerbudda Division ... ... 15 11 Chanda ... ... 1 0 Drug ... ... 8 6 Berar 50 37	
...	...	...	...	...	...	4	7	...	...	17	18		6
...	...	...	...	...	...	58	44	8	6	185	179		7
...	...	...	...	...	...	1	...	...	...	120	93		8
...	...	...	...	...	...	...	...	...	...	36	24		9
...	...	...	...	...	...	1	1	3	3	380	385		10
55	*67*	*1*	...	*170*	*158*	*334*	*262*	*4*	...	*541*	*631*	DOM includes— *Animist.* Jubbulpore ... ... 1 1 Udaipur ... ... 53 59 Jashpur 204 230	
51	59	...	...	95	94	...	...	...	...	198	269		11
...	...	...	...	75	64	283	240	4	...	184	190		12
...	...	1	...	...	...	26	14	...	...	10	17		13
...	...	...	...	...	...	6	6	...	...	99	104		14
34	8	...	...	...	...	9	2	...	...	50	51		15
...	...	*1,458*	*1,612*	...	...	*976*	*1,018*	*2*	*1*	*132*	*152*		
...	...	429	508	...	...	904	941	2	1	68	83		16
...	...	1,016	1,089	...	...	72	77	...	...	35	41		17
...	...	7	15	...	...	...	...	...	...	29	28		18
...	...	...	...	**3,011**	**2,994**	**88**	**68**	**11**	**7**	**2,009**	**1,910**		
...	...	...	...	774	759	75	61	2	1	1,076	1,056		19
...	...	...	...	690	715	...	...	...	...	628	585		20
...	...	...	...	1,508	1,447	4	2	...	...	205	253		21
...	...	...	...	39	73	9	5	9	6	10	16		22
15	**17**	**57**	**62**	...	...	**915**	**939**	**9**	...	**167**	**182**		
...	...	...	...	...	...	...	...	...	...	18	28		23
...	...	...	...	...	...	50	40	...	...	...	...		24
...	...	9	13	...	...	...	...	...	...	5	...		25
...	...	...	...	...	...	...	...	...	...	1	3		26
...	...	...	...	...	...	8	7	...	...	2	3		27
...	...	...	...	...	...	...	...	...	...	2	5		28
...	...	48	49	...	...	...	...	...	...	5	6		29
...	...	...	...	...	...	...	...	...	...	19	12		30
...	...	...	...	...	...	20	16	...	...	...	...		31
...	...	...	...	...	...	...	...	...	...	...	...		32
...	...	...	...	...	...	...	...	...	...	...	...		33
14	17	...	...	...	...	...	...	...	...	7	8		34
1	...	...	...	...	...	71	78	2	...	42	44		35
...	...	...	...	...	...	107	124	...	...	...	...		36
...	...	...	...	...	...	659	674	7	...	66	78		37

TABLE XIII.—Caste,

Serial No.	DISTRICT OR STATE.	GADARIA.		GANDA.				GANDHI.		GANDLI.		GARPAGARI.	
		HINDU.		HINDU.		ANIMIST.		HINDU.		HINDU.		HINDU.	
		Males.	Females.	Males.	Females.	Males.	Females.	Males.	Females.	Males.	Females.	Males.	Females.
		267	268	269	270	271	272	273	274	275	276	277	278
	Central Provinces and Berar ...	**20,244**	**19,963**	**72,379**	**75,595**	**1,906**	**1,907**	**170**	**164**	**1,414**	**1,499**	**4,500**	**4,548**
	C. P. British Districts and Berar ...	**18,080**	**17,730**	**44,180**	**46,613**	**133**	**141**	**170**	**164**	**1,414**	**1,494**	**4,497**	**4,542**
	C. P. British Districts	**17,980**	**17,682**	**44,178**	**46,613**	**133**	**141**	**6**	...	**1,360**	**1,437**	**3,056**	**3,153**
	JUBBULPORE DIVISION	*7,178*	*6,792*	*3*	*2*	...	...	...	...	...	...	*77*	*97*
1	Saugor	1,905	1,690	...	...	...	...	...	...	...	...	...	...
2	Damoh	1,309	1,295	...	...	...	...	...	...	...	...	...	...
3	Jubbulpore	3,399	3,259	...	...	...	...	...	...	...	...	...	...
4	Mandla	346	354	3	2	...	...	...	...	...	...	2	...
5	Seoni	219	194	...	...	...	...	...	...	...	...	75	97
	NERBUDDA DIVISION	*4,757*	*4,559*	*11*	*11*	...	...	...	...	...	...	*613*	*676*
6	Narsinghpur	944	898	...	...	...	...	...	...	...	...	...	...
7	Hoshangabad	1,467	1,358	...	...	...	...	...	...	...	...	...	...
8	Nimar	510	393	...	...	...	...	...	...	...	...	...	...
9	Betul	721	781	1	...	...	...	...	...	...	...	194	202
10	Chhindwara	1,115	1,159	10	11	...	...	...	...	...	...	419	474
	NAGPUR DIVISION	*224*	*147*	*107*	*137*	*3*	*2*	*6*	...	*1,345*	*1,428*	*2,364*	*2,377*
11	Wardha	33	22	...	...	...	...	6	...	1	...	369	374
12	Nagpur	160	109	...	...	...	...	...	...	51	38	1,113	1,092
13	Chanda	5	2	9	13	...	...	...	...	1,154	1,221	194	179
14	Bhandara	13	5	...	...	...	...	...	...	139	169	476	507
15	Balaghat	13	9	98	124	3	2	...	...	...	...	212	225
	CHHATTISGARH DIVISION	*5,831*	*6,154*	*44,057*	*46,463*	*130*	*139*	...	...	*15*	*9*	*2*	*3*
16	Raipur	1,997	2,078	27,537	28,025	30	30	...	...	12	5	2	3
17	Bilaspur	1,150	1,257	13,193	14,742	98	103	...	...	...	...	...	...
18	Drug	2,674	2,819	3,327	3,696	2	6	...	...	3	4	...	...
	Berar	**100**	**48**	**2**	...	...	...	**164**	**164**	**54**	**57**	**1,441**	**1,389**
19	Amraoti	71	29	...	...	...	...	59	37	...	...	756	681
20	Akola	23	18	...	...	...	...	28	43	...	...	336	353
21	Buldana	1	1	2	...	...	...	62	63	...	...	179	188
22	Yeotmal	5	...	...	...	...	...	15	21	54	57	170	167
	Feudatory States	**2,164**	**2,233**	**28,199**	**28,982**	**1,773**	**1,766**	...	..	...	**5**	**3**	**6**
23	Makrai	41	48	...	...	...	...	...	...	...	...	...	...
24	Bastar	10	21	2,447	2,509	19	15	...	...	...	...	...	...
25	Kanker	45	48	2,528	2,605	46	55	...	...	...	...	...	...
26	Nandgaon	833	828	588	642	...	...	...	...	...	...	...	...
27	Khairagarh	542	592	681	778	...	...	...	..	...	...	3	6
28	Chhuikhadan	255	274	77	93	...	...	...	...	...	...	...	...
29	Kawardha	169	162	296	343	4	2	...	...	...	...	...	...
30	Sakti	15	20	976	1,037	...	..	...	...	...	...	...	...
31	Raigarh	6	4	8,370	8,594	13	9	...	...	...	...	...	...
32	Sarangarh	...	...	5,252	5,372	...	..	...	...	...	...	...	...
33	Chang Bhakar	...	...	1	2	..	...	...	...	...	...	...	...
34	Korea	12	5	2	...	53	50	...	...	...	...	...	...
35	Surguja	221	222	1,720	1,721	29	33	...	...	...	...	...	...
36	Udaipur	2	2	634	605	1,108	1,117	...	...	...	...	...	...
37	Jashpur	13	7	4,618	4,681	501	485	...	...	...	5	...	...

Tribe, Race or Nationality.

GHASIA.		GHOSI.		GOLAR.		GOND.				Remarks.	Serial No.
Hindu.		Hindu.		Hindu.		Hindu.		Animist.			
Males.	Females.	Males.	Females.	Males.	Females.	Males.	Females.	Males.	Females.		
279	280	281	282	283	284	285	286	287	288	289	
20,881	22,261	4,999	4,740	8,080	8,630	177,982	189,275	960,175	1,006,461		
10,587	11,586	4,811	4,604	8,065	8,623	156,259	165,878	694,617	738,387		
10,586	11,586	4,809	4,604	5,432	5,855	141,178	150,461	665,492	708,669		
557	*638*	*3,757*	*3,619*	*373*	*433*	*27,309*	*27,936*	*207,279*	*219,604*	GADARIA includes— *Animist.* M. F. Mandla ... ... 1 0 Nerbudda Division ... ... 0 2 Bilaspur ... ... 1 0 *Arya.* Jubbulpore 5 3	
...	...	2,580	2,382	...	...	3,253	3,223	11,492	12,080		1
...	...	936	888	...	...	10,729	11,027	4,790	4,961		2
4	1	271	300	...	...	12,665	13,020	30,929	32,472		3
442	495	2	4	..	...	323	280	93,166	97,697		4
111	142	48	45	373	433	339	386	66,902	72,294		5
52	*53*	*991*	*963*	*463*	*672*	*11,842*	*11,958*	*161,128*	*172,394*	GANDHI includes— *Musalman.* Wardha ... ... 6 0 Berar ... ... 82 70 GANDLI includes— *Animist.* Yeotmal 0 1	
1	...	448	416	...	...	4,132	4,307	13,590	15,046		6
...	2	279	287	...	...	4,090	4,409	18,427	19,870		7
...	...	134	116	13	12	1,978	1,783	2,227	2,233		8
2	5	4	3	423	552	1,017	859	50,171	53,104		9
49	46	126	141	17	108	625	600	76,713	82,041		10
240	*258*	*16*	*13*	*4,606*	*4,750*	*21,133*	*21,990*	*154,735*	*162,580*	GHASIA includes— *Animist.* Mandla ... ... 170 172 Seoni ... ... 2 2 Chhindwara ... ... 30 21 Chhattisgarh Division ... ... 27 27 Feudatory States 475 509	
...	...	16	12	32	47	421	368	19,674	20,231		11
1	...	...	...	319	320	8,062	8,110	16,321	16,498		12
5	2	...	...	2,332	2,377	6,086	6,425	50,725	52,496		13
75	77	...	...	1,290	1,392	3,746	4,165	32,471	35,489		14
159	179	...	1	633	614	2,817	2,931	35,544	37,866		15
9,737	*10,637*	*15*	*9*	...	...	*80,895*	*88,568*	*142,350*	*154,291*	GHOSI includes— *Animist* Jashpur ... ... 117 41 *Musalman.* Saugor ... ... 0 4 Nerbudda Division 79 65	
3,533	3,869	5	3	...	...	24,711	27,304	76,289	83,088		16
5,404	5,865	10	6	...	...	44,842	48,407	22,341	23,677		17
800	903	...	...	...	...	11,342	12,857	43,720	47,526		18
1	...	2	...	2,633	2,768	15,081	15,417	29,125	29,718	GOLAR includes— *Animist.* Seoni ... ... 1 2 Betul ... ... 0 3 Nagpur ... ... 144 162 Chanda ... ... 5 0 Bhandara ... ... 321 327 Balaghat ... ... 57 23 Amraoti 829 855	
1	...	...	...	953	952	4,658	4,679	7,350	7,302		19
...	...	2	...	72	96	1,692	1,631	452	412		20
...	...	...	...	9	6	213	191	52	41		21
...	...	...	...	1,599	1,714	8,518	8,016	21,271	21,873		22
10,294	10,675	188	136	15	7	21,723	23,397	265,558	268,074	GOND includes— *Arya.* Hoshangabad... ... ... 1 1	
...	...	...	...	...	...	27	31	518	526		23
1,056	1,109	...	...	12	4	1,285	1,030	141,751	141,453		24
110	152	...	...	...	...	116	89	33,041	34,354		25
212	283	...	...	...	...	180	189	11,945	13,730		26
172	175	...	...	...	...	6,933	8,083	3,901	4,540		27
41	43	...	...	...	...	91	94	2,133	2,425		28
89	106	47	61	...	...	72	43	6,525	7,108		29
245	253	...	...	...	...	691	775	1,900	2,049		30
1,595	1,635	...	...	3	3	9,143	9,780	2,111	2,174		31
827	869	...	...	...	...	1,765	1,951	75	87		32
73	72	...	...	...	...	125	100	3,874	3,865		33
548	510	...	...	...	...	75	60	10,010	9,795		34
4,047	4,017	10	20	...	...	441	391	42,413	41,614		35
431	467	...	...	...	...	95	93	3,276	3,144		36
848	984	131	55	...	...	684	689	1,176	1,210		37

TABLE XIII.—Caste,

Serial No.	DISTRICT OR STATE.	GONDHALI.		GOSAIN.		GOWARI.				GUJAR.	
		Hindu.		Hindu.		Hindu.		Animist.		Hindu.	
		Males.	Females.	Males.	Females.	Males.	Females.	Males.	Females.	Males.	Females.
		290	291	292	293	294	295	296	297	298	299
	Central Provinces and Berar ...	1,810	1,767	22,107	20,165	74,747	77,756	2,553	2,524	28,607	27,191
	C. P. British Districts and Berar ...	1,810	1,767	20,791	18,909	74,714	77,719	2,553	2,524	28,130	26,740
	C. P. British Districts	272	243	13,462	12,814	60,427	62,508	2,497	2,482	27,656	26,327
	JUBBULPORE DIVISION	...	...	*2,279*	*2,218*	*2,418*	*2,531*	*297*	*296*	*463*	*348*
1	Saugor	...	...	326	286	...	...	...	...	222	151
2	Damoh	...	...	178	184	...	...	...	...	45	41
3	Jubbulpore	...	...	1,011	1,052	...	...	...	...	105	67
4	Mandla	...	...	208	183	21	5	...	...	14	12
5	Seoni	...	...	556	513	2,397	2,526	207	296	77	77
	NERBUDDA DIVISION	*28*	*31*	*3,987*	*3,613*	*1,909*	*1,979*	*1,600*	*1,603*	*27,018*	*25,774*
6	Narsinghpur	...	...	832	768	2	2	...	...	2,508	2,437
7	Hoshangabad	...	5	1,481	1,300	...	...	...	...	12,080	11,416
8	Nimar	6	10	699	593	4	2	...	...	11,956	11,453
9	Betul	22	16	432	427	538	554	1,278	1,305	46	20
10	Chhindwara	...	...	543	525	1,370	1,421	322	298	428	439
	NAGPUR DIVISION	*208*	*158*	*3,701*	*3,413*	*56,075*	*57,978*	*599*	*583*	*161*	*177*
11	Wardha	155	112	769	639	7,807	7,863	78	75	2	...
12	Nagpur	27	31	1,532	1,443	10,260	10,445	91	90	62	64
13	Chanda	25	15	330	311	5,347	5,456	253	239	...	...
14	Bhandara	1	...	587	537	21,031	22,002	92	100	96	113
15	Balaghat	...	...	483	483	11,630	12,212	85	79	1	...
	CHHATTISGARH DIVISION	*36*	*54*	*3,495*	*3,570*	*25*	*20*	*1*	...	*19*	*28*
16	Raipur	36	54	1,239	1,182	23	20	...	...	...	...
17	Bilaspur	...	...	1,445	1,564	...	...	...	...	19	28
18	Drug	...	...	811	824	2	...	1	...	...	...
	Berar	1,538	1,524	7,329	6,095	14,287	15,211	56	42	474	413
19	Amraoti	198	166	1,838	1,404	6,167	6,150	40	32	324	269
20	Akola	609	712	2,260	1,957	1,063	1,090	6	7	90	97
21	Buldana	420	414	1,598	1,359	99	81	...	...	47	44
22	Yeotmal	251	232	1,638	1,375	6,958	7,890	10	3	13	3
	Feudatory States	...	...	1,316	1,256	33	37	...	...	477	451
23	Makrai	...	...	5	2	...	...	...	...	451	425
24	Bastar	...	...	10	16	2	10	...	...	...	1
25	Kanker	...	...	61	62	1	...	...	...	...	...
26	Nandgaon	...	...	75	60	10	7	...	...	...	...
27	Khairagarh	...	...	145	146	3	4	...	...	...	1
28	Chhuikhadan	...	...	9	6	...	...	...	...	...	...
29	Kawardha	...	...	49	52	1	...	...	...	25	24
30	Sakti	...	...	8	8	...	...	...	...	...	...
31	Raigarh	...	...	46	49	...	...	...	...	...	...
32	Sarangarh	...	...	77	57	...	...	...	...	...	...
33	Chang Bhakar	...	...	11	5	...	...	...	...	...	...
34	Korea	...	...	94	96	...	...	...	...	...	...
35	Surguja	...	...	434	400	...	...	...	...	1	...
36	Udaipur	...	...	30	30	...	...	...	...	...	...
37	Jashpur	...	...	262	268	16	16	...	...	...	...

Tribe, Race or Nationality.

GURAO.		HALBA.		HALWAI.		HATGAR.		JANGAM.		Remarks.	Serial No.
Hindu.		Hindu.		Hindu.		Hindu.		Hindu.			
Males.	Females.	Males.	Females.	Males.	Females.	Males.	Females.	Males.	Females.		
300	301	302	303	304	305	306	307	308	309	310	
6,994	**7,178**	**48,836**	**51,375**	**1,597**	**1,382**	**7,189**	**7,236**	**1,836**	**1,765**		
6,988	**7,168**	**35,545**	**37,875**	**1,170**	**995**	**7,189**	**7,236**	**1,826**	**1,753**		
2,929	**3,127**	**33,760**	**36,056**	**971**	**795**	**152**	**165**	**696**	**686**		
5	*2*	*438*	*449*	*290*	*285*	...	...	*5*	*2*	Gosain includes— *Animist.* M. F. Mandla ... ... 3 0 Narsinghpur ... ... 3 1 *Arya.* Raipur ... ... 11 12 *Brahmo.* Jubbulpore ... ... 3 4 Narsinghpur ... ... 1 *Jain.* Berar 3 1	
4	2	26	31	6	7	...	...	1	...		1
...	...	...	...	8	8	...	...	...	...		2
...	...	3	1	150	142	...	...	4	2		3
1	...	3	4	38	39	...	...	...	...		4
...	...	396	413	88	89	...	...	...	...		5
532	*640*	*139*	*140*	*109*	*82*	*2*	*6*	*112*	*135*	Gowari includes— *Jain.* Nagpur 1 0	
...	...	...	...	3	1	...	...	...	...		6
78	104	...	...	6	9	...	...	16	17		7
379	435	127	140	34	19	2	6	38	64		8
19	39	1	...	3	2	...	...	21	23		9
56	62	1	...	63	51	...	...	37	31		10
2,347	*2,430*	*7,450*	*7,521*	*118*	*74*	*150*	*159*	*579*	*549*	Gujar includes— *Musalman.* Jubbulpore Division ... 43 8 Nimar ... ... 2 1 *Jain.* Akola 0 1	
771	808	388	346	10	8	42	50	173	159		11
845	820	331	352	84	56	11	10	102	100		12
483	490	1,222	1,107	14	3	94	95	286	202		13
209	259	4,891	4,946	10	7	3	4	37	28		14
39	53	618	680	...	...	...	...	1	...		15
45	*55*	*25,753*	*27,946*	*454*	*354*	...	...	...	...	Gurao includes— *Jain.* Amraoti 3 5	
23	27	2,186	2,313	239	163	...	...	...	...		16
7	9	1	...	193	175	...	...	...	...		17
15	19	23,566	25,633	22	16	...	...	...	...		18
4,059	**4,041**	**1,785**	**1,819**	**199**	**200**	**7,037**	**7,071**	**1,130**	**1,067**	Halba includes— *Animist* Mandla ... ... 1 0 Nagpur Division ... ... 11 18 Chhattisgarh Division ... 52 0 Berar ... ... 2 0 Feudatory States 47 47	
1,655	1,655	1,066	1,135	40	25	231	208	164	155		19
1,006	1,022	211	192	82	107	1,342	1,259	275	257		20
823	824	14	10	52	42	346	350	139	117		21
575	540	494	482	25	26	5,118	5,254	552	538		22
6	**10**	**13,291**	**13,500**	**427**	**387**	...	...	**10**	**12**	Halwai includes— *Musalman.* Akola ... .. 10 12 *Jain.* Amraoti ... ... 2 3 Hatgar includes— *Animist.* Yeotmal ... ... 1 0 Jangam includes— *Jain.* Chanda ... ... 2 1 Yeotmal 8 7	
...	...	...	...	...	...	...	...	...	...		23
...	...	7,956	7,884	5	...	...	...	10	12		24
...	...	4,276	4,453	2	3	...	...	...	...		25
...	...	1,002	1,110	9	9	...	...	...	...		26
4	6	36	47	6	1	...	...	...	...		27
...	...	1	1	...	...	...	...	...	...		28
...	...	...	...	12	19	...	...	...	...		29
...	...	...	...	...	...	...	...	...	...		30
2	4	...	...	59	46	...	...	...	...		31
...	...	9	...	10	11	...	...	...	...		32
...	...	...	...	...	...	...	...	...	...		33
...	...	...	...	10	12	...	...	...	...		34
...	...	1	5	286	250	...	...	...	...		35
...	...	...	...	1	...	...	...	...	...		36
...	...	...	...	27	36	...	...	...	...		37

TABLE XIII.—Caste,

Serial No.	DISTRICT OR STATE.	JAT.		JINGAR.		JOGI.		JOSHI.		JULAHA.		KAC	
		HINDU.		HINDU.		HINDU.		HINDU.		MUSALMAN.		HINDU.	
		Males.	Females.	Males.	Females.	Males.	Females.	Males.	Females.	Males.	Females.	Males.	Females.
		311	312	313	314	315	316	317	318	319	320	321	322
	Central Provinces and Berar ...	**5.753**	**4.206**	**950**	**936**	**7.753**	**7,649**	**2,831**	**3,075**	**2.340**	**1.858**	**801**	**891**
	C. P. British Districts and Berar ...	**5.738**	**4.190**	**945**	**932**	**6,866**	**6,750**	**2.823**	**3.061**	**1,675**	**1,269**	**732**	**808**
	C. P. British Districts	**5,093**	**3.852**	**248**	**256**	**4,722**	**4.682**	**1.923**	**2,006**	**1,361**	**1,076**	**559**	**578**
	JUBBULPORE DIVISION	*1,565*	*504*	*41*	*37*	*1,451*	*1,474*	*562*	*566*	*757*	*610*	*438*	*445*
1	Saugor	750	251	...	...	340	361	316	202	49	59	32	32
2	Damoh	43	30	1	...	94	83	131	133	5	...	84	73
3	Jubbulpore	600	169	3	2	288	275	92	114	691	539	316	333
4	Mandla	22	13	5	6	557	564	9	16	12	12	6	7
5	Seoni	44	41	32	29	174	191	14	11	...	...	...	...
	NERBUDDA DIVISION	*3,257*	*3,184*	*63*	*63*	*1,969*	*1,715*	*547*	*577*	*160*	*126*	*50*	*64*
6	Narsinghpur	496	439	11	8	273	249	135	136	3	1	47	59
7	Hoshangabad	2,406	2,438	2	1	956	803	185	157	54	10	1	3
8	Nimar	320	263	9	13	527	441	19	174	100	114	...	...
9	Betul	35	30	20	24	104	102	70	63	...	...	2	2
10	Chhindwara	30	14	21	17	109	120	58	47	3	1	...	...
	NAGPUR DIVISION	*233*	*161*	*106*	*102*	*347*	*262*	*556*	*571*	*410*	*321*	*54*	*48*
11	Wardha	117	96	4	5	44	43	294	377	...	3	32	42
12	Nagpur	61	28	34	47	39	30	142	87	319	280	8	2
13	Chanda	41	24	41	38	53	63	...	...	21	23	...	...
14	Bhandara	1	7	26	11	26	33	117	101	62	11	13	4
15	Balaghat	13	6	...	1	85	93	3	6	8	4	1	...
	CHHATTISGARH DIVISION	*16*	*3*	*39*	*54*	*1,055*	*1,231*	*258*	*292*	*34*	*19*	*17*	*21*
16	Raipur	8	2	22	42	174	188	82	96	11	11	...	1
17	Bilaspur	5	1	15	12	683	788	13	13	23	8	17	19
18	Drug	2	...	2	...	198	255	163	183	...	...	...	1
	Berar	**645**	**338**	**697**	**676**	**2.144**	**2.068**	**900**	**1.055**	**314**	**193**	**173**	**230**
19	Amraoti	255	142	169	146	416	392	221	213	158	144	84	120
20	Akola	218	113	248	267	832	795	25	16	111	39	35	48
21	Buldana	114	65	199	186	596	567	9	2	...	...	16	20
22	Yeotmal	58	18	81	77	300	314	645	824	45	10	38	42
	Feudatory States	**15**	**16**	**5**	**4**	**887**	**899**	**8**	**14**	**665**	**589**	**69**	**83**
23	Makrai	...	3	5	4	40	36	...	—	...	...	...	...
24	Bastar	...	...	...	...	102	105	—	—	2	4	1	1
25	Kanker	...	...	...	...	13	1	—	—	2	1	1	...
26	Nandgaon	5	8	...	...	60	53	...	...	2	3	61	72
27	Khairagarh	9	5	...	...	78	92	...	1	...	...	...	...
28	Chhuikhadan	...	...	...	...	1	3	...	...	...	...	...	...
29	Kawardha	...	...	...	...	379	387	...	...	...	—	...	...
30	Sakti	...	...	...	...	91	116	...	...	4	4	...	...
31	Raigarh	1	...	...	...	43	55	1	2	30	...	...	...
32	Sarangarh	...	...	...	...	12	14	...	...	...	...	...	...
33	Chang Bhakar	...	...	...	...	12	11	...	...	5	5	...	...
34	Korea	...	...	...	...	40	19	...	...	3	3	5	4
35	Surguja	...	...	...	...	16	7	7	11	560	504	1	5
36	Udaipur	...	...	...	—	...	...	...	—	...	...	...	1
37	Jashpur	...	...	...	...	...	...	...	...	57	65	...	...

Tribe, Race or Nationality.

HERA.		KACHHI.		KADERA.		KAHAR.		KALAR.			
MUSALMAN.		HINDU.		HINDU.		HINDU.		HINDU.		REMARKS.	
Males.	Females.	Males.	Females.	Males.	Females.	Males.	Females.	Males.	Females.		Serial No.
323	324	325	326	327	328	329	330	331	332	333	
561	591	60,287	59,266	1,114	1,155	11,883	11,474	96,426	99,024		
547	574	60,018	58,980	1,114	1,155	10,773	10,373	78,004	80,180		
544	570	59,355	58,715	1,112	1,154	10,409	10,153	68,224	70,841		
343	*340*	*45,191*	*44,692*	*449*	*479*	*628*	*577*	*9,138*	*9,359*		
80	79	20,383	20,249	215	231	50	31	1,301	1,304		1
...	...	7,976	7,674	105	112	3	...	1,216	1,256		2
105	107	13,866	13,920	110	117	249	107	3,360	3,367		3
17	22	1,974	1,930	3	...	13	11	702	768		4
141	132	992	919	16	19	313	338	2,559	2,694		5
58	*50*	*12,941*	*13,030*	*599*	*605*	*5,557*	*5,473*	*10,046*	*10,095*		
...	—	5,718	5,931	389	390	1,058	1,121	1,497	1,480		6
14	4	4,603	4,652	114	121	2,997	2,947	1,957	1,955		7
17	18	1,658	1,555	77	73	1,338	1,244	1,112	1,074		8
...	...	180	166	8	4	68	56	1,818	1,884		9
27	28	782	726	11	17	101	105	3,662	3,702		10
139	*177*	*724*	*608*	*9*	*22*	*1,684*	*1,599*	*29,026*	*30,088*		
...	...	107	84	...	...	85	45	1,788	1,758		11
...	...	482	434	...	...	508	465	4,923	4,963		12
40	52	26	12	...	...	176	144	4,417	4,446		13
62	88	56	51	...	...	579	540	13,773	14,416		14
37	37	53	27	9	22	336	405	4,125	4,505		15
4	*3*	*499*	*355*	*55*	*48*	*2,540*	*2,504*	*20,014*	*21,269*		
4	3	45	28	20	18	459	449	7,823	8,433		16
...	...	416	320	19	15	1,992	2,001	5,132	5,346		17
...	—	38	28	16	15	89	54	7,059	7,490		18
3	**4**	**663**	**265**	**2**	**1**	**364**	**220**	**9,780**	**9,339**		
...	—	349	103	2	1	249	170	4,067	3,880		19
...	...	57	29	...	...	61	26	2,064	1,949		20
3	4	24	21	...	...	16	5	909	874		21
...	...	233	112	...	...	38	19	2,740	2,636		22
14	**17**	**269**	**286**	...	...	**1,110**	**1,101**	**18,422**	**18,844**		
—	...	180	208	...	...	84	71	47	39		23
...	...	3	2	...	...	25	25	4,960	5,046		24
...	...	2	...	...	...	14	4	3,556	3,743		25
...	...	25	16	...	...	27	18	1,697	1,836		26
7	10	11	9	...	...	24	34	1,798	1,977		27
...	—	...	—	...	...	6	10	385	402		28
...	...	...	...	...	...	12	0	693	692		29
...	...	2	3	...	...	2	2	325	314		30
...	...	5	3	...	...	91	88	1,848	1,873		31
...	...	...	...	...	...	171	216	783	783		32
...	...	20	34	...	...	...	...	3	3		33
...	...	11	5	...	...	43	46	455	374		34
...	...	9	6	...	...	503	481	1,766	1,647		35
...	...	1	...	...	...	26	23	82	87		36
7	7	...	...	...	...	82	74	24	28		37

Remarks (333):

JAT includes—

	M.	F.
Musalman.		
Jubbulpore Division	68	33
Nimar	6	1
Amraoti	1	0
Arya.		
Raipur	1	0
Akola	0	1
Sikh.		
Saugor	340	38
Jubbulpore	340	30
Mandla	2	0
Nimar	1	0
Chanda	1	0
Khairagarh	5	0
Jain.		
Buldana	1	0

JOGI includes—

	M.	F.
Animist.		
Jubbulpore Division	4	2
Chhindwara	7	0
Feudatory States	23	10

JULAHA includes—

	M.	F.
Hindu.		
Jubbulpore	1	0
Nagpur Division	17	33
Yeotmal	37	4
Feudatory States	6	5

KACHHI includes—

	M.	F.
Animist.		
Jubbulpore Division	5	1
Chang Bhakar	0	1
Musalman.		
Amraoti	199	20
Yeotmal	215	93
Arya.		
Jubbulpore	2	0
Jain.		
Buldana	1	1

KADERA includes—

	M.	F.
Animist.		
Narsinghpur...	1	3

KAHAR includes—

	M.	F.
Animist.		
Narsinghpur...	1	1
Amraoti	6	9
Feudatory States	3	2
Sikh.		
Jubbulpore Division	10	3

KALAR includes—

	M.	F.
Animist.		
Mandla	3	2
Nerbudda Division	2	0
Nagpur Division	13	14
Chhattisgarh Division... ...	3	3
Berar	3	1
Feudatory States	17	11
Musalman.		
Surguja	12	10
Arya.		
Seoni	4	3
Drug	2	2
Jain.		
Chhindwara	5	5
Wardha	10	12
Nagpur	294	298
Chanda	50	48
Bhandara	48	39
Amraoti	36	24
Akola	1	3
Yeotmal	83	11

TABLE XIII.—Caste,

Serial No.	DISTRICT OR STATE.	KAMAR.		KANDH-KHOND.		KAONRA.		KAPEWAR OR KAPU.		KASAI.		KASAR.	
		ANIMIST.		HINDU.		HINDU.		HINDU.		MUSALMAN		HINDU.	
		Males.	Females.	Males.	Females.	Males.	Females.	Males.	Females.	Males.	Females.	Males.	Females.
		334	335	336	337	338	339	340	341	342	343	344	345
	Central Provinces and Berar ...	**3,542**	**3,896**	**4,643**	**4,944**	**7,791**	**7,548**	**9,131**	**9,358**	**2,060**	**2,045**	**10,210**	**9,965**
	C. P. British Districts and Berar ...	**3,432**	**3,754**	**3,547**	**3,705**	**7,782**	**7,544**	**7,210**	**7,492**	**2,060**	**2,045**	**8,540**	**8,239**
	C. P. British Districts	**3,432**	**3,754**	**3,547**	**3,705**	**7,782**	**7,544**	**4,877**	**5,215**	**1,176**	**1,217**	**5,034**	**4,938**
	JUBBULPORE DIVISION	...	...	...	...	*1*	...	...	...	*899*	*944*	*307*	*300*
1	Saugor	...	...	...	...	...	...	...	...	610	642	1	1
2	Damoh	...	...	...	...	...	...	...	...	106	84	6	5
3	Jubbulpore	...	...	...	...	1	...	...	...	159	173	2	2
4	Mandla	...	...	...	...	...	...	...	...	17	...	283	272
5	Seoni	...	...	...	...	...	...	...	...	7	45	15	20
	NERBUDDA DIVISION	...	...	...	...	*7,781*	*7,544*	*8*	*10*	*154*	*169*	*1,786*	*1,662*
6	Narsinghpur	...	...	...	...	7,454	7,293	...	...	...	1	96	94
7	Hoshangabad	...	...	...	...	66	68	...	...	10	25	565	519
8	Nimar	...	...	...	...	94	60	4	2	101	98	186	155
9	Betul	...	...	...	...	18	22	...	...	2	...	407	365
10	Chhindwara	...	...	...	...	149	101	4	8	41	45	532	529
	NAGPUR DIVISION	...	...	...	...	...	...	*4,843*	*5,196*	*80*	*81*	*1,324*	*1,289*
11	Wardha	...	...	...	...	...	...	26	51	53	50	443	415
12	Nagpur	...	...	...	...	...	...	147	102	22	20	440	505
13	Chanda	...	...	...	...	...	...	4,636	5,004	1	2	120	97
14	Bhandara		...	...	...	...	...	17	24	4	...	228	175
15	Balaghat	...	...	...	...	...	...	17	15	...	...	93	97
	CHHATTISGARH DIVISION	*3,432*	*3,754*	*3,547*	*3,705*	...	...	*26*	*9*	*43*	*23*	*1,617*	*1,687*
16	Raipur	3,432	3,753	3,198	3,281	...	...	13	2	32	23	875	920
17	Bilaspur	...	1	349	424	...	...	9	3	11	...	580	594
18	Drug	...	...	...	...	...	...	4	4	...	...	162	173
	Berar	...	...	...	...	...	...	**2,333**	**2,277**	**884**	**828**	**3,506**	**3,301**
19	Amraoti	...	...	...	...	...	...	...	...	377	341	966	848
20	Akola	...	...	...	...	...	...	41	...	266	233	943	905
21	Buldana	...	...	...	...	...	...	...	...	199	208	1,044	1,066
22	Yeotmal	...	...	...	...	...	...	2,292	2,277	42	46	553	482
	Feudatory States	**110**	**142**	**1,096**	**1,239**	**9**	**4**	**1,921**	**1,866**	...	...	**1,670**	**1,726**
23	Makrai	...	...	...	...	...	...	...	...	...	...	3	1
24	Bastar	9	18	...	...	...	...	1,921	1,866	...	...	110	93
25	Kanker	101	124	...	...	8	...	...	...	...	...	157	161
26	Nandgaon	...	...	...	...	...	...	...	...	...	...	77	91
27	Khairagarh	...	...	...	...	...	...	...	...	...	...	15	19
28	Chhuikhadan	...	...	...	...	...	...	...	...	...	...	1	3
29	Kawardha	...	...	...	...	...	...	...	...	...	...	31	46
30	Sakti	...	...	...	...	1	4	...	...	...	...	52	67
31	Raigarh	...	...	242	301	...	...	...	...	...	...	496	526
32	Sarangarh	...	...	840	937	...	...	...	...	...	...	12	19
33	Chang Bhakar	...	...	...	...	...	...	...	...	...	...	...	2
34	Korea	...	...	...	...	...	...	...	...	...	...	57	61
35	Surguja	...	...	2	1	...	...	...	...	...	...	399	399
36	Udaipur	...	...	...	...	...	...	...	...	...	...	83	70
37	Jashpur	...	...	12	...	...	...	...	...	...	...	177	168

Tribe, Race or Nationality.

KATIA.		KAWAR.				KAYASTH.		KEWAT.		
HINDU.		HINDU.		ANIMIST.		HINDU.		HINDU.		
Males.	Females.	Males.	Females.	Males.	Females.	Males.	Females.	Males.	Females.	Serial No.
346	347	348	349	350	351	352	353	354	355	
20,202	21,109	99,134	101,741	14,429	14,108	17,580	16,004	81,704	87,691	
19,881	20,756	44,430	46,024	34	13	16,079	14,736	66,699	71,739	
19,879	20,755	44,430	46,024	34	13	15,621	14,330	66,386	71,510	
5,887	*6,038*	*17*	*16*	...	...	*8,576*	*7,998*	*3,299*	*3,692*	
16	2	2	...	...	...	2,786	2,567	137	110	1
...	...	...	...	...	...	1,459	1,472	332	331	2
37	25	10	8	...	...	3,107	2,810	2,629	2,919	3
1,246	1,204	3	2	...	...	391	312	66	67	4
4,588	4,807	2	6	...	...	833	837	135	165	5
11,711	*12,250*	...	...	...	...	*4,017*	*3,811*	*753*	*658*	
958	1,143	...	...	...	...	2,204	2,126	608	628	6
3,619	3,602	...	...	...	...	881	922	11	5	7
34	17	...	...	...	...	249	192	10	3	8
1,608	1,673	...	...	...	...	221	142	6	6	9
5,497	5,725	...	...	...	...	462	429	48	16	10
1,990	*2,165*	*1,229*	*1,180*	*1*	...	*1,103*	*921*	*2,890*	*3,027*	
...	...	...	...	...	...	114	82	8	13	11
67	65	12	10	...	...	405	259	7	3	12
...	...	751	696	...	...	95	52	2,351	2,500	13
256	254	466	474	...	...	252	308	247	231	14
1,667	1,846	...	...	1	...	237	220	277	280	15
291	*302*	*43,184*	*44,828*	*33*	*13*	*1,925*	*1,600*	*59,454*	*64,233*	
35	38	13,302	14,481	24	10	663	515	24,580	26,220	16
149	157	26,849	27,085	7	3	798	677	19,200	20,602	17
107	107	3,033	3,262	2	...	464	408	15,674	17,351	18
2	1	...	...	...	...	458	406	313	229	
2	1	...	...	...	...	203	196	47	14	19
...	...	...	...	...	...	121	106	54	28	20
...	...	...	...	...	...	73	56	190	183	21
...	...	...	...	...	...	61	48	13	4	22
321	353	54,704	55,717	14,395	14,095	1,501	1,268	15,005	15,952	
...	...	...	...	...	...	26	17	...	...	23
71	74	110	100	6	4	176	186	808	832	24
...	...	51	59	3	...	48	52	1,223	1,215	25
...	1	4,312	4,827	...	...	278	207	2,985	3,363	26
58	63	3,391	3,847	2	4	252	243	2,420	2,701	27
...	...	140	177	...	...	72	83	431	485	28
172	190	5	4	...	...	110	120	686	747	29
...	...	1,845	1,979	4	...	27	25	652	670	30
...	1	17,994	18,776	12	6	102	94	2,348	2,409	31
...	...	211	199	...	...	20	14	1,907	2,020	32
...	...	1,067	1,008	25	17	13	5	63	76	33
...	1	37	27	3,739	3,704	49	21	87	78	34
20	23	20,712	20,147	57	46	210	65	1,204	1,148	35
...	...	198	201	10,555	10,308	27	11	90	91	36
...	...	4,631	4,366	2	6	91	35	101	117	37

REMARKS. (356)

	M.	F.
KAMAR includes—		
Hindu.		
Raipur	623	747
Feudatory States	91	115
KANDH or KHOND includes—		
Animist.		
Raipur	148	130
Raigarh	220	235
Jashpur	1	0
KAONRA includes—		
Animist.		
Narsinghpur...	1	0
Sakti	1	4
KAPEWAR or KAPU includes—		
Animist.		
Bastar	43	16
KASAR includes—		
Animist.		
Mandla	31	18
Feudatory States	80	108
Musalman.		
Nimar	1	0
Berar	36	36
Jain.		
Berar	29	56
KATIA includes—		
Animist.		
Jubbulpore Division	12	8
Nerbudda Division	61	57
Nagpur Division	6	2
Kawardha	3	0
KAYASTH includes—		
Arya.		
Jubbulpore Division	20	13
Nerbudda Division	8	11
Balaghat	1	1
Chhattisgarh Division... ...	12	11
Brahmo.		
Jubbulpore	1	0
Sikh.		
Saugor	0	1
KEWAT includes—		
Animist.		
Chanda	3	2
Chhattisgarh Division ...	9	8
Feudatory States	10	4

TABLE XIII.—Caste,

Serial No.	District or State.	Khangar. Hindu. Males.	Khangar. Hindu. Females.	Kharwar. Hindu. Males.	Kharwar. Hindu. Females.	Kharwar. Animist. Males.	Kharwar. Animist. Females.	Khatik. Hindu. Males.	Khatik. Hindu. Females.	Khatri. Hindu. Males.	Khatri. Hindu. Females.	Kir. Hindu. Males.	Kir. Hindu. Females.
		357	358	359	360	361	362	363	364	365	366	367	368
	Central Provinces and Berar ...	**6,422**	**6,393**	**8,734**	**9.344**	**795**	**778**	**6,315**	**6,281**	**2,683**	**2,288**	**3,526**	**3,185**
	C. P. British Districts and Berar ...	**6,403**	**6,370**	**1,971**	**2,037**	**192**	**209**	**6,261**	**6,247**	**2,645**	**2.252**	**3,526**	**3,185**
	C. P. British Districts	**6,318**	**6,282**	**1.963**	**2.027**	**192**	**209**	**3,551**	**3,566**	**1,824**	**1,577**	**3,519**	**3,169**
	Jubbulpore Division	*5,435*	*5,355*	*467*	*440*	*171*	*193*	*1,476*	*1,475*	*337*	*309*	...	...
1	Saugor	2,903	2,900	96	76	136	146	384	409	104	100	...	...
2	Damoh	1,050	1,066	308	361	35	47	198	181	46	49	...	...
3	Jubbulpore	1,398	1.345	3	2	...	...	780	780	173	113	...	...
4	Mandla	67	62	...	1	...	...	46	35	20	16	...	...
5	Seoni	17	12	...	...	...	...	68	70	44	31	...	...
	Nerbudda Division	*805*	*822*	*59*	*52*	*1*	...	*560*	*561*	*811*	*758*	*3,519*	*3,169*
6	Narsinghpur	494	509	11	5	...	...	94	112	108	122	453	399
7	Hoshangabad	260	280	...	...	...	...	123	101	252	231	2,773	2,461
8	Nimar	12	9	...	...	...	...	50	55	351	310	200	206
9	Betul	19	14	1	...	...	...	109	104	73	63	86	95
10	Chhindwara	20	10	47	47	1	...	184	189	27	32	7	8
	Nagpur Division	*39*	*34*	*4*	*5*	*1*	...	*1,470*	*1,489*	*555*	*443*	...	...
11	Wardha	16	14	...	...	...	...	380	408	156	110	...	...
12	Nagpur	20	18	2	3	...	...	729	708	237	167	...	...
13	Chanda	...	...	...	...	1	...	155	145	11	19	...	...
14	Bhandara	...	...	2	2	...	...	170	193	76	73	...	...
15	Balaghat	3	2	...	...	...	...	36	35	75	74	...	...
	Chhattisgarh Division	*39*	*41*	*1,433*	*1,530*	*19*	*16*	*45*	*41*	*71*	*67*	...	...
16	Raipur	9	3	175	191	...	...	2	1	35	27	...	...
17	Bilaspur	15	16	1,258	1,339	19	16	38	37	28	29	...	...
18	Drug	15	22	...	...	...	...	5	3	8	11	...	...
	Berar	**85**	**88**	**8**	**10**	...	...	**2.710**	**2.681**	**821**	**675**	**7**	**16**
19	Amraoti	50	55	2	2	...	...	1,825	1,766	458	386	7	16
20	Akola	30	30	1	...	...	...	446	443	155	127	...	...
21	Buldana	...	...	5	8	...	...	205	206	201	150	...	...
22	Yeotmal	5	3	...	...	...	...	234	266	7	12	...	...
	Feudatory States	**19**	**23**	**6.763**	**7.307**	**603**	**569**	**54**	**34**	**38**	**36**	...	...
23	Makrai	...	...	...	...	...	...	...	...	...	...	...	...
24	Bastar	2	...	...	...	...	...	2	...	...	...	...	...
25	Kanker	...	1	...	...	...	...	...	1	20	13	...	...
26	Nandgaon	10	10	...	...	...	...	1	...	12	13	...	...
27	Khairagarh	3	2	...	...	...	...	30	16	3	4	...	...
28	Chhuikhadan	...	...	...	...	...	...	...	...	...	...	...	...
29	Kawardha	2	3	...	...	...	...	...	...	...	...	...	...
30	Sakti	...	...	79	86	22	17	...	...	...	...	...	...
31	Raigarh	...	...	30	24	...	...	13	12	1	1	...	...
32	Sarangarh	...	...	8	11	...	...	...	...	1	2	...	...
33	Chang Bhakar	...	...	111	131	4	6	...	...	...	...	...	...
34	Korea	...	...	17	22	535	504	...	...	...	...	...	...
35	Surguja	2	7	5,894	6,308	18	21	...	...	1	3	...	...
36	Udaipur	...	—	12	15	23	20	...	...	...	...	...	...
37	Jashpur	...	...	612	620	1	1	8	5	...	...	...	...

Tribe, Race, or Nationality.

KIRAR.		KOHLI OR KOIRI.		KOL.				KOLAM.		Remarks.	Serial No.
Hindu.		Hindu.		Hindu.		Animist.		Animist.			
Males.	Females.	Males.	Females	Males.	Females.	Males.	Females.	Males.	Females.		
369	370	371	372	373	374	375	376	377	378	379	
24,036	**23,757**	**12,910**	**12,719**	**29,387**	**29,392**	**11,470**	**12,349**	**12,331**	**12,645**		
24,034	**23,750**	**11,243**	**11,176**	**28,884**	**28,937**	**8,874**	**9,790**	**12,331**	**12,645**		
23,499	**23,258**	**11,203**	**11,157**	**28,767**	**28,884**	**8,874**	**9,790**	**1,082**	**1,059**		
2,154	*2,188*	*2*	...	*21,542*	*23,137*	*8,548*	*9,645*	...	...	KHANGAR includes— M. F. *Animist.* Hoshangabad 1 0	
109	82	...	...	10	2	...	...	...	...		1
1	...	...	...	60	41	11	3	...	...		2
13	9	...	...	19,542	21,192	5,271	6,321	...	...		3
258	235	...	...	1,855	1,852	3,168	3,229	...	...		4
1,773	1,862	2	...	75	50	98	92	...	...		5
19,056	*18,822*	*3*	...	*4,149*	*2,909*	*308*	*133*	...	...	KHATIK includes— *Animist.* Jubbulpore 9 0	
6,046	5,897	...	...	326	305	6	7	...	...		6
5,204	5,155	...	...	168	199	27	16	...	...		7
...	...	...	...	49	101	...	...	...	...		8
4,808	4,831	...	...	1,397	947	2	1	...	...		9
2,998	2,939	3	...	2,209	1,357	273	108	...	...		10
2,289	*2,246*	*11,189*	*11,149*	*1,694*	*1,522*	*9*	*6*	*1,082*	*1,059*	KHATRI includes— *Musalman.*	
3	4	29	18	13	25	...	...	1,047	1,037	Nimar 3 4	11
2,172	2,105	53	13	187	135	...	...	35	22	*Arya.*	12
...	8	4,136	4,178	320	291	...	...	...	...	Jubbulpore Division 3 0	13
99	121	6,909	6,869	445	395	...	...	...	...	Nimar 11 6	14
15	8	62	71	729	676	9	6	...	...	Drug ... ... 1 0 *Sikh.* Jubbulpore Division ... ... 67 7 Nerbudda Division ... ... 5 3 Bilaspur ... ... 1 1 Raigarh 1 1	15
...	*2*	*9*	*8*	*1,332*	*1,316*	*9*	*7*	...	...	*Jain.*	
...	2	5	3	76	70	2	2	...	...	Buldana 1 0	16
...	...	4	5	1,291	1,228	7	5	...	...	KIRAR includes—	17
...	...	...	...	15	18	...	...	...	...	*Animist.* Betul ... ... 1 0 Surguja 1 0	18
535	**492**	**40**	**19**	**117**	**53**	...	...	**11,249**	**11,586**	KOHLI or KOIRI includes— *Animist.*	
532	492	16	12	71	49	...	...	61	59	Chanda 1 1	19
1	...	...	...	46	4	...	...	...	10	Korea 9 14	20
...	...	...	...	...	...	...	...	...	...		21
2	...	24	7	...	...	...	...	11,188	11,517		22
2	**7**	**1,667**	**1,543**	**503**	**455**	**2,596**	**2,559**	...	...	KOLAM includes— *Hindu.*	
...	...	...	...	...	...	...	...	...	...	Wardha 797 740	23
...	...	8	...	43	16	...	...	...	...	Nagpur 35 32	24
...	...	...	...	...	...	...	...	...	...	Amraoti 12 6	25
...	...	...	...	...	...	...	...	...	...	Akola 0 10	26
...	...	...	...	1	...	...	...	...	...	Yeotmal 3,330 3,407	27
...	...	...	...	...	...	...	...	...	...		28
...	...	...	...	2	1	...	...	...	...		29
...	...	...	...	5	...	...	...	...	...		30
...	...	...	...	1	...	...	...	...	...		31
...	...	...	...	1	...	...	...	...	...		32
...	...	...	...	38	37	2,457	2,436	...	...		33
...	...	358	361	284	273	113	90	...	...		34
2	7	1,278	1,165	128	127	20	18	...	...		35
...	...	...	...	...	...	6	15	...	...		36
...	...	23	17	...	1	...	...	...	...		37

TABLE XIII.—Caste,

Serial No.	DISTRICT OR STATE.	KOLI. Hindu. Males.	KOLI. Hindu. Females.	KOLTA. Hindu. Males.	KOLTA. Hindu. Females.	KOMTI. Hindu. Males.	KOMTI. Hindu. Females.	KORI. Hindu. Males.	KORI. Hindu. Females.	KOR… Hindu. Males.	KOR… Hindu. Females.
		380	381	382	383	384	385	386	387	388	389
	Central Provinces and Berar ...	**18.129**	**18.017**	**18.075**	**18.220**	**5.396**	**5.370**	**20.397**	**19.231**	**42.251**	**42,530**
	C. P. British Districts and Berar ...	**18.129**	**18.017**	**9.635**	**9.600**	**5.358**	**5.333**	**20.294**	**19.104**	**42.230**	**42.497**
	C. P. British Districts	**1.413**	**1.380**	**9.635**	**9.600**	**2.445**	**2.378**	**19.647**	**18.659**	**40.877**	**41.153**
	JUBBULPORE DIVISION	*3*	*2*	...	...	11	1	*12,960*	*13,130*	*17*	*14*
1	Saugor	3	2	...	...	1	1	4,601	4,558	...	...
2	Damoh	...	...	...	...	...	...	2,086	2,198	10	12
3	Jubbulpore	...	...	...	...	10	...	5,800	5,910	6	2
4	Mandla	...	...	...	...	...	...	231	212	...	...
5	Seoni	...	...	...	...	...	...	242	252	1	...
	NERBUDDA DIVISION	*1,232*	*1,229*	...	...	*8*	*15*	*3,512*	*3,087*	*40,493*	*40,782*
6	Narsinghpur	...	...	...	...	...	...	1,476	1,510	...	...
7	Hoshangabad	...	...	...	...	...	...	796	667	5,752	5,887
8	Nimar...	1,232	1,229	...	...	8	15	629	472	17,379	17,261
9	Betul	...	...	...	...	...	...	248	132	12,832	13,025
10	Chhindwara	...	...	...	...	...	...	363	306	4,530	4,609
	NAGPUR DIVISION	*178*	*149*	...	...	*2,426*	*2,361*	*2,156*	*1,444*	*363*	*348*
11	Wardha	142	111	...	...	242	355	107	83	312	311
12	Nagpur	...	...	...	...	103	126	1,637	1,068	51	37
13	Chanda	...	...	...	...	2,022	1,821	349	262	...	...
14	Bhandara	34	37	...	...	59	59	23	12	...	...
15	Balaghat	2	1	...	...	...	...	40	19	...	...
	CHHATTISGARH DIVISION	...	...	*9,635*	*9,600*	...	*1*	*1,019*	*998*	*4*	*9*
16	Raipur	...	...	6,541	6,440	...	...	195	170	...	1
17	Bilaspur	...	...	3,094	3,160	...	...	751	740	4	8
18	Drug	...	...	...	...	...	1	73	79	...	...
	Berar	**16.716**	**16.637**	...	—	**2.913**	**2.955**	**647**	**445**	**1.353**	**1,344**
19	Amraoti	4,170	4,041	...	...	82	71	312	228	1,124	1,116
20	Akola	4,875	4,738	...	...	115	120	154	78	59	60
21	Buldana	5,711	5,838	...	...	35	32	27	17	170	168
22	Yeotmal	1,960	2,020	...	...	2,681	2,732	154	122	...	...
	Feudatory States	...	...	**8.440**	**8.620**	**38**	**37**	**103**	**127**	**21**	**33**
23	Makrai	...	...	...	...	...	...	...	...	9	17
24	Bastar	...	...	...	...	38	37	6	17	12	15
25	Kanker	...	...	...	...	...	...	...	...	...	...
26	Nandgaon	...	...	1	2	...	...	5	3	...	...
27	Khairagarh	...	...	...	...	...	...	7	7	...	...
28	Chhuikhadan	...	...	...	...	...	...	...	...	...	...
29	Kawardha	...	...	...	...	...	...	8	1	...	...
30	Sakti	...	...	1	1	...	...	...	3	...	...
31	Raigarh	...	...	5,838	5,992	...	...	10	2	...	...
32	Sarangarh	...	...	2,509	2,527	...	...	3	1	...	...
33	Chang Bhakar	...	...	...	...	...	...	...	...	...	...
34	Korea	...	...	...	...	...	..	11	4	...	1
35	Surguja	..	...	26	31	...	...	46	54	...	...
36	Udaipur	...	...	63	67	...	...	...	28	...	...
37	Jashpur	...	...	2	...	...	...	7	7	...	...

Tribe, Race or Nationality.

KU.		KORWA.				KOSHTI.		KOSKATI.		Remarks.	Serial No.
Animist.		Hindu.		Animist.		Hindu.		Hindu.			
Males.	Females.	Males.	Females.	Males.	Females.	Males	Females	Males.	Females.		
390	391	392	393	394	395	396	397	398	399	400	
33,308	34.274	2,276	2,330	14.888	14.506	76.712	76,676	576	635		
31,880	32.930	417	453	2	4	72,219	72.072	576	635		
13,822	14.184	417	453	2	4	64,975	65,489	576	635		
2	...	...	*1*	...	...	*2,666*	*2,694*	...	...	Koli includes— M. F.	
...	...	...	...	...	...	494	505	...	...	*Musalman.*	1
1	...	...	...	...	...	201	200	...	...	Nimar 74 69	2
1	...	...	1	...	...	1,167	1,211	...	...	Amraoti 1 0	3
...	...	...	...	...	...	146	151	...	...		4
...	...	...	...	...	...	658	627	...	...		5
13,792	*14,163*	*1*	...	...	...	*2,818*	*2,823*	...	...	Kolta includes—	
...	...	...	...	...	...	361	386	...	...	*Animist.* Feudatory States 37 36	6
4,262	4,303	...	...	...	...	193	190	...	...		7
1,177	1,112	...	...	...	...	390	370	...	...		8
4,788	5,029	1	...	...	...	95	90	...	...		9
3,565	3,719	...	...	...	...	1,779	1,778	...	...		10
27	*21*	...	...	...	...	*41,594*	*41,170*	*574*	*635*	Komti includes—	
20	17	...	...	...	...	3,657	3,570	...	...	*Animist.*	11
5	4	...	...	...	...	21,311	20,960	8	10	Chanda 3 6	12
...	...	...	...	...	...	3,447	3,342	534	556	*Musalman.*	13
...	...	...	...	...	...	11,992	12,118	32	69	Amraoti 1 0	14
2	...	...	...		...	1,187	1,180	...	...		15
1	...	*416*	*452*	*2*	*4*	*17,897*	*18,802*	*2*	...	Kori includes—	
...	...	9	...	...	...	6,678	6,863	...	...	*Musalman.* Mandla 5 2	16
1	...	407	451	2	4	5,493	5,915	...	...	Narsinghpur 1 1	17
...	...	...	1	...	...	5,731	6,024	2	...		18
18.058	18,746	...	...	...	...	7.244	6.583	...	...	Koshti includes—	
17,946	18,641	...	...	...	...	4,207	3,774	...	...	*Animist.* Chanda 3 0	19
2	...	...	...	...	...	919	864	...	...	Drug 1 0	20
108	105	...	...	...	...	360	359	...	...	Yeotmal 0 1	21
2	...	...	...	...	...	1,758	1,586	...	...	Bastar 0 1	22
										Musalman. Nimar 2 0	
										Nagpur 2 0	
										Raipur 1 0	
1,428	1.344	1.859	1.877	14,886	14.502	4.493	4.604	...	...		
1,404	1,326	...	...	...	...	...	...	...	...		23
24	18	...	...	...	...	1,148	1,130	...	...		24
...	...	...	...	...	...	184	183	...	...		25
...	...	...	...	...	...	1,229	1,307	...	...		26
...	...	...	...	...	...	774	817	...	...		27
...	...	...	...	...	...	252	250	...	...		28
...	...	...	...	...	...	136	136	...	...		29
...	...	17	46	1	1	267	250	...	...		30
...	...	17	18	157	171	295	333	...	...		31
...	...	1	3	...	...	175	173	...	...		32
...	...	210	197	...	...	...	...	...	...		33
...	...	...	...	19	18	1	...	...	...		34
...	...	309	274	8,896	8,503	1	...	...	...		35
...	...	7	1	387	375	1	2	...	...		36
...	...	1,298	1,338	5,426	5,434	30	23	...	...		37

TABLE XIII.—Caste,

Serial No.	DISTRICT OR STATE.	KUMHAR. Hindu. Males.	KUMHAR. Hindu. Females.	KUNBI. Hindu. Males.	KUNBI. Hindu. Females.	KURAMWAR. Hindu. Males.	KURAMWAR. Hindu. Females.	KURMI. Hindu. Males.	KURMI. Hindu. Females.	LAKHERA. Hindu. Males.	LAKHERA. Hindu. Females.
		401	402	403	404	405	406	407	408	409	410
	Central Provinces and Berar ...	**60,054**	**58,466**	**682,737**	**673,997**	**1,890**	**1,902**	**150,109**	**152,479**	**1,430**	**1,427**
	C. P. British Districts and Berar ...	**51,355**	**49,919**	**681,888**	**673,211**	**1,890**	**1,902**	**141,379**	**143,432**	**1,406**	**1,410**
	C. P. British Districts	**39,482**	**39,694**	**284,166**	**283,086**	**1,890**	**1,901**	**141,341**	**143,399**	**1,321**	**1,329**
	JUBBULPORE DIVISION	*14,002*	*14,068*	*525*	*393*	...	...	*50,888*	*49,727*	*807*	*813*
1	Saugor	4,131	4,139	10	4	...	...	12,842	12,003	100	103
2	Damoh	2,619	2,578	3	3	...	...	12,577	11,845	116	134
3	Jubbulpore	5,079	5,104	192	79	...	...	17,710	18,058	452	431
4	Mandla	911	942	64	48	...	...	3,498	3,478	75	78
5	Seoni	1,202	1,305	256	259	...	...	4,261	4,343	55	67
	NERBUDDA DIVISION	*7,986*	*7,906*	*50,226*	*50,506*	...	...	*21,601*	*21,615*	*418*	*428*
6	Narsinghpur	1,633	1,654	31	32	...	...	3,061	3,085	45	37
7	Hoshangabad	2,468	2,437	291	237	...	...	10,176	10,253	96	92
8	Nimar	1,817	1,801	14,105	13,763	...	...	1,012	806	58	54
9	Betul	869	786	22,206	22,986	...	...	5,273	5,398	70	85
10	Chhindwara	1,199	1,228	13,503	13,488	...	...	2,079	2,073	149	160
	NAGPUR DIVISION	*7,125*	*6,917*	*232,744*	*231,464*	*1,889*	*1,898*	*445*	*358*	*67*	*67*
11	Wardha	1,319	1,174	43,904	42,849	...	...	55	62	14	9
12	Nagpur	2,144	2,106	82,687	81,812	4	5	55	10	2	2
13	Chanda	1,639	1,555	56,480	55,960	1,884	1,892	44	39	1	2
14	Bhandara	1,342	1,430	44,621	45,782	1	1	25	12	12	3
15	Balaghat	681	652	5,052	5,061	...	...	266	235	38	51
	CHHATTISGARH DIVISION	*10,369*	*10,803*	*671*	*723*	*1*	*3*	*68,407*	*71,699*	*29*	*21*
16	Raipur	5,168	5,319	367	363	1	3	24,494	24,987	4	3
17	Bilaspur	3,539	3,691	147	207	...	...	26,307	27,668	25	17
18	Drug	1,662	1,793	157	153	...	...	17,606	19,049	...	1
	Berar	**11,873**	**10,225**	**397,722**	**390,125**	...	**1**	**38**	**33**	**85**	**81**
19	Amraoti	3,873	3,013	102,327	97,491	...	...	36	33	30	31
20	Akola	3,506	3,095	113,050	110,453	...	...	...	...	38	33
21	Buldana	2,259	2,218	114,378	115,141	...	1	...	...	12	5
22	Yeotmal	2,235	1,809	67,967	67,040	...	...	2	...	5	12
	Feudatory States	**8,699**	**8,547**	**849**	**786**	...	...	**8,730**	**9,047**	**24**	**17**
23	Makrai	31	38	8	5	...	...	282	264	4	4
24	Bastar	1,310	1,223	540	532	...	...	352	328	7	1
25	Kanker	376	383	9	3	...	...	103	101	...	...
26	Nandgaon	807	811	42	51	...	...	575	555	...	1
27	Khairagarh	297	351	30	19	...	...	819	861	...	...
28	Chhuikhadan	95	94	1	...	...	...	160	181	...	...
29	Kawardha	134	155	2	...	...	...	3,245	3,549	...	...
30	Sakti	142	136	6	4	...	...	538	579	...	...
31	Raigarh	1,046	993	42	29	...	...	1,284	1,336	...	...
32	Sarangarh	405	453	80	71	...	...	533	546	...	...
33	Chang Bhakar	84	74	1	3	...	...	5	1	6	5
34	Korea	383	355	67	64	...	...	41	34	...	...
35	Surguja	2,751	2,652	...	...	...	...	741	673	...	...
36	Udaipur	266	275	9	1	...	...	15	8	...	...
37	Jashpur	1,072	1,054	3	4	...	...	37	31	7	6

Tribe, Race or Nationality.

LODHI.		LOHAR.		MADGI.		MAJHWAR.				MALA.		
HINDU.		HINDU.		HINDU.		HINDU.		ANIMIST.		HINDU.		
Males.	Females.	Males.	Females.	Males.	Females.	Males.	Females.	Males.	Females.	Males.	Females.	Serial No.
411	412	413	414	415	416	417	418	419	420	421	422	
155,922	157.978	91,183	90,407	4.243	4.331	4,969	4.880	2.227	2.134	7,085	6,613	
139,992	141,506	77,541	76,873	4.243	4.331	3.224	3.125	61	63	5.724	5,140	
138,860	140,501	68,016	68,273	2.776	2,829	3,224	3.125	61	63	4.900	4.438	
72,730	*72,461*	*17,838*	*17,641*	...	...	...	*2*	...	...	*403*	*408*	
21,813	21,050	4,526	4,275	...	...	...	...	..	...	18	8	1
20,864	20,979	2,033	1,962	...	...	...	...	...	...	...	...	2
24,130	24,339	5.769	5,609	...	...	...	2	...	...	355	381	3
3,029	3,193	2,621	2.727	...	...	...	...	...	...	20	17	4
2,894	2,900	2,889	3,068	...	...	...	...	...	...	10	2	5
28,522	*28,992*	*11,503*	*11,337*	...	...	...	...	...	...	*123*	*110*	
14,884	15,035	1,796	1.803	...	...	...	...	...	...	9	4	6
5,179	5,371	2,502	2,361	...	...	..	...	...	...	36	35	7
1,848	1,794	1.296	1,190	...	...	...	...	...	...	22	20	8
151	106	2,167	2,150	...	...	...	...	...	...	5	7	9
6,460	6,686	3,742	3,883	...	...	...	...	...	...	51	44	10
27,314	*27,937*	*23,203*	*22,770*	*2,776*	*2,829*	..	...	...	...	*4,317*	*3.882*	
544	525	2.063	1,862	...	...	...	...	...	...	50	35	11
4,523	4,372	5,513	5,262	59	75	...	...	...	...	661	664	12
119	52	5,516	5,414	2,681	2,719	...	...	...	...	3,105	3,126	13
11,407	11,875	7,249	7,263	36	85	...	...	...	...	42	37	14
10,721	11,163	2,862	2,069	...	...	...	...	...	...	459	20	15
10,294	*11,061*	*15,472*	*16,475*	...	...	*3,224*	*3,123*	*61*	*63*	*57*	*38*	
1,079	1.174	7,002	7.499	...	...	...	...	...	...	38	19	16
3,288	3,546	4,345	4,620	...	...	3,224	3,123	61	63	11	13	17
5,927	6,341	4,125	4,356	...	...	...	...	...	...	8	6	18
1.132	1,005	9.525	8,600	1,467	1.502	...	...	...	...	824	702	
685	631	2,929	2,585	...	...	...	...	...	...	64	42	19
193	148	1,788	1,480	...	...	...	...	...	...	127	127	20
23	20	1,550	1,400	...	...	...	...	...	...	64	47	21
231	206	3,258	3,126	1,467	1,502	...	...	...	..	569	486	22
15.930	16.472	13.642	13,534	...	...	1.745	1.755	2.166	2.071	1.361	1.473	
6	17	30	35	...	...	...	...	...	...	...	...	23
37	24	2,645	2,649	...	...	...	...	...	...	1,332	1,429	24
1	1	905	973	...	...	...	...	...	...	...	...	25
2,603	2,828	938	988	...	...	...	...	...	...	13	18	26
9,787	10,038	720	822	...	...	...	...	...		10	16	27
2,416	2,484	161	171	...	..	...	...	...	...	..	...	28
993	1,059	272	322	...	...	...	...	...	...	...	...	29
3	6	81	84	...	...	36	35	1	1	...	...	30
8	7	808	846	...	...	254	255	575	575	...	...	31
5	3	318	304	...	...	164	174	...	...	6	10	32
...	...	40	35	...	...	...	...	...	...	...	...	33
4	1	323	284	...	...	...	...	...	...	..	...	34
5	4	3,726	3,534	...	...	1,288	1,290	116	95	...	...	35
2	...	344	305	...	...	3	1	1,474	1.400	..	...	36
...	...	2,241	2,182	...	...	...	...	...	...	...	..	37

REMARKS. (423)

	M.	F.
KUMHAR includes—		
Animist.		
Jubbulpore	3	2
Nagpur Division	16	0
Chhattisgarh Division ...	1	2
Feudatory States ...	65	61
Jain.		
Berar	2	1
KUNBI includes—		
Animist.		
Nagpur Division	2	1
Korea	3	0
Jain.		
Nagpur Division... ...	0	2
Berar	7	5
KURMI includes—		
Animist.		
Jubbulpore Division ...	4	8
Bilaspur	3	3
Feudatory States ...	6	3
Arya.		
Saugor	1	0
Sikh.		
Jubbulpore	1	0
LAKHERA includes—		
Musalman.		
Nimar	1	0
Akola	2	0
LODHI includes—		
Animist.		
Jubbulpore Division ...	7	1
Hoshangabad	1	0
Bhandara	1	0
Korea	2	0
Musalman.		
Nimar	1	0
LOHAR includes—		
Animist.		
Saugor	4	1
Jubbulpore	133	122
Mandla	678	716
Seoni	153	167
Nerbudda Division ...	449	456
Nagpur Division ...	12	8
Chhattisgarh Division ...	142	148
Yeotmal	1	0
Feudatory States ...	1,482	1,523
Musalman.		
Nimar	53	33
Nagpur	3	0
Berar	1	18
Arya.		
Jubbulpore	1	1
Hoshangabad	1	0
Amraoti	4	4
Sikh.		
Saugor	1	1
Bhandara	1	0
Drug	2	1
Jain.		
Amraoti	1	0
MADGI includes—		
Animist		
Chanda	4	1
Yeotmal	2	3
MALA includes—		
Animist		
Chanda	1	1
Bastar	10	11
Musalman		
Khairagarh	0	1

TABLE XIII.—Caste,

Serial No.	DISTRICT OR STATE.	MALI.		MALLAH.		MANA.		MANBHAO.		MANG.		MANIHAR.	
		HINDU.		HINDU.		HINDU.		HINDU.		HINDU.		HINDU.	
		Males.	Females.	Males.	Females.	Males.	Females.	Males.	Females.	Males.	Females.	Males.	Females.
		424	425	426	427	428	429	430	431	432	433	434	435
	Central Provinces and Berar	**279.868**	**283,660**	**2.296**	**2.355**	**23,835**	**25,202**	**2.095**	**1.856**	**41.062**	**42.513**	**343**	**345**
	C. P. British Districts and Berar ...	**262.343**	**265,397**	**2,051**	**2,096**	**23,792**	**25.180**	**2,095**	**1,856**	**41,010**	**42,465**	**305**	**325**
	C. P. British Districts	**160.015**	**165,192**	**2.051**	**2,096**	**22.730**	**24,110**	**421**	**356**	**11.490**	**12,031**	**286**	**302**
	JUBBULPORE DIVISION	*10,018*	*10,625*	*932*	*945*	...	...	...	...	*129*	*98*	*234*	*242*
1	Saugor	603	626	1	1	...	...	...	...	13	6	43	34
2	Damoh	273	208	...	...	...	...	...	...	...	...	50	51
3	Jubbulpore	496	477	898	903	...	...	...	...	76	55	53	58
4	Mandla	2,679	2,725	31	38	...	...	...	...	...	...	4	6
5	Seoni	5,877	6,420	2	3	...	...	...	...	40	37	84	93
	NERBUDDA DIVISION	*14,327*	*14,711*	*876*	*904*	*7*	*5*	*28*	*31*	*2,190*	*2,269*	*28*	*39*
6	Narsinghpur	71	77	788	806	...	...	...	...	49	65	22	28
7	Hoshangabad	2,279	2,259	58	65	...	...	...	...	210	228	...	...
8	Nimar	4,479	4,523	25	33	...	...	4	4	494	502	5	9
9	Betul	2 796	2,902	3	...	2	...	3	5	684	715	...	...
10	Chhindwara	4,702	4,950	2	...	5	5	21	22	753	759	1	2
	NAGPUR DIVISION	*84,285*	*86,622*	*19*	*8*	*22,723*	*24,105*	*393*	*325*	*8,566*	*8,920*	...	...
11	Wardha	10,489	10,257	...	...	952	944	124	98	3,186	3,366	...	...
12	Nagpur	16,459	16,774	1	4	2,252	2,361	218	172	3,956	4,054	...	...
13	Chanda	18 343	18.447	10	1	16,495	17,151	12	8	573	582	...	...
14	Bhandara	14.928	15,420	6	3	1.317	1,443	39	47	710	772	...	...
15	Balaghat	24,066	25,724	2	...	1,707	2,206	...	...	141	146	...	...
	CHHATTISGARH DIVISION	*51,325*	*53,334*	*224*	*239*	...	...	...	...	*605*	*744*	*24*	*21*
16	Raipur	21,713	22,465	3	3	...	...	...	...	512	648	...	...
17	Bilaspur	17,836	18,536	117	128	...	...	...	...	49	53	24	21
18	Drug	11,776	12,333	104	108	...	...	...	...	44	43	...	...
	Berar	**102,328**	**100,205**	...	...	**1,062**	**1.070**	**1,674**	**1.500**	**29.520**	**30,434**	**19**	**23**
19	Amraoti	38,431	37,735	...	...	212	222	656	508	6,813	6,841	...	...
20	Akola	24,125	23,321	...	...	1	1	397	360	10,222	10,652	1	1
21	Buldana	25,131	24,961	...	...	2	...	399	386	7,215	7,434	18	22
22	Yeotmal	14,641	14,188	...	...	847	847	222	156	5,270	5,507	...	...
	Feudatory States	**17,525**	**18,263**	**245**	**259**	**43**	**22**	...	...	**52**	**48**	**38**	**20**
23	Makrai	127	120	...	...	...	...	...	...	5	6	...	...
24	Bastar	2,301	2,267	6	4	42	22	...	...	12	1	...	...
25	Kanker	1,929	1,963	...	...	...	...	...	...	25	33	...	...
26	Nandgaon	2,333	2.627	...	...	...	...	...	...	6	7	...	...
27	Khairagarh	2,205	2,362	...	...	...	...	...	...	4	1	...	...
28	Chhuikhadan	697	728	9	14	...	...	...	...	...	...	...	...
29	Kawardha	2,829	3,019	109	122	...	...	...	...	...	...	...	...
30	Sakti	1,053	1.008	...	...	...	...	...	...	...	...	...	...
31	Raigarh	1,806	1,797	...	...	1	...	...	...	...	...	...	...
32	Sarangarh	2,007	2.249	...	...	...	...	...	...	...	...	...	...
33	Chang Bhakar	1	...	...	...	...	...	...	...	...	...	...	...
34	Korea	47	36	...	...	...	...	...	...	...	...	5	5
35	Surguja	49	48	49	44	...	...	...	...	...	...	32	12
36	Udaipur	39	33	...	...	...	...	...	...	...	...	...	...
37	Jashpur	12	10	72	75	...	...	...	...	...	...	1	3

Tribe, Race or Nationality.

MARATHA.		MEHRA.		MEHTAR.		MHALI.		MOCHI.		NAGARCHI.	
HINDU.		HINDU.		HINDU.		HINDU.		HINDU.		HINDU.	
Males.	Females.	Males.	Females.	Males.	Females.	Males.	Females.	Males.	Females.	Males.	Females.
436	437	438	439	440	441	442	443	444	445	446	447
46.716	47,185	575,449	589.728	6,642	6,370	19,115	18.374	2.004	2.003	2.991	3.248
46,507	46,966	550,198	564,312	6.418	6,113	19,116	18,373	1,890	1.884	2,946	3.202
16.852	16,943	342,427	352.682	4,992	4,905	10,456	10,706	1.621	1,554	2.946	3.202
707	*693*	*37,943*	*28,748*	*1,336*	*1,280*	...	...	*396*	*395*	*976*	*1,066*
227	187	259	222	208	104	...	...	120	124	...	...
100	77	1,067	1.085	214	222	...	...	50	66	...	...
315	278	7,834	8,179	616	568	...	...	185	109	1	..
29	28	7,613	7.610	140	144	...	...	29	29	82	73
96	123	11,170	11,652	148	152	...	...	12	7	803	993
4,284	*3,939*	*54,635*	*56,136*	*1,288*	*1,164*	*268*	*269*	*427*	*399*	*452*	*473*
103	97	8,324	8,746	129	156	...	...	46	50	...	...
694	585	7,131	7.229	334	275	...	...	130	132	...	...
1,116	905	2,657	2,778	302	239	...	...	229	202	...	...
1,694	1,669	18,279	18,729	132	108	...	...	11	2	...	...
677	683	18,244	18,659	301	386	268	269	11	13	452	473
9,462	*9,739*	*233,651*	*245,961*	*1,945*	*1,954*	*10,188*	*10,437*	*289*	*273*	*1,378*	*1,477*
3,897	3.883	34,066	35,105	308	299	1,562	1.522	97	68	.	...
4,473	4,648	69,516	71,505	1,002	1,011	3,909	4,165	177	187	61	79
680	759	45.130	45,068	235	242	1,282	1,356	2	3	...	...
382	428	70,775	[illegible]	272	279	3,345	3,304	4	4	565	571
30	21	19,064	19,677	128	123	...	...	9	10	752	827
2,339	*2,572*	*21,293*	*22,837*	*433*	*507*	...	...	*509*	*488*	*150*	*156*
1,213	1,353	5.581	6,121	127	131	...	...	166	161	3	4
751	798	4 571	4,849	161	187	...	...	79	81	27	33
375	421	11.146	11,867	145	189	...	...	264	246	110	149
29,655	30,023	207,771	211.630	1.426	1.208	8,659	7,667	269	330	...	...
5,415	5.670	64,329	65,943	455	441	4,210	3,743	201	276	...	...
10,470	10,724	62.104	[illegible]	470	385	744	471	...	...	...	...
4,536	4.738	42,143	43,125	339	259	2,001	1.673	54	44	...	...
9,234	8,891	39,195	[illegible]	162	123	1,704	1,780	14	10	...	...
209	219	25,251	25.416	224	[illegible]	...	1	114	119	45	46
23	23	1	1	...	2	...	...	...	...	...	...
63	55	14,685	14.316	1	21	...	...	24	28	...	...
27	40	1,707	1,720	18	32	...	...	11	11	...	...
55	72	4.213	4,511	54	55	...	...	71	72	18	17
8	5	2,701	2,790	89	86	...	...	6	5	15	13
...	...	515	567	6	9	...	...	...	..	3	9
1	...	582	632	16	25	...	...	..	..	2	1
16	17	15	19	9	4	...	...	...	..	...	...
10	7	521	550	24	17	...	1	2	3	...	...
...	...	137	122	...	...	...	...	...	...	...	...
...	...	4	7	...	...	...	...	...	.	...	...
2	...	8	10	...	1	..	...	..	..	6	4
...	...	56	59	5	4	...	...	...	...	...	...
4	...	76	64	2	1	...	...	...	...	1	2
...	...	30	39	...	...	...	...	...	...	...	...

REMARKS. (448)

	M.	F.
MALI includes—		
Animist.		
Chhindwara	0	2
Nagpur Division	15	8
Chhattisgarh Division ...	4	6
Berar	27	25
Feudatory States	43	46
Musalman.		
Berar	104	106
Arya.		
Balaghat	0	1
Bilaspur	8	7
Akola	3	1
Jain.		
Amraoti	9	0
Buldana	5	12
Yeotmal	0	1
MALLAH includes—		
Animist.		
Betul	1	0
Drug	2	0
MANA includes—		
Animist.		
Nagpur Division.	15	8
MANBHAO includes—		
Jain.		
Berar	9	6
MANG includes—		
Animist.		
Wardha	1	1
Drug	1	0
Yeotmal	1	0
Kanker	16	16
Jain.		
Akola	0	1
MANIHAR includes—		
Musalman.		
Jubbulpore Division	37	34
Nerbudda Division	5	10
Bilaspur	9	11
Berar	19	23
Surguja	13	5
MARATHA includes—		
Arya.		
Nerbudda Division	6	5
Jain.		
Wardha	0	1
Akola	2	1
MEHRA includes—		
Animist.		
Jubbulpore Division	5	6
Nerbudda Division	18	11
Nagpur Division	36	30
Chhattisgarh Division ...	11	20
Berar	9	12
Feudatory States	203	[illegible]
Musalman.		
Akola	0	2
MEHTAR includes—		
Animist.		
Balaghat	1	0
Akola	5	4
Musalman.		
Jubbulpore Division	10	12
Nerbudda Division	28	34
Nagpur Division	29	25
Raipur	2	8
Berar	142	125
MHALI includes—		
Animist.		
Nagpur Division	2	0
Musalman.		
Akola	2	1
Jain.		
Wardha	3	2
Berar	7	3
MOCHI includes—		
Musalman.		
Saugor	0	1
Nimar	2	0
Nagpur	0	2
NAGARCHI includes—		
Animist.		
Jubbulpore Division	64	88
Chhindwara	324	350
Nagpur Division	92	101
Feudatory States	11	7
Musalman.		
Jubbulpore	.	0

TABLE XIII.—Caste,

Serial No.	DISTRICT OR STATE.	NAGASIA. Hindu. Males.	NAGASIA. Hindu. Females.	NAGASIA. Animist. Males.	NAGASIA. Animist. Females.	NAI. Hindu. Males.	NAI. Hindu. Females.	NIHAL OR NAHAL. Hindu. Males.	NIHAL OR NAHAL. Hindu. Females.	NIHAL OR NAHAL. Animist. Males.	NIHAL OR NAHAL. Animist. Females.
		449	450	451	452	453	454	455	456	457	458
	Central Provinces and Berar ...	**20.105**	**19.781**	**2.102**	**2.177**	**74.078**	**74.672**	**4.259**	**4.518**	**1.805**	**1.821**
	C. P. British Districts and Berar ...	**112**	**100**	...	...	**67.182**	**67.554**	**4.153**	**4.380**	**1,694**	**1.723**
	C. P. British Districts	**112**	**100**	...	...	**57.311**	**57.555**	**3.897**	**4.126**	**189**	**218**
	JUBBULPORE DIVISION	..	...	...	...	*19,228*	*19,141*	...	*1*	...	...
1	Saugor	...	...	...	...	6,541	6,456	...	...	...	...
2	Damoh	...	...	...	...	3,647	3,533	...	...	...	...
3	Jubbulpore	...	...	...	...	5,881	5,921	...	...	...	...
4	Mandla	...	...	...	...	870	897	...	...	...	...
5	Seoni	...	...	...	...	2,289	2,334	...	1	...	...
	NERBUDDA DIVISION	...	...	...	...	*13,630*	*13,256*	*3,892*	*4,123*	*187*	*212*
6	Narsinghpur	...	...	...	...	3,237	3,283	...	...	...	...
7	Hoshangabad	...	...	...	...	4,037	3,810	545	590	84	96
8	Nimar...	...	...	...	...	2,059	1,913	2,753	2,898	...	...
9	Betul	...	...	...	...	1,802	1,733	583	621	101	110
10	Chhindwara	...	...	...	...	2,495	2,517	11	14	2	6
	NAGPUR DIVISION	...	...	...	...	*8,601*	*8,290*	*5*	*2*	...	...
11	Wardha	...	...	...	...	1,484	1,455	...	...	...	...
12	Nagpur	...	...	...	...	1,825	1,528	5	2	...	...
13	Chanda	...		...	...	1,858	1,742	...	...	...	...
14	Bhandara	...	...	...	...	1,307	1,462	...	...	...	...
15	Balaghat	...	...	...	...	2,037	2,103	...	...	...	...
	CHHATTISGARH DIVISION	*112*	*100*	...	...	*15,852*	*16,868*	...	...	*2*	*6*
16	Raipur	...	..	...	...	5,964	6,335	...	...	2	6
17	Bilaspur	112	100	...	...	5,902	6,239	...	...	...	...
18	Drug	...	...	...	...	3,986	4,294	...	...	...	...
	Berar	...	...	...	...	**9,871**	**9,999**	**256**	**254**	**1.505**	**1.505**
19	Amraoti	...	...	...	...	1,421	1,386	9	5	1,466	1,476
20	Akola	..	...	...	...	4,093	4,185	2	4	...	...
21	Buldana	...	...	...	...	2,068	2.223	245	245	39	29
22	Yeotmal	...	...	...	...	2,289	2,205	...	...	...	...
	Feudatory States	**19.993**	**19.681**	**2.102**	**2.177**	**6.896**	**7,118**	**106**	**138**	**111**	**98**
23	Makrai	...	...	...	...	102	104	106	138	111	98
24	Bastar	...	...	...	...	146	121	...	...	...	...
25	Kanker	...	...	...	...	800	296	...	...	...	...
26	Nandgaon	...		...	...	990	997	...	...	...	...
27	Khairagarh	...		...	...	931	1,027	...	...	...	...
28	Chhuikhadan	...	...	...	...	194	191	...	...	...	...
29	Kawardha	...	...	...	...	393	434	...	...	...	...
30	Sakti	63	46	...	...	214	232	...	...	...	...
31	Raigarh	1,235	1,147	...	...	543	570	...	...	...	...
32	Sarangarh	1	...	...	...	206	327	...	...	...	...
33	Chang Bhakar	...	...	—	...	32	25	...	...	...	...
34	Korea — — ...	...	..	...	...	87	76	...	...	...	...
35	Surguja	10,659	10,464	479	464	2,374	2,438	...	...	...	...
36	Udaipur	2	2	1,613	1,700	153	132	...	—	...	...
37	Jashpur	8,033	8,022	10	13	141	148	...	...	...	...

Tribe, Race or Nationality.

ORAON.				OTARI.		PABIA.		PAIK.		PANKA.		REMARKS.	
HINDU.		ANIMIST.		HINDU.		HINDU.		HINDU.		HINDU.			
Males.	Females.	Males.	Females.	Males.	Females.	Males.	Females.	Males.	Females.	Males.	Females.		Serial No.
459	460	461	462	463	464	465	466	467	468	469	470	471	
2,501	2,508	39.415	38.675	1.271	1.363	4.529	4.807	1.548	1.643	104,032	110.862		
2,137	2.094	53	44	1.271	1,363	1,980	2,111	1,546	1.640	65.296	70,684		
2,137	2.094	53	44	693	731	1.980	2.111	1,546	1,640	65.292	70.684		
...	...	...	...	*23*	*17*	*14*	*14*	*6*	*5*	*11 365*	*11,711*		
...	...	...	...	...	...	...	...	...	...	21	33		1
...	...	...	...	...	...	...	...	...	...	396	417		2
...	...	...	...	...	...	3	11	6	5	1,057	1,004		3
...	...	...	...	...	...	11	3	...	...	8,706	8.913		4
...	...	...	...	23	17	...	...	...	...	1,185	1,254		5
...	...	...	...	*8*	*4*	...	...	...	...	*6*	*3*		
...	...	...	...	4	...	...	...	...	...	1	...		6
...	...	...	...	...	...	...	...	...	...	...	...		7
...	...	...	...	...	1	...	...	...	...	...	...		8
...	...	...	...	...	...	...	...	...	...	1	...		9
...	...	...	...	4	3	...	...	...	...	4	3		10
...	...	...	...	*662*	*710*	...	...	...	...	*1,573*	*1,632*		
...	...	...	...	45	78	...	...	...	...	...	...		11
...	...	...	...	49	47	...	...	...	...	27	20		12
...	...	...	...	249	246	...	...	...	...	46	49		13
...	...	...	...	253	252	...	...	...	...	40	53		14
...	...	...	...	66	87	...	...	...	...	1,451	1,510		15
2,157	*2,094*	*53*	*44*	...	...	*1,966*	*2,097*	*1,540*	*1,635*	*52,348*	*57,335*		
706	692	22	23	...	...	51	46	1,540	1,635	15,039	16,661		16
1,422	1,402	31	21	...	...	1,915	2,051	...	...	30,281	32,453		17
9	...	...	...	...	...	...	...	...	...	7,028	8,224		18
...	...	...	...	578	632	...	...	...	...	4	...		
...	...	...	...	182	241	...	...	...	...	4	...		19
...	...	...	...	139	157	...	...	...	...	...	...		20
...	...	...	...	120	106	...	...	...	...	...	...		21
...	...	...	...	137	128	...	...	...	...	...	...		22
364	414	39,362	38,631	...	...	2,549	2.696	2	3	38,736	40,178		
...	...	...	...	...	...	...	...	...	...	...	...		23
104	125	25	23	...	...	...	...	1	1	1,365	1,377		24
...	...	...	...	...	...	...	...	...	...	624	638		25
...	...	...	...	...	...	...	...	...	...	1,357	1,553		26
...	...	...	...	...	...	...	...	...	...	1,358	1,635		27
...	...	...	...	...	...	...	...	...	...	366	404		28
...	...	...	...	...	...	...	...	...	...	387	1,122		29
42	44	165	158	...	...	...	...	...	...	1,221	1,294		30
23	19	2,981	3,085	...	...	1,258	1.447	...	...	5,339	5,632		31
33	34	411	453	...	...	338	396	...	...	2,566	2,685		32
...	...	...	...	...	...	230	235	1	2	740	744		33
...	1	327	307	...	...	715	618	...	...	2,543	2,564		34
24	27	20.119	19,600	...	...	2	...	...	...	17,880	18,132		35
3	70	3,227	3,076	...	...	1	...	...	...	1,542	1,557		36
136	94	12,107	11,929	...	...	5	...	...	...	848	841		37

Remarks (471):

		M.	F.
NAI includes—			
Animist.			
Damoh	... ...	1	1
Feudatory States	... ...	124	99
Musalman.			
Jubbulpore Division	...	38	25
Nerbudda Division	...	31	28
Bilaspur	... ...	6	1
Berar	... ...	17	23
Feudatory States	... ...	22	27
Arya.			
Seoni	... ...	5	4
Chhindwara	... ...	6	3
Sikh			
Jubbulpore	... ...	2	0

Oraon. In Jashpur 36,363 Oraons have been recently converted into Christianity and have not been included with this caste. They have been shown as Indian Christians.

		M.	F.
OTARI includes—			
Animist.			
Nagpur Division	...	38	13
PABIA includes—			
Animist.			
Bilaspur	... ...	1	1
Feudatory States	... ...	32	40
PAIK includes—			
Animist.			
Raipur	... ...	39	35
PANKA includes—			
Animist.			
Jubbulpore Division	...	112	104
Balaghat	... ...	4	1
Chhattisgarh Division	...	4	5
Feudatory States	... ...	89	63

TABLE XIII.—Caste,

Serial No.	DISTRICT OR STATE.	PARDHAN.				PARDHI.		PASI.		PATWA.		RAJBHAR.	
		HINDU.		ANIMIST.		HINDU.		HINDU.		HINDU.		HINDU.	
		Males.	Females.	Males.	Females.	Males.	Females	Males.	Females.	Males.	Females.	Males.	Females.
		472	473	474	475	476	477	478	479	480	481	482	483
	Central Provinces and Berar ...	**12,203**	**12.967**	**45,508**	**47,952**	**6,506**	**6,384**	**2.496**	**2,143**	**3.470**	**3,603**	**2.256**	**2,247**
	C. P. British Districts and Berar ...	**11,026**	**11,730**	**44,879**	**47.242**	**6.232**	**6.119**	**2,455**	**2,109**	**3.243**	**3.362**	**1,978**	**2.028**
	C. P. British Districts	**6,790**	**7.201**	**39,786**	**42.000**	**1.965**	**2.000**	**1,997**	**1,711**	**2,990**	**3.097**	**1,946**	**1,996**
	JUBBULPORE DIVISION	*428*	*419*	*14,662*	*15,200*	*218*	*225*	*732*	*711*	*1,247*	*1,240*	*1,740*	*1,794*
1	Saugor	6	4	...	...	121	117	55	60	398	385	1	...
2	Damoh	...	...	...	...	10	10	11	6	200	204	...	1
3	Jubbulpore	133	140	850	913	7	10	637	621	397	422	1,094	1,134
4	Mandla	200	185	5,488	5,065	36	45	26	20	48	48	483	503
5	Seoni	89	90	8,324	9,222	44	43	3	4	204	181	162	156
	NERBUDDA DIVISION	*679*	*747*	*7,800*	*8,122*	*711*	*658*	*763*	*643*	*704*	*752*	*178*	*174*
6	Narsinghpur	86	102	826	873	48	50	26	28	350	398	143	152
7	Hoshangabad	367	420	604	688	240	228	459	408	302	322	...	...
8	Nimar	30	29	27	22	355	314	175	134	14	12	...	...
9	Betul	109	89	1,918	1,997	68	66	53	45	5	1	6	2
10	Chhindwara	87	107	4,425	4,542	...	...	50	28	33	19	29	20
	NAGPUR DIVISION	*3,931*	*3,972*	*16,867*	*17,608*	*490*	*532*	*386*	*263*	*166*	*205*	...	...
11	Wardha	748	812	3,320	3.450	241	285	28	14	5	7	...	...
12	Nagpur	1,974	1,994	1.242	1,290	70	65	229	179	73	110	...	...
13	Chanda	760	740	9 040	9,350	155	160	94	54	45	41	...	...
14	Bhandara	286	284	1,073	1,172	8	11	23	9	40	43	...	...
15	Balaghat	163	142	2,192	2,346	16	11	12	7	3	4	...	...
	CHHATTISGARH DIVISION	*1,752*	*2,063*	*457*	*470*	*546*	*585*	*116*	*94*	*873*	*900*	*28*	*28*
16	Raipur	486	541	124	129	137	169	33	31	378	418	3	...
17	Bilaspur	986	1 189	279	276	119	133	80	63	345	328	23	26
18	Drug	280	333	54	65	290	283	3	...	150	154	2	2
	Berar	**4,236**	**4.529**	**5,093**	**5.242**	**4.267**	**4,119**	**458**	**398**	**253**	**265**	**32**	**32**
19	Amraoti	243	226	207	221	1,455	1,394	220	221	144	130	29	30
20	Akola	29	87	18	15	857	820	136	90	67	62	...	...
21	Buldana	...	...	...	...	1,603	1,504	8	7	38	69	2	2
22	Yeotmal	3,964	4,216	4,868	5,006	352	401	94	80	4	4	1	...
	Feudatory States	**1,177**	**1.237**	**629**	**710**	**274**	**265**	**41**	**34**	**227**	**241**	**278**	**219**
23	Makrai	...	...	36	43	5	8	...	...	...	...	...	...
24	Bustar	212	219	78	96	99	87	...	...	8	7	...	..
25	Kanker	82	104	99	107	12	9	1	...	17	15	...	...
26	Nandgaon	50	62	18	24	48	41	4	1	26	31	...	...
27	Khairagarh	101	108	12	17	34	46	2	1	33	28	...	...
28	Chhuikhadan	...	...	...	...	10	9	...	...	9	7	...	...
29	Kawardha	89	124	...	2	62	60	...	...	21	22	6	14
30	Sakti	43	45	107	140	...	...	...	...	5	8	...	...
31	Raigarh	156	141	...	...	...	...	7	5	6	3	...	...
32	Sarangarh	15	6	...	...	4	5	...	...	...	...	...	...
33	Chang Bhakar	26	15	8	7	...	...	...	...	...	...	...	...
34	Korea	7	8	136	145	...	...	...	...	...	...	...	...
35	Surguja	390	399	105	100	...	...	22	22	97	119	...	...
36	Udaipur	...	...	30	29	...	...	...	...	3	...	...	...
37	Jashpur	6	6	...	...	...	...	5	5	2	1	272	205

Tribe, Race or Nationality.

Rajjhar or Lajjhar. Hindu Males.	Rajjhar or Lajjhar. Hindu Females.	Rajjhar or Lajjhar. Animist. Males.	Rajjhar or Lajjhar. Animist. Females.	Rajput Including Septs. Hindu. Males.	Rajput Including Septs. Hindu. Females.	Septs of Rajput. Bachhania. Males.	Septs of Rajput. Bachhania. Females.	Septs of Rajput. Bachhgoti. Males.	Septs of Rajput. Bachhgoti. Females.	Septs of Rajput. Baghel. Males.	Septs of Rajput. Baghel. Females.	Septs of Rajput. Bagri. Males.	Septs of Rajput. Bagri. Females.	Serial No.
484	485	486	487	488	489	490	491	492	493	494	495	496	497	
3.375	**3,623**	**274**	**282**	**223.581**	**217.6[illegible]0**	**147**	**104**	**75**	**39**	**1.784**	**1,873**	**3.662**	**3.754**	
3.375	**3.623**	**274**	**282**	**211,164**	**205.401**	**104**	**104**	**53**	**23**	**1.409**	**1.484**	**3,654**	**3,754**	
2,494	**2,700**	**274**	**282**	**191.780**	**187.374**	**104**	**104**	**53**	**23**	**1.303**	**1,393**	**3,653**	**3.754**	
596	*675*	...	*1*	*41,478*	*38,139*	...	...	*23*	*1*	*456*	*477*	*3,631*	*3,736*	
...	...	...	...	8,053	7,168	...	...	1	...	234	244	115	142	1
...	...	...	...	4,369	3,978	...	...	...	...	32	26	...	...	2
...	...	...	...	11,249	9,947	...	...	22	1	152	169	596	653	3
6	4	...	...	3,059	2,033	...	...	...	...	25	26	5	8	4
590	671	...	1	14,748	15,023	...	...	...	...	13	12	2,915	2,933	5
1,879	*2,009*	*274*	*281*	*59,856*	*57,547*	*104*	*104*	*18*	*9*	*445*	*442*	*18*	*18*	
220	239	1	...	6,710	6,741	...	...	...	...	36	37	...	...	6
383	401	272	279	26,951	26.165	68	58	2	...	294	297	14	13	7
3	...	...	...	16,170	15,371	36	46	6	...	87	78	4	5	8
621	684	1	2	4,331	3,950	...	...	10	9	12	15	...	..	9
652	685	...	...	5,694	5,311	...	...	...	...	16	15	...	...	10
13	*16*	...	...	*75,424*	*76,546*	...	...	...	...	*61*	*117*	*1*	...	
1	3	...	...	1,992	1,568	...	...	...	...	10	29	...	...	11
16	13	...	...	6,837	6,041	...	...	...	...	8	21	...	...	12
...	...	...	...	1,190	1,077	...	...	...	...	...	10	...	...	13
1	...	...	...	39.752	41,693	...	...	..	...	41	55	...	...	14
...	...	...	...	25,653	26,167	...	...	...	...	2	2	1	...	15
1	...	...	...	*15,022*	*16,132*	..	...	*12*	*13*	*341*	*357*	*3*	...	
...	...	...	...	3,543	3,287	...	...	6	6	164	149	...		16
1	...	...	--	7,613	7,829	...	...	4	7	107	117	3	...	17
...	...	...	...	3,866	4,016	...	...	2	...	70	91	...	...	18
881	**923**	...	...	**19,384**	**18,027**	..	...	...	...	**106**	**91**	**1**	...	
834	896	...	...	5,874	5,312	...	...	...	...	100	89	1	...	19
30	11	...	...	4.172	3,821	...	...	...	...	3	1	...	...	20
5	3	...	...	7,008	6,976	...	...	...	...	...	...	...	...	21
12	13	...	...	2,330	1,918	...	...	...	...	3	1	...	...	22
...	...	...	...	**12,417**	**12.249**	**43**	...	**22**	**16**	**375**	**389**	**8**	...	
...	...	...	...	664	641	43	...	...	...	6	12	...	...	23
...	...	...	...	5,118	4,976	...	—	...	...	29	35	...	...	24
...	...	...	...	432	444	...	...	...	...	22	24	...	...	25
...	...	...	...	932	924	...	..	...	...	64	79	...	...	26
...	...	...	...	1,550	1,679	...	...	..	...	78	88	...	...	27
...	...	...	...	109	114	...	...	...	...	4	1	...	--	28
...	...	...	...	700	785	...	...	...	...	21	5	...	...	29
...	...	...	...	82	90	...	...	...	...	1	2	...	...	30
...	...	...	...	475	419	...	...	21	16	52	55	...	...	31
...	...	...	...	173	204	...	...	...	...	10	11	.	...	32
...	...	...	...	85	60	..	...	...	...	8	5	...	...	33
...	...	...	...	299	213	...	...	...	...	8	2	...	...	34
...	...	...	...	1,072	1,070	...	...	...	...	63	62	8	...	35
...	...	...	...	191	144	...	...	1	...	5	...	...	...	36
...	...	...	...	535	486	...	...	...	...	4	8	...	...	37

Remarks. (498)

Pardhi includes—

	M.	F.
Animist.		
Jubbulpore Division	15	20
Hoshangabad	2	1
Wardha	32	31
Drug	77	74
Berar	38	42
Feudatory States	26	25
Musalman.		
Amraoti	0	1

Pasi includes—

	M.	F.
Animist		
Chhindwara	5	6
Wardha	5	1
Amraoti	0	3
Yeotmal	57	54
Jashpur	0	1

Patwa includes—

	M.	F.
Animist.		
Raigarh	1	0
Musalman.		
Nimar	1	6
Berar	5	7
Jain.		
Berar	20	48

Raijhar includes—

	M.	F.
Animist.		
Jubbulpore	3	2
Narsinghpur	29	23
Berar	31	28

Rajput includes—

	M.	F.
Animist.		
Nagpur Division	3	2
Bilaspur	1	0
Feudatory States	26	24
Yeotmal	0	1
Musalman.		
Saugor	98	5
Jubbulpore	373	5
Nimar	3	2
Raipur	41	0
Berar	30	41
Arya.		
Jubbulpore Division	15	19
Nerbudda Division	18	8
Nagpur Division	26	18
Chhattisgarh Division	10	6
Bastar	8	5
Sikh.		
Jubbulpore Division	42	4
Nerbudda Division	29	6
Nagpur Division	13	6
Chhattisgarh Division	41	9
Yeotmal	3	3
Feudatory States	6	0
Jain.		
Wardha	3	0
Chanda	0	1
Berar	4	1

TABLE XIII.—Caste,

Serial No.	DISTRICT OR STATE.	SEPTS OF													
		BAIS.		BANAPHAR.		BANAUDHIA.		BAKSARIA.		BARGUJAR.		BHADORIA.		BISEN.	
		Males.	Females.	Males.	Females.	Males.	Females.	Males.	Females.	Males.	Females.	Males.	Females.	Males.	Females.
		499	500	501	502	503	504	505	506	507	508	509	510	511	512
	Central Provinces and Berar ...	**8,355**	**7,841**	**403**	**433**	**166**	**175**	**1,960**	**2,225**	**79**	**67**	**500**	**510**	**492**	**433**
	C. P. British Districts and Berar ...	**7,311**	**6,801**	**287**	**306**	**154**	**152**	**1,253**	**1,436**	**79**	**67**	**493**	**507**	**438**	**366**
	C. P. British Districts	**7,201**	**6,697**	**284**	**306**	**154**	**152**	**1,252**	**1,436**	**79**	**67**	**493**	**505**	**438**	**366**
	JUBBULPORE DIVISION	*2,104*	*1,963*	*132*	*115*	...	...	*212*	*211*	*64*	*55*	*68*	*82*	*142*	*131*
1	Saugor	567	635	28	24	...	...	...	...	30	23	35	53	33	24
2	Damoh	240	219	15	18	...	...	...	...	11	11	4	5	8	5
3	Jubbulpore	1,032	934	62	55	...	...	9	10	23	21	23	15	99	102
4	Mandla	129	128	10	11	...	...	...	...	...	...	5	5	2	...
5	Seoni	136	146	7	7	...	...	203	201	...	...	1	4	...	...
	NERBUDDA DIVISION	*2,698*	*2,144*	*44*	*40*	...	...	*37*	*34*	*13*	*12*	*416*	*417*	*29*	*20*
6	Narsinghpur	372	387	28	25	...	...	...	...	13	12	42	30	11	7
7	Hoshangabad	1,967	1,433	1	...	...	...	...	...	...	...	353	371	4	3
8	Nimar	174	151	...	...	...	...	...	...	...	...	17	15	7	2
9	Betul	26	27	1	1	...	...	...	...	...	...	2	...	...	1
10	Chhindwara	159	146	14	14	...	...	37	34	...	...	2	1	7	7
	NAGPUR DIVISION	*358*	*519*	*14*	*1*	...	...	...	...	*2*	...	*7*	*5*	*74*	*32*
11	Wardha	77	63	1	1	...	...	...	...	...	...	5	5	...	3
12	Nagpur	118	165	12	...	...	...	...	...	...	...	2	...	64	11
13	Chanda	20	70	...	...	...	...	...	...	...	...	...	...	...	...
14	Bhandara	105	154	...	...	...	...	...	...	2	...	...	...	9	18
15	Balaghat	59	67	1	...	...	...	...	...	...	...	...	...	1	...
	CHHATTISGARH DIVISION	*2,011*	*2,072*	*104*	*150*	*154*	*152*	*1,003*	*1,191*	...	...	*2*	*1*	*193*	*183*
16	Raipur	629	637	20	26	13	34	2	9	...	...	...	...	47	51
17	Bilaspur	920	930	35	48	...	...	751	899	...	...	1	1	109	82
18	Drug	462	505	49	76	141	118	250	283	...	...	1	...	37	50
	Berar	**110**	**104**	**3**	...	...	...	**1**	...	...	...	...	**2**	...	...
19	Amraoti	68	80	...	...	...	...	1	...	...	...	...	...	...	...
20	Akola	2	2	3	...	...	...	...	...	...	...	...	2	...	...
21	Buldana	16	...	...	...	...	...	...	...	...	...	...	...	...	...
22	Yeotmal	24	22	...	...	...	...	...	...	...	...	...	...	...	...
	Feudatory States	**1,044**	**1,040**	**116**	**127**	**12**	**23**	**707**	**789**	...	...	**7**	**3**	**54**	**67**
23	Makrai	2	...	...	...	...	...	...	...	...	...	...	...	...	...
24	Bastar	153	145	2	3	...	...	...	...	...	...	...	...	3	1
25	Kanker	116	119	15	10	...	...	...	...	...	...	...	...	...	2
26	Nandgaon	168	165	39	52	10	15	...	...	...	...	...	...	8	7
27	Khairagarh	282	308	12	14	2	8	173	186	...	...	7	3	25	28
28	Chhuikhadan	19	18	7	8	...	...	...	...	...	...	...	...	...	...
29	Kawardha	16	29	4	7	...	...	534	603	...	...	...	...	2	2
30	Sakti	8	9	...	...	...	...	...	...	...	...	...	...	...	...
31	Raigarh	99	79	13	4	...	...	...	...	...	...	...	...	1	1
32	Sarangarh	44	56	12	9	...	...	...	...	...	...	...	...	6	8
33	Chang Bhakar	6	4	...	...	...	...	...	...	...	...	...	...	...	...
34	Korea	14	11	...	...	...	...	...	...	...	...	...	...	4	2
35	Surguja	63	47	7	16	...	...	...	...	...	...	...	...	2	12
36	Udaipur	47	43	2	...	...	...	...	...	...	...	...	...	3	4
37	Jashpur	7	7	3	4	...	...	...	...	...	...	...	...	...	...

Tribe, Race or Nationality.

RAJPUT—(contd.)

Bundela.		Chamar-gaur.		Chandel.		Chandravansi.		Chaonda.		Chauhan.		Daharia.		Deola.		Dhakar.		Dhundhere		
Males.	Females.	Males.	Females.	Males.	Females.	Males.	Females.	Males.	Females.	Males.	Females.	Males.	Females.	Males.	Females.	Males.	Females.	Males.	Females.	Serial No.
513	514	515	516	517	518	519	520	521	522	523	524	525	526	527	528	529	530	531	532	
1,089	1.049	448	365	1.501	1,478	92	46	118	127	7.352	5.970	277	269	26	24	2,244	3,872	66	75	
1.070	1.041	448	365	1,207	1.226	70	36	113	124	6.643	5.338	273	269	26	24	354	284	66	75	
911	842	446	361	1.153	1,142	67	36	113	124	6.410	5.150	273	269	26	24	354	284	66	75	
732	*673*	*180*	*108*	*317*	*251*	*15*	*16*	*12*	*13*	*1,059*	*947*	*5*	*3*	*23*	*23*	*34*	*23*	*66*	*72*	
613	402	19	13	148	134	3	6	12	13	543	463	...	...	23	23	31	15	37	33	1
43	73	21	18	24	24	...	...	...	...	50	59	5	3	...	...	...	..	...	...	2
71	102	3	2	129	68	5	7	...	...	367	340	...	...	...	...	2	8	4	13	3
5	5	14	13	11	17	7	3	...	...	49	42	...	...	...	...	...	...	...	...	4
...	...	123	62	5	8	...	...	...	...	50	43	...	...	...	...	1	...	25	26	5
108	*105*	*79*	*31*	*231*	*234*	*40*	*9*	*99*	*111*	*2,704*	*2,292*	...	...	*3*	...	*236*	*259*	...	*3*	
77	82	31	27	94	103	...	..	1	...	834	814	...	...	...	...	37	38	...	...	6
14	3	2	2	94	76	4	3	90	108	1,500	1,416	...	...	3	...	117	110	...	3	7
4	10	42	...	..	...	29	...	...	..	202	...	...	...	..	...	64	94	...	...	8
2	4	...	...	...	...	..	...	...	...	..	...	...	...	...	...	...	...	...	...	9
6	6	4	2	43	55	7	6	8	3	78	62	...	...	...	...	8	11	...	...	10
71	*47*	*180*	*216*	*172*	*156*	*4*	*8*	...	...	*531*	*566*	...	...	...	...	*6*	...	...	...	
46	...	...	..	146	164	...	...	...	...	125	132	..	...	...	...	3	...	...	...	11
...	...	...	...	24	17	...	...	...	...	121	134	...	...	...	...	...	..	...	...	12
19	45	...	...	1	2	...	...	...	..	53	38	...	...	..	...	3	...	...	...	13
...	...	180	216	1	2	4	8	...	...	198	206	...	...	...	...	...	...	...	...	14
6	2	..	...	...	1	..	...	...	...	34	55	...	...	..	...	...	...	...	...	15
5	*18*	*7*	*6*	*433*	*471*	*8*	*3*	*2*	...	*2,116*	*1,346*	*268*	*266*	...	*1*	*88*	*2*	...	...	
2	8	7	6	183	163	4	2	1	...	269	285	64	8	...	...	5	2	...	...	16
1	3	...	...	74	119	3	1	1	...	477	333	179	226	...	...	..	...	...	...	17
2	7	...	...	176	189	1	...	...	...	1,370	728	25	32	...	1	83	...	...	...	18
159	199	2	4	54	84	3	...	...	...	233	188	...	...	...	...	...	...	...	...	
11	8	2	4	20	77	2	...	...	...	133	115	...	...	...	...	...	...	...	...	19
1	34	...	...	33	6	...	...	...	...	47	51	...	...	...	..	...	...	...	...	20
147	157	...	...	1	1	..	...	...	...	29	9	...	...	...	..	...	...	...	...	21
...	...	...	...	...	...	1	...	...	...	24	13	...	...	...	...	...	...	...	...	22
19	8	...	...	294	252	22	10	5	3	709	632	4	...	...	...	1,890	3,588	...	...	
14	7	...	...	13	15	...	...	5	3	71	70	4	...	...	...	...	...	...	...	23
1	...	...	...	25	21	...	...	...	...	54	65	.	...	...	...	1,870	3,576	.	...	24
...	...	...	...	25	15	...	...	...	...	43	31	...	...	...	..	14	12	...	...	25
3	...	...	...	84	85	...	...	...	...	108	110	...	...	...	..	1	...	...	...	26
...	...	...	...	58	40	...	...	...	...	97	123	...	...	...	...	...	...	...	...	27
...	..	...	...	6	11	...	...	...	...	19	12	...	...	...	...	...	...	...	...	28
...	...	...	...	6	5	...	...	...	...	22	17	...	..	...	...	...	...	...	...	29
...	...	...	...	—	...	...	...	...	...	16	...	...	...	...	...	...	...	...	...	30
...	...	...	...	11	7	22	10	...	...	66	43	...	...	..	...	...	...	...	...	31
...	...	...	...	12	16	...	—	...	...	11	16	...	...	...	...	1	...	...	...	32
...	...	...	...	11	10	...	...	...	...	40	23	...	...	...	...	...	...	...	...	33
1	1	...	...	5	1	...	...	...	...	28	22	...	...	...	...	...	...	...	...	34
...	...	...	...	30	16	..	...	..	...	118	94	...	—	...	...	...	...	...	...	35
...	...	...	...	7	1	...	...	...	...	16	6	...	—	...	...	4	...	...	...	36
...	...	...	...	1	...	...	...	...	...	...	...	...	...	...	...	...	...	...	...	37

TABLE XIII.—Caste,

Serial No.	DISTRICT OR STATE.	SEPTS OF											
		DIKHIT.		GAHARWAR.		GAORAYR.		GAUR		GAUTAM.		GINNORA.	
		Males.	Females.	Males.	Females.	Males.	Females.	Males	Females.	Males.	Females.	Males.	Females.
		533	534	535	536	537	538	539	540	541	542	543	544
	Central Provinces and Berar ...	**467**	**420**	**629**	**527**	**3 017**	**2,818**	**3 287**	**2.629**	**697**	**623**	**559**	**459**
	C. P. British Districts and Berar ...	**405**	**335**	**366**	**287**	**3 017**	**2,818**	**3.261**	**2.612**	**531**	**479**	**559**	**459**
	C. P. British Districts	**405**	**335**	**341**	**268**	**3.017**	**2,818**	**3,166**	**2,612**	**526**	**477**	**559**	**459**
	JUBBULPORE DIVISION	*127*	*68*	*45*	*51*	*166*	*416*	*1,110*	*969*	*230*	*201*	...	...
1	Saugor	26	27	...	9	118	195	526	564	56	46	...	...
2	Damoh	1	...	...	...	...	...	57	62	3	12	...	...
3	Jubbulpore	96	39	39	36	43	214	408	335	165	138	...	...
4	Mandla	1	...	6	6	...	...	119	8	2	...	...	...
5	Seoni	3	2	...	...	5	7	...	...	4	5	...	...
	NERBUDDA DIVISION	*25*	*23*	*20*	*28*	*2,851*	*2,402*	*1,127*	*725*	*62*	*49*	*559*	*459*
6	Narsinghpur	5	3	6	9	2.106	2,139	438	405	26	22	...	...
7	Hoshangabad	17	17	2	4	724	261	349	243	5	4	448	415
8	Nimar	3	3	...	...	16	...	300	62	18	4	75	12
9	Betul	...	...	...	...	1	2	27	9	1	5	36	32
10	Chhindwara	...	...	12	15	4	...	4	6	12	14	...	...
	NAGPUR DIVISION	*20*	*25*	*117*	*38*	...	...	*835*	*861*	*44*	*64*	...	...
11	Wardha	4	8	4	7	...	...	14	2	13	6	...	...
12	Nagpur	5	5	11	4	...	...	16	11	3	14	...	...
13	Chanda	6	7	2	6	...	...	...	...	1	6	...	...
14	Bhandara	5	5	98	18	...	...	804	848	27	38	...	...
15	Balaghat	...	...	2	3	...	...	1	...	...	...	...	...
	CHHATTISGARH DIVISION ...	*233*	*219*	*159*	*151*	...	...	*94*	*57*	*190*	*163*	...	...
16	Raipur	42	37	90	92	...	...	29	18	52	62	...	...
17	Bilaspur	128	118	35	30	...	...	12	13	79	54	...	...
18	Drug	63	64	25	29	...	...	53	26	59	47	...	...
	Berar	...	...	**25**	**19**	...	...	**95**	...	**5**	**2**	...	...
19	Amraoti	...	...	20	19	...	...	...	...	3	2	...	...
20	Akola	...	...	5	...	...	...	89	...	...	...	...	...
21	Buldana	...	...	...	...	...	...	4	...	...	...	...	...
22	Yeotmal	...	...	...	...	...	...	2	...	2	...	...	...
	Feudatory States	**62**	**85**	**263**	**240**	...	...	**26**	**17**	**166**	**144**	...	...
23	Makrai	...	...	...	...	.	...	3	2	...	...	...	...
24	Bastar	5	5	18	6	...	..	2	...	13	9	...	...
25	Kanker	17	19	2	3	...	...	2	...	40	16	...	...
26	Nandgaon	4	4	10	12	...	...	5	3	17	13	...	...
27	Khairagarh	18	24	106	122	...	...	5	...	39	35	...	...
28	Chhuikhadan	9	6	7	9	...	...	5	5	...	...	...	...
29	Kawardha	...	...	7	19	...	...	2	7	...	.	...	...
30	Sakti	1	5	...	...	...	...	...	...	11	16	...	...
31	Raigarh	...	15	9	5	...	...	1	...	34	43	...	...
32	Sarangarh	2	2	16	13	...	...	...	...	1	...	...	...
33	Chang Bhakar	...	...	8	4	...	...	...	...	...	...	...	...
34	Korea	6	5	34	21	...	...	...	...	...	...	...	...
35	Surguja	...	...	44	26	...	...	1	...	2	4	...	...
36	Udaipur	...	...	2	...	...	...	...	...	9	8	...	...
37	Jashpur	...	...	...	...	...	...	...	...	...	...	...	...

Tribe, Race or Nationality.

RAJPUT—(*contd.*)

Gohil.		Hada.		Haihaiya-vansi.		Jadam.		Jaigan.		Jaiwar.		Jalkhedi.		Jangra.		Janwar.		
Males.	Females.	Males.	Females.	Males.	Females.	Males.	Females.	Males.	Females.	Males.	Females.	Males.	Females	Males.	Females.	Males.	Females.	Serial No.
545	546	547	548	549	550	551	552	553	554	555	556	557	558	559	560	561	562	
52	57	86	82	72	88	11,199	11,064	85	85	215	223	127	123	124	102	142	81	
52	57	72	71	71	73	11.180	11,051	85	85	215	223	106	95	124	102	141	78	
52	57	72	71	71	73	11,034	10.889	85	85	215	223	106	95	90	84	139	78	
...	...	*23*	*22*	*3*	*6*	*89*	*82*	*85*	*85*	*205*	*200*	...	...	*57*	*50*	*31*	*26*	
...	...	18	18	...	...	55	49	85	85	137	108	...	...	40	37	9	12	1
...	...	3	2	...	...	...	...	...	...	17	11	...	...	11	9	...	...	2
...	...	2	2	...	...	12	11	...	...	51	71	...	...	2	...	9	14	3
...	...	...	...	...	...	2	...	...	...	...	...	...	...	...	...	...	...	4
...	...	...	...	3	5	20	22	...	...	...	10	.	...	4	4	13	...	5
14	*14*	*12*	*18*	...	...	*10,689*	*10,782*	...	...	*10*	*21*	*106*	*95*	*19*	*32*	*72*	*13*	
...	...	1	1	...	...	174	209	...	...	5	14	...	...	2	14	...	...	6
...	...	5	7	...	...	8,597	8,810	...	...	5	7	26	32	17	18	...	...	7
...	...	6	10	...	...	1,725	1,621	...	...	...	...	80	63	...	...	2	3	8
11	11	...	...	...	...	33	16	...	...	...	...	...	...	...	...	66	10	9
3	3	...	...	...	...	160	126	...	...	...	...	...	...	...	...	4	...	10
33	*36*	...	...	...	...	*240*	*2*	...	...	...	...	...	...	...	...	*2*	*1*	
...	...	...	...	...	...	7	...	...	...	...	...	...	...	...	...	2	1	11
...	...	...	...	...	...	226	...	...	...	...	...	...	...	...	...	...	...	12
33	36	...	...	...	...	...	...	...	...	...	...	...	...	...	...	...	...	13
...	...	...	...	...	...	7	2	...	...	...	...	...	...	...	...	...	...	14
...	...	...	...	...	...	...	...	...	...	...	...	...	...	...	...	...	...	15
5	*7*	*37*	*31*	*68*	*68*	*16*	*23*	...	...	...	*2*	...	...	*14*	*2*	*34*	*38*	
...	...	6	10	68	68	6	4	...	...	...	1	...	...	...	...	17	12	16
5	7	28	18	...	...	10	18	...	...	...	...	...	...	14	2	4	9	17
...	...	3	3	...	...	...	1	...	...	...	1	...	...	...	...	13	17	18
...	...	...	...	...	...	146	162	...	...	...	...	...	...	34	18	2	...	
...	...	...	...	...	...	48	32	...	...	...	...	...	...	...	...	2	..	19
...	...	...	...	...	...	...	21	...	...	...	...	...	...	...	...	...	...	20
...	...	...	...	...	...	98	107	...	...	...	...	...	...	34	18	...	...	21
...	...	...	...	...	...	...	2	...	...	...	...	...	...	...	...	...	...	22
...	...	14	11	1	15	19	13	...	...	...	...	21	28	...	...	1	3	
...	...	...	...	...	...	17	13	...	...	...	...	21	28	...	...	...	...	23
...	...	...	...	...	...	...	...	...	...	...	...	...	...	...	...	...	...	24
...	...	10	9	...	...	...	...	...	...	...	...	...	...	...	...	...	...	25
...	...	...	...	...	...	1	...	...	...	...	...	...	...	...	...	...	...	26
...	...	...	...	...	...	...	...	...	...	...	...	...	...	...	...	1	3	27
...	...	...	...	...	...	...	...	...	...	...	...	...	...	...	...	...	...	28
...	...	...	...	...	...	...	...	...	...	...	...	...	...	...	...	...	...	29
...	...	...	...	...	...	...	...	...	...	...	...	...	...	...	...	...	...	30
...	...	...	...	...	11	...	...	...	...	...	...	...	...	...	...	...	...	31
...	...	...	...	...	...	...	...	...	...	...	...	...	...	...	...	...	...	32
...	...	4	2	1	4	...	...	...	...	...	...	...	...	...	...	...	...	33
...	...	...	...	...	...	...	...	...	...	...	...	...	...	...	...	...	...	34
...	...	...	...	...	...	...	...	...	...	...	...	...	...	...	...	...	...	35
...	...	...	...	...	...	1	...	...	...	...	...	...	...	...	...	...	...	36
...	...	...	...	...	...	...	...	...	...	...	...	...	...	...	...	...	...	37

TABLE XIII.—Caste,

Serial No.	DISTRICT OR STATE.	SEPTS OF — Jhola. Males.	Jhola. Females.	Kachhwaha. Males.	Kachhwaha. Females.	Kalam. Males.	Kalam. Females.	Kanaujia. Males.	Kanaujia. Females.	Karchuli. Males.	Karchuli. Females.
		563	564	565	566	567	568	569	570	571	572
	Central Provinces and Berar ...	49	60	1.389	1.387	456	350	2.085	2.104	123	140
	C. P. British Districts and Berar ...	49	60	1,357	1,349	441	344	2,063	2,063	107	121
	C. P. British Districts	49	60	1,344	1.330	441	344	2.058	2,058	107	121
	JUBBULPORE DIVISION	...	...	*436*	*365*	...	...	*1,639*	*1,603*	*50*	*53*
1	Saugor	...	...	260	241	...	...	27	23	15	9
2	Damoh	...	...	27	19	...	...	31	11	7	7
3	Jubbulpore	...	...	114	82	...	...	1,343	1,266	10	17
4	Mandla	...	...	11	8	...	...	...	...	...	...
5	Seoni	...	...	18	15	...	...	238	303	18	20
	NERBUDDA DIVISION	*49*	*60*	*815*	*879*	*441*	*344*	*240*	*258*	*20*	*15*
6	Narsinghpur	...	...	104	116	...	...	14	10	12	6
7	Hoshangabad	...	...	385	401	194	173	...	...	1	...
8	Nimar	49	60	303	350	247	171	1	1	...	...
9	Betul	...	...	15	4	...	...	...	...	7	9
10	Chhindwara	...	...	8	8	...	...	225	247	...	...
	NAGPUR DIVISION	...	...	*22*	*29*	...	...	*20*	*25*	*1*	*1*
11	Wardha	...	...	2	3	...	...	...	5	...	...
12	Nagpur	...	...	...	...	...	...	20	19	...	...
13	Chanda	...	...	...	...	...	...	...	...	...	...
14	Bhandara	...	...	20	26	...	...	...	1	...	1
15	Balaghat	...	...	...	...	...	...	...	...	1	...
	CHHATTISGARH DIVISION	...	...	*71*	*57*	...	...	*159*	*172*	*36*	*52*
16	Raipur	...	...	31	20	...	...	14	...	5	...
17	Bilaspur	...	...	37	35	...	...	79	82	31	51
18	Drug	...	...	3	2	...	...	66	90	...	1
	Berar	...	...	13	19	...	...	5	5	...	...
19	Amraoti	...	...	6	12	...	...	3	1	...	...
20	Akola	...	...	...	...	...	...	...	...	...	...
21	Buldana	...	...	7	7	...	...	2	4	...	...
22	Yeotmal	...	...	...	...	...	...	...	...	...	...
	Feudatory States	...	...	32	38	15	6	22	41	16	19
23	Makrai	...	...	1	7	15	6	...	...	...	...
24	Bastar	...	...	2	1	...	...	...	...	...	...
25	Kanker	...	...	1	...	...	...	...	...	...	...
26	Nandgaon	...	...	1	1	...	...	...	...	...	...
27	Khairagarh	...	...	3	2	...	...	5	8	...	...
28	Chhuikhadan	...	...	...	...	...	...	17	33	...	...
29	Kawardha	...	...	...	2	...	...	...	...	...	...
30	Sakti	...	...	6	5	...	...	...	...	...	...
31	Raigarh	...	...	1	...	...	...	...	...	5	1
32	Sarangarh	...	...	4	4	...	...	...	...	1	1
33	Chang Bhakar	...	...	...	...	...	...	...	...	...	...
34	Korea	...	...	5	5	...	...	...	...	...	...
35	Surguja	...	...	7	11	...	...	...	...	...	...
36	Udaipur	...	...	1	...	...	...	...	...	9	17
37	Jashpur	...	...	...	...	...	...	...	...	1	...

Tribe, Race or Nationality.

RAJPUT -(*contd.*)

Kesaria.		Khangar.		Kharwanch.		Khati.		Khichi.		Langar.		Mori.		Nagvanshi.		Nahar.		
Males.	Females.	Males.	Females.	Males.	Females.	Males.	Females.	Males.	Females.	Males.	Females.	Males.	Females.	Males.	Females.	Males.	Females.	Serial No.
573	574	575	576	577	578	579	580	581	582	583	584	585	586	587	588	589	590	
158	**171**	**211**	**263**	**177**	**149**	**188**	**200**	**161**	**112**	**84**	**70**	**754**	**696**	**205**	**197**	**86**	**88**	
99	**99**	**210**	**263**	**177**	**149**	**135**	**149**	**159**	**110**	**84**	**70**	**748**	**688**	**50**	**35**	**78**	**81**	
99	**99**	**210**	**263**	**177**	**149**	**135**	**149**	**157**	**110**	**84**	**70**	**719**	**652**	**50**	**35**	**78**	**81**	
1	..	*171*	*210*	*177*	*149*	*61*	*56*	*79*	*61*	*71*	*62*	*70*	*2*	...	...	*68*	*71*	
...	...	84	115	107	84	12	13	74	55	48	36	69	1	...	...	11	14	1
...	...	4	5	3	1	...	..	...	...	13	12	...	...	...	...	5	2	2
...	...	83	90	67	64	49	43	5	6	10	14	1	1	...	...	52	58	3
...	...	...	...	...	...	..	...	..	...	...	...	...	...	...	...	...	...	4
1	...	...	...	...	...	...	...	...	...	...	...	...	...	...	...	...	...	5
9	...	*33*	*43*	...	...	*16*	*19*	*67*	*32*	*13*	*5*	*630*	*565*	*3*	*6*	*10*	*7*	
...	...	29	42	...	...	16	19	7	7	7	5	2	1	...	...	10	7	6
...	...	...	...	...	...	...	...	9	9	...	..	247	264	-	...	...	...	7
...	...	2	1	...	...	...	...	9	13	4	...	381	300	...	...	...	...	8
...	...	...	...	...	...	...	...	42	3	...	...	...	...	3	6	...	...	9
9	...	2	...	...	...	...	...	...	—	2	...	...	...	...	...	...	..	10
...	...	*6*	*10*	...	...	*3*	*3*	*4*	*7*	...	...	...	*64*	...	...	...	...	
...	...	...	...	...	...	...	...	..	—	...	...	...	...	...	...	...	...	11
...	...	4	6	...	...	—	...	...	...	...	...	...	64	...	...	..	...	12
...	...	1	2	...	...	...	...	...	...	...	...	...	...	...	...	...	...	13
...	...	1	2	...	...	...	3	4	7	...	...	...	...	...	...	...	...	14
...	...	...	...	...	...	3	...	...	...	...	...	...	...	...	...	...	...	15
89	*99*	...	...	...	...	*55*	*71*	*7*	*10*	...	*3*	*19*	*21*	*47*	*29*	...	...	
29	13	...	...	...	...	13	9	...	1	...	...	14	10	45	29	...	...	16
34	55	...	...	..	...	5	8	7	9	...	...	4	6	1	...	...	...	17
26	31	...	...	...	...	37	54	...	..	...	3	1	5	1	...	...	...	18
...	...	...	...	...	...	...	...	**2**	...	...	...	**29**	**36**	...	...	...	...	
...	...	...	...	...	...	...	...	2	...	...	...	27	34	...	...	...	...	19
...	...	...	...	...	...	...	..	..	...	...	...	...	...	...	...	...	...	20
...	...	...	...	...	...	..	...	...	...	...	...	...	...	...	...	...	...	21
...	...	...	...	...	...	...	...	...	...	...	...	2	2	...	...	...	...	22
59	**72**	**1**	...	...	...	**53**	**51**	**2**	**2**	...	...	**6**	**8**	**155**	**162**	**8**	**7**	
...	...	...	...	...	...	...	...	...	...	...	...	4	4	...	...	...	...	23
...	...	...	...	...	...	...	...	...	..	...	...	...	...	1	...	8	7	24
5	10	...	...	...	...	8	10	...	...	...	...	...	...	44	32	...	...	25
12	11	...	...	...	...	43	40	...	...	...	...	...	...	10	15	...	...	26
25	30	...	...	...	...	...	...	...	..	...	...	2	4	76	93	...	...	27
6	7	...	...	...	...	...	...	...	...	...	...	...	...	...	...	...	...	28
...	...	...	...	...	...	...	...	...	...	...	...	...	...	...	...	...	...	29
...	...	...	...	...	...	...	...	...	...	...	...	...	...	...	...	...	...	30
1	1	...	...	...	...	...	...	...	...	...	...	...	...	16	12	...	...	31
...	...	...	...	...	...	...	...	...	...	...	...	...	...	...	...	..	...	32
...	...	...	.	...	...	...	...	...	...	...	...	..	...	...	...	...	...	33
...	...	...	...	...	...	...	...	2	2	...	...	...	...	...	...	...	...	34
...	...	...	...	...	..	2	1	...	...	...	...	...	...	4	4	...	...	35
...	...	1	...	...	...	...	...	...	...	...	...	...	...	...	...	...	...	36
10	13	—	...	...	...	...	...	...	...	...	...	...	...	4	6	...	...	37

TABLE XIII.—Caste,

Serial No.	DISTRICT OR STATE.	SEPTS OF									
		NANDVANSI.		NIKUMBH.		PAIJWAR.		PAIK.		PANWAR.	
		Males.	Females.	Males.	Females.	Males.	Females.	Males.	Females.	Males.	Females.
		591	592	593	594	595	596	597	598	599	600
	Central Provinces and Berar ...	76	100	339	267	78	71	320	265	73,812	77,396
	C. P. British Districts and Berar ...	76	100	325	245	78	71	320	265	73,544	77,190
	C. P. British Districts	76	100	322	244	78	71	320	265	72,927	76,640
	JUBBULPORE DIVISION	*66*	*60*	*2*	...	*73*	*61*	*282*	*234*	*10,605*	*10,614*
1	Saugor	2	...	2	...	73	61	191	103	523	373
2	Damoh	...	1	...	...	...	...	15	5	131	129
3	Jubbulpore	55	57	...	...	...	...	76	66	262	261
4	Mandla	2	1	...	...	...	...	...	...	24	18
5	Seoni	6	1	...	...	...	...	...	...	9,665	9,833
	NERBUDDA DIVISION	*4*	*40*	*320*	*244*	*5*	*10*	*5*	*5*	*1,821*	*1,646*
6	Narsinghpur	4	40	...	...	5	10	3	5	176	97
7	Hoshangabad	...	...	104	...	...	...	1	...	670	646
8	Nimar	...	...	204	235	...	...	...	...	709	606
9	Betul	...	...	12	9	...	...	1	...	101	87
10	Chhindwara	...	...	...	...	...	...	...	...	165	149
	NAGPUR DIVISION	...	...	...	...	...	...	2	...	*60,074*	*63,994*
11	Wardha	...	...	...	...	...	...	...	...	198	179
12	Nagpur	...	...	...	...	...	...	...	...	477	398
13	Chanda	...	...	...	...	...	...	...	...	97	89
14	Bhandara	...	...	...	...	...	...	...	...	36,424	38,179
15	Balaghat	...	...	...	...	...	...	2	...	22,878	25,149
	CHHATTISGARH DIVISION	*7*	...	...	...	...	...	*31*	*26*	*427*	*387*
16	Raipur	6	...	...	...	...	...	31	26	185	193
17	Bilaspur	1	...	...	...	...	...	...	...	110	104
18	Drug	...	...	...	...	...	...	...	...	132	90
	Berar	...	...	3	1	...	...	...	...	617	550
19	Amraoti	...	...	3	1	...	...	...	...	196	168
20	Akola	...	...	...	...	...	...	...	...	43	25
21	Buldana	...	...	...	...	...	...	...	...	131	137
22	Yeotmal	...	...	...	...	...	...	...	...	247	220
	Feudatory States ...	...	...	14	22	...	...	...	...	268	206
23	Makrai	...	...	13	22	...	...	...	...	32	20
24	Bastar	...	...	...	...	...	...	...	...	39	32
25	Kanker	...	...	...	...	...	...	...	...	12	17
26	Nandgaon	...	...	...	...	...	...	...	...	27	22
27	Khairagarh	...	...	...	...	...	...	...	...	63	52
28	Chhuikhadan	...	...	...	...	...	...	...	...	2	1
29	Kawardha	...	...	...	...	...	...	...	...	18	16
30	Sakti	...	...	...	...	...	...	...	...	6	10
31	Raigarh	...	...	...	...	...	...	...	...	...	2
32	Sarangarh	...	...	...	...	...	...	...	...	2	...
33	Chang Bhakar	...	...	...	...	...	...	...	...	...	...
34	Korea	...	...	1	...	...	...	...	...	4	4
35	Surguja	...	...	...	...	...	...	...	...	29	17
36	Udaipur	...	...	...	...	...	...	...	...	14	...
37	Jashpur	...	...	...	...	...	...	...	...	20	13

Tribe, Race or Nationality.

RAJPUT—*contd.*)

Parihar.		Phar-hara.		Purbia.		Raghuvansi.		Raikwar.		Rajput (*unspecified*).		Raksel.		Rana.		
Males.	Females.	Males.	Females.	Males.	Females.	Males.	Females.	Males.	Females.	Males.	Females.	Males.	Females.	Males.	Females.	Serial No.
601	602	603	604	605	606	607	608	609	610	611	612	613	614	615	616	
2,353	2,409	105	89	90	139	12,822	11,524	106	64	54,008	48,840	81	78	1,562	1,577	
2,136	2,191	87	69	90	139	12,744	11,460	97	60	49,354	45,931	24	3	1,557	1,572	
2,104	2,177	87	69	90	139	12,404	11,159	95	50	34,666	32,457	24	3	159	123	
1,303	*1,312*	...	...	...	...	*1,513*	*1,515*	*13*	...	*8,824*	*7,141*	*1*	*2*	*23*	*18*	
492	443	...	...	...	...	114	92	1	...	1,338	1,068	...	...	7	7	1
135	210	...	...	...	...	4	4	...	...	3,195	2,788	...	...	...	...	2
612	609	...	...	...	...	1,338	1,399	12	...	2,722	1,750	...	...	13	9	3
25	14	...	...	...	...	11	7	...	...	434	309	...	...	1	...	4
39	36	...	...	...	...	46	43	...	...	1,135	1,226	1	2	2	2	5
321	*372*	...	...	*90*	*139*	*8,411*	*8,066*	*52*	*28*	*12,313*	*13,360*	*1*	*1*	*86*	*56*	
172	171	...	...	...	...	625	588	51	23	591	640	1	1	1	...	6
83	83	...	...	25	40	4,091	3,876	1	3	2,729	3,173	...	...	...	...	7
13	64	...	...	...	...	158	152	...	...	6,820	7,254	...	...	83	54	8
13	7	...	...	...	...	1,084	952	...	2	1,071	954	...	...	2	2	9
40	47	...	...	65	99	2,453	2,498	...	...	1,602	1,339	...	...	...	...	10
135	*132*	...	...	...	...	*2,298*	*1,879*	*3*	*1*	*9,466*	*7,578*	...	...	*40*	*37*	
21	...	...	...	...	...	25	15	...	...	1,188	833	...	...	20	14	11
24	14	...	...	...	...	2,185	1,296	...	...	3,412	3,776	...	...	4	...	12
5	3	...	...	...	...	35	41	...	...	880	686	...	...	3	6	13
76	107	...	...	...	...	52	27	3	1	1,378	1,443	...	...		4	14
9	8	...	...	...	...	1	...	...	...	2,608	840	...	...	10	13	15
345	*361*	*87*	*69*	...	...	*182*	*169*	*27*	*21*	*3,563*	*4,378*	*22*	...	*10*	*12*	
36	43	...	...	...	...	121	106	...	...	1,011	930	5	...	...	...	16
272	297	26	14	...	...	25	27	23	19	2,285	2,382	3	...	7	7	17
37	21	61	55	...	...	36	36	4	2	267	1,066	14	...	3	5	18
32	14	...	...	...	...	340	301	2	10	14,689	13,474	...	...	1,398	1,449	
20	...	...	...	...	...	171	133	...	10	4,164	3,687	...	...	206	173	19
...	...	...	...	...	...	93	126	...	...	3,711	3,469	...	...	74	12	20
...	8	...	...	...	...	60	40	...	...	5,253	5,134	...	...	808	934	21
12	6	...	...	...	...	16	2	2	...	1,560	1,184	...	...	310	330	22
217	218	18	20	...	...	78	64	9	4	4,654	2,909	57	75	5	[illegible]	
2	...	...	...	...	...	...	...	...	...	162	256	...	...	...	...	23
22	20	...	...	...	...	3	4	...	...	2,779	954	...	...	...	...	24
6	12	...	...	...	...	6	4	...	...	3	61	2	1	...	...	25
18	14	18	20	...	...	27	28	...	...	157	119	3	8	5	3	26
102	107	...	...	...	...	3	2	9	4	166	177	28	24	...	2	27
8	2	...	...	...	...	...	...	...	...	...	1	...	...	...	...	28
18	32	...	...	...	...	1	...	...	...	43	36	...	...	...	...	29
1	1	...	...	...	...	...	...	...	...	10	19	...	...	...	...	30
1	4	...	...	...	...	2	2	...	...	99	73	...	...	...	...	31
...	7	...	...	...	...	...	...	...	...	38	40	...	...	...	...	32
...	1	...	...	...	...	...	...	...	...	...	...	...	...	...	...	33
3	2	...	...	...	...	24	11	...	...	129	107	1	...	...	...	34
28	16	...	...	...	...	4	4	...	...	600	657	19	33	...	...	35
7	...	...	...	...	...	3	3	...	...	37	45	4	9	...	...	36
1	...	...	...	...	...	5	6	...	...	431	364	...	...	...	...	37

TABLE XIII.—Caste,

Serial No.	DISTRICT OR STATE.	SEPTS OF											
		RATHAUR.		SAINI.		SAKARWAR.		SANWALYA.		SARASWAR.		SENGAR.	
		Males.	Females.	Males.	Females.	Males.	Females.	Males.	Females.	Males.	Females.	Males.	Females.
		617	618	619	620	621	622	623	624	625	626	627	628
	Central Provinces and Berar ...	**5,951**	**5,018**	**300**	**217**	**139**	**131**	**100**	**170**	**118**	**103**	**897**	**1,019**
	C. P. British Districts and Berar ...	**5,828**	**4,897**	**300**	**217**	**139**	**131**	**79**	**157**	**114**	**96**	**747**	**855**
	C. P. British Districts	**5,750**	**4,825**	**300**	**217**	**139**	**131**	**79**	**157**	**114**	**96**	**531**	**592**
	JUBBULPORE DIVISION	*2,620*	*1,825*	*237*	*170*	*39*	*36*	...	...	*103*	*75*	*320*	*338*
1	Saugor	218	212	34	26	5	2	...	...	63	46	97	83
2	Damoh	95	90	44	24	...	...	...	...	15	8	23	24
3	Jubbulpore	268	145	159	120	30	28	...	...	12	10	193	219
4	Mandla...	2,028	1,368	...	...	4	6	...	...	...	...	1	...
5	Seoni	11	10	...	...	...	...	...	...	13	11	6	12
	NERBUDDA DIVISION	*1,900*	*1,788*	*63*	*47*	*95*	*88*	*79*	*157*	*11*	*18*	*123*	*149*
6	Narsinghpur	108	133	46	38	33	33	...	...	9	11	77	74
7	Hoshangabad	694	662	...	...	50	48	53	79	...	...	31	34
8	Nimar	967	867	17	9	9	5	26	78	1	3	10	37
9	Betul	87	84	...	...	3	2	...	...	...	...	3	1
10	Chhindwara	44	42	...	...	...	...	...	...	1	4	2	3
	NAGPUR DIVISION...	*173*	*165*	...	...	*5*	*7*	...	...	...	*3*	*5*	*6*
11	Wardha	16	...	...	...	...	...	...	...	...	...	...	...
12	Nagpur...	31	31	...	...	...	...	...	...	...	...	...	4
13	Chanda...	2	...	...	...	5	7	...	...	...	3	2	...
14	Bhandara	119	129	...	...	...	...	...	...	...	...	3	2
15	Balaghat	5	5	...	...	...	...	...	...	...	...	...	...
	CHHATTISGARH DIVISION	*1,057*	*1,047*	...	...	...	...	...	...	...	...	*83*	*99*
16	Raipur	31	14	...	...	...	...	...	...	...	...	16	21
17	Bilaspur	930	943	...	...	...	...	...	...	...	...	49	42
18	Drug	96	90	...	...	...	...	...	...	...	...	18	36
	Berar	**78**	**72**	...	...	...	...	...	...	...	...	**216**	**263**
19	Amraoti	57	51	...	...	...	...	...	...	...	...	1	2
20	Akola	3	12	...	...	...	...	...	...	...	...	...	...
21	Buldana	12	8	...	...	...	...	...	...	...	...	215	260
22	Yeotmal	6	1	...	...	...	...	...	...	...	...	...	1
	Feudatory States	**123**	**121**	...	...	...	...	**21**	**13**	**4**	**7**	**150**	**164**
23	Makrai	21	6	...	...	...	...	21	13	...	...	...	...
24	Bastar	36	42	...	...	...	...	...	...	...	...	4	4
25	Kanker...	...	...	...	...	...	...	...	...	...	...	4	...
26	Nandgaon	...	...	...	...	...	...	...	...	...	...	42	40
27	Khairagarh	12	14	...	...	...	...	...	...	...	...	72	81
28	Chhuikhadan	...	...	...	...	...	...	...	...	...	...	...	...
29	Kawardha	1	...	...	...	...	...	...	...	...	...	5	6
30	Sakti	3	4	...	...	...	...	...	...	...	...	...	...
31	Raigarh	3	2	...	...	...	...	...	...	...	...	...	...
32	Sarangarh	3	1	...	...	...	...	...	...	...	...	3	7
33	Chang Bhakar	...	...	...	...	...	...	...	...	...	...	2	4
34	Korea	...	...	...	...	...	...	...	...	4	5	9	1
35	Surguja	3	5	...	...	...	...	...	...	...	2	...	1
36	Udaipur	5	...	...	...	...	...	...	...	...	...	9	8
37	Jashpur	36	47	...	...	...	...	...	...	...	...	...	4

Tribe, Race or Nationality.

RAJPUT— *concld.*)

Sinda.		Sirodia.		Sohner.		Solanki.		Somvansi.		Surki.		Suryavansi.		Tanwar.		Tomar.		
Males.	Females.	Males.	Females.	Males.	Females.	Males.	Females.	Males.	Females.	Males.	Females.	Males.	Females.	Males.	Females.	Males.	Females.	Serial No.
629	630	631	632	633	634	635	636	637	638	639	640	641	642	643	644	645	646	
105	**94**	**1,094**	**788**	**1.662**	**1.640**	**2.251**	**2.106**	**517**	**382**	**255**	**248**	**4.062**	**4.019**	**738**	**761**	**1,920**	**2,038**	
90	**82**	**1,047**	**734**	**1,479**	**1,475**	**2,217**	**2,075**	**406**	**284**	**235**	**228**	**3,974**	**3.905**	**726**	**746**	**1.904**	**2,035**	
90	**82**	**1,047**	**734**	**1,479**	**1,475**	**2,217**	**2,075**	**332**	**225**	**235**	**228**	**3,113**	**3.017**	**679**	**733**	**1.904**	**2,035**	
...	...	*122*	*107*	*2*	...	*443*	*422*	*52*	*47*	*155*	*140*	*181*	*78*	*2*	*2*	*239*	*214*	
...	...	90	96	...	...	364	349	...	...	...	...	10	17	2	2	172	150	1
...	...	6	6	...	...	...	...	...	...	...	...	38	39	...	...	33	36	2
...	...	21	3	1	...	77	71	49	35	148	137	17	6	...	...	24	21	3
...	...	5	2	1	...	...	...	3	12	7	3	110	13	...	...	...	...	4
...	...	...	...	...	...	2	2	...	...	...	...	6	3	...	...	10	7	5
90	*82*	*787*	*452*	*1,369*	*1,355*	*1,746*	*1,622*	*133*	*73*	*2*	...	*2,475*	*2,525*	*361*	*300*	*1,474*	*1,747*	
...	...	108	95	...	...	30	21	2	...	...	...	9	12	30	22	89	136	6
48	47	313	252	474	451	836	821	30	9	1	...	138	127	232	208	789	1,039	7
42	35	206	78	889	897	804	748	9	1	...	...	478	484	95	66	578	563	8
...	...	114	27	6	7	6	25	79	53	1	...	1,440	1,577	4	4	9	2	9
...	...	46	...	...	...	10	7	13	10	...	...	410	325	...	...	9	7	10
...	...	*3*	*35*	*7*	*16*	*14*	*19*	*75*	*53*	...	...	*241*	*226*	...	*4*	*25*	*29*	
...	...	...	...	...	...	12	14	3	5	...	...	49	77	...	2	1	...	11
...	...	...	30	...	...	2	2	37	19	...	...	30	...	...	...	1	...	12
...	...	1	2	...	...	...	...	3	1	...	...	5	3	...	...	4	14	13
...	...	...	...	6	16	...	3	32	28	...	...	150	142	...	2	...	...	14
...	...	2	3	1	...	...	...	...	...	...	...	7	4	...	...	19	15	15
...	...	*135*	*140*	*101*	*104*	*14*	*12*	*72*	*52*	*78*	*88*	*216*	*188*	*316*	*427*	*166*	*45*	
...	...	15	21	19	13	...	...	56	42	15	31	107	72	...	...	3	3	16
...	...	42	46	74	80	10	12	13	6	52	50	35	50	315	427	163	42	17
...	...	78	73	8	11	4	...	3	4	11	7	74	66	1	...	...	...	18
...	...	...	...	...	...	...	...	**74**	**59**	...	...	**861**	**888**	**47**	**13**	...	...	
...	...	...	...	...	...	...	...	30	24	...	...	530	577	47	13	...	...	19
...	...	...	...	...	...	...	...	...	...	...	...	65	60	...	...	...	...	20
...	...	...	...	...	...	...	...	43	35	...	...	148	117	...	...	...	...	21
...	...	...	...	...	...	...	...	1	...	...	...	118	134	...	...	...	...	22
15	**12**	**47**	**54**	**183**	**165**	**34**	**31**	**111**	**98**	**20**	**20**	**88**	**114**	**12**	**15**	**16**	**3**	
11	9	5	6	131	111	33	31	...	...	...	...	1	...	...	...	13	...	23
...	...	3	3	...	...	...	...	18	20	...	...	28	14	...	...	...	...	24
...	...	14	14	2	3	...	...	8	10	5	3	4	4	...	...	2	3	25
4	3	24	31	12	12	...	...	3	1	5	8	21	21	2	3	...	...	26
...	...	...	...	14	13	...	...	30	24	8	8	5	12	...	...	...	...	27
...	...	...	...	...	...	...	...	...	...	...	...	...	...	...	...	...	...	28
...	...	...	...	...	...	...	...	...	...	...	...	...	...	...	...	...	...	29
...	...	...	...	6	1	...	...	...	...	...	...	3	6	10	12	...	...	30
...	...	...	...	2	2	...	...	8	1	...	...	8	30	...	...	...	...	31
...	...	...	...	2	5	...	...	...	...	...	...	5	8	...	...	...	...	32
...	...	...	...	...	...	...	...	5	3	...	...	...	...	...	...	...	...	33
...	...	...	...	...	...	...	...	13	8	...	1	3	2	...	...	1	...	34
...	...	1	...	3	4	1	...	22	21	1	...	10	17	...	...	...	...	35
...	...	...	...	...	...	...	...	3	...	1	...	...	...	...	...	...	...	36
...	...	...	...	11	14	...	...	1	...	...	...	...	...	...	...	...	...	37

TABLE XIII.—Caste,

Serial No.	District or State.	Rajwar or Mowar. Hindu. Males.	Rajwar or Mowar. Hindu. Females.	Rajwar or Mowar. Animist. Males.	Rajwar or Mowar. Animist. Females.	Rangari. Hindu. Males.	Rangari. Hindu. Females.	Rautia. Hindu. Males.	Rautia. Hindu. Females.	Sali. Hindu. Males.	Sali. Hindu. Females.	Saon[i]. Hindu. Males.	Saon[i]. Hindu. Females.
		647	648	649	650	651	652	653	654	655	656	657	658
	Central Provinces and Berar ...	12,670	12.443	2,434	2.456	8 414	8.432	6,267	5.770	6.911	7.378	1,603	1.499
	C. P. British Districts and Berar ...	990	984	4	1	8.406	8.427	191	189	6 898	7.361	252	172
	C. P. British Districts	976	976	4	1	3,087	3.189	191	189	3.247	3,763	252	172
	JUBBULPORE DIVISION	...	*14*	...	...	*12*	*10*	...	...	*1*	*4*	...	...
1	Saugor	...	14	...	...	3	2	...	...	...	...	...	...
2	Damoh	...	...	...	...	...	...	...	...	...	...	...	...
3	Jubbulpore	...	...	...	...	...	...	...	...	...	...	...	...
4	Mandla	...	...	...	...	...	...	...	...	1	4	...	...
5	Seoni	...	...	...	...	9	8	...	...	...	...	...	...
	NERBUDDA DIVISION	...	...	...	...	*827*	*904*	...	...	*846*	*907*	...	...
6	Narsinghpur	...	...	...	...	...	...	...	...	...	...	...	...
7	Hoshangabad	...	...	...	...	5	1	...	...	1	...	...	...
8	Nimar	...	...	...	...	486	467	...	...	829	898	...	...
9	Betul	...	...	...	...	158	257	...	...	...	...	...	...
10	Chhindwara	...	...	...	...	178	179	...	...	16	9	...	...
	NAGPUR DIVISION	*2*	...	...	...	*2,239*	*2,264*	...	...	*2,247*	*2,689*	...	...
11	Wardha	...	...	...	...	632	581	...	...	227	254	...	...
12	Nagpur	2	...	...	...	916	934	...	...	235	246	...	...
13	Chanda	...	...	...	...	537	531	...	...	1,774	2,178	...	...
14	Bhandara	...	...	...	...	154	218	...	...	11	11	...	...
15	Balaghat	...	...	...	...	...	...	...	...	...	...	...	...
	CHHATTISGARH DIVISION	*974*	*962*	*4*	*1*	*9*	*11*	*191*	*189*	*153*	*163*	*252*	*172*
16	Raipur	1	...	...	...	7	7	...	...	152	163	...	...
17	Bilaspur	973	962	4	1	...	1	191	189	1	...	252	172
18	Drug	...	...	...	...	2	3	...	...	...	...	...	...
	Berar	14	8	...	...	5,319	5.238	...	...	3.651	3.598	...	...
19	Amraoti	14	8	...	...	1.357	1,348	...	...	1,416	1.332	...	...
20	Akola	...	...	...	...	988	899	...	...	733	721	...	...
21	Buldana	...	...	...	...	1,707	1.683	...	...	612	631	...	...
22	Yeotmal	...	...	...	...	1,267	1.308	...	...	890	914	...	...
	Feudatory States	11,680	11.459	2.430	2.455	8	5	6,076	5.581	13	17	1.351	1,327
23	Makrai	...	...	...	...	...	...	...	...	...	...	...	...
24	Bastar	...	...	...	...	3	5	...	...	...	...	...	...
25	Kanker	...	...	...	...	5	...	...	...	8	9	...	...
26	Nandgaon	...	...	...	...	...	...	...	...	4	8	...	...
27	Khairagarh	...	...	...	...	...	...	...	...	1	...	...	...
28	Chhuikhadan	...	...	...	...	...	...	...	...	...	...	...	...
29	Kawardha	...	...	...	...	...	...	...	...	...	...	...	...
30	Sakti	35	30	...	...	...	...	...	...	...	...	...	...
31	Raigarh	125	155	1	...	...	...	216	275	...	...	1	5
32	Sarangarh	356	333	...	...	...	...	...	...	...	...	...	...
33	Chang Bhakar	...	...	...	...	...	...	...	...	...	...	...	...
34	Korea	23	29	2,411	2.446	...	...	...	...	...	...	...	...
35	Surguja	11,093	10,846	16	8	...	...	759	197	...	...	1 305	1,292
36	Udaipur	5	...	1	...	...	...	16	14	...	...	2	5
37	Jashpur	43	67	1	1	...	...	5,085	5,095	...	...	43	25

Tribe, Race or Nationality.

TA.		SAWARA OR SAONR.		SUNAR.		SUNDI.		TAKARI.		TAMERA.		
ANIMIST.		HINDU.		HINDU.		HINDU.		HINDU.		HINDU.		
Males.	Females.	Males.	Females.	Males.	Females.	Males.	Females.	Males.	Females.	Males.	Females.	Serial No.
659	660	661	662	663	664	665	666	667	668	669	670	
3,695	**3.606**	**36,041**	**38.140**	**63 844**	**63,034**	**2.731**	**2,739**	**3.585**	**3,417**	**2.402**	**2.170**	
75	**143**	**27,725**	**29.188**	**61.520**	**60.873**	**561**	**533**	**3,585**	**3.417**	**2.295**	**2,102**	
75	**143**	**27,725**	**29.183**	**46.159**	**45,949**	**561**	**533**	**109**	**93**	**1.902**	**1.733**	
...	...	*12,993*	*13,739*	*11,059*	*10,594*	...	...	...	...	*1,106*	*995*	
...	...	9,062	9,465	2.622	2,477	...	...	...	...	379	308	1
..	...	3,243	3,462	1.427	1,302	...	...	...	...	169	171	2
...	...	684	812	4.107	4,169	...	...	...	...	435	403	3
...	...	4	...	892	850	...	...	...	...	55	46	4
...	—	...	...	2,041	2,096	...	...	...	...	68	67	5
...	...	*622*	*641*	*10,333*	*9,914*	*3*	...	*72*	*67*	*184*	*181*	
...	...	440	477	2.301	2,223	...	...	...	...	178	176	6
—	...	100	143	1,915	1,806	...	...	...	...	4	2	7
...	...	...	...	2,160	1,915	...	...	72	67	...	...	8
...	...	22	21	1,704	1,639	3	...	...	...	2	3	9
...	...	...	...	2,253	2,241	...	...	...	...	...	...	10
...	...	*1*	...	*18,090*	*18,331*	...	...	*36*	*25*	*14*	*14*	
...	...	...	...	2,402	2,463	...	...	...	...	4	5	11
...	...	...	...	5,079	5,036	...	...	18	...	...	...	12
...	...	1	...	2,403	2,399	...	...	18	25	...	...	13
...	...	...	...	5,785	5,928	...	...	...	...	...	...	14
...	...	...	...	2,121	2,555	...	...	...	...	10	9	15
75	*143*	*14,109*	*14,803*	*6,647*	*6,760*	*558*	*533*	*1*	*1*	*598*	*543*	
...	...	10.631	11,071	2,557	2,601	487	404	...	...	122	94	16
75	143	3,476	3,730	2,380	2,352	71	69	1	1	137	132	17
...	...	2	2	1,710	1,807	...	...	...	...	339	317	18
...	...	...	**5**	**15,361**	**14,924**	...	...	**3.476**	**3.324**	**393**	**369**	
...	—	...	5	5,149	4,888	...	...	1 104	1.085	102	107	19
...	...	...	...	4 178	4,107	...	...	1,720	1.603	159	139	20
...	...	...	...	3,395	3,380	...	...	594	569	102	100	21
...	...	...	...	2,639	2,543	..	...	58	67	30	23	22
3,620	**3.463**	**8,316**	**8.952**	**2,324**	**2.161**	**2.170**	**2,206**	...	...	**107**	**68**	
...	...	...	...	62	48	..	...	...	...	...	...	23
...	...	118	144	356	400	1,179	1,194	...	..	1	3	24
...	...	...	...	201	196	...	...	...	...	4	1	25
...	...	...	...	365	377	...	...	...	...	24	18	26
...	...	...	...	303	307	...	...	...	...	20	18	27
...	...	..	...	64	49	...	...	...	...	3	...	28
...	...	...	...	113	105	...	...	...	...	7	5	29
...	...	33	105	23	14	...	...	...	...	...	...	30
...	...	3,748	4,045	251	240	388	450	...	...	...	...	31
...	..	4,284	4,586	168	175	46	60	...	...	...	...	32
...	...	...	...	24	14	...	...	...	...	...	...	33
41	30	...	...	89	5	...	...	...	...	4	...	34
2,710	2,519	1	8	294	192	485	464	...	..	31	20	35
865	807	38	25	17	11	8	6	...	...	...	...	36
4	1	34	39	44	28	64	32	...	...	13	3	37

REMARKS. (671)

RANGARI includes—

	M.	F.
Musalman.		
Hoshangabad	4	1
Yeotmal	0	3
Sikh.		
Nagpur	33	17
Jain.		
Nagpur Division	4	4
Berar	31	30

RAUTIA includes—

Animist.		
Feudatory States	17	15

SALI includes—

Musalman.		
Nimar	1	0
Arya.		
Amraoti	2	1
Jain.		
Yeotmal	0	1

SAWARA OR SAONR includes—

Animist.		
Saugor...	488	504
Damoh	436	457
Nerbudda Division	8	3
Raipur	883	931
Feudatory States	52	49

SUNAR includes—

Animist		
Bastar	0	1
Musalman.		
Akola	1	0
Arya.		
Saugor...	1	0
Sikh.		
Saugor...	1	1
Jain		
Nagpur Division	7	4
Berar	10	9

SUNDI includes—

Animist.		
Feudatory States	7	9

TAKARI includes—

Musalman.		
Buldana	10	12

TAMERA includes—

Animist.		
Bilaspur	2	0

TABLE XIII.—Caste,

Serial No.	District or State.	Teli. Hindu. Males.	Teli. Hindu. Females.	Turi. Hindu. Males.	Turi. Hindu. Females.	Waddar. Hindu. Males.	Waddar. Hindu. Females.	Wanjari. Hindu. Males.	Wanjari. Hindu. Females.	Minor castes. Males.	Minor castes. Females.
		672	673	674	675	676	677	678	679	680	681
	Central Provinces and Berar ...	**427,126**	**442,244**	**2.037**	**2.016**	**6.551**	**6,318**	**16,815**	**16,899**	**61,734**	**61,219**
	C. P. British Districts and Berar ...	**379,849**	**393,013**	**235**	**266**	**6,486**	**6,260**	**16,815**	**16.899**	**49,271**	**48,917**
	C. P. British Districts	**339.803**	**354,135**	**235**	**266**	**2.480**	**2,569**	**448**	**479**	**33,564**	**33,519**
	JUBBULPORE DIVISION	*26,890*	*27,846*	...	...	*5*	...	...	...	*7,434*	*6,556*
1	Saugor	6.540	6,352	...	...	...	...	...	...	2.464	2,253
2	Damoh	3,562	3,728	...	...	...	...	...	...	728	675
3	Jubbulpore	8,894	9,298	...	...	5	...	...	...	2,651	2,399
4	Mandla	4,113	4,468	...	...	...	...	...	...	656	647
5	Seoni	3,781	3,9.9	...	...	...	...	...	...	925	882
	NERBUDDA DIVISION	*24,537*	*24,933*	...	...	*201*	*179*	*7*	*9*	*6,736*	*6,255*
6	Narsinghpur	3,451	3.552	...	...	...	...	...	...	1,145	1,092
7	Hoshangabad	4,311	4,356	...	...	...	...	...	...	1.354	1,021
8	Nimar	3,611	3,577	...	...	101	100	...	...	1,908	1,860
9	Betul	4,749	4,964	...	...	94	74	...	...	1,090	990
10	Chhindwara	8,405	8,489	...	...	6	5	7	9	1,229	1,292
	NAGPUR DIVISION	*100,498*	*101,883*	*1*	*1*	*2,374*	*2,390*	*440*	*470*	*11,645*	*11,716*
11	Wardha	22,586	22.426	...	...	370	392	130	172	1,750	1,712
12	Nagpur	33.594	33 541	1	1	176	137	...	...	2,392	2,162
13	Chanda	17,808	18,259	...	...	1,706	1,836	289	270	5.348	5,001
14	Bhandara	22,783	23,721	...	...	22	25	21	28	1,706	1,764
15	Balaghat	3,727	3,936	...	...	...	...	...	...	449	477
	CHHATTISGARH DIVISION	*187,588*	*199,469*	*234*	*266*	...	...	*1*	...	*7,769*	*8,693*
16	Raipur	85,934	91,046	182	198	...	...	...	...	2.474	2,629
17	Bilaspur	38,109	39,928	52	67	...	...	1	...	4,517	5.075
18	Drug	63,845	68,495	...	...	...	...	...	...	778	988
	Berar	**40.046**	**38,878**	...	...	**4,006**	**3.691**	**16.367**	**16.420**	**15.707**	**15.398**
19	Amraoti	15,715	14,965	...	...	382	364	167	155	2,807	2,068
20	Akola	8,110	7,936	...	...	586	455	5,292	5.818	4.704	4,347
21	Buldana	6,195	6,180	...	...	857	881	5.808	5.509	2.527	2,563
22	Yeotmal	10,026	9,791	...	...	2,181	1,991	5,100	4,848	5,669	5,820
	Feudatory States	**47.277**	**49.231**	**1.802**	**1.750**	**65**	**58**	...	...	**12 463**	**12,302**
23	Makrai	105	106	...	...	...	...	...	...	17	16
24	Bastar	825	670	...	...	65	58	...	...	1,274	844
25	Kanker	2,120	2.031	...	...	...	...	...	...	148	140
26	Nandgaon	16,533	17,744	...	...	...	...	...	...	163	165
27	Khairagarh	10,561	11,325	...	...	...	...	...	...	201	240
28	Chhuikhadan	1,900	2,042	...	...	...	...	...	...	44	47
29	Kawardha	4,465	4,749	...	...	...	...	...	...	33	71
30	Sakti	932	957	81	88	...	...	...	...	191	230
31	Raigarh	3,791	3,852	106	85	...	...	...	...	2,999	2,896
32	Sarangarh	2,569	2,633	123	126	...	...	...	...	683	966
33	Chang Bhakar	66	53	...	...	...	...	...	...	390	348
34	Korea	227	179	14	18	...	...	...	...	239	217
35	Surguja	2,800	2,578	758	751	...	...	...	...	2,638	2,627
36	Udaipur	65	52	37	41	...	...	...	...	299	289
37	Jashpur	318	265	683	641	...	...	...	...	3,144	3,204

Tribe, Race, or Nationality.

Unclassed.		Musalman.								Remarks.	Serial No.
		Shaikh.		Syed.		Moghal.		Pathan.			
Males.	Females.	Males.	Females.	Males.	Females.	Males.	Females.	Males.	Females.		
682	683	684	685	686	687	688	689	690	691	692	
162	**127**	**144,434**	**135,880**	**24,656**	**23,280**	**4,640**	**4,405**	**74,082**	**69,890**		
148	**114**	**140,072**	**131,704**	**23,953**	**22,516**	**4,441**	**4,214**	**71,320**	**67,067**		
106	**64**	**71 449**	**66,462**	**13,022**	**12,267**	**2,273**	**2,084**	**42,884**	**40,905**		
13	*10*	*18,890*	*17,088*	*3,229*	*2,779*	*465*	*418*	*13,624*	*12,537*	Teli includes—	
5	4	4,654	4,124	870	772	122	111	2,824	2 224	*Animist.* M. F. Mandla 1 0	1
2	3	1,516	1,380	406	350	50	48	1,144	1,140	Betul 1 1	2
1	1	9,068	8,067	1,274	1,038	201	158	4,863	4 263	Bhandara 2 0	3
4	2	1,375	1,241	232	174	45	49	1,055	972	Chhattisgarh Division 8 8	4
1	...	2,277	2,276	447	445	47	46	3,738	3,928	Yeotmal ... ... 0 1 Faudatory States 22 9	5.
										Musalman. Jubbulpore ... ... 1 0 Nimar ... ... 167 121 Chanda 1 0	
15	*9*	*20,651*	*19,018*	*3,615*	*3,424*	*664*	*538*	*12,218*	*11,447*	Berar 23 29	
...	...	1,905	1,780	433	402	89	60	1,536	1,640	*Arya.*	6.
5	3	3,731	3,455	1,034	970	205	195	3,661	3,673	Nimar 2 3	7
6	6	10,482	9,646	1,378	1,205	226	188	3,491	3,053	*Jain.*	8
2	...	1,964	1,652	281	256	64	39	1,391	1,089	Bhandara 0 2	9.
2	...	2,569	2,485	489	501	80	56	2,139	1,092		10
71	*44*	*23,073*	*21,951*	*4,002*	*3,810*	*636*	*619*	*11,070*	*10,620*	Turi includes—	
2	...	4,778	4,409	936	909	156	161	2,162	2,088	*Animist.* Sakti 14 13	11
34	34	10,565	9 691	1,528	1,389	212	196	3,826	3,481	Sar-ngarh 121 132	12
33	8	3,315	3,359	521	500	67	41	1,544	1,431	Korea 14 18	13
...	2	3,156	3,106	687	645	126	134	2,048	1,995	Surguja 15 13	14
2	...	1,259	1,296	330	358	75	87	1,490	1,625	Udaipur ... ... 37 41 Jashpur 585 566	15
7	*1*	*8,835*	*8,405*	*2,176*	*2,254*	*508*	*515*	*5,972*	*6,311*	Waddar includes—	
...	1	4,019	3 856	859	860	283	275	2,619	2,720	*Animist.* Bastar... ... ... 21 11	16
7	...	3,353	3,117	849	919	146	167	2,084	2,249		17
...	...	1,463	1,432	468	475	79	73	1,209	1,342		18
42	**50**	**68 623**	**65,242**	**10,931**	**10,249**	**2,168**	**2,130**	**28,436**	**26,162**		
29	29	20,060	19,256	3,163	2,935	742	681	8,334	7,428		19
6	6	20,777	19,821	3,373	3,157	616	624	8,420	7,701		20
4	9	16,465	15,506	2,199	2,106	617	502	6,656	6,348		21
3	6	11,321	10,650	2,196	2,051	293	323	5,026	4,625		22
14	**13**	**4,362**	**4,176**	**703**	**764**	**199**	**191**	**2,762**	**2,823**		
...	...	223	102	25	38	3	3	102	105		23
13	13	401	410	93	86	12	7	237	227		24
...	...	142	140	26	36	...	...	98	110		25
...	...	506	409	125	138	25	24	312	364		26
...	...	492	504	82	117	44	41	390	443		27
...	...	264	273	38	37	20	20	127	116		28
...	...	552	593	46	40	...	2	110	127		29
...	...	69	63	22	22	6	11	53	59		30
...	...	343	324	47	46	15	16	231	267		31
...	...	61	64	33	47	6	5	55	64		32
...	...	14	7	...	...	2	1	11	6		33
...	...	92	64	17	12	...	...	140	124		34
...	...	871	779	65	65	61	59	675	630		35
1	...	46	29	85	30	...	...	44	45		36
...	...	286	235	49	50	5	2	168	136		37

TABLE XIII.—Caste, Tribe, Race or Nationality.

Serial No.	DISTRICT OR STATE.	MUSALMAN—*concld.* Other Musalmans. Males.	Other Musalmans. Females.	CHRISTIAN. Males.	CHRISTIAN. Females.	BUDDHIST. Males.	BUDDHIST. Females.	JEW. Males.	JEW. Females.	PARSI. Males.	PARSI. Females.
		693	694	695	696	697	698	699	700	701	702
	Central Provinces and Berar ...	**7,643**	**5,856**	**39,208**	**34,193**	**8**	**1**	**78**	**47**	**1,052**	**705**
	C. P. British Districts and Berar ...	**6,699**	**5,022**	**19,731**	**14,966**	**8**	**1**	**78**	**47**	**1,031**	**697**
	C. P. British Districts	**4,449**	**2,994**	**18,210**	**13,664**	**8**	**1**	**54**	**41**	**710**	**487**
	JUBBULPORE DIVISION	*1,252*	*714*	*6,259*	*3,585*	*3*	...	*16*	*2*	*156*	*109*
1	Saugor	261	127	777	677	...	...	8	1	54	34
2	Damoh	167	131	337	100	...	...	...	...	9	3
3	Jubbulpore	549	236	4,554	2,326	2	...	8	1	77	59
4	Mandla	119	62	491	380	1	...	...	...	8	3
5	Seoni	156	158	100	102	—	...	...	...	8	10
	NERBUDDA DIVISION	*1,199*	*812*	*4,025*	*3,383*	*3*	*1*	*9*	*14*	*129*	*81*
6	Narsinghpur	128	104	315	156	...	...	...	...	4	4
7	Hoshangabad	179	115	1,[illegible]44	853	...	...	2	2	51	30
8	Nimar	210	102	1,904	1,790	1	...	7	12	68	47
9	Betul	327	208	274	273	...	...	...	...	4	...
10	Chhindwara	355	283	398	357	2	1	...	...	2	...
	NAGPUR DIVISION	*1,252*	*882*	*4,631*	*3,201*	2	...	*29*	*25*	*387*	*279*
11	Wardha	120	72	117	61	...	...	...	...	25	16
12	Nagpur	483	336	3,764	2,481	2	...	28	21	341	233
13	Chanda	270	181	304	237	...	...	1	4	5	19
14	Bhandara	227	174	250	288	...	...	...	..	8	1
15	Balaghat	152	119	196	134	...	...	...	...	8	10
	CHHATTISGARH DIVISION	*746*	*586*	*3,295*	*3,440*	...	...	...	...	*38*	*18*
16	Raipur	238	155	1,637	1,728	...	...	...	...	31	18
17	Bilaspur	306	293	971	1,040	...	...	...	...	7	...
18	Drug	142	138	687	672	...	...	...	...	...	...
	Berar	**2,250**	**2,028**	**1,521**	**1,303**	...	—	**24**	**6**	**321**	**210**
19	Amraoti	645	871	827	662	...	...	21	6	162	126
20	Akola	471	330	365	301	...	...	3	...	107	51
21	Buldana	646	489	183	195	...	...	...	...	43	29
22	Yeotmal	489	338	146	144	...	...	...	...	9	4
	Feudatory States	**944**	**834**	**19,477**	**19,227**	...	...	...	...	**21**	**8**
23	Makrai	8	10	...	...	...	...	...	...	...	...
24	Bastar	76	84	644	633	...	...	...	...	...	...
25	Kanker	25	20	5	5	—	...		...	...	...
26	Nandgaon	20	19	65	89	—	...	...	...	10	7
27	Khairagarh	39	40	132	120	—	...	...	...	8	...
28	Chhuikhadan	...	...	4	6	...	...	...	...	...	...
29	Kawardha	21	15	12	16	—	...	...	...	...	...
30	Sakti	2	1	7	7	—	...	...	...	2	1
31	Raigarh	18	11	27	24	...	...	...	...	...	...
32	Sarangarh	12	8	9	7	...	...	...	...	1	...
33	Chang Bhakar	5	4	...	—	...	...	...	...	...	...
34	Korea	31	20	3	1	...	...	...	...	...	...
35	Surguja	460	397	...	...	...	...	...	...	...	...
36	Udaipur	31	25	6	2	...	...	...	...	...	...
37	Jashpur	106	171	18,563	18,317	...	...	...	—	...	...

APPENDIX TO TABLE XIII.—Caste.

Detail of Minor Castes. (Column Nos. 680 and 681.)

NOTE.—H = Hindu ; A = Animist ; M = Musalman ; J = Jain ; Br. = Brahmo. Where a caste belongs to a single religion, the latter has been omitted in the last column.

CASTE.		TOTAL.			HINDU.		ANIMIST.		MUSALMAN.		DISTRIBUTION.
		Persons.	Males.	Females.	Males.	Females.	Males.	Females.	Males.	Females.	
Abdal	...	52	31	21	...	...	...	...	31	21	Hoshangabad. (31—21).
Akrmmasa	...	273	135	138	133	134	2	4	...	...	Mandla. H. (27—26). Hoshangabad. H. (3—3). Nagpur Division. H. (69—69). A. (1—1). Chhattisgarh Division. H. (9—12). A. (0—3). Berar. H. (22—20). Feudatory States. H. (3—4). A. (1—0).
Arab	...	138	77	61	...	...	...	...	77	61	Berar. (77—61).
Arakh	...	1,999	1,042	957	715	569	327	388	...	...	Jubbulpore Division. H. (93—91). Nerbudda Division. H (14—7). A. (10—8). Nagpur Division. H. (339—365). A. (317—380). Chhattisgarh Division. H. (11—3). Berar. H. (254—96). Feudatory States. H. (4—7).
Arora	...	26	19	7	19	7	...	...	...	...	Jubbulpore Division. (3—0). Chhindwara. (2—0). Nagpur Division. (9—4). Chhattisgarh Division. (5—3).
Arya	...	262	154	108	154	108	...	...	...	...	Saugor. *Arya* (20—11). Nerbudda Division. *Arya* (101—80). Nagpur Division. H. (4—3). *Arya* (12—9). Chhattisgarh Division. *Arya* (6—0). Berar. H. (1—2). *Arya* (10—3).
Asur	...	129	64	65	64	65	...	...	...	...	Feudatory States. (64—65).
Audhelia	...	880	455	425	455	425	...	...	...	...	Jubbulpore. (1—0). Raipur. (8—9). Bilaspur. (446—414). Raigarh. (0—2).
Babhan	...	4	2	2	2	2	...	...	...	...	Bilaspur. (1—0). Surguja. (1—2).
Bahurupi	...	483	242	241	242	241	...	...	...	...	Nimar. (4—9). Nagpur Division. (84—76). Berar. (154—156).
Balda	...	658	347	311	337	305	10	6	...	...	Chang Bhakar. H. (337—305). Korea. A. (10—6).
Balija	...	1,183	541	642	541	642	...	...	...	...	Jubbulpore Division. (77—76). Nerbudda Division. (24—29). Nagpur Division. (291—265). Chhattisgarh Division. (93—149). Berar. (38—51). Feudatory States. (18—72).
Balochi	...	60	40	20	...	...	...	...	40	20	Jubbulpore Division. (34—20). Nagpur. (5—0). Amraoti. (1—0).
Banka	...	16	9	7	9	7	...	...	...	...	Chanda. (5—2). Amraoti. (0—3). Bastar. (4—2).
Bari	...	1,192	685	507	685	507	...	...	...	...	Jubbulpore Division. (160—156). Nerbudda Division. (383—236). Chhattisgarh Division. (27—18). Feudatory States. (115—97).
Basdewa	...	2,458	1,242	1,216	1,242	1,216	...	...	...	...	Jubbulpore Division. (354—334). Nerbudda Division. (362—331). Nagpur Division. (53—45). Chhattisgarh Division. (226—251). Berar. (148—126). Feudatory States. (99—129).
Basta	...	709	344	365	344	365	...	...	...	...	Chanda. (343—365). Amraoti. (1—0).
Bhami	...	234	120	114	120	114	...	...	...	...	Nerbudda Division. (120—114).
Bhand	...	346	155	191	3	1	...	...	152	190	Jubbulpore Division. H. (1—0). M. (28—19). Nerbudda Division. H. (1—1). M. (12—11). Raipur. M. (1—1). Amraoti. H. (1—0). Akola. M. (106—156). Surguja. M. (6—3).
Bhar	...	44	43	1	43	1	...	...	...	...	Hoshangabad. (43—1).
Bharadi	...	2,252	1,164	1,088	1,164	1,088	...	...	...	...	Nimar. (7—9). Nagpur Division. (232—222). Berar. (925—857).

APPENDIX TO TABLE XIII.—Caste—(*contd.*)

CASTE.	Total. Persons.	Total. Males.	Total. Females.	Hindu. Males.	Hindu. Females.	Animist. Males.	Animist. Females.	Musalman. Males.	Musalman. Females.	Distribution.
Bhimma ...	439	200	239	117	156	83	83	...	...	Mandla. H. (7—8). A. (52—55). Seoni. A. (12—12). Betul. H. (3—0). Chhindwara. H. (7—10). Bilaspur. H. (14—17). A. (7—10). Feudatory States. H. (86—121). A. (12—6).
Bhisti ...	493	251	242	81	71	...	...	170	171	Saugor. M. (70—97). Jubbulpore. H. (5—0). M. (31—22). Nimar. M. (58—41). Betul. M. (2—0). Nagpur. H. (2—1). Bhandara. M. (0—5). Bilaspur. M. (1—0). Berar. H. (74—70). M. (8—6).
Bhogta ...	108	57	51	42	47	15	4	...	...	Bilaspur. H. (0—3). Feudatory States. H. (42—44). A (15—4).
Bhojak ...	2	1	1	1	1	...	...	...	...	Jubbulpore. (1—1).
Bhopa ...	89	51	38	45	35	6	3	...	...	Betul. H. (8—4). A. (6—3). Chhindwara. H. (3—0). Amraoti. H. (34—31).
Bilwar ...	35	14	21	14	21	...	...	...	...	Saugor. (3—1). Damoh. (11—16). Surguja. (0—4).
Bind ...	380	183	197	182	196	1	1	...	...	Nagpur. H. (2—0). Chhattisgarh Division. H. (136—145). Amraoti. H. (0—8). Feudatory States. H. (44—43). A. (1—1).
Binjhia ...	594	301	293	264	256	37	37	...	...	Chhattisgarh Division. H. (201—210). A. (26—16). Feudatory States. H. (63—46). A. (11—21).
Birhor ...	153	67	86	6	5	61	81	...	...	Feudatory States. H. (6—5). A. (61—81).
Biyar ...	1,117	563	554	514	525	49	29	...	...	Bilaspur. H. (154—171). A. (4—0). Berar. H. (90—88). Korea, A. (45—29). Surguja. H. (270—266).
Boya ...	1,065	516	549	516	549	...	...	...	...	Nagpur Division. (516—549).
Brahmo ...	23	13	10	13	10	..	...	...	...	Saugor. Br. (2—0). Mandla. Br. (2—0). Hoshangabad. Br. (1—0). Nagpur Division. H. (0—1). Br. (4—5). Bilaspur. Br. (2—4). Khairagarh. Br. (2—0).
Budhudkala ...	5	2	3	2	3	...	...	...	...	Chanda (2—3).
Chakar ...	36	27	9	27	9	...	...	...	...	Jubbulpore. (11—0). Nimar. (1—1). Berar. (15—8).
Chasa ...	10	10	...	10	...	...	..	...	..	Chhattisgarh Division. (10—0).
Chenchuwar ...	3	2	1	2	1	...	...	...	...	Nagpur. (2—1).
Chero ...	220	92	128	92	128	...	...	...	...	Mandla. (1—2). Bilaspur. (11—9). Feudatory States. (80—117)
Chisti ...	1	1	...	1	...	...	..	...	...	Saugor. (1—0).
Chitrkathi ...	1,487	729	758	729	758	...	...	...	...	Seoni. (8—10). Nagpur Division. (98—102). Berar. (623—646).
Cholian ...	4	4	...	4	...	...	...	...	...	Bastar. (4—0).
Chuhra ...	22	14	8	14	8	...	...	...	...	Saugor. (14—8).
Cutchi ...	2,079	1,745	334	97	33	...	...	1,648	301	Jubbulpore Division. H (7—6). M. (33—1). Nerbudda Division. H. (15—1). M. (174—34). Nagpur Division. H. (70—18). M. (309—27). Chhattisgarh Division. H. (5—8). M. (112—26). Berar. M. (1,007—198). Feudatory States. M. (13—15).
Daharia ...	957	485	472	483	472	2	...	...	...	Nerbudda Division. H. (7—2). A. (2—0). Nagpur. H. (9—5). Chhattisgarh Division H. (467—465).
Dangri ...	1,762	835	927	835	927	..	...	...	...	Nagpur Division. (608—671). Berar. (227—256).
Daphali ...	97	50	47	48	44	2	3	...	...	Jubbulpore Division. H. (19—22). Bilaspur. H. (17—14). Feudatory States. H. (12—8). A. (2—3).
Deulwar ...	128	64	64	64	64	...	...	...	...	Yeotmal. (64—64).
Devangan ...	56	31	25	31	25	...	...	...	...	Nagpur Division. (21—16). Bilaspur. (10—9).

APPENDIX TO TABLE XIII.—Caste—(*contd.*)

CASTE.	TOTAL.			HINDU.		ANIMIST.		MUSALMAN.		DISTRIBUTION.
	Persons.	Males.	Females.	Males.	Females.	Males.	Females.	Males.	Females.	
Devar ...	2,433	1,115	1,318	984	1,161	131	157	...	...	Chhattisgarh Division. Feudatory States. H. (621—685). H. (363—476). A. (58—83). A. (73—74).
Dhadi ...	206	159	137	44	46	...	...	115	91	Hoshangabad. Chhattisgarh Division. H. (1—3). H. (7—7). M. (44—39). Berar. Feudatory States. H. (33—32). H. (3—4). M. (62—41). M. (9—11).
Dhalgar ...	63	31	32	...	...	...	...	31	32	Jubbulpore Division. (31—32).
Dhami ...	53	24	29	24	29	...	...	...	...	Jubbulpore Division. Nimar. (21—24). (3—5).
Dharkar ...	326	173	153	143	137	30	16	...	...	Jubbulpore. Hoshangabad. Raipur. Feudatory States. H. (0—4). H. (3—2). H. (1—1). H. (139—130). A. (30—16).
Dumal ...	14	9	5	9	5	...	...	...	...	Chhattisgarh Division. (9—5).
Dusadh ...	269	154	115	147	110	7	5	...	...	Jubbulpore Division. Hoshangabad. Nagpur. H. (2—5). H. (3—0). H. (4—2). Feudatory States. H. (138—103). A. (7—5).
Ediga ...	14	5	9	5	9	...	...	...	...	Jubbulpore. Bastar. (4—1). (1—8).
Gadaba ...	658	322	336	33	35	289	301	...	...	Feudatory States. H. (33—35). A. (289—301).
Gadia ...	39	17	22	...	...	...	...	17	22	Mandla. (17—22).
Gakkad ...	8	8	...	8	...	...	...	...	...	Jubbulpore Division. (8—0).
Gandhmali ...	693	206	487	206	487	...	...	...	...	Chhattisgarh Division. Feudatory States. (73—305). (133—182).
Girasya ...	2	1	1	1	1	...	...	...	...	Amraoti. (1—1).
Gorkha ...	11	10	1	10	1	...	...	...	...	Damoh. Nerbudda Division. (1—0). (9—1).
Gosangi ...	211	84	127	84	127	...	...	...	...	Nagpur. Berar. (1—0). (83—127).
Guranda ...	3	2	1	2	1	...	...	...	...	Mandla. (2—1).
Hela ...	153	67	86	67	64	...	22	...	...	Nagpur Division. Bilaspur. Yeotmal. H. (21—18). H. (28—36). H. (18—10). A. (0—22).
Hirna ...	61	33	28	32	27	1	1	...	...	Bilaspur. Sakti. Surguja. H. (31—26). A. (1—1). H. (1—1).
Illia ...	3	1	2	1	...	...	...	...	2	Nagpur. Raipur. H. (1—0). M. (0—2).
Jasondhi ...	860	420	440	419	440	...	...	1	...	Jubbulpore Division. Nerbudda Division. H. (280—309). H. (127—124). M. (1—0). Nagpur Division. Amraoti. Bastar. H. (8—7). H. (3—0). H. (1—0).
Johri ...	315	135	180	135	180	...	...	...	...	Nagpur Division. Berar. (97—151). (38—29).
Jokhara ...	17	6	11	3	5	...	...	3	6	Nimar. H. (3—5). M. (3—6).
Kaicha ...	206	98	108	98	108	...	...	...	...	Hoshangabad. (98—108).
Kaikadi ...	2,311	1,104	1,207	1,101	1,205	3	2	...	...	Nimar. Nagpur Division. Berar. H. (90—92). H. (53—50). H. (958—1,063). A. (3—2).
Kaiwart ...	3	1	2	1	2	...	...	...	...	Khairagarh. (1—2).
Kakera ...	64	22	42	22	42	...	...	...	...	Jubbulpore Division. Balaghat. (4—19). (18—23).
Kalanga ...	1,754	872	882	872	882	...	...	...	...	Chhattisgarh Division. Feudatory States. (145—174). (727—708).
Kallan ...	77	11	66	11	66	...	...	...	...	Chanda. (11—66).
Kamad ...	4	4	...	4	...	...	...	...	...	Nimar. (4—0).
Kamathi ...	142	70	72	70	72	...	...	...	...	Nagpur. Drug. Berar. (54—62). (2—0). (14—10).
Kamma ...	84	26	58	26	58	...	...	...	...	Jubbulpore Division. Chhindwara. (9—5). (0—5). Nagpur Division. Chhattisgarh Division. Bastar. (10—16). (7—13). (0—19).
Kanadi ...	1,127	584	543	584	543	...	...	...	...	Nimar. Bilaspur. Berar. (2—5). (0—2). (582—536).

APPENDIX TO TABLE XIII.—Caste—(*contd.*)

CASTE.	Total.			Hindu.		Animist.		Musalman.		Distribution.
	Persons.	Males.	Females.	Males.	Females.	Males.	Females.	Males.	Females.	
Kangar ...	130	48	82	12	19	...	...	36	63	Nerbudda Division. Amraoti. Bastar. H. (9—10). H. (3—5). H. (0—4). M. (36—63).
Kanjar ...	416	212	204	209	200	1	1	2	3	Jubbulpore Division. Nerbudda Division. H. (138—123). H. (69—77). Balaghat. Bilaspur. Udaipur. Jashpur. M. (1—3). H. (1—0). A. (1—1). H. (1—0). M. (1—0).
Kapali ...	15	7	8	7	8	...	...	...	...	Seoni. Bilaspur. (1—2). (6—6).
• Karajgar ...	2	1	1	1	1	...	...	...	...	Yeotmal. (1—1).
Karan ...	963	547	416	503	368	44	48	...	...	Jubbulpore. Nerbudda Division. H. (0—1). H. (1—6). Chhattisgarh Division. Feudatory States. H. (115—107). H. (387—254). A. (44—48).
Kasbi ...	2,552	998	1,554	985	1,499	3	8	10	47	Jubbulpore Division. Nerbudda Division. H. (124—78). H. (115—155). A. (1—0). A. (2—7). M. (1—0). M. (7—26). J. (1—0). J. (1—0) Nagpur Division. Chhattisgarh Division. H. (92—100). H. (519—930). M. (1—8). Berar. Feudatory States. H. (61—80). H. (72—96). M. (1—13). A. (0—1).
Kathak ...	25	15	10	14	10	—	...	1	...	Jubbulpore Mandla. Narsinghpur. Nagpur. Amraoti. H. (2—4). M. (1—0). H. (8—6). H. (2—0). H. (2—0).
Kathilkar ...	19	6	13	6	13	...	...	...	...	Nagpur Division. Berar. (3—5). (3—8).
Khadia ...	747	331	416	330	416	1	...	...	...	Chhindwara. H. (330—416). A. (1—0).
Khadra ...	145	78	67	78	67	..	...	...	...	Chhattisgarh Division Feudatory States. (42—39). (36—28).
Khandait ...	18	14	4	14	4	...	...	...	...	Chanda. Raipur. Jashpur. (2—0). (1—0). (11—4).
Kharia ...	9,180	4,458	4,722	778	913	3,680	3,809	...	...	Chhattisgarh Division, Feudatory States. H. (651—714). H. (127—199) A. (56—70). A. (3,624—3,739).
Khawase ...	9	9	...	9	...	...	...	...	...	Saugor. (9—0).
Khoja ...	675	359	316	2	1	...	...	357	315	Jubbulpore Division. Nimar. Nagpur Division. M. (3—3). M. (1—0). H. (0—1). M. (185—172). Chhattisgarh Division. Berar. M. (16—8). H. (2—0). M. (150—128). Feudatory States. M. (2—4).
Kuchbandhia ...	940	479	461	467	448	12	13	...	...	Jubbulpore Division. Nerbudda Division. H. (214—196) H. (160—157). A. (12—13). Bhandara. Drug. Berar. H. (9—7). H. (1—0). H. (83—88).
Kumawat ...	2	2	...	2	...	...	...	...	...	Wardha. (2—0).
Kumrawat ...	1,716	879	837	879	837	...	...	...	...	Jubbulpore Division. Nerbudda Division. Amraoti. (600—608). (264—227). (13—1). Nandgaon. (2—1).
Kundera ...	120	46	74	46	74	...	...	...	...	Saugor. Nimar. Raipur. (44—55). (1—16). (1—3).
Kunjra ...	1,555	764	791	47	69	...	...	717	722	Jubbulpore Division. Nerbudda Division. H. (1—0). M. (85—72). M. (549—552). Nagpur Division. Chhattisgarh Division. H. (21—45). M. (12—11). M. (35—44). Berar. Feudatory States. H. (25—24). M. (36—43).
Kureshi ...	12	9	3	...	...	...	...	9	3	Jubbulpore. (9—3).
Kutubshahi ...	28	28	...	...	...	...	...	28	...	Jubbulpore. Hoshangabad. (17—0). (11—0).

APPENDIX TO TABLE XIII.—Caste—(*contd.*)

CASTE.	Total. Persons.	Total. Males.	Total. Females.	Hindu. Males.	Hindu. Females.	Animist. Males.	Animist. Females.	Musalman. Males.	Musalman. Females.	Distribution.
Lalbegi ...	2,573	1,418	1,155	1,223	986	...	...	195	160	Jubbulpore Division. H. (557—443). M. (130—119). J. (10—6). Nerbudda Division. H. (353—320). M. (24—24). Nagpur Division. H. (181—123). M. (37—24). Chhattisgarh Division. H. (32—35). Berar. H. (89—59). M. (4—2). Khairagarh. H. (1—0).
Lonari ...	2,077	1,030	1,047	1,030	1,047	...	...	...	...	Nimar. (127—121). Nagpur Division. (393—439). Berar. (510—487).
Londhari ...	35	15	20	7	7	...	...	8	13	Berar. H. (7—7). M. (8—13).
Mahli ...	276	144	132	63	51	81	81	...	...	Balaghat. H. (0—6). Feudatory States. H. (63—45) A. (81—81).
Mal ...	1,761	895	866	894	863	1	3	...	...	Nimar. H. (2—2). Feudatory States. H. (892—861). A. (1—3).
Malabari ...	2	2	...	2	...	...	...	...	...	Wardha. (2—0).
Malyar ...	118	70	48	58	45	12	3	...	...	Nerbudda Division. H. (5—0). Chanda. H. (3—1). Feudatory States. H. (50—44). A. (12—3).
Mangan ...	85	44	41	41	39	3	2	...	...	Saugor. H. (6—0). Chhattisgarh Division. H. (1—3). Feudatory States. H. (34—36). A. (3—2).
Mannewar ...	1,601	825	776	798	761	27	15	...	...	Jubbulpore. H. (2—0). Nerbudda Division. H. (1—9). Nagpur Division. H. (403—441). A. (26—15). Raipur. H. (5—1). Berar. H. (297—310). A. (1—0).
Marori ...	6	3	3	3	3	...	...	...	...	Bhandara. (3—3).
Meo ...	32	18	14	6	5	...	...	12	9	Saugor. H. (2—2). Nerbudda Division. H. (4—3). M (11—9). Jashpur. M. (1—0).
Mirasi ...	25	21	4	18	1	...	...	3	3	Jubbulpore Division. H. (18—1). Nimar. M. (3—3).
Munda ...	2,872	1,616	1,256	490	485	1,126	771	...	...	Nagpur. H. (24—14). Raipur. H. (31—12). A (22—8). Feudatory States. H. (435—450). A. (1,104—763).
Murha ...	2,572	1,254	1,318	1,235	1,293	19	25	...	...	Jubbulpore Division. H. (779—807). A. (0—8). Nerbudda Division. H. (438—466). A. (19—17). Raipur. H. (17—19). Surguja. H. (1—1).
Mutrasi ...	482	225	257	225	257	...	...	...	...	Nimar. (3—1). Nagpur Division. (210—244). Berar. (5—6). Bastar. (7—6).
Naikar ...	2,192	1,088	1,104	1,088	1,104	...	...	...	...	Jubbulpore. (3—1). Nagpur. (1—0). Berar. (1,080—1,100). Jashpur. (4—3).
Nanakshahi ...	329	214	115	214	115	...	...	...	...	Jubbulpore Division. H. (21—16). Nerbudda Division. H. (58—26). Nagpur Division. H. (34—26). Sikh (2—1). Drug. H. (1—0). Berar. H. (89—36). Sikh (4—2). J. (0—2). Jashpur. H. (5—6).
Naora ...	698	361	337	361	337	...	...	...	...	Nimar. (352—333). Raipur. (9—4).
Naru ...	2	1	1	1	1	...	...	...	...	Chhindwara. (1—1).
Nat ...	11,385	5,419	5,966	4,873	5,457	129	125	417	384	Jubbulpore Division. H. (538—675). M. (402—369). Nerbudda Division. H. (414—439). M. (15—15). Nagpur Division. H. (328—362). Chhattisgarh Division. H. (495—557). A. (34—31). Berar. H. (2,352—2,649). Feudatory States. H. (746—775). A. (95—94).
Nayar ...	1	1	...	1	...	...	...	...	...	Nagpur. (1—0).

APPENDIX TO TABLE XIII.—Caste—(*contd.*)

CASTE.		TOTAL.			HINDU.		ANIMIST.		MUSALMAN.		DISTRIBUTION.
		Persons.	Males.	Females.	Males.	Females.	Males.	Females.	Males.	Females.	
Nunia	...	3,336	1,719	1,617	1,703	1,607	16	10	...	...	Jubbulpore Division. H. (497—451). Nerbudda Division. H. (329—253). Nagpur Division. H. (125—100). Chhattisgarh Division. H. (637—690). A. (16—10). Berar. H. (6—10). Feudatory States. H. (109—103).
Od	...	2,175	1,065	1,110	999	1,040	60	62	6	8	Nagpur Division. H. (3—2). Chhattisgarh Division. H. (652—692). A. (17—14). Feudatory States. H. (344—346). A. (43—48). M. (6—8).
Ojha	...	5,468	2,705	2,763	1,234	1,269	1,470	1,494	1	...	Jubbulpore Division. H. (332—325). A. (293—290). Arya (19—10). Nerbudda Division. H. (469—472). A. (920—921). Nagpur Division. H. (246—291). A. (239—268). Chhattisgarh Division. H. (33—43). A. (9—6). Berar. H. (6—3). M. (1—0). Feudatory States. H. (129—125). A. (9—9).
Panchal	...	8,712	4,241	4,471	4,236	4,471	...	...	5	...	Mandla. H. (1—0). Nerbudda Division. H. (30—55). Nagpur Division. H. (2,901—3,068). Chhattisgarh Division. H. (13—13). Berar. H. (1,282—1,321). M. (5—0) Khairagarh. H. (9—14).
Pangul	...	1,854	941	913	941	913	...	...	...	...	Nimar. (2—2). Nagpur Division. (5—5). Berar. (934—906).
Paraiyan	...	224	122	102	122	102	...	...	...	...	Jubbulpore. (26—11). Nagpur. (87—89). Chhattisgarh Division. (0—2). Bastar. (9—0).
Parbhu	...	1,419	718	701	718	701	...	...	...	...	Jubbulpore Division. (13—12). Nerbudda Division. (25—31). Nagpur Division. (129—131). Chhattisgarh Division. (33—43). Berar. (512—480). Khairagarh. (6—4).
Pathrat	...	1,051	509	542	509	542	...	...	...	...	Saugor. (47—49). Nerbudda Division. (21—26). Nagpur Division. (30—21). Berar. (411—446).
Perki	...	3,968	1,877	2,091	1,876	2,091	1	...	...	...	Nagpur Division. H. (813—899). Raipur. H. (11—8). Berar. H. (1,050—1,180). A. (1—0). Kawardha. H. (2—4).
Pindari	...	146	69	77	48	49	...	...	21	28	Nerbudda Division. H. (2—0). M. (20—26). Nagpur Division, H. (21—17). Berar. H. (25—32). Makrai. M. (1—2).
Pustaki	...	160	78	82	78	82	...	...	...	...	Nagpur. (6—12). Berar. (72—70).
Ramosi	...	150	77	73	77	73	...	...	...	...	Nerbudda Division. (51—42). Raipur. (2—0). Berar. (24—31).
Rewari	...	38	28	10	28	10	...	...	...	...	Jubbulpore Division. (12—0). Nerbudda Division. (16—10).
Sadgop	...	6	3	3	3	3	...	...	...	...	Raipur. (3—3).
Sansia	...	1,106	528	578	499	553	29	25	...	...	Jubbulpore. H. (1—0). Chhattisgarh Division. H. (459—486). Feudatory States. H. (39—67). A. (29—25).
Santal	...	29	14	15	3	...	11	15	...	...	Chanda. H. (3—0). Feudatory States. A. (11—15).
Sargara	...	15	7	8	7	8	...	...	...	...	Hoshangabad. (7—8).
Satani	...	905	442	463	442	463	...	...	...	...	Chhindwara. (2—0). Nagpur Division. (212—240). Chhattisgarh Division. (89—88). Berar. (133—129). Bastar. (6—6).
Sewak	...	110	72	38	72	38	...	...	...	...	Nimar. (6—2). Raipur. (1—0). Berar. (65—36).
Shegar	...	580	267	313	236	281	...	...	31	32	Nagpur Division. H. (2—2). M. (31—32). Berar. H. (234—279).

APPENDIX TO TABLE XIII.—Caste—(*concld.*)

CASTE.		TOTAL.			HINDU.		ANIMIST.		MUSALMAN.		DISTRIBUTION.
		Persons.	Males.	Females.	Males.	Females.	Males.	Females.	Males.	Females.	
Siddi	...	42	17	25	2	3	...	...	15	22	Jubbulpore. Nimar. Wardha. Drug. M. (2—1). M. (1—0) M. (1—0). M. (0—1). Berar. H. (2—3). M. (11—20)
Sikh	...	1,174	819	355	738	328	...	...	81	27	Jubbulpore Division. Nerbudda Division. H. (17—14). H. (13—5). M. (70—12). Sikh (93—32). Sikh (278—36). Nagpur Division. Chhattisgarh Division. H. (10—5). H. (16—14). M. (11—15). Sikh (46—43). Sikh (122—42). Berar. Feudatory States. H. (12—8). H. (1—1). Sikh (70—65). Sikh (60—63).
Sikligar	...	451	225	226	206	215	...	...	19	11	Jubbulpore Division. Nerbudda Division. H. (67—68). H. (40—44). Nagpur Division. Berar. Bastar. H. (31—26) H. (60—70). H. (8—7). M. (19—11).
Solha	...	108	48	60	48	60	...	...	...	...	Chhattisgarh Division. Feudatory States. (26—43). (22—17).
Sonjhara	...	1,447	742	705	666	623	76	82	...	...	Jubbulpore Division. Nimar. Nagpur Division. H. (1—1). H. (0—3). H. (286—223) A. (50—51). Chhattisgarh Division. Feudatory States. H. (188—212). H. (191—184). A. (9—21). A. (17—10).
Sud	...	37	23	14	23	14	...	...	...	...	Chhattisgarh Division. (23—14).
Tanti	...	3	3	...	3	...	...	...	...	...	Raigarh. (3—0).
Tirmali	...	365	148	217	148	217	...	...	...	...	Betul. Bhandara. Berar. (2—1). (12—12). (134—204).
Tiyar	...	700	370	330	370	330	...	...	...	...	Chhattisgarh Division. Raigarh. (336—297). (34—33).
Uppari	...	29	9	20	9	20	...	...	...	...	Nagpur Division. (9—20).
Vaidya	...	97	51	46	51	46	...	...	...	...	Jubbulpore. Nerbudda Division. (5—12). (12—12). Nagpur Division. Chhattisgarh Division. (13—4). (13—13). Feudatory States. (8—5).
Velama	...	738	367	371	367	371	...	...	...	...	Nagpur Division. Chhattisgarh Division. (186—152). (16—10). Yeotmal. Bastar. (81—199). (84—10).
Vellalan	...	731	405	326	405	326	...	...	...	...	Jubbulpore Division. Nerbudda Division. (49—42). (8—6). Nagpur Division. Chhattisgarh Division. (229—194). (67—51). Berar. Feudatory States. (27—15). (25—18).
Waghya	...	71	31	40	31	40	...	...	...	...	Berar. (31—40).
Yerukala	...	78	47	31	47	31	...	...	...	...	Chanda. (47—31).

APPENDIX TO TABLE XIII.—Caste.

Detail of Unclassified Castes—(Column Nos. 682 and 683).

Caste.	Persons.	Males.	Females.	Distribution.
Ajmed	4	4	...	Nagpur Division, H. (4—0).
Aradbansi	1	1	...	Bilaspur, H. (1—0).
Ardi	3	3	...	Nimar, H. (2—0) ; Yeotmal, H. (1—0).
Bahika	1	...	1	Jubbulpore, H. (0—1).
Balsar	9	9	...	Amraoti, H. (9—0).
Banda	1	...	1	Chanda, H. (0—1).
Barat	1	1	...	Amraoti, H. (1—0).
Baradarwali	1	...	1	Nagpur, H. (0—1).
Bengali	70	32	38	Nagpur Division. H. (25—20) ; Nimar. H. (2—0). Berar. H. (5—18).
Bhawania	2	2	...	Amraoti, H. (2—0).
Bhorku	5	5	...	Amraoti, H. (5—0).
Bhorli	16	...	16	Amraoti, H. (0—16).
Bijaura	1	1	...	Saugor, H. (1—0).
Bong	4	4	...	Chanda, H. (4—0).
Bowak	1	1	...	Udaipur, H. (1—0).
Budhya	6	4	2	Nagpur, H. (4—2).
Champali...	1	...	1	Buldana, H. (0—1).
Chaumasi	3	...	3	Nagpur, H. (0—3).
Chiwaka	3	2	1	Chanda, A. (2—1).
Darud	2	...	2	Yeotmal, H. (0—2).
Dhamat	5	3	2	Buldana, H. (3—2).
Dhundhunia	26	13	13	Bastar, H. (13—13).
Dakei	3	2	1	Amraoti, H. (2—1).
Gadhincha	1	1	...	Amraoti, H. (1—0).
Gobi	2	...	2	Yeotmal, H. (0—2).
Gohni	1	1	...	Jubbulpore, H. (1—0).
Gunjwar	1	1	...	Yeotmal, H. (1—0).
Isab	2	2	...	Chhindwara, H. (2—0).
Jadia	1	1	...	Seoni, H. (1—0).
Jargal	5	2	3	Nerbudda Division, H. (2—3).
Jhanjar	1	1	...	Balaghat, H. (1—0).
Kadoria	2	2	...	Amraoti, H. (2—0).
Kajia	2	1	1	Chanda, H. (0—1) ; Amraoti, H. (1—0).
Kamekar...	1	1	...	Bilaspur, H. (1—0).
Kamnigir...	1	1	...	Betul, H. (1—0).
Kantharu	3	1	2	Yeotmal, H. (1—2).
Kateri	1	...	1	Saugor, H. (0—1).
Kathri	1	...	1	Raipur, H. (0—1).
Khokal	5	2	3	Damoh, H. (2—3).
Khujia	6	4	2	Mandla, H. (4—2).
Kileri	2	1	1	Saugor, H. (1—1).
Kodali	2	2	...	Chanda, A. (2—0).
Lahoti	9	3	6	Akola, H. (3—6).
Lasri	1	1	...	Amraoti, H. (1—0).
Mangwal...	7	6	1	Hoshangabad, H. (3—1); Akola, H. (3—0)
Melwat	7	...	7	Nagpur Division, H. (0—7).
Mijawal	1	1	...	Saugor, H. (1—0).
Makuti	2	2	...	Wardha, H. (2—0).
Musli	1	1	...	Chanda, H. (1—0).
Padat	5	5	...	Bilaspur, H. (5—0).
Parsapar	9	4	5	Chanda, H. (4—5).
Rairangi	7	2	5	Nimar, H. (2—5).
Rakapi	1	1	...	Amraoti, H. (1—0).
Raoka	1	1	...	Nagpur, H. (1—0).
Sathwara...	1	1	...	Betul, H. (1—0).
Sudra	3	2	1	Nagpur, H. (2—1).
Tapi	18	18	...	Chanda, H. (18—0).
Thob	4	2	2	Saugor, H. (2—2).
Virwa	3	1	2	Nagpur, H. (1—2).

TABLE XIV.

Civil condition by age for selected castes.

This table, like Table IX, deals not with the whole population but with certain selected castes in certain districts, or parts of districts, where they are specially numerous.

The figures in this table against 8 castes, *viz.*, Ahir, Bahna, Gond, Kawar, Kharwar, Kol, Oraon and Sawara do not agree with those in Table IX, as in this table figures for persons belonging to certain selected religions only have been included, while in Table IX figures for all religions have been taken.

TABLE XIV.—Civil condition

Caste, tribe or race.	Locality.	Sex.	Population dealt with.	Unmarried.						
				Total.	0—5.	5—12.	12—15	15—20.	20—40.	40 and over.
1	2	3	4	5	6	7	8	9	10	11
Ahir (Hindu)...	Province	Male ...	354 669	162.505	57,466	64,311	15,557	12,372	11,488	1,311
		Female ...	358.407	125.767	59,558	54,801	6,392	2,648	1,870	492
Ahir (Animist)	Province	Male ...	6.929	3.451	1,207	1,345	378	250	275	36
		Female ...	7.724	3.118	1,380	1,371	206	92	61	8
Andh ...	Berar ...	Male ...	25.561	10.455	4,505	4,236	815	525	335	39
		Female ...	26.815	8.892	4,603	2,792	153	172	787	385
Are ...	Chanda District ...	Male ...	1.123	606	143	213	106	66	72	6
		Female ...	1 163	502	159	190	44	67	25	8
Bahna (Muhammadan).	Total ...	Male ...	*14,367*	*6,866*	*2,380*	*2,515*	*716*	*594*	*598*	*63*
		Female ...	*14,397*	*4,734*	*2,348*	*2,135*	*175*	*35*	*35*	*7*
	Seoni	Male ...	1.410	718	229	200	79	66	48	6
		Female ...	1.390	483	223	221	27	10	2	...
	Chhindwara	Male ...	1.307	669	226	234	71	68	62	8
		Female ...	1.330	528	230	240	46	4	7	1
	Nerbudda Valley ...	Male ...	11.650	5.479	1.931	1,991	560	460	488	49
		Female ...	11.677	3 723	1,895	1,673	102	21	26	6
Baiga ...	Total ...	Male ...	*12,876*	*6,767*	*2,575*	*2,699*	*470*	*431*	*509*	*83*
		Female ...	*13,102*	*5,529*	*2,704*	*2,317*	*262*	*117*	*92*	*37*
	Jubbulpore	Male ...	1 099	589	238	214	37	43	47	10
		Female ...	1.124	474	241	180	19	18	14	2
	Mandla	Male ...	9.311	4.816	1,819	1,964	356	315	316	46
		Female ...	9 373	3.915	1,945	1,645	197	71	49	8
	Balaghat	Male ...	2.465	1.362	518	521	77	73	146	27
		Female ...	2.605	1.140	518	492	40	28	29	27
Bairagi ...	Province	Male ...	19.649	9 677	2,484	2,888	879	708	1,611	1,047
		Female ...	18 335	5.659	2,463	2,452	332	117	208	47
Balahi ...	Total ...	Male ..	*25,108*	*10,670*	*4,058*	*4,376*	*1,124*	*655*	*419*	*38*
		Female ...	*25,751*	*7,785*	*4,279*	*3,308*	*121*	*21*	*35*	*18*
	Hoshangabad	Male ...	9 927	4.295	1,539	1,696	499	335	213	13
		Female ...	10,215	2,981	1,608	1,275	65	13	18	7
	Nimar	Male ...	14.243	5.986	2,380	2.518	586	287	103	22
		Female ...	14.571	4.511	2,534	1.800	49	8	19	11
	Makrai	Male ...	938	389	139	162	39	33	13	3
		Female ...	965	293	142	143	7	...	1	...
Bania ...	Province	Male ...	100.683	45.157	11,820	15,037	5,165	4,662	6,906	1,567
		Female ...	94.137	26.114	12,109	12,129	1,040	250	404	182
Banjara ...	Total ...	Male ..	*67,343*	*34,980*	*10,967*	*12,018*	*3,315*	*3,275*	*4,840*	*567*
		Female ...	*63,293*	*22,989*	*10,129*	*8,931*	*1,312*	*712*	*1,246*	*359*
	Plateau Division ...	Male ..	4.844	2.791	739	840	257	313	559	78
		Female ...	4.535	1 685	634	798	162	50	30	11
	Maratha Division ...	Male ...	45.708	22,356	7,988	7,987	2,024	1,770	2,285	302
		Female ...	42 245	15.561	7,524	5,533	665	443	1,075	321
	Chhattisgarh Division ...	Male ...	5.400	3.124	733	1,131	324	351	524	61
		Female ...	6.087	2.155	831	951	201	99	62	11
	Nimar	Male ...	8.544	4 960	1,200	1.549	542	622	985	53
		Female ...	7,032	2.698	1,154	1,245	201	70	22	6
	Bastar	Male ...	2 847	1,749	298	505	160	219	488	73
		Female ...	2.394	890	286	402	83	50	57	10
Barai ...	Province	Male ...	29.640	10.975	3,837	4,486	969	758	756	169
		Female ...	29 518	7.329	4,144	2,718	152	91	99	125
Barhai ...	Province	Male ...	56.297	22.255	7.001	8,751	2,354	1,704	1,601	244
		Female ...	52.518	14.634	7,552	6,153	408	140	284	97
Basor ...	Nerbudda Valley ...	Male ...	15.542	7.383	2.702	2,994	548	490	601	48
		Female ...	15.789	5,473	2,823	2,408	160	42	33	7
Bedar ...	Akola	Male ...	680	311	94	113	31	32	38	3
		Female ...	801	224	111	96	9	1	6	1

by age for selected castes.

Married.							Widowed.						
Total.	0—5.	5—12.	12—15.	15—20.	20—40.	40 and over.	Total.	0—5.	5—12.	12—15.	15—20.	20—40.	40 and over.
12	13	14	15	16	17	18	19	20	21	22	23	24	25
177,367 181,333	293 619	4,221 10,155	5,147 9,422	12,054 19,671	100,507 110,446	55,145 31,020	14,797 51,307	8 30	116 214	99 218	334 398	5,412 9,305	8,828 41,142
3,219 3,734	8 10	51 111	44 150	159 426	1,863 2,457	1,054 580	259 872	... ...	2 2	1 1	4 8	110 181	142 680
14,315 13,887	54 592	475 1,949	566 831	913 1,640	7,821 7,178	4,486 1,607	791 4,036	... 99	11 32	9 94	15 58	264 784	402 2,969
489 481	2 2	27 50	20 40	66 63	281 206	134 54	28 180	... ...	... 3	... 5	1 2	12 63	15 107
6,843 *7,184*	*5* *9*	*96* *530*	*151* *409*	*378* *81.*	*4,096* *4,178*	*2,117* *1,095*	*655* *2,479*	... *1*	*1* *9*	*2* *9*	*7* *17*	*315* *493*	*433* *1,951*
645 698	1 ...	6 29	11 27	33 74	386 434	208 134	47 209	... ...	... 2	... ..	... ...	12 27	35 180
593 588	1 2	6 9	0 14	21 69	342 382	217 112	45 214	... 1	... ...	... 1	... ...	11 32	34 180
5,605 5,898	3 7	84 342	134 368	324 675	3,368 3,657	1,692 819	566 2,056	... ...	1 7	2 8	7 17	192 433	364 1,591
5,849 *6,333*	*10* *8*	*35* *99*	*51* *174*	*221* *636*	*3,524* *4,278*	*2,005* *1,149*	*259* *1,310*	... *4*	... *6*	*6* *2*	*9* *8*	*103* *237*	*139* *976*
482 511	1 ...	4 13	7 12	26 68	301 829	143 80	28 139	... ...	... ...	... ...	... 2	14 36	14 101
4,296 4,599	5 8	23 77	41 125	160 449	2,664 3,124	1,403 816	199 859	... 2	... 3	8 2	7 3	75 176	109 673
1,071 1,223	4 ...	8 9	6 37	35 113	559 820	459 244	32 242	... ...	... 2	... ...	2 3	14 35	16 202
8,800 8,978	37 25	185 467	191 475	542 942	4,582 5,237	3,263 1,832	1,172 3,698	1 ...	9 10	5 7	33 38	354 661	770 2,982
13,546 *14,238*	*9* *21*	*186* *1,047*	*456* *1,168*	*1,107* *1,872*	*7,597* *8,186*	*3,892* *1,944*	*892* *3,735*	*1* ...	*3* *14*	*2* *17*	*17* *43*	*267* *763*	*603* *2,891*
5,221 5,532	3 7	49 285	127 448	371 708	3,074 3,227	1,507 857	411 1,702	... ...	... 5	2 7	7 21	115 322	287 1,347
7,817 8,214	6 14	132 734	315 686	691 1,006	4,523 4,659	2,150 1,025	440 1,846	1 ...	3 9	... 10	9 19	137 407	290 1,401
508 492	... ...	4 28	14 34	45 68	300 300	145 62	41 180	... ...	... ...	... ...	1 3	15 34	25 143
47,964 45,502	101 235	674 3,330	1,436 3,596	3,714 6,709	26,023 24,041	16,016 6,991	7,562 22,521	3 23	37 131	72 192	169 496	2,228 6,200	5,053 15,389
29,305 *30,307*	*102* *868*	*544* *2,341*	*574* *1,389*	*1,316* *3,235*	*15,681* *17,884*	*11,088* *4,692*	*3,052* *8,997*	*5* *25*	*20* *52*	*36* *45*	*95* *80*	*895* *1,099*	*3,007* *7,093*
1,822 2,008	2 5	8 17	8 40	35 158	1,049 1,402	720 380	231 842	... 1	1 5	... 1	2 3	67 104	161 638
21,189 21,292	93 812	504 2,169	536 1,155	1,128 2,380	11,000 11,002	7,919 3,115	2,163 5,392	4 23	10 39	35 40	85 58	634 942	1,386 4,290
2,086 2,598	1 38	12 17	10 55	50 175	1,172 1,704	841 549	190 1,334	... 1	... 4	1 3	5 7	56 250	128 1,069
3,240 3,398	5 2	15 26	12 108	70 443	1,022 2,333	1,210 486	344 936	1 ...	... 4	... 3	1 9	91 102	251 758
968 1,011	1 6	5 13	8 31	27 82	520 723	308 156	130 493	... ...	... ...	... 1	2 3	47 151	81 338
16,687 16,872	35 162	630 2,413	819 1,170	1,440 2,032	8,492 8,408	5,271 2,681	1,978 5,317	... 8	28 60	43 60	72 86	630 1,084	1,205 4,019
30,950 29,054	53 190	555 2,054	990 2,011	2,410 3,317	16,335 15,472	10,607 5,110	3,092 8,830	3 8	21 86	28 82	79 121	945 1,570	2,016 6,054
7,626 8,182	13 20	149 473	187 388	506 855	4,496 5,178	2,275 1,208	533 2,134	... 1	1 6	4 9	12 24	201 405	315 1,629
324 368	... 2	3 10	5 29	20 44	155 213	141 61	45 209	... ...	... ...	... 3	... 5	18 52	27 149

TABLE XIV.—Civil condition

Caste, tribe or race.	Locality.	Sex.	Population dealt with.	Unmarried.						
				Total.	0—5.	5—12.	12—15.	15—20.	20—40.	40 and over.
1	2	3	4	5	6	7	8	9	10	11
Beldar ...	Total ...	Male ...	*3,167*	*1,375*	*455*	*456*	*141*	*137*	*174*	*15*
		Female ...	*3,098*	*929*	*431*	*371*	*61*	*39*	*18*	*9*
	Saugor	Male ...	521	249	93	83	18	17	35	3
		Female ...	447	143	75	60	3	1	2	2
	Jubbulpore	Male ...	586	243	87	56	30	25	42	3
		Female ...	563	133	70	57	5	...	1	...
	Nimar	Male ...	583	282	81	93	26	32	49	1
		Female ...	533	208	100	82	13	6	2	...
	Wardha	Male ...	981	383	130	142	39	34	35	3
		Female ...	1,097	305	129	93	33	31	13	6
	Nagpur	Male ...	496	221	64	82	28	29	13	5
		Female ...	458	146	57	79	7	1	...	1
Bhaina ...	Bilaspur	Male ..	6,498	3,380	1,182	1,357	267	269	258	47
		Female ...	6,696	2,763	1,238	1,186	158	96	79	6
Bhamta ...	Wardha	Male ...	558	194	74	68	24	15	11	2
		Female ...	549	134	60	56	5	3	1	...
Bharia (Bhumia).	Total ...	Male ...	*17,864*	*8,780*	*3,496*	*3,276*	*733*	*626*	*584*	*55*
		Female ...	*19,399*	*7,606*	*3,480*	*3,103*	*479*	*230*	*276*	*38*
	Jubbulpore	Male ...	12,882	6,195	2,506	2,352	528	436	332	31
		Female ...	14,100	5,395	2,560	2,136	342	148	178	22
	Narsinghpur	Male ...	1,230	600	225	236	45	52	41	1
		Female ...	1,314	503	232	228	24	5	10	4
	Chhindwara ...	Male ...	3,752	1,985	765	688	160	138	211	23
		Female ...	3,985	1,708	679	739	113	77	88	12
Bhat ...	Total ...	Male ...	*6,110*	*2,874*	*797*	*949*	*301*	*321*	*444*	*62*
		Female ...	*6,320*	*1,865*	*821*	*858*	*108*	*30*	*31*	*17*
	Nerbudda Valley ...	Male ...	3,976	1,957	502	628	205	231	351	40
		Female ...	3,963	1,170	500	558	62	14	21	15
	Nagpur	Male ...	795	325	90	111	42	31	35	16
		Female ...	818	217	115	91	9	1	1	...
	Raipur	Male ...	788	366	126	131	37	36	35	1
		Female	843	264	99	121	23	11	8	2
	Drug	Male ...	551	226	79	79	17	23	23	5
		Female ...	696	214	107	88	14	4	1	...
Bhil ...	Nimar	Male ...	11,804	5,119	1,867	2,238	599	250	128	28
		Female ...	11,933	4,066	2,059	1,880	85	20	16	6
Bhilala ...	Total ...	Male ...	*7,717*	*3,644*	*1,203*	*1,412*	*410*	*346*	*252*	*21*
		Female ...	*7,557*	*2,520*	*1,290*	*1,139*	*55*	*12*	*20*	*4*
	Hoshangabad	Male ...	1,393	634	177	232	77	74	68	6
		Female ...	1,340	368	184	173	7	1	2	1
	Nimar	Male ...	6,324	3,010	1,026	1,180	333	272	184	15
		Female ...	6,217	2,152	1,106	966	48	11	18	3
Bhoyar ...	Total ...	Male ...	*28,943*	*11,525*	*4,800*	*4,674*	*870*	*629*	*480*	*72*
		Female ...	*29,608*	*8,881*	*4,856*	*3,666*	*219*	*64*	*59*	*18*
	Betul	Male ...	11,256	4,938	1,853	1,921	439	344	345	36
		Female ...	11,536	3,851	1,988	1,633	148	44	30	8
	Chhindwara	Male ...	10,173	3,741	1,693	1,508	206	212	95	27
		Female ...	10,570	3,003	1,704	1,190	62	18	15	5
	Wardha	Male ...	5,850	2,167	970	950	169	53	20	5
		Female ...	5,855	1,550	880	636	7	2	13	3
	Nagpur	Male ...	1,664	679	284	295	56	20	20	4
		Female ...	1,647	477	275	197	2	...	1	2
Bhulia ...	Raipur	Male ...	1,441	832	248	290	104	105	73	3
		Female ...	1,372	619	248	274	57	36	3	1
Bhunjia ...	Raipur	Male ...	3,463	1,948	647	700	197	179	209	16
		Female ...	3,450	1,422	703	544	74	42	50	9

by age for selected castes.

Married.							Widowed.						
Total.	0—5.	5—12.	12—15.	15—20.	20—40.	40 and over.	Total.	0—5.	5—12.	12—15.	15—20.	20—40.	40 and over.
12	13	14	15	16	17	18	19	20	21	22	23	24	25
1,623	*5*	*20*	*43*	*88*	*895*	*569*	*166*	...	*1*	*1*	*6*	*40*	*118*
1,596	*3*	*113*	*129*	*146*	*951*	*255*	*573*	...	*3*	*7*	*3*	*105*	*455*
258	1	6	3	11	154	83	14	...	...	...	...	5	9
217	1	6	9	23	147	31	87	...	...	1	...	23	63
316	...	5	6	14	190	101	27	...	...	...	1	9	17
305	2	11	19	17	218	38	125	...	...	...	...	27	98
272	...	2	5	18	155	92	29	...	...	...	...	9	20
265	...	20	12	22	168	43	65	...	...	...	...	7	58
532	...	5	17	30	274	206	66	...	1	...	2	9	54
599	...	58	76	54	310	101	193	...	2	6	1	30	154
245	4	2	12	15	125	87	30	...	...	1	3	8	18
210	...	18	13	29	108	42	103	...	1	...	2	18	82
2,886	5	28	63	142	1,761	807	232	1	1	...	8	93	129
3,081	11	76	108	350	2,014	522	852	...	5	4	6	205	632
331	1	7	10	80	173	110	33	...	...	...	1	8	24
311	4	27	25	82	159	64	104	1	2	...	1	22	78
8,600	*8*	*47*	*86*	*437*	*5,475*	*2,553*	*478*	*1*	...	...	*4*	*185*	*288*
9,239	*8*	*126*	*238*	*951*	*6,369*	*1,547*	*2,554*	*3*	*1*	*4*	*7*	*477*	*2,062*
6,345	2	41	68	346	4,020	1,868	342	1	...	...	3	123	215
6,794	5	93	179	712	4,633	1,172	1,911	8	...	2	3	326	1,577
586	1	4	7	21	372	181	44	...	...	...	...	24	20
630	2	13	20	63	428	104	181	...	...	1	1	29	150
1,675	5	2	11	70	1,083	504	92	...	...	...	1	38	53
1,815	1	20	39	176	1,308	271	462	...	1	1	3	122	335
2,866	*4*	*31*	*54*	*197*	*1,583*	*997*	*370*	*1*	*1*	...	*4*	*111*	*253*
2,915	*5*	*149*	*156*	*316*	*1,731*	*561*	*1,537*	*2*	*4*	*8*	*11*	*391*	*1,121*
1,744	3	8	25	99	1,011	598	275	1	...	...	4	80	190
1,745	2	73	98	217	1,055	300	1,048	1	1	5	7	300	734
433	...	9	10	38	226	150	37	...	1	...	...	7	29
437	2	50	30	36	211	108	164	...	3	3	...	35	123
384	...	5	8	22	100	159	38	...	...	...	...	15	23
414	...	13	17	43	200	81	165	...	...	...	3	24	138
305	1	9	11	38	156	90	20	...	...	...	...	9	11
322	1	13	11	20	205	72	160	1	...	...	1	32	126
6,234	4	48	178	440	3,746	1,812	451	...	...	...	3	125	323
6,300	20	385	572	802	3,678	843	1,567	...	3	5	15	313	1,231
3,690	*3*	*15*	*44*	*234*	*2,233*	*1,163*	*353*	...	*1*	*1*	*2*	*122*	*257*
3,813	*9*	*152*	*301*	*557*	*2,294*	*500*	*1,221*	*1*	*2*	*2*	*10*	*246*	*963*
668	...	1	7	34	371	255	91	...	...	...	1	26	64
686	3	22	37	102	405	117	286	...	...	...	1	42	243
3,022	3	17	37	190	1,867	908	292	...	1	1	1	96	193
3,127	6	130	264	455	1,880	383	938	1	2	2	9	204	720
16,485	*64*	*800*	*743*	*1,336*	*7,985*	*5,557*	*938*	*1*	*11*	*10*	*18*	*213*	*680*
17,090	*155*	*1,996*	*1,123*	*1,743*	*9,026*	*3,044*	*3,637*	...	*17*	*25*	*17*	*509*	*3,070*
5,894	19	191	182	381	2,954	2,167	424	1	3	1	10	91	318
6,158	22	422	365	680	3,456	1,218	1,527	...	2	6	7	211	1,301
6,126	35	442	347	525	2,849	1,928	306	...	6	6	3	71	230
6,338	100	909	422	605	3,231	1,071	1,229	...	9	10	5	170	1,085
3,519	10	122	177	354	1,691	1,165	164	...	2	3	3	36	120
3,624	25	510	257	374	1,829	629	681	...	6	5	4	106	560
946	...	45	37	76	491	297	39	...	...	...	2	15	22
970	11	155	79	84	510	131	200	...	...	3	1	22	174
578	...	4	7	25	344	198	31	...	...	...	...	11	20
614	...	27	37	73	362	115	139	...	1	...	2	20	116
1,430	...	5	6	29	876	519	80	...	...	...	1	21	58
1,521	4	13	49	189	1,018	248	507	2	1	1	6	94	403

TABLE XIV.—Civil Condition

Caste, tribe or race.	Locality.	Sex.	Population dealt with.	Unmarried. Total.	0—5.	5—12.	12—15.	15—20.	20—40.	40 and over.
1	2	3	4	5	6	7	8	9	10	11
Bidur ...	Maratha Division ...	Male ...	8.507	3.844	1,113	1,374	489	371	417	80
		Female ...	8,684	2,324	1,157	965	113	15	52	22
Binjhwar ...	Total ...	Male ...	*22,893*	*11,593*	*4,038*	*4,053*	*1,167*	*1,192*	*1,040*	*103*
		Female ...	*23,422*	*9,300*	*3,831*	*3,769*	*809*	*473*	*260*	*69*
	Bhandara	Male ...	2.641	1.135	425	389	116	90	110	5
		Female ...	2,772	873	419	312	67	36	26	13
	Balaghat	Male ...	2.840	1.250	462	453	116	120	91	8
		Female ...	3,165	1,001	402	413	66	41	17	2
	Raipur	Male ...	12,022	6.439	2,159	2,192	704	750	578	56
		Female ...	12,276	5.254	2,053	2,119	550	328	169	35
	Bilaspur	Male ...	5,390	2,769	992	1,019	231	232	261	34
		Female ..	5,209	2,072	897	925	126	67	48	9
Bohra ...	Nimar	Male ...	703	303	98	109	26	39	27	4
		Female ...	642	318	70	110	101	27	9	1
Brahman ...	Province	Male ...	237,567	112,964	27,962	35,607	12,675	12,512	19,565	4,643
		Female	208,060	61,224	27,381	29,878	2,460	591	669	236
Chadar ...	Total ...	Male ...	*13,627*	*6,383*	*2,239*	*2,310*	*575*	*579*	*624*	*56*
		Female ...	*13,829*	*4,488*	*2,182*	*2,076*	*156*	*28*	*35*	*11*
	Saugor	Male ...	7,305	3.430	1,245	1,223	286	314	330	32
		Female ..	7.333	2.377	1,173	1,100	72	5	21	6
	Damoh	Male ...	3.516	1,651	557	617	150	142	162	17
		Female ...	3.681	1,220	564	577	51	14	9	5
	Jubbulpore	Male ...	1,327	623	198	227	66	63	65	4
		Female ...	1,359	453	206	224	19	1	3	...
	Narsinghpur	Male ..	1,479	679	239	243	67	60	67	3
		Female ...	1,456	438	239	175	14	8	2	...
Chamar ...	Province	Male ...	443,017	182.240	76,766	69,573	13,555	11,865	9,509	882
		Female ..	458,505	141.931	79,865	56,086	3,385	1,085	1,045	465
Chauhan ...	Bilaspur	Male ...	1.019	442	165	166	27	51	31	2
		Female ...	1.055	393	172	128	12	78	2	1
Chhipa ...	Jubbulpore	Male ...	637	259	108	101	21	18	10	1
		Female ...	726	219	97	106	14	1	...	1
Dahayat ...	Jubbulpore	Male ...	4.423	1.983	663	812	213	150	135	10
		Female ...	4,574	1,405	662	643	69	18	11	2
Dangi ...	Total ...	Male ...	*12,180*	*6.407*	*1,608*	*2,189*	*683*	*713*	*1,023*	*191*
		Female ...	*11,826*	*3,417*	*1,604*	*1,702*	*81*	*11*	*16*	*3*
	Saugor	Male ...	11.608	6.099	1,523	2,089	646	682	978	181
		Female ...	11.287	3,272	1,541	1,627	76	11	14	3
	Damoh	Male ...	572	308	85	100	37	31	45	10
		Female ...	539	145	63	75	5	...	2	...
Daraiba ...	Bilaspur	Male ...	1,179	535	151	214	67	55	41	7
		Female ...	1.334	451	203	199	25	14	4	6
Darji ...	Province	Male ...	26,109	10.952	3,551	4,153	1,228	945	905	170
		Female ...	25,173	6,898	3,583	2,896	193	69	100	57
Deswali ...	Total ...	Male ...	*3,599*	*1,682*	*360*	*624*	*192*	*182*	*214*	*20*
		Female ...	*3,422*	*943*	*362*	*524*	*41*	*3*	*3*	*10*
	Hoshangabad ...	Male	2.314	1,119	209	405	131	127	147	10
		Female ...	2.176	586	192	347	33	3	3	8
	Nimar	Male ...	1.285	563	151	219	61	55	67	10
		Female ..	1.246	357	170	177	8	...	...	2
Dhanagar ...	Total ...	Male ...	*9,225*	*3,445*	*1,439*	*1,439*	*313*	*143*	*111*	*20*
		Female ...	*9,184*	*2,366*	*1,330*	*780*	*56*	*11*	*56*	*33*
	Wardha	Male ...	3,598	1,287	551	512	121	52	41	10
		Female ...	3,466	791	476	214	17	7	48	29
	Nagpur	Male ...	3.721	1.515	561	671	149	66	59	9
		Female ...	3,844	1.036	554	454	19	3	4	2

by age for selected castes.

Married.							Widowed.						
Total.	0—5.	5—12.	12—15.	15—20.	20—40.	40 and over.	Total.	0—5.	5—12.	12—15.	15—20.	20—40.	40 and over.
12	13	14	15	16	17	18	19	20	21	22	23	24	25
4,002	5	38	87	287	2,094	1,511	661	3	7	5	26	219	401
4,251	35	402	310	557	2,144	803	2,109	15	20	14	57	475	1,528
10,425	*15*	*86*	*85*	*418*	*6,200*	*3,621*	*875*	...	*3*	...	*10*	*294*	*568*
10,753	*18*	*190*	*266*	*1,027*	*7,091*	*2,161*	*3,469*	*6*	*14*	*5*	*20*	*609*	*2,815*
1,378	7	20	6	62	772	511	128	...	1	...	...	26	101
1,406	5	45	52	143	855	306	493	5	5	...	5	108	370
1,469	...	10	23	81	858	497	121	...	...	...	2	34	85
1,573	3	33	55	176	994	312	591	...	1	1	3	97	489
5,127	4	7	15	118	3,183	1,800	456	...	1	...	4	171	280
5,301	7	22	45	388	3,771	1,068	1,721	...	4	3	9	290	1,415
2,451	4	49	41	157	1,387	813	170	...	1	...	4	63	102
2,473	3	90	114	320	1,471	475	664	1	4	1	3	114	541
330	...	6	19	27	138	140	70	...	...	...	12	14	44
219	1	2	7	25	110	74	105	...	1	7	10	36	51
107,402	181	1,337	2,207	6,022	58,568	38,187	17,201	4	57	69	238	4,643	12,195
95,666	320	5,709	7,422	13,414	52,529	16,272	51,170	17	229	306	902	14,382	35,244
6,621	*7*	*40*	*91*	*389*	*3,986*	*2,108*	*628*	...	...	*2*	*10*	*286*	*385*
6,906	*9*	*260*	*815*	*806*	*4,490*	*1,036*	*2,485*	...	*9*	*7*	*27*	*610*	*1,782*
3,525	3	18	40	201	2,111	1,152	350	...	...	...	7	124	219
3,658	4	157	177	424	2,348	548	1,298	...	6	4	8	341	939
1,719	...	11	20	94	1,077	517	146	...	...	1	2	46	97
1,812	2	41	62	217	1,221	260	649	...	1	3	10	167	468
643	3	5	12	44	387	192	61	...	...	1	...	29	31
658	2	26	37	84	400	109	248	...	...	...	4	58	186
734	1	6	19	50	411	247	66	...	...	...	1	27	38
778	1	36	39	81	521	100	240	...	2	...	5	44	189
244,798	663	8,904	7,375	16,759	135,368	75,729	15,979	11	173	140	545	5,594	9,516
258 792	1,423	17,919	13,267	27,522	151,924	46,737	57,782	75	310	153	438	9,671	47,135
536	...	14	9	88	296	179	41	...	1	...	...	18	22
459	1	33	24	57	249	95	203	...	1	...	1	36	165
345	1	10	17	30	198	89	33	...	...	1	1	12	19
371	2	34	18	54	213	50	136	...	...	...	...	31	105
2,266	1	58	79	171	1,333	624	174	...	2	...	4	58	110
2,399	7	124	124	286	1,515	343	770	...	1	7	5	164	593
5,099	*3*	*40*	*160*	*450*	*2,924*	*1,583*	*674*	...	...	*1*	*6*	*228*	*439*
5,203	*4*	*324*	*454*	*781*	*3,001*	609	*3,206*	*1*	*10*	*13*	*65*	*1,103*	*2,014*
4,860	3	30	150	424	2,801	1,443	649	...	...	1	6	224	418
4,956	4	305	465	750	2,855	577	3,059	1	10	12	61	1,064	1,911
239	...	1	10	26	123	79	25	...	...	...	...	4	21
247	...	19	19	31	146	32	147	...		1	4	39	103
586	...	9	16	52	310	190	58	...	1	...	2	22	33
658	3	36	46	94	378	102	225	...	...	6	9	63	147
13,493	21	178	389	1,011	7,381	4,513	1,664	–	17	14	48	476	1,109
13,559	83	1,198	947	1,626	7,487	2,218	4,716	2	48	84	61	970	3,601
1,718	...	*17*	*40*	*100*	*1,036*	*535*	*199*	...	*1*	*3*	*3*	*62*	*130*
1,840	*2*	*83*	*130*	*203*	*1,073*	*349*	*639*	...	*3*	*2*	*1*	*129*	*504*
1,061	...	11	19	54	641	396	134	...	...	...	1	42	91
1,180	2	40	76	121	677	264	410	...	3	2	1	84	320
657	...	6	21	46	395	189	66	...	1	3	2	20	39
660	...	43	54	82	396	85	229	...	...	...	...	45	184
5,359	*7*	*260*	*266*	*400*	*2,531*	*1,916*	*421*	...	*5*	*6*	*11*	*102*	*297*
5,417	*53*	*833*	*439*	*512*	*2,604*	977	*1,501*	...	*36*	*21*	*19*	*233*	*1,303*
2,109	5	51	72	164	1,058	759	202	...	2	2	2	55	141
2,054	14	334	170	219	999	318	621	...	17	13	4	108	479
2,049	1	71	89	103	958	767	157	...	...	1	7	87	112
2,179	10	254	178	228	1,034	475	629	...	4	5	14	95	511

TABLE XIV.—Civil condition

Caste, tribe or race.	Locality.	Sex.	Population dealt with.	Unmarried. Total.	0—5.	5—12.	12—15.	15—20.	20—40.	40 and over.
1	2	3	4	5	6	7	8	9	10	11
Dhanagar—(*concld.*)	Chanda	Male ...	1,906	643	317	246	43	25	11	1
		Female ...	1,874	439	300	112	20	1	4	2
Dhanuk ...	Narsinghpur ...	Male ...	2,411	1,121	436	420	97	99	64	5
		Female ...	2,583	890	429	404	33	14	7	3
Dhanwar ...	Bilaspur	Male ...	4,095	2,169	777	839	166	153	200	34
		Female ...	5,090	2,139	912	902	111	94	96	24
Dhimar ...	Province	Male ...	140,734	63,657	22,592	24,121	6,261	5,438	4,714	531
		Female ...	142,679	49,392	23,854	20,460	2,302	1,402	905	469
Dhobi ...	Province	Male ...	80,673	34,212	12,906	13,785	3,219	2,284	1,774	244
		Female ...	83,900	26,359	13,485	10,687	939	740	333	175
Dhuri ...	Bilaspur	Male ...	1,016	411	159	145	54	27	24	2
		Female ...	1,089	465	131	116	8	3	204	3
Dohor ...	Buldana	Male ...	1,508	618	272	272	37	23	12	2
		Female ...	1,447	396	281	103	5	2	5	...
Gadaria ...	Total ...	Male ...	*15,349*	*6,043*	*2,330*	*2,242*	*501*	*408*	*509*	*53*
		Female ...	*15,036*	*4,251*	*2,325*	*1,728*	*103*	*18*	*22*	*55*
	Nerbudda Valley ...	Male ...	9,528	3,920	1,432	1,475	337	275	375	26
		Female ...	8,882	2,562	1,365	1,120	48	7	12	10
	Chhattisgarh Division ...	Male ...	5,821	2,123	898	767	164	133	134	27
		Female ...	6,154	1,689	960	608	55	11	10	45
Ganda ...	Total ...	Male ...	*50,835*	*25,040*	*8,247*	*10,051*	*2,636*	*2,172*	*1,738*	*196*
		Female ...	*53,285*	*20,723*	*9,315*	*8,807*	*1,427*	*621*	*463*	*90*
	Chhattisgarh Division ...	Male ...	44,184	21,530	7,108	8,623	2,184	1,883	1,553	179
		Female ...	46,582	17,762	8,185	7,393	1,175	515	422	72
	Surguja	Male ...	1,559	769	266	313	102	53	32	3
		Female ...	1,555	650	245	330	39	20	11	5
	Jashpur	Male ...	5,091	2,741	873	1,115	350	236	153	14
		Female ...	5,148	2,311	885	1,084	213	86	30	13
Garpagari ...	Nagpur	Male ...	1,113	477	175	174	52	37	32	7
		Female ...	1,092	258	146	104	6	1	...	1
Ghasia ...	Chhattisgarh Division ...	Male ...	9,690	4,493	1,591	1,761	411	334	343	53
		Female ...	10,630	3,611	1,572	1,585	209	95	117	33
Ghosi ...	Total ...	Male ...	*3,914*	*1,927*	*607*	*688*	*201*	*210*	*202*	*19*
		Female ...	*3,682*	*1,165*	*585*	*635*	*28*	*8*	*7*	*2*
	Saugor	Male ...	2,530	1,227	400	410	131	144	130	12
		Female ...	2,378	770	386	359	16	4	4	1
	Damoh	Male ...	936	473	135	196	49	45	45	3
		Female ...	888	293	146	129	12	3	2	1
	Narsinghpur	Male ...	448	227	72	82	21	21	27	4
		Female ...	416	102	53	47	...	1	1	...
Golar ...	Yeotmal	Male ...	1,599	515	248	218	16	20	11	2
		Female ...	1,713	447	217	109	14	20	72	15
Gond (Hindu)	Province	Male ...	174,683	80,898	28,449	30,073	7,644	6,860	7,191	681
		Female ...	185,243	64,536	29,705	27,786	3,946	1,640	1,147	812
Gond (Animist)	Province	Male ...	910,853	456,582	154,346	171,472	45,339	41,333	40,332	3,760
		Female ...	956,761	379,417	161,633	161,052	30,032	16,205	8,893	1,602
Gosain ...	Total ...	Male ...	*10,176*	*4,802*	*1,421*	*1,656*	*473*	*429*	*639*	*285*
		Female ...	*9,777*	*3,002*	*1,397*	*1,314*	*153*	*33*	*34*	*71*
	Balaghat	Male ...	483	243	75	92	24	19	24	9
		Female ...	482	138	66	64	5	2	...	1
	Narsinghpur	Male ...	832	393	129	129	37	30	46	22
		Female ...	768	228	123	95	8	...	...	2
	Jubbulpore	Male ...	'1,011	491	149	167	39	53	54	29
		Female ...	1,052	389	140	167	20	4	4	54
	Hoshangabad	Male ...	1,481	715	197	238	93	71	81	35
		Female ...	i1,300	371	194	149	23	...	4	1

by age for selected castes.

Married.							Widowed.						
Total.	0—5.	5—12.	12—15.	15—20.	20—40.	40 and over.	Total.	0—5.	5—12.	12—15.	15—20.	20—40.	40 and over.
12	13	14	15	16	17	18	19	20	21	22	23	24	25
1,201	1	128	95	73	515	389	62	...	3	3	2	10	44
1,184	28	245	91	65	571	184	251	...	4	3	1	30	213
1.213	1	5	16	73	733	385	77	...	...	—	1	23	53
1.278	3	36	54	104	836	185	415	1	...	1	4	88	321
1.759	3	10	14	79	1,118	535	167	...	1	...	2	63	101
2.395	77	61	205	296	1,377	380	556	...	7	10	12	121	406
71,036	370	1,310	1,612	4,218	40,096	23,430	6.041	7	42	46	242	1,747	3,957
72,380	407	3,772	3,900	8,637	43,410	12,158	20.907	4	96	88	298	4,079	16,342
43,126	106	1,200	1,517	3,288	23,790	13,230	3.335	4	30	23	74	1,057	2,138
44,517	215	3,600	2,808	5,367	25,303	7,164	13.024	32	108	99	136	2,490	10,159
554	1	19	24	60	253	197	51	...	...	...	...	19	32
453	2	43	38	54	244	72	171	...	2	...	2	30	137
842	2	41	53	70	442	234	48	...	5	1	5	10	27
870	33	143	54	115	427	98	181	...	1	3	1	35	141
8,96[illegible]	*31*	*456*	*399*	*635*	*4,305*	*2,458*	*942*	...	*12*	*12*	*26*	*367*	*525*
8,661	*59*	*891*	*560*	*948*	*4,751*	*1,424*	*2,123*	*1*	*16*	*7*	*16*	*868*	*1,722*
4,993	13	266	224	888	2,042	1,405	615	...	3	6	18	235	853
5.086	57	487	360	558	2,856	750	1.234	...	9	7	10	231	977
3.371	18	220	175	302	1,603	993	327	...	9	6	8	182	172
3.575	32	404	191	385	1,808	665	890	1	6	...	6	132	745
24,257	*84*	*336*	*443*	*1,352*	*11,815*	*7,763*	*1,557*	*1*	*10*	*10*	*44*	*646*	*836*
25,441	*47*	*805*	*953*	*2,758*	*16,190*	*4,691*	*7,131*	*3*	*36*	*13*	*69*	*1,275*	*5,732*
21.337	84	322	401	1,232	12,566	6,782	1,317	1	9	8	38	548	713
22,490	45	751	843	2,447	14,275	4,129	6.330	3	27	6	32	1,077	5,185
731	...	7	14	40	425	245	59	...	1	...	1	25	32
722	1	22	31	68	457	143	183	...	1	2	10	38	132
2,179	...	7	28	80	1,327	737	171	...	...	2	5	73	91
2.229	1	30	78	243	1,458	419	608	...	8	5	17	168	415
593	1	6	14	42	301	229	43	...	...	2	2	10	29
635	3	63	31	71	349	118	199	...	...	6	...	33	160
4.865	5	81	89	283	2,887	1,529	332	1	...	...	12	137	182
5.523	10	184	201	571	3,588	969	1,496	...	1	1	9	271	1,214
1,785	*2*	*30*	*46*	*145*	*1,031*	*583*	*302*	...	...	*2*	...	*69*	*141*
1,841	*3*	*115*	*113*	*211*	*1,156*	*815*	*676*	...	...	*4*	*7*	*140*	*525*
1,162	1	13	31	94	691	332	141	...	...	...	...	44	97
1,173	...	68	74	137	735	159	435	...	...	4	5	70	347
427	1	12	6	37	227	144	36	...	...	...	...	9	27
442	..	25	22	50	291	54	153	...	...	...	1	37	115
196	...	5	9	12	117	57	25	...	...	2	...	6	17
226	3	22	17	24	130	30	88	...	...	...	1	24	63
1,022	6	97	79	74	522	244	62	...	...	2	...	24	86
946	62	189	50	88	450	107	320	...	7	4	4	75	280
86,087	141	918	1,479	4,615	48,744	30,190	7.698	10	34	89	201	2,637	4,777
91.696	278	2,557	3,372	9,588	58,317	17,584	29,011	16	92	86	240	5,251	23,326
422.649	540	3,378	5,322	18,040	243,623	151,737	31.622	24	124	207	686	11,380	19,251
451,028	1,356	9,750	14,810	44,318	294,023	85,[illegible]68	126,315	107	530	268	906	22,578	101,926
4,78[illegible]	*14*	*98*	*134*	*[illegible]*	*2,505*	*1,720*	*[illegible]*	...	*6*	*2*	*12*	*176*	*391*
4,936	*21*	*817*	*353*	*[illegible]*	*2,76[illegible]*	*93[illegible]*	*1,89[illegible]*	*2*	*12*	*6*	*12*	*351*	*1,456*
225	1	...	5	16	126	77	15	...	...	...	...	4	11
242	...	15	19	25	135	48	102	...	...	1	...	18	83
378	1	4	14	22	219	118	61	...	...	...	1	19	41
383	3	17	34	41	231	57	157	...	...	...	1	36	120
470	3	12	18	31	250	147	50	...	1	...	...	14	35
455	4	38	31	61	240	81	208	...	2	...	2	55	149
667	...	1	12	41	366	247	99	...	...	...	1	37	64
687	2	25	54	70	401	135	242	...	...	...	1	34	207

TABLE XIV.—Civil condition

Caste, tribe or race.	Locality.	Sex.	Population dealt with.	Unmarried.						
				Total.	0—5.	5—12.	12—15.	15—20.	20—40.	40 and over.
1	2	3	4	5	6	7	8	9	10	11
Gosain—(concld.)	Nagpur	Male ...	1.529	689	186	230	67	65	75	66
		Female ...	1.443	370	186	172	6	3	2	1
	Wardha	Male ...	769	353	87	102	33	35	47	49
		Female ...	639	174	89	68	9	2	4	2
	Bhandara	Male ...	587	276	64	92	32	22	46	20
		Female ...	537	148	68	67	6	3	3	1
	Raipur	Male ...	1.228	573	170	221	56	42	65	19
		Female ...	1.179	383	174	169	22	10	6	2
	Bilaspur	Male ...	1.445	697	243	248	62	59	65	20
		Female ...	1,553	554	234	259	38	8	10	5
	Drug	Male ...	811	372	121	136	30	33	36	16
		Female ...	824	247	123	104	16	1	1	2
Gowari ...	Maratha Division ...	Male ...	68,732	24.705	9,103	8,890	2,564	2.089	1,805	254
		Female ...	60.977	19.427	9,702	7,996	964	355	310	100
Gujar ...	Total ...	Male ...	*26,539*	*10,705*	*3,804*	*4,141*	*1,017*	*775*	*864*	*107*
		Female ...	*25,306*	*6,881*	*3,675*	*2,980*	*150*	*26*	*35*	*12*
	Narsinghpur	Male ...	2,503	1,039	331	308	100	98	106	6
		Female ...	2,437	642	312	298	22	3	5	2
	Hoshangabad ...	Male ...	12.030	5.208	1,601	1,935	574	485	475	48
		Female ...	11,416	3.186	1,505	1,440	100	17	20	8
	Nimar	Male ...	11,956	4,461	1,782	1,808	343	102	283	53
		Female ...	11,453	3,053	1,768	1,236	28	6	13	2
Gurao ...	Total ...	Male ...	*2,099*	*906*	*236*	*316*	*148*	*95*	*79*	*34*
		Female ...	*2,116*	*523*	*252*	*248*	*13*	*1*	*7*	*2*
	Nagpur	Male ...	845	370	95	136	62	42	29	6
		Female ...	820	206	105	95	3	1	1	1
	Wardha	Male ...	771	331	92	113	51	29	24	22
		Female ...	808	203	91	95	10	...	6	1
	Chanda	Male ...	483	204	49	67	32	24	26	6
		Female ...	488	114	56	58	...	...	...	...
Halba ...	Total ...	Male ...	*15,646*	*8,602*	*2,564*	*3,067*	*892*	*863*	*947*	*169*
		Female ...	*15,830*	*6,484*	*2,739*	*2,866*	*440*	*229*	*174*	*34*
	Chanda	Male ...	1.217	606	169	183	61	68	117	8
		Female ...	1,181	402	164	161	41	22	13	1
	Bastar	Male ...	7.966	4.496	1,260	1,716	478	453	553	36
		Female ...	7,883	3,337	1,422	1,460	191	116	124	24
	Kanker	Male ...	4.276	2.236	767	819	229	214	188	19
		Female ...	4.453	1.811	802	777	136	64	27	5
	Raipur	Male ...	2.186	1.164	368	349	124	128	89	106
		Female ...	2,313	934	351	470	72	27	10	4
Hatgar ...	Yeotmal	Male ...	5,117	1.824	740	695	127	134	117	11
		Female ...	5,254	1,275	670	389	23	32	130	31
Jat ...	Total ...	Male ...	*2,902*	*1,281*	*363*	*435*	*148*	*142*	*178*	*15*
		Female ...	*2,577*	*755*	*357*	*367*	*47*	*6*	*4*	*4*
	Narsinghpur ...	Male ...	496	261	62	84	34	34	46	1
		Female ...	439	125	53	64	4	1	3	...
	Hoshangabad	Male ...	2,406	1,020	301	351	114	108	132	14
		Female ...	2,438	660	304	303	43	5	1	4
Jogi ...	Total ...	Male ...	*1,492*	*742*	*222*	*478*	*86*	*71*	*70*	*15*
		Female ...	*1,367*	*453*	*192*	*191*	*34*	*12*	*11*	*3*
	Mandla	Male ...	557	307	93	119	29	20	37	9
		Female ...	564	201	84	91	14	9	3	...
	Hoshangabad	Male ...	935	435	120	150	57	51	33	6
		Female ...	803	242	108	100	20	3	8	3
Kachhi ...	Total ...	Male ...	*58,181*	*26,721*	*9,154*	*9,999*	*2,566*	*2,13*[illegible]	*2,300*	*172*
		Female ...	*57,749*	*18,578*	*9,329*	*8,319*	*615*	[illegible]	*129*	*31*

by age for selected castes.

Married.							Widowed.						
Total.	0—5.	5—12.	12—15.	15—20.	20—40.	40 and over.	Total.	0—5.	5—12.	12—15.	15—20.	20—40.	40 and over.
12	13	14	15	16	17	18	19	20	21	22	23	24	25
741	6	30	37	56	321	291	99	...	2	...	1	30	66
806	...	84	71	90	403	158	267	...	3	...	...	51	213
358	...	3	4	34	170	147	58	...	...	...	3	13	42
339	3	30	29	42	167	68	126	...	1	4	3	27	91
278	3	2	5	19	130	119	33	...	1	...	3	6	23
281	2	19	16	31	145	68	108	2	3	...	2	15	86
594	...	17	13	35	312	217	61	...	2	1	1	17	40
590	2	24	35	73	324	132	206	...	...	...	...	33	173
672	...	14	21	43	376	218	76	...	...	...	1	23	52
735	5	46	42	74	451	117	264	...	2	1	3	58	200
405	...	10	5	25	228	189	34	...	...	1	1	12	20
418	...	19	22	88	271	68	159	...	1	...	...	24	134
31,096	104	854	555	1,562	16,494	12,027	2,931	7	24	62	83	696	2,059
32,782	144	1,643	1,698	3,602	19,299	6,306	8,768	6	46	44	109	1,641	6,922
14,240	*10*	*466*	*812*	*1,297*	*7,473*	*4,182*	*1,691*	...	*4*	*13*	*30*	*435*	*1,116*
14,377	*32*	*1,394*	*1,280*	*1,765*	*7,612*	*2,301*	*4,045*	*1*	*16*	*13*	*21*	*722*	*3,275*
1,340	1	49	51	98	704	437	124	...	...	...	2	36	86
1,360	5	104	113	166	739	233	435	...	1	2	3	60	300
6,147	5	145	328	538	3,263	1,868	725	...	2	7	13	221	482
6,159	12	449	516	728	3,402	1,052	2,071	1	6	6	10	374	1,674
6,753	4	272	433	661	3,506	1,877	742	...	2	6	15	171	548
6,858	15	841	651	864	3,471	1,016	1,542	...	9	5	8	279	1,241
1,050	*1*	*15*	*12*	*56*	*524*	*445*	*135*	*4*	...	*2*	*1*	*27*	*105*
1,079	*4*	*92*	*94*	*140*	*528*	*221*	*514*	...	*6*	*7*	*6*	*92*	*405*
405	1	16	7	23	200	158	70	4	...	1	1	11	53
415	1	38	32	49	218	77	199	...	...	3	1	47	148
393	...	1	1	22	196	173	47	...	...	1	...	12	34
410	1	30	40	63	180	96	195	...	3	2	4	32	154
258	...	1	4	13	128	112	21	...	...	...	...	4	47
254	2	24	22	28	130	48	120	...	2	2	1	13	102
6,622	*10*	*35*	*78*	*255*	*3,963*	*2,286*	*521*	...	*1*	*1*	*6*	*156*	*327*
6,889	*9*	*130*	*261*	*818*	*4,559*	*1,132*	*2,457*	*2*	*15*	*5*	*23*	*622*	*1,790*
558	1	5	3	13	314	222	53	...	1	...	...	11	41
532	3	15	15	61	340	98	247	...	3	2	2	49	191
3,230	5	13	31	114	1,974	1,093	240	...	...	...	4	77	159
3,436	2	59	130	425	2,303	517	1,110	1	6	2	12	342	747
1,877	2	14	31	90	1,119	612	163	...	...	1	2	68	92
1,925	3	34	80	239	1,244	325	717	1	6	1	6	162	541
957	2	3	9	29	555	359	65	...	...	...	...	30	35
996	1	12	36	93	672	182	383	...	...	...	3	69	311
2,980	8	138	143	222	1,480	980	313	...	4	8	17	93	191
3,069	100	546	197	324	1,511	389	910	4	17	4	11	157	717
1,431	*5*	*52*	*57*	*115*	*778*	*434*	*190*	...	*10*	*5*	*6*	*67*	*102*
1,475	*9*	*105*	*91*	*175*	*848*	*248*	*619*	...	*2*	*2*	*4*	*101*	*510*
189	...	2	1	10	109	67	46	...	...	...	...	16	30
215	...	11	15	30	118	41	99	...	...	...	1	9	89
1,242	5	50	56	105	669	357	144	...	10	5	6	51	72
1,258	9	94	76	142	730	207	520	...	2	2	3	92	421
661	...	*7*	*14*	*41*	*361*	*235*	*89*	*1*	*7*	*3*	*3*	*31*	*45*
704	...	*21*	*46*	*65*	*446*	*136*	*230*	...	*2*	...	*5*	*40*	*170*
235	...	...	2	7	143	83	15	...	...	...	...	9	6
275	...	4	13	25	187	46	88	...	1	...	1	17	69
426	...	7	12	34	218	155	74	1	7	3	3	22	38
429	...	17	33	40	250	80	132	...	1	...	7	23	101
28,679	*22*	*456*	*780*	*1,965*	*17,006*	*8,157*	*2,731*	*2*	*10*	*9*	*33*	*910*	*1,757*
29,455	*72*	*1,503*	*1,747*	*3,607*	*15,397*	*4,142*	*9,716*	*3*	*19*	*33*	*93*	*2,297*	*7,271*

TABLE XIV.—Civil condition

Caste, tribe or race.	Locality.	Sex.	Population dealt with.	Unmarried. Total	0—5.	5—12.	12 - 15.	15—20.	20—40.	40 and over.
1	2	3	4	5	6	7	8	9	10	11
Kachhi—(*concld.*)	Nerbudda Valley ...	Male ... Female ...	54.204 53.981	24,913 17,368	8,587 8,771	9,332 7,804	2,398 551	2,266 104	2.178 111	152 27
	Plateau Division ...	Male ... Female ...	3,977 3,768	1.808 1.210	567 558	667 545	168 64	167 21	212 18	27 4
Kahar ...	Total ...	Male ... Female ...	*5,388* *5,312*	*2,541* *1,830*	*872* *933*	*953* *808*	*287* *61*	*200* *5*	*156* *13*	*73* *7*
	Narsinghpur	Male ... Female ...	1.053 1.121	481 384	177 206	179 165	47 8	41 1	30 1	1 3
	Hoshangabad	Male ... Female ...	2.997 2,947	1.438 1,045	505 521	534 460	161 45	102 7	87 9	49 3
	Nimar	Male ... Female ...	1.338 1,244	622 401	190 206	240 183	79 8	57 ...	33 3	23 1
Kalar ...	Province	Male ... Female ...	96.393 98,902	41.838 31.209	14,681 15,317	16,153 13,462	3,972 1,317	3,231 529	3,388 434	413 150
Kasar ...	Total ...	Male ... Female ...	*883* *920*	*367* *210*	*106* *102*	*125* *98*	*59* *1*	*39* *1*	*35* *8*	3 ...
	Wardha	Male ... Female ...	443 415	186 91	54 43	63 42	27 ...	18 ...	23 6	1 ...
	Nagpur	Male ... Female ...	440 505	181 119	52 59	62 56	32 1	21 1	12 2	2 ...
Katia ...	Plateau Division ...	Male ... Female ...	14.600 15,254	7,334 5.908	2,498 2,512	2,877 2,716	703 395	614 174	580 92	62 19
Kawar (Hindu)	Total ...	Male ... Female ...	*43,781* *45,453*	*22,385* *18,476*	*7,157* *7,528*	*8,485* *8,009*	*2,184* *1,501*	*2,136* *819*	*2,078* *474*	*345* *145*
	Chanda	Male ... Female ...	751 696	308 259	132 140	113 99	21 10	28 8	13 2	1 ...
	Chhattisgarh Division ...	Male ... Female ...	43.030 44.757	22.077 18,217	7,025 7,388	8,372 7,910	2,163 1,491	2,108 811	2,065 472	344 145
Kayasth ...	Province	Male ... Female ...	17.580 15.991	8.864 5.397	2,112 2,181	2,903 2,618	1,046 389	1,119 112	1,458 68	226 29
Kewat ...	Total ...	Male ... Female ...	*5,874* *5,993*	*2,375* *1,873*	*977* *1,001*	*869* *771*	*183* *62*	*151* *15*	*146* *18*	*49* *6*
	Jubbulpore	Male ... Female ...	2.657 2,867	1.079 921	423 413	410 436	94 48	77 12	70 9	5 3
	Narsinghpur	Male ... Female ...	868 628	330 221	100 103	131 107	13 8	20 1	27 1	39 1
	Chanda	Male ... Female ...	2,349 2,498	966 731	454 485	328 228	76 6	54 2	49 8	5 2
Kharwar (Hindu).	Total ...	Male ... Female ...	*1,859* *1,957*	*888* *762*	*280* *320*	*355* *356*	*96* *49*	*81* *17*	*71* *16*	*5* *4*
	Bilaspur	Male ... Female ...	1,247 1,337	584 526	200 225	235 238	49 33	52 13	43 13	5 4
	Jashpur	Male ... Female ...	612 620	304 236	80 95	120 118	47 16	29 4	28 3	... ...
Khangar ...	Total ...	Male ... Female ...	*5,845* *5,818*	*2,824* *1,792*	*834* *763*	*1,021* *845*	*283* *82*	*303* *10*	*346* *20*	*37* *3*
	Saugor	Male ... Female ...	2,903 2.900	1.365 896	451 420	485 435	135 23	123 3	150 5	21 1
	Damoh	Male ... Female ...	1,050 1,066	509 346	149 100	200 155	43 21	45 4	65 6	7 ...
	Jubbulpore	Male ... Female ...	1,398 1,345	721 413	172 175	248 193	84 35	114 3	100 5	3 2
	Narsinghpur	Male ... Female ...	494 507	229 137	62 68	88 62	21 3	21 ...	31 4	6 ...
Kharia ...	Total ...	Male ... Female ...	*3,100* *3,168*	*1,777* *1,720*	*635* *660*	*763* *726*	*199* *159*	*123* *64*	*52* *34*	*5* *7*

by age for selected castes.

Married.							Widowed.						
Total.	0—5.	5—12.	12—15.	15—20.	20—40.	40 and over.	Total.	0—5.	5—12.	12—15.	15—20.	20—40.	40 and over.
12	13	14	15	16	17	18	19	20	21	22	23	24	25
26,702	20	424	737	1,808	15,870	7,848	2,589	2	10	8	29	872	1,668
27,521	75	1,396	1,658	3,356	17,219	3,817	9,092	3	17	30	91	2,184	6,767
1,977	2	32	43	165	1,136	599	192	...	...	1	4	68	119
1,934	4	107	89	251	1,178	305	624	...	2	3	2	113	504
3,668	*2*	*22*	*49*	*181*	*1,598*	*811*	*189*	...	...	...	...	*46*	*148*
2,730	*2*	*110*	*151*	*363*	*1,620*	*475*	*762*	*3*	*1*	*1*	*9*	*171*	*577*
541	1	6	12	40	305	177	31	...	...	...	...	10	21
587	...	21	28	75	372	91	150	...	...	...	1	24	125
1,453	1	16	24	92	864	456	106	—	...	...	...	21	85
1,529	2	50	80	198	905	204	373	1	1	...	1	81	289
664	...	...	13	49	424	178	52	...	...	...	—	15	37
604	...	39	43	89	343	90	239	2	...	1	7	66	163
50,000	84	1,497	1,701	3,535	26,871	16,312	4,555	7	28	32	118	1,360	8,010
51,901	214	3,885	3,331	5,902	29,434	9,135	15,792	12	82	78	153	2,903	12,564
444	...	*6*	*5*	*22*	*260*	*151*	*72*	...	...	...	*3*	*17*	*63*
485	*5*	*61*	*47*	*64*	*244*	*67*	*232*	...	*1*	*3*	*2*	*49*	*167*
217	...	4	2	9	125	77	40	...	...	...	2	9	29
225	4	26	21	33	109	32	99	...	1	3	1	21	73
227	...	2	3	13	135	74	32	...	...	...	1	8	23
263	1	35	26	31	135	35	123	...	...	...	1	28	94
6,787	5	62	108	351	3,990	2,271	479	1	1	5	13	173	286
7,331	8	206	264	754	4,845	1,254	2,015	...	4	4	10	350	1,647
19,918	*26*	*252*	*327*	*1,036*	*11,844*	*6,943*	*1,475*	*2*	*5*	*6*	*12*	*400*	*1,050*
20,529	*30*	*562*	*667*	*2,138*	*13,117*	*4,015*	*6,148*	*2*	*6*	*7*	*43*	*1,170*	*5,220*
420	3	2	7	11	240	157	23	...	...	...	...	6	17
345	1	3	16	32	235	58	92	...	...	1	1	16	74
19,498	23	250	320	1,015	11,104	6,786	1,455	2	8	6	12	394	1,039
20,184	29	559	651	2,106	12,882	3,957	6,356	2	6	6	42	1,154	5,146
7,597	9	45	78	396	4,508	2,561	1,119	1	4	4	16	852	742
7,013	14	214	432	1,038	4,217	1,098	3,581	...	8	7	52	896	2,618
2,970	*3*	*66*	*100*	*211*	*1,720*	*870*	*229*	...	*4*	*2*	*3*	*70*	*150*
3,170	*5*	*365*	*194*	*364*	*1,902*	*440*	*950*	...	*3*	*4*	*23*	*201*	*719*
1,351	3	30	48	109	794	367	127	...	4	2	1	41	79
1,478	3	96	86	146	937	210	466	...	1	1	2	123	341
309	...	4	7	20	162	116	29	...	...	...	...	18	16
331	...	9	21	28	208	65	76	...	1	1	...	8	66
1,310	...	32	46	82	764	387	73	...	...	...	2	16	55
1,361	2	160	87	190	757	165	406	...	1	2	21	70	312
905	*1*	*16*	*9*	*55*	*503*	*334*	*66*	...	...	...	...	*24*	*42*
920	...	*15*	*53*	*103*	*664*	*182*	*275*	...	*1*	*1*	*3*	*66*	*204*
618	1	14	8	34	338	223	45	...	...	...	...	18	27
629	...	14	28	74	377	136	182	...	1	...	1	38	142
287	...	2	1	18	165	101	21	...	...	...	...	6	15
291	...	4	25	29	187	46	93	...	...	1	2	28	62
2,730	*1*	*17*	*33*	*141*	*1,610*	*913*	*301*	...	...	*1*	*3*	*103*	*194*
2,809	*2*	*75*	*141*	*368*	*1,839*	*391*	*1,317*	...	*7*	*4*	*5*	*312*	*886*
1,385	...	7	20	76	824	458	153	...	...	...	3	40	104
1,428	2	42	69	203	916	196	576	...	3	2	6	158	407
488	...	3	8	29	277	171	53	...	—	...	...	23	30
516	...	10	21	71	338	76	204	...	2	...	1	49	152
612	1	6	7	21	372	205	65	...	...	...	...	26	39
621	...	15	33	70	418	85	311	...	2	1	...	79	229
235	...	1	3	15	137	79	30	...	...	1	...	8	21
244	...	11	18	24	157	34	126	...	...	1	1	26	98
1,129	...	*2*	*35*	*115*	*607*	*370*	*194*	...	...	*2*	*7*	*68*	*117*
1,108	...	*6*	*17*	*118*	*718*	*244*	*345*	...	*1*	*2*	*28*	*95*	*219*

TABLE XIV.—Civil condition

Caste, tribe or race.	Locality.	Sex.	Population dealt with.	Unmarried.						
				Total.	0—5.	5—12.	12—15.	15—20.	20—40.	40 and over.
1	2	3	4	5	6	7	8	9	10	11
Kharia—(*concld.*)	Raigarh ...	Male ...	1,478	833	318	298	97	77	39	4
		Female ...	1,484	719	304	296	60	33	20	6
	Jashpur ...	Male ...	1,622	944	317	465	102	46	13	1
		Female ...	1,684	1,001	356	500	99	31	14	1
Khatik ...	Jubbulpore ...	Male ...	768	367	126	147	36	20	29	3
		Female ...	776	269	135	109	14	3	8	...
Kir ...	Hoshangabad ...	Male ...	2,773	1,373	417	480	156	152	156	12
		Female ...	2,461	825	398	379	32	9	5	2
Kirar ...	Total	Male ...	*23,267*	*10,339*	*3,461*	*3,870*	*1,085*	*861*	*955*	*109*
		Female ...	*23,031*	*7,146*	*3,416*	*3,233*	*342*	*83*	*49*	*21*
	Plateau Division	Male ...	9,845	4,655	1,579	1,804	478	367	376	51
		Female ...	9,874	3,516	1,617	1,603	214	46	26	10
	Narsinghpur	Male ...	6,046	2,549	885	868	222	230	314	30
		Female ...	5,897	1,584	819	674	57	19	11	4
	Hoshangabad	Male ...	5,204	2,250	711	867	272	199	194	7
		Female ...	5,155	1,473	734	666	60	8	6	5
	Nagpur ...	Male ...	2,172	885	286	331	113	65	69	21
		Female ...	2,105	572	246	296	11	11	6	2
Kohli ...	Total	Male ...	*11,044*	*4,541*	*1,635*	*1,777*	*407*	*287*	*382*	*53*
		Female ...	*11,046*	*2,959*	*1,651*	*1,263*	*40*	*9*	*16*	*10*
	Chanda ...	Male ...	4,135	1,677	643	618	140	85	155	30
		Female ...	4,177	1,095	628	448	6	3	6	4
	Bhandara ...	Male ...	6,909	2,864	992	1,159	261	202	227	23
		Female ...	6,869	1,894	1,023	815	34	6	10	6
Kol (Hindu)...	Total	Male ...	*21,769*	*10,336*	*4,117*	*4,004*	796	*707*	*651*	*61*
		Female ...	*23,415*	*8,773*	*4,187*	*3,749*	507	*163*	*147*	*20*
	Jubbulpore ...	Male ...	19,542	9,251	3,731	3,548	708	643	507	54
		Female ...	21,189	7,857	3,749	3,335	461	153	136	19
	Mandla ...	Male ...	1,855	897	336	365	74	49	64	5
		Female ...	1,852	753	368	334	35	7	9	...
	Chota Nagpur States	Male ...	372	188	56	87	14	15	20	2
		Female ...	374	163	76	76	11	3	2	1
Kol (Animist)	Total	Male ...	*11,028*	*5,498*	*2,147*	*2,289*	*458*	*327*	*224*	*53*
		Female ...	*12,105*	*4,842*	*2,250*	*2,216*	*234*	*72*	*59*	*11*
	Jubbulpore ...	Male ...	5,268	2,657	1,100	1,113	228	143	68	5
		Female ...	6,321	2,448	1,145	1,131	123	20	22	7
	Mandla ...	Male ...	3,168	1,499	612	618	109	77	73	10
		Female ...	3,229	1,300	657	555	53	16	12	3
	Chota Nagpur States	Male ...	2,592	1,342	435	559	121	107	83	38
		Female ...	2,555	1,094	448	526	58	36	25	1
Koli ...	Berar ...	Male ...	16,715	6,123	2,406	2,403	561	392	202	66
		Female ...	16,637	3,971	2,515	1,318	34	36	45	25
Kolta ...	Raigarh ...	Male ...	5,838	2,107	829	1,070	145	40	17	6
		Female ...	5,992	1,730	871	824	17	7	7	4
Komti ...	Chanda ...	Male ...	2,019	1,001	276	241	145	95	199	45
		Female ...	1,821	439	195	192	27	4	14	7
Kori ...	Nerbudda Valley	Male ...	15,339	6,580	2,283	2,482	548	532	673	62
		Female ...	15,282	4,681	2,380	2,053	140	30	51	9
Korku ...	Total	Male ...	*37,307*	*24,279*	*8,488*	*9,003*	*2,377*	*2,012*	*2,230*	*169*
		Female ...	*47,73[illegible]*	*20,292*	*9,024*	*8,362*	*1,624*	*799*	*524*	*59*
	Hoshangabad ...	Male ...	10,014	5,007	1,633	1,811	541	486	518	18
		Female ...	10,190	3,959	1,806	1,606	291	156	94	6
	Amraoti ...	Male ...	1,124	448	126	131	37	33	107	14
		Female ...	1,116	348	156	136	21	11	15	9
	Nimar ...	Male ...	18,549	9,452	3,407	3,592	961	730	704	49
		Female ...	18,368	7,802	3,471	3,387	569	221	141	13

by age for selected castes.

Married.							Widowed.						
Total.	0—5.	5—12.	12—15.	15—20.	20—40.	40 and over.	Total.	0—5.	5—12.	12—15.	15—20.	20—40.	40 and over.
12	13	14	15	16	17	18	19	20	21	22	23	24	25
602	...	...	...	15	378	209	43	...	...	...	...	16	27
619	...	3	9	71	422	114	146	...	...	...	2	20	115
527	...	2	35	100	229	161	151	...	...	2	7	52	90
484	...	3	8	47	208	130	199	...	1	2	26	66	104
368	...	7	6	25	212	118	33	...	...	...	...	14	19
373	...	15	22	45	285	56	134	...	...	...	3	35	96
1,271	2	7	6	39	739	478	129	...	...	...	1	41	87
1,309	...	26	61	183	846	243	327	...	...	...	1	53	273
11,807	*7*	*326*	*465*	*934*	*6,282*	*3,803*	*1,121*	...	*4*	*8*	*20*	*353*	*736*
12,305	*35*	*842*	*824*	*1,419*	*7,049*	*2,133*	*3,581*	*4*	*14*	*10*	*19*	*595*	*2,939*
4,826	4	68	122	328	2,542	1,762	364	...	2	1	3	103	255
4,988	4	202	296	593	2,905	988	1,370	...	4	1	2	198	1,165
3,139	...	135	174	272	1,712	840	358	...	1	5	6	117	229
3,341	13	342	226	376	1,912	472	972	...	3	2	4	184	779
2,693	...	104	139	232	1,485	733	261	...	1	...	7	89	164
2,798	8	200	215	347	1,614	414	884	...	1	2	8	176	697
1,149	3	19	30	92	543	462	138	...	...	2	4	44	88
1,178	13	98	87	108	618	259	355	4	6	5	5	37	298
6,007	*15*	*270*	*260*	*389*	*3,005*	*2,065*	*496*	...	*12*	*9*	*1*	*131*	*343*
6,129	*55*	*728*	*421*	*669*	*3,397*	*859*	*1,938*	...	*8*	*7*	*25*	*379*	*1,509*
2,256	3	102	101	122	1,108	820	202	...	7	4	...	51	140
2,331	19	265	169	250	1,306	322	751	...	1	1	3	127	619
3,751	12	168	159	267	1,900	1,245	294	...	5	5	1	80	208
3,798	36	463	252	419	2,091	537	1,177	...	7	6	22	252	890
10,745	*13*	*109*	*165*	*565*	*6,650*	*3,243*	*686*	...	...	*2*	*14*	*229*	*443*
11,460	*10*	*250*	*368*	*1,167*	*7,714*	*1,951*	*3,182*	...	*6*	*3*	*13*	*643*	*2,518*
9,678	12	96	140	513	5,067	2,950	613	...	...	2	14	204	393
10,404	10	224	339	1,055	6,981	1,795	2,928	...	5	2	11	579	2,331
907	1	9	21	40	595	235	51	...	...	...	...	22	29
888	...	21	24	91	624	128	211	...	1	1	1	55	153
160	...	4	4	6	88	58	24	...	...	...	...	3	21
168	...	5	5	21	109	28	43	...	...	...	...	9	34
5,236	*9*	*79*	*85*	*356*	*3,204*	*1,493*	*304*	...	...	*2*	*6*	*94*	*203*
5,519	*19*	*157*	*214*	*651*	*3,844*	*954*	*1,444*	*1*	*1*	*1*	*12*	267	*1,162*
2,469	3	37	42	104	1,479	744	142	...	...	...	1	31	110
2,992	6	76	98	321	1,935	556	881	...	...	...	7	138	736
1,584	5	19	26	100	908	436	85	...	...	...	2	28	55
1,617	4	52	64	168	1,104	225	312	1	...	...	2	50	259
1,173	1	23	17	92	727	313	77	...	...	2	2	35	38
1,210	9	29	52	142	805	173	251	...	1	1	3	79	167
9,588	59	230	363	761	4,841	3,334	1,004	2	5	12	63	320	602
9,713	79	1,446	508	1,149	4,908	1,533	2,953	1	40	40	40	619	2,213
3,493	2	120	274	383	1,804	910	238	...	...	...	2	77	159
3,516	3	337	369	420	1,800	572	746	...	2	3	2	131	608
784	15	20	34	61	856	298	234	9	10	26	35	22	132
742	3	79	76	100	357	127	640	...	2	4	7	170	451
7,942	8	97	148	412	4,830	2,441	817	...	3	5	12	306	491
7,835	19	368	382	838	5,137	1,091	2,768	...	6	9	24	592	2,135
21,630	*19*	*59*	*144*	*617*	*12,690*	*8,101*	*1,398*	...	*6*	*8*	*21*	*572*	*991*
22,631	*44*	*203*	*609*	*2,352*	*15,313*	*4,011*	*4,905*	*5*	*11*	*10*	*30*	*819*	*4,030*
4,655	3	11	25	121	2,747	1,748	352	...	1	...	2	96	253
4,907	7	40	123	475	3,389	873	1,324	...	5	...	3	222	1,094
585	1	1	41	73	227	242	91	...	5	6	10	28	42
641	2	23	67	131	255	163	127	...	...	6	13	32	76
8,681	7	28	50	240	5,273	3,083	416	...	...	1	5	105	305
8,883	17	96	284	988	6,013	1,485	1,683	3	3	3	3	271	1,400

TABLE XIV.—Civil condition

Caste, tribe or race.	Locality.	Sex.	Population dealt with.	UNMARRIED. Total.	0—5.	5—12.	12—15.	15—20.	20—40.	40 and over.
1	2	3	4	5	6	7	8	9	10	11
Korku—(concld.)	Betul	Male ...	17,620	9,372	3,322	3,460	838	754	901	88
		Female ...	18,054	8,183	3,591	3,233	643	411	274	31
Koshti ...	Total ...	Male ...	68,453	29,283	9,602	11,434	2,884	2,483	2,600	390
		Female ...	68,337	21,688	9,892	8,658	1,738	666	447	287
	Jubbulpore	Male ...	1,156	522	219	190	37	38	34	4
		Female ...	1,195	454	219	215	11	6	3	...
	Chhattisgarh Division ...	Male ...	17,893	7,272	2,853	2,860	655	488	379	37
		Female ...	18,799	5,738	3,069	2,347	231	40	35	16
	Maratha Division ...	Male ...	47,635	20,707	6,245	8,088	2,127	1,883	2,021	343
		Female ...	46,565	14,885	6,341	5,822	1,450	605	399	268
	Chhindwara	Male ...	1,769	782	285	280	65	74	66	6
		Female ...	1,778	611	263	274	46	15	10	3
Koskati ...	Chanda	Male ...	534	235	77	87	24	24	22	1
		Female ...	556	110	71	37	...	2	...	...
Kumbar ...	Province	Male ...	60,047	25,004	8,855	9,702	2,348	1,949	1,894	256
		Female ...	58,454	18,392	9,493	7,588	681	269	275	86
Kunbi ...	Total ...	Male ...	675,302	237,066	92,918	94,053	21,211	12,947	13,260	2,657
		Female ...	666,698	147,370	90,567	49,040	1,876	1,761	3,189	937
	Maratha Division ...	Male ...	625,398	217,827	85,745	85,967	19,603	11,756	12,218	2,538
		Female ...	616,461	134,638	83,282	43,904	1,721	1,722	3,103	906
	Chhindwara	Male ...	13,503	5,002	1,906	2,145	380	378	160	33
		Female ...	13,488	2,935	1,810	1,076	19	3	12	15
	Nimar	Male ...	14,195	5,237	1,859	2,220	460	315	337	46
		Female ...	13,763	3,277	1,877	1,332	24	9	31	4
	Betul	Male ...	22,206	9,000	3,408	3,721	768	498	535	70
		Female ...	22,986	6,520	3,598	2,728	112	27	43	12
Kuramwar ...	Chanda	Male ...	1,884	658	225	278	61	39	49	6
		Female ...	1,892	374	257	95	9	6	6	1
Kurmi ...	Total ...	Male ...	141,079	58,132	21,535	22,390	5,198	4,170	4,351	498
		Female ...	143,232	41,294	21,986	17,246	1,420	263	271	108
	Nerbudda Valley ...	Male ...	57,295	25,391	8,153	9,639	2,600	2,195	2,542	262
		Female ...	56,006	16,416	8,285	7,311	611	89	89	31
	Plateau Division ...	Male ...	15,377	6,559	2,250	2,563	699	491	497	59
		Female ...	15,527	4,862	2,292	2,230	226	43	50	21
	Chhattisgarh Division ...	Male ...	68,407	26,182	11,122	10,188	1,899	1,484	1,312	177
		Female ...	71,699	20,016	11,400	7,705	583	131	132	56
Lodhi ...	Province	Male ...	155,174	73,372	24,425	27,292	7,243	6,350	7,364	698
		Female ...	157,200	50,712	24,128	22,894	2,571	643	376	100
Lohar ...	Province	Male ...	90,929	41,501	14,098	16,143	4,223	3,487	3,057	493
		Female ...	90,382	31,759	14,776	13,313	1,810	864	814	182
Madgi ...	Chanda	Male ...	2,677	1,348	460	481	142	141	95	23
		Female ...	2,718	1,007	508	398	53	26	14	8
Majhwar ...	Total ...	Male ...	2,881	1,610	478	618	172	169	165	8
		Female ...	2,786	1,284	502	613	96	42	27	4
	Surguja	Male ...	1,404	770	230	313	96	76	54	1
		Female ...	1,385	637	249	321	47	9	11	...
	Udaipur	Male ...	1,477	840	248	305	76	93	111	7
		Female ...	1,401	647	253	292	49	33	16	4
Mala ...	Chanda	Male ...	1,935	1,274	170	158	475	370	33	68
		Female ...	1,885	485	238	137	57	23	25	10
Mali ...	Province	Male ...	279,589	104,740	42,969	41,516	8,393	5,984	4,965	913
		Female ...	281,643	74,955	43,396	26,622	2,279	1,133	997	528
Mallah ...	Total ...	Male ...	1,686	817	314	335	57	45	59	4
		Female ...	1,709	659	312	308	24	9	4	2
	Jubbulpore	Male ...	898	442	188	157	38	30	29	...
		Female ...	903	355	164	165	18	5	1	2

by age for selected castes.

Married.							Widowed.						
Total.	0—5.	5—12.	12—15.	15—20.	20—40.	40 and over.	Total.	0—5.	5—12.	12—15.	15—20.	20—40.	40 and over.
12	13	14	15	16	17	18	19	20	21	22	23	24	25
7,709	8	19	28	183	4,443	3,028	539	...	...	1	4	143	391
8,100	18	43	135	758	5,656	1,490	1,771	2	3	1	11	294	1,460
35,540	110	909	985	2,037	18,927	12,669	3,630	31	40	28	107	1,009	2,415
35,517	315	2,836	2,272	4,231	18,943	6,920	11,132	216	287	334	307	1,627	8,361
585	1	2	8	30	813	231	49	...	...	...	...	15	34
550	...	26	29	50	308	137	191	...	...	1	...	27	108
10,026	26	472	414	839	5,327	2,948	595	...	11	4	22	175	383
10,578	90	904	684	1,216	5,835	1,789	2,483	...	7	6	9	327	2,134
24,039	82	416	548	1,129	12,826	9,038	2,889	30	27	24	82	790	1,930
23,459	224	1,788	1,514	2,867	12,275	4,791	8,221	216	276	327	293	1,238	5,871
890	1	19	18	39	401	352	97	1	2	...	3	23	68
930	1	58	45	98	525	203	237	...	4	...	5	35	193
273	...	1	9	13	143	107	28	...	...	...	...	8	18
296	1	42	20	23	165	45	150	...	1	1	1	23	124
32,217	95	1,101	1,089	2,339	17,403	10,190	2,826	3	29	30	87	895	1,782
31,173	227	2,759	1,996	3,497	17,486	5,208	8,889	4	69	44	91	1,790	6,891
324,170	2,252	16,349	18,902	30,023	186,850	140,394	44,066	39	520	597	1,351	12,982	28,577
402,931	6,725	61,565	27,540	43,541	193,519	71,091	116,347	224	1,949	1,245	1,653	20,857	90,419
366,024	2,226	15,542	17,488	27,924	172,167	130,677	41,547	37	505	581	1,303	12,257	26,864
373,616	6,600	58,022	25,309	40,330	177,493	65,796	108,207	222	1,896	1,191	1,580	19,558	83,760
7,791	9	268	444	468	3,736	2,856	720	1	5	4	18	209	488
8,337	58	1,367	584	806	3,928	1,594	2,216	1	32	16	22	308	1,837
7,996	11	188	413	667	4,324	2,308	982	...	4	5	20	291	642
8,054	34	888	699	1,027	4,207	1,199	2,432	1	7	17	26	501	1,880
12,369	0	351	557	964	6,023	4,468	837	1	6	7	10	225	588
12,974	27	1,288	888	1,378	6,891	2,502	3,492	...	14	21	25	490	2,942
1,148	...	61	104	95	543	345	78	...	2	5	3	18	50
1,114	17	220	76	141	518	142	404	...	1	3	2	94	304
76,479	157	3,886	3,664	6,859	40,389	21,524	6,468	3	79	57	140	2,120	4,069
78,642	469	7,542	5,500	9,580	43,249	12,302	23,296	5	105	80	187	4,353	18,563
28,861	38	1,045	1,325	2,545	15,862	8,046	3,043	1	21	18	56	981	1,966
29,768	118	2,300	2,224	3,740	17,159	4,227	9,822	3	37	41	90	2,219	7,432
8,143	9	189	277	674	4,395	2,590	675	...	4	6	22	217	426
8,147	19	610	534	984	4,002	1,308	2,518	1	9	9	20	463	2,016
39,475	110	2,652	2,062	3,640	20,132	10,879	2,750	2	54	33	62	922	1,077
40,727	332	4,632	2,742	4,856	21,488	6,677	10,956	1	62	30	77	1,671	9,115
75,104	121	2,005	2,685	5,776	41,157	23,360	6,698	2	35	54	103	2,059	4,445
79,417	230	4,644	4,012	9,669	46,888	13,065	27,071	19	103	110	269	6,223	20,347
45,388	127	889	1,351	3,226	24,643	15,152	4,040	10	43	106	278	1,186	2,417
45,889	275	2,716	2,555	5,191	26,805	8,347	12,734	24	81	138	259	2,335	9,807
1,198	6	29	40	97	592	434	131	...	4	22	11	42	52
1,292	8	85	66	200	607	232	419	...	3	13	45	104	254
1,201	4	13	9	39	659	477	76	...	...	1	...	19	50
1,231	7	13	35	109	817	237	281	1	—	...	7	74	199
597	2	11	7	20	821	236	37	...	...	1	...	10	26
621	6	8	26	44	418	119	127	...	...	...	4	34	89
604	2	2	2	10	338	241	33	...	...	...	...	9	24
600	1	5	12	65	399	118	154	1	...	...	3	40	110
479	5	17	93	113	117	134	182	...	19	29	35	43	56
1,204	2	33	466	163	468	72	196	...	1	11	47	34	103
159,267	550	6,214	7,775	12,646	78,880	53,202	15,582	110	230	208	445	4,557	10,032
161,338	1,735	20,107	10,399	17,870	81,150	80,077	45,350	54	646	429	644	7,494	36,083
775	...	9	20	61	453	230	94	...	...	...	...	24	66
800	2	34	63	71	518	112	250	—	...	...	1	56	193
													8
412	...	2	8	27	244	131	44	...	...	...	...	16	12
406	1	20	23	39	264	69	142	...	...	...	1	28	13

TABLE XIV.—Civil condition

Caste, tribe or race.	Locality.	Sex.	Population dealt with.	Unmarried. Total.	0—5.	5—12.	12—15.	15—20.	20—40.	40 and over.
1	2	3	4	5	6	7	8	9	10	11
Mallah—(concld.)	Narsinghpur	Male ...	788	375	126	181	10	15	30	4
		Female ...	806	304	148	143	6	4	3	...
Mana ...	Nagpur Division ...	Male ...	20,985	8,645	3,386	3,353	841	582	419	64
		Female ...	21,864	6,325	3,494	2,565	162	30	47	27
Mang ...	Maratha Division ...	Male ...	37,943	15,466	6,415	6,098	1,231	788	767	167
		Female ...	39,207	11,326	6,570	3,984	193	136	340	97
Maratha ...	Province	Male ...	46,701	19,002	5,740	6,740	2,039	1,909	2,154	420
		Female ...	47,178	12,625	6,169	5,132	456	233	481	154
Mehra ...	Province	Male ...	575,028	249,238	97,499	95,055	22,325	17,967	14,683	1,709
		Female ...	589,355	189,433	98,824	74,428	7,729	3,308	4,035	1,109
Mehtar ...	Total ...	Male ...	*9,558*	*4,373*	*1,610*	*1,559*	*418*	*355*	*464*	*67*
		Female ...	*9,291*	*3,300*	*1,454*	*1,485*	*186*	*89*	*80*	*7*
	Nerbudda Valley ...	Male ...	6,948	3,156	1,114	1,109	310	256	326	41
		Female ...	6,720	2,304	1,030	1,008	97	40	37	2
	Nagpur	Male ...	1,447	587	220	184	51	45	73	14
		Female ...	1,363	490	218	184	42	17	25	4
	Raipur	Male ...	1,163	630	176	266	57	54	65	12
		Female ...	1,211	506	206	203	46	32	18	1
Mhali ...	Maratha Division ...	Male ...	18,843	7,029	2,598	2,880	667	438	369	77
		Female ...	18,103	4,647	2,037	1,775	99	48	66	22
Nai ...	Province	Male ...	72,797	30,708	10,591	12,220	3,175	2,342	2,113	207
		Female ...	73,293	22,216	10,973	0,772	855	293	244	79
Oraon (Animist).	Total ...	Male ...	*38,720*	*21,177*	*6,889*	*9,452*	*2,595*	*1,66[illegible]*	*652*	*87*
		Female ...	*37,994*	*17,377*	*7,282*	*7,464*	*1,278*	*877*	*306*	*170*
	Raigarh	Male ...	2,981	1,692	603	600	199	156	65	3
		Female ...	3,085	1,581	602	682	141	70	24	2
	Chota Nagpur States ...	Male ...	35,739	19,485	6,226	8,786	2,396	1,406	587	84
		Female ...	34,909	15,796	6,620	6,782	1,137	807	282	168
Oraon (Christian).	Jashpur	Male ...	18,302	10,734	3,717	4,278	1,422	875	402	40
		Female ...	18,060	9,114	3,940	3,970	760	304	111	29
Paik ...	Raipur	Male ...	1,540	895	265	323	107	101	91	8
		Female ...	1,635	741	291	334	58	28	25	5
Panka ...	Total ...	Male ...	*63,643*	*27,020*	*10,366*	*10,476*	*2,220*	*1,960*	*1,778*	*220*
		Female ...	*69,336*	*21,723*	*11,151*	*9,037*	*832*	*277*	*334*	*92*
	Mandla	Male ...	8,706	4,283	1,519	1,079	380	351	325	29
		Female ...	8,913	3,390	1,579	1,476	214	75	37	9
	Seoni	Male ...	1,185	592	184	224	69	49	59	7
		Female ...	1,254	457	190	209	30	6	11	5
	Balaghat	Male ...	1,451	746	240	260	53	81	93	19
		Female ...	1,510	540	240	248	31	10	9	2
	Chhattisgarh Division ...	Male ...	52,300	21,399	8,423	8,313	1,718	1,479	1,301	165
		Female ...	57,659	17,336	9,136	7,104	557	180	277	76
Rajbhar ...	Jubbulpore	Male ...	1,091	486	153	209	48	53	20	3
		Female ...	1,134	314	159	132	13	5	4	1
Rajjhar or Lajjhar.	Total ...	Male ...	*1,867*	*827*	*288*	*259*	*95*	*76*	*65*	*11*
		Female ...	*2,038*	*773*	*343*	*306*	*57*	*16*	*17*	*34*
	Seoni	Male ...	590	250	73	90	30	24	19	8
		Female ...	672	245	98	109	22	7	8	1
	Hoshangabad	Male ...	655	290	121	102	20	24	14	3
		Female ...	680	267	132	107	15	5	6	2
	Betul	Male ...	622	287	94	97	36	28	32	...
		Female ...	686	261	113	90	20	4	3	31
Rajput ...	Province	Male ...	223,103	96,904	29,747	34,086	9,891	8,962	12,394	1,824
		Female ...	217,220	64,194	30,668	28,126	3,301	928	[illegible]54	257
Rangari ...	Total ...	Male ...	*1,118*	*470*	*141*	*180*	*[illegible]*	*52*	*38*	*7*
		Female ...	*1,048*	*252*	*116*	*116*	*3*	*3*	*5*	*10*

by age for selected castes.

Married.							Widowed.						
Total.	0—5.	5—12.	12—15.	15—20.	20—40.	40 and over.	Total.	0—5.	5—12.	12—15.	15—20.	20—40.	40 and over.
12	13	14	15	16	17	18	19	20	21	22	23	24	25
363 394	... 1	7 24	18 40	24 32	209 254	105 43	50 108	... ...	... ...	... ...	... ...	12 28	38 80
11,544 11,914	38 35	165 925	207 705	870 1,246	5,889 6,766	4,285 2,147	796 3,625	8 1	3 15	4 24	14 13	166 428	601 3,084
21.075 22.224	95 476	680 2,808	935 1,405	1,543 2,987	11,003 11,401	6,819 3,152	1.402 5,657	15 15	33 127	32 41	46 149	392 1,200	884 4,119
24.481 23,659	92 314	463 2,194	601 1,716	1,278 2,956	12,692 11,841	9,355 4,038	3.218 10,894	3 24	31 75	26 120	68 221	881 2,015	2,209 7,830
303.895 315,835	925 2,517	6,328 25,825	9,378 18,315	18,677 36,393	101,063 175,408	107,524 57,377	21.895 84,087	48 104	146 860	289 1,040	565 2,529	5,801 15,145	15,046 64,400
4,53[illegible] *4,60[illegible]*	*6* *10*	*94* *217*	*89* *185*	*200* *510*	*2,590* *2,774*	*1,653* *866*	*653* *1,432*	... ...	*4* *2*	*3* *4*	*26* *12*	*308* *407*	*317* *1,007*
3.336 3,310	4 9	67 162	68 152	144 328	1,958 2,030	1,095 629	456 1,106	... ...	... 2	... 2	10 8	224 320	216 774
692 679	2 1	21 50	18 19	42 122	328 365	281 122	168 194	... ...	3 ...	3 2	10 3	67 48	85 141
504 573	... ...	6 5	3 14	14 60	304 379	177 115	29 132	... ...	1 ...	... ...	... 1	12 30	16 92
10.698 10.277	18 92	288 1,310	302 748	790 1,220	5,607 5,205	3,003 1,701	1.116 3.179	... 1	14 35	14 26	21 43	321 621	746 2,453
38.450 38.986	97 271	1,041 3,285	1.460 2,580	3,025 4,477	20,791 21,833	12,030 6,540	3.639 12,091	11 23	28 72	75 62	93 137	1,139 2,238	2.293 9,550
16,28[illegible] *17,029*	*58* *73*	*195* *340*	*797* *768*	*1,031* *3,030*	*8,272* *9,934*	*5,932* *2,558*	*1,266* *3,558*	... *4*	*46* *19*	*57* *53*	*222* *465*	*480* *1,124*	*411* *1,920*
1.230 1.270	... 1	8 4	9 24	41 135	776 808	396 238	59 234	... ...	... ...	... 1	1 2	18 50	40 181
15,058 15.759	58 72	190 342	788 744	900 2,885	7,496 9,066	5,530 2,650	1.196 3,354	... 4	40 19	87 52	221 406	471 1,074	371 1,739
7.224 7.345	... ...	20 111	72 263	327 843	4,357 4,701	2,448 1,427	344 1,601	... ...	2 4	6 12	9 24	113 307	214 1,254
618 660	... 1	2 6	2 14	14 112	405 437	195 90	27 234	... ...	... ...	... ...	... ...	6 49	21 185
34,065 *36,741*	*68* *93*	*735* *1,815*	*799* *1,565*	*2,126* *3,686*	*19,351* *22,633*	*10,963* *6,952*	*2,657* *10,592*	*5* *12*	*20* *38*	*16* *20*	*85* *66*	*1,097* *1,820*	*1,334* *8,944*
4.144 4.490	6 10	50 124	60 133	173 509	2,500 2,958	1,286 756	279 1,033	1 1	... 2	3 2	4 5	118 230	153 787
569 636	1 2	7 18	9 21	32 66	329 408	191 121	24 161	... ...	... 1	... ...	... 1	14 23	10 136
658 749	2 2	8 17	4 24	23 82	374 483	247 141	47 221	... ...	... ...	1 1	1 ...	15 37	30 183
28,694 30,846	59 79	673 1,659	717 1,875	1,898 3,029	16,118 18,734	9,229 5,970	2,207 9.477	4 11	20 35	12 17	80 52	950 1,524	1,141 7,838
558 570	... ...	13 44	17 27	50 72	345 354	133 73	47 250	... ...	2 ...	... 1	... 1	17 67	28 181
979 *964*	*4* *2*	*10* *29*	*16* *30*	*30* *99*	*663* *647*	*355* *157*	*61* *301*	... ...	... ...	... ...	... *2*	*18* *42*	*43* *257*
310 330	... 1	... 10	4 10	7 30	179 205	120 74	30 97	... ...	... ...	... ...	... 1	11 6	19 90
354 343	4 1	10 19	10 15	20 38	211 222	99 48	11 70	... ...	... ...	... ...	... ...	2 10	9 60
315 291	... ...	... ...	2 5	3 31	174 220	136 35	20 134	... ...	... ...	— ...	... 1	5 26	15 107
114,124 111,179	317 575	4,001 8,706	4,131 7,829	7,787 13,223	59,900 60,906	37,988 19,940	12,075 41,847	11 60	67 202	85 244	261 550	3,520 9,218	8,131 31,578
544 *569*	*1* *1*	*5* *53*	*17* *33*	*35* *63*	*261* *315*	*226* *105*	*104* *227*	... ...	... *2*	... *1*	*2* *4*	*27* *45*	*76* *175*

TABLE XIV.—Civil condition

Caste, tribe or race.	Locality.	Sex.	Population dealt with.	Unmarried. Total.	0–5.	5–12.	12–15.	15–20.	20–40.	40 and over.
1	2	3	4	5	6	7	8	9	10	11
Bangari—(concld.)	Nimar	Male ...	486	202	55	86	22	26	9	4
		Female ...	467	115	57	55	2	...	...	1
	Wardha	Male ...	632	268	86	94	30	26	29	3
		Female ...	581	137	58	61	1	3	5	9
Sali ...	Total ...	Male ...	*1,602*	*583*	*220*	*209*	*66*	*27*	*49*	*12*
		Female ...	*1,647*	*401*	*212*	*150*	*13*	*7*	*12*	*7*
	Amraoti	Male ...	990	343	141	111	38	17	26	10
		Female ...	1,016	236	125	83	10	4	8	6
	Buldana	Male ...	612	240	79	96	28	10	23	2
		Female ...	631	165	87	67	3	3	4	1
Sawara (Hindu).	Total ...	Male ...	*11,381*	*5,491*	*2,228*	*2,143*	*397*	*350*	*333*	*41*
		Female ...	*12,212*	*4,741*	*2,436*	*1,996*	*196*	*47*	*61*	*6*
	Saugor	Male ...	8,574	4,149	1,714	1,605	291	257	251	31
		Female ...	8,951	3,462	1,828	1,440	115	27	49	3
	Damoh	Male ...	2,807	1,342	514	538	106	93	81	10
		Female ...	3,261	1,279	607	556	81	20	12	3
Sunar ...	Province	Male ...	63,830	27,549	8,061	10,684	3,045	2,376	2,350	433
		Female ...	63,034	18,240	9,010	8,145	560	206	230	89
Takari ...	Akola	Male ...	1,720	787	270	307	89	71	45	5
		Female ...	1,603	512	252	215	15	17	8	5
Teli ...	Province	Male ...	427,124	164,263	70,609	65,417	12,660	8,250	6,321	997
		Female ...	442,212	123,097	70,985	46,266	2,957	943	1,348	598
Waddar ...	Yeotmal	Male ...	2,181	1,149	456	398	101	84	98	12
		Female ...	1,991	816	402	297	29	17	59	12
Wanjari ...	Berar	Male ...	16,367	7,270	2,885	2,602	607	506	611	59
		Female ...	16,420	5,057	2,661	1,682	184	153	243	134
Anglo-Indian (or Eurasian).	Province	Male ...	1,883	1,290	232	230	188	229	361	41
		Female ...	1,605	946	254	233	132	148	149	30
Indian Christian (other than Oraon converts).	Province	Male ...	13,576	7,680	2,052	2,310	936	1,282	1,019	81
		Female ...	12,642	5,981	2,002	1,967	688	792	395	47

by age for selected castes.

Married.							Widowed.						
Total.	0—5.	5—12.	12—15.	15—20.	20—40.	40 and over.	Total.	0—5.	5—12.	12—15.	15—20.	20—40.	40 and over.
12	13	14	15	16	17	18	19	20	21	22	23	24	25
253	1	4	14	18	121	95	31	...	...	...	2	9	20
259	...	22	19	23	151	44	93	...	1	...	1	20	71
291	...	1	3	17	140	130	73	...	...	...	...	18	55
310	1	81	13	40	164	61	134	...	1	1	3	25	104
870	2	9	26	62	423	345	149	...	1	1	5	37	105
86[illegible]	2	117	55	107	446	135	375	...	5	5	6	63	300
538	1	4	17	40	257	219	109	...	...	...	4	30	75
549	1	67	35	66	280	100	231	...	3	8	3	83	189
332	1	5	9	22	166	129	40	...	1	1	1	7	30
319	1	50	23	41	166	38	147	...	2	2	3	29	111
6,658	6	24	45	272	3,550	1,655	832	...	1	...	5	106	220
6,066	6	119	215	679	4,232	815	1,405	2	4	3	10	375	1,011
4,184	3	19	38	213	2,671	1,240	241	...	1	...	5	77	158
4,461	5	101	172	530	3,108	545	1,028	2	8	2	5	288	728
1,374	3	5	10	56	879	418	91	...	...	...	...	29	62
1,605	1	18	43	149	1,124	270	377	...	1	1	5	87	283
32,649	189	555	1,090	2,564	17,230	11,012	3,632	6	22	39	120	1,090	2,855
32,744	210	3,070	2,388	4,186	17,439	5,451	12,050	10	91	131	238	2,626	8,954
881	2	6	11	49	476	337	52	...	...	...	...	15	37
873	13	63	53	106	475	163	218	8	...	...	5	46	159
245,382	812	11,911	12,407	21,593	123,908	74,751	17,479	21	217	209	455	5,455	11,122
255,211	2,258	28,857	17,667	28,051	133,743	44,685	63,904	65	589	470	640	9,005	52,535
940	5	23	24	67	476	345	92	...	1	1	...	34	56
917	37	100	36	91	550	103	258	...	1	...	15	49	193
8,396	36	335	439	546	4,294	2,746	701	...	9	14	32	240	406
8,950	225	1,127	748	1,238	4,290	1,313	2,413	2	47	118	152	408	1,086
535	...	...	...	3	275	257	58	...	2	...	1	15	40
520	2	2	2	31	373	110	139	...	...	...	1	26	112
5,444	4	36	96	220	3,620	1,459	452	2	4	...	9	172	265
5,232	5	136	141	829	3,448	673	1,429	...	3	5	14	344	1,063

TABLE XV.—Occupation or means of livelihood.

Part A.—General Table.

TABLE XV.—Occupation or means

	CLASS ...	...						CLASS A.—PRODUCTION			
	SUB-CLASS ...	...						...			
	ORDER ...	...						...			
		TOTAL POPULATION.						TOTAL			
Serial number.	DISTRICT, CITY OR STATE.	Total workers and dependants.	Actual workers. Total. Males.	Actual workers. Total. Females.	Actual workers. Partially agriculturists. Males.	Actual workers. Partially agriculturists. Females.	Dependants.	Total workers and dependants.	Actual workers. Total. Males.	Actual workers. Total. Females.	Actual workers. Partially agricul[turists]. Males.
	1	2	3	4	5	6	7	8	9	10	11
	Central Provinces and Berar ...	**16,033,310**	**5,266,491**	**4,266,409**	**170,424**	**72,343**	**6,500,410**	**12,782,215**	**4,118,917**	**3,690,363**	**26,964**
	C. P. British Districts and Berar ...	**13,916,308**	**4,607,093**	**3,760,178**	**160,615**	**68,989**	**5,549,037**	**10,949,684**	**3,549,104**	**3,252,874**	**25,052**
	C. P. British Districts ...	**10,859,146**	**3,548,572**	**3,008,991**	**128,554**	**58,709**	**4,301,583**	**8,555,552**	**2,747,712**	**2,577,821**	**21,991**
	JUBBULPORE DIVISION	*2,431,064*	*784,735*	*614,897*	*35,412*	*11,109*	*1,021,432*	*1,810,171*	*574,676*	*513,821*	*3,480*
1	Saugor ...	541,410	180,008	127,273	11,916	3,752	234,120	376,160	122,998	100,824	855
2	Damoh ...	333,047	106,509	72,530	8 790	2,205	154,008	239,882	76,078	57,376	777
3	Jubbulpore ...	745,892	240,047	180,410	10,856	3,977	325,435	513,931	159,187	143,704	1,314
	JUBBULPORE CITY ...	*100,651*	*37,365*	*9,933*	*142*	*21*	*53,354*	*3,026*	*2,702*	*1,121*	*13*
4	Mandla ...	405,234	128,784	115,974	2,181	626	160,476	349,101	109,079	105,393	452
5	Seoni ...	395,481	129,387	118,710	1,660	400	147,384	331,097	107,333	106,524	82
	NERBUDDA DIVISION	*2,031,477*	*696,221*	*548,350*	*22,256*	*10,616*	*836,906*	*1,572,431*	*514,804*	*463,501*	*2,181*
6	Narsinghpur ...	325,677	105,035	81,404	6,446	3,290	139,238	232,237	75,077	63,495	711
7	Hoshangabad ...	457,395	154,918	104,060	6,318	2,527	198,417	313,126	105,117	82,208	512
8	Nimar ...	391,071	134,629	100,235	2,995	984	156,207	288,874	96,346	86,468	236
9	Betul ...	390,386	130,959	115,388	3,398	2,464	144,039	315,575	102,281	100,906	446
10	Chhindwara ...	510,948	170,680	147,263	3,098	1,351	190,005	422,619	135,083	130,634	276
	NAGPUR DIVISION ...	*3,109,53[illegible]*	*1,049,619*	*907,346*	*45,936*	*29,229*	*1,152,973*	*2,327,297*	*768,720*	*762,819*	*10,929*
11	Wardha ...	450,796	160,938	125,206	4,617	1,841	173,652	357,572	121,208	112,456	867
12	Nagpur ...	809,901	279,291	223,943	7,381	3,069	306,667	519,756	174,347	174,288	844
	NAGPUR CITY ...	*101,416*	*36,053*	*14,843*	*371*	*28*	*50,520*	*5,713*	*1,866*	*1,124*	*14*
13	Chanda ...	677,544	224,737	200,028	19,171	14,280	252,779	520,805	170,261	168,934	6,095
14	Bhandara ...	773,677	256,477	237,793	13,740	8,031	279,407	605,102	197,431	201,627	2,622
15	Balaghat ...	388,920	128,076	120,376	4,027	2,C0[illegible]	140,468	324,062	105,473	105,515	501
	CHHATTISGARH DIVISION	*3,246,767*	*1,018,097*	*938,394*	*21,950*	*7,755*	*1,290,272*	*2,845,653*	*889,513*	*837,380*	*5,401*
16	Raipur ...	1,324,856	420,260	387,489	9,020	3,637	517,107	1,144,073	362,868	341,426	2,869
17	Bilaspur ...	1,146,223	351,371	314,940	7,807	3,009	479,912	1,024,395	310,933	286,205	1,666
18	Drug ...	775,688	246,466	235,960	4,223	1,109	293,253	677,185	215,712	209,749	866
	Berar ...	**3,057,162**	**1,058,521**	**751,187**	**32,061**	**10,280**	**1,247,454**	**2,394,132**	**801,392**	**675,053**	**3,061**
19	Amraoti ...	875,904	304,082	192,026	9,113	3,829	379,796	668,389	225,602	166,410	1,594
20	Akola ...	788,863	277,217	188,479	9,906	2,721	323,167	615,810	208,728	169,053	465
21	Buldana ...	669,182	227,695	169,709	8,707	2,714	271,778	519,812	171,974	152,584	462
22	Yeotmal ...	723,213	249,527	200,973	4,335	1,516	272,713	589,921	195,088	187,006	540
	Feudatory States ...	**2,117,002**	**659,398**	**506,231**	**9,809**	**3,354**	**951,373**	**1,832,531**	**569,813**	**437,489**	**1,912**
23	Makrai ...	15,021	4,931	4,043	134	19	6,047	11,562	3,728	3,556	13
24	Bastar ...	433,310	135,802	117,279	777	286	180,229	381,328	119,537	101,865	98
25	Kanker ...	127,014	40,800	38,014	279	157	48,200	110,200	35,288	33,693	42
26	Nandgaon ...	167,362	51,785	49,629	838	304	65,948	140,321	42,853	43,782	127
27	Khairagarh ...	155,471	49,133	44,383	762	248	61,955	120,007	41,006	38,135	145
28	Chhuikhadan ...	31,150	9,521	7,918	180	32	13,711	25,150	7,775	9,507	21
29	Kawardha ...	77,654	24,486	22,521	560	139	30,647	66,364	21,026	19,812	122
30	Sakti ...	34,547	10,415	9,298	192	76	14,834	31,159	9,242	8,426	58
31	Raigarh ...	218,860	68,153	59,349	1,918	854	91,358	183,918	57,558	49,910	546
32	Sarangarh ...	102,071	31,443	23,961	899	261	46,667	86,363	27,240	18,663	234
33	Chang Bhakar ...	24,421	8,434	7,032	173	91	8,955	21,200	7,302	6,109	7
34	Korea ...	62,107	20,064	14,615	284	53	27,428	53,830	17,193	12,587	70
35	Surguja ...	428,706	127,680	46,196	794	127	254,827	386,790	113,999	41,923	70
36	Udaipur ...	64,853	20,072	13,873	189	53	31,408	56,029	17,337	11,218	40
37	Jashpur ...	174,458	56,679	48,620	1,821	654	69,159	149,310	48,729	41,243	319

# of livelihood, Part A.—General Table.

OF RAW MATERIALS.

CLASS A.		Sub-Class I.—Exploitation of the surface of the earth. — Total Sub-Class I.						Order I.—Pasture and Agriculture. — Total Order I.						
...ially ...turists	Dependants.	Total workers and dependants.	Actual workers. Total.		Actual workers. Partially agriculturists		Dependants.	Total workers and dependants.	Actual workers. Total.		Actual workers. Partially agriculturists		
Females.			Males.	Females.	Males.	Females.			Males.	Females.	Males.	Females.	Serial number.
12	13	14	15	16	17	18	19	20	21	22	23	24	
15,887	**4,972,935**	**12,752,240**	**4,106,968**	**3,682,691**	**26,615**	**15,719**	**4,962,581**	**12,618,871**	**4,055,214**	**3,660,479**	**13,424**	**8,148**	
15,230	**4,147,706**	**10,919,927**	**3,537,214**	**3,245,282**	**24,711**	**15,079**	**4,137,431**	**10,793,698**	**3,487,904**	**3,224,441**	**11,787**	**7,586**	
13,985	**3,230,019**	**8,526,379**	**2,735,996**	**2,570,354**	**21,656**	**13,835**	**3,220,029**	**8,416,840**	**2,693,749**	**2,551,410**	**10,421**	**7,054**	
2,114	*731,675*	*1,808,437*	*674,034*	*513,449*	*3,450*	*2,101*	*730,964*	*1,803,344*	*571,804*	*512,549*	*3,211*	*2,023*	
612	152,338	375,760	122,888	100,700	840	603	152,160	375,346	122,738	100,670	807	594	1
447	106,428	239,755	76,070	57,334	774	440	106,351	239,049	76,026	57,320	771	446	2
791	211,040	512,806	158,683	143,512	1,294	791	210,611	512,280	158,460	143,459	1,273	789	3
2	*4,303*	*7,960*	*2,693*	*1,092*	*13*	*2*	*4,175*	*7,786*	*2,627*	*1,086*	*12*	*2*	
242	134,629	349,038	109,064	105,370	451	241	134,598	346,278	108,150	104,825	316	181	4
20	117,240	331,088	107,329	106,521	82	20	117,238	328,791	106,430	106,269	44	13	5
2,557	*593,520*	*1,567,525*	*512,905*	*463,758*	*2,093*	*2,532*	*591,535*	*1,558,170*	*509,058*	*461,730*	*1,621*	*2,371*	
766	93,665	229,487	73,987	63,044	654	742	92,456	228,837	73,681	63,015	590	741	6
415	125,801	313,024	105,080	82,182	512	415	125,702	310,966	104,214	82,042	349	380	7
147	106,060	288,860	96,343	86,468	230	147	106,049	287,493	95,676	86,409	163	133	8
1,073	112,298	315,524	102,256	100,987	446	1,072	112,281	313,583	101,535	100,614	400	1,015	9
156	156,002	420,630	135,239	130,104	241	156	155,287	417,291	133,952	129,656	119	102	10
7,482	*795,758*	*2,305,135*	*759,699*	*756,802*	*10,722*	*7,379*	*788,637*	*2,281,606*	*731,011*	*743,596*	*1,362*	*1,384*	
466	123,900	357,564	121,205	112,453	866	466	123,906	352,145	119,083	111,703	148	59	11
659	171,121	510,263	170,274	171,592	749	611	168,397	500,424	166,487	170,254	358	345	12
1	*2,724*	*5,674*	*1,852*	*1,124*	*14*	*1*	*2,698*	*5,394*	*1,778*	*1,063*	*9*	*1*	
4,680	181,610	519,104	169,457	168,032	6,002	4,680	180,715	492,683	159,663	162,965	360	429	13
1,345	206,044	509,217	195,173	199,981	2,540	1,315	204,062	574,883	185,190	193,479	381	408	14
323	113,074	318,900	103,590	103,844	475	208	111,556	311,473	100,583	102,405	120	45	15
1,834	*1,118,760*	*2,845,269*	*889,358*	*837,312*	*5,391*	*1,823*	*1,118,593*	*2,834,716*	*881,876*	*833,229*	*4,327*	*1,376*	
960	439,779	1,143,797	362,745	341,308	2,866	959	439,654	1,133,064	359,151	339,387	2,202	685	16
657	427,257	1,024,360	310,918	286,201	1,666	657	427,240	1,019,891	309,265	285,358	1,318	537	17
217	251,724	677,113	215,605	209,719	859	207	251,609	670,863	213,400	208,484	677	154	18
1,245	**917,687**	**2,393,548**	**801,218**	**674,928**	**3,055**	**1,244**	**917,402**	**2,376,838**	**794,155**	**673,031**	**1,366**	**532**	
838	276,577	668,483	225,561	166,309	1,501	837	276,523	662,605	223,064	165,481	829	405	19
68	238,029	615,537	208,657	168,978	463	68	237,902	612,814	207,456	168,782	172	35	20
118	195,254	519,657	171,917	152,558	461	118	195,182	518,360	171,369	152,427	309	60	21
221	207,827	589,871	195,083	186,993	540	221	207,795	583,080	192,266	186,341	56	32	22
657	**825,229**	**1,832,313**	**569,754**	**437,409**	**1,904**	**640**	**825,150**	**1,825,173**	**567,310**	**436,038**	**1,637**	**562**	
...	4,278	11,562	3,728	3,550	13	...	4,278	11,460	3,678	3,553	12	...	23
58	159,926	381,323	119,534	101,864	98	58	150,925	380,204	119,183	101,709	57	57	24
38	41,219	110,178	35,275	33,690	42	38	41,213	109,254	34,967	33,519	31	37	25
69	53,686	140,315	42,852	43,782	127	69	53,681	139,232	42,456	43,656	80	64	26
71	49,866	128,997	41,001	38,134	144	71	40,862	128,269	40,717	38,045	122	68	27
4	10,868	25,142	7,770	6,504	21	4	10,868	24,955	7,704	6,490	17	4	28
40	25,526	66,364	21,026	19,812	122	40	25,526	65,872	20,854	19,735	114	37	29
6	13,431	31,159	9,242	8,486	58	6	13,431	31,122	9,227	8,485	55	6	30
152	76,450	183,900	57,556	49,900	546	152	76,444	183,290	57,365	49,728	515	115	31
31	40,460	86,363	27,240	18,663	234	31	40,400	86,052	27,118	18,530	215	22	32
24	7,789	21,200	7,302	6,100	7	24	7,789	21,144	7,282	6,087	5	23	33
15	24,050	53,820	17,192	12,587	70	15	24,050	53,814	17,187	12,587	67	15	34
9	230,868	386,790	113,999	41,923	70	9	230,868	386,732	113,975	41,913	70	9	35
8	27,474	55,946	17,326	11,182	40	8	27,438	55,817	17,301	11,156	37	4	36
132	59,338	149,245	48,711	41,217	312	115	59,317	147,930	48,316	40,839	240	101	37

TABLE XV.—Occupation or means

Serial number.	CLASS ... / SUB-CLASS ... / ORDER ... / DISTRICT, CITY OR STATE.	... / ... / ... / Order I.—Pasture and Agriculture. Total Order I—(concld.) Dependants.	CLASS A.—PRODUCTION. Sub-Class I. Exploitation. Order I.—Pasture. Sub-Order (a).— Total Sub-Order (a.) Total workers and dependants.	Actual workers. Total. Males.	Actual workers. Total. Females.	Partially agriculturists. Males.	Partially agriculturists. Females.	Dependants.	1.—Income from rent of agricultural land. Total workers and dependants.	Actual workers. Total. Males.	Actual workers. Total. Females.	Partially agriculturists. Males.	Partially agriculturists. Females.	Dependants.
	1	25	26	27	28	29	30	31	32	33	34	35	36	37
	Central Provinces and Berar ...	**4,903,178**	**12,051,933**	**3,782.755**	**3.561.762**	**575**	**23**	**4.707 416**	**129,911**	**32,142**	**25,782**	...	...	**71.987**
	C. P. British Districts and Berar ...	**4,081,353**	**10,330,646**	**3,258.403**	**3,145,066**	**557**	**22**	**3,927,177**	**122,417**	**30.888**	**25,221**	...	...	**66,308**
	C. P. British Districts	**3,171,681**	**8,011,974**	**2,499,097**	**2,476,763**	**528**	**22**	**3.036,114**	**80,948**	**22.199**	**12,546**	...	...	**46,203**
	JUBBULPORE DIVISION	*717,991*	*1,712,307*	*532,357*	*493,579*	*137*	...	*650,141*	*14,479*	*3,655*	*1,229*	...	...	*9,595*
1	Saugor ..	151,938	354,718	113,091	96,281	47	...	145,316	3,361	877	322	...	...	2,102
2	Damoh ...	106,297	223,714	69,235	53,759	24	...	100,720	2,926	795	271	...	...	1,860
3	Jubbulpore ...	210,361	488,083	148,471	138,317	58	...	201,205	5,607	1,335	413	...	...	3,850
	JUBBULPORE CITY ...	*4,073*	*5,304*	*1,707*	*730*	*5*	...	*2,807*	*773*	*167*	*34*	...	...	*672*
4	Mandla ...	138,308	328,573	101,370	101,006	6	...	126,197	1,473	378	96	...	...	999
5	Seoni ...	116,092	317,219	100,120	104,510	2	...	112,583	1,112	270	127	...	...	715
	NERBUDDA DIVISION...	*587,376*	*1,481,225*	*471,095*	*444,703*	*70*	*4*	*565,368*	*22,269*	*6,734*	*3,092*	...	...	*12,393*
6	Narsinghpur ...	92,141	213,356	67,238	58,431	25	...	87,687	4,364	1,234	585	.	...	2,545
7	Hoshangabad ...	124,710	293,823	96,224	77,500	30	...	120,039	8,549	2,011	1,106	...	...	4,842
8	Nimar ...	105,408	276,375	90,569	84,580	...	4	101,226	2,722	811	424	...	...	1,487
9	Betul ...	111,434	295,200	91,842	96,668	3	...	106,690	4,130	1,253	621	...	...	2,256
10	Chhindwara ...	153,683	402,471	125,222	127,523	6	...	149,720	2,504	875	356	...	..	1,273
	NAGPUR DIVISION ...	*756,701*	*2,132,762*	*670,681*	*732,599*	*217*	*3*	*739,182*	*33,097*	*9,059*	*7,125*	...	...	*16,913*
11	Wardha ...	121,354	330,520	112,502	110,197	43	...	116,821	7,122	2,429	810	..	...	3,883
12	Nagpur ...	163,683	472,059	148,748	166,278	59	2	157,033	9,631	3,118	1,097	...	...	5,416
	NAGPUR CITY. ...	*2,556*	*3,568*	*1,153*	*708*	*6*	...	*1,707*	*371*	*92*	*46*	...	...	*234*
13	Chanda ...	170,055	468,052	144,078	160,900	40	1	163,005	2,201	681	261	...	...	1,259
14	Bhandara ...	193,214	551,052	100,650	193,878	68	...	187,524	12,904	2,490	4,823	...	...	5,641
15	Balaghat ...	108,395	302,079	95,703	101,337	7	...	105,039	1,149	341	134	...	...	674
	CHHATTISGARH DIVISION.	*1,109,613*	*2,685,680*	*825,034*	*805,523*	*104*	*15*	*1,055,123*	*11,103*	*2,701*	*1,100*	..	...	*7,302*
16	Raipur ...	435,426	1,071,105	334,019	325,718	47	15	411,368	4,327	1,166	362	...	—	2,799
17	Bilaspur ...	425,268	982,103	294,403	277,488	41	...	410,272	3,274	814	497	...	...	1,963
18	Drug ...	248,919	632,412	196,612	202,317	16	...	233,483	3,502	721	241	...	...	2,540
	Berar ...	**909,672**	**2.318.672**	**759,306**	**668.303**	**29**	...	**891.063**	**41.469**	**8.689**	**12.675**	...	...	**20.105**
19	Amraoti ...	274,009	612,702	212,807	163,091	1	...	266,804	8,709	2,694	939	...	...	5,157
20	Akola ...	236,576	601,405	200,246	167,862	1	...	233,207	14,983	2,336	7,115	...	...	5,532
21	Buldana ...	194,163	507,955	164,166	151,702	27	...	192,087	10,347	1,505	3,920	...	..	4,922
22	Yeotmal ...	204,479	566,610	182,087	185,648	...	...	198,875	7,349	2,154	701	...		4,494
	Feudatory States ...	**821.825**	**1.721,287**	**524.352**	**416.696**	**18**	**1**	**780 239**	**7.494**	**1.254**	**561**	...	...	**5.679**
23	Makrai ...	4,235	10,624	3,354	3,273	...	...	3,997	14	5	2	...	...	7
24	Bastar ...	159,422	364,013	113,158	97,872	...	1	152,983	178	52	15	...	...	111
25	Kanker ...	40,763	101,835	32,159	31,497	2	...	38,179	136	40	9	...	...	87
26	Nandgaon ...	53,120	126,913	36,128	41,351	6	...	49,434	55	13	0	...	...	36
27	Khairagarh ...	49,507	115,569	34,289	36,033	2	...	45,247	3,465	855	471	...	...	2,139
28	Chhuikhadan ...	10,761	22,320	6,550	6,183	...	...	9,587	18	2	3	...	...	8
29	Kawardha ...	25,288	61,402	19,106	18,821	1	...	23,475	130	34	23	...	...	73
30	Sakti ...	13,410	30,281	8,583	8,355	1	...	13,043	...	...	...	...	...	...
31	Raigarh ...	76,197	173,978	54,070	47,689	...	...	72,019	35	9	2	...	...	24
32	Sarangarh ...	40,304	82,212	25,451	18,004	2	...	38,757	12	2	2	...	...	8
33	Chang Bhakar ...	7,775	19,255	6,313	5,769	...	...	7,173	32	14	3	...	...	21
34	Korea ...	24,040	50,040	15,340	11,954	4	...	22,446	115	57	12	...	...	46
35	Surguja ...	230,838	372,877	100,379	40,633	...	...	222,866	281	98	2	...	...	181
36	Udaipur ...	27,390	51,714	15,900	10,526	...	...	25,288	93	59	7	..	...	27
37	Jashpur ...	58,775	138,254	43,972	38,530	...	...	55,746	2,929	14	4	...	...	2,911

# of livelihood, Part A.—General Table.

OF RAW MATERIALS—(*continued*).

of the surface of the earth—(*continued*).

and agriculture—(*continued*).

Ordinary cultivation.

2.—Ordinary Cultivators.						3—Agents, Managers of landed estates (not Planters), clerks, rent collectors, etc.						4.—Farm servants and field labourers.			
Total workers and dependants.	Actual workers. Total. Males.	Actual workers. Total. Females.	Actual workers. Partially agriculturists. Males.	Actual workers. Partially agriculturists. Females.	Dependants.	Total workers and dependants.	Actual workers. Total. Males.	Actual workers. Total. Females.	Actual workers. Partially agriculturists. Males.	Actual workers. Partially agriculturists. Females.	Dependants.	Total workers and dependants.	Actual workers. Total. Males.	Actual workers. Total. Females.	Serial number.
38	39	40	41	42	43	44	45	46	47	48	49	50	51	52	
7,472,405	**2,350,713**	**1,756,106**	...	..	**3,365,586**	**18,862**	**7,473**	**364**	**575**	**23**	**11,025**	**4,430,755**	**1,392,427**	**1,779,510**	
6,146,166	**1,946,335**	**1,462,362**	...	...	**2,737,469**	**18,086**	**7,184**	**352**	**557**	**22**	**10,550**	**4,043,977**	**1,273,996**	**1,657,131**	
5,149,115	**1,602,693**	**1,361,254**	...	...	**2,185,168**	**17,354**	**6,789**	**347**	**528**	**22**	**10,218**	**2,764,557**	**867,416**	**1,102,616**	
1,093,824	*343,972*	*261,955*	...	...	*486,594*	*3,243*	*1,305*	*30*	*137*	...	*1,905*	*601,761*	*188,352*	*230,662*	
218,384	69,195	44,533	...	...	90,656	875	370	1	47	...	502	137,100	42,649	51,425	1
135,190	43,456	18,014	...	...	73,720	647	199	4	24	...	444	84,951	24,785	35,470	2
304,157	93,516	71,072	...	...	139,569	1,202	579	21	58	...	662	177,057	53,041	66,811	3
3,078	*1,087*	*352*	...	...	*1,639*	*294*	*93*	...	*5*	...	*203*	*1,159*	*361*	*344*	
246,044	76,457	72,525	...	...	97,062	179	52	...	6	...	127	80,877	24,488	28,385	4
194,049	61,348	55,814	...	...	76,887	282	108	4	2	...	170	121,776	38,394	48,571	5
897,043	*284,931*	*213,342*	...	...	*399,770*	*3,461*	*1,293*	*61*	*70*	*4*	*2,107*	*558,452*	*178,087*	*229,267*	
119,613	37,617	22,912	...	...	59,084	552	196	4	25	...	352	88,827	28,191	34,930	6
156,158	50,282	27,067	...	...	78,809	2,104	818	45	36	...	1,246	127,012	42,518	49,342	7
165,989	55,540	43,604	...	...	69,836	155	37	12	...	4	106	104,509	34,172	40,540	8
196,105	61,584	55,160	...	...	79,361	370	125	...	3	...	245	94,595	28,880	40,887	9
256,178	79,890	63,509	...	...	112,680	280	122	...	6	...	158	143,500	44,326	63,568	10
1,186,435	*379,055*	*332,092*	...	...	*475,288*	*5,632*	*2,256*	*54*	*217*	*3*	*3,332*	*907,598*	*250,311*	*398,328*	
129,668	43,568	22,186	...	...	63,914	909	334	3	43	...	572	201,821	66,171	87,198	11
226,359	75,807	52,086	...	...	98,466	1,615	683	22	59	2	910	234,454	69,140	113,073	12
1,299	*475*	*102*	..	...	*722*	*368*	*131*	*2*	*6*	...	*245*	*1,530*	*465*	*559*	
282,727	89,884	83,222	...	...	109,621	1,150	417	5	40	1	734	181,968	53,006	77,421	13
343,585	106,446	109,249	...	...	127,890	1,391	531	9	68	...	851	193,082	60,183	79,806	14
204,096	63,350	65,358	...	...	75,388	561	291	15	7	...	255	96,273	31,721	35,830	15
1,972,813	*594,735*	*554,862*	...	...	*823,216*	*5,018*	*1,932*	*202*	*104*	*15*	*2,884*	*696,746*	*225,666*	*249,359*	
749,339	228,313	212,727	...	...	308,299	2,723	1,067	148	47	15	1,508	314,716	103,473	112,481	16
792,611	235,220	212,340	...	..	345,051	1,517	562	33	41	...	922	184,761	57,807	64,018	17
430,863	131,202	129,795	...	...	169,866	778	303	21	16	...	454	197,269	64,386	72,260	18
997,051	**343,642**	**101,108**	...	...	**552,301**	**732**	**395**	**5**	**29**	..	**332**	**1,279,420**	**406,580**	**554,515**	
258,050	81,743	16,935	..	...	159,372	62	16	2	1	...	44	375,800	128,354	145,215	19
270,731	94,019	31,502	...	...	145,210	67	18	3	1	...	46	315,624	103,873	120,242	20
254,745	87,691	38,121	...	...	128,933	356	223	...	27	..	133	242,507	74,747	109,661	21
213,525	80,189	14,550	...	...	118,786	247	138	...	...	...	109	345,489	99,606	170,397	22
1,326,239	**404,378**	**293,744**	...	...	**628,117**	**776**	**289**	**12**	**18**	**1**	**475**	**386,778**	**118,431**	**122,379**	
7,056	2,130	2,048	...	...	2,878	20	4	...	...	...	25	8,525	1,215	1,223	23
285,670	88,608	75,281	...	...	121,787	80	24	3	...	1	53	78,079	24,474	22,573	24
72,875	22,674	21,242	...	...	28,959	88	37	4	2	...	47	28,736	9,408	10,242	25
82,523	23,030	23,820	...	...	34,767	117	48	2	6	...	67	44,218	12,131	17,523	26
73,143	22,000	21,070	...	...	30,061	199	88	1	2	...	110	38,762	11,340	14,485	27
14,663	4,222	3,505	...	...	6,840	26	5	...	...	...	21	7,618	2,321	2,585	28
46,665	14,481	13,448	...	...	18,736	29	10	...	1	...	19	14,578	4,581	5,350	29
24,193	6,973	6,377	...	...	10,843	25	2	...	1	...	23	6,063	1,908	1,978	30
133,857	40,952	34,762	...	...	58,143	55	13	...	...	...	42	40,031	13,096	13,125	31
55,938	17,116	9,600	..	...	29,126	9	4	...	2	...	5	26,253	8,329	8,306	32
12,556	4,492	2,852	...	...	5,212	...	...	...	...	...	...	6,061	1,807	2,914	33
36,894	11,700	7,372	...	...	17,816	61	35	...	4	...	26	12,070	3,842	4,570	34
315,504	92,216	80,506	...	...	192,872	37	10	2	...	...	25	56,965	17,055	10,123	35
43,736	13,325	8,379	...	...	22,032	18	9	...	...	...	9	7,867	2,507	2,140	36
120,870	39,541	33,200	...	...	48,039	3	...	...	...	...	3	14,452	4,417	5,242	37

TABLE XV.—Occupation or means

Serial number.	CLASS ... / SUB-CLASS ... / ORDER ...	CLASS A— PRODUCTION / Sub-Class I.—Exploitation / Order I.—Pasture / Sub-Order (a).— / Details of Group Number 4.											
		4.—Farm servants and field labourers.			(a).—Farm servants.						(b).—Field labourers.		
		Actual workers. Partially agriculturists.		Dependants.	Total workers and dependants.	Actual workers. Total.		Actual workers. Partially agriculturists.		Dependants.	Total workers and dependants.	Actual. Total.	
	DISTRICT, CITY OR STATE.	Males.	Females.			Males.	Females.	Males.	Females.			Males.	Females.
	1	53	54	55	56	57	58	59	60	61	62	63	64
	Central Provinces and Berar ...	...	...	**1,258,818**	**1,088,365**	**552,208**	**94,448**	...	...	**441,709**	**3,342,390**	**840,219**	**1,685,062**
	C. P. British Districts and Berar ...	...	...	**1,112,850**	**923,233**	**485,403**	**74,683**	...	...	**363,147**	**3,120,744**	**788,593**	**1,582,448**
	C. P. British Districts ...	...	...	**794,525**	**783,239**	**410,438**	**58,574**	...	...	**314,227**	**1,981,318**	**456,978**	**1,044,042**
	JUBBULPORE DIVISION	...	...	*157,747*	*86,432*	*45,482*	*3,313*	...	...	*37,037*	*615,339*	*137,570*	*227,349*
1	Saugor ...	...	...	43,026	14,750	8,014	440	...	...	6,296	122,350	34,635	50,985
2	Damoh ...	...	...	24,696	5,741	2,913	145	...	...	2,683	79,210	21,872	35,325
3	Jubbulpore ...	...	...	57,205	14,795	7,343	567	...	...	6,885	162,262	45,698	66,244
	JUBBULPORE CITY ...	...	...	*454*	*141*	*83*	*2*	...	...	*56*	*1,018*	*278*	*349*
4	Mandla ...	...	...	28,009	11,372	5,480	446	...	...	5,446	60,505	19,003	27,939
5	Seoni ...	...	...	34,811	39,774	21,732	1,715	...	...	16,327	82,002	16,662	46,856
	NERBUDDA DIVISION	...	...	*151,098*	*120,078*	*70,004*	*3,771*	...	...	*46,298*	*438,379*	*108,088*	*235,496*
6	Narsinghpur ...	...	...	25,706	11,181	6,411	188	...	...	4,582	77,646	21,780	34,742
7	Hoshangabad ...	...	...	35,152	25,563	14,885	474	...	...	10,204	101,449	27,633	48,868
8	Nimar ...	...	...	29,797	12,974	7,724	434	...	...	4,816	91,535	26,448	40,106
9	Betul ...	...	...	24,828	23,648	13,978	748	...	...	8,922	70,947	14,902	40,139
10	Chhindwara ...	...	...	35,615	46,707	27,006	1,927	...	...	17,774	96,802	17,320	61,641
	NAGPUR DIVISION ...	...	...	*233,969*	*264,962*	*153,312*	*8,996*	...	...	*102,654*	*642,636*	*126,999*	*334,332*
11	Wardha ...	...	...	48,452	53,247	32,207	461	...	...	20,579	148,574	33,964	86,737
12	Nagpur ...	...	...	52,241	66,653	40,305	1,877	...	...	24,471	167,801	28,835	111,190
	NAGPUR CITY ...	...	...	*506*	*579*	*212*	*154*	...	...	*213*	*951*	*253*	*405*
13	Chanda ...	...	...	51,451	36,410	20,423	1,187	...	...	14,800	145,558	32,673	76,234
14	Bhandara ...	...	...	53,093	63,850	35,900	3,382	...	...	24,568	120,232	24,283	76,424
15	Balaghat ...	...	...	28,722	44,802	24,477	2,080	...	...	18,236	51,471	7,244	33,741
	CHHATTISGARH DIVISION.	...	...	*221,721*	*311,772*	*141,640*	*42,494*	...	...	*127,638*	*384,973*	*84,026*	*206,865*
16	Raipur ...	...	...	98,762	143,781	69,559	12,688	...	...	61,534	170,935	33,914	99,793
17	Bilaspur ...	...	...	62,336	61,936	25,107	11,746	...	...	25,083	122,825	32,700	52,872
18	Drug ...	...	...	60,623	106,055	46,974	18,060	...	...	41,021	91,214	17,412	54,200
	Berar ...	...	...	**318,325**	**139,994**	**74,965**	**16,109**	...	...	**48,920**	**1,139,426**	**331,615**	**538,406**
19	Amraoti ...	...	...	102,231	41,663	17,696	10,844	...	...	13,123	334,137	110,658	184,371
20	Akola ...	...	...	82,509	13,963	7,306	3,158	...	...	3,499	301,661	96,567	126,084
21	Buldana ...	...	...	58,099	10,895	7,562	230	...	...	3,103	231,612	67,185	109,431
22	Yeotmal ...	...	...	75,486	73,473	42,401	1,877	...	...	29,195	272,016	57,205	168,520
	Feudatory States ...	...	...	**145,968**	**165,132**	**66,805**	**19,765**	...	...	**78,562**	**221,646**	**51,626**	**102,614**
23	Makrai ...	...	...	1,087	124	88	...	...	...	36	3,401	1,127	1,223
24	Bastar ...	...	...	31,032	24,639	10,531	3,395	...	...	10,713	53,440	13,943	19,178
25	Kanker ...	...	...	9,086	13,210	7,063	637	...	...	5,510	15,496	2,345	9,605
26	Nandgaon ...	...	...	14,564	20,301	9,166	545	...	...	10,590	23,917	2,965	16,078
27	Khairagarh ...	...	...	12,937	24,818	8,424	6,756	...	...	9,638	13,944	2,016	7,729
28	Chhuikhadan ...	...	...	2,712	3,589	1,612	77	...	...	1,900	4,029	709	2,508
29	Kawardha ...	...	...	4,647	6,432	2,568	1,518	...	...	2,346	8,146	2,013	3,832
30	Sakti ...	...	...	2,177	2,577	1,093	276	...	...	1,211	3,486	818	1,702
31	Raigarh ...	...	...	13,810	4,567	1,270	1,306	...	...	1,985	35,464	11,820	11,819
32	Sarangarh ...	...	...	9,618	15,075	6,372	1,138	...	...	7,565	11,178	1,957	7,168
33	Chang Bhakar ...	...	...	1,940	1,647	788	201	...	...	658	5,014	1,019	2,713
34	Korea ...	...	...	4,558	1,224	367	102	...	...	755	11,746	3,475	4,468
35	Surguja ...	...	...	29,787	36,043	12,887	1,942	...	...	21,214	20,922	4,168	8,181
36	Udaipur ...	...	...	3,220	3,570	1,598	315	...	...	1,663	4,291	909	1,825
37	Jashpur ...	...	...	4,793	7,280	2,975	1,557	...	...	2,748	7,172	1,442	3,685

# of livelihood, Part A.—General Table.

OF RAW MATERIALS—(*continued*).

of the surface of the earth—(*continued*).

and agriculture—(*continued*).

Ordinary cultivation.—(*concluded*).			Sub-Order (*b*).—Growers of special products and market gardening.													
			Total Sub-Order (*b*).						5.—Tea, coffee, cinchona, and indigo plantations.						6.—Fruit, flower, etc., growers	
WORKERS.				ACTUAL WORKERS.						ACTUAL WORKERS.						
Partially agriculturists.		Dependants.	Total workers and dependants.	Total.		Partially agriculturists.		Dependants.	Total workers and dependants.	Total.		Partially agriculturists.		Dependants.	Total workers and dependants.	Serial number.
Males.	Females.			Males.	Females.	Males.	Females.			Males.	Females.	Males.	Females.			
65	66	67	68	69	70	71	72	73	74	75	76	77	78	79	80	
...	...	**817,109**	**52,827**	**16,784**	**15,489**	**2,246**	**1,311**	**20,554**	**487**	**327**	**84**	**3**	**1**	**76**	**52,340**	
...	...	**749,703**	**45,849**	**14,859**	**12,997**	**2,108**	**1,174**	**17,993**	**482**	**322**	**84**	**3**	**1**	**76**	**45,367**	
...	...	**480,298**	**43,531**	**14,099**	**12,423**	**2,032**	**1,154**	**17,009**	**473**	**318**	**84**	**3**	**1**	**71**	**43,058**	
...	...	*150,110*	*16,711*	*5,306*	*4,541*	*1,136*	*539*	*6,864*	*44*	*38*	*3*	...	...	*9*	*16,667*	
...	...	30,730	3,362	968	1,001	241	137	1,303	4	4	...	...	...	...	3,358	1
...	...	22,013	4,897	1,387	1,561	323	171	1,949	1	1	...	...	...	...	4,896	2
...	...	50,320	6,294	2,298	1,312	554	210	2,684	26	15	3	...	...	8	6,268	3
...	...	*395*	*929*	*425*	*45*	*3*	*1*	*456*	*7*	...	...	...	...	*7*	*922*	
...	...	22,563	1,501	416	470	9	9	615	6	6	...	...	...	...	1,405	4
...	...	18,484	657	237	197	9	2	223	7	6	...	...	...	1	650	5
...	...	*104,800*	*4,714*	*1,592*	*1,085*	*215*	*100*	*2,037*	*9*	*7*	*2*	...	...	...	*4,705*	
...	...	21,124	1,216	414	254	68	25	548	3	3	...	...	...	...	1,213	6
...	...	24,948	1,661	607	283	87	15	771	2	1	1	...	...	...	1,659	7
...	...	24,081	525	203	116	27	1	206	2	2	...	...	...	...	523	8
...	...	15,906	534	125	212	22	50	197	2	1	1	...	...	...	532	9
...	...	17,841	778	243	220	14	9	315	...	...	...	...	...	...	778	10
...	...	*131,305*	*7,572*	*2,515*	*2,155*	*205*	*228*	*2,899*	*45*	*31*	*3*	...	...	*11*	*7,527*	
...	...	27,873	588	231	59	3	...	298	...	...	...	...	...	...	588	11
...	...	27,770	2,720	1,012	689	33	24	1,019	6	...	1	...	...	5	2,714	12
...	...	*293*	*515*	*211*	*75*	...	...	*229*	...	...	...	...	...	...	*515*	
...	...	36,651	1,031	322	383	44	34	376	...	...	...	...	...	...	1,031	13
...	...	28,525	2,725	776	949	114	159	1,000	8	2	...	...	...	6	2,717	14
...	...	10,486	508	174	128	14	11	206	31	29	2	...	...	...	477	15
...	...	*94,053*	*14,534*	*4,686*	*4,639*	*470*	*297*	*5,209*	*375*	*248*	*76*	*3*	*1*	*51*	*14,159*	
...	...	37,228	7,416	2,306	2,417	220	154	2,693	16	7	6	...	...	3	7,400	16
...	...	37,253	1,802	621	664	82	59	517	308	199	62	1	1	47	1,494	17
...	...	19,602	5,316	1,759	1,558	168	84	1,999	51	42	8	2	...	1	5,265	18
...	...	**269,405**	**2,318**	**760**	**574**	**76**	**20**	**984**	**9**	**4**	...	...	...	**5**	**2,309**	
...	...	89,108	1,460	491	320	48	1	649	8	3	...	...	...	5	1,452	19
...	...	79,010	343	88	121	9	12	134	1	1	...	...	...	...	342	20
...	...	54,906	381	110	130	19	7	141	...	...	...	...	...	...	381	21
...	...	46,291	134	71	3	...	...	60	...	...	...	...	...	...	134	22
...	...	**67,406**	**6,978**	**1,925**	**2,492**	**138**	**137**	**2,561**	**5**	**5**	...	...	...	...	**6,973**	
...	...	1,051	128	75	...	3	...	53	...	...	...	...	...	...	128	23
...	...	20,319	717	101	451	17	33	165	...	...	...	...	...	...	717	24
...	...	3,546	1,053	295	360	9	15	398	...	...	...	...	...	...	1,053	25
...	...	3,974	1,573	445	504	32	43	624	1	1	...	...	...	...	1,572	26
...	...	3,299	2,333	729	693	48	20	911	...	...	...	...	...	...	2,333	27
...	...	812	441	148	51	7	3	242	...	...	...	...	...	...	441	28
...	...	2,301	89	...	57	...	...	32	...	...	...	...	...	...	89	29
...	...	966	20	5	11	1	1	4	3	3	...	...	...	...	17	30
...	...	11,825	218	54	105	18	8	59	...	...	...	...	...	...	218	31
...	...	2,053	276	8	247	1	4	21	...	...	...	...	...	...	276	32
...	...	1,282	17	13	...	1	...	4	1	1	...	...	...	...	16	33
...	...	3,803	4	3	1	1	...	...	...	...	...	...	...	...	4	34
...	...	8,578	65	30	4	...	...	31	...	...	...	...	...	...	65	35
...	...	1,557	24	11	5	...	...	8	...	...	...	...	...	...	24	36
...	...	2,045	20	8	3	...	1	9	...	...	...	...	...	...	20	37

TABLE XV.—Occupation or means

Serial number.	CLASS ... / SUB-CLASS ... / ORDER ...	CLASS A.—PRODUCTION / Sub-Class I.—Exploitation / Order I.—Pasture										
		Sub-Order (*b*).—Growers of special products and market gardening—(*concld.*)					Sub-Order (*c*).—					
		6.—Fruit, flower, vegetable, betel vine, areca-nut, etc., growers.					Total Sub-Order (*c*).					
	DISTRICT, CITY OR STATE.	ACTUAL WORKERS. Total. Males.	ACTUAL WORKERS. Total. Females.	Partially agriculturists. Males.	Partially agriculturists. Females.	Dependants.	Total workers and dependants.	ACTUAL WORKERS. Total. Males.	ACTUAL WORKERS. Total. Females.	Partially agriculturists. Males.	Partially agriculturists. Females.	Dependants.
	1	81	82	83	84	85	86	87	88	89	90	91
	Central Provinces and Berar ...	**16,457**	**15,405**	**2,243**	**1,310**	**20,478**	**81,462**	**21,079**	**30,474**	**2.738**	**4.098**	**29.909**
	C. P. British Districts and Berar ...	**14,537**	**12,913**	**2,105**	**1,173**	**17,917**	**72,304**	**18,628**	**27.544**	**2,602**	**4.008**	**26,132**
	C. P. British Districts ...	**13,781**	**12,339**	**2,029**	**1,153**	**16,938**	**63,704**	**15,621**	**488**	**1,935**	**3,609**	**22,595**
	JUBBULPORE DIVISION	*5,274*	*4,538*	*1,136*	*539*	*6,855*	*18,769*	*4,861*	*6,404*	*744*	*965*	*7,514*
1	Saugor ...	964	1,001	241	137	1,393	6,782	1,707	2,473	303	375	2,602
2	Damoh ...	1,386	1,561	323	171	1,949	3,404	879	1,085	151	206	1,440
3	Jubbulpore ...	2,283	1,309	554	210	2,676	4,785	1,197	1,689	245	346	1,890
	JUBBULPORE CITY.	*435*	*48*	*3*	*1*	*449*	*974*	*399*	*195*	*4*	*1*	*480*
4	Mandla ...	410	470	9	9	615	1,890	576	493	40	38	821
5	Seoni ...	231	197	9	2	222	1,908	492	664	5	...	752
	NERBUDDA DIVISION.	*1,585*	*1,083*	*218*	*100*	*2,037*	*23,050*	*4,987*	*10,991*	*693*	*1,874*	*7,072*
6	Narsinghpur ...	411	254	68	25	548	6,672	1,457	3,273	356	653	1,942
7	Hoshangabad ...	606	282	87	15	771	6,097	1,303	3,460	148	354	1,928
8	Nimar ...	201	116	27	1	206	3,454	1,073	1,008	38	65	1,378
9	Betul ...	124	211	22	50	197	4,214	687	2,445	137	765	1,082
10	Chhindwara ...	243	220	14	9	315	2,013	467	804	14	37	742
	NAGPUR DIVISION.	*2,484*	*2,155*	*205*	*228*	*2,888*	*12,815*	*3,396*	*4,695*	*311*	*591*	*4,824*
11	Wardha ...	231	59	3	...	298	1,695	424	674	14	13	597
12	Nagpur ...	1,012	688	83	24	1,014	4,932	1,159	2,154	114	262	1,619
	NAGPUR CITY.	*211*	*75*	...	—	*229*	*498*	*113*	*170*	*3*	...	*215*
13	Chanda ...	322	333	44	34	376	2,513	647	762	35	158	1,104
14	Bhandara ...	774	949	114	150	994	2,477	598	963	110	152	916
15	Balaghat ...	145	126	14	11	206	1,198	408	142	38	6	588
	CHHATTISGARH DIVISION.	*4,438*	*4,563*	*467*	*296*	*5,158*	*9,070*	*2,487*	*3,398*	*187*	*179*	*3,186*
16	Raipur ...	2,299	2,411	220	154	2,690	4,257	1,413	1,199	90	62	1,645
17	Bilaspur ...	422	602	81	58	470	3,687	778	1,665	88	115	1,244
18	Drug ...	1,717	1,550	166	84	1,998	1,126	296	534	9	2	296
	Berar ...	**756**	**574**	**76**	**20**	**979**	**8,600**	**3,007**	**2,056**	**667**	**399**	**3,537**
19	Amraoti ...	488	320	48	1	644	5,522	2,024	1,335	589	367	2,163
20	Akola ...	87	121	9	12	134	1,490	447	377	11	10	608
21	Buldana ...	110	130	19	7	141	879	286	263	59	19	330
22	Yeotmal ...	71	3	...	...	60	709	250	81	8	3	378
	Feudatory States ...	**1,920**	**2,492**	**138**	**137**	**2,561**	**9,158**	**2,451**	**2,930**	**136**	**90**	**3.777**
23	Makrai ...	75	...	3	...	53	414	89	243	8	...	82
24	Bastar ...	101	451	17	33	165	766	292	119	5	...	355
25	Kanker ...	295	360	9	15	398	816	217	405	7	2	194
26	Nandgaon ...	444	504	32	43	624	449	74	278	4	8	99
27	Khairagarh ...	729	698	48	29	911	844	100	444	33	30	210
28	Chhuikhadan ...	148	51	7	3	242	50	7	25	...	1	18
29	Kawardha ...	...	57	...	...	32	410	104	119	2	1	187
30	Sakti ...	2	11	1	1	4	161	46	31	12	3	84
31	Raigarh ...	54	105	18	8	59	865	241	251	2	13	373
32	Sarangarh ...	8	247	1	4	21	302	82	100	19	4	120
33	Chang Bhakar ...	12	...	1	...	4	19	10	...	...	...	9
34	Korea ...	3	1	1	...	...	935	281	239	16	7	415
35	Surguja ...	30	4	...	...	31	2,344	598	426	21	3	1,820
36	Udaipur ...	11	5	...	...	8	117	28	37	...	—	52
37	Jashpur ...	8	3	...	1	9	666	192	215	7	18	259

# of livelihood, Part A.—General Table.

OF RAW MATERIALS—(*continued*).

of the surface of the earth—(*continued*).

and agriculture—(*continued*).

Forestry. | Sub-Order (*d*).—Raising of farm stock.

7.—Forest officers, rangers, guards, etc.						8.—Wood cutters: firewood, lac, catechu, rubber, etc., collectors & charcoal burners.						Total Sub-Order (*d*).						
Total workers and dependants.	Actual workers. Total. Males.	Actual workers. Total. Females.	Actual workers. Partially agriculturists. Males.	Actual workers. Partially agriculturists. Females.	Dependants.	Total workers and dependants.	Actual workers. Total. Males.	Actual workers. Total. Females.	Actual workers. Partially agriculturists. Males.	Actual workers. Partially agriculturists. Females.	Dependants.	Total workers and dependants.	Actual workers. Total. Males.	Actual workers. Total. Females.	Actual workers. Partially agriculturists. Males.	Actual workers. Partially agriculturists. Females.	Dependants.	Serial number.
92	93	94	95	96	97	98	99	100	101	102	103	104	105	106	107	108	109	
13,948	**5,061**	**416**	**169**	**59**	**8,471**	**67,514**	**16,018**	**30,058**	**2,569**	**4,039**	**21,438**	**432,534**	**234,569**	**52,725**	**7,865**	**2,716**	**145,240**	
12,492	**4,493**	**402**	**143**	**59**	**7,597**	**59,812**	**14,135**	**27,142**	**2,459**	**3,949**	**18,535**	**344,790**	**195,989**	**38,806**	**6,520**	**2,382**	**109,995**	
11,111	**3,969**	**336**	**124**	**59**	**6,806**	**52,593**	**11,652**	**25,152**	**1,811**	**3,550**	**15,789**	**297,529**	**164,908**	**36,710**	**5,926**	**2,269**	**95,911**	
3,144	*1,035*	*20*	*16*	...	*2,059*	*15,626*	*3,816*	*6,384*	*735*	*965*	*5,425*	*54,523*	*29,349*	*7,722*	*1,194*	*539*	*17,452*	
726	224	6	3	...	496	6,056	1,483	2,467	300	375	2,106	10,459	6,967	912	216	82	2,580	1
643	166	3	...	...	474	2,761	713	1,082	151	206	966	7,634	4,525	921	273	69	2,188	2
514	175	2	6	...	337	4,271	1,022	1,687	239	346	1,562	13,110	6,489	2,141	416	233	4,480	3
330	*62*	...	...	...	*174*	*735*	*237*	*195*	*4*	*1*	*306*	*579*	*196*	*113*	...	...	*370*	
671	262	...	5	...	409	1,219	314	493	35	38	412	14,313	5,787	2,856	261	134	5,670	4
590	208	9	2	...	373	1,318	284	655	3	...	379	9,007	5,581	892	28	11	2,534	5
3,003	*1,060*	*47*	*18*	*2*	*1,896*	*20,047*	*3,927*	*10,944*	*675*	*1,872*	*5,176*	*49,172*	*31,353*	*4,894*	*640*	*393*	*12,895*	
242	71	..	2	...	171	6,430	1,386	3,273	354	658	1,771	7,593	4,572	1,067	141	63	1,964	6
913	271	40	1	...	602	5,784	1,032	3,426	147	354	1,326	8,777	6,080	729	78	11	1,969	7
762	297	1	4	1	464	2,692	776	1,002	34	64	914	7,138	3,830	710	98	63	2,598	8
495	204	4	6	1	287	3,719	483	2,441	131	764	795	13,635	8,881	1,289	238	200	3,465	9
591	217	2	5	...	372	1,422	250	802	9	37	870	12,029	8,020	1,109	85	56	2,900	10
3,356	*1,298*	*132*	*64*	*55*	*1,956*	*9,429*	*1,998*	*4,563*	*247*	*530*	*2,863*	*78,416*	*54,517*	*4,436*	*626*	*463*	*19,473*	
229	82	55	6	1	92	1,406	342	619	8	12	505	10,342	5,931	773	88	46	3,638	11
509	227	5	10	...	277	4,423	932	2,149	104	262	1,342	20,713	15,568	1,133	147	57	4,012	13
125	*43*	*2*	*3*	...	*80*	*873*	*70*	*163*	...	...	*135*	*813*	*298*	*110*	...	*1*	*405*	
1,239	427	64	17	54	748	1,274	220	608	18	104	356	21,048	14,616	943	241	236	5,489	13
784	305	3	24	...	476	1,693	293	960	86	152	440	18,625	14,164	689	89	95	3,772	14
625	257	5	7	...	363	573	211	137	31	6	225	7,688	4,238	888	61	28	2,562	15
1,575	*576*	*137*	*26*	*2*	*865*	*7,493*	*1,911*	*3,261*	*161*	*177*	*2,330*	*115,418*	*49,659*	*19,668*	*3,466*	*885*	*46,021*	
921	344	7	18	...	570	3,336	1,069	1,192	72	62	1,075	51,171	21,404	10,052	1,845	454	19,715	16
285	117	1	6	...	167	3,402	661	1,664	82	115	1,077	32,238	13,462	5,541	1,137	363	13,285	17
372	115	120	2	2	128	754	181	405	7	...	168	32,009	14,793	4,075	484	68	13,141	18
1,381	**524**	**66**	**19**	...	**791**	**7,219**	**2,483**	**1,990**	**648**	**399**	**2,746**	**47,261**	**31,081**	**2,096**	**594**	**113**	**14,084**	
571	201	63	9	...	307	4,951	1,829	1,272	580	367	1,856	12,916	7,742	733	191	37	4,441	19
178	61	3	4	...	114	1,312	386	374	7	10	552	9,574	6,674	422	151	18	2,478	20
207	105	...	6	...	102	672	181	263	53	19	228	9,144	6,807	382	204	34	2,005	21
425	157	...	...	...	268	284	98	81	8	3	110	15,627	9,858	609	48	29	5,160	22
1,456	**568**	**14**	**26**	...	**874**	**7,702**	**1,883**	**2,916**	**110**	**90**	**2,903**	**87,744**	**38,580**	**13,919**	**1,345**	**334**	**35,245**	
10	4	1	...	...	5	404	85	242	8	...	77	300	160	37	1	...	103	23
463	204	8	3	...	251	303	88	111	2	...	104	14,708	5,612	3,267	35	23	5,919	24
226	78	3	6	...	145	590	139	402	1	2	49	5,544	2,294	1,256	13	20	1,994	25
115	46	1	2	...	68	334	28	375	2	8	31	10,297	5,809	1,525	38	13	2,963	26
72	37	...	...	...	35	772	153	444	33	30	175	9,523	5,509	875	39	9	3,139	27
21	4	...	...	...	17	29	3	25	...	1	1	2,144	939	231	10	...	914	28
187	41	...	2	...	96	273	63	119	...	1	91	3,971	1,644	738	111	36	1,589	29
38	10	...	1	...	28	123	36	31	11	3	56	660	253	89	41	2	279	30
198	76	...	1	...	122	667	165	251	1	13	251	8,229	3,000	1,483	495	94	3,746	31
91	27	...	8	...	64	211	55	100	11	4	56	3,162	1,577	179	193	14	1,406	32
...	...	...	...	...	...	19	10	...	...	...	9	1,853	946	318	4	23	589	33
16	11	...	1	...	5	919	270	289	15	7	410	2,835	1,263	393	46	8	1,179	34
40	14	...	1	...	26	2,304	584	426	20	3	1,294	11,446	3,908	856	49	6	6,622	35
25	12	1	...	...	12	92	16	36	...	...	40	3,992	1,362	588	37	4	2,012	36
4	4	...	1	...	...	662	188	215	6	18	259	8,990	4,144	2,085	233	82	2,761	37

TABLE XV.—Occupation or means

Serial number.	CLASS ... / SUB-CLASS ... / ORDER ... / DISTRICT, CITY OR STATE.	CLASS A.—PRODUCTION. Sub-Class I.—Exploitation. Order I.—Pasture. Sub-Order (d).—Raising. 9.—Cattle and buffalo breeders and keepers. Total workers and dependants.	9.—Actual workers. Total. Males.	9.—Actual workers. Total. Females.	9.—Actual workers. Partially agriculturists. Males.	9.—Actual workers. Partially agriculturists. Females.	9.—Dependants.	10.—Sheep, goat and pig breeders. Total workers and dependants.	10.—Actual workers. Total. Males.	10.—Actual workers. Total. Females.	10.—Actual workers. Partially agriculturists. Males.	10.—Actual workers. Partially agriculturists. Females.	10.—Dependants.	11.—Breeders of other animals (horses, mules, camels, asses, etc.). Total workers and dependants.	11.—Actual workers. Total. Males.	11.—Actual workers. Total. Females.	11.—Actual workers. Partially agriculturists. Males.	11.—Actual workers. Partially agriculturists. Females.	11.—Dependants.
	1	110	111	112	113	114	115	116	117	118	119	120	121	122	123	124	125	126	127
	Central Provinces and Berar ...	**33,789**	**7,814**	**15,415**	**879**	**1,068**	**10,560**	**3,311**	**1,912**	**313**	**61**	**15**	**1,086**	**381**	**190**	**27**	**5**	**...**	**164**
	C. P. British Districts and Berar ...	**30,790**	**7,336**	**13,541**	**836**	**1,025**	**9,913**	**3,174**	**1,839**	**297**	**59**	**15**	**1,038**	**355**	**177**	**27**	**4**	**...**	**151**
	C. P. British Districts ...	**26,542**	**5,982**	**12,624**	**699**	**970**	**7,956**	**2,895**	**1,697**	**284**	**59**	**11**	**914**	**292**	**144**	**26**	**4**	**...**	**122**
	JUBBULPORE DIVISION	*4,813*	*1,199*	*1,539*	*253*	*149*	*2,075*	*678*	*220*	*174*	*28*	*8*	*284*	*82*	*46*	...	*1*	...	*36*
1	Saugor ...	1,535	420	464	100	60	651	98	45	21	3	...	32	14	11	...	...	...	3
2	Damoh ...	951	253	228	83	28	470	205	29	78	4	4	98	13	7	...	...	...	6
3	Jubbulpore ...	1,449	323	501	31	40	625	296	120	56	21	4	120	37	15	...	1	...	22
	JUBBULPORE CITY ...	*276*	*35*	*95*	...	...	*143*	...	...	...	...	...	...	*17*	*6*	...	...	...	*11*
4	Mandla ...	591	136	233	16	16	222	31	8	7	...	...	16	...	...	...	...	...	...
5	Seoni ...	287	67	113	3	5	107	48	18	12	...	...	18	18	13	...	...	...	5
	NERBUDDA DIVISION.	*5,810*	*1,460*	*1,776*	*221*	*182*	*2,584*	*537*	*238*	*52*	*15*	*3*	*247*	*121*	*45*	*23*	*1*	...	*53*
6	Narsinghpur ...	369	77	195	13	17	97	247	93	34	5	3	120	26	12	...	...	...	14
7	Hoshangabad ...	1,670	443	412	39	7	815	81	57	3	...	...	21	30	23	...	...	...	7
8	Nimar ...	1,916	516	508	50	52	892	78	31	5	1	...	42	11	6	...	...	...	5
9	Betul ...	1,563	349	502	111	94	622	36	14	7	4	...	15	5	1	...	...	...	4
10	Chhindwara ...	202	65	69	8	12	158	95	43	3	5	...	49	49	3	23	1	...	23
	NAGPUR DIVISION ...	*6,695*	*2,126*	*2,090*	*142*	*345*	*2,477*	*1,383*	*1,121*	*13*	*3*	...	*249*	*74*	*47*	*1*	*2*	...	*26*
11	Wardha ...	1,282	250	523	12	41	450	82	50	...	...	...	23	20	13	...	...	...	16
12	Nagpur ...	2,006	670	553	17	23	783	473	445	3	...	...	25	28	24	...	2	...	4
	NAGPUR CITY ...	*484*	*80*	*90*	...	*1*	*314*	...	...	...	...	...	...	*1*	*1*	...	...	...	...
13	Chanda ...	2,125	723	511	106	179	891	810	609	...	3	...	201	1	1	...	...	...	...
14	Bhandara ...	901	435	261	6	80	205	17	7	10	...	...	...	7	4	1	...	...	2
15	Balaghat ...	431	50	242	1	13	139	1	1	...	...	...	...	9	5	...	...	...	4
	CHHATTISGARH DIVISION.	*9,224*	*1,186*	*7,319*	*103*	*294*	*820*	*297*	*118*	*45*	*13*	...	*134*	*15*	*6*	*2*	...	...	*7*
16	Raipur ...	4,801	95	4,403	7	175	213	192	96	22	11	...	74	7	5	...	...	...	2
17	Bilaspur ...	1,988	208	1,480	33	94	300	82	20	12	2	...	50	4	1	2	...	...	1
18	Drug ...	2,435	882	1,240	63	25	307	23	2	11	...	...	10	4	...	...	...	...	4
	Berar ...	**4,248**	**1,374**	**917**	**137**	**55**	**1,957**	**279**	**142**	**13**	**...**	**4**	**124**	**63**	**33**	**1**	**...**	**...**	**29**
19	Amraoti ...	1,655	458	330	66	16	867	79	60	2	...	...	17	33	13	...	...	...	20
20	Akola ...	960	188	207	10	3	565	132	41	8	...	4	83	4	2	...	...	...	2
21	Buldana ...	885	524	84	45	9	277	50	33	1	...	...	16	19	13	1	...	...	5
22	Yeotmal ...	748	204	296	10	27	248	18	8	2	...	...	8	7	5	...	...	...	2
	Feudatory States ...	**2,999**	**478**	**1,874**	**43**	**43**	**647**	**137**	**73**	**16**	**2**	**...**	**48**	**26**	**13**	**...**	**1**	**...**	**13**
23	Makrai ...	4	...	3	...	...	1	9	4	...	...	...	5	4	2	...	...	...	2
24	Bastar ...	472	194	124	2	...	154	...	...	...	...	...	...	2	1	...	...	...	1
25	Kanker ...	110	15	85	...	1	16	22	...	14	...	...	8	5	...	...	...	...	5
26	Nandgaon ...	532	9	489	...	12	34	13	1	2	...	...	10	1	1	...	...	...	...
27	Khairagarh ...	570	68	302	9	9	110	20	14	...	1	...	6	1	1	...	...	...	...
28	Chhuikhadan ...	180	...	179	...	...	1	...	...	...	...	...	...	...	...	...	...	...	...
29	Kawardha ...	276	...	254	...	15	22	...	...	...	...	...	...	...	...	...	...	...	...
30	Sakti ...	...	...	...	...	...	...	1	1	...	1	...	...	...	...	...	...	...	...
31	Raigarh ...	...	...	...	...	...	...	...	...	...	...	...	...	...	...	...	...	...	...
32	Sarangarh ...	20	...	20	...	...	...	66	51	...	...	...	15	...	...	...	...	...	...
33	Chang Bhakar ...	244	60	68	...	4	116	6	2	...	...	...	4	...	...	...	...	...	...
34	Korea ...	154	...	128	...	2	26	...	...	...	...	...	...	...	...	...	...	...	...
35	Surguja ...	169	87	6	28	...	76	...	...	...	...	...	...	13	8	...	1	...	5
36	Udaipur ...	149	33	49	4	...	67	...	...	...	...	...	...	...	...	...	...	...	...
37	Jashpur ...	113	12	77	...	...	24	...	...	...	...	...	...	...	...	...	...	...	...

# of livelihood, Part A.—General Table.

OF RAW MATERIALS—(continued).

of the surface of the earth—(continued).

and agriculture—(concluded). of farm stock—(concluded). 12.—Herdsmen, shepherds, goatherds, etc.						Total Sub-Order (e).—Raising of small animals. 13.—Birds, bees, silk-worms, etc.						Order 2.—Fishing and hunting. Total Order 2.						
Total workers and dependants.	Actual workers. Total. Males.	Actual workers. Total. Females.	Partially agriculturists. Males.	Partially agriculturists. Females.	Dependants	Total workers and dependants.	Actual workers. Total. Males.	Actual workers. Total. Females.	Partially agriculturists. Males.	Partially agriculturists. Females	Dependants.	Total workers and dependants.	Actual workers. Total. Males.	Actual workers. Total. Females.	Partially agriculturists. Males.	Partially agriculturists. Females.	Dependants.	Serial number.
128	129	130	131	132	133	134	135	136	137	138	139	140	141	142	143	144	145	
396,053	224,653	36,970	6,920	1,633	133,430	115	27	29	...	...	59	133,389	51,754	22,212	13,191	7,571	59,403	
310,471	186,637	24,941	5,621	1,342	98,893	109	25	28	...	...	56	126,229	49,310	20,841	12,924	7,493	56,078	
267,800	157,105	23,776	5,164	1,288	86,919	102	24	26	...	...	52	109,539	42,247	18,944	11,23[illegible]	6,781	48,848	
48,950	*27,884*	*6,009*	*933*	*372*	*15,057*	*34*	*11*	*3*	...	...	*20*	*6,103*	*2,230*	*900*	*259*	*78*	*2,973*	
8,812	6,491	427	113	22	1,894	25	5	3	...	...	17	414	150	30	42	9	228	1
6,465	4,230	615	186	37	1,614	...	...	...	...	...	...	106	44	2	3	...	54	2
11,326	6,031	1,584	363	189	3,713	8	5	...	...	...	3	526	223	53	21	2	250	3
286	*152*	*[illegible]*	...	...	*110*	...	...	...	...	...	...	*[illegible]*	*66*	*12*	...	...	*109*	
13,691	5,643	2,616	245	118	5,432	1	1	...	...	...	...	2,760	914	551	135	60	1,295	4
8,65[illegible]	5,483	767	25	6	2,404	...	...	...	...	...	...	2,297	809	252	88	7	1,146	5
42,704	*29,650*	*3,043*	*408*	*208*	*10,011*	*9*	*1*	*4*	...	...	*4*	*9,355*	*3,847*	*1,049*	*472*	*161*	*4,459*	
6,951	4,390	82[illegible]	123	43	1,738	...	...	...	...	...	...	650	306	29	68	1	315	6
6,990	5,557	314	89	4	1,125	8	...	4	...	...	4	2,058	866	140	163	35	1,052	7
5,133	3,277	197	47	11	1,659	1	1	..	...	...	...	1,367	667	59	73	14	641	8
12,031	9,517	690	123	106	2,824	...	—	...	...	...	...	1,941	721	373	46	57	847	9
11,593	7,909	1,014	71	44	2,670	...	—	...	...	...	...	3,339	1,287	448	122	54	1,604	10
70,264	*51,231*	*2,332*	*479*	*117*	*16,721*	*43*	*2*	*18*	...	...	*23*	*73,530*	*28,688*	*12,906*	*9,360*	*6,095*	*31,936*	
8,999	5,609	250	76	5	3,140	...	...	...	...	...	...	5,419	2,117	750	718	407	2,552	11
18,206	14,429	577	128	34	3,200	...	...	...	...	...	...	9,839	3,787	1,338	396	206	4,714	12
325	*217*	*20*	...	...	*91*	...	...	...	...	...	...	*250*	*77*	*61*	*5*	...	*112*	
18,112	13,283	432	132	57	4,397	30	...	18	...	—	21	26,421	9,794	5,967	5,732	4,260	10,660	13
17,700	13,718	417	83	6	3,565	4	2	...	...	...	2	24,834	9,983	3,502	2,159	900	10,849	14
7,247	4,182	646	60	15	2,419	...	...	...	...	...	...	7,517	3,007	1,349	355	253	3,161	15
105,882	*48,350*	*12,403*	*3,350*	*591*	*45,130*	*16*	*10*	*1*	...	...	*5*	*20,561*	*7,482*	*4,089*	*1,164*	*447*	*8,980*	
46,171	21,208	5,537	1,827	279	19,426	15	9	1	...	...	5	9,833	3,504	2,011	664	274	4,228	16
30,164	13,233	4,047	1,102	269	12,884	1	1	...	...	...	...	4,468	1,653	843	318	120	1,972	17
29,547	13,909	2,818	421	43	12,820	—	...	...	...	...	...	6,250	2,235	1,235	182	53	2,780	18
42,671	29,532	1,165	457	54	11,974	7	1	2	...	...	4	16,690	7,063	1,897	1,689	712	7,730	
11,144	7,211	401	125	21	3,537	5	...	2	...	...	3	5,872	2,497	918	762	432	2,463	19
8,478	6,443	247	135	6	1,828	2	1	..	...	...	1	2,723	1,201	190	291	33	1,326	20
8,190	6,237	240	150	25	1,707	...	...	...	...	...	...	1,208	548	131	152	58	619	21
14,854	9,641	311	38	2	4,902	—	...	.	...	...	...	6,791	2,817	652	484	189	3,322	22
84,582	38,016	12,029	1,299	291	34,537	6	2	1	...	...	3	7,140	2,444	1,371	267	78	3,325	
283	151	34	1	...	95	...	...	...	...	...	...	96	50	3	1	...	43	23
14,324	5,417	8,143	33	29	5,764	—	...	...	...	...	...	1,020	371	155	41	1	503	24
5,401	2,279	1,157	13	19	1,965	6	2	1	...	...	3	924	308	171	11	1	445	25
9,751	5,708	1,034	38	1	2,919	...	...	...	...	...	...	1,083	396	126	47	5	501	26
8,932	5,426	483	29	...	3,023	...	...	...	...	...	...	728	284	89	22	3	355	27
1,964	990	52	10	...	913	...	...	...	...	...	...	187	66	14	4	...	107	28
3,695	1,641	484	111	21	1,567	...	...	...	—	...	...	492	172	77	8	3	243	29
630	292	8-	40	2	279	...	...	...	...	...	...	37	15	1	3	...	21	30
8,229	3,000	1,483	495	94	3,746	...	—	...	...	...	...	610	191	172	31	37	247	31
3,076	1,526	150	193	14	1,391	...	...	...	...	...	...	411	122	133	19	9	156	32
1,603	884	250	4	19	469	...	...	...	...	...	...	50	20	22	2	1	14	33
2,631	1,203	265	46	6	1,153	...	...	...	...	...	...	15	5	...	3	...	10	34
11,264	3,873	850	20	6	6,541	...	...	...	...	...	...	58	24	4	...	...	20	35
3,843	1,829	539	33	4	1,975	...	...	...	...	...	...	99	25	26	3	4	48	36
6,677	4,182	2,006	238	82	2,737	...	...	...	...	...	...	1,315	395	378	72	14	542	37

TABLE XV.—Occupation or means

Serial number	CLASS ...	CLASS A.—PRODUCTION															
	SUB-CLASS ...	Sub-Class I.– Exploitation of the surface of the earth— (*concluded*).												Sub-Class II.—			
	ORDER ...	Order 2.—Fishing and hunting— (*concluded*).															
		14.—Fishing.						15.—Hunting.						Total			
	DISTRICT, CITY OR STATE.	Total workers and dependants.	Actual workers. Total. Males.	Actual workers. Total. Females.	Actual workers. Partially agriculturists. Males.	Actual workers. Partially agriculturists. Females.	Dependants.	Total workers and dependants.	Actual workers. Total. Males.	Actual workers. Total. Females.	Actual workers. Partially agriculturists. Males.	Actual workers. Partially agriculturists. Females.	Dependants.	Total workers and dependants.	Actual workers. Total. Males.	Actual workers. Total. Females.	Actual workers. Partially. Males.
	1	146	147	148	149	150	151	152	153	154	155	156	157	158	159	160	161
	Central Provinces and Berar ...	**127,244**	**49,312**	**21,446**	**13,058**	**7,539**	**56 486**	**6,125**	**2,442**	**766**	**133**	**32**	**2,917**	**29,975**	**11,949**	**7,672**	**349**
	C. P. British Districts and Berar ...	**120,781**	**47,083**	**20,253**	**12,797**	**7,461**	**53,445**	**5,448**	**2,227**	**588**	**127**	**32**	**2,633**	**29,757**	**11,890**	**7,592**	**341**
	C. P. British Districts ...	**106,249**	**40,963**	**18,499**	**11,143**	**6,764**	**46,787**	**3,290**	**1,284**	**446**	**92**	**17**	**1,561**	**29,173**	**11,716**	**7,467**	**335**
	JUBBULPORE DIVISION	*5,532*	*1,973*	*835*	*206*	*70*	*2,721*	*571*	*257*	*62*	*33*	*8*	*252*	*1,724*	*641*	*372*	*30*
1	Saugor ...	210	77	6	10	1	127	204	73	30	82	8	101	400	110	118	6
2	Damoh ...	77	28	3	3	...	46	29	16	5	...	...	8	127	8	42	3
3	Jubbulpore ...	458	107	53	21	2	208	68	20	...	...	...	42	1,125	504	192	20
	JUBBULPORE CITY ...	*124*	*49*	*12*	...	...	*63*	*56*	*17*	...	...	...	*39*	*60*	*9*	*23*	*1*
4	Mandla ...	2,659	873	536	134	60	1,250	101	41	15	1	...	45	63	16	17	1
5	Seoni ...	2,128	798	240	38	7	1,090	169	101	12	...	...	56	9	4	3	...
	NERBUDDA DIVISION	*8,820*	*3,639*	*972*	*457*	*160*	*4,209*	*536*	*208*	*77*	*15*	*1*	*250*	*4,906*	*1,599*	*1,016*	*85*
6	Narsinghpur ...	582	274	12	68	1	296	68	32	17	...	...	19	2,750	1,090	451	55
7	Hoshangabad ...	1,752	751	108	152	34	893	306	115	32	11	1	159	102	37	26	...
8	Nimar ...	1,350	659	59	72	14	632	17	8	...	1	...	9	14	3	...	...
9	Betul ...	1,808	674	345	43	57	789	183	47	28	3	...	58	51	25	9	...
10	Chhindwara ...	3,328	1,281	448	122	54	1,590	11	6	...	...	...	5	1,989	744	530	35
	NAGPUR DIVISION ...	*72,629*	*28,342*	*12,816*	*9,342*	*6,093*	*31,465*	*901*	*340*	*90*	*12*	*2*	*471*	*22,159*	*9,021*	*6,017*	*207*
11	Wardha ...	5,054	1,978	711	713	407	2,365	365	139	39	5	...	187	8	3	2	1
12	Nagpur ...	9,699	3,738	1,311	394	260	4,650	140	49	27	2	...	64	9,493	4,073	2,696	95
	NAGPUR CITY ...	*273*	*76*	*61*	*5*	...	*136*	*7*	*1*	...	...	...	*6*	*39*	*13*	...	...
13	Chanda ...	26,175	9,688	5,062	5,729	4,260	10,525	246	100	5	3	...	135	1,701	804	2	3
14	Bhandara ...	24,207	9,945	3,485	2,157	907	10,777	127	38	17	2	2	72	5,865	2,258	1,646	82
15	Balaghat ...	7,494	2,999	1,347	355	253	3,148	23	8	2	...	...	13	5,072	1,883	1,671	26
	CHHATTISGARH DIVISION.	*19,263*	*7,003*	*3,873*	*1,132*	*441*	*8,392*	*1,263*	*479*	*216*	*32*	*6*	*585*	*384*	*155*	*62*	*10*
16	Raipur ...	9,393	3,424	1,911	655	268	4,056	440	170	100	9	6	170	276	123	28	3
17	Bilaspur ...	4,086	1,511	801	295	120	1,774	382	142	42	23	...	198	36	15	4	...
18	Drug ...	5,789	2,068	1,161	182	53	2,500	401	167	74	...	...	220	72	17	30	7
	Berar ...	**14,532**	**6,120**	**1,754**	**1,654**	**697**	**6,658**	**2,158**	**943**	**143**	**35**	**15**	**1,072**	**584**	**174**	**125**	
19	Amraoti ...	5,406	2,274	904	751	431	2,228	472	223	14	11	1	235	106	41	11	3
20	Akola ...	1,906	878	117	269	19	971	757	323	79	22	14	355	273	71	75	2
21	Buldana ...	926	370	119	150	58	437	372	178	12	2	...	182	155	67	26	1
22	Yeotmal ...	6,234	2,598	614	484	189	3,022	557	219	38	...	...	300	50	5	13	...
	Feudatory States ...	**6,463**	**2,229**	**1,193**	**261**	**78**	**3,041**	**677**	**215**	**178**	**6**	...	**284**	**218**	**59**	**80**	**8**
23	Makrai ...	87	45	3	...	...	39	9	5	...	1	...	4	...	...	...	...
24	Bastar ...	920	338	114	41	1	468	109	33	41	...	...	35	5	3	1	...
25	Kanker ...	844	283	155	11	1	406	80	25	10	...	...	39	22	13	8	...
26	Nandgaon ...	997	366	101	47	5	530	86	30	25	...	...	31	6	1	...	...
27	Khairagarh ...	671	264	72	20	3	335	57	20	17	2	...	20	10	5	1	1
28	Chhuikhadan ...	170	62	12	4	...	96	17	4	2	...	...	11	8	5	3	...
29	Kawardha ...	385	142	56	8	3	187	107	30	21	...	...	56	...	...	...	...
30	Sakti ...	37	15	1	3	...	21	...	...	...	...	...	...	...	...	...	...
31	Raigarh ...	541	164	155	31	37	222	60	27	17	...	...	25	18	2	10	...
32	Sarangarh ...	401	119	133	19	9	149	10	3	...	...	...	7	...	...	...	...
33	Chang Bhakar ...	55	19	22	2	1	14	1	1	...	...	...	...	...	...	...	...
34	Korea ...	...	...	...	...	...	...	15	5	...	3	...	10	1	1	...	...
35	Surguja ...	26	11	2	...	...	13	32	13	2	...	...	17	...	...	...	...
36	Udaipur ...	74	21	23	3	4	30	25	4	3	...	...	18	83	11	36	...
37	Jashpur ...	1,255	380	344	72	14	531	60	15	34	...	...	11	65	18	26	7

# of livelihood. Part A.—General Table.

OF RAW MATERIALS—(*continued*).

Extraction of minerals.

Sub-Class II.		Order 3.—Mines.																			
Sub-Class II.		Total Order 3.						16.—Coal mines and petroleum wells.						17.—Mines and metallic minerals (gold, iron, manganese, etc.).							
Partially agriculturists.		Total workers and dependants.	Actual workers.				Dependants.	Total workers and dependants.	Actual workers.				Dependants.	Total workers and dependants.	Actual workers.				Dependants.	Serial number.
			Total.		Partially agriculturists.				Total.		Partially agriculturists.				Total.		Partially agriculturists.			
Females.	Dependants.		Males.	Females.	Males.	Females.			Males.	Females.	Males.	Females.			Males.	Females.	Males.	Females.		
162	163	164	165	166	167	168	169	170	171	172	173	174	175	176	177	178	179	180	181	
168	**10,354**	**27,423**	**10,910**	**7,205**	**279**	**157**	**9,308**	**6,117**	**2,569**	**840**	**69**	**18**	**2,708**	**21,306**	**8,341**	**6,365**	**210**	**139**	**6,600**	
151	**10,275**	**27,237**	**10,863**	**7,139**	**271**	**140**	**9,235**	**6,105**	**2,569**	**828**	**69**	**7**	**2,708**	**21,132**	**8,294**	**6,311**	**202**	**133**	**6,527**	
150	**9,990**	**27,080**	**10,813**	**7,113**	**271**	**139**	**9,154**	**6,078**	**2,547**	**828**	**69**	**7**	**2,698**	**21,007**	**8,266**	**6,285**	**202**	**132**	**6,456**	
11	*711*	*365*	*112*	*59*	*1*	*1*	*169*	*140*	*17*	*65*	...	...	*58*	*225*	*95*	*24*	*1*	*1*	*106*	
9	172	51	11	7	...		38	...	...	...	...	...	...	51	11	7	...	...	33	1
1	77	2	1	...	...	...	1	...	...	...	...	...	...	2	1	...	...	...	1	2
...	429	244	82	65	...	...	97	140	17	65	...	...	58	104	65	...	...	...	39	3
...	*21*	*11*	*1*	...	...	...	*10*	*5*	...	...	...	...	*5*	*6*	*1*	...	...	...	*5*	
1	31	63	15	17	1	1	31	...	...	...	...	...	...	63	15	17	1	1	31	4
...	2	5	3	...	...	...	2	...	...	...	...	...	...	5	3	...	...	...	2	5
25	*1,991*	*4,605*	*1,757*	*979*	*60*	*25*	*1,869*	*4,160*	*1,659*	*756*	*56*	*7*	*1,718*	*445*	*65*	*223*	*4*	*17*	*154*	
24	1,209	2,697	1,072	438	52	24	1,187	2,655	1,070	420	52	7	1,165	42	2	18	..	17	22	6
...	39	18	8	4	...	...	6	3	...	...	...	...	3	15	8	4	...	—	3	7
...	11	...	...	...	...	—	...	...	...	...	...	...	...	...	...	...	...	...	—	8
1	17	48	24	8	...	...	16	46	24	8	...	...	14	2	...	...	...	—	2	9
...	715	1,842	653	529	8	...	660	1,456	505	328	4	—	533	388	58	201	4	...	127	10
103	*7,121*	*21,976*	*8,903*	*6,004*	*202*	*103*	*7,069*	*1,752*	*832*	*3*	*13*	...	*917*	*20,224*	*8,071*	*6,001*	*189*	*103*	*6,152*	
...	3	8	3	2	1	...	3	...	...	...	...	...	...	8	3	2	1	...	3	11
48	2,724	9,374	3,902	2,694	91	48	2,688	1	1	...	...	...	...	9,373	3,991	2,694	91	48	2,688	12
...	*26*	*35*	*9*	...	...	...	*26*	*1*	*1*	...	—	...	...	*34*	*5*	—	...	...	*26*	
...	895	1,682	789	2	3	...	891	1,674	782	2	...	—	890	8	7	...	3	...	1	13
30	1,981	5,869	2,249	1,646	81	30	1,974	70	49	1	13	...	20	5,799	2,200	1,645	68	30	1,954	14
25	1,518	5,043	1,870	1,660	26	25	1,513	7	...	...	...	—	7	5,096	1,870	1,660	26	25	1,506	15
11	*167*	*134*	*41*	*41*	*8*	*11*	*52*	*21*	*9*	*4*	...	...	*8*	*113*	*32*	*37*	*8*	*11*	*44*	
1	125	58	23	14	1	1	21	4	4	...	...	...	...	54	19	14	1	1	21	16
...	17	20	5	2	...	...	13	13	4	2	...	...	7	7	1	...	...	...	6	17
10	25	56	13	25	7	10	18	4	1	2	...	...	1	52	12	23	7	10	17	18
1	**285**	**157**	**50**	**26**	...	**1**	**81**	**32**	**22**	...	...	...	**10**	**125**	**28**	**26**	...	**1**	**71**	
1	54	86	28	11	...	1	47	...	...	...	...	...	...	86	28	11	...	1	47	19
...	127	71	22	15	...	...	34	32	22	...	...	...	10	39	...	15	...	...	24	20
...	72	...	—	...	...	...	...	...	...	...	...	...	...	...	...	...	...	...	...	21
...	32	...	...	...	...	...	...	...	...	...	...	...	...	...	...	...	...	...	...	22
17	**79**	**186**	**47**	**66**	**8**	**17**	**73**	**12**	...	**12**	...	**11**	...	**174**	**47**	**54**	**8**	**6**	**73**	
...	...	...	...	...	...	...	...	...	...	...	...	...	...	—	...	...	...	...	...	23
...	1	3	2	1	...	...	...	...	...	...	...	...	...	3	2	1	...	...	...	24
...	6	20	13	1	...	...	6	...	...	...	...	...	...	20	13	1	...	...	6	25
...	5	1	...	...	...	...	1	...	...	...	...	...	...	1	...	...	...	...	1	26
...	4	5	2	...	1	...	3	...	...	...	...	...	...	5	2	...	1	...	3	27
...	...	...	...	...	...	...	...	...	...	...	...	...	...	...	—	...	...	...	...	28
...	...	...	...	...	...	...	...	...	...	...	...	...	...	...	...	...	...	...	...	29
...	...	...	...	...	...	...	...	...	...	...	...	...	...	...	...	...	...	...	...	30
...	6	10	2	2	...	...	6	...	...	...	...	...	...	10	2	2	...	...	6	31
...	...	...	...	...	...	...	...	...	...	...	...	...	...	...	...	...	...	...	...	32
...	...	...	...	...	...	...	...	...	...	...	...	...	...	...	...	...	...	...	...	33
...	...	1	1	...	...	...	...	...	...	...	...	...	...	1	1	...	...	...	...	34
...	...	...	...	...	...	...	...	...	...	...	...	...	...	...	...	...	...	...	...	35
...	36	83	11	36	...	...	36	...	...	...	...	...	...	83	11	36	...	...	36	36
17	21	63	16	26	7	17	21	12	...	12	...	11	...	51	16	14	7	6	21	37

TABLE XV.—Occupation or means

Serial number.	CLASS ... / SUB-CLASS ... / ORDER ... / DISTRICT, CITY OR STATE.	CLASS A.—PRODUCTION OF RAW MATERIALS—(concluded). Sub-Class II.—Extraction of minerals—(concluded). Total Order 4.—Quarries of hard rocks. 18.—Other minerals (jade, diamonds, limestone, etc.). Total workers and dependants.	Actual workers. Total. Males.	Actual workers. Total. Females.	Actual workers. Partially agriculturists. Males.	Actual workers. Partially agriculturists. Females.	Dependants.	Order 5.—Salt, etc. Total Order 5. Total workers and dependants.	Actual workers. Total. Males.	Actual workers. Total. Females.	Actual workers. Partially agriculturists. Males.	Actual workers. Partially agriculturists. Females.	Dependants.	19.—Rock, sea and marsh salt. Total workers and dependants.	Actual workers. Total. Males.	Actual workers. Total. Females.	Actual workers. Partially agriculturists. Males.	Actual workers. Partially agriculturists. Females.	Dependants.	20.—Extrac alum and soluble. Total workers and dependants.	Actual Total. Males.	Actual Total. Females.
	1	182	183	184	185	186	187	188	189	190	191	192	193	194	195	196	197	198	199	200	201	202
	Central Provinces and Berar ...	**1,892**	**844**	**216**	**65**	**2**	**832**	**660**	**195**	**251**	**5**	**9**	**214**	**3**	**1**	...	**1**	...	**2**	**657**	**194**	**251**
	C. P. British Districts and Berar ...	**1,883**	**839**	**216**	**65**	**2**	**828**	**637**	**188**	**237**	**5**	**9**	**212**	**3**	**1**	...	**1**	...	**2**	**634**	**187**	**237**
	C. P. British Districts ...	**1,544**	**743**	**146**	**59**	**2**	**655**	**549**	**160**	**208**	**5**	**9**	**181**	**3**	**1**	...	**1**	...	**2**	**546**	**159**	**208**
	JUBBULPORE DIVISION	*981*	*437*	*125*	*26*	*1*	*439*	*378*	*102*	*158*	*3*	*9*	*115*	—	...	...	...	...	...	*378*	*102*	*156*
1	Saugor ...	184	57	28	6	...	99	165	42	83	...	9	40	...	...	...	...	...	...	165	42	83
2	Damoh ...	103	7	31	3	1	65	22	...	11	...	...	11	...	...	...	...	...	...	22	...	11
3	Jubbulpore ...	694	363	66	17	...	265	187	59	61	3	...	67	—	...	...	...	...	...	187	59	61
	JUBBULPORE CITY ...	*7*	*1*	...	*1*	...	*6*	*42*	*7*	*23*	...	...	*12*	...	...	...	...	...	...	*42*	*7*	*23*
4	Mandla ...	...	...	...	...	...	...	—	...	...	...	—	...	...	...	...	...	...	...	...	...	...
5	Seoni ...	...	—	...	...	...	...	4	1	3	...	.	...	...	...	...	...	...	...	4	1	3
	NERBUDDA DIVISION	*189*	*106*	*2*	*27*	*1*	*81*	*112*	*36*	*35*	*1*	...	*41*	*1*	...	...	...	...	*1*	*111*	*36*	*35*
6	Narsinghpur ...	2	2	...	..	...	...	51	16	13	1	...	22	...	...	...	...	...	...	51	16	13
7	Hoshangabad ...	24	9	...	...	...	15	60	20	22	...	...	18	...	...	...	...	...	...	60	20	22
8	Nimar ...	14	8	...	...	...	11	...	...	...	—	...	—	—	...	...	...	...	...	...	...	...
9	Betul ...	3	1	1	...	1	1	...	...	...	...	...	...	...	...	...	...	—	...	...	...	...
10	Chhindwara ...	146	91	1	27	...	54	1	...	...	...	...	1	1	...	...	...	—	1	...	...	...
	NAGPUR DIVISION ...	*181*	*117*	*13*	*4*	—	*51*	*2*	*1*	...	*1*	...	*1*	*2*	*1*	...	*1*	—	*1*	...	..	...
11	Wardha ...	..	...	...	...	...	...	...	...	...	...	...	...	...	...	...	...	...	...	...	...	...
12	Nagpur ...	119	81	2	4	...	36	—	...	...	...	...	...	—	...	.	...	...	...	...	...	...
	NAGPUR CITY ...	*4*	*4*	...	...	—	...	...	...	...	...	...	...	...	...	...	...	...	...	...	...	...
13	Chanda ...	19	15	...	...	...	4	...	...	...	...	...	...	...	...	...	...	...	...	...	...	...
14	Bhandara ...	14	8	...	...	—	6	2	1	...	1	...	1	2	1	...	1	...	1	...	...	—
15	Balaghat ...	29	13	11	...	—	5	...	...	...	...	...	...	...	...	...	...	...	...	..	—	—
	CHHATTISGARH DIVISION.	*193*	*93*	*6*	*2*	...	*94*	*57*	*21*	*15*	...	...	*21*	...	...	...	...	...	...	*57*	*21*	*15*
16	Raipur ...	179	85	6	2	...	88	39	15	8	...	...	16	...	...	...	...	...	...	39	15	8
17	Bilaspur ...	11	7	...	...	...	4	5	3	2	...	...	...	...	...	...	...	...	...	5	3	2
18	Drug ...	3	1	...	...	...	2	13	3	5	...	...	5	...	...	...	...	—	...	13	3	5
	Berar ...	**339**	**96**	**70**	**6**	...	**173**	**88**	**28**	**29**	...	...	**31**	...	...	...	...	...	...	**88**	**28**	**29**
19	Amraoti ...	20	13	...	3	...	7	.	...	...	...	...	...	..	...	...	...	...	...	...	...	...
20	Akola ...	114	21	31	2	—	62	88	28	29	...	...	31	—	—	...	...	...	.	88	28	29
21	Buldana ...	155	57	20	1	...	72	...	..	...	...	...	...	...	—	...	...	...	...	...	...	...
22	Yeotmal ...	50	5	13	...	...	32	...	...	...	...	...	...	...	...	...	...	...	...	...	...	...
	Feudatory States ...	**9**	**5**	...	...	...	**4**	**23**	**7**	**14**	...	...	**2**	...	...	...	—	...	...	**23**	**7**	**14**
23	Makrai ..	...	—	—	...	...	...	...	...	...	...	..	...	...	...	...	..	...	...	...	...	—
24	Bastar ...	2	1	...	...	...	1	...	...	...	...	...	...	...	...	...	...	...	...	...	...	...
25	Kanker ...	—	...	...	...	...	...	2	..	2	...	...	...	...	...	...	...	...	...	2	...	2
26	Nandgaon ...	4	1	...	...	...	3	1	...	...	...	...	1	...	.	...	...	...	...	1	...	...
27	Khairagarh ...	1	1	...	...	...	...	4	2	1	—	...	1	...	...	...	...	—	...	4	2	1
28	Chhuikhadan ...	...	...	..	...	...	...	8	5	3	—	...	...	...	...	...	...	...	...	8	5	3
29	Kawardha ...	...	...	...	..	...	...	...	...	...	...	...	...	...	...	...	...	...	...	...	...	...
30	Sakti ...	...	...	...	...	—	...	...	.	...	—	...	...	...	...	...	...	...	...	...	...	...
31	Raigarh ...	...	...	...	...	...	...	8	...	8	...	...	...	...	...	...	...	...	...	8	...	8
32	Sarangarh ...	...	...	...	...	...	...	...	...	...	...	...	..	...	...	...	...	...	...	...	...	...
33	Chang Bhakar ...	...	...	...	...	...	...	..	...	...	...	...	...	...	...	...	...	...	...	...	...	...
34	Korea ...	...	...	...	...	—	...	...	...	...	...	...	...	...	...	...	...	...	...	...	—	...
35	Surguja ...	...	...	...	—	—	...	—	...	..	...	...	...	...	...	...	...	...	...	...	...	...
36	Udaipur ...	...	—	...	—	—	...	—	..	...	...	..	...	...	...	...	...	...	...	...	...	...
37	Jashpur ...	2	2	...	...	...	...	...	...	...	...	...	...	...	...	...	...	...	—	—	...	...

# of livelihood. Part A.—General Table.

...tion of saltpetre, other substances in water.			CLASS B.—PREPARATION AND SUPPLY OF MATERIAL SUBSTANCES.												
			Total Class B.						Sub-Class III.—Industry. Total Sub-Class III.						
WORKERS.				ACTUAL WORKERS.						ACTUAL WORKERS.					
Partially agriculturists.		Dependants.	Total workers and dependants.	Total.		Partially agriculturists.		Dependants.	Total workers and dependants.	Total.		Partially agriculturists.		Dependants.	Serial Number.
Males.	Females.			Males.	Females.	Males.	Females.			Males.	Females.	Males.	Females.		
203	204	205	206	207	208	209	210	211	212	213	214	215	216	217	
4	**9**	**212**	**2,427,166**	**839,991**	**465,142**	**106,499**	**49,461**	**1,122,033**	**1,613,813**	**551,175**	**337,776**	**83,446**	**39,140**	**724,862**	
4	**9**	**210**	**2,210,067**	**772,863**	**409,849**	**100,844**	**47,048**	**1,027,355**	**1,455,206**	**503,476**	**295,524**	**78,886**	**37,213**	**656,206**	
4	**9**	**179**	**1,746,794**	**599,014**	**347,334**	**81,484**	**39,095**	**800,446**	**1,178,602**	**399,436**	**252,147**	**66,594**	**31,452**	**527,019**	
3	*9*	*115*	*450,276*	*158,394*	*73,837*	*25,309*	*6,595*	*223,995*	*295,943*	*100,262*	*51,313*	*21,853*	*5,364*	*144,368*	
...	9	40	123,655	42,560	18,610	8,793	2,030	62,485	84,065	29,345	13,558	7,887	1,760	41,162	1
...	...	11	69,924	23,550	9,800	6,744	1,187	36,574	50,389	17,288	6,869	6,096	994	26,232	2
3	...	67	166,372	55,045	27,172	7,472	2,645	84,155	101,494	33,918	17,293	6,005	1,909	50,283	3
...	...	*12*	*59,995*	*19,752*	*6,794*	*75*	*17*	*33,449*	*33,625*	*11,018*	*4,044*	*15*	*15*	*17,563*	
...	...	...	41,848	14,743	8,603	1,159	381	18,502	25,332	8,140	5,979	933	351	11,213	4
...	..	...	48,477	16,496	9,702	1,141	352	22,279	34,663	11,571	7,614	932	341	15,478	5
1	...	*40*	*392,625*	*139,724*	*70,051*	*15,037*	*6,735*	*182,323*	*252,885*	*86,331*	*48,698*	*11,923*	*5,443*	*117,356*	
1	...	22	70,241	22,593	13,901	4,327	2,042	33,747	50,597	16,400	10,624	3,650	1,688	28,573	6
...	...	18	106,896	36,706	17,456	4,367	1,677	52,734	68,168	23,441	11,486	3,578	1,170	33,241	7
...	...	...	81,794	30,090	12,099	1,992	733	39,605	53,838	18,980	10,159	1,445	648	24,699	8
...	...	...	60,041	23,093	12,755	2,228	1,254	24,193	33,730	11,665	7,695	1,714	1,132	14,370	9
...	...	...	73,626	27,242	13,840	2,123	1,029	32,544	46,552	16,345	8,734	1,536	805	21,473	10
...	...	...	*618,056*	*216,423*	*126,766*	*30,146*	*20,667*	*274,567*	*431,098*	*150,794*	*96,707*	*28,818*	*16,495*	*183,597*	
...	...	...	75,185	28,531	10,011	2,545	1,172	36,643	47,608	18,420	7,018	1,615	817	22,170	11
...	...	...	222,807	78,489	42,229	4,414	2,153	102,085	154,838	54,781	32,294	3,075	1,666	67,763	12
...	...	...	*69,377*	*24,397*	*10,879*	*155*	*26*	*34,101*	*46,671*	*16,331*	*7,859*	*81*	*15*	*21,431*	
...	..	...	128,445	43,661	27,693	11,285	9,302	57,001	91,982	31,062	20,966	9,592	7,507	39,004	13
...	...	...	141,233	48,492	33,550	9,170	6,457	59,191	100,012	34,151	26,435	7,064	5,150	39,426	14
...	...	...	50,390	17,250	13,283	2,781	1,583	19,857	36,708	12,380	9,994	2,467	1,346	14,334	15
...	...	*21*	*285,864*	*90,473*	*76,630*	*10,993*	*6,098*	*118,761*	*193,676*	*61,549*	*55,489*	*9,005*	*4,150*	*81,693*	
...	...	16	130,360	40,671	36,211	4,535	2,366	53,478	91,227	27,590	27,280	3,785	1,994	38,407	16
...	...	...	86,753	28,290	21,509	4,239	1,975	36,954	57,351	17,976	15,556	3,392	1,552	23,819	17
...	...	5	68,751	21,512	18,910	2,219	757	28,329	50,098	15,983	12,643	1,828	604	21,472	18
...	...	**31**	**463,273**	**173,849**	**62,515**	**19,360**	**7,953**	**226,909**	**276,604**	**104,040**	**43,377**	**12,292**	**5,761**	**129,187**	
...	...	...	144,984	53,110	20,417	5,171	2,225	71,458	84,359	31,096	13,278	2,884	1,295	39,990	19
...	...	31	120,697	46,121	16,269	6,095	2,329	58,307	69,906	26,626	11,111	4,005	1,725	32,169	20
...	...	...	102,181	36,444	14,509	5,478	2,415	51,228	62,893	22,655	10,778	3,766	1,982	29,460	21
...	...	...	95,415	38,174	11,320	2,616	984	45,921	50,446	23,603	8,215	1,637	759	27,568	22
...	...	**2**	**217,099**	**67,128**	**55,293**	**5,655**	**2,413**	**94,678**	**158,607**	**47,699**	**42,252**	**4,580**	**1,927**	**68,656**	
...	...	...	2,236	754	398	89	17	1,084	1,580	563	327	73	15	690	23
...	...	...	44,114	13,344	14,006	584	221	16,764	31,574	9,314	10,444	450	183	11,816	24
...	...	...	12,940	4,064	3,560	183	112	5,316	10,019	3,129	2,816	141	92	4,074	25
...	...	1	20,120	6,754	4,463	496	189	8,903	14,271	4,080	3,459	392	159	6,123	26
...	...	1	18,500	5,710	4,450	411	160	8,436	11,638	3,494	3,031	335	142	5,013	27
...	...	...	4,168	1,245	1,041	117	25	1,882	3,004	948	773	100	23	1,373	28
...	...	...	7,673	2,334	2,044	249	84	3,295	5,324	1,621	1,404	206	76	2,290	29
...	...	...	2,249	756	560	75	58	933	1,508	441	462	58	57	605	30
...	...	...	25,299	7,464	7,548	543	589	10,287	17,256	4,898	5,495	457	371	6,863	31
...	...	...	10,615	2,654	4,121	479	197	3,840	7,252	1,725	3,073	322	125	2,454	32
...	...	...	2,514	864	754	130	57	896	1,888	660	500	116	36	728	33
...	...	...	6,240	2,158	1,448	172	37	2,639	4,677	1,459	1,196	118	30	2,022	34
...	...	...	32,536	10,355	8,075	647	113	19,100	25,200	7,718	2,429	449	86	15,053	35
...	...	...	6,863	2,039	1,838	114	42	2,986	5,717	1,612	1,593	96	41	2,512	36
...	...	...	20,936	6,683	5,992	1,306	512	8,311	17,700	5,428	5,250	1,347	491	7,031	37

TABLE XV.—Occupation or means

Serial number.	CLASS ...	CLASS B.—PREPARATION AND SUPPLY												
	SUB-CLASS ...													
	ORDER ...	Order 6.—Textiles.												
		Total Order 6.						21.—Cotton ginning, cleaning and pressing.						
	DISTRICT, CITY OR STATE.	Total workers and dependants.	ACTUAL WORKERS. Total.		ACTUAL WORKERS. Partially agriculturists.		Dependants.	Total workers and dependants.	ACTUAL WORKERS. Total.		ACTUAL WORKERS. Partially agriculturists.		Dependants.	Total workers and dependants.
			Males.	Females.	Males.	Females.			Males.	Females.	Males.	Females.		
	1	218	219	220	221	222	223	224	225	226	227	228	229	230
	Central Provinces and Berar ...	**443.730**	**150.288**	**117.089**	**18,223**	**14,106**	**176.353**	**47,261**	**17,595**	**9,515**	**1,733**	**870**	**20,151**	**350.540**
	C. P. British Districts and Berar ...	**390.379**	**133.797**	**102.588**	**16,811**	**13,436**	**153.996**	**47,110**	**17,562**	**9,438**	**1,730**	**870**	**20.110**	**299.635**
	C. P. British Districts ...	**340.850**	**115.885**	**91,298**	**15,395**	**12,560**	**133.667**	**25,632**	**9,792**	**4.962**	**1,075**	**406**	**10.878**	**276.114**
	JUBBULPORE DIVISION	*40,369*	*13,926*	*9,245*	*2,406*	*1,144*	*17,195*	*4,504*	*1,653*	*531*	*533*	*86*	*2,300*	*31,534*
1	Saugor ...	10.719	3,616	2,707	679	321	4,396	1,416	514	175	261	51	607	7,582
2	Damoh ...	4,949	1,635	966	524	117	2,348	1,011	360	55	190	16	587	3,171
3	Jubbulpore ..	12,566	4,566	2,452	805	446	5,548	1,788	674	243	74	19	871	9,402
	JUBBULPORE CITY ...	*5,749*	*2,159*	*1,002*	...	*1*	*2,588*	*866*	*217*	*194*	...	...	*455*	*4,544*
4	Mandla ...	4,883	1,588	1,295	244	155	2,000	54	18	9	5	...	27	4,653
5	Seoni ...	7,252	2,621	1,828	154	105	2,003	235	78	30	3	...	118	6,726
	NERBUDDA DIVISION	*53,624*	*18,287*	*12,418*	*2,568*	*1,564*	*21,919*	*6,660*	*2,259*	*1,318*	*406*	*125*	*3,053*	*40,100*
6	Narsinghpur ...	7,869	2,562	2,076	809	502	3,231	1,131	449	97	191	30	585	5,731
7	Hoshangabad ...	11,237	3,994	2,209	591	283	5,034	1,658	538	321	100	35	799	8,432
8	Nimar ...	14,207	4,849	3,636	354	216	5,722	3,223	1,074	781	81	40	1,368	8,769
9	Betul ..	7,855	2,732	1,986	424	510	3,137	56	15	19	3	7	22	6,975
10	Chhindwara ...	11,456	4,150	2,511	390	353	4,795	592	213	100	31	13	279	10,193
	NAGPUR DIVISION ...	*178,919*	*61,910*	*47,395*	*7,645*	*7,799*	*69,611*	*13,414*	*5,748*	*3,210*	*131*	*96*	*6,456*	*145,152*
11	Wardha ...	13,348	5,279	2,336	211	136	5,728	6,129	2,535	956	30	10	2,638	6,323
12	Nagpur ...	71,619	25,297	17,936	456	557	28,386	6,132	2,852	860	73	21	2,420	54,626
	NAGPUR CITY ...	*28,770*	*10,724*	*5,505*	*61*	*12*	*12,541*	*4,075*	*2,041*	*451*	*31*	...	*1,583*	*18,539*
13	Chanda ...	38,182	12,387	10,497	4,333	4,449	15,208	823	254	310	7	60	259	34,630
14	Bhandara ...	42,282	14,461	12,520	2,021	2,080	15,301	184	66	39	2	...	79	36,688
15	Balaghat ...	13,493	4,486	4,100	624	577	4,898	146	41	45	10	5	60	12,885
	CHHATTISGARH DIVISION.	*68,938*	*21,762*	*22,234*	*2,776*	*1,753*	*24,942*	*1,054*	*72*	*918*	*5*	*99*	*69*	*59,325*
16	Raipur ..	33,260	10,284	11,035	1,193	923	11,941	973	63	852	5	97	58	29,830
17	Bilaspur ...	17,510	5,601	5,485	1,184	614	6,424	52	3	45	...	2	4	13,485
18	Drug ...	18,168	5,877	5,714	399	216	6,577	29	6	16	..	...	7	16,063
	Berar ...	**49,529**	**17,912**	**11,288**	**1.416**	**876**	**20.329**	**21.478**	**7,770**	**4.476**	**655**	**464**	**9.232**	**23.521**
19	Amraoti ...	17,637	6,210	3,901	406	144	7,520	6,028	2,312	1,325	179	64	3,291	9,184
20	Akola ...	13,269	4,870	2,859	471	325	5,540	6,546	2,430	1,418	250	225	2,698	5,754
21	Buldana ...	10,428	3,495	2,921	207	201	4,012	5,156	1,918	1,101	82	47	2,137	3,791
22	Yeotmal ...	8,201	3,337	1,607	332	206	3,257	2,848	1,110	632	144	128	1,106	4,792
	Feudatory States ...	**53,351**	**16,491**	**14,503**	**1.412**	**670**	**22,357**	**151**	**33**	**77**	**3**	...	**41**	**50,905**
23	Makrai ...	231	97	23	17	...	111	36	10	14	3	...	12	187
24	Bastar ...	12,649	3,959	3,861	157	65	4,829	28	...	28	—	...	...	12,462
25	Kanker ...	3,386	1,119	936	27	19	1,331	1	...	1	...	...	...	3,326
26	Nandgaon ...	6,332	2,202	1,647	87	56	2,483	19	1	8	...	...	10	5,887
27	Khairagarh ...	2,967	941	888	62	31	1,138	26	6	13	..	...	7	2,718
28	Chhuikhadan ...	1,161	365	364	19	2	432	2	1	1	...	...	—	918
29	Kawardha ...	1,232	384	473	22	20	375	2	1	...	...	...	1	1,025
30	Sakti ...	312	100	100	21	16	112	...	...	...	...	...	...	191
31	Raigarh ...	4,790	1,368	1,470	105	49	1,952	16	12	...	...	...	4	4,222
32	Sarangarh ...	2,369	655	878	75	67	836	4	...	4	—	...	...	2,249
33	Chang Bhakar ...	410	110	120	14	6	162	...	...	...	...	...	...	410
34	Korea ...	576	175	126	18	4	275	3	...	2	...	...	1	553
35	Surguja ...	7,548	2,275	642	87	20	4,651	2	1	...	...	...	1	7,492
36	Udaipur ...	2,406	637	691	67	23	1,078	...	—	...	...	...	—	2,359
37	Jashpur ...	6,982	2,095	2,295	634	298	2,532	12	1	6	...	...	5	6,906

# of livelihood. Part A.—General Table.

OF MATERIAL SUBSTANCES—(*continued*).

Sub-Class III.—Industry—(*continued*).

22.—Cotton-spinning, sizing and weaving. Actual workers. Total. Males.	22.—Actual workers. Total. Females.	22.—Actual workers. Partially agriculturists. Males.	22.—Actual workers. Partially agriculturists. Females.	22.—Dependants.	Details of Group 22. (a)—Cotton-spinning. Total workers and dependants.	(a) Actual workers. Total. Males.	(a) Actual workers. Total. Females.	(a) Actual workers. Partially agriculturists. Males.	(a) Actual workers. Partially agriculturists. Females.	(a) Dependants.	(b)—Cotton sizing. Total workers and dependants.	(b) Actual workers. Total. Males.	(b) Actual workers. Total. Females.	(b) Actual workers. Partially agriculturists. Males.	(b) Actual workers. Partially agriculturists. Females.	(b) Dependants.	Serial number.
231	232	233	234	235	236	237	238	239	240	241	242	243	244	245	246	247	
117,635	**95,418**	**14,789**	**11,485**	**137,487**	**37,983**	**3,581**	**27,448**	**342**	**3,064**	**6,954**	**1,867**	**383**	**761**	**18**	**192**	**723**	
101,808	**81,772**	**13,431**	**10,845**	**116,055**	**33,579**	**3,216**	**24,471**	**325**	**2,933**	**5,892**	**1,509**	**383**	**539**	**18**	**131**	**587**	
93,379	**75,991**	**12,892**	**10,630**	**106,744**	**29,621**	**2,869**	**21,435**	**303**	**2,853**	**5,317**	**1,102**	**116**	**524**	**11**	**127**	**462**	
10,855	*7,731*	*1,657*	*955*	*12,949*	*1,999*	*100*	*1,551*	*18*	*243*	*335*	*245*	*50*	*75*	*11*	*22*	*120*	
2,506	2,105	320	229	2,969	529	25	394	4	102	110	91	1	27	...	16	63	1
1,079	739	291	89	1,353	332	33	249	2	47	50	2	1	1	...	...	...	2
3,440	1,927	661	392	4,035	783	31	594	12	90	158	140	44	42	11	6	54	3
1,811	*800*	...	*1*	*1,933*	*357*	*3*	*270*	...	...	*84*	*42*	*10*	*16*	...	...	*22*	
1,508	1,249	227	143	1,896	40	8	22	...	3	15	6	2	3	...	...	1	4
2,319	1,711	140	105	2,096	315	8	292	...	1	15	6	2	2	...	...	2	5
14,155	*9,380*	*1,915*	*1,159*	*16,566*	*4,256*	*801*	*2,180*	*85*	*33[illegible]*	*1,305*	*6*	*3*	...	...	...	*3*	
1,824	1,610	515	364	2,297	761	142	525	66	131	94	6	3	...	...	...	3	6
3,115	1,545	475	224	3,772	360	4	331	...	32	25	...	...	...	...	...	...	7
3,083	2,264	216	122	3,422	1,786	278	721	...	11	787	...	...	...	...	...	...	8
2,440	1,721	374	432	2,805	119	5	109	...	38	5	...	...	...	...	...	...	9
3,684	2,240	335	317	4,269	1,200	372	494	19	120	394	...	...	...	...	...	...	10
49,300	*40,419*	*7,182*	*6,970*	*55,408*	*18,606*	*1,792*	*13,512*	*159*	*1,930*	*3,403*	*773*	*63*	*408*	...	*90*	*307*	
2,416	1,197	127	98	2,710	845	44	229	...	27	72	...	...	...	...	...	...	11
18,347	15,270	323	463	21,009	10,588	634	7,843	14	331	2,111	410	34	113	...	...	265	12
6,834	*4,699*	*15*	*1[illegible]*	*8,006*	*2,777*	*130*	*1,730*	...	*11*	*937*	*94*	*34*	*1*	...	...	*69*	
11,644	9,066	4,156	3,830	13,920	3,003	150	2,439	10	789	405	...	...	...	...	...	...	13
12,604	10,954	1,970	2,022	13,130	4,427	918	2,916	133	767	593	357	20	295	...	90	42	14
4,289	3,902	607	562	4,634	143	37	85	2	22	21	11	9	...	...	...	2	15
19,070	*18,431*	*2,133*	*1,237*	*21,827*	*4,830*	*176*	*4,192*	*41*	*345*	*462*	*73*	...	*41*	...	*9*	*32*	
9,494	9,367	1,030	679	10,909	3,615	127	3,226	40	256	262	...	...	...	...	...	...	16
4,310	4,044	772	383	5,072	721	30	518	...	65	173	73	...	41	...	9	32	17
5,257	5,020	336	175	5,786	494	19	448	1	27	27	...	...	...	—	...	...	18
8,429	**5,781**	**539**	**215**	**9,811**	**3,958**	**347**	**3,036**	**22**	**80**	**575**	**407**	**267**	**15**	**7**	**4**	**126**	
3,220	2,327	160	40	3,628	2,025	150	1,678	10	23	107	32	11	5	...	4	16	19
2,030	1,290	127	67	2,428	543	104	258	7	28	181	...	...	...	...	...	...	20
1,151	1,317	67	46	1,325	983	82	786	5	9	115	323	220	...	...	...	97	21
2,013	849	179	56	1,930	407	11	814	...	20	82	52	30	10	7	...	12	22
15,827	**13,646**	**1,358**	**640**	**21,432**	**4,404**	**365**	**2,977**	**17**	**131**	**1,062**	**358**	...	**222**	...	**61**	**136**	
84	8	14	...	95	1	...	1	...	...	...	...	...	...	...	...	...	23
3,913	3,800	157	65	4,749	1,698	215	1,262	4	8	216	...	...	...	...	...	...	24
1,087	928	25	19	1,311	380	...	219	..	...	161	...	...	...	...	...	...	25
2,074	1,497	66	42	2,316	35	3	31	...	6	1	...	...	...	...	...	...	26
860	811	57	30	1,047	6	...	5	...	...	1	...	...	...	...	...	...	27
297	284	15	1	337	1	...	1	...	...	...	...	...	...	...	...	...	28
350	399	22	17	276	20	1	17	...	5	2	...	...	...	...	...	...	29
63	50	11	7	69	2	1	1	...	...	...	...	...	...	...	...	...	30
1,187	1,271	98	41	1,764	12	...	10	—	1	2	...	...	...	...	...	...	31
650	808	75	67	796	447	109	217	7	1	121	...	...	...	...	...	...	32
119	129	14	6	162	5	1	...	...	...	4	...	...	...	...	...	...	33
167	120	18	4	266	53	...	52	...	3	1	...	...	...	...	...	...	34
2,268	602	87	20	4,622	110	1	54	...	—	55	...	...	...	...	...	...	35
629	684	67	23	1,046	209	11	177	...	5	21	...	...	...	...	...	...	36
2,079	2,251	632	298	2,576	1,430	23	930	16	102	477	358	...	222	...	61	136	37

TABLE XV.—Occupation or means

Serial No.	CLASS ... / SUB-CLASS ... / ORDER ...	CLASS B.—PREPARATION AND SUPPLY / Sub-Class III.— / Order 6.— / Details of Group 22—(*concluded*).											
		(c) Cotton weaving.						(d) Cotton and silk weaving.					
	DISTRICT, CITY OR STATE.	Total workers and dependants.	Actual workers. Total.		Actual workers. Partially agriculturists.		Dependants.	Total workers and dependants.	Actual workers. Total.		Actual workers. Partially agriculturists.		Dependants.
			Males.	Females.	Males.	Females.			Males.	Females.	Males.	Females.	
	1	248	249	250	251	252	253	254	255	256	257	258	259
	Central Provinces and Berar ...	**308,614**	**112,842**	**66,918**	**14,424**	**8,229**	**128,854**	**2,076**	**829**	**291**	**5**	...	**956**
	C. P. British Districts and Berar ...	**262,471**	**97,380**	**56,471**	**13,083**	**7,781**	**108,620**	**2,076**	**829**	**291**	**5**	...	**956**
	C. P. British Districts ...	**243,320**	**89,565**	**53,743**	**12,573**	**7,650**	**100,012**	**2,071**	**829**	**289**	**5**	...	**953**
	JUBBULPORE DIVISION.	*29,207*	*10,667*	*6,095*	*1,635*	*693*	*12,445*	*83*	*37*	*10*	...	...	*36*
1	Saugor ...	6,948	2,482	1,678	325	111	2,788	14	...	6	...	...	8
2	Damoh ...	2,837	1,045	489	289	42	1,303	...	...	...	...	...	...
3	Jubbulpore ...	8,414	3,329	1,287	638	296	3,798	65	36	4	...	...	25
	JUBBULPORE CITY ...	*4,086*	*1,762*	*520*	...	*1*	*1,503*	*60*	*36*	...	...	...	*24*
4	Mandla ...	4,603	1,502	1,224	227	140	1,877	4	1	...	...	...	3
5	Seoni ...	6,405	2,309	1,417	149	104	2,679	...	...	...	...	...	...
	NERBUDDA DIVISION	*35,291*	*13,156*	*7,040*	*1,830*	*1,127*	*15,095*	*517*	*195*	*160*	...	...	*162*
6	Narsinghpur ...	4,964	1,679	1,085	449	233	2,200	...	...	...	...	...	...
7	Hoshangabad ...	8,072	3,111	1,214	475	192	3,747	...	...	...	...	...	...
8	Nimar ...	6,466	2,610	1,383	216	111	2,473	517	195	160	...	...	162
9	Betul ...	6,856	2,444	1,612	374	394	2,800	...	...	...	...	...	...
10	Chhindwara ...	8,933	3,312	1,740	316	197	3,875	...	...	...	...	...	...
	NAGPUR DIVISION ...	*124,399*	*46,850*	*26,410*	*7,018*	*4,950*	*51,139*	*1,469*	*595*	*119*	*5*	...	*755*
11	Wardha ...	5,978	2,372	968	127	71	2,638	...	...	...	...	...	...
12	Nagpur ...	42,352	17,203	7,205	307	132	17,944	1,276	470	109	2	...	691
	NAGPUR CITY ...	*16,090*	*5,680*	*2,800*	*11*	*1*	*6,550*	*578*	...	*105*	...	...	*470*
13	Chanda ...	31,627	11,485	6,627	4,146	3,047	13,515	...	...	...	...	...	...
14	Bhandara ...	31,904	11,666	7,743	1,837	1,160	12,495	...	...	...	...	...	...
15	Balaghat ...	12,538	4,124	3,867	602	540	4,547	193	119	10	3	...	64
	CHHATTISGARH DIVISION.	*53,823*	*18,892*	*14,198*	*2,097*	*880*	*21,333*	*2*	*2*	...	...	...	...
16	Raipur ...	26,215	9,367	6,141	990	423	10,707	...	...	...	...	...	...
17	Bilaspur ...	12,039	4,287	3,485	772	300	4,867	2	2	...	...	...	...
18	Drug ...	15,569	5,238	4,572	335	148	5,759	...	...	...	...	...	...
	Berar ...	**19,151**	**7,815**	**2,728**	**510**	**131**	**8,808**	**5**	...	**2**	...	...	**3**
19	Amraoti ...	7,127	3,068	641	156	19	3,415	...	...	...	...	...	...
20	Akola ...	5,211	1,032	1,032	120	39	2,247	...	...	...	...	...	...
21	Buldana ...	2,480	843	527	62	37	1,110	5	...	2	...	...	3
22	Yeotmal ...	4,333	1,072	525	172	36	1,836	...	...	...	...	...	...
	Feudatory States ...	**46,143**	**15,462**	**10,447**	**1,341**	**448**	**20,234**	...	...	...	...	...	...
23	Makrai ...	186	84	7	14	...	95	...	...	...	...	...	...
24	Bastar ...	10,769	3,698	2,538	153	57	4,533	...	...	...	...	...	...
25	Kanker ...	2,946	1,087	700	25	19	1,150	...	...	...	...	...	...
26	Nandgaon ...	5,852	2,071	1,466	66	36	2,315	...	...	...	...	...	...
27	Khairagarh ...	2,712	860	806	57	30	1,040	...	...	...	...	...	...
28	Chhuikhadan ...	917	207	283	15	1	337	...	...	...	...	...	...
29	Kawardha ...	1,005	349	382	22	12	274	...	...	...	...	...	...
30	Sakti ...	189	62	58	11	7	69	...	...	...	...	...	...
31	Raigarh ...	4,210	1,187	1,261	98	40	1,762	...	...	...	...	...	...
32	Sarangarh ...	1,802	541	586	68	66	675	...	...	...	...	...	...
33	Chang Bhakar ...	405	118	129	14	6	158	...	...	...	...	...	...
34	Korea ...	500	167	68	18	1	265	...	...	...	...	...	...
35	Surguja ...	7,382	2,267	548	87	20	4,567	...	...	...	...	...	...
36	Udaipur ...	2,150	618	507	67	19	1,025	...	...	...	...	...	...
37	Jashpur ...	5,118	2,056	1,099	626	135	1,963	...	...	...	...	...	...

# of livelihood, Part A.—General Table.

OF MATERIAL SUBSTANCES—(*continued*).

Industry—(*continued*).

Textiles—(*continued*).

23.—Jute spinning, pressing and weaving.						24.—Rope, twine and string.						25.—Other fibres (cocoanut, aloes, flax, hemp, straw, etc.)						
Total workers and dependants.	Actual workers. Total. Males.	Actual workers. Total. Females.	Actual workers. Partially agriculturists. Males.	Actual workers. Partially agriculturists. Females.	Dependants.	Total workers and dependants.	Actual workers. Total. Males.	Actual workers. Total. Females.	Actual workers. Partially agriculturists. Males.	Actual workers. Partially agriculturists. Females.	Dependants.	Total workers and dependants.	Actual workers. Total. Males.	Actual workers. Total. Females.	Actual workers. Partially agriculturists. Males.	Actual workers. Partially agriculturists. Females.	Dependants.	Serial No.
260	261	262	263	264	265	266	267	268	269	270	271	272	273	274	275	276	277	
2,129	**795**	**569**	**145**	**76**	**765**	**3,676**	**1,065**	**1,322**	**147**	**194**	**1,289**	**1,345**	**399**	**428**	**91**	**165**	**518**	
1,953	**758**	**535**	**142**	**76**	**660**	**3,440**	**1,005**	**1,252**	**146**	**194**	**1,183**	**1,296**	**396**	**401**	**91**	**165**	**499**	
1,537	**549**	**474**	**103**	**58**	**514**	**2,837**	**854**	**1,003**	**117**	**159**	**980**	**1,167**	**372**	**361**	**86**	**164**	**434**	
361	*194*	*110*	*5*	*6*	*133*	*451*	*169*	*165*	*21*	*5*	*133*	*185*	*61*	*19*	*3*	*1*	*105*	
68	22	21	2	6	25	251	80	92	18	3	79	94	31	13	3	1	50	1
5	4	...	...	...	1	32	7	18	3	2	7	18	7	2	...	...	9	2
120	41	41	2	...	44	108	30	36	...	...	36	72	24	2	...	...	46	3
16	*6*	*1*	...	...	*9*	*8*	*3*	*1*	...	...	*4*	*16*	*1*	*2*	...	...	*13*	
33	15	2	...	...	16	7	5	...	...	...	2	2	...	2	...	...	...	4
129	46	46	1	...	37	83	41	22	...	...	20	2	2	...	...	...	...	5
805	*279*	*251*	*86*	*38*	*278*	*1,196*	*336*	*436*	*56*	*103*	*425*	*377*	*168*	*77*	*50*	*35*	*132*	
294	110	93	51	16	91	488	133	172	48	89	183	2	1	1	...	...	...	6
113	34	35	5	7	44	403	117	156	5	7	130	20	11	...	...	...	9	7
32	11	9	...	...	12	187	81	76	...	4	80	345	148	76	50	38	121	8
235	85	62	17	15	88	32	20	8	1	3	4	2	2	...	...	...	...	9
131	39	52	7	...	40	86	34	24	2	...	28	8	6	...	...	...	2	10
193	*53*	*47*	*17*	*8*	*63*	*747*	*239*	*264*	*31*	*42*	*254*	*550*	*126*	*235*	*32*	*128*	*156*	
4	3	...	...	...	1	218	68	79	4	...	71	32	1	23	1	21	8	11
52	42	...	3	...	10	179	50	64	3	1	65	257	68	95	5	23	94	12
...	...	...	...	...	...	*117*	*34*	*40*	...	...	*43*	...	...	...	...	...	...	
111	29	42	11	5	40	133	47	44	23	29	42	197	31	100	23	79	66	13
13	5	2	...	...	6	183	45	66	2	12	72	64	26	20	3	2	18	14
13	4	3	3	8	6	34	19	11	2	...	4	...	...	...	...	...	...	15
178	*69*	*66*	*1*	*1*	*53*	*413*	*121*	*135*	*6*	*9*	*157*	*52*	*14*	*27*	*1*	...	*11*	
6	2	3	1	...	1	122	40	31	4	7	51	40	9	24	1	...	7	16
31	6	12	...	1	13	253	71	91	1	2	91	9	3	3	...	...	3	17
141	51	51	...	...	39	38	10	13	1	...	15	3	2	...	...	...	1	18
416	**209**	**61**	**39**	**23**	**146**	**603**	**151**	**249**	**29**	**35**	**203**	**129**	**24**	**40**	**5**	**1**	**65**	
297	158	46	38	18	91	316	58	132	8	12	126	8	3	...	...	...	5	19
18	8	6	...	5	4	66	40	5	12	1	21	14	6	2	4	...	6	20
101	43	7	1	...	51	119	39	41	6	...	30	86	7	32	...	1	47	21
...	...	...	...	...	...	102	14	71	8	22	17	21	8	6	1	...	7	22
176	**37**	**34**	**3**	...	**105**	**236**	**60**	**70**	**1**	...	**106**	**49**	**3**	**27**	...	...	**19**	
...	...	...	...	...	...	...	...	...	...	...	...	...	...	...	...	...	...	23
33	4	8	...	...	21	25	8	9	...	...	13	1	4	...	...	...	...	24
22	9	4	1	...	9	6	2	1	...	...	8	...	...	...	...	...	...	25
4	4	...	...	...	...	3	...	1	...	...	2	...	...	...	...	...	...	26
...	...	...	...	...	...	10	7	1	...	...	2	3	...	3	...	...	...	27
13	4	4	1	...	5	...	...	...	...	...	...	...	...	...	...	...	...	28
51	...	10	...	...	35	10	2	...	...	...	8	...	...	...	...	...	...	29
...	...	...	...	...	...	...	...	...	...	...	...	...	...	...	...	...	...	30
27	5	...	...	...	22	90	31	31	...	...	28	36	...	24	...	...	12	31
...	...	...	...	...	...	...	...	...	...	...	...	...	...	...	...	...	...	32
...	...	...	...	...	...	...	...	...	...	...	...	...	...	...	...	...	...	33
15	7	1	...	...	7	...	...	...	...	...	...	...	...	...	...	...	...	34
6	2	...	...	...	4	35	4	17	...	...	14	7	...	...	...	...	7	35
...	...	...	...	...	...	46	6	6	...	...	32	...	...	...	...	...	...	36
5	2	1	1	...	2	11	8	4	1	...	4	2	2	...	...	...	...	37

TABLE XV.—Occupation or means

Serial No.	CLASS ... / SUB-CLASS ... / ORDER ...	CLASS B.—PREPARATION AND SUPPLY / Sub-Class III.— / Order 6.—											
		26.—Wool carders and spinners, weavers of woollen blankets, carpets, etc.						27.—Silk spinners and weavers.					
	DISTRICT, CITY OR STATE.	Total workers and dependants.	Actual workers. Total.		Actual workers. Partially agriculturists.		Dependants.	Total workers and dependants.	Actual workers. Total.		Actual workers. Partially agriculturists.		Dependants.
			Males.	Females.	Males.	Females.			Males.	Females.	Males.	Females.	
	1	278	279	280	281	282	283	284	285	286	287	288	289
	Central Provinces and Berar ...	**14,178**	**4,018**	**4,282**	**676**	**878**	**5,878**	**18,903**	**6,974**	**4,122**	**574**	**413**	**7,807**
	C. P. British Districts and Berar ...	**13,162**	**3,716**	**3,951**	**646**	**859**	**5,495**	**18,159**	**6,757**	**3,849**	**557**	**402**	**7,553**
	C. P. British Districts ...	**11,236**	**3,038**	**3,446**	**513**	**724**	**4,752**	**17,777**	**6,541**	**3,844**	**556**	**402**	**7,392**
	JUBBULPORE DIVISION	*2,519*	*799*	*550*	*185*	*80*	*1,140*	*335*	*119*	*35*	...	...	*181*
1	Saugor ...	1,212	404	269	66	31	539	85	22	32	...	...	31
2	Damoh ...	461	111	106	39	10	244	...	—	...	...	...	...
3	Jubbulpore ...	695	234	170	68	28	291	241	95	...	...	...	146
	JUBBULPORE CITY ...	*40*	*13*	*3*	...	...	*24*	*241*	*95*	...	...	...	*146*
4	Mandla ...	110	38	20	12	11	52	9	2	3	...	...	4
5	Seoni ...	32	12	6	...	...	14	...	...	...	...	...	...
	NERBUDDA DIVISION ...	*1,491*	*424*	*431*	*43*	*55*	*636*	*590*	*224*	*341*	*6*	*45*	*325*
6	Narsinghpur ...	203	37	97	3	3	69	1	1	...	1	...	...
7	Hoshangabad ...	564	156	141	5	10	267	1	1	...	..	...	..
8	Nimar ...	3	3	...	...	...	...	837	211	302	...	12	324
9	Betul ...	406	143	141	26	29	212	40	9	30	3	24	1
10	Chhindwara ...	225	85	52	9	13	88	11	2	9	1	9	...
	NAGPUR DIVISION ..	*3,265*	*691*	*1,099*	*148*	*466*	*1,479*	*12,714*	*4,964*	*2,162*	*66*	*73*	*5,591*
11	Wardha ...	198	78	17	25	6	103	228	96	18	...	...	114
12	Nagpur ...	827	290	139	31	47	398	7,587	3,219	790	4	2	3,578
	NAGPUR CITY ...	*1*	...	*1*	...	...	...	*5,678*	*2,691*	*285*	*4*	—	*3,699*
13	Chanda ...	1,862	218	800	57	398	844	330	120	115	57	48	95
14	Bhandara ...	376	102	143	35	15	131	4,403	1,496	1,195	5	23	1,712
15	Balaghat ...	5	3	...	...	...	2	166	33	41	...	...	92
	CHHATTISGARH DIVISION.	*3,958*	*1,124*	*1,336*	*137*	*123*	*1,498*	*3,838*	*1,231*	*1,309*	*485*	*284*	*1,295*
16	Raipur ...	1,490	413	515	42	59	562	790	257	242	110	81	201
17	Bilaspur ...	582	166	207	33	23	210	3,045	975	1,067	375	203	1,008
18	Drug ...	1,885	545	614	62	41	726	3	2	...	...	...	1
	Berar ...	**1,926**	**678**	**505**	**133**	**135**	**743**	**382**	**216**	**5**	**1**	...	**161**
19	Amraoti ...	242	70	31	10	3	141	340	216	2	1	...	122
20	Akola ...	589	272	73	74	25	244	36	...	1	...	...	35
21	Buldana ...	1,003	305	380	48	107	309	1	...	1	...	...	...
22	Yeotmal ...	92	31	12	1	...	49	5	...	1	...	...	4
	Feudatory States ...	**1,016**	**302**	**331**	**30**	**19**	**383**	**744**	**217**	**273**	**17**	**11**	**254**
23	Makrai ...	8	3	1	...	...	4	...	...	...	...	...	...
24	Bastar ...	...	...	...	...	...	...	98	38	14	...	...	46
25	Kanker ...	30	20	2	1	...	8	1	1	...	...	...	...
26	Nandgaon ...	419	123	141	21	14	155	...	...	...	...	...	...
27	Khairagarh ...	203	65	60	5	1	78	5	3	...	...	...	2
28	Chhuikhadan ...	228	63	75	3	1	90	...	...	...	...	.	...
29	Kawardha ...	126	27	51	...	3	48	...	...	...	...	...	...
30	Sakti ...	...	...	...	...	...	...	121	37	41	10	9	43
31	Raigarh ...	...	...	...	...	...	...	397	132	143	7	2	122
32	Sarangarh ...	...	...	...	...	...	...	116	5	71	...	...	40
33	Chang Bhakar ...	...	...	...	...	...	...	...	...	...	...	...	...
34	Korea ...	1	...	1	...	...	...	3	1	1	...	—	1
35	Surguja ...	...	...	...	...	...	...	3	—	3	...	...	...
36	Udaipur ...	...	...	...	...	...	...	...	...	...	...	...	...
37	Jashpur ...	1	1	...	...	...	...	...	...	...	...	...	...

# of livelihood, Part A.—General Table.

OF MATERIAL SUBSTANCES.—(*continued*).

Industries—(*continued*).

Textiles—(*continued*).

Details of Group 27.

(*a*) Silk spinners.						(*b*) Silk weavers.						(*c*) Tassar weavers (whether combined or not combined with silk or cotton weaving).						
Total workers and dependants.	Actual workers. Total.		Actual workers. Partially agriculturists		Dependants.	Total workers and dependants.	Actual workers. Total.		Actual workers. Partially agriculturists.		Dependants.	Total workers and dependants.	Actual workers. Total.		Actual workers. Partially agriculturists.		Dependants.	Serial No
	Males.	Females.	Males.	Females.			Males.	Females.	Males.	Females.			Males.	Females.	Males.	Females.		
290	291	292	293	294	295	296	297	298	299	300	301	302	303	304	305	306	307	
4,239	**696**	**2.593**	**116**	**223**	**950**	**10.496**	**4.989**	**494**	**8**	**12**	**5,013**	**4,168**	**1.289**	**1.035**	**450**	**178**	**1.844**	
4,140	**696**	**2.529**	**116**	**223**	**915**	**10,331**	**4.878**	**491**	**6**	**12**	**4.962**	**3,688**	**1.183**	**829**	**435**	**167**	**1,676**	
3.831	**501**	**2,525**	**115**	**223**	**805**	**10,260**	**4.857**	**490**	**6**	**12**	**4.913**	**3,686**	**1.183**	**829**	**435**	**167**	**1.674**	
33	...	*32*	...	...	*1*	*265*	*115*	*3*	...	...	*144*	*37*	*1*	...	...	...	*36*	
32	...	31	...	...	1	53	22	1	...	...	30	...	...	...	...	...	...	1
...	...	...	...	...	...	...	...	...	...	...	...	...	...	...	...	...	...	2
...	...	...	...	...	...	208	95	...	...	...	113	33	...	...	...	...	33	3
...	...	...	...	...	...	*208*	*95*	...	...	...	*113*	*33*	...	...	...	...	*33*	
1	...	1	...	...	...	4	1	2	...	...	1	4	1	...	...	...	3	4
...	...	...	...	...	...	...	...	...	...	...	...	...	...	...	...	...	...	5
276	*37*	*136*	*4*	*9*	*103*	*546*	*157*	*174*	...	*12*	*215*	*65*	*30*	*31*	*1*	*24*	*7*	
...	...	...	...	...	...	...	...	...	...	...	...	1	1	...	1	...	...	6
...	...	...	...	...	...	...	...	...	...	...	...	1	1	...	...	...	...	7
261	31	127	...	...	103	541	152	174	...	12	215	35	28	1	...	...	6	8
4	4	...	3	...	...	5	5	...	...	...	...	31	...	30	...	24	1	9
11	2	9	1	9	...	...	...	...	...	...	...	—	...	...	...	...	...	10
2,632	*351*	*1,655*	*57*	*70*	*616*	*9,436*	*4,577*	*313*	*6*	...	*4,546*	*656*	*36*	*191*	*3*	*3*	*429*	
...	...	...	...	...	...	228	96	18	...	...	114	...	...	...	...	...	...	11
784	57	443	...	2	284	6,311	3,162	191	4	...	2,958	492	...	156	...	...	336	12
184	*55*	*97*	...	...	*32*	*5,494*	*2,636*	*191*	*4*	...	*2,667*	—	...	...	—	...	...	
246	93	84	54	45	69	...	...	...	...	...	...	84	27	31	3	3	20	13
1,517	182	1,001	3	23	244	2,886	1,314	104	2	...	1,468	...	...	...	...	...	...	14
75	19	37	...	...	19	11	5	...	...	...	6	80	9	4	...	...	67	15
900	*113*	*702*	*54*	*144*	*85*	*13*	*5*	...	...	...	*8*	*2,925*	*1,116*	*607*	*431*	*140*	*1,202*	
269	111	79	54	21	79	...	...	...	...	...	...	521	146	163	56	60	212	16
631	2	623	...	123	6	10	3	...	...	...	7	2,404	970	444	375	80	990	17
...	...	...	...	...	...	3	2	...	...	...	1	...	...	...	...	...	...	18
309	**195**	**4**	**1**	...	**110**	**71**	**21**	**1**	...	...	**49**	**2**	...	...	—	...	**2**	
305	195	2	1	...	108	35	21	...	...	...	14	...	...	...	...	...	...	19
...	...	...	...	...	...	36	...	1	...	...	35	...	...	...	...	...	...	20
1	...	1	...	...	...	...	...	...	...	...	...	...	...	...	...	...	...	21
3	...	1	...	...	2	—	...	...	...	...	—	2	...	...	...	...	2	22
99	...	**64**	...	...	**35**	**165**	**111**	**3**	**2**	...	**51**	**480**	**106**	**206**	**15**	**11**	**168**	
...	...	...	...	...	...	...	...	...	...	...	...	...	...	...	...	...	...	23
...	...	...	...	...	...	...	...	...	...	...	...	98	38	14	...	...	46	24
...	...	...	...	...	...	...	...	...	...	...	...	1	1	...	—	...	...	25
...	...	...	...	...	...	...	...	...	...	...	...	...	—	...	...	...	...	26
...	...	...	...	...	...	...	...	...	...	...	...	5	3	...	...	...	2	27
...	...	...	...	...	...	...	...	...	...	...	...	...	...	...	...	...	...	28
...	...	...	...	...	...	...	...	...	...	...	...	...	...	...	...	...	...	29
...	...	...	...	...	...	...	...	...	...	...	...	121	37	41	10	9	43	30
...	...	...	...	...	...	162	111	...	2	...	51	235	21	143	5	2	71	31
99	...	64	...	...	35	...	...	...	...	...	...	17	5	7	...	...	6	32
...	...	...	...	...	...	...	...	...	...	...	...	...	...	...	...	...	...	33
...	...	...	...	...	...	...	...	...	...	...	...	3	1	1	...	...	1	34
...	...	...	...	...	...	3	...	3	...	...	...	...	...	...	...	...	...	35
...	...	...	...	...	...	...	...	...	...	...	...	...	...	...	...	...	...	36
...	...	...	...	...	...	...	...	...	...	...	...	...	...	...	...	...	...	37

TABLE XV.—Occupation or means

Serial No.	CLASS ... / SUB-CLASS ... / ORDER ...	CLASS B.—PREPARATION AND SUPPLY — Sub-Class III.— Order 6.—																	
		28.—Hair, camel and horse hair, bristles work, brush-makers, etc.						29.—Persons occupied with feathers.						30.—Dyeing, bleaching, printing, preparation and sponging of textiles.					
	DISTRICT, CITY OR STATE.	Total workers and dependants.	Actual workers. Total. Males.	Actual workers. Total. Females.	Actual workers. Partially agriculturists. Males.	Actual workers. Partially agriculturists. Females.	Dependants.	Total workers and dependants.	Actual workers. Total. Males.	Actual workers. Total. Females.	Actual workers. Partially agriculturists. Males.	Actual workers. Partially agriculturists. Females.	Dependants.	Total workers and dependants.	Actual workers. Total. Males.	Actual workers. Total. Females.	Actual workers. Partially agriculturists. Males.	Actual workers. Partially agriculturists. Females.	Dependants.
	1	308	309	310	311	312	313	314	315	316	317	318	319	320	321	322	323	324	325
	Central Provinces and Berar.	**219**	**94**	**65**	**1**	...	**60**	**6**	**4**	...	...	...	**2**	**3.923**	**1,205**	**1,058**	**39**	**23**	**1.665**
	C.P. British Districts and Berar.	**172**	**87**	**30**	**1**	...	**52**	**6**	**4**	..	...	...	**2**	**3.899**	**1,200**	**1,043**	**39**	**25**	**1,656**
	C. P. British Districts.	**165**	**83**	**30**	**1**	...	**52**	**6**	**4**	...	...	...	**2**	**3.359**	**932**	**1.001**	**31**	**22**	**1,426**
	JUBBULPORE DIVISION	*4*	*4*	...	...	...	*4*	...	...	...	...	...	...	*425*	*102*	*83*	*2*	*8*	*243*
1	Saugor ...	2	...	...	...	...	2	...	...	...	...	...	...	9	5	...	...	...	4
2	Damoh ...	1	...	...	...	...	1	...	...	...	...	...	...	250	58	46	1	...	146
3	Jubbulpore ...	3	2	...	...	...	1	...	...	...	...	...	...	120	16	32	...	7	72
	JUBBULPORE CITY ...	*3*	*2*	...	...	...	*1*	...	...	...	...	...	...	*15*	*9*	...	...	...	*6*
4	Mandla ...	...	..	...	...	...	...	...	...	...	...	...	...	6	2	1	...	1	3
5	Seoni ...	2	2	...	...	...	...	...	...	...	...	..	...	43	21	4	1	...	18
	NERBUDDA DIVISION...	*38*	*19*	*7*	*1*	...	*12*	...	...	.	...	...	...	*251*	*102*	*45*	*5*	*1*	*104*
6	Narsinghpur ...	13	5	6	...	...	2	...	...	..	...	...	...	6	2	...	...	—	4
7	Hoshangabad ...	6	5	...	...	...	1	...	...	...	..	...	...	38	15	11	1	...	12
8	Nimar ...	...	...	...	...	...	...	...	...	..	...	...	...	19	4	...	...	...	15
9	Betul ...	7	3	1	...	...	3	...	...	...	...	...	...	12	6	4	...	...	2
10	Chhindwara ...	12	6	...	1	...	6	...	...	...	...	...	...	176	75	30	4	1	71
	NAGPUR DIVISION ...	*99*	*45*	*22*	...	...	*33*	...	...	...	...	..	—	*2,659*	*650*	*857*	*21*	*13*	*1,052*
11	Wardha ...	17	6	7	...	...	4	...	...	...	...	...	...	149	49	39	1	1	61
12	Nagpur ...	5	2	1	...	...	2	...	.	...	...	...	...	1,856	413	694	14	—	749
	NAGPUR CITY ...	...	...	...	...	...	—	...		...	...	...	...	*344*	*117*	*23*	*1*	...	*204*
13	Chanda ...	37	17	3	...	...	17	...	...	...	...	...	...	39	27	...	...	...	12
14	Bhandara ...	40	19	11	...	...	10	...	...	...	...	...	...	301	94	77	4	5	130
15	Balaghat ...	...	...	...	...	...	...	...	...	...	...	...	...	244	97	47	2	7	100
	CHHATTISGARH DIVISION.	*20*	*16*	*1*	...	...	*3*	*6*	*4*	...	...	...	*2*	*91*	*45*	*16*	*3*	...	*27*
16	Raipur ...	5	4	...	...	...	1	...	.	...	...	...	...	4	2	1	...	...	1
17	Bilaspur ...	15	12	1	...	...	2	...	...	...	...	...	...	87	46	15	3	...	26
18	Drug ...	...	...	...	...	...	...	6	4	...	...	...	2	...	—	...	...	...	...
	Berar ...	**7**	**4**	...	...	...	**3**	...	...	...	—	...	...	**540**	**268**	**42**	**8**	**1**	**230**
19	Amraoti ...	1	1	...	...	...	...	...	...	...	...	...	...	174	114	14	3	1	46
20	Akola ...	...	...	...	...	...	...	...	...	...	...	...	...	...	...	...	...	...	...
21	Buldana ...	6	3	—	...	...	3	...	...	...	...	...	...	65	2	2	1	...	61
22	Yeotmal ...	...	...	—	...	...	...	...	...	...	...	...	...	301	152	20	4	...	123
	Feudatory States ...	**47**	**7**	**35**	...	...	**5**	...	...	...	...	...	...	**24**	**5**	**10**	...	...	**9**
23	Makrai ...	...	...	...	...	...	...	...	...	...	...	...	...	...	...	...	...	...	...
24	Bastar ...	2	...	2	...	...	...	...	...	...	...	...	...	...	...	...	...	...	...
25	Kanker ...	...	...	...	...	...	...	...	...	...	...	...	...	...	...	...	...	...	...
26	Nandgaon ...	...	...	...	...	...	...	...	...	...	...	...	...	...	...	...	...	...	...
27	Khairagarh ...	...	...	...	...	...	...	...	...	...	...	...	...	2	...	...	...	...	2
28	Chhuikhadan ...	...	...	...	...	...	...	...	...	...	...	...	...	...	...	...	...	...	...
29	Kawardha ...	...	...	...	—	...	...	...	...	...	...	...	...	18	4	7	...	...	7
30	Sakti ...	...	...	...	...	...	...	...	...	...	...	...	...	...	...	...	—	...	...
31	Raigarh ...	...	...	...	...	...	...	...	...	...	...	...	...	2	1	1	...	...	...
32	Sarangarh ...	...	...	...	...	...	...	...	...	...	—	...	...	...	—	...	...	...	...
33	Chang Bhakar ...	...	...	...	...	...	...	...	...	...	...	...	...	...	...	...	...	...	...
34	Korea ...	—	...	...	...	...	...	...	..	—	...	...	...	1	...	1	...	...	...
35	Surguja ...	...	—	...	...	—	...	...	...	...	...	...	...	...	...	...	...	...	...
36	Udaipur ...	...	...	...	...	...	...	...	...	—	...	...	...	1	...	1	...	...	...
37	Jashpur ...	45	7	33	...	...	5	...	...	...	...	...	...	...	...	...		...	...

# of livelihood, Part A.—General Table.

OF MATERIAL SUBSTANCES—(*continued*).

Industry—(*continued*).

Textiles—(*concluded*).						Order 7.—Hides, skins and hard materials from the animal kingdom.												
31.—Other (lace, crape, embroideries, fringes, etc.,) and insufficiently described textile industries.						Total Order 7.						32.—Tanners, curriers, leather dressers and dyers, etc.						
Total workers and dependants.	Actual workers. Total.		Actual workers. Partially agriculturists.		Dependants.	Total workers and dependants.	Actual workers. Total.		Actual workers. Partially agriculturists.		Dependants.	Total workers and dependants.	Actual workers. Total.		Actual workers. Partially agriculturists.		Dependants.	Serial No.
	Males.	Females.	Males.	Females.			Males.	Females.	Males.	Females.			Males.	Females.	Males.	Females.		
326	327	328	329	330	331	332	333	334	335	336	337	338	339	340	341	342	343	
1,550	**504**	**315**	**28**	**2**	**731**	**13,787**	**4,987**	**1,814**	**1,013**	**283**	**6,986**	**8,972**	**3,427**	**1,004**	**793**	**138**	**4,541**	
1,547	**504**	**315**	**28**	**2**	**728**	**12,990**	**4,732**	**1,706**	**983**	**268**	**6,552**	**8,643**	**3,318**	**965**	**777**	**138**	**4,360**	
1,020	**341**	**186**	**21**	...	**493**	**11,056**	**3,920**	**1,444**	**865**	**212**	**5,692**	**7,212**	**2,704**	**790**	**672**	**96**	**3,718**	
11	*4*	*1*	...	...	*6*	*4,090*	*1,429*	*384*	*483*	*32*	*2,277*	*3,195*	*1,161*	*229*	*446*	*21*	*1,805*	
...	...	...	...	...	...	977	233	123	33	1	621	966	229	121	33	1	616	1
...	...	...	...	...	...	2,096	927	55	414	18	1,114	1,936	849	55	407	18	1,032	2
11	4	1	...	...	6	199	63	13	33	3	123	62	19	4	4	...	39	3
6	*2*	*1*	...	...	*3*	*49*	*6*	*4*	...	...	*39*	*36*	*5*	*4*	...	...	*27*	
...	...	...	...	...	...	393	69	139	2	10	185	99	19	32	1	2	48	4
...	...	...	...	...	...	425	137	54	1	...	234	132	45	17	1	...	70	5
816	*292*	*132*	*7*	...	*392*	*3,249*	*1,185*	*429*	*159*	*86*	*1,635*	*1,860*	*757*	*198*	*92*	*25*	*905*	
...	...	...	...	...	...	650	255	76	71	14	319	621	241	76	64	14	304	6
2	2	...	...	...	...	265	73	9	16	3	183	55	22	2	1	...	31	7
792	284	128	7	...	380	899	359	103	16	14	437	753	316	94	16	10	343	8
...	...	...	...	...	...	489	141	134	37	44	214	8	1	1	...	...	6	9
22	6	4	...	...	12	946	357	107	19	11	482	423	177	25	11	4	221	10
193	*44*	*53*	*14*	...	*96*	*1,288*	*464*	*249*	*79*	*63*	*575*	*299*	*114*	*89*	*12*	*16*	*96*	
45	27	...	14	...	18	118	35	21	1	...	62	65	17	21	1	...	27	11
98	14	23	...	...	61	341	126	53	8	17	162	74	54	3	4	...	17	12
16	*7*	*3*	...	...	*6*	*25*	*4*	*1*	...	...	*20*	*13*	*1*	*1*	...	...	*11*	
20	...	17	...	...	3	141	48	4	17	4	89	38	10	...	3	...	28	13
30	4	13	...	...	13	153	54	46	15	14	53	49	11	30	4	13	8	14
...	...	...	...	...	...	535	201	125	38	18	209	73	22	35	...	3	16	15
...	...	...	...	...	...	*2,429*	*842*	*382*	*144*	*41*	*1,205*	*1,858*	*672*	*274*	*122*	*31*	*912*	
...	...	...	...	...	...	1,001	398	114	78	18	489	794	343	70	61	10	381	16
...	...	...	...	...	...	908	231	217	40	21	460	767	215	174	40	19	378	17
...	...	...	...	...	...	520	213	51	26	2	256	297	114	30	21	2	153	18
527	**163**	**129**	**7**	**2**	**235**	**1,934**	**812**	**262**	**118**	**56**	**860**	**1,431**	**614**	**175**	**105**	**42**	**642**	
141	49	22	1	...	70	601	246	85	40	18	270	420	185	57	32	17	178	19
246	78	64	4	2	104	480	219	57	49	8	204	400	212	28	49	1	160	20
100	27	33	2	...	40	728	310	65	29	18	353	531	200	41	24	12	200	21
40	9	10	...	...	21	125	37	55	...	12	33	80	17	49	...	12	14	22
3	...	...	...	...	**3**	**797**	**255**	**108**	**30**	**15**	**434**	**329**	**109**	**39**	**16**	...	**181**	
...	...	...	...	...	...	...	...	...	...	...	...	...	...	...	...	...	...	23
...	...	...	...	...	...	23	6	8	...	...	9	7	...	7	...	...	...	24
...	...	...	...	...	...	115	40	19	3	4	56	84	30	12	3	...	42	25
...	...	...	...	...	...	49	15	8	1	...	26	49	15	8	1	...	26	26
...	...	...	...	...	...	247	88	11	13	...	148	140	47	8	7	...	85	27
...	...	...	...	...	...	...	...	...	...	...	...	...	...	...	...	...	...	28
...	...	...	...	...	...	19	10	...	...	...	9	4	...	...	...	...	4	29
...	...	...	...	...	...	...	...	...	...	...	...	...	...	...	...	...	...	30
...	...	...	...	...	...	2	1	...	...	...	1	...	...	...	...	...	...	31
...	...	...	...	...	...	166	52	34	8	3	80	2	1	...	...	...	1	32
...	...	...	...	...	...	...	...	...	...	...	...	...	...	...	...	...	...	33
...	...	...	...	...	...	58	7	15	...	7	36	11	2	4	...	...	5	34
3	...	...	...	...	3	49	17	2	...	...	30	5	...	...	...	...	5	35
...	...	...	...	...	...	67	19	11	5	1	37	27	14	...	5	...	13	36
...	...	...	...	...	...	2	...	...	...	...	2	...	...	...	...	...	...	37

TABLE XV.—Occupation or means

	CLASS ...	CLASS B.—PREPARATION AND SUPPLY																	
	SUB-CLASS ...	Sub-class III.—																	
	ORDER ...	Order 7.—Hides, skins and hard materials from the animal kingdom—(*concluded*).																	
		33.—Makers of leather articles, such as trunks, water bags, etc.*						34.—Furriers.						35.—Bone, ivory, horn, shell, etc., workers.					
		Total workers and dependants.	Actual workers. Total.		Actual workers. Partially agriculturists.		Dependants.	Total workers and dependants.	Actual workers. Total.		Actual workers. Partially agriculturists.		Dependants.	Total workers and dependants.	Actual workers. Total.		Actual workers. Partially agriculturists.		Dependants.
Serial No.	DISTRICT, CITY OR STATE.		Males.	Females.	Males.	Females.			Males.	Females.	Males.	Females.			Males.	Females.	Males.	Females.	
	1	344	345	346	347	348	349	350	351	352	353	354	355	356	357	358	359	360	361
	Central Provinces and Berar.	**4.623**	**1,533**	**751**	**220**	**138**	**2,339**	**36**	...	**6**	...	...	**30**	**156**	**27**	**53**	...	**7**	**76**
	C. P. British Districts and Berar.	**4,155**	**1,387**	**682**	**206**	**123**	**2,086**	**36**	...	**6**	...	...	**30**	**156**	**27**	**53**	...	**7**	**76**
	C. P. British Districts	**3,724**	**1,211**	**604**	**193**	**109**	**1,909**	**6**	...	**4**	—	...	**2**	**114**	**5**	**46**	...	**7**	**63**
	JUBBULPORE DIVISION	*877*	*266*	*145*	*57*	*11*	*466*	—	...	...	...	...	...	*18*	*2*	*10*	...	...	*6*
1	Saugor ...	11	4	2	...	...	5	...	...	...	...	...	...	...	...	...	...	...	...
2	Damoh ...	160	78	...	7	...	82	...	...	...	...	...	...	...	...	...	...	...	...
3	Jubbulpore ...	137	44	9	29	3	84	...	...	...	...	...	...	...	...	...	...	...	...
	JUBBULPORE CITY ...	*13*	*1*	...	...	—	*13*	...	...	...	...	...	...	...	...	...	...	...	...
4	Mandla ...	294	50	107	1	8	137	...	...	...	...	...	...	...	...	...	...	...	...
5	Seoni ...	275	90	27	—	...	158	...	...	...	...	...	...	18	2	10	...	...	6
	NERBUDDA DIVISION	*1,3·9*	*428*	*231*	*67*	*55*	*730*	...	...	...	...	...	...	...	...	...	...	...	...
6	Narsinghpur ...	29	14	...	7	...	15	...	...	...	...	...	...	...	...	...	...	...	...
7	Hoshangabad ...	210	51	7	15	3	152	...	...	...	...	...	...	...	...	...	...	...	...
8	Nimar ...	140	43	9	...	4	94	...	...	...	...	...	...	...	...	...	...	...	...
9	Betul ...	481	140	133	37	44	208	...	...	...	...	...	...	...	...	...	...	...	...
10	Chhindwara ...	523	180	82	8	7	201	...	...	...	...	...	...	...	...	...	...	...	...
	NAGPUR DIVISION ...	*920*	*358*	*144*	*67*	*37*	*425*	...	...	...	...	...	...	*69*	*2*	*16*	...	...	*51*
11	Wardha ...	53	18	...	...	...	35	...	...	...	...	...	...	...	...	...	...	...	...
12	Nagpur ...	198	70	34	4	17	94	...	...	...	...	...	...	69	2	16	...	...	51
	NAGPUR CITY ...	*11*	*2*	...	...	...	*9*	...	...	...	...	...	...	*1*	*1*	...	...	...	...
13	Chanda ...	103	38	4	14	4	61	...	...	...	...	...	...	...	...	...	...	...	...
14	Bhandara ...	104	43	16	11	1	45	...	...	...	...	...	...	...	...	...	...	...	...
15	Balaghat ...	462	179	90	38	15	193	...	...	...	...	...	...	...	...	...	...	...	...
	CHHATTISGARH DIVISION.	*535*	*169*	*84*	*23*	*3*	*255*	*6*	...	*4*	...	...	*2*	*27*	*1*	*20*	...	*7*	*6*
16	Raipur ...	181	55	26	17	1	100	6	...	4	...	...	2	20	...	14	...	7	6
17	Bilaspur ...	134	15	37	...	2	82	...	...	...	...	...	...	7	1	6	...	...	...
18	Drug ...	223	99	21	5	...	103	...	...	...	...	...	...	...	...	...	...	...	...
	Berar ...	**431**	**176**	**78**	**13**	**14**	**177**	**30**	...	**2**	...	...	**28**	**42**	**22**	**7**	...	...	**13**
19	Amraoti ...	173	60	27	8	1	80	...	...	...	...	...	...	8	1	1	...	...	6
20	Akola ...	47	5	26	...	7	16	30	...	2	...	...	28	3	2	1	...	...	...
21	Buldana ...	190	103	24	5	6	63	...	...	...	...	...	...	7	7	...	...	...	...
22	Yeotmal ...	21	8	1	...	...	12	...	...	...	...	...	...	24	12	5	...	...	7
	Feudatory States ...	**468**	**146**	**69**	**14**	**15**	**253**	...	...	...	...	...	...	...	...	...	...	...	...
23	Makrai ...	...	...	...	...	...	...	...	...	...	...	...	...	...	...	...	...	...	...
24	Bastar ...	16	6	1	...	...	9	...	...	...	...	...	...	...	...	...	...	...	...
25	Kanker ...	31	10	7	...	4	14	...	...	...	...	...	...	...	...	...	...	...	...
26	Nandgaon ...	...	...	...	...	...	...	...	...	...	...	...	...	...	...	...	...	...	...
27	Khairagarh ...	107	41	3	6	...	63	...	...	...	...	...	...	...	...	...	...	...	...
28	Chhuikhadan ...	...	...	...	...	...	...	...	...	...	...	...	...	...	...	...	...	...	...
29	Kawardha ...	15	10	...	...	...	5	...	...	...	...	...	...	...	...	...	...	...	...
30	Sakti ...	...	...	...	...	...	...	...	...	...	...	...	...	...	...	...	...	...	...
31	Raigarh ...	2	1	...	...	...	1	...	...	...	...	...	...	...	...	...	...	...	...
32	Sarangarh ...	164	51	34	8	3	79	...	...	...	...	...	...	...	...	...	...	...	—
33	Chang Bhakar ...	...	...	...	...	...	...	...	...	...	...	...	...	...	...	...	...	...	...
34	Korea ...	47	5	11	...	7	31	...	...	...	...	...	...	...	...	...	...	...	...
35	Surguja ...	44	17	2	...	...	25	...	...	...	...	...	...	...	...	...	...	...	...
36	Udaipur ...	40	5	11	...	1	24	...	...	...	...	...	...	...	...	...	...	...	...
37	Jashpur ...	2	...	...	...	...	2	...	...	...	...	...	...	...	...	...	...	...	...

# of livelihood, Part A.—General Table.

OF MATERIAL SUBSTANCES—(*continued*).

Industry—(*continued*).

Order 8.—Wood.																		
Total order 8.						36.—Sawyers, carpenters, turners and joiners, etc.						37.—Basket-makers and other industries of woody material, including leaves.						
Total workers and dependants.	Actual workers. Total.		Actual workers. Partially agriculturists.		Dependants.	Total workers and dependants.	Actual workers. Total.		Actual workers. Partially agriculturists.		Dependants.	Total workers and dependants.	Actual workers. Total.		Actual workers. Partially agriculturists.		Dependants.	Serial No.
	Males.	Females.	Males.	Females.			Males.	Females.	Males.	Females.			Males.	Females.	Males.	Females.		
362	363	364	365	306	367	368	369	370	371	372	373	374	375	376	377	378	379	
196,762	**69,929**	**35,588**	**9,600**	**4,483**	**91,245**	**98,329**	**41,933**	**1,280**	**5,885**	**140**	**55,116**	**98,433**	**27,996**	**34,308**	**3,715**	**4,343**	**36,129**	
178,729	**64,046**	**31,340**	**9,290**	**4,364**	**83,348**	**94,773**	**40,069**	**1,174**	**5,825**	**133**	**53,530**	**83,956**	**23,977**	**30,166**	**3,465**	**4,231**	**29,813**	
138,240	**47,162**	**27,393**	**7,286**	**3,130**	**63,685**	**65,037**	**26,363**	**906**	**4,639**	**98**	**37,768**	**73,203**	**20,799**	**26,487**	**2,647**	**3,032**	**25,917**	
41,417	*13,658*	*8,257*	*2,618*	*741*	*19,502*	*14,110*	*6,304*	*233*	*1,193*	*21*	*8,573*	*27,307*	*8,351*	*8,024*	*1,420*	*720*	*10,929*	
12,174	4,330	1,843	1,055	197	6,001	5,003	1,951	75	508	4	2,977	7,171	2,379	1,768	547	193	3,024	1
7,843	2,621	1,164	867	195	4,058	2,356	746	14	302	2	1,596	5,487	1,875	1,150	565	193	2,402	2
13,763	4,191	3,048	591	297	6,524	4,743	1,708	67	345	15	2,968	9,020	2,488	2,081	246	282	3,556	3
2,759	*1,000*	*272*	*1*	*1*	*1,487*	*1,555*	*747*	*10*	*1*	*1*	*1,101*	*901*	*253*	*264*	...	...	*356*	
4,248	1,417	1,234	68	14	1,507	677	322	52	9	...	303	3,571	1,095	1,182	59	14	1,294	4
3,389	1,099	968	32	38	1,322	1,331	577	25	29	...	729	2,058	522	948	3	38	593	5
31,452	*10,621*	*6,762*	*1,592*	*559*	*15,155*	*18,492*	*7,215*	*186*	*1,254*	*17*	*11,092*	*12,946*	*3,306*	*5,577*	*335*	*572*	*4,063*	
7,980	2,352	1,951	385	196	3,677	3,705	1,326	23	294	6	2,356	4,275	1,026	1,928	91	190	1,321	6
9,794	3,170	1,625	483	123	4,999	6,342	2,286	62	380	3	3,994	3,452	884	1,568	44	120	1,005	7
4,641	1,725	606	190	70	2,310	3,067	1,281	55	144	2	1,731	1,574	444	551	52	68	579	8
4,318	1,483	935	335	173	1,900	2,270	966	25	205	6	1,279	2,048	517	910	130	107	621	9
4,705	1,791	645	243	27	2,269	3,108	1,356	20	222	...	1,732	1,597	435	625	21	27	537	10
46,846	*17,062*	*8,197*	*2,734*	*1,559*	*21,556*	*28,075*	*11,886*	*305*	*2,110*	*55*	*15,887*	*18,767*	*6,176*	*7,892*	*674*	*1,504*	*5,699*	
6,686	2,838	375	302	59	3,473	5,773	2,507	57	288	12	3,149	913	271	318	14	47	324	11
13,502	5,190	1,480	657	98	6,826	10,414	4,894	141	607	11	5,879	3,088	796	1,345	50	87	947	12
1,673	*622*	*119*	*2*	...	*932*	*1,306*	*616*	*14*	*2*	...	*776*	*367*	*106*	*105*	...	...	*156*	
11,836	4,177	1,930	1,040	580	5,723	5,758	2,240	62	575	29	3,456	6,078	1,937	1,874	474	551	2,267	13
10,651	3,605	2,819	605	585	4,227	5,073	2,185	28	577	3	2,860	5,578	1,420	2,791	88	582	1,367	14
4,170	1,252	1,581	111	237	1,337	1,060	500	17	63	...	543	3,110	752	1,564	48	237	794	15
18,540	*5,931*	*5,177*	*297*	*241*	*7,442*	*4,357*	*1,958*	*183*	*83*	*5*	*3,216*	*14,183*	*3,963*	*4,994*	*215*	*236*	*5,326*	
9,099	3,055	2,925	161	148	3,719	2,347	1,102	66	38	3	1,179	7,352	1,953	2,859	123	145	2,540	16
6,112	1,957	1,457	108	87	2,098	1,494	635	82	25	2	777	4,618	1,322	1,375	83	85	1,021	17
2,729	909	795	28	6	1,025	516	221	35	19	...	260	2,213	688	760	9	6	705	18
40,489	**16,884**	**3,947**	**2,004**	**1,234**	**19,658**	**29,736**	**13,706**	**268**	**1,186**	**35**	**15,782**	**10,753**	**3,178**	**3,679**	**818**	**1,199**	**3,896**	
10,995	4,428	942	300	154	5,625	8,652	3,752	118	321	26	4,782	2,343	676	824	45	128	843	19
9,394	4,062	1,060	573	361	4,272	6,730	3,250	46	316	2	3,440	2,658	812	1,014	257	359	832	20
10,580	4,079	1,415	700	632	5,086	6,360	2,880	50	302	5	3,430	4,211	1,199	1,356	458	627	1,656	21
9,520	4,315	530	305	87	4,075	7,979	3,824	45	247	2	4,110	1,541	491	485	58	85	565	22
18,033	**5,883**	**4,248**	**310**	**119**	**7,902**	**3,556**	**1,864**	**106**	**60**	**7**	**1,586**	**14,477**	**4,019**	**4,142**	**250**	**112**	**6,316**	
287	90	55	12	...	142	167	60	3	12	...	104	120	30	62	—	...	38	23
2,330	1,064	535	7	14	731	1,175	821	17	1	1	337	1,155	243	518	6	13	394	24
804	270	249	1	1	375	101	40	1	...	...	60	793	230	248	1	1	315	25
660	207	168	11	8	285	262	101	4	6	...	157	398	109	164	5	8	128	26
665	223	171	3	13	271	258	112	4	3	...	142	407	111	167	...	13	129	27
106	34	25	2	1	47	57	20	...	2	...	87	49	14	25	...	1	10	28
696	289	65	6	...	343	544	243	24	5	...	277	152	45	41	1	...	66	29
440	115	131	3	14	194	30	11	—	1	...	19	410	104	131	2	14	175	30
2,627	817	620	37	17	1,190	404	197	6	2	...	201	2,222	620	614	35	17	989	31
353	113	82	20	...	158	61	26	2	5	...	33	292	87	80	15	...	125	32
382	114	125	15	1	143	7	1	3	...	...	3	375	113	122	15	1	140	33
1,558	476	421	16	5	661	10	7	...	...	...	3	1,548	469	421	16	5	658	34
3,104	902	402	50	19	1,800	164	63	3	5	...	98	2,940	839	399	45	19	1,702	35
900	305	283	4	2	312	31	15	...	...	...	16	869	290	283	4	2	296	36
3,031	865	916	123	24	1,250	285	147	39	18	6	99	2,746	718	877	105	18	1,151	37

TABLE XV.—Occupation or means

Serial No.	CLASS ... / SUB-CLASS ... / ORDER ...	CLASS B.—PREPARATION AND SUPPLY														
		Sub-Class III.—														
		Order 9.—														
		Total order 9.						38.—Forging and rolling of iron and other metals.						39.—Plough and implement		
	DISTRICT, CITY OR STATE.	Total workers and dependants.	Actual workers. Total.		Actual workers. Partially agriculturists.		Dependants.	Total workers and dependants.	Actual workers. Total.		Actual workers. Partially agriculturists.		Dependants.	Total workers and dependants.	Actual workers. Total.	
			Males.	Females.	Males.	Females.			Males.	Females.	Males.	Females.			Males.	Females.
	1	380	381	382	383	384	385	386	387	388	389	390	391	392	393	394
	Central Provinces and Berar.	**140,451**	**49,617**	**15,153**	**7,682**	**1,524**	**75,681**	**4,400**	**1,286**	**1,019**	**83**	**22**	**2,095**	**17,002**	**5,835**	**1,667**
	C.P. British Districts and Berar.	**113,264**	**41,030**	**10,277**	**7,090**	**1,381**	**61,957**	**1,634**	**484**	**409**	**67**	**12**	**741**	**13,819**	**4,737**	**1,195**
	C P. British Districts	**96,514**	**34,707**	**8,941**	**6,626**	**1,291**	**52,866**	**1,634**	**484**	**409**	**67**	**12**	**741**	**13,806**	**4,730**	**1,195**
	JUBBULPORE DIVISION	*24,055*	*8,301*	*1,588*	*1,586*	*134*	*14,166*	*143*	*46*	*30*	*6*	...	*67*	*5,047*	*1,758*	*288*
1	Saugor ...	5,418	1,970	203	379	8	3,245	78	29	13	6	...	36	1,808	633	42
2	Damoh ...	3,116	1,039	109	333	8	1,968	1	1	...	...	...	...	407	128	8
3	Jubbulpore ...	8,177	2,836	362	467	38	4,979	3	...	3	...	...	...	827	243	24
	JUBBULPORE CITY ...	*3,477*	*1,253*	*21*	*6*	...	*2,203*	...	...	...	...	...	...	*96*	...	...
4	Mandla ...	4,059	1,274	683	240	68	2,102	61	16	14	...	...	31	813	287	145
5	Seoni ...	3,285	1,182	231	167	12	1,872	...	...	...	...	...	...	1,192	467	69
	NERBUDDA DIVISION ...	*19,459*	*6,867*	*1,829*	*896*	*250*	*10,793*	*7*	*1*	*2*	...	...	*4*	*3,106*	*1,091*	*255*
6	Narsinghpur ...	3,860	1,292	183	202	6	2,395	...	...	...	...	...	...	1,214	407	39
7	Hoshangabad ...	4,461	1,597	171	219	10	2,693	6	...	2	...	...	4	103	30	4
8	Nimar ...	2,160	796	188	99	13	1,176	...	...	...	...	...	...	174	44	18
9	Betul ...	4,114	1,445	823	213	153	1,846	...	...	...	...	...	...	949	401	146
10	Chhindwara ...	4,885	1,737	464	163	68	2,684	1	1	...	...	...	...	666	200	48
	NAGPUR DIVISION ...	*29,062*	*11,581*	*2,262*	*2,764*	*689*	*15,219*	*19*	*13*	*1*	*3*	...	*5*	*572*	*197*	*54*
11	Wardha ...	2,682	1,117	208	92	41	1,357	1	1	...	...	...	...	1	1	...
12	Nagpur ...	7,221	2,887	578	299	137	3,756	1	1	...	...	...	...	63	8	3
	NAGPUR CITY ...	*879*	*314*	*14*	*2*	...	*551*	...	...	...	...	...	...	...	...	...
13	Chanda ...	7,417	2,830	829	1,006	382	3,758	15	10	...	3	...	5	147	1	41
14	Bhandara ...	8,195	3,413	387	939	89	4,395	...	...	...	...	...	...	106	50	5
15	Balaghat ...	3,547	1,334	260	428	40	1,953	2	1	1	...	...	...	255	137	5
	CHHATTISGARH DIVISION.	*23,909*	*7,958*	*3,262*	*1,380*	*218*	*12,689*	*1,465*	*422*	*376*	*58*	*12*	*665*	*5,081*	*1,684*	*598*
16	Raipur ...	10,397	3,418	1,485	637	100	5,494	510	147	102	44	10	259	2,762	990	288
17	Bilaspur ...	6,423	2,214	1,060	452	85	3,149	941	274	271	13	2	396	815	258	139
18	Drug ...	7,089	2,326	717	291	33	4,046	14	1	3	1	...	10	1,504	436	171
	Berar ..	**16,750**	**6,323**	**1,336**	**464**	**90**	**9,091**	...	...	...	...	...	...	**13**	**7**	...
19	Amraoti ...	4,867	1,859	399	132	39	2,609	...	...	...	...	...	...	...	...	...
20	Akola ..	3,447	1,284	294	132	18	1,869	...	...	...	...	...	...	...	...	...
21	Buldana ...	3,431	1,216	255	106	13	1,960	...	...	...	...	...	...	...	...	...
22	Yeotmal ...	5,005	1,964	388	91	20	2,653	...	...	...	...	...	...	13	7	...
	Feudatory States ...	**27,187**	**8,587**	**4,876**	**592**	**143**	**13,724**	**2,766**	**802**	**610**	**16**	**10**	**1,354**	**3,183**	**1,098**	**472**
23	Makrai ...	48	19	8	2	...	21	...	...	...	...	...	...	...	...	...
24	Bastar ...	6,126	1,906	1,499	20	16	2,721	577	174	154	...	...	249	70	27	11
25	Kanker ...	1,510	493	326	15	3	691	97	20	40	...	...	31	543	107	62
26	Nandgaon ...	1,430	475	84	70	1	871	3	7	...	1	...	...	305	145	...
27	Khairagarh ...	1,334	445	86	49	...	803	2	1	...	...	...	1	24	4	6
28	Chhuikhadan ...	308	108	20	9	2	180	...	...	...	...	...	...	137	48	6
29	Kawardha ...	595	180	101	35	11	314	73	9	30	...	...	34	4	...	1
30	Sakti ...	181	57	25	8	2	99	...	...	...	...	...	...	2	2	...
31	Raigarh ...	2,793	858	644	77	5	1,291	1	1	...	...	...	...	493	132	146
32	Sarangarh ...	539	177	98	89	6	264	...	...	...	...	...	...	17	11	...
33	Chang Bhakar ...	382	159	78	32	12	145	53	22	13	1	2	18	5	...	...
34	Korea ...	1,050	337	235	21	8	478	271	4	155	...	7	112	25	3	5
35	Surguja ...	5,996	1,789	523	45	4	3,684	717	190	50	1	...	462	432	182	3
36	Udaipur ...	1,099	333	211	1	5	555	532	181	97	...	...	254	401	104	74
37	Jashpur ...	3,790	1,251	939	157	68	1,600	440	185	62	13	1	193	725	273	158

# of livelihood, Part A.—General Table.

OF MATERIAL SUBSTANCES—(*continued*).

Industry—(*continued*).

Metals.

...agricultural makers. — Workers. Partially agriculturists. Males.	...agricultural makers. — Workers. Partially agriculturists. Females.	...agricultural makers. — Dependants.	40.—Makers of arms, guns, etc. — Total workers and dependants.	40. — Actual workers. Total. Males.	40. — Actual workers. Total. Females.	40. — Actual workers. Partially agriculturists. Males.	40. — Actual workers. Partially agriculturists. Females.	40. — Dependants.	41.—Other workers in iron and makers of implements and tools, principally or exclusively of iron. — Total workers and dependants.	41. — Actual workers. Total. Males.	41. — Actual workers. Total. Females.	41. — Actual workers. Partially agriculturists. Males.	41. — Actual workers. Partially agriculturists. Females.	41. — Dependants.	42.—Workers in brass, copper and bell-metal. — Total workers and dependants.	42. — Actual workers. Total. Males.	42. — Actual workers. Total. Females.	42. — Actual workers. Partially agriculturists. Males.	42. — Actual workers. Partially agriculturists. Females.	42. — Dependants.	Serial No.
395	396	397	398	399	400	401	402	403	404	405	406	407	408	409	410	411	412	413	414	415	
1.131	**183**	**9,500**	**1.753**	**672**	**7**	**1**	...	**1.074**	**91.522**	**33.103**	**9.674**	**5.931**	**1.173**	**48.745**	**23.007**	**7.786**	**2.593**	**489**	**118**	**12.628**	
1,023	**164**	**7,887**	**1,661**	**621**	**7**	**1**	...	**1.033**	**74.785**	**27.861**	**6.723**	**5.570**	**1.068**	**40.201**	**18.714**	**6.444**	**1.751**	**384**	**109**	**10,519**	
1,023	**164**	**7,881**	**1.641**	**616**	**7**	**1**	...	**1.018**	**60.428**	**22.417**	**5.617**	**5.159**	**995**	**32.394**	**17.166**	**5,868**	**1,565**	**338**	**95**	**9.733**	
457	*31*	*3,001*	*1,610*	*610*	*7*	*1*	...	*993*	*11,619*	*4,037*	*860*	*1,008*	*86*	*6,732*	*4,913*	*1,601*	*373*	*78*	*17*	*2,959*	
173	2	1,133	10	2	...	...	...	8	1,824	719	71	195	3	1,034	1,537	534	74	5	3	929	1
49	2	271	...	...	...	...	...	...	1,846	620	60	273	2	1,157	833	273	41	11	4	519	2
104	7	560	1,592	605	7	1	...	980	3,747	1,324	174	280	23	2,240	1,542	505	127	54	8	910	3
...	...	*96*	*1,569*	*601*	*4*	...	...	*964*	*1,296*	*495*	*12*	*6*	...	*786*	*370*	*116*	*5*	...	...	*349*	
53	15	381	8	3	...	...	...	5	2,484	753	419	182	51	1,312	680	210	105	5	2	385	4
78	5	656	...	...	...	...	...	...	1,718	612	136	79	7	970	321	79	26	3	...	216	5
228	*50*	*1,760*	*30*	*6*	...	...	...	*24*	*11,645*	*4,116*	*1,240*	*598*	*182*	*6,189*	*4,472*	*1,557*	*314*	*69*	*14*	*2,610*	
124	3	768	17	5	...	...	...	12	1,093	371	45	56	3	677	1,501	497	98	21	...	906	6
9	...	60	3	...	...	...	...	3	2,911	1,075	99	192	10	1,737	1,330	450	62	18	...	827	7
5	...	112	...	...	...	...	...	...	1,630	618	147	94	13	865	313	123	20	...	...	170	8
72	39	402	10	1	...	...	...	9	2,520	803	580	120	99	1,128	540	217	80	12	11	243	9
18	8	418	...	...	...	...	...	...	3,391	1,249	360	127	57	1,782	788	270	54	18	3	464	10
50	*34*	*321*	*1*	...	...	...	...	*1*	*25,038*	*10,087*	*1,894*	*2,637*	*596*	*13,017*	*3,825*	*1,070*	*272*	*73*	*47*	*1,483*	
...	...	...	...	...	...	...	...	...	2,437	1,008	204	80	41	1,225	117	55	...	2	...	62	11
...	1	52	1	...	...	...	...	1	6,468	2,646	556	287	131	3,206	448	141	16	12	5	291	12
...	...	...	...	...	...	...	...	...	*636*	*231*	*11*	*-*	...	*393*	*82*	*22*	*2*	...	...	*58*	
...	31	105	...	...	...	...	...	...	6,538	2,562	697	983	326	3,279	604	236	61	20	13	307	13
10	1	51	...	...	...	...	...	...	6,740	2,838	253	898	68	3,640	1,250	487	127	31	20	636	14
40	1	113	...	...	...	...	...	...	2,845	1,033	184	380	30	1,628	406	151	68	8	9	187	15
288	*49*	*2,799*	...	...	...	...	...	...	*12,236*	*4,177*	*1,623*	*916*	*131*	*6,436*	*4,887*	*1,640*	*606*	*118*	*17*	*2,701*	
200	20	1,484	...	...	...	...	...	...	4,824	1,550	784	348	56	2,490	2,107	710	264	45	5	1,193	16
43	25	418	...	...	...	...	...	...	3,174	1,137	444	344	51	1,593	1,457	537	194	52	7	726	17
45	4	897	...	...	...	...	...	...	4,238	1,490	395	224	24	2,353	1,323	393	148	21	5	782	18
...	...	**6**	**20**	**5**	...	...	...	**15**	**14.357**	**5.444**	**1.106**	**411**	**73**	**7.807**	**1.548**	**576**	**186**	**46**	**14**	**786**	
...	...	...	...	...	...	...	...	...	4,179	1,587	352	103	36	2,240	418	186	27	28	1	205	19
...	...	...	...	...	...	...	...	...	2,858	1,074	227	125	13	1,557	388	132	57	7	5	190	20
...	...	...	11	5	...	...	...	6	2,892	1,019	227	98	12	1,646	321	121	18	5	...	182	21
...	...	6	9	...	...	...	...	9	4,428	1,764	300	85	12	2,384	421	137	84	6	8	200	22
108	**19**	**1,613**	**92**	**51**	...	...	...	**41**	**16.737**	**5,242**	**2,951**	**361**	**105**	**8,544**	**4,293**	**1,342**	**842**	**105**	**9**	**2.109**	
...	...	...	...	...	...	...	...	...	40	18	8	2	...	20	...	...	...	...	...	...	23
1	...	32	84	48	...	...	...	36	4,029	1,216	1,035	21	16	1,778	1,363	430	298	4	...	626	24
10	2	314	...	...	...	...	...	...	683	251	158	2	1	274	193	49	66	3	...	78	25
22	...	160	...	...	...	...	...	...	865	240	62	32	1	557	227	75	27	21	...	125	26
...	...	14	...	...	...	...	...	...	,143	401	42	49	...	700	150	34	38	...	...	78	27
6	2	83	3	2	...	...	...	1	105	37	7	3	...	61	63	21	7	...	...	35	28
...	...	3	...	...	...	...	...	...	402	154	51	35	10	257	56	17	19	...	1	20	29
...	...	...	...	...	...	...	...	...	51	19	11	3	2	21	128	36	14	5	...	78	30
13	4	215	...	...	...	...	...	...	1,482	456	393	7	...	631	754	231	106	55	1	417	31
1	...	6	...	...	...	...	...	...	375	126	66	34	5	183	146	39	32	4	1	75	32
...	...	5	...	...	...	...	...	...	304	133	64	31	10	107	20	4	1	...	...	15	33
...	1	17	...	...	...	...	...	...	636	270	56	10	...	301	118	51	19	2	...	48	34
6	...	247	5	1	...	...	...	4	4,264	1,220	402	29	4	2,642	578	190	59	9	...	329	35
1	3	223	...	...	...	...	...	...	60	11	13	...	...	36	106	37	27	...	2	42	36
48	7	294	...	...	...	...	...	...	2,232	672	584	94	56	976	391	119	120	2	4	143	37

TABLE XV.—Occupation or means

CLASS ... CLASS B.—PREPARATION AND SUPPLY

SUB-CLASS ... Sub-Class III.—

ORDER ... Order 9.—Metals—(*concluded*). | Order 10.—

Serial No.	DISTRICT, CITY OR STATE.	43.—Workers in other metals (tin, zinc, lead, quick-silver, etc.). Total workers and dependants	Actual workers. Total. Males.	Actual workers. Total. Females.	Actual workers. Partially agriculturists. Males.	Actual workers. Partially agriculturists. Females.	Dependants.	44.—Workers in mints, die-sinkers, etc. Total workers and dependants.	Actual workers. Total. Males.	Actual workers. Total. Females.	Actual workers. Partially agriculturists. Males.	Actual workers. Partially agriculturists. Females.	Dependants.	Total order 10. Total workers and dependants.	Actual workers. Total. Males.	Actual workers. Total. Females.	Actual workers. Partially agriculturists. Males.	Actual workers. Partially agriculturists. Females.	Dependants.
	1	416	417	418	419	420	421	422	423	424	425	426	427	428	429	430	431	432	433
	Central Provinces and Berar ...	**2,570**	**817**	**193**	**11**	**28**	**1,560**	**197**	**118**	...	**36**	...	**79**	**98,595**	**34,172**	**27,282**	**4,670**	**2,560**	**37,141**
	C. P. British Districts and Berar ...	**2,454**	**765**	**192**	**9**	**28**	**1,497**	**197**	**118**	...	**36**	...	**79**	**88,375**	**30,920**	**24,421**	**4,039**	**2,341**	**33,034**
	C. P. British Districts ...	**1,642**	**474**	**148**	**2**	**25**	**1,020**	**197**	**118**	...	**36**	...	**79**	**69,090**	**23,394**	**19,508**	**3,189**	**1,818**	**26,188**
	JUBBULPORE DIVISION.	*537*	*133*	*30*	...	...	*369*	*191*	*116*	...	*36*	...	*75*	*24,303*	*7,833*	*6,371*	*1,358*	*633*	*10,100*
1	Saugor	161	53	3	...	...	105	...	...	...	...	...	...	6,112	1,097	1,655	591	292	2,460
2	Damoh	29	8	...	...	...	21	...	...	...	...	...	...	4,108	1,253	993	344	129	1,862
3	Jubbulpore ...	280	55	27	...	...	207	177	104	...	28	...	73	9,734	3,116	2,378	353	199	4,240
	JUBBULPORE CITY ...	*125*	*35*	...	...	...	*90*	*18*	...	...	...	...	*18*	*2,620*	*724*	*459*	...	...	*1,437*
4	Mandla	13	5	...	...	...	8	...	...	...	...	...	...	1,767	557	535	34	12	675
5	Seoni	40	12	...	...	...	28	14	12	...	8	...	2	2,583	910	810	36	11	863
	NERBUDDA DIVISION.	*319*	*95*	*18*	*1*	*4*	*206*	*1*	*1*	...	...	...	...	*14,315*	*5,004*	*3,986*	*321*	*182*	*5,325*
6	Narsinghpur ...	44	12	1	1	...	31	...	...	...	...	...	...	3,331	1,110	913	102	54	1,308
7	Hoshangabad ...	99	33	4	...	...	62	...	...	...	...	...	...	4,206	1,484	1,194	115	78	1,528
8	Nimar ...	42	10	3	...	...	29	1	1	...	...	...	...	2,720	951	705	68	38	1,064
9	Betul ...	95	23	8	...	4	64	...	...	...	...	...	...	1,754	664	503	16	5	587
10	Chhindwara ...	39	17	2	...	...	20	...	...	...	...	...	...	2,304	795	671	20	7	838
	NAGPUR DIVISION ...	*612*	*213*	*41*	*1*	*12*	*358*	*5*	*1*	...	...	...	*4*	*17,692*	*6,356*	*4,963*	*860*	*595*	*6,383*
11	Wardha	120	52	4	1	...	70	...	...	...	...	...	...	2,677	1,052	676	90	55	949
12	Nagpur	239	90	3	...	...	146	1	1	...	...	...	...	5,548	1,872	1,547	91	73	2,129
	NAGPUR CITY ...	*160*	*60*	*1*	...	...	*99*	*1*	*1*	...	...	...	...	*642*	*189*	*169*	...	...	*294*
13	Chanda	113	21	30	...	12	62	...	...	...	...	...	...	3,623	1,318	1,025	334	252	1,280
14	Bhandara ...	95	38	2	...	...	55	4	...	...	...	...	4	4,104	1,508	1,159	285	162	1,437
15	Balaghat ...	39	12	2	...	...	25	...	...	...	...	...	...	1,740	606	546	60	53	588
	CHHATTISGARH DIVISION.	*179*	*33*	*59*	...	*9*	*87*	...	...	...	...	...	...	*12,779*	*4,201*	*4,198*	*650*	*308*	*4,380*
16	Raipur	134	19	47	...	9	68	...	...	...	...	...	...	5,400	1,821	1,815	290	104	1,764
17	Bilaspur	36	8	12	...	...	16	...	...	...	...	...	...	4,307	1,359	1,372	241	132	1,576
18	Drug	9	6	...	...	...	3	...	...	...	...	...	...	3,072	1,021	1,011	119	72	1,040
	Berar	**812**	**291**	**44**	**7**	**3**	**477**	...	...	...	...	...	...	**19,285**	**7,526**	**4,913**	**850**	**523**	**6,846**
19	Amraoti	270	86	20	2	2	164	...	...	...	...	...	...	6,349	2,676	1,459	310	140	2,214
20	Akola	201	78	10	...	...	113	...	...	...	...	...	...	5,358	2,014	1,425	258	152	1,919
21	Buldana	207	71	10	5	1	126	...	...	...	...	...	...	3,702	1,284	1,074	190	182	1,344
22	Yeotmal	134	56	4	...	...	74	...	...	...	...	...	...	3,876	1,552	955	83	49	1,369
	Feudatory States ...	**116**	**52**	**1**	**2**	...	**63**	...	...	...	...	...	...	**10,220**	**3,252**	**2,861**	**631**	**219**	**4,107**
23	Makrai	2	1	...	...	...	1	...	...	...	...	...	...	67	19	23	...	...	25
24	Bastar	3	2	1	...	...	...	...	...	...	...	...	...	1,579	502	444	139	43	633
25	Kanker	...	...	...	...	...	...	...	...	...	...	...	...	770	237	278	32	28	255
26	Nandgaon ...	30	6	...	...	...	24	...	...	...	...	...	...	597	221	201	16	2	175
27	Khairagarh ...	15	5	...	...	...	10	...	...	...	...	...	...	783	247	204	27	24	272
28	Chhuikhadan ...	...	...	...	...	...	...	...	...	...	...	...	...	238	69	68	7	2	101
29	Kawardha ...	...	...	...	...	...	...	...	...	...	...	...	...	308	101	95	14	6	112
30	Sakti	...	...	...	...	...	...	...	...	...	...	...	...	125	52	38	6	3	35
31	Raigarh	63	35	...	2	...	28	...	...	...	...	...	...	1,302	416	424	53	27	462
32	Sarangarh ...	1	1	...	...	...	...	...	...	...	...	...	...	483	113	225	21	4	145
33	Chang Bhakar ...	...	...	...	...	...	...	...	...	...	...	...	...	155	49	44	8	3	62
34	Korea ...	...	...	...	...	...	...	...	...	...	...	...	...	222	80	73	20	...	69
35	Surguja ...	...	...	...	...	...	...	...	...	...	...	...	...	1,839	675	205	86	21	1,059
36	Udaipur ...	...	...	...	...	...	...	...	...	...	...	...	...	286	88	81	9	3	117
37	Jashpur ...	2	2	...	...	...	...	...	...	...	...	...	...	1,409	483	398	193	53	585

# of livelihood, Part A.—General Table.

OF MATERIAL SUBSTANCES—*(continued)*.

Industry *(continued)*.

Ceramics.

45.—Makers of glass and crystal ware. Total workers and dependants.	45. Actual workers. Total. Males.	45. Actual workers. Total. Females.	45. Actual workers. Partially agriculturists. Males.	45. Actual workers. Partially agriculturists. Females.	45. Dependants.	46.—Makers of porcelain and crockery. Total workers and dependants.	46. Actual workers. Total. Males.	46. Actual workers. Total. Females.	46. Actual workers. Partially agriculturists. Males.	46. Actual workers. Partially agriculturists. Females.	46. Dependants.	47.—Potters and earthen pipe and bowl makers. Total workers and dependants.	47. Actual workers. Total. Males.	47. Actual workers. Total. Females.	47. Actual workers. Partially agriculturists. Males.	47. Actual workers. Partially agriculturists. Females.	47. Dependants.	Serial No.
434	435	436	437	438	439	440	441	442	443	444	445	446	447	448	449	450	451	
1,630	**568**	**354**	**49**	**23**	**708**	**49**	**29**	...	**2**	...	**20**	**76,785**	**25,836**	**21,637**	**4,078**	**2,214**	**29,312**	
1,522	**524**	**339**	**45**	**23**	**659**	**46**	**26**	...	**2**	...	**20**	**67,717**	**22,965**	**19,159**	**3,463**	**2,008**	**25,593**	
1,508	**514**	**339**	**45**	**23**	**655**	**25**	**12**	...	...	...	**13**	**52,325**	**17,260**	**14,987**	**2,760**	**1,562**	**20,078**	
865	*301*	*157*	*31*	*19*	*330*	*20*	*9*	...	...	...	*11*	*19,680*	*6,194*	*5,190*	*1,300*	*607*	*8,296*	
197	77	19	...	...	101	...	...	...	...	...	...	5,367	1,726	1,471	584	288	2,170	1
72	11	32	...	...	29	...	...	...	...	...	...	3,688	1,146	850	338	120	1,692	2
496	182	106	29	15	208	20	9	...	...	...	11	7,573	2,287	1,963	313	175	3,323	3
110	*48*	*10*	...	...	*52*	*20*	*9*	...	...	...	*11*	*1,336*	*242*	*267*	...	...	*537*	
33	9	7	...	...	17	...	...	...	...	...	...	1,372	430	405	33	12	537	4
70	22	23	2	4	25	...	...	...	...	...	...	1,080	605	501	32	6	574	5
265	*119*	*27*	*6*	...	*119*	...	...	...	...	...	...	*10,310*	*3,439*	*2,868*	*244*	*135*	*3,906*	
196	86	23	1	...	87	...	...	...	...	...	...	2,731	871	780	86	51	1,074	6
40	10	4	...	...	20	...	...	...	...	...	...	3,409	1,202	958	97	63	1,249	7
17	13	...	5	...	4	...	...	...	...	...	...	1,698	574	438	39	15	680	8
9	7	...	...	...	2	...	...	...	...	...	...	1,006	376	319	8	1	401	9
3	3	...	...	...	...	...	...	...	...	...	...	1,276	410	304	14	5	496	10
133	*87*	*37*	*2*	...	*69*	*5*	*3*	...	...	...	*2*	*11,602*	*4,097*	*3,285*	*590*	*443*	*4,120*	
...	...	...	...	...	...	...	...	...	...	...	...	1,549	563	418	49	27	568	11
5	1	...	...	...	4	1	1	...	...	...	...	3,252	1,151	836	40	23	1,265	12
1	*1*	...	...	...	...	...	...	...	...	...	...	*341*	*108*	*68*	...	...	*165*	
106	34	32	2	...	40	3	1	...	...	...	2	2,860	972	833	283	210	1,055	13
10	2	...	...	...	8	1	1	...	...	...	...	2,573	961	771	167	127	841	14
12	...	5	...	...	7	...	...	...	...	...	...	1,208	450	427	51	49	391	15
242	*57*	*88*	*6*	*4*	*97*	...	...	...	...	...	...	*10,933*	*3,530*	*3,647*	*636*	*373*	*3,756*	
93	24	28	2	1	41	...	...	...	...	...	...	4,380	1,432	1,508	290	184	1,440	16
96	16	38	4	3	42	...	...	...	...	...	...	3,700	1,109	1,192	229	123	1,339	17
58	17	22	...	...	14	...	...	...	...	...	...	2,853	920	947	117	71	977	18
14	**10**	...	...	...	**4**	**21**	**14**	...	**2**	...	**7**	**15,392**	**5,705**	**4,172**	**703**	**446**	**5,515**	
...	...	...	...	...	...	...	...	...	...	...	...	4,833	1,920	1,182	243	103	1,731	19
3	2	...	...	...	1	...	...	...	...	...	...	4,152	1,481	1,181	223	129	1,487	20
...	...	...	...	...	...	21	14	...	2	...	7	3,273	1,116	998	175	179	1,159	21
11	8	...	...	...	3	...	...	...	...	...	...	3,134	1,188	808	62	35	1,138	22
108	**44**	**15**	**4**	..	**49**	**3**	**3**	...	...	...	...	**9,068**	**2,871**	**2,478**	**615**	**206**	**3,719**	
...	...	...	...	...	...	...	...	...	...	...	...	67	19	23	...	...	25	23
2	2	...	...	...	...	...	...	...	...	...	...	1,563	495	438	139	43	630	24
9	5	3	...	...	1	...	...	...	...	...	...	484	166	142	32	26	176	25
6	1	2	...	...	3	...	...	...	...	...	...	497	170	182	15	2	145	26
17	8	4	...	...	5	...	...	...	...	...	...	535	161	178	21	19	196	27
29	...	6	...	...	23	...	...	...	...	...	...	178	58	50	6	1	64	28
19	10	...	...	...	9	...	...	...	...	...	...	259	81	93	14	6	85	29
...	...	...	...	...	...	...	...	...	...	...	...	96	35	31	6	3	30	30
...	...	...	...	...	...	3	3	...	...	...	...	1,150	378	372	53	23	409	31
...	...	...	...	...	...	...	...	...	...	...	...	474	109	224	18	4	141	32
...	...	...	...	...	...	...	...	...	...	...	...	150	47	43	8	3	60	33
...	...	...	...	...	...	...	...	...	...	...	...	211	74	68	20	...	69	34
...	...	...	...	...	...	...	...	...	...	...	...	1,727	538	180	86	21	1,003	35
...	...	...	...	...	...	...	...	...	...	...	...	272	87	69	9	3	116	36
26	18	...	4	...	8	...	...	...	...	...	...	1,398	453	379	188	52	584	37

TABLE XV.—Occupation or means

Serial No.	CLASS ... / SUB-CLASS ... / ORDER ... — DISTRICT, CITY OR STATE.	CLASS B.—PREPARATION AND SUPPLY; Sub-Class III.—; Order 10.—Ceramics—(concluded). 48.—Brick and tile makers. Total workers and dependants.	Actual workers. Total. Males.	Actual workers. Total. Females.	Actual workers. Partially agriculturists. Males.	Actual workers. Partially agriculturists. Females.	Dependants.	49.—Others (mosaic, talc, mica, alabaster, etc., workers). Total workers and dependants.	Actual workers. Total. Males.	Actual workers. Total. Females.	Actual workers. Partially agriculturists. Males.	Actual workers. Partially agriculturists. Females.	Dependants.	Order 11.—Chemical products. Total order 11. Total workers and dependants.	Actual workers. Total. Males.	Actual workers. Total. Females.	Actual workers. Partially agriculturists. Males.	Actual workers. Partially agriculturists. Females.	Dependants.
	1	452	453	454	455	456	457	458	459	460	461	462	463	464	465	466	467	468	469
	Central Provinces and Berar ...	**20.128**	**7.739**	**5.291**	**541**	**323**	**7,098**	**3**	...	...	...	...	**3**	**37,041**	**10,501**	**12.225**	**1.962**	**1.291**	**14.315**
	C. P. British Districts and Berar...	**19.087**	**7.405**	**4.923**	**529**	**310**	**6,759**	**3**	...	...	...	...	**3**	**33.037**	**9,531**	**10,442**	**1,825**	**1.107**	**13,064**
	C. P. British Districts ...	**15.229**	**5.608**	**4.182**	**384**	**233**	**5.439**	**3**	...	...	...	...	**3**	**32.127**	**9.171**	**10,352**	**1,784**	**1.106**	**12,604**
	JUBBULPORE DIVISION.	*3,736*	*1,339*	*995*	*27*	*17*	*1,413*	...	...	...	...	...	...	*10,378*	*2,896*	*3,199*	*648*	*422*	*4,353*
1	Saugor ...	548	194	165	7	4	189	...	...	...	...	...	...	3,162	959	833	238	98	1,370
2	Damoh ...	348	96	111	6	3	141	...	...	...	...	...	...	1,877	539	543	173	77	795
3	Jubbulpore ...	1,645	638	309	11	9	698	...	...	...	...	...	...	2,557	660	826	139	136	1,071
	JUBBULPORE CITY...	*1,154*	*425*	*192*	...	...	*537*	...	...	...	...	...	...	*338*	*102*	*34*	...	*1*	*202*
4	Mandla ...	362	118	123	1	...	121	...	...	...	...	...	...	676	170	232	26	19	274
5	Seoni ...	833	283	286	2	1	264	...	...	...	...	...	...	2,206	568	765	72	92	873
	NERBUDDA DIVISION.	*3,837*	*1,446*	*1,094*	*71*	*47*	*1,297*	*3*	...	...	...	...	*3*	*11,342*	*3,327*	*3,513*	*411*	*246*	*4,502*
6	Narsinghpur ...	404	153	104	15	3	147	...	...	...	...	...	...	1,973	545	628	116	55	800
7	Hoshangabad ...	757	272	232	18	15	253	...	...	...	...	...	...	1,908	586	525	65	33	797
8	Nimar ...	1,005	364	267	24	23	374	...	...	...	...	...	...	1,520	539	270	63	26	705
9	Betul ...	649	281	184	8	4	184	...	...	...	...	...	...	3.069	807	1,168	101	82	1,094
10	Chhindwara ...	1,022	376	307	6	2	330	3	...	...	...	...	3	2,872	850	916	66	50	1,106
	NAGPUR DIVISION...	*6,052*	*2,219*	*1,631*	*268*	*153*	*2,202*	...	...	...	...	...	...	*4,453*	*1,640*	*832*	*511*	*226*	*1,981*
11	Wardha ...	1,128	489	258	41	28	381	...	...	...	...	...	...	389	102	49	7	4	178
12	Nagpur ...	2,290	719	711	51	50	860	...	...	...	...	...	...	927	330	81	24	1	516
	NAGPUR CITY ...	*300*	*80*	*91*	...	...	*129*	...	...	...	...	...	...	*219*	*60*	*7*	*1*	...	*152*
13	Chanda ...	654	311	160	49	36	183	...	...	...	...	...	...	155	65	34	23	25	56
14	Bhandara ...	1,520	544	388	118	35	588	...	...	...	...	...	...	1,384	505	276	173	46	603
15	Balaghat ...	460	156	114	9	4	190	...	...	...	...	...	...	1,508	578	392	284	149	628
	CHHATTISGARH DIVISION.	*1,604*	*614*	*463*	*18*	*16*	*527*	...	...	...	...	...	...	*5,854*	*1,308*	*2,808*	*214*	*213*	*1,738*
16	Raipur ...	927	365	279	8	9	283	...	...	...	...	...	...	2,814	539	1,434	114	109	841
17	Bilaspur ...	511	174	142	8	6	195	...	...	...	...	...	...	1,173	300	570	39	64	303
18	Drug ...	166	75	42	2	1	49	...	...	...	...	...	...	1,867	469	804	61	40	594
	Berar ...	**3.858**	**1.797**	**741**	**145**	**77**	**1.320**	...	...	...	...	...	...	**910**	**360**	**90**	**41**	**1**	**460**
19	Amraoti ...	1,516	756	277	67	37	483	...	...	...	...	...	...	242	105	29	19	1	108
20	Akola ...	1,203	531	241	35	23	431	...	...	...	...	...	...	115	56	3	4	...	56
21	Buldana ...	408	154	76	22	3	178	...	...	...	...	...	...	246	80	22	10	...	144
22	Yeotmal ...	731	356	147	21	14	228	...	...	...	...	...	...	307	119	36	8	...	152
	Feudatory States.	**1,041**	**334**	**368**	**12**	**13**	**339**	...	...	...	...	...	...	**4,004**	**970**	**1.783**	**137**	**184**	**1,251**
23	Makrai ...	...	...	...	...	...	...	...	...	...	...	...	...	95	27	32	3	...	36
24	Bastar ...	14	5	6	...	...	3	...	...	...	...	...	...	111	28	47	3	2	36
25	Kanker ...	277	66	133	...	2	78	...	...	...	...	...	...	377	96	137	15	18	144
26	Nandgaon ...	94	50	17	1	...	27	...	...	...	...	...	...	605	169	228	27	12	208
27	Khairagarh ...	231	78	82	6	5	71	...	...	...	...	...	...	680	151	318	30	18	211
28	Chhuikhadan ...	31	11	6	1	1	14	...	...	...	...	...	...	164	41	61	11	8	62
29	Kawardha ...	30	10	2	...	...	18	...	...	...	...	...	...	158	22	88	3	2	48
30	Sakti ...	29	17	7	...	...	5	...	...	...	...	...	...	19	3	13	...	2	3
31	Raigarh ...	140	35	52	...	4	53	...	...	...	...	...	...	505	93	382	12	101	90
32	Sarangarh ...	9	4	1	3	...	4	...	...	...	...	...	...	396	43	312	7	8	41
33	Chang Bhakar ...	5	2	1	...	...	2	...	...	...	...	...	...	78	28	21	3	1	29
34	Korea ...	11	6	5	...	...	...	...	...	...	...	...	...	124	33	49	4	1	42
35	Surguja ...	112	37	25	...	...	50	...	...	...	...	...	...	547	219	51	14	6	277
36	Udaipur ...	14	1	12	...	...	1	...	...	...	...	...	...	15	3	6	...	...	6
37	Jashpur ...	44	12	19	1	1	13	...	...	...	...	...	...	70	14	38	5	5	18

# of livelihood. Part A.—General Table.

OF MATERIAL SUBSTANCES—*continued*).

Industry—(*continued*).

properly so called, and analogous.

50.—Manufacture of matches and explosive materials.						51.—Manufacture of aerated and mineral waters.						52.—Manufacture of dyes, paint and ink.						
Total workers and dependants.	Actual workers. Total. Males.	Actual workers. Total. Females.	Actual workers. Partially agriculturists. Males.	Actual workers. Partially agriculturists. Females.	Dependants.	Total workers and dependants.	Actual workers. Total. Males.	Actual workers. Total. Females.	Actual workers. Partially agriculturists. Males.	Actual workers. Partially agriculturists. Females.	Dependants.	Total workers and dependants.	Actual workers. Total. Males.	Actual workers. Total. Females.	Actual workers. Partially agriculturists. Males.	Actual workers. Partially agriculturists. Females.	Dependants.	Serial No.
470	471	472	473	474	475	476	477	478	479	480	481	482	483	484	485	486	487	
1.400	**460**	**251**	**53**	**16**	**689**	**50**	**27**	...	**2**	...	**23**	**33**	**8**	**11**	...	**7**	**14**	
1.382	**454**	**249**	**53**	**16**	**679**	**49**	**26**	...	**2**	...	**23**	**32**	**8**	**10**	...	**7**	**14**	
1.303	**435**	**242**	**51**	**16**	**626**	**41**	**19**	...	**2**	...	**22**	**20**	**6**	**8**	...	**7**	**6**	
618	*175*	*112*	*28*	*8*	*331*	*10*	*3*	...	...	...	*7*	*7*	*3*	...	...	...	*4*	
205	58	39	10	1	108	8	1	...	...	...	7	...	...	...	...	...	...	1
142	39	26	10	3	77	...	...	...	...	...	...	...	...	...	...	...	...	2
200	55	35	8	4	119	2	2	...	...	...	...	3	2	...	...	...	1	3
62	*15*	*2*	...	...	*35*	*2*	*2*	...	...	...	...	*3*	*2*	...	...	...	*1*	
17	8	1	...	...	8	...	...	...	...	...	...	...	...	...	...	...	...	4
45	15	11	...	...	19	...	...	...	...	...	...	4	1	...	...	...	3	5
260	*108*	*40*	*11*	*7*	*123*	*6*	*3*	...	...	...	*3*	...	...	...	...	...	...	
100	44	13	11	7	52	...	...	...	...	...	...	...	...	...	...	...	...	6
63	30	4	2	...	29	5	2	...	...	...	3	...	...	...	...	...	...	7
2	...	1	...	...	1	...	...	...	...	...	...	...	...	...	...	...	...	8
61	19	11	...	...	31	1	1	...	...	...	...	...	...	...	...	...	...	9
31	10	11	1	...	10	...	...	...	...	...	...	...	...	...	...	...	...	10
83	*30*	*3*	*7*	...	*50*	*22*	*10*	...	*2*	...	*13*	*11*	*2*	*7*	...	*7*	*2*	
6	1	...	...	...	5	...	...	...	...	...	...	...	...	...	...	...	...	11
58	22	...	7	...	36	21	9	...	2	...	12	4	2	...	...	...	2	12
18	*10*	...	...	...	*8*	*18*	*6*	...	*1*	...	*7*	*1*	...	...	...	...	*1*	
3	...	...	...	...	3	...	...	...	...	...	...	7	...	7	...	7	...	13
8	4	1	...	...	3	...	...	...	...	...	...	...	...	...	...	...	...	14
8	3	2	...	...	3	1	1	...	...	...	...	...	...	...	...	...	...	15
336	*127*	*57*	*2*	*1*	*123*	*3*	*3*	...	...	...	...	*2*	*1*	*1*	...	...	...	
55	19	...	...	...	36	3	3	...	...	...	...	1	...	1	...	...	...	16
281	108	87	2	1	86	...	...	...	...	...	...	1	1	...	...	...	...	17
..	...	...	...	...	...	...	...	...	...	...	...	...	...	...	...	...	...	18
79	**19**	**7**	**2**	...	**53**	**8**	**7**	...	...	...	**1**	**12**	**2**	**2**	...	...	**8**	
19	4	2	...	...	13	8	7	...	...	...	1	7	...	1	...	...	6	19
35	8	3	2	...	24	...	...	...	...	...	...	1	1	...	...	...	...	20
24	6	2	...	...	10	...	...	...	...	...	...	4	1	1	...	...	2	21
1	1	...	...	...	...	...	...	...	...	...	...	...	...	...	...	...	...	22
18	**6**	**2**	...	...	**10**	**1**	**1**	...	...	...	...	**1**	...	**1**	...	...	...	
7	2	1	...	...	4	...	...	...	...	...	...	...	...	...	...	...	...	23
...	...	...	...	...	...	...	...	...	...	...	...	...	...	...	...	...	...	24
...	...	...	...	...	...	...	...	...	...	...	...	...	...	...	...	...	...	25
...	...	...	...	...	...	...	...	...	...	...	...	...	...	...	...	...	...	26
...	...	...	...	...	...	...	...	...	...	...	...	1	...	1	...	...	...	27
...	...	...	...	...	...	...	...	...	...	...	...	...	...	...	...	...	...	28
...	...	...	...	...	...	...	...	...	...	...	...	...	...	...	...	...	...	29
...	...	...	...	...	...	...	...	...	...	...	...	...	...	...	...	...	...	30
...	...	...	...	...	...	1	1	...	...	...	...	...	...	...	...	...	...	31
...	...	...	...	...	...	...	...	...	...	...	...	...	...	...	...	...	...	32
...	...	...	...	...	...	...	...	...	...	...	...	...	...	...	...	...	...	33
6	2	1	...	...	3	...	...	...	...	...	...	...	...	...	...	...	...	34
5	2	...	...	...	3	...	...	...	...	...	...	...	...	...	...	...	...	35
...	...	...	...	...	...	...	...	...	...	...	...	...	...	...	...	...	...	36
...	...	...	...	...	...	...	...	...	...	...	...	...	...	...	...	...	...	37

TABLE XV.—Occupation or means

CLASS ... CLASS B.—PREPARATION AND SUPPLY

SUB-CLASS ... Sub-Class III.—

ORDER ... Order 11.—Chemical products properly so called, and analogous—(*concluded*).

Serial No	DISTRICT, CITY OR STATE.	53.—Manufacture and refining of vegetable and mineral oils.						54.—Manufacture of paper, cardboard and papier maché.						55.—Others (soap, candles, lac, cutch, perfumes and miscellaneous drugs).					
		Total workers and dependants.	Actual workers. Total.		Actual workers. Partially agriculturists.		Dependants.	Total workers and dependants.	Actual workers. Total.		Actual workers. Partially agriculturists.		Dependants.	Total workers and dependants.	Actual workers. Total.		Actual workers. Partially agriculturists.		Dependants.
			Males.	Females.	Males.	Females.			Males.	Females.	Males.	Females.			Males.	Females.	Males.	Females.	
	1	488	489	490	491	492	493	494	495	496	497	498	499	500	501	502	503	504	505
	Central Provinces and Berar ...	**33,872**	**9,422**	**11,595**	**1,858**	**1,236**	**12,855**	**58**	**30**	**4**	**5**	...	**24**	**1,628**	**554**	**364**	**44**	**32**	**710**
	C. P. British Districts and Berar ...	**30.122**	**8,577**	**9,838**	**1,725**	**1,053**	**11,707**	**52**	**24**	**4**	**1**	...	**24**	**1,400**	**442**	**341**	**44**	**31**	**617**
	C. P. British Districts ...	**29,569**	**8,339**	**9,803**	**1,706**	**1,053**	**11,427**	**52**	**24**	**4**	**1**	...	**24**	**1,142**	**348**	**295**	**24**	**30**	**499**
	JUBBULPORE DIVISION.	*9,551*	*2,675*	*2,982*	*613*	*355*	*3,891*	*15*	*5*	*3*	...	...	*7*	*277*	*33*	*102*	*7*	*29*	*143*
1	Saugor ...	2,900	893	782	228	97	1,225	...	...	...	...	...	...	49	7	12	...	...	30
2	Damoh ...	1,700	495	500	163	74	705	15	5	3	...	...	7	20	...	14	...	...	6
3	Jubbulpore ...	2,213	593	738	130	110	882	...	...	...	...	...	...	130	8	53	1	22	69
	JUBBULPORE CITY ...	*251*	*82*	*26*	...	*1*	*143*	...	...	...	...	...	...	*30*	*1*	*6*	...	...	*23*
4	Mandla ...	598	145	214	20	13	230	...	...	...	...	...	...	61	17	17	6	6	27
5	Seoni ...	2,140	552	748	72	91	840	...	...	...	...	...	...	17	...	6	...	1	11
	NERBUDDA DIVISION...	*11,017*	*3,203*	*3,467*	*396*	*238*	*4,347*	*11*	*5*	*1*	*1*	...	*7*	*42*	*15*	*5*	...	*1*	*22*
6	Narsinghpur ...	1,844	495	615	105	48	734	...	...	...	...	...	...	20	6	...	...	...	14
7	Hoshangabad ...	1,829	549	519	63	33	761	...	...	...	...	...	...	11	5	2	...	...	4
8	Nimar ...	1,500	535	274	62	26	697	11	3	1	1	...	7	1	1	...	...	...	...
9	Betul ...	3,002	785	1,157	101	82	1,060	...	...	...	...	...	...	5	2	...	...	...	3
10	Chhindwara ...	2,836	839	902	65	49	1,095	...	...	...	...	...	...	5	1	3	...	1	1
	NAGPUR DIVISION ...	*3,625*	*1,360*	*645*	*499*	*215*	*1,623*	...	...	...	...	...	...	*709*	*235*	*177*	*3*	...	*294*
11	Wardha ...	252	121	17	7	4	114	...	...	...	...	...	...	131	40	32	...	...	59
12	Nagpur ...	648	241	22	15	1	385	...	...	...	...	...	...	196	56	59	...	...	81
	NAGPUR CITY ...	*178*	*43*	*6*	...	...	*129*	...	...	...	...	...	...	*9*	*1*	*1*	...	...	*7*
13	Chanda ...	137	60	25	22	18	52	...	...	...	...	...	...	8	5	2	1	...	1
14	Bhandara ...	1,050	382	208	172	46	469	...	...	...	...	...	...	317	119	67	1	...	131
15	Balaghat ...	1,532	556	373	283	149	603	...	...	...	...	...	...	57	18	17	1	...	22
	CHHATTISGARH DIVISION.	*5,373*	*1,098*	*2,709*	*198*	*212*	*1,566*	*26*	*16*	...	...	...	*10*	*114*	*63*	*11*	*14*	...	*40*
16	Raipur ...	2,710	499	1,424	109	109	787	...	...	...	...	...	...	45	18	9	5	...	18
17	Bilaspur ...	822	146	481	28	63	195	...	...	...	...	...	...	69	45	2	9	...	22
18	Drug ...	1,841	453	804	61	40	584	26	16	...	...	...	10	...	...	...	...	...	...
	Berar ...	**553**	**238**	**35**	**19**	...	**280**	...	...	...	...	...	...	**258**	**94**	**46**	**20**	**1**	**118**
19	Amraoti ...	94	37	8	...	...	49	...	...	...	...	...	...	114	57	18	19	1	39
20	Akola ...	63	43	...	2	...	20	...	...	...	...	...	...	16	4	...	...	...	12
21	Buldana ...	215	73	19	10	...	123	...	...	...	...	...	...	3	...	...	...	...	3
22	Yeotmal ...	181	85	8	7	...	88	...	...	...	...	...	...	125	33	28	1	...	64
	Feudatory States ...	**3,750**	**845**	**1,757**	**133**	**183**	**1,148**	**6**	**6**	...	**4**	...	...	**228**	**112**	**23**	...	**1**	**93**
23	Makrai ...	88	25	31	3	...	32	...	...	...	...	...	...	...	...	...	...	...	...
24	Bastar ...	111	28	47	8	2	36	...	...	...	...	...	...	...	...	...	...	...	...
25	Kanker ...	377	96	137	15	18	144	...	...	...	...	...	...	...	...	...	...	...	...
26	Nandgaon ...	605	109	228	27	12	208	...	...	...	...	...	...	...	...	...	...	...	...
27	Khairagarh ...	676	148	317	30	18	211	2	2	...	...	...	...	1	1	...	...	...	...
28	Chhuikhadan ...	164	41	61	11	8	62	...	...	...	...	...	...	...	...	...	...	...	...
29	Kawardha ...	158	22	88	3	2	48	...	...	...	...	...	...	...	...	...	...	...	...
30	Sakti ...	19	3	13	...	2	3	...	...	...	...	...	...	...	...	...	...	...	...
31	Raigarh ...	563	91	382	12	101	90	...	...	...	...	...	...	1	1	...	...	...	...
32	Sarangarh ...	396	43	312	7	8	41	...	...	...	...	...	...	...	...	...	...	...	...
33	Chang Bhakar ...	58	22	15	3	1	21	...	...	...	...	...	...	20	6	6	...	...	8
34	Korea ...	114	31	44	4	...	39	...	...	...	...	...	...	4	...	4	...	1	...
35	Surguja ...	350	109	51	10	6	190	4	4	...	4	...	...	188	104	...	...	...	84
36	Udaipur ...	15	3	6	...	...	6	...	...	...	...	...	...	...	...	...	...	...	...
37	Jashpur ...	56	14	25	5	5	17	...	...	...	...	...	...	14	...	13	...	...	1

# of livelihood, Part A.—General Table.

OF MATERIAL SUBSTANCES—(*continued*).

Industry—(*continued*).

Order 12.—Food industries.																		
Total order 12.						56.—Rice pounders and huskers and flour grinders.						57.—Bakers and biscuit makers.						
Total workers and dependants.	Actual workers. Total. Males.	Actual workers. Total. Females.	Partially agriculturists. Males.	Partially agriculturists. Females.	Dependants.	Total workers and dependants.	Actual workers. Total. Males.	Actual workers. Total. Females.	Partially agriculturists. Males.	Partially agriculturists. Females.	Dependants.	Total workers and dependants.	Actual workers. Total. Males.	Actual workers. Total. Females.	Partially agriculturists. Males.	Partially agriculturists. Females.	Dependants.	Serial No.
506	507	508	509	510	511	512	513	514	515	516	517	518	519	520	521	522	523	
105,538	**22,078**	**47,265**	**1.466**	**3,726**	**36,195**	**25,275**	**1,696**	**18,068**	**193**	**1.275**	**5,511**	**593**	**160**	**126**	**8**	**1**	**307**	
88,036	**18.553**	**38,534**	**1.237**	**3.493**	**30.949**	**20.408**	**1,299**	**14.635**	**144**	**1,142**	**4,474**	**465**	**138**	**58**	...	...	**269**	
68,331	**13.300**	**33.127**	**823**	**3,205**	**21.904**	**15.848**	**1.103**	**11,454**	**141**	**1,059**	**3.291**	**406**	**117**	**56**	...	...	**233**	
16,322	*3,812*	*6,232*	*155*	*160*	*6,275*	*4,509*	*317*	*3,461*	*6*	*66*	*1,031*	*231*	*66*	*27*	...	...	*188*	
6,343	1,693	2,098	95	73	2,552	1,408	85	1,032	4	33	201	74	15	15	...	...	44	1
1,811	191	901	3	25	719	818	41	581	...	22	196	3	...	3	...	...	...	2
5,450	1,347	1,978	33	45	2,125	2,003	165	1,473	3	11	455	134	50	5	...	...	79	3
3,009	*735*	*853*	...	*11*	*1,391*	*976*	*29*	*693*	...	*11*	*254*	*126*	*47*	*8*	...	...	*76*	
1,302	335	526	16	8	441	238	5	177	1	...	56	11	1	3	...	...	7	4
1,416	246	729	8	12	441	252	21	198	...	...	33	9	...	1	...	...	8	5
10,570	*2,247*	*4,653*	*86*	*266*	*3,970*	*3,209*	*233*	*2,352*	*4*	*80*	*694*	*67*	*19*	*16*	...	...	*83*	
1,980	279	1,172	9	69	535	1,177	86	878	2	43	213	1	1	...	...	...	...	6
3,053	590	1,331	17	68	1,132	882	62	662	2	17	158	42	9	13	...	...	20	7
3,010	823	929	48	66	1,264	518	34	357	...	1	127	6	1	3	...	...	2	8
1,164	230	570	6	16	355	320	22	253	...	8	45	14	7	...	...	...	7	9
1,651	316	651	6	46	684	312	29	232	...	11	51	4	1	...	...	...	3	10
23,699	*4,203*	*12,889*	*312*	*2,355*	*6,566*	*5,910*	*475*	*4,255*	*124*	*905*	*1,174*	*75*	*29*	*6*	...	...	*45*	
2,770	804	598	44	46	1,314	455	42	346	2	13	67	3	1	2	...	...	...	11
6,230	1,482	2,383	34	138	2,874	1,068	64	604	3	6	310	58	22	3	...	...	33	12
1,513	*556*	*395*	*3*	...	*860*	*420*	*11*	*245*	...	...	*161*	*25*	*10*	*1*	...	...	*17*	
3,634	520	2,265	105	554	849	999	137	652	69	148	210	11	2	...	...	...	9	13
8,681	1,119	5,925	119	1,533	1,637	3,152	210	2,379	50	714	563	6	4	...	...	...	2	14
2,209	219	1,658	10	114	302	236	25	187	...	23	24	...	...	...	...	...	...	15
17,540	*3,037*	*9,413*	*270*	*335*	*5,090*	*1,920*	*75*	*1,353*	*5*	*9*	*492*	*30*	*3*	*5*	...	...	*19*	
8,534	1,309	4,901	133	191	2,324	788	33	597	5	5	158	23	...	6	...	...	17	16
6,399	1,320	2,958	110	168	2,121	1,021	35	667	...	4	319	3	2	...	...	...	1	17
2,007	408	1,554	27	36	645	111	7	89	...	...	15	4	1	2	...	...	1	18
19,705	**5.253**	**5,407**	**414**	**288**	**9,045**	**4,560**	**196**	**3,181**	**3**	**83**	**1,183**	**59**	**21**	**2**	...	...	**36**	
6,284	1,702	1,456	142	62	3,126	1,705	58	1,030	2	27	611	50	18	...	...	...	32	19
5,050	1,350	1,508	145	104	2,192	1,278	61	926	...	24	291	4	1	2	...	...	1	20
5,092	1,270	1,509	110	60	2,313	1,119	36	893	...	21	190	1	...	...	...	...	1	21
3,279	931	934	17	62	1,414	458	41	326	1	11	91	4	2	...	...	...	2	22
17,502	**3.525**	**8,731**	**229**	**233**	**5.246**	**4.867**	**397**	**3.433**	**49**	**133**	**1.037**	**128**	**22**	**68**	**8**	**1**	**38**	
60	18	32	...	4	10	7	2	4	...	...	1	...	...	...	...	...	...	23
6,848	1,197	3,685	80	23	1,966	2,480	53	2,075	5	2	352	101	16	57	8	1	28	24
1,617	424	578	19	3	615	137	49	28	13	2	60	2	1	1	...	...	...	25
1,209	298	668	10	27	333	69	4	56	...	2	9	3	...	2	...	...	1	26
1,102	222	575	7	14	305	187	3	150	...	1	28	5	2	...	...	...	1	27
160	21	104	3	1	35	24	1	11	...	...	4	...	...	...	...	...	...	28
357	58	156	4	1	144	21	3	9	...	...	9	...	...	...	...	...	...	29
190	41	94	2	6	55	...	...	...	...	...	...	...	...	...	...	...	...	30
2,204	450	1,144	40	131	610	729	73	530	18	117	136	1	...	...	...	...	1	31
1,342	197	870	19	10	275	29	2	26	...	...	1	...	...	...	...	...	...	32
33	...	24	...	1	9	33	...	24	...	1	9	...	...	...	...	...	...	33
207	60	109	1	2	38	112	6	98	...	...	8	...	...	...	...	...	...	34
1,019	280	256	16	...	477	582	87	216	...	...	279	2	2	...	...	...	...	35
263	60	114	...	...	89	24	1	13	...	...	10	...	...	...	...	...	...	36
792	193	323	22	10	276	483	113	189	18	8	131	14	1	8	—	...	5	37

TABLE XV.—Occupation or means

Serial No.	CLASS ... / SUB-CLASS ... / ORDER ...	CLASS B.—PREPARATION AND SUPPLY / Sub-Class III.— / Order 12.—Food																	
		58.—Grain parchers, etc.						59.—Butchers.						60.—Fish curers.					
	DISTRICT, CITY OR STATE.	Total workers and dependants.	Actual workers. Total.		Actual workers. Partially agriculturists.		Dependants.	Total workers and dependants.	Actual workers. Total.		Actual workers. Partially agriculturists.		Dependants.	Total workers and dependants.	Actual workers. Total.		Actual workers. Partially agriculturists.		Dependants.
			Males.	Females.	Males.	Females.			Males.	Females.	Males.	Females.			Males.	Females.	Males.	Females.	
	1	524	525	526	527	528	529	530	531	532	533	534	535	536	537	538	539	540	541
	Central Provinces and Berar ...	**32,061**	**4,118**	**20,476**	**378**	**1,924**	**7,467**	**18,953**	**6,137**	**2,022**	**365**	**78**	**10,794**	**90**	**68**	...	**9**	...	**22**
	C. P. British Districts and Berar ...	**26,422**	**3,299**	**17,087**	**316**	**1,856**	**6,036**	**18,794**	**6,100**	**2,009**	**365**	**78**	**10,685**	**90**	**68**	...	**9**	...	**22**
	C. P. British Districts ...	**23,041**	**2,439**	**15,733**	**271**	**1,715**	**4,869**	**10,260**	**3,338**	**1,397**	**90**	**23**	**5,545**	...	...	...	...	...	...
	JUBBULPORE DIVISION.	*1,26[illegible]*	*160*	*741*	*15*	*2[illegible]*	*303*	*[illegible],610*	*1,405*	*9[illegible]3*	*2[illegible]*	*7*	*2,25[illegible]*	...	...	...	...	...	...
1	Saugor	152	45	49	9	9	58	3,101	1,030	707	20	4	1,364	...	...	...	...	...	...
2	Damoh	10	...	4	...	...	6	298	10	125	...	3	163	...	...	...	...	...	...
3	Jubbulpore ...	292	68	63	1	2	161	863	245	84	1	...	534	...	...	...	...	...	...
	JUBBULPORE CITY ...	*220*	*46*	*4[illegible]*	...	...	*130*	*735*	*192*	*80*	...	...	*403*	...	...	...	...	...	...
4	Mandla	204	8	159	2	5	37	146	54	23	...	...	69	...	...	...	...	...	...
5	Seoni	606	39	466	3	12	101	202	70	4	3	...	128	...	...	...	...	...	...
	NERBUDDA DIVISION.	*2,487*	*323*	*1,56[illegible]*	*20*	*160*	*600*	*1,399*	*472*	*125*	*15*	*5*	*902*	...	...	...	...	...	...
6	Narsinghpur ...	245	25	171	2	23	49	58	14	4	...	...	40	...	...	...	...	...	...
7	Hoshangabad ...	765	112	473	9	45	180	277	83	5	...	...	189	...	...	...	...	...	...
8	Nimar ...	780	141	380	8	56	253	542	180	42	12	2	320	...	...	...	...	...	...
9	Betul	288	16	230	...	7	36	244	78	44	1	...	122	...	...	...	...	...	...
10	Chhindwara ...	409	29	208	1	29	82	378	117	30	2	3	231	...	...	...	...	...	...
	NAGPUR DIVISION ...	*8,005*	*583*	*6,135*	*49*	*1,163*	*1,277*	*3,088*	*988*	*260*	*43*	*11*	*1,530*	...	...	...	...	...	...
11	Wardha	437	86	151	10	29	200	802	268	73	19	3	461	...	...	...	...	...	...
12	Nagpur	1,798	181	1,313	2	117	304	1,547	491	116	12	8	940	...	...	...	...	...	...
	NAGPUR CITY ...	*157*	*56*	*3[illegible]*	...	...	*69*	*530*	*169*	*29*	...	...	*33[illegible]*	...	...	...	...	...	...
13	Chanda	1,408	117	1,087	14	290	190	273	89	20	3	...	164	...	...	...	...	...	...
14	Bhandara ...	2,688	105	2,279	17	634	304	373	100	34	8	...	239	...	...	...	...	...	...
15	Balaghat ...	1,679	94	1,315	6	84	270	93	40	17	1	...	36	...	...	...	...	...	...
	CHHATTISGARH DIVISION.	*11,256*	*1,373*	*7,283*	*187*	*36[illegible]*	*2,629*	*1,083*	*469*	*69*	*8*	...	*546*	...	...	...	...	...	...
16	Raipur	5,010	672	3,944	92	170	1,303	286	80	16	...	...	190	...	...	...	...	...	...
17	Bilaspur ...	3,422	498	1,990	78	159	925	718	377	25	7	...	316	...	...	...	...	...	...
18	Drug	1,944	208	1,340	17	35	401	79	12	28	1	...	39	...	...	...	...	...	...
	Berar	**3,381**	**860**	**1,354**	**45**	**141**	**1,167**	**8,514**	**2,762**	**612**	**275**	**55**	**5,140**	**90**	**68**	...	**9**	...	**22**
19	Amraoti	518	204	98	8	3	210	3,118	1,054	245	108	27	1,819	...	...	...	...	...	...
20	Akola	909	221	408	23	63	280	2,192	681	146	72	17	1,365	85	66	...	9	...	19
21	Buldana	1,196	316	412	13	27	468	1,986	611	136	84	10	1,230	5	2	...	...	...	3
22	Yeotmal	758	119	436	1	48	203	1,218	416	85	11	1	717	...	...	...	...	...	...
	Feudatory States ...	**5,639**	**819**	**3,389**	**62**	**68**	**1,431**	**159**	**37**	**13**	...	...	**109**	...	...	...	...	...	...
23	Makrai ...	33	...	28	...	4	5	6	3	...	...	...	3	...	...	...	...	...	...
24	Bastar	433	54	269	2	...	110	18	5	1	...	...	12	...	...	...	...	...	...
25	Kanker	701	122	331	3	1	248	2	...	2	...	...	...	...	...	...	...	...	...
26	Nandgaon ...	678	28	547	6	23	103	43	8	...	...	...	35	...	...	...	...	...	...
27	Khairagarh ...	475	26	358	1	11	91	62	17	6	...	...	39	...	...	...	...	...	...
28	Chhuikhadan ...	98	5	80	...	1	13	4	1	...	...	...	3	...	...	...	...	...	...
29	Kawardha ...	151	9	105	1	1	37	5	...	...	...	...	5	...	...	...	...	...	...
30	Sakti	136	18	85	2	6	33	7	2	1	...	...	4	...	...	...	...	...	...
31	Raigarh	1,192	268	553	17	9	371	12	1	8	...	...	8	...	...	...	...	...	...
32	Sarangarh ...	1,234	172	819	19	10	243	...	...	...	...	...	...	...	...	...	...	...	...
33	Chang Bhakar ...	...	...	...	...	...	...	...	...	...	...	...	...	...	...	...	...	...	...
34	Korea	25	2[illegible]	...	1	...	5	...	...	...	...	...	...	...	...	...	...	...	...
35	Surguja	73	27	18	7	...	28	...	...	...	...	...	...	...	...	...	...	...	...
36	Udaipur	189	45	91	...	...	53	...	...	...	...	...	...	...	...	...	...	...	...
37	Jashpur	221	25	105	3	2	91	...	...	...	...	...	...	...	...	...	...	...	...

# of livelihood, Part A.—General Table.

OF MATERIAL SUBSTANCES—(*continued*).

Industry—(*continued*).

industries—(*continued*).

61.—Butter, cheese and ghee makers.						62.—Makers of sugar, molasses and gur.						63.—Sweetmeat makers, preparers of jam and condiments, etc.						
Total workers and dependants.	ACTUAL WORKERS.				Dependants.	Total workers and dependants.	ACTUAL WORKERS.				Dependants.	Total workers and dependants.	ACTUAL WORKERS.				Dependants.	Serial No.
	Total.		Partially agriculturists.				Total.		Partially agriculturists.				Total.		Partially agriculturists.			
	Males.	Females.	Males.	Females.			Males.	Females.	Males.	Females.			Males.	Females.	Males.	Females.		
542	543	544	545	546	547	548	549	550	551	552	553	554	555	556	557	558	559	
2,172	**525**	**619**	**90**	**50**	**1.028**	**242**	**81**	**119**	...	**1**	**42**	**13,314**	**4,486**	**2,879**	**185**	**295**	**5,949**	
2,165	**525**	**618**	**90**	**50**	**1.022**	**242**	**81**	**119**	...	**1**	**42**	**12,605**	**4,216**	**2.754**	**178**	**295**	**5,635**	
2,159	**523**	**618**	**89**	**50**	**1,018**	**158**	**15**	**112**	...	**1**	**31**	**10.323**	**3.234**	**2.572**	**118**	**290**	**4,517**	
1,148	*304*	*376*	*66*	*30*	*468*	*108*	...	*88*	...	—	*20*	*3,485*	*1,251*	*536*	*38*	*28*	*1,708*	
547	159	146	53	26	242	...	...	...	...	...	...	1,018	356	132	9	1	531	1
108	15	48	2	...	45	108	...	88	...	...	20	441	122	52	1	...	267	2
109	12	63	...	4	34	...	...	...	...	...	...	1,543	580	208	24	27	686	3
1	...	—	...	...	*1*	...	...	...	...	...	...	*757*	*338*	*49*	...	...	*370*	
364	109	119	10	...	136	...	...	...	...	...	...	169	82	16	2	...	71	4
20	9	...	...	...	11	...	...	...	...	—	...	314	103	58	2	...	158	5
805	*200*	*193*	*24*	*16*	*412*	*43*	*10*	*24*	...	*1*	*9*	*2,496*	*885*	*310*	*22*	*3*	*1,304*	
115	35	43	4	3	37	20	7	4	...	...	9	352	104	69	1	...	179	6
183	5	83	...	5	95	...	...	...	...	...	...	826	283	90	5	1	456	7
380	157	50	20	7	164	...	—	...	...	...	...	670	263	54	8	...	353	8
...	...	...	...	...	...	3	3	...	...	...	...	283	108	36	5	1	139	9
127	3	8	...	1	116	20	...	20	...	1	...	365	127	61	3	1	177	10
167	*10*	*34*	...	*4*	*123*	*7*	*5*	...	...	...	*2*	*2,723*	*560*	*1,423*	*35*	*249*	*740*	
...	...	...	...	...	...	1	1	...	...	...	...	320	101	20	7	...	145	11
165	9	34	...	4	122	1	1	...	—	...	...	487	218	34	3	...	235	12
...	...	...	...	...	...	*1*	*1*	...	...	...	...	*119*	*49*	*3*	...	...	*67*	
...	...	...	...	...	...	1	1	...	...	...	...	704	67	472	8	107	165	13
...	...	...	...	...	...	...	...	...	...	...	...	988	81	758	16	135	149	14
2	1	...	...	...	1	4	2	...	...	...	2	218	33	139	1	7	46	15
39	*9*	*15*	...	...	*15*	...	...	...	—	...	...	*1,616*	*538*	*313*	*23*	*10*	*765*	
28	2	15	...	—	11	...	—	...	...	...	...	811	285	164	7	6	362	16
11	7	...	...	—	4	...	...	...	...	...	...	623	191	121	15	3	311	17
...	...	...	...	...	—	...	...	...	...	...	...	182	62	28	1	1	92	18
6	**2**	...	**1**	...	**4**	**84**	**66**	**7**	—	...	**11**	**2.282**	**982**	**182**	**60**	**5**	**1,118**	
3	2	...	1	...	1	14	1	7	...	...	6	587	250	37	5	4	300	19
3	...	—	...	...	3	65	63	...	...	...	2	356	181	17	40	...	158	20
...	...	...	...	...	...	5	2	...	...	...	3	681	264	58	12	...	359	21
...	...	...	—	...	...	...	...	...	...	—	...	658	287	70	8	1	301	22
7	...	**1**	...	...	**6**	...	...	...	...	...	...	**709**	**270**	**125**	**7**	...	**314**	
...	...	...	...	...	...	...	...	...	...	...	...	23	13	...	...	...	10	23
...	...	...	...	...	...	...	...	...	...	...	...	27	11	5	...	...	11	24
...	...	...	...	...	...	...	...	...	...	...	...	16	5	5	...	...	6	25
...	...	...	...	...	...	...	...	...	...	...	...	64	33	7	...	...	24	26
...	...	...	...	...	...	...	...	...	...	...	...	80	32	17	...	...	40	27
...	...	...	...	...	...	...	...	...	...	...	...	5	3	1	...	...	1	28
...	...	...	...	...	...	...	...	...	...	...	...	100	28	12	1	...	60	29
...	...	...	...	...	...	...	...	...	...	...	...	14	5	3	...	...	6	30
...	...	...	...	...	...	...	...	...	...	...	...	105	42	29	3	...	34	31
...	...	...	...	...	...	...	...	...	...	...	...	51	14	23	...	...	14	32
...	...	...	...	...	...	...	...	...	...	...	...	...	...	...	...	...	...	33
...	...	...	...	...	...	...	...	...	...	...	...	7	4	1	...	...	2	34
7	...	1	...	...	6	...	...	...	...	...	...	150	57	12	2	...	81	35
...	...	...	...	...	...	...	...	...	...	...	...	18	10	...	...	...	8	36
...	...	...	...	...	...	...	...	...	...	...	...	40	13	10	1	...	17	37

TABLE XV.—Occupation or means

	CLASS ...	CLASS B.—PREPARATION AND SUPPLY																	
	SUB-CLASS ...	Sub-Class III.—																	
	ORDER ...	Order 12.—Food Industries—(concluded).																	
		64.—Brewers and distillers.						65. —Toddy drawers.						66.—Manufacturers of tobacco, opium and ganja.					
	DISTRICT, CITY OR STATE.	Total workers and dependants.	Actual workers. Total.		Actual workers. Partially agriculturists.		Dependants.	Total workers and dependants.	Actual workers. Total.		Actual workers. Partially agriculturists.		Dependants.	Total workers and dependants.	Actual workers. Total.		Actual workers. Partially agriculturists.		Dependants.
Serial No.			Males.	Females.	Males.	Females.			Males.	Females.	Males.	Females.			Males.	Females.	Males.	Females.	
	1	560	561	562	563	564	565	566	567	568	569	570	571	572	573	574	575	576	577
	Central Provinces and Berar ...	**6,933**	**2,239**	**1,938**	**157**	**74**	**2.756**	**1.494**	**655**	**52**	**37**	**5**	**787**	**4,411**	**1,913**	**966**	**44**	**23**	**1,532**
	C. P. British Districts and Berar ...	**1,632**	**607**	**343**	**59**	**46**	**682**	**1,488**	**653**	**51**	**37**	**5**	**784**	**3.725**	**1,567**	**860**	**39**	**20**	**1,298**
	C. P. British Districts ...	**1,492**	**540**	**339**	**57**	**46**	**613**	**1,171**	**521**	**27**	**22**	**4**	**623**	**3,453**	**1,470**	**819**	**35**	**17**	**1,164**
	Jubbulpore Division.	*414*	*212*	*35*	*5*	*1*	*167*	...	...	...	...	...	...	*253*	*93*	*35*	...	...	*126*
1	Saugor ...	...	...	...	...	...	...	...	...	...	...	...	...	43	4	17	...	...	22
2	Damoh ...	22	...	...	...	...	22	...	...	...	...	...	...	3	3	...	...	...	...
3	Jubbulpore ...	218	133	6	4	1	79	...	...	...	...	...	...	198	85	16	...	...	97
	Jubbulpore City ...	*43*	*27*	...	...	...	*16*	...	...	...	...	...	...	*161*	*66*	*14*	...	...	*81*
4	Mandla ...	170	76	20	1	...	65	...	...	...	...	...	...	...	...	...	...	...	...
5	Seoni ...	4	3	...	...	...	1	...	...	...	...	...	...	9	1	2	...	...	6
	Nerbudda Division.	*56*	*31*	...	*1*	...	*25*	*16*	*7*	*1*	...	...	*8*	*159*	*67*	*35*	...	...	*84*
6	Narsinghpur ...	...	...	...	...	...	...	...	...	...	...	...	...	18	7	3	...	...	8
7	Hoshangabad ...	40	22	...	1	...	18	...	...	...	...	...	...	35	14	5	...	...	16
8	Nimar ...	1	1	...	...	...	...	4	4	...	...	...	...	115	42	28	...	...	45
9	Betul ...	1	1	...	...	...	...	4	1	...	...	...	3	7	3	1	...	...	3
10	Chhindwara ...	14	7	...	...	...	7	8	2	1	...	...	5	14	1	1	...	...	12
	Nagpur Division ...	*359*	*61*	*150*	*6*	*35*	*148*	*1,143*	*509*	*26*	*22*	*4*	*609*	*2,118*	*981*	*528*	*38*	*16*	*609*
11	Wardha ...	9	...	...	...	...	9	738	301	6	6	1	431	5	4	...	...	...	1
12	Nagpur ...	71	3	33	2	...	35	295	142	20	7	3	133	749	351	136	5	...	262
	Nagpur City ...	*1*	...	...	...	...	*1*	...	...	...	...	...	...	*557*	*259*	*85*	*3*	...	*213*
13	Chanda ...	92	35	25	2	...	32	109	65	...	9	...	44	42	7	9	...	...	26
14	Bhandara ...	157	3	92	...	35	62	2	1	...	...	...	1	1,315	615	383	28	15	317
15	Balaghat ...	30	20	...	2	...	10	...	...	...	...	...	...	7	4	...	...	...	3
	Chhattisgarh Division.	*663*	*230*	*157*	*45*	*10*	*273*	*11*	*5*	...	...	...	*6*	*893*	*329*	*218*	*2*	*2*	*346*
16	Raipur ...	327	90	85	28	9	143	...	...	...	...	...	...	352	138	74	1	1	140
17	Bilaspur ...	188	66	39	9	1	83	11	5	...	...	...	6	402	139	107	1	1	156
18	Drug ...	148	71	30	8	...	47	...	...	...	...	...	...	139	52	37	...	...	50
	Berar ...	**140**	**67**	**4**	**2**	...	**69**	**317**	**132**	**24**	**15**	**1**	**161**	**272**	**97**	**41**	**4**	**3**	**134**
19	Amraoti ...	17	7	...	1	...	10	195	83	17	15	1	99	77	25	20	2	...	32
20	Akola ...	75	41	1	...	...	33	68	31	1	...	...	26	20	4	2	1	...	14
21	Buldana ...	5	4	...	...	...	1	...	...	...	...	...	...	94	35	10	1	2	49
22	Yeotmal ...	43	15	3	1	...	25	54	18	5	...	...	30	81	33	9	...	1	39
	Feudatory States ...	**5,301**	**1,632**	**1,595**	**98**	**28**	**2,074**	**6**	**2**	**1**	...	...	**3**	**686**	**346**	**106**	**5**	**3**	**234**
23	Makrai ...	...	...	...	...	...	...	...	...	...	...	...	...	...	...	...	...	...	...
24	Bastar ...	3,759	1,046	1,272	65	20	1,441	...	...	...	...	...	...	30	12	6	...	...	12
25	Kanker ...	754	244	211	3	...	299	2	...	...	...	...	2	3	3	...	...	...	...
26	Nandgaon ...	89	33	14	2	1	42	...	...	...	...	...	...	353	192	42	2	1	119
27	Khairagarh ...	39	22	5	3	...	12	...	...	...	...	...	...	245	120	33	3	2	92
28	Chhuikhadan ...	22	5	4	3	...	13	...	...	...	...	...	...	7	6	...	...	...	1
29	Kawardha ...	77	17	27	2	...	33	...	...	...	...	...	...	3	1	2	...	...	...
30	Sakti ...	30	14	4	...	...	12	...	...	...	...	...	...	3	2	1	...	...	...
31	Raigarh ...	127	58	19	13	5	50	...	...	...	...	...	...	38	8	20	...	...	10
32	Sarangarh ...	27	9	1	...	...	17	...	...	...	...	...	...	1	...	1	...	...	...
33	Chang Bhakar ...	...	...	...	...	...	...	...	...	...	...	...	...	...	...	...	...	...	...
34	Korea ...	63	30	10	...	2	23	...	...	...	...	...	...	...	...	...	...	...	...
35	Surguja ...	205	113	9	7	...	83	...	...	...	...	...	...	...	...	...	...	...	...
36	Udaipur ...	30	3	9	...	...	18	...	...	...	...	...	...	2	1	1	...	...	...
37	Jashpur ...	79	38	10	...	...	31	4	2	1	...	...	1	1	1	...	...	...	...

# of livelihood, Part A.—General Table.

OF MATERIAL SUBSTANCES—*(continued)*.

Industry—*(continued)*.

Order 13.—Industries of dress and the toilet.																		
Total order 13.						67.—Hat, cap and turban makers.						68.—Tailors, milliners, dressmakers and darners, embroiderers on linen.						
Total workers and dependants.	Actual workers.				Dependants.	Total workers and dependants.	Actual workers.				Dependants.	Total workers and dependants.	Actual workers.				Dependants.	Serial No.
	Total.		Partially agriculturists.				Total.		Partially agriculturists.				Total.		Partially agriculturists.			
	Males.	Females.	Males.	Females.			Males.	Females.	Males.	Females.			Males.	Females.	Males.	Females.		
578	579	580	581	582	583	584	585	586	587	588	589	590	591	592	593	594	595	
371,735	**136,158**	**55,486**	**30,604**	**9,592**	**180,091**	**7,573**	**2,569**	**1,483**	**9**	...	**3,521**	**59,741**	**19,605**	**12,762**	**1,567**	**935**	**27,374**	
352,127	**129,923**	**52,208**	**29,576**	**9,282**	**169,996**	**7,570**	**2,568**	**1,482**	**9**	...	**3,520**	**58,136**	**19,088**	**12,518**	**1,546**	**931**	**26,532**	
278,436	**101,200**	**41,207**	**25,127**	**7,361**	**136,029**	**7,171**	**2,469**	**1,333**	**7**	...	**3,369**	**45,112**	**14,433**	**9,764**	**1,267**	**701**	**20,915**	
93,921	*34,631*	*10,288*	*11,572*	*1,870*	*49,002*	*61*	*16*	*6*	...	...	*29*	*15,119*	*5,076*	*1,851*	*546*	*96*	*8,192*	
28,724	11,093	2,900	4,501	710	14,722	...	...	...	...	...	...	3,850	1,297	460	138	30	2,093	1
19,308	7,193	1,527	3,244	359	10,588	...	...	...	...	...	...	2,194	754	150	87	15	1,290	2
30,013	10,925	2,922	3,258	668	16,166	41	10	6	...	...	25	5,759	2,030	490	258	33	3,239	3
5,964	*2,057*	*494*	*6*	*1*	*3,353*	*40*	*9*	*6*	...	...	*25*	*2,007*	*694*	*216*	*1*	...	*1,097*	
5,814	1,886	1,057	229	68	2,871	7	6	...	...	...	1	1,058	322	174	32	9	562	4
10,062	3,584	1,823	341	65	4,655	3	...	...	...	...	3	2,258	673	577	31	8	1,008	5
79,407	*28,546*	*12,697*	*4,907*	*1,799*	*38,164*	*7,035*	*2,405*	*1,325*	*1*	...	*3,304*	*10,706*	*3,320*	*2,930*	*193*	*142*	*4,456*	
18,149	6,435	2,985	1,793	745	8,729	1	1	...	...	...	...	2,459	785	530	72	43	1,144	6
25,365	9,242	3,419	1,900	531	12,704	36	14	1	...	...	21	2,953	945	723	52	24	1,285	7
16,473	6,037	2,582	404	162	7,854	6,990	2,390	1,319	1	...	3,281	1,537	550	350	18	15	637	8
7,013	2,599	1,307	369	142	3,107	6	1	3	...	...	2	1,206	378	411	22	24	417	9
12,407	4,233	2,404	441	219	5,770	2	2	...	...	...	...	2,551	662	916	29	36	972	10
72,453	*26,856*	*13,118*	*5,578*	*2,912*	*32,479*	*84*	*44*	*4*	*6*	...	*36*	*16,493*	*5,093*	*4,534*	*470*	*445*	*6,866*	
10,661	4,135	1,842	591	413	4,684	22	19	1	6	...	2	2,202	678	609	30	57	915	11
22,669	8,114	4,201	920	590	10,354	60	25	3	...	...	32	5,230	1,552	1,446	51	49	2,232	12
3,875	*1,341*	*487*	*3*	...	*2,047*	*53*	*20*	*2*	...	...	*31*	*1,275*	*392*	*171*	...	...	*712*	
17,304	6,200	3,352	2,020	1,169	7,752	...	...	...	...	...	...	3,613	1,095	978	163	184	1,540	13
15,493	5,942	2,619	1,744	595	6,932	2	...	...	...	...	2	3,651	1,182	1,044	166	133	1,425	14
6,326	2,465	1,104	603	145	2,757	...	...	...	...	...	...	1,797	586	457	60	25	754	15
32,655	*11,117*	*5,154*	*2,770*	*780*	*16,384*	*1*	*1*	...	...	...	...	*2,794*	*944*	*449*	*56*	*16*	*1,401*	
12,300	4,195	2,025	1,031	256	6,080	...	...	...	...	...	...	1,295	384	230	8	8	681	16
9,270	3,205	1,555	951	330	4,510	1	1	...	...	...	...	1,058	415	143	45	6	500	17
11,085	3,717	1,574	788	185	5,794	...	...	...	...	...	...	441	145	76	5	7	220	18
73,691	**28,723**	**11,001**	**4,449**	**1,921**	**33,967**	**399**	**99**	**149**	**2**	...	**151**	**13,026**	**4,655**	**2,754**	**279**	**230**	**5,617**	
22,652	8,530	3,651	963	505	10,471	192	17	116	...	...	59	4,631	1,067	919	101	52	2,045	19
17,944	7,161	2,418	1,459	496	8,365	18	5	1	1	...	12	2,788	1,032	482	65	47	1,274	20
16,158	6,311	2,481	1,461	659	7,306	25	5	12	...	...	8	2,927	985	696	92	103	1,240	21
16,937	6,721	2,451	566	261	7,765	164	72	20	1	...	72	2,680	971	657	21	28	1,052	22
19,608	**6,235**	**3,278**	**1,028**	**310**	**10,095**	**3**	**1**	**1**	...	...	**1**	**1,603**	**517**	**244**	**21**	**4**	**842**	
582	221	120	32	11	241	...	...	...	...	...	...	75	21	24	...	...	30	23
979	317	225	9	10	437	...	...	...	...	...	...	169	40	65	...	...	64	24
779	258	150	23	15	371	...	...	...	...	...	...	113	30	30	...	...	53	25
2,477	800	344	147	53	1,333	—	...	...	...	...	...	218	78	25	2	...	115	26
2,614	823	451	133	39	1,340	...	...	...	...	...	...	214	74	15	2	...	125	27
689	210	105	46	7	374	...	...	...	...	...	...	29	12	2	...	...	15	28
1,580	476	354	120	36	750	...	...	...	...	...	...	99	27	7	...	...	65	29
147	44	42	15	14	61	...	...	...	...	...	...	5	1	2	...	...	2	30
1,672	498	417	94	38	757	...	...	...	...	...	...	103	41	5	2	1	57	31
893	240	280	85	23	373	...	...	...	...	...	...	65	23	16	3	...	26	32
408	170	77	41	12	161	...	...	...	...	...	...	19	11	3	6	1	5	33
679	245	70	35	2	364	...	—	...	...	...	...	37	16	1	2	...	20	34
4,532	1,448	272	142	16	2,812	3	1	1	...	...	1	367	113	20	2	...	234	35
486	121	131	9	7	234	...	...	...	...	...	...	25	8	7	...	...	10	36
1,091	364	240	97	27	487	...	...	...	...	...	...	65	22	22	2	2	21	37

TABLE XV.—Occupation or means

Serial No.	CLASS ... / SUB-CLASS ... / ORDER ...	CLASS B.—PREPARATION AND SUPPLY OF															
		Sub-Class III.—															
		Order 13.—Industries of															
		69.—Shoe, boot and sandal makers.						70.—Other industries pertaining to dress, gloves, socks, gaiters, belts, buttons, umbrellas, canes, etc.						71.—Washing, cleaning			
	DISTRICT, CITY OR STATE.	Total workers and dependants.	Actual workers. Total.		Actual workers. Partially agriculturists.		Dependants.	Total workers and dependants.	Actual workers. Total.		Actual workers. Partially agriculturists.		Dependants.	Total workers and dependants.	Actual work[ers]. Total.		Parti[ally] agri[cul]tur[ists].
			Males.	Females.	Males.	Females.			Males.	Females.	Males.	Females.			Males.	Females.	Males.
	1	596	597	598	599	600	601	602	603	604	605	606	607	608	609	610	611
	Central Provinces and Berar ...	**121,606**	**45,265**	**13,812**	**12,447**	**3,010**	**62,529**	**1,688**	**391**	**716**	**24**	**18**	**581**	**82,521**	**25,527**	**25,233**	**6,212**
	C. P. British Districts and Berar ...	**114,898**	**43,070**	**13,011**	**12,216**	**2,982**	**58,817**	**1,214**	**270**	**559**	**19**	**14**	**385**	**77,507**	**24.165**	**23.390**	**5,859**
	C. P. British Districts ...	**94,779**	**35,221**	**10,252**	**11,008**	**2,358**	**49,306**	**1,178**	**261**	**558**	**17**	**14**	**359**	**58,337**	**17.762**	**18,186**	**4,681**
	JUBBULPORE DIVISION.	*33,557*	*14,760*	*2,090*	*6,673*	*410*	*21,737*	*327*	*99*	*106*	*12*	*7*	*122*	*19,692*	*5,900*	*5,644*	*1,840*
1	Saugor ...	11,212	4,546	211	2,490	54	6,455	44	16	11	3	...	17	6,833	2,104	1,969	846
2	Damoh ...	8,929	3,452	106	2,173	41	5,371	3	1	...	...	...	2	4,229	1,243	1,231	429
3	Jubbulpore ...	12,205	4,607	647	1,865	290	6,951	...	...	...	...	...	...	6,037	1,739	1,640	459
	JUBBULPORE CITY ...	*1,276*	*398*	*35*	*3*	*1*	*843*	...	...	...	...	...	...	*1,505*	*443*	*237*	*2*
4	Mandla ...	3,098	1,005	596	72	19	1,497	106	56	65	9	7	75	522	170	150	39
5	Seoni ...	3,143	1,150	530	64	6	1,463	84	26	30	...	...	28	2,071	644	654	67
	NERBUDDA DIVISION	*29,181*	*10,590*	*3,535*	*2,419*	*879*	*15,056*	*210*	*77*	*59*	*4*	...	*74*	*15,357*	*4,801*	*4,701*	*830*
6	Narsinghpur ...	6,797	2,469	788	1,005	346	3,540	1	...	...	...	...	1	5,026	1,475	1,652	305
7	Hoshangabad ...	12,473	4,583	1,280	1,121	315	6,610	15	5	1	...	...	9	4,669	1,470	1,400	287
8	Nimar ...	3,252	1,183	436	146	96	1,633	41	11	9	...	...	21	2,021	732	454	31
9	Betul ...	2,672	936	421	51	51	1,315	...	...	...	...	...	...	1,171	377	403	47
10	Chhindwara ...	3,987	1,419	610	96	71	1,958	153	61	49	4	...	43	2,500	747	792	100
	NAGPUR DIVISION ...	*18,181*	*6,673*	*3,477*	*1,383*	*959*	*8,031*	*112*	*26*	*25*	...	*4*	*61*	*15,482*	*4,931*	*4,908*	*1,257*
11	Wardha ...	2,368	964	382	96	76	1,022	18	2	6	...	...	10	2,588	864	837	189
12	Nagpur ...	5,627	1,996	1,242	164	268	2,380	58	18	8	...	...	37	4,793	1,468	1,476	235
	NAGPUR CITY ...	*608*	*207*	*62*	...	...	*339*	*39*	*10*	...	...	...	*29*	*1,057*	*352*	*261*	*1*
13	Chanda ...	5,153	1,964	861	757	307	2,328	...	...	...	...	...	...	4,615	1,434	1,494	487
14	Bhandara ...	3,890	1,341	766	277	209	1,789	4	...	...	...	...	4	2,388	804	736	261
15	Balaghat ...	1,137	408	226	89	39	503	32	6	16	...	4	10	1,098	361	360	85
	CHHATTISGARH DIVISION.	*8,830*	*3,198*	*1,160*	*533*	*110*	*4,482*	*529*	*59*	*368*	*1*	*3*	*102*	*7,776*	*2,130*	*2,938*	*754*
16	Raipur ...	2,578	985	328	170	37	1,265	178	20	131	...	...	27	3,184	871	1,240	278
17	Bilaspur ...	2,497	859	360	169	50	1,278	170	22	98	...	3	50	2,350	647	877	275
18	Drug ...	3,755	1,354	462	194	23	1,939	181	17	139	1	...	25	2,242	612	821	201
	Berar ...	**20,119**	**7,849**	**2,759**	**1,208**	**624**	**9,511**	**36**	**9**	**1**	**2**	...	**26**	**19,170**	**6,403**	**5,204**	**1,178**
19	Amraoti ...	4,827	1,847	710	213	87	2,270	17	3	...	...	...	14	6,566	2,117	1,857	277
20	Akola ...	5,000	1,884	742	382	182	2,374	4	1	1	...	...	2	4,480	1,544	1,163	414
21	Buldana ...	5,305	2,155	715	471	259	2,525	12	3	...	2	...	9	3,714	1,233	1,010	332
22	Yeotmal ...	4,897	1,963	592	142	96	2,342	3	2	...	...	...	1	4,410	1,509	1,165	155
	Feudatory States ...	**6,708**	**2,195**	**801**	**231**	**28**	**3,712**	**474**	**121**	**157**	**5**	**4**	**196**	**5,014**	**1,362**	**1,843**	**353**
23	Makrai ...	283	105	61	6	...	117	9	6	...	...	...	3	91	27	34	12
24	Bastar ...	385	135	56	4	1	194	10	...	8	...	...	2	245	65	89	4
25	Kanker ...	11	2	5	...	...	4	7	3	2	...	...	2	251	66	101	14
26	Nandgaon ...	573	187	76	25	5	310	33	2	21	...	1	10	551	146	201	57
27	Khairagarh ...	538	166	98	2	...	274	44	5	32	...	...	7	624	164	258	40
28	Chhuikhadan ...	263	80	34	21	...	149	5	1	4	...	...	...	120	29	47	8
29	Kawardha ...	521	153	159	12	7	209	18	...	13	...	...	5	388	102	136	48
30	Sakti ...	6	6	...	1	...	...	...	...	...	...	...	...	78	17	39	7
31	Raigarh ...	103	28	15	5	1	60	9	4	1	1	...	4	942	252	363	44
32	Sarangarh ...	45	13	6	3	...	26	4	1	3	...	...	...	495	119	255	37
33	Chang Bhakar ...	344	139	70	31	10	135	...	...	...	...	...	...	8	3	4	1
34	Korea ...	501	176	39	29	...	286	43	23	1	...	...	19	60	18	21	3
35	Surguja ...	2,760	886	124	84	4	1,750	64	12	15	1	1	37	561	179	91	21
36	Udaipur ...	62	17	...	1	...	45	108	24	29	3	...	55	239	56	90	4
37	Jashpur ...	313	102	58	7	...	153	120	40	28	...	2	52	361	119	114	53

# of livelihood, Part A.—General Table.

MATERIAL SUBSTANCES—(*continued*).

Industry—(*continued*).

dress and the toilet—(*concluded*).

... and dyeing. Actual workers. Partially agriculturists. Females.	... and dyeing. Dependants.	72.—Barbers, hair dressers and wig makers. Total workers and dependants.	72. Actual workers. Total. Males.	72. Actual workers. Total. Females.	72. Actual workers. Partially agriculturists. Males.	72. Actual workers. Partially agriculturists. Females.	72. Dependants.	73.—Other industries connected with the toilet (tattooers, shampooers, bath houses, etc.) Total workers and dependants.	73. Actual workers. Total. Males.	73. Actual workers. Total. Females.	73. Actual workers. Partially agriculturists. Males.	73. Actual workers. Partially agriculturists. Females.	73. Dependants.	Order 14.—Furniture industries. Total order 14. Total workers and dependants.	Total order 14. Actual workers. Total. Males.	Total order 14. Actual workers. Total. Females.	Total order 14. Actual workers. Partially agriculturists. Males.	Total order 14. Actual workers. Partially agriculturists. Females.	Total order 14. Dependants.	Serial No.
612	613	614	615	616	617	618	619	620	621	622	623	624	625	626	627	628	629	630	631	
5,433	**31,761**	**97,906**	**42,750**	**968**	**10,345**	**167**	**54,188**	**700**	**51**	**512**	...	**29**	**137**	**259**	**86**	**13**	**1**	...	**160**	
5,173	**29,952**	**92,262**	**40,712**	**861**	**9,927**	**154**	**50,689**	**538**	**50**	**387**	...	**28**	**101**	**255**	**83**	**13**	**1**	...	**159**	
4,143	**22,889**	**71,326**	**31,005**	**727**	**8,147**	**117**	**39,594**	**533**	**49**	**387**	...	**28**	**97**	**181**	**71**	**9**	...	...	**101**	
1,809	*8,145*	*19,876*	*8,508*	*375*	*2,501*	*41*	*10,694*	*269*	*22*	*167*	...	*8*	*86*	*104*	*31*	*7*	...	...	*66*	
616	2,760	6,724	3,130	234	1,015	10	3,360	61	...	24	...	...	37	79	25	5	...	...	40	1
280	1,755	3,941	1,743	30	555	16	2,168	12	...	10	...	1	2	...	...	...	...	...	...	2
331	2,658	5,850	2,517	76	676	14	3,266	112	22	63	...	...	27	22	6	2	...	...	14	3
...	*825*	*1,135*	*552*	...	...	...	*593*	*1*	*1*	...	...	...	...	*22*	*6*	*2*	...	...	*15*	
26	202	863	327	16	76	...	520	70	...	56	...	7	14	...	...	...	...	...	...	4
50	773	2,480	1,091	18	179	1	1,380	14	...	14	...	...	...	3	...	...	...	...	8	5
757	*5,855*	*16,763*	*7,333*	*54*	*1,460*	*11*	*9,376*	*125*	*17*	*95*	...	*10*	*13*	*22*	*14*	...	...	...	*8*	
348	1,899	3,853	1,705	3	351	1	2,145	12	...	12	...	7	...	14	8	...	...	...	6	6
189	1,799	5,196	2,209	14	440	3	2,973	23	16	...	...	...	7	5	4	...	...	...	1	7
51	835	2,632	1,171	14	208	...	1,447	...	...	...	...	...	...	1	1	...	...	...	...	8
63	391	1,887	907	4	249	1	976	71	...	65	...	3	6	...	...	...	...	...	...	9
106	961	3,195	1,341	19	212	6	1,835	19	1	18	...	...	...	2	1	...	...	...	1	10
1,466	*5,645*	*22,010*	*10,059*	*93*	*2,762*	*26*	*11,834*	*91*	*6*	*85*	...	*10*	*3*	*49*	*25*	*2*	...	...	*22*	
280	887	3,463	1,608	7	270	...	1,848	...	...	...	...	...	...	3	3	...	...	...	...	11
260	1,849	6,884	3,050	22	470	4	3,812	17	5	9	...	3	3	41	20	...	...	...	21	12
...	*454*	*841*	*359*	*1*	*2*	...	*451*	*2*	*1*	...	...	...	*1*	...	...	...	...	...	...	
607	1,687	3,922	1,707	18	613	11	2,197	1	...	1	...	...	...	4	1	2	...	...	1	13
243	848	5,516	2,615	37	1,040	9	2,864	36	...	36	...	1	...	...	...	...	...	...	...	14
70	377	2,225	1,103	9	369	1	1,113	37	1	36	...	6	...	1	1	...	...	...	...	15
611	*2,708*	*12,677*	*4,781*	*206*	*1,424*	*40*	*7,690*	*48*	*4*	*43*	...	...	*1*	*6*	*1*	...	...	...	*5*	
206	1,073	5,029	1,935	60	575	11	3,034	36	...	36	...	...	...	...	...	...	...	...	...	16
257	826	3,182	1,257	70	462	23	1,855	12	4	7	...	...	1	5	...	...	...	...	5	17
149	800	4,406	1,589	76	387	6	2,801	...	...	...	...	...	...	1	1	...	...	...	...	18
1,030	**7,563**	**20,936**	**9,707**	**134**	**1,780**	**37**	**11,095**	**5**	**1**	...	...	...	**4**	**74**	**12**	**4**	**1**	...	**58**	
361	2,592	6,419	2,879	49	372	5	3,491	...	...	...	...	...	...	19	8	...	...	...	11	19
259	1,773	5,649	2,694	29	597	8	2,926	5	1	...	...	...	4	31	...	1	...	...	31	20
275	1,462	4,085	1,930	39	564	22	2,116	...	...	...	...	...	...	22	3	3	1	...	15	21
135	1,736	4,783	2,204	17	247	2	2,562	...	...	...	...	...	...	2	1	...	...	...	1	22
260	**1,809**	**5,844**	**2,038**	**107**	**418**	**13**	**3,499**	**162**	**1**	**125**	...	**1**	**36**	**4**	**3**	...	...	...	**1**	
11	30	124	62	1	14	...	61	...	...	...	...	...	...	...	...	...	...	...	...	23
9	91	164	77	1	1	...	86	6	...	6	...	...	...	...	...	...	...	...	...	24
15	84	389	157	4	9	...	228	8	...	8	...	...	...	...	...	...	...	...	...	25
46	204	1,102	387	21	63	1	694	...	...	...	...	...	...	3	2	...	...	...	1	26
39	202	1,146	414	1	80	...	731	48	...	47	...	...	1	...	...	...	...	...	...	27
7	44	250	88	...	17	...	162	22	...	18	...	...	4	1	1	...	...	...	...	28
27	150	554	194	30	60	2	321	...	...	...	...	...	...	...	...	...	...	...	...	29
14	22	57	20	...	7	...	37	1	...	1	...	...	...	...	...	...	...	...	...	30
36	327	456	173	2	42	...	281	59	...	31	...	...	28	...	...	...	...	...	...	31
23	121	284	84	...	42	...	200	...	...	...	...	...	...	...	...	...	...	...	...	32
1	1	37	17	...	3	...	20	...	...	...	...	...	...	...	...	...	...	...	...	33
1	21	29	11	...	1	...	18	9	1	8	...	1	...	...	...	...	...	...	...	34
4	291	773	257	18	34	7	498	4	...	3	...	...	1	...	...	...	...	...	...	35
7	93	48	16	3	1	...	29	4	...	2	...	...	2	...	...	...	...	...	...	36
20	128	231	81	67	35	3	133	1	...	1	...	...	...	...	...	...	...	...	...	37

TABLE XV.—Occupation or means

CLASS ... CLASS B.—PREPARATION AND SUPPLY

SUB-CLASS ... Sub-Class III.—

ORDER ... Order 11.—Furniture industries—(*concluded*).

Serial No.	DISTRICT, CITY OR STATE.	74.—Cabinet makers, carriage painters, etc. — Total workers and dependants.	74 — Actual workers — Total — Males.	74 — Actual workers — Total — Females.	74 — Actual workers — Partially agriculturists — Males.	74 — Actual workers — Partially agriculturists — Females.	74 — Dependants.	75.—Upholsterers, tent makers, etc. — Total workers and dependants.	75 — Actual workers — Total — Males.	75 — Actual workers — Total — Females.	75 — Actual workers — Partially agriculturists — Males.	75 — Actual workers — Partially agriculturists — Females.	75 — Dependants.	Total order 15. — Total workers and dependants.	Total order 15 — Actual workers — Total — Males.	Total order 15 — Actual workers — Total — Females.	Total order 15 — Actual workers — Partially agriculturists — Males.	Total order 15 — Actual workers — Partially agriculturists — Females.	Total order 15 — Dependants.
	1	632	633	634	635	636	637	638	639	640	641	642	643	644	645	646	647	648	649
	Central Provinces and Berar ...	**169**	**66**	**5**	**1**	...	**98**	**90**	**20**	**8**	...	...	**62**	**81,564**	**30,430**	**13,486**	**2,470**	**932**	**37,648**
	C. P. British Districts and Berar ...	**165**	**63**	**5**	**1**	...	**97**	**90**	**20**	**8**	...	...	**62**	**79,450**	**29,780**	**12,887**	**2,462**	**932**	**36,783**
	C. P British Districts ...	**128**	**51**	**5**	...	...	**72**	**53**	**20**	**4**	...	...	**29**	**51,672**	**19,253**	**8,921**	**938**	**295**	**23,498**
	JUBBULPORE DIVISION	*92*	*30*	*5*	...	...	*57*	*12*	*1*	*2*	...	...	*9*	*14,439*	*5,076*	*1,551*	*199*	*32*	*7,207*
1	Saugor ...	79	25	5	...	...	49	...	...	...	...	...	...	3,308	1,120	263	101	8	1,911
2	Damoh ...	...	...	...	...	...	...	...	...	...	...	...	...	1,530	640	87	27	3	794
3	Jubbulpore ...	10	5	...	...	...	5	12	1	2	...	...	9	8,374	2,781	1,091	38	17	3,902
	JUBBULPORE CITY ...	*10*	*5*	...	...	...	*5*	*12*	*1*	*2*	...	...	*9*	*3,766*	*1,329*	*812*	*1*	...	*2,118*
4	Mandla ...	...	...	...	...	...	...	...	...	...	...	...	...	625	301	38	32	...	286
5	Seoni ...	3	...	...	...	...	3	...	...	...	...	...	...	602	210	72	1	4	314
	NERBUDDA DIVISION...	*22*	*14*	...	...	...	*8*	...	...	...	...	...	...	*8,334*	*3,443*	*1,179*	*159*	*49*	*3,712*
6	Narsinghpur ...	14	8	...	...	...	6	...	...	...	...	...	...	712	256	63	19	2	393
7	Hoshangabad ...	5	4	...	...	...	1	...	...	...	...	...	...	2,161	849	278	41	...	1,034
8	Nimar ...	1	1	...	...	...	...	...	...	...	...	...	...	3,161	1,156	615	46	33	1,390
9	Betul ...	...	...	...	...	...	...	...	...	...	...	...	...	1,041	528	120	42	5	393
10	Chhindwara ...	2	1	...	...	...	1	...	...	...	...	...	...	1,259	654	108	11	9	502
	NAGPUR DIVISION ...	*8*	*6*	...	...	...	*2*	*41*	*19*	*2*	...	...	*20*	*24,776*	*9,634*	*5,081*	*479*	*159*	*10,561*
11	Wardha ...	3	3	...	...	...	...	...	...	...	...	...	...	3,981	1,406	749	114	59	1,826
12	Nagpur ...	2	1	...	...	...	1	39	19	...	...	...	20	14,109	5,245	3,169	154	50	5,695
	NAGPUR CITY ...	...	...	...	...	...	...	...	...	...	...	...	...	*3,925*	*1,366*	*738*	*5*	*3*	*1,521*
13	Chanda ...	2	1	...	...	...	1	2	...	2	...	...	...	3,813	1,297	787	113	67	1,729
14	Bhandara ...	...	...	...	...	...	...	...	...	...	...	...	...	2,096	812	303	88	10	981
15	Balaghat ...	1	1	...	...	...	...	...	...	...	...	...	...	777	374	73	10	3	330
	CHHATTISGARH DIVISION.	*6*	*1*	...	...	...	*5*	...	...	...	...	...	...	*4,128*	*1,600*	*510*	*101*	*25*	*2,018*
16	Raipur ...	...	...	...	...	...	...	...	...	...	...	...	...	2,343	875	284	39	13	1,184
17	Bilaspur ...	5	...	...	...	...	5	...	...	...	...	...	...	1,239	482	157	55	10	600
18	Drug ...	1	1	...	...	...	...	...	...	...	...	...	...	546	243	69	7	2	234
	Berar ...	**37**	**12**	...	**1**	...	**25**	**37**	...	**4**	...	...	**33**	**27,778**	**10,527**	**3,966**	**1,524**	**637**	**13,285**
19	Amraoti ...	19	8	...	...	...	11	...	...	...	...	...	...	6,085	2,090	848	251	124	3,147
20	Akola ...	...	...	...	...	...	...	31	...	1	...	...	30	7,737	3,098	1,181	555	241	3,463
21	Buldana ...	16	3	...	1	...	13	6	...	3	...	...	3	7,131	2,651	845	594	211	3,635
22	Yeotmal ...	2	1	...	...	...	1	...	...	...	...	...	...	6,825	2,693	1,092	124	61	3,040
	Feudatory States ...	**4**	**3**	...	...	...	**1**	...	...	...	...	...	...	**2,114**	**650**	**599**	**8**	...	**885**
23	Makrai ...	...	...	...	...	...	...	...	...	...	...	...	...	65	24	20	...	...	21
24	Bastar ..	...	...	...	...	...	...	...	...	...	...	...	...	225	88	20	3	...	117
25	Kanker ...	...	...	...	...	...	...	...	...	...	...	...	...	229	73	97	...	...	59
26	Nandgaon ...	3	2	...	...	...	1	...	...	...	...	...	...	142	79	6	1	...	57
27	Khairagarh ...	...	...	...	...	...	...	...	...	...	...	...	...	466	131	153	1	...	182
28	Chhuikhadan ...	1	1	...	...	...	...	...	...	...	...	...	...	47	11	9	...	...	27
29	Kawardha ...	...	...	...	...	...	...	...	...	...	...	...	...	146	47	14	1	...	85
30	Sakti ...	...	...	...	...	...	...	...	...	...	...	...	...	23	7	13	...	...	13
31	Raigarh ...	...	...	...	...	...	...	...	...	...	...	...	...	200	56	61	...	...	93
32	Sarangarh ...	...	...	...	...	...	...	...	...	...	...	...	...	74	8	13	1	...	53
33	Chang Bhakar ...	...	...	...	...	...	...	...	...	...	...	...	...	21	8	2	1	...	11
34	Korea ...	...	...	...	...	...	...	...	...	...	...	...	...	83	16	56	...	...	11
35	Surguja ...	...	...	...	...	...	...	...	...	...	...	...	...	196	47	80	...	...	69
36	Udaipur ...	...	...	...	...	...	...	...	...	...	...	...	...	108	25	44	...	...	39
37	Jashpur ...	...	...	...	...	...	...	...	...	...	...	...	...	80	30	21	...	...	29

# of livelihood, Part A.—General Table.

OF MATERIAL SUBSTANCES—(*continued*).

Industry—(*continued*).

Order 15.—Building industries.

76.—Lime burners, cement workers.						77.—Excavators, plinth builders and well-sinkers.						78.—Stone and marble workers, masons and bricklayers.						
Total workers and dependants.	Actual workers.				Dependants.	Total workers and dependants.	Actual workers.				Dependants.	Total workers and dependants.	Actual workers.				Dependants.	Serial No.
	Total.		Partially agriculturists.				Total.		Partially agriculturists.				Total.		Partially agriculturists.			
	Males.	Females.	Males.	Females.			Males.	Females.	Males.	Females.			Males.	Females.	Males.	Females.		
650	651	652	653	654	655	656	657	658	659	660	661	662	663	664	665	666	667	
4,530	**1,470**	**1,315**	**72**	**29**	**1,745**	**3,902**	**1,385**	**1,093**	**16**	**22**	**1,424**	**70,158**	**26,483**	**10,656**	**2,274**	**850**	**33,019**	
4,465	**1,449**	**1,290**	**72**	**29**	**1,726**	**3,849**	**1,373**	**1,070**	**16**	**22**	**1,406**	**68,406**	**25,905**	**10,198**	**2,267**	**850**	**32,303**	
3,987	**1,296**	**1,245**	**57**	**22**	**1,446**	**3,269**	**1,338**	**1,004**	**16**	**21**	**927**	**42,666**	**16,062**	**6,447**	**827**	**238**	**20,157**	
3,303	*1,049*	*1,106*	*36*	*10*	*1,149*	*303*	*40*	*131*	*2*	*11*	*130*	*10,061*	*3,359*	*736*	*160*	*11*	*5,436*	
195	82	49	14	5	64	5	1	1	...	1	3	3,006	1,033	212	87	2	1,761	1
62	14	19	6	3	29	11	5	5	...	...	1	1,446	627	56	21	...	763	2
3,036	952	1,034	16	2	1,050	224	7	118	...	10	99	4,564	1,799	379	21	5	2,386	3
30	*13*	...	...	...	*23*	*5*	...	...	...	...	*5*	*3,545*	*1,311*	*316*	*1*	...	*1,915*	
1	1	...	...	...	...	60	26	8	2	...	26	459	217	21	30	...	221	4
10	...	4	...	...	6	2	1	...	...	...	1	586	213	68	1	4	305	5
278	*112*	*64*	*7*	*1*	*102*	*139*	*84*	*6*	*9*	...	*40*	*7,688*	*3,143*	*1,106*	*140*	*48*	*3,439*	
17	7	3	1	1	7	...	...	...	...	...	...	694	248	60	18	1	386	6
117	51	43	...	...	23	3	1	...	...	...	2	1,933	734	235	39	...	964	7
62	20	8	...	...	34	70	62	...	6	...	8	2,957	1,048	606	39	33	1,303	8
34	19	6	6	...	9	7	2	1	...	...	4	990	504	113	36	5	370	9
48	15	4	...	...	29	49	19	4	8	...	26	1,108	606	92	8	9	407	10
313	*110*	*49*	*7*	*10*	*157*	*2,831*	*1,206*	*862*	*5*	*8*	*753*	*21,11.*	*7,661*	*4,135*	*438*	*157*	*9,523*	
99	29	9	...	...	61	4	4	...	...	...	...	3,040	1,256	711	104	45	1,673	11
115	45	12	3	3	58	2,702	1,163	825	4	8	714	11,077	3,929	2,324	130	39	4,824	12
63	*29*	*3*	...	...	*31*	*3*	*3*	...	...	...	...	*3,812*	*1,319*	*735*	*4*	*3*	*1,758*	
22	8	9	1	4	5	33	12	6	1	...	15	3,708	1,266	769	110	68	1,683	13
51	15	10	1	1	20	36	14	19	...	...	3	1,995	777	[illegible]	87	9	950	14
26	13	3	2	2	10	46	13	12	...	...	21	692	343	56	7	1	293	15
94	*25*	*26*	*7*	*1*	*41*	*17*	[illegible]	*5*	...	*4*	*4*	*3,505*	*1,469*	*477*	*59*	*22*	*1,559*	
52	18	9	7	...	25	...	...	...	...	...	...	2,130	782	274	30	13	1,088	16
27	5	16	...	1	6	...	...	...	...	...	...	1,200	474	140	55	9	586	17
13	2	1	...	...	10	17	8	5	...	2	4	466	213	63	4	...	190	18
478	**153**	**45**	**15**	**7**	**280**	**580**	**35**	**66**	...	**1**	**479**	**25,740**	**9,843**	**3,751**	**1,440**	**612**	**12,146**	
217	80	9	1	2	128	23	6	...	...	...	17	5,726	1,989	888	229	122	2,949	19
63	22	10	3	...	81	489	2	44	...	1	443	6,958	2,963	1,104	541	229	2,891	20
177	41	25	11	4	111	68	27	22	...	...	19	6,567	2,414	772	555	204	3,381	21
21	10	1	...	1	10	...	...	...	...	...	...	6,489	2,527	1,037	115	57	2,025	22
65	**21**	**25**	...	...	**19**	**53**	**12**	**23**	...	...	**18**	**1,752**	**578**	**458**	**7**	...	**716**	
...	...	...	...	...	...	...	...	...	...	...	...	65	24	20	...	...	21	23
10	4	2	...	...	4	10	2	3	...	...	5	183	77	15	3	...	91	24
...	...	...	...	...	...	15	4	11	...	...	...	214	69	86	...	...	59	25
...	...	...	...	...	...	...	...	...	...	...	...	140	79	6	1	...	55	26
6	1	1	...	...	4	...	...	...	...	...	...	439	120	152	...	...	167	27
...	...	...	...	...	...	...	...	...	...	...	...	47	11	9	...	...	27	28
1	...	...	...	...	1	13	3	4	...	...	6	125	44	9	1	...	72	29
3	...	3	...	...	...	...	...	...	...	...	...	20	7	...	...	...	13	30
17	8	8	...	...	1	...	...	...	...	...	...	113	46	6	...	...	61	31
7	...	6	...	...	1	...	...	...	...	...	...	67	8	7	1	...	52	32
...	...	...	...	...	...	...	...	...	...	...	...	13	8	1	1	...	4	33
...	...	...	...	...	...	15	3	5	...	...	7	67	12	51	...	...	4	34
21	8	5	...	...	8	...	...	...	...	...	...	172	39	75	...	...	58	35
...	...	...	...	...	...	...	...	...	...	...	...	7	4	...	...	...	3	36
...	...	...	...	...	...	...	...	...	...	...	...	80	30	21	...	...	29	37

TABLE XV.—Occupation or means

Serial No.	CLASS … / SUB-CLASS … / ORDER … / DISTRICT, CITY OR STATE.	CLASS B.—PREPARATION AND SUPPLY / Sub-Class III.— / Order 15.—Building industries—(concld.) / 79.—Others (thatchers, building contractors, house-painters, tilers, plumbers, locksmiths, etc.). Total workers and dependants.	Actual workers. Total. Males.	Actual workers. Total. Females.	Actual workers. Partially agriculturists. Males.	Actual workers. Partially agriculturists. Females.	Dependants.	Order 16.—Construction of / Total order 16. Total workers and dependants.	Actual workers. Total. Males.	Actual workers. Total. Females.	Actual workers. Partially agriculturists. Males.	Actual workers. Partially agriculturists. Females.	Dependants.	80.—Cart, carriage, palki, etc., makers and wheelwrights. Total workers and dependants.	Actual workers. Total. Males.	Actual workers. Total. Females.	Actual workers. Partially agriculturists. Males.	Actual workers. Partially agriculturists. Females.	Dependants.
	1	668	669	670	671	672	673	674	675	676	677	678	679	680	681	682	683	684	685
	Central Provinces and Berar …	**2,974**	**1,092**	**422**	**108**	**31**	**1,460**	**1,056**	**380**	**77**	**28**	**4**	**599**	**423**	**160**	**13**	**15**	…	**250**
	C. P. British Districts and Berar …	**2,730**	**1,053**	**329**	**107**	**31**	**1,348**	**883**	**301**	**67**	**23**	**4**	**515**	**251**	**81**	**4**	**10**	…	**166**
	C. P. British Districts …	**1,750**	**557**	**225**	**38**	**14**	**968**	**577**	**180**	**23**	**18**	…	**374**	**239**	**77**	**4**	**10**	…	**158**
	JUBBULPORE DIVISION.	*767*	*98*	*177*	*1*	…	*423*	*186*	*48*	*4*	*9*	…	*134*	*77*	*9*	…	*6*	…	*63*
1	Saugor …	97	13	1	…	…	83	76	19	2	4	…	55	34	4	…	4	…	30
2	Damoh …	11	3	7	…	…	1	22	4	…	2	…	18	8	…	…	…	…	8
3	Jubbulpore …	550	23	160	1	…	367	60	10	…	3	…	50	30	3	…	2	…	27
	JUBBULPORE CITY …	*182*	*5*	*2*	…	…	*175*	*37*	*6*	…	…	…	*31*	*15*	*1*	…	…	…	*14*
4	Mandla …	105	57	9	…	…	39	16	7	1	…	…	8	…	…	…	…	…	…
5	Seoni …	4	2	…	…	…	2	12	8	1	…	…	3	5	2	…	…	…	3
	NERBUDDA DIVISION.	*239*	*104*	*4*	*3*	…	*131*	*213*	*61*	*6*	*8*	…	*146*	*71*	*26*	*1*	*3*	…	*44*
6	Narsinghpur …	1	1	…	…	…	…	40	20	3	3	…	17	23	11	1	2	…	11
7	Hoshangabad …	108	63	…	2	…	45	9	5	…	…	…	4	2	2	…	…	…	…
8	Nimar …	72	26	1	1	…	45	29	20	1	…	…	8	13	11	…	…	…	2
9	Betul …	4	3	…	…	…	1	43	10	2	1	…	31	13	1	…	1	…	12
10	Chhindwara …	54	11	3	…	…	40	92	6	…	4	…	86	20	1	…	…	…	19
	NAGPUR DIVISION …	*530*	*257*	*42*	*29*	*14*	*231*	*80*	*37*	*6*	…	…	*37*	*37*	*16*	…	…	…	*21*
11	Wardha …	238	117	29	10	14	92	13	6	4	…	…	3	…	…	…	…	…	…
12	Nagpur …	215	108	8	17	…	99	48	23	…	…	…	25	33	13	…	…	…	20
	NAGPUR CITY …	*47*	*15*	…	*1*	…	*32*	*36*	*16*	…	…	…	*20*	*30*	*12*	…	…	…	*18*
13	Chanda …	50	21	3	1	…	26	3	1	1	…	…	1	1	1	…	…	…	…
14	Bhandara …	14	6	…	…	…	8	15	6	1	…	…	8	2	1	…	…	…	1
15	Balaghat …	13	5	2	1	…	6	1	1	…	…	…	…	1	1	…	…	…	…
	CHHATTISGARH DIVISION.	*214*	*98*	*2*	*6*	…	*114*	*98*	*34*	*7*	*1*	…	*57*	*54*	*26*	*3*	*1*	…	*25*
16	Raipur …	152	75	1	2	…	76	57	18	6	1	…	33	28	13	2	1	…	13
17	Bilaspur …	12	3	1	…	…	8	21	7	…	…	…	14	6	4	…	…	…	2
18	Drug …	50	20	…	3	…	30	20	9	1	…	…	10	20	9	1	…	…	10
	Berar …	**980**	**496**	**104**	**69**	**17**	**380**	**306**	**121**	**44**	**5**	**4**	**141**	**12**	**4**	…	…	…	**8**
19	Amraoti …	119	65	1	21	…	53	38	17	5	…	…	16	8	7	…	…	…	6
20	Akola …	227	106	23	11	11	98	106	37	26	4	4	43	…	…	…	…	…	…
21	Buldana …	319	169	26	28	3	124	120	46	13	1	…	61	4	2	…	…	…	2
22	Yeotmal …	315	156	54	9	3	105	42	21	…	…	…	21	…	…	…	…	…	…
	Feudatory States …	**244**	**39**	**93**	**1**	…	**112**	**173**	**79**	**10**	**5**	…	**84**	**172**	**79**	**9**	**5**	…	**84**
23	Makrai …	…	…	…	…	…	…	…	…	…	…	…	…	…	…	…	…	…	…
24	Bastar …	22	5	…	…	…	17	148	63	8	5	…	77	147	63	7	5	…	77
25	Kanker …	…	…	…	…	…	…	…	…	…	…	…	…	…	…	…	…	…	…
26	Nandgaon …	2	…	…	…	…	2	4	4	…	…	…	…	4	4	…	…	…	…
27	Khairagarh …	21	10	…	1	…	11	2	2	…	…	…	…	2	2	…	…	…	…
28	Chhuikhadan …	…	…	…	…	…	…	…	…	…	…	…	…	…	…	…	…	…	…
29	Kawardha …	7	…	1	…	…	6	…	…	…	…	…	…	…	…	…	…	…	…
30	Sakti …	…	…	…	…	…	…	1	…	…	…	…	1	1	…	…	…	…	1
31	Raigarh …	79	2	47	…	…	30	1	1	…	…	…	…	1	1	…	…	…	…
32	Sarangarh …	…	…	…	…	…	…	…	…	…	…	…	…	…	…	…	…	…	…
33	Chang Bhakar …	8	…	1	…	…	7	…	…	…	…	…	…	…	…	…	…	…	…
34	Korea …	1	1	…	…	…	…	…	…	…	…	…	…	…	…	…	…	…	…
35	Surguja …	3	…	…	…	…	3	…	…	…	…	…	…	…	…	…	…	…	…
36	Udaipur …	101	21	44	…	…	36	…	…	…	…	…	…	…	…	…	…	…	…
37	Jashpur …	…	…	…	…	…	…	17	9	2	…	…	6	17	9	2	…	…	6

# of livelihood, Part A.—General Table.

OF MATERIAL SUBSTANCES—*(continued)*.

Industry—*(continued)*.

means of Transport.

Total order 17.—Production and transmission of physical forces (heat, light, electricity, motive power, etc.).

81.—Saddlers, harness-makers, whip and lash makers.						82.—Ship and boat builders.						83.—Gas works, electric light and ice factories.						
Total workers and dependants.	Actual workers. Total. Males.	Actual workers. Total. Females.	Actual workers. Partially agriculturists. Males.	Actual workers. Partially agriculturists. Females.	Dependants.	Total workers and dependants.	Actual workers. Total. Males.	Actual workers. Total. Females.	Actual workers. Partially agriculturists. Males.	Actual workers. Partially agriculturists. Females.	Dependants.	Total workers and dependants.	Actual workers. Total. Males.	Actual workers. Total. Females.	Actual workers. Partially agriculturists. Males.	Actual workers. Partially agriculturists. Females.	Dependants.	Serial No.
686	687	688	689	690	691	692	693	694	695	696	697	698	699	700	701	702	703	
632	**220**	**64**	**13**	**4**	**348**	**1**	...	...	...	...	**1**	**45**	**28**	**1**	**1**	...	**16**	
631	**220**	**63**	**13**	**4**	**348**	**1**	...	...	...	...	**1**	**42**	**25**	**1**	**1**	...	**16**	
337	**103**	**19**	**8**	...	**215**	**1**	...	...	...	...	**1**	**36**	**22**	**1**	**1**	...	**13**	
109	*39*	*4*	*5*	...	*66*	...	...	...	...	...	...	*7*	*1*	...	...	...	*6*	
42	15	2	...	...	25	...	...	...	...	...	...	...	...	...	...	...	...	1
14	4	...	2	...	10	...	...	...	...	...	...	...	...	...	...	...	...	2
30	7	...	1	...	28	...	...	...	...	...	...	...	...	...	...	...	...	3
22	*5*	...	...	...	*17*	...	...	...	...	...	...	...	...	...	...	...	...	
16	7	1	...	...	8	...	...	...	...	...	...	...	...	...	...	...	...	4
7	6	1	...	...	...	...	...	...	...	...	...	7	1	...	...	...	6	5
142	*35*	*5*	*5*	...	*102*	...	...	...	...	...	...	*6*	*2*	...	...	...	*4*	
17	9	2	1	...	6	...	...	...	...	...	...	1	1	...	...	...	...	6
7	3	...	...	...	4	...	...	...	...	...	...	3	1	...	...	...	2	7
16	9	1	...	...	6	...	...	...	...	...	...	2	...	...	...	...	2	8
30	9	2	...	...	19	...	...	...	...	...	...	...	...	...	...	...	...	9
72	5	...	4	...	67	...	...	...	...	...	...	...	...	...	...	...	...	10
42	*21*	*6*	...	...	*16*	*1*	...	...	...	...	*1*	*17*	*14*	...	*1*	...	*3*	
18	6	4	...	...	3	...	...	...	...	...	...	...	...	...	...	...	...	11
14	10	...	...	...	4	1	...	...	...	...	1	10	7	...	1	...	3	12
6	*4*	...	...	...	*2*	...	...	...	...	...	...	*5*	*6*	...	...	...	*2*	
2	...	1	...	...	1	...	...	...	...	...	...	6	6	...	...	...	...	13
13	5	1	...	...	7	...	...	...	...	...	...	...	...	...	...	...	...	14
...	...	...	...	...	...	...	...	...	...	...	...	1	1	...	...	...	...	15
44	*5*	*4*	...	...	*35*	...	...	...	...	...	...	*6*	*5*	*1*	...	...	...	
20	5	4	...	...	20	...	...	...	...	...	...	4	4	...	...	...	...	16
15	3	...	...	...	12	...	...	...	...	...	...	2	1	1	...	...	...	17
...	...	...	...	...	...	...	...	...	...	...	...	...	...	...	...	...	...	18
294	**117**	**44**	**5**	**4**	**133**		...	...	...	...	...	**6**	**3**	...	...	...	**3**	
30	15	5	...	...	10	...	...	...	...	...	...	6	3	...	...	...	3	19
106	37	26	4	4	43	...	...	...	...	...	...	...	...	...	...	...	...	20
110	44	13	1	...	50	...	...	...	...	...	...	...	...	...	...	...	...	21
42	21	...	...	...	21	...	...	...	...	...	...	...	...	...	...	...	...	22
1	...	**1**	...	...	...	...	...	...	...	...	...	**3**	**3**	...	...	...	...	
...	...	...	...	...	...	...	...	...	...	...	...	...	...	...	...	...	...	23
1	...	1	...	...	...	...	...	...	...	...	...	...	...	...	...	...	...	24
...	...	...	...	...	...	...	...	...	...	...	...	...	...	...	...	...	...	25
...	...	...	...	...	...	...	...	...	...	...	...	...	...	...	...	...	...	26
...	...	...	...	...	...	...	...	...	...	...	...	...	...	...	...	...	...	27
...	...	...	...	...	...	...	...	...	...	...	...	...	...	...	...	...	...	28
...	...	...	...	...	...	...	...	...	...	...	...	...	...	...	...	...	...	29
...	...	...	...	...	...	...	...	...	...	...	...	...	...	...	...	...	...	30
...	...	...	...	...	...	...	...	...	...	...	...	2	2	...	...	...	...	31
...	...	...	...	...	...	...	...	...	...	...	...	...	...	...	...	...	...	32
...	...	...	...	...	...	...	...	...	...	...	...	...	...	...	...	...	...	33
...	...	...	...	...	...	...	...	...	...	...	...	...	...	...	...	...	...	34
...	...	...	...	...	...	...	...	...	...	...	...	...	...	...	...	...	...	35
...	...	...	...	...	...	...	...	...	...	...	...	1	1	...	...	...	...	36
...	...	...	...	...	...	...	...	...	...	...	...	...	...	...	...	...	...	37

TABLE XV.—Occupation or means

Serial No.	CLASS ... / SUB-CLASS ... / ORDER ...	CLASS B.—PREPARATION AND SUPPLY — Sub-Class III.— — Order 18.—Industries of luxury and those pertaining to literature																	
		Total order 18.						84.—Printers, lithographers, engravers, etc.						85.—Newspaper and magazine managers and editors, journalists, etc.					
	DISTRICT, CITY OR STATE.	Total workers and dependants.	Actual workers. Total. Males.	Actual workers. Total. Females.	Partially agriculturists. Males.	Partially agriculturists. Females.	Dependants.	Total workers and dependants.	Actual workers. Total. Males.	Actual workers. Total. Females.	Partially agriculturists. Males.	Partially agriculturists. Females.	Dependants.	Total workers and dependants.	Actual workers. Total. Males.	Actual workers. Total. Females.	Partially agriculturists. Males.	Partially agriculturists. Females.	Dependants.
	1	704	705	706	707	708	709	710	711	712	713	714	715	716	717	718	719	720	721
	Central Provinces and Berar ...	**97,469**	**34,532**	**4,254**	**5,459**	**338**	**58,683**	**1,881**	**686**	**23**	**10**	...	**1,170**	**29**	**6**	**3**	...	**2**	**20**
	C. P. British Districts and Berar ...	**93,209**	**33,011**	**3,828**	**5,295**	**318**	**56,370**	**1,788**	**652**	**18**	**10**	...	**1,118**	**29**	**6**	**3**	...	**2**	**20**
	C. P. British Districts ...	**69,853**	**24,432**	**3,229**	**4,299**	**191**	**42,192**	**1,677**	**601**	**17**	**8**	...	**1,059**	**25**	**6**	**3**	...	**2**	**16**
	JUBBULPORE DIVISION.	*17,492*	*5,850*	*1,103*	*704*	*61*	*10,539*	*285*	*102*	*2*	...	...	*181*	*1*	*1*	...	...	...	...
1	Saugor ...	4,512	1,497	247	157	17	2,768	51	17	1	...	...	33	1	1	...	...	...	...
2	Damoh ...	2,412	845	109	112	5	1,458	3	2	1	...	...	...	...	...	...	...	...	...
3	Jubbulpore ...	6,454	2,140	450	275	37	3,864	231	83	...	...	...	148	...	...	...	...	...	...
	JUBBULPORE CITY ...	*2,693*	*906*	*66*	*1*	...	*1,621*	*230*	*83*	...	...	...	*147*	...	...	...	...	...	...
4	Mandla ...	1,214	438	126	43	...	650	...	...	...	...	...	...	...	...	...	...	...	...
5	Seoni ...	2,900	930	171	117	2	1,799	...	...	...	...	...	...	...	...	...	...	...	...
	NERBUDDA DIVISION	*15,750*	*5,412*	*471*	*710*	*15*	*9,807*	*220*	*76*	*11*	*1*	...	*133*	...	...	...	...	...	...
6	Narsinghpur ...	2,704	873	109	111	9	1,722	53	19	...	...	...	34	...	...	...	...	...	...
7	Hoshangabad ...	3,495	1,133	97	113	...	2,265	36	15	...	1	...	21	...	...	...	...	...	...
8	Nimar ...	3,711	1,323	165	145	4	2,223	95	25	10	...	...	60	...	...	...	...	...	...
9	Betul ...	2,528	892	38	170	2	1,598	9	5	...	...	...	4	...	...	...	...	...	...
10	Chhindwara ...	3,312	1,191	62	171	...	2,059	27	12	1	...	...	14	...	...	...	...	...	...
	NAGPUR DIVISION ...	*27,474*	*10,102*	*576*	*2,484*	*74*	*16,796*	*1,137*	*412*	*4*	*7*	...	*721*	*24*	*5*	*3*	...	*2*	*16*
11	Wardha ...	3,821	1,383	36	163	2	2,402	57	29	...	...	...	28	10	...	3	...	2	7
12	Nagpur ...	9,880	3,309	166	431	5	6,405	1,047	372	3	6	...	672	12	5	...	...	...	7
	NAGPUR CITY ...	*2,339*	*766*	*45*	*14*	...	*1,528*	*984*	*322*	*3*	*6*	...	*659*	*11*	*4*	...	...	...	*7*
13	Chanda ...	5,372	2,084	96	587	19	3,192	15	6	1	...	...	8	2	...	...	...	...	2
14	Bhandara ...	6,426	2,541	223	1,013	38	3,662	13	3	...	1	...	10	...	...	...	...	...	...
15	Balaghat ...	1,975	785	55	290	10	1,135	5	2	...	...	...	3	...	...	...	...	...	...
	CHHATTISGARH DIVISION.	*9,137*	*3,068*	*1,079*	*392*	*41*	*4,990*	*35*	*11*	...	...	...	*24*	...	...	...	...	...	...
16	Raipur ...	3,959	1,280	477	105	12	2,202	35	11	...	...	...	24	...	...	...	...	...	...
17	Bilaspur ...	3,207	1,125	410	210	21	1,672	...	...	...	...	...	—	...	...	...	...	...	...
18	Drug ...	1,971	663	192	77	8	1,116	...	...	...	...	...	...	...	...	...	...	...	...
	Berar ...	**23.356**	**8.579**	**599**	**996**	**127**	**14,178**	**111**	**51**	**1**	**2**	...	**59**	**4**	...	...	...	...	**4**
19	Amraoti ...	7,436	2,808	284	252	105	4,344	52	25	1	1	...	26	...	...	...	...	...	...
20	Akola ...	6,248	2,235	140	351	15	3,873	21	14	...	...	...	7	4	...	...	...	...	4
21	Buldana ...	4,681	1,681	95	282	6	2,935	18	2	...	1	...	16	...	...	...	...	...	...
22	Yeotmal ...	4,991	1,855	80	111	1	3,056	20	10	...	...	...	10	...	...	...	...	...	...
	Feudatory States ...	**4,260**	**1,521**	**426**	**164**	**20**	**2,313**	**93**	**36**	**5**	...	...	**52**	...	...	...	...	...	...
23	Makrai ...	92	33	1	7	...	58	...	...	...	...	...	...	...	...	...	...	...	...
24	Bastar ...	455	156	80	21	10	219	9	3	...	...	...	6	...	...	...	...	...	...
25	Kanker ...	271	100	25	6	1	146	13	8	...	...	...	5	...	...	...	...	...	...
26	Nandgaon ...	544	176	40	15	...	328	51	17	...	...	...	34	...	...	...	...	...	...
27	Khairagarh ...	500	159	44	9	2	207	1	...	...	...	...	1	...	...	...	...	...	...
28	Chhuikhadan ...	188	80	5	3	...	103	...	...	...	...	...	...	...	...	...	...	...	...
29	Kawardha ...	165	40	24	1	...	101	...	...	...	...	...	...	...	...	...	...	...	...
30	Sakti ...	46	16	5	2	...	25	...	...	...	...	...	...	...	...	...	...	...	...
31	Raigarh ...	755	322	38	33	...	395	18	7	5	...	...	6	...	...	...	...	...	...
32	Sarangarh ...	291	100	7	38	...	184	...	...	...	...	...	...	...	...	...	...	...	...
33	Chang Bhakar ...	19	13	...	2	...	6	...	...	...	...	...	...	...	...	...	...	...	...
34	Korea ...	117	29	42	2	1	46	...	...	...	...	...	...	...	...	...	...	...	...
35	Surguja ...	359	157	14	9	...	188	...	...	...	...	...	...	...	...	...	...	...	...
36	Udaipur ...	72	17	18	1	...	37	1	1	...	...	...	...	...	...	...	...	...	...
37	Jashpur ...	386	123	83	15	6	180	...	...	...	...	...	...	...	...	...	...	...	...

# of livelihood, Part A.—General Table.

OF MATERIAL SUBSTANCES—*(continued).*

Industry—*(continued).*

and the arts and sciences—*(continued).*

86.—Bookbinders and stitchers, envelope-makers, etc.						87.—Makers of musical instruments.						88.—Makers of watches and clocks, and optical, photographic and surgical instruments.						
Total workers and dependants.	Actual workers.				Dependants.	Total workers and dependants.	Actual workers.				Dependants.	Total workers and dependants.	Actual workers.				Dependants.	Serial No.
	Total.		Partially agriculturists.				Total.		Partially agriculturists.				Total.		Partially agriculturists.			
	Males.	Females.	Males.	Females.			Males.	Females.	Males.	Females.			Males.	Females.	Males.	Females.		
722	723	724	725	726	727	728	729	730	731	732	733	734	735	736	737	738	739	
680	**225**	**17**	**9**	...	**438**	**1,258**	**408**	**201**	**42**	**10**	**649**	**435**	**136**	**3**	...	...	**296**	
676	**223**	**17**	**9**	...	**436**	**884**	**280**	**158**	**27**	**6**	**446**	**397**	**134**	...	...	...	**263**	
609	**207**	**16**	**9**	...	**386**	**802**	**251**	**153**	**22**	**6**	**398**	**302**	**104**	...	...	...	**198**	
393	*115*	*9*	*9*	...	*367*	*93*	*32*	*10*	*1*	...	*61*	*130*	*45*	...	...	...	*85*	
55	13	...	9	...	42	12	6	2	...	...	4	22	8	...	...	...	14	1
30	12	...	...	...	18	15	5	4	...	...	6	24	12	...	...	...	12	2
241	70	4	...	...	167	37	10	...	1	...	27	81	25	...	...	...	56	3
228	*65*	*4*	...	...	*153*	*18*	*4*	...	...	...	*14*	*81*	*25*	...	...	...	*66*	
14	6	1	...	...	7	29	11	4	...	...	14	...	...	...	...	...	...	4
54	17	4	...	...	33	...	...	...	...	...	...	3	...	...	...	...	3	5
81	*27*	*6*	...	...	*45*	*13*	*6*	...	...	...	*8*	*43*	*15*	...	...	...	*25*	
33	10	4	...	...	10	2	2	...	...	...	...	7	3	...	...	...	4	6
28	10	1	...	...	12	7	...	...	...	...	7	24	6	...	...	...	18	7
6	1	...	...	...	5	...	...	...	...	...	...	9	6	...	...	...	3	8
11	2	...	...	...	9	...	...	...	...	...	...	...	...	...	...	...	...	9
8	4	1	...	...	3	4	3	...	...	...	1	3	...	...	...	...	3	10
101	*43*	*1*	...	...	*56*	*80*	*28*	*9*	...	...	*43*	*96*	*39*	...	...	...	*60*	
9	4	...	...	...	5	40	14	6	...	...	20	13	1	...	...	...	12	11
63	26	...	...	...	37	30	8	3	...	...	19	67	30	...	...	...	37	12
68	*23*	...	...	...	*36*	*19*	*5*	*2*	...	...	*12*	*39*	*15*	...	...	...	*21*	
5	2	...	...	...	3	10	6	...	...	...	4	8	2	...	...	...	6	13
23	12	1	...	...	10	...	...	...	...	...	...	8	3	...	...	...	5	14
1	...	...	...	...	1	...	...	...	...	...	...	...	...	...	...	...	...	15
33	*18*	...	...	...	*15*	*616*	*186*	*134*	*21*	*6*	*296*	*33*	*8*	...	...	...	*25*	
23	14	...	...	...	9	229	74	39	11	3	116	24	5	...	...	...	16	16
3	2	...	...	...	1	330	106	69	10	2	155	9	3	...	...	...	6	17
7	2	...	...	...	5	57	6	25	...	1	25	...	...	...	...	...	...	18
67	**16**	**1**	...	...	**50**	**82**	**29**	**5**	**5**	...	**48**	**95**	**30**	...	...	...	**65**	
43	10	...	...	...	33	41	20	4	4	...	17	42	10	...	...	...	26	19
15	4	...	...	...	11	20	1	...	...	...	10	35	7	...	...	...	28	20
2	...	1	...	...	1	3	1	...	...	...	2	5	2	...	...	...	3	21
7	2	...	...	...	5	18	7	1	1	...	10	13	5	...	...	...	8	22
4	**2**	...	...	...	**2**	**374**	**128**	**43**	**15**	**4**	**203**	**38**	**2**	**3**	...	...	**33**	
...	...	...	...	...	...	...	...	...	...	...	...	...	...	...	...	...	...	23
2	1	...	...	...	1	...	...	...	...	...	...	...	...	...	...	...	...	24
1	1	...	...	...	...	5	2	1	...	...	2	...	...	...	...	...	...	25
...	...	...	...	...	...	...	...	...	...	...	...	...	...	...	...	...	...	26
1	...	...	...	...	1	26	8	6	1	...	12	...	...	...	...	...	...	27
...	...	...	...	...	...	...	...	...	...	...	...	...	...	...	...	...	...	28
...	...	...	...	...	...	...	...	...	...	...	...	2	1	...	...	...	1	29
...	...	...	...	...	...	2	1	1	...	...	...	1	...	...	...	...	1	30
...	...	...	...	...	...	21	11	...	1	...	10	29	...	3	...	...	25	31
...	...	...	...	...	...	43	10	1	...	...	32	...	...	...	...	...	...	32
...	...	...	...	...	...	1	...	...	...	...	1	...	...	...	...	...	...	33
...	...	...	...	...	...	21	5	4	...	...	12	...	...	...	...	...	...	34
...	...	...	...	...	...	26	10	4	...	...	12	...	...	...	...	...	...	35
...	...	...	...	...	...	7	8	...	...	...	4	6	1	...	...	...	5	36
...	...	...	...	...	...	222	78	26	13	4	118	...	...	...	...	...	...	37

TABLE XV.—Occupation or means

Serial No.	CLASS ... / SUB-CLASS ... / ORDER ...	CLASS B.—PREPARATION AND SUPPLY — Sub-Class III.— Order 18.—Industries of luxury and those pertaining to literature																	
		89.—Workers in precious stones and metals, enamellers, imitation jewellery makers, gilders, etc.						90.—Makers of bangles, rosaries, bead and other necklaces, spangles, lingams and sacred threads.						91.—Toy, kite, cage, fishing tackle, etc., makers, taxidermists, etc.					
	DISTRICT, CITY OR STATE.	Total workers and dependants.	Actual workers. Total. Males.	Actual workers. Total. Females.	Actual workers. Partially agriculturists. Males.	Actual workers. Partially agriculturists. Females.	Dependants.	Total workers and dependants.	Actual workers. Total. Males.	Actual workers. Total. Females.	Actual workers. Partially agriculturists. Males.	Actual workers. Partially agriculturists. Females.	Dependants.	Total workers and dependants.	Actual workers. Total. Males.	Actual workers. Total. Females.	Actual workers. Partially agriculturists. Males.	Actual workers. Partially agriculturists. Females.	Dependants.
	1	740	741	742	743	744	745	746	747	748	749	750	751	752	753	754	755	756	757
	Central Provinces and Berar ...	**82,773**	**29,559**	**1,539**	**5,151**	**235**	**51,675**	**9,040**	**3,040**	**2,187**	**234**	**79**	**3,813**	**851**	**208**	**251**	**13**	**8**	**392**
	C. P. British Districts and Berar ...	**80,017**	**28,585**	**1,391**	**5,010**	**223**	**50.041**	**8,093**	**2,677**	**1,962**	**226**	**75**	**3.454**	**840**	**202**	**251**	**13**	**8**	**387**
	C. P British Districts ...	**57,697**	**20,314**	**1,016**	**4,033**	**105**	**36,367**	**7,882**	**2,631**	**1,909**	**225**	**75**	**3,342**	**450**	**104**	**96**	**2**	**2**	**250**
	JUBBULPORE DIVISION.	*12,503*	*4,206*	*233*	*570*	*14*	*8,062*	*3,620*	*1,184*	*779*	*124*	*46*	*1,657*	*245*	*52*	*58*	...	*1*	*139*
1	Saugor ...	3,285	1,098	22	120	4	2,105	906	313	185	28	13	408	124	11	35	...	...	78
2	Damoh ...	1,746	583	21	94	2	1,141	519	213	69	18	2	237	48	9	12	...	1	27
3	Jubbulpore ...	4,050	1,351	62	205	7	2,637	1,624	503	370	69	30	751	72	32	6	...	...	34
	JUBBULPORE CITY ...	*1,491*	*491*	*15*	*1*	...	*985*	*375*	*144*	*36*	...	...	*195*	*59*	*25*	*8*	..	...	*28*
4	Mandla ...	1,050	387	77	40	...	586	113	33	40	3	...	40	4	...	4	...	...	...
5	Seoni ...	2,373	780	51	111	1	1,533	458	122	115	6	1	221	1	...	1	...	...	...
	NERBUDDA DIVISION.	*14,121*	*4,823*	*147*	*692*	*10*	*9,151*	*1,160*	*409*	*285*	*17*	*4*	*466*	*53*	*16*	*15*	...	*1*	*19*
6	Narsinghpur ...	2,810	747	21	106	6	1,542	272	84	72	5	2	116	26	7	12	...	1	7
7	Hoshangabad ...	3,070	900	12	111	...	2,074	296	99	81	1	...	119	8	3	8	...	...	2
8	Nimar ...	3,205	1,148	53	134	2	2,604	373	136	98	11	2	130	18	4	4	...	...	10
9	Betul ...	2,455	856	28	170	2	1,571	46	22	10	...	...	14	1	1	...	...	...	...
10	Chhindwara ...	3,075	1,082	33	171	...	1,960	170	68	24	...	...	78	...	...	...	...	...	...
	NAGPUR DIVISION ...	*25,175*	*9,243*	*464*	*2,467*	*70*	*15,467*	*671*	*264*	*81*	*17*	*2*	*826*	*99*	*27*	*13*	*2*	...	*59*
11	Wardha ...	3,642	1,323	23	163	...	2,206	9	2	1	...	...	6	35	7	3	...	...	25
12	Nagpur ...	8,327	2,738	141	425	5	5,448	204	82	10	...	...	112	57	15	9	...	...	33
	NAGPUR CITY ...	*1,032*	*816*	*32*	*8*	...	*684*	*106*	*25*	*5*	...	...	*73*	*32*	*10*	*4*	...	...	*20*
13	Chanda ...	5,133	1,975	68	571	19	3,090	193	87	27	14	...	79	5	5	...	2	...	...
14	Bhandara ...	6,229	2,478	189	1,011	36	3,557	164	42	34	1	2	78	...	...	...	...	...	..
15	Balaghat ...	1,850	730	44	297	10	1,076	111	51	9	2	...	51	2	...	1	...	...	1
	CHHATTISGARH DIVISION.	*6,594*	*2,039*	*172*	*304*	*11*	*3,687*	*2,431*	*774*	*764*	*67*	*23*	*898*	*49*	*16*	*6*	...	...	*33*
16	Raipur ...	2,477	813	92	73	1	1,572	1,094	330	339	21	8	416	46	10	5	...	...	31
17	Bilaspur ...	1,991	744	45	164	7	1,202	860	262	294	36	11	304	3	...	1	...	...	2
18	Drug ...	1,430	482	35	67	3	913	477	173	131	10	4	173	...	...	...	...	...	...
	Berar ...	**22,320**	**8.271**	**375**	**977**	**118**	**13,674**	**211**	**46**	**53**	**1**	...	**112**	**390**	**98**	**155**	**11**	**6**	**137**
19	Amraoti ...	6,968	2,647	207	245	104	4,114	79	13	14	...	...	52	183	63	52	2	1	68
20	Akola ...	5,984	2,174	78	347	9	3,732	46	12	7	1	...	21	106	14	52	3	3	40
21	Buldana ...	4,513	1,641	43	275	4	2,829	56	12	19	...	...	25	63	12	32	6	2	19
22	Yeotmal ...	4,855	1,806	47	110	1	2,990	36	9	13	...	...	14	38	9	19	...	...	10
	Feudatory States ...	**2,756**	**974**	**148**	**141**	**12**	**1,634**	**947**	**363**	**225**	**8**	**4**	**359**	**11**	**6**	...	...	...	**5**
23	Makrai ...	88	30	1	7	...	57	4	2	...	...	...	1	...	...	...	...	...	...
24	Bastar ...	421	146	73	21	10	202	19	6	6	...	...	7	...	..	...	...	...	...
25	Kanker ..	219	74	12	5	...	133	38	15	12	1	1	6	...	...	...	...	...	...
26	Nandgaon ...	889	129	4	15	...	256	18	29	36	...	...	34	...	...	...	..	...	...
27	Khairagarh ...	398	125	8	6	2	261	71	26	30	2	...	21	...	...	...	...	...	...
28	Chhuikhadan ...	94	34	1	2	...	59	76	42	3	1	...	34	...	...	...	...	...	...
29	Kawardha ...	127	33	4	1	...	90	26	6	20	...	...	10	...	...	...	...	...	...
30	Sakti ...	36	12	...	2	...	18	13	3	4	...	...	6	...	...	...	...	...	...
31	Raigarh ...	361	130	15	20	...	207	316	162	15	3	...	130	...	...	...	...	...	...
32	Sarangarh ...	225	80	...	37	...	145	23	10	6	1	...	7	...	...	...	...	...	...
33	Chang Bhakar ...	18	13	...	2	...	5	...	..	...	...	...	...	...	...	...	...	...	...
34	Korea ...	38	24	...	2	...	14	58	...	38	...	1	20	...	...	...	...	...	...
35	Surguja ...	206	94	...	9	..	115	118	52	10	...	...	57	5	1	...	...	...	4
36	Udaipur ...	30	11	...	1	...	19	28	1	18	...	...	9	...	...	...	...	...	...
37	Jashpur ..	105	26	30	2	...	53	49	14	27	...	2	8	6	5	...	...	...	1

# of livelihood, Part A.—General Table.

OF MATERIAL SUBSTANCES—(continued).																		
Industry—(concluded).												Sub-Class IV.—Transport.						
and the arts and sciences—(concluded).						Total order 19.—Industries concerned with refuse matter.												
92.—Others including managers, persons other than performers employed in theatres and other places of public entertainment, employés of public societies, race-course service, huntsmen, etc.						93.—Sweepers, scavengers, dust and sweeping contractors.						Total Sub-Class IV.						
Total workers and dependants.	Actual workers.				Dependants.	Total workers and dependants.	Actual workers.				Dependants.	Total workers and dependants.	Actual workers				Dependants.	Serial No.
	Total.		Partially agriculturists.				Total.		Partially agriculturists.				Total.		Partially agriculturists.			
	Males.	Females.	Males.	Females.			Males.	Females.	Males.	Females.			Males.	Females.	Males	Females.		
758	759	760	761	762	763	764	765	766	767	768	769	770	771	772	773	774	775	
522	**262**	**30**	...	**4**	**230**	**25,781**	**7,989**	**8,043**	**267**	**301**	**9,749**	**217,961**	**90,713**	**27,030**	**3,090**	**991**	**100,218**	
485	**252**	**28**	...	**4**	**205**	**24,430**	**7,744**	**7,214**	**253**	**287**	**9,472**	**203,897**	**85,177**	**25,405**	**2,939**	**931**	**93,315**	
409	**214**	**19**	...	**1**	**176**	**21,639**	**6,739**	**6,694**	**243**	**283**	**8,206**	**173,031**	**71,644**	**23,052**	**2,290**	**606**	**78,335**	
217	*108*	*12*	...	...	*97*	*8,764*	*2,720*	*2,531*	*120*	*126*	*3,513*	*43,949*	*17,318*	*4,372*	*642*	*132*	*22,359*	
56	30	2	...	...	24	2,406	784	670	54	44	1,012	10,333	3,904	982	151	37	5,857	1
28	9	2	...	...	17	1,317	392	415	53	58	510	5,025	1,824	637	94	24	2,563	2
118	66	8	...	...	44	4,125	1,277	1,171	10	23	1,677	19,895	7,748	1,453	344	65	10,094	3
113	*66*	*8*	...	...	*39*	*2,243*	*705*	*489*	...	...	*1,049*	*10,684*	*3,941*	*705*	*21*	...	*6,038*	
4	1	...	...	...	8	335	98	113	...	...	124	5,567	2,496	747	38	4	2,324	4
11	2	...	...	...	9	521	169	162	3	...	190	3,129	1,156	553	15	2	1,420	5
59	*42*	*3*	...	...	*14*	*5,826*	*1,915*	*1,755*	*106*	*95*	*2,156*	*53,374*	*24,171*	*7,775*	*425*	*120*	*21,125*	
1	1	...	...	...	...	1,319	412	465	30	36	442	3,854	1,474	202	70	16	2,177	6
22	10	...	—	...	12	2,206	713	628	68	41	865	13,903	5,635	1,179	96	5	7,080	7
5	3	...	—	—	2	1,298	401	353	6	6	544	8,305	3,833	480	17	27	3,092	8
6	6	...	...	...	...	342	125	109	—	...	108	16,128	7,712	3,640	176	65	4,770	9
25	22	3	...	...	...	661	264	200	2	15	197	11,184	5,517	2,270	66	7	3,397	10
91	*43*	*1*	...	...	*48*	*4,391*	*1,409*	*1,204*	*7*	*15*	*1,775*	*49,360*	*19,674*	*6,760*	*693*	*207*	*22,920*	
6	3	...	—	...	3	458	140	124	...	2	194	5,127	2,088	377	85	51	2,712	11
78	33	...	...	...	40	2,684	879	694	...	...	1,111	20,206	7,736	2,524	172	13	9,940	12
57	*21*	...	...	...	*86*	*1,468*	*418*	*357*	...	...	*663*	*11,840*	*3,867*	*1,252*	*9*	*1*	*6,331*	
1	1	...	...	...	...	442	128	138	5	6	170	9,864	4,008	1,633	192	100	4,223	13
5	3	...	...	...	2	532	185	157	2	7	190	9,263	3,778	1,246	183	32	4,239	14
6	2	1	...	...	3	275	77	91	...	...	107	4,900	2,114	980	61	5	1,800	15
48	*22*	*3*	...	*1*	*17*	*3,658*	*695*	*1,204*	*10*	*45*	*759*	*26,345*	*10,581*	*4,142*	*580*	*147*	*11,626*	
31	14	2	...	...	15	1,459	394	729	3	30	336	13,137	4,780	2,632	182	56	5,725	16
11	8	1	...	1	2	775	174	314	2	11	287	9,950	4,212	1,206	257	87	4,541	17
...	...	...	...	...	...	424	127	161	5	4	136	3,252	1,589	304	91	4	1,359	18
76	**38**	**9**	...	**3**	**29**	**2,791**	**1,005**	**520**	**10**	**4**	**1,266**	**30,866**	**13,533**	**2,353**	**649**	**325**	**14,980**	
28	14	6	...	...	8	1,154	414	214	2	3	520	9,978	4,268	387	147	27	5,323	19
23	9	3	...	3	11	727	245	139	4	1	348	10,434	4,587	1,612	300	294	4,235	20
21	11	...	...	—	10	574	220	80	4	...	265	5,570	2,304	216	123	1	3,050	21
4	4	...	...	...	...	336	117	87	...	...	132	4,878	2,374	138	79	3	2,300	22
37	**10**	**2**	...	...	**25**	**1,351**	**245**	**829**	**14**	**14**	**277**	**14,064**	**5,536**	**1,625**	**151**	**60**	**6,903**	
...	...	...	...	...	...	44	15	13	...	—	16	31	13	1	...	...	17	23
4	...	1	...	...	3	101	28	32	...	...	41	2,276	917	316	6	2	1,013	24
...	...	...	...	...	...	65	19	21	...	...	25	323	133	36	1	...	154	25
5	1	...	...	...	4	120	41	60	1	...	28	1,923	755	104	22	1	1,064	26
3	2	...	...	...	1	178	62	70	1	1	46	2,904	1,142	200	20	1	1,643	27
15	4	1	...	...	10	32	8	12	...	...	12	79	38	6	2	...	35	28
...	...	...	...	...	...	68	15	35	...	...	18	198	86	35	...	...	77	29
...	...	...	...	...	...	24	6	11	1	...	7	243	139	11	6	...	93	30
10	3	...	...	...	7	834	16	295	...	9	28	2,956	1,036	566	30	33	1,354	31
...	...	...	...	...	—	346	27	274	9	4	45	394	126	107	4	13	161	32
...	...	...	...	...	...	...	...	...	...	...	...	115	62	16	3	1	37	33
...	...	...	...	...	...	8	1	...	1	...	2	646	289	62	9	1	295	34
...	...	...	—	...	...	11	3	2	...	...	6	1,258	514	63	28	8	681	35
...	...	...	...	...	—	14	3	3	...	...	8	262	112	84	1	...	116	36
...	...	...	...	...	...	2	1	1	1	...	...	366	174	59	13	...	183	37

TABLE XV.—Occupation or means

	CLASS ...	CLASS B.—PREPARATION AND SUPPLY																	
	SUB-CLASS ...	Sub-Class IV.—																	
	ORDER ...	Order 20.—Transport																	
		Total order 20.						94.—Harbour works, dock-yards and pilots.						95.—Shipowners and their employés, ship brokers, ships' officers, engineers, mariners and firemen.					
		Total workers and dependants.	Actual workers. Total.		Actual workers. Partially agriculturists.		Dependants.	Total workers and dependants.	Actual workers. Total.		Actual workers. Partially agriculturists.		Dependants.	Total workers and dependants.	Actual workers. Total.		Actual workers. Partially agriculturists.		Dependants.
Serial No.	DISTRICT, CITY OR STATE.		Males.	Females.	Males.	Females.			Males.	Females.	Males.	Females.			Males.	Females.	Males.	Females.	
	1	776	777	778	779	780	781	782	783	784	785	786	787	788	789	790	791	792	793
	Central Provinces and Berar ...	**6,154**	**2,732**	**1,126**	**126**	**64**	**2,296**	**3**	**3**	...	...	...	...	**5**	**3**	...	**1**	...	**2**
	C. P. British Districts and Berar ...	**5,999**	**2,676**	**1,104**	**125**	**64**	**2,219**	**3**	**3**	...	...	...	...	**5**	**3**	...	**1**	...	**2**
	C. P. British Districts ...	**5,829**	**2,578**	**1,102**	**110**	**64**	**2,149**	**3**	**3**	...	...	...	...	**5**	**3**	...	**1**	...	**2**
	JUBBULPORE DIVISION.	*550*	*259*	*57*	*11*	*2*	*234*	...	...	...	...	...	...	*1*	...	...	...	...	*1*
1	Saugor ...	17	4	...	...	...	13	...	...	...	...	...	...	...	...	...	...	...	...
2	Damoh ...	80	36	4	1	...	40	...	...	...	...	...	...	...	...	...	...	...	...
3	Jubbulpore ...	343	165	40	7	1	135	...	...	...	...	...	...	1	...	...	...	...	1
	JUBBULPORE CITY ...	*14*	*2*	...	...	...	*12*	...	...	...	...	...	...	*1*	...	...	...	...	*1*
4	Mandla ...	38	20	2	2	...	16	...	...	...	...	...	...	...	...	...	...	...	...
5	Seoni ...	72	34	11	1	1	27	...	...	...	...	...	...	...	...	...	...	...	...
	NERBUDDA DIVISION	*374*	*164*	*20*	*6*	...	*190*	...	...	...	...	...	...	*3*	*2*	...	*1*	...	*1*
6	Narsinghpur ...	45	23	...	3	...	22	...	...	...	...	...	...	3	2	...	1	...	1
7	Hoshangabad ...	235	102	19	1	...	114	...	...	...	...	...	...	...	...	...	...	...	...
8	Nimar ...	88	37	1	2	...	50	...	...	...	...	...	...	...	...	...	...	...	...
9	Betul ...	1	1	...	...	...	...	...	...	...	...	...	...	...	...	...	...	...	...
10	Chhindwara ...	5	1	...	...	...	4	...	...	...	...	...	...	...	...	...	...	...	...
	NAGPUR DIVISION ...	*4,096*	*1,706*	*907*	*71*	*62*	*1,483*	*3*	*3*	...	...	...	...	**1**	**1**	...	...	...	...
11	Wardha ...	24	14	...	...	...	10	3	3	...	...	...	...	...	...	...	...	...	...
12	Nagpur ...	220	52	13	3	...	155	...	...	...	...	...	...	...	...	...	...	...	...
	NAGPUR CITY ...	*67*	*19*	...	...	...	*48*	...	...	...	...	...	...	...	...	...	...	...	...
13	Chanda ...	2,032	799	507	59	59	726	...	...	...	...	...	...	1	1	...	...	...	...
14	Bhandara ...	1,587	755	376	5	3	456	...	...	...	...	...	...	...	...	...	...	...	...
15	Balaghat ...	233	86	11	4	...	136	...	...	...	...	...	...	...	...	...	...	...	...
	CHHATTISGARH DIVISION.	*809*	*449*	*118*	*22*	...	*242*	...	...	...	...	...	...	...	...	...	...	...	...
16	Raipur ...	159	87	7	1	...	65	...	...	...	...	...	...	...	...	...	...	...	...
17	Bilaspur ...	78	26	10	2	...	42	...	...	...	...	...	...	...	...	...	...	...	...
18	Drug ...	572	336	101	19	...	135	...	...	...	...	...	...	...	...	...	...	...	...
	Berar ...	**170**	**98**	**2**	**15**	...	**70**	...	...	...	...	...	...	...	...	...	...	...	...
19	Amraoti ...	2	2	...	...	...	...	...	...	...	...	...	...	...	...	...	...	...	...
20	Akola ...	103	70	...	15	...	33	...	...	...	...	...	...	...	...	...	...	...	...
21	Buldana ...	...	...	...	...	...	...	...	...	...	...	...	...	...	...	...	...	...	...
22	Yeotmal ...	65	26	2	...	...	37	...	...	...	...	...	...	...	...	...	...	...	...
	Feudatory States ...	**155**	**56**	**22**	**1**	...	**77**	...	...	...	...	...	...	...	...	...	...	...	...
23	Makrai ...	...	...	...	...	...	...	...	...	...	...	...	...	...	...	...	...	...	...
24	Bastar ...	118	43	19	...	...	56	...	...	...	...	...	...	...	...	...	...	...	...
25	Kanker ...	2	2	...	...	...	...	...	...	...	...	...	...	...	...	...	...	...	...
26	Nandgaon ...	8	6	...	...	...	2	...	...	...	...	...	...	...	...	...	...	...	...
27	Khairagarh ...	...	...	...	...	...	...	...	...	...	...	...	...	...	...	...	...	...	...
28	Chhuikhadan ...	...	...	...	...	...	...	...	...	...	...	...	...	...	...	...	...	...	...
29	Kawardha ...	...	...	...	...	...	...	...	...	...	...	...	...	...	...	...	...	...	...
30	Sakti ...	...	...	...	...	...	...	...	...	...	...	...	...	...	...	...	...	...	...
31	Raigarh ...	3	1	2	...	...	...	...	...	...	...	...	...	...	...	...	...	...	...
32	Sarangarh ...	...	...	...	...	...	...	...	...	...	...	...	...	...	...	...	...	...	...
33	Chang Bhakar ...	4	1	1	...	...	2	...	...	...	...	...	...	...	...	...	...	...	...
34	Korea ...	...	—	...	...	...	...	...	...	...	...	...	...	...	...	...	...	...	...
35	Surguja ...	12	2	...	1	...	10	...	...	...	...	...	...	...	...	...	...	...	...
36	Udaipur ...	4	1	...	...	...	3	...	...	...	...	...	...	...	...	...	...	...	...
37	Jashpur ...	4	...	...	...	...	4	...	...	...	...	...	...	...	...	...	...	...	...

# of livelihood, Part A.—General Table.

OF MATERIAL SUBSTANCES— *(continued).*

Transport— *(continued).*

by water. | Order 21.—Transport by road.

96.—Persons employed on the maintenance of streams, rivers and canals (including construction).						97.—Boat owners, boatmen and towmen.						Total order 21.						
Total workers and dependants.	Actual workers. Total. Males.	Actual workers. Total. Females.	Actual workers. Partially agriculturists. Males.	Actual workers. Partially agriculturists. Females.	Dependants.	Total workers and dependants.	Actual workers. Total. Males.	Actual workers. Total. Females.	Actual workers. Partially agriculturists. Males.	Actual workers. Partially agriculturists. Females.	Dependants.	Total workers and dependants.	Actual workers. Total. Males.	Actual workers. Total. Females.	Actual workers. Partially agriculturists. Males.	Actual workers. Partially agriculturists. Females.	Dependants.	Serial No.
794	795	796	797	798	799	800	801	802	803	804	805	806	807	808	809	810	811	
4,985	**2,247**	**1,081**	**90**	**64**	**1,657**	**1,161**	**479**	**45**	**35**	...	**637**	**119,004**	**48,255**	**15,836**	**2,303**	**611**	**54,913**	
4,970	**2,239**	**1,078**	**90**	**64**	**1,653**	**1,021**	**431**	**26**	**34**	...	**564**	**108,256**	**43,989**	**14,313**	**2,181**	**551**	**49,954**	
4,969	**2,238**	**1,078**	**90**	**64**	**1,653**	**852**	**334**	**24**	**19**	...	**494**	**85,797**	**34,058**	**13,062**	**1,583**	**462**	**38,677**	
416	*203*	*55*	*6*	*2*	*158*	*133*	*56*	*2*	*5*	...	*75*	*26,115*	*9,916*	*3,559*	*505*	*128*	*12,340*	
6	1	...	...	...	6	11	3	...	...	...	8	4,780	1,831	768	110	37	2,181	1
71	32	4	1	...	35	9	4	...	...	...	5	3,673	1,286	622	87	23	1,765	2
269	140	40	4	1	89	73	25	...	3	...	48	11,628	4,323	1,300	275	64	6,005	3
8	*1*	...	...	...	*7*	*5*	*1*	...	...	...	*4*	*5,815*	*1,958*	*650*	*20*	...	*3,207*	
2	...	...	...	...	2	36	20	2	2	...	14	3,853	1,768	641	24	4	1,444	4
68	30	11	1	1	27	4	4	...	...	...	...	2,181	708	528	9	...	945	5
17	*10*	...	...	...	*7*	*354*	*152*	*20*	*5*	...	*182*	*15,649*	*6,600*	*1,918*	*221*	*70*	*7,131*	
1	1	...	...	...	...	41	20	...	2	...	21	2,024	770	180	60	15	1,065	6
12	6	...	...	...	6	223	96	19	1	...	108	4,840	1,977	545	57	2	2,318	7
3	2	...	...	...	1	85	35	1	2	...	49	3,630	1,560	423	9	27	1,647	8
1	1	...	...	...	...	...	...	...	...	...	...	2,427	1,076	374	57	22	977	9
...	...	...	...	...	...	5	1	...	...	...	4	2,728	1,217	387	38	4	1,124	10
3,785	*1,699*	*907*	*64*	*62*	*1,279*	*307*	*103*	...	*7*	...	*204*	*26,375*	*10,216*	*4,496*	*456*	*126*	*11,663*	
...	...	...	...	...	...	21	11	...	...	...	10	3,415	1,339	330	68	51	1,740	11
175	44	13	...	...	118	45	8	...	3	...	37	11,082	4,155	1,925	128	11	5,002	12
65	*19*	...	...	...	*46*	*2*	...	...	...	...	*2*	*5,948*	*1,997*	*1,024*	*5*	...	*2,927*	
1,828	727	507	56	59	594	203	71	...	8	...	132	4,963	2,021	857	100	38	2,085	13
1,563	746	376	4	8	441	24	9	...	1	...	15	4,009	1,508	640	122	21	1,861	14
219	82	11	4	...	126	14	4	...	...	...	10	2,006	1,193	744	38	5	969	15
751	*426*	*116*	*20*	...	*209*	*55*	*23*	*2*	*2*	...	*33*	*17,658*	*7,326*	*2,789*	*401*	*135*	*7,543*	
127	74	5	1	...	48	32	13	2	...	...	17	9,513	3,626	1,650	159	56	4,237	16
65	22	10	2	...	33	13	4	...	...	...	9	5,963	2,645	951	185	78	2,367	17
550	330	101	17	...	128	13	6	...	2	...	7	2,182	1,055	188	57	4	939	18
1	**1**	...	...	...	...	**169**	**97**	**2**	**15**	...	**70**	**22,459**	**9,931**	**1,251**	**598**	**89**	**11,277**	
1	1	...	...	...	...	1	1	...	...	...	...	6,790	2,970	268	138	27	3,557	19
...	...	...	...	...	...	103	70	...	15	...	33	7,429	3,272	704	274	58	3,453	20
...	...	...	...	...	...	...	...	...	...	...	...	3,832	1,530	149	111	1	2,153	21
...	...	...	...	...	...	65	26	2	...	...	37	4,408	2,159	135	75	3	2,114	22
15	**8**	**3**	...	...	**4**	**140**	**48**	**19**	**1**	...	**73**	**10,748**	**4,266**	**1,523**	**122**	**60**	**4,959**	
...	...	...	...	...	...	...	...	...	...	...	...	11	8	1	...	...	2	23
...	...	...	...	...	...	118	43	19	...	...	56	1,883	757	293	4	2	833	24
...	...	...	...	...	...	2	2	...	...	...	...	271	116	33	1	...	122	25
...	...	...	...	...	...	...	...	...	...	...	...	1,534	601	80	21	1	844	26
8	6	...	...	...	2	...	...	...	...	...	...	1,453	504	180	13	1	670	27
...	...	...	...	...	...	...	...	...	...	...	...	68	34	6	2	...	28	28
...	...	...	...	...	...	...	...	...	...	...	...	179	81	35	...	...	63	29
...	...	...	...	...	...	...	...	...	...	...	...	112	55	9	1	...	48	30
3	1	2	...	...	...	...	...	...	...	...	...	2,352	790	536	24	33	1,026	31
...	...	...	...	...	...	...	...	...	...	...	...	373	120	107	4	13	146	32
4	1	1	...	...	2	...	...	...	...	...	...	109	60	15	3	1	34	33
...	...	...	...	...	...	...	...	...	...	...	...	643	287	62	8	1	294	34
...	...	...	...	...	...	12	2	...	1	...	10	1,220	505	61	27	8	654	35
...	...	...	...	...	...	4	1	...	...	...	3	192	88	34	1	...	70	36
...	...	...	...	...	...	4	...	...	...	...	4	348	170	53	13	...	125	37

TABLE XV.—Occupation or means

Serial No.	CLASS / SUB-CLASS / ORDER	CLASS B.—PREPARATION AND SUPPLY; Sub-Class IV.—; Order 21.—Transport																	
		98.—Persons employed on the construction and maintenance of roads and bridges.						99.—Cart owners, drivers, coachmen, stable boys, tramway, mail carriage, etc., managers and employés excluding private servants).						100.—Palki, etc., bearers and owners.					
	DISTRICT, CITY OR STATE.	Total workers and dependants.	Actual workers. Total. Males.	Actual workers. Total. Females.	Actual workers. Partially agriculturists. Males.	Actual workers. Partially agriculturists. Females.	Dependants.	Total workers and dependants.	Actual workers. Total. Males.	Actual workers. Total. Females.	Actual workers. Partially agriculturists. Males.	Actual workers. Partially agriculturists. Females.	Dependants.	Total workers and dependants.	Actual workers. Total. Males.	Actual workers. Total. Females.	Actual workers. Partially agriculturists. Males.	Actual workers. Partially agriculturists. Females.	Dependants.
	1	812	813	814	815	816	817	818	819	820	821	822	823	824	825	826	827	828	829
	Central Provinces and Berar ...	**40,592**	**14.592**	**11.530**	**635**	**447**	**14.470**	**46,720**	**20,704**	**841**	**1.173**	**25**	**25,175**	**1.768**	**807**	**34**	**77**	**1**	**927**
	C. P. British Districts and Berar ...	**37,270**	**13.606**	**10.515**	**617**	**408**	**13.149**	**43.450**	**19,205**	**757**	**1,134**	**25**	**23,488**	**1.595**	**723**	**33**	**68**	**1**	**839**
	C. P. British Districts ...	**34.574**	**12,483**	**9,891**	**554**	**364**	**12.200**	**27.670**	**12.173**	**552**	**866**	**14**	**14.945**	**1.400**	**610**	**33**	**50**	**1**	**757**
	JUBBULPORE DIVISION.	*9,690*	*3,235*	*2,836*	*181*	*106*	*3,621*	*7,202*	*3,064*	*91*	*170*	*6*	*4,047*	*70*	*34*	...	...	...	*36*
1	Saugor ...	1,979	736	453	63	30	790	1,268	543	19	29	...	706	13	9	...	...	...	4
2	Damoh ...	1,707	473	539	33	20	695	889	347	10	38	...	532	...	...	...	...	...	...
3	Jubbulpore ...	3,506	1,231	930	77	53	1,345	3,933	1,619	37	87	5	2,277	56	24	...	...	...	32
	JUBBULPORE CITY ...	*1,763*	*535*	*461*	*1*	...	*767*	*2,542*	*959*	*20*	*15*	...	*1,563*	*50*	*15*	...	...	...	*32*
4	Mandla ...	1,429	599	411	3	3	419	381	211	13	12	1	157	...	...	...	...	...	...
5	Seoni ...	1,069	194	503	5	...	372	731	344	12	4	...	375	1	1	...	...	...	...
	NERBUDDA DIVISION	*6,036*	*2,311*	*1,667*	*63*	*66*	*2,058*	*5,872*	*2,643*	*90*	*122*	*3*	*3,139*	...	...	...	...	...	...
6	Narsinghpur ...	479	193	132	21	15	154	593	227	7	21	...	359	...	...	...	...	...	...
7	Hoshangabad ...	1,811	652	489	13	1	670	1,782	788	20	43	1	974	...	...	...	...	...	...
8	Nimar ...	1,338	503	392	...	26	443	1,263	555	17	5	1	691	...	...	...	...	...	...
9	Betul ...	1,089	406	331	21	20	352	1,205	574	33	35	1	598	...	...	...	...	...	...
10	Chhindwara ...	1,319	557	323	7	4	439	1,029	499	13	18	...	517	...	...	...	...	...	...
	NAGPUR DIVISION ...	*11,639*	*4,318*	*3,254*	*122*	*119*	*3,967*	*8,779*	*3,700*	*170*	*248*	*1*	*4,909*	*32*	*11*	...	...	...	*21*
11	Wardha ...	745	180	282	3	48	273	1,707	687	14	58	...	1,006	...	...	...	...	...	...
12	Nagpur ...	3,909	1,510	1,083	16	10	1,316	4,031	1,645	96	86	1	2,290	25	11	...	...	...	14
	NAGPUR CITY ...	*1,615*	*679*	*345*	...	...	*588*	*2,111*	*753*	*64*	*4*	...	*1,294*	*4*	*4*	...	...	...	...
13	Chanda ...	2,794	1,128	772	58	38	894	1,508	651	18	34	...	839	...	...	...	...	...	...
14	Bhandara ...	2,075	729	491	33	17	855	973	399	10	50	...	564	7	...	...	...	...	7
15	Balaghat ...	2,016	771	616	13	1	629	660	318	32	14	...	210	...	...	...	...	...	...
	CHHATTISGARH DIVISION.	*7,309*	*2,621*	*2,134*	*189*	*78*	*2,654*	*5,817*	*2,766*	*201*	*126*	*4*	*2,860*	*1,398*	*565*	*33*	*60*	*1*	*700*
16	Raipur ...	3,993	1,252	1,456	51	47	1,285	3,489	1,531	69	65	2	1,889	554	276	26	22	1	252
17	Bilaspur ...	2,659	1,075	557	127	28	1,027	1,638	848	88	42	1	702	182	66	...	2	...	116
18	Drug ...	657	294	121	11	3	242	690	387	44	19	1	259	562	223	7	20	...	332
	Berar ...	**2.696**	**1.123**	**624**	**63**	**44**	**949**	**15,780**	**7.032**	**205**	**468**	**11**	**8.543**	**195**	**113**	...	**18**	...	**82**
19	Amraoti ...	673	263	160	11	22	250	4,691	2,048	63	110	4	2,580	32	10	...	5	...	13
20	Akola ...	989	379	251	38	22	359	5,138	2,302	95	211	4	2,741	18	17	...	3	...	1
21	Buldana ...	453	170	123	5	...	154	2,427	960	16	86	...	1,451	145	77	...	10	...	68
22	Yeotmal ...	581	305	90	9	...	186	3,524	1,722	31	61	3	1,771	...	...	...	...	...	...
	Feudatory States ...	**3.322**	**986**	**1.015**	**18**	**39**	**1,321**	**3,270**	**1.499**	**84**	**39**	...	**1,687**	**173**	**84**	**1**	**9**	...	**88**
23	Makrai ...	7	5	...	...	...	2	3	2	1	...	...	...	...	...	...	...	...	...
24	Bastar ...	253	42	110	...	...	101	1,015	522	19	2	...	474	...	...	...	...	...	...
25	Kanker ...	90	30	19	1	...	35	90	47	3	...	...	49	28	15	...	...	...	13
26	Nandgaon ...	246	90	74	3	1	82	788	322	10	17	...	456	9	2	...	...	...	7
27	Khairagarh ...	366	127	108	...	1	131	503	226	8	12	...	269	29	20	...	...	...	9
28	Chhuikhadan ...	42	19	4	2	...	19	23	13	1	...	...	9	2	1	1	...	...	...
29	Kawardha ...	115	31	20	...	...	55	41	29	5	...	...	7	11	11	...	...	...	...
30	Sakti ...	66	35	2	1	...	29	26	14	...	...	...	12	...	...	...	...	...	...
31	Raigarh ...	1,393	378	461	10	24	554	543	224	14	5	...	305	...	...	...	...	...	...
32	Sarangarh ...	223	53	106	1	13	64	145	65	1	3	...	79	...	...	...	...	...	...
33	Chang Bhakar ...	5	2	...	...	...	3	...	...	...	...	...	...	...	...	...	...	...	...
34	Korea ...	150	40	51	...	...	59	...	...	...	...	...	...	...	...	...	...	...	...
35	Surguja ...	216	47	20	...	...	149	13	6	...	...	...	7	19	9	...	2	...	10
36	Udaipur ...	74	37	20	...	...	17	28	17	...	...	...	11	38	14	...	1	...	24
37	Jashpur ...	76	44	11	...	...	21	43	12	22	...	...	9	37	12	...	6	...	25

# of livelihood, Part A.—General Table.

OF MATERIAL SUBSTANCES—(*continued*).

Transport—(*continued*).

by road—(*concluded*). | Order 22.—Transport by rail.

101.—Pack elephant, camel, mule, ass and bullock owners and drivers. Total workers and dependants.	101. Actual workers. Total. Males.	101. Actual workers. Total. Females.	101. Actual workers. Partially agriculturists. Males.	101. Actual workers. Partially agriculturists. Females.	101. Dependants.	102.—Porters and messengers. Total workers and dependants.	102. Actual workers. Total. Males.	102. Actual workers. Total. Females.	102. Actual workers. Partially agriculturists. Males.	102. Actual workers. Partially agriculturists. Females.	102. Dependants.	Total order 22. Total workers and dependants.	Total order 22. Actual workers. Total. Males.	Total order 22. Actual workers. Total. Females.	Total order 22. Actual workers. Partially agriculturists. Males.	Total order 22. Actual workers. Partially agriculturists. Females.	Total order 22. Dependants.	Serial No.
830	831	832	833	834	835	836	837	838	839	840	841	842	843	844	845	846	847	
8,164	**3,595**	**802**	**186**	**35**	**3,767**	**21,760**	**8,557**	**2,629**	**232**	**103**	**10,574**	**84,167**	**36,315**	**10,038**	**551**	**316**	**37,814**	
5,884	**2,547**	**609**	**145**	**23**	**2,728**	**20,057**	**7,908**	**2,399**	**217**	**94**	**9,750**	**81,669**	**35,349**	**9,967**	**528**	**316**	**36,353**	
5,744	**2,484**	**599**	**136**	**23**	**2,661**	**16,409**	**6,308**	**1,987**	**177**	**60**	**8,114**	**74,719**	**32,409**	**8,869**	**506**	**80**	**33,441**	
4,120	*1,766*	*818*	*101*	*15*	*2,036*	*6,033*	*1,819*	*614*	*58*	*1*	*2,600*	*15,866*	*6,339*	*463*	*107*	*2*	*8,573*	
281	122	34	9	7	125	1,239	421	262	9	...	556	5,034	1,997	214	38	...	2,823	1
669	310	51	12	8	308	408	156	22	4	...	230	1,129	442	10	3	1	077	2
1,425	491	58	73	5	876	2,708	958	275	38	1	1,475	7,081	2,966	111	54	...	4,004	3
59	*25*	...	...	...	*34*	*1,401*	*421*	*169*	*1*	...	*811*	*4,318*	*1,808*	*54*	*1*	...	*2,456*	
1,660	809	163	7	...	697	374	149	54	2	...	171	1,430	593	104	8	...	733	4
70	34	12	...	...	36	304	135	1	...	...	168	691	341	14	4	1	336	5
598	*297*	*70*	*18*	*1*	*231*	*3,143*	*1,349*	*91*	*19*	...	*1,703*	*35,976*	*16,827*	*5,835*	*185*	*60*	*13,311*	
185	86	7	5	...	92	767	264	43	13	...	460	1,541	596	14	3	1	932	6
51	44	...	...	...	7	1,196	493	36	1	...	667	8,319	3,328	614	37	8	4,377	7
26	16	3	2	...	7	1,003	486	11	2	...	500	4,364	2,133	56	4	...	2,175	8
54	31	9	...	1	14	77	65	1	1	...	13	13,521	6,563	3,271	118	43	3,087	9
282	120	51	11	...	111	98	41	...	2	...	57	8,231	4,208	1,883	26	3	2,140	10
346	*115*	*97*	*12*	*4*	*134*	*5,679*	*2,072*	*975*	*74*	*7*	*2,632*	*16,567*	*6,874*	*1,353*	*131*	*19*	*8,340*	
13	5	1	...	...	7	950	467	23	7	3	460	1,491	602	47	13	...	842	11
5	5	...	...	...	...	3,112	984	746	27	...	1,382	7,714	3,088	584	26	2	4,042	12
4	*4*	...	...	...	...	*2,214*	*557*	*612*	*1*	...	*1,045*	*4,485*	*1,555*	*226*	*4*	*1*	*2,707*	
...	...	...	...	...	...	661	242	67	8	...	352	2,411	1,024	267	81	9	1,120	13
32	21	...	1	...	11	922	359	139	32	4	424	3,350	1,394	230	50	8	1,726	14
296	84	96	11	4	116	34	20	...	...	...	14	1,601	766	225	11	...	610	15
650	*306*	*114*	*5*	*3*	*260*	*2,554*	*1,065*	*307*	*31*	*52*	*1,179*	*6,811*	*2,369*	*1,225*	*80*	*9*	*3,217*	
383	142	66	3	1	175	1,094	425	33	18	5	636	2,832	810	970	13	...	1,048	16
223	130	34	2	2	53	1,261	520	272	12	47	469	3,699	1,452	245	65	9	2,002	17
74	28	14	...	...	32	199	123	2	1	...	74	280	98	10	2	...	172	18
140	**63**	**10**	**9**	...	**67**	**3,648**	**1,600**	**412**	**40**	**34**	**1,636**	**6,950**	**2,940**	**1,098**	**22**	**236**	**2,912**	
106	48	5	6	...	57	1,289	597	35	6	1	657	2,767	1,100	122	5	...	1,545	19
28	17	2	...	...	9	1,256	557	356	22	32	343	2,548	1,106	908	6	236	534	20
4	3	...	3	...	1	803	314	10	7	1	479	1,504	668	67	9	...	774	21
3	...	...	...	...	...	300	132	11	5	...	157	131	71	1	2	...	56	22
2,280	**1,048**	**193**	**41**	**12**	**1,039**	**1,703**	**649**	**230**	**15**	**9**	**824**	**2,498**	**966**	**71**	**23**	...	**1,461**	
...	...	...	...	...	...	1	1	...	...	...	...	...	...	...	...	...	...	23
417	130	76	1	2	211	198	63	88	1	...	47	...	...	...	...	...	...	24
48	15	11	...	...	22	6	3	...	...	...	3	3	...	...	...	...	8	25
...	...	...	...	...	...	491	187	5	1	...	299	326	181	15	...	...	180	26
19	7	4	...	...	8	536	214	69	1	...	253	1,453	512	20	12	...	921	27
...	...	...	...	...	...	1	1	...	...	...	...	...	...	...	...	...	...	28
7	6	1	...	...	...	5	4	...	...	...	1	...	...	...	...	...	...	29
...	...	...	...	...	...	20	6	7	...	...	7	123	80	2	5	...	41	30
108	68	19	...	...	16	313	120	42	9	9	151	570	233	28	6	...	309	31
5	2	...	...	...	3	...	...	...	...	...	...	...	...	...	...	...	...	32
104	58	15	3	1	31	...	...	...	...	...	...	...	...	...	...	...	...	33
487	246	11	8	1	230	6	1	...	...	...	5	...	...	...	...	...	...	34
904	409	33	25	8	462	68	34	8	...	...	26	...	...	...	...	...	...	35
50	20	14	...	...	16	2	...	...	...	...	2	17	10	...	...	...	7	36
130	87	9	4	...	40	56	15	11	3	...	30	6	...	6	...	...	...	37

TABLE XV.—Occupation or means

Serial No.	CLASS ... SUB-CLASS ... ORDER ...	CLASS B.—PREPARATION AND SUPPLY																	
		Sub-Class IV.—Transport—(*concluded*).																	
		Order 22.—Transport by rail—(*concluded*).												Total order 23.—Post Office, Telegraph and Telephone services.					
		103.—Railway employés of all kinds other than construction coolies.						104.—Labourers employed on railway construction.						105.—Post Office, Telegraph and Telephone services.					
	DISTRICT, CITY OR STATE.	Total workers and dependants.	Actual workers. Total.		Actual workers. Partially agriculturists.		Dependants.	Total workers and dependants.	Actual workers. Total.		Actual workers. Partially agriculturists.		Dependants.	Total workers and dependants.	Actual workers. Total.		Actual workers. Partially agriculturists.		Dependants.
			Males.	Females.	Males.	Females.			Males.	Females.	Males.	Females.			Males.	Females.	Males.	Females.	
	1	848	849	850	851	852	853	854	855	856	857	858	859	860	861	862	863	864	865
	Central Provinces and Berar.	**37,983**	**15,160**	**797**	**284**	**26**	**22,026**	**46,184**	**21,155**	**9,241**	**267**	**290**	**15,788**	**8,636**	**3,411**	**30**	**110**	...	**5,195**
	C. P. British Districts and Berar.	**36,276**	**14,554**	**779**	**268**	**26**	**20,943**	**45,393**	**20,795**	**9,188**	**260**	**290**	**15,410**	**7,973**	**3,163**	**21**	**105**	...	**4,789**
	C. P. British Districts.	**32,840**	**13,184**	**490**	**256**	**13**	**19,166**	**41,879**	**19,225**	**8,379**	**250**	**67**	**14,275**	**6,686**	**2,599**	**19**	**91**	...	**4,068**
	JUBBULPORE DIVISION	*11,405*	*4,705*	*80*	*66*	*2*	*6,614*	*3,957*	*1,631*	*367*	*41*	...	*1,959*	*1,912*	*704*	*3*	*19*	...	*1,212*
1	Saugor ...	3,237	1,396	32	23	...	1,809	1,797	601	182	15	...	1,014	502	162	...	3	...	340
2	Damoh ...	939	330	8	2	1	601	190	112	2	1	...	76	143	60	1	3	...	82
3	Jubbulpore ...	5,707	2,363	33	29	...	3,311	1,374	603	78	25	...	693	843	294	2	8	...	547
	JUBBULPORE CITY ...	*3,615*	*1,546*	*8*	*1*	...	*2,064*	*700*	*262*	*46*	...	...	*392*	*537*	*173*	*1*	...	...	*363*
4	Mandla ...	1,030	405	9	8	...	616	400	188	95	...	...	117	240	115	...	4	...	131
5	Seoni ...	495	214	4	4	1	277	196	127	10	...	...	59	185	73	...	1	...	112
	NERBUDDA DIVISION	*9,886*	*3,943*	*86*	*80*	...	*5,857*	*26,090*	*12,884*	*5,752*	*105*	*50*	*7,454*	*1,375*	*580*	*2*	*10*	...	*793*
6	Narsinghpur ...	786	312	1	2	...	473	755	283	13	1	1	459	244	86	...	4	...	158
7	Hoshangabad ...	4,390	1,604	38	18	...	2,748	3,920	1,724	576	19	3	1,029	509	228	1	1	...	280
8	Nimar ...	2,959	1,151	30	3	...	1,778	1,405	982	26	1	...	397	223	103	...	2	...	120
9	Betul ...	978	501	10	36	...	467	12,543	6,062	3,261	82	43	3,220	179	72	1	1	...	106
10	Chhindwara ...	773	375	7	21	...	391	7,458	3,833	1,876	5	3	1,749	220	91	...	2	...	129
	NAGPUR DIVISION ...	*8,455*	*3,383*	*130*	*70*	*2*	*4,945*	*8,109*	*3,491*	*1,223*	*61*	*17*	*3,395*	*2,332*	*875*	*4*	*35*	...	*1,410*
11	Wardha ...	955	416	11	12	...	528	536	186	36	1	...	314	197	83	...	4	...	114
12	Nagpur ...	4,105	1,601	65	10	1	2,439	3,609	1,487	519	16	1	1,603	1,190	441	2	15	...	747
	NAGPUR CITY ...	*2,782*	*1,017*	*40*	*4*	...	*1,725*	*1,706*	*535*	*186*	...	*1*	*982*	*837*	*296*	*2*	...	...	*539*
13	Chanda ...	670	230	15	5	1	425	1,741	794	252	26	8	695	458	164	2	2	...	292
14	Bhandara ...	2,032	757	35	37	...	1,240	1,318	637	195	13	8	486	317	121	...	6	...	196
15	Balaghat ...	696	379	4	6	...	313	905	387	221	5	...	297	160	69	...	8	...	91
	CHHATTISGARH DIVISION.	*3,084*	*1,150*	*188*	*40*	*9*	*1,750*	*3,723*	*1,219*	*1,037*	*40*	...	*1,467*	*1,070*	*437*	*10*	*27*	...	*633*
16	Raipur ...	982	442	16	4	...	524	1,850	377	954	9	...	519	633	248	5	9	...	380
17	Bilaspur ...	1,844	613	165	34	9	1,066	1,855	839	80	31	...	936	219	89	...	5	...	130
18	Drug ...	262	95	7	2	...	160	18	3	3	...	...	12	218	100	5	13	...	113
	Berar ...	**3,436**	**1,370**	**289**	**12**	**13**	**1,777**	**3,514**	**1,570**	**809**	**10**	**223**	**1,135**	**1,287**	**564**	**2**	**14**	...	**721**
19	Amraoti ...	1,869	710	58	2	...	1,101	898	390	64	3	...	444	419	196	2	4	...	221
20	Akola ...	754	310	215	4	13	229	1,794	796	693	2	223	305	354	139	...	5	...	215
21	Buldana ...	771	330	16	5	...	425	733	333	51	4	...	349	240	111	...	3	...	129
22	Yeotmal ...	42	20	...	1	...	22	89	51	1	1	...	37	274	118	...	2	...	156
	Feudatory States ...	**1,707**	**606**	**18**	**16**	...	**1,083**	**791**	**360**	**53**	**7**	...	**378**	**863**	**248**	**9**	**5**	...	**406**
23	Makrai ...	...	...	...	...	...	...	...	...	...	...	...	...	20	5	...	...	...	16
24	Bastar ...	...	...	...	...	...	...	...	...	...	...	...	...	275	117	4	2	...	154
25	Kanker ...	3	...	...	...	...	3	...	...	...	...	...	...	47	15	3	...	...	29
26	Nandgaon ...	160	61	3	...	...	96	166	70	12	...	...	84	55	17	...	1	...	38
27	Khairagarh ...	1,229	400	12	12	...	817	224	112	8	...	...	104	88	36	...	1	...	52
28	Chhuikhadan ...	...	...	...	...	...	...	...	...	...	...	...	...	11	4	...	...	...	7
29	Kawardha ...	...	...	...	...	...	...	...	...	...	...	...	...	19	5	...	...	...	14
30	Sakti ...	106	73	1	4	...	32	17	7	1	1	...	9	8	4	...	...	...	4
31	Raigarh ...	192	62	2	...	...	128	378	171	26	6	...	181	31	12	...	...	...	19
32	Sarangarh ...	...	...	...	...	...	...	...	...	...	...	...	...	21	6	...	...	...	15
33	Chang Bhakar ...	...	...	...	...	...	...	...	...	...	...	...	...	2	1	...	...	...	1
34	Korea ...	...	...	...	...	...	...	...	...	...	...	...	...	3	2	...	1	...	1
35	Surguja ...	...	...	...	...	...	...	...	...	...	...	...	...	26	7	2	...	...	17
36	Udaipur ...	17	10	...	...	...	7	...	...	...	...	...	...	40	13	...	...	...	36
37	Jashpur ...	...	...	...	...	...	...	6	...	6	...	...	...	8	4	...	...	...	4

# of livelihood, Part A.—General Table.

OF MATERIAL SUBSTANCES—(*continued*).

Sub-Class V.—Trade. Total Sub-Class V. Total workers and dependants.	Actual workers. Total. Males.	Actual workers. Total. Females.	Actual workers. Partially agriculturists. Males.	Actual workers. Partially agriculturists. Females.	Dependants.	Total order 24.—Banks, establishments of credit, exchange and insurance. 106.—Bank Managers, money-lenders, exchange and insurance agents, money changers and brokers and their employés. Total workers and dependants.	Actual workers. Total. Males.	Actual workers. Total. Females.	Actual workers. Partially agriculturists. Males.	Actual workers. Partially agriculturists. Females.	Dependants.	Total order 25.—Brokerage, commission and export. 107.—Brokers; commission agents, commercial travellers, ware-house owners and employés. Total workers and dependants.	Actual workers. Total. Males.	Actual workers. Total. Females.	Actual workers. Partially agriculturists. Males.	Actual workers. Partially agriculturists. Females.	Dependants.	Serial No.
866	867	868	869	870	871	872	873	874	875	876	877	878	879	880	881	882	883	
595,392	**198,103**	**100.336**	**19.963**	**9,330**	**296.953**	**85,479**	**32,427**	**2 293**	**3,682**	**286**	**50,759**	**6.959**	**2,211**	**177**	**120**	**13**	**4.571**	
550,964	**184,210**	**88,920**	**19,019**	**8,904**	**277,834**	**81,611**	**30,922**	**2,056**	**3,544**	**267**	**48,633**	**6,692**	**2,117**	**166**	**116**	**13**	**4.409**	
395,161	**127,934**	**72,135**	**12,600**	**7,037**	**195.092**	**56,104**	**21,231**	**1,526**	**2,032**	**196**	**33,347**	**4,742**	**1,576**	**121**	**70**	**4**	**3,045**	
110,384	*34,914*	*18,202*	*2,814*	*1,099*	*57,265*	*16,378*	*5,956*	*593*	*392*	*30*	*9,839*	*1,559*	*537*	*66*	*16*	*1*	*986*	
29,257	9,221	4,070	755	224	15,966	5,035	1,684	196	168	13	3,155	292	84	2	5	...	206	1
14,510	4,438	2,294	554	160	7,778	2,605	862	86	115	8	1,657	124	32	2	1	...	90	2
44,983	13,379	8,420	1,123	671	23,178	6,363	2,321	219	76	5	3,823	1,148	406	62	9	1	680	3
16,686	*4,793*	*2,046*	*39*	*2*	*9,848*	*4,044*	*1,457*	*112*	*17*	...	*2,475*	*536*	*202*	*31*	*3*	...	*293*	
10,944	4,107	1,877	188	26	4,965	1,329	705	71	15	3	553	13	9	...	...	...	4	4
10,685	3,760	1,535	194	9	5,381	1,040	384	21	18	1	641	12	6	...	1	...	6	5
86,332	*28,724*	*13,571*	*2,659*	*1,172*	*44,048*	*15,054*	*5,725*	*373*	*601*	*129*	*8,956*	*948*	*299*	*11*	*8*	...	*635*	
15,790	4,718	3,074	607	339	7,997	1,993	658	49	88	4	1,286	433	116	5	4	...	312	6
24,825	7,630	4,791	693	502	12,404	3,697	1,339	107	121	107	2,251	350	122	2	3	...	226	7
19,051	7,277	1,460	530	58	10,914	6,307	2,478	94	241	7	3,735	149	53	1	1	...	89	8
10,185	3,716	1,414	339	57	5,053	1,058	417	54	40	2	587	3	2	...	...	...	1	9
15,800	5,380	2,830	521	217	7,674	1,999	833	69	111	9	1,097	16	6	3	...	...	7	10
137,592	*45,958*	*23,299*	*5,632*	*3,965*	*68,344*	*19,029*	*7,136*	*327*	*829*	*31*	*11,567*	*1,541*	*572*	*26*	*38*	*2*	*943*	
22,456	8,073	2,616	845	304	11,761	3,485	1,273	40	195	11	2,172	111	45	...	2	...	66	11
47,754	15,972	7,411	1,167	474	24,376	6,721	2,548	160	280	7	4,004	786	271	17	9	...	498	12
12,360	*4,148*	*1,763*	*65*	*9*	*6,449*	*1,077*	*435*	*30*	*31*	*2*	*612*	*490*	*149*	*3*	*3*	...	*335*	
26,042	8,501	5,094	1,451	1,680	12,964	4,094	1,491	75	172	11	2,528	288	104	6	17	2	178	13
31,954	10,563	5,865	1,922	1,266	15,526	4,173	1,550	27	169	1	2,590	339	148	1	9	...	190	14
8,782	2,750	2,301	258	232	3,717	556	273	16	15	1	267	17	4	2	1	...	11	15
60,834	*18,343*	*17,053*	*1,452*	*801*	*25,435*	*5,643*	*2,416*	*233*	*210*	*6*	*2,995*	*667*	*164*	*18*	*8*	*1*	*481*	
25,990	8,301	6,341	563	310	11,340	2,893	1,204	102	104	2	1,587	540	130	5	6	...	405	16
19,443	6,102	4,747	590	330	8,594	1,819	838	78	82	3	908	88	20	8	1	...	51	17
15,401	3,941	5,963	300	140	5,498	931	378	53	24	1	500	30	9	5	1	1	25	18
155.802	**56,276**	**16,785**	**6,419**	**1.867**	**82,742**	**25.507**	**9.691**	**530**	**1.512**	**71**	**15,286**	**1,950**	**541**	**4**	**46**	**9**	**1,364**	
50,642	17,740	6,757	2,140	908	26,140	6,478	2,579	155	297	18	3,744	185	49	2	4	...	134	19
40,357	14,908	3,540	1.790	310	21,903	7,970	2,998	148	546	24	4,824	597	162	1	9	...	434	20
33,712	11,485	3,515	1,589	432	18,712	6,566	2,276	170	491	20	4,120	674	157	11	13	1	506	21
31,091	12,137	2,967	900	222	15,967	4,498	1,838	57	178	9	2,596	494	173	31	20	8	290	22
44.426	**13,893**	**11,416**	**944**	**426**	**19.119**	**3,868**	**1.505**	**237**	**138**	**19**	**2,126**	**267**	**94**	**11**	**4**	...	**162**	
625	178	70	10	2	377	169	52	6	12	1	111	...	...	...	...	...	...	23
10,284	3,113	3,240	128	30	3,905	420	184	27	6	...	209	54	30	1	2	...	2	24
2,596	802	709	41	2	1,088	173	76	19	5	1	78	...	...	...	...	...	...	25
3,924	1,310	900	82	29	1,716	325	184	25	6	...	116	43	2	4	...	...	37	26
4,064	1,074	1,210	56	17	1,780	230	93	10	3	...	127	35	2	2	...	...	13	27
995	259	262	15	2	474	123	36	7	2	...	80	...	...	...	...	...	...	28
2,151	627	605	42	8	919	155	56	13	7	...	86	...	...	...	...	...	...	29
498	170	87	11	1	235	15	6	...	...	...	9	4	1	...	...	...	3	30
5,067	1,530	1,487	56	185	2,070	204	69	12	2	...	123	118	40	...	2	...	78	31
2,060	803	941	153	50	1,225	265	84	1	24	...	180	...	...	...	...	...	...	32
511	142	238	11	20	131	15	14	...	...	...	1	...	...	...	...	...	...	33
917	410	185	45	6	322	103	53	8	9	3	42	...	...	...	...	...	...	34
6,078	2,123	583	170	19	3,372	1,567	562	80	56	14	916	1	...	...	...	...	1	35
884	315	211	17	1	358	31	14	1	1	...	16	...	...	...	...	...	...	36
2,861	1,031	683	106	21	1,147	73	22	19	5	...	32	12	1	4	...	...	7	37

TABLE XV.—Occupation or means

Serial No.	CLASS ... / SUB-CLASS ... / ORDER ...	CLASS B.—PREPARATION AND SUPPLY / Sub-Class V.— Total order 26.—Trade in textiles. 108.—Trade in piece-goods, wool, cotton, silk, hair and other textiles.						Total order 27.—Trade in skins, leather and furs. 109.—Trade in skins, leather, furs, feathers, horns, etc.						Total order 28.—Trade in wood. 110.—Trade in wood (not firewood), cork, bark, etc.					
	DISTRICT, CITY OR STATE.	Total workers and dependants.	Actual workers. Total. Males.	Actual workers. Total. Females.	Actual workers. Partially agriculturists. Males.	Actual workers. Partially agriculturists. Females.	Dependants.	Total workers and dependants.	Actual workers. Total. Males.	Actual workers. Total. Females.	Actual workers. Partially agriculturists. Males.	Actual workers. Partially agriculturists. Females.	Dependants.	Total workers and dependants.	Actual workers. Total. Males.	Actual workers. Total. Females.	Actual workers. Partially agriculturists. Males.	Actual workers. Partially agriculturists. Females.	Dependants.
	1	884	885	886	887	888	889	890	891	892	893	894	895	896	897	898	899	900	901
	Central Provinces and Berar.	**51,946**	**19,279**	**3,324**	**1,612**	**234**	**29,343**	**8,338**	**3,179**	**690**	**403**	**92**	**4,469**	**6,890**	**2,371**	**1,200**	**667**	**356**	**3,319**
	C. P. British Districts and Berar.	**49,365**	**18,410**	**3,081**	**1,562**	**229**	**27,874**	**7,313**	**2,783**	**586**	**372**	**83**	**3,944**	**6,543**	**2,251**	**1,154**	**653**	**356**	**3,138**
	C. P. British Districts.	**31,895**	**11,299**	**2,407**	**961**	**209**	**18,189**	**5,390**	**2,030**	**509**	**249**	**73**	**2,851**	**2,949**	**1,039**	**670**	**106**	**19**	**1,240**
	JUBBULPORE DIVISION.	*6,654*	*2,172*	*275*	*156*	*20*	*4,203*	*899*	*319*	*45*	*25*	...	*533*	*1,196*	*293*	*415*	*12*	*6*	*488*
1	Saugor ...	1,746	504	47	42	5	1,195	350	135	6	19	...	209	78	37	10	2	...	31
2	Damoh ...	771	222	29	30	1	520	57	15	1	...	...	41	23	1	8	...	...	14
3	Jubbulpore ...	2,614	837	95	56	11	1,682	301	76	14	3	...	211	1,013	207	392	10	6	414
	JUBBULPORE CITY	*1,120*	*291*	*24*	...	*1*	*805*	*163*	*39*	*5*	...	...	*116*	*679*	*61*	*241*	...	...	*277*
4	Mandla ...	605	259	48	19	3	299	111	60	18	1	...	33	47	25	1	...	...	21
5	Seoni ...	918	351	59	9	...	509	80	33	9	2	...	38	35	23	4	...	...	8
	NERBUDDA DIVISION.	*7,375*	*2,665*	*414*	*261*	*60*	*4,298*	*864*	*300*	*66*	*22*	*15*	*499*	*485*	*219*	*15*	*25*	...	*248*
6	Narsinghpur ...	926	300	25	48	1	595	270	85	23	8	...	162	62	22	...	2	...	40
7	Hoshangabad ...	1,650	540	66	32	4	1,053	78	25	4	1	...	49	203	85	8	10	...	110
8	Nimar ...	1,715	642	88	49	15	985	70	27	3	...	...	49	95	40	2	2	...	53
9	Betul ...	1,160	513	62	58	4	594	42	19	2	3	...	21	61	29	6	7	...	26
10	Chhindwara ...	1,906	667	173	74	36	1,066	305	144	33	10	18	218	64	43	2	7	...	19
	NAGPUR DIVISION	*13,377*	*4,764*	*1,116*	*410*	*89*	*7,497*	*2,194*	*835*	*245*	*139*	*51*	*1,111*	*753*	*355*	*109*	*45*	*11*	*319*
11	Wardha ...	3,100	1,200	123	142	11	1,780	228	138	3	32	...	87	175	105	6	9	...	64
12	Nagpur ...	6,530	2,247	574	173	34	3,709	769	258	132	15	2	379	332	113	84	9	9	135
	NAGPUR CITY ...	*1,487*	*341*	*237*	*2*	...	*909*	*135*	*34*	*1*	...	...	*50*	*134*	*44*	*11*	*1*	...	*79*
13	Chanda ...	971	363	54	35	7	554	560	210	44	47	28	315	89	52	8	5	1	29
14	Bhandara ...	2,169	691	288	47	29	1,190	510	177	55	47	16	278	131	58	7	21	1	66
15	Balaghat ...	598	257	77	13	8	264	118	52	14	8	5	52	56	27	4	1	...	25
	CHHATTISGARH DIVISION.	*4,459*	*1,695*	*599*	*135*	*40*	*2,195*	*1,439*	*576*	*145*	*58*	*4*	*709*	*485*	*172*	*126*	*21*	*2*	*185*
16	Raipur ...	1,811	763	104	55	7	884	739	294	70	33	2	375	143	45	44	2	...	54
17	Bilaspur ...	1,671	542	324	64	31	805	404	170	32	12	1	202	319	112	83	17	2	124
18	Drug ...	1,007	390	111	15	2	506	290	112	46	8	1	132	23	15	1	2	...	7
	Berar ...	**17,470**	**7,111**	**674**	**601**	**20**	**9,685**	**1,928**	**753**	**77**	**123**	**10**	**1,093**	**3,594**	**1,212**	**484**	**547**	**337**	**1,898**
19	Amraoti ...	5,552	2,217	202	154	6	3,133	537	235	37	30	3	265	3,038	1,001	390	512	305	1,647
20	Akola ...	4,459	1,897	127	226	3	2,435	467	177	18	10	2	272	216	96	9	25	...	111
21	Buldana ...	4,035	1,616	213	137	5	2,206	556	189	17	62	4	350	215	77	50	9	10	88
22	Yeotmal ..	3,424	1,381	132	84	6	1,911	363	152	5	21	1	206	125	38	35	1	16	52
	Feudatory States	**2,581**	**869**	**248**	**50**	**5**	**1,469**	**1,025**	**396**	**104**	**31**	**9**	**525**	**347**	**120**	**46**	**14**	...	**181**
23	Makrai ...	46	15	...	...	...	31	...	...	...	...	...	...	1	...	1	...	...	...
24	Bastar ...	697	205	100	4	1	386	281	115	38	1	...	128	118	38	17	9	...	63
25	Kanker ...	266	75	50	7	3	141	106	37	23	3	1	46	2	1	...	...	...	1
26	Nandgaon ...	247	101	16	1	...	130	95	34	11	2	1	50	7	4	...	...	...	3
27	Khairagarh ...	128	20	12	...	...	87	59	24	2	10	...	33	57	22	1	1	...	34
28	Chhuikhadan ...	52	20	5	...	...	27	26	8	...	...	...	18	...	...	...	...	...	...
29	Kawardha ...	224	90	17	12	...	117	11	6	1	1	...	4	...	...	...	...	...	...
30	Sakti ...	45	22	1	2	...	22	14	4	1	2	...	9	3	1	...	1	...	2
31	Raigarh ...	249	92	7	2	...	150	170	64	7	...	1	99	70	33	...	3	...	37
32	Sarangarh ...	61	25	4	2	...	32	28	9	2	3	...	17	5	...	5	...	...	...
33	Chang Bhakar ...	26	11	6	2	...	9	27	13	4	3	4	10	...	...	...	...	...	...
34	Korea ...	84	49	1	7	...	34	2	2	...	...	...	...	...	...	...	...	...	...
35	Surguja ...	195	87	7	4	...	101	78	28	4	2	2	46	80	18	22	...	...	40
36	Udaipur ...	42	18	2	...	...	22	70	34	4	2	...	32	...	...	...	...	...	...
37	Jashpur ...	219	30	9	7	1	180	58	18	7	2	...	33	4	3	...	...	...	1

# of livelihood, Part A.—General Table.

OF MATERIAL SUBSTANCES—(*continued*).

Trade—(*continued*).

Total order 29.—Trade in metals. 111.—Trade in metals, machinery, knife, tool, etc., sellers. Total workers and dependants.	Actual workers. Total. Males.	Actual workers. Total. Females.	Partially agriculturists. Males.	Partially agriculturists. Females.	Dependants.	Total order 30.—Trade in pottery. 112.—Trade in pottery. Total workers and dependants.	Actual workers. Total. Males.	Actual workers. Total. Females.	Partially agriculturists. Males.	Partially agriculturists. Females.	Dependants.	Total order 31.—Trade in chemical products. 113.—Trade in chemical products (drugs, dyes, paints, petroleum, explosives, etc.) Total workers and dependants.	Actual workers. Total. Males.	Actual workers. Total. Females.	Partially agriculturists. Males.	Partially agriculturists. Females.	Dependants.	Serial No.
902	903	904	905	906	907	908	909	910	911	912	913	914	915	916	917	918	919	
1,851	584	329	33	8	938	1,546	415	595	47	68	536	8,612	2,803	1,831	133	74	3,978	
1,220	433	118	25	6	669	1,411	385	538	33	66	488	6,885	2,189	1,412	116	67	3,284	
974	352	76	21	6	546	981	220	432	24	59	329	5,274	1,714	1,057	101	40	2,503	
395	*140*	*37*	*3*	...	*218*	*560*	*83*	*200*	*12*	*61*	*217*	*659*	*245*	*105*	*12*	*7*	*339*	
134	41	4	...	...	89	226	68	58	12	12	110	149	50	32	5	5	67	1
31	16	...	1	...	15	40	2	22	...	...	16	51	25	12	...	1	14	2
196	67	30	1	...	99	272	6	170	...	39	96	352	119	34	6	...	199	3
76	*31*	*4*	*1*	...	*41*	*12*	*3*	...	...	...	*9*	*76*	*21*	*6*	...	...	*49*	
19	10	8	...	...	6	9	2	5	...	...	2	25	10	6	...	...	9	4
15	6	...	1	...	9	13	5	5	...	...	3	112	41	21	1	1	50	5
259	*108*	*7*	*6*	*1*	*174*	*176*	*46*	*98*	*7*	*3*	*31*	*921*	*261*	*169*	*21*	*10*	*491*	
25	6	1	...	...	18	3	...	3	...	1	...	252	60	59	12	5	124	6
133	39	...	2	...	94	1	...	...	...	...	1	217	47	49	5	2	121	7
54	24	1	1	...	20	7	1	6	...	...	...	277	97	6	...	...	174	8
21	14	...	...	...	7	12	...	8	...	...	4	56	10	30	1	1	16	9
56	25	5	2	1	26	153	46	81	7	2	27	119	38	25	3	2	50	10
152	*60*	*11*	*3*	*1*	*81*	*179*	*50*	*63*	*4*	*5*	*66*	*1,357*	*418*	*276*	*26*	*10*	*663*	
28	15	3	...	...	10	50	17	21	1	...	12	167	32	62	1	4	73	11
54	22	4	1	...	32	46	2	12	...	...	32	337	111	40	13	4	180	12
82	*12*	*1*	...	...	*19*	*9*	*1*	...	...	...	[illegible]	*90*	*26*	[illegible]	...	...	*56*	
23	6	...	1	...	17	13	...	11	...	...	2	227	67	24	4	...	130	13
41	15	4	1	1	22	70	31	19	3	5	20	234	103	32	5	1	90	14
2	2	...	...	...	...	...	...	...	...	...	...	302	105	112	2	1	175	15
134	*45*	*21*	*10*	*4*	*73*	*66*	*41*	*11*	*1*	...	*14*	*2,307*	*796*	*507*	*43*	*13*	*1,016*	
28	9	2	4	...	17	11	3	2	...	...	6	1,259	380	338	25	7	541	16
84	29	15	6	4	45	6	6	...	...	...	...	721	256	132	18	5	335	17
21	6	4	...	...	11	49	32	9	1	...	8	327	154	37	...	1	136	18
246	81	42	4	...	123	430	165	106	9	7	159	1,611	475	355	15	27	781	
115	30	35	3	...	50	225	82	54	9	6	89	625	198	119	12	25	312	19
23	10	1	...	...	12	33	9	3	...	...	21	390	117	96	2	2	177	20
79	23	5	1	...	51	83	28	30	...	1	25	342	79	66	1	...	197	21
29	18	1	...	...	10	89	46	19	...	...	24	250	81	74	...	...	95	22
631	151	211	8	2	269	135	80	57	14	2	48	1,727	614	419	17	7	694	
...	...	...	...	...	...	...	...	...	...	...	...	...	...	...	...	...	...	23
284	60	118	2	2	100	90	14	48	11	...	37	900	348	218	8	1	423	24
37	17	11	...	...	1	[illegible]	...	[illegible]	...	2	...	446	130	145	3	5	160	25
21	6	...	...	...	15	[illegible]	4	1	...	...	1	52	17	19	...	...	10	26
1	1	...	...	...	...	2	...	1	...	...	1	39	6	17	...	1	10	27
5	2	...	...	...	3	...	...	...	...	...	...	13	5	7	...	...	2	28
...	...	...	...	...	...	...	...	...	...	...	...	5	...	4	...	...	1	29
3	2	1	1	...	...	...	...	...	...	...	...	6	...	...	...	...	6	30
27	14	1	1	...	12	17	7	4	...	...	6	18	9	8	...	...	6	31
14	5	1	...	...	8	...	...	...	...	...	...	10	6	1	1	...	3	32
42	...	14	...	...	28	...	...	...	...	...	...	...	...	...	...	...	...	33
51	8	20	4	...	17	...	...	...	...	...	...	121	78	5	[illegible]	...	36	34
120	29	82	...	...	65	8	5	...	3	...	3	18	1	...	...	...	17	35
6	3	...	...	...	3	...	...	...	...	...	...	7	7	...	...	...	...	36
14	4	7	...	...	3	...	...	...	...	...	...	2	2	...	1	...	...	37

TABLE XV.—Occupation or means

Serial No.	CLASS / SUB-CLASS / ORDER / DISTRICT, CITY OR STATE.	CLASS B.—PREPARATION AND SUPPLY. Sub-Class V.— Order 32.—Hotels, cafés, restaurants, etc. Total order 32. Total workers and dependants.	Total order 32. Actual workers. Total. Males.	Total order 32. Actual workers. Total. Females.	Total order 32. Actual workers. Partially agriculturists. Males.	Total order 32. Actual workers. Partially agriculturists. Females.	Total order 32. Dependants.	114—Vendors of wine, liquors, aerated waters, etc. Total workers and dependants.	114. Actual workers. Total. Males.	114. Actual workers. Total. Females.	114. Actual workers. Partially agriculturists. Males.	114. Actual workers. Partially agriculturists. Females.	114. Dependants.	115—Owners and managers of hotels, cookshops, sarais, etc., and their employés. Total workers and dependants.	115. Actual workers. Total. Males.	115. Actual workers. Total. Females.	115. Actual workers. Partially agriculturists. Males.	115. Actual workers. Partially agriculturists. Females.	115. Dependants.
	1	920	921	922	923	924	925	926	927	928	929	930	931	932	933	934	935	936	937
	Central Provinces and Berar.	**13,794**	**4,874**	**1,450**	**426**	**68**	**7,470**	**12,520**	**4,408**	**1,351**	**417**	**65**	**6,761**	**1,274**	**466**	**99**	**9**	**3**	**709**
	C. P. British Districts and Berar.	**12,084**	**4,426**	**907**	**384**	**58**	**6,751**	**10,823**	**3,964**	**808**	**375**	**55**	**6,051**	**1,261**	**462**	**99**	**9**	**3**	**700**
	C. P. British Districts.	**9,010**	**3,278**	**814**	**286**	**53**	**4,918**	**8,102**	**2,915**	**754**	**278**	**50**	**4,433**	**908**	**363**	**60**	**8**	**3**	**485**
	JUBBULPORE DIVISION	*1,723*	*616*	*199*	*43*	*8*	*907*	*1,470*	*524*	*187*	*41*	*6*	*759*	*252*	*92*	*12*	*2*	...	*143*
1	Saugar ...	224	75	14	1	...	135	194	66	11	1	...	117	30	9	3	...	...	18
2	Damoh ...	87	34	2	3	...	51	74	29	2	3	...	43	13	5	...	...	...	8
3	Jubbulpore ...	505	169	45	16	6	291	362	115	37	16	6	210	143	54	8	...	...	81
	JUBBULPORE CITY ...	*245*	*82*	*5*	...	...	*158*	*144*	*48*	...	...	...	*96*	*101*	*34*	*5*	...	...	*62*
4	Mandla ...	610	225	98	15	1	287	564	213	98	14	1	253	46	12	...	1	...	34
5	Seoni ...	296	113	40	8	1	143	270	101	39	7	1	136	20	12	1	1	...	7
	NERBUDDA DIVISION	*1,976*	*702*	*139*	*60*	*3*	*1,135*	*1,848*	*652*	*132*	*59*	*2*	*1,064*	*128*	*50*	*7*	*1*	*1*	*71*
6	Narsinghpur ...	172	54	16	8	...	102	152	47	16	8	...	89	20	7	...	...	...	13
7	Hoshangabad ...	369	130	12	10	1	227	332	117	11	9	...	204	37	13	1	1	1	23
8	Nimar ...	559	185	36	10	...	338	529	175	30	10	...	324	30	10	6	...	...	14
9	Betul ...	422	136	36	13	2	250	405	129	36	13	2	240	17	7	...	...	...	10
10	Chhindwara ...	454	197	39	19	...	218	430	184	39	19	...	207	24	13	...	...	...	11
	NAGPUR DIVISION ...	*4,149*	*1,517*	*309*	*148*	*31*	*2,323*	*3,772*	*1,361*	*273*	*146*	*30*	*2,13*[illegible]	*377*	*156*	*36*	*2*	*1*	*185*
11	Wardha ...	926	357	51	33	16	518	847	332	43	32	15	472	79	25	8	1	1	46
12	Nagpur ...	1,209	437	65	24	1	707	1,007	353	41	23	1	613	202	84	24	1	...	94
	NAGPUR CITY ...	*353*	*131*	*21*	*2*	...	*211*	*223*	*71*	*3*	*1*	...	*149*	*130*	*50*	*12*	*1*	...	*62*
13	Chanda ...	1,025	363	80	57	7	573	1,004	354	86	57	7	562	21	9	1	...	...	11
14	Bhandara ...	705	263	54	25	2	388	665	241	52	25	2	372	40	22	2	...	...	16
15	Balaghat ...	284	97	50	9	5	137	249	81	41	9	5	119	35	16	1	...	...	18
	CHHATTISGARH DIVISION	*1,163*	*443*	*167*	*35*	*11*	*553*	*1,012*	*378*	*162*	*32*	*10*	*472*	*151*	*65*	*5*	*3*	*1*	*81*
16	Raipur ...	471	187	45	10	5	239	360	142	40	9	4	177	111	44	5	1	1	62
17	Bilaspur ...	306	157	37	10	...	172	343	145	37	9	...	161	23	12	...	1	...	11
18	Drug ...	326	90	85	15	6	142	309	90	85	14	6	134	17	9	...	1	...	8
	Berar ...	**3,074**	**1,146**	**93**	**98**	**5**	**1,833**	**2,721**	**1,049**	**54**	**97**	**5**	**1,618**	**353**	**99**	**39**	**1**	...	**215**
19	Amraoti ...	905	313	46	24	1	636	806	275	17	24	1	514	189	38	20	...	...	122
20	Akola ...	669	261	22	23	3	386	595	234	15	22	3	346	74	27	7	1	...	40
21	Buldana ...	576	184	12	20	...	380	514	161	9	20	...	341	62	20	3	...	...	39
22	Yeotmal ...	834	300	13	31	1	431	806	370	13	31	1	417	28	14	...	...	...	14
	Feudatory States ...	**1,710**	**448**	**543**	**42**	**10**	**719**	**1,697**	**444**	**543**	**42**	**10**	**710**	**13**	**4**	...	...	...	**9**
23	Makrai ...	38	14	3	...	...	21	38	14	3	...	...	21	...	...	...	...	...	...
24	Bastar ...	701	100	321	12	5	280	700	100	321	12	5	279	1	...	...	...	...	1
25	Kanker ...	154	28	62	...	...	64	154	28	62	...	...	64	...	...	...	...	...	...
26	Nandgaon ...	76	20	16	1	...	40	74	19	16	1	...	39	2	1	...	...	...	1
27	Khairagarh ...	136	41	35	7	2	60	131	30	35	7	2	57	5	2	...	...	...	3
28	Chhuikhadan ...	...	...	...	...	...	...	...	...	...	...	...	...	...	...	...	...	...	...
29	Kawardha ...	68	34	7	...	...	28	65	33	7	...	...	25	4	1	...	...	...	3
30	Sakti ...	1	1	...	...	...	...	1	1	...	...	...	...	...	...	...	...	...	...
31	Raigarh ...	87	32	24	2	...	31	87	32	24	2	...	31	...	...	...	...	...	...
32	Sarangarh ...	67	21	11	6	...	35	66	21	11	6	...	34	1	...	...	...	...	1
33	Chang Bhakar ...	22	9	8	5	1	5	22	9	8	5	1	5	...	...	...	...	...	...
34	Korea ...	72	32	13	2	1	27	72	32	13	2	1	27	...	...	...	...	...	...
35	Surguja ...	102	50	3	4	...	49	102	50	3	4	...	49	...	...	...	...	...	...
36	Udaipur ...	62	22	10	1	1	30	62	22	10	1	1	30	...	...	...	...	...	...
37	Jashpur ...	123	44	30	2	...	49	123	44	30	2	...	49	...	...	...	...	...	...

# of livelihood, Part A.—General Table.

OF MATERIAL SUBSTANCES—*(continued)*.

Trade—*(continued)*.

Order 33.—Other trade in food-stuffs.																		
Total order 33.						116. – Fish dealers.						117.—Grocers and sellers of vegetable oil, salt and other condiments.						
Total workers and dependants.	Actual workers. Total. Males.	Actual workers. Total. Females.	Actual workers. Partially agriculturists. Males.	Actual workers. Partially agriculturists. Females.	Dependants.	Total workers and dependants.	Actual workers. Total. Males.	Actual workers. Total. Females.	Actual workers. Partially agriculturists. Males.	Actual workers. Partially agriculturists. Females.	Dependants.	Total workers and dependants.	Actual workers. Total. Males.	Actual workers. Total. Females.	Actual workers. Partially agriculturists. Males.	Actual workers. Partially agriculturists. Females.	Dependants.	Serial No.
938	939	940	941	942	943	944	945	946	947	948	949	950	951	952	953	954	955	
335,583	**105,277**	**75,580**	**10,906**	**7,140**	**154.726**	**3,365**	**682**	**1,747**	**81**	**929**	**936**	**138,280**	**45,343**	**27,339**	**5,096**	**2,493**	**65,598**	
309,410	**97,349**	**67,840**	**10,372**	**6.934**	**144,221**	**3,276**	**668**	**1,698**	**81**	**928**	**910**	**128,182**	**42,115**	**24,367**	**4.918**	**2,430**	**61,700**	
232,562	**70,567**	**56,382**	**7,549**	**5,818**	**105,613**	**2,464**	**323**	**1 611**	**34**	**896**	**530**	**90,545**	**28,011**	**20,656**	**3,315**	**2,071**	**41,878**	
68,496	*20,506*	*14,393*	*1,849*	*872*	*33,293*	*157*	*56*	*47*	*2*	*2*	*55*	*25,485*	*7,774*	*5,509*	*733*	*284*	*12,805*	
17,414	5,439	3,176	386	178	8,799	...	...	...	...	...	...	7,905	2,451	1,458	180	92	3,996	1
9,393	2,819	1,943	333	128	4,631	9	...	1	...	1	8	5,212	1,575	1,108	193	69	2,529	2
27,913	7,890	6,793	855	544	13,230	131	43	45	2	1	43	7,594	2,185	1,906	233	117	3,503	3
7,818	*1,998*	*1,399*	*15*	...	*4,421*	*114*	*36*	*41*	...	...	*37*	*801*	*213*	*82*	...	...	*506*	
7,141	2,405	1,356	129	17	3,880	1	...	1	...	...	...	2,259	715	588	23	3	956	4
6,635	2,253	1,130	146	5	3,252	16	12	...	...	...	4	2,518	848	449	104	3	1,221	5
50,357	*15,722*	*10,990*	*1,520*	*897*	*23,675*	*266*	*131*	*20*	*4*	...	*126*	*18,484*	*6,050*	*3,622*	*626*	*161*	*8,818*	
10,281	2,987	2,624	403	324	4,670	1	1	...	...	...	...	4,000	1,275	961	142	43	1,764	6
16,214	4,650	4,256	482	388	7,308	24	4	2	...	...	18	4,972	1,582	983	206	50	2,407	7
8,498	3,048	981	194	34	4,469	19	4	3	...	...	12	3,001	1,079	454	66	13	1,558	8
6,248	2,145	1,072	179	48	3,031	14	3	4	...	...	7	2,245	762	431	50	9	1,052	9
9,146	2,892	2,057	262	103	4,197	208	100	11	4	...	88	4,170	1,352	793	160	46	2,031	10
77,794	*24,496*	*18,198*	*3,351*	*3,121*	*35,100*	*1,630*	*95*	*1,342*	*7*	*862*	*193*	*34,635*	*10,937*	*7,491*	*1,671*	*1,457*	*16,106*	
10,971	3,789	1,811	317	170	5,371	32	7	2	1	2	23	6,047	2,193	888	178	99	2,966	11
25,068	7,924	5,385	529	324	11,759	198	60	73	3	44	56	10,639	3,006	2,330	204	187	5,213	12
6,590	*2,339*	*1,352*	*20*	*7*	*3,199*	*42*	*17*	*14*	...	...	*17*	*1,736*	*531*	*253*	*6*	*2*	*942*	
15,077	4,501	4,242	857	1,542	6,334	1,198	4	1,119	1	797	81	7,910	2,633	1,666	595	496	3,611	13
21,148	6,750	4,935	1,503	1,176	9,463	169	12	135	2	12	22	7,770	2,405	1,922	514	520	3,449	14
5,530	1,532	1,825	175	209	2,172	38	3	19	...	6	11	2,162	610	685	90	155	867	15
35,885	*9,543*	*12,796*	*799*	*628*	*13,546*	*411*	*52*	*202*	*21*	*32*	*157*	*12,039*	*3,250*	*4,034*	*285*	*169*	*4,768*	
14,129	4,113	4,019	292	262	5,397	61	...	48	...	11	13	5,550	1,557	1,933	124	88	2,066	16
11,527	3,214	3,376	302	244	4.937	391	45	142	20	21	144	3,494	914	1,100	79	45	1,481	17
10,229	2,216	4,801	205	122	3,212	11	7	12	1	...	...	2,989	779	1,001	82	36	1,200	18
76.848	**26.782**	**11,458**	**2.823**	**1,116**	**38.608**	**812**	**345**	**87**	**47**	**32**	**380**	**37,637**	**14.104**	**3,711**	**1,603**	**359**	**19,822**	
25,661	8,535	4,714	920	467	12,412	530	275	44	39	24	211	10,091	3,787	1,441	420	137	5,463	19
19,301	7,081	2,400	773	200	9,901	118	56	4	7	1	58	9,507	3,759	791	408	82	4,958	20
15,507	5,217	2,282	657	305	8,068	24	4	2	1	1	18	7,529	2,682	688	399	94	4,152	21
16,229	5,949	2,058	473	144	8,227	140	10	37	...	6	93	9,010	3,877	791	327	40	5,242	22
26.173	**7.928**	**7,740**	**534**	**206**	**10,505**	**89**	**14**	**49**	...	**1**	**26**	**10.098**	**3,228**	**2,972**	**178**	**63**	**3.898**	
328	84	50	4	1	194	...	...	...	...	...	...	173	52	10	3	1	111	23
5,470	1,615	2,023	62	25	1,832	61	8	37	...	...	16	2,055	650	711	9	...	69	24
958	323	279	19	7	350	...	...	...	...	...	...	334	97	105	7	3	132	25
2,511	805	601	67	22	1,106	1	...	1	...	1	...	650	204	166	9	10	28	26
2,829	670	962	19	14	1,191	...	...	...	...	...	...	635	176	100	5	6	328	27
661	168	188	12	2	305	...	...	...	...	...	...	124	33	39	...	...	63	28
1,544	417	507	22	8	620	...	...	...	...	...	...	418	145	75	8	1	228	29
291	111	50	5	1	130	...	...	...	...	...	...	63	16	12	4	...	21	30
3,309	1,032	1,027	44	61	1,810	15	5	8	..	...	2	967	205	534	4	12	222	31
1,447	319	690	72	25	429	...	...	...	...	...	...	679	152	332	16	3	198	32
331	78	190	1	15	63	...	...	...	...	...	...	143	44	62	...	5	37	33
334	137	96	14	1	101	...	...	...	...	...	...	66	38	15	2	...	13	34
3,507	1,210	858	99	3	1,939	7	1	...	...	...	6	1,736	635	223	28	2	876	35
575	177	181	12	...	217	...	...	...	...	...	...	317	74	142	...	...	101	36
2,018	770	530	82	20	712	5	...	3	...	...	2	1,674	707	386	81	20	581	37

TABLE XV.—Occupation or means

Serial No.	CLASS ... / SUB-CLASS ... / ORDER ...	CLASS B.—PREPARATION AND SUPPLY / Sub-Class V.— / Order 33.—Other trade in														
		118.—Sellers of milk, butter, ghee, poultry, eggs, etc.						119.—Sellers of sweetmeats, sugar, gur and molasses.						120.—Cardamom, betel fruit and areca nut		
			Actual workers.						Actual workers.						Actual	
			Total.		Partially agriculturists.				Total.		Partially agriculturists.				Total.	
	District, City or State.	Total workers and dependants.	Males.	Females.	Males.	Females.	Dependants.	Total workers and dependants.	Males.	Females.	Males.	Females.	Dependants.	Total workers and dependants.	Males.	Females.
	1	956	957	958	959	960	961	962	963	964	965	966	967	968	969	970
	Central Provinces and Berar.	**14.769**	**3.187**	**5.823**	**350**	**218**	**5,759**	**7.273**	**2.655**	**940**	**123**	**64**	**3,678**	**51,932**	**14,915**	**15,852**
	C.P. British Districts and Berar.	**11.804**	**2.600**	**4.592**	**269**	**185**	**4.812**	**7.187**	**2.631**	**919**	**121**	**64**	**3.637**	**49.108**	**14,098**	**14,856**
	C.P. British Districts.	**10.121**	**2.220**	**4.011**	**249**	**166**	**3.890**	**4.406**	**1.560**	**694**	**80**	**60**	**2,152**	**35.607**	**10,045**	**10,965**
	Jubbulpore Division.	*3,385*	*947*	*743*	*103*	*48*	*1,095*	*622*	*131*	*59*	*3*	*3*	*392*	*11,778*	*3,339*	*3,157*
1	Saugor ...	1,462	401	374	56	38	687	218	40	36	...	3	142	2,091	980	723
2	Damoh ...	320	104	58	23	3	158	47	21	9	1	...	17	1,870	536	489
3	Jubbulpore ...	1,258	340	220	17	4	608	265	60	33	2	...	172	5,371	1,344	1,529
	Jubbulpore City ...	*976*	*364*	*133*	*6*	...	*679*	*188*	*21*	*21*	...	...	*146*	*2,684*	*559*	*596*
4	Mandla ...	305	92	73	8	3	140	68	10	6	...	...	52	638	223	153
5	Seoni ...	43	10	18	...	...	15	24	10	5	...	...	9	908	250	263
	Nerbudda Division.	*2,182*	*590*	*512*	*57*	*28*	*1,080*	*920*	*373*	*121*	*12*	*1*	*436*	*7,434*	*2,184*	*2,284*
6	Narsinghpur ...	474	90	172	10	11	203	171	69	39	2	1	63	2,086	512	753
7	Hoshangabad ...	1,002	303	178	22	2	521	60	27	10	3	...	32	2,854	850	844
8	Nimar ...	143	26	34	1	1	83	428	181	56	...	...	101	768	237	166
9	Betul ...	151	33	55	6	11	63	130	40	9	4	...	81	792	304	224
10	Chhindwara ...	412	129	73	18	3	210	122	56	7	3	...	59	934	281	297
	Nagpur Division ...	*1,961*	*570*	*510*	*81*	*40*	*881*	*2,606*	*934*	*855*	*51*	*61*	*1,218*	*11,777*	*3,409*	*3,689*
11	Wardha ...	277	88	50	5	2	139	420	171	21	3	...	228	1,800	530	632
12	Nagpur ...	787	252	142	10	...	393	1,053	412	101	18	5	540	5,134	1,421	1,500
	Nagpur City ...	*392*	*103*	*79*	*1*	...	*210*	*307*	*126*	*16*	*1*	...	*165*	*1,568*	*390*	*353*
13	Chanda ...	472	63	249	18	34	100	415	165	64	17	6	186	1,741	534	548
14	Bhandara ...	357	148	51	45	4	158	540	102	160	13	41	218	1,097	631	613
15	Balaghat ...	68	19	18	3	...	31	77	24	12	...	...	41	1,045	293	337
	Chhattisgarh Division.	*2,590*	*113*	*2,246*	*7*	*50*	*231*	*359*	*112*	*136*	*14*	*5*	*121*	*4,618*	*1,113*	*1,885*
16	Raipur ...	330	51	191	4	8	88	155	46	72	9	2	37	833	193	397
17	Bilaspur ...	237	39	131	...	19	67	139	40	42	3	2	57	1,607	420	579
18	Drug ...	2,023	23	1,924	3	20	76	65	26	12	2	1	27	2,178	500	909
	Berar ...	**1,683**	**380**	**581**	**20**	**19**	**722**	**2,781**	**1.071**	**225**	**41**	**4**	**1 485**	**13,501**	**4,053**	**3,891**
19	Amraoti ...	401	80	86	1	5	235	1,405	543	74	27	1	788	5,839	1,651	1,962
20	Akola ...	403	99	205	11	12	159	801	202	100	6	2	403	3,639	1,158	859
21	Buldana ...	435	119	122	4	...	194	311	124	12	6	...	175	2,503	751	689
22	Yeotmal ...	384	82	168	4	2	134	264	112	33	2	1	119	1,520	493	389
	Feudatory States ...	**2,965**	**587**	**1,231**	**81**	**31**	**1,147**	**86**	**24**	**21**	**2**	...	**41**	**2,824**	**817**	**996**
23	Makrai ...	2	2	...	...	...	...	...	...	...	...	...	...	91	14	32
24	Bastar ...	607	84	337	1	10	186	1	...	1	...	...	...	490	159	180
25	Kanker ...	3	2	...	...	...	1	4	...	...	...	...	4	388	148	86
26	Nandgaon ...	56	3	50	...	3	3	2	1	1	1	...	...	460	171	116
27	Khairagarh ...	387	13	337	1	3	37	5	2	1	...	...	...	201	36	116
28	Chhuikhadan ...	45	15	3	3	...	27	25	4	9	...	...	10	143	27	73
29	Kawardha ...	243	2	231	...	2	10	11	1	2	...	...	8	209	68	59
30	Sakti ...	2	...	2	...	...	...	2	2	...	1	...	...	6	3	2
31	Raigarh ...	115	35	25	1	...	55	15	...	7	...	..	8	292	81	79
32	Sarangarh ...	10	...	10	...	2	...	...	...	—	...	...	...	386	89	182
33	Chang Bhakar ...	125	...	113	...	10	12	...	...	...	...	...	...	23	...	13
34	Korea ...	73	19	35	9	1	19	18	9	...	...	...	9	1	1	...
35	Surguja ...	1,234	395	65	58	...	774	4	4	...	...	...	...	61	5	28
36	Udaipur ...	18	13	...	8	...	5	—	...	...	...	...	...	9	4	5
37	Jashpur ...	45	4	23	...	...	18	3	1	...	...	...	2	64	11	25

# of livelihood, Part A.—General Table.

OF MATERIAL SUBSTANCES—(*continued*).

Trade—(*continued*).

food stuffs—(*continued*).

leaf, vegetables, sellers.			121.—Grain and pulse dealers.						122.—Tobacco, opium, ganja, etc., sellers.						123.—Dealers in sheep, goats and pigs.						
WORKERS.				ACTUAL WORKERS.						ACTUAL WORKERS.						ACTUAL WORKERS.					
Partially agriculturists.				Total.		Partially agriculturists.				Total.		Partially agriculturists.				Total.		Partially agriculturists.			
Males.	Females.	Dependants.	Total workers and dependants.	Males.	Females.	Males.	Females.	Dependants.	Total workers and dependants.	Males.	Females.	Males.	Females.	Dependants.	Total workers and dependants.	Males.	Females.	Males.	Females.	Dependants.	Serial No.
971	972	973	974	975	976	977	978	979	980	981	982	983	984	985	986	987	988	989	990	991	
1,766	**1,292**	**21,165**	**79,630**	**26,452**	**12,126**	**2,127**	**769**	**41,0[illegible]2**	**18,676**	**6,399**	**3,123**	**513**	**211**	**9,154**	**1,444**	**526**	**95**	**48**	**5**	**823**	
1,625	**1,257**	**20 154**	**71,535**	**23,776**	**10,331**	**2,012**	**731**	**37,428**	**17,142**	**5,939**	**2,659**	**498**	**181**	**8,544**	**1,433**	**523**	**91**	**48**	**5**	**819**	
1,145	**927**	**14,597**	**61,526**	**20,216**	**9,882**	**1,716**	**707**	**31,428**	**13,933**	**4,565**	**2,547**	**338**	**176**	**6,821**	**1,180**	**416**	**85**	**33**	**[illegible]**	**679**	
33[illegible]	*225*	*5,282*	*19,407*	*6,287*	*2,383*	*371*	*19*	*10,797*	*1,690*	*577*	*19[illegible]*	*10*	*6*	*931*	*470*	*169*	*21*	*13*	...	*280*	
73	18	1,288	4,084	1,297	453	54	7	2,334	434	167	39	...	1	232	33	14	2	3	...	17	1
75	50	845	1,578	478	231	34	2	869	235	52	31	2	1	152	66	22	7	1	...	37	2
164	152	2,498	7,451	2,231	922	172	36	4,298	558	168	74	6	3	316	320	103	7	9	...	210	3
3	...	*1,329*	*2,115*	*605*	*275*	*2*	...	*1,235*	*215*	*66*	*7*	...	...	*149*	*143*	*27*	*1*	...	...	*115*	
10	5	262	3,528	1,254	427	80	2	1,847	150	72	18	1	1	69	22	10	...	...	...	12	4
10	...	389	2,760	967	350	31	2	1,449	304	122	30	1	...	152	20	20	5	...	...	4	5
241	*243*	*2,966*	*14,21[illegible]*	*4,712*	*1,675*	*326*	*29*	*7,925*	*1,995*	*666*	*165*	*30*	*3*	*1,164*	*261*	*110*	*16*	*2*	*2*	*135*	
91	107	821	2,416	668	361	58	8	1,387	350	125	37	4	...	188	28	17	1	...	...	10	6
90	90	1,160	3,976	1,242	488	72	6	2,240	483	139	39	5	...	305	91	33	3	1	...	55	7
12	13	365	3,591	1,320	237	108	7	2,028	276	98	20	5	...	158	36	18	6	1	...	12	8
34	15	264	2,310	795	289	48	7	1,227	438	142	27	10	...	200	40	11	3	...	2	20	9
14	18	356	1,925	681	204	40	1	1,040	448	102	42	6	3	244	66	31	3	...	...	32	10
461	*330*	*4,729*	*16,620*	*5,579*	*3,409*	*767*	*505*	*7,632*	*5,980*	*2,243*	*504*	*208*	*50*	*3,233*	*330*	*80*	*20*	*15*	*3*	*230*	
74	57	698	1,142	382	38	16	...	722	762	308	35	22	2	419	30	10	4	2	1	25	11
89	52	2,204	4,404	1,728	825	44	7	1,851	1,590	600	97	31	6	803	190	61	6	13	...	123	12
4	*3*	*815*	*2,037*	*953*	*476*	*4*	...	*605*	*274*	*84*	*21*	*3*	*2*	*169*	*12*	*3*	...	...	...	*9*	
111	108	659	1,638	601	150	57	19	887	903	385	82	40	13	526	88	...	9	...	2	79	13
153	98	753	7,810	2,465	1,754	609	450	3,591	2,130	778	181	92	25	1,171	7	4	1	...	...	2	14
34	15	415	1,626	408	642	31	29	581	505	172	109	17	4	224	6	5	...	...	...	1	15
111	*139*	*1,620*	*11,281*	*3,695*	*2,512*	*262*	*134*	*5,071*	*4,265*	*1,079*	*1,686*	*90*	*117*	*1,509*	*119*	*67*	*28*	*3*	...	*33*	
7	7	243	4,714	1,580	957	97	54	2,171	2,424	650	1,012	50	92	762	30	13	4	...	...	13	16
52	89	606	4,579	1,464	1,083	112	50	2,082	1,017	227	337	29	18	453	57	31	5	3	...	21	17
52	38	769	1,988	648	522	53	20	818	827	202	337	11	7	288	32	13	19	...	...	...	18
480	**330**	**5,557**	**10,009**	**3,560**	**449**	**296**	**24**	**6,000**	**3,209**	**1,374**	**112**	**160**	**5**	**1,723**	**253**	**107**	**6**	**15**	...	**140**	
203	129	2,226	3,294	1,101	184	60	4	2,000	1,360	622	38	100	1	700	75	21	2	3	...	52	19
110	66	1,630	2,941	1,071	126	110	4	1,744	555	245	16	14	2	294	83	47	1	7	...	35	20
119	115	1,063	2,204	831	79	73	4	1,294	616	196	22	25	...	396	48	18	1	3	...	20	21
48	20	638	1,570	557	60	44	12	953	678	311	36	21	2	331	47	21	2	2	...	24	22
141	**35**	**1,011**	**8,095**	**2,676**	**1,795**	**115**	**38**	**3,624**	**1,534**	**460**	**464**	**15**	**30**	**610**	**11**	**3**	**4**	...	...	**4**	
1	...	45	48	12	8	...	...	28	13	4	...	...	...	9	...	...	...	...	...	...	23
23	2	151	1,735	564	584	28	11	587	401	140	160	1	2	191	6	2	4	...	...	...	24
12	2	154	180	60	67	...	2	53	47	14	21	...	...	12	...	...	...	...	...	...	25
30	4	173	1,165	364	229	21	4	572	175	60	37	6	1	78	1	1	...	...	...	...	26
2	...	40	1,309	404	280	9	2	706	170	45	59	2	3	66	4	...	...	...	...	4	27
2	2	43	281	78	57	7	...	146	41	11	13	...	...	17	...	...	...	...	...	...	28
12	2	82	591	183	133	2	3	275	42	18	7	...	...	17	...	...	...	...	...	...	29
...	...	1	189	79	21	...	1	89	30	11	7	...	...	12	...	...	...	...	...	...	30
11	15	132	1,588	580	248	24	13	751	304	88	104	2	21	112	...	...	...	...	...	...	31
47	8	115	175	51	63	3	1	61	111	26	40	4	3	45	...	...	...	...	...	...	32
...	...	10	20	16	...	1	...	4	20	18	2	...	...	...	...	...	...	...	...	...	33
...	...	...	160	61	43	3	...	56	16	9	3	...	...	4	...	...	...	...	...	...	34
...	...	28	287	88	13	13	1	186	24	9	2	...	...	18	...	...	...	...	...	...	35
...	...	...	195	79	32	4	...	84	29	2	2	...	...	25	...	...	...	...	...	...	36
1	...	28	83	48	8	...	...	27	21	5	7	...	...	9	...	...	...	...	...	...	37

TABLE XV.—Occupation or means

Serial No.	CLASS ...	CLASS B.—PREPARATION AND SUPPLY																	
	SUB-CLASS ...	Sub-Class V.—																	
	ORDER ...	Order 33.—Other trade in food stuffs—(*concluded*).						Total order 34.—Trade in clothing and toilet articles.						Order 35.—Trade					
		124.—Dealers in hay, grass and fodder.						125.—Trade in ready made clothing and other articles of dress and the toilet (hats, umbrellas, socks, ready made shoes, perfumes, etc.)						Total order 35.					
	DISTRICT, CITY OR STATE.	Total workers and dependants.	ACTUAL WORKERS. Total. Males.	ACTUAL WORKERS. Total. Females.	Partially agriculturists. Males.	Partially agriculturists. Females.	Dependants.	Total workers and dependants.	ACTUAL WORKERS. Total. Males.	ACTUAL WORKERS. Total. Females.	Partially agriculturists. Males.	Partially agriculturists. Females.	Dependants.	Total workers and dependants.	ACTUAL WORKERS. Total. Males.	ACTUAL WORKERS. Total. Females.	Partially agriculturists. Males.	Partially agriculturists. Females.	Dependants.
	1	992	993	994	995	996	997	998	999	1000	1001	1002	1003	1004	1005	1006	1007	1008	1009
	Central Provinces and Berar.	**20,214**	**5,118**	**8,535**	**802**	**1,161**	**6,561**	**6,450**	**2,064**	**1,009**	**161**	**77**	**3,377**	**5,614**	**1,909**	**837**	**145**	**107**	**2,968**
	C. P. British Districts and Berar.	**19,743**	**4,999**	**8,327**	**800**	**1,153**	**6,417**	**6,379**	**2,033**	**992**	**160**	**77**	**3,354**	**5,448**	**1,732**	**821**	**130**	**107**	**2,895**
	C. P. British Districts.	**12,780**	**3,211**	**5,931**	**639**	**810**	**3,638**	**3,052**	**972**	**457**	**78**	**44**	**1,623**	**3,137**	**1,068**	**356**	**66**	**27**	**1,713**
	JUBBULPORE DIVISION.	*5,496*	*1,577*	*2,257*	*281*	*255*	*1,662*	*759*	*213*	*70*	*47*	*24*	*476*	*235*	*103*	*11*	*3*	...	*123*
1	Saugor ...	287	93	91	20	19	103	164	53	6	16	...	105	67	8	8	...	...	51
2	Damoh ...	56	31	9	4	2	16	129	37	1	16	...	91	1	1	...	1	...	...
3	Jubbulpore ...	4,965	1,416	2,057	250	231	,492	412	101	56	14	24	255	11	3	2	...	...	6
	JUBBULPORE CITY.	*679*	*207*	*240*	*7*	...	*232*	*200*	*45*	*19*	...	...	*133*	*11*	*3*	*2*	...	...	*6*
4	Mandla ...	161	29	90	7	3	42	9	6	...	...	...	3	35	27	...	...	...	8
5	Seoni ...	27	8	10	...	...	9	45	16	7	1	...	22	124	65	1	2	...	58
	NERBUDDA DIVISION.	*4,627*	*916*	*2,672*	*222*	*430*	*1,039*	*373*	*161*	*45*	*8*	*4*	*175*	*300*	*97*	*53*	...	*2*	*156*
6	Narsinghpur ...	755	221	300	96	154	234	38	17	2	...	...	19	89	42	1	...	...	46
7	Hoshangabad ...	2,743	470	1,700	81	240	564	49	21	...	...	...	28	77	5	25	...	...	47
8	Nimar ...	146	79	5	1	...	62	109	65	5	6	...	39	33	11	7	...	...	15
9	Betul ...	128	55	31	27	4	42	34	15	7	...	...	12	16	10	...	...	...	6
10	Chhindwara ...	855	91	627	17	32	137	148	43	28	2	4	77	91	20	20	...	2	42
	NAGPUR DIVISION	*2,457*	*649*	*925*	*136*	*123*	*883*	*1,723*	*525*	*316*	*21*	*15*	*882*	*1,421*	*466*	*243*	*46*	*23*	*713*
11	Wardha ...	392	100	141	16	7	151	441	134	60	5	3	247	374	122	78	13	16	174
12	Nagpur ...	1,073	285	302	27	23	486	632	238	72	3	...	322	547	162	134	14	4	251
	NAGPUR CITY ...	*531*	*126*	*141*	*1*	...	*264*	*159*	*79*	*6*	*1*	...	*104*	*69*	*21*	*6*	*1*	...	*42*
13	Chanda ...	622	116	361	12	68	145	260	60	64	7	7	136	260	96	25	7	3	139
14	Bhandara ...	362	145	118	75	25	99	303	56	101	6	5	146	153	57	5	9	...	91
15	Balaghat ...	8	3	3	...	...	2	87	37	19	...	...	31	87	20	1	2	...	57
	CHHATTISGARH DIVISION.	*200*	*69*	*77*	*6*	*2*	*54*	*192*	*73*	*29*	*2*	*1*	*90*	*1,172*	*401*	*49*	*18*	*2*	*722*
16	Raipur ...	20	17	5	1	...	4	100	34	10	...	1	56	856	301	40	3	1	515
17	Bilaspur ...	66	34	7	4	...	25	58	30	7	2	...	21	73	17	9	5	1	47
18	Drug ...	108	18	65	1	2	25	34	9	12	...	...	13	243	83	...	10	...	160
	Berar ...	**6,963**	**1,788**	**2,396**	**161**	**343**	**2,779**	**3,327**	**1,061**	**535**	**82**	**33**	**1,731**	**2,311**	**664**	**465**	**64**	**80**	**1,182**
19	Amraoti ...	2,066	455	883	67	166	728	870	280	141	15	2	449	774	180	157	8	15	428
20	Akola ...	1,284	356	309	30	31	620	1,163	381	154	41	6	628	609	164	138	14	25	307
21	Buldana ...	1,897	492	667	33	91	738	727	232	128	18	7	367	644	160	143	36	40	332
22	Yeotmal ...	1,716	486	537	25	55	693	567	168	112	8	18	287	284	142	27	6	...	115
	Feudatory States	**471**	**119**	**208**	**2**	**8**	**144**	**71**	**31**	**17**	**1**	...	**23**	**166**	**77**	**16**	**15**	...	**73**
23	Makrai ...	1	...	...	...	...	1	...	...	...	...	...	...	...	...	...	...	...	...
24	Bastar ...	24	8	9	...	...	7	10	1	5	...	...	4	59	17	10	7	...	28
25	Kanker ...	2	2	...	...	...	...	3	1	...	...	...	2	23	13	...	1	...	10
26	Nandgaon ...	1	1	...	...	...	...	7	4	...	1	...	3	6	5	...	...	...	1
27	Khairagarh ...	...	...	...	...	...	...	10	3	5	...	...	2	40	15	...	2	...	25
28	Chhuikhadan ...	...	...	...	...	...	...	...	...	...	...	...	...	1	1	...	...	...	...
29	Kawardha ...	...	...	...	...	...	...	3	3	...	...	...	...	...	...	...	...	...	...
30	Sakti ...	...	...	...	...	...	...	8	5	...	...	...	3	...	...	...	...	...	...
31	Raigarh ...	73	29	22	2	...	22	14	5	2	...	...	7	7	4	...	...	...	3
32	Sarangarh ...	86	1	72	...	8	13	...	...	...	...	...	...	15	11	...	5	...	4
33	Chang Bhakar ...	...	...	...	...	...	...	1	1	...	...	...	...	...	...	...	...	...	...
34	Korea ...	...	...	...	...	...	...	2	...	2	...	...	...	15	11	...	...	...	4
35	Surguja ...	154	73	27	...	...	54	13	8	3	...	...	2	...	...	...	...	...	...
36	Udaipur ...	7	5	...	...	...	2	...	...	...	...	...	...	...	...	...	...	...	...
37	Jashpur ...	123	...	78	...	...	45	...	...	...	...	...	...	...	...	...	...	...	...

# of livelihood, Part A.—General Table.

OF MATERIAL SUBSTANCES—*(continued)*.

Trade—*(continued)*.

in furniture. | Total order 36.—Trade in building materials.

126.—Trade in furniture, carpets, curtains and bedding.						127.—Hardware, cooking utensils, porcelain, crockery, glassware, bottles, articles for gardening, the cellar, etc.						128.—Trade in building materials (stones, bricks, plaster, cement, sand, tiles, thatch, etc.)						
Total workers and dependants.	Actual workers. Total. Males.	Actual workers. Total. Females.	Actual workers. Partially agriculturists. Males.	Actual workers. Partially agriculturists. Females.	Dependants.	Total workers and dependants.	Actual workers. Total. Males.	Actual workers. Total. Females.	Actual workers. Partially agriculturists. Males.	Actual workers. Partially agriculturists. Females.	Dependants.	Total workers and dependants.	Actual workers. Total. Males.	Actual workers. Total. Females.	Actual workers. Partially agriculturists. Males.	Actual workers. Partially agriculturists. Females.	Dependants.	Serial No.
1010	1011	1012	1013	1014	1015	1016	1017	1018	1019	1020	1021	1022	1023	1024	1025	1026	1027	
1,592	**318**	**585**	**55**	**97**	**689**	**4,022**	**1,491**	**252**	**90**	**10**	**2,279**	**1,955**	**660**	**288**	**92**	**60**	**1,007**	
1,592	**318**	**585**	**55**	**97**	**689**	**3,856**	**1,414**	**236**	**75**	**10**	**2,206**	**1,939**	**652**	**286**	**92**	**60**	**1,001**	
598	**133**	**238**	**19**	**23**	**227**	**2,539**	**935**	**118**	**47**	**4**	**1,486**	**730**	**241**	**148**	**56**	**49**	**341**	
7	*3*	*1*	...	...	*3*	*231*	*101*	*10*	*3*	...	*120*	*177*	*63*	*30*	*28*	*13*	*94*	
1	1	...	...	...	...	66	7	8	...	...	51	42	10	8	2	...	24	1
...	...	...	...	...	...	1	1	...	1	...	...	96	30	16	26	13	41	2
5	1	1	...	...	2	6	2	1	...	...	3	38	4	5	...	...	29	3
6	*1*	*1*	...	...	*3*	*6*	*2*	*1*	...	...	*3*	*23*	*2*	*5*	...	...	*16*	
...	...	...	...	...	...	35	27	...	...	...	8	1	...	1	...	...	...	4
1	1	...	...	...	...	123	64	1	2	...	58	...	...	...	...	...	...	5
85	*10*	*41*	...	*2*	*38*	*217*	*87*	*13*	...	...	*118*	*65*	*25*	*6*	*7*	...	*32*	
1	1	...	...	...	...	88	41	1	...	...	46	...	...	...	...	...	...	6
56	...	23	...	...	27	27	5	2	...	...	20	...	...	...	...	...	...	7
3	...	3	...	...	...	30	11	4	...	...	15	19	3	...	...	...	16	8
...	...	...	...	...	...	16	10	...	...	...	6	30	15	...	6	...	15	9
35	9	15	...	2	11	50	20	5	...	...	31	16	10	5	1	...	1	10
479	*118*	*180*	*19*	*20*	*181*	*942*	*348*	*63*	*26*	*3*	*531*	*464*	*145*	*103*	*21*	*35*	*206*	
118	22	65	7	16	26	261	100	13	6	...	148	80	39	21	6	4	29	11
321	76	115	11	4	130	226	86	19	3	...	121	271	87	57	12	29	127	12
45	*6*	*4*	*1*	...	*34*	*26*	*16*	*2*	...	...	*5*	*87*	*18*	*5*	...	...	*61*	
33	17	...	1	...	16	227	79	25	6	3	123	26	8	11	1	2	12	13
12	3	...	...	...	9	141	54	5	9	...	82	64	14	14	2	...	36	14
...	...	...	...	...	...	87	29	1	2	...	57	4	2	...	...	...	2	15
23	*2*	*16*	...	*1*	*5*	*1,149*	*399*	*33*	*18*	*1*	*717*	*34*	*16*	*10*	...	*1*	*9*	
19	2	12	...	...	5	837	290	28	3	1	510	15	13	...	...	...	2	16
4	...	4	...	1	...	60	17	5	5	...	47	15	2	6	...	1	7	17
...	...	...	...	...	...	243	83	...	10	...	160	4	...	4	...	...	...	18
994	**185**	**347**	**36**	**74**	**462**	**1,317**	**479**	**118**	**28**	**6**	**720**	**1,209**	**411**	**138**	**36**	**11**	**660**	
341	51	125	4	15	165	433	138	32	4	...	263	396	137	52	10	3	207	19
297	59	113	6	20	125	312	105	25	8	5	182	230	58	32	3	3	140	20
286	40	107	24	39	130	358	129	36	12	1	193	165	50	13	2	3	102	21
70	35	2	2	...	38	214	107	25	4	...	82	418	160	41	21	2	211	22
...	...	...	...	...	...	**166**	**77**	**16**	**15**	...	**73**	**16**	**8**	**2**	...	...	**6**	
...	...	...	...	...	...	...	...	...	...	...	...	...	...	...	...	...	...	23
...	...	...	...	...	...	59	17	16	7	...	26	1	...	1	...	...	...	24
...	...	...	...	...	...	23	13	...	1	...	10	...	...	...	...	...	...	25
...	...	...	...	...	...	6	5	...	...	...	1	...	...	...	...	...	...	26
...	...	...	...	...	...	40	15	...	2	...	25	...	...	...	...	...	...	27
...	...	...	...	...	...	1	1	...	...	...	...	...	...	...	...	...	...	28
...	...	...	...	...	...	...	...	...	...	...	...	...	...	...	...	...	...	29
...	...	...	...	...	...	...	...	...	...	...	...	...	...	...	...	...	...	30
...	...	...	...	...	...	7	4	...	...	...	3	...	...	...	...	...	...	31
...	...	...	...	...	...	15	11	...	5	...	4	6	5	...	...	...	1	32
...	...	...	...	...	...	...	...	...	...	...	...	...	...	...	...	...	...	33
...	...	...	...	...	...	15	11	...	...	...	4	3	1	...	...	...	2	34
...	...	...	...	...	...	...	...	...	...	...	...	6	2	1	...	...	3	35
...	...	...	...	...	...	...	...	...	...	...	...	...	...	...	...	...	...	36
...	...	...	...	...	...	...	...	...	...	...	...	...	...	...	...	...	...	37

TABLE XV.—Occupation or means

Serial No.	CLASS ... / SUB-CLASS ... / ORDER ...	CLASS B.—PREPARATION AND SUPPLY — Sub-Class V.—																	
		Total order 37.—Trade in means of transport.						Total order 38.—Trade in fuel.						Order 39.—Trade in articles					
		129.—Dealers and hirers of elephants, camels, horses, cattle, asses, mules, etc.; sellers (not makers) of carriages, saddlery, etc.						130.—Dealers in firewood, charcoal, coal, cowdung, etc.						Total order 39.					
	DISTRICT, CITY OR STATE.	Total workers and dependants.	Actual workers. Total. Males.	Actual workers. Total. Females.	Partially agriculturists. Males.	Partially agriculturists. Females.	Dependants.	Total workers and dependants.	Actual workers. Total. Males.	Actual workers. Total. Females.	Partially agriculturists. Males.	Partially agriculturists. Females.	Dependants.	Total workers and dependants.	Actual workers. Total. Males.	Actual workers. Total. Females.	Partially agriculturists. Males.	Partially agriculturists. Females.	Dependants.
	1	1028	1029	1030	1031	1032	1033	1034	1035	1036	1037	1038	1039	1040	1041	1042	1043	1044	1045
	Central Provinces and Berar.	**10,622**	**4,170**	**488**	**403**	**17**	**5,964**	**5,257**	**1,322**	**1,978**	**130**	**206**	**1,957**	**32,275**	**9,758**	**7,092**	**564**	**290**	**15,425**
	C. P. British Districts and Berar.	**9,859**	**3,869**	**399**	**388**	**16**	**5,591**	**4,475**	**1,227**	**1,570**	**127**	**167**	**1,678**	**29,765**	**9,125**	**6,102**	**555**	**285**	**14,538**
	C. P. British Districts.	**8,295**	**3,137**	**354**	**308**	**14**	**4,804**	**2,803**	**661**	**1,173**	**88**	**130**	**969**	**19,886**	**5,617**	**4,968**	**307**	**207**	**9,281**
	JUBBULPORE DIVISION	*3,873*	*1,446*	*165*	*140*	*12*	*2,262*	*699*	*148*	*266*	*14*	*4*	*285*	*4,585*	*1,233*	*1,151*	*57*	*50*	*2,171*
1	Saugor ...	2,041	741	83	84	1	1,217	250	26	137	1	4	87	930	217	268	12	6	445
2	Damoh ...	424	139	22	13	8	263	50	17	10	1	...	23	494	139	128	14	10	227
3	Jubbulpore ...	862	310	28	39	3	524	372	92	113	12	...	107	1,617	411	333	23	31	873
	JUBBULPORE CITY ...	*37*	*8*	...	...	...	*29*	*322*	*64*	*109*	...	...	*149*	*537*	*157*	*45*	...	...	*330*
4	Mandla ...	206	114	16	2	...	70	3	2	...	...	...	1	691	195	243	5	2	253
5	Seoni ...	340	142	16	2	...	182	24	11	6	...	...	7	858	271	209	3	1	373
	NERBUDDA DIVISION	*1,679*	*680*	*43*	*69*	*2*	*956*	*432*	*116*	*187*	*18*	*38*	*129*	*4,365*	*1,308*	*875*	*38*	*3*	*2,122*
6	Narsinghpur ...	292	107	5	14	...	180	31	17	3	12	...	11	897	223	252	8	3	422
7	Hoshangabad ...	387	171	12	22	...	204	41	12	14	...	...	15	1,252	404	231	4	...	617
8	Nimar ...	510	204	14	12	1	202	247	56	114	1	...	77	789	260	90	7	...	439
9	Betul ...	323	123	9	18	...	191	23	2	9	...	...	12	582	221	117	10	...	244
10	Chhindwara ...	167	75	3	3	1	89	90	29	47	5	38	14	845	200	185	9	...	400
	NAGPUR DIVISION ...	*2,057*	*766*	*102*	*64*	...	*1,189*	*1,048*	*294*	*323*	*56*	*86*	*431*	*6,121*	*1,834*	*1,171*	*137*	*80*	*3,116*
11	Wardha ...	127	50	1	4	...	70	207	48	79	23	32	80	1,235	399	153	21	9	683
12	Nagpur ...	388	178	8	21	...	202	554	158	160	6	31	230	2,079	629	349	17	6	1,101
	NAGPUR CITY ...	*44*	*9*	*2*	...	...	*33*	*253*	*93*	*20*	...	...	*140*	*624*	*210*	*49*	*2*	...	*366*
13	Chanda ...	869	278	40	18	...	551	95	12	48	3	2	35	923	238	270	41	54	415
14	Bhandara ...	261	101	19	18	...	141	167	69	32	28	20	60	1,327	418	252	32	8	657
15	Balaghat ...	412	150	34	3	...	219	25	7	4	...	...	14	557	150	147	26	3	260
	CHHATTISGARH DIVISION.	*680*	*245*	*44*	*35*	...	*397*	*624*	*103*	*397*	*1*	*3*	*124*	*4,795*	*1,182*	*1,751*	*75*	*77*	*1,872*
16	Raipur ...	222	72	11	8	...	139	258	27	138	...	1	98	2,200	565	743	22	26	892
17	Bilaspur ...	250	104	19	24	...	136	247	75	149	1	1	24	1,362	360	306	40	33	606
18	Drug ...	208	69	14	3	...	122	119	1	110	...	1	2	1,233	257	602	12	13	374
	Berar ...	**1,564**	**732**	**45**	**80**	**2**	**787**	**1,672**	**566**	**397**	**39**	**37**	**709**	**9,899**	**3,508**	**1,134**	**248**	**78**	**5,257**
19	Amraoti ...	453	180	5	7	...	268	669	263	100	30	15	306	3,305	1,121	483	92	30	1,699
20	Akola ...	243	122	2	19	1	119	523	182	123	8	12	218	2,511	851	207	62	24	1,453
21	Buldana ...	418	173	9	48	1	236	135	14	73	...	1	48	2,396	804	267	78	21	1,327
22	Yeotmal ...	450	257	29	6	...	164	345	107	101	1	9	137	1,687	732	177	16	3	778
	Feudatory States ...	**763**	**301**	**89**	**15**	**1**	**373**	**782**	**95**	**408**	**3**	**39**	**279**	**2,510**	**633**	**990**	**9**	**5**	**887**
23	Makrai ...	...	...	...	...	...	...	...	...	...	...	...	...	32	5	10	...	...	18
24	Bastar ...	306	125	48	2	...	133	95	28	36	...	...	31	509	145	205	4	2	158
25	Kanker ...	9	7	1	...	...	1	113	1	5	...	...	107	251	50	109	2	1	93
26	Nandgaon ...	42	17	1	1	1	24	120	25	77	3	3	18	339	80	120	...	1	130
27	Khairagarh ...	49	26	...	4	...	28	41	2	37	...	...	2	289	60	122	1	...	107
28	Chhuikhadan ...	19	7	...	1	...	12	6	1	5	...	...	...	89	13	50	...	...	26
29	Kawardha ...	8	4	...	...	...	4	1	...	1	...	...	...	100	13	49	...	...	38
30	Sakti ...	15	4	6	...	...	5	1	...	1	...	...	...	35	9	10	...	...	16
31	Raigarh ...	26	13	1	...	...	12	165	21	89	...	2	55	306	67	155	...	...	86
32	Sarangarh ...	3	1	1	...	...	1	132	14	114	...	34	4	120	81	49	...	...	40
33	Chang Bhakar ...	...	...	...	...	...	...	...	...	...	...	...	...	35	9	16	...	...	10
34	Korea ...	28	7	3	...	...	18	...	...	...	...	...	...	81	15	31	...	1	35
35	Surguja ...	55	15	6	...	...	34	83	...	27	...	...	56	207	97	30	2	...	80
36	Udaipur ...	33	18	2	...	...	13	...	...	...	...	...	...	55	19	11	...	...	25
37	Jashpur ...	170	57	20	7	...	93	25	3	16	...	...	6	60	20	24	...	...	16

# of livelihood, Part A.—General Table.

OF MATERIAL SUBSTANCES—(continued).

Trade—(continued).

of luxury and those pertaining to letters and the arts and sciences.

131.—Dealers in precious stones, jewellery (real and imitation), clocks, optical instruments, etc.						132.—Dealers in common bangles, bead necklaces, fans, small articles, toys, hunting and fishing tackle, flowers, etc.						133.—Publishers, booksellers, stationers, dealers in music, pictures, musical instruments and curiosities.						
Total workers and dependants.	Actual workers.				Dependants.	Total workers and dependants.	Actual workers.				Dependants.	Total workers and dependants.	Actual workers.				Dependants.	Serial No.
	Total.		Partially agriculturists.				Total.		Partially agriculturists.				Total.		Partially agriculturists.			
	Males.	Females.	Males.	Females.			Males.	Females.	Males.	Females.			Males.	Females.	Males.	Females.		
1046	1047	1048	1049	1050	1051	1052	1053	1054	1055	1056	1057	1058	1059	1060	1061	1062	1063	
1,649	**616**	**286**	**53**	**27**	**747**	**29,391**	**8,676**	**6,777**	**492**	**263**	**13,938**	**1,235**	**466**	**29**	**19**	...	**740**	
1,585	**584**	**282**	**53**	**27**	**719**	**26,945**	**8,075**	**5,791**	**483**	**258**	**13,079**	**1,235**	**466**	**29**	**19**	...	**740**	
1,056	**364**	**187**	**46**	**27**	**505**	**18,105**	**4,976**	**4,762**	**249**	**180**	**8,367**	**705**	**277**	**19**	**12**	...	**409**	
169	*82*	*26*	*2*	...	*81*	*4,283*	*1,114*	*1,151*	*55*	*50*	*2,018*	*113*	*37*	*4*	...	...	*72*	
53	22	7	1	...	24	843	186	257	11	6	400	34	9	4	...	...	21	1
14	1	1	...	...	12	477	137	127	14	10	213	3	1	...	...	...	2	2
46	21	3	1	...	22	1,505	367	330	22	31	808	66	23	...	...	...	43	3
26	*12*	*1*	...	...	*13*	*460*	*127*	*47*	...	...	*256*	*49*	*15*	...	...	...	*31*	
10	5	5	...	...	...	676	188	228	5	2	250	5	2	...	...	...	3	4
66	33	10	...	...	23	782	236	199	3	1	347	5	2	...	...	...	3	5
200	*76*	*16*	*5*	...	*105*	*4,053*	*1,229*	*857*	*31*	*3*	*1,967*	*112*	*63*	*2*	*2*	...	*47*	
19	9	1	1	...	9	873	211	251	7	3	411	5	3	...	...	...	2	6
63	21	9	...	...	33	1,148	365	222	4	...	561	41	18	...	...	...	23	7
77	30	1	...	...	46	663	199	88	5	...	376	49	31	1	2	...	17	8
11	2	5	...	...	4	565	213	112	10	...	240	6	6	...	...	...	...	9
30	14	...	4	...	16	804	241	184	5	...	379	11	5	1	...	...	5	10
512	*162*	*110*	*39*	*27*	*240*	*5,327*	*1,556*	*1,051*	*90*	*53*	*2,720*	*252*	*116*	*10*	*5*	...	*156*	
109	33	29	1	...	47	1,087	352	120	20	9	615	39	14	4	...	...	21	11
152	42	22	2	...	88	1,779	525	324	12	6	930	148	62	3	3	...	83	12
110	*32*	*15*	...	...	*60*	*416*	*139*	*25*	...	...	*249*	*95*	*39*	*3*	*2*	...	*56*	
139	37	37	24	20	65	741	186	230	15	28	325	43	15	8	2	...	25	13
69	24	17	...	1	28	1,212	373	235	20	7	604	46	21	...	3	...	25	14
43	26	5	12	...	12	508	120	142	14	3	246	6	4	...	...	...	2	15
155	*44*	*35*	...	...	*76*	*4,442*	*1,077*	*1,703*	*73*	*74*	*1,662*	*198*	*61*	*3*	*2*	...	*134*	
99	35	18	...	...	46	2,011	488	722	22	28	801	90	42	3	...	...	45	16
53	7	16	...	...	30	1,222	342	380	38	33	500	87	11	...	2	...	76	17
3	2	1	...	...	...	1,209	247	601	13	13	361	21	8	...	...	...	13	18
529	**220**	**95**	**7**	...	**214**	**8,840**	**3,099**	**1,029**	**234**	**78**	**4,712**	**530**	**189**	**10**	**7**	...	**331**	
270	87	69	1	...	114	2,843	960	406	89	30	1,477	190	74	8	2	...	108	19
86	39	10	4	...	87	2,321	775	196	55	24	1,350	104	37	1	3	...	66	20
54	28	...	2	...	26	2,217	738	267	75	21	1,212	127	38	...	1	...	89	21
119	66	16	...	...	37	1,459	626	160	15	3	673	109	40	1	1	...	68	22
64	**32**	**4**	...	...	**28**	**2,446**	**601**	**986**	**9**	**5**	**859**	...	...	...	...	...	...	
...	...	...	...	...	...	33	5	10	...	...	18	...	...	...	...	...	...	23
2	2	...	...	...	...	506	143	201	4	2	158	...	...	...	...	...	...	24
2	2	...	...	...	...	249	48	108	2	1	93	...	...	...	...	...	...	25
17	4	3	...	...	10	322	76	117	...	1	129	...	...	...	...	...	...	26
...	...	...	...	...	...	280	60	122	1	...	107	...	...	...	...	...	...	27
...	...	...	...	...	...	89	13	50	...	...	26	...	...	...	...	...	...	28
...	...	...	...	...	...	100	13	49	...	...	38	...	...	...	...	...	...	29
...	...	...	...	...	...	35	9	10	...	...	10	...	...	...	...	...	...	30
...	...	...	...	...	...	308	67	155	...	...	86	...	...	...	...	...	...	31
5	2	1	...	...	2	115	29	48	...	...	38	...	...	...	...	...	...	32
...	...	...	...	...	...	85	9	10	...	...	10	...	...	...	...	...	...	33
16	4	...	...	...	12	65	11	31	...	1	23	...	...	...	...	...	...	34
22	18	...	...	...	4	185	79	30	2	...	76	...	...	...	...	...	...	35
...	...	...	...	...	...	55	19	11	...	...	25	...	...	...	...	...	...	36
...	...	...	...	...	...	60	20	24	...	...	16	...	...	...	...	...	...	37

TABLE XV.—Occupation or means

Serial No.	CLASS ...	CLASS B.—PREPARATION AND SUPPLY																	
	SUB-CLASS ...	Sub-Class V.—																	
	ORDER ...	Total Order 40.—Trade in refuse matter.						Order 41.—Trade											
		134.—Dealers in rags, stable refuse, etc.						Total order 41.						135.—Shop-keepers otherwise unspecified.					
	DISTRICT, CITY OR STATE.	Total workers and dependants.	Actual workers. Total. Males.	Actual workers. Total. Females.	Partially agriculturists. Males.	Partially agriculturists. Females.	Dependants.	Total workers and dependants.	Actual workers. Total. Males.	Actual workers. Total. Females.	Partially agriculturists. Males.	Partially agriculturists. Females.	Dependants.	Total workers and dependants.	Actual workers. Total. Males.	Actual workers. Total. Females.	Partially agriculturists. Males.	Partially agriculturists. Females.	Dependants.
	1	1064	1065	1066	1067	1068	1069	1070	1071	1072	1073	1074	1075	1076	1077	1078	1079	1080	1081
	Central Provinces and Berar.	**597**	**299**	**5**	**18**	...	**293**	**11,624**	**4,601**	**1,170**	**421**	**234**	**5,853**	**5,189**	**2,094**	**490**	**62**	**142**	**2,605**
	C. P. British Districts and Berar.	**593**	**296**	**4**	**18**	...	**293**	**9,972**	**4,011**	**888**	**372**	**113**	**5,073**	**4,730**	**1,916**	**305**	**61**	**21**	**2,509**
	C. P. British Districts.	**528**	**266**	**3**	**17**	...	**259**	**6,869**	**2,666**	**682**	**281**	**89**	**3,521**	**3,264**	**1,306**	**255**	**31**	**20**	**1,703**
	JUBBULPORE DIVISION	*120*	*36*	...	...	...	*84*	*1,356*	*514*	*80*	*6*	*1*	*761*	*944*	*352*	*42*	...	...	*550*
1	Saugor ...	9	2	...	...	...	7	106	47	15	...	...	44	5	3	...	...	...	2
2	Damoh ...	...	...	...	...	...	...	134	38	12	...	...	84	58	10	...	...	...	48
3	Jubbulpore ...	105	33	...	...	...	72	889	327	35	3	1	527	825	307	34	...	...	484
	JUBBULPORE CITY ...	*105*	*33*	...	...	...	*72*	*794*	*293*	*32*	...	*1*	*469*	*772*	*256*	*31*	...	...	*455*
4	Mandla ...	...	...	...	...	...	...	95	54	11	2	...	30	36	25	6	...	...	5
5	Seoni ...	6	1	...	...	...	5	131	48	7	...	...	76	20	7	2	...	...	11
	NERBUDDA DIVISION	*1*	...	...	...	...	*1*	*641*	*222*	*86*	*16*	*2*	*333*	*361*	*57*	*69*	*3*	*2*	*305*
6	Narsinghpur ...	1	...	...	...	...	1	25	10	6	...	...	9	1	...	...	...	...	1
7	Hoshangabad ...	...	...	...	...	...	...	98	40	5	1	...	53	49	19	5	...	...	25
8	Nimar ...	...	...	...	...	...	...	210	83	12	6	1	115	123	32	6	...	1	85
9	Betul ...	...	...	...	...	...	...	83	45	2	3	...	36	18	10	...	...	...	2
10	Chhindwara ...	...	...	...	...	...	...	225	44	61	6	1	120	170	20	58	3	1	92
	NAGPUR DIVISION ...	*407*	*230*	*3*	*17*	...	*174*	*3,812*	*1,493*	*355*	*247*	*75*	*1,964*	*1,581*	*669*	*75*	*37*	*8*	*837*
11	Wardha ...	...	...	...	...	...	...	727	304	104	41	28	319	147	78	2	...	...	67
12	Nagpur ...	15	8	3	...	...	4	1,417	579	140	41	23	698	898	403	41	11	7	454
	NAGPUR CITY ...	...	...	...	...	...	...	*403*	*167*	*13*	*2*	...	*223*	*365*	*154*	*13*	*2*	...	*201*
13	Chanda ...	392	222	...	17	...	170	1,448	525	83	162	23	840	468	158	27	15	1	283
14	Bhandara ...	...	...	...	...	...	...	163	62	24	3	1	77	38	19	5	1	...	14
15	Balaghat ...	...	...	...	...	...	...	57	23	4	...	...	30	30	11	...	...	...	19
	CHHATTISGARH DIVISION.	...	...	...	...	...	...	*1,061*	*437*	*161*	*13*	*11*	*463*	*375*	*195*	*69*	*1*	*10*	*111*
16	Raipur ...	...	...	...	...	...	...	321	161	16	4	...	144	111	77	8	...	...	26
17	Bilaspur ...	...	...	...	...	...	...	419	166	82	6	10	171	228	95	56	1	9	77
18	Drug ...	...	...	...	...	...	...	321	110	63	3	1	148	39	26	5	...	1	8
	Berar ...	**65**	**30**	**1**	**1**	...	**34**	**3,103**	**1,345**	**206**	**91**	**24**	**1,552**	**1,466**	**610**	**50**	**30**	**1**	**806**
19	Amraoti ...	1	1	...	...	...	...	762	336	65	13	7	361	250	108	11	5	...	131
20	Akola ...	2	1	1	...	...	...	861	341	55	29	5	465	496	169	19	4	1	308
21	Buldana ...	62	28	...	1	...	34	470	169	26	15	7	275	272	109	6	5	...	157
22	Yeotmal ...	...	...	...	...	...	...	1,010	499	60	34	5	451	448	224	14	16	...	210
	Feudatory States ...	**4**	**3**	**1**	...	...	...	**1,652**	**590**	**282**	**49**	**121**	**780**	**459**	**178**	**185**	**1**	**121**	**96**
23	Makrai ...	...	...	...	...	...	...	10	8	...	...	...	2	8	6	...	...	...	2
24	Bastar ...	...	...	...	...	...	...	171	87	18	3	...	66	102	57	15	1	...	30
25	Kanker ...	...	...	...	...	...	...	54	37	2	1	...	15	33	20	...	...	...	7
26	Nandgaon ...	...	...	...	...	...	...	29	2	10	...	...	17	28	2	9	...	...	17
27	Khairagarh ...	3	3	...	...	...	...	116	53	4	3	...	59	19	14	...	...	...	5
28	Chhuikhadan ...	...	...	...	...	...	...	...	...	...	...	...	...	...	...	...	...	...	...
29	Kawardha ...	...	...	...	...	...	...	31	4	6	1	...	21	...	...	...	...	...	...
30	Sakti ...	1	...	1	...	...	...	56	10	16	...	...	30	...	...	...	...	...	...
31	Raigarh ...	...	...	...	...	...	...	238	28	155	...	121	55	173	...	156	...	121	18
32	Sarangarh ...	...	...	...	...	...	...	796	272	53	40	...	471	...	...	...	...	...	...
33	Chang Bhakar ...	...	...	...	...	...	...	12	7	...	...	...	5	8	6	...	...	...	2
34	Korea ...	...	...	...	...	...	...	21	17	...	...	...	4	20	16	...	...	...	4
35	Surguja ...	...	...	...	...	...	...	32	11	1	...	...	20	9	3	...	...	...	6
36	Udaipur ...	...	...	...	...	...	...	3	3	...	1	...	...	1	1	...	...	...	...
37	Jashpur ...	...	...	...	...	...	...	83	51	17	...	...	15	58	47	6	...	...	5

# of livelihood, Part A.—General Table.

OF MATERIAL SUBSTANCES.—(*concluded*).

Trade—(*concluded*).

of other sorts.

136.—Itinerant traders, pedlars, hawkers, etc.						137.—Conjurors, acrobats, fortune-tellers, reciters, exhibitors of curiosities and wild animals.						138.—Other trades (including farmers of pounds, tolls and markets).						
Total workers and dependants.	Actual workers.				Dependants.	Total workers and dependants.	Actual workers.				Dependants.	Total workers and dependants.	Actual workers.				Dependants.	Serial No.
	Total.		Partially agriculturists.				Total.		Partially agriculturists.				Total.		Partially agriculturists.			
	Males.	Females.	Males.	Females.			Males.	Females.	Males.	Females.			Males.	Females.	Males.	Females.		
1082	1083	1084	1085	1086	1087	1088	1089	1090	1091	1092	1093	1094	1095	1096	1097	1098	1099	
49	**21**	**1**	**2**	...	**27**	**5,461**	**2,194**	**614**	**336**	**83**	**2,653**	**925**	**292**	**65**	**21**	**9**	**568**	
49	**21**	**1**	**2**	...	**27**	**4,290**	**1,792**	**518**	**288**	**83**	**1,980**	**903**	**282**	**64**	**21**	**9**	**557**	
12	**7**	**1**	...	...	**4**	**3,063**	**1,198**	**376**	**242**	**68**	**1,489**	**530**	**155**	**50**	**8**	**1**	**325**	
1	*1*	...	...	...	...	*253*	*125*	*30*	*2*	...	*12[illegible]*	*127*	*36*	*8*	*3*	*1*	*83*	
1	1	...	...	...	...	65	34	10	...	...	21	35	9	5	...	...	21	1
...	...	...	...	...	...	61	24	10	...	...	27	15	4	2	...	...	9	2
...	...	...	...	...	...	24	9	...	...	...	15	40	11	1	3	1	28	3
...	...	...	...	...	...	*7*	*3*	...	...	...	*4*	*15*	*4*	*1*	...	*1*	*10*	
...	...	...	...	...	...	51	26	5	2	...	20	8	3	...	...	...	5	4
...	...	...	...	...	...	82	32	5	...	...	45	29	9	...	...	...	20	5
1	...	*1*	...	...	...	*136*	*75*	*9*	*10*	...	*49*	*143*	*57*	*7*	*3*	...	*79*	
...	...	...	...	...	...	14	6	6	...	...	7	10	4	...	...	...	6	6
...	...	...	...	...	...	20	10	...	...	...	10	29	11	...	1	...	18	7
1	...	1	...	...	...	24	22	1	4	...	1	62	20	4	2	...	29	8
...	...	...	...	...	...	36	18	...	3	...	18	20	11	2	...	...	16	9
...	...	...	...	...	...	42	22	2	3	...	18	13	2	1	...	...	10	10
10	*6*	...	...	...	*4*	*2,043*	*775*	*253*	*218*	*67*	*1,013*	*178*	*40*	*27*	*2*	...	*111*	
6	5	...	...	...	1	527	208	93	40	28	220	47	13	9	1	...	25	11
3	...	...	...	...	3	427	161	85	30	16	181	89	15	14	...	...	60	12
...	...	...	...	...	...	*22*	*11*	...	...	...	*11*	*13*	*2*	...	...	...	*11*	
...	...	...	...	...	...	950	362	52	147	22	542	24	5	4	...	...	15	13
1	1	...	...	...	...	106	35	19	1	1	52	18	7	...	1	...	11	14
...	...	...	...	...	...	27	12	4	...	...	11	...	...	...	...	...	...	15
...	...	...	...	...	...	*601*	*217*	*84*	*17*	*1*	*306*	*83*	*29*	*5*	...	...	*52*	
...	...	...	...	...	...	178	73	8	4	...	97	32	11	...	...	...	21	16
...	...	...	...	...	...	167	64	18	5	1	85	24	7	8	...	...	9	17
...	...	...	...	...	...	250	80	58	3	...	118	20	4	...	...	...	22	18
37	**14**	...	**2**	...	**23**	**1.227**	**594**	**142**	**46**	**15**	**491**	**373**	**127**	**14**	**13**	**8**	**232**	
...	...	...	...	...	...	408	198	52	5	7	157	104	80	1	3	...	77	19
1	1	...	...	...	...	252	110	36	10	4	100	112	55	...	6	...	57	20
27	11	...	2	...	16	76	26	8	4	...	42	95	23	12	4	7	60	21
9	2	...	...	...	7	491	254	45	18	4	192	62	19	1	...	1	42	22
...	...	...	...	...	...	**1,171**	**402**	**96**	**48**	...	**673**	**22**	**10**	**1**	...	...	**11**	
...	...	...	...	...	...	2	2	...	...	...	...	...	...	...	...	...	...	23
...	...	...	...	...	...	69	30	3	2	...	36	...	...	...	...	...	...	24
...	...	...	...	...	...	20	10	2	1	...	8	1	1	...	...	...	...	25
...	...	...	...	...	...	1	...	1	...	...	...	...	...	...	...	...	...	26
...	...	...	...	...	...	79	31	3	8	...	45	18	8	1	...	...	9	27
...	...	...	...	...	...	...	...	...	...	...	...	...	...	...	...	...	...	28
...	...	...	...	...	...	81	4	6	1	...	21	...	...	...	...	...	...	29
...	...	...	...	...	...	56	10	16	...	...	30	...	...	...	...	...	...	30
...	...	...	...	...	...	62	27	...	...	...	35	3	1	...	...	...	2	31
...	...	...	...	...	...	796	272	53	40	...	471	...	...	...	...	...	...	32
...	...	...	...	...	...	4	1	...	...	...	3	...	...	...	...	...	...	33
...	...	...	...	...	...	1	1	...	...	...	...	...	...	...	...	...	...	34
...	...	...	...	...	...	23	8	1	...	...	14	...	...	...	...	...	...	35
...	...	...	...	...	...	2	2	...	1	...	...	...	...	...	...	...	...	36
...	...	...	...	...	...	25	4	11	...	...	10	...	...	...	...	...	...	37

TABLE XV.—Occupation or means

Serial No.	CLASS / SUB-CLASS / ORDER	CLASS C.—PUBLIC ADMINISTRATION												
		Sub-Class VI.—												
		Order 41.—Trade of other sorts— (*concluded*).												
		Total Class C.						Total Sub-Class VI.						
	DISTRICT, CITY OR STATE.	Total workers and dependants.	Actual workers. Total. Males.	Actual workers. Total. Females.	Actual workers. Partially agriculturists. Males.	Actual workers. Partially agriculturists. Females.	Dependants.	Total workers and dependants.	Actual workers. Total. Males.	Actual workers. Total. Females.	Actual workers. Partially agriculturists. Males.	Actual workers. Partially agriculturists. Females.	Dependants.	Total workers and dependants
	1	1100	1101	1102	1103	1104	1105	1106	1107	1108	1109	1110	1111	1112
	Central Provinces and Berar.	**522,515**	**197,785**	**31,162**	**30,855**	**2,710**	**293.568**	**173,740**	**70,418**	**2.577**	**14,756**	**389**	**100,745**	**11,321**
	C.P. British Districts and Berar.	**483,353**	**183,838**	**27,782**	**28,944**	**2,584**	**271,733**	**157,311**	**65,046**	**1,973**	**13,567**	**360**	**90,292**	**11,286**
	C. P. British Districts	**345,622**	**128,149**	**23,033**	**20,769**	**2,089**	**194.440**	**112,739**	**45,355**	**1,637**	**11.680**	**315**	**65,747**	**11,207**
	JUBBULPORE DIVISION	*91,882*	*35,098*	*6,412*	*4,78[illegible]*	*585*	*50,372*	*33,004*	*15,709*	*259*	*2,898*	*36*	*17,036*	*9,157*
1	Saugor ...	24,567	9,208	1,835	1,628	280	13.434	8,316	4,073	33	1,012	3	4,210	2,605
2	Damoh ...	12,871	4,099	1,415	791	192	7,357	3,036	1,003	16	273	3	2,017	6
3	Jubblupore ...	33,381	14,314	1,765	1,427	70	17,302	13,642	7,804	59	890	15	5,779	6,524
	JUBBULPORE CITY ...	*17,217*	*8,028*	*426*	*57*	*1*	*8,163*	*7,834*	*5,857*	...	*30*	...	*1,977*	*6,452*
4	Mandla ...	9,918	3,403	614	526	20	5,901	4,084	1,351	97	418	12	2,636	16
5	Seoni ...	11,145	3,984	783	410	14	6,378	3,926	1,478	54	307	[illegible]	2,394	6
	NERBUDDA DIVISION	*75,879*	*27,141*	*3,590*	*3,994*	*253*	*45,148*	*22,593*	*8,129*	*163*	*2,341*	*26*	*14,601*	*238*
6	Narsinghpur ...	14,512	4,614	796	1,030	62	9,102	4,310	1,352	11	594	3	2,947	...
7	Hoshangabad ...	22,275	7,656	898	1,026	40	13,721	5,918	2,034	21	504	...	3,863	197
8	Nimar ...	15,297	6,182	652	661	43	8,463	4,309	1,721	13	371	2	2,575	74
9	Betul ...	10,100	3,742	510	665	50	5,854	3,434	1,223	44	477	12	2,167	...
10	Chhindwara ...	13,689	4,947	734	612	79	8.008	4,922	1,799	74	395	9	3,049	17
	NAGPUR DIVISION ...	*106,213*	*41,003*	*6,105*	*6,902*	*726*	*59,102*	*31,337*	*12,729*	*348*	*2,917*	*67*	*18,260*	*1,742*
11	Wardha ...	16,280	6,521	743	993	134	9,016	3,962	1,603	16	194	8	2,343	1
12	Nagpur ...	40,780	16,171	2,421	1,894	181	22,188	9,902	4,612	127	826	7	5,163	1,725
	NAGPUR CITY ...	*13,140*	*4,655*	*427*	*169*	*1*	*8,025*	*1,840*	*790*	*28*	*49*	...	*1,022*	*134*
13	Chanda ...	18,606	7,023	906	1,615	170	10,677	6,179	2,261	54	558	24	3,864	3
14	Bhandara ...	20,295	7,48[illegible]	1,273	1,728	161	11,539	8,019	3,003	67	978	19	4,949	9
15	Balaghat ...	10,252	3,805	765	672	80	5,682	3,275	1,250	84	361	9	1,941	4
	CHHATTISGARH DIVISION.	*71,648*	*24,907*	*6,923*	*5,055*	*495*	*39,818*	*25,505*	*8,788*	*867*	*3,527*	*186*	*15,850*	*20*
16	Raipur ...	32,080	11,153	2,019	2,402	194	18,608	11,678	4.038	809	1,735	68	7,331	11
17	Bilaspur ...	20,795	7,658	2,274	1,011	229	10,863	6,657	2,396	306	1,072	102	3,955	6
18	Drug ...	18,173	6,096	1,730	1,072	72	10,347	7,170	2,354	252	720	16	4,564	3
	Berar ...	**137,731**	**55,689**	**4.749**	**8,175**	**495**	**77.293**	**44.572**	**19,691**	**336**	**1,887**	**45**	**24.545**	**79**
19	Amraoti ...	40,588	16,003	1,864	2,003	180	22,721	11,021	5,053	116	384	14	5,852	38
20	Akola ...	37,087	15,425	1,226	2,773	137	20,436	11,495	5,334	76	712	11	6,085	24
21	Buldana ...	34,367	13,473	895	2,418	105	19,999	12,052	5,024	92	602	17	6,936	15
22	Yeotmal ...	25,688	10,788	764	981	64	14,137	10,004	4,280	52	189	3	5,672	2
	Feudatory States ...	**39,162**	**13,947**	**3,380**	**1.911**	**126**	**21.835**	**16.429**	**5,372**	**604**	**1,189**	**29**	**10.453**	**35**
23	Makrai ...	884	378	20	32	2	486	333	128	7	4	...	198	4
24	Bastar ...	4,045	1,439	281	76	4	2,325	1,941	666	87	35	1	1,188	1
25	Kanker ...	2,441	956	278	50	5	1,207	1.270	467	162	34	5	641	18
26	Nandgaon ...	4,578	1,621	420	206	43	2,537	1,864	623	89	125	14	1,152	11
27	Khairagarh ...	4,937	1,648	412	198	15	2,877	1,881	608	34	104	1	1,239	...
28	Chhuikhadan ...	1,285	403	57	39	...	825	475	126	...	20	...	349	...
29	Kawardha ...	2,520	834	202	192	11	1,484	994	331	52	131	3	611	...
30	Sakti ...	760	277	138	46	10	354	89	30	1	12	...	58	...
31	Raigarh ...	5,265	1,706	468	616	12	3,091	2,830	753	24	567	4	2,053	...
32	Sarangarh ...	3,173	1,039	264	174	7	1,870	1,518	471	12	74	...	1,035	...
33	Chang Bhakar ...	447	183	72	31	4	187	85	30	12	6	...	43	...
34	Korea ...	1,007	433	95	33	...	479	418	139	21	9	...	258	...
35	Surguja ...	4,920	1,914	295	69	4	2,720	1,931	720	64	13	1	1,147	...
36	Udaipur ...	1,177	431	104	34	3	642	486	136	23	27	...	327	..
37	Jashpur ...	1,710	685	274	115	6	751	314	144	16	28	...	154	1

# of livelihood, Part A.—General Table.

AND LIBERAL ARTS.

Public Force.

Order 42.—Army. Total order 42. Actual workers. Total. Males.	Total order 42. Actual workers. Total. Females.	Total order 42. Actual workers. Partially agriculturists. Males.	Total order 42. Actual workers. Partially agriculturists. Females.	Total order 42. Dependants.	139.—Army (Imperial). Total workers and dependants.	139. Actual workers. Total. Males.	139. Actual workers. Total. Females.	139. Actual workers. Partially agriculturists. Males.	139. Actual workers. Partially agriculturists. Females.	139. Dependants.	140.—Army (Native States). Total workers and dependants.	140. Actual workers. Total. Males.	140. Actual workers. Total. Females.	140. Actual workers. Partially agriculturists. Males.	140. Actual workers. Partially agriculturists. Females.	140. Dependants.	Total order 43.—Navy. 141.—Navy. Total workers and dependants.	141. Actual workers. Total. Males.	141. Actual workers. Total. Females.	141. Actual workers. Partially agriculturists. Males.	141. Actual workers. Partially agriculturists. Females.	141. Dependants.	Serial No.
1113	1114	1115	1116	1117	1118	1119	1120	1121	1122	1123	1124	1125	1126	1127	1128	1129	1130	1131	1132	1133	1134	1135	
9,084	**31**	**468**	...	**2,206**	**10,103**	**8,035**	**31**	**468**	...	**2,037**	**1,218**	**1,049**	...	...	...	**169**	**16**	...	**4**	...	...	**12**	
9,066	**31**	**468**	...	**2,189**	**10,099**	**8,031**	**31**	**468**	...	**2,037**	**1,187**	**1,035**	...	...	...	**152**	**12**	...	...	...	...	**12**	
9,040	**31**	**467**	...	**2,136**	**10,025**	**8,008**	**31**	**467**	...	**1,986**	**1,182**	**1,032**	...	...	...	**150**	...	...	...	...	...	...	
7,431	*14*	*462*	...	*1,712*	*7,996*	*6,418*	*14*	*463*	...	*1,563*	*1,161*	*1,013*	...	...	...	*148*	...	...	...	...	...	...	
1,994	14	439	...	507	1,991	1,474	14	439	...	503	614	520	...	...	...	94	...	...	...	...	...	...	1
5	...	...	...	1	6	5	...	...	...	1	...	...	...	...	...	...	...	...	...	...	...	...	2
5,411	...	23	...	1,113	5,978	4,910	...	23	...	1,059	546	492	...	...	...	54	...	...	...	...	...	...	3
5,361	...	*23*	...	*1,091*	*5,918*	*4,879*	...	*23*	...	*1,039*	*533*	*452*	...	...	...	*52*	...	...	...	...	...	...	
15	...	2	..	1	15	14	...	2	...	1	1	1	...	...	...	...	...	...	...	...	...	...	4
6	...	...	...	...	6	6	...	...	...	...	...	...	...	...	...	...	...	...	...	...	...	...	5
216	*3*	*2*	...	*69*	*267*	*197*	*3*	*2*	...	*67*	*21*	*19*	...	...	...	*2*	...	...	...	...	...	...	
...	...	...	...	...	...	...	...	...	...	...	...	...	...	...	...	...	...	...	...	...	...	...	6
143	...	1	...	54	176	124	...	1	...	52	21	19	...	...	...	2	...	...	...	...	...	...	7
66	2	...	...	6	74	66	2	...	...	6	...	...	...	...	...	...	...	...	...	...	...	...	8
...	...	...	...	...	...	...	...	...	...	...	...	...	...	...	...	...	...	...	...	...	...	...	9
7	1	1	...	9	17	7	1	1	...	9	...	...	...	...	...	...	.	...	...	...	...	...	10
1,381	*14*	...	...	*337*	*1,742*	*1,381*	*14*	...	...	*337*	...	...	...	...	...	...	...	...	...	...	...	...	
1	...	...	...	...	1	1	...	...	...	...	...	...	...	...	...	...	...	...	...	...	...	...	11
1,374	14	...	...	337	1,725	1,374	14	...	...	337	...	...	...	...	...	...	...	...	...	...	...	...	12
101	...	...	...	*23*	*124*	*101*	...	...	...	*23*	...	...	...	...	...	...	...	...	...	...	...	...	
3	...	...	...	...	3	3	...	...	...	...	...	...	...	...	...	...	...	...	...	...	...	...	13
2	...	...	...	7	9	2	...	...	...	7	...	...	...	...	...	...	...	...	...	...	...	...	14
1	...	...	...	3	4	1	...	...	...	3	...	...	...	...	...	...	...	...	...	...	...	...	15
12	...	*1*	...	*8*	*20*	*12*	...	*1*	...	*8*	...	...	...	...	...	...	...	...	...	...	...	...	
7	...	1	...	4	11	7	...	1	...	4	...	...	...	...	...	...	...	...	...	...	...	...	16
5	...	...	...	1	6	5	...	...	...	1	...	...	...	...	...	...	...	...	...	...	...	...	17
...	...	...	...	3	3	...	...	...	...	3	...	...	..	...	...	...	...	...	...	...	...	...	18
26	...	**1**	...	**53**	**74**	**23**	...	**1**	...	**51**	**5**	**8**	...	...	...	**2**	**12**	...	...	...	...	**12**	
15	...	...	...	23	33	12	...	...	...	21	5	8	...	...	...	2	...	...	...	...	...	...	19
4	...	1	...	20	24	4	...	1	...	20	...	...	...	...	...	...	12	...	...	...	...	12	20
5	.	...	...	10	15	5	...	...	...	10	...	...	...	...	...	...	...	...	...	...	...	...	21
2	...	...	...	...	2	2	...	...	...	...	...	...	...	...	...	...	...	...	...	...	...	...	22
18	...	...	...	**17**	**4**	**4**	...	...	...	...	**31**	**14**	...	...	...	**17**	**4**	...	**4**	...	...	...	
4	...	...	...	...	4	4	...	...	...	...	...	...	...	...	...	...	...	...	...	...	...	...	23
...	...	...	...	1	...	...	...	...	...	...	1	...	...	...	...	1	4	...	4	...	...	...	24
10	...	...	...	8	...	...	...	...	...	...	18	10	...	...	...	8	...	...	...	...	...	...	25
3	...	...	...	8	...	...	...	...	...	...	11	3	...	...	...	8	...	...	...	...	...	...	26
...	...	...	...	...	...	...	...	...	...	...	...	...	...	...	...	...	...	...	...	...	...	...	27
...	...	...	...	...	...	...	...	...	...	...	...	...	...	...	...	...	...	...	...	...	...	...	28
...	...	...	...	...	...	...	...	...	...	...	...	...	...	...	...	...	...	...	...	...	...	...	29
...	...	...	...	...	...	...	...	...	...	...	...	...	...	...	...	...	...	...	...	...	...	...	30
...	...	...	...	...	...	...	...	...	...	...	...	...	...	...	...	...	...	...	...	...	...	...	31
...	...	...	...	...	...	...	...	...	...	...	...	...	...	...	...	...	...	...	...	...	...	...	32
...	...	...	...	...	...	...	...	...	...	...	...	...	...	...	...	...	...	...	...	...	...	...	33
...	...	...	...	...	...	...	...	...	...	...	...	...	...	...	...	...	...	...	...	...	...	...	34
...	...	...	...	...	...	...	...	...	...	...	...	...	...	...	...	...	...	...	...	...	...	...	35
...	...	...	...	...	...	...	...	...	...	...	...	...	...	...	...	...	...	...	...	...	...	...	36
1	...	...	...	...	...	...	...	...	...	...	1	1	...	...	...	...	...	...	...	...	...	...	37

TABLE XV.—Occupation or means

Serial No.	CLASS ... / SUB-CLASS ... / ORDER ...	CLASS C.—PUBLIC ADMINISTRATION / Sub-Class VI.—Public Force / Order 44.—														
		Total order 44.						142.—Police.						143.—Village		
	DISTRICT, CITY OR STATE.	Total workers and dependants.	Actual workers. Total. Males.	Actual workers. Total. Females.	Actual workers. Partially agriculturists. Males.	Actual workers. Partially agriculturists. Females.	Dependants.	Total workers and dependants.	Actual workers. Total. Males.	Actual workers. Total. Females.	Actual workers. Partially agriculturists. Males.	Actual workers. Partially agriculturists. Females.	Dependants.	Total workers and dependants.	Actual. Total. Males.	Actual. Total. Females.
	1	1136	1137	1138	1139	1140	1141	1142	1143	1144	1145	1146	1147	1148	1149	1150
	Central Provinces and Berar.	**162,403**	**61,334**	**2,542**	**14,288**	**389**	**98,527**	**32,533**	**12,410**	**133**	**272**	**2**	**19,990**	**129,870**	**48,924**	**2,409**
	C. P. British Districts and Berar.	**146,013**	**55,980**	**1,942**	**13,099**	**360**	**88,091**	**28,635**	**10,967**	**74**	**221**	**1**	**17,594**	**117,378**	**45,013**	**1,868**
	C. P. British Districts.	**101,532**	**36,315**	**1,606**	**11,213**	**315**	**63,611**	**23,537**	**8,969**	**54**	**180**	**1**	**14,514**	**77,995**	**27,346**	**1,552**
	JUBBULPORE DIVISION	*23,847*	*8,338*	*245*	*2,431*	*36*	*15,324*	*7,031*	*2,621*	*14*	*24*	...	*4,446*	*16,766*	*5,657*	*231*
1	Saugor ...	5,711	2,079	19	573	3	3,613	2,237	802	13	7	...	1,422	3,474	1,277	6
2	Damoh ...	3,030	998	16	273	3	2,016	934	326	...	3	...	608	2,096	672	16
3	Jubbulpore ...	7,118	2,393	59	867	15	4,606	2,207	870	1	12	...	1,426	4,821	1,523	58
	JUBBULPORE CITY ...	*1,332*	*496*	...	*7*	...	*836*	*1,343*	*486*	...	*6*	...	*857*	*39*	*10*	...
4	Mandla ...	4,068	1,396	97	411	12	2,635	842	335	...	2	...	507	3,226	1,001	97
5	Seoni ...	3,920	1,472	54	307	3	2,394	771	288	...	...	...	483	3,149	1,184	54
	NERBUDDA DIVISION	*22,605*	*7,913*	*160*	*2,339*	*26*	*14,532*	*5,397*	*2,016*	*8*	*22*	...	*3,374*	*17,208*	*5,898*	*153*
6	Narsinghpur ...	4,310	1,352	11	594	3	2,947	1,036	333	1	3	...	702	3,274	1,019	10
7	Hoshangabad ...	5,721	1,891	21	503	...	3,809	1,476	529	1	4	...	946	4,245	1,362	20
8	Nimar ...	4,235	1,655	11	371	2	2,569	963	435	...	2	...	528	3,272	1,220	11
9	Betul ...	3,434	1,223	44	477	12	2,167	870	330	2	11	...	532	2,564	887	42
10	Chhindwara ...	4,905	1,792	73	394	9	3,040	1,052	382	4	2	...	666	3,853	1,410	69
	NAGPUR DIVISION ...	*29,595*	*11,348*	*334*	*2,917*	*67*	*17,913*	*6,938*	*2,770*	*13*	*87*	*1*	*4,165*	*22,647*	*8,558*	*321*
11	Wardha ...	3,961	1,602	16	194	8	2,343	692	268	1	7	1	423	3,269	1,334	15
12	Nagpur ...	8,177	3,238	113	826	7	4,826	2,778	1,213	8	56	...	1,557	5,399	2,025	105
	NAGPUR CITY ...	*1,716*	*659*	*28*	*49*	...	*999*	*1,536*	*63*	*3*	*48*	...	*896*	*180*	*51*	*25*
13	Chanda ...	6,176	2,258	54	558	24	3,864	1,650	621	2	7	...	1,027	4,526	1,637	52
14	Bhandara ...	8,010	3,001	67	978	10	4,942	1,162	402	...	11	...	760	6,848	2,599	67
15	Balaghat ...	3,271	1,249	84	361	9	1,938	606	266	2	6	...	398	2,605	963	82
	CHHATTISGARH DIVISION.	*25,485*	*8,776*	*867*	*3,526*	*186*	*15,842*	*4,111*	*1,563*	*19*	*47*	...	*2,439*	*21,374*	*7,213*	*848*
16	Raipur ...	11,667	4,031	309	1,734	68	7,327	1,903	795	2	42	...	1,106	9,764	3,236	307
17	Bilaspur ...	6,651	2,391	306	1,072	102	3,954	1,205	392	14	4	...	709	5,446	1,999	292
18	Drug ...	7,167	2,354	252	720	16	4,561	1,003	376	3	1	...	624	6,164	1,978	249
	Berar ...	**44,481**	**19,665**	**336**	**1,886**	**45**	**24,480**	**5,098**	**1,998**	**20**	**41**	...	**3,080**	**39,383**	**17,667**	**318**
19	Amraoti ...	10,983	5,038	116	384	14	5,829	1,321	542	16	3	...	763	9,662	4,496	100
20	Akola ...	11,459	5,330	76	711	11	6,053	1,310	517	1	21	...	798	10,143	4,813	75
21	Buldana ...	12,037	5,019	92	602	17	6,926	1,125	436	3	13	...	686	10,912	4,583	89
22	Yeotmal ...	10,002	4,278	52	189	3	5,672	1,336	503	...	4	...	833	8,666	3,775	52
	Feudatory States ...	**16,390**	**5,354**	**600**	**1,189**	**29**	**10,436**	**3,898**	**1,443**	**59**	**51**	**1**	**2,396**	**12,492**	**3,911**	**541**
23	Makrai ...	329	124	7	4	...	198	160	52	...	...	...	108	169	72	7
24	Bastar ...	1,936	666	83	35	1	1,187	744	285	4	4	...	455	1,192	381	79
25	Nanker ...	1,252	457	162	34	5	633	240	81	37	1	1	122	1,012	370	125
26	Kandgaon ...	1,853	620	89	125	14	1,144	491	165	...	...	...	326	1,362	455	89
27	Khairagarh ...	1,881	608	34	104	1	1,239	375	137	...	2	...	238	1,506	471	34
28	Chhuikhadan ...	475	126	...	20	...	349	143	34	...	...	...	109	332	92	...
29	Kawardha -	994	331	52	131	3	611	181	44	...	1	...	137	813	287	52
30	Sakti ...	89	30	1	12	...	58	78	25	...	9	...	53	11	5	1
31	Raigarh ...	2,830	753	24	567	4	2,053	366	116	...	...	...	250	2,464	637	24
32	Sarangarh ...	1,518	471	12	74	...	1,035	141	49	...	9	...	92	1,377	422	12
33	Chang Bhakar ...	85	30	12	6	...	43	1	...	...	...	...	1	84	30	12
34	Korea ...	418	139	21	9	...	258	36	18	...	1	...	18	382	121	21
35	Surguja ...	1,931	720	64	13	1	1,147	638	312	6	5	...	320	1,293	408	58
36	Udaipur ...	480	130	23	27	...	327	102	37	...	...	...	65	394	94	23
37	Jashpur ...	313	143	16	28	...	154	202	88	12	21	...	102	111	55	4

# of livelihood, Part A.—General Table.

AND LIBERAL ARTS—(*continued*).

—(*concluded*). | Sub-Class VII.—Public Administration.

Police. | Order 45.—Public Administration.

watchmen. | Total Sub-Class VII and Order 45. | 144.—Service of the State. | 145.—Service of Native and Foreign States.

Workers. Partially agriculturists. Males.	Workers. Partially agriculturists. Females.	Dependants.	Total Sub-Class VII and Order 45. Total workers and dependants.	Actual workers. Total. Males.	Actual workers. Total. Females.	Actual workers. Partially agriculturists. Males.	Actual workers. Partially agriculturists. Females.	Dependants.	144. Total workers and dependants.	Actual workers. Total. Males.	Actual workers. Total. Females.	Actual workers. Partially agriculturists. Males.	Actual workers. Partially agriculturists. Females.	Dependants.	145. Total workers and dependants.	Actual workers. Total. Males.	Actual workers. Total. Females.	Actual workers. Partially agriculturists. Males.	Actual workers. Partially agriculturists. Females.	Dependants.	Serial No.
1151	1152	1153	1154	1155	1156	1157	1158	1159	1160	1161	1162	1163	1164	1165	1166	1167	1168	1169	1170	1171	
14,016	**387**	**78,537**	**102,207**	**34,770**	**1,367**	**3,778**	**68**	**66,070**	**49,346**	**17,012**	**322**	**675**	**15**	**32,012**	**4,601**	**1,693**	**159**	**146**	**1**	**2,749**	
12,878	**359**	**70,497**	**96,482**	**32,664**	**1,206**	**3,604**	**67**	**62,612**	**49,245**	**16,975**	**322**	**675**	**15**	**31,948**	**292**	**117**	**2**	**6**	...	**173**	
11,033	**314**	**49,097**	**61,226**	**20,837**	**624**	**1,239**	**17**	**40,265**	**31,624**	**10,883**	**140**	**345**	**10**	**20,601**	**267**	**107**	...	**4**	...	**160**	
2,407	*30*	*10,575*	*15,224*	*4,756*	*116*	*219*	...	*10,363*	*7,728*	*2,462*	*16*	*59*	...	*5,244*	*94*	*15*	...	...	...	*76*	
566	3	2,191	4,149	1,219	4	97	...	2,926	1,673	549	1	18	...	1,123	18	8	...	...	...	10	1
270	3	1,408	2,010	603	7	26	...	1,400	1,111	365	2	13	...	744	33	3	...	...	...	30	2
855	15	3,240	5,619	1,864	93	91	...	3,662	3,247	1,052	8	23	...	2,187	39	7	...	...	...	32	3
1	...	*29*	*3,134*	*1,056*	*5*	*7*	...	*2,073*	*2,437*	*741*	*5*	*5*	...	*1,653*	*13*	...	...	...	...	*13*	
406	12	2,128	1,578	527	8	20	...	1,043	700	228	4	2	...	477	...	...	...	...	...	...	4
307	3	1,911	1,868	542	4	15	...	1,322	988	274	1	3	...	713	4	...	...	...	...	4	5
2,317	*26*	*11,156*	*14,677*	*4,566*	*54*	*374*	...	*10,057*	*6,497*	*2,091*	*7*	*53*	...	*4,399*	*53*	*27*	...	...	...	*56*	
591	3	2,245	2,908	790	7	85	...	2,111	1,198	366	3	9	...	829	21	5	...	...	...	16	6
499	...	2,863	4,604	1,451	84	119	...	3,119	1,730	529	...	9	...	1,201	18	11	...	...	...	7	7
369	2	2,041	2,822	983	2	76	...	1,887	1,271	404	1	9	...	866	41	11	...	...	...	30	8
466	12	1,635	2,052	724	4	60	...	1,324	1,060	415	3	15	...	642	1	...	...	...	...	1	9
392	9	2,374	2,291	668	7	28	...	1,610	1,238	377	...	11	...	861	2	...	...	...	...	2	10
2,830	*66*	*13,745*	*20,857*	*7,435*	*365*	*417*	*4*	*13,056*	*13,149*	*4,672*	*57*	*204*	*1*	*8,390*	*2*	*2*	...	...	...	...	
187	7	1,920	3,102	1,187	46	60	1	1,860	2,067	788	28	44	...	1,251	...	...	...	...	...	...	11
770	7	3,269	9,272	3,435	139	180	2	5,698	6,234	2,223	48	95	...	3,963	...	...	...	...	...	...	12
1	...	*104*	*4,990*	*1,786*	*27*	*63*	...	*3,177*	*3,874*	*1,299*	*14*	*62*	...	*2,561*	...	...	...	...	...	...	
551	24	2,837	3,861	1,376	31	100	1	2,454	2,338	835	7	40	1	1,496	...	...	...	...	...	...	13
967	19	4,182	3,150	928	140	51	...	2,087	1,690	534	1	22	...	1,155	...	...	...	...	...	...	14
355	9	1,540	1,472	517	7	11	...	948	820	292	3	3	...	525	2	2	...	...	...	...	15
3,479	*156*	*13,313*	*10,464*	*3,575*	*91*	*199*	*13*	*6,799*	*4,250*	*1,652*	*30*	*29*	*9*	*2,565*	*84*	*60*	...	*5*	...	*25*	
1,692	68	6,221	5,094	1,623	45	84	1	3,428	2,078	700	8	10	...	1,370	35	21	...	1	...	14	16
1,068	102	3,155	2,892	1,073	89	71	2	1,780	1,124	540	10	16	...	565	6	5	...	2	...	1	17
719	10	3,987	2,482	882	15	35	9	1,585	1,048	403	12	4	9	633	47	34	...	2	...	13	18
1,845	**45**	**21,400**	**35,256**	**12,327**	**582**	**2,365**	**20**	**22,347**	**17,621**	**6,092**	**182**	**330**	**5**	**11,347**	**25**	**10**	**2**	**1**	...	**13**	
381	14	5,006	10,006	3,227	317	427	15	6,552	5,772	1,864	80	50	...	3,830	...	...	...	...	...	...	19
690	11	5,255	10,309	3,795	150	808	27	6,856	5,480	1,946	51	165	3	3,483	5	5	...	...	...	...	20
589	17	6,240	9,124	3,282	87	888	7	5,755	3,740	1,336	40	91	2	2,364	20	5	2	1	...	13	21
185	3	4,839	5,727	2,023	22	244	3	3,682	2,628	956	11	15	...	1,661	...	...	...	...	...	...	22
1,138	**28**	**8,040**	**5,725**	**2,106**	**161**	**174**	**1**	**3,458**	**101**	**37**	...	...	...	**64**	**4,309**	**1,576**	**157**	**140**	**1**	**2,576**	
4	...	90	218	90	...	17	...	128	3	1	...	...	...	2	124	59	...	4	...	65	23
31	1	732	832	301	10	6	1	521	15	9	...	...	...	6	620	192	8	5	1	420	24
33	4	511	407	166	2	6	...	231	1	1	...	...	...	...	292	111	2	4	...	179	25
125	14	818	626	211	4	9	...	411	1	...	...	...	...	1	385	137	4	5	...	244	26
102	1	1,001	706	187	4	12	...	515	60	12	...	...	...	48	435	119	4	5	...	312	27
20	...	240	207	54	1	...	...	152	7	6	...	...	...	1	124	20	1	...	...	97	28
130	3	474	365	105	...	6	...	200	...	...	...	...	...	...	198	55	...	4	...	143	29
2	...	5	108	82	2	8	...	60	5	3	...	...	...	2	60	19	2	5	...	45	30
567	4	1,805	402	135	97	9	...	170	...	...	...	...	...	...	288	80	97	7	...	111	31
65	...	943	247	62	...	17	...	185	...	...	...	...	...	...	247	62	...	17	...	185	32
[illegible]	...	42	176	71	3	18	...	102	3	3	...	...	...	...	173	68	3	18	...	102	33
8	...	240	176	100	1	11	...	66	...	...	...	...	...	...	166	101	1	11	...	63	34
10	1	827	715	343	13	22	...	359	...	...	...	...	...	...	695	382	12	22	...	351	35
27	...	202	240	111	...	2	...	120	4	1	...	...	...	2	195	89	...	2	...	108	36
7	...	52	305	129	24	31	...	152	2	...	...	...	...	2	290	126	23	31	...	150	37

TABLE XV.—Occupation or means

Serial No.	CLASS ... / SUB-CLASS ... / ORDER ... / DISTRICT, CITY OR STATE.	CLASS C.—PUBLIC ADMINISTRATION. Sub-Class VII.—Public Administration—(concluded). Order 45.—Public Administration—(concluded). 146.—Municipal and other local (not village) service. Total workers and dependants.	Actual workers. Total. Males.	Actual workers. Total. Females.	Actual workers. Partially agriculturists. Males.	Actual workers. Partially agriculturists. Females.	Dependants.	147.—Village officials and servants other than watchmen. Total workers and dependants.	Actual workers. Total. Males.	Actual workers. Total. Females.	Actual workers. Partially agriculturists. Males.	Actual workers. Partially agriculturists. Females.	Dependants.	Total Sub- … Total workers and dependants.	Actual … Total. Males.	Actual … Total. Females.
	1	1172	1173	1174	1175	1176	1177	1178	1179	1180	1181	1182	1183	1184	1185	1186
	Central Provinces and Berar	**11,928**	**4.196**	**518**	**127**	**15**	**7,214**	**36,332**	**11,869**	**368**	**2,830**	**37**	**24.095**	**234,704**	**89,413**	**26.045**
	C. P. British Districts and Berar.	**11,737**	**4,109**	**516**	**125**	**15**	**7,112**	**35,208**	**11.463**	**366**	**2.798**	**37**	**23,379**	**217,844**	**82,988**	**23,454**
	C. P. British Districts.	**9,684**	**3,417**	**313**	**99**	**2**	**5,954**	**19,651**	**5,930**	**171**	**790**	**5**	**13,550**	**163,197**	**60.235**	**19,768**
	JUBBULPORE DIVISION	*2,296*	*863*	*46*	*19*	...	*1,357*	*5,106*	*1,406*	*64*	*171*	...	*3,646*	*41,051*	*15,005*	*6,764*
1	Saugor ...	712	255	3	8	..	455	1,745	407	...	71	...	1,338	11,304	3,798	1,742
2	Damoh ...	244	52	...	...	...	192	622	183	5	13	...	434	7,603	2,436	1,375
3	Jubbulpore ...	963	406	41	7	...	516	1,370	309	44	61	...	927	12,855	4,355	1,470
	JUBBULPORE CITY ...	*613*	*293*	*9*	*2*	...	*317*	*81*	*21*	...	...	...	*60*	*5,155*	*1,460*	*297*
4	Mandla ...	122	56	...	3	...	66	747	243	4	15	...	500	4,046	1,487	457
5	Seoni ...	254	94	2	1	...	158	622	174	1	11	...	447	5,243	1,924	720
	NERBUDDA DIVISION	*2,884*	*783*	*41*	*19*	...	*1,464*	*5,509*	*1,665*	*6*	*302*	...	*4,135*	*36,775*	*14,016*	*3,357*
6	Narsinghpur ...	376	114	2	6	...	260	1,313	305	2	70	...	1,000	7,036	2,407	747
7	Hoshangabad ...	901	331	33	4	...	537	1,955	580	1	106	...	1,374	11,302	4,047	800
8	Nimar ...	542	186	1	1	...	355	968	332	...	60	...	630	7,864	3,482	616
9	Betul ...	171	68	...	3	...	103	820	241	1	48	...	578	4,427	1,735	453
10	Chhindwara ...	298	84	5	5	...	209	753	207	2	12	...	544	6,146	2,397	641
	NAGPUR DIVISION ...	*3,516*	*1,318*	*219*	*35*	...	*1,979*	*4,190*	*1,446*	*57*	*178*	*3*	*2,657*	*50,731*	*19,579*	*5,181*
11	Wardha ..	478	182	11	2	...	285	557	217	7	23	1	333	8,813	3,645	663
12	Nagpur ...	1,945	796	61	25	...	1,088	1,093	416	30	60	2	647	19,799	7,563	1,993
	NAGPUR CITY ...	*1,074*	*464*	*13*	*11*	...	*597*	*42*	*23*	...	...	...	*19*	*5,291*	*1,799*	*342*
13	Chanda ...	409	152	6	5	...	251	1,114	380	18	61	...	707	8,024	3,220	811
14	Bhandara ...	595	151	139	2	...	305	865	238	...	27	...	627	8,742	3,450	1,044
15	Balaghat ...	89	37	2	1	...	50	561	186	2	7	...	373	5,353	1,995	670
	CHHATTISGARH DIVISION.	*1,584*	*453*	*7*	*26*	*2*	*1,134*	*4,536*	*1,413*	*54*	*139*	*2*	*3,079*	*34,630*	*12,335*	*5,566*
16	Raipur .	1,010	253	1	2	...	756	1,971	649	34	71	1	1,288	15,090	5,355	2,187
17	Bilaspur ...	483	172	4	22	2	307	1,279	347	19	37	1	913	11,100	4,138	1,022
18	Drug ...	91	28	2	2	...	61	1,296	417	1	31	...	878	8,450	2,842	1,457
	Berar ...	**2.053**	**692**	**203**	**26**	**13**	**1.158**	**15,557**	**5,533**	**195**	**2,008**	**32**	**9.829**	**54.647**	**22.753**	**3,686**
19	Amraoti ...	722	194	108	5	...	420	3,601	1,179	120	361	15	2,293	18,173	7,329	1,345
20	Akola ...	666	249	85	11	13	332	4,158	1,595	20	632	9	2,543	14,375	6,075	963
21	Buldana .	431	161	7	8	...	263	4,933	1,780	38	788	5	3,115	12,527	5,019	696
22	Yeotmal ...	234	88	3	2	...	143	2,867	979	8	227	3	1,878	9,572	4,330	682
	Feudatory States ...	**191**	**87**	**2**	**2**	...	**102**	**1.124**	**406**	**2**	**82**	...	**716**	**16.860**	**6.425**	**2.591**
23	Makrai ...	...	...	...	...	...	...	91	30	...	13	...	61	324	156	7
24	Bastar ...	80	4	2	...	...	38	117	60	...	1	...	57	1,240	467	180
25	Kanker ...	7	2	...	...	...	5	107	52	...	2	...	57	755	317	110
26	Nandgaon ...	8	7	...	...	...	1	232	67	...	4	...	165	2,060	781	323
27	Khairagarh ...	1	1	...	...	...	...	210	55	...	7	...	155	2,310	839	370
28	Chhuikhadan ...	2	1	...	...	...	1	74	21	...	...	...	53	585	217	65
29	Kawardha ...	1	1	...	...	...	...	166	49	...	2	...	117	1,100	397	150
30	Sakti ...	5	1	...	...	...	4	24	9	...	3	...	15	571	214	134
31	Raigarh ...	79	28	...	2	...	51	35	27	...	...	...	8	2,033	818	347
32	Sarangarh ...	...	...	...	...	...	...	...	...	...	...	...	...	1,398	506	252
33	Chang Bhakar ...	...	...	...	...	...	...	...	...	...	...	...	...	181	82	57
34	Korea ...	...	...	...	...	...	...	11	8	...	...	...	3	413	185	73
35	Surguja ...	8	6	...	...	...	2	12	5	1	...	...	6	2,283	851	218
36	Udaipur ...	...	...	...	...	...	...	41	20	...	...	...	21	450	183	81
37	Jashpur ...	...	...	...	...	...	...	4	3	1	...	...	...	1,001	412	234

# of livelihood, Part A.—General Table.

AND LIBERAL ARTS—(*continued*).

Sub-Class VIII.—Professions and liberal arts.

Order 46.—Religion.

Class VIII. Workers. Partially agriculturists. Males.	Class VIII. Workers. Partially agriculturists. Females.	Class VIII. Dependants.	Total order 46. Total workers and dependants.	Total order 46. Actual workers. Total. Males.	Total order 46. Actual workers. Total. Females.	Total order 46. Actual workers. Partially agriculturists. Males.	Total order 46. Actual workers. Partially agriculturists. Females.	Total order 46. Dependants.	148.—Priests, ministers, etc. Total workers and dependants.	148. Actual workers. Total. Males.	148. Actual workers. Total. Females.	148. Actual workers. Partially agriculturists. Males.	148. Actual workers. Partially agriculturists. Females.	148. Dependants.	149.—Religious mendicants, inmates of monasteries, etc. Total workers and dependants.	149. Actual workers. Total. Males.	149. Actual workers. Total. Females.	Serial No.
1187	1188	1189	1190	1191	1192	1193	1194	1195	1196	1197	1198	1199	1200	1201	1202	1203	1204	
11,994	**2.213**	**119,246**	**129.490**	**50,234**	**16.112**	**6,548**	**909**	**63.144**	**11,406**	**4,141**	**156**	**942**	**18**	**7.109**	**103,762**	**41,667**	**15.154**	
11,448	**2,117**	**111,402**	**118,698**	**46,144**	**14,117**	**6.207**	**854**	**58.437**	**10.786**	**3,875**	**143**	**908**	**18**	**6.768**	**94.933**	**38,440**	**13,239**	
7,638	**1,723**	**83,194**	**86,74[illegible]**	**32,380**	**11,835**	**4,280**	**716**	**42,530**	**9,390**	**3,270**	**124**	**787**	**17**	**5,996**	**66,08[illegible]**	**25,896**	**11,095**	
1,593	*651*	*21,28[illegible]*	*25,374*	*9,005*	*3,861*	*1,84[illegible]*	*23[illegible]*	*13,50[illegible]*	*4,846*	*1,694*	*51*	*424*	[illegible]	*3,101*	*17,114*	*6,307*	*3,615*	
498	277	5,764	7,215	2,631	1,049	429	70	3,530	1,593	514	11	141	1	1,068	4,720	1,777	985	1
486	189	3,792	5,520	1,891	893	405	94	2,741	1,278	430	13	103	4	835	3,711	1,318	859	2
434	54	7,030	7,555	2,573	1,123	355	54	3,851	1,295	497	10	76	2	782	4,752	1,673	1,019	3
1[illegible]	*1*	*3,39[illegible]*	*1,82[illegible]*	*456*	*137*	*9*	*1*	*1,21[illegible]*	*677*	*267*	*11*	*6*	*1*	*399*	*306*	*96*	*63*	
80	13	2,102	2,416	869	352	72	10	1,195	380	124	9	33	1	247	1,767	690	320	4
86	11	2,594	2,662	1,041	445	28	1	1,170	300	129	2	11	...	169	2,164	849	429	5
1,231	*250*	*19,50[illegible]*	*20,506*	*8,084*	*2,031*	*880*	*114*	*10,40[illegible]*	*2,039*	*66[illegible]*	*1[illegible]*	*157*	*3*	*1,359*	*15,646*	*6,545*	*1,566*	
342	58	3,882	4,427	1,550	590	281	48	2,278	1,163	381	10	119	3	772	2,550	965	507	6
393	48	6,455	6,630	2,500	474	312	25	3,650	534	157	1	24	...	370	5,138	2,005	451	7
208	41	3,810	4,706	2,170	374	100	26	2,102	90	37	3	...	...	50	4,132	1,947	336	8
110	37	2,241	1,833	719	257	61	7	857	58	34	...	6	...	24	1,547	622	231	9
177	70	3,108	2,910	1,139	317	72	8	1,454	194	53	4	8	...	137	2,273	1,000	281	10
3,461	*61[illegible]*	*25,671*	*18,56[illegible]*	*7,66[illegible]*	*2,159*	*1,162*	*20[illegible]*	*9,011*	*617*	*223*	[illegible]	*50*	...	*359*	*16,169*	*6,749*	*2,019*	
718	125	4,509	3,640	1,513	270	182	13	1,803	116	44	3	11	...	69	3,326	1,372	252	11
857	171	10,248	6,558	2,820	632	380	41	3,100	97	28	1	6	...	68	5,686	2,558	583	12
45	*1*	*3,150*	*1,353*	*550*	*8[illegible]*	*14*	*1*	*711*	*24*	*9*	...	...	...	*16*	*937*	*456*	*57*	
905	148	3,987	3,302	1,310	404	290	64	1,588	39	5	...	...	...	30	2,850	1,186	435	13
680	135	4,248	3,411	1,377	501	214	51	1,541	151	65	...	14	...	84	2,948	1,177	478	14
294	71	2,688	1,877	642	292	96	33	945	212	75	1	19	...	138	1,353	456	270	15
1,3[illegible]	*27[illegible]*	*16,739*	*22,005*	*7,629*	*3,794*	*883*	*16[illegible]*	*10,580*	*1,88[illegible]*	*691*	*50*	*150*	*6*	*1,147*	*17,150*	*6,395*	*3,692*	
573	104	7,548	9,496	3,252	1,523	394	57	4,723	734	249	17	42	2	408	7,230	2,654	1,449	16
457	124	5,040	7,227	2,644	1,472	285	84	3,109	573	223	16	53	...	334	5,973	2,250	1,303	17
312	4[illegible]	4,151	5,278	1,731	799	205	21	2,748	581	219	17	61	4	345	3,953	1,391	750	18
3,815	**394**	**28,208**	**31,953**	**13,764**	**2,282**	**1.927**	**138**	**15.907**	**1,396**	**605**	**19**	**121**	**1**	**772**	**28,848**	**12,544**	**2.144**	
1,164	158	9,404	9,406	4,002	700	428	25	4,703	565	250	10	52	1	299	8,212	3,523	657	19
1,210	101	7,337	8,726	3,767	656	509	51	4,302	353	187	6	38	...	100	7,953	3,408	606	20
903	77	6,812	8,300	3,378	510	613	45	4,412	206	83	1	20	...	121	7,749	3,183	491	21
538	58	4,560	5,523	2,617	416	287	17	2,490	.272	78	2	11	...	192	4,934	2,430	396	22
546	**96**	**7.844**	**10,792**	**4,090**	**1,995**	**341**	**55**	**4,707**	**620**	**266**	**13**	**34**	...	**341**	**8,829**	**3,227**	**1,915**	
11	2	157	217	127	2	10	...	88	7	5	...	...	...	2	180	114	2	23
34	2	593	707	261	129	31	2	317	19	9	1	1	...	9	466	174	103	24
9	...	326	454	184	92	2	...	174	28	12	1	...	...	15	407	165	90	25
72	20	962	1,219	484	194	40	12	541	76	27	4	2	...	49	958	300	187	26
82	14	1,107	1,404	547	202	48	4	655	232	60	2	20	...	164	1,039	405	195	27
19	...	319	346	120	37	11	...	189	104	38	1	3	...	65	222	78	34	28
55	[illegible]	613	806	207	122	39	5	417	...	...	...	...	...	...	806	200	122	29
20	10	221	464	170	118	19	9	170	7	7	...	1	...	...	456	103	117	30
40	8	808	1,573	633	320	34	8	611	12	6	...	...	...	6	1,246	480	326	31
83	7	640	1,081	358	244	47	6	479	12	7	...	...	...	5	865	286	240	32
7	4	42	166	74	52	6	4	40	...	...	...	...	...	...	156	66	52	33
13	...	155	233	101	80	4	...	82	24	19	1	...	...	4	205	78	49	34
34	3	1,214	1,091	379	174	12	1	538	64	49	...	4	...	15	984	303	174	35
5	8	180	205	108	79	2	3	108	2	2	...	...	...	...	288	105	79	36
56	6	445	740	277	171	27	1	292	83	23	3	3	...	7	519	180	152	37

TABLE XV.—Occupation or means

Serial No.	CLASS ... / SUB-CLASS ... / ORDER ...	CLASS C.—PUBLIC ADMINISTRATION — Sub-Class VIII.—Professions — Order 46.—Religion—(concluded).																	
		149.—Religious mendicants, inmates of monasteries, etc.—(concluded).			150.—Catechists, readers, church and mission service.						151.—Temple, burial or burning ground service, pilgrim conductors, circumcisers.						Total		
	DISTRICT, CITY OR STATE.	Actual workers.—(concluded). Partially agriculturists. Males.	Partially agriculturists. Females.	Dependants.	Total workers and dependants.	Actual workers. Total. Males.	Actual workers. Total. Females.	Partially agriculturists. Males.	Partially agriculturists. Females.	Dependants.	Total workers and dependants.	Actual workers. Total. Males.	Actual workers. Total. Females.	Partially agriculturists. Males.	Partially agriculturists. Females.	Dependants.	Total workers and dependants.	Actual. Total. Males.	Actual. Total. Females.
	1	1205	1206	1207	1208	1209	1210	1211	1212	1213	1214	1215	1216	1217	1218	1219	1220	1221	1222
	Central Provinces and Berar.	**5,041**	**863**	**46,941**	**6,780**	**910**	**511**	**26**	...	**5,359**	**7,542**	**3,516**	**291**	**539**	**28**	**3,735**	**14,429**	**4,028**	**66**
	C. P. British Districts and Berar.	**4,838**	**810**	**43,254**	**6,440**	**810**	**462**	**16**	...	**5,168**	**6,539**	**3,019**	**273**	**445**	**26**	**3,247**	**14,021**	**3,927**	**65**
	C. P. British Districts.	**3,084**	**683**	**29,094**	**5,730**	**692**	**406**	**9**	...	**4,632**	**5,540**	**2,522**	**210**	**400**	**16**	**2,808**	**11,194**	**3,226**	**48**
	JUBBULPORE DIVISION	*513*	*225*	*7,159*	*1,807*	*180*	*120*	*1*	...	*1,507*	*1,607*	*824*	*72*	*110*	*2*	*711*	*2,400*	*666*	*11*
1	Saugor ...	246	76	1,958	818	42	20	1	...	256	584	298	32	40	2	254	480	141	...
2	Damoh ...	269	90	1,534	264	13	9	...	...	242	273	130	12	32	...	131	186	43	...
3	Jubbulpore ...	246	52	2,060	970	99	73	...	...	798	538	304	15	33	...	219	1,003	283	10
	JUBBULPORE CITY ...	*3*	...	*147*	*728*	*70*	*61*	...	...	*602*	*132*	*58*	*4*	...	...	*67*	*650*	*151*	...
4	Mandla ...	37	9	751	186	21	10	...	...	155	83	34	7	2	...	42	249	78	...
5	Seoni ...	15	1	880	69	5	8	...	...	56	129	58	6	2	...	65	482	121	1
	NERBUDDA DIVISION	*639*	*102*	*7,235*	*1,196*	*190*	*91*	*3*	...	*915*	*1,626*	*657*	*46*	*87*	*2*	*593*	*4,071*	*1,175*	*13*
6	Narsinghpur ..	120	44	1,024	195	19	10	1	...	166	512	185	12	41	1	316	804	188	5
7	Hoshangabad ...	261	25	2,682	355	71	20	1	...	264	603	273	2	26	...	328	1,497	422	1
8	Nimar ...	153	25	1,849	203	49	12	1	...	141	281	137	22	6	1	122	551	183	...
9	Betul ...	49	7	604	133	27	25	...	...	81	95	36	1	6	...	58	606	207	4
10	Chhindwara ...	50	8	980	310	24	23	...	...	263	133	56	5	8	...	68	553	178	2
	NAGPUR DIVISION ...	*1,020*	*196*	*7,101*	*852*	*150*	*73*	*1*	...	*619*	*1,224*	*581*	*61*	*55*	*6*	*632*	*3,390*	*920*	*21*
11	Wardha ...	163	12	1,701	38	21	1	1	...	16	100	70	13	7	1	77	569	145	4
12	Nagpur ...	359	41	2,545	428	84	34	...	...	310	347	150	14	15	...	183	1,335	368	16
	NAGPUR CITY ...	*14*	*1*	*413*	*335*	*63*	*23*	...	...	*250*	*63*	*27*	*1*	...	...	*36*	*457*	*175*	...
13	Chanda ...	272	63	1,235	260	30	21	...	...	209	207	85	8	18	1	114	274	53	1
14	Bhandara ...	180	50	1,293	60	12	7	...	...	41	258	110	10	20	1	123	673	204	...
15	Balaghat ...	52	30	627	66	12	11	...	...	43	240	101	10	25	3	135	539	150	...
	CHHATTISGARH DIVISION.	*606*	*150*	*7,269*	*1,878*	*163*	*121*	*4*	...	*1,591*	*1,054*	*480*	*31*	*118*	*6*	*578*	*1,333*	*462*	*4*
16	Raipur ...	268	50	3,127	853	62	39	...	...	752	681	287	18	84	5	370	648	207	4
17	Bilaspur ...	198	83	2,330	466	54	57	4	...	355	215	119	6	30	1	90	353	129	...
18	Drug ...	140	17	1,812	550	47	25	...	...	484	188	74	7	4	...	107	332	120	...
	Berar ..	**1,754**	**127**	**14,160**	**710**	**118**	**56**	**7**	...	**536**	**999**	**497**	**63**	**45**	**10**	**439**	**2,827**	**701**	**17**
19	Amraoti ...	302	22	4,032	249	30	18	1	...	201	377	193	15	13	2	171	1,084	252	9
20	Akola ...	536	43	3,945	138	20	13	3	...	105	281	152	37	22	8	92	714	189	1
21	Buldana ...	590	45	4,075	180	42	9	2	...	129	165	69	9	1	...	87	561	127	4
22	Yeotmal ...	200	17	2,108	143	26	16	1	...	101	174	83	2	9	...	89	408	133	3
	Feudatory States ...	**203**	**53**	**3,687**	**340**	**100**	**49**	**10**	...	**191**	**1,003**	**497**	**18**	**94**	**2**	**488**	**408**	**101**	**1**
23	Makrai ..	10	...	64	...	...	...	...	...	...	30	8	...	...	...	22	37	7	...
24	Bastar ...	14	1	189	132	30	21	8	...	81	90	48	4	8	1	38	26	7	...
25	Kanker ...	1	...	150	...	...	...	...	...	...	17	7	1	1	...	9	51	19	...
26	Nandgaon ...	27	12	418	12	5	5	...	...	2	173	96	5	20	...	72	39	3	...
27	Khairagarh ...	18	4	439	13	7	5	...	...	1	120	69	...	10	...	51	105	19	...
28	Chhuikhadan ...	8	...	115	10	2	2	...	...	6	10	7	...	...	...	3	14	5	...
29	Kawardha ...	39	5	412	5	1	...	...	...	4	1	...	...	...	...	1	10	1	...
30	Sakti ...	18	9	176	...	...	...	...	...	...	1	...	1	...	...	...	3	1	...
31	Raigarh ...	8	8	471	2	1	...	...	...	1	273	137	3	26	...	133	87	20	...
32	Sarangarh ...	21	5	339	...	...	...	...	...	...	204	65	4	26	1	135	2	2	...
33	Chang Bhakar ...	6	4	38	...	...	...	...	...	...	10	8	...	...	...	2	...	...	...
34	Korea ...	3	...	78	...	...	...	...	...	...	4	4	...	1	...	...	4	3	...
35	Surguja ...	8	1	507	...	...	...	...	...	...	43	27	...	...	...	16	17	8	...
36	Udaipur ...	2	3	104	...	...	...	...	...	...	5	1	...	...	...	4	1	1	...
37	Jashpur ...	20	1	187	166	54	16	2	...	96	22	20	...	2	...	2	12	5	1

# of livelihood, Part A.—General Table.

AND LIBERAL ARTS—(*continued*).

and liberal arts—(*continued*).

Order 47.—Law.																Order 48.—Medicine.					
order 47.			152.—Lawyers of all kinds, including kazis, law agents and mukhtiars.						153.—Lawyers' clerks, petition-writers, etc.						Total order 48.						
Workers.			Total workers and dependants.	Actual workers.				Dependants.	Total workers and dependants.	Actual workers.				Dependants.	Total workers and dependants.	Actual workers.				Dependants.	Serial No.
Partially agriculturists.		Dependants.		Total.		Partially agriculturists.				Total.		Partially agriculturists.				Total.		Partially agriculturists.			
Males.	Females.			Males.	Females.	Males.	Females.			Males.	Females.	Males.	Females.			Males.	Females.	Males.	Females.		
1223	1224	1225	1226	1227	1228	1229	1230	1231	1232	1233	1234	1235	1236	1237	1238	1239	1240	1241	1242	1243	
539	**3**	**10,335**	**9,757**	**2,720**	**54**	**390**	**3**	**6,983**	**4,672**	**1,308**	**12**	**149**	...	**3,352**	**17,426**	**3,440**	**6,855**	**172**	**1,178**	**7,131**	
521	**3**	**10,029**	**9,495**	**2,657**	**53**	**379**	**3**	**6,785**	**4,526**	**1,270**	**12**	**142**	...	**3,244**	**16,459**	**3,229**	**6,512**	**162**	**1,150**	**6,718**	
383	**1**	**7,920**	**8,058**	**2,371**	**42**	**305**	**1**	**5,645**	**3,136**	**855**	**6**	**78**	...	**2,275**	**13,518**	**2,544**	**5,687**	**137**	**930**	**5,337**	
56	...	*1,723*	*1,499*	*446*	*11*	*44*	...	*1,042*	*901*	*220*	...	*15*	...	*681*	*3,250*	*665*	*1,184*	*33*	*290*	*1,481*	
11	...	339	218	68	...	6	...	150	262	73	...	5	...	185	1,110	149	505	6	186	456	1
7	...	143	49	16	...	5	...	33	137	27	...	2	...	110	691	75	413	4	91	208	2
28	...	710	714	209	10	25	...	405	289	74	...	8	...	215	954	323	87	21	...	544	3
6	...	*529*	*455*	*96*	...	*6*	...	*359*	*228*	*52*	...	...	...	*176*	*650*	*197*	*26*	...	...	*427*	
5	...	171	185	60	...	4	...	125	64	18	...	1	...	46	190	64	28	1	2	112	4
5	...	360	383	93	1	4	...	289	141	28	...	1	...	121	320	54	150	1	8	110	5
152	*1*	*2,881*	*3,129*	*942*	*12*	*126*	*1*	*2,176*	*942*	*236*	...	*26*	...	*766*	*2,023*	*419*	*723*	*19*	*122*	*881*	
25	...	611	675	140	5	27	...	454	225	48	...	2	...	177	242	52	75	5	11	181	6
55	...	1,074	1,195	364	1	45	...	830	102	55	...	6	...	244	581	104	144	10	21	281	7
13	...	268	381	119	...	7	...	270	102	64	...	6	...	58	371	118	68	1	4	195	8
33	1	455	502	181	4	25	1	577	105	20		4	...	78	344	63	165	2	28	122	9
22	...	373	404	118	2	14	...	204	143	40	...	5	...	100	427	50	275	...	58	104	10
123	...	*2,449*	*2,351*	*602*	*15*	*35*	...	*1,764*	*1,065*	*315*	*6*	*34*	...	*655*	*5,527*	*1,076*	*2,334*	*66*	*426*	*2,113*	
18	...	420	310	75	4	12	...	231	255	70	...	6	...	185	741	161	327	10	107	312	11
47	...	951	876	150	10	25	...	607	455	101	6	18	...	284	2,305	446	918	9	124	947	12
9	...	*254*	*261*	*80*	...	*6*	...	*181*	*190*	*95*	...	*3*	...	*101*	*713*	*222*	*166*	*1*	...	*456*	
...	...	220	192	81	1	...	...	100	82	22	...	...	...	60	948	210	208	22	77	445	13
51	...	405	491	155	...	50	...	850	182	41	...	1	...	133	152	110	461	22	88	325	14
10	...	369	512	142	...	15	...	870	27	8	...	1	...	15	547	60	355	2	85	143	15
55	...	*567*	*1,045*	*381*	*4*	*46*	...	*664*	*284*	*51*	...	*6*	...	*203*	*2,625*	*390*	*1,390*	*20*	*98*	*845*	
14	...	437	525	170	4	12	...	340	119	31	...	2	...	88	1,190	200	524	11	28	400	16
15	...	224	210	91	...	14	...	125	137	36	...	4	...	95	648	124	270	6	25	248	17
20	...	200	304	114	...	20	...	190	26	12	...	...	...	10	790	60	550	3	25	124	18
138	**2**	**2,109**	**1,437**	**286**	**11**	**74**	**2**	**1,140**	**1,300**	**415**	**6**	**64**	...	**969**	**2,841**	**685**	**875**	**25**	**220**	**1,381**	
57	1	823	612	127	7	40	1	478	472	126	2	17	...	345	1,830	285	470	7	110	619	19
20	...	524	290	56	...	17	...	240	416	128	1	13	...	284	864	145	152	10	41	208	20
29	1	430	270	44	4	13	1	228	285	88	...	10	...	202	510	181	74	5	22	255	21
20	...	332	255	56	...	8	...	194	215	74	8	15	...	138	557	128	173	2	41	250	22
18	...	**306**	**262**	**63**	**1**	**11**	...	**198**	**146**	**38**	...	**7**	...	**108**	**967**	**211**	**248**	**10**	**28**	**413**	
1	...	30	37	7	...	1	...	30	...	...	...	...	...	...	26	2	5	...	2	15	23
1	...	15	10	1	...	...	...	5	10	6	...	1	...	10	113	55	9	...	...	60	24
5	...	82	88	16	...	4	...	21	15	4	...	1	...	5	40	14	5	...	...	22	25
1	...	36	20	5	...	1	...	17	19	...	...	...	...	15	220	86	114	1	17	60	26
...	...	80	81	15	—	...	...	65	24	6	...	...	...	15	210	27	134	2	8	55	27
...	...	9	11	8	...	...	...	5	2	2	...	...	...	1	23	4	10	...	...	5	28
...	...	9	4	1	...	...	...	5	6	—	...	...	...	4	55	25	15	2	...	41	29
1	...	2	2	...	...	...	...	2	1	1	...	1	...	...	24	2	10	1	1	5	30
6	...	67	40	9	...	4	...	31	47	11	...	2	...	30	100	50	8	...	...	65	31
2	...	...	...	...	...	...	...	...	2	2	...	2	...	...	52	15	...	2	...	17	32
...	...	...	...	...	...	...	...	...	...	...	...	...	...	...	3	1	...	...	...	...	33
1	...	1	2	2	...	1	...	...	2	1	...	...	...	1	12	6	5	2	...	5	34
...	...	9	5	4	...	...	...	1	12	4	...	...	...	5	8	4	2	...	...	2	35
...	...	...	...	...	...	...	...	...	1	1	...	...	...	...	17	4	1	...	...	11	36
...	...	6	12	6	1	...	...	6	...	...	...	...	...	...	41	6	7	2	...	25	37

TABLE XV.—Occupation or means

CLASS ... CLASS C.—PUBLIC ADMINISTRATION

SUB-CLASS ... Sub-Class VIII.—Profession

ORDER ... Order 48.—Medicine—(*concluded*). | Total order 49.—Instruction.

154.—Medical practitioners of all kinds, including dentists, oculists and veterinary surgeons. (columns 1244–1249)

155.—Midwives, vaccinators, compounders, nurses, masseurs, etc. (columns 1250–1255)

156.—Professors and teachers of all kinds,* and clerks and servants connected with education. (columns 1256–1261)

Serial No.	DISTRICT, CITY OR STATE.	154. Total workers and dependants.	Actual workers. Total. Males.	Actual workers. Total. Females.	Partially agriculturists. Males.	Partially agriculturists. Females.	Dependants.	155. Total workers and dependants.	Actual workers. Total. Males.	Actual workers. Total. Females.	Partially agriculturists. Males.	Partially agriculturists. Females.	Dependants.	156. Total workers and dependants.	Actual workers. Total. Males.	Actual workers. Total. Females.	Partially agriculturists. Males.	Partially agriculturists. Females.	Dependants.
	1	1244	1245	1246	1247	1248	1249	1250	1251	1252	1253	1254	1255	1256	1257	1258	1259	1260	1261
	Central Provinces and Berar.	**6,713**	**2,284**	**183**	**127**	**5**	**4,246**	**10,713**	**1,156**	**6,672**	**45**	**1,173**	**2,885**	**29,648**	**11,391**	**1,019**	**502**	**7**	**17,238**
	C. P. British Districts and Berar.	**6,442**	**2,186**	**174**	**123**	**2**	**4,082**	**10,017**	**1,043**	**6,338**	**39**	**1,148**	**2,636**	**27,890**	**10,543**	**955**	**457**	**6**	**16,392**
	C. P. British Districts.	**4,925**	**1,629**	**149**	**105**	**1**	**3,147**	**8,593**	**915**	**5,488**	**32**	**929**	**2,190**	**20,944**	**7,962**	**853**	**290**	**4**	**12,129**
	JUBBULPORE DIVISION.	*1,184*	*349*	*6*	*8*	...	*829*	*2,096*	*316*	*1,178*	*25*	*290*	*602*	*5,691*	*1,933*	*337*	*51*	...	*3,431*
1	Saugor ...	365	87	...	4	...	278	745	62	505	2	189	178	1,536	496	74	10	...	966
2	Damoh ...	100	36	1	3	...	63	591	39	412	1	91	140	790	273	26	6	...	491
3	Jubbulpore ...	560	172	3	1	...	385	394	151	84	20	...	159	2,079	704	175	16	...	1,200
	JUBBULPORE CITY	*442*	*131*	*2*	...	...	*309*	*208*	*66*	*33*	...	...	*118*	*1,063*	*307*	*95*	*1*	...	*661*
4	Mandla ...	79	27	2	...	...	50	120	37	21	1	2	62	549	215	21	8	...	313
5	Seoni ...	80	27	...	...	...	53	246	27	156	1	8	63	737	245	41	5	...	451
	NERBUDDA DIVISION.	*695*	*223*	*18*	*18*	...	*452*	*1,330*	*196*	*705*	*1*	*122*	*423*	*4,903*	*1,822*	*158*	*53*	...	*2,863*
6	Narsinghpur ...	120	43	...	5	...	77	222	39	79	...	11	104	1,019	308	41	11	...	610
7	Hoshangabad ...	233	62	6	10	...	165	208	44	138	...	21	110	1,579	547	65	4	...	907
8	Nimar ...	178	66	11	1	...	101	201	52	57	...	4	92	1,067	445	29	6	...	503
9	Betul ...	75	26	...	2	...	49	209	37	159	1	28	73	549	204	12	12	...	333
10	Chhindwara ...	87	26	1	...	...	60	340	24	272	...	58	44	689	318	11	20	...	360
	NAGPUR DIVISION	*2,318*	*816*	*115*	*62*	*1*	*1,358*	*3,169*	*255*	*2,319*	*3*	*425*	*695*	*5,851*	*2,307*	*207*	*110*	*4*	*3,337*
11	Wardha ...	303	123	15	10	...	225	428	28	312	...	107	88	931	433	8	25	...	490
12	Nagpur ...	962	304	50	9	...	602	1,347	140	862	...	124	345	2,163	773	142	34	1	1,248
	NAGPUR CITY ...	*394*	*121*	*31*	*1*	...	*252*	*382*	*101*	*86*	...	...	*203*	*799*	*255*	*53*	*9*	...	*491*
13	Chanda ...	530	178	13	20	1	330	418	32	280	2	76	106	1,013	386	20	24	...	607
14	Bhandara ...	420	163	9	22	...	248	572	33	452	...	83	87	1,096	486	26	20	...	590
15	Balaghat ...	143	47	22	1	...	74	404	22	313	1	35	60	648	235	11	7	3	402
	CHHATTISGARH DIVISION.	*630*	*252*	*10*	*17*	...	*378*	*1,998*	*138*	*1,356*	*3*	*92*	*464*	*4,499*	*1,840*	*151*	*77*	...	*2,508*
16	Raipur ...	396	104	4	10	...	232	794	46	520	1	38	228	2,232	858	61	40	...	1,813
17	Bilaspur ...	144	51	2	4	...	91	504	73	274	2	29	157	1,337	590	70	23	...	671
18	Drug ...	90	31	4	3	...	55	700	20	502	...	25	79	930	380	20	14	...	524
	Berar ...	**1,517**	**557**	**25**	**18**	**1**	**935**	**1,424**	**128**	**850**	**7**	**219**	**446**	**6,946**	**2,581**	**102**	**167**	**2**	**4,263**
19	Amraoti ...	502	195	18	6	1	379	738	40	458	1	115	240	2,086	733	30	29	...	1,323
20	Akola ...	204	100	3	8	...	191	270	44	149	2	41	77	1,862	708	43	64	1	1,111
21	Buldana ...	367	157	3	1	...	207	143	24	71	4	22	48	1,766	658	10	60	1	1,098
22	Yeotmal ...	264	105	1	3	...	158	273	20	172	...	41	81	1,232	482	19	14	...	731
	Feudatory States.	**271**	**98**	**9**	**4**	**3**	**164**	**696**	**113**	**334**	**6**	**25**	**249**	**1,758**	**848**	**64**	**45**	**1**	**846**
23	Makrai ...	18	...	5	...	2	13	8	2	...	...	...	6	28	12	...	...	...	16
24	Bastar ...	31	17	1	...	...	13	82	21	8	...	...	53	119	56	4	...	...	59
25	Kanker ...	2	1	...	...	...	1	44	13	9	...	...	22	135	68	5	2	...	62
26	Nandgaon ...	30	13	3	1	1	14	190	22	110	...	10	52	337	149	8	3	...	180
27	Khairagarh ...	30	13	...	1	...	23	180	14	134	1	8	32	203	90	2	2	...	111
28	Chhuikhadan ..	8	2	...	...	...	6	15	2	10	...	...	3	81	43	3	...	...	35
29	Kawardha ...	38	11	...	2	...	27	45	12	19	...	...	14	122	50	1	2	...	71
30	Sakti ...	...	...	...	...	...	...	23	2	16	1	1	5	68	33	...	3	...	30
31	Raigarh ...	53	20	...	...	...	33	53	10	8	...	...	35	195	106	3	...	...	86
32	Sarangarh ...	12	9	...	...	...	3	20	6	...	2	...	14	181	83	7	26	1	91
33	Chang Bhakar ...	1	1	...	...	...	...	...	...	...	...	...	...	4	4	...	1	...	...
34	Korea ...	5	3	...	...	...	2	7	3	3	2	...	1	20	18	...	...	...	8
35	Surguja ...	1	1	...	...	...	...	7	3	2	...	...	2	84	51	...	...	...	33
36	Udaipur ...	9	2	...	...	...	7	8	2	2	...	...	4	98	59	...	3	...	30
37	Jashpur ...	27	5	...	2	...	22	14	1	7	...	...	6	83	26	31	3	...	25

* Except law, medicine, music, dancing and drawing.

# of livelihood, Part A.—General Table.

AND LIBERAL ARTS—(*continued*).

and liberal arts—(*continued*).

Order 50.—Letters and arts and sciences.

Total order 50.						157.—Public scribes, stenographers, etc.						158.—Architects, surveyors, engineers and their employés.						
Total workers and dependants.	Actual workers.				Dependants.	Total workers and dependants.	Actual workers.				Dependants.	Total workers and dependants.	Actual workers.				Dependants.	Serial No.
	Total.		Partially agriculturists.				Total.		Partially agriculturists.				Total.		Partially agriculturists.			
	Males.	Females.	Males.	Females.			Males.	Females.	Males.	Females.			Males.	Females.	Males.	Females.		
1202	1203	1204	1205	1206	1207	1268	1269	1270	1271	1272	1273	1274	1275	1276	1277	1278	1279	
43.711	**20,320**	**1,893**	**4,233**	**116**	**21,398**	**25**	**8**	**1**	**6**	...	**16**	**7,495**	**2,900**	**167**	**250**	...	**4,428**	
40,776	**19,145**	**1,805**	**4,101**	**104**	**19,826**	**25**	**8**	**1**	**6**	...	**16**	**7,204**	**2,797**	**153**	**244**	...	**4,254**	
30,796	**14,123**	**1,395**	**2,543**	**72**	**15,278**	**25**	**8**	**1**	**6**	...	**16**	**6,338**	**2,494**	**136**	**233**	...	**3,708**	
4,300	*1,756*	*371*	*106*	*16*	*2,199*	*1*	...	...	...	...	*1*	*1,491*	*495*	*7*	*17*	...	*980*	
963	381	115	37	9	407	...	...	...	...	...	...	317	118	...	13	...	190	1
410	154	43	4	4	213	...	...	...	...	...	...	210	83	1	2	...	132	2
1,264	472	75	14	...	717	1	...	...	...	...	1	623	106	...	2	...	427	3
934	*325*	*40*	*2*	...	*560*	*1*	...	...	...	...	*1*	*536*	*100*	...	*2*	...	*370*	
633	261	61	3	1	311	...	...	...	...	...	...	177	61	...	...	...	116	4
1,036	408	77	47	2	491	...	...	...	...	...	...	158	40	6	...	...	112	5
5,372	*2,453*	*343*	*122*	*19*	*2,476*	*4*	...	...	...	...	*4*	*1,237*	*596*	*21*	*11*	...	*610*	
444	219	23	17	...	202	...	...	...	...	...	...	251	126	2	10	...	123	6
1,065	466	116	13	3	483	4	...	...	...	...	4	378	194	9	...	...	175	7
1,161	516	145	28	11	500	...	...	...	...	...	...	142	48	7	...	...	87	8
1,035	540	21	1	1	474	...	...	...	...	...	...	305	162	3	...	...	140	9
1,567	712	38	63	4	817	...	...	...	...	...	...	151	66	...	1	...	85	10
17,041	*7,920*	*460*	*2,001*	*17*	*8,661*	*20*	*8*	*1*	*6*	...	*11*	*3,081*	*1,194*	*98*	*195*	...	*1,70[illegible]*	
2,876	1,403	54	483	5	1,419	...	...	...	...	...	...	138	57	1	5	...	80	11
7,434	3,158	285	387	5	3,991	14	2	1	...	...	11	1,820	542	91	14	...	1,190	12
1,399	*591*	*101*	*12*	...	*1,207*	*2*	*1*	*1*	...	...	...	*1,400*	*399*	*57*	*1[illegible]*	...	*913*	
2,427	1,267	83	567	2	1,127	...	...	...	...	...	...	654	452	1	175	...	201	13
2,562	1,193	56	391	5	1,313	...	...	...	...	...	...	239	70	1	3	...	168	14
1,742	899	32	170	...	811	6	6	...	6	...	...	101	78	1	2	...	117	15
4,177	*2,013*	*231*	*315*	*20*	*1,943*	...	...	...	...	...	...	*869*	*200*	*13*	*6*	...	*350*	
1,522	832	75	120	9	615	...	...	...	...	...	...	341	103	...	1	...	238	16
1,535	643	104	125	11	788	...	...	...	...	...	...	87	38	...	2	...	46	17
1,120	539	42	70	...	539	...	...	...	...	...	...	141	65	13	3	...	63	18
9,980	**5,022**	**410**	**1,558**	**32**	**4,548**	...	...	...	...	...	...	**866**	**303**	**17**	**11**	...	**546**	
4,268	2,107	130	643	19	2,031	...	...	...	...	...	...	257	97	2	4	...	158	19
2,510	1,267	111	511	8	1,132	...	...	...	...	...	...	365	129	11	6	...	228	20
1,390	675	98	190	8	617	...	...	...	...	...	...	163	45	4	...	...	114	21
1,812	973	71	208	...	768	...	...	...	...	...	...	81	35	...	1	...	40	22
2,935	**1,175**	**188**	**132**	**12**	**1,572**	...	...	...	...	...	...	**291**	**103**	**14**	**6**	...	**174**	
12	8	...	...	...	4	...	...	...	...	...	...	3	1	...	...	...	2	23
275	105	38	2	...	132	...	...	...	...	...	...	134	52	8	1	...	74	24
71	32	4	...	...	35	...	...	...	...	...	...	38	17	4	...	...	17	25
251	110	2	18	...	139	...	...	...	...	...	...	41	13	...	2	...	28	26
388	156	32	30	2	200	...	...	...	...	...	...	24	6	...	1	...	18	27
121	45	5	8	...	71	...	...	...	...	...	...	17	3	2	...	...	12	28
139	56	8	12	3	78	...	...	...	...	...	...	6	1	...	1	...	5	29
18	8	...	2	...	10	...	...	...	...	...	...	12	4	...	1	...	8	30
72	29	7	...	...	36	...	...	...	...	...	...	3	1	...	...	...	2	31
102	48	1	6	...	53	...	...	...	...	...	...	4	1	...	...	...	3	32
10	3	5	...	...	2	...	...	...	...	...	...	...	...	...	...	...	...	33
138	57	20	6	...	61	...	...	...	...	...	...	...	...	...	...	...	...	34
1,083	400	42	22	2	632	...	...	...	...	...	...	5	3	...	...	...	2	35
39	11	...	...	...	28	...	...	...	...	...	...	4	1	...	...	...	3	36
216	98	24	24	5	94	...	...	...	...	...	...	...	...	...	...	...	...	37

TABLE XV.—Occupation or means

Serial No.	DISTRICT, CITY OR STATE.	CLASS C.—PUBLIC ADMINISTRATION AND LIBERAL ARTS—(concluded). Sub-Class VIII.—Professions and liberal arts—(concluded). Order 50.—Letters and arts and sciences—(concluded). 159.—Others (authors, photographers, artists, sculptors, astronomers, meteorologists, botanists, astrologers, etc.)						160.—Music composers and masters, players on all kinds of musical instruments (not military), singers, actors and dancers.						Total Sub-Class IX.—Persons living on their income. Total order 51.—Persons living principally on their income. 161.—Proprietors (other than of agricultural land) fund and scholarship holders and pensioners.					
		Total workers and dependants.	Actual workers. Total.		Partially agriculturists.		Dependants.	Total workers and dependants.	Actual workers. Total.		Partially agriculturists.		Dependants.	Total workers and dependants.	Actual workers. Total.		Partially agriculturists.		Dependants.
			Males.	Females.	Males.	Females.			Males.	Females.	Males.	Females.			Males.	Females.	Males.	Females.	
	1	1280	1281	1282	1283	1284	1285	1286	1287	1288	1289	1290	1291	1292	1293	1294	1295	1296	1297
	Central Provinces and Berar.	**1,451**	**555**	**162**	**40**	**1**	**734**	**34,740**	**16,857**	**1,663**	**3,937**	**115**	**16,220**	**11,864**	**3,184**	**1,173**	**327**	**40**	**7,507**
	C. P. British Districts and Berar.	**1,372**	**524**	**142**	**34**	**1**	**706**	**32,175**	**15,816**	**1,509**	**3,817**	**103**	**14,850**	**11,716**	**3,140**	**1,149**	**325**	**40**	**7,427**
	C. P. British Districts.	**964**	**373**	**82**	**15**	...	**509**	**23,469**	**11,248**	**1,176**	**2,289**	**72**	**11,045**	**8,460**	**2,222**	**1,004**	**217**	**34**	**5,234**
	JUBBULPORE DIVISION.	*237*	*130*	*2*	*4*	...	*115*	*2,577*	*1,115*	*362*	*84*	*10*	*1,097*	*2,603*	*629*	*873*	*51*	*5*	*1,701*
1	Saugor ...	45	20	...	...	...	25	601	243	115	24	9	243	798	208	50	21	...	534
2	Damoh ...	30	11	2	...	...	17	164	60	40	2	4	64	222	57	17	6	...	148
3	Jubbulpore ...	152	85	...	3	...	67	488	191	75	9	...	222	1,265	201	143	12	1	831
	JUBBULPORE CITY	*98*	*47*	...	...	...	*51*	*299*	*112*	*49*	...	...	*138*	*1,094*	*249*	*124*	*2*	...	*721*
4	Mandla ...	7	1	...	...	...	6	449	190	61	3	1	189	210	38	52	4	4	120
5	Seoni ...	8	3	...	1	...	...	875	425	71	46	2	379	108	35	5	8	...	68
	NERBUDDA DIVISION	*86*	*37*	*1*	*2*	...	*45*	*3,955*	*1,820*	*321*	*109*	*19*	*1,814*	*1,634*	*430*	*116*	*45*	*1*	*938*
6	Narsinghpur ...	9	4	...	...	...	5	184	80	21	7	...	74	258	65	31	9	...	162
7	Hoshangabad ...	9	3	...	...	...	6	674	299	107	13	3	298	451	124	43	9	...	284
8	Nimar ...	28	11	...	2	...	17	991	457	138	26	11	306	302	96	21	6	...	185
9	Betul ...	23	8	...	...	...	15	707	370	18	1	1	319	193	62	9	12	1	122
10	Chhindwara ...	17	11	1	...	...	5	1,399	635	37	62	4	727	330	83	12	12	...	235
	NAGPUR DIVISION ...	*608*	*203*	*79*	*9*	...	*332*	*13,362*	*6,615*	*285*	*1,787*	*17*	*6,562*	*3,385*	*957*	*216*	*107*	*6*	*2,115*
11	Wardha ...	110	34	24	1	...	52	2,628	1,312	20	477	5	1,287	403	86	18	12	...	299
12	Nagpur ..	326	112	37	6	...	177	5,265	2,502	156	307	5	2,607	1,807	561	162	31	1	1,084
	NAGPUR CITY ...	*162*	*48*	*9*	...	...	*95*	*315*	*143*	*4*	...	...	*195*	*1,019*	*310*	*30*	*12*	...	*679*
13	Chanda ...	128	48	12	2	...	68	1,645	767	20	390	2	858	542	100	10	48	2	372
14	Bhandara ...	33	5	6	...	...	22	2,200	1,118	40	391	5	1,123	384	107	22	10	3	255
15	Balaghat ...	11	4	...	...	...	7	1,534	816	31	162	...	687	152	43	4	6	...	105
	CHHATTISGARH DIVISION.	*33*	*13*	...	...	...	*20*	*3,575*	*1,795*	*208*	*309*	*20*	*1,572*	*1,035*	*206*	*399*	*11*	*22*	*430*
16	Raipur ...	23	10	...	...	...	13	1,158	719	75	119	9	364	818	137	380	4	21	301
17	Bilaspur ...	4	1	...	...	...	3	1,444	604	104	123	11	736	146	51	13	6	...	82
18	Drug ...	6	2	...	...	...	4	973	472	29	67	...	472	71	18	6	1	1	47
	Berar ...	**408**	**151**	**60**	**19**	**1**	**197**	**8,706**	**4,568**	**333**	**1,528**	**31**	**3,805**	**3,256**	**918**	**145**	**108**	**6**	**2,193**
19	Amraoti ...	255	89	36	16	1	130	3,756	1,921	92	623	15	1,743	1,298	394	86	30	2	818
20	Akola ...	100	39	22	3	...	39	2,045	1,102	78	502	8	865	908	221	31	43	...	656
21	Buldana ...	15	6	...	...	...	9	1,212	624	94	196	8	494	664	148	20	25	4	496
22	Yeotmal ...	38	17	2	...	...	19	1,603	921	69	207	...	703	386	155	8	10	...	223
	Feudatory States	**79**	**31**	**20**	**6**	...	**28**	**2,565**	**1,041**	**154**	**120**	**12**	**1,370**	**148**	**44**	**24**	**2**	...	**80**
23	Makrai ...	3	1	...	...	...	2	6	6	...	...	...	...	13	4	6	...	...	3
24	Bastar ...	19	...	19	...	...	...	122	53	11	1	...	58	32	5	4	1	...	23
25	Kanker ...	...	...	...	...	...	...	33	15	...	2	...	18	11	6	4	1	...	1
26	Nandgaon ...	2	1	...	...	...	1	208	96	2	16	...	110	22	6	4	...	...	12
27	Khairagarh ...	5	3	...	1	...	2	359	147	32	28	2	18	34	14	4	...	...	16
28	Chhuikhadan ...	...	...	...	...	...	...	104	42	3	8	...	59	18	6	1	...	...	11
29	Kawardha ...	...	...	-	...	...	...	133	55	8	11	3	70	1	1	...	...	...	...
30	Sakti ...	...	...	...	...	...	...	6	4	...	1	...	2	6	1	1	...	...	4
31	Raigarh ...	...	...	...	...	...	...	60	28	7	...	...	34	...	...	...	...	...	...
32	Sarangarh ...	50	26	1	5	...	23	48	21	...	1	...	27	10	...	...	...	...	10
33	Chang Bhakar ...	...	...	...	...	...	...	10	3	5	...	...	2	...	...	...	...	...	...
34	Korea ...	...	...	...	...	...	...	138	57	20	6	...	61	...	...	...	...	...	...
35	Surguja ...	...	...	...	...	...	...	1,078	409	42	22	2	630	...	...	...	...	...	...
36	Udaipur ...	...	...	...	...	...	...	35	10	...	...	...	25	1	1	—	...	..	...
37	Jashpur ...	...	...	...	...	...	...	210	98	24	24	5	94	...	...	...	.	...	—

of livelihood, Part A.—General Table.

CLASS D.—MISCELLANEOUS.																		
Sub-Class X.—Domestic service.																		
Order 52.—Domestic service.																		
Total Class D.						Total Sub-Class X and Order 52.						162.—Cooks, water-carriers, door-keepers, watchmen and other in-door servants.						
Total workers and dependants.	Actual workers.				Dependants.	Total workers and dependants.	Actual workers.				Dependants.	Total workers and dependants.	Actual workers.				Dependants.	Serial No.
	Total.		Partially agriculturists.				Total.		Partially agriculturists.				Total.		Partially agriculturists.			
	Males.	Females.	Males.	Females.			Males.	Females.	Males.	Females.			Males.	Females.	Males.	Females.		
1298	1299	1300	1301	1302	1303	1304	1305	1306	1307	1308	1309	1310	1311	1312	1313	1314	1315	
301.414	109.798	79,742	6,106	4.285	111,874	160,995	56,128	47,165	2,901	3.166	57,702	145,710	49,203	46,416	2.784	3,158	50,091	
273,204	101,288	69.673	5.775	4,127	102.243	142,792	51,043	40.013	2,691	3,082	51,736	131,095	45,517	39,602	2,590	3,074	45,976	
211.178	73,697	60.803	4,810	3,540	76,678	112,263	36,351	36,815	2,288	2,804	39,097	101,798	31,540	36,419	2,200	2,796	33,839	
68,738	22,563	20,777	1,535	1,817	25,390	42,512	12,601	14,523	1,416	1,656	15,3[illegible]8	38,634	10,569	14,496	1,410	1,650	13,319	
17,028	5,152	6,004	640	830	5,872	12,271	3,402	4,831	500	783	3,978	11,259	3,074	4,820	500	783	3,365	1
10,370	2,782	3,939	487	469	3,649	7,476	1,869	3,217	416	440	2,390	7,375	1,822	3,217	414	440	2,336	2
32,208	11,501	7,769	643	471	12,938	18,418	6,153	4,548	480	385	7,717	16,007	4,989	4,544	478	385	6,474	3
15,413	6,253	1,591	3	1	7,539	9,119	3,526	801	...	1	4,792	6,848	2,431	799	...	1	3,013	
4,367	1,559	1,364	44	33	1,444	1,700	511	640	18	30	540	1,539	452	644	16	30	463	4
4,762	1,574	1,701	21	14	1,487	2,647	606	1,278	2	9	763	2,484	532	1,271	2	9	681	5
40,569	14,552	10,908	1,044	1,041	15,109	19,524	6,367	6,764	441	810	6,695	19,162	6,011	6,749	440	809	6,402	
8,687	2,751	3,212	378	420	2,724	5,947	1,610	2,532	263	371	1,804	5,849	1,564	2,533	263	371	1,752	6
15,098	5,439	3,498	41[illegible]	384	6,161	7,432	2,380	2,352	147	344	2,700	7,233	2,284	2,350	147	344	2,506	7
6,100	2,011	1,010	100	61	2,079	1,773	731	333	6	9	700	1,721	688	332	6	9	701	8
4,664	1,843	1,127	60	87	1,094	1,804	656	512	7	40	636	1,613	564	501	6	39	548	9
7,014	2,508	2,055	87	87	2,451	2,868	990	1,034	18	40	844	2,746	911	1,033	18	40	802	10
58,272	23,373	11,653	960	355	23,236	24,369	10,348	4,019	217	148	10,007	22,699	9,420	4,008	203	148	9,171	
10,759	4,078	1,997	212	69	4,084	3,757	1,840	479	54	18	1,432	3,630	1,771	479	53	18	1,380	11
26,562	10,284	5,008	22[illegible]	70	11,272	13,397	5,375	2,153	65	57	5,869	12,236	4,796	2,146	63	57	5,294	12
18,155	5,106	2,412	33	1	5,667	7,970	3,049	1,289	28	...	3,635	7,252	2,689	1,285	26	...	3,281	
9,688	3,792	2,495	226	119	3,401	2,562	1,132	542	44	33	888	2,416	1,055	541	37	33	814	13
7,047	3,071	1,349	220	68	2,633	2,830	1,182	467	46	28	1,181	2,607	1,053	466	43	28	1,086	14
4,210	1,548	813	73	22	1,855	1,823	808	378	8	12	637	1,716	745	376	7	12	505	15
43,602	13,204	17,466	471	328	12,933	25,552	7,040	11,509	214	190	7,009	21,353	5,240	11,166	147	183	4,947	
17,743	5,568	6,033	114	117	5,242	11,602	3,296	4,984	77	88	3,323	9,717	2,480	4,813	54	84	2,424	16
14,280	4,490	4,952	201	148	4,838	7,032	2,129	2,628	110	71	2,275	5,494	1,478	2,499	73	69	1,517	17
11,579	3,146	5,580	66	63	2,853	6,922	1,615	3,897	27	31	1,411	6,142	1,282	3,854	20	30	1,008	18
62,026	27,591	8,870	1.465	587	25,565	30.529	14,692	3,198	403	278	12.639	29.297	13,977	3,183	380	278	12,137	
21,747	9,307	3,335	345	77	9,046	11,854	5,315	1,372	92	25	5,107	11,418	5,082	1,372	80	25	4,964	19
15,260	6,043	1,931	573	187	6,395	7.734	3,807	745	178	42	3,182	7,540	3,677	745	177	42	3,124	20
12,822	5,804	1,721	349	70	5,297	6,545	3,393	375	99	15	2,777	6,172	3,108	373	93	15	2,631	21
12,188	5,477	1,883	198	247	4,828	4,390	2,177	700	34	196	1,513	4,161	2,050	698	34	196	1,418	22
28,210	8,510	10,069	331	158	9,631	18,203	5,085	7,152	210	84	5,966	14,615	3.686	6.814	194	84	4,115	
338	71	60	...	...	199	18[illegible]	52	34	...	...	97	141	35	34	...	...	72	23
3,823	1,482	1,127	19	3	1,214	2,215	836	671	9	...	708	1,066	680	670	9	...	609	24
1,433	492	483	4	2	458	1,087	321	353	1	1	303	885	247	353	...	1	285	25
2,343	557	964	9	3	822	1,406	335	711	6	1	452	1,300	242	711	6	1	350	26
2,931	769	1,880	8	2	770	2,394	542	1,226	7	1	620	1,944	453	907	7	1	524	27
547	98	313	3	2	136	400	41	295	1	2	64	869	25	295	1	2	49	28
1,007	202	463	0	4	342	798	188	366	2	3	244	722	154	366	2	3	202	29
870	140	114	13	2	116	121	41	54	...	2	26	84	19	54	...	2	11	30
4,378	1,425	1,423	213	101	1,530	3,334	1,024	1,147	138	58	1,163	2,401	657	1,123	128	58	621	31
1,920	510	913	12	26	497	1,080	209	651	9	8	220	924	142	650	8	8	132	32
265	85	97	5	6	83	132	38	54	5	3	40	114	31	51	5	3	32	33
1,080	288	490	9	1	260	763	165	410	7	...	188	655	123	409	7	...	123	34
4,448	1,412	903	8	1	2,138	2,427	751	466	5	1	1,210	1,707	487	464	4	1	756	35
784	205	212	1	...	306	534	196	110	1	...	222	289	110	98	...	...	81	36
2,502	632	1,111	21	4	759	1,287	340	508	19	4	343	1,106	275	569	17	4	262	37

TABLE XV.—Occupation or means

CLASS ...		Class D.—Miscel																	
SUB-CLASS ...		Sub-Class X.—Domestic service—(concluded).						Sub-Class XI.—Insufficiently											
ORDER ...		Order 52.—Domestic service—(concluded).						Order 53.—General terms which do not											
		163.—Private grooms, coachmen, dog boys, etc.						Total Sub-Class XI and Order 53.						164.—Manufacturers, business-men and contractors otherwise unspecified.					
		Total workers and dependants.	Actual workers. Total.		Actual workers. Partially agriculturists.		Dependants.	Total workers and dependants.	Actual workers. Total.		Actual workers. Partially agriculturists.		Dependants.	Total workers and dependants.	Actual workers. Total.		Actual workers. Partially agriculturists.		Dependants.
Serial No.	DISTRICT, CITY OR STATE.		Males.	Females.	Males.	Females.			Males.	Females.	Males.	Females.			Males.	Females.	Males.	Females.	
	1	1316	1317	1318	1319	1320	1321	1322	1323	1324	1325	1326	1327	1328	1329	1330	1331	1332	1333
	Central Provinces and Berar.	**15,285**	**6,925**	**749**	**117**	**8**	**7,611**	**37,729**	**11,722**	**10,194**	**245**	**86**	**15,813**	**2,401**	**774**	**16**	**46**	**1**	**1,611**
	C. P. British Districts and Berar.	**11,697**	**5,526**	**411**	**101**	**8**	**5,760**	**35,449**	**11,164**	**9,441**	**177**	**83**	**14,844**	**2,389**	**767**	**16**	**45**	**1**	**1,606**
	C. P. British Districts.	**10,465**	**4,811**	**396**	**88**	**8**	**5,258**	**33,093**	**10,249**	**8,965**	**143**	**79**	**13,879**	**1,917**	**613**	**16**	**32**	**1**	**1,288**
	JUBBULPORE DIVISION	*3,828*	*1,732*	*27*	*6*	...	*2,069*	*12,084*	*3,776*	*3,095*	*35*	*40*	*5,214*	*388*	*103*	*4*	*7*	...	*281*
1	Saugor ...	1,012	388	11	...	...	613	1,314	321	515	3	...	478	20	10	...	...	...	10
2	Damoh ...	101	47	...	2	...	54	1,370	282	388	2	4	700	47	8	...	1	...	39
3	Jubbulpore ...	2,411	1,164	4	2	...	1,243	8,161	2,696	1,895	27	36	3,570	279	69	4	5	...	208
	JUBBULPORE CITY ...	*2,276*	*1,095*	*2*	...	...	*1,179*	*4,540*	*1,614*	*621*	*2*	...	*2,305*	*195*	*36*	...	*2*	...	*157*
4	Mandla ...	141	59	5	2	...	77	601	150	204	2	...	247	15	4	...	...	...	11
5	Seoni ...	163	74	7	...	...	82	638	326	93	1	...	219	27	12	...	1	...	15
	NERBUDDA DIVISION	*662*	*356*	*15*	*1*	*1*	*291*	*4,513*	*1,550*	*1,205*	*30*	*12*	*1,758*	*188*	*58*	*1*	...	...	*129*
6	Narsinghpur ...	98	46	...	...	...	52	327	93	131	7	1	103	6	5	...	...	...	1
7	Hoshangabad ...	199	96	2	...	...	101	777	281	179	5	...	317	33	14	...	...	...	19
8	Nimar ...	52	43	1	...	...	8	1,024	339	246	1	...	439	62	20	...	...	...	42
9	Betul ...	191	92	11	1	1	88	544	215	124	8	9	205	21	6	1	...	...	14
10	Chhindwara ...	122	79	1	...	...	42	1,841	622	525	9	2	694	66	13	...	...	...	53
	NAGPUR DIVISION ...	*1,770*	*923*	*11*	*14*	...	*836*	*12,161*	*3,536*	*3,269*	*63*	*9*	*5,356*	*1,040*	*377*	*6*	*23*	...	*657*
11	Wardha ...	127	75	...	1	...	52	2,003	636	608	10	1	759	83	35	...	2	...	48
12	Nagpur ...	1,161	579	7	2	...	575	6,716	1,880	1,908	26	5	2,928	539	194	4	4	...	341
	NAGPUR CITY ...	*718*	*360*	*1*	*2*	...	*357*	*2,959*	*801*	*796*	*4*	...	*1,358*	*251*	*51*	*1*	*1*	...	*198*
13	Chanda ...	152	77	1	7	...	74	1,986	711	564	16	3	711	212	90	1	10	...	121
14	Bhandara ...	223	129	1	3	...	93	459	135	127	5	...	197	110	38	...	3	...	72
15	Balaghat ...	107	63	2	1	...	42	997	174	62	6	...	761	96	20	1	4	...	75
	CHHATTISGARH DIVISION.	*4,205*	*1,800*	*334*	*67*	*7*	*2,053*	*4,335*	*1,388*	*1,396*	*15*	*18*	*1,551*	*301*	*75*	*6*	*2*	*1*	*221*
16	Raipur ...	1,886	816	171	23	4	890	1,255	443	331	4	...	481	167	18	...	...	...	149
17	Bilaspur ...	1,538	651	120	37	2	758	1,733	514	539	9	4	680	36	8	1	1	...	27
18	Drug ...	781	333	43	7	1	405	1,347	431	526	2	14	390	98	49	4	1	1	45
	Berar ...	**1,232**	**715**	**15**	**13**	...	**502**	**2,356**	**915**	**476**	**34**	**4**	**965**	**472**	**154**	...	**13**	...	**318**
19	Amraoti ...	436	233	...	6	...	203	734	270	124	20	2	340	157	45	...	1	...	114
20	Akola ...	188	130	...	1	...	58	424	221	26	6	...	177	120	46	...	4	...	74
21	Buldana ...	373	225	2	6	...	146	561	149	229	7	2	183	79	28	...	7	...	51
22	Yeotmal ...	235	127	13	...	...	95	637	275	97	1	...	265	116	37	...	1	...	79
	Feudatory States ...	**3,588**	**1,399**	**338**	**16**	...	**1,851**	**2,280**	**558**	**753**	**68**	**3**	**969**	**12**	**7**	...	**1**	...	**5**
23	Makrai ...	42	17	...	...	...	25	1	...	...	...	...	1	...	...	...	...	...	...
24	Bastar ...	250	150	1	...	...	99	280	71	90	...	...	119	...	...	...	...	...	...
25	Kanker ...	152	74	...	1	...	78	1	1	...	...	...	...	1	1	...	...	...	...
26	Nandgaon ...	189	93	...	...	...	96	404	86	109	...	...	146	...	...	...	...	...	...
27	Khairagarh ...	450	89	259	...	...	102	27	14	...	...	...	13	2	1	...	...	...	1
28	Chhuikhadan ...	31	16	...	...	...	15	...	...	...	...	...	...	...	...	...	...	...	...
29	Kawardha ...	76	34	...	...	...	42	12	8	4	1	...	1	3	3	...	1	...	...
30	Sakti ...	37	22	...	...	...	15	45	12	19	...	...	14	...	...	...	...	...	...
31	Raigarh ...	933	367	24	10	...	542	221	90	...	64	...	122	3	...	...	...	...	3
32	Sarangarh ...	156	67	1	1	...	88	2	2	...	...	...	...	...	...	...	...	...	...
33	Chang Bhakar ...	18	7	3	...	...	8	26	8	12	...	3	6	...	...	...	...	...	...
34	Korea ...	108	42	1	...	...	65	2	1	...	...	...	1	...	...	...	...	...	...
35	Surguja ...	720	264	2	1	...	454	506	121	84	3	...	301	2	2	...	...	...	...
36	Udaipur ...	245	86	18	1	...	141	52	...	46	...	...	6	...	...	...	...	...	...
37	Jashpur ...	181	71	29	2	...	81	700	132	320	...	...	239	1	...	...	...	...	1

# of livelihood, Part A.—General Table.

laneous— (*continued*).

described occupations. | Sub-Class XII.—Unproductive.

indicate a definite occupation.

165.—Cashiers, accountants, book-keepers, clerks and other employés in unspecified offices, warehouses and shops.						166.—Mechanics otherwise unspecified.						167.—Labourers and workmen otherwise unspecified.						Total Sub-Class XII.			
Total workers and dependants.	Actual workers. Total. Males.	Actual workers. Total. Females.	Partially agriculturists. Males.	Partially agriculturists. Females.	Dependants.	Total workers and dependants.	Actual workers. Total. Males.	Actual workers. Total. Females.	Partially agriculturists. Males.	Partially agriculturists. Females.	Dependants.	Total workers and dependants.	Actual workers. Total. Males.	Actual workers. Total. Females.	Partially agriculturists. Males.	Partially agriculturists. Females.	Dependants.	Total workers and dependants.	Actual workers. Total. Males.	Actual workers. Total. Females.	Serial No.
1334	1335	1336	1337	1338	1339	1340	1341	1342	1343	1344	1345	1346	1347	1348	1349	1350	1351	1352	1353	1354	
4,865	**1,838**	**344**	**113**	**2**	**2,683**	**1,012**	**349**	**72**	**1**	**2**	**591**	**29,451**	**8,761**	**9,762**	**85**	**81**	**10,928**	**102,690**	**41,948**	**22,383**	
4,410	**1,676**	**334**	**47**	**2**	**2,400**	**1,009**	**346**	**72**	**1**	**2**	**591**	**27,641**	**8,375**	**9,019**	**84**	**78**	**10,247**	**94,963**	**39,081**	**20,219**	
4,000	**1,472**	**326**	**43**	**2**	**2,202**	**966**	**321**	**70**	**1**	**1**	**575**	**26,210**	**7,843**	**8,553**	**67**	**75**	**9,814**	**65,822**	**27,097**	**15,023**	
1,178	*474*	*16*	*5*	...	*688*	*536*	*158*	...	...	...	*378*	*9,982*	*3,040*	*3,075*	*23*	*40*	*3,867*	*14,139*	*6,192*	*3,159*	
66	19	...	1	...	47	...	...	...	...	...	...	1,228	292	515	2	...	421	3,443	1,369	658	1
63	16	2	1	...	45	...	...	...	...	...	...	1,200	258	386	...	4	616	1,524	631	334	2
980	406	7	2	...	567	536	158	...	...	...	378	6,366	2,063	1,884	20	36	2,419	5,629	2,652	1,326	3
875	*359*	*1*	...	...	*515*	*536*	*158*	...	...	...	*378*	*2,931*	*1,059*	*520*	...	...	*1,352*	*1,754*	*1,143*	*269*	
52	27	5	1	...	20	...	...	...	...	...	...	534	119	190	1	...	216	2,066	898	511	4
17	6	2	...	...	9	...	...	...	...	...	...	594	308	91	...	...	105	1,477	642	330	5
457	*239*	*9*	*13*	...	*219*	*13*	*7*	...	...	...	*6*	*3,855*	*1,256*	*1,196*	*17*	*12*	*1,404*	*16,233*	*6,635*	*2,939*	
24	12	...	3	...	12	7	1	...	...	...	6	200	75	131	4	1	84	2,413	1,048	548	6
65	40	...	5	...	25	...	...	...	...	...	...	679	227	179	...	...	273	6,889	2,778	967	7
175	93	1	1	...	81	6	6	...	...	...	...	781	220	245	...	...	316	2,300	941	437	8
81	32	7	...	...	42	...	...	...	...	...	...	442	177	116	8	9	149	2,310	972	491	9
112	52	1	4	...	59	...	...	...	...	...	...	1,663	557	524	5	2	582	2,305	896	496	10
1,797	*673*	*34*	*24*	...	*1,090*	*410*	*155*	*70*	*1*	*1*	*185*	*5,914*	*2,331*	*3,159*	*15*	*5*	*3,434*	*21,752*	*9,394*	*4,365*	
246	93	1	5	...	152	36	7	...	...	...	29	1,638	501	607	3	1	530	4,909	2,196	910	11
1,137	423	25	17	...	689	363	141	70	1	1	152	4,677	1,122	1,809	4	4	1,746	6,449	3,029	944	12
405	*150*	*4*	...	...	*251*	*244*	*117*	...	*1*	...	*127*	*2,060*	*453*	*791*	*2*	...	*816*	*2,230*	*1,256*	*327*	
185	86	5	...	...	94	3	2	...	...	...	1	1,586	533	558	6	3	495	5,140	1,940	1,389	13
132	58	2	2	...	72	8	5	...	...	...	3	200	34	125	...	...	50	3,758	1,754	749	14
97	13	1	...	...	83	...	...	...	...	...	...	804	141	60	2	...	603	1,396	566	373	15
565	*96*	*267*	*1*	*2*	*205*	*7*	*1*	...	...	...	*6*	*3,159*	*1,216*	*1,134*	*12*	*15*	*1,119*	*13,709*	*4,776*	*4,560*	
93	43	—	1	...	50	3	1	...	...	...	2	992	381	331	3	...	280	4,885	1,829	1,018	16
89	28	8	...	...	53	4	...	...	...	...	4	1,604	478	530	8	4	596	5,515	1,847	1,785	17
380	25	259	...	2	102	...	...	...	...	...	...	863	357	263	1	11	243	3,309	1,100	1,157	18
410	**204**	**8**	**4**	...	**198**	**43**	**25**	**2**	...	**1**	**16**	**1,431**	**532**	**466**	**17**	**3**	**433**	**29,141**	**11,984**	**5,196**	
79	39	2	2	...	38	27	15	1	...	1	11	471	173	121	17	1	177	9,159	3,782	1,830	19
94	50	1	2	...	43	8	6	...	...	...	2	202	110	25	...	...	58	7,111	2,915	1,160	20
53	11	1	...	...	41	3	1	1	...	...	1	426	109	227	...	2	90	5,716	2,262	1,117	21
184	104	4	...	...	76	5	3	...	...	...	2	332	131	93	...	...	108	7,155	3,025	1,080	22
455	**162**	**10**	**66**	...	**283**	**3**	**3**	...	...	...	...	**1,810**	**386**	**743**	**1**	**3**	**681**	**7,727**	**2,867**	**2,164**	
1	...	...	...	...	1	...	...	...	...	...	...	...	...	...	...	...	...	155	19	35	23
67	24	8	...	...	35	...	...	...	...	...	...	213	47	82	...	...	84	1,328	575	366	24
...	...	...	...	...	...	...	...	...	...	...	...	...	...	...	...	...	...	395	170	130	25
37	5	1	...	...	31	...	...	...	...	...	...	367	84	168	...	...	115	441	133	84	26
21	10	...	...	...	11	3	3	...	...	...	...	1	...	...	...	...	1	510	213	160	27
...	...	...	...	—	...	...	...	...	...	...	...	...	...	...	...	...	...	147	57	18	28
...	...	...	...	...	...	...	...	...	...	...	...	10	5	4	...	...	1	286	96	93	29
1	...	...	...	...	1	...	...	...	...	...	...	44	12	19	...	...	13	204	87	41	30
210	93	...	64	...	117	...	...	...	...	...	...	8	6	...	...	...	2	823	302	276	31
...	...	...	...	...	...	...	...	...	...	...	...	2	2	...	...	...	...	838	200	262	32
...	...	...	...	...	...	...	...	...	...	...	...	26	8	12	...	3	6	107	39	31	33
...	...	...	...	...	...	...	...	...	...	...	...	2	1	...	...	...	1	265	114	80	34
100	18	1	2	...	81	...	...	...	...	...	...	404	101	83	1	...	220	1,515	540	353	35
...	...	...	...	...	...	...	...	...	...	...	...	52	...	46	...	...	6	198	69	51	36
18	12	...	...	...	6	...	...	...	...	...	...	681	120	329	...	...	232	516	154	184	37

TABLE XV.—Occupation or means of livelihood. Part A.— General Table.

Serial No.	CLASS ... / SUB-CLASS ... / ORDER ...	CLASS D.—MISCELLANEOUS—(concluded). Sub-Class XII.—Unproductive—(concluded). Total Sub-Class XII—(concluded).			Total order 54.—Inmates of jails, asylums and hospitals. 168.—Inmates of jails, asylums and hospitals.						Total order 55.—Beggars, vagrants and prostitutes. 169.—Beggars, vagrants, procurers, prostitutes, receivers of stolen goods, cattle-poisoners.						Serial No.
	DISTRICT, CITY OR STATE.	Actual workers—(concluded) Partially agriculturists.		Dependants.	Total workers and dependants.	Actual workers. Total.		Actual workers. Partially agriculturists.		Dependants.	Total workers and dependants.	Actual workers. Total.		Actual workers. Partially agriculturists.		Dependants.	
		Males.	Females.			Males.	Females.	Males.	Females.			Males.	Females.	Males.	Females.		
	1	1355	1356	1357	1358	1359	1360	1361	1362	1363	1364	1365	1366	1367	1368	1369	
	Central Provinces and Berar	**2,960**	**1.033**	**38,359**	**3.856**	**2,893**	**208**	**11**	...	**755**	**98.834**	**39.055**	**22,175**	**2,949**	**1,033**	**37,604**	
	C. P. British Districts and Berar.	**2,907**	**962**	**35,663**	**3.341**	**2,487**	**192**	**11**	...	**662**	**91,622**	**36,594**	**20.027**	**2,896**	**962**	**35,001**	
	C. P. British Districts.	**1,879**	**657**	**23,702**	**3.009**	**2,228**	**177**	**11**	...	**604**	**62,813**	**24,869**	**14.846**	**1,868**	**657**	**23,098**	
	JUBBULPORE DIVISION	*334*	*121*	*4,788*	*1,011*	*882*	*59*	...	...	*70*	*13,128*	*5,310*	*3,100*	*334*	*121*	*4,718*	
1	Saugor ...	137	47	1,416	64	53	5	...	...	6	3,379	1,316	653	137	47	1,410	1
2	Damoh ...	69	16	559	43	43	...	...	...	...	1,481	588	334	69	16	559	2
3	Jubbulpore ...	136	50	1,651	781	680	44	...	...	57	4,848	1,972	1,282	136	50	1,594	3
	JUBBULPORE CITY ...	*1*	...	*342*	*780*	*650*	*44*	...	...	*56*	*974*	*463*	*225*	*1*	...	*286*	
4	Mandla ...	24	3	657	57	49	4	...	...	4	2,009	849	507	24	3	653	4
5	Seoni ...	18	5	505	66	57	6	...	...	3	1,411	585	324	18	5	502	5
	NERBUDDA DIVISION.	*573*	*219*	*6,655*	*209*	*161*	*25*	...	...	*23*	*16,023*	*6,474*	*2,914*	*573*	*219*	*6,635*	
6	Narsinghpur ...	108	48	817	24	1	...	...	...	23	2,389	1,047	548	108	48	794	6
7	Hoshangabad ...	261	42	3,144	75	70	5	...	...	...	6,814	2,708	962	261	42	3,144	7
8	Nimar ...	99	52	931	71	65	6	...	...	...	2,238	876	431	99	52	931	8
9	Betul ...	45	38	853	7	...	7	...	...	...	2,309	972	484	45	38	853	9
10	Chhindwara ...	60	39	913	32	25	7	...	...	...	2,273	871	489	60	39	913	10
	NAGPUR DIVISION ...	*680*	*197*	*7,883*	*1,645*	*1,100*	*82*	*11*	...	*306*	*20,194*	*8,394*	*4,283*	*669*	*197*	*7,517*	
11	Wardha ...	148	50	1,893	29	14	...	...	...	15	4,970	2,182	910	148	50	1,878	11
12	Nagpur ...	138	14	2,476	1,296	960	46	...	...	290	5,153	2,069	898	138	14	2,186	12
	NAGPUR CITY ...	*1*	*1*	*637*	*1,295*	*959*	*46*	...	...	*290*	*925*	*297*	*281*	*1*	*1*	*347*	
13	Chanda ...	166	83	1,802	54	38	13	...	...	3	5,086	1,911	1,876	166	83	1,799	13
14	Bhandara ...	160	40	1,255	114	88	...	11	...	26	3,644	1,666	749	158	40	1,229	14
15	Balaghat ...	59	10	457	55	...	23	...	...	32	1,341	566	350	59	10	425	15
	CHHATTISGARH DIVISION.	*242*	*120*	*4,373*	*341*	*85*	*11*	...	...	*145*	*13,468*	*4,691*	*4,549*	*242*	*120*	*4,228*	
16	Raipur ...	33	29	1,438	74	20	2	...	...	52	4,811	1,809	1,616	33	29	1,386	16
17	Bilaspur ...	172	73	1,883	123	65	9	...	...	40	5,392	1,782	1,776	172	73	1,834	17
18	Drug ...	37	18	1,052	44	...	...	...	...	44	3,265	1,100	1,157	37	18	1,008	18
	Berar ...	**1.028**	**305**	**11.961**	**332**	**259**	**15**	...	...	**58**	**28.809**	**11,725**	**5,181**	**1,028**	**305**	**11,903**	
19	Amraoti ...	233	50	3,538	255	188	15	...	...	52	8,904	3,594	1,824	233	50	3,486	19
20	Akola ...	380	145	3,036	6	...	...	...	...	6	7,105	2,915	1,160	380	145	3,030	20
21	Buldana ...	243	69	2,337	...	...	...	...	...	...	5,716	2,262	1,117	243	69	2,837	21
22	Yeotmal ...	163	51	3,050	71	71	...	...	...	...	7,084	2,954	1,080	163	51	3,050	22
	Feudatory States ...	**53**	**71**	**2,696**	**515**	**406**	**16**	...	...	**93**	**7,212**	**2,461**	**2,148**	**53**	**71**	**2,603**	
23	Makrai ...	...	...	101	...	...	...	...	...	...	155	19	35	...	...	101	23
24	Bastar ...	10	3	387	149	145	4	...	...	...	1,179	430	362	10	3	387	24
25	Kanker ...	3	1	95	44	43	1	...	...	...	351	127	129	3	1	95	25
26	Nandgaon ...	3	2	224	123	27	4	...	...	92	318	106	80	3	2	132	26
27	Khairagarh ...	1	1	137	28	27	1	...	...	...	482	186	159	1	1	137	27
28	Chhuikhadan ...	2	1	72	13	13	...	...	...	...	134	44	18	2	1	72	28
29	Kawardha ...	3	1	97	12	10	1	...	...	1	274	86	92	3	1	96	29
30	Sakti ...	13	...	76	15	14	1	...	...	...	189	73	40	13	...	76	30
31	Raigarh ...	11	43	245	...	...	...	...	...	...	823	302	276	11	43	245	31
32	Sarangarh ...	3	18	277	17	17	...	...	...	...	821	282	262	3	18	277	32
33	Chang Bhakar ...	...	...	37	5	4	1	...	...	...	102	35	30	...	...	37	33
34	Korea ...	2	1	71	25	24	1	...	...	...	240	90	79	2	1	71	34
35	Surguja ...	...	...	622	84	82	2	...	...	...	1,431	458	351	...	...	622	35
36	Udaipur ...	...	...	78	...	...	...	...	...	...	198	69	51	...	...	78	36
37	Jashpur ...	2	...	177	...	...	...	...	...	...	515	154	184	2	...	177	37

TABLE XV.—Occupation or means of livelihood. Part B.—Subsidiary occupations of Agriculturists.—Actual workers only.

TABLE XV.—Occupation or means of livelihood. Part B.—

(1) RENT

Serial No.	District or State.	Total number of rent receivers (actual workers). Males.	Females.	Number of actual workers who returned subsidiary occupations. (a) Agricultural. Males.	Females.	(b) Non-agricultural. Males.	Females.	Details of subsidiary — Rent payers. Males.	Females.	Agricultural labourers. Males.	Females.	Servants of all kinds. Males.	Females.	Money-lenders and grain dealers. Males.	Females.	Other of all Males.
	1	2	3	4	5	6	7	8	9	10	11	12	13	14	15	16
	Central Provinces and Berar.	**33,142**	**25,782**	**9,264**	**2,845**	**6,993**	**1,674**	**3,615**	**551**	**5,649**	**2,294**	**685**	**24**	**827**	**93**	**962**
	C. P. British Districts and Berar.	**30,888**	**25,221**	**9,119**	**2,821**	**6,829**	**1,662**	**3,484**	**528**	**5,635**	**2,293**	**683**	**24**	**784**	**93**	**898**
	C. P. British Districts	**22,199**	**12,546**	**7,629**	**2,386**	**3,882**	**920**	**3,336**	**508**	**4,293**	**1,878**	**241**	...	**431**	**64**	**476**
	JUBBULPORE DIVISION	*3,655*	*1,229*	*1,828*	*355*	*398*	*177*	*1,594*	*247*	*234*	*105*	*12*	...	*130*	*37*	*50*
1	Saugor ...	877	322	412	91	153	40	325	42	87	40	1	...	49	6	19
2	Damoh ...	796	271	431	71	80	110	360	45	71	26	...	...	29	21	9
3	Jubbulpore ...	1,335	413	775	159	106	23	733	126	42	33	4	...	30	8	12
4	Mandla ...	378	96	174	32	35	1	156	32	18	...	5	...	9	1	6
5	Seoni ...	270	127	36	2	24	3	20	2	16	...	2	...	3	1	4
	NERBUDDA DIVISION...	*6,784*	*3,092*	*2,442*	*846*	*1,124*	*177*	*786*	*130*	*1,656*	*710*	*37*	...	*109*	*10*	*132*
6	Narsinghpur ...	1,234	585	484	161	200	43	239	42	245	119	5	...	29	1	10
7	Hoshangabad ...	2,611	1,106	1,058	310	429	68	272	38	786	278	7	...	31	6	73
8	Nimar ...	811	424	142	74	102	6	82	7	60	67	8	...	24	...	6
9	Betul ...	1,253	621	523	177	245	43	127	27	396	150	14	...	15	3	37
10	Chhindwara ...	875	356	235	112	148	17	66	16	169	96	3	...	10	...	6
	NAGPUR DIVISION ...	*9,059*	*7,125*	*2,873*	*1,050*	*2,121*	*510*	*626*	*59*	*2,247*	*991*	*154*	...	*115*	*12*	*275*
11	Wardha ...	2,429	810	787	228	406	28	88	3	699	225	12	...	22	3	92
12	Nagpur ...	3,118	1,097	1,290	466	1,003	189	325	27	965	439	36	...	66	4	114
13	Chanda ...	681	261	128	72	333	69	41	15	87	57	117	...	7	...	15
14	Bhandara ...	2,490	4,823	532	255	315	203	95	6	437	249	14	...	17	2	49
15	Balaghat ...	341	134	136	20	64	21	77	8	59	21	5	...	3	3	5
	CHHATTISGARH DIVISION.	*2,701*	*1,100*	*486*	*141*	*239*	*56*	*330*	*72*	*156*	*69*	*8*	...	*87*	*5*	*19*
16	Raipur ...	1,166	362	234	65	100	44	128	15	106	50	6	...	18	3	14
17	Bilaspur ...	814	497	162	48	69	7	147	45	15	3	1	...	38	...	3
18	Drug ...	721	241	90	28	70	5	55	12	35	16	1	...	31	2	2
	Berar ...	**8,689**	**12,675**	**1,490**	**435**	**2,947**	**742**	**148**	**20**	**1,342**	**415**	**442**	**24**	**353**	**29**	**422**
19	Amraoti ...	2,694	939	820	164	1,751	651	67	10	753	154	279	17	180	12	192
20	Akola ...	2,336	7,115	300	121	449	20	27	3	273	118	37	2	39	4	58
21	Buldana ...	1,505	3,920	179	71	328	45	15	3	164	68	43	4	63	11	84
22	Yeotmal ...	2,154	701	191	79	419	26	39	4	152	75	83	1	71	2	88
	Feudatory States ...	**1,254**	**561**	**145**	**24**	**164**	**12**	**131**	**23**	**14**	**1**	**2**	...	**43**	...	**64**
23	Makrai ...	5	2	...	...	1	...	...	...	...	...	...	...	1	...	...
24	Bastar ...	52	15	21	3	5	1	21	3	...	...	...	...	...	...	2
25	Kanker ...	40	9	14	3	11	...	13	3	1	...	...	...	1	...	2
26	Nandgaon ...	13	6	5	3	5	...	4	3	1	...	1	...	1	...	...
27	Khairagarh ...	855	471	8	1	54	7	3	...	5	1	...	...	22	...	5
28	Chhuikhadan ...	2	3	...	...	1	...	...	...	...	...	...	...	...	...	...
29	Kawardha ...	34	23	8	1	4	2	3	1	...	...	...	...	...	...	...
30	Sakti ...	...	...	...	...	...	...	...	...	...	...	...	...	...	...	...
31	Raigarh ...	9	2	3	...	...	...	3	...	...	...	...	...	...	...	...
32	Sarangarh ...	2	2	1	...	...	...	1	...	...	...	...	...	...	...	...
33	Chang Bhakar ..	14	3	14	3	...	...	14	3	...	...	...	...	...	...	...
34	Korea ...	57	12	22	8	1	...	21	8	1	...	...	...	...	...	1
35	Surguja ...	98	2	43	...	81	2	37	...	6	...	1	...	18	...	54
36	Udaipur ...	59	7	2	...	1	...	2	...	...	...	...	...	...	...	...
37	Jashpur ...	14	4	9	2	...	...	9	2	...	...	...	...	...	...	...

Subsidiary occupations of Agriculturists.—Actual workers only.

RECEIVERS.

OCCUPATIONS RETURNED.

... traders ... kinds.	Priests.		Clerks of all kinds (not Government servants).		School-masters.		Lawyers.		Estate Agents and Managers.		Medical practitioners.		Artisans.		Others.		Serial No.
Females.	Males.	Females.	Males.	Females.	Males.	Females.	Males.	Females.	Males.	Females.	Males.	Females.	Males.	Females.	Males.	Females.	
17	18	19	20	21	22	23	24	25	26	27	28	29	30	31	32	33	
209	183	12	105	4	57	2	26	...	27	3	34	3	552	35	3,535	1,289	
207	180	12	105	4	56	2	26	...	26	3	33	3	552	35	3,486	1,279	
175	101	2	48	...	23	...	23	...	16	...	10	3	353	20	2,160	656	
12	*25*	...	*4*	...	*1*	...	*2*	...	*1*	...	*1*	...	*12*	1	*170*	127	
1	10	...	2	...	1	...	...	...	...	...	...	...	4	1	67	32	1
11	6	...	1	...	...	...	...	...	...	...	...	...	4	...	31	78	2
...	6	...	1	...	...	...	...	...	1	...	1	...	3	...	48	15	3
...	3	...	...	...	...	...	2	...	...	...	...	...	...	...	10	...	4
...	...	...	...	...	...	...	...	...	...	...	...	...	1	...	14	2	5
26	*34*	*1*	*21*	...	*7*	...	*18*	...	*6*	...	...	...	*102*	*4*	*659*	*136*	
5	18	1	4	...	1	...	5	...	...	...	...	...	10	1	118	35	6
8	9	...	8	...	1	...	5	...	5	...	...	...	21	1	260	53	7
2	...	...	3	...	2	...	2	...	...	...	...	...	5	1	62	3	8
9	1	...	...	...	2	...	6	...	1	...	...	...	27	1	142	30	9
2	6	...	6	...	1	...	...	...	...	...	...	...	39	...	77	15	10
111	*33*	*1*	*23*	...	*15*	...	*3*	...	*7*	...	*9*	*3*	*223*	*12*	*1,234*	*371*	
7	3	...	11	...	6	...	...	...	3	...	5	2	56	1	196	15	11
60	9	1	7	...	8	...	1	...	3	...	3	...	110	2	646	122	12
3	4	...	4	...	...	...	...	...	...	...	...	1	21	1	165	64	13
38	14	...	...	...	1	...	1	...	1	...	1	...	23	5	194	158	14
3	3	...	1	...	...	...	1	...	...	...	...	...	13	3	33	12	15
26	*9*	...	...	...	...	...	...	...	*2*	...	...	...	*16*	*3*	*98*	*22*	
22	5	...	...	...	...	...	...	...	1	...	...	...	10	1	46	18	16
1	2	...	...	...	...	...	...	...	...	...	...	...	1	2	24	4	17
3	2	...	...	...	...	...	...	...	1	...	...	...	5	...	28	...	18
32	79	10	57	4	33	2	3	...	10	3	23	...	199	15	1,326	623	
13	46	5	30	4	21	2	2	...	10	1	19	...	134	7	838	590	19
3	15	1	17	...	6	...	...	...	...	...	3	...	18	...	256	10	20
7	3	...	3	...	3	...	1	...	...	2	1	...	18	8	109	13	21
9	15	4	7	...	3	...	...	...	...	...	...	...	29	...	123	10	22
2	3	...	...	...	1	...	...	...	1	...	1	...	...	...	49	10	
...	...	...	...	...	...	...	...	...	...	...	...	...	...	...	...	...	23
...	...	...	...	...	...	...	...	...	...	...	...	...	...	...	3	1	24
...	...	...	...	...	...	...	...	...	...	...	1	...	...	...	7	...	25
...	...	...	...	...	...	...	...	...	...	...	...	...	...	...	3	...	26
...	...	...	...	...	...	...	...	...	1	...	...	...	...	...	24	7	27
...	2	...	...	...	...	...	...	...	...	...	...	...	...	...	1	...	28
...	...	...	...	...	...	...	...	...	...	...	...	...	...	...	2	2	29
...	1	...	...	...	1	...	...	...	...	...	...	...	...	...	...	...	30
...	...	...	...	...	...	...	...	...	...	...	...	...	...	...	...	...	31
...	...	...	...	...	...	...	...	...	...	...	...	...	...	...	...	...	32
...	...	...	...	...	...	...	...	...	...	...	...	...	...	...	...	...	33
...	...	...	...	...	...	...	...	...	...	...	...	...	...	...	...	...	34
...	...	...	...	...	...	...	...	...	...	...	...	...	...	...	8	...	35
2	...	...	...	...	...	...	...	...	...	...	...	...	...	...	1	...	36
...	...	...	...	...	...	...	...	...	...	...	...	...	...	...	...	...	37

TABLE XV.—Occupation or means of livelihood.—Part B.—

(2) RENT

Serial No.	DISTRICT OR STATE.	Total number of rent payers (actual workers).		NUMBER OF ACTUAL WORKERS WHO RETURNED SUBSIDIARY OCCUPATIONS.				DETAILS OF SUBSIDIARY				
				(a) Agricultural.		(b) Non-agricultural.		Rent receivers.		Agricultural labourers.		General
		Males.	Females.	Males.	Females.	Males.	Females.	Males.	Females.	Males.	Females.	Males.
	1	2	3	4	5	6	7	8	9	10	11	12
	Central Provinces and Berar.	**2,350,713**	**1,756,106**	**81,046**	**86,566**	**242,919**	**94,540**	**23,362**	**3,117**	**57,684**	**83,449**	**11,312**
	C. P. British Districts and Berar.	**1,946,335**	**1,462,362**	**78,679**	**85,653**	**215,484**	**78,319**	**22,124**	**2,999**	**56,555**	**82,654**	**10,845**
	C. P. British Districts ...	**1,602,693**	**1,361,254**	**65,752**	**77,529**	**185,553**	**75,046**	**21,175**	**1,988**	**44,577**	**75,541**	**9,727**
	JUBBULPORE DIVISION ...	*343,972*	*261,958*	*17,772*	*8,601*	*39,529*	*9,176*	*6,732*	*635*	*11,040*	*7,967*	*1,173*
1	Saugor ...	69,195	44,533	3,581	1,240	7,970	1,384	1,900	171	1,612	1,069	112
2	Damoh ...	43,456	18,014	3,959	1,302	6,718	1,233	1,563	146	2,396	1,156	280
3	Jubbulpore ...	93,516	71,072	8,361	5,279	17,452	4,685	1,989	244	6,372	5,035	444
4	Mandla ...	76,457	72,525	993	507	4,717	1,405	555	39	438	468	312
5	Seoni ...	61,348	55,814	878	273	2,666	469	656	34	222	239	25
	NERBUDDA DIVISION ...	*284,931*	*212,352*	*12,376*	*20,069*	*27,045*	*9,033*	*3,848*	*339*	*8,438*	*19,730*	*3,068*
6	Narsinghpur ...	37,617	22,912	2,569	1,172	5,361	1,491	1,010	108	1,559	1,064	947
7	Hoshangabad ...	50,282	27,067	1,353	461	5,510	1,028	610	59	743	402	338
8	Nimar ...	55,549	43,604	1,030	1,046	3,126	470	537	29	493	1,017	455
9	Betul ...	61,584	55,160	5,367	11,962	8,301	5,206	642	75	4,725	11,887	850
10	Chhindwara ...	70,809	63,599	1,957	5,428	4,686	748	1,049	68	908	5,360	478
	NAGPUR DIVISION ...	*379,055*	*332,092*	*13,925*	*36,250*	*43,412*	*16,412*	*4,045*	*384*	*9,880*	*35,896*	*2,776*
11	Wardha ...	43,568	22,186	1,649	6,555	4,166	397	266	31	1,283	6,524	59
12	Nagpur ...	75,807	52,080	2,896	7,535	7,804	2,247	1,303	100	1,503	7,435	358
13	Chanda ...	89,884	83,222	5,542	18,512	11,275	5,490	531	51	5,011	18,461	974
14	Bhandara ...	106,446	109,240	3,009	3,451	13,663	5,527	1,313	151	1,696	3,300	675
1	Balaghat ...	63,350	65,358	920	227	6,504	2,751	632	51	297	170	710
	CHHATTISGARH DIVISION ...	*594,735*	*554,862*	*21,779*	*12,579*	*75,568*	*40,436*	*6,550*	*631*	*15,229*	*11,948*	*2,710*
16	Raipur ...	228,313	212,727	6,577	3,921	32,123	18,473	2,577	239	4,000	3,682	1,869
17	Bilaspur ...	235,220	212,340	11,660	7,946	32,990	17,912	1,924	228	9,736	7,718	772
18	Drug ...	131,202	129,795	3,542	712	10,440	4,040	2,040	164	1,493	548	69
	Berar ...	**343,642**	**101,108**	**12,927**	**8,124**	**29,931**	**3,273**	**949**	**1,011**	**11,978**	**7,113**	**1,118**
19	Amraoti ...	81,743	16,935	2,312	2,081	12,208	1,924	270	58	2,042	2,023	877
20	Akola ...	94,019	31,502	3,936	1,374	6,946	688	325	25	3,611	1,349	94
21	Buldana ...	87,691	38,121	6,334	4,174	6,551	554	134	914	6,200	3,260	116
22	Yeotmal ...	80,189	14,550	345	495	4,167	107	220	14	125	481	31
	Feudatory States ...	**404,378**	**293,744**	**2,367**	**913**	**27,435**	**16,221**	**1,238**	**118**	**1,129**	**795**	**467**
23	Makrai ...	2,130	2,048	6	1	133	5	1	...	5	1	...
24	Bastar ...	88,608	75,281	128	31	5,904	5,685	113	17	15	14	2
25	Kauker ...	22,674	21,242	263	55	2,401	3,358	211	29	52	26	1
26	Nandgaon ...	23,936	23,820	413	86	1,871	1,058	280	15	133	71	213
27	Khairagarh ...	22,006	21,076	77	13	1,816	558	15	2	62	11	192
28	Chhuikhadan ...	4,222	3,595	96	3	340	100	80	...	16	3	...
29	Kawardha ...	14,481	13,448	134	40	974	617	97	16	37	24	...
30	Sakti ...	6,973	6,377	318	286	1,313	869	6	1	312	286	3
31	Raigarh ...	40,952	34,762	331	158	4,040	1,998	137	22	194	136	7
32	Sarangarh ...	17,116	9,696	92	56	2,181	549	11	1	81	56	19
33	Chang Bhakar ...	4,492	2,852	92	5	429	101	58	...	34	5	...
34	Korea ...	11,700	7,372	97	92	758	142	80	4	17	88	7
35	Surguja ...	92,216	30,506	71	20	3,069	378	27	1	44	19	8
36	Udaipur ...	13,325	8,379	137	31	809	137	86	6	51	25	...
37	Jashpur ...	39,541	33,290	112	36	1,391	666	36	4	76	32	15

Subsidiary occupations of Agriculturists.—Actual workers only.[1]

PAYERS.

OCCUPATIONS RETURNED.

labourers.	Government employés of all kinds.		Money-lenders and grain dealers.		Other traders of all kinds.		Fishermen and boatmen.		Cattle-breeders and milkmen.		Village watchmen.		Weavers.		Serial No.
Females.	Males.	Females.	Males.	Females.	Males.	Females.	Males.	Females.	Males.	Females.	Males.	Females.	Males.	Females.	
13	14	15	16	17	18	19	20	21	22	23	24	25	26	27	
7,927	6,215	125	13,875	1,938	36,363	18,187	11,162	3,690	4.914	2,689	4.351	171	15.537	5.959	
7,517	6.010	116	13.165	1.815	32,380	15,794	10.455	3.548	4,388	2.422	3.837	142	11,897	4,519	
6,454	3,215	61	9,802	1,688	25,753	15.347	10,073	3,530	3,914	2,370	3,270	136	11,511	4.466	
1,020	*626*	*6*	*2,087*	*201*	*3,636*	*1,038*	*1,082*	*204*	*1,059*	*333*	*642*	*17*	*1,296*	*400*	
50	148	2	417	29	1,104	178	7	...	400	62	80	...	60	14	1
133	34	...	400	100	515	263	14	...	173	30	51	...	58	6	2
583	233	3	749	46	1,387	377	228	6	315	181	227	3	409	114	3
208	128	1	233	16	320	131	690	194	122	39	173	10	555	228	4
52	83	...	288	10	301	79	143	4	49	21	111	4	154	38	5
2,315	*625*	*7*	*1,901*	*86*	*3,568*	*777*	*309*	*18*	*641*	*264*	*597*	*8*	*832*	*153*	
496	105	...	366	13	506	170	145	7	75	83	41	...	72	9	6
234	87	...	446	17	893	184	53	8	76	18	67	...	47	4	7
109	140	1	309	15	451	29	30	...	80	37	182	2	37	9	8
1,368	142	...	370	24	1,074	194	27	2	357	106	192	6	267	90	9
108	142	6	410	17	644	191	54	6	47	20	115	...	409	41	10
1,519	*852*	*23*	*3,338*	*835*	*8,993*	*4,581*	*2,287*	*993*	*577*	*229*	*585*	*17*	*2,289*	*762*	
7	257	4	503	24	1,048	82	102	10	121	18	38	2	63	2	11
50	104	4	789	32	1,696	1,024	138	3	147	43	114	5	151	4	12
538	189	14	356	16	2,267	1,419	1,171	682	183	130	178	1	836	392	13
291	162	...	1,503	620	3,184	1,597	707	237	88	31	101	5	863	203	14
633	140	1	187	143	798	450	109	55	38	7	154	4	376	161	15
1,594	*1,112*	*25*	*2,476*	*566*	*9,556*	*8,961*	*6,395*	*2,315*	*1,637*	*1,544*	*1,446*	*94*	*7,094*	*3,151*	
1,019	307	2	953	194	2,318	2,766	2,777	1,311	519	674	630	12	3,180	1,546	16
537	514	19	1,072	292	5,396	4,723	2,654	781	806	754	638	77	3,220	1,408	17
38	291	4	451	80	1,840	1,472	964	223	222	116	178	5	694	137	18
1,063	2,795	55	3,363	127	6,627	447	382	18	474	52	567	6	386	53	
711	911	24	921	44	2,351	173	284	17	261	38	259	3	143	23	19
315	757	20	991	47	1,500	84	35	...	86	10	88	1	123	9	20
34	485	11	888	24	1,684	153	36	1	46	2	136	2	61	21	21
3	642	...	563	12	1,092	37	27	...	81	2	84	...	59	...	22
410	205	9	710	123	3,983	2,393	707	142	526	267	514	38	3,640	1,440	
...	12	...	13	1	8	...	...	...	5	...	5	...	1	...	23
2	21	1	103	10	1,865	1,640	71	12	106	112	103	4	813	322	24
3	18	2	60	10	123	51	89	53	11	17	46	7	94	54	25
200	12	...	70	5	101	28	94	16	50	31	65	5	160	87	26
96	11	...	60	4	76	3	118	4	45	17	82	1	92	33	27
...	1	...	1	...	22	6	19	2	...	2	5	...	13	...	28
1	2	...	27	4	453	272	35	5	30	35	9	...	27	16	29
...	17	...	36	8	38	23	43	...	...	7	88	2	192	186	30
63	20	...	112	34	113	28	6	7	...	...	13	...	690	286	31
...	13	6	68	20	574	236	150	5	2	3	6	...	802	17	32
...	1	...	8	5	87	34	52	24	12	1	7	3	38	13	33
...	5	...	10	8	61	10	...	...	15	7	14	...	112	19	34
5	55	...	130	10	242	31	3	1	182	5	81	11	510	64	35
...	...	...	17	...	123	8	4	7	46	3	13	2	215	50	36
40	17	...	9	3	97	23	17	6	22	27	27	1	372	293	37

TABLE XV.—Occupation or means of livelihood. Part B.—Subsidiary occupations of Agriculturists.—Actual workers only.

(2) RENT PAYERS—(*concluded*).

Serial No.	DISTRICT OR STATE.	DETAILS OF SUBSIDIARY OCCUPATIONS—(*concluded*).											
		Barbers.		Oil-pressers.		Washermen.		Potters.		Blacksmiths and carpenters.		Others.	
		Males.	Females.	Males.	Females.	Males.	Females.	Males.	Females.	Males.	Females.	Males.	Females.
	1	28	29	30	31	32	33	34	35	36	37	38	39
	Central Provinces and Berar.	**8,657**	**182**	**10,378**	**8,350**	**5,775**	**3,962**	**4,301**	**2,391**	**9,626**	**652**	**100,453**	**38,310**
	C. P. British Districts and Berar.	**8,040**	**166**	**8,793**	**7,175**	**5,122**	**3,571**	**3,211**	**1,897**	**8,868**	**449**	**88,473**	**29,188**
	C. P. British Districts.	**7,111**	**150**	**8,284**	**7,093**	**4,679**	**3,494**	**2,980**	**1,860**	**8,080**	**438**	**77,154**	**27,959**
	JUBBULPORE DIVISION.	*1,933*	*73*	*1,446*	*802*	*1,229*	*627*	*655*	*340*	*2,312*	*70*	*20,354*	*4,059*
1	Saugor ...	478	27	235	104	267	121	171	66	492	4	4,005	727
2	Damoh ...	274	...	200	54	177	47	105	39	374	12	4,063	549
3	Jubbulpore ...	882	38	670	507	574	328	34[illegible]	205	967	27	9,967	2,267
4	Mandla ...	128	7	152	83	114	84	9	20	246	23	1,526	361
5	Seoni ...	171	1	180	54	97	47	29	10	233	4	793	145
	NERBUDDA DIVISION	*723*	*8*	*541*	*229*	*250*	*106*	*157*	*35*	*1,346*	*37*	*12,456*	*4,987*
6	Narsinghpur ...	132	...	85	31	59	30	41	6	268	1	2,519	636
7	Hoshangabad ...	147	1	80	29	54	7	27	9	313	5	2,882	517
8	Nimar ...	156	...	127	23	20	13	51	16	148	9	925	207
9	Betul ...	144	4	87	47	35	20	15	4	256	16	4,545	3,415
10	Chhindwara ...	144	3	162	99	82	36	23	3	361	6	1,615	212
	NAGPUR DIVISION	*1,303*	*13*	*1,852*	*1,330*	*660*	*398*	*210*	*101*	2,238	*85*	*15,452*	*5,626*
11	Wardha ...	215	...	98	72	114	81	34	2	226	1	1,288	86
12	Nagpur ...	317	2	242	124	130	45	13	3	431	7	3,174	901
13	Chanda ...	220	1	378	313	134	81	29	17	550	43	3,810	1,843
14	Bhandara ...	382	2	713	636	218	166	30	42	799	18	4,169	1,679
15	Balaghat ...	169	8	361	185	64	25	95	37	232	16	3,011	1,017
	CHHATTISGARH DIVISION.	*3,152*	*56*	*4,445*	*4,732*	*2,540*	*2,363*	*1,959*	*1,381*	*2,184*	*246*	*28,862*	*13,397*
16	Raipur ...	1,095	12	1,885	2,096	778	859	1,010	722	783	114	14,019	7,146
17	Bilaspur ...	1,549	33	1,603	2,104	1,232	1,182	867	558	1,138	112	11,446	5,272
18	Drug ...	508	11	957	532	530	322	82	101	263	20	3,397	979
	Berar ...	**929**	**16**	**509**	**82**	**443**	**77**	**231**	**37**	**788**	**11**	**11,319**	**1,229**
19	Amraoti ...	271	11	173	34	136	25	112	27	239	7	5,330	787
20	Akola ...	207	2	107	12	182	17	59	4	174	2	2,542	165
21	Buldana ...	251	2	129	30	72	25	29	4	194	1	2,424	244
22	Yeotmal ...	200	1	100	6	53	10	31	2	181	1	1,023	33
	Feudatory States	**617**	**16**	**1,585**	**1,175**	**653**	**391**	**1,090**	**494**	**758**	**203**	**11,980**	**9,122**
23	Makrai ...	3	...	2	...	5	...	...	...	7	...	72	4
24	Bastar ...	5	...	20	23	19	13	231	118	159	99	2,386	3,329
25	Kankar ...	28	3	150	122	36	21	60	43	28	5	1,651	2,961
26	Nandgaon ...	88	...	165	169	57	51	10	26	45	1	726	439
27	Khairagarh ...	63	...	163	61	67	28	16	8	31	...	830	303
28	Chhuikhadan ...	16	...	31	9	16	8	...	...	5	...	211	73
29	Kawardha ...	26	7	92	149	30	52	3	7	40	6	200	63
30	Sakti ...	69	...	86	120	49	65	41	44	42	14	609	400
31	Raigarh ...	122	...	620	423	123	91	157	69	59	19	2,024	978
32	Sarangarh ...	59	...	133	71	79	29	111	20	63	3	596	139
33	Chang Bhakar ...	3	...	6	5	3	1	...	...	4	...	208	15
34	Korea ...	16	...	14	2	23	2	59	16	35	2	387	81
35	Surguja ...	101	6	66	12	90	15	243	83	133	27	1,225	108
36	Udaipur ...	12	...	7	...	31	2	33	6	16	5	292	54
37	Jashpur ...	6	...	10	9	25	13	120	54	91	22	563	175

TABLE XV.—Occupation or means of livelihood. Part B.—Subsidiary occupations of Agriculturists.—Actual workers only.

(3) AGRICULTURAL LABOURERS.

Serial No.	DISTRICT OR STATE.	Total number of agricultural labourers (actual workers only).		Number of actual workers who returned subsidiary occupations. (a) Agricultural.		Number of actual workers who returned subsidiary occupations. (b) Non-agricultural.		Details of subsidiary occupations returned. Rent receivers.		Details of subsidiary occupations returned. Rent payers.		Details of subsidiary occupations returned. General labourers.		Serial No.
		Males.	Females.	Males.	Females.	Males.	Females.	Males.	Females.	Males.	Females.	Males.	Females.	
	1	2	3	4	5	6	7	8	9	10	11	12	13	
	Central Provinces and Berar.	**1,392,427**	**1,779,510**	**13,692**	**5,227**	**44,910**	**49,027**	**5,947**	**936**	**7,745**	**4,291**	**5,347**	**6,405**	
	C. P. British Districts and Berar.	**1,273,996**	**1,657,131**	**13,300**	**5,104**	**43,367**	**46,193**	**5,913**	**924**	**7,387**	**4,180**	**5,211**	**6,204**	
	C. P. British Districts.	**867,416**	**1,102,616**	**12,242**	**4,602**	**30,355**	**37,129**	**5,545**	**824**	**6,697**	**3,778**	**4,928**	**5,763**	
	JUBBULPORE DIVISION	*183,352*	*230,662*	*2,196*	*951*	*8,675*	*5,876*	*343*	*74*	*1,853*	*877*	*889*	*1,697*	
1	Saugor ...	42,649	51,425	299	145	3,665	1,568	83	27	216	118	178	123	1
2	Damoh ...	24,785	35,470	254	91	2,291	960	72	28	182	63	131	60	2
3	Jubbulpore ...	53,041	66,811	1,518	666	3,069	2,689	152	18	1,366	648	352	1,244	3
4	Mandla ...	24,483	28,385	69	41	527	570	11	...	58	41	228	255	4
5	Seoni ...	38,394	48,571	56	8	123	89	25	1	31	7	...	15	5
	NERBUDDA DIVISION...	*178,087*	*229,267*	*1,339*	*857*	*6,095*	*9,175*	*753*	*152*	*586*	*705*	*1,311*	*2,330*	
6	Narsinghpur ...	28,191	34,930	344	353	2,047	2,034	128	30	216	323	576	958	6
7	Hoshangabad ...	42,518	49,342	438	138	1,398	1,795	250	64	188	74	145	448	7
8	Nimar ...	34,172	40,540	47	24	645	282	29	12	18	12	136	11	8
9	Betul ...	28,880	40,887	328	118	1,486	4,192	244	41	84	77	249	789	9
10	Chhindwara ...	44,326	63,568	182	224	519	872	102	5	80	219	205	124	10
	NAGPUR DIVISION ...	*280,311*	*393,325*	*4,450*	*1,307*	*10,264*	*14,924*	*3,224*	*529*	*1,226*	*778*	*2,295*	*1,287*	
11	Wardha ...	66,171	87,198	958	213	1,583	1,384	751	92	207	121	79	83	11
12	Nagpur ...	69,140	113,073	1,980	569	2,852	5,406	1,583	252	397	317	1,389	318	12
13	Chanda ...	53,096	77,421	670	327	2,829	4,448	354	93	316	234	438	431	13
14	Bhandara ...	60,183	79,806	733	168	2,409	3,074	477	83	256	85	265	201	14
15	Balaghat ...	31,721	35,830	109	30	591	612	59	9	50	21	127	254	15
	CHHATTISGARH DIVISION.	*225,666*	*249,359*	*4,257*	*1,487*	*5,321*	*7,154*	*1,225*	*69*	*3,032*	*1,418*	*430*	*449*	
16	Raipur ...	103,473	112,481	1,735	626	2,685	4,054	594	36	1,141	590	355	320	16
17	Bilaspur ...	57,807	64,618	1,461	620	1,801	2,382	271	5	1,190	615	48	89	17
18	Drug ...	64,386	72,260	1,061	241	835	718	360	28	701	213	27	40	18
	Berar ...	**406,580**	**554,515**	**1,058**	**502**	**13,012**	**9,064**	**368**	**100**	**690**	**402**	**283**	**441**	
19	Amraoti ...	128,354	145,216	333	197	5,110	4,338	106	16	227	181	84	54	19
20	Akola ...	108,873	129,242	325	91	3,952	1,807	108	33	217	58	108	240	20
21	Buldana ...	74,747	109,661	350	83	2,530	2,094	127	41	223	42	73	92	21
22	Yeotmal ...	99,606	170,397	60	181	1,420	825	27	10	23	121	18	55	22
	Feudatory States ...	**118,431**	**122,379**	**392**	**123**	**1,543**	**2,834**	**34**	**12**	**358**	**111**	**136**	**201**	
23	Makrai ...	1,215	1,223	...	...	43	45	...	...	...	...	6	...	23
24	Bastar ...	24,474	22,573	11	...	410	880	8	...	3	...	1	...	24
25	Kanker ...	9,406	10,242	5	1	227	716	3	1	2	...	...	...	25
26	Nandgaon ...	12,131	17,523	60	15	199	348	6	1	61	14	63	171	26
27	Khairagarh ...	11,340	14,485	39	9	187	340	8	...	36	9	55	20	27
28	Chhuikhadan ...	2,321	2,585	8	...	41	37	...	...	8	...	...	...	28
29	Kawardha ...	4,581	5,350	9	16	36	80	6	9	3	7	1	...	29
30	Sakti ...	1,908	1,978	124	75	78	63	...	...	124	75	1	...	30
31	Raigarh ...	13,006	13,125	48	2	42	77	1	...	47	2	1	1	31
32	Sarangarh ...	8,329	8,300	42	3	66	47	3	1	39	2	2	...	32
33	Chang Bhakar ...	1,807	2,914	...	...	30	11	...	...	...	...	...	...	33
34	Korea ...	3,842	4,570	1	1	50	100	...	...	1	1	1	9	34
35	Surguja ...	17,055	10,123	5	...	77	42	1	...	4	...	4	...	35
36	Udaipur ...	2,507	2,140	16	1	42	24	...	...	16	1	1	...	36
37	Jashpur ...	4,417	5,242	15	...	15	24	1	...	14	...	...	...	37

TABLE XV.—Occupation or means of livelihood. Part B.—

(3) AGRICULTURAL

Serial No.	DISTRICT OR STATE.	DETAILS OF SUBSIDIARY											
		Village watchmen.		Cattle-breeders and milkmen.		Mill-hands.		Fishermen and boatmen.		Rice-pounders.		Traders of all kinds.	
		Males.	Females.	Males.	Females.	Males.	Females.	Males.	Females.	Males.	Females.	Males.	Females.
	1	14	15	16	17	18	19	20	21	22	23	24	25
	Central Provinces and Berar.	**530**	**83**	**527**	**608**	**152**	**250**	**2,158**	**1,295**	**650**	**1,140**	**3,223**	**5,011**
	C.P. British Districts and Berar.	**507**	**80**	**515**	**567**	**151**	**250**	**2,094**	**1,267**	**649**	**1,073**	**3,168**	**4,941**
	C.P. British Districts.	**103**	**26**	**264**	**452**	**18**	**150**	**1,607**	**1,109**	**564**	**956**	**2,374**	**4,422**
	JUBBULPORE DIVISION.	*6*	*10*	*64*	*38*	*4*	1	*117*	*11*	*4*	*5*	*162*	*41*
1	Saugor ...	...	...	33	20	1	...	31	...	1	3	4	6
2	Damoh ...	1	3	15	3	...	1	2	...	1	...	71	12
3	Jubbulpore ...	2	4	13	12	1	...	38	3	...	...	78	16
4	Mandla ...	1	3	2	3	...	...	29	7	...	1	7	6
5	Seoni ...	1	...	1	...	2	...	17	1	2	1	2	1
	NERBUDDA DIVISION.	*15*	*3*	*69*	*58*	*8*	*148*	*150*	*57*	*4*	*28*	*253*	*284*
6	Narsinghpur ...	2	...	28	23	...	...	53	14	...	9	65	83
7	Hoshangabad ...	...	...	11	7	4	...	50	1	3	17	89	36
8	Nimar ...	7	1	14	15	3	2	35	4	...	2	40	4
9	Betul ...	3	...	9	8	...	145	3	...	1	...	35	37
10	Chhindwara ...	5	2	7	5	1	1	9	38	...	...	24	124
	NAGPUR DIVISION ...	*47*	*4*	*81*	*137*	*6*	...	*455*	*613*	*527*	*906*	*1,453*	*2,200*
11	Wardha ...	11	1	20	43	2	...	103	107	...	1	362	247
12	Nagpur ...	15	...	23	41	1	...	79	118	9	8	152	875
13	Chanda ...	16	...	19	37	3	...	180	242	105	189	221	411
14	Bhandara ...	5	2	18	12	...	...	97	99	413	706	684	625
15	Balaghat ...	...	1	1	4	...	...	20	47	...	2	34	42
	CHHATTISGARH DIVISION.	*36*	*9*	*50*	*219*	...	*1*	*855*	*425*	*29*	*17*	*506*	*1,897*
16	Raipur ...	5	1	16	129	...	...	403	233	...	6	180	1,286
17	Bilaspur ...	10	1	32	69	...	1	335	167	28	6	238	506
18	Drug ...	21	7	2	21	...	...	117	28	1	5	88	105
	Berar ...	**404**	**54**	**251**	**115**	**133**	**100**	**487**	**158**	**85**	**117**	**794**	**519**
19	Amraoti ...	122	22	117	58	19	65	235	113	76	110	202	135
20	Akola ...	147	17	82	32	90	26	138	3	8	3	249	79
21	Buldana ...	99	13	27	5	14	7	68	18	1	4	120	206
22	Yeotmal ...	30	2	25	20	10	2	46	24	...	...	133	99
	Feudatory States ...	**23**	**3**	**12**	**41**	**1**	...	**64**	**28**	**1**	**67**	**55**	**70**
23	Makrai ...	6	...	...	...	...	...	...	...	...	4	...	...
24	Bastar ...	6	...	6	8	...	...	9	2	1	23	15	14
25	Kanker ...	7	2	3	2	...	...	...	1	...	1	2	16
26	Nandgaon ...	...	...	2	11	1	...	16	2	...	2	7	22
27	Khairagarh ...	...	1	...	16	...	...	7	...	...	...	9	11
28	Chhuikhadan ...	...	...	...	...	...	...	3	1	...	...	...	...
29	Kawardha ...	...	...	1	2	...	...	4	1	...	...	...	...
30	Sakti ...	1	...	...	...	...	...	5	2	...	...	8	...
31	Raigarh ...	...	...	...	...	...	...	1	...	...	37	...	...
32	Sarangarh ...	...	...	...	1	...	...	2	...	...	...	17	7
33	Chang Bhakar ...	2	...	...	1	...	...	6	4	...	...	...	...
34	Korea ...	1	...	...	...	...	...	...	...	...	...	...	...
35	Surguja ...	...	...	...	...	...	...	...	...	...	...	2	...
36	Udaipur ...	...	...	...	...	...	...	7	15	...	...	...	...
37	Jashpur ...	...	...	...	...	...	...	4	...	...	...	...	...

Subsidiary occupations of Agriculturists.—Actual workers only.

LABOURERS—(*concluded*).

OCCUPATIONS RETURNED—(*concluded*).

Oil-pressers.		Weavers.		Potters.		Leather workers.		Washermen.		Blacksmiths and carpenters.		Others.		Serial No.
Males.	Females.	Males.	Females.	Males.	Females.	Males.	Females.	Males.	Females.	Males.	Females.	Males.	Females.	
26	27	28	29	30	31	32	33	34	35	36	37	38	39	
489	556	1,437	913	414	346	3,197	490	978	1,042	748	160	25,060	30,728	
449	527	1,366	867	404	337	3,130	452	914	992	703	150	24,106	28,486	
292	393	1,108	712	287	231	2,931	226	605	740	355	84	14,919	21,865	
35	*33*	*255*	*91*	*51*	*73*	*2,587*	*59*	*234*	*183*	*45*	*1*	*4,220*	*3,628*	
8	6	48	14	26	33	991	19	74	61	14	1	1,256	1,282	1
15	14	62	9	17	18	1,140	22	36	38	11	...	789	780	2
8	14	135	64	8	21	450	16	107	73	13	...	1,864	1,222	3
3	3	9	3	...	1	1	...	11	7	4	...	232	281	4
1	1	4	1	...	...	5	2	6	4	3	...	79	63	5
47	*50*	*264*	*113*	*62*	*45*	*207*	*75*	*59*	*70*	*44*	*7*	*3,602*	*5,905*	
9	16	37	30	31	33	158	41	24	19	7	...	1,057	808	6
15	11	61	11	6	2	30	23	22	14	7	...	955	1,225	7
1	1	80	11	10	6	15	8	5	8	9	2	290	207	8
15	8	27	28	11	2	2	2	1	4	8	4	1,122	3,165	9
7	14	59	32	4	2	2	1	7	25	13	1	178	503	10
79	*134*	*316*	*243*	*152*	*45*	*48*	*81*	*97*	*207*	*184*	*51*	*4,491*	*9,017*	
11	14	43	46	42	15	3	36	28	44	30	3	849	744	11
46	63	35	11	37	6	7	21	38	123	49	35	972	3,787	12
2	27	160	151	5	2	23	16	9	19	52	9	1,590	2,914	13
19	27	69	32	50	16	10	8	22	18	41	3	716	1,825	14
1	3	9	2	18	6	5	...	...	3	12	1	364	247	15
131	*171*	*270*	*267*	*23*	*63*	*39*	*11*	*215*	*230*	*82*	*26*	*2,606*	*3,313*	
54	86	179	175	6	3	42	9	90	137	59	20	1,296	1,649	16
21	42	50	54	4	10	25	2	50	80	14	5	946	1,350	17
56	43	41	38	12	55	22	...	75	63	9	...	364	313	18
157	134	258	155	117	106	199	226	309	252	348	66	9,187	6,621	
79	67	48	48	70	53	67	114	166	72	166	59	3,567	3,368	19
38	20	82	21	17	29	51	30	81	76	79	4	2,782	1,218	20
31	20	68	67	19	17	57	63	41	55	54	2	1,858	1,525	21
9	18	60	19	11	7	24	19	19	49	49	1	980	510	22
40	29	71	46	10	9	67	38	64	50	45	10	954	2,242	
1	...	5	...	1	...	1	...	...	...	...	...	23	41	23
3	1	8	5	...	...	6	...	...	...	6	4	349	823	24
13	9	4	3	3	3	...	...	11	7	2	1	182	671	25
6	6	2	3	1	4	11	...	15	20	2	...	73	107	26
10	6	...	5	4	2	4	...	14	6	3	...	81	273	27
...	...	...	1	...	...	1	...	1	3	...	...	86	32	28
4	4	1	1	...	...	...	...	...	3	...	...	25	69	29
3	2	7	7	...	...	3	...	6	6	...	2	49	44	30
...	1	5	6	...	...	...	...	4	2	...	...	31	30	31
...	...	10	1	...	...	4	...	5	1	...	...	26	37	32
...	...	3	1	...	...	...	...	3	...	16	3	...	2	33
...	...	10	3	1	...	...	4	1	...	1	...	35	84	34
...	...	5	2	...	...	37	34	2	...	...	...	27	6	35
...	...	5	...	...	...	...	...	...	...	15	...	14	9	36
...	...	6	8	...	...	...	...	2	2	...	...	3	14	37

TABLE XV.—Occupation or means of livelihood.

Part D.—Distribution by Religion.

TABLE XV.—Occupation or means of livelihood.

Part D.—Distribution by Religion.

Group No.	OCCUPATION.	Total number of workers and dependants.	Distribution by Religion.					
			Hindus.	Animists.	Musalmans.	Christians.	Jains.	Others.
1	2	3	4	5	6	7	8	9
	Central Provinces and Berar	16,033,310	12,807,874	2,490,355	585,029	73,401	71,417	5,234
	A.—Production of raw materials	12,782,215	10,081,372	2,388,514	250,069	44,821	16,893	546
	I.—Exploitation of the surface of the earth ...	12,752,240	10,058,372	2,383,363	248,499	44,677	16,851	478
	1.—Pasture and agriculture	12,618,871	9,926,800	2,381,877	248,194	44,671	16,851	478
	(a)—Ordinary cultivation	12,051,933	9,439,059	2,315,986	236,044	43,601	16,788	455
1	Income from rent of agricultural land	129,911	115,441	5,716	7,471	19	1,167	97
2	Ordinary cultivators	7,472,405	5,845,474	1,447,057	129,027	38,211	12,338	298
3	Agents, managers of landed estates (not planters), clerks, rent-collectors, etc.	18,862	14,275	976	3,479	42	73	17
4	Farm servants and field-labourers	4,430,755	3,463,869	862,237	96,067	5,329	3,210	43
	Farm servants	1,088,365	781,328	290,622	14,519	1,298	587	11
	Field-labourers	3,342,390	2,682,541	571,615	81,548	4,031	2,623	32
	(b)—Growers of special products and market gardening.	52,827	51,262	837	522	204	2	...
5	Tea, coffee, cinchona and indigo plantations ...	487	415	51	13	8	...	...
6	Fruit, flower, vegetable, betel, vine, areca nut, etc., growers.	52,340	50,847	786	509	196	2	...
	(c)—Forestry	81,462	52,981	21,282	7,019	145	12	23
7	Forest Officers, rangers, guards, etc.	13,948	8,156	1,295	4,363	107	7	20
8	Wood-cutters; firewood, lac, catechu, rubber, etc., collectors, and charcoal burners.	67,514	44,825	19,987	2,656	38	5	3
	(d)—Raising of farm stock	432,534	383,438	43,757	4,569	721	49	...
9	Cattle and buffalo breeders and keepers	33,789	32,563	279	936	...	11	...
10	Sheep, goat and pig breeders	3,311	3,188	70	47	6	...	...
11	Breeders of other animals (horses, mules, camels, asses, etc.)	381	142	6	231	2	...	...
12	Herdsmen, shepherds, goatherds, etc.	395,053	347,545	43,402	3,355	713	38	...
13	**(e)—Raising of small animals** (birds, bees, silkworms, etc.)	115	60	15	40	...	...	...
	2.—Fishing and Hunting	133,369	131,572	1,486	305	6	...	...
14	Fishing	127,244	126,200	852	187	5	...	...
15	Hunting	6,125	5,372	634	118	1	...	...
	II.—Extraction of minerals	29,975	23,000	5,151	1,570	144	42	68
	3.—Mines	27,423	21,153	4,622	1,405	135	40	68
16	Coal mines and petroleum wells	6,117	4,406	1,049	562	31	27	40
17	Mines and metallic minerals (gold, iron, manganese, etc.)	21,300	16,745	3,573	843	104	13	28
18	**4.—Quarries of hard rocks** (other minerals, jade, diamonds, limestone, etc.)	1,892	1,268	506	107	9	2	...
	5.—Salt, etc.	660	579	23	58	...	...	...
19	Rock, sea and marsh salt	3	...	1	2	...	...	...
20	Extraction of saltpetre, alum and other substances soluble in water.	657	579	22	56	...	...	...
	B.—Preparation and supply of material substances.	2,427,166	2,068,991	73,441	223,201	7,604	51,887	2,142
	III.—Industry	1,613,813	1,461,846	46,148	99,253	2,873	3,047	646
	6.—Textiles	443,730	405,647	2,753	33,627	1,068	231	354

TABLE XV.—Occupation or means of livelihood.
Part D.—Distribution by Religion.

Group No.	OCCUPATION.	Total number of workers and dependants.	Distribution by Religion. Hindus.	Animists.	Musalmans.	Christians	Jains.	Others.
1	2	3	4	5	6	7	8	9
21	Cotton-ginning, cleaning and pressing	47,261	30,535	444	15,770	142	201	169
22	Cotton-spinning, sizing and weaving	350,540	331,284	1,813	16,292	915	51	185
	Cotton-spinning	37,983	34,705	295	2,777	27	42	137
	Cotton-sizing	1,867	1,805	4	58	...	...	...
	Cotton-weaving	308,614	292,795	1,514	13,360	888	9	43
	Cotton and silk weaving	2,076	1,979	...	97	...	...	...
23	Jute spinning, pressing and weaving ...	2,129	2,029	27	70	...	3	...
24	Rope, twine and string ...	3,676	3,025	386	265	...	...	...
25	Other fibres (cocoanut, aloes, flax, hemp, straw, etc.,	1,345	1,320	19	4	...	2	...
26	Wool carders and spinners, weavers of woollen blankets, carpets, etc.	14,178	14,130	3	45	...	...	...
27	Silk spinners and weavers ...	18,903	18,503	3	386	11	...	...
	Silk spinners ...	4,239	4,092	...	136	11	...	...
	Silk weavers ...	10,496	10,286	...	210	...	...	...
	Tassar weavers (whether combined or not combined with silk or and cotton weaving).	4,168	4,125	3	40	...	...	...
28	Hair, camel and horse hair, bristles work, brush makers, etc.	219	168	45	6	...	...	...
29	Persons occupied with feathers	6	6	...	...	...	...	...
30	Dyeing, bleaching, printing, preparation and sponging of textiles.	3,923	3,388	12	499	...	24	...
31	Other (lace, crape, embroideries, fringes, etc.), and insufficiently described textile industries.	1,550	1,259	1	290	...	...	...
	7.—Hides, skins and hard materials from the animal kingdom.	**13,787**	**13,498**	**40**	**238**	**11**	...	...
32	Tanners, curriers, leather dressers and dyers, etc. ...	8,972	8,897	7	65	3	...	...
33	Makers of leather articles, such as trunks, water bags, etc.	4,623	4,524	17	74	8	...	...
34	Furriers	36	36	...	...	...	...	...
35	Bone, ivory, horn, shell, etc., workers	156	41	16	99	...	...	...
	8.—Wood	**196,762**	**169,480**	**25,088**	**1,446**	**592**	**53**	**103**
36	Sawyers, carpenters, turners and joiners, etc. ...	98,329	91,836	4,585	1,204	560	41	103
37	Basket-makers and other industries of woody material, including leaves.	98,433	77,644	20,503	242	32	12	...
	9.—Metals	**140,451**	**127,508**	**8,157**	**4,421**	**246**	**27**	**92**
38	Forging and rolling of iron and other metals ...	4,400	2,700	1,692	7	1	...	...
39	Plough and agricutural implement makers ...	17,002	16,143	755	104	...	...	...
40	Makers of arms, guns, etc.	1,753	1,008	88	513	67	...	77
41	Other workers in iron and makers of implements and tools, principally or exclusively of iron.	91,522	84,621	5,105	1,632	145	4	15
42	Workers in brass, copper and bell-metal ...	23,007	22,147	460	359	26	15	...
43	Workers in other metals (tin, zinc, lead, quicksilver, etc.)	2,570	707	57	1,791	7	8	...
44	Workers in mints, die-sinkers, etc. ...	197	182	...	15	...	...	...
	10.—Ceramics	**98,595**	**96,221**	**902**	**1,454**	**17**	**1**	...
45	Makers of glass and crystal ware	1,630	805	6	815	4	...	...
46	Makers of porcelain and crockery	49	10	...	39	...	...	...
47	Potters and earthen pipe and bowl makers ..	76,785	76,411	198	163	13	...	...
48	Brick and tile makers	20,128	18,992	698	437	...	1	...
49	Others (mosaic, talc, mica, alabaster, etc., workers)	3	3	...	...	...	...	...
	11.—Chemical products properly so called, and analogous.	**37,041**	**35,791**	**358**	**870**	**2**	**16**	**4**
50	Manufacture of matches and explosive materials ...	1,400	1,026	39	331	1	3	...
51	Manufacture of aerated and mineral waters ...	50	35	1	14	...	...	...
52	Manufacture of dyes, paint and ink	33	19	...	14	...	...	...
53	Manufacture and refining of vegetable and mineral oils.	33,872	33,540	18	300	1	...	4
54	Manufacture of paper, cardboard and papier-maché,	58	46	...	12	...	...	...
55	Others (soap, candles, lac, cutch, perfumes and miscellaneous drugs).	1,628	1,125	300	190	...	13	...
	12.—Food Industries	**105,538**	**84,696**	**4,187**	**15,434**	**97**	**1,113**	**11**
56	Rice pounders and huskers and flour-grinders ...	25,275	19,638	2,913	2,412	36	272	4
57	Bakers and biscuit-makers	593	152	3	402	22	14	...
58	Grain parchers, etc.	32,061	31,788	177	84	2	10	...

TABLE XV.—Occupation or means of livelihood.

Part D.—Distribution by Religion.

Group No.	OCCUPATION.	Total number of workers and dependants.	DISTRIBUTION BY RELIGION.					
			Hindus.	Animists.	Musalmans.	Christians.	Jains.	Others.
1	2	3	4	5	6	7	8	9
59	Butchers	18,953	7,883	447	10,607	16	...	...
60	Fish-curers	90	85	...	5	...	...	...
61	Butter, cheese and ghee makers	2,172	2,040	119	12	1	...	...
62	Makers of sugar, molasses and gur	242	237	...	5	...	...	...
63	Sweetmeat-makers, preparers of jam and condiments, etc.	13,314	12,080	80	339	9	806	...
64	Brewers and distillers	6,933	6,435	384	106	1	...	7
65	Toddy-drawers	1,404	1,440	10	44	...	...	...
66	Manufacturers of tobacco, opium and ganja ...	4,411	2,918	54	1,418	10	11	...
	13.—Industries of dress and the toilet ...	**371.735**	**342,521**	**703**	**26,807**	**313**	**1,387**	**4**
67	Hat, cap and turban makers	7,573	572	6	6,995	...	...	...
68	Tailors, milliners, dressmakers and darners, embroiderers on linen.	59,741	46,563	307	11,326	212	1,332	1
69	Shoe, boot and sandal makers	121,606	121,377	32	146	51	...	...
70	Other industries pertaining to dress, gloves, socks, gaiters, belts, buttons, umbrellas, canes, etc.	1,688	1,463	133	92	...	...	...
71	Washing, cleaning and dyeing	82,521	75,272	23	7,169	23	31	3
72	Barbers, hair-dressers and wig-makers ...	97,900	96,862	60	937	27	20	...
73	Other industries connected with the toilet (tattooers, shampooers, bath-houses, etc.)	700	412	142	142	...	4	...
	14.—Furniture industries	**259**	**166**	...	**93**	...	...	...
74	Cabinet makers, carriage painters, etc.	169	116	...	53	...	...	...
75	Upholsterers, tent-makers, etc.	90	50	...	40	...	...	...
	15.—Building industries	**81,564**	**69 668**	**3,276**	**8,452**	**127**	**31**	**10**
76	Lime-burners, cement-workers ...	4,530	3,410	441	671	2	1	5
77	Excavators, plinth-builders and well-sinkers ...	3,902	2,896	416	588	...	...	2
78	Stone and marble workers, masons and bricklayers ...	70,158	60,934	2,167	6,903	122	30	2
79	Others (thatchers, building contractors, house painters, tilers, plumbers, locksmiths, etc.)	2,974	2,428	252	290	3	...	1
	16.—Construction of means of transport ...	**1.056**	**844**	**121**	**87**	**4**	...	...
80	Cart, carriage, palki, etc., makers and wheelwrights	423	260	113	46	4	...	...
81	Saddlers, harness-makers, whip and lash makers ...	632	583	8	41	...	...	...
82	Ship and boat builders	1	1	...	...	...	...	...
83	**17.—Production and transmission of physical forces (heat, light, electricity, motive powers, etc.) (Gas works, electric light and ice factories).**	**45**	**35**	**1**	...	**9**	...	...
	18.—Industries of luxury and those pertaining to literature and the arts and sciences.	**97,469**	**91.927**	**503**	**4.604**	**256**	**138**	**41**
84	Printers, lithographers, engravers, etc. ...	1,881	1,132	14	430	233	38	34
85	Newspaper and magazine managers and editors, journalists, etc.	29	17	10	1	...	1	...
86	Book-binders and stitchers, envelope makers, etc. ...	[illegible]	536	...	143	1	...	...
87	Makers of musical instruments	[illegible]	1,114	72	63	...	9	...
88	Makers of watches and clocks and optical, photographic and surgical instruments.	43	262	...	153	15	...	5
89	Workers in precious stones and metals, enamellers, imitation jewellery makers, gilders, etc.	82,773	82,056	27	606	...	82	2
90	Makers of bangles, rosaries, bead and other necklaces, spangles, lingams and sacred threads.	9,040	[illegible],790	368	2,880	1	1	...
91	Toy, kite, cage, fishing tackle, etc., makers, taxidermists, etc.	851	705	1	142	1	2	...
92	Others, including managers, persons other than performers employed in theatres and other places of public entertainment, employés of public societies, race-course service, huntsmen, etc.	522	315	11	186	5	5	...
93	**19.—Industries concerned with refuse matter ...** (Sweepers, scavengers, dust and sweeping contractors).	**25.781**	**2[illegible],844**	**59**	**1,720**	**131**	...	**27**

TABLE XV.—Occupation or means of livelihood.
Part D.—Distribution by Religion.

Group No.	OCCUPATION.	Total number of workers and dependants.	DISTRIBUTION BY RELIGION. Hindus.	Animists.	Musalmans.	Christians.	Jains.	Others.
1	2	3	4	5	6	7	8	9
	IV.—Transport.	**217,961**	**172,979**	**13,393**	**26,045**	**3,921**	**726**	**897**
	20.—Transport by water	**6,154**	**5,455**	**374**	**244**	**39**	**4**	**38**
94	Harbour works, dockyards, and pilots	3	3	...	...	...	...	...
95	Shipowners and their employés, shipbrokers, ships' officers, engineers, mariners and firemen.	6	4	...	1	...	...	...
96	Persons employed on the maintenance of streams, rivers and canals (including construction).	4,985	4,378	315	211	39	4	38
97	Boat owners, boatmen and towmen	1,161	1,070	59	32	...	...	...
	21.—Transport by Road	**119,004**	**95,029**	**8,152**	**14,918**	**348**	**511**	**46**
98	Persons employed on the construction and maintenance of roads and bridges.	40,592	33,618	5,097	1,763	20	63	31
99	Cart owners and drivers, coachmen, stable boys, tramway, mail carriage, etc., managers and employés (excluding private servants).	46,720	34,556	1,375	10,383	221	171	14
100	Palki, etc., bearers and owners	1,768	1,680	83	5	...	...	...
101	Pack elephant, camel, mule, ass and bullock owners and drivers.	8,164	6,774	513	621	2	254	...
102	Porters and messengers	21,760	18,401	1,084	2,140	105	23	1
	22.—Transport by Rail	**84,167**	**66,007**	**4,288**	**9,720**	**3,191**	**164**	**797**
103	Railway employés of all kinds other than construction coolies.	37,983	26,353	935	6,729	3,028	156	782
104	Labourers employed on railway construction ...	46,184	39,654	3,353	2,991	163	8	15
105	**23.—Post Office, Telegraph and Telephone services.**	**8,636**	**6,488**	**579**	**1,163**	**343**	**47**	**16**
	V.—Trade	**595,392**	**434,166**	**13,900**	**97,903**	**710**	**48,114**	**599**
106	**24.—Banks, establishments of credit, exchange and insurance.** (Bank managers, money lenders, exchange and insurance agents, money changers and brokers and their employés).	**85,479**	**62,760**	**791**	**13,444**	**49**	**8,330**	**105**
107	**25.—Brokerage, commission and export** (Brokers, commission agents, commercial travellers, warehouse owners and employés).	**6,959**	**5,673**	**99**	**650**	**12**	**516**	**9**
108	**26.—Trade in textiles.** (Trade in piece-goods, wool, cotton, silk, hair and other textiles).	**51,946**	**32,554**	**201**	**10,952**	**8**	**8,070**	**161**
109	**27.—Trade in skins, leather and furs.** (Feathers, horns, etc.).	**8,338**	**6,595**	**57**	**1,650**	**33**	**3**	...
110	**28.—Trade in wood** (not firewood), cork, bark, etc.	**6,890**	**2,884**	**2,750**	**1,225**	**4**	**17**	**10**
111	**29.—Trade in metals.** (Machinery, knife, tool, etc., sellers).	**1,851**	**1,130**	**99**	**592**	...	**27**	**3**
112	**30.—Trade in Pottery**	**1,546**	**1,436**	**8**	**93**	...	**9**	...
113	**31.—Trade in chemical products** (drugs, dyes, paints, petroleum, explosives, etc.)	**8,612**	**6,443**	**784**	**1,289**	**7**	**75**	**14**
	32.—Hotels, cafes, restaurants, etc. ...	**13,794**	**11,454**	**406**	**1,634**	**107**	**97**	**96**
114	Vendors of wine, liquors, aerated waters, etc. ...	12,520	10,898	388	1,024	29	88	93
115	Owners and managers of hotels, cookshops, sarais, etc., and their employés.	1,274	556	18	610	78	9	3
	33.—Other trade in food stuffs	**335,583**	**261,642**	**6,112**	**37,220**	**174**	**30,330**	**105**
116	Fish-dealers	3,365	3,205	23	137	...	...	...
117	Grocers and sellers of vegetable oil, salt and other condiments.	138,280	103,550	848	12,418	40	21,409	15
118	Sellers of milk, butter, ghee, poultry, eggs, etc. ...	14,709	13,150	69	955	13	581	1
119	Sellers of sweetmeats, sugar, gur and molasses ...	7,273	6,249	21	639	...	318	46
120	Cardamom, betel-leaf, vegetables, fruit and areca nut sellers.	51,982	42,855	413	8,545	4	111	4

TABLE XV.—Occupation or means of livelihood.
Part D.—Distribution by Religion.

Group No.	OCCUPATION.	Total number of workers and dependants.	Distribution by Religion. Hindus.	Animists.	Musalmans.	Christians.	Jains.	Others.
1	2	3	4	5	6	7	8	9
121	Grain and pulse dealers	79,630	64,712	590	6,848	66	7,413	35
122	Tobacco, opium, ganja, etc., sellers	18,676	12,879	432	4,908	3	450	4
123	Dealers in sheep, goats and pigs	1,444	1,128	4	312	...	...	...
124	Dealers in hay, grass and fodder	20,214	13,914	3,706	2,498	48	48	...
125	34.—**Trade in clothing and toilet articles** [ready-made clothing and other articles of dress and the toilet (hats, umbrellas, socks, ready-made shoes, perfumes, etc.)]	6,450	2,529	41	3,724	1	149	6
	35.—**Trade in furniture**	5,614	5,258	74	244	4	34	...
126	Trade in furniture, carpets, curtains and bedding ...	1,592	1,413	14	161	4	...	...
127	Hardware, cooking utensils, porcelain, crockery, glassware, bottles, articles for gardening, the cellar, etc.	4,022	3,845	60	83	...	34	...
128	36.—**Trade in building materials** (stones, bricks, plaster, cement, sand, tiles, thatch, etc.).	1,955	1,227	18	706	2	2	...
129	37.—**Trade in means of transport** (dealers and hirers of elephants, camels, horses, cattle, asses, mules, etc.); sellers (not makers) of carriages, saddlery etc.	10,622	6,127	278	4,172	25	20	...
130	38.—**Trade in fuel** (dealers in firewood, charcoal, coal, cowdung, etc.).	5,257	3,675	571	942	65	4	...
	39.—**Trade in articles of luxury and those pertaining to letters and the arts and sciences**	32,275	14,507	227	17,199	131	187	24
131	Dealers in precious stones, jewellery (real and imitation), clocks, optical instruments, etc.	1,649	1,285	112	161	20	70	1
132	Dealers in common bangles, bead necklaces, fans, small articles, toys, hunting and fishing tackle, flowers, etc.	29,391	12,569	110	16,590	14	101	7
133	Publishers, booksellers, stationers, dealers in music, pictures, musical instruments, and curiosities.	1,235	653	5	448	97	16	16
134	40.—**Trade in refuse matter** (dealers in rags, stable refuse, etc.).	597	471	...	124	...	2	...
	41.—**Trade of other sorts**	11,624	7,801	1,384	2,043	88	242	66
135	Shop-keepers otherwise unspecified	5,189	3,512	107	1,235	75	197	63
136	Itinerant traders, pedlars, hawkers, etc. ...	49	31	1	17	...	...	...
137	Conjurors, acrobats, fortune-tellers, reciters, exhibitors of curiosities and wild animals.	5,461	3,537	1,269	639	6	9	1
138	Other trades (including farmers of pounds, tolls and markets).	925	721	7	152	7	36	2
	C.—Public administration and liberal arts ...	522,515	436,840	12,923	62,429	16,468	1,531	2,324
	VI.—Public force	173,740	141,651	6,140	19,486	5,157	50	1,256
	42.—**Army**	11,321	2,672	5	3,039	4,428	1	1,176
139	Army (Imperial)	10,103	2,644	...	3,030	4,428	1	...
140	Army (Native States)	1,218	28	5	9	...	...	1,176
141	43.—**Navy**	16	16	...	...	...	...	...
	44.—**Police**	162,403	138,963	6,135	16,447	729	49	80
142	Police	32,533	19,095	554	12,241	518	45	80
143	Village watchmen	129,870	119,868	5,581	4,206	211	4	...
	VII.—45.—Public Administration ...	102,207	79,120	1,710	19,809	932	369	267
144	Service of the State	49,340	34,541	507	13,014	858	217	179
145	Service of Native and Foreign States	4,601	3,492	288	806	12	3	...
146	Municipal and other local (not village) service ...	11,928	8,525	85	3,181	34	31	72
147	Village officials and servants other than watchmen ...	36,332	32,562	830	2,778	28	118	16

TABLE XV.—Occupation or means of livelihood.
Part D.—Distribution by Religion.

Group No.	OCCUPATION.	Total number of workers and dependants.	DISTRIBUTION BY RELIGION.					
			Hindus.	Animists.	Musalmans.	Christians.	Jains.	Others.
1	2	3	4	5	6	7	8	9
	VIII.—Professions and liberal Arts... ...	**234,704**	**198,872**	**4,984**	**19,699**	**9,384**	**1,001**	**764**
	46.—Religion	**129,490**	**113,713**	**1,634**	**7,381**	**6,296**	**235**	**231**
148	Priests, ministers, etc.	11,406	10,978	6	357	21	7	37
149	Religious mendicants, inmates of monasteries, etc....	103,762	96,206	977	6,880	9	156	25
150	Catechists, readers, Church and Mission service ...	6,780	276	30	64	6,246	...	164
151	Temple, burial or burning ground service, pilgrim conductors, circumcisers.	7,542	6,253	621	571	20	72	5
	47.—Law	**14,429**	**11,959**	**99**	**1,991**	**75**	**192**	**113**
152	Lawyers of all kinds, including Kazis, Law agents and mukhtiars.	9,757	8,111	43	1,328	71	128	76
153	Lawyers' clerks, petition-writers, etc.	4,672	3,848	56	663	4	64	37
	48.—Medicine	**17,426**	**14,039**	**325**	**2,539**	**402**	**53**	**68**
154	Medical practitioners of all kinds, including dentists, oculists and veterinary surgeons.	6,713	4,766	58	1,490	294	48	57
155	Midwives, vaccinators, compounders, nurses, masseurs, etc.	10,713	9,273	267	1,049	108	5	11
156	**49.—Instruction.** (Professors and teachers of all kinds,* and clerks and servants connected with education.)	**29,648**	**22,884**	**291**	**4,099**	**1,836**	**462**	**76**
	50.—Letters and arts and sciences ...	**43,711**	**36,277**	**2,635**	**3,689**	**775**	**59**	**276**
157	Public scribes, stenographers, etc.	25	23	...	...	2	...	...
158	Architects, surveyors, engineers, and their employés.	7,495	5,264	135	1,247	548	37	264
159	Others (authors, photographers, artists, sculptors, astronomers, meteorologists, botanists, astrologers, etc.)	1,451	1,161	19	194	60	8	9
160	Music composers and masters, players on all kinds of musical instruments (not military), singers, actors and dancers.	34,740	29,820	2,481	2,248	165	14	8
161	**IX. 51.—Persons living principally on their income** [Proprietors (other than of agricultural land), fund and scholarship holders and pensioners].	**11,864**	**7,197**	**89**	**3,435**	**995**	**111**	**37**
	D.—Miscellaneous	**301,414**	**230,671**	**15,477**	**49,330**	**4,608**	**1,106**	**222**
	X. 52.—Domestic service	**160,995**	**127,621**	**6,745**	**21,945**	**3,754**	**826**	**104**
162	Cooks, water-carriers, door-keepers, watchmen and other in-door servants.	145,710	114,698	6,373	20,017	3,696	824	102
163	Private grooms, coachmen, dog boys, etc. ...	15,285	12,923	372	1,928	58	2	2
	XI. 53.—Insufficiently described occupations—General terms which do not indicate a definite occupation.	**37,729**	**30,046**	**2,522**	**4,309**	**619**	**147**	**86**
164	Manufacturers, business men and contractors otherwise unspecified.	2,401	1,532	14	694	79	43	39
165	Cashiers, accountants, book-keepers, clerks and other employés in unspecified offices, warehouses and shops.	4,865	3,433	184	847	358	11	32
166	Mechanics otherwise unspecified	1,012	822	7	72	98	2	11
167	Labourers and workmen otherwise unspecified ...	20,451	24,25[illegible]	2,317	2,696	84	91	4
	XII.—Unproductive	**102,690**	**73,004**	**6,210**	**23,076**	**235**	**133**	**32**
168	**54.—Inmates of jails, asylums and hospitals...**	**3,856**	**3,090**	**303**	**277**	**157**	**4**	**25**
169	**55.—Beggars, vagrants, prostitutes** (procurers, receivers of stolen goods, cattle-poisoners).	**98,834**	**69,914**	**5,907**	**22,799**	**78**	**129**	**7**

* Except law, medicine, music, dancing and drawing.

TABLE XV.—Occupation or means of livelihood.

Part D.—Distribution by Religion.

CITIES.

TABLE XV.—Occupation or means of livelihood.

Part D.—Distribution by Religion.

Serial No.	OCCUPATION.	Jubbulpore City. Total number of workers and dependants.	Jubbulpore City. Distribution by Religion. Hindus.	Animists.	Musalmans.	Christians.	Jains.	Others.	Nagpur City. Total number of workers and dependants.	Nagpur City. Distribution by Religion. Hindus.	Animists.	Musalmans.	Christians.	Jains.	Others.
1	2	3	4	5	6	7	8	9	10	11	12	13	14	15	16
	Total Population ...	100,651	68,902	195	23,032	6,310	1,364	848	101,415	80,141	1,365	14,589	3,960	624	736
	A.—Production of raw materials.	8,026	7,178	53	690	20	83	2	5,713	4,953	321	348	61	7	23
	I.—Exploitation of the surface of the earth.	7,966	7,129	53	689	10	83	2	5,674	4,944	317	345	57	7	4
	1.—Pasture and Agriculture	7,786	6,964	38	689	10	83	2	5,394	4,671	317	338	57	7	4
	(a)—Ordinary cultivation	5,304	4,725	29	464	1	83	2	3,568	3,017	248	259	33	7	4
1	Income from rent of agricultural land.	773	630	...	86	...	56	1	371	310	...	46	14	1	—
2	Ordinary cultivators ...	3,078	2,828	12	217	1	19	1	1,299	1,126	13	147	5	4	4
3	Agents, managers of landed estates (not planters), clerks, rent-collectors, etc.	294	205	...	81	...	8	...	368	318	1	35	14	...	—
4	Farm servants and field-labourers	1,159	1,062	17	80	...	...	...	1,530	1,263	234	31	...	2	...
	Farm servants ...	141	109	5	27	...	...	...	579	438	117	24	...	...	...
	Field-labourers ...	1,018	953	12	53	...	...	...	951	825	117	7	...	2	...
	(b)—Growers of special products and market gardening.	929	882	...	38	9	...	...	515	458	22	21	14	...	...
5	Tea, coffee, cinchona and indigo plantations.	7	...	...	7	...	...	...	...	...	...	...	...	...	...
6	Fruit, flower, vegetable, betel, vine, areca nut, etc., growers.	922	882	...	31	9	...	...	515	458	22	21	14	...	...
	(c)—Forestry ...	974	808	7	159	...	...	...	498	423	36	31	8	...	...
7	Forest officers, rangers, guards, etc.	236	129	...	107	...	...	...	125	103	...	17	5	...	...
8	Wood-cutters; firewood, lac, catechu, rubber, etc., collectors and charcoal burners.	738	679	7	52	...	...	...	373	320	36	14	3	...	...
	(d)—Raising of farm stock	579	549	2	28	...	...	...	813	773	11	27	2	...	...
9	Cattle and buffalo breeders and keepers.	276	270	...	6	...	...	...	484	478	...	6	...	...	...
10	Sheep, goat and pig breeders ...	...	...	...	...	...	...	...	...	...	...	...	...	...	...
11	Breeders of other animals (horses, mules, camels, asses, etc.)	17	8	...	9	...	...	...	1	...	...	1	...	...	...
12	Herdsmen, shepherds, goatherds, etc.	286	271	2	13	...	...	...	328	295	11	20	2	...	...
13	**(e)—Raising of small animals** Birds, bees, silkworms, etc.	...	...	...	...	...	...	...	...	...	...	...	...	...	...
	2.—Fishing and hunting ...	180	165	15	...	...	...	...	280	273	...	7	...	...	...
14	Fishing	124	124	...	...	...	...	...	273	273	...	...	...	...	...
15	Hunting	56	41	15	...	...	...	...	7	...	...	7	...	...	...
	II.—Extraction of minerals	60	49	...	1	10	...	...	39	9	4	3	4	...	19
	3.—Mines ...	11	...	...	1	10	...	...	35	9	...	3	4	...	19
16	Coal mines and pretroleum wells	5	...	...	...	5	...	...	1	...	...	1	...	...	...
17	Mines and metallic minerals (gold, iron, manganese, etc.).	6	...	...	1	5	...	...	34	9	...	2	4	...	19
18	**4.—Quarries of hard rocks.** Other minerals (jade, diamonds, limestone, etc.)	7	7	...	...	...	...	...	4	...	4	...	...	...	...

TABLE XV.—Occupation or means of livelihood.
Part D.—Distribution by Religion.

Serial No.	OCCUPATION.	Jubbulpore City. Total number of workers and dependants.	Jubbulpore City. Hindus.	Jubbulpore City. Animists.	Jubbulpore City. Musalmans.	Jubbulpore City. Christians.	Jubbulpore City. Jains.	Jubbulpore City. Others.	Nagpur City. Total number of workers and dependants.	Nagpur City. Hindus.	Nagpur City. Animists.	Nagpur City. Musalmans.	Nagpur City. Christians.	Nagpur City. Jains.	Nagpur City. Others.
1	2	3	4	5	6	7	8	9	10	11	12	13	14	15	16
	5.—Salt, etc. ...	**42**	**42**	...	...	...	...	...	...	...	...	...	...	...	...
19	Rock, sea and marsh salt ...	...	...	...	...	...	...	...	...	...	...	...	...	...	...
20	Extraction of saltpetre, alum and other substances soluble in water.	42	42	...	...	...	...	...	...	...	...	...	...	...	...
	B.—Preparation and supply of material substances.	**59,995**	**43,484**	**78**	**13,888**	**1,121**	**1,206**	**218**	**69,377**	**56,763**	**665**	**9,786**	**1,069**	**528**	**566**
	III.—Industry ...	**32,625**	**24,542**	**31**	**7,635**	**246**	**41**	**130**	**45,671**	**38,749**	**293**	**5,861**	**419**	**96**	**253**
	6.—Textiles ...	**5,749**	**2,966**	...	**2,743**	**37**	...	**3**	**28,770**	**24,957**	**84**	**3,382**	**58**	**58**	**231**
21	Cotton-ginning, cleaning and pressing.	806	452	...	414	...	...	..	4,075	3,574	57	291	8	47	98
22	Cotton spinning, sizing and weaving.	4,544	2,426	...	2,078	37	...	3	18,539	15,461	27	2,868	50	...	133
	Cotton spinnng ...	357	113	...	244	...	...	...	2,777	2,527	2	119	...	...	129
	Cotton sizing ...	42	42	...	...	...	...	...	94	85	4	5	...	...	...
	Cotton weaving ...	4,085	2,271	...	1,774	37	...	3	15,090	12,271	21	2,744	50	...	4
	Cotton and silk weaving	60	...	...	60	...	...	...	578	578	...	...	...	...	...
23	Jute spinning, pressing and weaving	10	10	...	...	...	...	...	...	...	...	...	...	...	...
24	Rope, twine and string ...	8	6	...	2	...	...	...	117	116	...	1	...	...	...
25	Other fibres (cocoanut, aloes, flax, hemp, straw, etc.)	16	16	...	...	...	...	...	...	...	...	...	...	...	...
26	Wool carders and spinners, weavers of woollen blankets, carpets, etc.	40	36	...	4	...	...	...	1	1	...	...	...	...	...
27	Silk spinners and weavers ...	241	...	...	241	...	...	...	5,678	5,648	...	30	...	...	...
	Silk spinners ...	...	...	...	...	...	...	...	184	156	...	28	...	...	...
	Silk weavers ...	208	...	...	208	...	...	...	5,494	5,492	...	2	...	...	...
	Tassar weavers whether combined or not combined with silk or cotton weaving.	33	...	...	33	...	...	...	...	...	...	...	...	...	...
28	Hair, camel and horse hair, bristles work, brush makers, etc.	3	3	...	...	...	...	...	...	...	...	...	...	...	...
29	Persons occupied with feathers	...	...	...	...	...	...	...	...	...	...	...	...	...	...
30	Dyeing, bleaching, printing, preparation and sponging of textiles.	15	15	...	...	...	...	...	344	151	...	182	...	11	...
31	Other (lace, crape, embroideries, fringes, etc.) and insufficiently described textile industries.	6	2	...	4	...	...	...	16	6	...	10	...	...	...
	7.—Hides, skins and hard materials from the animal kingdom.	**49**	**44**	...	**2**	**3**	...	...	**25**	**17**	...	**8**	...	...	...
32	Tanners, curriers, leather dressers and dyers, etc.	36	33	...	...	3	...	...	13	12	...	1	...	...	...
33	Makers of leather articles, such as trunks, water bags, etc.	13	11	...	2	...	...	...	11	4	...	7	...	...	...
34	Furriers ...	...	...	...	...	...	...	...	...	...	...	...	...	...	...
35	Bone, ivory, horn, shell, etc., workers.	...	...	...	...	...	...	...	1	1	...	...	...	...	...
	8.—Wood ...	**2,759**	**2,575**	**5**	**105**	**37**	...	**37**	**1,673**	**1,595**	**20**	**30**	**24**	...	**4**
36	Sawyers, carpenters, turners and joiners, etc.	1,858	1,676	5	103	37	...	37	1,306	1,229	20	29	24	...	4
37	Basket-makers and other industries of woody material including leaves.	901	899	...	2	...	...	...	367	366	...	1	...	...	...
	9.—Metals ...	**3,477**	**2,587**	**4**	**728**	**72**	...	**86**	**879**	**558**	**13**	**270**	**38**	...	...
38	Forging and rolling of iron and other metals.	...	...	...	...	...	...	...	...	...	...	...	...	...	...
39	Plough and agricultural implement makers.	96	96	...	...	...	...	...	...	...	...	...	...	...	...
40	Makers of arms, guns, etc. ...	1,569	944	4	477	67	...	77	...	...	...	...	...	...	...
41	Other workers in iron and makers of implements and tools principally or exclusively of iron.	1,296	1,127	...	155	5	...	9	636	513	5	89	29	...	...

TABLE XV.—Occupation or means of livelihood.

Part D.—Distribution by Religion.

Serial No.	OCCUPATION.	Jubbulpore City. Total number of workers and dependants.	Jubbulpore City. Distribution by Religion. Hindus.	Animists.	Musalmans.	Christians.	Jains.	Others.	Nagpur City. Total number of workers and dependants.	Nagpur City. Distribution by Religion. Hindus.	Animists.	Musalmans.	Christians.	Jains.	Others.
1	2	3	4	5	6	7	8	9	10	11	12	13	14	15	16
42	Workers in brass, copper and bell-metal.	370	370	...	...	...	...	...	82	38	...	37	7	...	...
43	Workers in other metals (tin, zinc, lead, quicksilver, etc.)	128	32	...	96	...	...	...	160	7	8	143	2	...	...
44	Workers in mints, die-sinkers, etc.	18	18	...	...	...	...	...	1	...	...	1	...	...	...
	10.—Ceramics ...	**2,620**	**2,459**	**6**	**147**	**8**	...	...	**642**	**618**	**10**	**14**	...	...	...
45	Makers of glass and crystal ware	110	82	...	24	4	...	...	1	...	...	1	...	...	...
46	Makers of porcelain and crockery.	20	7	...	13	...	...	...	...	...	...	...	...	...	...
47	Potters and earthen pipe and bowl makers.	1,336	1,252	6	74	4	...	...	341	341	...	...	...	...	...
48	Brick and tile makers ...	1,154	1,118	...	36	...	...	...	300	277	10	13	...	...	...
49	Others (mosaic, talc, mica, alabaster, etc., workers).	...	...	...	...	...	...	...	...	...	...	...	...	...	...
	11.—Chemical products properly so called and analogous.	**338**	**313**	...	**25**	...	...	...	**219**	**195**	...	**24**	...	...	...
50	Manufacture of matches and explosive materials.	52	43	...	9	...	...	...	18	6	...	12	...	...	...
51	Manufacture of aerated and mineral waters.	2	1	...	1	...	...	...	13	6	...	7	...	...	...
52	Manufacture of dyes, paint and ink.	3	3	...	...	...	...	...	1	1	...	...	...	...	...
53	Manufacture and refining of vegetable and mineral oils.	251	248	...	3	...	...	...	178	178	...	...	...	...	...
54	Manufacture of paper, cardboard and papier-maché.	...	...	...	...	...	...	...	...	...	...	...	...	...	...
55	Others (soap, candles, lac, cutch, perfumes and miscellaneous drugs).	30	18	...	12	...	...	...	9	4	...	5	...	...	...
	12.—Food industries ...	**3,009**	**2.093**	**5**	**862**	**12**	**37**	...	**1,813**	**1,089**	**14**	**650**	**40**	**20**	...
56	Rice-pounders and huskers and flour-grinders.	976	829	5	127	...	15	...	420	350	2	43	21	4	...
57	Bakers and biscuit makers ...	126	...	...	121	4	1	...	28	1	...	9	18	...	...
58	Grain-parchers, etc. ...	220	220	...	...	...	...	...	157	156	...	1	...	...	...
59	Butchers	735	251	...	484	...	...	...	530	366	...	164	...	...	...
60	Fish-curers	...	...	...	...	...	...	...	...	...	...	...	...	...	...
61	Butter, cheese and ghee makers	1	...	...	1	...	...	...	...	...	...	...	...	...	...
62	Makers of sugar, molasses and gur.	...	...	...	...	...	...	...	1	1	...	...	...	...	...
63	Sweetmeat makers, preparers of jam and condiments, etc.	747	695	...	23	8	21	...	119	107	...	6	...	6	...
64	Brewers and distillers ...	43	35	...	8	...	...	...	1	1	...	...	...	...	...
65	Toddy drawers ...	...	...	...	...	...	...	...	...	...	...	...	...	...	...
66	Manufacturers of tobacco, opium and ganja.	161	63	...	98	...	...	...	557	107	12	427	1	10	...
	13.—Industries of dress and the toilet.	**5,964**	**4,217**	...	**1,724**	**23**	...	...	**3,875**	**3,270**	**2**	**584**	**12**	**4**	**3**
67	Hat, cap and turban makers ...	40	15	...	25	...	...	...	53	8	...	45	...	...	...
68	Tailors, milliners, dress-makers and darners, embroiderers on linen.	2,007	995	...	995	17	...	...	1,275	904	...	355	12	4	...
69	Shoe, boot and sandal makers ...	1,276	1,207	...	9	...	...	...	608	599	...	9	...	...	...
70	Other industries pertaining to dress gloves, socks, gaiters, belts, buttons, umbrellas, canes, etc.	...	...	...	...	...	...	...	39	32	...	7	...	...	...
71	Washing, cleaning and dyeing...	1,506	1,016	...	483	6	...	...	1,057	912	2	140	...	...	3
72	Barbers, hair-dressers and wig-makers.	1,135	924	...	211	...	...	...	841	815	...	26	...	...	...
73	Other industries connected with the toilet (tattooers, shampooers, bath-houses, etc.)	1	...	...	1	...	...	...	2	...	...	2	...	...	...
	14.—Furniture industries	**22**	**13**	...	**9**	...	...	...	...	...	...	...	...	...	...
74	Cabinet-makers, carriage painters, etc.	10	10	...	...	...	...	...	...	...	...	...	...	...	...
75	Upholsterers, tent-makers, etc.	12	3	...	9	...	...	...	...	...	...	...	...	...	...
	15.—Building industries ...	**3,765**	**2,923**	**11**	**821**	**10**	...	...	**3,925**	**3,501**	**146**	**257**	**20**	**1**	...
76	Lime-burners, cement workers...	36	28	...	8	...	...	...	63	15	8	39	...	1	...

TABLE XV.—Occupation or means of livelihood.
Part D.—Distribution by Religion.

Serial No.	OCCUPATION.	Jubbulpore City. Total number of workers and dependants.	Jubbulpore City. Distribution by Religion. Hindus.	Animists.	Musalmans.	Christians.	Jains.	Others.	Nagpur City. Total number of workers and dependants.	Nagpur City. Distribution by Religion. Hindus.	Animists.	Musalmans.	Christians.	Jains.	Others.
1	2	3	4	5	6	7	8	9	10	11	12	13	14	15	16
77	Excavators, plinth builders and well sinkers.	5	...	...	5	...	...	...	3	...	3	...	...	...	...
78	Stone and marble workers, masons and bricklayers.	3,542	2,721	11	800	10	...	...	3,812	3,451	135	206	20	...	...
79	Others (thatchers, building contractors, house painters, tilers, plumbers, locksmiths, etc.)	182	174	...	8	...	...	...	47	35	...	12	...	...	...
	16.—Construction of means of transport.	**37**	**13**	...	**20**	**4**	...	...	**36**	**17**	...	**19**	...	...	...
80	Cart, carriage, palki, etc., makers and wheelwrights.	15	1	...	10	4	...	...	30	12	...	18	...	...	...
81	Saddlers, harness-makers, whip and lash makers.	22	12	...	10	...	...	...	6	5	...	1	...	...	...
82	Ship and boat builders ...	...	...	...	...	...	...	...	...	...	...	...	...	...	...
83	**17.—Production and transmission of physical forces (heat, light, electricity, motive power, etc.)** Gas work, electric light and ice factory.	...	...	...	...	...	...	...	**8**	**6**	...	**2**	...	...	...
	18.—Industries of luxury and those pertaining to literature and the arts and sciences.	**2,593**	**2,169**	...	**397**	**19**	**4**	**4**	**2,338**	**1,570**	**4**	**515**	**227**	**13**	**9**
84	Printers, lithographers, engravers, etc.	230	132	...	82	14	...	2	984	512	4	239	218	5	6
85	Newspaper and magazine managers and editors, journalists, etc.	...	...	...	...	...	...	...	11	10	...	1	...	...	...
86	Book binders and stitchers, envelope makers, etc.	223	211	...	12	...	...	...	58	10	...	47	1	...	...
87	Makers of musical instruments...	18	4	...	14	...	...	...	19	19	...	...	...	...	...
88	Makers of watches and clocks and optical, photographic and surgical instruments.	81	46	...	28	5	...	2	39	10	...	20	6	...	3
89	Workers in precious stones and metals, enamellers, imitation jewellery makers, gilders, etc.	1,491	1,485	...	6	...	...	...	1,032	941	...	83	...	8	...
90	Makers of bangles, rosaries, bead and other necklaces, spangles, lingams and sacred threads.	378	247	...	131	...	...	...	106	14	...	92	...	...	...
91	Toy, kite, cage, fishing tackle, etc., makers, taxidermists, etc.	59	19	...	38	...	2	...	32	9	...	23	...	...	...
92	Others including managers, persons other than performers employed in theatres, and other places of public entertainment, employés of public societies, race-course service, huntsmen, etc.	113	25	...	86	...	2	...	57	45	...	10	2	...	...
93	**19.—Industries concerned with refuse matter.** (Sweepers, scavengers, dust and sweeping contractors).	**2,243**	**2,170**	...	**52**	**21**	...	...	**1,468**	**1,356**	...	**106**	...	...	**6**
	IV.—Transport ...	**10,684**	**7,339**	**17**	**2,478**	**785**	**12**	**53**	**11,340**	**8,609**	**305**	**1,622**	**539**	**9**	**256**
	20.—Transport by water...	**14**	**12**	...	**2**	...	...	...	**67**	**59**	...	**8**	...	...	...
94	Harbour works, dockyards and pilots.	...	...	...	...	...	...	...	...	...	...	...	...	...	...
95	Shipowners and their employés, shipbrokers, ships' officers, engineers, mariners and firemen.	1	...	...	1	...	...	...	...	...	...	...	...	...	...
96	Persons employed on the maintenance of streams, rivers and canals (including construction).	8	7	...	1	...	...	...	65	57	...	8	...	...	...
97	Boat-owners, boatmen and towmen.	5	5	...	...	...	...	...	2	2	...	...	...	...	...
	21.—Transport by road ...	**5,815**	**4,343**	**16**	**1,433**	**5**	**9**	**9**	**5,948**	**5,097**	**188**	**628**	**35**	...	...
98	Persons employed on the construction and maintenance of roads and bridges.	1,763	1,377	9	364	...	7	6	1,615	1,522	55	38	...	...	...

TABLE XV.—Occupation or means of livelihood.
Part D.—Distribution by Religion.

Serial No.	OCCUPATION.	Jubbulpore City. Total number of workers and dependants.	Distribution by Religion. Hindus.	Animists.	Musalmans.	Christians.	Jains.	Others.	Nagpur City. Total number of workers and dependants.	Distribution by Religion. Hindus.	Animists.	Musalmans.	Christians.	Jains.	Others.
1	2	3	4	5	6	7	8	9	10	11	12	13	14	15	16
99	Cart-owners and drivers, coachmen, stable boys, tramway, mail, carriage, etc., managers and employés (excluding private servants).	2,542	1,712	6	815	5	1	3	2,111	1,578	69	461	3	...	...
100	Palki, etc., bearers and owners	50	50	...	...	...	...	...	4	4	...	...	...	...	...
101	Pack elephant, camel, mule, ass and bullock owners and drivers.	59	42	...	17	...	...	...	4	...	...	4	...	...	...
102	Porters and messengers ...	1,401	1,162	1	237	...	1	...	2,214	1,993	64	125	32	...	...
	22.—Transport by rail ...	4,318	2,652	1	924	695	2	44	4,488	2,829	110	894	397	8	250
103	Railway employés of all kinds other than construction coolies.	3,618	2,043	...	838	691	2	44	2,782	1,424	48	655	397	8	250
104	Labourers employed on railway construction.	700	600	1	86	4	...	...	1,706	1,405	62	239	...	...	...
105	**23.—Post Office, Telegraph and Telephone services.**	537	332	...	119	85	1	...	837	624	7	92	107	1	6
	V.—Trade ...	16,686	11,603	30	3,775	90	1,153	35	12,366	9,405	67	2,303	111	423	57
106	**24.—Banks, establishments of credit, exchange and insurance** (Bank managers, money-lenders, exchange and insurance agents, money changers and brokers and their employés).	4,044	2,988	8	679	2	355	12	1,077	828	3	123	28	85	9
107	**25.—Brokerage commission and export.** (Brokers, Commission agents, commercial travellers warehouse owners and employés.)	526	409	...	74	3	38	2	490	467	...	15	...	8	...
108	**26.—Trade in texiles.** (Trade in piece-goods, wool, cotton, silk, hair and other textiles.)	1,120	373	...	207	...	538	2	1,487	1,070	8	282	...	124	3
109	**27.—Trade in skins, leather and furs** (feathers, horns, etc.)	163	60	...	103	...	...	...	13.	95	...	37	...	3	...
110	**28.—Trade in wood** (not firewood), cork, bark, etc.	579	501	...	78	...	...	...	134	33	...	98	3	...	...
111	**29.—Trade in metals** (machinery, knife, tool, etc., sellers).	76	26	...	48	...	...	2	32	19	...	12	...	...	1
112	**30.—Trade in pottery ...**	12	9	...	3	...	...	...	9	5	...	4	...	...	...
113	**31.—Trade in chemical products** (drugs, dies, paints, petroleum, explosives, etc).	76	39	...	36	...	1	...	90	32	1	53	...	4	...
	32.—Hotels, cafes, restaurants, etc.	245	14.	...	58	32	4	2	3. 3	223	...	94	11	6	19
114	Vendors of wine, liquors, aerated waters, etc.	144	117	...	13	11	1	2	22	184	...	15	...	6	18
115	Owners and managers of hotels, cookshops, sarais, etc., and their employés.	101	32	...	45	21	3	...	13	39	...	79	11	...	1
	33.—Other trade in food stuffs	7,818	6,082	19	1,513	3	191	10	6,890	5,782	39	877	3	183	6
116	Fish dealers	114	97	...	17	...	...	...	48	48	...	...	...	...	...

TABLE XV.—Occupation or means of livelihood.
Part D.—Distribution by Religion.

Serial No.	OCCUPATION.	Jubbulpore City. Total number of workers and dependants.	Jubbulpore City. Distribution by Religion. Hindus.	Animists.	Musalmans.	Christians.	Jains.	Others.	Nagpur City. Total number of workers and dependants.	Nagpur City. Distribution by Religion. Hindus.	Animists.	Musalmans.	Christians.	Jains.	Others.
1	2	3	4	5	6	7	8	9	10	11	12	13	14	15	16
117	Grocers and sellers of vegetable oil, salt and other condiments.	801	698	...	69	...	28	6	1,720	1,393	1	214	...	118	...
118	Sellers of milk, butter, ghee, poultry, eggs, etc.	970	948	...	16	3	9	...	392	372	1	19	...	...	...
119	Sellers of sweetmeats, sugar, gur and molasses.	188	156	...	6	...	26	...	307	282	...	13	...	12	...
120	Cardamom, betel-leaf, vegetables, fruit and areca nut sellers.	2,584	1,802	13	767	...	2	...	1,563	1,251	13	272	...	27	...
121	Grain and pulse dealers ...	2,118	1,601	2	389	...	122	4	2,037	1,941	1	70	1	18	6
122	Tobacco, opium, ganja, etc., sellers.	215	120	...	91	...	4	...	274	76	1	191	2	4	...
123	Dealers in sheep, goats and pigs.	143	143	...	...	...	...	...	12	4	...	8	...	...	...
124	Dealers in hay, grass and fodder	679	517	4	158	...	...	...	531	415	22	90	...	4	...
125	**34.—Trade in clothing and toilet articles** (ready-made clothing and other articles of dress, and the toilet, hats, umbrellas, socks, ready-made shoes, perfumes, etc).	**200**	**87**	...	**108**	...	**4**	**1**	**189**	**106**	**3**	**75**	...	**5**	...
	35.—Trade in furniture ...	**11**	**5**	...	...	...	**6**	...	**69**	**58**	...	**11**	...	...	...
126	Trade in furniture, carpets, curtains and bedding.	5	5	...	...	...	...	...	43	40	...	3	...	...	...
127	Hardware, cooking utensils, porcelain, crockery, glassware, bottles, articles for gardening, the cellar, etc.	6	...	...	...	...	6	...	26	18	...	8	...	...	...
128	**36.—Trade in building materials** (stones, bricks, plaster, cement, sand, tiles, thatch, etc.)	**23**	**22**	...	...	**1**	...	...	**87**	**17**	...	**69**	**1**	...	...
129	**37.—Trade in means of transport.** Dealers and hirers of elephants, camels, horses, cattle, asses, mules, etc.; sellers (not makers) of carriage, saddlery etc.	**37**	**11**	...	**15**	**11**	...	...	**44**	**16**	...	**26**	**2**	...	...
130	**38.—Trade in fuel.** Dealers in firewood, charcoal, coal, cowdung, etc.	**322**	**256**	...	**66**	...	...	...	**253**	**204**	**7**	**42**	...	...	...
	39.—Trade in articles of luxury and those pertaining to letters and the arts and sciences.	**535**	**95**	**3**	**416**	**11**	**9**	**1**	**624**	**223**	...	**357**	**27**	**2**	**15**
131	Dealers in precious stones, jewellery (real and imitation), clocks, optical instruments, etc.	26	18	...	...	...	7	1	110	53	...	39	18	...	...
132	Dealers in common bangles, beads, necklaces, fans, small articles, toys, hunting and fishing tackle, flowers, etc.	460	50	3	401	4	2	...	416	125	...	275	9	...	7
133	Publishers, book-sellers, stationers, dealers in music, pictures, musical instruments and curiosities.	49	27	...	15	7	...	...	98	45	...	43	...	2	8
134	**40.—Trade in refuse matter.** (Dealers in rags, stable refuse, etc.)	**105**	...	...	**105**	...	...	...	...	...	...	...	...	...	...
	41.—Trades of other sorts ...	**794**	**491**	...	**266**	**27**	**7**	**3**	**403**	**226**	**6**	**128**	**36**	**3**	**4**
135	Shopkeepers otherwise unspecified.	772	487	...	260	24	...	1	368	213	6	119	27	...	3

TABLE XV.—Occupation or means of livelihood.
Part D.—Distribution by Religion.

Serial No.	OCCUPATION.	Jubbulpore City. Total number of workers and dependants.	Jubbulpore City. Distribution by Religion. Hindus.	Animists.	Musalmans.	Christians.	Jains.	Others.	Nagpur City. Total number of workers and dependants.	Nagpur City. Distribution by Religion. Hindus.	Animists.	Musalmans.	Christians.	Jains.	Others.
1	2	3	4	5	6	7	8	9	10	11	12	13	14	15	16
136	Itinerant traders, pedlars, hawkers, etc.	...	...	...	...	...	...	...	...	...	...	...	...	...	...
137	Conjurors, acrobats, fortune-tellers, reciters, exhibitors of curiosities and wild animals.	7	2	...	5	...	...	...	22	6	...	9	5	1	1
138	Other trades (including farmers of pounds, tolls and markets).	15	2	...	1	3	7	2	13	7	...	...	4	2	...
	C.—Public administration and liberal arts.	**17,217**	**7,470**	**24**	**4,672**	**4.383**	**48**	**620**	**13.140**	**8,693**	**55**	**2,402**	**1,835**	**41**	**114**
	VI.—Public Force ...	**7,834**	**1.728**	**13**	**2.524**	**3.034**	...	**535**	**1,840**	**1 087**	...	**601**	**234**	**4**	**14**
	42.—Army	**6,452**	**983**	...	**1,923**	**3,012**	...	**534**	**124**	**29**	...	**11**	**84**	...	...
139	Army (Imperial)	5,918	983	...	1,923	3,012	...	...	124	29	...	11	84	...	...
140	Army (Native States) ...	534	...	...	...	...	...	534	...	...	...	...	...	...	...
141	**43.—Navy**	...	...	...	...	...	...	...	...	...	...	...	...	...	...
	44.—Police	**1.382**	**745**	**13**	**601**	**22**	...	**1**	**1,716**	**1.058**	...	**490**	**150**	**4**	**14**
142	Police	1,343	718	9	593	22	...	1	1,536	881	...	487	150	4	14
143	Village watchmen	39	27	4	8	...	...	...	180	177	...	3	...	...	...
	VII. 45.—Public administration.	**3,134**	**2.251**	**5**	**789**	**51**	**14**	**24**	**4,990**	**3,714**	**21**	**782**	**442**	**10**	**21**
144	Service of the State ...	2,427	1,728	3	613	46	13	24	3,874	2,841	19	560	429	7	18
145	Service of Native and Foreign States.	13	8	...	5	...	...	...	...	...	...	...	...	...	...
146	Municipal and other local (not village) service.	613	435	2	171	5	...	...	1,074	844	2	212	13	2	...
147	Village officials and servants other than watchmen.	81	80	...	...	...	1	...	42	29	...	10	...	...	3
	VIII.—Professions and liberal arts.	**5,155**	**2,968**	**6**	**1,067**	**1.034**	**19**	**61**	**5,291**	**3.429**	**34**	**789**	**947**	**21**	**71**
	46.—Religion	**1,828**	**968**	**6**	**129**	**715**	**6**	**4**	**1,353**	**808**	**2**	**193**	**320**	**15**	**14**
148	Priests, ministers, etc. ...	677	666	3	4	...	...	4	24	7	...	4	...	...	13
149	Religious mendicants, inmates of monasteries, etc.	306	188	...	118	...	...	...	927	763	2	147	...	15	...
150	Catechists, readers, Church and Mission service.	723	7	...	1	715	...	...	338	3	...	16	318	...	1
151	Temple, burial or burning ground service, pilgrim conductors, circumcisers.	122	107	3	6	...	6	...	64	36	...	26	2	...	...
	47.—Law	**680**	**477**	...	**185**	**8**	**2**	**7**	**457**	**397**	...	**30**	**8**	...	**22**
152	Lawyers of all kinds, including Kazis, Law agents and mukhtiars.	455	345	...	93	9	1	7	261	219	...	13	7	...	22
153	Lawyers' clerks, petition-writers, etc.	225	132	...	92	...	1	...	196	178	...	17	1	...	...
	48.—Medicine ...	**650**	**350**	...	**196**	**76**	**2**	**26**	**783**	**542**	**2**	**160**	**69**	**2**	**8**
154	Medical practitioners of all kinds including dentists, oculists and veterinary surgeons.	442	235	...	109	75	1	22	394	242	1	94	47	2	8

TABLE XV.—Occupation or means of livelihood.
Part D.—Distribution by Religion.

Serial No.	OCCUPATION.	Jubbulpore City. Total number of workers and dependants.	Jubbulpore City. Distribution by Religion. Hindus.	Animists.	Musalmans.	Christians.	Jains.	Others.	Nagpur City. Total number of workers and dependants.	Nagpur City. Distribution by Religion. Hindus.	Animists.	Musalmans.	Christians.	Jains.	Others.
1	2	3	4	5	6	7	8	9	10	11	12	13	14	15	16
155	Midwives, vaccinators, compounders, nurses, masseurs, etc.	208	115	...	87	1	1	4	389	300	1	66	22	...	...
156	**49.—Instruction.** Professors and teachers of all kinds* and clerks and servants connected with education.	**1,063**	**619**	...	**260**	**167**	**9**	**8**	**799**	**401**	...	**111**	**274**	**3**	**10**
	50.—Letters and arts and sciences.	**934**	**554**	...	**297**	**67**	...	**16**	**1,899**	**1,280**	**30**	**295**	**276**	**1**	**17**
157	Public scribes, stenographers, etc.	1	...	...	...	1	...	...	2	2	...	...	...	...	...
158	Architects, surveyors, engineers and their employés.	536	339	...	135	53	...	9	1,400	992	8	226	160	1	13
159	Others (authors, photographers, artists, sculptors, astronomers, meteorologists, botanists, astrologers, etc).	98	69	...	14	11	...	4	152	107	...	22	19	...	4
160	Music composers and masters, players on all kinds of musical instruments (not military), singers, actors and dancers.	299	146	...	148	2	...	3	345	179	22	47	97	...	...
161	**IX. 51.—Persons living Principally on their income.** (Proprietors (other than of agricultural land), fund and scholarship holders and pensioners).	**1,094**	**523**	...	**292**	**264**	**15**	...	**1,019**	**463**	...	**330**	**212**	**6**	**8**
	D.—Miscellaneous ...	**15,413**	**10,770**	**40**	**3,782**	**786**	**27**	**8**	**13,185**	**9,732**	**324**	**2,053**	**995**	**48**	**33**
	X 52.—Domestic service ...	**9,119**	**6,136**	**3**	**2,245**	**713**	**15**	**7**	**7,976**	**5,738**	**161**	**1,418**	**606**	**42**	**11**
162	Cooks, water-carriers, doorkeepers, watchmen and other in-door servants.	6,843	4,111	3	1,996	713	13	7	7,258	5,095	161	1,366	583	42	11
163	Private grooms, coachmen, dog-boys, etc.	2,276	2,025	...	249	...	2	...	718	643	...	52	23	...	...
	XI. 53.—Insufficiently described occupations. General terms which do not indicate a definite occupation.	**4,540**	**3,385**	**6**	**1,067**	**69**	**12**	**1**	**2,989**	**2,304**	**138**	**178**	**345**	**3**	**21**
164	Manufacturers, business men and contractors, otherwise unspecified.	195	89	...	63	32	10	1	280	181	...	79	16	1	3
165	Cashiers, accountants, bookkeepers, clerks and other employés in unspecified offices, warehouses and shops.	878	521	1	333	23	...	...	405	135	...	3	254	...	13
166	Mechanics otherwise unspecified.	536	536	...	...	...	...	...	244	147	4	24	64	...	5
167	Labourers and workmen otherwise unspecified.	2,931	2,239	5	671	14	2	...	2,000	1,841	134	72	11	2	...
	XII.—Unproductive ...	**1,754**	**1,249**	**31**	**470**	**4**	...	...	**2,220**	**1,690**	**25**	**457**	**44**	**3**	**1**
168	**54.—Inmates of jails, asylums and hospitals.**	**780**	**737**	**27**	**13**	**3**	...	...	**1,295**	**1,089**	**18**	**156**	**30**	**1**	**1**
169	**55.—Beggars, vagrants, prostitutes** (procurers, receivers of stolen goods, cattle-poisoners.)	**974**	**512**	**4**	**457**	**1**	...	...	**925**	**601**	**7**	**301**	**14**	**2**	...

* Except law, medicine, music, dancing and drawing.

TABLE XV-E.—Statistics of Industries.

Part I.—Provincial Summary.

TABLE XV-E.—Statistics of Industries.

Description of Factory, Mine, etc. A.—Mills in which mechanical power is used. B.—Mills in which mechanical power is not used.	Classification of factory, etc., according to number of persons employed (including management).	Number of factories.	Total number of persons employed.		CLASSIFICATION			
					Direction, supervision and clerical work.			
					Europeans and Anglo-Indians.		Indians.	
			Males.	Females.	Males.	Females.	Males.	Females.
1	2	3	4	5	6	7	8	9
	Grand Total ...	**307**	**38,077**	**18,541**	**151**	**3**	**2,478**	**47**
Mines	......	**45**	**8,918**	**5,884**	**41**	**1**	**237**	**6**
Collieries and Coal Mines (one Government).	Total ...	*5*	*2,309*	*715*	*15*	...	*102*	...
	Total A ...	*4*	*2,274*	*700*	*15*	...	*101*	...
A	From 200 to 400 persons	1	159	79	...	...	3	...
A	400 and over ...	3	2,115	621	15	...	98	...
B	50 to 100 persons ...	1	35	15	...	...	1	...
Manganese	Total ...	*40*	*6,609*	*5,169*	*26*	*1*	*135*	*6*
A	400 and over ...	5	2,029	1,368	3	...	24	...
	Total B ...	*35*	*4,580*	*3,801*	*23*	*1*	*111*	*6*
B	20 to 50 persons ...	6	100	107	1	1	10	...
B	50 to 100 persons ...	7	319	180	2	...	28	2
B	100 to 200 persons ...	10	805	681	9	...	20	4
B	200 to 400 persons ...	8	1,083	1,034	8	...	24	...
B	400 and over ...	4	2,273	1,799	3	...	29	...
Quarries of hard rocks ...	......	**7**	**511**	**277**	**2**	...	**16**	...
	Total B ...	*5*	*342*	*204*	*2*	...	*13*	...
Limestone Quarries ... B	50 to 100 persons ...	3	150	85	...	...	5	...
B	100 to 200 persons ...	2	192	119	2	...	8	...
Stone Quarries ... B	100 to 200 persons ...	2	169	73	...	...	3	...
Textile Industries (a) Cotton ...	...	**163**	**18,419**	**8,546**	**10**	...	**1,439**	**32**
Cotton-ginning, cleaning and pressing mills.	Total A ...	*153*	*7,895*	*5,696*	*1*	...	*66[illegible]*	*19*
A	From 20 to 50 persons	24	662	119	1	...	88	7
A	50 to 100 persons	80	3,202	2,620	...	...	271	2
A	100 to 200 persons	43	3,232	2,422	...	...	237	6
A	200 to 400 persons	6	799	535	...	...	72	4
Cotton-spinning, weaving and other mills.	Total A ...	*10*	*10,534*	*2,850*	*9*	...	*771*	*13*
	From 200 to 400 persons	1	305	41	...	...	28	...
	400 and over ...	9	10,219	2,809	9	...	743	13
Leather and other Industries ...	...	**2**	**68**	**27**	...	...	**7**	**2**
Leather Factory ... B	50 to 100 persons ...	1	45	23	...	...	6	...
Gut Factory ... B	20 to 50 persons ...	1	23	4	...	...	1	2
Wood, etc., Industries	...	**3**	**161**	**31**	**3**	**1**	**11**	**1**
Carpentry Works ... A	50 to 100 persons ...	1	66	...	2	...	6	...

Part I.—Provincial Summary.

Of persons employed.								Nature of mechanical power.	State of business. (1) Much brisker than usual. (2) Brisker than usual. (3) Somewhat brisker than usual. (4) Normal. (5) Somewhat slacker than usual. (6) Slacker than usual. (7) Much slacker than usual.
Skilled workmen.				Unskilled labourers.					
Europeans and Anglo-Indians.		Indians.		Age 14 and over.		Under 14.			
Males.	Females.	Males.	Females.	Males.	Females.	Males.	Females.		
10	11	12	13	14	15	16	17	18	19
137	...	11.846	1,825	21,110	15,086	2,350	1,580	Steam ... 208 Oil ... 4 Water ... 2 214	(1) ... 1, (2) ... 13, (3) ... 13, (4) ... 89, (5) ... 28, (6) ... 90, (7) ... 73. Total ... 307.
9	...	1,370	8	6,774	5,488	487	381	...	...
3	...	*1,211*	...	*930*	*694*	*46*	*21*	...	...
3	...	*1,207*	...	*900*	*679*	*45*	*21*	...	...
...	...	147	...	5	79	4	...	Steam ... 1	(5) ... 1.
3	...	1,060	...	895	600	44	21	Steam ... 3	(2) ... 1, (3) ... 1, (6) ... 1.
...	...	4	...	30	15	...	...	...	(4) ... 1.
6	...	*159*	*6*	*5,844*	*4,795*	*439*	*360*	...	...
2	...	62	...	1,877	1,209	61	69	Steam ... 5	(4) ... 4, (6) ... 1.
4	...	*97*	*6*	*3,967*	*3,495*	*372*	*291*	...	...
...	...	17	6	69	99	3	1	...	(4) ... 3, (5) ... 1, (7) ... 2.
1	...	10	...	213	146	65	32	...	(4) ... 2, (5) ... 2, (6) ... 2, (7) ... 1.
2	...	3	...	698	624	73	53	...	(1)...1, (2) ... 1, (4)...6, (5) ... 1, (6) ... 1.
1	...	16	...	946	963	88	71	...	(2) ... 1, (4) ... 5, (5) ... 1, (7) ... 1.
...	...	51	2	2,041	1,663	149	134	...	(2) ... 1, (3) ... 1, (4) ... 2
...	...	77	...	369	220	47	57	...	...
...	...	*85*	...	*273*	*161*	*30*	*43*	...	...
...	...	14	...	113	65	18	20	...	(6) ... 2, (7) ... 1.
...	...	10	...	160	96	12	23	...	(4) ... 2.
...	...	53	...	96	59	17	14	...	(6) ... 1, (7) ... 1.
1	...	7,461	1,749	8,728	6,266	780	499	...	...
...	...	*1,356*	...	*5,610*	*5,324*	*231*	*353*	...	...
...	...	169	...	383	92	21	20	Steam ... 24	(4) ... 6, (5) ... 2, (6) ... 8, (7) ... 8.
...	...	540	... *1*	2,262	2,490	129	128	Steam ... 79 Water ... 1	(2) ... 2, (4) ... 7, (5)...4, (6)...38, (7)...29.
...	...	557	...	2,357	2,315	81	101	Steam ... 42 Oil ... 1	(4) ... 11, (5) ... 3, (6) ... 11, (7) ... 18.
...	...	119	...	608	427	...	104	Steam ... 6	(4) ... 2, (5) ... 2, (6) ... 2.
1	...	*6,076*	*1,749*	*3,118*	*942*	*549*	*146*	...	...
...	...	138	32	90	9	49	...	Steam ... 1 ...	(6) ... 1.
1	...	5,938	1,717	3,028	933	500	146	Steam ... 9 ...	(4) ...1, (5) ... 1, (6) ... 5, (7) ... 2.
...	...	...	...	60	23	1	2	...	...
...	...	...	...	39	22	...	1	...	(5) ... 1.
...	...	...	...	21	1	1	1	...	(6) ... 1.
...	...	63	1	58	17	26	11	...	...
...	...	21	...	37	...	...	...	Steam ... 1 ...	(7) ... 1.

TABLE XV-E.—Statistics of Industries.

Description of Factory, Mine, etc. A.—Mills in which mechanical power is used. B.—Mills in which mechanical power is not used.		Classification of factory, etc., according to number of persons employed (including management).	Number of factories.	Total Number of persons employed.		CLASSIFICATION				
						Direction, supervision and clerical work.				
						Europeans and Anglo-Indians.		Indians.		
				Males.	Females.	Males.	Females.	Males.	Females.	
1		2	3	4	5	6	7	8	9	
	B	*Total B* ...	*2*	*95*	*31*	*1*	*1*	*5*		*1*
		20 to 50 persons ...	1	42	...	...	...	4	...	
		50 to 100 persons ...	1	53	31	1	1	1		1
Metal Industries ...		... ...	3	1,754	28	39	...	101	...	
Gun-Carriage Factory (Govt.)	A	400 and over ...	1	1,525	...	38	...	88	...	
Olphert's Metallic Paint Works	A	20 to 50 persons ...	1	22	20	1	...	3	...	
Machinery and Engineering Workshop (Government).	A	200 to 400 persons ...	1	207	8	...	...	10	...	
Glass and Earthenware Industries		... ...	8	1,089	529	5	...	61	...	
Glass Factory ...	A	100 to 200 persons ...	1	134	54	...	...	11	...	
Pottery Works ...	A	*Total A* ...	*2*	*591*	*139*	*3*	...	33	...	
		200 to 400 persons ...	1	214	63	1	...	13	...	
		400 and over ...	1	377	66	2	...	20	...	
Brick and Tile Factory ...		... ...	*5*	*364*	*346*	*2*	...	*17*	...	
	A	400 and over ...	1	194	251	2	...	5	...	
	B	*Total B* ...	*4*	*170*	*95*	...	...	*12*	...	
		20 to 50 persons ...	1	27	6	...	...	4	...	
		50 to 100 persons ...	2	75	43	...	...	6	...	
		100 to 200 persons ...	1	68	46	...	...	2	...	
Industries connected with chemical products.		... ...	11	424	368	...	...	34		6
Match Factory ...	A	200 to 400 persons ...	1	133	73	...	...	10	...	
Oil Mills ...	A	20 to 50 persons ...	3	86	2	...	...	16	...	
Lac Factory ...	B	*Total B* ...	5	*166*	*148*	...	...	*5*	...	
		20 to 50 persons ...	1	12	12	...	...	1	...	
		50 to 100 persons ...	4	154	136	...	...	4	...	
Harra Factory ...	B	*Total B* ...	*2*	*39*	*145*	...	...	*3*		*6*
		20 to 50 persons ...	1	2	31	...	...	...	...	
		100 to 200 persons ...	1	37	114	...	...	3		6
Food Industries ...	...	... ...	27	3,295	1,950	13	...	382	...	
Flour and Oil Mill ...	A	20 to 50 persons ...	1	11	20	...	...	1	...	
Jerked Meat Works ...	B	*Total B* ...	*8*	*1,424*	*1,105*	*2*	...	*45*	...	
		20 to 50 persons ...	4	75	57	...	...	6	...	
		50 to 100 persons ...	1	44	42	...	...	2	...	
		100 to 200 persons ...	1	79	53	...	...	10	...	
		200 to 400 persons ...	1	233	117	...	...	25	...	
		400 and over ...	1	993	830	2	...	2	...	
Dairy Farm (Government)	A	20 to 50 persons ...	1	40	5	5	...	4	...	
Grass Farm (Government)	B	20 to 50 persons ...	1	42	...	...	...	2	...	
Brewery	A	20 to 50 persons ...	1	41	...	...	...	3	...	
Distilleries ...	A	*Total A* ...	*5*	*288*	*25*	*5*	...	*30*	...	
		20 to 50 persons ...	3	95	...	2	...	11	...	
		50 to 100 persons ...	1	71	10	2	...	14	...	
		100 to 200 persons ...	1	122	15	1	...	5	...	

Part I.—Provincial Summary.

OF PERSONS EMPLOYED.								Nature of mechanical power.	State of business. (1) Much brisker than usual. (2) Brisker than usual. (3) Somewhat brisker than usual. (4) Normal. (5) Somewhat slacker than usual. (6) Slacker than usual. (7) Much slacker than usual.
Skilled workmen.				Unskilled labourers.					
Europeans and Anglo-Indians.		Indians.		Age 14 and over.		Under 14.			
Males.	Females.	Males.	Females.	Males.	Females.	Males.	Females.		
10	11	12	13	14	15	16	17	18	19
...	...	*42*	*1*	*21*	*17*	*26*	*11*	...	...
...	...	37	...	1	...	...	...	...	(2) ... 1.
...	...	5	1	20	17	26	11	...	(2) ... 1.
39	...	1,058	...	480	28	37	...	...	...
36	...	954	...	380	...	29	...	Electricity generated by Steam 1.	(4) ... 1.
...	...	4	...	14	20	...	...	Water ... 1	(7) ... 1.
3	...	100	...	86	8	8	...	Steam ... 1	(4) ... 1.
1	...	259	59	659	399	104	71	—	...
1	...	71	35	23	16	28	3	Oil Engine ... 1	(2) ... 1.
...	...	*137*	*1*	*398*	*121*	*20*	*7*	...	...
...	...	37	1	155	57	8	5	Steam ... 1	(4) ... 1.
...	...	100	...	243	64	12	2	Steam ... 1	(3) ... 1.
...	...	*51*	*23*	*238*	*262*	*56*	*61*	...	...
...	...	2	...	162	229	23	22	Steam ... 1	(4) ... 1.
...	...	*49*	*23*	*76*	*33*	*33*	*39*	...	...
...	...	7	...	14	4	2	2	...	(7) ... 1.
...	...	24	11	28	11	17	21	...	(4) ... 1, (5) ... 1.
...	...	18	12	34	18	14	16	...	(4) ... 1.
...	...	76	7	261	296	53	59	...	...
...	...	5	...	95	61	23	12	Steam ... 1	(3) ... 1.
...	...	11	...	59	2	...	...	Steam ... 3	(6) ... 1, (7) ... 2.
...	...	*60*	*7*	*97*	*137*	*4*	*4*	...	...
...	...	7	1	4	11	...	...	...	(7) ... 1.
...	...	53	6	93	126	4	4	...	(4) ... 1, (5) ... 1, (6) ... 1, (7) ... 1.
...	...	...	...	*10*	*96*	*26*	*43*	...	...
...	...	...	...	2	25	...	6	...	(6) ... 1.
...	...	...	...	8	71	26	37	...	(4) ... 1.
1	...	282	1	1,948	1,507	669	442	...	...
...	...	5	...	5	20	...	...	Steam ... 1	(4) ... 1.
...	...	*115*	*1*	*816*	*748*	*448*	*356*	...	...
...	...	...	...	42	43	27	14	...	(6) ... 3, (7) ... 1.
...	...	...	...	20	21	22	21	...	(4) ... 1.
...	...	...	...	56	53	13	...	...	(7) ... 1.
...	...	25	1	171	114	12	2	...	(5) ... 1.
...	...	88	...	527	517	374	319	...	(4) ... 1.
...	...	...	...	31	5	...	...	Steam ... 1	(3) ... 1.
...	...	7	...	33	...	...	...	...	(2) ... 1.
1	...	5	...	32	...	...	...	Steam ... 1	(4) ... 1.
...	...	*48*	...	*205*	*25*	...	...	...	...
...	...	10	...	72	...	...	...	Steam ... 3	(3) ... 2, (7) ... 1.
...	...	18	...	37	10	...	...	Steam ... 1	(3) ... 1.
...	...	20	...	96	15	...	...	Steam ... 1	(3) ... 1.

TABLE XV-E,—Statistics of Industries.

Description of Factory, Mine, etc. A.—Mills in which mechanical power is used. B.—Mills in which mechanical power is not used.	Classification of factory, etc., according to number of persons employed (including management).	Number of factories.	Total number of persons employed.		CLASSIFICATION — Direction, supervision and clerical work.			
					Europeans and Anglo-Indians.		Indians.	
			Males.	Females.	Males.	Females.	Males.	Females.
1	2	3	4	5	6	7	8	9
Water-Works (Government) A	Total A ...	*2*	*835*	*658*	*1*	...	*7*	...
	50 to 100 persons ...	1	54	37	...	...	2	...
	400 and over ...	1	781	621	1	...	5	...
...								
Tobacco Factories ... B	Total B ...	*8*	*614*	*137*	...	...	*290*	...
	20 to 50 persons ...	3	77	13	...	...	1	...
	50 to 100 persons ...	3	151	78	...	...	5	...
	100 to 200 persons ...	1	54	46	...	...	2	...
	200 to 400 persons ...	1	332	...	...	...	282	...
Furniture Industries —	...	**4**	**253**	**4**	**1**	...	**12**	...
A	50 to 100 persons ...	1	92	...	...	...	5	...
B	Total B ...	*3*	*161*	*4*	*1*	...	*7*	...
	20 to 50 persons ...	1	23	4	1	...	...	...
	50 to 100 persons ...	2	138	...	...	...	7	...
Industries connected with building Lime Works and Kilns.	...	**17**	**970**	**817**	**8**	...	**40**	...
A	Total A ...	*8*	*632*	*508*	*3*	...	*24*	...
	20 to 50 persons ...	1	23	11	...	...	2	...
	50 to 100 persons ...	1	42	46	...	...	1	...
	100 to 200 persons ...	4	320	245	1	...	6	...
	200 to 400 persons ...	2	247	206	2	...	15	...
B	Total B ...	*9*	*338*	*309*	*5*	...	*16*	...
	20 to 50 persons ...	5	86	87	3	...	5	...
	50 to 100 persons ...	2	73	93	...	...	4	...
	100 to 200 persons ...	2	179	129	2	...	7	...
Construction of means of transport	...	**13**	**1,697**	**80**	**18**	**1**	**82**	...
Railway Workshops (Engineering)	...	11	1,504	78	11	...	73	...
A	Total A ...	*8*	*1,268*	*78*	*10*	...	*64*	...
	20 to 50 persons ...	2	85	2	1	...	9	...
	50 to 100 persons ...	2	111	12	3	...	11	...
	100 to 200 persons ...	2	284	12	2	...	11	...
	200 to 400 persons ...	1	175	26	3	...	10	...
	400 and over ...	1	613	26	1	...	23	...
B	Total B ...	*3*	*236*	...	*1*	...	*9*	...
	20 to 50 persons ...	1	41	...	...	...	3	...
	50 to 100 persons ...	1	54	...	...	...	3	...
	100 to 200 persons ...	1	141	...	1	...	3	...
Tramway Workshop A	100 to 200 persons ...	1	139	1	...	...	6	...
Telegraph Department Workshop A (Government).	50 to 100 persons ...	1	60	1	7	1	3	...
Production and transmission of physical forces. Railway Gas Factory. A	20 to 50 persons ...	1	23	...	...	...	2	...
Industries of Luxury. Printing Presses (one Government). B	Total B ...	3	495	...	11	...	54	...
	20 to 50 persons ...	1	42	...	1	...	3	...
	50 to 100 persons ...	1	77	...	...	...	5	...
	200 to 400 persons ...	1	376	...	10	...	46	...

Part I.—Provincial Summary.

OF PERSONS EMPLOYED.									
Skilled workmen.				Unskilled labourers.				Nature of mechanical power.	State of business. (1) Much brisker than usual. (2) Brisker than usual. (3) Somewhat brisker than usual. (4) Normal. (5) Somewhat slacker than usual. (6) Slacker than usual. (7) Much slacker than usual.
Europeans and Anglo-Indians.		Indians.		Age 14 and over.		Under 14.			
Males.	Females.	Males.	Females.	Males.	Females.	Males.	Females.		
10	11	12	13	14	15	16	17	18	19
...	...	*54*	...	*618*	*602*	*155*	*56*	...	...
...	...	17	...	30	31	5	6	Steam ... 1	(6) ... 1.
...	...	37	...	588	571	150	50	Steam ... 1	(6) ... 1.
...	...	*60*	...	*205*	*107*	*66*	*30*	...	...
...	...	...	...	55	11	21	2	...	(4) ... 2, (5) ... 1.
...	...	...	...	113	60	33	18	...	(4) ... 2, (5) ... 1.
...	...	...	...	40	36	12	10	...	(4) ... 1.
...	...	50	...	...	...	...	...	...	(4) ... 1.
...	...	178	...	62	4	...	...	...	...
...	...	66	...	21	...	...	...	Oil ... 1	(4) ... 1.
...	...	*112*	...	*41*	*4*	...	...	...	...
...	...	8	...	14	4	...	...	...	(4) ... 1.
...	...	104	...	27	...	...	...	...	(3) ... 1, (4) ... 1.
2	...	83	...	752	760	85	57	...	...
4	...	*52*	...	*492*	*475*	*59*	*33*	...	...
...	...	5	...	16	11	...	...	Steam ... 1	(6) ... 1.
...	...	4	...	33	41	4	5	Steam ... 1	(6) ... 1.
2	...	32	...	240	217	39	28	Steam ... 4	(5) ... 2, (6) ... 2.
...	...	11	...	203	206	16	...	Steam ... 2	(4) ... 1, (6) ... 1.
...	...	*31*	...	*260*	*285*	*26*	*24*	...	...
...	...	7	...	61	63	10	24	...	(4) ... 3, (5) ... 1, (6) ... 1.
...	...	9	...	60	93	...	...	...	(4) ... 1, (6) ... 1.
...	...	15	...	139	129	16	...	...	(4) ... 1, (5) ... 1.
81	...	577	...	873	78	66	1	...	...
51	...	520	...	798	77	56	1	...	...
43	...	*456*	...	*678*	*77*	*17*	*1*	...	...
...	...	29	...	46	2	...	...	Steam ... 2	(3) ... 2.
...	...	31	...	66	12	...	...	Steam ... 1	(3) ... 1.
								Oil Engine (electrical) ... 1	(4) ... 1.
37	...	78	...	154	11	2	1	Steam ... 2	(4) ... 2.
6	...	32	...	124	26	...	...	Steam ... 1	(2) ... 1.
...	...	286	...	288	26	15	...	Steam ... 1	(4) ... 1.
8	...	*64*	...	*115*	...	*39*	...	...	...
...	...	5	...	...	...	33	...	...	(2) ... 1.
...	...	9	...	36	...	6	...	...	(4) ... 1.
8	...	50	...	79	...	...	...	...	(4) ... 1.
...	...	55	...	62	1	10	...	Steam ... 1	(4) ... 1.
30	...	2	...	18	...	...	...	Steam ... 1	(4) ... 1.
...	...	11	...	10	...	...	...	Steam ... 1	(2) ... 1.
3	...	351	...	76	...	...	...	...	...
...	...	20	...	18	...	...	...	...	(6) ... 1.
...	...	28	...	44	...	...	...	...	(4) ... 1.
3	...	303	...	14	...	...	...	...	(4) ... 1.

TABLE XV-E.—Statistics of Industries. Part II.—Distribution by districts.

TABLE XV-E.—Statistics of Industries. Part II.—Distribution by districts.

Description of Factory, Mine, etc.	District.	Number of factories.	Total number of persons employed.		Classification of persons employed.												Remarks.
					Direction, supervision and clerical work.				Skilled workmen.				Unskilled labourers.				
					Europeans and Anglo-Indians.		Indians.		Europeans and Anglo-Indians.		Indians.		Age 14 and over.		Under 14.		
			Males.	Females.	Males.	Females.	Males.	Females.	Males.	Females.	Males.	Females.	Males.	Females.	Males.	Females.	
1	2	3	4	5	6	7	8	9	10	11	12	13	14	15	16	17	18
	Grand Total	**307**	**38,077**	**18,541**	**151**	**3**	**2,478**	**47**	**137**	...	**11,846**	**1,825**	**21,110**	**15,086**	**2,355**	**1,580**	
Mines ...	...	**45**	**8,918**	**5,884**	**41**	**1**	**237**	**6**	**9**	...	**1,370**	**8**	**6,774**	**5,488**	**487**	**381**	
Collieries ...	Chanda ...	1	725	...	3	...	26	...	...	...	382	...	314	...	...	...	
Ditto ...	Narsinghpur	1	1,077	461	9	...	67	...	...	...	668	...	301	440	32	21	
Ditto ...	Betul ...	1	35	15	...	...	1	...	...	...	4	...	30	15	...	...	
Ditto ...	Chhindwara	2	472	239	3	...	8	...	3	...	157	...	285	239	16	...	
Manganese ...	Chhindwara	1	6	26	...	...	...	...	...	...	4	...	2	26	...	...	
Ditto ...	Balaghat ...	13	2,220	1,780	10	...	52	...	2	...	80	8	1,914	1,609	171	163	
Ditto ...	Nagpur ...	12	2,299	1,528	5	1	37	6	2	...	61	...	2,058	1,412	136	109	
Ditto ...	Bhandara ...	14	2,075	1,835	11	...	46	...	2	...	14	...	1,870	1,747	132	88	
Quarries of hard rock.	...	**7**	**511**	**277**	**2**	...	**16**	...	...	...	**77**	...	**369**	**220**	**47**	**57**	
Limestone Quarries ...	Jubbulpore...	4	307	189	2	...	12	...	...	...	21	...	247	148	25	41	
Ditto ...	Hoshangabad	1	35	15	...	...	1	...	...	...	3	...	20	13	5	2	
Stone Quarry ...	Jubbulpore...	1	83	55	...	...	2	...	...	...	28	...	46	49	7	6	
Ditto ...	Hoshangabad	1	86	18	...	...	1	...	...	...	25	...	50	10	10	8	
Textile Industries.	...	**163**	**18,419**	**8,546**	**10**	...	**1,439**	**32**	**1**	...	**7,461**	**1,749**	**8,728**	**6,266**	**780**	**499**	
(a) Cotton.																	
Cotton-ginning, cleaning and pressing mills.	Wardha ...	27	1,015	939	...	...	76	...	...	...	178	...	710	917	51	22	
Ditto ...	Hoshangabad	5	222	165	...	...	20	...	...	...	65	...	131	162	6	3	
Ditto ...	Chhindwara	1	16	40	...	...	2	...	...	...	2	...	12	40	...	...	
Ditto ...	Nimar ...	18	691	432	...	...	61	8	...	...	163	...	436	379	31	45	
Ditto ...	Nagpur ...	15	783	576	1	...	81	...	...	...	124	...	499	476	78	100	
Ditto ...	Chanda ...	1	95	69	...	...	6	...	...	...	10	...	79	69	...	...	
Ditto ...	Amraoti ...	19	1,041	704	...	...	103	4	...	...	194	...	689	621	55	79	
Ditto ...	Akola ...	34	1,832	1,240	...	...	158	...	...	...	311	...	1,353	1,240	10	...	
Ditto ...	Yeotmal ...	11	530	469	...	...	46	...	...	...	78	...	406	409	...	...	
Ditto ...	Buldana ...	22	1,670	1,062	...	...	115	7	...	...	260	...	1,295	951	...	104	
Cotton-spinning, and weaving mills.	Jubbulpore ...	1	572	114	1	...	60	...	...	...	250	88	151	6	110	20	
Ditto ...	Nimar ...	1	691	139	1	...	42	3	...	...	33	...	574	134	41	2	
Ditto ...	Wardha ...	3	2,267	646	1	...	103	...	1	...	687	222	1,176	347	239	77	
Ditto (and dyeing and bleaching).	Nagpur ...	1	3,918	965	2	...	336	10	...	...	2,899	717	681	238	...	...	
Ditto (and dyeing)	Amraoti ...	1	699	140	...	...	67	...	...	...	476	109	96	11	60	20	
Ditto ...	Akola ...	2	1,083	276	...	...	54	...	...	...	767	152	179	124	83	...	
Ditto ...	Nandgaon State.	1	1,294	570	4	...	49	...	...	...	964	461	261	82	16	27	
Leather and other Industries.	...	**2**	**68**	**27**	...	...	**7**	**2**	...	...	...	...	**60**	**23**	**1**	**2**	
Leather Factory ...	Raipur ...	1	46	23	...	...	6	...	...	...	...	...	30	22	...	1	
Gut Factory ...	Damoh ...	1	23	4	...	...	1	2	...	...	...	...	21	1	1	1	
Wood, etc., Industries	...	**3**	**161**	**31**	**3**	**1**	**11**	**1**	...	...	**63**	**1**	**58**	**17**	**26**	**11**	
Carpentry works (and weaving).	Jubbulpore...	1	53	31	1	1	1	1	...	...	5	1	20	17	26	11	
Ditto (and joining)	Hoshangabad	1	66	...	2	...	6	...	...	...	21	...	37	...	...	...	
Ditto ...	Akola ...	1	42	...	...	...	4	...	...	...	37	...	1	...	...	...	
Metal Industries ...	...	**3**	**1,754**	**28**	**39**	...	**101**	...	**39**	...	**1,058**	...	**480**	**28**	**37**	...	
Gun-Carriage Factory	Jubbulpore...	1	1,525	...	38	...	88	...	36	...	954	...	380	...	29	...	
Olphert's Metallic Paint Works.	Ditto ...	1	22	20	1	...	3	...	...	...	4	...	14	20	...	...	
Machinery and Engineering Workshops (P.W.D.)	Nagpur ...	1	207	8	...	...	10	...	3	...	100	...	86	8	8	...	
Glass and Earthenware Industries.	...	**8**	**1,089**	**529**	**5**	...	**61**	...	**1**	...	**259**	**59**	**659**	**399**	**104**	**71**	
Glass Factory ...	Jubbulpore...	1	134	54	...	...	11	...	1	...	71	35	23	16	28	3	
Pottery Works ...	Ditto ...	2	501	129	3	...	33	...	...	...	137	1	398	121	20	7	
Brick and Tile Factory	Ditto ...	3	295	327	2	...	10	...	...	...	34	23	196	247	53	57	
Ditto ...	Hoshangabad	1	42	13	...	...	3	...	...	...	10	...	28	11	1	2	
Ditto ...	Bhandara ...	1	27	6	...	...	4	...	...	...	7	...	14	4	2	2	
Industries connected with Chemical products.	...	**11**	**424**	**368**	...	...	**34**	**6**	...	...	**76**	**7**	**261**	**298**	**53**	**59**	
Match Factory ...	Bilaspur ...	1	133	73	...	...	10	...	...	...	5	...	95	61	23	12	
Oil Mills ...	Wardha ...	1	22	...	...	...	4	...	...	...	4	...	14	...	...	...	
Ditto ...	Amraoti ...	2	64	2	...	...	12	...	...	...	7	...	45	2	...	...	

TABLE XV-E.—Statistics of Industries. Part II.—Distribution by districts.

Description of Factory, Mine, etc.	District.	Number of factories.	Total number of persons employed. Males.	Total number of persons employed. Females.	Direction, supervision and clerical work. Europeans and Anglo-Indians. Males.	Europeans and Anglo-Indians. Females.	Indians. Males.	Indians. Females.	Skilled workmen. Europeans and Anglo-Indians. Males.	Europeans and Anglo-Indians. Females.	Indians. Males.	Indians. Females.	Unskilled labourers. Age 14 and over. Males.	Age 14 and over. Females.	Under 14. Males.	Under 14. Females.	Remarks.
1	2	3	4	5	6	7	8	9	10	11	12	13	14	15	16	17	18
Lac Factories ...	Bhandara ...	4	154	136	...	...	4	...	...	...	53	6	93	126	4	4	
Ditto ...	Bilaspur ...	1	12	12	...	...	1	...	...	...	7	1	4	11	...	...	
Harra Factory ...	Bhandara ...	1	2	31	...	...	...	...	...	...	...	...	2	25	...	6	
Ditto ...	Raipur ...	1	37	114	...	...	3	6	...	...	...	...	8	71	26	37	
Food Industries ...	...	27	3,295	1,950	13	...	382	...	1	...	282	1	1,948	1,507	669	442	
Flour and Oil Mill ...	Jubbulpore...	1	11	20	...	...	1	...	...	...	5	...	5	20	...	...	
Jerked Meat Works (and the disposal of the hide, guts, bones and fat of slaughtered cattle).	Saugor ...	3	1,305	1,006	2	...	37	...	...	...	113	1	754	684	399	321	
Ditto ...	Damoh ...	5	119	99	...	...	8	...	...	...	...	...	62	64	49	35	
Dairy Farms (Military)	Jubbulpore...	1	40	5	5	...	4	...	...	...	...	...	31	5	...	...	
Grass Farm (Military)	Ditto ...	1	42	...	...	...	2	...	...	...	7	...	33	...	...	...	
Brewery, Flour Mills, Malting and Ice Factory.	Ditto ...	1	41	...	...	...	3	...	1	...	5	...	32	...	...	...	
Distilleries ...	Ditto ...	2	154	15	3	...	10	...	...	...	23	...	118	15	...	...	
Ditto ...	Seoni ...	1	20	...	...	...	3	...	...	...	2	...	15	...	...	...	
Ditto ...	Nagpur ...	1	71	10	2	...	14	...	...	...	18	...	37	10	...	...	
Ditto ...	Akola ...	1	43	...	...	...	3	...	...	...	5	...	35	...	...	...	
Water-Works. (Reservoir tank construction.)	Nagpur ...	2	835	658	1	...	7	...	...	...	54	...	618	602	155	56	
Tobacco (Biri) Factory	Jubbulpore ...	1	332	...	...	...	282	...	...	...	50	...	...	...	...	...	
Ditto ...	Nagpur ...	1	40	...	...	...	...	...	...	...	...	...	25	...	15	...	
Ditto ...	Bhandara ...	6	242	137	...	...	8	...	...	...	...	...	183	107	51	30	
Furniture Industries	...	4	253	4	1	...	12	...	...	...	178	...	62	4	...	...	
Furniture and Painting Workshop.	Jubbulpore ...	1	23	4	1	...	...	...	...	...	8	...	14	4	...	...	
Coach and Furniture Workshop.	Nagpur ...	1	79	...	...	...	3	...	...	...	70	...	6	...	...	...	
Ditto ...	Raipur ...	2	151	...	...	...	9	...	...	...	100	...	42	...	...	...	
Industries connected with building.	...	17	970	817	8	...	40	...	2	...	83	...	752	760	85	57	
Lime Works and Kilns	Jubbulpore ...	16	943	796	8	...	40	...	2	...	83	...	725	743	85	53	
Ditto ...	Hoshangabad	1	27	21	...	...	...	...	...	...	...	...	27	17	...	4	
Construction of means of transport.	...	13	1,697	80	18	1	82	...	81	...	577	...	873	78	66	1	
Railway Workshop (Engineering).	Saugor ...	1	54	...	...	...	3	...	...	...	9	...	36	...	6	...	
Railway Workshop (Locomotive).	Jubbulpore...	2	281	3	2	...	9	...	37	...	77	...	156	3	...	...	
Ditto ...	Mandla ...	1	41	...	1	...	8	...	...	...	21	...	11	...	...	...	
Ditto ...	Hoshangabad	2	234	37	6	...	18	...	6	...	44	...	160	37	...	...	
Ditto ...	Nagpur ...	2	757	35	2	...	28	...	8	...	337	...	365	34	17	1	
Ditto ...	Bhandara ...	2	85	2	...	...	4	...	...	...	13	...	35	2	33	...	
Ditto ...	Raipur ...	1	52	1	...	...	3	...	...	...	19	...	30	1	...	...	
Tramway Workshop	Bhandara ...	1	133	1	...	...	6	...	...	...	55	...	62	1	10	...	
Telegraph Department Workshop.	Nagpur ...	1	60	1	7	1	3	...	30	...	2	...	18	...	...	...	
Production and transmission of physical forces. Railway Gas Factory.	Bhandara ...	1	23	...	...	...	2	...	...	...	11	...	10	...	...	...	
Industries of Luxury	...	3	495	...	11	...	54	...	3	...	351	...	76	...	...	...	
Printing Presses ...	Jubbulpore...	1	77	...	...	...	5	...	...	...	28	...	44	...	...	...	
Ditto ...	Nagpur ...	2	418	...	11	...	49	...	3	...	323	...	32	...	...	...	

TABLE XV-E.—Statistics of Industries. Part III.—Particulars as to ownership of Factories, etc.

TABLE XV-E.—Statistics of Industries. Part III.—Particulars as to ownership of Factories, etc.

Description of Factory, etc.	Number of factories, etc.	Number owned by Companies of which the Directors are: Europeans or Anglo-Indians.	Number owned by Companies of which the Directors are: Indians.	Number owned by Companies of which the Directors are: Of both races.	Number privately owned by: Europeans and Anglo-Indians.	Number privately owned by Indians: Total.	Arora.	Bahna.	Bania.	Barai.	Barhai.	Brahman.	Kalar.	Kayasth.	Khatri.	Kirar.	Kurmi.	Madrasi (Telugu).	Maratha.	Musalman.	Prabhu.	Parsi.
1	2	3	4	5	6	7	8	9	10	11	12	13	14	15	16	17	18	19	20	21	22	23
Grand Total ...	307	55	78	4	14	156	1	1	92	1	2	14	2	1	1	1	4	2	1	17	1	15
Mines	45	19	3	...	2	21	...	...	9	...	...	5	...	...	...	...	...	1	...	...	...	6
Collieries (one Govt.) ...	5	4	...	...	1	...	...	...	...	...	...	...	...	...	...	...	...	...	...	...	...	...
Manganese ...	40	15	3	...	1	21	...	...	9	...	...	5	...	...	...	...	...	1	...	...	...	6
Quarries of hard rock ...	7	...	1	...	1	5	1	-	—	1	...	1	...	...	...	...	...	1	...	1	...	...
Limestone Quarries ...	5	...	1	...	1	3	...	...	...	1	...	1	...	...	...	...	...	1	...	...	...	...
Stone Quarries	2	...	...	...	...	2	1	...	...	...	...	...	...	...	...	...	...	...	...	1	...	...
Textile Industries ...	163	7	62	1	...	93	...	1	73	...	...	4	...	...	...	...	1	...	...	7	1	6
Cotton-ginning, cleaning and pressing mills.	153	5	56	1	...	91	...	1	71	...	...	4	...	...	...	...	1	...	...	7	1	6
Cotton-spinning, weaving and other mills.	10	2	6	...	...	2	...	...	2	...	...	...	...	...	...	...	...	...	...	...	...	...
Leather and other Industries	2	...	...	...	1	1	...	...	...	...	...	...	...	...	...	...	...	...	...	1	...	...
Leather Factory ...	1	...	...	...	...	1	...	...	...	...	...	...	...	...	...	...	...	...	...	1	...	...
Gut Factory ...	1	...	...	...	1	...	...	...	...	...	...	...	...	...	...	...	...	...	...	...	...	...
Wood, etc., Industries. Carpentry Works.	3	...	...	...	3	...	...	...	...	...	...	...	...	...	...	...	...	...	...	...	...	...
Metal Industries ...	3	2	...	...	1	...	...	...	...	...	...	...	...	...	...	...	...	.	...	...	...	...
Gun-Carriage Factory (Govt.)...	1	1	...	...	...	...	...	...	...	...	...	...	...	...	...	...	...	...	...	...	...	...
Olphert's Metallic Paint Works	1	...	...	...	1	...	...	...	...	...	...	...	...	...	...	...	...	...	...	...	...	...
Machinery and Engineering Workshop (Govt.)	1	1	...	...	...	...	...	...	...	...	...	...	...	...	...	...	...	...	...	...	...	...
Glass and Earthenware Industries.	8	2	...	1	1	4	...	...	2	...	1	...	...	...	...	...	1	...	...	...	...	...
Glass Factory ...	1	...	...	...	...	1	...	...	1	...	...	...	...	...	...	...	...	...	...	...	...	...
Pottery Works ...	2	1	...	1	...	...	...	...	...	...	...	...	...	...	...	...	...	...	...	...	...	...
Brick and Tile Factory ...	5	1	...	...	1	3	...	...	1	...	1	...	...	...	...	...	1	...	...	...	...	...
Industries connected with chemical products.	11	1	2	—	...	8	...	...	5	...	...	...	...	...	...	...	2	...	...	1	..	...
Match Factory	1	...	...	...	...	1	...	...	...	...	...	...	...	...	...	...	1	...	...	...	...	...
Oil Mills	3	1	2	...	...	...	...	...	...	...	...	...	...	...	...	...	...	...	...	...	...	...
Lac Factory	5	...	...	...	...	5	...	...	4	...	...	...	...	...	...	...	...	...	...	1	...	...
Harra Factory	2	...	...	...	...	2	...	...	1	...	...	...	...	...	...	...	1	...	...	...	...	...
Food Industries	27	7	6	2	...	12	...	...	1	—	...	...	2	...	...	1	...	...	1	7	...	...
Flour and Oil Mills ...	1	...	1	...	...	...	...	...	...	...	...	...	...	...	...	...	...	...	...	...	...	...
Jerked Meat Works ...	8	...	3	2	...	3	...	...	...	...	...	...	...	...	...	...	...	...	...	3	...	...
Dairy Farm (Govt.) ...	1	1	...	...	...	...	...	...	...	...	...	...	...	...	...	...	...	...	...	...	...	...
Grass Farm (do.) ...	1	1	...	...	...	...	...	...	...	...	...	...	...	...	...	...	...	...	...	...	...	...
Brewery	1	1	...	...	...	...	...	...	...	...	...	...	...	...	...	...	...	...	...	...	...	...
Distilleries	5	2	2	...	...	1	...	...	...	...	...	...	1	...	...	...	...	...	...	...	...	...
Water-Works (Govt.) ...	2	2	...	...	...	...	...	...	...	...	...	...	...	...	...	...	...	...	...	...	...	...
Tobacco Factory	8	...	...	...	...	8	...	...	1	...	...	...	1	...	...	1	...	...	1	4	...	...
Furniture Industries Furniture Works. ...	4	1	1	...	...	2	...	...	...	...	...	...	...	...	...	...	...	...	...	...	...	2
Industries connected with building. Lime Works and Kilns.	17	1	2	...	4	10	...	...	2	...	1	4	...	1	1	...	...	...	...	...	...	1
Construction of means of transport.	13	13	...	...	...	...	...	...	...	...	...	...	...	...	...	...	...	...	—	...	...	...
Railway Workshops ...	11	11	...	...	...	...	...	...	...	...	...	...	...	...	...	...	...	...	...	...	...	...
Tramway Workshop ...	1	1	...	...	...	...	...	...	...	...	...	...	...	...	...	...	...	...	...	...	...	...
Telegraph Department Workshop. (Govt.)	1	1	...	...	...	...	...	...	...	...	...	...	...	...	...	...	...	...	...	...	...	...
Production and transmission of physical forces. Railway Gas Factory.	1	1	...	...	...	...	...	...	...	...	...	...	...	...	...	...	...	...	...	...	...	...
Industries of Luxury Printing Presses. ...	3	1	1	...	1	...	...	...	...	...	...	...	...	...	...	...	...	...	...	...	...	...

Factories and mines belonging to Government are included in col. 3.

TABLE XV-E.—Statistics of Industries. Part IV.— Caste or race of Managers of Factories, &c.

TABLE XV-E.—Statistics of Industries. Part IV.—Caste or race of Managers of Factories, &c.

Description of Factory, etc.	Number of factories.	Number managed by: Europeans and Anglo-Indians.	Indians: Total.	Bania.	Barhai.	Bohra.	Brahman.	Cutchi.	Darji.	Gond.	Gosain.	Kalar.	Kamma.	Kayasth.	Khatri.	Khoja.	Kirar.	Kurmi.	Lodhi.	Maratha.	Musalman.	Parsi.	Sikh.	Telanga.	Teli.	Vidur.
1	2	3	4	5	6	7	8	9	10	11	12	13	14	15	16	17	18	19	20	21	22	23	24	25	26	27
Grand Total ...	307	74	233	67	1	4	73	1	1	1	1	2	1	4	4	3	1	6	1	5	19	29	2	4	1	2
Mines	45	25	20	2	...	2	5	...	...	...	...	1	...	...	...	...	—	—	1	...	3	4	...	2	...	...
Collieries (one Govt.) ...	5	5	...	...	...	...	...	...	...	...	...	...	...	...	...	...	...	...	...	...	...	...	...	...	...	...
Manganese	40	20	20	2	...	2	5	...	...	...	...	1	...	...	...	...	...	...	1	...	3	4	...	2	...	...
Quarries of hard rock ...	7	2	5	...	...	...	2	...	...	...	...	...	1	1	...	...	...	...	...	...	1	...	...	...	...	...
Limestone Quarries ...	5	2	3	...	...	...	1	...	...	...	...	...	1	1	...	...	...	...	...	...	...	...	...	...	...	...
Stone Quarries	2	...	2	...	...	...	1	...	...	...	...	...	...	...	...	...	...	...	...	...	1	...	...	...	...	...
Textile Industries ...	163	11	152	57	...	2	54	...	1	...	1	...	...	...	1	2	...	5	...	4	3	18	...	1	1	2
Cotton-ginning, cleaning and pressing mills.	153	7	146	57	...	2	51	...	1	...	1	...	...	...	1	2	...	5	...	4	3	15	...	1	1	2
Cotton-spinning, weaving and other mills.	10	4	6	...	...	...	3	...	...	...	...	...	...	...	...	...	...	...	...	...	...	3	...	...	...	...
Leather and other Industries.	2	1	1	...	...	...	...	...	...	...	...	...	...	...	...	1	...	...	...	...	...	...	...	...	...	...
Leather Factory	1	...	1	...	...	...	...	...	...	...	...	...	...	...	...	1	...	...	...	...	...	...	...	...	...	...
Gut Factory	1	1	...	...	...	...	...	...	...	...	...	...	...	...	...	...	...	...	...	...	...	...	...	...	...	...
Wood, etc., Industries ... Carpentry Works.	3	3	...	...	...	...	...	...	...	...	...	...	...	...	...	...	...	...	...	...	...	...	...	...	...	...
Metal Industries ...	3	2	1	...	...	...	...	...	...	...	...	...	...	1	...	...	...	...	...	...	...	—	...	...	...	...
Gun-Carriage Factory (Govt.) ...	1	1	...	...	...	...	...	...	...	...	...	...	...	...	...	...	...	...	...	...	...	...	...	...	...	...
Olphert's metalic paint works	1	1	...	...	...	...	...	...	...	...	...	...	...	...	...	...	...	...	...	...	...	...	...	...	...	...
Machinery and Engineering Workshop (Govt.)	1	...	1	...	...	...	...	...	...	...	...	...	...	1	...	...	...	...	...	...	...	...	...	...	...	...
Glass and Earthenware Industries.	8	4	4	1	1	...	...	...	...	...	...	...	...	...	...	.	...	1	..	...	...	1	...	...	...	...
Glass Factory	1	...	1	...	...	...	...	...	...	...	...	...	...	...	...	...	...	...	...	...	...	1	...	...	...	...
Pottery Works	2	2	...	...	...	...	...	...	...	...	...	...	...	...	...	...	...	...	...	...	...	...	...	...	...	...
Brick and Tile Factory ...	5	2	3	1	1	...	...	...	...	...	...	...	...	...	...	...	...	1	...	...	...	...	...	...	...	...
Industries connected with chemical products.	11	1	10	4	...	...	5	...	...	...	...	...	...	...	...	...	...	...	...	...	1	...	...	...	...	...
Match Factory	1	...	1	...	...	...	1	...	...	...	...	...	...	...	...	...	...	...	...	...	...	...	...	...	...	...
Oil Mills	3	1	2	...	...	...	2	...	...	...	...	...	...	...	...	...	...	...	...	...	...	...	...	...	...	...
Lac Factory	5	...	5	3	...	...	1	...	...	...	...	...	...	...	...	...	...	...	...	...	1	...	...	...	...	...
Harra Factory	2	...	2	1	...	...	1	...	...	...	...	...	...	...	...	...	...	...	...	...	...	...	...	...	...	...
Food Industries	27	7	20	1	...	...	1	1	...	...	...	1	...	...	2	...	1	...	...	1	10	2	...	...	...	...
Flour and Oil Mills ...	1	...	1	...	...	...	1	...	...	...	...	...	...	...	...	...	...	...	...	...	...	...	...	...	...	...
Jerked Meat Works ...	8	1	7	...	...	...	...	...	...	...	...	...	...	...	...	...	...	...	...	...	7	...	...	...	...	...
Dairy Farm (Govt.) ...	1	1	...	...	...	...	...	...	...	...	...	...	...	...	...	...	...	...	...	...	...	...	...	...	...	...
Grass Farm (do.) ...	1	1	...	...	...	...	...	...	...	...	...	...	...	...	...	...	...	...	...	...	...	...	...	...	...	...
Brewery	1	1	...	...	...	...	...	...	...	...	...	...	...	...	...	...	...	...	...	...	...	...	...	...	...	...
Distilleries	5	3	2	...	...	...	...	...	...	...	...	...	...	...	...	...	...	...	...	...	...	2	...	...	...	...
Water-Works (Govt.) ...	2	...	2	...	...	...	...	...	...	...	...	...	...	...	2	...	...	...	...	...	...	...	...	...	...	...
Tobacco Factory	8	...	8	1	...	...	...	1	...	...	...	1	...	...	...	...	1	...	...	1	3	...	...	...	...	...
Furniture Industries. Furniture Works.	4	1	3	...	...	...	...	...	...	...	...	...	...	...	...	...	...	...	...	...	...	3	...	...	...	...
Industries connected with building. Lime Works and Kilns.	17	5	12	2	...	...	6	...	...	1	...	...	...	2	...	...	...	...	...	...	...	1	...	...	...	...
Construction of means of transport.	13	10	3	...	...	...	—	...	...	...	...	...	...	...	1	...	...	...	—	...	...	...	1	1	...	..
Railway Workshops ...	11	8	3	...	...	...	...	...	...	...	...	...	...	...	1	...	...	...	...	...	...	...	1	1	...	...
Tramway Workshop ...	1	1	...	...	...	...	...	...	...	...	...	...	...	...	...	...	...	...	...	...	...	...	...	...	...	...
Telegraph Department Workshop (Govt.)	1	1	...	...	...	...	...	...	...	...	...	...	...	...	...	...	...	...	...	...	...	...	...	...	...	...
Production and transmission of physical forces. Railway Gas Factory.	1	...	1	...	...	...	...	...	...	...	...	...	...	—	...	...	...	...	...	...	...	...	1	...	...	...
Industries of Luxury ... Printing Presses.	3	2	1	...	...	...	...	...	...	...	...	..	...	...	...	...	...	...	...	...	1	...	...	...	...	...

TABLE XVI.—Occupation by Selected Castes, Tribes or Races.

This table shows the occupations of 101 principal castes. At the end an appendix gives the principal occupations of minor industrial castes.

It may be explained that the total strength of a caste in this Table does not necessarily tally with that in Table XIII, as the latter includes figures added in the course of classification.

TABLE XVI.—Occupation by

Caste, tribe or race.	Traditional occupation.	Population dealt with. — Actual workers. — Males.	Population dealt with. — Actual workers. — Females.	Population dealt with. — Dependants. — Males.	Population dealt with. — Dependants. — Females.	Number of actual workers whose traditional caste occupation was returned as their — Principal means of livelihood. — Males.	Principal means of livelihood. — Females.	Subsidiary means of livelihood. — Males.	Subsidiary means of livelihood. — Females.	Number of actual workers returning their traditional occupation as their principal means of livelihood who had some subsidiary occupation. — Males.	Females.
1	2	3	4	5	6	7	8	9	10	11	12
Ahir											
Province ...	Graziers ...	237,780	197,413	123,820	168,720	86,311	40,925	9,543	4,251	6,476	2,907
Andh											
Berar ...	Agriculturists ...	17,464	17,437	8,007	9,378	12,278	9,372	52	27	352	163
Bahna ...	Cotton Carders ...	11.287	8,169	6.484	9.723	2.495	1.006	664	92	1.134	215
Nerbudda Valley ...	...	7,627	5,549	4,069	6,153	1,888	608	579	72	972	165
Seoni ...	...	871	711	540	682	149	41	14	...	12	...
Nagpur ...	...	1,414	928	986	1,582	261	251	30	18	84	34
Chhindwara ...	...	1,375	981	883	1,300	197	106	32	2	66	16
Baiga ...	Agriculturists ...	7.822	7,863	5,053	5,239	4.551	4.074	16	4	366	239
Jubbulpore ...	...	645	654	454	470	340	343	1	1	50	35
Mandla ...	...	5,649	5,615	3,662	3,758	3,691	3.176	13	3	249	162
Balaghat ...	...	1,528	1,594	937	1,011	520	555	2	...	67	42
Bairagi											
Province ...	Devotees ...	13,648	7,868	6,001	10,967	6,498	2,672	1,360	239	539	116
Balahi ...	Cotton-weavers ...	16.761	15.719	8.347	10.032	1,549	460	156	31	421	151
Hoshangabad ...	...	6,767	6,147	3,160	4,068	800	228	72	...	217	56
Nimar ...	...	9,352	8,942	4,801	5,629	662	221	70	31	182	95
Makrai ...	...	642	630	206	335	87	11	14	...	22	...
Bania											
Province ...	Traders ...	63,967	18,442	36,716	75,695	38,585	8,964	4,405	401	6,718	408
Banjara ...	Pack bullock-carriers.	44,720	36,541	22,623	25.752	2.578	1.021	154	106	164	64
Plateau Division ...	...	3,371	2,605	1,473	1,080	655	214	24	8	23	8
Maratha Division ...	...	20,852	24,815	15,850	17,430	762	159	10	8	86	24
Chhattisgarh Division	...	3,602	3,604	1,798	2,483	385	169	70	74	21	16
Nimar ...	...	5,836	4,284	2,708	2,748	5	...	...	...	2	...
Bastar ...	...	2,059	1,233	788	1,101	770	479	44	16	32	16
Barai											
Province ...	Betel-leaf growers	19,404	14,479	10,230	15,030	7,006	7,102	1.338	658	969	467
Barhai											
Province ...	Carpenters ...	37,378	19,870	18,911	32,648	28,153	1,017	2,911	72	4,4[illegible]	107
Basor											
Nerbudda Valley ...	Bamboo Workers ...	9,725	9,158	5,817	6,031	7,669	6,800	494	389	2,876	1,610
Beldar ...	Earth Workers ...	2,163	1,666	1,004	1,432	1,085	528	51	10	99	64
Saugor ...	...	332	222	189	225	142	52	4	1	5	1
Jubbulpore ...	...	429	318	157	245	103	71	8	...	3	...
Nimar ...	...	404	314	171	210	310	221	2	1	27	31
Wardha ...	...	667	623	314	474	317	115	24	8	44	28
Nagpur ...	...	331	189	165	261	213	69	13	...	20	4
Bhaina											
Bilaspur ...	Agriculturists ...	4,019	3,777	2,479	2,919	2,726	2,364	34	13	151	86
Bharia (Bhumia) ...	Agriculturists ...	11,347	11,143	6,517	8.256	3.552	3.116	130	53	669	460
Jubbulpore ...	...	8,124	7,833	4,758	6,267	1,291	966	107	52	451	325
Narsinghpur ...	...	787	781	443	533	285	247	21	1	148	113
Chhindwara ...	...	2,436	2,529	1,316	1,456	1,976	1,908	2	...	73	22

Selected Castes, Tribes or Races.

Recorded principal occupation of actual workers.															
I.—Exploitation of the surface of the soil.												II.—Extraction of Minerals.			
Income from rent of land.		Cultivators of all kinds		Agents and managers of landed estates, planters, forest officers and their clerks, rent collectors, etc.		Field labourers, wood-cutters, etc.		Raisers of live-stock, milk-men and herdsmen.		Fishing and hunting.		Owners, managers, clerks, etc.		Labourers.	
Males.	Females.	Males.	Females.	Males.	Females.	Males.	Females.	Males.	Females.	Males.	Females.	Males.	Females.	Males.	Females.
13	14	15	16	17	18	19	20	21	22	23	24	25	26	27	28
413	531	92,176	77,440	496	...	43,450	58,728	...	...	38	5	7	1	328	132
...	...	...	...	4	...	4,506	7,872	488	60	...	...	...	...	...	...
40	14	3,034	1,711	38	...	2,930	4.220	295	17	3	...	3	...	47	8
17	6	1,998	1,141	24	...	2,195	3,055	216	16	3	...	2	...	29	3
5	...	201	184	3	...	213	360	11	1	...	...	...	...	...	...
11	7	314	140	1	...	176	334	34	...	...	...	...	...	10	3
7	1	431	246	10	...	346	462	34	...	...	...	1	...	8	2
...	...	...	...	19	...	2,834	3,543	88	14	1	...	...	...	...	...
...	...	...	...	...	...	230	281	2	...	...	...	...	...	...	...
...	...	...	...	18	...	1,816	2,350	66	13	1	...	...	...	...	...
...	...	...	...	1	...	779	912	20	1	...	...	...	...	...	...
182	283	5,751	3,359	53	...	349	701	52	2	...	...	...	...	1	1
49	14	3,799	3,280	1	...	8,650	11,636	786	11	1	...	...	...	...	...
26	8	563	890	1	...	4,005	5,348	520	3	1	...	...	...	...	...
23	6	3,164	2,825	...	...	4,200	5,734	234	7	...	...	...	...	...	...
...	...	72	59	...	...	385	554	32	1	...	...	...	...	...	...
827	507	13,671	3,105	210	2	2,935	3,767	179	22	1	...	14	2	56	13
136	48	16,183	8,079	19	...	18,139	23,684	3,371	349	3	...	1	...	5	1
9	10	907	774	7	...	854	1,053	254	22	1	...	...	...	3	1
120	36	10,500	3,655	6	...	14,427	20,081	2,235	208	...	...	1	...	2	...
4	...	1,131	1,101	3	...	693	658	252	23	2	...	...	...	...	...
3	2	3,488	2,467	1	...	2,038	1,778	138	4	...	...	...	...	...	...
...	...	151	82	2	...	127	114	492	92	...	...	...	...	...	...
127	49	6,705	2,452	35	2	3,767	4,120	131	11	...	3	6	...	7	1
206	96	5,326	4,653	10	...	2,162	13,372	427	19	9	...	1	...	24	16
...	...	351	216	23	...	865	1,635	152	51	...	...	...	...	...	...
18	4	250	140	11	...	233	687	13	1	...	...	...	...	19	1
...	...	21	13	9	...	38	81	1	...	...	...	...	...	5	...
...	...	23	15	1	...	33	76	5	1	...	...	...	...	...	...
...	...	15	21	...	...	18	45	1	...	...	...	...	...	...	...
12	1	165	69	1	...	126	421	6	...	...	...	...	...	14	1
6	3	26	22	...	...	18	64	...	...	...	...	...	...	...	...
...	...	...	...	...	...	1,197	1,345	77	16	...	...	...	...	...	...
...	...	...	...	14	...	6,842	7,418	268	48	4	...	2	—	146	135
...	...	...	...	11	...	6,201	6,509	161	14	1	...	2	...	145	133
...	...	...	...	...	...	404	476	29	11	3	...	...	...	1	1
...	...	...	...	3	...	237	433	78	23	...	...	...	...	...	1

TABLE XVI.—Occupation by

Caste, tribe or race.	Traditional occupation.	Recorded principal occupation													
		III.—Industries.				IV.—Transport.				V.—Trade.		VI.—Public force.			
		Owners, managers, clerks, etc.		Artisans and other workmen.		Owners, managers, ships' officers, etc.		Labourers, boatmen, carters, palki-bearers, etc.				Commissioned and gazetted officers.		Others.	
		Males.	Females.	Males.	Females.	Males.	Females.	Males.	Females.	Males.	Females.	Males.	Females.	Males.	Females.
1	2	29	30	31	32	33	34	35	36	37	38	39	40	41	42
Ahir															
Province ...	Graziers ...	35	1	2,169	1,803	73	5	8,886	787	2,098	1,902	9	...	512	...
Andh															
Berar ...	Agriculturists	...	...	51	23	...	...	2	...	31	27	...	...	5	...
Bahna ...	Cotton Carders	...	...	332	428	8	...	343	61	1,294	516	...	...	23	...
Nerbudda Valley ...	...	...	...	264	376	4	...	256	27	466	179	...	...	21	...
Seoni ...	...	...	...	6	9	...	...	15	3	155	88	...	...	...	...
Nagpur ...	...	...	...	41	26	3	...	30	5	470	140	...	...	...	...
Chhindwara ...	...	...	...	21	17	1	...	42	26	203	103	...	...	2	...
Baiga ...	Agriculturists	...	...	192	118	...	...	18	5	62	78	...	...	2	...
Jubbulpore ...	...	...	...	41	25	...	...	13	1	...	1	...	...	1	...
Mandla ...	...	...	...	14	17	...	...	4	3	14	32	...	...	1	...
Balaghat ...	...	...	...	137	76	...	...	1	1	48	45	...	...	...	...
Bairagi															
Province ...	Devotees ...	5	...	62	50	4	...	63	10	218	198	...	...	27	...
Balahi ...	Cotton-weavers	...	...	144	35	1	...	170	45	97	65	...	...	967	...
Hoshangabad ...	...	...	...	38	8	1	...	87	23	45	17	...	...	247	...
Nimar ...	...	...	...	106	27	...	...	83	22	52	48	...	...	656	...
Makrai ...	...	...	...	...	...	...	...	...	...	...	...	...	...	64	...
Bania															
Province ...	Traders ...	104	26	1,827	1,077	114	2	695	100	1,361	171	6	...	91	...
Banjara ...	Pack bullock-carriers.	2	...	432	657	11	6	358	130	2,735	2,112	...	...	28	...
Plateau Division ...	...	...	...	79	228	1	...	64	48	405	228	...	...	...	...
Maratha Division ...	...	1	...	281	229	10	...	201	6	774	188	...	...	18	...
Chhattisgarh Division	...	1	...	31	120	...	6	65	63	947	1,377	...	...	10	...
Nimar ...	...	...	...	23	6	...	...	25	11	94	5	...	...	...	...
Bastar ...	...	...	...	18	74	...	...	3	2	455	314	...	...	...	...
Barai															
Province ...	Betel-leaf growers.	2	...	159	122	8	...	139	22	678	457	...	...	38	...
Barhai															
Province ...	Carpenters ...	6	...	396	279	21	3	135	39	134	106	...	...	12	...
Basor															
Nerbudda Valley ...	Bamboo Workers	...	...	37	59	...	...	39	20	41	21	...	...	273	1
Beldar ...	Earth Workers	4	...	289	147	...	...	46	35	121	85	...	...	1	...
Saugor ...	...	...	...	78	32	...	...	15	17	5	14	...	...	1	...
Jubbulpore ...	...	...	...	126	82	...	...	28	10	85	57	...	...	...	...
Nimar ...	...	...	...	43	17	...	...	2	5	11	4	...	...	...	...
Wardha ...	...	...	...	24	2	...	...	...	1	7	2	...	...	...	...
Nagpur ...	...	4	...	18	14	...	...	1	2	13	8	...	...	...	...
Bhaina															
Bilaspur ...	Agriculturists	...	...	2	26	...	...	5	1	3	6	...	...	...	...
Bharia (Bhumia) ...	Agriculturists	...	...	208	170	1	...	164	61	58	104	...	...	15	2
Jubbulpore ...	...	...	...	148	136	1	...	73	9	24	30	...	...	7	...
Narsinghpur ...	...	...	...	31	25	...	...	2	...	31	19	...	...	...	...
Chhindwara ...	...	...	...	29	9	...	...	89	52	3	55	...	...	8	2

Selected Castes, Tribes or Races.

OF ACTUAL WORKERS—(*concluded*).

VII.—Public Administration.				VIII.—Arts and Professions.						IX.—Persons living on their income.		X.—Domestic service.		XI.—Contractors, clerks, cashiers, etc., otherwise unspecified.		XII.—Labourers unspecified.		XIII.—Beggars, prostitutes, criminals and inmates of jails and asylums.	
Gazetted officers.		Others.		Religious.		Lawyers, doctors and teachers.		Others.											
Males.	Females.	Males.	Females.	Males.	Females.	Males.	Females.	Males.	Females.	Males.	Females.	Males.	Females.	Males.	Females.	Males.	Females.	Males.	Females.
43	44	45	46	47	48	49	50	51	52	53	54	55	56	57	58	59	60	61	62
2	...	915	19	82	25	176	20	173	110	71	10	3,312	13,871	78	14	502	669	468	406
...	...	47	...	...	1	3	...	3	...	...	...	14	44	1	...	16	22	15	10
...	...	79	1	...	...	54	6	4	1	5	1	135	61	2	...	89	98	34	20
...	...	38	...	...	...	9	5	3	1	3	...	89	40	2	...	72	77	28	15
...	...	4	...	...	...	8	...	1	...	1	...	8	4	...	...	1	10	...	2
...	...	11	...	...	...	24	1	...	...	1	...	24	9	...	...	2	5	1	1
...	...	26	1	...	...	13	...	...	...	...	1	14	8	...	...	14	6	5	2
...	...	9	2	24	4	...	...	4	1	...	...	4	7	...	...	10	10	4	7
...	...	5	...	...	1	...	...	1	...	...	...	1	...	...	...	1	1	1	1
...	...	4	2	13	...	...	...	2	1	...	...	...	6	...	...	2	9	3	6
...	...	...	...	11	3	...	...	1	...	...	...	3	1	...	...	7	...	...	...
1	...	67	3	...	...	100	5	57	3	11	7	78	34	14	1	11	10	35	20
...	...	397	2	2	...	1	10	9	72	...	...	29	36	1	...	24	19	84	34
...	...	313	2	2	...	...	10	1	50	...	...	16	34	...	...	15	4	26	16
...	...	84	...	...	...	1	...	6	17	...	...	13	2	1	...	9	15	58	18
...	...	...	...	...	...	...	...	2	5	...	...	...	...	...	...	...	...	...	...
2	...	493	...	130	15	547	24	130	19	332	111	1,950	260	211	11	190	137	306	107
...	...	88	...	14	6	30	4	20	20	5	2	242	172	16	4	110	180	194	66
...	...	1	...	...	...	4	1	1	...	...	...	30	5	8	...	8	15	14	6
...	...	78	...	1	1	25	2	17	2	5	2	135	74	7	2	93	149	146	21
...	...	6	...	11	5	...	1	2	18	...	...	46	32	...	2	2	5	11	24
...	...	3	...	...	...	1	...	...	...	...	...	7	2	...	...	3	8	7	1
...	...	...	...	2	...	...	...	...	...	...	...	18	59	1	...	4	3	10	14
4	...	164	1	7	1	154	7	10	3	17	3	109	38	27	4	66	69	38	12
...	...	60	...	7	1	38	3	12	4	3	7	73	73	36	...	41	134	86	48
...	...	...	...	...	...	...	...	110	756	...	...	100	33	...	...	16	13	43	53
...	...	9	...	...	...	7	4	...	...	2	1	12	4	8	...	11	24	24	5
...	...	1	...	...	...	...	...	...	...	...	...	4	...	1	...	...	12	11	1
...	...	1	...	...	...	5	4	...	...	...	1	4	...	...	...	8	...	7	1
...	...	...	...	...	...	...	...	...	...	...	...	...	...	8	...	1	1	...	...
...	...	3	...	...	...	1	...	...	...	1	...	2	3	1	...	1	7	...	2
...	...	4	...	...	...	1	...	...	...	1	...	2	1	3	...	1	4	6	1
...	...	...	...	1	...	...	...	...	...	...	...	4	16	...	...	...	...	4	3
...	...	2	1	1	1	1	...	...	...	...	...	24	55	4	...	24	24	17	8
...	...	2	...	1	1	...	...	...	...	...	...	17	11	4	...	20	19	15	5
...	...	...	...	...	...	...	...	...	...	...	...	...	...	...	...	1	2	...	...
...	...	...	1	...	...	1	...	...	...	...	...	7	44	...	...	3	3	2	3

TABLE XVI.—Occupation by

Caste, tribe or race.	Traditional occupation.	Population dealt with.				Number of actual workers whose traditional caste occupation was returned as their				Number of actual workers returning their traditional occupation as their principal means of livelihood who had some subsidiary occupation.	
		Actual workers.		Dependants.		Principal means of livelihood.		Subsidiary means of livelihood.			
		Males.	Females.	Males.	Females.	Males.	Females.	Males.	Females.	Males.	Females.
1	2	3	4	5	6	7	8	9	10	11	12
Bhat ...	Genealogists ...	**4,227**	**2,689**	**1,883**	**3,631**	**1,464**	**813**	**195**	**44**	**180**	**57**
Nerbudda Valley ...	...	2,753	1,507	1,223	2,366	720	430	120	32	108	47
Nagpur ...	...	554	433	241	385	201	37	27	...	22	2
Raipur ...	...	547	364	241	479	350	223	36	5	37	8
Drug ...	...	373	295	178	401	178	123	12	7	13	...
Bhil											
Nimar ...	Agriculturists ...	7,881	7,589	3,923	4,344	3,350	2,840	41	3	96	78
Bhilala ...	Agriculturists ...	**5,114**	**4,385**	**2,603**	**3,172**	**2,763**	**2,321**	**7**	**2**	**71**	**17**
Hoshangabad ...	...	1,000	736	393	604	221	125	2	...	8	2
Nimar ...	...	4,114	3,649	2,210	2,568	2,542	2,196	5	2	63	15
Bhoyar ...	Agriculturists ...	**19,379**	**18,538**	**9,564**	**11,070**	**12,549**	**9,907**	**51**	**23**	**573**	**951**
Betul ...	...	7,625	7,236	3,631	4,300	4,817	4,701	10	16	365	501
Chhindwara ...	...	6,894	6,503	3,271	3,977	5,022	4,029	39	...	148	360
Wardha ...	...	3,846	3,731	2,004	2,124	2,187	882	1	3	44	23
Nagpur ...	...	1,014	978	658	669	523	296	1	4	16	67
Bhunjia											
Raipur ...	Agriculturists ...	2,232	1,751	1,231	1,698	1,378	1,038	16	24	207	105
Bidur											
Maratha Division ...	Writers ...	5,035	2,387	3,472	6,207	367	...	25	...	44	...
Binjhwar ...	Agriculturists ...	**15,139**	**14,172**	**7,742**	**9,239**	**7,215**	**6,385**	**143**	**55**	**805**	**495**
Bhandara ...	...	1,859	1,772	782	1,009	134	225	11	18	...	...
Balaghat ...	...	1,973	2,091	855	1,063	182	192	20	17	64	47
Raipur ...	...	7,865	7,220	4,157	5,050	4,086	3,524	92	14	485	226
Bilaspur ...	...	3,442	3,089	1,948	2,120	2,813	2,444	20	6	256	222
Brahman											
Province ...	Priests ...	152,691	40,238	84,876	167,822	16,767	2,679	3,368	192	3,000	149
Chadar ...	Village Watchmen	**8,978**	**7,609**	**4,649**	**6,220**	**1,749**	**20**	**90**	**1**	**386**	**4**
Saugor ...	...	4,808	4,149	2,497	3,184	737	5	45	...	186	2
Damoh ...	...	2,341	1,996	1,175	1,685	258	8	16	1	84	...
Jubbulpore ...	...	867	676	460	683	597	5	27	...	74	2
Narsinghpur ...	...	962	788	517	668	157	2	2	...	42	...
Chamar											
Province ...	Leather Workers ...	288,544	269,200	154,473	189,305	47,401	15,489	19,836	2,191	12,985	3,026
Dahayait											
Jubbulpore ...	Village Watchmen	2,792	2,327	1,631	2,247	760	38	132	6	307	10
Dangi ...	Agriculturists ...	**8,127**	**4,044**	**4,053**	**7,782**	**6,946**	**3,252**	**47**	**7**	**471**	**50**
Saugor ...	...	7,771	3,925	3,837	7,362	6,668	3,180	45	7	431	48
Damoh ...	...	356	119	216	420	278	72	2	...	40	2
Darji											
Province ...	Tailors ...	17,394	10,029	8,715	15,144	13,037	6,616	613	231	1,189	645
Deswali ...	Agriculturists ...	**2,538**	**2,003**	**1,061**	**1,419**	**1,605**	**1,236**	...	...	**62**	**26**
Hoshangabad ...	...	1,618	1,185	696	991	980	632	...	...	43	11
Nimar ...	...	920	818	365	428	625	604	...	...	19	15

Selected Castes, Tribes or Races.

Recorded principal occupation of actual workers.															
I.—Exploitation of the surface of the soil.												II.—Extraction of Minerals.			
Income from rent of land.		Cultivators of all kinds.		Agents and managers of landed estates, planters, forest officers and their clerks, rent collectors, etc.		Field labourers, wood-cutters, etc.		Raisers of live-stock, milkmen and herdsmen.		Fishing and hunting.		Owners, managers, clerks, etc.		Labourers.	
Males.	Females.	Males.	Females.	Males.	Females.	Males.	Females.	Males.	Females.	Males.	Females.	Males.	Females.	Males.	Females.
13	14	15	16	17	18	19	20	21	22	23	24	25	26	27	28
52	18	1,252	739	33	...	451	774	56	6	...	...	1	...	23	11
39	9	958	481	13	...	354	400	39	2	...	...	...	...	4	3
9	8	106	82	11	...	73	250	12	...	...	...	1	...	19	8
3	...	100	85	9	...	8	27	3	4	...	...	...	...	...	...
1	1	88	91	...	...	16	37	2	...	...	...	...	...	...	...
...	...	...	...	6	...	3,988	4,713	282	2	1	...	...	...	...	...
...	...	...	...	3	...	1,999	2,010	214	3	2	...	1	...	...	...
...	...	...	...	...	...	640	584	89	3	1	...	...	...	...	...
...	...	...	...	3	...	1,353	1,426	125	...	1	...	1	...	...	...
...	...	...	...	3	...	5,424	8,280	932	13	1	...	...	...	3	1
...	...	...	...	1	...	1,999	2,241	560	5	1	...	...	...	...	...
...	...	...	...	1	...	1,506	2,534	221	5	...	...	...	...	3	1
...	...	...	...	1	...	1,488	2,844	115	2	...	...	...	...	...	...
...	...	...	...	...	...	431	661	36	1	...	...	...	...	...	...
...	...	...	...	25	...	655	535	34	3	11	6	...	...	...	...
93	63	1,218	422	53	...	867	1,218	80	3	2	...	3	2	3	2
...	...	...	...	14	1	5,917	6,555	417	168	944	644	...	...	62	63
...	...	...	...	1	1	933	1,120	174	9	391	264	...	...	8	5
...	...	...	...	7	...	1,002	1,239	34	145	552	379	...	...	54	58
...	...	...	...	6	...	3,413	3,507	194	6	1	1	...	...	...	...
...	...	...	...	...	...	569	599	15	8	...	...	...	...	...	...
4,164	1,323	61,191	20,427	2,228	...	7,489	5,368	814	199	...	...	94	...	177	24
22	7	1,852	1,634	...	...	3,903	5,312	462	34	13	...	...	...	4	2
9	3	1,181	1,071	...	...	2,187	2,796	240	10	1	...	...	...	...	...
3	3	435	256	...	...	1,100	1,514	178	14	12	...	...	...	1	...
6	...	78	176	...	...	129	460	4	6	...	...	...	...	...	...
4	1	158	131	...	...	478	542	34	4	...	...	...	...	3	2
478	8	145,609	140,842	125	7	77,556	103,260	3,669	165	9	8	...	...	608	500
5	1	952	1,012	9	1	790	1,003	42	3	...	...	...	...	42	38
...	...	...	...	11	1	797	718	270	4	...	...	...	...	...	...
...	...	...	...	11	1	741	675	262	4	...	...	...	...	...	...
...	...	...	...	...	...	56	43	8	...	...	...	...	...	...	...
49	36	1,726	892	25	1	1,157	2,045	70	9	...	...	1	...	9	2
...	...	...	...	5	...	725	738	124	9	...	...	...	...	...	...
...	...	...	...	3	...	493	531	79	9	...	...	...	...	...	...
...	...	...	...	2	...	232	207	45	...	...	...	...	...	...	...

TABLE XVI.—Occupation by

RECORDED PRINCIPAL OCCUPATION

Caste, tribe or race.	Traditional occupation.	III.—Industries.				IV.—Transport.				V.—Trade.		VI.—Public Force.			
		Owners, managers, clerks, etc.		Artisans and other workmen.		Owners, managers, ships' officers, etc.		Labourers, boatmen, carters, palki-bearers, etc.				Commissioned and gazetted officers.		Others.	
		Males.	Females.	Males.	Females.	Males.	Females.	Males.	Females.	Males.	Females.	Males.	Females.	Males.	Females.
1	2	29	30	31	32	33	34	35	36	37	38	39	40	41	42
Bhat ...	Genealogists ...	3	...	66	49	3	...	55	11	140	82	...	...	39	...
Nerbudda Valley ...	...	3	...	50	41	...	...	44	5	81	41	...	...	29	...
Nagpur ...	...	...	...	11	6	1	...	0	...	39	13	...	...	3	...
Raipur ...	...	...	...	3	2	1	...	2	...	15	18	...	...	5	...
Drug ...	...	...	...	2	...	1	...	3	6	5	10	...	...	2	...
Bhil															
Nimar ...	Agriculturists	...	...	37	6	...	...	33	8	42	5	...	...	108	...
Bhilala ...	Agriculturists	...	...	27	5	...	...	15	3	28	5	...	...	11	...
Hoshangabad ...	...	...	...	15	5	...	...	8	2	10	4	...	...	1	...
Nimar ...	...	...	...	12	...	...	...	7	1	18	1	...	...	10	...
Bhoyar ...	Agriculturists	...	...	1 06	28	...	...	86	52	118	221	...	...	4	...
Betul ...	...	...	...	42	18	...	...	58	28	82	218	...	...	3	...
Chhindwara ...	...	...	...	42	8	...	...	28	9	17	2	...	...	1	...
Wardha ...	...	...	...	16	...	...	...	...	...	9	1	...	...	...	...
Nagpur ...	...	...	...	6	2	...	...	...	15	10	...	...	...	...	...
Bhunjia															
Raipur ...	Agriculturists	...	...	60	71	...	...	1	7	55	74	...	...	...	...
Bidur															
Maratha Division ...	Writers ...	20	...	218	93	18	...	51	3	945	198	2	...	57	...
Binjhwar ...	Agriculturists	...	1	127	112	2	2	102	30	68	71	...	...	93	...
Bhandara ...	...	...	1	62	42	1	...	57	17	33	21	...	...	2	...
Balaghat ...	...	...	...	32	25	...	...	30	11	9	6	...	...	...	...
Raipur ...	...	...	...	14	33	1	2	14	2	17	24	...	...	90	...
Bilaspur ...	...	...	...	19	12	...	...	1	...	9	20	...	...	1	...
Brahman															
Province ...	Priests ...	416	8	2,760	952	1,213	3	3,445	208	11,570	1,486	12	...	3,615	...
Chadar ...	Village Watchmen.	6	...	706	457	14	...	109	6	45	65	...	...	...	...
Saugor ...	...	3	...	299	191	14	...	72	3	25	31	...	...	...	...
Damoh ...	...	3	...	278	164	...	...	19	1	5	12	...	...	...	...
Jubbulpore ...	...	...	...	29	24	...	...	6	1	8	1	...	...	...	...
Narsinghpur ...	...	...	...	100	78	...	...	12	1	7	21	...	...	...	...
Chamar															
Province ...	Leather Workers	11	12	3,318	2,089	8	...	3,870	1,913	2,120	1,524	...	...	289	27
Dahayat															
Jubbulpore ...	Village Watchmen.	...	...	39	44	...	...	51	2	30	20	...	...	...	...
Dangi ...	Agriculturists	...	...	12	24	...	...	21	1	22	20	...	...	1	...
Saugor ...	...	...	...	10	22	...	...	21	1	16	19	...	...	1	...
Damoh ...	...	...	...	2	2	...	...	...	...	6	1	...	...	...	...
Darji															
Province ...	Tailors ...	4	2	173	194	13	...	52	10	714	133	...	...	28	...
Deswali ...	Agriculturists	1	...	10	6	...	...	32	...	8	5	...	...	1	...
Hoshangabad ...	...	...	...	8	6	...	...	32	...	3	...	...	...	...	...
Nimar ...	...	1	...	2	...	...	...	...	...	5	5	...	...	1	...

Selected Castes, Tribes or Races.

OF ACTUAL WORKERS—(*concluded*).

VII.—Public Administration.				VIII.—Arts and Professions.						IX.—Persons living on their income.		X.—Domestic service.		XI.—Contractors, clerks, cashiers, etc., otherwise unspecified.		XII.—Labourers, unspecified.		XIII.—Beggars, prostitutes, criminals and inmates of jails and asylums.	
Gazetted officers.		Others.		Religious.		Lawyers, doctors and teachers.		Others.											
Males.	Females.	Males.	Females.	Males.	Females.	Males.	Females.	Males.	Females.	Males.	Females.	Males.	Females.	Males.	Females.	Males.	Females.	Males.	Females.
43	44	45	46	47	48	49	50	51	52	53	54	55	56	57	58	59	60	61	62
1	...	65	1	258	60	39	6	51	18	9	2	49	18	7	7	19	29	91	45
1	...	23	...	212	49	21	4	41	18	9	2	28	7	5	...	11	17	62	28
...	...	19	...	1	...	5	...	6	...	...	...	4	7	1	...	1	10	25	12
...	...	18	...	...	...	9	...	8	...	...	...	7	4	...	...	2	...	...	1
...	...	5	1	45	11	4	2	1	...	...	...	10	...	1	7	5	2	4	4
...	...	4	...	2	2	...	...	4	2	2	...	6	...	...	...	12	9	4	2
...	...	4	...	6	11	...	...	...	...	1	...	30	22	...	...	4	3	6	2
...	...	...	...	...	...	...	...	...	...	...	...	8	11	...	...	2	...	4	2
...	...	4	...	6	11	...	...	...	...	1	...	27	11	...	...	2	3	2	...
...	...	17	...	...	...	33	...	3	...	2	...	60	20	9	...	6	3	23	13
...	...	11	...	...	...	20	...	2	...	...	...	21	18	3	...	2	...	3	7
...	...	5	...	...	...	4	...	...	...	...	...	23	1	1	...	4	3	16	2
...	...	1	...	...	...	8	...	1	...	...	...	14	1	5	...	...	...	1	1
...	...	...	...	...	...	1	...	...	...	2	...	2	...	...	...	...	...	3	3
...	...	1	...	1	...	...	...	...	...	1	...	4	10	...	...	2	7	4	...
...	...	356	59	16	6	152	3	14	5	13	2	323	204	62	2	41	57	61	45
...	...	21	...	28	4	6	3	1	12	1	...	64	70	19	4	17	31	21	16
...	...	7	...	...	3	2	1	...	10	...	...	15	20	18	...	11	28	10	5
...	...	8	...	25	...	3	...	...	2	...	...	29	25	1	4	4	3	1	2
...	...	6	...	3	1	1	...	...	...	1	...	7	22	...	...	2	...	9	8
...	...	...	...	...	...	...	2	1	...	...	...	13	3	...	...	...	...	1	1
104	...	9,982	105	11,586	5,530	5,030	156	874	31	950	169	5,987	1,044	651	22	481	204	1,091	300
...	...	...	...	...	...	6	1	3	4	1	2	32	16	1	2	30	33	20	14
...	...	...	...	...	...	3	1	1	4	1	1	15	12	1	2	2	10	11	9
...	...	...	...	...	...	1	...	1	...	...	...	11	1	...	...	23	21	4	2
...	...	...	...	...	...	1	...	...	...	...	...	2	1	...	...	4	1	3	1
...	...	...	...	...	...	1	...	1	...	...	1	4	2	...	...	1	1	2	2
...	...	...	...	82	35	...	...	93	1,304	16	7	1,474	359	14	13	801	886	993	757
...	...	...	...	...	...	4	...	1	...	1	1	13	6	8	...	89	66	11	2
...	...	5	...	1	1	5	1	...	...	...	1	27	15	...	...	4	4	5	2
...	...	4	...	1	1	3	1	...	...	...	1	25	15	...	...	4	4	4	1
...	...	1	...	...	...	2	...	...	...	...	...	2	...	...	...	...	...	1	1
1	...	107	...	8	1	87	4	19	2	13	3	...	...	19	5	26	43	47	31
...	...	5	...	...	...	...	...	...	...	...	2	9	3	...	...	9	2	4	2
...	...	2	...	...	...	...	...	...	...	...	2	6	2	...	...	9	2	3	1
...	...	3	...	...	...	...	...	...	...	...	...	3	1	...	...	...	...	1	1

TABLE XVI.—Occupation by

Caste, tribe or race.	Traditional occupation.	Population dealt with.				Number of actual workers whose traditional caste occupation was returned as their				Number of actual workers returning their traditional occupation as their principal means of livelihood who had some subsidiary occupation.	
		Actual workers.		Dependants.		Principal means of livelihood.		Subsidiary means of livelihood.			
		Males.	Females.	Males.	Females.	Males.	Females.	Males.	Females.	Males.	Females.
1	2	3	4	5	6	7	8	9	10	11	12
Dhanagar ...	Shepherds ...	**7,195**	**6,459**	**3,318**	**3,978**	**2,800**	**953**	**185**	**47**	**330**	**218**
Wardha ...	...	2,534	2,102	1,064	1,274	536	61	23	10	56	18
Nagpur ...	...	2,517	2,376	1,204	1,469	1,407	625	75	32	112	129
Chanda ...	...	1,269	1,131	637	743	641	238	71	4	152	58
Nimar ...	...	506	379	215	301	46	8	5	...	2	...
Chhindwara ...	...	369	381	198	192	170	21	11	1	8	13
Dhanuk											
Narsinghpur ...	Labourers ...	1,567	1,659	844	924	1,047	1,233	126	157	40	27
Dhanwar											
Bilaspur ...	Agriculturists ...	3,012	2,842	1,083	2,248	1,154	1,011	38	16	280	218
Dhimar											
Province ...	Water-bearers ...	92,870	86,000	47,864	56,079	45,425	27,451	6,710	3,695	13,024	8,379
Dhobi											
Province ...	Washermen ...	53,139	50,400	27,534	33,500	20,795	22,063	6,801	5,222	6,764	5,234
Gadaria ...	Shepherds ...	**10,245**	**8,043**	**5,104**	**6,993**	**3,876**	**1,981**	**704**	**160**	**1,454**	**266**
Nerbudda Valley ...	...	6,320	4,477	3,208	4,407	2,599	1,320	433	103	690	217
Chhattisgarh Division	...	3,925	3,566	1,896	2,584	1,277	661	271	57	764	49
Ganda ...	Cotton-Weavers ...	**32,645**	**30,516**	**18,189**	**22,769**	**5,289**	**5,633**	**2,020**	**1,661**	**1,297**	**843**
Chhattisgarh Division	...	28,488	27,306	15,696	19,270	3,198	3,733	1,624	1,429	727	598
Surguja ...	...	914	309	645	1,246	283	113	38	10	18	2
Jashpur ...	...	3,243	2,901	1,848	2,247	1,808	1,787	358	222	552	243
Ghasia											
Chhattisgarh Division	Labourers ...	6,270	6,402	3,420	4,228	3,064	4,010	120	113	143	217
Ghosi ...	Graziers ...	**2,551**	**1,855**	**1,363**	**1,827**	**218**	**77**	**62**	**3**	**8**	**15**
Saugor ...	...	1,687	1,313	843	1,065	160	55	43	3	4	15
Damoh ...	...	586	326	350	562	27	5	12	...	2	...
Narsinghpur ...	...	278	216	170	200	31	17	7	...	2	...
Golar											
Yeotmal ...	Graziers ...	1,089	1,121	510	592	128	3	1	...	1	...
Gond											
Province ...	Agriculturists ...	714,958	601,139	370,578	450,865	441,625	415,567	3,058	2,734	28,672	28,291
Gosain ...	Devotees ...	**6,857**	**4,145**	**3,319**	**5,632**	**2,812**	**939**	**443**	**102**	**313**	**72**
Balaghat ...	...	304	215	179	267	112	61	11	3	15	3
Narsinghpur ...	...	568	343	264	425	132	58	36	6	23	3
Jubbulpore ...	...	637	422	374	630	124	61	18	6	12	5
Hoshangabad ...	...	1,018	543	463	757	428	84	44	2	68	10
Nagpur ...	...	1,072	678	457	765	660	138	39	2	73	16
Wardha ...	...	575	276	194	363	352	52	20	...	28	8
Bhandara ...	...	415	271	172	260	234	87	20	10	28	15
Raipur ...	...	800	444	428	735	204	146	114	17	36	4
Bilaspur ...	...	927	651	518	902	262	160	90	33	19	8
Drug ...	...	541	302	270	522	214	92	51	23	11	...
Gowari											
Maratha Division ...	Graziers ...	41,673	39,260	17,059	21,708	8,073	712	119	19	76	39

Selected Castes, Tribes or Races.

Recorded principal occupation of actual workers.															
I.—Exploitation of the surface of the soil.												II.—Extraction of Minerals.			
Income from rent of land.		Cultivators of all kinds.		Agents and managers of landed estates, planters, forest officers and their clerks, rent collectors, etc.		Field labourers, wood-cutters, etc.		Raisers of live-stock, milkmen and herdsmen.		Fishing and hunting.		Owners, managers, clerks, etc.		Labourers.	
Males.	Females.	Males.	Females.	Males.	Females.	Males.	Females.	Males.	Females.	Males.	Females.	Males.	Females.	Males.	Females.
13	14	15	16	17	18	19	20	21	22	23	24	25	26	27	28
63	25	2,045	1,476	5	...	1,683	3,561	...	...	1	...	...	...	13	3
45	16	864	381	...	...	905	1,678	...	...	...	...	...	...	...	...
12	4	494	453	1	...	334	1,071	...	...	1	...	...	...	8	3
2	...	409	430	1	...	124	366	...	...	...	...	...	...	5	...
2	3	153	103	3	...	184	218	...	...	...	...	...	...	...	...
2	2	135	109	...	...	40	228	...	...	...	...	...	...	...	...
4	2	431	344	2	...	...	...	40	3	...	...	...	...	...	...
...	...	...	...	5	...	1,095	1,191	43	20	148	153	...	...	...	...
148	146	20,614	15,606	190	...	14,220	24,590	1,895	192	2,115	612	20	1	244	139
230	71	18,730	15,424	...	...	10,194	11,847	1,070	74	2	1	1	...	64	18
22	41	2,837	2,411	30	...	1,226	1,648	...	...	...	...	1	...	12	2
4	40	1,528	1,134	23	...	777	1,058	...	...	...	...	1	...	12	2
18	1	1,309	1,277	7	...	449	590	...	...	...	...	...	...	...	...
8	9	12,727	12,064	30	...	8,305	10,507	2,244	1,309	...	6	1	...	3	5
8	9	11,315	11,152	30	...	8,028	10,288	1,981	1,212	...	6	...	...	3	5
...	...	370	97	...	...	68	30	146	51	...	...	1	...	...	...
...	...	1,042	815	...	...	209	189	117	46	...	...	...	...	...	...
43	1	1,594	1,545	67	2	...	...	92	17	5	...	...	...	...	...
23	7	1,606	1,135	8	...	548	567	...	...	...	...	...	...	...	...
16	4	1,057	86[illegible]	4	...	365	349	...	...	...	...	...	...	...	...
7	2	403	190	1	...	95	114	...	...	...	...	...	...	...	...
...	1	146	76	8	...	88	104	...	...	...	...	...	...	...	...
7	1	356	15	...	...	489	1,03[illegible]	...	...	...	...	...	...	...	...
...	...	...	...	931	15	224,387	253,927	24,168	2,328	193	43	4	...	1,582	1,324
72	75	2,837	1,710	38	6	520	1,183	83	8	2	2	2	...	5	2
...	9	120	96	3	...	11	17	1	...	...	...	...	...	1	...
10	7	254	117	...	1	137	149	12	2	...	...	...	...	2	2
5	26	387	235	6	4	67	73	4	...	...	...	...	...	...	...
26	7	312	142	4	...	174	288	25	3	...	...	...	...	...	...
14	8	222	110	6	1	30	363	28	2	...	...	2	...	2	...
7	3	149	47	...	...	34	160	4	...	...	...	...	...	...	...
3	...	120	113	5	...	13	56	3	1	...	...	...	...	...	...
3	5	421	237	5	...	11	20	3	...	...	...	...	...	...	...
2	10	572	422	3	...	32	33	2	...	2	2	...	...	...	...
2	...	280	185	6	...	11	12	1	...	...	...	...	...	...	...
93	23	6,178	5,123	70	...	24,454	31,622	...	...	4	4	2	...	257	289

TABLE XVI.—Occupation by

RECORDED PRINCIPAL OCCUPATION

Caste, tribe or race.	Tradition, occupation.	III.—Industries. Owners, managers, clerks, etc. Males.	III.—Industries. Owners, managers, clerks, etc. Females.	III.—Industries. Artisans and other workmen. Males.	III.—Industries. Artisans and other workmen. Females.	IV.—Transport. Owners, managers, ships' officers, etc. Males.	IV.—Transport. Owners, managers, ships' officers, etc. Females.	IV.—Transport. Labourers, boatmen, carters, palki-bearers, etc. Males.	IV.—Transport. Labourers, boatmen, carters, palki-bearers, etc. Females.	V.—Trade. Males.	V.—Trade. Females.	VI.—Public Force. Commissioned and gazetted officers. Males.	VI.—Public Force. Commissioned and gazetted officers. Females.	VI.—Public Force. Others. Males.	VI.—Public Force. Others. Females.
1	2	29	30	31	32	33	34	35	36	37	38	39	40	41	42
Dhanagar ...	Shepherds ...	...	...	**213**	**325**	...	...	**49**	**5**	**210**	**67**	...	...	**17**	...
Wardha ...	...	...	...	23	28	...	...	7	...	50	9	...	...	2	...
Nagpur ...	...	...	...	84	195	...	...	7	3	101	7	...	...	11	...
Chanda ...	...	...	...	30	43	...	...	7	...	37	50	...	...	4	...
Nimar ...	...	...	...	70	39	...	...	27	2	15	1	...	...	...	...
Chhindwara ...	...	...	...	6	20	...	...	1	...	7	...	...	...	...	...
Dhanuk															
Narsinghpur ...	Labourers ...	...	...	...	...	...	...	...	...	39	74	...	...	...	...
Dhanwar															
Bilaspur ...	Agriculturists...	...	...	478	350	...	...	16	...	47	98	...	...	...	...
Dhimar															
Province ...	Water-bearers...	6	...	1,897	6,578	56	5	2,105	673	2,487	9,115	...	...	115	...
Dhobi															
Province ...	Washermen ...	13	...	405	176	8	...	597	116	340	186	...	...	26	...
Gadaria ...	Shepherds ...	**2**	**2**	**1,300**	**1,562**	**19**	**18**	**304**	**43**	**343**	**203**	...	...	**20**	...
Nerbudda Valley ...	...	2	2	707	688	19	18	257	31	231	145	...	...	15	...
Chhattisgarh Division	...	...	...	593	874	...	...	47	12	112	58	...	...	5	...
Ganda ...	Cotton-Weavers	...	**2**	**113**	**102**	...	**1**	**151**	**117**	**203**	**251**	...	...	**1,911**	...
Chhattisgarh Division	...	...	2	111	91	...	1	150	116	193	236	...	...	1,874	...
Surguja ...	...	...	...	...	5	...	...	1	1	7	8	...	...	11	...
Jashpur ...	...	...	...	2	6	...	...	...	...	3	7	...	...	26	...
Ghasia															
Chhattisgarh Division	Labourers ...	...	...	...	...	1	...	53	98	239	465	...	...	...	...
Ghosi	Graziers ...	...	...	**5**	**27**	...	...	**62**	**5**	**34**	**27**	...	...	**2**	...
Saugor ...	...	...	...	4	7	...	...	36	3	20	19	...	...	1	...
Damoh ...	...	...	...	1	7	...	...	23	1	9	4	...	...	...	...
Narsinghpur ...	...	...	...	...	13	...	...	3	1	5	4	...	...	1	...
Golar															
Yeotmal ...	Graziers ...	...	...	13	3	...	...	3	...	10	5	...	...	...	...
Gond															
Province ...	Agriculturists...	29	...	5,549	5,650	52	7	5,572	2,148	3,107	4,423	...	...	521	78
Gosain ...	Devotees ...	...	...	**36**	**63**	...	...	**34**	**3**	**126**	**112**	...	...	**12**	...
Balaghat ...	...	...	...	2	1	...	...	2	...	16	20	...	...	1	...
Narsinghpur ...	...	...	...	...	3	...	...	6	...	7	3	...	...	...	...
Jubbulpore ...	...	...	...	8	7	...	...	5	1	6	7	...	...	...	...
Hoshangabad ...	...	...	...	5	9	...	...	9	1	6	3	...	...	2	...
Nagpur ...	...	...	...	10	32	...	...	4	1	25	10	...	...	2	...
Wardha ...	...	...	...	2	...	...	...	3	...	8	4	...	...	...	...
Bhandara ...	...	...	...	1	3	...	...	...	...	12	8	...	...	1	...
Raipur ...	...	...	...	4	3	...	...	3	...	25	23	...	...	...	...
Bilaspur ...	...	...	...	4	5	...	...	2	...	12	17	...	...	5	...
Drug ...	...	...	...	...	...	...	...	...	...	9	8	...	...	1	...
Gowari															
Maratha Division ...	Graziers ...	5	...	892	590	24	...	404	88	346	235	...	...	24	...

Selected Castes, Tribes or Races.

OF ACTUAL WORKERS—(*concluded*).

VII.—Public Administration.				VIII.—Arts and Professions.						IX.—Persons living on their income.		X.—Domestic service.		XI.—Contractors, clerks, cashiers, etc., otherwise unspecified.		XII.—Labourers unspecified.		XIII.—Beggars, prostitutes, criminals and inmates of jails and asylums.	
Gazetted officers.		Others.		Religious.		Lawyers, doctors and teachers.		Others.											
Males.	Females.	Males.	Females.	Males.	Females.	Males.	Females.	Males.	Females.	Males.	Females.	Males.	Females.	Males.	Females.	Males.	Females.	Males.	Females.
43	44	45	46	47	48	49	50	51	52	53	54	55	56	57	58	59	60	61	62
...	...	8	...	1	...	10	...	...	2	...	2	30	13	3	1	12	23	32	3
...	...	2	...	...	...	2	...	...	...	...	1	13	3	...	...	2	13	3	2
...	...	5	...	...	...	7	...	...	...	...	1	11	4	3	1	7	6	24	...
...	...	1	...	1	...	...	...	...	...	...	...	3	3	...	...	...	...	4	1
...	...	...	...	...	...	...	...	...	2	...	...	3	3	...	...	2	...	1	...
...	...	...	...	...	...	1	...	...	...	...	...	...	...	...	...	1	1	...	...
...	...	...	...	...	...	...	...	1	...	...	...	...	1	2	...	...	...	1	2
...	...	...	...	4	...	...	...	1	...	...	...	18	13	...	...	2	5	1	1
1	...	371	11	32	2	152	26	55	32	24	15	...	...	50	10	363	500	285	200
...	...	111	...	37	39	64	...	65	9	5	...	...	...	11	1	98	94	264	281
...	...	38	...	6	1	6	3	3	9	3	...	71	23	12	1	49	37	65	58
...	...	30	...	4	...	3	2	2	1	1	...	39	14	4	...	42	17	20	5
...	...	8	...	2	1	3	1	1	8	2	...	32	9	8	1	7	20	45	53
...	...	9	...	19	10	10	...	1,220	154	1	6	107	107	12	...	66	74	216	159
...	...	...	...	19	10	10	...	1,200	154	1	6	91	87	11	...	55	58	210	140
...	...	...	...	...	...	...	...	20	...	...	...	3	2	1	...	2	2	1	...
...	...	9	...	...	...	...	...	...	...	...	...	13	27	...	...	9	14	5	10
...	...	20	...	1	...	4	2	18	64	17	6	1,012	134	1	...	...	...	39	58
...	...	3	...	2	...	1	...	...	1	...	...	22	6	...	...	13	2	4	1
...	...	2	...	2	...	1	...	...	1	...	...	15	3	...	...	1	2	3	1
...	...	1	...	...	...	...	...	...	...	...	...	7	3	...	...	12	...	...	...
...	...	...	...	...	...	...	...	...	...	...	...	...	...	...	...	...	...	1	...
...	...	34	...	...	...	1	...	...	...	...	...	5	2	...	...	15	42	28	15
5	...	804	15	533	184	200	10	264	140	55	22	2,971	2,787	105	35	926	1,335	1,309	1,092
2	...	87	...	...	...	70	5	8	3	5	3	61	10	7	...	11	8	27	13
...	...	13	...	...	...	15	...	...	2	1	...	1	...	4	...	...	...	1	...
...	...	...	...	...	...	1	...	1	...	1	...	2	...	...	...	...	...	3	1
2	...	3	...	...	...	1	...	1	...	...	2	3	...	1	...	7	4	7	2
...	...	2	...	...	...	6	3	...	...	...	...	15	1	...	...	1	...	3	2
...	...	48	...	...	...	6	1	3	...	...	...	8	2	...	...	...	3	2	1
...	...	5	...	...	...	3	1	...	...	...	...	[illegible]	2	1	...	2	...	2	1
...	...	3	...	...	...	6	...	...	1	1	...	10	...	1	...	...	1	2	1
...	...	8	...	...	...	12	...	2	...	...	...	6	2	...	...	1	...	2	2
...	...	3	...	...	...	16	...	1	...	1	1	5	...	...	...	...	...	3	1
...	...	2	...	...	...	4	...	...	...	1	...	8	3	...	...	...	...	2	2
...	...	165	...	5	6	34	1	12	17	2	5	374	313	21	3	131	175	107	63

TABLE XVI.—Occupation by

Caste, tribe or race.	Traditional occupation.	Population dealt with. Actual workers. Males.	Population dealt with. Actual workers. Females.	Population dealt with. Dependants. Males.	Population dealt with. Dependants. Females.	Number of actual workers whose traditional caste occupation was returned as their Principal means of livelihood. Males.	Principal means of livelihood. Females.	Subsidiary means of livelihood. Males.	Subsidiary means of livelihood. Females.	Number of actual workers returning their traditional occupation as their principal means of livelihood who had some subsidiary occupation. Males.	Females.
1	2	3	4	5	6	7	8	9	10	11	12
Gujar ...	Herdsmen ...	**17,804**	**12,245**	**8,735**	**13,061**	**790**	**33**	**11**	**13**	**11**	**4**
Narsinghpur ...	...	1,758	1,283	745	1,154	126	14	2	...	2	1
Hoshangabad ...	...	8,084	4,087	3,996	7,329	554	19	9	13	8	3
Nimar ...	...	7,962	6,875	3,994	4,578	110	...	...	...	1	...
Gurao ...	Temple Servants ...	**1,344**	**759**	**755**	**1,357**	**142**	**90**	**11**	**2**	**16**	**10**
Wardha ...	...	498	274	273	534	25	21	5	2	3	2
Nagpur ...	...	528	299	317	521	86	54	6	...	12	5
Chanda ...	...	318	186	165	302	31	15	...	...	1	3
Halba ...	Agriculturists ...	**9,856**	**8,505**	**5,789**	**7,325**	**6,529**	**5,327**	**50**	**21**	**457**	**864**
Raipur ...	...	1,315	1,241	871	1,072	933	853	2	10	59	24
Chanda ...	...	824	784	393	397	531	541	2	3	46	69
Bastar ...	...	4,964	3,828	3,002	4,057	3,499	2,512	13	5	163	384
Kanker ...	...	2,753	2,652	1,523	1,801	1,566	1,421	33	3	189	387
Hatgar											
Yeotmal ...	Shepherds ...	3,534	3,027	1,583	2,227	122	21	22	...	6	...
Jat ...	Agriculturists ...	**1,948**	**1,211**	**954**	**1,666**	**1,410**	**891**	**12**	**7**	**81**	**4**
Narsinghpur ...	...	305	99	191	346	202	46	9	1	29	2
Hoshangabad ...	...	1,643	1,112	763	1,320	1,208	845	3	6	52	2
Kachhi ...	Vegetable Growers	**38,333**	**32,403**	**19,848**	**25,346**	**3,977**	**4,572**	**2,599**	**1,733**	**843**	**556**
Nerbudda Valley ...	...	35,646	30,327	18,558	23,654	3,759	4,165	2,432	1,656	826	549
Plateau Division ...	...	2,687	2,076	1,290	1,692	218	407	167	77	17	7
Kahar ...	Palki-bearers ...	**4,796**	**4,201**	**2,572**	**3,112**	**121**	...	**33**	...	**24**	...
Narsinghpur ...	...	703	691	350	430	97	...	32	...	20	...
Hoshangabad ...	...	1,937	1,679	1,060	1,268	21	...	...	...	4	...
Nimar ...	...	883	714	455	530	3	...	...	...	...	...
Bilaspur ...	...	1,273	1,117	707	884	...	...	1	...	...	...
Kalar											
Province ...	Distillers ...	62,491	49,628	33,002	49,274	4,143	2,447	1,299	450	562	136
Katia ...	Spinners ...	**12,476**	**11,637**	**6,701**	**8,452**	**1,399**	**803**	**243**	**60**	**295**	**194**
Plateau Division ...	...	9,425	8,991	5,175	6,263	961	601	224	43	164	142
Narsinghpur ...	...	641	634	317	509	64	70	7	5	23	21
Hoshangabad ...	...	2,410	2,012	1,209	1,680	374	132	12	12	108	31
Kawar ...	Agriculturists ...	**28,050**	**26,443**	**15,764**	**19,023**	**22,954**	**21,737**	**115**	**49**	**1,063**	**419**
Chanda ...	...	513	448	238	248	355	310	...	...	...	...
Chhattisgarh Division...	...	27,537	25,995	15,526	18,775	22,599	21,418	115	49	1,063	419
Kayasth											
Province ...	Writers ...	10,321	1,936	7,259	14,055	3,203	...	115	...	291	...
Kewat ...	Boatmen ...	**3,713**	**3,645**	**1,861**	**2,348**	**30**	...	**19**	...	**23**	...
Jubbulpore ...	...	1,717	1,719	840	1,148	4	...	9	...	3	...
Narsinghpur ...	...	416	385	252	243	...	...	10	...	...	...
Chanda ...	...	1,580	1,541	769	957	26	...	...	...	20	...
Khangar ...	Village Watchmen...	**3,868**	**2,967**	**1,977**	**2,851**	**298**	**7**	**40**	...	**120**	**1**
Saugor ...	...	1,934	1,534	969	1,366	214	6	27	...	88	1
Damoh ...	...	677	490	373	570	57	1	4	...	24	...
Narsinghpur ...	...	324	262	170	245	8	...	2	...	2	...
Jubbulpore ...	...	933	681	465	664	19	...	7	...	6	...

Selected Castes, Tribes or Races.

RECORDED PRINCIPAL OCCUPATION OF ACTUAL WORKERS.

I.—Exploitation of the surface of the soil.												II.—Extraction of Minerals.			
Income from rent of land.		Cultivators of all kinds.		Agents and managers of landed estates, planters, forest officers and their clerks, rent collectors, etc.		Field labourers, wood-cutters, etc.		Raisers of live-stock, milk-men and herdsmen.		Fishing and hunting.		Owners, managers, clerks, etc.		Labourers.	
Males.	Females.	Males.	Females.	Males.	Females.	Males.	Females.	Males.	Females.	Males.	Females.	Males.	Females.	Males.	Females.
13	14	15	16	17	18	19	20	21	22	23	24	25	26	27	28
291	**375**	**13,371**	**9,090**	**14**	...	**2,987**	**2,608**	...	...	...	...	...	...	**4**	**1**
28	13	1,188	805	3	...	388	420	...	...	...	...	...	...	4	1
191	316	5,202	2,149	11	...	1,932	1,518	...	...	...	...	...	...	...	...
72	40	6,981	6,136	...	...	667	664	...	...	...	...	...	...	...	...
22	**14**	**289**	**126**	**4**	**2**	**163**	**285**	**24**	**1**	...	...	...	...	**2**	...
11	5	107	29	...	...	106	157	2	1	...	...	...	...	...	...
9	6	101	48	...	...	40	82	17	...	...	...	...	...	2	...
2	3	81	49	4	2	17	40	5	...	...	...	...	...	...	...
...	...	...	...	**45**	**1**	**2,451**	**2,585**	**266**	**40**	**21**	...	...	...	**1**	...
...	...	...	...	7	...	277	350	57	2	...	...	...	...	...	...
...	...	...	...	2	...	161	184	21	1	...	...	...	...	1	...
...	...	...	...	27	...	1,021	806	79	34	21	...	...	...	...	...
...	...	...	...	9	1	992	1,155	109	3	...	...	...	...	...	...
75	**32**	**2,053**	**318**	**2**	...	**1,147**	**2,620**	...	...	...	...	...	...	**1**	...
...	...	...	...	**1**	...	**339**	**276**	**88**	**2**	...	...	...	...	**1**	...
...	...	...	...	...	...	62	38	14	2	...	...	...	...	1	...
...	...	...	...	1	...	277	243	74	...	...	...	...	...	...	...
111	**61**	**19,574**	**14,689**	**20**	...	**10,895**	**11,433**	**814**	**51**	**1**	...	...	...	**63**	**32**
108	59	17,028	13,519	13	...	10,586	11,116	795	40	1	...	...	...	45	22
3	2	1,646	1,170	7	...	300	317	19	2	...	...	...	...	18	10
10	**3**	**1,829**	**1,334**	**14**	**1**	**821**	**1,040**	**108**	**10**	**973**	**70**	...	...	**4**	**2**
4	1	274	175	...	...	188	204	26	6	20	3	...	...	4	2
6	2	468	218	7	...	373	465	45	1	463	28	...	...	...	...
...	...	86	56	6	1	151	242	27	3	409	7	...	...	...	...
...	...	1,001	885	1	...	109	129	10	...	72	32	...	...	...	...
508	614	35,816	20,017	131	11	12,182	14,231	1,164	56	3	...	4	...	164	61
22	...	**5,217**	**4,690**	**35**	...	**3,276**	**5,096**	**325**	**18**	**1**	**1**	...	...	**157**	**136**
10	...	4,585	4,302	26	...	2,111	3,507	253	12	1	1	...	...	72	87
...	...	74	53	1	...	222	331	1	4	...	...	...	...	85	49
12	...	558	335	8	...	943	1,258	63	2	...	...	...	...	...	...
...	...	...	...	**12**	**2**	**4,576**	**4,494**	**235**	**17**	**12**	**3**	...	...	...	...
...	...	...	...	...	...	131	121	20	...	2	...	...	...	...	...
...	...	...	...	12	2	4,445	4,373	215	17	10	3	...	...	...	...
294	106	2,905	781	252	31	618	585	31	5	1	...	13	...	32	4
8	**8**	**1,003**	**1,012**	**12**	...	**737**	**970**	**120**	**15**	**1,226**	**1,193**	...	...	**23**	**7**
8	7	648	671	1	...	551	733	40	3	4	9	...	...	20	7
...	1	162	155	...	...	110	80	5	...	1	20	...	...	...	...
...	...	153	186	11	...	76	157	75	12	1,221	1,155	...	...	2	...
11	**7**	**1,327**	**980**	**9**	...	**1,350**	**1,650**	**162**	**13**	...	...	...	...	**22**	**5**
4	3	641	549	3	...	637	842	96	6	...	...	...	...	1	...
2	2	160	88	1	...	282	330	87	4	...	...	...	...	...	...
...	1	72	39	4	...	162	168	18	...	...	...	...	...	18	5
5	1	454	304	1	...	269	301	16	3	...	...	...	...	3	...

TABLE XVI.—Occupation by

RECORDED PRINCIPAL OCCUPATION

Caste, tribe or race.	Traditional occupation.	III.—Industries.				IV.—Transport.				V.—Trade.		VI.—Public Force.			
		Owners, managers, clerks, etc.		Artisans and other workmen.		Owners, managers, ships' officers, etc.		Labourers, boatmen, carters, palki-bearers, etc.				Commissioned and gazetted officers.		Others.	
		Males.	Females.	Males.	Females.	Males.	Females.	Males.	Females.	Males.	Females.	Males.	Females.	Males.	Females.
1	2	29	30	31	32	33	34	35	36	37	38	39	40	41	42
Gujar ...	Herdsmen ...	6	...	61	63	...	...	120	9	63	21	...	...	3	...
Narsinghpur ...	...	...	...	4	15	...	...	8	...	2	1	...	...	...	...
Hoshangabad ...	...	1	...	18	37	...	...	82	4	34	16	...	...	2	...
Nimar ...	...	5	...	39	11	...	...	30	5	27	4	...	...	1	...
Gurao ...	Temple Servants	5	...	77	64	5	...	22	...	298	125	...	...	8	...
Wardha ...	...	3	...	42	18	3	...	...	...	92	25	...	...	2	...
Nagpur ...	...	2	...	25	31	2	...	4	...	135	50	...	...	2	...
Chanda ...	...	...	...	10	15	...	...	18	...	71	50	...	...	4	...
Halba ...	Agriculturists	...	...	90	280	1	...	87	14	127	185	...	...	44	5
Raipur ...	...	...	...	5	15	...	...	19	2	7	10	...	...	...	...
Chanda ...	...	...	...	7	...	1	...	9	2	46	52	...	...	1	...
Bastar ...	...	...	...	65	229	...	...	52	7	61	101	...	...	38	3
Kanker ...	...	...	...	13	36	...	...	7	3	13	22	...	...	5	2
Hatgar															
Yeotmal ...	Shepherds ...	...	...	15	13	...	...	14	...	23	4	...	...	...	...
Jat ...	Agriculturists	...	7	28	10	...	...	22	2	21	13	...	...	10	...
Narsinghpur ...	...	...	...	4	4	...	...	4	1	5	10	...	...	2	...
Hoshangabad ...	...	...	7	24	6	...	...	18	1	16	3	...	...	8	...
Kachhi ...	Vegetable Growers.	1	...	730	511	5	...	911	163	407	416	...	...	36	...
Nerbudda Valley ...	...	1	...	650	493	2	...	686	90	341	371	...	...	24	...
Plateau Division ...	...	...	...	80	18	3	...	225	73	66	45	...	...	12	...
Kahar ...	Palki-bearers...	...	...	132	449	2	4	88	14	228	505	...	...	2	...
Narsinghpur ...	...	...	...	1	46	...	...	2	...	24	50	...	...	...	...
Hoshangabad ...	...	...	...	65	153	1	...	43	6	99	296	...	...	...	...
Nimar ...	...	...	...	63	249	...	...	32	6	85	123	...	...	2	...
Bilaspur ...	...	...	...	3	1	1	4	11	2	20	27	...	...	...	...
Kalar															
Province ...	Distillers ...	45	...	927	479	11	...	1,109	188	4,670	2,120	9	...	60	...
Katia ...	Spinners ...	...	...	248	340	...	...	346	133	441	316	...	...	874	37
Plateau Division ...		...	...	153	110	...	...	186	69	300	230	...	...	699	30
Narsinghpur ...	...	...	...	48	69	...	...	32	23	40	23	...	...	39	3
Hoshangabad ...	...	...	...	47	161	...	...	128	41	101	54	...	...	136	4
Kawar ...	Agriculturists	...	...	87	46	...	...	21	4	27	64	...	...	3	...
Chanda ...	...	...	...	...	...	...	...	...	...	1	5	...	...	...	...
Chhattisgarh Division	...	...	...	87	46	...	...	21	4	26	59	...	...	3	...
Kayasth															
Province ...	Writers ...	22	2	258	146	71	2	225	23	533	131	11	...	275	...
Kewat ...	Boatmen ...	...	...	281	237	...	...	87	9	94	119	...	...	...	...
Jubbulpore ...	...	...	...	153	123	...	...	83	7	85	91	...	...	...	...
Narsinghpur ...	...	...	...	127	113	...	...	2	...	8	7	...	...	...	...
Chanda ...	...	...	...	1	1	...	...	2	2	1	21	...	...	...	...
Khangar ...	Village Watchmen.	1	...	87	108	...	...	180	30	95	76	...	...	89	...
Saugor ...	...	...	...	49	41	...	...	97	16	29	38	...	...	54	...
Damoh ...	...	...	...	22	27	...	...	30	6	20	1	...	...	26	...
Narsinghpur ...	...	...	...	5	17	...	...	16	1	11	23	...	...	2	...
Jubbulpore ...	...	1	...	11	23	...	...	37	7	35	14	...	...	7	...

Selected Castes, Tribes or Races.

OF ACTUAL WORKERS—*(concluded)*.

VII.—Public Administration.				VIII.—Arts and Professions.						IX.—Persons living on their income.		X.—Domestic service.		XI.—Contractors, clerks, cashiers, etc., otherwise unspecified.		XII.—Labourers unspecified.		XIII.—Beggars, prostitutes, criminals and inmates of jails and asylums.	
Gazetted officers.		Others.		Religious.		Lawyers, doctors and teachers.		Others.											
Males.	Females.	Males.	Females.	Males.	Females.	Males.	Females.	Males.	Females.	Males.	Females.	Males.	Females.	Males.	Females.	Males.	Females.	Males.	Females.
43	44	45	46	47	48	49	50	51	52	53	54	55	56	57	58	59	60	61	62
...	...	11	1	...	...	10	...	8	1	1	...	34	21	1	...	4	11	25	11
...	...	...	...	...	...	1	...	...	...	...	...	2	5	1	...	...	1	3	2
...	...	6	1	...	...	5	...	2	1	1	...	26	16	...	...	3	2	14	8
...	...	5	...	...	...	4	...	6	...	...	...	6	...	...	...	1	8	8	1
...	...	76	3	...	...	55	1	4	...	3	2	105	33	14	...	11	9	15	4
...	...	25	...	...	...	24	...	...	...	3	2	41	11	2	...	7	4	3	1
...	...	29	2	...	...	13	...	4	...	...	...	42	10	8	...	3	4	4	3
...	...	22	1	...	...	18	1	...	...	...	...	22	3	4	...	1	1	8	...
...	...	52	...	5	1	15	1	3	...	1	...	45	45	1	1	46	13	28	7
...	...	3	...	...	...	1	...	3	...	...	...	2	1	...	...	1	8	...	...
...	...	4	...	...	...	...	...	...	...	1	...	4	2	1	...	33	2	1	...
...	...	33	...	4	1	8	...	...	...	...	...	25	36	...	1	12	3	19	5
...	...	12	...	1	...	6	1	...	...	...	...	14	6	...	...	...	...	6	2
...	...	48	...	...	...	2	...	3	...	...	...	10	14	2	...	11	4	6	1
...	...	7	...	1	...	2	...	...	1	1	...	9	5	1	...	1	...	6	4
...	...	4	...	1	...	1	...	...	1	1	...	...	...	1	...	...	...	3	2
...	...	3	...	...	...	1	...	...	...	...	...	9	5	...	...	1	...	3	2
...	...	62	...	7	...	23	3	17	5	5	4	200	87	12	6	338	311	124	59
...	...	49	...	6	...	19	3	14	4	5	4	178	82	11	4	318	293	107	63
...	...	13	...	1	...	4	...	3	1	...	...	22	5	1	2	20	18	17	6
...	...	15	1	1	...	10	...	11	1	...	...	406	757	6	...	10	7	5	3
...	...	3	...	...	...	1	...	4	...	...	...	45	194	...	...	...	1	1	...
...	...	3	...	1	...	...	...	7	...	...	...	329	507	3	...	2	1	1	2
...	...	5	...	...	...	1	...	...	1	...	...	9	23	...	...	4	3	...	...
...	...	4	1	...	...	8	...	...	...	...	...	23	33	3	...	4	2	3	1
2	...	281	1	10	...	213	6	29	2	31	14	558	123	119	12	170	155	132	91
...	...	16	...	1	...	13	1	6	2	7	1	45	24	10	...	16	26	21	13
...	...	7	...	1	...	7	1	2	1	6	...	17	5	4	...	10	23	14	3
...	...	3	...	...	...	1	...	4	...	1	...	11	5	4	...	3	1	...	3
...	...	6	...	...	...	5	...	...	1	...	1	17	14	2	...	3	2	7	7
...	...	10	...	7	3	7	...	...	...	4	...	58	30	...	2	12	21	25	20
...	...	...	...	...	...	...	...	...	...	...	...	1	...	...	...	...	...	3	3
...	...	10	...	7	3	7	...	...	...	4	...	57	30	...	2	12	21	22	17
17	...	594	...	12	1	469	7	36	8	101	16	186	31	63	1	63	38	36	18
...	...	10	2	4	...	2	...	...	...	1	...	26	35	6	1	35	35	8	2
...	...	6	2	...	...	2	...	...	...	1	...	24	31	6	1	35	33	6	1
...	...	...	...	...	...	...	...	...	...	...	...	1	...	...	...	...	...	...	...
...	...	4	...	4	...	...	...	...	...	...	...	1	4	...	...	...	2	2	1
...	...	68	...	...	...	22	2	7	7	10	1	35	18	2	...	62	54	31	9
...	...	42	...	...	...	11	1	3	5	4	...	21	11	1	...	15	13	12	3
...	...	9	...	...	...	2	...	2	...	3	1	7	3	...	...	12	14	5	4
...	...	8	...	...	...	...	...	2	2	1	...	1	3	1	...	...	3	...	...
...	...	9	...	...	...	9	1	...	...	2	...	6	1	...	...	35	24	14	2

TABLE XVI.—Occupation by

Caste, tribe or race.	Traditional occupation.	Population dealt with. — Actual workers. — Males.	Population dealt with. — Actual workers. — Females.	Population dealt with. — Dependants. — Males.	Population dealt with. — Dependants. — Females.	Number of actual workers whose traditional caste occupation was returned as their Principal means of livelihood. — Males.	Principal means of livelihood. — Females.	Subsidiary means of livelihood. — Males.	Subsidiary means of livelihood. — Females.	Number of actual workers returning their traditional occupation as their principal means of livelihood who had some subsidiary occupation. — Males.	Females.
1	2	3	4	5	6	7	8	9	10	11	12
Kharia ...	Agriculturists ...	**1,790**	**1,683**	**1,310**	**1,485**	**1,034**	**864**	**29**	**14**	**125**	**80**
Raigarh ...	...	861	824	617	660	359	27:	29	14	121	77
Jashpur ...	...	929	859	693	825	675	591	...	...	4	3
Kharwar ...	Agriculturists ...	**1,190**	**1,050**	**683**	**918**	**787**	**643**	**43**	**8**	**263**	**216**
Bilaspur ...	...	764	749	496	598	498	463	25	3	215	202
Jashpur ...	...	426	301	187	320	289	180	18	5	48	14
Kir ...	Agriculturists ...	**2,197**	**1,717**	**1,029**	**1,143**	**1,210**	**831**	**141**	**48**	**338**	**151**
Narsinghpur ...	...	285	242	168	157	166	141	26	12	39	54
Hoshangabad ...	...	1,912	1,475	861	986	1,044	690	115	36	299	97
Kirar ...	Agriculturists ...	**15,727**	**12,423**	**7,540**	**10,608**	**11,649**	**8,255**	**72**	**9**	**711**	**377**
Plateau Division ...	...	6,540	5,195	3,305	4,679	4,975	3,379	7	3	229	219
Narsinghpur ...	...	4,131	3,456	1,915	2,441	3,044	2,570	15	2	299	127
Hoshangabad ...	...	3,595	2,656	1,609	2,499	2,571	1,586	41	3	93	24
Nagpur ...	...	1,461	1,116	711	989	1,059	720	9	1	90	7
Kohli ...	Agriculturists ...	**7,247**	**6,517**	**3,797**	**4,529**	**6,099**	**5,604**	**40**	**5**	**829**	**273**
Chanda ...	...	2,739	2,424	1,396	1,753	2,222	1,981	5	2	313	168
Bhandara ...	...	4,508	4,093	2,401	2,776	3,877	3,623	35	3	516	105
Kol ...	Agriculturists ...	**20,851**	**22,245**	**11,946**	**13,276**	**3,038**	**2,195**	**494**	**148**	**770**	**440**
Jubbulpore ...	...	15,614	17,404	9,196	10,107	1,538	1,152	464	146	647	406
Mandla ...	...	3,183	3,029	1,840	2,052	547	499	2	1	42	34
Chota Nagpur States	...	2,054	1,812	910	1,117	953	544	28	1	81	...
Koli											
Berar ...	Fishermen ...	10,606	9,761	6,109	6,870	606	136	1	...	110	9
Kolta											
Raigarh ...	Agriculturists ...	3,759	3,065	2,079	2,927	3,511	2,840	2	...	73	34
Komti											
Chanda ...	Traders	1,330	295	689	1,520	865	228	83	4	260	27
Kori											
Nerbudda Valley ...	Cotton Weavers ...	10,351	8,394	4,988	6,888	4,242	3,173	358	160	978	648
Korku ...	Agriculturists ...	**30,583**	**29,345**	**16,724**	**18,383**	**16,409**	**13,852**	**60**	**30**	**3,517**	**2,958**
Hoshangabad ...	...	6,724	6,217	3,290	3,973	2,897	2,150	30	17	677	270
Nimar ...	...	11,943	11,340	6,606	7,028	6,340	5,591	1	...	612	577
Betul ...	...	11,389	11,228	6,231	6,826	6,993	5,740	26	13	2,205	2,110
Amraoti ...	...	527	560	597	556	179	371	3	...	23	1
Koshti ...	Cotton Weavers ...	**45,398**	**40,124**	**24,103**	**29,210**	**36,550**	**32,217**	**1,593**	**999**	**1,848**	**1,428**
Jubbulpore ...	...	749	612	407	583	571	285	...	...	7	1
Seoni ...	...	439	409	219	218	419	391	...	...	...	...
Chhindwara ...	...	1,173	1,086	596	692	1,052	993	5	...	48	76
Nimar ...	...	253	200	137	170	230	182	1	...	...	...
Maratha Division ...	...	31,290	26,518	16,345	20,047	25,691	21,877	289	117	601	663
Chhattisgarh Division	...	11,494	11,299	6,399	7,500	8,587	8,489	1,298	882	1,192	688
Kumhar											
Province ...	Potters	40,024	33,339	20,023	25,115	29,056	24,650	5,023	2,716	4,279	2,510

Selected Castes, Tribes or Races.

RECORDED PRINCIPAL OCCUPATION OF ACTUAL WORKERS.

I.—Exploitation of the surface of the soil.												II.—Extraction of Minerals.			
Income from rent of land.		Cultivators of all kinds.		Agents and managers of landed estates, planters, forest officers and their clerks, rent collectors, etc.		Field labourers, wood-cutters, etc.		Raisers of live-stock, milk-men and herdsmen.		Fishing and hunting.		Owners, managers, clerks, etc.		Labourers.	
Males.	Females.	Males.	Females.	Males.	Females.	Males.	Females.	Males.	Females.	Males.	Females.	Males.	Females.	Males.	Females.
13	14	15	16	17	18	19	20	21	22	23	24	25	26	27	28
...	...	...	...	1	...	614	651	13	14	...	...	...	...	...	...
...	...	...	...	1	...	302	462	5	4	...	...	...	...	...	...
...	...	...	...	...	...	222	189	8	10	...	...	...	...	...	...
...	...	...	...	1	...	194	221	33	8	...	...	...	...	...	...
...	...	...	...	1	...	174	213	7	1	...	...	...	...	...	...
...	...	...	...	...	...	20	8	20	7	...	...	...	...	...	...
...	...	...	...	...	...	834	840	116	6	1	...	...	...	1	...
...	...	...	...	...	...	97	89	18	3	...	...	...	...	1	...
...	...	...	...	...	...	737	751	98	3	1	...	...	...	...	...
...	...	...	...	15	3	3,006	3,265	653	37	2	...	...	...	3	1
...	...	...	...	6	...	1,003	1,701	319	6	2	...	...	...	2	...
...	...	...	...	4	...	821	627	237	23	...	...	...	...	1	...
...	...	...	...	2	...	951	1,030	18	6	...	...	...	...	...	...
...	...	...	...	3	3	108	347	79	2	...	...	...	...	...	1
...	...	...	...	7	4	776	865	210	3	2	...	...	...	41	17
...	...	...	...	...	...	380	430	79	...	1	...	...	...	...	...
...	...	...	...	7	4	300	435	131	3	1	...	...	...	41	17
...	...	...	...	5	...	14,651	18,016	617	74	2	7	...	...	446	442
...	...	...	...	5	...	11,653	14,496	320	30	...	...	...	...	446	442
...	...	...	...	...	...	2,120	2,381	163	8	...	...	...	...	...	...
...	...	...	...	...	...	878	1,139	128	30	2	7	...	...	...	...
44	51	3,623	1,055	4	...	5,123	8,120	257	3	...	...	...	...	1	...
...	...	...	...	1	...	218	177	1	...	...	...	...	...	...	...
8	2	304	44	11	1	25	5	1	...	1	...	1	...	...	...
4	3	631	492	41	...	2,118	3,106	214	18	5	...	...	...	86	64
...	...	...	...	24	...	12,275	14,854	1,086	76	15	...	...	...	5	2
...	...	...	...	11	...	3,302	3,899	384	23	5	...	...	...	...	...
...	...	...	...	4	...	5,292	5,064	190	7	...	...	...	...	...	...
...	...	...	...	9	...	3,396	5,141	502	36	10	...	...	...	5	2
...	...	...	...	...	...	284	150	10	10	...	...	...	...	...	...
80	29	3,783	2,697	19	...	2,499	3,649	169	21	17	...	2	...	10	5
...	...	3	7	1	...	54	210	...	...	...	...	...	...	...	...
...	...	1	...	...	...	6	3	1	...	...	...	...	...	...	...
11	...	9	4	...	...	12	20	1	...	...	...	1	...	4	...
...	...	2	1	1	...	4	6	1	...	...	...	...	...	...	...
58	21	1,350	585	13	...	2,220	3,068	152	21	17	...	1	...	6	5
11	8	2,412	2,100	4	...	203	342	14	...	...	...	...	...	...	...
119	84	7,330	4,981	41	2	1,720	2,848	337	62	16	...	...	...	14	3

TABLE XVI.—Occupation by

RECORDED PRINCIPAL OCCUPATION

CASTE, TRIBE OR RACE.	Traditional occupation.	III.—Industries.				IV.—Transport.				V.—Trade.		VI.—Public Force.			
		Owners, managers, clerks, etc.		Artisans and other workmen.		Owners, managers, ships' officers, etc.		Labourers, boatmen, carters, palki-bearers, etc.				Commissioned and gazetted officers.		Others.	
		Males.	Females.	Males.	Females.	Males.	Females.	Males.	Females.	Males.	Females.	Males.	Females.	Males.	Females.
1	2	29	30	31	32	33	34	35	36	37	38	39	40	41	42
Kharia ...	Agriculturists ...	...	...	98	62	...	...	9	12	2	17	...	...	...	...
Raigarh ...	...	...	...	97	61	...	...	5	6	2	17	...	...	...	...
Jashpur ...	...	...	...	1	1	...	...	4	6	...	...	...	...	...	...
Kharwar ...	Agriculturists ...	...	...	140	165	...	...	2	...	7	1	...	...	8	...
Bilaspur ...	...	...	...	76	69	...	...	2	...	3	1	...	...	...	...
Jashpur ...	...	...	...	64	96	...	...	...	...	4	...	...	...	8	...
Kir ...	Agriculturists ...	...	...	5	3	...	...	7	3	16	28	...	...	...	...
Narsinghpur ...	...	...	...	...	3	...	...	...	...	1	5	...	...	...	...
Hoshangabad ...	...	...	...	5	...	...	...	7	3	15	23	...	...	...	...
Kirar ...	Agriculturists ...	...	...	59	40	4	...	102	23	108	58	...	...	5	...
Plateau Division ...	...	...	...	30	5	2	...	72	21	29	12	...	...	...	...
Narsinghpur ...	...	...	...	3	10	...	...	2	1	3	9	...	...	1	...
Hoshangabad ...	...	...	...	3	16	...	...	12	1	9	3	...	...	3	...
Nagpur ...	...	...	...	23	3	2	...	16	...	67	34	...	...	1	...
Kohli ...	Agriculturists ...	...	...	20	1	1	...	12	6	34	9	...	...	1	...
Chanda ...	...	...	...	13	...	1	...	11	6	12	4	...	...	1	...
Bhandara ...	...	...	...	7	1	...	...	1	...	22	5	...	...	...	...
Kol ...	Agriculturists ...	...	...	838	750	58	3	440	175	317	222	...	...	13	...
Jubbulpore ...	...	...	...	743	675	...	3	287	85	263	207	...	...	5	...
Mandla ...	...	...	...	85	46	58	...	92	46	51	10	...	...	8	...
Chota Nagpur States	...	...	...	10	29	...	...	61	44	3	5	...	...	...	...
Koli															
Berar ...	Fishermen ...	...	1	20[illegible]	110	2	...	28	5	141	140	...	...	23	...
Kolta															
Raigarh ...	Agriculturists ...	1	...	6	27	...	...	2	...	7	19	...	...	1	...
Komti															
Chanda ...	Traders ...	...	...	10	4	...	...	41	1	...	...	...	...	3	...
Kori															
Nerbudda Valley ...	Cotton-weavers...	3	1	898	532	16	1	697	371	212	240	...	...	99	...
Korku ...	Agriculturists ...	...	...	258	152	...	1	212	184	166	130	...	...	13	...
Hoshangabad ...	...	...	...	31	29	...	1	65	43	4	32	...	...	...	...
Nimar ...	...	...	...	42	14	...	...	14	4	28	50	...	...	9	...
Betul ...	...	...	...	159	97	...	...	133	137	110	39	...	...	4	...
Amraoti ...	...	...	...	26	12	...	...	...	...	15	9	...	...	...	...
Koshti ...	Cotton-weavers...	2	...	348	325	11	...	130	78	1,099	514	...	...	23	...
Jubbulpore ...	...	...	...	90	87	...	...	5	1	13	8	...	...	3	...
Seoni ...	...	...	...	3	5	...	...	3	...	5	7	...	...	...	...
Chhindwara ...	...	...	...	4	4	...	...	6	7	52	52	...	...	5	...
Nimar ...	...	...	...	2	...	...	...	[illegible]	8	4	3	...	...	1	...
Maratha Division ...	...	2	...	220	194	10	...	84	45	908	200	...	...	13	...
Chhattisgarh Division.	...	...	...	29	35	1	...	29	17	117	244	...	...	1	...
Kumhar															
Province ...	Potters ...	3	4	482	294	16	...	266	143	277	142	1	...	10	...

Selected Castes, Tribes or Races.

OF ACTUAL WORKERS—(*concluded*).

VII.—Public Administration.				VIII.—Arts and Professions.						IX.—Persons living on their income.		X.—Domestic service.		XI.—Contractors, clerks, cashiers, etc., otherwise unspecified.		XII.—Labourers unspecified.		XIII.—Beggars, prostitutes, criminals and inmates of jails and asylums.	
Gazetted officers.		Others.		Religious.		Lawyers, doctors and teachers.		Others.											
Males.	Females.	Males.	Females.	Males.	Females.	Males.	Females.	Males.	Females.	Males.	Females.	Males.	Females.	Males.	Females.	Males.	Females.	Males.	Females.
43	44	45	46	47	48	49	50	51	52	53	54	55	56	57	58	59	60	61	62
...	...	...	...	...	...	...	...	...	...	...	...	...	30	...	...	18	30	1	3
...	...	...	...	...	...	...	...	...	...	...	...	...	...	...	...	...	...	...	1
...	...	...	...	...	...	...	...	...	...	...	...	...	30	...	...	18	30	1	2
...	...	4	...	...	...	4	...	1	...	...	...	9	9	...	...	...	1	...	2
...	...	1	...	...	...	...	...	...	...	...	...	2	1	...	...	...	...	...	1
...	...	3	...	...	...	4	...	1	...	...	...	7	8	...	...	...	1	...	1
...	...	...	...	...	...	...	...	...	...	...	1	5	1	...	...	1	1	1	3
...	...	...	...	...	...	...	...	...	...	...	...	...	...	...	...	1	1	1	...
...	...	...	...	...	...	...	...	...	...	...	1	5	1	...	...	...	...	...	3
...	...	18	1	1	...	17	1	2	...	1	...	35	15	6	1	25	11	16	12
...	...	3	...	...	...	3	...	...	...	...	...	12	6	4	...	14	4	4	1
...	...	1	1	...	...	5	...	...	...	...	...	5	8	1	...	...	1	3	5
...	...	1	...	1	...	6	1	...	...	...	...	8	5	...	...	...	3	7	5
...	...	13	...	...	...	3	...	2	...	1	...	10	1	1	1	11	3	2	1
...	...	9	...	1	...	11	...	1	...	2	...	11	2	4	...	...	...	5	6
...	...	6	...	1	...	2	...	...	...	...	...	5	...	3	...	...	...	2	3
...	...	3	...	...	...	9	...	1	...	2	...	6	2	1	...	...	...	3	3
...	...	17	...	1	1	1	...	2	3	1	...	35	21	31	22	251	273	87	41
...	...	8	...	...	1	1	...	2	1	1	...	21	13	...	1	240	262	75	36
...	...	7	...	...	...	...	...	...	2	...	...	6	2	31	21	8	11	7	3
...	...	2	...	1	...	...	...	...	...	...	...	8	6	...	...	3	...	5	2
...	...	224	1	7	...	20	...	21	8	3	...	168	20	5	...	27	82	19	29
...	...	2	...	...	...	6	...	...	...	...	...	1	1	...	...	...	...	2	1
...	...	35	1	...	...	8	...	...	...	...	...	6	2	7	...	1	3	3	4
...	...	86	2	2	...	12	3	10	15	7	3	660	45	14	...	217	285	77	40
...	...	25	...	3	...	6	...	3	2	2	...	45	63	8	...	15	17	13	12
...	...	7	...	1	...	...	...	2	...	2	...	7	36	1	...	1	1	3	3
...	...	5	...	...	...	1	...	...	1	...	...	8	4	1	...	6	...	3	5
...	...	12	...	2	...	5	...	1	1	...	...	28	22	...	...	8	11	3	2
...	...	1	...	...	...	...	...	...	...	...	...	2	1	6	...	...	5	4	2
...	...	130	5	12	1	14	5	12	1	13	7	199	150	25	5	84	322	167	93
...	...	3	...	...	...	2	2	...	...	...	3	1	...	...	...	...	7	3	2
...	...	1	...	...	...	...	...	...	...	...	...	...	...	...	...	...	...	...	3
...	...	8	...	...	...	1	...	...	...	...	...	6	2	...	...	3	4	3	...
...	...	3	...	...	...	2	...	...	...	...	...	...	...	...	...	...	...	...	...
...	...	84	4	9	...	5	3	12	1	11	3	171	135	23	1	72	288	152	67
...	...	30	1	3	1	4	...	...	...	2	1	21	13	2	4	9	23	[illegible]	21
...	...	34	2	...	1	20	1	11	1	8	9	117	40	12	1	58	62	50	48

TABLE XVI.—Occupation by

Caste, tribe or race.	Traditional occupation.	Population dealt with: Actual workers. Males.	Actual workers. Females.	Dependants. Males.	Dependants. Females.	Number of actual workers whose traditional caste occupation was returned as their Principal means of livelihood. Males.	Principal means of livelihood. Females.	Subsidiary means of livelihood. Males.	Subsidiary means of livelihood. Females.	Number of actual workers returning their traditional occupation as their principal means of livelihood who had some subsidiary occupation. Males.	Females.
1	2	3	4	5	6	7	8	9	10	11	12
Kunbi ...	Agriculturists ...	**465,522**	**350,264**	**209,780**	**316,434**	**261,931**	**141,923**	**1,930**	**403**	**20,417**	**21,466**
Maratha Division ...	...	431,003	319,604	194,395	296,857	240,307	124,267	1,823	352	18,430	18,364
Chhindwara ...	...	9,350	8,395	4,153	5,093	5,381	3,630	50	32	408	1,041
Nimar ...	...	9,737	7,022	4,458	5,841	6,558	5,167	3	4	316	72
Betul ...	...	15,432	14,343	6,774	8,643	9,685	8,859	54	15	1,263	1,089
Kuranwar Chanda ...	Shepherds ...	1,321	1,232	563	660	1,108	1,002	27	4	520	301
Kurmi ...	Agriculturists ...	**91,108**	**70,469**	**49,971**	**72,763**	**71,277**	**53,932**	**596**	**223**	**6,283**	**1,842**
Nerbudda Valley ...	...	37,410	25,044	19,885	30,962	27,848	17,572	302	52	2,885	595
Plateau Division ...	...	10,405	8,512	4,972	7,015	7,817	5,988	23	28	807	541
Chhattisgarh Division ...	...	43,293	36,913	25,114	34,786	35,612	30,372	271	143	2,591	706
Lodhi Province ...	Agriculturists ...	101,650	83,802	53,524	73,308	74,140	59,189	537	149	5,715	1,806
Lohar Province ...	Ironsmiths ...	58,769	41,850	32,160	48,532	35,770	10,232	4,859	589	7,514	1,337
Madgi Chanda ...	Leather-workers ...	1,623	1,528	1,054	1,100	1,250	372	64	13	592	205
Majhwar ...	Labourers ...	**1,824**	**668**	**1,057**	**2,118**	**437**	**275**	**9**	**8**	**9**	**1**
Surguja ...	...	888	62	516	1,323	203	32	2	...	...	...
Udaipur ...	...	936	606	541	795	234	243	7	8	9	1
Mala Chanda ...	Labourers ...	1,157	1,014	778	871	611	640	122	134	35	50
Mali Province ...	Vegetables and fruit-growers.	188,117	166,380	91,472	115,263	13,153	14,871	9,093	6,790	1,985	1,348
Mallah ...	Boatmen ...	**1,023**	**916**	**663**	**793**	**3**	...	...	...	...	...
Jubbulpore ...	...	541	464	357	439	3	...	...	...	...	...
Narsinghpur ...	...	482	452	306	354	...	...	...	...	...	...
Mana Nagpur Division ...	Agriculturists ...	14,641	14,366	6,344	7,498	6,410	6,220	53	11	659	2,294
Mang Maratha Division ...	Native Musicians...	26,097	25,193	11,840	14,014	7,048	382	2,632	127	3,302	308
Maratha Province ...	Soldiers ...	32,050	17,280	14,651	29,898	1,104	...	150	...	157	...
Mehra or Mahar Province ...	Cotton-weavers ...	385,050	367,407	189,978	221,948	47,430	36,337	5,820	2,755	10,104	8,248
Mehtar ...	Scavengers ...	**6,319**	**5,460**	**3,239**	**3,834**	**4,948**	**4,261**	**145**	**124**	**421**	**281**
Nerbudda Valley ...	...	4,682	3,945	2,266	2,775	3,894	3,306	143	122	414	276
Nagpur ...	...	881	778	566	585	843	744	...	...	2	1
Raipur ...	...	756	737	407	474	211	211	2	2	5	4
Mhali Maratha Division ...	Barbers ...	12,943	8,401	5,900	9,612	9,625	...	1,315	...	2,304	...
Nai Province ...	Barbers ...	47,685	33,339	25,112	39,954	31,947	...	7,861	...	8,935	...
Oraon ...	Agriculturists ...	**22,218**	**14,709**	**16,683**	**23,489**	**19,700**	**11,834**	**54**	**80**	**380**	**240**
Raigarh ...	...	1,722	1,636	1,282	1,468	1,182	1,025	16	12	235	142
Chota Nagpur States ...	...	20,496	13,073	15,401	22,021	18,518	10,809	38	68	145	98

Selected Castes, Tribes or Races.

RECORDED PRINCIPAL OCCUPATION OF ACTUAL WORKERS.

I.—Exploitation of the surface of the soil.												II.—Extraction of Minerals.			
Income from rent of land.		Cultivators of all kinds.		Agents and managers of landed estates, planters, forest officers and their clerks, rent collectors, etc.		Field labourers, wood-cutters, etc.		Raisers of live-stock, milkmen and herdsmen.		Fishing and hunting.		Owners, managers, clerks, etc.		Labourers.	
Males.	Females.	Males.	Females.	Males.	Females.	Males.	Females.	Males.	Females.	Males.	Females.	Males.	Females.	Males.	Females.
13	14	15	16	17	18	19	20	21	22	23	24	25	26	27	28
...	...	...	...	433	35	160,194	200,10[illegible]	17,051	648	78	6	16	1	449	208
...	...	...	...	386	34	150,729	187,954	15,779	637	77	[illegible]	15	1	446	207
...	...	...	...	12	...	3,202	4,598	252	...	...	...	1	...	3	1
...	...	...	...	7	1	2,086	2,356	64	2	1	...	...	...	...	...
...	...	...	...	28	...	4,177	5,197	956	9	...	...	...	...	...	...
...	...	11	5	...	...	16	35	...	...	...	...	...	...	...	...
...	...	...	...	172	4	14,532	14,985	1,678	83	4	3	1	...	54	14
...	...	...	...	78	4	6,582	6,785	1,188	55	...	1	...	...	30	8
...	...	...	...	37	...	1,545	2,250	270	8	...	...	1	...	15	6
...	...	...	...	57	...	6,405	5,941	220	20	4	2	...	...	...	...
...	...	...	...	97	2	20,599	22,557	2,704	146	2	...	18	...	258	149
118	195	11,837	12,402	41	5	5,550	17,335	843	74	7	6	1	...	147	76
4	1	120	235	...	...	178	816	17	...	...	...	...	...	...	...
...	...	1,375	378	...	...	...	...	4	3	1	6	...	...	...	...
...	...	683	27	...	...	...	...	...	2	...	...	...	...	...	...
...	...	692	351	...	...	...	...	4	1	1	6	...	...	...	...
6	...	446	320	...	...	...	...	24	8	...	...	...	...	...	...
1,503	1,042	98,294	67,608	200	...	62,233	77,475	3,585	109	2	9	...	...	242	203
3	...	651	471	...	...	242	320	10	1	...	...	...	...	1	1
1	...	359	288	...	...	124	150	5	...	...	...	...	...	1	1
2	...	292	183	...	...	118	170	5	1	...	...	...	...	...	...
...	...	...	...	33	...	6,527	8,056	1,249	7	2	1	...	...	11	4
30	15	874	362	11	...	11,564	17,770	878	37	64	5	...	...	33	19
622	406	14,332	4,063	132	2	8,041	10,281	530	47	...	...	8	...	22	5
1,368	470	89,104	68,558	402	...	162,589	234,199	16,160	2,100	257	4	...	2	2,890	2,028
1	...	233	160	5	...	274	281	78	18	...	...	...	...	1	...
...	...	46	30	4	...	134	145	53	13	...	...	...	...	1	...
...	...	...	...	...	...	...	...	3	...	...	...	...	...	...	...
1	...	187	130	1	...	140	136	22	5	...	...	...	...	...	...
104	89	2,065	1,838	4	...	565	5,183	191	13	...	...	...	...	10	5
162	90	12,335	11,688	41	3	1,416	10,269	400	36	1	...	...	...	12	8
...	...	...	...	1	...	1,835	2,178	367	277	...	...	...	...	...	...
...	...	...	...	...	...	395	511	2	8	...	...	...	...	...	...
...	...	...	...	1	...	1,440	1,667	365	274	...	...	...	...	...	...

TABLE XVI.—Occupation by

Caste, tribe or race.	Traditional occupation.	Recorded principal occupation													
		III.—Industries.				IV.—Transport.				V.—Trade.		VI.—Public Force.			
		Owners, managers, clerks, etc.		Artisans and other workmen.		Owners, managers, ships' officers, etc.		Labourers, boatmen, carters, palki-bearers, etc.				Commissioned and gazetted officers.		Others.	
		Males.	Females.	Males.	Females.	Males.	Females.	Males.	Females.	Males.	Females.	Males.	Females.	Males.	Females.
1	2	29	30	31	32	33	34	35	36	37	38	39	40	41	42
Kunbi ...	Agriculturists..	71	2	6,099	2,735	86	4	3,669	585	4,226	985	...	...	596	...
Maratha Division ...	...	69	2	5,465	2,503	81	4	3,047	352	3,895	828	...	..	576	...
Chhindwara ...	...	...	...	104	70	2	...	144	12	85	28	...	...	4	...
Nimar ...	...	2	...	427	137	2	...	272	126	158	45	...	...	9	...
Betul ...	...	...	...	103	25	1	...	206	95	88	84	...	...	7	...
Kuramwar Chanda ...	Shepherds ...	...	...	39	159	...	...	3	...	132	19	...	...	...	...
Kurmi ...	Agriculturists...	2	...	556	395	21	2	1,116	143	574	512	...	...	76	...
Nerbudda Valley ...	...	1	...	332	258	4	...	648	72	201	135	...	...	31	...
Plateau Division ...	...	...	...	112	37	6	2	268	56	130	70	...	...	29	...
Chhattisgarh Division.	...	1	...	112	100	11	...	200	15	243	208	...	...	16	...
Lodhi Province ...	Agriculturists...	39	...	944	561	14	5	1,118	128	608	552	...	...	60	...
Lohar Province ...	Ironsmiths ...	32	4	3,207	627	26	7	365	116	278	270	2	...	39	...
Madgi Chanda ...	Leather-workers	...	...	...	7	...	...	5	1	3	3	...	...	2	...
Majhwar ...	Labourers ...	...	...	...	...	...	...	1	...	1	2	...	...	...	...
Surguja ..	...	...	...	...	...	...	...	...	...	...	...	...	...	...	...
Udaipur ...	...	...	...	...	...	...	...	1	...	1	2	...	...	...	...
Mala Chanda ...	Labourers ...	...	...	...	...	...	...	3	4	11	3	...	...	1	...
Mali Province ...	Vegetables and fruit-growers.	20	4	2,053	1,241	35	1	1,142	270	2,378	2,343	...	...	164	...
Mallah ...	Boatmen ...	...	...	83	58	...	...	5	...	6	53	6	...	...	...
Jubbulpore ...	...	...	...	23	8	...	...	5	...	2	5	6	...	...	...
Narsinghpur ...	...	...	...	60	50	...	...	...	...	4	48	...	...	...	...
Mana Nagpur Division ...	Agriculturists	1	...	164	33	2	...	34	5	74	8	...	...	7	...
Mang Maratha Division ..	Native Musicians.	3	...	2,190	2,996	...	...	137	52	735	1,194	...	...	730	...
Maratha Province ...	Soldiers ...	62	...	1,677	876	52	...	1,437	116	968	384	...	...	89	...
Mehra or Mahar Province ...	Cotton-weavers	80	13	12,767	8,985	270	5	9,798	4,223	9,170	6,059	...	...	24,961	10
Mehtar ...	Scavengers ...	...	1	534	415	...	...	45	94	35	99	...	...	...	...
Nerbudda Valley ...	...	...	1	339	271	...	...	40	1	20	59	...	...	...	...
Nagpur ...	...	...	...	23	27	...	...	...	...	1	1	...	...	...	...
Raipur ...	...	...	...	172	117	...	...	5	93	14	39	...	...	...	...
Mhali Maratha Division ...	Barbers ...	1	...	87	853	5	...	19	5	60	200	...	...	14	...
Nai Province ...	Barbers ...	5	1	254	3,207	9	...	128	58	241	294	1	...	67	...
Oraon ...	Agriculturists...	...	...	164	141	...	...	36	43	45	57	1	...	6	...
Raigarh ...	...	...	...	116	73	...	...	5	7	20	16	...	...	...	...
Chota Nagpur States	...	...	...	48	68	...	...	31	36	25	41	1	...	6	...

Selected Castes, Tribes or Races.

OF ACTUAL WORKERS—*(concluded)*

VII.—Public Administration.				VIII.—Arts and Professions.						IX.—Persons living on their income.		X.—Domestic service.		XI.—Contractors, clerks, cashiers, etc., otherwise unspecified.		XII.—Labourers unspecified.		XIII.—Beggars, prostitutes, criminals and inmates of jails and asylums.	
Gazetted officers.		Others.		Religious.		Lawyers, doctors and teachers.		Others.											
Males.	Females.	Males.	Females.	Males.	Females.	Males.	Females.	Males.	Females.	Males.	Females.	Males.	Females.	Males.	Females.	Males.	Females.	Males.	Females.
43	44	45	46	47	48	49	50	51	52	53	54	55	56	57	58	59	60	61	62
2	...	3,325	14	110	16	769	12	229	80	187	59	3,298	1,029	246	16	1,129	1,309	1,328	492
2	...	3,228	13	107	16	720	11	181	75	183	59	3,108	903	232	9	1,071	1,248	1,299	475
...	...	47	1	3	...	18	...	4	...	2	...	46	12	7	...	29	38	4	5
...	...	17	...	...	...	11	...	12	4	...	...	72	58	3	...	21	21	15	5
...	...	33	...	...	...	20	1	32	1	2	...	72	56	4	7	8	2	10	7
...	...	...	...	...	...	1	...	...	...	...	...	...	4	2	...	...	1	9	7
3	...	216	5	23	2	127	8	18	8	42	...	303	154	17	4	152	123	144	97
...	...	60	4	3	...	32	6	11	1	7	...	145	51	8	...	110	65	82	27
1	...	36	1	2	...	36	1	1	...	4	...	54	37	5	...	12	28	24	10
2	...	120	...	18	2	59	1	6	2	31	...	104	66	4	4	30	30	38	60
1	...	130	1	12	4	62	6	18	5	16	5	328	176	18	...	206	226	199	90
...	...	75	2	6	1	53	7	13	6	6	12	134	120	29	2	82	197	108	94
...	...	3	...	...	...	...	...	2	5	4	...	2	3	...	...	16	69	11	17
...	...	...	...	1	...	...	...	...	...	...	...	1	3	1	...	...	...	2	1
...	...	...	...	...	...	...	...	...	...	...	...	1	...	...	...	...	...	1	1
...	...	...	...	1	...	...	...	...	...	...	...	...	3	1	...	...	...	1	...
...	...	23	...	...	...	...	1	1	1	...	...	9	1	...	...	...	...	22	36
1	...	632	...	63	41	285	9	84	33	35	17	1,151	363	85	11	395	481	382	249
...	...	...	...	1	...	...	...	...	...	...	...	2	...	...	...	7	12	3	...
...	...	...	...	1	...	...	...	...	...	...	...	1	...	...	...	7	12	3	...
...	...	...	...	...	...	...	...	...	...	...	...	1	...	...	...	...	...	...	...
...	...	23	...	1	...	12	...	3	3	3	...	41	10	8	...	11	7	25	12
...	...	80	12	43	22	1	...	77	1,279	2	...	154	156	11	1	92	167	728	724
...	...	973	...	45	12	248	22	154	71	86	29	725	527	92	13	211	190	355	236
...	...	33	...	64	53	317	90	473	710	48	11	2,701	931	103	25	500	581	3,460	1,944
...	...	...	...	...	...	1	1	23	41	...	...	76	6[illegible]	2	...	19	4	44	20
...	...	...	...	...	...	...	1	22	38	...	...	74	62	2	...	19	2	34	16
...	...	...	...	...	...	1	...	...	1	...	...	2	1	...	...	...	2	8	2
...	...	...	...	...	...	...	...	1	2	...	...	...	2	...	...	...	...	2	2
...	...	52	1	2	...	20	25	5	25	3	1	65	263	6	1	10	2	24	19
...	...	140	3	24	14	126	11	33	70	14	3	206	7,410	12	...	34	85	76	89
...	...	1	...	...	2	2	...	...	...	...	...	36	87	1	7	12	32	11	51
...	...	...	...	...	...	...	...	...	...	...	...	2	1	...	...	...	...	...	...
...	...	1	...	...	2	2	...	...	...	...	...	34	86	1	7	12	32	11	51

TABLE XVI.—Occupation by

Caste, tribe or race.	Traditional occupation.	Population dealt with				Number of actual workers whose traditional caste occupation was returned as their				Number of actual workers returning their traditional occupation as their principal means of livelihood who had some subsidiary occupation.	
		Actual workers.		Dependants.		Principal means of livelihood.		Subsidiary means of livelihood.			
		Males.	Females.	Males.	Females.	Males.	Females.	Males.	Females.	Males.	Females.
1	2	3	4	5	6	7	8	9	10	11	12
Paik											
Raipur ...	Soldiers ...	972	592	568	1,043	79	...	7	...	...	...
Panchal											
Maratha Division ...	Ironsmiths ...	2,656	1,259	1,523	3,126	1,450	445	43	...	152	14
Panka ...	Cotton-weavers ...	**41,762**	**40,865**	**21,880**	**28,471**	**5,483**	**5,003**	**3,312**	**96**	**696**	**417**
Mandla ...	...	5,527	5,115	3,179	3,798	456	491	166	87	51	31
Seoni ...	...	788	798	397	450	18	9	3	...	...	...
Balaghat ...	...	961	929	490	581	21	7	1	...	1	...
Chhattisgarh Division	...	34,486	34,023	17,814	23,636	4,988	4,496	3,142	9	644	386
Patwa ...	Silk-workers ...	**1,585**	**1,302**	**851**	**1,232**	**932**	**735**	**135**	**69**	**129**	**41**
Nerbudda Valley ...	...	1,033	787	622	876	588	355	53	16	104	33
Chhattisgarh Division	...	552	515	229	356	344	380	82	53	25	8
Rajjhar or Lajjhar ...	Labourers ...	**1,243**	**1,300**	**624**	**738**	**821**	**1,010**	**19**	**8**	**31**	**104**
Seoni ...	...	374	436	216	236	276	354	...	...	...	...
Hoshangabad ...	...	418	385	237	295	239	330	10	5	28	16
Betul ...	...	451	479	171	207	306	326	9	3	3	88
Rajput											
Province ...	Soldiers ...	151,843	100,822	71,260	116,398	3,955	...	78	...	465	...
Sali ...	Silk-weavers ...	**1,066**	**1,096**	**536**	**551**	**686**	**652**	**17**	**14**	**68**	**12**
Amraoti ...	...	633	666	357	350	279	296	17	14	63	12
Buldana ...	...	433	430	179	201	407	356	...	...	5	...
Sawara or Saonr ...	Agriculturists ...	**16,906**	**16,378**	**9,508**	**11,351**	**8,003**	**7,081**	**142**	**78**	**455**	**211**
Saugor ...	...	5,659	5,677	3,403	3,788	2,084	1,845	53	23	119	76
Damoh ...	...	2,051	2,093	1,192	1,369	723	561	14	40	141	44
Chhattisgarh Division	...	9,196	8,608	4,913	6,194	5,196	4,675	75	9	195	91
Sunar											
Province ...	Goldsmiths ...	40,567	15,081	23,263	47,953	27,892	1,405	3,555	67	4,094	113
Takari											
Akola ...	Grinding Mill Repairers.	1,210	977	510	626	216	83	86	21	105	21
Teli											
Province ...	Oil-pressers ...	276,889	250,944	150,235	191,268	19,066	20,847	11,140	8,598	5,410	3,252
Waddar											
Yeotmal ...	Earthworkers ...	1,359	1,085	822	906	816	305	7	11	22	10
Wanjari ...											
Berar ...	Carriers ...	11,820	9,925	4,547	6,495	195	235	7	...	72	6
Europeans ...											
Province ...	...	4,893	375	554	1,511	...	...	...	...	...	...
Anglo-Indians											
Province ...	...	950	194	933	1,411	...	...	...	...	...	...
Indian Christians											
Province ...	...	18,641	14,036	13,237	16,666	...	...	...	...	...	...

Selected Castes, Tribes or Races.

Recorded principal occupation of actual workers.															
I.—Exploitation of the surface of the soil.												II.—Extraction of Minerals.			
Income from rent of land.		Cultivators of all kinds.		Agents and managers of landed estates, planters, forest officers and their clerks, rent collectors, etc.		Field labourers, wood-cutters, etc.		Raisers of live-stock, milk-men and herdsmen.		Fishing and hunting.		Owners, managers, clerks, etc.		Labourers.	
Males.	Females.	Males.	Females.	Males.	Females.	Males.	Females.	Males.	Females.	Males.	Females.	Males.	Females.	Males.	Females.
13	14	15	16	17	18	19	20	21	22	23	24	25	26	27	28
2	...	646	333	12	...	143	126	11	...	2	...	...	...	...	...
11	5	131	182	5	...	88	398	10	1	...	...	...	...	...	...
26	19	19,530	20,456	9	...	10,500	13,580	506	178	...	3	...	...	3	12
1	...	2,726	2,791	...	...	1,234	1,578	242	145	...	2	...	...	...	...
1	1	299	307	...	...	328	459	30	5	...	...	...	...	...	...
...	...	468	508	...	...	279	328	15	7	...	...	...	...	3	10
24	18	16,037	16,850	9	...	8,659	11,215	210	21	...	1	...	...	...	2
9	8	247	144	3	...	69	43	6	...	...	...	...	...	3	4
7	1	92	51	3	...	52	27	6	...	...	...	...	...	3	4
2	8	155	93	...	...	17	16	...	...	...	...	...	...	...	...
4	2	345	168	...	1	...	...	51	3	...	...	...	...	...	...
...	...	80	78	...	...	...	...	15	...	...	...	...	...	...	...
2	...	171	37	...	1	...	...	3	...	...	...	...	...	...	...
2	2	94	53	...	...	...	...	33	3	...	...	...	...	...	...
1,991	939	96,872	70,496	904	3	26,640	24,274	3,570	177	45	8	14	...	218	60
3	9	72	3	...	...	97	162	2	...	...	...	...	...	...	...
3	9	67	2	...	...	97	161	2	...	...	...	...	...	...	...
...	...	5	1	...	...	...	1	...	...	...	...	...	...	...	...
...	...	...	...	11	...	7,684	8,454	648	250	7	2	3	...	3	22
...	...	...	...	4	...	2,907	3,247	327	235	...	...	3	...	...	17
...	...	...	...	1	...	1,159	1,464	92	6	...	...	...	...	...	...
...	...	...	...	6	...	3,618	3,743	220	9	7	2	...	...	3	5
267	139	7,191	5,703	65	...	1,609	6,025	171	43	...	...	1	...	21	8
6	1	212	55	...	...	667	832	36	1	...	...	...	...	...	...
2,673	948	157,396	136,361	141	15	70,745	82,566	6,129	241	2	7	8	...	344	97
...	...	12	2	...	...	107	513	38	6	...	...	...	...	...	...
40	20	5,614	3,224	...	...	5,051	6,189	586	47	10	2	...	...	...	...
...	...	3	1	26	1	...	...	...	...	...	...	22	...	...	...
1	2	1	3	9	...	...	...	...	...	...	...	8	...	...	...
11	1	13,111	11,818	369	4	189	173	119	212	12	...	2	1	27	16

TABLE XVI.—Occupation by

Caste, tribe or race.	Traditional occupation.	Recorded principal occupation													
		III.—Industries.				IV.—Transport.				V.—Trade.		VI.—Public Force.			
		Owners, managers, clerks, etc.		Artisans and other workmen.		Owners, managers, ships' officers, etc.		Labourers, boatmen, carters, palki-bearers, etc.				Commissioned and gazetted officers.		Others.	
		Males.	Females.	Males.	Females.	Males.	Females.	Males.	Females.	Males.	Females.	Males.	Females.	Males.	Females.
1	2	29	30	31	32	33	34	35	36	37	38	39	40	41	42
Paik															
Raipur ...	Soldiers ...	1	...	21	60	...	...	7	3	16	48	...	...	...	...
Panchal															
Maratha Division ...	Ironsmiths ...	...	...	823	123	...	...	6	2	36	42	...	...	3	...
Panka ...	Cotton-weavers...	...	...	88	74	5	1	514	234	486	736	...	...	3,655	42
Mandla ...	...	...	...	30	12	...	...	70	28	84	27	...	...	615	16
Seoni ...	...	...	...	7	5	...	...	1	1	2	...	...	...	80	...
Balaghat ...	...	...	...	10	2	...	...	17	8	17	18	...	...	16	...
Chhattisgarh Division.	...	...	...	41	55	5	1	426	197	383	691	...	...	2,944	26
Patwa ...	Silk-workers ...	...	...	90	80	...	...	9	1	198	279	...	...	...	...
Nerbudda Valley ...	...	...	...	83	74	...	...	8	1	181	270	...	...	...	...
Chhattisgarh Division.	...	...	...	7	6	...	...	1	...	17	9	...	...	...	...
Rajjhar or Lajjhar...	Labourers ...	1	...	...	...	...	...	6	...	7	112	...	...	...	...
Seoni ...	...	...	...	...	...	...	...	2	...	...	...	...	...	...	...
Hoshangabad ...	...	...	...	...	...	...	...	1	...	2	17	...	...	...	...
Betul ...	...	1	...	...	...	...	...	3	...	5	95	...	...	...	...
Rajput															
Province ...	Soldiers ...	67	2	3,170	1,360	317	10	3,872	514	4,386	1,723	6	...	355	...
Sali ...	Silk weavers ...	...	...	104	182	...	...	2	...	72	65	...	...	...	...
Amraoti ...	...	...	...	100	178	...	...	2	...	57	...	...	...	...	...
Buldana ...	...	...	...	4	4	...	...	...	...	15	65	...	...	...	...
Sawara or Saonr ...	Agriculturists ...	...	...	160	160	...	...	60	13	191	277	...	...	43	...
Saugor ...	...	...	...	135	102	...	...	30	4	139	162	...	...	4	...
Damoh ...	...	...	...	8	18	...	...	8	1	21	20	...	...	3	...
Chhattisgarh Division.	...	...	...	17	40	...	...	22	8	31	95	...	...	36	...
Sunar															
Province ...	Goldsmiths ...	20	...	1,223	672	17	...	120	30	974	632	1	...	64	...
Takari															
Akola ...	Grinding Mill Repairers.	...	...	4	1	...	...	4	...	6	1	...	...	...	...
Teli															
Province ...	Oil-pressers ...	35	5	3,367	1,940	101	1	3,981	964	9,472	5,060	...	...	172	...
Waddar															
Yeotmal ...	Earth-workers ...	...	...	249	100	...	...	22	20	105	62	...	...	...	...
Wanjari															
Berar ...	Carriers ...	...	...	81	35	1	...	27	45	73	30	...	...	5	...
Europeans															
Province ...	...	82	...	...	...	378	6	...	...	40	1	211	...	3,602	...
Anglo-Indians															
Province ...	...	56	4	...	...	217	3	...	...	8	...	6	...	38	...
Indian Christians															
Province ...	...	47	1	1,044	331	148	3	220	142	142	29	12	...	59	...

Selected Castes, Tribes or Races.

OF ACTUAL WORKERS—(*concluded*).

VII.—Public Administration.				VIII.—Arts and Professions.						IX.—Persons living on their income.		X.—Domestic service.		XI.—Contractors, clerks, cashiers, etc., otherwise unspecified.		XII.—Labourers unspecified.		XIII.—Beggars, prostitutes, criminals and inmates of jails and asylums.	
Gazetted officers.		Others.		Religious.		Lawyers, doctors and teachers.		Others.											
Males.	Females.	Males.	Females.	Males.	Females.	Males.	Females.	Males.	Females.	Males.	Females.	Males.	Females.	Males.	Females.	Males.	Females.	Males.	Females.
43	44	45	46	47	48	49	50	51	52	53	54	55	56	57	58	59	60	61	62
...	...	1	...	1	1	4	...	2	...	...	...	16	11	5	...	...	...	3	6
...	...	10	...	2	1	14	2	3	5	1	2	46	27	4	...	2	14	12	10
...	...	98	...	42	19	96	4	39	19	2	...	273	113	14	5	65	60	328	307
...	...	11	...	2	2	6	...	7	...	1	...	7	6	2	...	8	5	25	12
...	...	2	...	...	...	...	...	1	7	...	...	2	1	...	...	...	...	17	3
...	...	64	...	...	3	1	...	...	5	...	...	14	7	...	...	7	3	29	23
...	...	21	...	40	14	80	4	31	7	1	...	250	90	12	5	50	52	257	269
...	...	3	...	1	...	9	1	...	...	...	3	3	1	...	...	...	...	3	2
...	...	2	...	...	...	3	...	...	...	...	2	2	1	...	...	...	...	3	1
...	...	1	...	1	...	6	1	...	...	...	1	1	...	...	...	...	...	...	1
...	...	...	...	...	...	...	...	...	...	...	...	8	4	...	...	...	...	...	...
...	...	...	...	...	...	...	...	...	...	...	...	1	4	...	...	...	...	...	...
...	...	...	...	...	...	...	...	...	...	...	...	...	...	...	...	...	...	...	...
...	...	...	...	...	...	...	...	...	...	...	...	7	...	...	...	...	...	...	...
25	...	1,583	...	104	13	746	37	247	52	172	61	1,768	480	268	9	412	261	641	331
...	...	3	...	...	...	2	...	1	...	...	...	7	2	...	...	1	7	14	14
...	...	3	...	...	...	2	...	1	...	...	...	7	1	...	...	1	5	12	14
...	...	...	...	...	...	...	...	...	...	...	...	...	1	...	...	...	2	2	...
...	...	3	...	...	1	5	...	1	3	...	...	27	62	...	...	30	32	27	21
...	...	1	...	...	...	...	...	...	3	...	...	13	40	...	...	6	12	6	10
...	...	...	...	...	...	1	...	...	...	...	...	4	3	...	...	18	15	13	5
...	...	2	...	...	1	4	...	1	...	...	...	10	19	...	...	6	5	8	6
5	...	181	...	22	1	205	12	16	12	34	20	182	178	37	5	57	106	120	84
...	...	47	...	...	...	1	...	...	...	...	...	8	...	...	...	3	2	...	1
3	...	466	...	50	11	124	12	50	13	58	11	1,049	334	124	1	770	1,059	645	445
...	...	1	...	...	...	1	...	...	...	...	...	...	13	...	...	2	48	5	10
...	...	45	...	1	...	3	...	[illegible]	1	...	...	33	20	...	...	16	54	26	14
129	...	130	3	145	188	45	96	11	1	53	38	2	30	7	...	...	...	1	4
35	...	360	21	16	22	116	44	[illegible]	12	52	55	15	20	4	1	...	...	1	1
3	...	353	3	538	270	448	261	223	52	179	58	1,233	541	24	21	86	63	30	36

APPENDIX TO TABLE XVI.

Occupations of minor Industrial Castes.

Serial No.	Caste, Tribe or Race.	Traditional occupation.	Locality.	Population dealt with: Actual workers.	Population dealt with: Dependants.	Principal occupations of actual workers.
	1	2	3	4	5	6
1	Agaria ...	Iron-smelters ...	Chhattisgarh Division.	1,589	1,033	Iron-smelters (994), agriculturists (375), field-labourers, wood-cutters, etc. (176), others (44).
2	Besta ...	Fishermen ...	Chanda ...	407	301	Fishermen (205), agriculturists (78), artisans and other workmen (40), field-labourers, wood-cutters, etc. (37), others (47).
3	Bharbhunja	Grain-parchers ...	Raipur ...	129	218	Grain-parchers (69), agriculturists (35), others (25).
4	Bhulia ...	Cotton-weavers ...	Raipur ...	1,757	1,056	Cotton-weavers (1,230), agriculturists (460), others (67).
5	Chhipa ...	Cotton-painters ...	Jubbulpore ...	737	626	Cotton-painters (547), agriculturists (67), artisans and other workmen (30), traders (30), others (63).
			Narsinghpur ...	392	390	Cotton-painters (285, labourers in the extraction of minerals (22), others (85).
6	Chitari ...	Painters ...	Maratha Division	534	420	Painters (234), field-labourers, wood-cutters, etc. (145), agriculturists (73), others (82).
7	Dhuri ...	Grain-parchers ...	Bilaspur ...	1,253	852	Grain-parchers (42), agriculturists (1,016), field-labourers, wood-cutters, etc. (126), others (69).
8	Dohor ...	Leather-workers ...	Buldana ...	1,820	1,135	Leather-workers (888), field-labourers, wood-cutters, etc. (760), agriculturists (120), others (52).
9	Gandhi ...	Perfumers ...	Maratha Division	57	81	Perfumers (20), others (37).
10	Gandli ...	Oil-pressers ...	Chanda ...	1,368	1,007	Oil-pressers (307), agriculturists (748), field-labourers, wood-cutters, etc. (143), traders (103), others (67).
11	Jingar ...	Saddle-makers ...	Maratha Division	816	739	Saddle-makers (491), artisans and other workmen (108), traders (90), field-labourers, wood-cutters, etc. (88), others (39).
12	Kachera ...	Glass bangle-makers	Province ...	1,311	914	Glass bangle-makers (793), agriculturists (236), field-labourers, wood-cutters, etc. (139), traders (94), others (49).
13	Kadera ...	Gunpowder-makers	Nerbudda Valley...	1,230	820	Gunpowder-makers (475), field-labourers, wood-cutters, etc. (533), agriculturists (72), traders (39), others (111).
14	Kasar ...	Brass-workers ...	Wardha ...	419	439	Brass-workers (102), traders (111), field-labourers, wood-cutters, etc. (77), agriculturists (75), others (54).
			Nagpur ...	371	574	Brass-workers (126), traders (122), agriculturists (48), field-labourers, wood-cutters, etc. (19), others (56).
15	Khatik ...	Butchers ...	Jubbulpore ...	687	857	Butchers (380), traders (217), others (90).
16	Koskati ...	Kosa-weavers ...	Chanda ...	699	391	Kosa-workers (580), others (119).
17	Kundera ...	Lacquerers ...	Nerbudda Valley...	35	67	Lacquerers (13), others (22).
18	Lakhera ...	Lac bangle-makers	Nerbudda Valley...	1,002	714	Lac bangle-makers (817), traders (78), agriculturists (46), others (61).
19	Lonari ...	Salt manufacturers	Berar ...	663	334	Salt manufacturers (24), field-labourers, wood-cutters, etc. (427), traders (75), agriculturists (71), artisans and other workmen (49), others (17).
20	Mochi ...	Book-binders ...	Nerbudda Valley ...	716	787	Book-binders (181), artisans and other workmen (270), labourers, carters, palki-bearers, etc. (112), traders (44), others (109).
21	Otari ...	Bell-metal castors	Maratha Division	1,374	886	Bell-metal casters (997), field-labourers, wood-cutters, etc. (191), agriculturists (100), others (86).
22	Pathrat ...	Stone-workers ...	Maratha Division	520	356	Stone-workers (207), field-labourers, wood-cutters, etc. (268), others (45).
23	Rangari ...	Dyers ...	Nimar ...	551	402	Dyers (318), traders (56), artisans and other workmen (36), labourers, carters, palki-bearers, etc. (35), field-labourers, wood-cutters, etc. (34), agriculturists (28), others (44).
			Wardha ...	635	578	Dyers (241), field-labourers, wood-cutters, etc. (152), traders (110), agriculturists (75), others (57).
24	Sonjhara ...	Gold-washers ...	Chhattisgarh Division.	274	156	Gold-washers (90), agriculturists (119), others (65).
25	Tamera ...	Coppersmiths ...	Saugor ...	250	437	Coppersmiths (227), others (23).
			Jubbulpore ...	313	518	Coppersmiths (231), agriculturists (30), traders (23), others (29).
			Maratha Division	364	407	Coppersmiths (238), field-labourers, wood-cutters, etc. (60), artisans and other workmen (27), others (39).

TABLE XVII.

Territorial Distribution of the Christian Population by Sect and Race.

TABLE XVII.—Territorial Distribution of the

Serial number.	DISTRICT OR STATE.	ALL DENOMINATIONS. Distribution by race. Total. Persons.	Total. Males.	Total. Females.	European and allied races. Males.	European and allied races. Females.	Anglo-Indian. Males.	Anglo-Indian. Females.	Indian. Males.	Indian. Females.	ANGLICAN COMMUNION. Distribution by race. Total. Persons.	Total. Males.	Total. Females.	European and allied races. Males.	European and allied races. Females.	Anglo-Indian. Males.	Anglo-Indian. Females.	Indian. Males.	Indian. Females.
	1	2	3	4	5	6	7	8	9	10	11	12	13	14	15	16	17	18	19
	Central Provinces and Berar ...	**73,401**	**39,208**	**34,193**	**5,447**	**1,886**	**1,883**	**1,605**	**31,878**	**30,702**	**8,240**	**5,593**	**2,647**	**3,939**	**1,045**	**752**	**682**	**902**	**920**
	C. P. British Districts and Berar ...	**34,697**	**19,731**	**14,966**	**5,395**	**1,853**	**1,812**	**1,531**	**12,524**	**11,582**	**8,119**	**5,528**	**2,591**	**3,910**	**1,031**	**722**	**643**	**896**	**917**
	C. P. British Districts .	**31,874**	**18,210**	**13,664**	**5,299**	**1,755**	**1,656**	**1,382**	**11,255**	**10,527**	**7,839**	**5,368**	**2,471**	**3,860**	**1,001**	**630**	**573**	**878**	**897**
	JUBBULPORE DIVISION ...	*9,845*	*6,259*	*3,586*	*3,395*	*938*	*404*	*482*	*2,460*	*2,165*	*4,941*	*3,455*	*1,486*	*2,663*	*604*	*165*	*189*	*628*	*693*
1	Saugor ...	1,454	777	677	196	134	80	88	501	455	292	190	102	150	66	40	36	...	...
2	Damoh ...	437	337	100	21	14	16	25	300	61	36	21	15	10	4	4	6	7	5
3	Jubbulpore ...	6,880	4,554	2,326	3,130	766	260	329	1,164	1,231	3,929	2,882	1,047	2,467	519	117	136	298	392
4	Mandla ...	871	491	380	35	20	39	27	417	333	669	351	318	27	14	4	8	320	296
5	Seoni ...	202	100	102	13	4	9	13	78	85	15	11	4	8	1	...	3	3	...
	NERBUDDA DIVISION ...	*7,463*	*4,025*	*3,438*	*458*	*286*	*78*	*82*	*3,489*	*3,070*	*477*	*282*	*195*	*230*	*140*	*29*	*27*	*23*	*28*
6	Narsinghpur	471	315	156	22	15	14	12	279	129	30	19	11	17	10	2	1	...	...
7	Hoshangabad	1,897	1,044	853	277	170	26	20	741	654	284	166	118	133	87	16	17	17	14
8	Nimar ...	3,793	1,994	1,799	87	80	27	31	1,880	1,738	84	55	29	39	16	11	7	5	6
9	Betul ...	547	274	273	33	32	4	3	237	238	39	20	19	19	15	...	...	1	4
10	Chhindwara	755	398	357	39	39	7	7	352	311	40	22	18	22	12	...	2	...	4
	NAGPUR DIVISION ...	*7,832*	*4,631*	*3,201*	*1,276*	*372*	*1,040*	*693*	*2,315*	*2,136*	*2,096*	*1,445*	*648*	*878*	*190*	*371*	*308*	*199*	*150*
11	Wardha ...	178	117	61	10	4	22	15	85	42	21	13	8	8	4	3	3	2	1
12	Nagpur ...	6,245	3,764	2,481	1,180	322	935	607	1,649	1,552	1,775	1,255	520	820	164	333	285	102	71
13	Chanda ...	541	304	237	28	16	13	14	263	207	171	95	76	17	7	8	6	70	63
14	Bhandara ...	538	250	288	15	9	65	50	170	223	88	57	31	9	3	24	14	24	14
15	Balaghat ...	330	196	134	43	21	5	1	148	112	41	28	13	24	12	3	...	1	1
	CHHATTISGARH DIVISION ...	*6,735*	*3,295*	*3,440*	*170*	*159*	*134*	*125*	*2,991*	*3,156*	*335*	*183*	*142*	*90*	*67*	*65*	*49*	*28*	*26*
16	Raipur ...	3,365	1,637	1,728	49	55	15	11	1,573	1,602	87	47	40	32	26	10	6	5	8
17	Bilaspur ...	2,011	971	1,040	102	93	112	112	757	835	212	120	92	54	38	52	42	14	12
18	Drug ...	1,359	687	672	19	11	7	2	661	659	26	16	10	4	3	3	1	9	6
	Berar ...	**2,823**	**1,521**	**1,302**	**96**	**98**	**156**	**149**	**1,269**	**1,055**	**280**	**160**	**120**	**50**	**30**	**92**	**70**	**18**	**20**
19	Amraoti ...	1,489	827	662	36	53	88	114	703	495	172	87	85	24	21	53	51	10	13
20	Akola ...	666	365	301	23	23	34	13	308	265	58	37	21	12	8	22	6	3	7
21	Buldana ...	378	183	195	23	8	25	14	135	173	30	23	7	13	1	9	6	1	...
22	Yeotmal ...	290	146	144	14	14	9	8	123	122	20	13	7	1	...	8	7	4	...
	Feudatory States ...	**36,704**	**19,477**	**19,227**	**52**	**33**	**71**	**74**	**19,354**	**19,120**	**121**	**65**	**56**	**29**	**14**	**30**	**39**	**6**	**8**
23	Makrai ...	...	...	...	...	...	...	...	...	...	...	...	...	...	...	...	...	...	...
24	Bastar ...	1,277	644	633	6	5	...	...	638	628	6	4	2	4	2	...	...	...	...
25	Kanker ...	10	5	5	...	...	...	...	5	5	...	...	...	...	...	...	...	...	...
26	Nandgaon ...	154	65	89	10	10	...	...	55	79	8	5	3	4	3	...	...	1	...
27	Khairagarh ...	252	132	120	32	17	64	71	36	32	101	52	49	19	8	30	39	3	2
28	Chhuikhadan	10	4	6	...	...	...	...	4	6	...	...	...	...	...	...	...	...	...
29	Kawardha ...	28	12	16	...	...	...	...	12	16	...	...	...	...	...	...	...	...	...
30	Sakti ...	14	7	7	...	...	4	3	3	4	...	...	...	...	...	...	...	...	...
31	Raigarh ...	51	27	24	1	...	1	...	25	24	...	...	...	...	...	...	...	...	...
32	Sarangarh ..	16	9	7	...	...	...	...	9	7	1	...	1	...	...	...	...	...	1
33	Chang Bhakar	...	...	...	...	...	...	...	...	...	...	...	...	...	...	...	...	...	...
34	Korea ...	4	3	1	...	...	...	...	3	1	2	2	...	...	...	...	...	2	...
35	Surguja ...	...	...	—	...	...	...	...	...	...	...	...	...	...	...	...	...	...	...
36	Udaipur ...	8	6	2	2	1	2	...	2	1	2	1	1	1	1	...	...	...	...
37	Jashpur ...	36,880	18,563	18,317	1	...	...	...	18,562	18,317	1	1	...	1	...	...	...	...	—

Christian Population by Sect and Race.

Armenian — Total — Persons	Armenian — Total — Males	Armenian — Total — Females	Armenian — European and allied races — Males	Armenian — European and allied races — Females	Armenian — Anglo-Indian — Males	Armenian — Anglo-Indian — Females	Armenian — Indian — Males	Armenian — Indian — Females	Baptist — Total — Persons	Baptist — Total — Males	Baptist — Total — Females	Baptist — European and allied races — Males	Baptist — European and allied races — Females	Baptist — Anglo-Indian — Males	Baptist — Anglo-Indian — Females	Baptist — Indian — Males	Baptist — Indian — Females	Congregationalist — Total — Persons	Congregationalist — Total — Males	Congregationalist — Total — Females	Serial number
20	21	22	23	24	25	26	27	28	29	30	31	32	33	34	35	36	37	38	39	40	
10	3	7	1	4	...	...	2	3	1,170	584	586	17	14	11	8	556	564	10	6	4	
10	3	7	1	4	...	...	2	3	1,068	531	537	16	14	9	7	506	516	10	6	4	
7	3	4	1	1	...	...	2	3	915	444	471	16	8	8	7	420	456	7	5	2	
...	...	...	...	...	...	...	...	...	*98*	*46*	*52*	*9*	*2*	*5*	*6*	*32*	*44*	*4*	*2*	*2*	
...	...	...	...	...	...	...	...	...	12	7	5	1	...	5	4	1	1	...	...	...	1
...	...	...	...	...	...	...	...	...	...	...	...	...	...	...	...	...	...	...	...	...	2
...	...	...	...	...	...	...	...	...	43	20	23	8	2	...	2	12	19	...	...	...	3
...	...	...	...	...	...	...	...	...	43	19	24	...	...	...	...	19	24	4	2	2	4
...	...	...	...	...	...	...	...	...	...	...	...	...	...	...	...	...	...	...	...	...	5
...	...	...	...	...	...	...	...	...	*37*	*18*	*19*	*5*	*6*	*1*	...	*12*	*13*	...	...	...	
...	...	...	...	...	...	...	...	...	...	...	...	...	...	...	...	...	...	...	...	...	6
...	...	...	...	...	...	...	...	...	30	16	14	5	3	1	...	10	11	...	...	...	7
...	...	...	...	...	...	...	...	...	...	...	...	...	...	...	...	...	...	...	...	...	8
...	...	...	...	...	...	...	...	...	3	...	3	...	3	...	...	...	...	...	...	...	9
...	...	...	...	...	...	...	...	...	4	2	2	...	...	...	...	2	2	...	...	...	10
2	*1*	*1*	*1*	*1*	...	...	...	...	*119*	*69*	*50*	*2*	...	*1*	*1*	*66*	*49*	*1*	*1*	...	
...	...	...	...	...	...	...	...	...	5	2	3	...	...	...	...	2	3	...	...	...	11
2	1	1	1	1	...	...	...	...	111	65	46	2	...	1	1	62	45	1	1	...	12
...	...	...	...	...	...	...	...	...	...	...	...	...	...	...	...	...	...	...	...	...	13
...	...	...	...	...	...	...	...	...	3	2	1	...	...	...	...	2	1	...	...	...	14
...	...	...	...	...	...	...	...	...	...	...	...	...	...	...	...	...	...	...	...	...	15
5	*2*	*3*	...	...	...	...	*2*	*3*	*661*	*311*	*350*	...	...	*1*	...	*310*	*350*	*2*	*2*	...	
...	...	...	...	...	...	...	...	...	535	254	281	...	...	...	...	254	281	...	...	...	16
...	...	...	...	...	...	...	...	...	109	46	63	...	...	1	...	45	63	2	2	...	17
5	2	3	...	...	...	...	2	3	17	11	6	...	...	...	...	11	6	...	...	...	18
3	...	3	...	3	...	...	...	...	153	87	66	...	6	1	...	86	60	3	1	2	
...	...	...	...	...	...	...	...	...	83	48	35	...	3	...	...	48	32	...	...	...	19
...	...	...	...	...	...	...	...	...	41	22	19	...	2	1	...	21	17	1	...	1	20
3	...	3	...	3	...	...	...	...	28	17	11	...	...	...	...	17	11	2	1	1	21
...	...	...	...	...	...	...	...	...	1	...	1	...	1	...	...	...	...	...	...	...	22
...	...	...	...	...	...	...	...	...	102	53	49	1	...	2	1	50	48	...	...	...	
...	...	...	...	...	...	...	...	...	...	...	...	...	...	...	...	...	...	...	...	...	23
...	...	...	...	...	...	...	...	...	24	11	13	...	...	...	...	11	13	...	...	...	24
...	...	...	...	...	...	...	...	...	10	5	5	...	...	...	...	5	5	...	...	...	25
...	...	...	...	...	...	...	...	...	...	...	...	...	...	...	...	...	...	...	...	...	26
...	...	...	...	...	...	...	...	...	2	1	1	1	...	...	1	...	...	...	...	...	27
...	...	...	...	...	...	...	...	...	...	...	...	...	...	...	...	...	...	...	...	...	28
...	...	...	...	...	...	...	...	...	...	...	...	...	...	...	...	...	...	...	...	...	29
...	...	...	...	...	...	...	...	...	2	2	...	...	...	2	...	...	...	...	...	...	30
...	...	...	...	...	...	...	...	...	49	25	24	...	...	...	...	25	24	...	...	...	31
...	...	...	...	...	...	...	...	...	15	9	6	...	...	...	...	9	6	...	...	...	32
...	...	...	...	...	...	...	...	...	...	...	...	...	...	...	...	...	...	...	...	...	33
...	...	...	...	...	...	...	...	...	...	...	...	...	...	...	...	...	...	...	...	...	34
...	...	...	...	...	...	...	...	...	...	...	...	...	...	...	...	...	...	...	...	...	35
...	...	...	...	...	...	...	...	...	...	...	...	...	...	...	...	...	...	...	...	...	36
...	...	...	...	...	...	...	...	...	...	...	...	...	...	...	...	...	...	...	...	...	37

TABLE XVII.—Territorial Distribution of the

Serial number.	DISTRICT OR STATE.	CONGREGATIONALIST. Distribution by race. European and allied races. Males.	European and allied races. Females.	Anglo-Indian. Males.	Anglo-Indian. Females.	Indian. Males.	Indian. Females.	GREEK. Distribution by race. Total. Persons.	Total. Males.	Total. Females.	European and allied races. Males.	European and allied races. Females.	Anglo-Indian. Males.	Anglo-Indian. Females.	Indian. Males.	Indian. Females.	LUTHERAN. Distribution by caste. Total. Persons.	Total. Males.	Total. Females.	European and allied races. Males.	European and allied races. Females.	Anglo-Indian. Males.	Anglo-Indian. Females.	Indian. Males.	Indian. Females.
	1	41	42	43	44	45	46	47	48	49	50	51	52	53	54	55	56	57	58	59	60	61	62	63	64
	Central Provinces and Berar ...	4	4	2	...	...	...	13	11	2	10	2	...	...	1	...	5,799	2,815	2,984	31	40	2	1	2,782	2,943
	C. P. British Districts and Berar ...	4	4	2	...	...	...	13	11	2	10	2	...	...	1	...	1,598	790	808	31	40	2	1	757	767
	C. P. British Districts ...	3	2	2	...	...	...	8	8	...	7	...	...	...	1	...	1,593	787	806	30	38	2	1	755	767
	Jubbulpore Division ...	*2*	*2*	...	...	...	...	*3*	*3*	...	*2*	...	...	...	1	...	*435*	*187*	*248*	*6*	*6*	*1*	...	*181*	*242*
1	Saugor ...	...	...	...	...	...	...	...	...	...	...	...	...	...	...	...	422	185	237	5	6	...	...	180	231
2	Damoh ...	...	...	...	...	...	...	...	...	...	...	...	...	...	...	...	...	...	...	...	...	...	...	...	...
3	Jubbulpore ...	...	...	...	...	...	...	3	3	...	2	...	...	...	1	...	9	...	9	...	...	...	...	...	9
4	Mandla ...	2	2	...	...	...	...	...	...	...	...	...	...	...	...	...	4	2	2	...	...	1	...	1	2
5	Seoni ...	...	...	...	...	...	...	...	...	...	...	...	...	...	...	...	...	...	...	...	...	...	...	...	...
	Nerbudda Division ...	...	...	...	...	...	...	*4*	*4*	...	*4*	...	...	...	...	...	*1,026*	*527*	*499*	*18*	*29*	...	...	*509*	*470*
6	Narsinghpur ...	...	...	...	...	...	...	...	...	...	...	...	...	...	...	...	8	6	2	...	...	...	...	6	2
7	Hoshangabad	...	...	...	...	...	...	...	...	...	...	...	...	...	...	...	1	1	...	...	...	...	...	1	...
8	Nimar ...	...	...	...	...	...	...	4	4	...	4	...	...	...	...	...	2	...	2	...	...	...	...	...	2
9	Betul ...	...	...	...	...	...	...	...	...	...	...	...	...	...	...	...	383	187	196	6	10	...	...	181	186
10	Chhindwara	...	...	...	...	...	...	...	...	...	...	...	...	...	...	...	632	333	299	12	19	...	...	321	280
	Nagpur Division ...	*1*	...	...	...	...	...	*1*	*1*	...	*1*	...	...	...	...	...	*9*	*6*	*3*	*3*	*2*	*1*	*1*	*2*	...
11	Wardha ...	...	...	...	...	...	...	...	...	...	...	...	...	...	...	...	...	...	...	...	...	...	...	...	...
12	Nagpur ...	1	...	...	...	...	...	1	1	...	1	...	...	...	...	...	8	5	3	3	2	1	1	1	...
13	Chanda ...	...	...	...	...	...	...	...	...	...	...	...	...	...	...	...	...	...	...	...	...	...	...	...	...
14	Bhandara ...	...	...	...	...	...	...	...	...	...	...	...	...	...	...	...	...	...	...	...	...	...	...	...	...
15	Balaghat ...	...	...	...	...	...	...	...	...	...	...	...	...	...	...	...	1	1	...	...	...	...	...	1	...
	Chhattisgarh Division ...	...	...	*2*	...	...	...	...	...	...	...	...	...	...	...	...	*123*	*67*	*56*	*4*	*1*	...	...	*63*	*55*
16	Raipur ..	...	...	...	...	...	...	...	...	...	...	...	...	...	...	...	42	24	18	...	...	...	...	24	18
17	Bilaspur ...	...	...	2	...	...	...	...	...	...	...	...	...	...	...	...	74	39	35	4	1	...	...	35	34
18	Drug ...	...	...	...	...	...	...	...	...	...	...	...	...	...	...	...	7	4	3	...	...	...	...	4	3
	Berar ...	1	2	...	...	...	...	5	3	2	3	2	...	...	...	...	5	3	2	1	2	...	...	2	...
19	Amraoti ...	...	...	...	...	...	...	...	...	...	...	...	...	...	...	...	5	3	2	1	2	...	...	2	...
20	Akola ...	...	1	...	...	...	...	4	2	2	2	2	...	...	...	...	...	...	...	...	...	...	...	...	...
21	Buldana ..	1	1	...	...	...	...	1	1	...	1	...	...	...	...	...	...	...	...	...	...	...	...	...	...
22	Yeotmal ...	...	...	...	...	...	...	...	...	...	...	...	...	...	...	...	...	...	...	...	...	...	...	...	...
	Feudatory States ...	...	...	...	...	...	...	...	...	...	...	...	...	...	...	...	4,201	2,025	2,176	...	...	...	...	2,025	2,176
23	Makrai ...	...	...	...	...	...	...	...	...	...	...	...	...	...	...	...	...	...	...	...	...	...	...	...	...
24	Bastar ...	...	...	...	...	...	...	...	...	...	...	...	...	...	...	...	...	...	...	...	...	...	...	...	...
25	Kanker ...	...	...	...	...	...	...	...	...	...	...	...	...	...	...	...	...	...	...	...	...	...	...	...	...
26	Nandgaon ...	...	...	...	...	...	...	...	...	...	...	...	...	...	...	...	...	...	...	...	...	...	...	...	...
27	Khairagarh	...	...	...	...	...	...	...	...	...	...	...	...	...	...	...	...	...	...	...	...	...	...	...	...
28	Chhuikhadan	...	...	...	...	...	...	...	...	...	...	...	...	...	...	...	...	...	...	...	...	...	...	...	...
29	Kawardha ...	...	...	...	...	...	...	...	...	...	...	...	...	...	...	...	...	...	...	...	...	...	...	...	...
30	Sakti ...	...	...	...	...	...	...	...	...	...	...	...	...	...	...	...	...	...	...	...	...	...	...	...	...
31	Raigarh ...	...	...	...	...	...	...	...	...	...	...	...	...	...	...	...	...	...	...	...	...	...	...	...	...
32	Sarangarh ...	...	...	...	...	...	...	...	...	...	...	...	...	...	...	...	...	...	...	...	...	...	...	...	...
33	Chang Bhakar	...	...	...	...	...	...	...	...	...	...	...	...	...	...	...	...	...	...	...	...	...	...	...	...
34	Korea ...	...	...	...	...	...	...	...	...	...	...	...	...	...	...	...	...	...	...	...	...	...	...	...	...
35	Surguja ...	...	...	...	...	...	...	...	...	...	...	...	...	...	...	...	...	...	...	...	...	...	...	...	...
36	Udaipur ...	...	...	...	...	...	...	...	...	...	...	...	...	...	...	...	...	...	...	...	...	...	...	...	...
37	Jashpur ...	...	...	...	...	...	...	...	...	...	...	...	...	...	...	...	4,201	2,025	2,176	...	...	...	...	2,025	2,176

Christian Population by Sect and Race.

METHODIST.									MINOR PROTESTANT DENOMINATIONS.									
DISTRIBUTION BY RACE.									DISTRIBUTION BY RACE.									
TOTAL.			European and allied races.		Anglo-Indian.		Indian.		TOTAL.			European and allied races.		Anglo-Indian.		Indian.		
Persons.	Males.	Females.	Males.	Females.	Males.	Females.	Males.	Females.	Persons.	Males.	Females.	Males.	Females.	Males.	Females.	Males.	Females.	Serial number.
65	66	67	68	69	70	71	72	73	74	75	76	77	78	79	80	81	82	
4,713	2,509	2,204	258	107	27	29	2,224	2,068	2,752	1,423	1,329	59	70	5	4	1,359	1,255	
3,479	1,889	1,590	252	99	24	29	1,613	1,462	2,655	1,394	1,261	57	66	5	4	1,332	1,191	
3,140	1,706	1,434	247	85	20	28	1,439	1,321	2,229	1,186	1,043	45	53	1	2	1,140	988	
1,013	*509*	*504*	*193*	*51*	*14*	*16*	*303*	*437*	*432*	*333*	*99*	*13*	*12*	...	*1*	*320*	*86*	
16	9	7	5	3	...	...	4	4	21	12	9	1	...	...	...	11	9	1
2	...	2	...	...	...	...	...	2	344	286	58	7	9	...	1	279	48	2
985	493	492	187	47	14	16	292	429	65	33	32	5	3	...	...	28	29	3
9	6	3	—	1	...	...	6	2	2	2	...	...	...	...	...	2	—	4
1	1	...	1	...	...	...	...	...	—	...	...	...	...	...	...	...	—	5
1,289	*758*	*531*	*7*	*13*	...	...	*751*	*518*	*43*	*22*	*21*	*3*	*1*	...	...	*19*	*20*	
372	261	111	1	3	...	...	260	108	...	...	...	...	...	...	...	...	...	6
55	28	27	5	7	...	...	23	20	4	3	1	3	1	...	...	...	...	7
831	440	391	1	3	...	...	439	388	3	...	3	...	...	...	...	...	3	8
28	26	2	...	...	...	...	26	2	36	19	17	...	...	...	...	19	17	9
3	3	...	...	...	...	...	3	...	...	...	...	...	...	...	...	...	...	10
578	*319*	*259*	*47*	*17*	*4*	*9*	*265*	*233*	*11*	*6*	*5*	...	*1*	...	...	*6*	*4*	
...	—	...	...	—	—	...	—	...	...	...	...	...	...	...	...	...	...	11
182	111	71	38	14	3	4	70	53	5	4	1	...	1	...	...	4	...	12
163	81	82	...	1	...	5	81	76	...	...	...	...	...	...	...	...	...	13
46	24	22	...	...	1	...	23	22	...	...	...	...	...	...	...	...	...	14
187	103	84	9	2	...	...	94	82	6	2	4	...	...	...	...	2	4	15
260	*120*	*140*	...	*4*	*2*	*3*	*118*	*133*	*1,745*	*825*	*918*	*29*	*39*	*1*	*1*	*795*	*878*	
170	73	97	...	4	...	1	73	92	589	261	328	4	14	...	...	257	314	16
16	12	4	...	...	1	1	11	3	1,047	489	558	23	21	1	1	465	536	17
74	35	39	...	...	1	1	34	38	107	75	32	2	4	...	...	73	28	18
339	183	156	5	14	4	1	174	141	426	208	218	12	13	4	2	192	203	
9	4	5	...	...	...	1	4	4	160	66	94	3	4	4	...	59	90	19
167	75	92	1	3	1	...	73	89	238	124	114	1	6	...	...	123	108	20
5	4	1	...	...	3	...	1	1	25	15	10	5	3	...	2	10	5	21
158	100	58	4	11	...	...	96	47	3	3	...	3	...	...	...	...	...	22
1,234	620	614	6	8	3	...	611	606	97	29	68	2	4	...	...	27	64	
...	...	...	...	...	...	...	...	...	...	...	...	...	...	...	...	...	...	23
1,202	605	597	1	...	...	...	604	597	...	...	...	...	...	...	...	...	...	24
4	2	2	2	2	...	...	...	...	...	...	...	...	...	...	...	...	...	25
16	8	8	3	6	3	...	2	2	86	24	62	2	4	...	...	22	58	26
10	4	6	...	...	...	...	4	6	11	5	6	...	...	...	...	5	6	27
2	1	1	...	...	...	...	1	1	...	...	...	...	...	...	...	...	...	28
...	...	...	...	...	...	...	...	...	...	...	...	...	...	...	...	...	...	29
...	...	...	...	...	...	...	...	...	...	...	...	...	...	...	...	...	...	30
...	...	...	...	...	...	...	...	...	...	...	...	...	...	...	...	...	...	31
...	...	...	...	...	...	...	...	...	...	...	...	...	...	...	...	...	...	32
...	...	...	...	...	...	...	...	...	...	...	...	...	...	...	...	...	...	33
...	...	...	...	...	...	...	...	...	...	...	...	...	...	...	...	...	...	34
...	...	...	...	...	...	...	...	...	...	...	...	...	...	...	...	...	...	35
...	...	...	...	...	...	...	...	...	...	...	...	...	...	...	...	...	...	36
...	...	...	...	...	...	...	...	...	...	...	...	...	...	...	...	...	...	37

TABLE XVII.—Territorial Distribution of the

Serial number.	DISTRICT OR STATE.	PRESBYTERIAN.									QUAKER.									ROMAN		
		Distribution by race.									Distribution by race.									Distribution		
		Total.			European and allied races.		Anglo-Indian.		Indian.		Total.			European and allied races.		Anglo-Indian.		Indian.		Total.		
		Persons.	Males.	Females.	Males.	Females.	Males.	Females.	Males.	Females.	Persons.	Males.	Females.	Males.	Females.	Males.	Females.	Males.	Females.	Persons.	Males.	Females.
	1	83	84	85	86	87	88	89	90	91	92	93	94	95	96	97	98	99	100	101	102	103
	Central Provinces and Berar ...	**4,152**	**2,086**	**2,066**	**98**	**43**	**24**	**24**	**1,964**	**1,999**	**1,160**	**607**	**553**	**7**	**11**	**1**	**1**	**599**	**541**	**44,552**	**23,164**	**21,388**
	C. P. British Districts and Berar ...	**4,144**	**2,081**	**2,063**	**96**	**43**	**24**	**24**	**1,961**	**1,996**	**1,160**	**607**	**553**	**7**	**11**	**1**	**1**	**599**	**541**	**11,630**	**6,495**	**5,135**
	C. P. British Districts ...	**4,037**	**2,022**	**2,015**	**90**	**42**	**22**	**22**	**1,910**	**1,951**	**1,160**	**607**	**553**	**7**	**11**	**1**	**1**	**599**	**541**	**10,504**	**5,837**	**4,667**
	JUBBULPORE DIVISION ...	*245*	*129*	*116*	*30*	*8*	*5*	*2*	*91*	*106*	*19*	*3*	*16*	...	...	...	...	*3*	*16*	*2,538*	*1,554*	*1,034*
1	Saugor ...	36	20	16	3	1	1	2	16	13	...	...	...	...	...	...	...	...	...	644	347	297
2	Damoh ...	1	1	...	1	...	...	...	...	...	...	...	...	...	...	...	...	...	...	53	28	25
3	Jubbulpore ...	45	29	16	25	4	3	...	1	12	17	2	15	...	...	...	...	2	15	1,733	1,064	669
4	Mandla ...	9	9	...	1	...	4	...	4	...	...	...	...	...	...	...	...	...	...	130	100	30
5	Seoni ...	154	70	84	...	3	...	...	70	81	2	1	1	...	...	...	...	1	1	28	15	13
	NERBUDDA DIVISION ...	*70*	*41*	*29*	*18*	*8*	*1*	*3*	*22*	*18*	*1,135*	*600*	*535*	*4*	*10*	...	...	*596*	*525*	*3,363*	*1,763*	*1,600*
6	Narsinghpur	2	1	1	1	1	...	...	...	...	...	...	...	...	...	...	...	...	...	55	26	29
7	Hoshangabad	29	19	10	9	2	...	...	10	8	1,126	595	531	4	10	...	...	591	521	365	213	152
8	Nimar ...	21	14	7	7	3	...	...	7	4	9	5	4	...	...	...	...	5	4	2,829	1,472	1,357
9	Betul ...	9	4	5	1	2	1	3	2	...	...	...	...	...	...	...	...	...	...	49	18	31
10	Chhindwara	9	3	6	...	...	...	...	3	6	...	...	...	...	...	...	...	...	...	65	34	31
	NAGPUR DIVISION ...	*727*	*361*	*366*	*26*	*17*	*12*	*17*	*323*	*332*	...	...	...	...	...	...	...	...	...	*4,013*	*2,257*	*1,756*
11	Wardha ...	69	50	19	1	...	...	...	49	19	...	...	...	...	...	...	...	...	...	80	49	31
12	Nagpur ...	410	203	207	18	12	8	12	177	183	...	...	...	...	...	...	...	...	...	3,534	1,986	1,548
13	Chanda ...	58	42	16	4	1	...	...	38	15	...	...	...	...	...	...	...	...	...	148	85	63
14	Bhandara ...	185	62	123	3	3	4	5	55	115	...	...	...	...	...	...	...	...	...	180	86	94
15	Balaghat ...	5	4	1	...	1	...	...	4	...	...	...	...	...	...	...	...	...	...	71	51	20
	CHHATTISGARH DIVISION ...	*2,995*	*1,491*	*1,504*	*16*	*9*	*1*	...	*1,474*	*1,495*	*6*	*4*	*2*	*3*	*1*	*1*	*1*	...	...	*540*	*263*	*277*
16	Raipur ...	1,734	883	851	8	7	1	...	874	844	5	3	2	3	1	...	1	...	...	198	91	107
17	Bilaspur ...	182	89	93	3	...	...	...	86	93	1	1	...	...	...	1	...	...	...	313	156	157
18	Drug ...	1,079	519	560	5	2	...	...	514	558	...	...	...	...	...	...	...	...	...	29	16	13
	Berar ...	**107**	**59**	**48**	**6**	**1**	**2**	**2**	**51**	**45**	...	...	...	...	...	...	...	...	...	**1,126**	**658**	**468**
19	Amraoti ...	19	9	10	2	1	...	...	7	9	...	...	...	...	...	...	...	...	...	938	540	398
20	Akola ...	5	5	...	1	...	...	...	4	...	...	...	...	...	...	...	...	...	...	102	61	41
21	Buldana ...	71	39	32	1	...	2	2	36	30	...	...	...	...	...	...	...	...	...	60	44	16
22	Yeotmal ...	12	6	6	2	...	...	...	4	6	...	...	...	...	...	...	...	...	...	26	13	13
	Feudatory States ...	**8**	**5**	**3**	**2**	...	...	...	**3**	**3**	...	...	...	...	...	...	...	...	...	**32,922**	**16,669**	**16,253**
23	Makrai ...	...	...	...	...	...	...	...	...	...	...	...	...	...	...	...	...	...	...	...	...	...
24	Bastar ...	...	...	...	...	...	...	...	...	...	...	...	...	...	...	...	...	...	...	45	24	21
25	Kanker ...	...	...	...	...	...	...	...	...	...	...	...	...	...	...	...	...	...	...	...	...	...
26	Nandgaon ...	1	1	...	1	...	...	...	...	...	...	...	...	...	...	...	...	...	...	55	33	22
27	Khairagarh ...	2	2	...	1	...	...	...	1	...	...	...	...	...	...	...	...	...	...	107	56	51
28	Chhuikhadan	...	...	...	...	...	...	...	...	...	...	...	...	...	...	...	...	...	...	...	...	...
29	Kawardha ...	...	...	...	...	...	...	...	...	...	...	...	...	...	...	...	...	...	...	26	11	15
30	Sakti ...	5	2	3	...	...	...	...	2	3	...	...	...	...	...	...	...	...	...	2	1	1
31	Raigarh ...	...	...	...	...	...	...	...	...	...	...	...	...	...	...	...	...	...	...	1	1	...
32	Sarangarh ...	...	...	...	...	...	...	...	...	...	...	...	...	...	...	...	...	...	...	...	...	...
33	Chang Bhakar	...	...	...	...	...	...	...	...	...	...	...	...	...	...	...	...	...	...	...	...	...
34	Korea ...	...	...	...	...	...	...	...	...	...	...	...	...	...	...	...	...	...	...	2	1	1
35	Surguja ...	...	...	...	...	...	...	...	...	...	...	...	...	...	...	...	...	...	...	...	...	...
36	Udaipur ...	...	...	...	...	...	...	...	...	...	...	...	...	...	...	...	...	...	...	6	5	1
37	Jashpur ...	...	...	...	...	...	...	...	...	...	...	...	...	...	...	...	...	...	...	32,678	16,537	16,141

Christian Population by Sect and Race.

CATHOLIC.						SECT NOT RETURNED.												INDEFINITE BELIEFS.									
By race.									Distribution by race.									Distribution by race.						
European and allied races.		Anglo-Indian.		Indian.		Total.			European and allied races.		Anglo-Indian.		Indian.		Total.			European and allied races.		Anglo-Indian.		Indian.		
Males.	Females.	Males.	Females.	Males.	Females.	Persons.	Males.	Females.	Males.	Females.	Males.	Females.	Males.	Females.	Persons.	Males.	Females.	Males.	Females.	Males.	Females.	Males.	Females.	Serial number.
104	105	106	107	108	109	110	111	112	113	114	115	116	117	118	119	120	121	122	123	124	125	126	127	
993	520	1,041	831	21,130	20,037	808	390	418	14	22	18	24	358	372	22	17	5	16	4	...	1	1	...	
984	513	1,007	800	4,504	3,822	789	379	410	11	22	16	21	352	367	22	17	5	16	4	...	1	1	...	
968	490	955	727	3,914	3,450	413	220	193	9	20	15	20	196	153	22	17	5	16	4	...	1	1	...	
472	*252*	*211*	*265*	*871*	*514*	*61*	*33*	*28*	*2*	*1*	...	...	*31*	*27*	*5*	*5*	...	*5*	...	...	...	...	...	
29	57	34	46	284	194	10	6	4	1	1	...	...	5	3	1	1	...	1	...	...	...	...	...	1
2	1	12	18	14	6	...	...	...	...	...	...	...	...	...	1	1	...	1	...	...	...	...	...	2
434	191	126	175	504	303	49	20	23	...	...	...	...	26	23	2	2	...	2	...	...	...	...	...	3
5	3	30	19	65	8	1	...	1	...	...	...	...	...	1	...	...	...	...	...	...	...	...	...	4
2	...	9	10	4	3	1	1	...	1	...	...	...	...	...	1	1	...	1	...	...	...	...	...	5
160	*76*	*47*	*52*	*1,550*	*1,472*	*13*	*7*	*6*	...	...	...	...	*7*	*6*	*6*	*3*	*3*	*3*	*3*	...	...	...	...	
8	1	12	11	11	17	4	2	2	...	...	...	...	2	2	...	...	...	...	...	...	...	...	...	6
115	60	9	12	89	80	...	...	...	...	...	...	...	...	...	3	3	...	3	...	...	...	...	...	7
30	5	16	24	1,420	1,328	7	4	3	...	...	...	...	4	3	3	...	3	...	3	...	...	...	...	8
7	2	3	...	8	29	...	...	...	...	...	...	...	...	...	...	...	...	...	...	...	...	...	...	9
5	8	7	5	22	18	2	1	1	...	...	...	...	1	1	...	...	...	...	...	...	...	...	...	10
306	*143*	*645*	*355*	*1,306*	*1,255*	*267*	*154*	*113*	*4*	*1*	*6*	*2*	*144*	*110*	*8*	*8*	...	*7*	...	...	...	*1*	...	
1	...	17	12	31	19	2	2	...	...	...	2	...	...	...	1	1	...	...	...	...	...	1	...	11
288	127	586	304	1,112	1,117	210	126	84	2	1	3	...	121	83	6	6	...	6	...	...	...	...	...	12
6	7	5	3	74	53	...	...	...	...	...	...	...	...	...	1	1	...	1	...	...	...	...	...	13
2	3	35	35	49	56	36	19	17	1	...	1	2	17	15	...	...	...	...	...	...	...	...	...	14
9	6	2	1	40	13	19	7	12	1	...	...	...	6	12	...	...	...	...	...	...	...	...	...	15
24	*19*	*52*	*52*	*187*	*206*	*72*	*26*	*46*	*3*	*18*	*9*	*18*	*14*	*10*	*3*	*1*	*2*	*1*	*1*	...	*1*	...	...	
2	2	4	2	85	103	3	1	2	...	...	...	...	1	2	2	...	2	...	1	...	1	...	...	16
17	17	48	50	91	90	54	16	38	...	16	6	18	10	4	1	1	...	1	...	...	...	...	...	17
5	...	...	...	11	13	15	9	6	3	2	3	...	3	4	...	...	...	...	...	...	...	...	...	18
16	23	52	73	590	372	376	159	217	2	2	1	1	156	214	...	...	...	...	...	...	...	...	...	
6	22	31	62	503	314	108	70	33	...	...	...	...	70	33	...	...	...	...	...	...	...	...	...	19
6	1	10	7	45	33	50	39	11	...	...	...	...	39	11	...	...	...	...	...	...	...	...	...	20
2	...	10	3	32	13	153	39	114	...	...	1	1	38	113	...	...	...	...	...	...	...	...	...	21
2	...	1	1	10	12	70	11	59	2	2	...	...	9	57	...	...	...	...	...	...	...	...	...	22
9	7	34	31	16,626	16,215	19	11	8	3	...	2	3	6	5	...	...	...	...	...	...	...	...	...	
...	...	...	...	...	...	...	...	...	...	...	...	...	...	...	...	...	...	...	...	...	...	...	...	23
1	3	...	...	23	18	...	...	...	...	...	...	...	...	...	...	...	...	...	...	...	...	...	...	24
...	...	...	...	...	...	...	...	...	...	...	...	...	...	...	...	...	...	...	...	...	...	...	...	25
1	1	...	...	32	21	...	...	...	...	...	...	...	...	...	...	...	...	...	...	...	...	...	...	26
6	3	31	31	19	17	13	8	5	2	...	...	...	6	5	...	...	...	...	...	...	...	...	...	27
...	...	...	...	...	...	...	...	...	...	...	...	...	...	...	...	...	...	...	...	...	...	...	...	28
...	...	...	...	11	15	...	...	...	...	...	...	...	...	...	...	...	...	...	...	...	...	...	...	29
...	...	...	...	1	1	5	2	3	...	...	2	3	...	...	...	...	...	...	...	...	...	...	...	30
...	...	1	...	...	...	1	1	...	1	...	...	...	...	...	...	...	...	...	...	...	...	...	...	31
...	...	...	...	...	...	...	...	...	...	...	...	...	...	...	...	...	...	...	...	...	...	...	...	32
...	...	...	...	...	...	...	...	...	...	...	...	...	...	...	...	...	...	...	...	...	...	...	...	33
...	...	...	...	1	1	...	...	...	...	...	...	...	...	...	...	...	...	...	...	...	...	...	...	34
...	...	...	...	...	...	...	...	...	...	...	...	...	...	...	...	...	...	...	...	...	...	...	...	35
1	...	2	...	2	1	...	...	...	...	...	...	...	...	...	...	...	...	...	...	...	...	...	...	36
...	...	...	...	16,537	16,141	...	...	...	...	...	...	...	...	...	...	...	...	...	...	...	...	...	...	37

TABLE XVIII.

Europeans, Armenians and Anglo-Indians by Race and Age.

This table shows the distribution by districts and States. Details for the two cities of Jubbulpore and Nagpur are given under their districts in brackets. Figures for cities are included in the district totals.

TABLE XVIII.—Europeans, Armenians and

Serial number.	DISTRICT OR STATE.	TOTAL.			EUROPEAN AND													
					BRITISH SUBJECTS.													
					All ages.			0—12.		12—15.		15—30.		30—50.		50 and over.		
		Persons.	Males.	Females.	Persons.	Males.	Females.	Males.	Females.	Males.	Females.	Males.	Females.	Males.	Females.	Males.	Females.	
	1	2	3	4	5	6	7	8	9	10	11	12	13	14	15	16	17	
	Central Provinces and Berar	**10,821**	**7,330**	**3,491**	**7,033**	**5,323**	**1,710**	**448**	**489**	**60**	**66**	**3,579**	**479**	**1,094**	**555**	**142**	**121**	
	C. P. British Districts and Berar ...	**10,591**	**7,207**	**3,384**	**6,957**	**5,274**	**1,683**	**440**	**481**	**60**	**65**	**3,565**	**470**	**1,073**	**546**	**136**	**121**	
	C. P. British Districts ...	**10,092**	**6,955**	**3,137**	**6,808**	**5,191**	**1,617**	**423**	**468**	**60**	**64**	**3,553**	**450**	**1,025**	**519**	**130**	**116**	
	JUBBULPORE DIVISION ...	*5,219*	*3,799*	*1,420*	*4,276*	*3,367*	*909*	*246*	*286*	*47*	*42*	*2,422*	*259*	*552*	*257*	*71*	*65*	
1	Saugor	498	276	222	310	183	127	31	39	4	11	66	37	74	35	8	5	
2	Damoh	76	37	30	24	16	8	3	2	...	...	6	1	5	5	2	...	
3	Jubbulpore	4,485	3,390	1,095	3,871	3,120	751	209	238	42	31	2,332	216	477	209	60	57	
	Jubbulpore City ...	*4,378*	*3,336*	*1,042*	*3,822*	*3,094*	*728*	*208*	*231*	*41*	*31*	*2,323*	*211*	*463*	*196*	*59*	*53*	
4	Mandla	121	74	47	54	35	19	2	7	1	...	12	4	19	6	1	2	
5	Seoni	39	22	17	17	13	4	...	...	...	...	6	1	7	2	...	1	
	NERBUDDA DIVISION ...	*904*	*536*	*365*	*656*	*410*	*246*	*71*	*64*	*5*	*4*	*144*	*71*	*155*	*86*	*32*	*19*	
6	Narsinghpur	63	36	27	34	21	13	3	6	...	...	5	3	11	3	2	1	
7	Hoshangabad	502	303	199	438	273	165	51	42	4	3	102	51	95	54	21	15	
8	Nimar	175	114	61	80	60	26	12	4	1	1	23	8	20	11	4	2	
9	Betul	72	37	35	50	28	22	4	5	...	...	5	2	17	15	2	...	
10	Chhindwara	92	46	46	48	28	20	1	7	...	...	9	7	15	5	3	1	
	NAGPUR DIVISION ...	*3,381*	*2,316*	*1,065*	*1,606*	*1,272*	*335*	*75*	*75*	*6*	*13*	*950*	*57*	*225*	*131*	*16*	*24*	
11	Wardha	51	32	19	14	10	4	...	2	...	...	5	1	5	1	..	...	
12	Nagpur	3,044	2,115	929	1,463	1,179	284	62	72	5	13	924	75	177	105	11	19	
	Nagpur City ...	*1,691*	*1,043*	*648*	*261*	*165*	*96*	*13*	*13*	*2*	...	*95*	*24*	*49*	*52*	*6*	*7*	
13	Chanda	71	41	30	43	28	15	3	...	...	...	7	4	17	11	1	...	
14	Bhandara	145	80	65	24	15	9	2	2	...	...	2	...	11	6	...	1	
15	Balaghat	70	48	22	61	40	21	8	2	1	...	12	7	15	8	4	4	
	CHHATTISGARH DIVISION ...	*588*	*304*	*284*	*271*	*142*	*129*	*32*	*40*	*2*	*6*	*37*	*33*	*60*	*43*	*11*	*8*	
16	Raipur	130	64	66	80	40	40	6	11	2	2	10	9	17	16	5	2	
17	Bilaspur	419	214	205	173	89	84	25	29	...	3	21	21	37	25	6	6	
18	Drug	39	26	13	18	13	5	1	...	...	...	6	3	6	2	...	...	
	Berar	**499**	**252**	**247**	**149**	**83**	**66**	**17**	**13**	...	**1**	**12**	**20**	**48**	**27**	**6**	**5**	
19	Amraoti	291	124	167	60	31	29	4	6	...	1	4	6	20	14	3	2	
20	Akola	93	57	36	34	17	17	5	3	...	...	2	7	9	4	1	3	
21	Buldana	70	48	22	27	21	6	5	...	...	...	4	3	11	3	1	...	
22	Yeotmal	45	23	22	28	14	14	3	4	...	...	2	4	8	6	1	...	
	Feudatory States	**230**	**123**	**107**	**76**	**49**	**27**	**8**	**8**	...	**1**	**14**	**9**	**21**	**9**	**6**	...	
23	Makrai	...	...	...	...	...	...	...	...	...	...	...	...	...	...	...	...	
24	Bastar	11	6	5	8	5	3	...	...	...	...	3	2	1	1	1	...	
25	Kanker	...	...	...	...	...	...	...	...	...	...	...	...	...	...	...	...	
26	Nandgaon	20	10	10	14	8	6	1	1	...	1	3	2	4	2	...	...	
27	Khairagarh	184	66	88	49	32	17	7	7	...	...	7	5	13	5	5	...	
28	Chhuikhadan	...	...	...	...	...	...	...	...	...	...	...	...	...	...	...	...	
29	Kawardha	...	...	...	...	...	...	...	...	...	...	...	...	...	...	...	...	
30	Sakti	7	4	3	...	...	...	...	...	...	...	...	...	...	...	...	...	
31	Raigarh	2	2	...	1	1	...	...	...	...	...	1	...	...	...	...	...	
32	Sarangarh	...	...	...	...	...	...	...	...	...	...	...	...	...	...	...	...	
33	Chang Bhakar	...	...	...	...	...	...	...	...	...	...	...	...	...	...	...	...	
34	Korea	...	...	...	...	...	...	...	...	...	...	...	...	...	...	...	...	
35	Surguja	...	...	...	...	...	...	...	...	...	...	...	...	...	...	...	...	
36	Udaipur	5	4	1	3	2	1	...	...	...	...	...	...	2	1	...	...	
37	Jashpur	1	1	...	1	1	...	...	...	...	...	...	...	1	...	...	...	

Anglo-Indians by Race and Age.

ALLIED RACES.													ANGLO-INDIANS.													
OTHERS.													All ages.			0—12.		12—15.		15—30.		30—50.		50 and over.		Serial number.
All ages.			0—12.		12—15.		15—30.		30—50.		50 and over.															
Persons.	Males.	Females.	Males.	Females.	Males.	Females.	Males.	Females.	Males.	Females.	Males.	Females.	Persons.	Males.	Females.	Males.	Females.	Males.	Females.	Males.	Females.	Males.	Females.	Males.	Females.	
18	19	20	21	22	23	24	25	26	27	28	29	30	31	32	33	34	35	36	37	38	39	40	41	42	43	
300	**124**	**176**	**11**	**11**	**1**	...	**29**	**42**	**67**	**95**	**16**	**28**	**3,488**	**1,883**	**1,605**	**525**	**533**	**137**	**97**	**587**	**507**	**490**	**331**	**144**	**137**	
291	**121**	**170**	**11**	**10**	**1**	...	**27**	**39**	**67**	**94**	**15**	**27**	**3,343**	**1,812**	**1,531**	**494**	**504**	**136**	**95**	**570**	**487**	**470**	**316**	**142**	**129**	
246	**108**	**138**	**8**	**10**	**1**	...	**25**	**29**	**60**	**78**	**14**	**21**	**3,033**	**1,656**	**1,382**	**456**	**456**	**134**	**86**	**532**	**442**	**412**	**280**	**122**	**118**	
57	*25*	*29*	*2*	*2*	...	...	*6*	*5*	*19*	*19*	*2*	*3*	*886*	*404*	*482*	*141*	*170*	*22*	*36*	*116*	*142*	*97*	*105*	*25*	*29*	
20	13	7	...	1	...	...	4	1	8	4	1	1	168	80	88	25	27	2	5	24	25	22	24	7	7	1
11	5	6	1	...	...	...	...	1	4	5	...	...	41	16	25	3	8	...	3	10	10	3	2	...	2	2
25	10	15	1	1	...	...	1	3	7	9	1	2	589	260	329	91	116	20	28	69	95	61	71	19	19	3
25	*10*	*15*	*1*	*1*	...	...	*1*	*3*	*7*	*9*	*1*	*2*	*551*	*252*	*299*	*81*	*107*	*16*	*26*	*64*	*86*	*49*	*63*	*17*	*17*	
1	...	1	...	...	...	...	...	...	...	1	...	...	66	39	27	17	12	...	...	12	11	8	4	2	...	4
...	...	...	...	...	...	...	...	...	...	...	...	...	22	9	13	5	7	...	...	1	1	3	4	...	1	5
85	*45*	*40*	*5*	*3*	...	...	*11*	*7*	*24*	*23*	*5*	*7*	*160*	*73*	*82*	*20*	*31*	*2*	*2*	*27*	*26*	*24*	*14*	*5*	*9*	
3	1	2	...	...	...	...	...	...	1	1	...	1	26	14	12	3	4	2	2	4	2	4	4	1	...	6
9	4	5	1	...	...	...	...	1	2	3	1	1	55	28	29	7	14	...	...	6	5	11	5	2	5	7
31	27	4	...	...	...	...	9	1	15	2	3	1	58	27	31	7	11	...	...	12	13	7	4	1	3	8
15	5	10	1	1	...	...	...	3	3	4	1	2	7	4	3	3	2	...	...	...	1	1	...	...	...	9
30	11	19	3	2	...	...	2	2	3	13	3	2	14	7	7	...	...	...	...	5	5	1	1	1	1	10
43	*4*	*39*	...	*3*	...	...	*3*	*5*	*1*	*24*	...	*7*	*1,733*	*1,040*	*693*	*239*	*201*	*103*	*41*	*356*	*244*	*251*	*134*	*81*	*73*	
...	...	...	...	...	...	...	...	...	...	...	...	...	37	22	15	6	3	...	...	7	8	8	4	1	...	11
39	1	38	...	3	...	...	...	4	1	24	...	7	1,542	935	607	222	175	102	39	320	208	216	118	75	67	12
35	...	*35*	...	*2*	...	...	...	*4*	...	*23*	...	*7*	*1,395*	*875*	*517*	*205*	*151*	*95*	*30*	*310*	*165*	*197*	*105*	*65*	*63*	
1	...	1	...	...	...	...	...	1	...	...	...	...	27	13	14	4	4	...	...	3	8	5	2	1	...	13
...	...	...	...	...	...	...	...	...	...	...	...	...	121	65	56	16	19	1	2	25	19	19	10	4	6	14
3	3	...	...	...	...	...	3	...	...	...	...	...	6	5	1	1	...	...	...	1	1	3	...	...	...	15
55	*25*	*30*	*1*	*2*	*1*	...	*6*	*12*	*16*	*12*	*4*	*4*	*259*	*134*	*125*	*46*	*54*	*7*	*7*	*33*	*30*	*40*	*27*	*5*	*7*	
24	9	15	1	2	1	...	3	6	2	6	2	1	26	15	11	1	3	...	...	2	3	11	3	1	2	16
22	13	9	...	...	...	...	1	3	11	4	1	2	224	112	112	45	51	7	7	29	27	27	23	4	4	17
12	6	6	...	...	...	...	2	3	3	2	1	1	9	7	2	...	...	...	...	2	...	2	1	3	1	18
45	**13**	**32**	**3**	...	...	...	**2**	**10**	**7**	**16**	**1**	**6**	**305**	**156**	**149**	**33**	**48**	**2**	**9**	**38**	**45**	**58**	**36**	**20**	**11**	
20	5	24	...	...	...	...	...	6	5	12	...	6	202	88	114	25	39	2	8	20	34	29	23	12	10	19
12	6	6	3	...	...	...	1	3	1	3	1	...	47	34	13	11	5	...	...	6	4	12	3	5	1	20
4	2	2	...	...	...	...	1	1	1	1	...	...	39	25	14	1	3	...	...	9	4	13	7	2	...	21
...	...	...	...	...	...	...	...	...	...	...	...	...	17	9	8	1	1	...	1	3	3	4	3	1	...	22
9	**3**	**6**	...	**1**	...	...	**2**	**3**	...	**1**	**1**	**1**	**145**	**71**	**74**	**31**	**29**	**1**	**2**	**17**	**20**	**20**	**15**	**2**	**8**	
...	...	...	...	...	...	...	...	...	...	...	...	...	...	...	...	...	...	...	...	...	...	...	...	...	...	23
3	1	2	...	1	...	...	1	1	...	...	...	...	...	...	...	...	...	...	...	...	...	...	...	...	...	24
...	...	...	...	...	...	...	...	...	...	...	...	...	...	...	...	...	...	...	...	...	...	...	...	...	...	25
6	2	4	...	...	...	...	1	2	...	1	1	1	...	...	...	...	...	...	...	...	...	...	...	...	...	26
...	...	...	...	...	...	...	...	...	...	...	...	...	136	64	71	30	28	1	2	16	19	15	15	2	7	27
...	...	...	...	...	...	...	...	...	...	...	...	...	...	...	...	...	...	...	...	...	...	...	...	...	...	28
...	...	...	...	...	...	...	...	...	...	...	...	...	...	...	...	...	...	...	...	...	...	...	...	...	...	29
...	...	...	...	...	...	...	...	...	...	...	...	...	7	4	3	1	1	...	...	...	1	2	...	...	...	30
...	...	...	...	...	...	...	...	...	...	...	...	...	1	1	...	...	...	...	...	1	...	...	...	...	...	31
...	...	...	...	...	...	...	...	...	...	...	...	...	...	...	...	...	...	...	...	...	...	...	...	...	...	32
...	...	...	...	...	...	...	...	...	...	...	...	...	...	...	...	...	...	...	...	...	...	...	...	...	...	33
...	...	...	...	...	...	...	...	...	...	...	...	...	...	...	...	...	...	...	...	...	...	...	...	...	...	34
...	...	...	...	...	...	...	...	...	...	...	...	...	...	...	...	...	...	...	...	...	...	...	...	...	...	35
...	...	...	...	...	...	...	...	...	...	...	...	...	2	2	...	...	...	...	...	...	...	2	...	...	...	36
...	...	...	...	...	...	...	...	...	...	...	...	...	...	...	...	...	...	...	...	...	...	...	...	...	...	37

PROVINCIAL TABLE I.

Area and Population of Tahsils, Cities and large Towns.

In this Table the area and population of the Tahsils of the Central Provinces, the Taluks of Berar and of two cities, and ten large towns are shown. The figures for Zamindaris are given separately under the Tahsil to which they belong. The figures of the cities and towns are shown above the Tahsil to which they belong and are not included in the Tahsil figures.

PROVINCIAL TABLE I.—Area and Popula

Tahsil, Taluk, Zamindaris or Township.	Area in square miles.	Number of Towns.	Number of Villages.	Number of occupied houses.	Population 1911 Persons.	Population 1911 Males.	Population 1911 Females.	Population 1901 (both sexes).	Percentage of variation 1901 to 1911.	Percentage of variation 1891 to 1901.	Number of persons per square mile in 1911.
1	2	3	4	5	6	7	8	9	10	11	12
C. P. British Districts and Berar.	99,823	112	39,005	2,858,302	13,916,308	6,930,392	6,985,916	11,971,452	+16·24	—8·26	139
C. P. British Districts.	82,057	65	33,156	2,203,068	10,859,146	5,379,778	5,479,368	9,217,436	+17·81	—9·20	132
Jubbulpore Division.	18,953	12	8,794	505,706	2,421,064	1,210,980	1,210,084	2,081,480	+16·31	—12·35	128
SAUGOR DISTRICT...	*3,963*	*5*	*1,809*	*115,712*	*541,410*	*276,233*	*265,177*	*469,479*	*+15·32*	*—20·41*	*137*
Saugor Town ...	...	1	...	9,911	45,908	24,330	21,578	42,330	+8·45	—5·25	179
Saugor Tahsil ...	1,064	...	485	31,675	144,782	73,350	71,432	124,069	+16·69	—23·78	
Khurai Tahsil ...	940	2	476	24,163	111,070	56,923	54,147	93,788	+18·43	—25·57	118
Rehli Tahsil ...	1,254	2	580	32,249	157,815	79,894	77,921	136,463	+15·65	—19·34	126
Banda Tahsil ...	704	...	268	17,714	81,835	41,736	40,099	72,829	+12·37	—16·47	116
DAMOH DISTRICT...	*2,816*	*1*	*1,148*	*68,597*	*333,047*	*168,060*	*164,987*	*285,326*	*+16·73*	*—12·37*	*118*
Damoh Tahsil ...	1,797	1	713	43,233	210,898	106,237	104,661	183,316	+15·05	—0·44	117
Hatta Tahsil ...	1,019	...	435	25,364	122,149	61,823	60,326	102,010	+19·74	—21·33	120
JUBBULPORE DISTRICT.	*3,912*	*4*	*2,350*	*164,794*	*745,892*	*373,173*	*372,719*	*680,585*	*+9·60*	*—9·05*	*191*
Jubbulpore City ...	...	1	—	23,560	100,651	56,035	44,616	90,533	+11·18	+6·91	234
Jubbulpore Tahsil...	1,117	1	735	36,289	161,206	79,911	81,295	145,316	+10·93	—9·03	
Sihora Tahsil ...	1,181	1	734	44,825	204,869	100,254	104,615	186,424	+9·89	—12·46	173
Murwara Tahsil ...	1,190	1	522	37,467	181,699	88,450	93,249	161,673	+12·39	—6·71	153
Patan Tahsil ...	424	...	359	22,644	97,467	48,523	48,944	96,639	+·86	—17·73	230
MANDLA DISTRICT	*5,057*	*1*	*1,918*	*74,877*	*405,234*	*200,872*	*204,362*	*318,381*	*+27·25*	*—6·48*	*80*
Mandla Tahsil ...	2,536	1	1,033	43,138	222,169	110,000	112,169	178,752	+24·29	—8·35	88
Dindori Tahsil ...	2,521	...	885	31,739	183,065	90,872	92,193	139,629	+31·11	—3·98	73
SEONI DISTRICT ...	*3,206*	*1*	*1,569*	*81,726*	*395,481*	*192,642*	*202,839*	*327,709*	*+20·65*	*—11·61*	*123*
Seoni Tahsil ...	1,648	1	722	45,871	224,805	109,149	115,656	192,364	+16·86	—12·28	136
Lakhnadon Tahsil...	1,558	...	847	35,855	170,676	83,493	87,183	135,345	+26·10	—10·65	110
Nerbudda Division	18,388	17	6,438	418,852	2,081,477	1,043,239	1,038,238	1,785,008	+16·61	—5·21	113
NARSINGHPUR DISTRICT.	*1,976*	*3*	*1,009*	*69,433*	*325,677*	*161,795*	*163,882*	*315,518*	*+3·22*	*—14·45*	165
Narsinghpur Tahsil	1,068	2	558	32,563	153,482	76,004	77,388	150,305	+2·11	—13·97	144
Gadarwara Tahsil...	908	1	451	36,870	172,195	85,701	86,494	165,213	+4·23	—14·94	190
HOSHANGABAD DISTRICT.	*3,682*	*6*	*1,326*	*93,979*	*457,395*	*230,632*	*226,763*	*446,645*	*+2·41*	*—9·55*	*124*
Hoshangabad Tahsil	774	2	312	25,559	128,166	64,936	63,230	125,071	+2·47	—9·24	166
Harda Tahsil ...	1,125	1	385	24,984	129,915	65,673	64,242	128,918	+·77	—8·11	115
Sohagpur Tahsil ...	1,261	2	435	28,659	134,447	67,434	67,013	126,863	+6·82	—10·06	107
Seoni-Malwa Tahsil	522	1	194	14,777	64,867	32,589	32,278	66,793	—2·88	—11·9	124
NIMAR DISTRICT...	*4,227*	*2*	*1,019*	*74,066*	*391,071*	*200,765*	*190,306*	*337,173*	*+19·53*	*+14·33*	*93*
Khandwa Town ...	...	1	...	4,540	21,604	11,511	10,093	19,401	+11·36	+24·45	110
Khandwa Tahsil ...	1,871	...	473	31,701	183,744	93,810	89,934	141,825	+29·56	+8·75	
Burhanpur Town...	...	1	...	4,836	22,777	11,624	11,153	33,341	—31·68	+3·38	95
Burhanpur Tahsil...	1,138	...	228	16,836	84,946	43,730	41,216	59,592	+42·55	+21·33	
Harsud Tahsil ...	1,218	...	318	16,153	78,000	40,090	37,910	73,014	+6·83	+24·16	64
BETUL DISTRICT ...	*3,872*	*2*	*1,242*	*75,789*	*390,386*	*194,163*	*196,223*	*287,807*	*+35·64*	*—11·87*	*101*
Betul Tahsil ...	1,802	2	481	30,781	150,493	75,755	74,738	111,440	+35·04	...	84
Multai Tahsil ...	969	...	394	28,732	154,525	76,184	78,341	118,9·1	+29·90	...	159
Bhainsdohi Tahsil	1,101	...	367	16,276	85,368	42,224	43,144	57,416	+48·68	...	78

tion of Tahsils, Cities and large Towns.

Tahsil, Taluk, Zamindaris or Township.	Area in square miles.	Number of: Towns.	Number of: Villages.	Number of occupied houses.	Population. 1911. Persons.	Population. 1911. Males.	Population. 1911. Females.	Population. 1901 (both sexes).	Percentage of variation. 1901 to 1911.	Percentage of variation. 1891 to 1901.	Number of persons per square mile in 1911.
1	2	3	4	5	6	7	8	9	10	11	13
Chhindwara District.	*4,631*	*4*	*1,842*	*105,585*	*516,948*	*255,884*	*261,064*	*407,865*	*+26·74*	*+·11*	*113*
Chhindwara Tahsil Khalsa.	1,925	1	947	58,962	287,717	141,654	146,068	236,716	+26·91	+3·56	149
Chhindwara Tahsil Zamindaris.	1,597	...	491	15,599	77,744	38,858	38,886	60,001	+29·57	—11·83	49
Sausar Tahsil ...	1,109	3	404	31,024	151,487	75,372	76,115	121,148	+25·04	+·58	137
Nagpur Division...	**22.677**	**29**	**7,796**	**628,606**	**3.109.838**	**1,548,737**	**1,561,101**	**2,659,286**	**+16·94**	**—8·59**	**137**
Wardha District	*2,425*	*7*	*920*	*99,211*	*459,796*	*231,871*	*227,925*	*385,103*	*+19·40*	*—3·93*	*189*
Wardha Tahsil ...	800	4	318	38,609	177,534	89,318	88,216	152,565	+16·37	—3·57	210
Arvi Tahsil ...	890	2	308	35,546	166,172	84,203	81,969	137,737	+20·64	+5·00	187
Hinganghat Tahsil	729	1	294	25,056	116,090	58,350	57,740	94,801	+22·46	—14·95	159
Nagpur District...	*3,840*	*12*	*1,659*	*167,374*	*809,901*	*408,848*	*401,055*	*751,844*	*+7·72*	*—·79*	*211*
Nagpur City ...	...	1	...	23,175	101,415	53,696	47,719	127,734	—20·60	...	
Kamptee Town ...	...	1	...	3,912	17,155	9,348	7,807	38,888	—55·89	...	} 308
Nagpur Tahsil ...	810	...	373	26,745	130,965	65,649	65,316	105,150	+24·55	...	
Ramtek Tahsil ...	897	1	389	29,972	145,147	72,560	72,587	119,461	+21·50	...	162
Umrer Tahsil ...	969	1	427	27,306	144,930	72,064	72,866	123,580	+17·28	...	150
Katol Tahsil ...	617	3	293	30,654	142,713	71,330	71,383	124,443	+14·68	...	231
Saoner Tahsil ...	547	5	207	25,610	127,576	64,196	63,380	112,588	+13·31	...	233
Chanda District...	*9,312*	*5*	*2,419*	*134,556*	*677,544*	*337,540*	*340,004*	*533,857*	*+26·91*	*—14·65*	*73*
Chanda Town ...	...	1	...	4,025	19,866	10,077	9,789	17,803	+11·59	+10·06	} 132
Chanda Tahsil ...	1,174	...	397	26,053	134,660	67,526	67,134	103,237	+30·43	—11·23	
Warora Tahsil ...	1,282	2	440	32,149	158,546	79,458	79,088	134,547	+17·84	—6·94	124
Brahmapuri Tahsil	897	2	349	30,063	150,818	74,194	76,624	115,049	+31·09	—20·09	168
Garhchiroli Tahsil Khalsa.	1,457	...	312	20,223	97,705	47,980	49,725	72,993	+33·86	—25·46	67
Garhchiroli Tahsil Zamindaris.	1,413	...	432	8,935	46,175	23,377	22,798	34,793	+32·71	—36·31	33
Sironcha Tahsil Khalsa.	489	...	109	5,727	32,353	15,982	16,371	31,607	+2·36	+26·28	66
Ahiri Zamindari ...	2,600	...	380	6,781	37,421	18,946	18,475	23,858	+56·84	—10·65	14
Bhandara District.	*3,965*	*4*	*1,633*	*148,920*	*773,677*	*380,014*	*393,663*	*663,062*	*+16·68*	*—10·74*	*195*
Bhandara Tahsil...	1,088	3	509	44,476	235,445	116,472	118,973	204,153	+15·33	—10·96	216
Tirora Tahsil Khalsa	559	1	371	44,356	229,249	112,310	116,939	130,944	+75·07	—12·97	410
Tirora Tahsil Zamindaris.	769	...	204	21,436	109,028	53,239	55,789	160,570	—32·09	—12·79	142
Sakoli Tahsil Khalsa	839	...	302	26,223	137,056	66,977	70.079	124,054	+10·48	—4·78	163
Sakoli Tahsil Zamindaris.	710	...	247	12,429	62,899	31,016	31,883	43,341	+45·13	—11·00	89
Balaghat District.	*3,132*	*1*	*1,135*	*78,545*	*388,920*	*190,469*	*198,451*	*325,390*	*+19·52*	*—14·38*	*124*
Balaghat Tahsil Khalsa.	949	1	417	41,807	208,251	101,681	106,570	179,952	+15·73	—19·04	219
Balaghat Tahsil Zamindaris.	439	...	186	14,005	75,380	36,635	38,745	59,189	+27·35	—13·10	172
Baihar Tahsil Khalsa.	1,260	...	477	20,106	95,783	47,470	48,313	69,185	+38·44	—8·86	76
Baihar Tahsil Zamindaris.	484	...	55	1,937	9,506	4,683	4,823	17,064	—44·29	+6·86	20
Chhattisgarh Division.	**22,039**	**7**	**10,128**	**649.904**	**3.246.767**	**1.576.822**	**1.669,945**	**2.691.662**	**+20·62**	**—9·81**	**147**
Raipur District	*9,776*	*3*	*4,371*	*271,504*	*1,324,856*	*645,186*	*679,670*	*1,096,858*	*+20·79*	*—2·50*	*136*
Raipur Town ...	...	1	...	7,517	35,335	18.038	17,297	32,114	+10·03	+35·17	} 249
Raipur Tahsil ...	1,010	1	485	46,925	217,440	104,909	112,531	214,400	+1·42	—6·50	
Mahasamund Tahsil Khalsa.	645	...	292	22,526	102,934	49,672	53,262	96,300	+6·89	+11·13	160
Mahasamund Tahsil Zamindaris.	4,584	...	1,870	76,186	410,350	202,791	207,559	301,775	+35·98	+10·28	90
Baloda Bazar Tahsil Khalsa.	1,618	...	811	61,653	286,266	138,569	147,697	224,809	+27·84	—17·94	177
Baloda Bazar Tahsil Zamindaris.	315	...	197	9,555	51,159	25,788	25,371	39,254	+30·33	—12·20	162
Dhamtari Tahsil ...	1,598	1	616	47,142	221,372	105,419	115,953	188,206	+17·62	—2·46	139

PROVINCIAL TABLE I.—Area and Population of Tahsils, Cities and large Towns.

TAHSIL, TALUK, ZAMINDARIS OR TOWNSHIP.	Area in square miles.	Number of Towns.	Number of Villages.	Population. Number of occupied houses.	1911. Persons.	1911. Males.	1911. Females.	1901 (both sexes).	Percentage of variation. 1901 to 1911.	Percentage of variation. 1891 to 1901.	Number of persons per square mile in 1911.
1	2	3	4	5	6	7	8	9	10	11	12
Bilaspur District	*7,618*	*3*	*3,345*	*218,760*	*1,146,223*	*558,477*	*587,746*	*918,491*	*+24·79*	*—12·24*	*160*
Bilaspur Town ..	...	1	...	4,784	19,850	9,983	9,867	18,937	+4·82	+70·27	240 (Bilaspur Town and Tahsil Khalsa)
Bilaspur Tahsil Khalsa.	1,135	1	596	52,685	252,043	121,186	130,857	302,978 (Khalsa and Zamindaris)	+25·85	...	
Bilaspur Tahsil Zamindaris.	1,976	...	493	24,242	127,755	64,615	63,140				65
Mungeli Tahsil Khalsa.	940	1	555	31,681	145,195	68,839	76,356	177,116 (Khalsa and Zamindaris)	+21·30	...	154
Mungeli Tahsil Zamindaris.	512	...	347	15,093	69,656	33,628	36,028				136
Janjgir Tahsil Khalsa.	1,303	...	741	63,467	376,829	183,038	193,791	419,460 (Khalsa and Zamindaris)	+26·76	...	289
Janjgir Tahsil Zamindaris.	1,752	...	613	26,808	154,895	77,188	77,707				88
Drug District ...	*4,645*	*1*	*2,512*	*159,640*	*775,688*	*373,159*	*402,539*	*676,313*	*+14·69*	*—16·78*	*167*
Drug Tahsil Khalsa	924	1	507	46,640	220,723	105,520	115,203	209,302 (Khalsa and Zamindaris)	+17·83	...	239
Drug Tahsil Zamindaris.	140	...	69	5,290	25,068	12,339	13,029				185
Bemetara Tahsil Khalsa.	952	...	604	43,263	208,755	99,450	109,305	240,843 (Khalsa and Zamindaris)	+11·07	...	219
Bemetara Tahsil Zamindaris.	614	...	281	12,262	58,742	28,808	29,939				96
Sanjari Tahsil Khalsa.	891	...	481	31,763	158,961	76,329	82,632	226,108 (Khalsa and Zamindaris)	+15·65	...	178
Sanjari Tahsil Zamindaris	1,124	...	570	20,422	102,539	50,718	51,821				91
Berar ...	**17,766**	**47**	**5,849**	**655,234**	**3,057,162**	**1,550,614**	**1,506,548**	**2,754,016**	**+11·01**	**—4·95**	**172**
Amraoti District	*4,733*	*20*	*1,627*	*187,331*	*875,904*	*447,216*	*428,688*	*809,499*	*+8·20*	*—4·72*	*185*
Amraoti Town ...	...	1	...	6,218	34,270	18,147	16,123	34,216	+·16	+18·21	282 (Amraoti Town and Taluk)
Amraoti Taluk ...	672	4	264	32,975	154,902	79,593	75,309	141,341	+9·59	—8·55	
Morsi Taluk ...	623	5	229	33,971	154,144	78,470	75,674	143,734	+7·24	—5·67	247
Chandur Taluk ...	855	4	303	46,635	204,133	104,343	99,790	102,805	+5·88	—2·68	239
Ellichpur Town...	469 (Ellichpur Town and Taluk)	1	...	3,279	13,909	7,027	6,882	26,082	—46·67	—3·08	305 (Ellichpur Town and Taluk)
Ellichpur Taluk...		4	248	25,786	128,954	65,822	63,132	119,953	+7·50	+·31	
Daryapur Taluk ...	505	1	245	28,026	129,534	65,799	63,735	114,698	+12·93	—6·41	256
Melghat Taluk ...	1,609	...	338	10,431	56,058	28,015	28,043	36,670	+52·87	—21·73	35
Akola District...	*4,097*	*12*	*1,481*	*171,040*	*788,863*	*400,893*	*387,970*	*754,187*	*+4·60*	*—·55*	*193*
Akola Town ...	739 (Akola Town and Taluk)	1	...	5,311	25,826	14,006	11,820	29,289	—11·82	+36·42	212 (Akola Town and Taluk)
Akola Taluk ...		1	202	28,988	130,891	66,350	64,541	120,933	+8·23	+3·79	
Akot Taluk ...	521	3	212	28,958	137,874	70,393	67,481	137,683	+·14	—·03	265
Balapur Taluk ...	551	3	166	24,434	111,550	56,234	55,316	103,878	+7·39	+2·58	202
Basim Taluk ...	1,046	1	327	35,621	165,606	83,266	82,340	153,320	+8·01	—13·50	158
Mangrul Taluk ...	630	1	206	20,873	95,130	48,108	47,022	91,062	+4·47	+10·45	151
Murtizapur Taluk	610	2	278	26,955	121,986	62,536	59,450	118,022	+3·36	—2·99	200
Buldana District	*3,731*	*9*	*1,174*	*144,586*	*669,183*	*337,179*	*332,003*	*614,373*	*+8·92*	*—9·52*	*179*
Chikhli Taluk ...	1,009	3	274	32,474	145,633	72,674	72,959	129,590	+12·38	—13·66	144
Mehkar Taluk ...	1,027	1	313	26,614	142,067	70,858	71,209	121,409	+17·02	—20·88	138
Khamgaon Taluk...	442	2	133	25,117	101,068	51,969	49,099	102,948	—1·83	+3·17	229
Jalgaon Taluk ...	461	1	161	20,087	91,372	46,238	45,134	87,192	+4·79	—10·84	198
Malkapur Taluk ...	792	2	293	39,394	189,042	95,440	93,602	173,234	+9·13	—2·61	239
Yeotmal District	*5,205*	*6*	*1,667*	*152,357*	*723,213*	*365,326*	*357,887*	*575,957*	*+25·57*	*—5·60*	*139*
Yeotmal Taluk ...	908	1	302	33,879	150,891	76,313	74,578	124,031	+21·66	—·32	166
Kelapur Taluk ...	1,086	...	310	26,907	130,797	65,120	65,677	103,657	+26·18	—2·14	120
Wun Taluk ...	862	1	297	22,317	108,070	55,508	52,562	82,562	+30·90	—2·50	125
Darwha Taluk ...	1,064	2	339	39,160	181,281	91,670	89,611	156,679	+15·70	+·06	170
Pusad Taluk ...	1,285	2	310	30,425	152,174	76,715	75,459	109,028	+39·57	—21·27	118

PROVINCIAL TABLE II.

Population of Tahsils, Cities and large Towns by Religion and Education.

In this Table the population of the Tahsils of the Central Provinces and the Taluks of Berar and of two cities and ten large towns is shown by the four principal religions. The figures for zamindari areas are given separately under the Tahsils to which they belong. The figures of the cities and towns are shown above the Tahsil to which they belong and are not included in the Tahsil figures. Literacy is shown for the same areas for certain main age periods, but the Tahsil figures include only Hindu, Animist and Muhammadan literates as literacy for the Christian and minor religions was not sorted for smaller units than the District.

PROVINCIAL TABLE II.—Population of Tahsils,

TAHSIL, TALUK, ZAMINDARIS OR TOWN-SHIP.	DISTRIBUTION BY RELIGION.						
	HINDU (BRAHMANIC).		ANIMIST.		MUSALMAN.		CHRIS
	Males.	Females.	Males.	Females.	Males.	Females.	Males.
1	2	3	4	5	6	7	8
Jubbulpore Division	**875,450**	**868,312**	**257,700**	**273,220**	**53,341**	**48,611**	**6,259**
SAUGOR DISTRICT	*240,356*	*231,294*	*12,154*	*12,770*	*13,632*	*12,203*	*777*
Saugor Town	17,677	16,116	6	5	5,054	4,406	312
Saugor Tahsil	68,641	66,963	143	163	2,315	2,208	199
Khurai do.	51,870	49,604	110	113	2,666	2,367	247
Rehli do.	63,232	61,262	11,605	12,200	2,750	2,353	19
Banda do.	38,936	37,349	290	289	847	814	...
DAMOH DISTRICT	*152,873*	*150,316*	*5,461*	*5,654*	*5,680*	*5,322*	*337*
Damoh Tahsil	94,796	93,638	4,438	4,599	3,831	3,623	328
Hatta do.	58,077	56,678	1,023	1,055	1,849	1,699	9
JUBBULPORE DISTRICT	*298,484*	*300,476*	*44,113*	*47,430*	*22,117*	*19,222*	*4,554*
Jubbulpore City	37,334	31,568	118	77	12,827	10,205	4,349
Jubbulpore Tahsil	57,455	58,222	19,927	20,593	1,847	1,813	42
Sihora do.	88,523	92,400	8,295	8,858	2,901	2,827	15
Murwara do.	70,936	73,675	13,982	15,987	2,993	2,890	125
Patan do.	44,230	44,611	1,791	1,915	1,549	1,487	23
MANDLA DISTRICT	*77,986*	*77,020*	*118,656*	*123,605*	*3,329*	*3,013*	*491*
Mandla Tahsil	50,253	50,081	56,617	59,267	2,334	2,175	442
Dindori do.	27,733	26,939	62,039	64,338	995	838	49
SEONI DISTRICT	*105,751*	*109,206*	*77,316*	*83,761*	*8,583*	*8,851*	*100*
Seoni Tahsil	67,074	70,073	36,516	39,728	5,030	5,309	86
Lakhnadon Tahsil	38,677	39,133	40,800	44,033	3,553	3,542	14
Nerbudda Division	**790,633**	**777,858**	**193,920**	**206,214**	**49,450**	**45,928**	**4,025**
NARSINGHPUR DISTRICT... ...	*138,622*	*139,436*	*15,714*	*17,278*	*5,888*	*5,819*	*315*
Narsinghpur Tahsil	64,066	64,728	7,477	8,286	3,545	3,549	278
Gadarwara do.	74,556	74,708	8,237	8,992	2,343	2,270	37
HOSHANGABAD DISTRICT... ...	*193,785*	*188,990*	*24,157*	*25,758*	*10,640*	*10,159*	*1,044*
Hoshangabad Tahsil	52,724	50,811	8,955	9,506	2,635	2,310	387
Harda do	57,941	56,613	3,732	3,743	3,411	3,341	246
Sohagpur Tahsil	55,638	54,471	8,055	8,872	3,238	3,184	206
Seoni-Malwa do.	27,482	27,095	3,415	3,637	1,356	1,324	205
NIMAR DISTRICT	*174,111*	*165,919*	*3,434*	*3,369*	*20,109*	*18,319*	*1,894*
Khandwa Town	7,319	6,338	5	3	3,587	3,225	336
Khandwa Tahsil	86,477	83,343	588	581	4,871	4,282	1,492
Burhanpur Town	6,119	6,025	...	...	5,454	5,090	11
Burhanpur Tahsil	38,471	36,460	403	380	4,542	4,172	94
Harsud do.	35,725	33,753	2,438	2,405	1,655	1,550	61
BETUL DISTRICT	*129,817*	*129,501*	*58,947*	*62,228*	*4,354*	*3,495*	*274*
Betul Tahsil	44,638	43,157	28,230	29,468	2,427	1,698	193
Multai do.	61,325	62,638	13,273	14,146	1,204	1,191	43
Bhainsdehi do.	23,854	23,706	17,444	18,614	723	606	38
CHHINDWARA DISTRICT	*154,298*	*154,032*	*91,668*	*97,581*	*8,459*	*8,136*	*398*
Chhindwara Tahsil Khalsa ...	91,900	92,948	43,476	47,052	5,173	5,093	346
Chhindwara Tahsil Zamindaris ...	10,107	9,407	27,952	28,794	659	554	40
Sausar Tahsil	52,291	51,677	20,240	21,735	2,627	2,489	12

Cities and large Towns by Religion and Education.

...TIAN.	OTHERS.		NUMBER OF LITERATE PERSONS.					
			0—15.		15—20.		20 AND OVER.	
Females.	Males.	Females.	Males.	Females.	Males.	Females.	Males.	Females.
9	10	11	12	13	14	15	16	17
3,585	**18,230**	**16,356**	**13,620**	**1,652**	**12,505**	**1,086**	**72,236**	**3,869**
677	*9,314*	*8,233*	*3,196*	*414*	*3,189*	*326*	*17,906*	*970*
302	1,281	689	898	131	822	123	4,410	311
158	2,052	1,945	542	31	583	24	2,894	80
213	2,030	1,850	519	48	486	38	3,193	122
4	2,288	2,102	514	40	499	30	3,112	78
...	1,663	1,647	207	18	313	17	1,639	64
100	*3,709*	*3,595*	*2,423*	*166*	*1,869*	*86*	*10,418*	*405*
92	2,844	2,709	1,148	84	959	50	5,418	217
8	865	886	909	32	633	17	3,739	73
2,326	*3,905*	*3,265*	*5,534*	*811*	*5,154*	*544*	*30,964*	*1,978*
1,961	1,407	805	2,109	537	1,824	407	12,882	1,539
47	640	620	486	17	494	10	2,947	50
9	520	521	1,047	25	1,065	29	5,958	115
278	414	419	1,283	85	1,144	31	5,727	96
31	924	900	436	27	472	6	2,469	34
380	*410*	*344*	*1,221*	*111*	*1,068*	*56*	*5,825*	*215*
341	354	305	837	81	731	40	3,854	118
39	56	39	339	11	291	1	1,670	30
102	*892*	*919*	*1,846*	*148*	*1,210*	*74*	*7,120*	*301*
91	443	455	759	47	755	22	4,461	150
11	449	464	412	70	383	32	2,275	98
3,438	**5,211**	**4,800**	**11,382**	**712**	**10,118**	**564**	**63,061**	**2,060**
156	*1,256*	*1,203*	*1,942*	*123*	*2,144*	*99*	*11,405*	*398*
129	728	701	914	70	962	61	5,408	238
27	528	502	908	86	1,014	25	5,443	100
853	*1,006*	*1,008*	*3,317*	*189*	*3,040*	*194*	*18,009*	*643*
842	235	261	920	49	811	24	4,848	158
196	343	349	991	44	920	28	5,274	75
203	297	283	745	33	694	25	4,088	91
112	131	110	517	14	489	13	2,883	41
1,799	*1,117*	*900*	*2,580*	*179*	*2,231*	*150*	*16,134*	*504*
322	264	205	462	82	390	92	2,602	209
1,380	382	348	1,030	38	1,059	22	7,213	94
11	40	27	210	20	156	12	1,531	58
41	220	163	489	29	368	18	2,861	78
45	211	157	250	2	162	5	1,474	27
273	*771*	*726*	*1,401*	*66*	*1,032*	*46*	*7,592*	*239*
203	267	212	627	26	420	21	3,501	116
37	339	329	585	25	442	6	2,852	30
33	165	185	124	2	115	3	1,137	14
357	*1,061*	*965*	*2,208*	*155*	*1,671*	*75*	*9,618*	*376*
322	759	658	1,122	63	886	26	4,809	115
32	100	99	136	7	104	1	692	19
8	202	211	890	13	587	10	3,650	33

PROVINCIAL TABLE II.—Population of Tahsils,

Tahsil, Taluk, Zamindaris or Township.	Distribution by Religion.						
	Hindu (Brahmanic).		Animist.		Musalman.		Chris
	Males.	Females.	Males.	Females.	Males.	Females.	Males.
1	2	3	4	5	6	7	8
Nagpur Division	**1,315,027**	**1,322,886**	**177,747**	**186,428**	**46,883**	**44,570**	**4,631**
WARDHA DISTRICT	*197,583*	*193,450*	*23,549*	*24,282*	*9,331*	*8,843*	*117*
Wardha Tahsil	76,495	75,367	8,527	8,821	3,602	3,364	98
Arvi do.	70,488	68,132	9,691	9,951	3,620	3,508	2
Hinganghat Tahsil	50,600	49,981	5,331	5,510	2,109	1,971	17
NAGPUR DISTRICT	*365,125*	*360,274*	*17,870*	*18,133*	*20,047*	*18,387*	*3,764*
Nagpur City	42,187	37,954	703	662	7,854	6,735	2,158
Kamptee Town	5,430	5,004	46	47	2,533	2,306	1,295
Nagpur Tahsil	59,404	59,164	3,920	3,996	1,958	1,818	31
Ramtek do.	62,142	62,135	8,515	8,724	1,645	1,487	76
Umrer do.	68,060	68,839	2,159	2,116	1,567	1,604	151
Katol Tahsil	67,565	67,591	1,106	1,151	2,312	2,314	3
Saoner do.	60,337	59,587	1,421	1,437	2,178	2,123	50
CHANDA DISTRICT	*269,465*	*270,248*	*61,161*	*63,195*	*6,205*	*5,967*	*304*
Chanda Town	8,955	8,730	183	200	719	683	142
Chanda Tahsil	54,876	54,269	11,777	12,082	840	762	24
Warora do.	69,888	69,403	7,327	7,458	1,939	1,957	2
Brahmapuri Tahsil	65,839	67,751	7,202	7,786	1,129	1,063	8
Garhchiroli Tahsil Khalsa ...	39,420	40,732	7,935	8,369	618	622	3
Garhchiroli Tahsil Zamindaris ...	9,838	9,043	13,171	13,421	348	310	...
Sironcha Tahsil Khalsa	14,690	15,013	849	964	359	313	84
Ahiri Zamindari	5,959	5,298	12,717	12,906	253	257	15
BHANDARA DISTRICT	*337,336*	*348,007*	*34,669*	*37,755*	*7,434*	*7,273*	*250*
Bhandara Tahsil	105,789	107,898	7,508	7,911	2,873	2,811	185
Tirora Tahsil Khalsa	100,619	104,320	9,431	10,405	2,121	2,069	26
Tirora Tahsil Zamindaris	47,878	49,940	4,467	4,989	859	832	25
Sakoli Tahsil Khalsa	59,305	61,661	6,508	7,244	1,082	1,085	12
Sakoli Tahsil Zamindaris ...	23,744	24,188	6,755	7,206	499	476	2
BALAGHAT DISTRICT	*145,519*	*150,877*	*40,495*	*43,063*	*3,866*	*4,100*	*196*
Balaghat Tahsil Khalsa	84,656	88,406	13,847	14,852	2,747	3,001	86
Balaghat Tahsil Zamindaris ...	32,959	34,751	3,166	3,409	501	578	4
Baihar Tahsil Khalsa	24,770	24,437	21,959	23,294	595	489	106
Baihar Tahsil Zamindaris ...	3,134	3,283	1,526	1,508	23	32	...
Chhattisgarh Division	**1,398,430**	**1,479,781**	**154,705**	**167,126**	**18,920**	**18,541**	**3,295**
RAIPUR DISTRICT	*549,378*	*577,119*	*85,106*	*92,194*	*8,393*	*8,122*	*1,637*
Raipur Town	14,421	13,775	127	106	2,962	2,920	278
Raipur Tahsil	99,464	106,518	4,278	4,775	917	1,010	187
Mahasamund Tahsil Khalsa ...	40,413	43,146	8,590	9,522	608	553	15
Mahasamund Tahsil Zamindaris ...	151,721	153,600	49,235	52,209	1,511	1,427	244
Baloda Bazar Tahsil Khalsa ...	136,154	145,395	532	502	1,162	1,069	630
Baloda Bazar Tahsil Zamindaris ...	25,410	25,022	152	166	214	177	12
Dhamtari Tahsil	81,795	89,663	22,192	24,914	1,019	960	271
BILASPUR DISTRICT	*524,724*	*552,614*	*25,455*	*26,970*	*7,049*	*6,915*	*971*
Bilaspur Town	8,106	7,932	41	25	1,410	1,386	382
Bilaspur Tahsil Khalsa	107,677	115,928	12,002	13,333	1,352	1,449	132
Bilaspur Tahsil Zamindaris ...	53,795	52,423	9,928	9,976	779	615	87
Mungeli Tahsil Khalsa	67,344	74,824	652	688	506	601	238
Mungeli Tahsil Zamindaris ...	32,352	34,062	804	851	444	501	13
Janjgir Tahsil Khalsa	180,382	191,067	852	902	1,607	1,674	79
Janjgir Tahsil Zamindaris ...	75,068	75,778	1,176	1,195	891	689	40
DRUG DISTRICT	*324,328*	*350,048*	*44,144*	*47,962*	*3,478*	*3,504*	*687*
Drug Tahsil Khalsa	95,423	103,725	8,801	10,351	1,060	968	54
Drug Tahsil Zamindaris ...	11,058	12,172	1,198	1,305	65	84	1
Bemetara Tahsil Khalsa ...	91,881	100,719	6,267	7,240	715	727	526
Bemetara Tahsil Zamindaris ...	21,397	21,909	6,882	7,524	478	468	2
Sanjari Tahsil Khalsa	70,779	76,794	4,694	5,072	637	634	64
Sanjari Tahsil Zamindaris ...	33,790	34,729	16,302	16,410	523	628	40

Cities and large Towns by Religion and Education.

...TIAN.	OTHERS.		NUMBER OF LITERATE PERSONS.					
			0—15.		15—20.		20 AND OVER.	
Females.	Males.	Females.	Males.	Females.	Males.	Females.	Males.	Females.
9	10	11	12	13	14	15	16	17
3,201	**4,449**	**4,016**	**15,500**	**1,286**	**12,268**	**831**	**80.618**	**3,261**
61	*1,291*	*1,259*	*2,899*	*123*	*2,481*	*76*	*15,742*	*336*
51	596	613	1,272	53	1,085	35	6,568	154
2	402	376	1,047	42	823	24	5,299	80
8	293	270	494	17	494	13	3,316	40
2,481	*2,037*	*1,783*	*5,924*	*843*	*4,375*	*483*	*29,791*	*2,036*
1,802	794	566	1,361	514	1,257	316	9,068	1,338
419	44	31	232	143	171	63	2,240	237
16	336	322	606	43	533	25	3,220	101
46	182	195	813	20	471	23	3,675	74
170	127	137	905	53	647	27	3,382	110
1	344	326	646	12	583	4	3,601	50
27	210	206	1,288	49	743	16	4,018	65
237	*405*	*357*	*2,027*	*112*	*1,635*	*90*	*11,834*	*304*
95	78	63	361	21	284	51	1,602	87
15	9	6	390	21	267	11	2,252	40
16	276	254	501	23	405	8	2,911	52
18	16	6	381	9	323	2	2,497	30
...	4	2	247	8	204	7	1,394	28
...	20	24	51	2	51	...	430	4
81	...	...	32	3	29	4	264	9
12	2	2	31	...	41	...	300	4
238	*326*	*340*	*2,776*	*116*	*2,286*	*116*	*15,639*	*344*
224	117	120	1,215	58	789	38	5,547	136
32	113	113	793	14	730	9	4,023	68
21	10	7	209	5	291	4	1,721	6
7	70	82	460	3	337	11	2,023	25
4	16	9	113	3	108	1	841	8
134	*390*	*277*	*1,874*	*98*	*1,491*	*68*	*7,632*	*241*
47	345	264	1,181	60	883	39	4,555	132
3	5	4	320	5	253	6	1,191	14
84	40	9	314	6	311	8	1,530	32
...	...	—	18	...	5	...	42	1
3,440	**1,472**	**1.057**	**7,970**	**776**	**8,133**	**619**	**44,793**	**1,703**
1,725	*672*	*507*	*3,616*	*407*	*3,558*	*312*	*19,000*	*828*
278	250	212	984	220	737	123	3,709	440
184	63	44	471	21	512	7	2,793	35
10	46	31	259	22	315	7	1,501	27
275	80	48	465	18	568	11	3,083	48
647	91	84	473	14	511	7	3,175	31
6	...	...	90	4	118	1	562	14
328	142	88	793	67	671	31	3,701	91
1,040	*278*	*207*	*2,846*	*256*	*2,873*	*233*	*15,615*	*614*
493	44	31	318	109	241	123	1,839	228
140	23	7	571	21	582	12	2,875	80
98	26	28	147	5	175	3	1,281	13
217	39	20	394	81	394	37	1,982	64
9	15	5	129	5	159	11	790	26
46	118	102	1,020	33	1,034	25	4,832	88
37	13	8	255	41	202	17	1,702	52
672	*522*	*343*	*1,508*	*114*	*1,702*	*69*	*10,275*	*261*
44	182	120	571	20	692	18	3,924	63
...	17	8	17	...	39	1	263	...
574	61	45	353	10	419	8	2,517	25
5	44	33	73	3	76	1	522	8
41	155	91	339	51	329	17	1,982	55
8	63	46	100	5	79	1	603	23

PROVINCIAL TABLE II.—Population of Tahsils.

TAHSIL, TALUK, ZAMINDARIS OR TOWNSHIP.			DISTRIBUTION BY RELIGION.						
			HINDU (BRAHMANIC).		ANIMIST.		MUSALMAN.		CHRIS
			Males.	Females.	Males.	Females.	Males.	Females.	Males.
1			2	3	4	5	6	7	8
Berar	—	...	**1,352,396**	**1,315,713**	**63,095**	**64,766**	**123,453**	**115,212**	**1,521**
AMRAOTI DISTRICT	...	...	*377,352*	*360,942*	*23,193*	*28,993*	*37,896*	*35,415*	*827*
Amraoti Town	...	...	13,860	12,155	8	7	3,855	3,581	50
Amraoti Taluk	...	...	70,445	66,999	913	886	7,593	6,769	220
Morsi do.	...	...	71,046	68,686	1,506	1,590	5,321	4,842	7
Chandur do. ...	...	...	95,170	91,204	2,832	2,921	5,398	4,839	17
Ellichpur Town	...	...	4,553	4,298	75	48	2,373	2,508	...
Ellichpur Taluk	...	...	58,077	55,835	739	697	6,440	6,183	216
Daryapur do.	...	...	59,357	57,521	193	190	5,799	5,710	200
Melghat do.	...	...	4,844	4,244	21,932	22,654	1,117	983	117
AKOLA DISTRICT	...	—	*360,644*	*350,381*	*491*	*443*	*36,342*	*33,806*	*365*
Akola Town	...	...	10,285	8,606	71	60	3,305	2,933	143
Akola Taluk	...	...	61,484	60,021	90	85	4,410	4,082	102
Akot do. ...	...	...	62,575	60,181	152	139	7,393	6,887	9
Balapur do. ...	...	...	49,658	48,806	...	...	6,282	6,240	1
Basim do. ...	...	...	77,264	76,399	6	5	4,948	4,790	84
Mangrul do.	...	...	44,540	43,732	10	10	3,351	3,050	2
Murtizapur do.	...	...	54,838	52,636	162	144	6,658	5,824	24
BULDANA DISTRICT	...	...	*305,993*	*302,616*	*204*	*178*	*28,435*	*26,833*	*183*
Chikhli Taluk...	...	...	65,480	66,012	2	...	6,495	6,304	42
Mehkar do. ...	...	...	65,698	66,307	17	21	4,392	4,203	30
Khamgaon Taluk	...	...	46,854	44,489	11	7	4,632	4,140	84
Jalgaon do.	...	...	42,420	41,507	169	144	3,641	3,479	2
Malkapur do.	...	...	85,541	84,301	5	6	9,275	8,696	25
YEOTMAL DISTRICT	...	...	*308,407*	*301,774*	*34,203*	*35,152*	*20,780*	*19,169*	*146*
Yeotmal Taluk	...	...	59,207	57,261	12,585	13,087	3,863	3,618	52
Kelapur do.	...	...	52,100	52,465	10,521	10,921	2,237	2,081	43
Wun do.	...	...	44,292	41,770	9,350	9,313	1,752	1,397	7
Darwha do.	...	—	82,549	80,949	1,746	1,830	6,941	6,432	6
Pusad do.	...	...	70,250	69,329	...	1	5,987	5,641	38

Printed at the Pioneer Press, by GEO. SIM, No. 1591.—30-12-12.

Cities and large Towns by Religion and Education.

...TIAN.	Others.		Number of literate persons.					
			0—15.		15—20.		20 and over.	
Females.	Males.	Females.	Males.	Females.	Males.	Females.	Males.	Females.
9	10	11	12	13	14	15	16	17
1,302	10,149	9,555	12,954	981	13,009	735	95,549	2,385
662	*2,943*	*2,676*	*4,074*	*409*	*4,796*	*278*	*33,902*	*991*
43	374	337	641	171	900	104	4,470	370
281	422	374	783	72	811	56	5,942	141
5	500	551	711	16	662	13	5,046	60
17	926	809	640	10	851	15	6,508	71
...	26	28	103	4	42	6	525	12
103	350	314	626	28	704	17	5,230	43
54	250	260	504	22	606	15	4,602	61
159	5	3	88	1	44	1	517	11
301	*3,051*	*3,039*	*3,915*	*275*	*3,361*	*211*	*25,945*	*533*
95	202	126	443	124	410	81	2,835	115
70	264	283	873	17	553	12	3,969	13
4	264	270	818	40	708	44	6,033	90
...	293	270	368	17	377	15	2,960	70
104	969	1,042	479	14	439	4	3,329	46
2	205	228	342	12	270	7	1,974	23
26	854	820	434	24	474	23	3,772	107
196	*2,364*	*2,192*	*2,916*	*179*	*2,950*	*143*	*20,828*	*518*
26	655	617	500	46	517	22	3,756	108
26	721	652	396	16	426	5	2,790	28
188	388	325	600	62	547	61	4,124	141
...	6	4	491	14	434	11	2,955	70
5	594	594	828	37	919	35	6,349	137
144	*1,791*	*1,648*	*2,049*	*118*	*1,902*	*104*	*14,874*	*343*
86	606	526	612	79	584	48	4,053	142
4	210	206	437	3	286	5	2,269	24
5	107	77	265	6	178	6	1,673	14
10	428	390	361	13	454	12	3,758	88
39	440	449	298	1	317	5	2,453	9